COLLINS
COBUILD

DICTIONARY OF
PHRASAL
VERBS

**THE UNIVERSITY
OF BIRMINGHAM**

**COLLINS
COBUILD**

HarperCollins*Publishers*

first edition 1989

© HarperCollins Publishers 1989

latest reprint 2001

HarperCollins Publishers
Westerhill Road, Bishopbriggs, Glasgow G64 2QT

ISBN 0-00-370265-0 paperback

Collins®, COBUILD®, and Bank of English® are registered
trademarks of HarperCollins Publishers Limited

www.cobuild.collins.co.uk

Corpus Acknowledgements

We would like to acknowledge the assistance of the many hundreds of individuals and
companies who have kindly given permission for copyright material to be used in The Bank
of English. The written sources include many national and regional newspapers in Britain
and overseas; magazine and periodical publishers; and book publishers in Britain, the United
States, and Australia. Extensive spoken data has been provided by radio and television
broadcasting companies; research workers at many universities and other institutions; and
numerous individual contributors. We are grateful to them all.

Note

Entered words that we have reason to believe constitute trademarks have been designated
as such. However, neither the presence nor the absence of such designation should be
regarded as affecting the legal status of any trademark.

A catalogue record for this book is available
from the British Library.

Computer typeset by C R Barber & Partners, Wrotham, England

Printed and bound in Great Britain by Omnia Books Limited, Glasgow, G64

Editorial Team

Editor in Chief
John Sinclair

Editorial Director
Patrick Hanks

Senior Editor
Rosamund Moon

Editors
Stephen Bullon
Ramesh Krishnamurthy

Assistant Editors
Elaine Pollard
Deborah Yuill

Computer Officer
Tim Lane

Secretarial Staff
Sue Smith
Joanne Brown

HarperCollins Publishers
Annette Capel
Lorna Heaslip
Douglas Williamson

The original project design was done by Helen Liebeck,
and we would like to thank her for her exceptional
contribution. We would also like to thank Sheila Dignen
for work on the Particles Index and editorial assistance;
Alex Collier for work on the Particles Index and
computational and editorial assistance; Katy Shaw and
Janet Whitcut for their detailed reading of the text;
Jeremy Clear for his formative comments at the
planning stage; Ela Bullon for her work on the
synonyms and antonyms; Malcolm Goodale for revisions
to the Particles Index; Henri Béjoint and Ken Church
for comments and advice.

Foreword

THIS DICTIONARY concentrates on one particular aspect of the grammar and vocabulary of English: combinations of verbs with adverbial or prepositional particles. They are extremely common in English.

These combinations are generally called *phrasal verbs*. They are often a particular problem for learners of English. There are several reasons for this. One reason is that in many cases, even though students may be familiar with both the verb in the phrasal verb and with the particle, they may not understand the meaning of the combination, since it can differ greatly from the meanings of the two words used independently. For example, *make, put, out,* and *off* are all very common words which students will encounter in their first weeks of learning English, and yet the combinations *make out* and *put off* are not transparent. *Make out* can mean 'perceive' or 'imply', and *put off* can mean 'postpone' or 'deter', amongst other meanings: these meanings are unrelated to the meanings of the individual words in the combinations. The fact that phrasal verbs often have a number of different meanings adds to their complexity.

There are some particular grammatical problems associated with phrasal verbs. For example, there are restrictions on the positions in which an adverb can be placed in relation to the object of a verb. Some particles, such as *about, over, round,* and *through* can be used as both adverbs and prepositions in particular phrasal verbs combinations, although in other combinations they are used either adverbially or prepositionally. Some phrasal verbs are not normally used with pronouns as objects, others are normally only used with pronouns as objects. The Extra Column of this dictionary gives detailed information about the grammatical behaviour of phrasal verbs: see pages ix-xvi.

There are other difficulties, such as the fact that there are frequently strong collocational associations between phrasal verbs and other words. Thus, in some cases a particular word or small set of words is the only one normally found as the subject or object of a particular verb. We show on page viii how the explanations in the dictionary give guidance on this.

It is often said that phrasal verbs tend to be rather 'colloquial' or 'informal' and more appropriate to spoken English than written, and even that it is better to avoid them and choose single-word equivalents or synonyms instead. Yet in many cases phrasal verbs and their synonyms have different ranges of use, meaning, or collocation, so that a single-word synonym cannot be substituted appropriately for a phrasal verb. Single-word synonyms are often much more formal in style than phrasal verbs, so that they seem out of place in many contexts, and students using them run the risk of sounding pompous or just unnatural. We include notes on synonyms and antonyms to help with this.

The set of English phrasal verbs is constantly growing and changing. New combinations appear and spread. Yet these new combinations are rarely made on a random basis, but form patterns which can to some extent be anticipated. Particles often have particular meanings which they contribute to a variety of combinations, and which are productive: that is, these fixed meanings are used in order to create new combinations. This dictionary contains an index of the particles, showing the different meanings and listing the phrasal verbs containing those meanings. In this way, you can understand the patterns underlying the combinations, and you can see the relationship in meaning between, for example, *cool off, ease off,* and *wear off,* or between *hook up*, *join up*, and *link up*.

The Collins COBUILD Dictionary of Phrasal Verbs lists over three thousand combinations of verbs with adverbs or prepositions, explaining over five and a half thousand different meanings. These are the combinations which are in common use in everyday modern English. We can make this statement with confidence because the dictionary has been based on a detailed computational study of the extensive Birmingham Collection of English Texts, now part of The Bank of English.

What sorts of item can you expect to find in this dictionary? Different people have different definitions of 'phrasal verb', and different ideas about which particles can be used to form phrasal verbs. The following list contains all the particles which we use in this dictionary:

aback	around	between	of	through
about	as	beyond	off	to
above	aside	by	on	together
across	at	down	onto	towards
after	away	for	out	under
against	back	forth	over	up
ahead	before	forward	overboard	upon
along	behind	from	past	with
among	below	in	round	without
apart	beneath	into		

In addition, there are cases of combinations with two particles, such as *out of* and *in with*.

The headwords included in this dictionary range from combinations the meanings of which are highly unpredictable to reasonably predictable ones. In between these extremes are combinations which have reasonably predictable meanings reinforced by habitual collocation. There is a general shading of meaning from one extreme to the other, but it is possible to point to four main types of combination of verbs with particles.

1 combinations where the meaning of the whole cannot be understood by knowing the meanings of the individual verbs and particles. Examples are *go off* (= 'explode'), *put off* (= 'postpone'), and *turn down* (= 'reject').

2 combinations where the verb is always used with a particular preposition or adverb, and is not normally found without it. Examples are *refer to* and *rely on*. We also include similar cases where a verb is always used with a particular preposition or adverb in a particular meaning.

3 combinations where the particle does not change the meaning of the verb, but is used to suggest that the action described by the verb is performed thoroughly, completely, or continuously. For example, in *spread out*, the verb *spread* has its basic meaning, and the adverb *out* adds ideas of direction and thoroughness. In *link up*, the particle *up* adds an idea of completeness to the idea of connection. In *slave away* and *slog away*, the particle *away* adds an idea of continuousness to the idea of hard work. These combinations are sometimes called 'completive-intensives'.

4 combinations where the verb and particle both have meanings which may be found in other combinations and uses, but where there is overwhelming evidence in our data that they occur together. For example, in the combination *fight back*, the verb *fight* has the same meaning that it normally does in isolation, and *back* is used in a similar way in other combinations such as *phone back* and *strike back*. Yet *fight* and *back* frequently occur together in our data, and we have decided to treat this as a unit in the dictionary. Such combinations are sometimes called 'literal phrasal verbs'. In addition, we mention as the first meaning of *come out*

'leave a place' and of *go up,* 'move to a higher position'. These meanings can of course be easily understood. However, *come out* has nineteen meanings altogether in this dictionary and *go up* has thirteen: most of these are not transparent and cannot be understood so easily. We do not give literal meanings and combinations for all verbs. We have, however, widened the scope of our coverage in the cases of thirty-eight common verbs which occur in a large number of combinations with different particles, and which have many non-transparent meanings. These verbs are especially problematic for students of English. The thirty-eight verbs are:

break	fall	kick	make	put	stay
bring	get	knock	move	run	stick
call	give	lay	pass	send	take
cast	go	lie	play	set	talk
come	hang	live	pull	sit	throw
cut	hold	look	push	stand	turn
do	keep				

We include in this dictionary fixed expressions with verbs and particles, together with the word *it*: for example, *go for it* and *step on it.* We do not include other fixed expressions with verbs and particles: for example, *keep up with the Joneses, push up the daisies,* and *skate on thin ice.* These are idioms, rather than phrasal verbs, and they are included in a companion volume, the Collins COBUILD Dictionary of English Idioms (forthcoming).

The following table summarizes the combinations which we include and those which we do not.

example	phrasal verb type	included?	category no.	reason
We really went to town.	idiom	no		*town* is part of the idiom
The town went up.	non-literal	yes	**go up 10**	new meaning = 'explode'
The number refers to the day.	fixed particle	yes	**refer to 3**	*refer* always occurs with *to*
It's going along fine.	completive	yes	**go along 4**	particle reinforces verb
Thomas hit back.	semi-literal	yes	**hit back 1**	frequent occurrence
We went up the hill.	literal	yes	**go up 1**	common verb and particle
Don't walk on the grass.	literal	no		meaning is clear

This dictionary gives extensive information about phrasal verbs in English. The facts are presented in a very simple way, with plenty of real examples. We hope you find this book useful. We would be pleased to hear your comments and criticisms, which are tremendously useful to us in improving the range of COBUILD dictionaries.

John Sinclair
Editor in Chief
Professor of Modern English Language,
University of Birmingham

Rosamund Moon
Senior Editor

A Guide to the Use
of the Dictionary

Finding phrasal verbs and meanings

The order of entries is alphabetical, according to the verb in the phrasal verb headword. Phrasal verbs which contain the same verb but different particles are arranged in alphabetical order of the particle. So that the order of phrasal verbs beginning with *n* is:

naff off
nail down
nail up
name after
name for
narrow down
nestle up
nibble at
nod off
nose about
nose around
nose out
notch up
note down
number among

Note, for example, that all the phrasal verbs containing the verb *go* are explained before phrasal verbs containing other verbs beginning with the letters *go-*, such as *goad* and *gouge*.

Some phrasal verb combinations contain two particles. In the dictionary, combinations like this, where the second particle is compulsory, are listed as phrasal verb headwords, in their correct alphabetical place in the sequence:

get out
get out of
get over
get over with
get round
get round to
get through

Other phrasal verbs are typically, but not always, used with a second particle. In these cases, the second particle is mentioned in the definition and shown as an optional structure in the Extra Column, but it does not appear in the phrasal verb headword. *Onto* is a special problem as it can be spelled both as one word and as two. We show both spellings if it is a phrasal verb headword in its own right.

get on to, get onto

In other cases where *-to* is optional, we mention it in the explanation, and in the Extra Column as *+to*, but not in the actual headword. Phrasal verbs with *into* are treated separately from ones with *in*, even though there may be little difference in meaning.

Many phrasal verbs have more than one meaning. The different meanings are usually arranged in order of frequency, so that the commonest ones come first. Different meanings are nearly always explained in separate paragraphs.

Verb forms and spelling

1 All the forms or inflections of a verb are given in bold letters at the beginning of each sequence of phrasal verbs containing that verb. They are listed in the order: base form, third person form of the present tense (-s form), present participle (-ing form), past tense (-ed form), and past participle (-n form) if this is different from the past tense form. If there are alternative spellings for a form, both spellings are given. For example:

fill, fills, filling, filled
give, gives, giving, gave, given
go, goes, going, went, gone
leap, leaps, leaping, leaped/leapt
put, puts, putting

All other irregularities are explained in a note after the forms.

2 If a verb has two spellings, for example if it is spelled differently in British English and American English, this is mentioned in a note after the forms.

plough, ploughs, ploughing, ploughed
Plough is also spelled **plow** in American English.

Explanations

The explanations of phrasal verbs are in simple English. They do not just tell you about the meaning of the phrasal verb, but also show you how it is typically used: what kinds of word collocate with it, what kind of thing is usually mentioned as the subject or object of the verb, and what sort of sentence structure it is used in. For example, the explanation for **map out** says:

If you **map out** a plan or task, you work out in detail how you will do it.

This tells you that a person is usually mentioned as the subject of the verb, whereas the object is usually a word which is similar in meaning to *plan* or *task*. In the same way, the explanation for the first meaning of **keep on** says:

If you **keep on** doing something, you continue to do it and do not stop.

This tells you that you usually use the phrasal verb with the -ing form of a verb. This kind of grammatical information is also given in the Extra Column.

Examples

The dictionary contains a large number of examples taken from the Birmingham Collection of English Texts. They show how speakers and writers of English actually use phrasal verbs. These examples are chosen to illustrate the grammatical patterns associated with the phrasal verbs, and they are generally arranged in the same order as the patterns appear in the Extra Column.

Style and usage

Phrasal verbs are generally more common in spoken or informal English than in written or formal English. When phrasal verbs are only found in very informal contexts, we state this in the explanation. Similarly, we tell you when a particular phrasal verb is only used in formal or technical contexts, or when it is found mainly in either British English or American English.

Synonyms and antonyms

Synonyms are words which mean almost the same as each other, and antonyms are words which mean the opposite. In this dictionary, we give notes on synonyms and antonyms after the explanation and examples. They are introduced by the symbol ●. There are very few cases where two words or expressions mean exactly the same as each other, but you should be able to substitute the synonyms which we give in most contexts, without greatly changing the meaning. We often give another phrasal verb as a synonym, and in this case, you can look up the other word to find out about any differences between them: there may be differences in grammar as well as slight differences in meaning. Many phrasal verbs have synonyms which are single words, but these words are much more formal. The synonym notes give information about this, and about other differences in usage. The antonyms which we give are usually other phrasal verbs, and in most cases these pairs of antonyms describe opposite processes, such as *putting on* and *taking off*, or *coming in* and *going out*.

Derived words

It is quite common in English for nouns and adjectives to be formed by combining verbs and particles, and they are often very closely related to phrasal verbs. For example, if someone makes a *getaway*, they *get away* from a place in a hurry, perhaps after committing a crime. Sometimes the order of verb and particle is reversed: an *off-putting* person is someone who *puts* you *off* or causes you to dislike them. Sometimes both orders are found: *break-out* and *outbreak* are both linked to the phrasal verb *break out*. In this dictionary, we give such nouns and adjectives in the entries for the phrasal verb combinations, so that *getaway* is explained in the entry for **get away**. If they are closely linked with a meaning of the phrasal verb, they appear in the same paragraph, after the examples and any synonym notes, and they are introduced by the symbol ►. If there is not such a clear link, they appear in a paragraph on their own.

Cross-references

Sometimes, verbs can be used with different particles, but the phrasal verb combinations may mean exactly the same as each other. For example, you can often substitute *about* or *around* for *round* without changing the meaning at all. In such cases, we treat the identical meanings together at the commonest form, and put a cross-reference at the less common ones. There may be a difference in formality between the variations: *upon* is generally more formal than *on*, and we mention this in the cross-reference.

The Particles Index

At the end of this dictionary is an index to the particles occurring in the phrasal verbs which we have included. This index explains the common meanings that particles contribute to phrasal verb combinations, and lists the phrasal verbs in which those meanings appear. New phrasal verbs are continually being created, and you may hear or read a combination which we have not included. By using the index, you should be able to understand the meaning of many such new combinations.

Grammar notes in the Extra Column

In this dictionary, grammatical information is given in the Extra Column, to the right of the explanations. The Extra Column shows all the ways in which phrasal verbs are normally used, setting out each pattern on a separate line, with the most frequent patterns first. The following pages explain the meanings of the abbreviations and words in the Extra Column, and how to use the information.

Grammatical information about phrasal verbs is given as a series of patterns. In each pattern, we state the word classes of the words in order, linking them together with +. We use / to indicate alternatives.

The following abbreviations are used in the patterns. They are given in alphabetical order. ADV, N, PREP, PRON, REFL and V are the most important abbreviations as they are used in the basic patterns to give information about verb transitivity and the particles. We explain the meaning of structures with prepositions such as +*to* or +*with* after the other abbreviations. See also pages xiii-xvi, which give further information about phrasal verb syntactic patterns.

A   means adjunct. An adjunct consists of an adverb or prepositional phrase, and usually expresses time, place, manner, or condition. A is used in WITH A or +A to indicate that you use the phrasal verb with an adjunct in addition to the particle in the phrasal verb itself. An example is **go down** 3 which is labelled V+ADV: USUALLY+A: EG *I have to go down to Brighton.*

ADJ   means adjective and it is used in WITH ADJ or +ADJ to indicate that you use an adjective after the phrasal verb.

ADJECTIVE   is used in the Extra Column to indicate that a derived word is used as an adjective.

ADV   means adverb or adverbial particle. It usually refers to the adverb in the phrasal verb headword, but we also sometimes use it when mentioning following structures. ADV/PREP means that the particle can be used as an adverb or preposition, but that it is more often used as an adverb. We usually use this notation when we need to simplify a long list of patterns.

C   means complement. A complement consists of an adjective or noun group, and adds information about the subject of the verb, or sometimes its object. C is used in WITH C or +C to indicate that you use the phrasal verb with a complement.

ERGATIVE   is used to refer to a group of verbs which can be either transitive or intransitive. If the verb is transitive, it links a subject and object, describing how the subject affects or causes a change in the object. If it is intransitive, the subject is the thing that is affected or changed, and there may be no mention of what causes the change. The subject of the verb when it is intransitive refers to the same person or thing as the object of the verb when it is transitive. An example is **pull out** 3: EG *We've invested too much money and manpower to pull out now . . . He pulled his party out of the coalition.*

if   is used in + *if* to indicate that you use the phrasal verb with a clause beginning with the conjunction *if.* An example is **make out** 2 which includes the pattern V+ADV+*if*: EG *I can't make out if Nell likes him or not.*

IMPERATIVE   is used in patterns such as IMPERATIVE: V+ADV to indicate that the phrasal verb is always used in the imperative or in reported imperatives, for example after the verb *tell.* It is used in ALSO IMPERATIVE to indicate that the phrasal verb is often used in the imperative. The imperative form of a verb is its base form, and there is no subject. You use imperatives when you are giving orders, making invitations, reacting to someone else's actions or words, and so on.

-ING   is used in WITH -ING or +-ING to indicate that you use the phrasal verb in a structure with the present participle, or -*ing* form, of another verb. An example is **end up 2** which includes the pattern **V+ADV: WITH -ING** EG *We ended up taking a taxi there.*

it   is used in **V+***it***+ADV** or **V+***it***+PREP** to indicate that the object of the verb must be the pronoun *it.* Note that you cannot use these structures in the passive. An example is **sweat out 1:** EG *He sweated it out to the end.* We give the pattern **V+PREP+***it* when the preposition must be followed by *it.* In these cases, *it* does not have a specific meaning, but is often used to refer vaguely to the general situation. Such expressions are often regarded as idioms, but we include them here for the sake of completeness.

N   means noun group: that is, a phrase consisting of a noun and perhaps a determiner such as *a* or *the* and an adjective. The noun group may also consist of an indefinite pronoun such as *someone, everybody,* or *nothing,* but not a personal pronoun or reflexive pronoun, as these are referred to as **PRON** or **REFL:** see below.

We use **N** in order to show that a verb is transitive, and where you put the adverb in the headword in relation to the object of the verb: **N** refers to the object of the verb. Very often, two possible positions are indicated with two patterns, **V+ADV+N** and **V+N+ADV.** You usually follow the pattern **V+ADV+N** when you want to give a special focus or emphasis to the noun group, for example because the noun group contains new information. You usually follow the pattern **V+N+ADV** when you do not want to give special focus to the noun group, for example because the noun group contains information that has already been given. It is often the case that you follow the pattern **V+ADV+N** when the object or **N** is a long noun group or has a relative clause dependent on it, and you follow the pattern **V+N+ADV** when the object or **N** is fairly short, perhaps consisting of only one or two words. This is because we tend to use short noun groups when we are referring to something which has already been mentioned or whose identity is clear in the situation.

If the particle in the headword is a preposition, you almost always put the object of the verb between the verb and the prepositional phrase, and this is coded as **V+N+PREP.**

Transitive phrasal verbs can be used in the passive unless the Extra Column says **NO PASSIVE.**

N COUNT   is used in the Extra Column to indicate that a derived word is used as a count or countable noun. This means that you can use it in the plural and that if you use it in the singular, you must use a determiner such as *a or the* in front of it. We do not give the plural form unless the -*s* ending is added to the middle of the word rather than to the end.

NEGATIVE   is used in **WITH NEGATIVE** to indicate that you use the phrasal verb in a negative structure. This can mean that the verb is used in the negative, or that the clause contains a negative structure using words such as *hardly, scarcely, or never.* An example is **dream of 1** which is labelled **V+PREP: WITH NEGATIVE:** EG *I wouldn't dream of asking my mother to look after her.*

N PLURAL   is used in the Extra Column to indicate that a derived word is only used in the plural. It does not have a singular form, and you use it with a plural verb.

N SING   is used in the Extra Column to indicate that a derived word does not have a plural form, and that you must use a determiner such as *a* or *the* in front of it. You use it with a singular verb.

NUMBER   is used in **WITH NUMBER** to indicate that you use a number after the phrasal verb.

N UNCOUNT   is used in the Extra Column to indicate that a derived word is used as an uncount or uncountable noun. This means that it does not have a plural form, and that you cannot use it after *a* or *one*. You use it with a singular verb.

PASSIVE   is used in **USUALLY PASSIVE** to indicate that the phrasal verb is usually used in the passive.
It is also used in **NO PASSIVE** to indicate that the phrasal verb is never used in the passive, although it contains a transitive verb.
It is used in **HAS PASSIVE** after a notation such as **V+PREP** or **V+ADV+PREP** in order to indicate that although the verb is intransitive, you can use it in the passive, with the object of the preposition becoming the subject of the verb.
If a phrasal verb is always passive, its pattern is given as **PASSIVE**: **V+ADV**, and so on. We do not mention any object because a verb does not have an object when it is passive.

PREP   means preposition or prepositional particle. You need to put a noun group after the preposition. **PREP/ADV** means that the particle can be used as a preposition or adverb, but that it is more often used as a preposition. We usually use this notation when we need to simplify a long list of patterns.

PRON   means personal pronoun. As the personal pronoun is the object of the verb, you use the object form. The object forms are *me, you, him, her, it, one, us,* and *them.*
If you use a personal pronoun as the object of the verb, you always put it between the verb and its particle.

QUOTE   is used in **+QUOTE** to indicate that you use the phrasal verb as a reporting verb, with direct speech or a quote. An example is **point out 2** which includes the pattern **V+ADV+QUOTE**: EG *'It's a golden opportunity, really,' Johnson pointed out.*

RECIPROCAL   is used to refer to a group of verbs which refer to a relationship or connection between two people or two groups as part of their meaning. If only one person or group is mentioned as the subject of the verb, then you mention the other one after the preposition *with*. You can also mention both people or groups as the subject of the verb. In this case, you do not use the preposition *with*, although you sometimes use the adverb *together*. An example is **join up 1:** EG *We joined up with two young men and went along to a road-house ... The two families joined up for the rest of the holiday.*

REFL   means reflexive pronoun. The reflexive pronouns are *myself, yourself, himself, herself, itself, oneself, ourselves, yourselves,* and *themselves.* You use a reflexive pronoun when the object of the verb refers to the same person or thing as the subject of the verb, and you put it between the verb and its particle.
We give the pattern **V+PREP+REFL** when the preposition must be followed by a reflexive pronoun.

REPORT   is used in **+REPORT** to indicate that you use the phrasal verb as a reporting verb, with indirect speech or a reported clause, usually beginning with the conjunction *that*. An example is **find out 1** which includes the pattern **V+ADV+REPORT**: EG *I've just found out that I won't have to start until Wednesday.*

to-INF   is used in **+ *to*-INF** or **WITH *to*-INF** to indicate that you use the phrasal verb in a structure with *to* and the infinitive, or base form, of another verb. An example is **set out 2** which has the pattern **V+ADV+*to*-INF**: EG *This chapter sets out to explain some of the relevant terms and principles.*

V   means verb. It refers to the verb in the phrasal verb headword. You normally need to use a subject with the verb, unless the verb is imperative.

VERB   is used in **WITH VERB** to indicate that you use another verb after the phrasal verb.

WH   is used in **+WH** to indicate that you use the phrasal verb with a clause beginning with a **WH**-word: *who, what, when, where, whom, whose, how, why, which,* or *whether. An example is* **make out 2** which includes the pattern **V+ADV+WH**: EG *Sylvia could not make out how it had happened.*

to, with, from, on, etc   The patterns sometimes mention a particular preposition. In these cases, the phrasal verb is often used with the preposition in the structures mentioned. For example, the Extra Column notes may say **USUALLY+*to*** or **ALSO+*of*** to indicate that a phrasal verb is usually followed by *to*, or often followed by *of*.

Phrasal Verb
Syntactic Patterns

You can find out how to use phrasal verbs grammatically by looking at the patterns in the Extra Column. Most phrasal verbs have two or more patterns. The Extra Column shows all the possible patterns, with each pattern appearing on a separate line. They are mainly given in frequency order: that is, the commonest pattern appears first. However, we group transitive patterns separately from intransitive ones. The patterns are usually separated by a comma (,) or sometimes with **OR**. An example is **give up 2**, which is labelled:

    V+ADV+N,
    V+PRON+ADV,
    V+ADV

The patterns give information on the following points:

1 Verb transitivity

Verbs can be transitive or intransitive: that is, some verbs have objects and others do not.

If the verb is transitive, the pattern will include **N, PRON**, or **REFL**, and you need to use an object with the verb. Examples are **take out** 3 which includes the pattern V+N+ADV, **add up** 1, which includes the pattern V+ADV+N, **call in** 1 which includes the pattern V+PRON+ADV, and **shut away** 2, which is labelled V+REFL+ADV.

V+N+ADV means that the verb has an object (N), and that the object must come in front of the adverb (ADV): EG *I took Andrea out to dinner one evening.*

V+ADV+N means that the verb has an object (N), and that the object comes after the adverb (ADV): EG *First, add up all your regular payments.*

V+PRON+ADV means that the verb must have an object which can be a personal pronoun (PRON), and that the object comes in front of the adverb (ADV): EG *They called me in for questioning.*

V+REFL+ADV means that the verb has an object which must be a reflexive pronoun (REFL), and that the object must come in front of the adverb (ADV): EG *I shut myself away in a library that night and wrote a letter.*

You can use transitive phrasal verbs in the passive unless the Extra Column includes the note NO PASSIVE.

If the verb is intransitive, the pattern will not include N, PRON, or REFL. For example, the pattern given at **shut up** 1 is V+ADV, so you know that the verb does not have an object.

If the verb is sometimes transitive and sometimes intransitive, both transitive and intransitive patterns will be given in the Extra Column.

A few phrasal verbs are ditransitive. That is, they are used with two objects: a direct object and an indirect object. The patterns for ditransitive phrasal verbs include both objects. The first object mentioned is the indirect one and the second is the direct object. For example, **hand back** 1 includes the pattern V+PRON+ADV+N. This means that the adverb comes between the indirect object, which must be a pronoun, and the direct object, which must be a full noun group. EG *The girl handed him back his card.*

2 Word-classes of particles

The particles in phrasal verbs are sometimes adverbial and sometimes prepositional. If the particle is a preposition, you need a noun group after it. This noun group is called a prepositional object: do not confuse it with the object of a verb.

If the particle is an adverb, the pattern will include ADV. If the particle is a preposition, the pattern will include PREP. Examples are: **move off,** which is labelled V+ADV: EG *The fleet of cars prepared to move off.* . . and **rely on** 1, which is labelled V+PREP: EG *She is forced to rely on her mother's money.*

If the particle can be used either as an adverb or a preposition, then this is shown as two separate patterns. An example is **come in** 1 which is labelled V+ADV, V+PREP. This means that the particle *in* can be used as an adverb: EG *Jeremy came in looking worried.* . . or as a preposition: EG *'Come in the house,' she said.*

In cases where there is a large number of patterns, we sometimes combine the patterns and say: ADV/PREP or PREP/ADV. This means that the particle can be either an adverb or a preposition. The order of the two particles reflects their frequency: the more frequent of the two is placed first. An example is **put on** 4 which includes the pattern V+N+ADV/PREP: EG *She put lipstick on before every class.* . . *They must have put ointment on my burns.*

If there are two particles in the phrasal verb, the Extra Column will say ADV+PREP or ADV+ADV in the same order as the two particles. Examples are: **catch up with,** where *up* is an adverb and *with* is a preposition, and **put back on,** where both *back* and *on* are adverbs.

3 Positioning of particles

If the verb is transitive, you need to know where to put the particle in relation to the object. Does the particle come between the verb and the object of the verb, or does it follow the object?

You can see where to put the particle by looking at the order of elements in the patterns. Each possible position for the particle is shown. For example, if the Extra Column has V+ADV+N, you put the particle between the verb and its object. An example is **clean out 1**: EG *I was cleaning out my desk at the office.*

If it has V+N+ADV, you put the particle after the object. **Clean out 1** also has the pattern V+N+ADV: EG *I spent three days cleaning our flat out.*

If several patterns are given for a phrasal verb, you can follow any of them. In most cases, an adverb can come in front of or after the object, as in **clean out 1**. You choose where to put the object and adverb in relation to one another according to whether the object contains new information or whether it refers to something that is already known. The explanation of the abbreviation N on page xi gives guidance on this.

Some phrasal verbs are only found in one pattern, for example **put up 6**, which is labelled simply V+ADV+N: EG *We had put up a fierce struggle.* If only one pattern is given, you should follow that pattern.

If the object is a pronoun, then you always put the adverb after the object. This is shown as V+PRON+ADV. An example is **set down 1**: EG *The Colonel lifted his cup, glared at it, set it down again.*

4 Additional structures

In many cases, there are particular structures which you have to use with the phrasal verb. The Extra Column shows this information after listing the patterns. Usually this information is introduced by a colon (:). An example is **stick at 3**, which is labelled V+PREP: WITH NEGATIVE. This means that the verb is intransitive, has a preposition, and is always used in the negative or with a negative word somewhere near it.

If a structure is not compulsory, we indicate this with USUALLY or ALSO. USUALLY means that the phrasal verb is usually used in this structure. ALSO means that this structure often occurs, but is optional. Examples are **head back,** which is labelled V+ADV: USUALLY+A, and **lock out 2,** which is labelled V+REFL+ADV: ALSO+*of.* **Head back** is usually, though not always, followed by an adjunct of some kind, and **lock out** is often followed by a prepositional phrase beginning with *of.*

The following sequences of patterns are the commonest ones which occur in the Collins Cobuild Dictionary of Phrasal Verbs. Sequences of patterns have been counted as a single type if the only difference between them is the order in which they are listed, or the particular compulsory structure which is mentioned. All these patterns occur twenty or more times. This means that a very few basic pattern types account for most cases.

In each case, the frequency of the pattern is given, followed by the notation as it might appear in the Extra Column, and an explanation of the notation.

1267	V+ADV+N, V+N+ADV, V+PRON+ADV	transitive verb with adverb, adverb may follow or precede object
1148	V+ADV	intransitive verb with adverb
581	V+PREP	intransitive verb with preposition

255	V+PREP: HAS PASSIVE	intransitive verb with preposition. The verb can have a passive, with the object of the preposition becoming the subject of the passive verb
215	V+N+PREP, V+PRON+PREP	transitive verb with preposition
194	V+N+ADV, V+PRON+ADV	transitive verb with adverb, the adverb must follow the object
192	V+ADV+PREP	intransitive verb with adverb and preposition
130	V+ADV, V+PREP	intransitive verb with particle which can function as an adverb or a preposition
97	V+ADV+N, V+PRON+ADV	transitive verb with adverb: the adverb must precede object when the object is a full noun group, and follow it if it is a personal pronoun
92	V+ADV, V+N+ADV, V+PRON+ADV, V+ADV+N: ERGATIVE	ergative verb with adverb, adverb may precede or follow object when present (See notes above on ERGATIVE)
73	V+ADV+N	transitive verb with adverb and full noun group as object: adverb must precede object
64	PASSIVE: V+ADV	passive verb with adverb. The verb is always passive, and the particle is an adverb.
52	V+ADV: WITH A [etc]	intransitive verb with adverb and a compulsory following structure such as an adjunct.
25	PASSIVE: V+PREP	passive with a preposition. The verb is always passive, and the particle is a preposition.
25	V+ADV, V+N+ADV, V+PRON+ADV: ERGATIVE	ergative verb with adverb, adverb can come only after the object when present (see notes above on ERGATIVE)
24	V+N+ADV+PREP, V+PRON+ADV+PREP	transitive verb with adverb followed by preposition; object can be noun group or pronoun and must come in front of the adverb.
24	V+ADV+N, V+N+ADV	transitive verb with adverb and full noun group as object: adverb may precede or follow object
23	V+N+PREP	transitive verb with preposition and full noun group as object of verb
20	V+N+PREP, V+PRON+PREP, V+REFL+PREP	transitive verb with preposition; object can be noun group, pronoun, or reflexive pronoun and must come in front of the preposition.

Corpus Acknowledgements

We wish to thank the following, who have kindly given permission for the use of copyright material in the Birmingham Collection of English Texts.

Associated Business Programmes Ltd for: *The Next 200 Years* by Herman Kahn with William Brown and Leon Martel first published in Great Britain by Associated Business Programmes Ltd 1977 © Hudson Institute 1976. David Attenborough and William Collins Sons & Co Ltd for: *Life on Earth* by David Attenborough first published by William Collins Sons & Co Ltd 1979 © David Attenborough Productions Ltd 1979. James Baldwin for: *The Fire Next Time* by James Baldwin published in Great Britain by Michael Joseph Ltd 1963 © James Baldwin 1963. B T Batsford Ltd for: *Witchcraft in England* by Christina Hole first published by B T Batsford Ltd 1945 © Christina Hole 1945. Michael Billington for: 'Lust at First Sight' by Michael Billington in the *Illustrated London News* July 1981 and 'Truffaut's Tolerance' by Michael Billington in the *Illustrated London News* August 1981. Birmingham International Council For Overseas Students' Aid for: BICOSA Information Leaflets 1981. Basil Blackwell Publishers Ltd for: *Breaking the Mould? The Birth and Prospects of the Social Democratic Party* by Ian Bradley first published by Martin Robertson & Co Ltd 1981 © Ian Bradley 1981. *Seeing Green (The Politics of Ecology Explained)* by Jonathon Porritt first published by Basil Blackwell Publisher Ltd 1984 © Jonathon Porritt 1984. Blond & Briggs Ltd for: *Small is Beautiful* by E F Schumacher first published in Great Britain by Blond & Briggs Ltd 1973 © E F Schumacher 1973. The Bodley Head Ltd for: *The Americans (Letters from America 1969-1979)* by Alistair Cooke first published by Bodley Head Ltd 1979 © Alistair Cooke 1979. *Baby and Child Care* by Dr Benjamin Spock published in Great Britain by The Bodley Head Ltd 1955 © Benjamin Spock MD 1945, 1946, 1957, 1968, 1976, 1979. *What's Wrong With The Modern World?* by Michael Shanks first published by The Bodley Head Ltd 1978 © Michael Shanks 1978. *Future Shock* by Alvin Toffler first published in Great Britain by The Bodley Head Ltd 1970 © Alvin Toffler 1970. *Zen and the Art of Motorcycle Maintenance* by Robert M Pirsig first published in Great Britain by The Bodley Head Ltd 1974 © Robert M Pirsig 1974. *Marnie* by Winston Graham first published by the Bodley Head Ltd 1961 © Winston Graham 1961. *You Can Get There From Here* by Shirley MacLaine first published in Great Britain by The Bodley Head Ltd 1975 © Shirley MacLaine 1975. *It's An Odd Thing, But ...* by Paul Jennings first published by Max Reinhardt Ltd 1971 © Paul Jennings 1971. *King of the Castle (Choice and Responsibility in the Modern World)* by Gai Eaton first published by the Bodley Head Ltd 1977 © Gai Eaton 1977. *Revolutionaries in Modern Britain* by Peter Shipley first published by The Bodley Head Ltd 1976 © Peter Shipley 1976. *The Prerogative of the Harlot (Press Barons and Power)* by Hugh Cudlipp first published by The Bodley Head Ltd 1980 © Hugh Cudlipp 1980. *But What About The Children (A Working Parents' Guide to Child Care)* by Judith Hann first published by The Bodley Head Ltd 1976 © Judith Hann 1976. *Learning to Read* by Margaret Meek first published by The Bodley Head Ltd 1982 © Margaret Meek 1982. Bolt & Watson for: *Two is Lonely* by Lynne Reid Banks first published by Chatto & Windus 1974 © Lynne Reid Banks 1974. The British and Foreign Bible Society with William Collins Sons & Co Ltd for: *Good News Bible (with Deuterocanonical Books/Apocrypha)* first published by The British and Foreign Bible Society with William Collins Sons & Co Ltd 1979 © American Bible Society: Old Testament 1976, Deuterocanonical Books/Apocrypha 1979, New Testament 1966, 1971, 1976 © Maps, British and Foreign Bible Society 1976, 1979. The British Council for: *How to Live in Britain (The British Council's Guide for Overseas Students and Visitors)* first published by The British Council 1952 © The British Council 1984. Mrs R Bronowski for: *The Ascent of Man* by J Bronowski published by Book Club Associates by arrangement with The British Broadcasting Corporation 1977 © J Bronowski 1973. Alison Busby for: *The Death of Trees* by Nigel Dudley first published by Pluto Press Ltd 1985 © Nigel Dudley 1985. Tony Buzan for: *Make The Most of your Mind* by Tony Buzan first published by Colt Books Ltd 1977 © Tony Buzan 1977. Campbell Thomson & McLaughlin Ltd for: *Ring of Bright Water* by Gavin Maxwell first published by Longmans Green & Co 1960, published in Penguin Books Ltd 1976 © The Estate of Gavin Maxwell 1960. Jonathan Cape Ltd for: *Manwatching (A Field Guide to Human Behaviour)* by Desmond Morris first published in Great Britain by Jonathan Cape Ltd 1977 © Text, Desmond Morris 1977 © Compilation, Elsevier Publishing

Projects SA, Lausanne, and Jonathan Cape Ltd, London 1977. *Tracks* by Robyn Davidson first published by Jonathan Cape Ltd 1980 © Robyn Davidson 1980. *In the Name of Love* by Jill Tweedie first published by Jonathan Cape Ltd 1979 © Jill Tweedie 1979. *The Use of Lateral Thinking* by Edward de Bono first published by Jonathan Cape 1967 © Edward de Bono 1967. *Trout Fishing in America* by Richard Brautigan first published in Great Britain by Jonathan Cape Ltd 1970 © Richard Brautigan 1967. *The Pendulum Years: Britain and the Sixties* by Bernard Levin first published by Jonathan Cape Ltd 1970 © Bernard Levin 1970. *The Summer Before The Dark* by Doris Lessing first published in Great Britain by Jonathan Cape Ltd 1973 © Doris Lessing 1973. *The Boston Strangler* by Gerold Frank first published in Great Britain by Jonathan Cape Ltd 1967 © Gerold Frank 1966. *I'm OK - You're OK* by Thomas A Harris MD first published in Great Britain as The Book of Choice by Jonathan Cape Ltd 1970 © Thomas A Harris MD, 1967, 1968, 1969. *The Vivisector* by Patrick White first published by Jonathan Cape Ltd 1970 © Patrick White 1970. *The Future of Socialism* by Anthony Crosland first published by Jonathan Cape Ltd 1956 © C A R Crosland 1963. *Funeral in Berlin* by Len Deighton first published by Jonathan Cape Ltd 1964 © Len Deighton 1964. Chatto & Windus Ltd for: *A Postillion Struck by Lightning* by Dirk Bogarde first published by Chatto & Windus Ltd 1977 © Dirk Bogarde 1977. *Nuns and Soldiers* by Iris Murdoch published by Chatto & Windus Ltd 1980 © Iris Murdoch 1980. *Wounded Knee (An Indian History of the American West)* by Dee Brown published by Chatto & Windus Ltd 1978 © Dee Brown 1970. *The Virgin in the Garden* by A S Byatt published by Chatto & Windus Ltd 1978 © A S Byatt 1978. *A Story Like The Wind* by Laurens van der Post published by Clarke Irwin & Co Ltd in association with The Hogarth Press Ltd 1972 © Laurens van der Post 1972. *Brave New World* by Aldous Huxley published by Chatto & Windus Ltd 1932 © Aldous Huxley and Mrs Laura Huxley 1932, 1960. *The Reivers* by William Faulkner first published by Chatto & Windus Ltd 1962 © William Faulkner 1962. *Cider With Rosie* by Laurie Lee published by The Hogarth Press 1959 © Laurie Lee 1959 *The Tenants* by Bernard Malamud first published in Great Britain by Chatto & Windus Ltd 1972 © Bernard Malamud 1971. *Kinflicks* by Lisa Alther first published in Great Britain by Chatto & Windus Ltd 1976 © Lisa Alther 1975. William Collins Sons & Co Ltd for: *The Companion Guide to London* by David Piper published by William Collins Sons & Co Ltd 1964 © David Piper 1964. *The Bedside Guardian 29* edited by W L Webb published by William, Collins & Sons Ltd 1980 © Guardian Newspapers Ltd 1980. *Bear Island* by Alistair MacLean first published by William Collins Sons & Co Ltd 1971 © Alistair MacLean 1971. *Inequality in Britain: Freedom, Welfare and the State* by Frank Field first published by Fontana Paperbacks 1981 © Frank Field 1981. *Social Mobility* by Anthony Heath first published by Fontana Paperbacks 1981©Anthony Heath 1981. *Yours Faithfully* by Gerald Priestland first published by Fount Paperbacks 1979 © British Broadcasting Corporation 1977, 1978. *Power Without Responsibility: The Press and Broadcasting in Britain* by James Curran and Jean Seaton first published by Fontana Paperbacks 1981 © James Curran and Jean Seaton 1981. *The Times Cookery Book* by Katie Stewart first published by William Collins Sons & Co Ltd 1972 © Times Newspapers Ltd. *Friends from the Forest* by Joy Adamson by Collins and Harvill Press 1981 © Elsa Limited 1981. *The Media Mob* by Barry Fantoni and George Melly first published by William Collins Sons & Co Ltd 1980 © Text, George Melly 1980 © Illustrations, Barry Fantoni 1980. *Shalom (a collection of Australian and Jewish Stories)* compiled by Nancy Keesing first published by William Collins Publishers Pty Ltd 1978 © William Collins Sons &Co Ltd 1978. *The Bedside Guardian 31* edited by W L Webb first published by William Collins Sons & Co Ltd 1982 © Guardian Newspapers Ltd 1982. *The Bedside Guardian 32* edited by W L Webb first published by William Collins Sons & Co Ltd 1983 © Guardian Newspapers Ltd 1983. *Design for the Real World* by Victor Papanek first published in Great Britain by Thames & Hudson Ltd 1972 © Victor Papanek 1971. *Food For Free* by Richard Mabey first published by William Collins Sons & Co Ltd 1972 © Richard Mabey 1972. *Unended Quest* by Karl Popper (first published as Autobiography of Karl Popper in The Philosophy of Karl Popper in The Library of Philosophers edited by Paul Arthur Schlipp by the Open Court Publishing Co 1974) published by Fontana Paperbacks 1976 © The Library of Living Philosophers Inc 1974 © Karl R Popper 1976. *My Mother My Self* by Nancy Friday first published in Great Britain by Fontana Paperbacks 1979 © Nancy Friday 1977. *The Captain's*

Diary by Bob Willis first published by Willow Books/William Collins Sons & Co Ltd 1984 © Bob Willis and Alan Lee 1984 © New Zealand Scorecards, Bill Frindall 1984. *The Bodywork Book* by Esme Newton-Dunn first published in Great Britain by Willow Books/William Collins Sons & Co Ltd 1982 © TVS Ltd/Esme Newton-Dunn 1982. *Collins' Encyclopaedia of Fishing in The British Isles* edited by Michael Prichard first published by William Collins Sons & Co Ltd 1976 © William Collins Sons & Co Ltd 1976. *The AAA Runner's Guide* edited by Heather Thomas first published by William Collins Sons & Co Ltd 1983 © Sackville Design Group Ltd 1983. *Heroes and Contemporaries* by David Gower with Derek Hodgson first published by William Collins Sons & Co Ltd 1983 © David Gower Promotions Ltd 1983. *The Berlin Memorandum* by Adam Hall first published by William Collins Sons & Co Ltd 1965 © Jonquil Trevor 1965. *Arlott on Cricket: His Writings on the Game* edited by David Rayvern Allen first published by William Collins (Willow Books) 1984 © John Arlott 1984. *A Woman in Custody* by Audrey Peckham first published by Fontana Paperbacks 1985 © Audrey Peckham 1985. *Play Golf with Peter Alliss* by Peter Alliss published by the British Broadcasting Corporation 1977 © Peter Alliss and Renton Laidlaw 1977. Curtis Brown Ltd for: *The Pearl* by John Steinbeck first published by William Heinemann Ltd 1948 © John Steinbeck 1948. *An Unfinished History of the World* by Hugh Thomas first published in Great Britain by Hamish Hamilton Ltd 1979 © Hugh Thomas 1979, 1981. *The Winter of our Discontent* by John Steinbeck first published in Great Britain by William Heinemann Ltd 1961 © John Steinbeck 1961. *Burr* by Gore Vidal first published in Great Britain by William Heinemann Ltd 1974 © Gore Vidal 1974. *Doctor on the Job* by Richard Gordon first published by William Heinemann Ltd 1976 © Richard Gordon Ltd 1976. *Andre Deutsch Ltd for: How to be an Alien* by George Mikes first published by Andre Deutsch Ltd 1946 © George Mikes and Nicholas Bentley 1946. *Jaws* by Peter Benchley first published in Great Britain by Andre Deutsch Ltd 1974 © Peter Benchley 1974. *A Bend in the River* by V S Naipaul first published by Andre Deutsch Ltd 1979 © V S Naipaul 1979. *Couples* by John Updike first published by Andre Deutsch Ltd 1968 © John Updike 1968. *Games People Play* by Eric Berne published in Great Britain by Andre Deutsch Ltd 1966 © Eric Berne 1964. *The Age of Uncertainty* by John Kenneth Galbraith first published by The British Broadcasting Corporation and Andre Deutsch Ltd 1977 © John Kenneth Galbraith 1977. The Economist Newspaper Ltd for: *The Economist* (9-15 May 1981 and 22-28 August 1981) © published by The Economist Newspaper Ltd 1981. Faber & Faber Ltd for: *Lord of the Flies* by William Golding first published by Faber & Faber Ltd 1954 © William Golding 1954. *The Complete Book of Self-Sufficiency* by John Seymour first published in Great Britain by Faber & Faber Ltd 1976 © Text, John Seymour 1976, 1977 © Dorling Kindersley Ltd 1976, 1977. *Conversations with Igor Stravinsky* by Igor Stravinsky and Robert Craft first published by Faber & Faber Ltd 1959 © Igor Stravinsky 1958,1959. John Farquharson Ltd for: *The Moon's A Balloon* by David Niven published in Great Britain by Hamish Hamilton Ltd 1971 © David Niven 1971. John Gaselee for: 'Going it Alone' by John Gaselee in the *Illustrated London News* July 1981 and 'The Other Car's Fault' by John Gaselee in the *Illustrated London News* August 1981. Glidrose Publications Ltd for: *The Man with the Golden Gun* by Ian Fleming first published by Jonathan Cape Ltd © Glidrose Productions Ltd 1965. Victor Gollancz Ltd for: *The Next Horizon* by Chris Bonnington published by Victor Gollancz Ltd 1976 © Chris Bonnington 1973. *Summerhill: A Radical Approach to Education* by A S Neill first published by Victor Gollancz Ltd 1962 © A S Neill 1926, 1932, 1937, 1953, 1961 (US permission by Hart Publishing Inc). *Lucky Jim* by Kingsley Amis first published by Victor Gollancz Ltd 1954 © Kingsley Amis 1953. *The Mighty Micro (The Impact of the Computer Revolution)* by Christopher Evans first published by Victor Gollancz Ltd 1979 © Christopher Evans 1979. *The Longest Day* by Cornelius Ryan published by Victor Gollancz Ltd 1960 © Cornelius Ryan 1959. *Asking for Trouble (Autobiography of a Banned Journalist)* by Donald Woods published by Victor Gollancz Ltd 1980 © Donald Woods 1980. *The Turin Shroud* by Ian Wilson first published in Great Britain by Victor Gollancz Ltd 1978 © Ian Wilson 1978. *Murdo and Other Stories* by Iain Crichton Smith published by Victor Gollancz Ltd 1981 © Iain Crichton Smith 1981. *The Class Struggle in Parliament* by Eric S Heffer published by Victor Gollancz Ltd 1973 © Eric S Heffer 1973. *A Presumption of Innocence (The Amazing Case of Patrick Meehan)* by Ludovic Kennedy published by Victor Gollancz Ltd 1976 © Ludovic Kennedy 1976. *The Treasure of Sainte Foy* by MacDonald Harris published by Victor Gollancz Ltd 1980 © MacDonald Harris 1980. *A Long Way to Shiloh* by Lionel Davidson first published by Victor Gollancz Ltd 1966 © Lionel Davidson 1966. *Education After School* by Tyrrell

Burgess first published by Victor Gollancz Ltd 1977 © Tyrrell Burgess 1977. *The View From Serendip* by Arthur C Clarke published by Victor Gollancz Ltd 1978 © Arthur C Clarke 1967, 1968, 1970, 1972, 1974, 1976, 1977. *On Wings of Song* by Thomas M Disch published by Victor Gollancz Ltd 1979 © Thomas M Disch 1979. *The World of Violence* by Colin Wilson published by Victor Gollancz Ltd 1963 © Colin Wilson 1963. *The Lightning Tree* by Joan Aiken published by Victor Gollancz Ltd 1980 © Joan Aiken Enterprises 1980. *Russia's Political Hospitals* by Sidney Bloch and Peter Reddaway published by Victor Gollancz Ltd 1977 © Sidney Bloch and Peter Reddaway 1977. *Unholy Loves* by Joyce Carol Oates first published in Great Britain by Victor Gollancz Ltd 1980 © Joyce Carol Oates 1979. *Consenting Adults (or The Duchess will be Furious)* by Peter De Vries published by Victor Gollancz Ltd 1981 © Peter De Vries 1980. *The Passion of New Eve* by Angela Carter published by Victor Gollancz Ltd 1977 © Angela Carter 1977. Gower Publishing Co Ltd for: *Solar Prospects (The Potential for Renewable Energy)* by Michael Flood first published in Great Britain by Wildwood House Ltd in association with Friends of the Earth Ltd 1983 © Michael Flood. *Voiceless Victims* by Rebecca Hall first published in Great Britain by Wildwood House Ltd 1984 © Rebecca Hall 1984. Graham Greene and Laurence Pollinger Ltd for: *The Human Factor* by Graham Greene first published by The Bodley Head Ltd 1978 © Graham Greene 1978. Syndication Manager, The Guardian, for: *The Guardian* (12 May 1981, 7 September 1981 and 15 September 1981) © published by Guardian Newspapers Ltd 1981. Hamlyn for: *How to Play Rugby* by David Norrie published by The Hamlyn Publishing Group Ltd 1981 © The Hamlyn Publishing Group Ltd 1981. *How to Play Badminton* by Pat Davies first published by The Hamlyn Publishing Group Ltd 1979 © The Hamlyn Publishing Group Ltd 1979. Margaret Hanbury for: *Crisis and Conservation: Conflict in the British Countryside* by Charlie Pye-Smith and Chris Rose first published by Pelican/Penguin Books Ltd 1984 © Charlie Pye-Smith and Chris Rose 1984. Paul Harrison for: *Inside the Third World* by Paul Harrison first published in Great Britain by The Harvester Press Ltd 1980 © Paul Harrison 1979. A M Heath & Co Ltd for: *Rembrandt's Hat* by Bernard Malamud published by Chatto & Windus Ltd 1982 © Bernard Malamud 1968, 1972, 1973. William Heinemann Ltd for: *It's an Old Country* by J B Priestley first published in Great Britain by William Heinemann Ltd 1967 © J B Priestley 1967. Heinemann Educational Books Ltd and Gower Publishing Co Ltd for: *The Environmental Crisis (A Handbook for all Friends of the Earth)* edited by Des Wilson first published by Heinemann Educational Books Ltd 1984 © Foreword, David Bellamy 1984 © Individual Chapters, the Author of the Chapter 1984 © In the selection and all other matters Des Wilson 1984. The Controller, Her Majesty's Stationery Office, for: Department of Health and Social Security leaflets published by Her Majesty's Stationery Office 1981 © The Crown. David Higham Associates Ltd for: 'Two Peruvian Projects' by E R Chamberlain in the *Illustrated London News* September 1981. *Akenfield: Portrait of an English Village* by Ronald Blythe first published by Allen Lane, Penguin Books Ltd 1969 © Ronald Blythe 1969. *The Far Pavillions* by M M Kaye first published by Allen Lane/Penguin Books Ltd 1978 © M M Kaye 1978. *Staying On* by Paul Scott first published by William Heinemann Ltd 1977 © Paul Scott 1977. *Let Sleeping Vets Lie* by James Herriot first published by Michael Joseph Ltd 1973 © James Herriot 1973. *The Midwich Cuckoos* by John Wyndham first published in Great Britain by Michael Joseph Ltd 1957 © The Estate of John Wyndham 1957. *The Girl in a Swing* by Richard Adams first published in Great Britain by Allen Lane in Penguin Books Ltd 1980 © Richard Adams 1980. Dr K B Hindley for: 'Hot Spots of the Deep' by Dr K B Hindley in the *Illustrated London News July* 1981. Hodder and Stoughton Ltd for: *Supernature* by Lyall Watson first published by Hodder & Stoughton Ltd 1973 © Lyall Watson 1973. *Tinker Tailor Soldier Spy* by John Le Carre first published by Hodder & Stoughton Ltd 1974 © Le Carre Productions 1974. The Editor, Homes and Gardens, for: *Homes and Gardens* (October 1981) (Number 4 Volume 63) © published by IPC Magazines Ltd 1981. Hughes Massie Ltd for: *Elephants Can Remember* by Agatha Christie first published by William Collins Sons & Co Ltd 1972 © Agatha Christie Mallowan. Hutchinson Publishing Group Ltd for: *An Autobiography* by Angela Davis published in Great Britain by Hutchinson & Co Publishers Ltd by arrangement with Bantam Books Inc 1975 © Angela Davis 1974. *The Day of the Jackal* by Frederick Forsyth published in Great Britian by Hutchinson & Co Publishers Ltd 1971 © Frederick Forsyth 1971. *Roots* by Alex Haley first published in Great Britain by Hutchinson & Co Publishers Ltd 1977 © Alex Haley 1976. *The Climate of Treason* by Andrew Boyle first published by Hutchinson & Co Publishers Ltd 1979 © Andrew Boyle 1979. *The Collapsing Universe: The Story of Black Holes* by Isaac Asimov first published by Hutchinson & Co Publishers Ltd 1977 © Isaac Asimov. *XPD* by Len Deighton published by Book Club Associates by arrangement with Hutchinson & Co Publishers Ltd 1981 © Len Deighton 1981. *Show Jumping with Harvey Smith* by Harvey Smith first published by Stanley Paul & Co Ltd 1979 © Tyne-Tees Television Ltd, A Member of the Trident Group 1979. *2001: A Space Odyssey* by Arthur C Clarke first published by Hutchinson & Co Publishers Ltd 1968 © Arthur C Clarke and Polaris Productions Inc 1968 © Epilogue material, Serendip BV 1982, 1983. The Illustrated London News and Sketch Ltd for: *The Illustrated London News* (July 1981, August 1981 and September 1981) © published by the Illustrated London News and Sketch Ltd 1981. The Editor, International Herald Tribune, for: *International Herald Tribune* (25-26 July 1981) © published by International Herald Tribune with The New York Times and The Washington Post 1981. Michael Joseph Ltd for: *Chronicles of Fairacre: Village School* by Miss Read first published in Great Britain by Michael Joseph Ltd 1964 © Miss Read 1955, 1964. *Fire Fox* by Craig Thomas first published in Great Britain by Michael Joseph Ltd 1977 © Craig Thomas 1977. William Kimber & Co Ltd for: *Exodus* by Leon Uris originally published in Great Britain by Alan Wingate Ltd 1959 © Leon Uris 1958. Kogan Page Ltd for: *How to Save the World (Strategy for World Conservation)* by Robert Allen first published by Kogan Page Ltd 1980 © IUCN-UNEP-WWF 1980. Marketing Department, Lloyds Bank PLC, for: *Lloyds Bank Leaflets* (1981) © published by Lloyds Bank PLC 1981. Macmillan Publishers Ltd for: *Appropriate Technology: Technology with a Human Face* by P D Dunn first published by the Macmillan Press Ltd 1978 © P D Dunn 1978. John Murray Publishers Ltd for: *A Backward Place* by Ruth Prawer Jhabvala first published by John Murray Publishers Ltd 1965 © R Prawer Jhabvala 1965. *Food For All The Family* by Magnus Pyke first published by John Murray Publishers Ltd 1980 © Magnus Pyke 1980. *Simple Movement* by Laura Mitchell and Barbara Dale first published by John Murray Publishers Ltd 1980 © Laura Mitchell and Barbara Dale 1980. *Civilisation: A Personal View* by Kenneth Clark first published by the British Broadcasting Corporation and John Murray Publishers Ltd 1969 © Kenneth Clark 1969. The Editor, National Geographic, for: *National Geographic* January, February and March (1980) © published by The National Geographic Society 1979, 1980. The National Magazine Co Ltd for: *Cosmopolitan* (May 1981 and July 1981) © published by the National Magazine Co Ltd 1981. Neilson Leisure Group Ltd for: *NAT Holidays' 'Caravans and Tents in the Sun'* (Summer 1983) holiday brochure. Newsweek Inc for: *Newsweek* (11 May 1981, 27 July 1981 and August 1981) © published by Newsweek Inc 1981. The Associate Editor, Now!, for: *Now!* (14-20 November 1980) © published by Cavenham Communications Ltd 1980. Harold Ober Associates Inc for: *The Boys from Brazil* by Ira Levin first published by Michael Joseph Ltd 1976 © Ira Levin 1976. Edna O'Brien and A M Heath & Co Ltd for: *August is a Wicked Month* by Edna O'Brien first published by Jonathan Cape Ltd 1965 © Edna O'Brien 1965. Pan Books Ltd for: *Dispatches* by Michael Herr first published in Great Britain by Pan Books Ltd 1978 © Michael Herr 1968, 1969, 1970, 1977. *Health and Safety at Work* by Dave Eva and Ron Oswald first published by Pan Books Ltd 1981 © Dave Eva, Ron Oswald and the Workers' Educational Association 1981. *Democracy at Work* by Patrick Burns and Mel Doyle first published by Pan Books Ltd 1981 © Patrick Burns,Mel Doyle and the Workers' Educational Association 1981. *Diet for Life (A Cookbook for Arthritics)* by Mary Laver and Margaret Smith first published by Pan Books Ltd 1981 © Mary Laver and Margaret Smith 1981. Penguin Books Ltd for: *Inside the Company: CIA Diary* by Philip Agee first published in Allen Lane/Penguin Books Ltd 1975 © Philip Agee 1975. Penguin Books Ltd and Spare Ribs Ltd for: *Spare Rib Reader* edited by Marsha Rowe first published in Penguin Books Ltd 1982 © Spare Ribs Ltd 1982. A D Peters & Co Ltd for: 'The Dark Side of Israel' by Norman Moss in Illustrated London News July 1981, 'Aftermath of Osirak' by Norman Moss in the *Illustrated London News* August 1981 and 'Turning Point for Poland' by Norman Moss in the *Illustrated London News* September 1981. 'Recent Fiction' by Sally Emerson in the *Illustrated London News* July 1981, August 1981 and September 1981. *The Complete Upmanship* by Stephen Potter first published in Great Britain by Rupert Hart-Davis Ltd 1970 © Stephen Potter. Elaine Pollard for: Personal Letters 1981 donated by Elaine Pollard. Laurence Pollinger Ltd for: *A Glastonbury Romance* by John Cowper Powys first published by MacDonald & Co Ltd 1933. Murray Pollinger for: *Kiss Kiss* by Roald Dahl published in Great Britain by Michael Joseph Ltd 1960 © Roald Dahl 1962. *Can You Avoid Cancer?* by Peter Goodwin first published by the British Broadcasting Corporation 1984 © Peter Goodwin 1984. Preston Travel Ltd for: Preston Sunroutes 'Camping and Self-Catering' (April to October 1983)

holiday brochure. Punch Publications Ltd for: *Punch* (6 May 1981, 29 July 1981, 12 August 1981, 26 August 1981 and 9 September 1981) © published by Punch Publications Ltd 1981. Radala and associates for: *The Naked Civil Servant* by Quentin Crisp first published by Jonathan Cape Ltd 1968 © Quentin Crisp 1968. The Rainbird Publishing Group Ltd for: *The Making of Mankind* by Richard E Leakey first published in Great Britain by Michael Joseph Ltd 1981 © Sherma BV 1981. Robson Books Ltd for: *The Punch Book of Short Stories* 3 selected by Alan Coren first published in Great Britain by Robson Books Ltd in association with Punch Publications Ltd 1981 © Robson Books Ltd 1981.*The Best of Robert Morley* by Robert Morley first published in Great Britain by Robson Books Ltd 1981 © Robert Morley 1981. Deborah Rogers Ltd for: 'Picasso's Late Works' by Edward Lucie-Smith in the *Illustrated London News* July 1981, 'David Jones at the Tate' by Edward Lucie-Smith in the *Illustrated London News* August 1981 and 'Further Light on Spanish Painting' by Edward Lucie-Smith in the *Illustrated London News* September 1981. *The Godfather* by Mario Puzo first published in Great Britain by William Heinemann Ltd 1969 © Mario Puzo 1969. Routledge & Kegan Paul Ltd for: *How To Pass Examinations* by John Erasmus first published by Oriel Press Ltd 1967 © Oriel Press Ltd 1980. *Daisy, Daisy* by Christian Miller first published by Routledge & Kegan Paul Ltd 1980 © Christian Miller 1980. *The National Front* by Nigel Fielding first published by Routledge & Kegan Paul Ltd 1981 © Nigel Fielding 1981. *The Myth of Home Ownership* by Jim Kemeny first published by Routledge & Kegan Paul Ltd 1980 © J Kemeny 1981. *Absent With Cause (Lessons of Truancy)* by Roger White first published by Routledge & Kegan Paul Ltd 1980 © Roger White 1980. *The Powers of Evil (in Western Religion, Magic and Folk Belief)* by Richard Cavendish first published by Routledge & Kegan Paul Ltd 1975 © Richard Cavendish 1975. *Crime and Personality* by H J Eysenck first published by Routledge & Kegan Paul Ltd 1964 © H J Eysenck 1964, 1977. Martin Secker & Warburg Ltd for: *Changing Places* by David Lodge first published in England by Martin Secker & Warburg Ltd 1975 © David Lodge 1975. *The History Man* by Malcolm Bradbury first published by Martin Secker & Warburg 1975 © Malcolm Bradbury 1975. *Humboldt's Gift* by Saul Bellow first published in England by The Alison Press/Martin Secker & Warburg Ltd 1975 © Saul Bellow 1973, 1974, 1975. *Wilt* by Tom Sharpe first published in England by Martin Secker & Warburg Ltd 1976 © Tom Sharpe 1976. *The Last Days of America* by Paul E Erdman first published in England by Martin Secker & Warburg Ltd 1981 © Paul E Erdman 1981. *Autumn Manoeuvres* by Melvyn Bragg first published in England by Martin Secker & Warburg Ltd 1978 © Melvyn Bragg 1978. *The Act of Being* by Charles Marowitz first published in England by Martin Secker & Warburg Ltd 1978 © Charles Marowitz 1978. *As If By Magic* by Angus Wilson first published in England by Martin Secker & Warburg Ltd 1973 © Angus Wilson 1973. *All the President's Men* by Carl Bernstein and Bob Woodward first published in England by Martin Secker & Warburg Ltd 1974 © Carl Bernstein and Bob Woodward 1974. *The Myth of the Nation and the Vision of Revolution* by J L Talmon first published by Martin Secker & Warburg Ltd 1981 © J L Talmon 1980. *Animal Farm* by George Orwell first published by Martin Secker & Warburg 1945 © Eric Blair 1945. Anthony Sheil Associates Ltd for: *Daniel Martin* by John Fowles first published in Great Britain by Jonathan Cape Ltd 1977 © J R Fowles Ltd 1977. *Love Story* by Erich Segal published by Hodder & Stoughton Ltd 1970 © Erich Segal 1970. Sidgwick & Jackson Ltd for: *The Third World War* by General Sir John Hackett and others first published in Great Britain by Sidgwick & Jackson Ltd 1978 © General Sir John Hackett 1978. *Superwoman* by Shirley Conran first published by Sidgwick & Jackson Ltd 1975 © Shirley Conran 1975, 1977. *An Actor and His Time* by John Gielgud first published in Great Britain by Sidgwick & Jackson Ltd 1979 © John Gielgud, John Miller and John Powell 1979 © Biographical Notes, John Miller 1979. Simon & Schuster for: *Our Bodies Ourselves (A Health Book by and for Women)* by the Boston Women's Health Book Collective (British Edition by Angela Phillips and Jill Rakusen) published in Allen Lane and Penguin Books Ltd 1978 © The Boston Women's Health Collective Inc 1971, 1973, 1976 © Material for British Edition, Angela Phillips and Jill Rakusen 1978. Souvenir Press Ltd for: *The Bermuda Triangle* by Charles Berlitz (An Incredible Saga of Unexplained Disappearances) first published in Great Britain by Souvenir Press Ltd 1975 © Charles Berlitz 1974. Souvenir Press Ltd and Michael Joseph Ltd for: *Airport* by Arthur Hailey first published in Great Britain by Michael Joseph Ltd in association with Souvenir Press Ltd 1968 © Arthur Hailey Ltd 1968. Sunmed Holidays Ltd for: 'Go Greek' (Summer 1983) holiday brochure. Maurice Temple Smith Ltd for: *Friends of the Earth Pollution Guide* by Brian Price published by Maurice Temple Smith Ltd 1983 © Brian Price 1983. Maurice Temple Smith and Gower Publishing Co Ltd for: *Working the Land (A New Plan for a Healthy Agriculture)* by Charlie Pye-Smith and Richard North first published by Maurice Temple Smith Ltd 1984 © Charlie Pye-Smith and Richard North 1984. Times Newspapers Ltd for: *The Sunday Times Magazine* (13 January 1980, 20 January 1980 and 11 May 1980) © published by Times Newspapers Ltd 1981. *The Times* (7 September 1981) © published by Times Newspapers Ltd 1981. Twenty's Holidays for: 'The Best 18-33 Holidays' (Winter 1982/83) holiday brochure. University of Birmingham for: Living in Birmingham (1984) © published by The University of Birmingham 1984. Birmingham University Overseas Student Guide © The University of Birmingham. Working with Industry and Commerce © published by The University of Birmingham 1984. University of Birmingham Prospectus (June 1985) © published by The University of Birmingham 1985. University of Birmingham Library Guide © published by The University of Birmingham. University of Birmingham Institute of Research and Development (1984) © published by the University of Birmingham 1984. Biological Sciences at The University of Birmingham (1985) © published by The University of Birmingham 1985. History at the University of Birmingham (1985) © published by the University of Birmingham 1985. Faculty of Arts Handbook (1984-85) © published by The University of Birmingham 1984. Virago Press Ltd for: *Benefits* by Zoe Fairbairns published by Virago Press Ltd 1979 © Zoe Fairbairns 1979. *Simple Steps to Public Life* by Pamela Anderson, Mary Stott and Fay Weldon published in Great Britain by Virago Press Ltd 1980 © Action Opportunities 1980. *Tell Me A Riddle* by Tillie Olsen published by Virago Press Ltd 1980 © this edition Tillie Olsen 1980. A P Watt (& Sons) Ltd for: *The Glittering Prizes* by Frederic Raphael first published in Great Britain by Penguin Books Ltd 1976 © Volatic Ltd 1976. *Then and Now* by W Somerset Maugham first published by William Heinemann Ltd 1946 © W Somerset Maugham 1946. *The Language of Clothes* by Alison Lurie published by William Heinemann Ltd 1981 © Alison Lurie 1981. 'Herschel Commemorative' by Patrick Moore in the *Illustrated London News* July 1981. 'The Outermost Giant' by Patrick Moore in the *Illustrated London News* August 1981. 'Cosmic Bombardment' by Patrick Moore in the *Illustrated London News* September 1981. Weidenfeld & Nicolson Ltd for: 'The Miraculous Toy' by Susan Briggs in the *Illustrated London News* August 1981. *The Needle's Eye* by Margaret Drabble first published by Weidenfeld & Nicolson Ltd 1972 © Margaret Drabble 1972. *Success Without Tears: A Woman's Guide to the Top* by Rachel Nelson first published in Great Britain by Weidenfeld & Nicolson Ltd 1979 © Rachel Nelson 1979. *Education in the Modern World* by John Vaizey published by Weidenfeld & Nicolson Ltd 1967 © John Vaizey 1967. *Rich Man, Poor Man* by Irwin Shaw first published in Great Britain by Weidenfeld & Nicolson Ltd 1970 © Irwin Shaw 1969, 1970. *Lolita* by Vladimir Nabokov first published in Great Britain by Weidenfeld & Nicolson Ltd 1959 © Vladimir Nabokov 1955, 1959, 1968, © G P Putnam's Sons 1963 © McGraw-Hill International Inc 1971. *The Third World* by Peter Worsley first published by Weidenfeld & Nicolson Ltd 1964 © Peter Worsley 1964, 1967. *Portrait of a Marriage* by Nigel Nicolson published by Weidenfeld & Nicolson Ltd 1973 © Nigel Nicolson 1973. *The Dogs Bark: Public People and Private Places* by Truman Capote first published in Great Britain by Weidenfeld & Nicolson Ltd 1974 © Truman Capote 1974. *Great Planning Disasters* by Peter Hall first published in Great Britain by George Weidenfeld & Nicolson Ltd 1980 © Peter Hall 1980. The Writers and Readers Publishing Co-operative Ltd for: *Working with Words, Literacy Beyond School* by Jane Mace published by The Writers and Readers Publishing Co-operative Ltd 1979 © Jane Mace 1979. *The Alienated: Growing Old Today* by Gladys Elder OAP published by The Writers and Readers Publishing Co-operative Ltd 1977 © Text, The Estate of Gladys Elder 1977 © Photographs, Mike Abrahams 1977. *Beyond the Crisis in Art* by Peter Fuller published by The Writers and Readers Publishing Co-operative Ltd 1980 © Peter Fuller 1980. *The War and Peace Book* by Dave Noble published by The Writers and Readers Publishing Co-operative Ltd 1977 © Dave Noble 1977. *Tony Benn: A Political Biography* by Robert Jenkins first published by The Writers and Readers Publishing Co-operative Ltd 1980 © Robert Jenkins 1980. *Nuclear Power for Beginners* by Stephen Croall and Kaianders Sempler first published by The Writers and Readers Publishing Co-operative Ltd 1978 © Text, Stephen Croall 1978, 1980 © Illustrations Kaianders Sempler 1978, 1980. Yale University Press for: *Life in the English Country House: A Social and Architectural History* by Mark Girouard published by Yale University Press Ltd, London 1978 © Yale University 1978. The British Broadcasting Corporation for transcripts of radio transmissions of 'Kaleidoscope', 'Any Questions', 'Money Box' and 'Arts and Africa' 1981 and 1982. The British Broadcasting Corporation and Mrs Shirley Williams for transcripts of television interviews with Mrs Shirley Williams 1979. Dr B L Smith, School of Mathematics and Physical Sciences, University of Sussex for programmes on Current Affairs, Science and The Arts originally broadcast on Radio Sussex 1979 and 1980 © B L Smith. The following people in the University of Birmingham: Professor J McH Sinclair, Department of English, for his tapes of informal conversation (personal collection). Mr R Wallace, formerly Department of Accounting and Finance, and Ms D Houghton, Department of English, for transcripts of his accountancy lectures. Dr B K Gazey, Department of Electrical Engineering and Dr M Montgomery, University of Strathclyde, Department of English, for a transcript of Dr Gazey's lecture. Dr L W Poel, Department of Plant Biology, and Dr M Montgomery, University of Strathclyde, Department of English, for a transcript of Dr Poel's lecture. Professor J G Hawkes, formerly Department of Plant Biology, for recordings of his lectures. Dr M S Snaith, Department of Transportation for recordings of his lectures. Dr M P Hoey, Department of English, and Dr M Cooper, The British Council, for a recording of their discussion on discourse analysis. Ms A Renouf, Department of English, for recordings of job and academic interviews 1977. Mr R H Hubbard, formerly a B Phil (Ed) student, Faculty of Education, for his research recordings of expressions of uncertainty 1978-79. Mr A E Hare, formerly a B Phil (Ed) student, Faculty of Education, for his transcripts of telephone conversations 1978. Dr A Tsui, formerly Department of English, for her recordings of informal conversation. Mr J Couperthwaite, formerly Department of English, for a recording of informal conversation 1981. Ms C Emmott, M Litt student, Department of English, for a recording of informal conversation 1981. Mrs B T Atkins for the transcript of an account of a dream 1981. The British Council for 'Authentic Materials Numbers 1-28' 1981. Professor M Hammerton and Mr K Coghill, Department of Psychology, University of Newcastle-upon-Tyne, for tape recordings of their lectures 1981. Mr G P Graveson, formerly research student, University of Newcastle, for his recordings of teacher discussion 1977. Mr W R Jones, formerly research student, University of Southampton, for his recordings of classroom talk. Mr Ian Fisher, formerly BA student, Newcastle Polytechnic, for his transcripts of interviews on local history 1981. Dr N Coupland, formerly PhD student, Department of English, UWIST, for his transcripts of travel agency talk 1981. Professor D B Bromley, Department of Psychology, University of Liverpool, for his transcript of a research recording. Mr Brian Lawrence, formerly of Saffron Walden County High School, for a tape of his talk on 'The British Education System' 1979.

Every effort has been made to trace the copyright holders, but if any have been inadvertently overlooked the publishers will be pleased to make the necessary acknowledgments at the first opportunity.

A a

abide, abides, abiding, abided

abide by. If you **abide by** a law, an agreement, or a decision, you accept it and behave in accordance with it. EG *Germany and Russia agreed informally to abide by the agreement... Both parties must agree to abide by the court's decision.* ● **Observe** and **respect** mean almost the same as **abide by,** and **flout** means the opposite.

V+PREP:
HAS PASSIVE

accede, accedes, acceding, acceded

accede to. If you **accede to** someone's request or opinion, you allow it or agree with it, usually rather unwillingly; a formal word. EG *He was upset by my refusal to accede to his request... To accede to such a contention would set a dangerous precedent.*

V+PREP:
HAS PASSIVE

account, accounts, accounting, accounted

account for. 1 If you **account for** something that has happened or that you have done, you explain how it happened or why you did it. EG *He was always prepared to account for his actions... This cannot be accounted for in such a straightforward way.*

V+PREP:
HAS PASSIVE

2 If someone or something can **be accounted for,** people know where they are or what has happened to them. EG *There was no means of ensuring that all of them were accounted for... A sizeable sum of money could not be accounted for... Mrs White is accounted for. Dr and Mrs Gill aren't... 'Everyone here?'—'All accounted for.'—'All right, pay attention.'*

V+PREP:
HAS PASSIVE,
USUALLY PASSIVE

3 If something **accounts for** a particular part or proportion of something, it forms that part or proportion of the whole. EG *Children's needs account for a good part of the family budget... Tea accounted for three fifths of Sri Lanka's exports... 50 percent of 1974 manufacturing sales were accounted for by foreign-owned enterprises.*

V+PREP:
HAS PASSIVE

4 If a sum of money **is accounted for,** it has been included in a budget. EG *Grants for each student must be accounted for by the issuing authority... Indeed, the B-bomber is barely accounted for in existing defence budgets.* ● **Budget for** means almost the same as **account for.**

V+PREP:
HAS PASSIVE,
USUALLY PASSIVE

5 To **account for** someone or something also means to defeat or destroy them; an old-fashioned use. EG *...an identical shot to the identical ball which accounted for him on Friday... We were helped immeasurably by a run-out which accounted for Salim.*

V+PREP:
HAS PASSIVE

acquaint, acquaints, acquainting, acquainted

acquaint with. 1 If you **are acquainted with** something, you know about it and are familiar with it; a fairly formal use. EG *Students became acquainted with all aspects of biology before choosing the course... He was well acquainted with sorrow, disappointment, and loneliness... She had acquainted herself with our technology... I will acquaint you with the facts.*

V+N+PREP,
V+PRON+PREP,
V+REFL+PREP:
USUALLY PASSIVE

2 If you **are acquainted with** someone, you know them slightly but they are not a close friend; a fairly formal use. EG *I hear you're acquainted with Jerry Pierce... Mrs Grunblatt used to be acquainted with a painter.*

PASSIVE:
V+PREP

act, acts, acting, acted

act on. If you **act on** or **upon** advice or information, you do what has

V+PREP:
HAS PASSIVE

been advised or suggested. EG *Why didn't you act on my warning?...
They were content to provide information on which others could
act... The recommendations could not, for reasons of finance, be
fully acted on... ...acting upon his advice... We must use these powers
and act upon them.*

act out. 1 When you **act out** your feelings or ideas, you express   V+ADV+N,
them in your behaviour, especially as a means of relieving nervous   V+PRON+ADV
tension or emotion. EG *Children act out their frustration in temper
tantrums.*

2 If you **act out** an event which has happened, you copy the actions   V+ADV+N,
which took place and make them into a play. EG *The teacher gets the*   V+PRON+ADV
students to act out some historic event.

act up. 1 If something is **acting up**, it is not working properly; an   V+ADV
informal use. EG *Her washing machine was acting up again.* ● **Play
up** means almost the same as **act up**.

2 If a child is **acting up**, they are behaving badly; an informal use. EG   V+ADV
I'm sorry he had to act up like this. ● **Play up** means almost the
same as **act up**.

act upon. See act on: **act upon** is more formal.

add, adds, adding, added

add in. If you **add** something **in**, you include it as a part of   V+ADV+N,
something else. EG *We had to add in a couple of extra scenes... If you*   V+PRON+ADV,
add in his gains of last year he'd made no less than £20,000.   V+N+ADV

add on. If you **add** something **on**, you attach it to something else or   V+ADV+N,
include it as part of something else. EG *If the tip hasn't been added*   V+PRON+ADV,
on, you will see the words 'service not included'... They add on about   V+N+ADV
nine per cent for service.

add together. 1 If you **add together** several numbers, you calcu-   V+N+ADV,
late their total. EG *If you add these two numbers together what do*   V+PRON+ADV,
you get?... These amounts are added together to produce the total   V+ADV+N
*earnings... To work out the number of units, add together all your
contributions.* ● **Add up** means almost the same as **add together**.

2 If you **add** several things **together**, you put them all in one place so   V+N+ADV,
that they are combined. EG *...adding the eggs and butter together in a*   V+PRON+ADV,
bowl... She got one pail of boiling water and one of cold water and   V+ADV+N
added them together in a tub. ● **Mix** means almost the same as **add
together**.

add up. 1 If you **add up** several numbers, you calculate their total. EG   V+N+ADV,
We add all the marks up... First, add up all your regular payments.   V+ADV+N,
● **Add together** means almost the same as **add up**.   V+PRON+ADV

2 If you say that facts or events **add up**, you mean that you can   V+ADV
understand their significance. EG *It all added up. I became aware
that Halliday was the thief.*

add up to. 1 If numbers or amounts **add up to** a particular total,   V+ADV+PREP
they result in that total. EG *This adds up to 75,000 miles of new
streets.* ● **Amount to** means almost the same as **add up to**.

2 You talk about things **adding up** to something when they result in   V+ADV+PREP
it or suggest it. EG *This adds up to a formidable list of qualifications...
Most of the evidence adds up to the clear conclusion that human
beings are able to control their feelings... ...the shapes, the glowing
colours; they all seem to add up to a work of art.*

adhere, adheres, adhering, adhered

adhere to. 1 If you **adhere to** a rule or agreement, you act in the   V+PREP:
way that it says you should. EG *...their failure to adhere to the*   HAS PASSIVE
warder's instructions... The fire regulations have been adhered to.

2 If you **adhere to** an opinion or belief, you support or hold it. EG   V+PREP

Many people adhered to this view... ...idealists who adhered to the principles expounded by Professor Read.

admit, admits, admitting, admitted

admit of. If an event or situation **admits of** something, it makes it possible for that thing to happen; a formal expression. EG *The relevant statute admitted of one interpretation only.* ● **Allow** means almost the same as **admit of.**

V+PREP

agree, agrees, agreeing, agreed

agree with. 1 If a particular food or drink does not **agree with** you, it gives you indigestion; an informal use. EG *My milk didn't seem to agree with the baby.* ● **Upset** means almost the same as **not agree with.**

V+PREP: WITH NEGATIVE

2 If something **agrees with** you, it makes you feel healthy and contented; a rather old-fashioned use. EG *The sea air really agrees with her.* ● **Suit** means almost the same as **agree with.**

V+PREP

aim, aims, aiming, aimed

aim at. 1 If you **aim at** something, you plan or hope to achieve it. EG *We should aim at two-thirds of the average wage... ...aiming at a higher production level... All Fair Rent Associations aim at helping people with real housing needs... ...a fresh package of public spending cuts aimed at bringing down the government borrowing requirements.*

V+PREP: HAS PASSIVE

2 If an action or activity **is aimed** at someone, it is intended to help them or affect them in some way. EG *I knew that all this publicity was not really aimed at me as an individual... Many of the devices are aimed at people with lumbago.* ● **Be directed at** means almost the same as **be aimed at.**

V+N+PREP, V+PRON+PREP: USUALLY PASSIVE

allow, allows, allowing, allowed

allow for. 1 When you **allow for** something such as a problem, delay, or expense in your planning, you make sure that you have enough time, money, or resources in order to deal with it if it occurs. EG *If you are self-employed, allow for tax and national insurance... ...long-term fixed-price contracts which did not allow for the escalation of costs.*

V+PREP: HAS PASSIVE

2 If you **allow for** something that does not yet exist, you take action or make plans so that it will be possible. EG *Pasta can be frozen, but should be undercooked to allow for the reheating... His original plans allowed for meadows and a lake for recreation.*

V+PREP

allude, alludes, alluding, alluded

allude to. If you **allude to** something, you mention it in an indirect way; a fairly formal expression. EG *They very soon learned not to allude to the subject in the presence of their father... ...a controversial question to which we may briefly allude... This is only rarely alluded to in even indirect terms.* ● **Refer to** means almost the same as **allude to.**

V+PREP: HAS PASSIVE

amount, amounts, amounting, amounted

amount to. 1 If you say that something **amounts to** a particular sum or number, you mean that its total is that quantity. EG *...very high fees which amount to £2,000... ...her entire fortune, which amounted by then to a considerable sum of money... ...a huge infantry force which with reserves amounted to 200,000 men.* ● **Add up to** and **total** mean almost the same as **amount to.**

V+PREP

2 If you say that an idea, feeling, statement, action, etc **amounts to** something, you mean that it seems like that to you. EG *His attitude towards her amounted to loathing... The proposals amount to a new*

V+PREP

charter for the mentally ill... The message amounted to little more than personal regards.

3 If you say that something **amounts to** little, you mean that it is V+PREP unimportant, and if you say that it **amounts to** a great deal, you mean that it is important. EG *The trouble had amounted to hardly anything... It had never amounted to much.*

angle, angles, angling, angled

angle for. If you are **angling for** something, you try to make V+PREP someone offer it to you without asking for it directly. EG *He got the invitation to Washington he had been angling for... I am quite sure she was not angling for some sort of reconciliation.* ● **Fish for** means almost the same as **angle for.**

answer, answers, answering, answered

answer back. If someone, especially a child, **answers** you **back** or V+ADV, **answers back,** they speak rudely to you when you have spoken to V+N+ADV, them; an informal expression. EG *What do you do with a child who answers back?... He answered back vehemently... At first I couldn't resist the temptation to answer teachers back.*

answer for. **1** If you say that someone has something to **answer** V+PREP **for,** you mean that they have done something bad and should be held responsible for it. EG *The cosmetic industry has much to answer for... If they start terror tactics the entire army will have to answer for his actions... I think the motorist has a lot to answer for. He expects too much.*

2 If you can **answer for** someone or for a quality of theirs, you mean V+PREP that you are sure they are reliable and trustworthy, or have that quality. EG *I can answer for his loyalty.* ● **Vouch for** means almost the same as **answer for.**

answer to. **1** If someone or something **answers to** a particular V+PREP description, they have the characteristics described. EG *He knew of several boys who might answer to that description.* ● **Fit** means almost the same as **answer to.**

2 If something **answers to** your needs or requirements, it will fill V+PREP your needs. EG *The Militia must have had something that answered to our national military needs.* ● **Satisfy** means almost the same as **answer to.**

3 When someone **answers to** a person who has authority over them, V+PREP they give them the information that is officially required; a formal use. EG *The young couple line up to enter the wedding tent after answering to the official scribe.*

apprise, apprises, apprising, apprised

apprise of. When you **apprise** someone **of** something, you inform V+PRON+PREP, them about it; a formal expression. EG *I apprised him of the political* V+N+PREP *situation in Washington.* ● **Tell** is a more general word for **apprise of.**

approve, approves, approving, approved

approve of. **1** If you **approve of** an action, event, or suggestion, you V+PREP: are pleased about it. EG *My grandfather did not approve of my* HAS PASSIVE *father's marriage... His return to the office was widely approved of.*

2 If you **approve of** someone or something, you like and admire V+PREP: them. EG *He did not approve of my pictures... ...the desire to be loved* HAS PASSIVE *and approved of.*

argue, argues, arguing, argued

argue down. If you **argue** someone **down,** you succeed in getting V+N+ADV, them to accept your point of view during an argument; used mainly V+PRON+ADV, V+ADV+N in American English. EG *When we're discussing·politics, I can always argue him down.*

argue out. When you **argue out** an idea or plan, you discuss in detail all the aspects and possible consequences of it in order to reach a decision. EG *Our proposals were argued out in meetings that seemed never to end... We would discuss it and argue it out in the church.* ● **Thrash out** is a more informal expression for **argue out.**   V+ADV+N, V+PRON+ADV, V+N+ADV

argue out of. If you **argue** someone **out of** doing something, you persuade them not to do it. EG *He argued a homosexual clergyman out of suicide... Bill tried to argue him out of it for a while.* ● **Talk out of** is a less formal expression for **argue out of.**   V+N+ADV+PREP, V+PRON+ADV+PREP

arse, arses, arsing, arsed

arse about. You say that someone **is arsing about** or **around** when they are behaving in a silly and irritating way instead of getting on with what they are supposed to be doing; an informal and rude expression. ● **Muck about** is an informal but less rude expression for arse about.   V+ADV

arse around. See arse about.

ask, asks, asking, asked

ask after. If you **ask after** someone, you ask for information about them, for example how they are and if they are well, or what they are doing at the present time. EG *She asked after my father... She asked after his health... If anyone should ask after me, say I'm at the Thunderbird hotel.* ● **Inquire after** means almost the same as **ask after.**   V+PREP

ask around. If you **ask around** when you need help with something, you ask several people, usually people you do not know, to help you. EG *She asked around but no-one seemed to know where the little boy had gone... I asked around the village to see if any of the old men would like to come with me.*   V+ADV, V+PREP

ask for. 1 If you **ask for** something, you say that you would like to have it. EG *She asked for a drink of water... The publisher asked for time to think it over... Send it by recorded delivery and ask for a receipt.* ● **Request** is a more formal word for **ask for.**   V+PREP: HAS PASSIVE

2 If you **ask for** someone when you are making a phone call, you say that you would like to speak to them. EG *Call the town hall and ask for the pest controller... He rang the office and asked for Cynthia.*   V+PREP

3 If you say that someone **asks for** something unpleasant such as a punishment, trouble, or other problems, or if you say that they **ask for** it, you mean that they behave in a way that makes it more likely or possible for those things to occur. EG *To plan a route all in one go was asking for trouble. It was obviously a better idea to do it in bits... He had no business crawling like that out of the dark. He was batty. He asked for it... When I reported the attack they said 'Are you sure you didn't ask for it?'*   V+PREP, V+PREP+it

ask in. If you **ask** someone **in,** you invite them to come into the room or building that you are in. EG *The vicar went across the hall to ask Mrs. Daniels in... Gerald had gone out for a while. Mr Sutton asked me in... ...neighbours that ask you in for coffee every now and again.*   V+N+ADV, V+PRON+ADV

ask into. If you **ask** someone **into** a place. you invite them to come in. EG *It gave me an excuse to ask him into the cabin... They asked me into their classrooms to watch them teach... Mr Coles asked me into his office.*   V+N+PREP, V+PRON+PREP

ask out. If you **ask** someone **out,** you invite them to go somewhere with you. EG *Every few weeks he and his wife would ask Brody and*   V+N+ADV, V+PRON+ADV, V+ADV+N

Ellen out to dinner... It had to be a cheap restaurant, since he was asking her out... I kept being asked out by men.

ask over. If you **ask** someone **over**, you invite them to come and   V+PRON+ADV,
visit you. EG *One evening he asked me over to inspect the house... He*   V+N+ADV:
asked us over to his flat... What if he asks you over for the evening?   ALSO+*to*

ask round. If you **ask** someone **round**, you invite them to come and   V+PRON+ADV,
visit you; a fairly informal expression. EG *I hoped he'd ask me round*   V+N+ADV:
to his pad... 'She's asked me round on Friday,' said the Count... I'll   ALSO+*to*
ask Sylvia Wicks round for a drink.

aspire, aspires, aspiring, aspired

aspire to. If you **aspire to** something, you have a strong ambition to   V+PREP:
achieve it. EG *Edward Heath has always aspired to leadership... She*   HAS PASSIVE
had achieved none of the height she had aspired to.

attend, attends, attending, attended

attend to. 1 If you **attend to** something such as a problem, you deal   V+PREP:
with it. EG *I had two items of business to attend to before I could*   HAS PASSIVE
relax... Everyone has his own affairs to attend to... If we do not
attend to the problem, it will certainly grow. ● **See to** means almost
the same as **attend to.**

2 If you **attend to** someone who needs something, you help them or   V+PREP:
look after them. EG *I see now that I should have attended to her*   HAS PASSIVE
myself... Henry was attended to in a competent manner... It can, too
easily, be assumed that one is attending to them when one is merely
fussing.

auction, auctions, auctioning, auctioned

auction off. If furniture or property **is auctioned off,** you get rid of   V+N+ADV,
it by selling it at an auction. EG *The furniture was auctioned off... We*   V+ADV+N,
auctioned off all my grandad's war memorabilia.   V+PRON+ADV

average, averages, averaging, averaged

average out. When you **average out** a set of numbers, you work   V+N+ADV,
out the average or approximate figure. EG *We find that, averaging it*   V+PRON+ADV,
out, only 8,000 chairs could have been purchased... We sort of   V+ADV+N
averaged out the estimates.

average out at. If a set of numbers **averages out at** a particular   V+ADV+PREP
figure, that figure is the average for the set of numbers. EG *'How*
many hours do you work?' 'I suppose it averages out at about 40 a
week.'

B b

back, backs, backing, backed

back away. 1 If you **back away** from someone or something, you   V+ADV:
move slowly backwards away from them, usually because you are   ALSO+*from*
nervous or frightened. EG *The waitress, having put the tray down,*
rose and backed away... They moved towards each other, then they
backed away... He was vaguely aware of the fur-coated woman
backing away from him. ● **Retreat** is a more formal word for **back**
away.

2 If you **back away** from an idea or suggestion, you avoid supporting   V+ADV:
it or commenting on it, and try to dissociate yourself from it. EG *The*   ALSO+*from*

administration appeared to back away from official criticism of the Prime Minister.

back down. If you **back down** on something, you accept someone else's point of view or agree to do what they want you to do, even though you do not really want to. EG *Eventually he backed down on the question of seating... ...but the men refused to back down... ...asserting his authority and making them back down.* ● **Give in** means almost the same as **back down**.

V+ADV:
ALSO+*on*

back off. If you **back off**, you try to avoid a fight or difficult situation by moving away or not becoming involved in it. If you tell some one to **back off**, you are telling them not to interfere with something you are doing. EG *Brody was ready for a fight, but he backed off... They backed off, handing him what money they had... A part of him was always backing off from these events... Back off, or I shoot!* ● **Withdraw** is a more formal word for **back off**.

V+ADV:
ALSO IMPERATIVE

back onto. If a building **backs onto** something, the back of it faces in that direction. EG *...the Gardens and the houses backing onto them.*

V+PREP

back out. 1 If you **back out** of an arrangement, you decide not to do something you had previously agreed to do. EG *You can't back out now. A deal's a deal... They openly express the worry that the Japanese will back out of the agreements.* ● **Pull out** means almost the same as **back out**.

V+ADV:
ALSO+*of*

2 If you **back out** or **back** your car **out**, you move your car backwards out of a confined space, such as a garage or a parking place. EG *Joe threw the car into gear and backed out... Harold backed out of the parking lot.*

V+ADV,
V+N+ADV,
V+PRON+ADV:
ALSO+*of*

back up. 1 If you **back up** a statement, you supply evidence to prove that it is true or reasonable. EG *The more bills you can include to back up your claim, the happier the finance department will be... He backed this up with a few horrifying anecdotes... Their demands for independence were backed up with quotes from western political writers.* ● **Support** means almost the same as **back up**.

V+ADV+N,
V+PRON+ADV,
V+N+ADV

2 If you **back** someone **up**, you give them help or support them. EG *They asked local administrators to back them up... ...a Soviet regime backed up by an armed workers' militia... He had loyally backed one of their number up in his false statement... Baker said later that he would back up Goldwater in whatever he decided to do.* ● **Support** means almost the same as **back up**. ▶ **Back-up** is extra help or support from people or machines, which you need in order to be able to achieve what you want. EG *...the tremendous computer back-up which each mission required... We don't really need any back-up, do we? We solve our own problems.* ▶ If you have something such as a second piece of equipment or set of plans as **back-up**, you have arranged for it to be available for use in case the first one does not work. EG *Use a conventional heating system as back-up... ...the sheer strength of the back-up crew of 25 actors.* ● **Stand-by** means almost the same as **back-up**.

V+PRON+ADV,
V+N+ADV,
V+ADV+N

N UNCOUNT

N UNCOUNT

3 If you **back up** when you are driving, you move your car backwards a little way. EG *I backed up three hundred yards to the entrance... You back up the car and I'll get the suitcases... I can't back it up. I can't get it into reverse gear.* ● **Reverse** means almost the same as **back up**.

V+ADV,
V+ADV+N,
V+N+ADV,
V+PRON+ADV

4 If you **back up**, you walk backwards a little way. EG *She backed up a few steps, then ran at the water.* ● **Retreat** is a more formal word for **back up**.

V+ADV

bag, bags, bagging, bagged

bag up. If you **bag up** something, you put it into bags. EG *Bag up as*   V+ADV+N,
many of the leaves as you can... We'll bag them up tonight and they   V+PRON+ADV,
can be delivered tomorrow.   V+N+ADV

bail, bails, bailing, bailed

Bail is also spelled **bale** in paragraphs 2, 3 and 4.

bail out. 1 If you **bail out** someone who is in custody, you pay bail on   V+N+ADV,
their behalf so that they can be released. EG *I went down to the Hall*   V+PRON+ADV,
of Justice to bail my friend out... Look, can you come down here and   V+ADV+N
bail me out?

2 If you **bail** someone **out,** you help them out of a difficult situation.   V+PRON+ADV,
EG *We need government assistance to bail us out should things go*   V+ADV+N,
wrong... Their sole mission in Vietnam was to bail out Marines in   V+N+ADV
trouble... ...a financial package designed to bail out the Missile
Development Corporation. ● **Rescue** means almost the same as **bail**
out.

3 If you **bail out** of an aircraft, you jump out of it with a parachute   V+ADV:
because it is damaged and likely to crash. EG *One pilot was seen to*   ALSO+of
bail out... Were they bomber crews that had bailed out?

4 If you **bail out** a small boat, or if you **bail** water **out** of it, you   V+ADV+N,
remove water from the inside of it using a container, often because   V+N+ADV,
the boat is leaking or sinking. EG *...bailing out the rain water from*   V+PRON+ADV,
the bottom of the boat... Quickly! You bail the water out and I'll   V+ADV
paddle... We couldn't bail out fast enough and were forced to
abandon it.

balance, balances, balancing, balanced

balance against. When you **balance** one thing **against** another,   V+N+PREP,
you assess the importance of the first thing in relation to the second.   V+PRON+PREP
EG *...balancing the assumptions of Marxist theory against the values*
and needs of a government... Conflicting claims and interests had to
be balanced one against the other. ● **Set against** means almost the
same as **balance against.**

balance out. If two or more things **balance out,** they are equal in   V+ADV
amount or value. EG *If I am overdrawn one month, it should*
theoretically balance out in the following months. ● **Even out** means
almost the same as **balance out.**

balance up. When things **balance up** or when you **balance** them   V+ADV,
up, they become equal in amount or value, or you make them equal.   V+ADV+N,
EG *How the forces balance up is really a matter of opinion... The*   V+N+ADV,
Clearing House is where the major banks daily balance up their   V+PRON+ADV
claims on each other.

bale, bales, baling, baled

Bale is another spelling for **bail.**

balk, balks, balking, balked

Balk is also spelled **bauk.**

balk at. If you **balk at** something, you are very reluctant to do it or   V+PREP
to let it happen. EG *I balked at cleaning the lavatory... The adminis-*
tration does not baulk at such a prospect. ● **Jib at** means almost the
same as **balk at.**

balls, ballses, ballsing, ballsed

balls up. If you **balls** something **up,** you spoil it by making a lot of   V+PRON+ADV,
mistakes; a very informal expression, used to express annoyance. EG   V+ADV+N,
Watton, you've ballsed it all up... Don't balls up the next one!... ...the   V+N+ADV
way you balls things up. ● **Cock up, mess up,** and **botch** mean almost
the same as **balls up.** ▶ A **balls-up** is something that is done very   N COUNT

badly because of mistakes or carelessness; a very informal word. EG *Our union, in a classic balls-up, voted both ways... ...the man who could sort out other people's balls-ups.* ● **Cock-up** means almost the same as **balls-up.**

band, bands, banding, banded

band together. If people **band together,** they meet and act together as a group in order to try and achieve something. EG *Everywhere, small groups of women banded together to talk about liberation... More and more people are banding themselves together to get things done... Producing countries have been successful recently in banding their interests together.* ● **Unite** means almost the same as **band together.**

V+ADV,
V+REFL+ADV,
V+N+ADV,
V+PRON+ADV,
V+ADV+N:
NO PASSIVE

bandage, bandages, bandaging, bandaged

bandage up. If you **bandage up** a wound or part of someone's body, you wrap it up completely in a bandage. EG *...to bandage up a patient's leg... I bandaged him up with a rag.* ● **Bind up** means almost the same as **bandage up.**

V+ADV+N,
V+PRON+ADV,
V+N+ADV

bandy, bandies, bandying, bandied

bandy about. 1 When people **bandy** words **about** or **around,** they use them a lot without paying much attention to their meanings. EG *We bandy about such phrases as 'the moral fabric' of a society... ...just another label for journalists to bandy about... Abstruse terms and jargon are bandied around by experts.*

V+ADV+N,
V+N+ADV,
V+PRON+ADV

2 If ideas **are bandied about** or **around,** a lot of people hear and talk about them. EG *The idea was bandied about that legislation might help to curb the militants... Various suggestions were bandied around by the younger members.*

PASSIVE:
V+ADV

bandy around. See bandy about.

bang, bangs, banging, banged

bang about. 1 If you **bang** something **about** or **around,** you treat it very roughly and risk damaging it; an informal use. EG *Don't bang your vacuum cleaner about—it's a sensitive machine... If you have a tendency to bang things around, take more time.* ● **Bash about** means almost the same as **bang about.**

V+N+ADV,
V+PRON+ADV

2 If you **bang about** in a place, you move around doing things noisily; an informal use. EG *We listened to her singing while she banged about in the kitchen... I heard her banging about and beating the walls.* ● **Clatter about** means almost the same as **bang about.**

V+ADV,
V+PREP

3 If something **bangs about,** it moves around rapidly and knocks into things that are nearby. EG *The contents of the case were prevented from banging about... I heard a tennis ball banging about.*

V+ADV

4 If a person **has been banged about** or **around,** someone has attacked them and hit them several times. EG *She had been terrorized and banged around badly.* ● **Bash about** means almost the same as **bang about.**

V+N+ADV,
V+PRON+ADV,
V+ADV+N:
USUALLY PASSIVE

bang around. 1 If you **bang around** from one place to another, you move from one to the other without staying anywhere for very long; an informal use. EG *After the divorce, Mark moved East and began banging around from job to job.*

V+ADV:
WITH A

2 See bang about 1, 4.

bang away. If you **bang away** when you hit something, you continue hitting it noisily and with a lot of energy. EG *He used the knocker vigorously. Nothing happened. He banged away even harder... He keeps banging away at the guy.*

V+ADV:
USUALLY+A

bang down. If you **bang** something **down,** you put it down violently so that it makes a loud noise. EG *He banged the window down...*

V+N+ADV,
V+ADV+N,
V+PRON+ADV

'Pride be hanged' said the old woman, banging his supper plate down in front of him... He banged down the phone angrily. ● **Slam down** means almost the same as **bang down.**

bang into. If you **bang into** someone, you bump against them accidentally. EG *You couldn't turn round without banging into her... ...the cars banging into each other.* v+PREP

bang on. If you **bang on** about something, you talk or write about it repeatedly for a long time in an uninteresting or boring way. EG *...an unusual treat to read a contemporary American authoress who is not banging on interminably about some freaky minority fancy.* v+ADV; ALSO+*about*

bang out. 1 If you **bang out** a tune on a piano, you play it noisily and rather badly; an informal use. EG *He was banging out 'Au Clair de la Lune' for all he was worth.* v+ADV+N, v+N+ADV; v+PRON+ADV

2 If you **bang out** something that you have written on a typewriter, or on a computer keyboard, you type it very quickly and noisily; an informal use. EG *...bent over my typewriter in the press tent, banging out a couple of thousand words... I managed to bang a few pages out last night.* v+ADV+N, v+N+ADV, v+PRON+ADV

bang up. If someone **is banged up,** they are in prison; an informal expression. EG *He was banged up for fifteen years.* ● **Be imprisoned** is a more formal expression for **be banged up.** PASSIVE: v+ADV

bank, banks, banking, banked

bank on. If you **bank on** a situation, you rely on it and expect to get some advantage out of it. EG *Green Cross is clearly banking on these advantages to outweigh the drawbacks... Don't bank on it.* ● **Count on** and **bet on** mean almost the same as **bank on,** and **rely on** is a less informal expression. v+PREP

bank up. 1 To **bank up** something solid such as earth or sand means to pile it into a mound or against a wall. EG *The storm had banked up the snow against the front door.* ● **Build up** means almost the same as **bank up.** ▶ Something solid which is **banked-up** is piled up into a mound. EG *...threatening, banked-up clouds on the horizon.* v+ADV+N, v+N+ADV; v+PRON+ADV

ADJECTIVE

2 If you **bank up** a fire, you put a large quantity of coal onto it so that it will keep burning for a long time. EG *Mother nursed the fire with skill, banking it up every night and blowing hard on the coals.* v+PRON+ADV, v+N+ADV, v+ADV+N

bargain, bargains, bargaining, bargained

bargain for. If something happens that you had not **bargained for** or **bargained on,** you did not expect it to happen. If it happens more than you **bargained for,** it happens to a greater extent than you expected. EG *This was one complication he had not bargained for... They went more slowly than Ralph had bargained for... Some of them might get more than they bargained for... I hadn't bargained on taking the kids as well.* ● **Reckon on** means almost the same as **bargain for,** and **anticipate** is a more formal word. v+PREP: HAS PASSIVE

bargain on. See **bargain for.**

barge, barges, barging, barged

barge in. If you **barge in,** you rudely interrupt what someone else is doing or saying. EG *I'm sorry, I won't barge in again... If anyone barged in, it was you, not her... They went barging in late at night.* v+ADV

barge into. 1 If you **barge into** a place, you rush or push into it in a rough and rude way. EG *Most women would have come barging into the kitchen with ironic or unhelpful suggestions... You don't barge into the garage as you did in the old mechanic's institute.* v+PREP

2 If you **barge into** a conversation, you rudely interrupt the person who is speaking. EG *Renate spoke stiffly to her when she barged into these conversations.* ● **Butt in** means almost the same as **barge into.** v+PREP

3 If you **barge into** someone, you bump against them rather roughly and rudely while you are walking. EG *I hate shopping in town—people are always barging into you.* ● **Jostle** means almost the same as **barge into.**   `V+PREP`

barge through. If you **barge through** a crowd of people, you push past them rudely. EG *I got up from my seat, my drink half finished, and barged through the ladies with their lagers... ...barging through the yelling crowd.* ● **Push through** means almost the same as **barge through.**   `V+PREP`

bark, barks, barking, barked

bark out. If you **bark out** an order, you shout it out loudly and suddenly. EG *Bill Fry stood on the bridge, barking out orders through a megaphone... 'Company, halt,' he barked out.*   `V+ADV+N,`
`V+ADV+QUOTE,`
`V+PRON+ADV`

base, bases, basing, based

base on. If something **is based on** or **upon** another thing, it takes its general form, subject, or nature from that other thing. EG *The new agreement is based on the original United Nations proposal... ...movies based on Britain and British life... I base all my characters on someone... ...the images upon which we base our behaviour.*   `V+N+PREP,`
`V+PRON+PREP:`
`USUALLY PASSIVE`

base upon. See **base on: base upon** is more formal.

bash, bashes, bashing, bashed

bash about. If you **bash** something **about,** you treat it very roughly and risk damaging it. EG *It's rather bashed about... ...keeping it in running order and not bashing it about.* ● **Bang about** means almost the same as **bash about.**   `V+N+ADV,`
`V+PRON+ADV`

bash in. 1 If you **bash** something **in,** you break it or damage it by hitting it very hard. EG *The doors had to be broken down, or the windows bashed in... I'll bash your silly head in.*
2 See **bash up.**   `V+N+ADV,`
`V+PRON+ADV,`
`V+ADV+N`

bash on. If you **bash on** with a task, you carry on doing it, often in a rather unenthusiastic way. EG *I'd better bash on with this report.* ● **Get on** means almost the same as **bash on.**   `V+ADV:`
`ALSO+with`

bash up. If someone **bashes up** a person or thing, or **bashes** them **in,** they attack them violently and hurt or damage them. EG *Her son seemed to feel the need to bash up things and wreck things... Kill the pig! Bash him in!*   `V+ADV+N,`
`V+PRON+ADV,`
`V+N+ADV`

batten, battens, battening, battened

batten down. If you **batten** something **down,** you make it secure by fixing pieces of wood across it or by closing it firmly. EG *...a ship battened down for a storm.*   `V+N+ADV,`
`V+ADV+N,`
`V+PRON+ADV`

batten on. If someone **battens on** another person, they live comfortably or become successful by using that person's money or position in society for their own benefit. EG *He got round my mother and battened on her... ...the village women on whom he had battened.* ● **Sponge off** means almost the same as **batten on.**   `V+PREP`

batter, batters, battering, battered

batter down. To **batter down** something such as a door means to hit it repeatedly and hard so that it breaks and falls down. EG *...mud walls that the rains have battered down.* ● **Break down** means almost the same as **batter down.**   `V+ADV+N,`
`V+N+ADV,`
`V+PRON+ADV`

baulk, baulks, baulking, baulked

Baulk is another spelling for **balk.**

bawl, bawls, bawling, bawled

bawl out. 1 If someone **bawls** you **out,** they tell you off angrily; an   `V+N+ADV,`

informal use. EG *I was used to being bawled out at school for not*   V+ADV+N,
doing homework... Schultzy wasn't there to bawl him out... Just for   V+PRON+ADV
my benefit he bawled out a junior clerk.

2 If you **bawl** something **out**, you shout or sing it very loudly and   V+ADV+N,
rather harshly. EG *...hecklers bawling out, 'What about pensions?'...*   V+N+ADV,
They bawl out the lusty old favourites.   V+PRON+ADV, V+ADV+QUOTE

bear, bears, bearing, bore, borne

bear down on. If something large **bears down on** or **upon** some-   V+ADV+PREP
one or something, it moves quickly towards them in a threatening
way. EG *We struggled to turn the boat as the wave bore down on us.*

bear down upon. See bear down on: bear down upon is more
formal.

bear on. If a fact or situation **bears on** or **upon** something, it is   V+PREP
relevant to it or affects it; a formal expression. EG *Certain facts*
bearing on the choice of time should be carefully considered...
Government was only one of the forces bearing on the lives of the
inhabitants... The group would require an analysis of existing activi-
ties which bear upon the problems.

bear out. If someone or something **bears out** what you are saying,   V+PRON+ADV,
they support what you are saying. EG *She provided a strong counter-*   V+ADV+N,
argument, with some witnesses to bear her out... The machine did   V+N+ADV
not in fact bear out the claims made for it... Harris's assertion is
hardly borne out by the facts.

bear up. 1 If you **bear up** when experiencing difficulties or prob-   V+ADV
lems, you remain cheerful and show courage in spite of them. EG
You have to bear up under the strain.

2 If something **does** not **bear up**, it is not good enough or accurate   V+ADV
enough when you examine it carefully. EG *The results just don't bear*
up at all. ● **Stand up** means almost the same as **bear up.**

bear upon. See bear on: bear upon is even more formal.

beat, beats, beating, beaten

beat down. 1 When the sun **beats down**, it is very hot and bright. EG   V+ADV
The sun was beating down on the fields.

2 When the rain **beats down**, it rains very hard. EG *...torrential rains*   V+ADV
that beat down on her like hailstones. ● **Pour down** means almost
the same as **beat down.**

3 When you **beat** someone **down**, you force them to accept a lower   V+PRON+ADV,
price for something that they are selling you. EG *I beat him down*   V+ADV+N,
from £500 to £400. ● **Knock down** means almost the same as **beat**   V+N+ADV
down.

beat off. If you **beat off** someone who is opposing or attacking you,   V+ADV+N,
you prevent them from winning or overcoming you. EG *...beating off*   V+PRON+ADV
the opposition.

beat on. If someone **beats on** you, they hit or kick you many times   V+PREP
so that you are badly hurt; used in American English. EG *...beating on*
Lamin... They were dragged and beaten on.

beat out. 1 If you **beat out** sounds on a drum, you make the sounds   V+ADV+N,
by hitting the drum. EG *The drummers walked among them, beating*   V+N+ADV,
out a rhythm to match their movements... The lookout drummer   V+PRON+ADV
beat out the news.

2 If you **beat out** a fire, you stop it burning by hitting it with a   V+N+ADV,
blanket, brush, or other object. ● **Extinguish** is a more formal word   V+ADV+N,
for **beat out.**   V+PRON+ADV

beat up. 1 If someone **beats** you **up**, they hit or kick you many times   V+PRON+ADV,
so that you are badly hurt. EG *They beat her up in the street... I'd beat*   V+ADV+N,
up anybody who made a pass at you... He told us that he had been   V+N+ADV
beaten up by the police. ● **Bash up** means almost the same as **beat**

up. ▶ If someone gives you a **beating up,** they hit or kick you many N SING times so that you are badly hurt. EG *I can honestly tell you that I've never seen any beating-up or torture.*

2 Something that is **beat-up** or **beaten-up** is old and in bad condition. ADJECTIVE EG *...broken television set, empty bottles, or beat-up old armchair... ...a beaten-up yellow mini.*

beat up on. If someone **beats up on** you, they hit or kick you many V+ADV+PREP times so that you are badly hurt; used in American English. EG *You couldn't beat up on a guy who looked that sick... You can't beat up on a little kid like that.*

beaver, beavers, beavering, beavered

beaver away. If someone is **beavering away,** they are working V+ADV very hard at a job. EG *He beavers away, putting up one house after another.* ● **Slog away** means almost the same as **beaver away.**

become, becomes, becoming, became
The form **become** is used in the present tense and is the past participle of the verb.

become of. If you wonder what **has become of** someone or V+PREP something, you wonder where they are and what has happened to them. If you wonder what will **become of** them, you wonder about their future. EG *What a terrific cheek he had, that chap Boon. I wonder what became of him... Whatever became of that gold watch you used to have?*

bed, beds, bedding, bedded

bed down. 1 If you **bed** someone **down,** you put them to bed. EG V+N+ADV, *...after the kids were bedded down.*   V+ADV+N, V+PRON+ADV

2 If you **bed down** in a place where you do not normally sleep, you V+ADV sleep there, for example because you are travelling or are in an unusual situation. EG *Servants no longer bedded down in the drawing room.* ● **Doss down** is a more informal expression for **bed down.**

3 When soil or another substance **beds down,** it becomes firm, so V+ADV that further movement or use will not shake it loose. EG *...in order to allow the loose fibres to bed down.* ● **Settle** means almost the same as **bed down.**

bed out. If you **bed out** young plants, you take them from the pot or V+ADV+N, seed tray where they have been growing and plant them in the V+PRON+ADV, ground. ● **Plant out** means almost the same as **bed out.**   V+N+ADV

beef, beefs, beefing, beefed

beef up. If you **beef** something **up,** you strengthen it or make it V+ADV+N, more interesting, significant, or important. EG *They had beefed up* V+N+ADV, *the early evening news programme.*   V+PRON+ADV

beg, begs, begging, begged

beg off. If someone **begs off,** they say apologetically that they are V+ADV, unable to do something that they had agreed to do. EG *They arranged* V+PREP *another meeting but I begged off.* ● **Cry off** means almost the same as **beg off.**

begin, begins, beginning, began, begun

begin by. See **begin with.**

begin with. 1 If you **begin with** something, or **begin by** doing it, you V+PREP deal with it or do it first. EG *The broadcast began with close-up film of babies crying... We decided that we would begin with something familiar.*

2 If something that is printed or written **begins with** a particular V+PREP letter, word, or sentence, this letter, word, or sentence is its first part. EG *Think of all the names beginning with D.*

believe, believes, believing, believed

believe in. 1 If you **believe in** God or things such as fairies or v+PREP
miracles, you feel sure that they exist. EG *I don't believe in ghosts... I*
believe in reincarnation.

2 If you **believe in** an idea or policy, you are in favour of it because v+PREP
you think it is right. EG *...all those who believe in democracy... Do you*
believe in public expenditure cuts?... You believed in giving every-
body access to all the information. ● **Support** means almost the
same as **believe in,** and **oppose** means the opposite.

3 If you **believe in** someone or in something that they are doing, you v+PREP
have confidence in them and think that they will be successful. EG *No*
one would believe in us or what we were doing. ● **Trust** means
almost the same as **believe in.**

belly, bellies, bellying, bellied

belly out. When a large piece of fabric such as the sail of a ship v+ADV
bellies out, it becomes rounded because the wind is filling it. EG *The*
child pulled on a rope and the canvas bellied out. ● **Billow** means
almost the same as **belly out.**

belong, belongs, belonging, belonged

belong to. 1 If something **belongs to** someone, it is owned by them v+PREP
or associated with them. EG *This land does not belong to the*
university... He had taken some valuables belonging to another
person... ...a myth belonging to some tribe in Western Australia... He
recognized the voice as belonging to a senior foreman.

2 If you say that something **belongs to** a person or thing, you mean v+PREP
that they have it, do it, or control it. EG *The last word belonged to the*
chairwoman... The future belonged to automation.

3 If someone **belongs to** a club, an organization, or a group, they are v+PREP
a member of it. EG *The majority of the nation did not belong to trade*
unions... She belongs to the Labour Party.

4 If someone or something **belongs to** a particular type or category, v+PREP
they are of that type or in that category. EG *...several million bats,*
belonging to eight different species... Henry and I belong to very
different generations.

5 If someone or something **belongs to** a particular place or time, v+PREP
they come from that place or time. EG *His wife belongs to the*
village... They have a strong sense of belonging to a farm... Today's
children belong to an age of films.

belt, belts, belting, belted

belt out. If you **belt out** a song, you sing or play it very loudly; an v+ADV+N,
informal expression. EG *She was belting out 'My Way' at the top of* V+PRON+ADV,
her voice. V+N+ADV

belt up. 1 If you tell someone to **belt up,** you tell them to stop v+ADV:
talking; a very informal and impolite use. ● **Shut up** means almost ALSO IMPERATIVE
the same as **belt up.**

2 When you **belt up** while travelling in a car or a plane, you fasten v+ADV
yourself into the seat with a safety belt.

bend, bends, bending, bent

bend down. If you **bend down** when you are standing up, you move v+ADV
the top part of your body downwards. EG *He asked me to bend down*
so that he could stand on my shoulders.

bend over. If you **bend over,** you move the top part of your body v+ADV,
downwards and forwards. EG *She had to bend over sharply because* V+PREP
the roof was so low... He watched them bend over the documents to
sign them.

bet, bets, betting

The form **bet** is used in the present tense and is the past tense and past participle of the verb.

bet on. 1 If you **bet on** something happening, you expect it to happen. EG *Just don't bet on old Arnold gaining a lot of ground with her... That is something which few people would have been prepared to bet on ten years ago.* ● **Bank on** and **count on** mean almost the same as **bet on**. `V+PREP`

2 If you **bet on** something, you rely on it and expect it to help you. EG *Wall Street is betting on Britain's Grand Metropolitan, which has long wanted to expand its U.S.holdings.* ● **Bank on** and **count on** mean almost the same as **bet on**. `V+PREP`

bind, binds, binding, bound

bind over. If someone **is bound over** by a court or a judge, they are given an order and are legally obliged to do as the order says for a particular period of time. EG *The magistrate bound him over to keep the peace.* `V+PRON+ADV, V+N+ADV`

bind up. If you **bind up** a wound, you wrap a bandage around it to stop it bleeding or to protect it; an old-fashioned expression. EG *...bathing it, dressing it, feeding it, binding up its wounds... 'Bind that up, nurse' said the doctor when he arrived.* ● **Bandage up** means almost the same as **bind up**. `V+ADV+N, V+PRON+ADV, V+N+ADV`

bind up with. If something **is bound up with** a particular problem, situation, or activity, it is closely connected with the problem, situation, or activity. EG *All this was bound up with what was happening in Egypt... Wanting her was bound up with the notion of changing her.* `PASSIVE: V+ADV+PREP`

bitch, bitches, bitching, bitched

bitch up. If you **bitch** something **up**, you ruin or spoil it; an informal expression. EG *I was bitching up my marriage and your daughter's life... She couldn't bitch up the relationship of two people she liked.* `V+ADV+N, V+N+ADV, V+PRON+ADV`

bite, bites, biting, bit, bitten

bite back. If you **bite back** a remark or feeling, you stop yourself from saying it or showing it. EG *The word 'Sorry' rises to Morris's lips, but he bites it back... He poured some more soda into his glass, biting back his anger.* ● **Suppress** is a more formal word for **bite back**, and **choke back** means almost the same. `V+PRON+ADV, V+ADV+N, V+N+ADV: NO PASSIVE`

bite into. If an object **bites into** something firm, it cuts or presses into its surface. EG *His collar was biting into his neck.* `V+PREP: HAS PASSIVE`

black, blacks, blacking, blacked

black out. 1 If you **black out**, you lose consciousness for a short time. EG *Marianne told me you blacked out... I was able, before blacking out, to note that he had a gun.* ● **Pass out** means almost the same as **black out**. ▸ A **blackout** is a temporary loss of consciousness or memory. EG *I started having these memory lapses, blackouts they're called... ...an element of danger for someone prone to blackouts.* `V+ADV` `N COUNT`

2 If a room or a building **is blacked out**, it is made completely dark by someone switching off all the lights and covering the windows. EG *The room had been blacked out.* ▸ A **blackout** is a period of time when the electricity supply to a place stops completely. EG *The blackout was caused by the failure of the Northeast power station... ...a fifteen-hour power blackout.* ● **Power cut** means almost the same as a **blackout**. ▸ The **blackout** is a period of time during a war when buildings and streets are kept as dark as possible at night, so `V+ADV+N, V+N+ADV, V+PRON+ADV` `N COUNT` `N SING`

that enemy aircraft cannot see them and bomb them. EG *They used to get very cross if I prevented them from getting home before the blackout.*

3 If people **black out** a television or radio programme, they prevent it being broadcast, usually in protest against something. EG *...blacking out tonight's episode of 'Dallas'.* ▸ A **blackout** is the prevention of the broadcasting of a radio or television programme. EG *The radio blackout would last only an hour.* ▸ A news **blackout** is the prevention of the reporting of news about a particular event. EG *Talks had been held under a news blackout.*
V+ADV+N,
V+N+ADV,
V+PRON+ADV

N COUNT

N COUNT

4 If you **black out** a feeling or an emotion, you hide it and refuse to think about it. EG *He was not only living in the past, but he blacked out all subsequent reality... ...blacking out the sense of danger.*
● **Block out** means almost the same as **black out**.
V+ADV+N,
V+PRON+ADV

blare, blares, blaring, blared

blare out. When a device such as a radio or record player is **blaring out** noise or music, it produces loud noise or music. You can also say that loud noise or music **blares out**. EG *A radio was blaring out the news... Loud hailers blared out 'Keep in line! Keep in line!'... Indian music had been blaring out all evening... The first movement of the Emperor Concerto blared out.*
V+ADV+N,
V+ADV+QUOTE,
V+ADV :
ERGATIVE

blast, blasts, blasting, blasted

blast away. **1** If someone **blasts away** with a gun or if a gun **blasts away**, they fire the gun continuously for a period of time. EG *...riding up and down Wall Street, blasting away with a six-shooter in each hand... The big ships blasted away five to six miles offshore.*
V+ADV :
ALSO+with

2 When something such as a radio or music band is **blasting away**, it plays music very loudly for a period of time. EG *The marching bands were still blasting away.* ● **Blare out** means almost the same as **blast away**.
V+ADV

blast off. When a space rocket **blasts off**, it leaves the ground at the start of a journey into space. EG *...blasting off to commence its two-year mission.* ▸ **Blast-off** is the moment when a rocket leaves the ground and rises into the air. EG *A Saturn V blast-off is the most magnificent spectacle.* ● **Lift-off** means almost the same as **blast-off**.
V+ADV :
USUALLY+A

N UNCOUNT

blast out. When something such as a radio or a music band **blasts out** music or noise, or when music or noise is **blasting out**, very loud music or noise is produced. EG *The band blasts out its version of the school song... ...four more of the shrieks blasted out.* ● **Blare out** and **blast away** mean almost the same as **blast out**.
V+ADV+N,
V+ADV :
ERGATIVE

blaze, blazes, blazing, blazed

blaze away. **1** If a fire or flame is **blazing away**, it is burning very strongly and brightly. EG *It's terribly unhealthy in here with the stoves blazing away like that.*
V+ADV

2 If a light **blazes away**, it shines very brightly. EG *The signs outside the motels, hotels, and night clubs blaze away.*
V+ADV

3 If someone **blazes away** with a gun, they fire the gun rapidly and continuously for a period of time. EG *The Captain continued to blaze away with his machine gun... The police burst into the building blazing away with their guns... He was amazed to see one man calmly standing up, blazing away with a Sten gun... He came out, blazing away.* ● **Blast away** means almost the same as **blaze away**.
V+ADV :
ALSO+with

4 If someone **blazes away**, they talk very loudly for a period of time and do not allow anyone else to interrupt them; used in American English. EG *The ante-room was empty, except for Miss Saunders*
V+ADV

blazing away... This American senator will blaze away the whole evening. ● **Sound off** means almost the same as **blaze away**.

blaze up. If a fire **blazes up**, it suddenly begins to burn strongly and   V+ADV
brightly. EG *...pouring great jugs of oil over it, to make it blaze up as rapidly as possible when lit.*

blend, blends, blending, blended

blend in. If something **blends in** with its surroundings, it is so   V+ADV:
similar to the surroundings in appearance that it becomes difficult   ALSO+*with*
to see it separately. EG *I could not see them—they blended in so well with the landscape... A submarine is often not picked up by radar, as it will often blend in with the ocean floor... Their coloration allows them to blend in.*

blend into. If something **blends into** something in the background,   V+PREP
it it is so similar to the background in appearance or sound that it is difficult to see or hear separately. EG *The clothes are deliberately chosen to blend into their surroundings... Tree snakes are bright green, but they blend so well into foliage... The words of the driver blending into the roar of the engine.* ● **Merge into** means almost the same as **blend into**.

bliss, blisses, blissing, blissed

bliss out. If something **blisses** you **out**, it makes you extremely   V+PRON+ADV,
happy; used mainly in American English. EG *It was my chosen*   V+N+ADV,
profession. I was good at it. It blissed me out, as Eddie used to say.   V+ADV+N
▶ Someone who is **blissed-out** is extremely happy; used mainly in   ADJECTIVE
American English. EG *...blissed-out babies and mothers.*

block, blocks, blocking, blocked

block in. 1 If you **block** someone **in**, you park your car so close to   V+PRON+ADV,
their car that they cannot drive away. EG *Eric was late because I*   V+N+ADV,
blocked him in by mistake.   V+ADV+N

2 If you **block in** a figure that is drawn only with an outline, you fill it   V+ADV+N,
in by covering the area inside the figure with paint, ink, or pencil. EG   V+PRON+ADV,
Let me have another look at it after you've blocked in the buildings.   V+N+ADV
● **Shade in** and **colour in** mean almost the same as **block in**.

block off. When you **block off** a road or the entrance to a building,   V+ADV+N,
you put something across it and cover it completely so that nothing   V+N+ADV,
can pass through it. EG *The soldiers blocking off the jail were in*   V+PRON+ADV
position... I got off the bus and the road was blocked off. ● **Close off**
and **seal off** mean almost the same as **block off**, and **obstruct** is a
more formal word.

block out. 1 Something that **blocks out** light from a place prevents   V+ADV+N,
it from entering. EG *...satellites that would block out sunlight.* ● **Shut**   V+N+ADV,
out means almost the same as **block out**, and **exclude** is a more   V+PRON+ADV
formal word.

2 If something **blocks out** something else, it is in front of it so that   V+ADV+N,
you cannot see it. EG *The trees almost successfully block out the*   V+PRON+ADV
brick houses... The woman wore her bonnet well forward, blocking out her view of the world on both sides. ● **Obscure** is a more formal
word for **block out**.

3 If someone **blocks out** something such as news or information,   V+ADV+N,
they prevent other people from hearing about it. EG *Governments*   V+PRON+ADV
can try to block out unwelcome ideas from abroad. ● **Suppress** is a
more formal word for **block out**.

4 If you **block out** a feeling or an idea, you try not to think about it.   V+ADV+N,
EG *...dissatisfaction blurring, even blocking out that appreciation...*   V+PRON+ADV
They attempt to withdraw from it, to block it out. ● **Shut out** means
almost the same as **block out**, and **suppress** is a more formal word.

block up. 1 If you **block up** something, you close it up completely so that nothing can get through it. EG *Never block up ventilators... Drains must be left clear, so don't let leaves block them up.* ● **Obstruct** is a more formal word for **block up.**

V+ADV+N,
V+PRON+ADV,
V+N+ADV

2 If something **blocks up,** it becomes covered or filled and nothing can pass through it. EG *The sink keeps blocking up.*

V+ADV

blot, blots, blotting, blotted

blot out. 1 If one thing **blots out** another thing, it hides it or stops it from being seen or heard. EG *The resulting dust cloud could have blotted out the sun... ...a dry monotonous rustling that blotted out all other sounds... One side of his face was blotted out by a large purple birthmark.*

V+ADV+N,
V+PRON+ADV,
V+N+ADV

2 If a particular idea, experience, or feeling that you have **blots out** all other ones, it is the only one that you can think about. EG *The money had blotted out everything else... Panic wells up and blots out your real abilities.* ● **Obscure** is a more formal word for **blot out.**

V+ADV+N,
V+PRON+ADV

3 If you try to **blot out** a memory or thought, you try not to think of it. EG *...casting around for something that will blot out his failures as President... 'The way to blot him out,' I said, 'is not to think about him'.* ● **Block out** means almost the same as **blot out.**

V+ADV+N,
V+PRON+ADV,
V+N+ADV

blot up. If you **blot up** a small amount of liquid, you remove it by pressing something absorbent onto it. EG *She blotted up the juice from the beans with her bread.* ● **Mop up** means almost the same as **blot up.**

V+ADV+N,
V+PRON+ADV,
V+N+ADV

blow, blows, blowing, blew, blown

blow about. If things **blow about** or **around** in the wind, or if they are **blown about** or **around,** the wind moves them around in different directions. EG *She got terribly blown about... My papers had been blown about, and some were missing... ...all that dust blowing around.*

V+N+ADV,
V+PRON+ADV,
V+ADV:
ERGATIVE,
USUALLY PASSIVE

blow around. See **blow about.**

blow away. 1 If something **blows away** or if the wind **blows** it **away,** the wind moves it away from the place where it was. EG *It turned into dust and blew away when he turned his back... The wind blew his papers away... Use near an open window to blow away fumes.*

V+ADV,
V+N+ADV,
V+ADV+N,
V+PRON+ADV:
ERGATIVE

2 If you **blow** something **away,** you blow on it so that it moves away from the place where it was. EG *Shake them in your hand and blow the husks away.*

V+N+ADV,
V+PRON+ADV,
V+ADV+N:
NO PASSIVE

3 If a bomb or explosion **blows away** part of your body, it removes it or destroys it. EG *...a marine whose face had been blown away.*

V+N+ADV,
V+PRON+ADV,
V+ADV+N

blow back. If something **blows back** or **is blown back,** the wind moves it back in the direction it was coming from. EG *The tear-gas that we'd fired was blowing back over our positions... The ashes blew back into Ralph's face from the dying fire... The wind blew all the smoke back down the chimney.*

V+ADV,
V+N+ADV,
V+PRON+ADV,
V+ADV+N:
ERGATIVE,
USUALLY+A

blow down. If something **blows down** or **is blown down,** the wind makes it fall to the ground. EG *...deckchairs and tents which had blown down in the storm... Several trees had been blown down... The tent was blown down during the gale.* ● **Blow over** means almost the same as **blow down.**

V+ADV,
V+ADV+N,
V+N+ADV,
V+PRON+ADV:
ERGATIVE

blow off. 1 If something **blows off** or **is blown off,** it is removed from a place by the wind. EG *Your hat won't blow off... Roofs were blown off... He was blown off his horse.*

V+ADV/PREP,
V+N+ADV/PREP,
V+PRON+ADV/PREP:
ERGATIVE

2 If a bomb or explosion **blows off** a part of your body, it removes it. EG *I didn't want my head blown off... He probably would have blown his hand off if he'd fired it.*

V+N+ADV,
V+PRON+ADV,
V+ADV+N

blow out. 1 When a person or the wind **blows out** a flame or fire, they stop it burning. EG *Rudolph blew out the candles... The wind almost blew out the flame.* ● **Extinguish** is a more formal word for **blow out**, and **put out** means almost the same. `V+ADV+N, V+N+ADV, V+PRON+ADV`

2 If a storm **blows** itself **out**, it comes to an end. EG *This little duststorm will blow itself out soon enough... Eventually the storm blew itself out.* `V+REFL+ADV`

3 A **blow-out** is 3.1 a meal that is larger than you normally have; an informal use. EG *Have a blow-out on your birthday.* ● **Binge** means almost the same as **blow-out**. 3.2 a sudden loss of air from a tyre because the tyre has burst; an informal use. EG *My car had a blow-out.* ● **Puncture** means almost the same as **blow-out**. 3.3 a sudden uncontrolled rush of oil or gas from a well. `N COUNT` `N COUNT` `N COUNT`

blow over. 1 If something such as an argument or some trouble **blows over**, it comes to an end and is forgotten about. EG *The row has blown over... Gary told me that it would blow over and that I shouldn't worry so much.* `V+ADV`

2 When a storm **blows over**, it becomes less fierce and ends. ● **Die down** means almost the same as **blow over**. `V+ADV`

3 If something **is blown over**, the wind makes it fall to the ground. EG *All lightweight structures were blown over.* ● **Blow down** means almost the same as **blow over**. `V+N+ADV, V+PRON+ADV, V+ADV+N`

blow up. 1 If you **blow** something **up** or if it **blows up**, it is destroyed by an explosion. EG *He was going to blow the place up... They now have enough nuclear weapons to blow themselves up many times over... The battleship Maine has been blown up in Havana Harbour... One of the submarines blew up and sank.* `V+N+ADV, V+REFL+ADV, V+ADV+N, V+PRON+ADV, V+ADV: ERGATIVE`

2 If you **blow up**, you lose your temper and become very angry; an informal use. EG *It takes considerable character not to blow up.* ● **Explode** is a more formal word for **blow up**. `V+ADV`

3 If a difficult or dangerous situation **blows up**, it begins suddenly and unexpectedly. EG *Then this murder case blew up, and we had to drop it... Occasionally trouble blew up; challenges were exchanged... The situation blew up in Miller's face when a demonstration turned into a riot.* `V+ADV`

4 If you **blow up** something such as a balloon or a tyre, you fill it with air. EG *We spent the afternoon blowing up balloons for the party.* ● **Inflate** is a more formal word for **blow up**. `V+ADV+N, V+N+ADV, V+PRON+ADV`

5 If you **blow up** a photograph or picture, you print a larger copy of it. EG *Once the photos had been blown up, the gun in his hand was clearly visible.* ● **Enlarge** is a more formal word for **blow up**. ▷ A **blow-up** is an enlargement of a photograph or picture. `V+N+ADV, V+PRON+ADV, V+ADV+N` `N COUNT`

6 If a storm **blows up**, the weather becomes stormy. EG *We were warned of a storm blowing up off the East coast.* ● **Get up** means almost the same as **blow up**, and **die down** means the opposite. `V+ADV`

bluff, bluffs, bluffing, bluffed

bluff into. If you **bluff** someone **into** doing something, you persuade them to do it by telling them something that is not true. EG *He wanted to try to bluff them into thinking that he was being stern.* `V+PRON+PREP, V+N+PREP`

blunder, blunders, blundering, blundered

blunder about. If you **blunder about** or **around**, you move about in a clumsy or uncertain way, for example because you cannot see properly. EG *I can't blunder about without specs... They screamed and blundered about... She was blundering around the kitchen.* `V+ADV, V+PREP`

blunder around. See **blunder about**.

blunder through. If you **blunder through** an exam or other activity, you manage to finish it although you are not all sure `V+PREP, V+ADV` whether what you are doing is right. EG *He blundered through the exercises somehow.* ● **Muddle though** means almost the same as **blunder through.**

blurt, blurts, blurting, blurted

blurt out. If you **blurt** something **out**, you say it suddenly, without thinking about it. EG *The astounded Reichert could only blurt out 'Where have you come from?'... I blurted out that I had got a job... Frank blurted out the news of Sir James's arrival... I hadn't intended to blurt it out.*

V+ADV+QUOTE,
V+ADV+REPORT,
V+ADV+N,
V+PRON+ADV,
V+N+ADV

board, boards, boarding, boarded

board out. If you **board out** someone who is in your care, you send them to stay with someone else for a period of time. EG *Almost half of all children in care were boarded out with foster parents.*

V+N+ADV,
V+PRON+ADV,
V+ADV+N

board up. If you **board up** a door or window, you fasten boards over it so that it is covered up. EG *Shopkeepers were boarding up their windows... Some of the old shops were boarded up.*

V+ADV+N,
V+N+ADV,
V+PRON+ADV

bob, bobs, bobbing, bobbed

bob about. If something **bobs about** or **around,** it moves gently up and down, like something floating on water. EG *John's head was bobbing about among the fishing boats... They bobbed around like corks.*

V+ADV

bob around. See **bob about.**

bob up. 1 If something **bobs up,** it suddenly floats to the surface after it has been under water. EG *Suddenly an object bobbed up from below the surface.*

V+ADV

2 If someone **bobs up,** they appear or reappear suddenly. EG *Here and there at the cliff top soldiers bobbed up.* ● **Pop up** means almost the same as **bob up.**

V+ADV

bog, bogs, bogging, bogged

bog down. If you **are bogged down** in a task, you are not progressing quickly because you are being too careful or spending too much time on minor problems. EG *The outsider is not bogged down by a particular way of doing things... Don't get bogged down in details.*

PASSIVE:
V+ADV

bog off. If you tell someone to **bog off,** you are telling them rudely to go away; a very informal expression which some people find rude and offensive.

V+ADV:
ALSO IMPERATIVE

boil, boils, boiling, boiled

boil away. When a liquid that is being heated **boils away,** it changes into steam or vapour. EG *...causing the engine to overheat and the water to boil away... They cooked it until the water was boiled away.* ● **Evaporate** is a more formal word for **boil away.**

V+ADV

boil down. 1 When you **boil down** a liquid, you boil it until it decreases in amount, because some of it has changed into steam or vapour. EG *Boil the sauce down until it is really thick... A panful of spinach boils down to virtually nothing.*

V+N+ADV,
V+PRON+ADV,
V+ADV+N,
V+ADV:
ERGATIVE

2 If you **boil down** an amount of information, you keep only the most important parts and details. EG *...sorting through data and boiling it down.* ● **Condense** means almost the same as **boil down,** and **pad out** means the opposite.

V+PRON+ADV,
V+N+ADV,
V+ADV+N

boil down to. If you say that a situation, issue, or question **boils down to** a particular thing, you mean that this is the most important aspect of it. EG *What it all seemed to boil down to was money... The question boils down to one of social priorities.*

V+ADV+PREP

boil over. 1 When a liquid that is being heated **boils over,** it rises

V+ADV

and flows over the edge of its container. EG *The milk's boiling over...*   V+ADV
The kettle had boiled over.

2 If a situation in which people are very angry **boils over,** they   V+ADV
become so angry that the situation gets out of control. EG *The*
simmering quarrel between the opposing parties boiled over...
Sleepy as he was, his temper promptly boiled over again.

boil up. 1 When you **boil up** a liquid, you heat it until it boils. EG *If the*   V+ADV+N,
insides of aluminium pans discolour, boil up some water in them   V+N+ADV,
V+PRON+ADV
with a squeezed lemon... I kept a stockpot last winter and boiled it
up every day... When the juice is boiled up with sugar it forms jelly.

2 If you say that anger **boils up** in you, you mean that you suddenly   V+ADV
feel very angry. EG *The feeling of fury boils up in them.*

bolster, bolsters, bolstering, bolstered

bolster up. To **bolster up** someone or something means to support   V+ADV+N
them or help them. EG *...a strike fund to bolster up employees*
fighting their employers... To bolster up their case, they quoted a
speech by Ray Gun.

bolt, bolts, bolting, bolted

bolt down. If you **bolt down** your food, you eat it very quickly; an   V+ADV+N,
informal expression. EG *...bolting down his lunch and rushing off to*   V+N+ADV,
V+PRON+ADV
the airport.

bomb, bombs, bombing, bombed

bomb along. If you **bomb along,** you move or travel very quickly;   V+PREP,
an informal expression. EG *We went bombing along the motorway at*   V+ADV
90 mph.

bomb out. If a building is **bombed out** or if people in a building are   PASSIVE:
bombed out, the building is completely destroyed by a bomb. EG   V+ADV
Their factories were bombed out... ...people bombed out in the war.

bone, bones, boning, boned

bone up on. If you **bone up on** a subject, you revise it; an informal   V+ADV+PREP
expression. EG *He had been boning up on French history.* ● **Swot up**
on means almost the same as **bone up on.**

book, books, booking, booked

book in. 1 When you **book in,** you announce that you have arrived at   V+ADV
a hotel and sign your name in a register. EG *It was too late to go*
shopping, so he booked in at the Ritz Hotel. ● **Check in** means
almost the same as **book in,** and **check out** means the opposite.

2 When you **book** someone **in,** you arrange for them to stay   V+PRON+ADV,
somewhere such as a hotel. You can also say that you **book** someone   V+N+ADV
in when you arrange for them to register for something such as a
course, event, or appointment. EG *I had booked us in at a hotel in*
Torquay... The theatre company had already booked them in for
another show long before we arrived on the scene... She booked Mr
Bashton in to see the doctor on Tuesday.

book into. 1 When you **book into** a hotel, you inform the reception-   V+PREP
ist that you have arrived and sign your name in a register. EG *He had*
booked into the Warsaw Hotel. ● **Check into** means almost the same
as **book into.**

2 When you **book** someone **into** a hotel, you arrange for a room to be   V+N+PREP,
reserved for them there. EG *He had been booked into this hotel by*   V+PRON+PREP
the travel agent.

book up. 1 If you **book up** for something such as a course, event, or   V+ADV:
other organized activity, you arrange to take part in it. EG *'Can I help*   ALSO+*for*
you?'—'Yes, I want to book up for what you have on the window'...
We've still got time to book up for the French course.

2 If something such as a hotel, concert, plane, or course **is booked up**, it has no rooms, seats, or tickets left. EG *Ski resorts have been booked up for weeks... Are they fully booked up?... There are no more flights available to East London tonight. They're booked up.*   PASSIVE: V+ADV

boom, booms, booming, boomed

boom out. When someone **booms out** something or when their voice **booms out**, they speak in a very loud, deep voice. EG *He boomed out: 'Good evening ladies and gentlemen!'... A great voice boomed out the words which announced their arrival.*   V+ADV+QUOTE, V+ADV+N: NO PASSIVE

boot, boots, booting, booted

boot out. If someone is **booted out** of a job or a place, they are forced to leave it; an informal expression. EG *No wonder Gertrude booted me out... The member who made that speech was booted out by Conservative Party leaders.* ● **Kick out** means almost the same as **boot out**, and **expel** is a more formal word.   V+PRON+ADV, V+N+ADV, V+ADV+N: ALSO+*of*

border, borders, bordering, bordered

border on. **1** A country that **borders on** another country is next to that country and shares a border with it. EG *Soviet territory facing the West borders on Poland, Czechoslovakia, and Hungary.*   V+PREP

2 When you say that something **borders on** a particular state or condition, you mean that it is almost in that state or condition. EG *I was in a state of excitement bordering on insanity... Their rough treatment of each other bordered on brutality.* ● **Verge on** means almost the same as **border on**.   V+PREP

bore, bores, boring, bored

bore into. If someone's eyes **bore into** you, they are staring intensely at you. EG *Vorster's eyes bored into me. He said 'We are at war. You cannot afford to refuse.'*   V+PREP

botch, botches, botching, botched

botch up. If you **botch up** a piece of work, you do it very badly or clumsily. EG *He really botched up the last job he did for us.*   V+ADV+N, V+PRON+ADV, V+N+ADV

bottle, bottles, bottling, bottled

bottle out. If you **bottle out** just before doing something difficult or frightening, you lose your courage at the last moment, and do not do it; an informal expression used in British English. EG *She'll bottle out when she sees the other competitors.* ● **Chicken out** means almost the same as **bottle out**.   V+ADV: ALSO+*of*

bottle up. **1** If you **bottle up** a strong feeling, you deliberately do not express it for a long time, although you find this very difficult. EG *All the rage that had been bottled up in him for so long flooded out in a torrent of abuse.*   V+ADV+N, V+PRON+ADV, V+N+ADV

2 If you **bottle up** a liquid, you transfer it from a large container into several smaller bottles. EG *Bottle up that Benylin and put it on the shelves... She's in the cellar, bottling the home-made wine up... All the ginger beer was bottled up and ready for the party.*   V+ADV+N, V+N+ADV, V+PRON+ADV

bottom, bottoms, bottoming, bottomed

bottom out. When something that was getting worse or decreasing **bottoms out**, it stops doing so and remains steady. EG *Even if the recession has bottomed out, it will not help the unemployed... Death rates have not bottomed out by any means... ...bottoming out of the downward spiral.* ● **Level out** means almost the same as **bottom out**.   V+ADV

bounce, bounces, bouncing, bounced

bounce back. If you **bounce back** after a disappointing or unpleasant experience, you return quickly to your normal activities or to   V+ADV your previous level of enthusiasm or success. EG *You'll bounce back, don't worry... My bet is he'll bounce right back.* ● **Recover** is a more general word for **bounce back.**

bow, bows, bowing, bowed

bow down. If you **bow down,** you bow very low in order to show great respect. EG *The servants were commanded to bow down.* V+ADV: ALSO+*to*

bow out. If you **bow out** of something, you stop doing it or taking part in it, often in order to allow someone else to take your place. EG *We may do one more performance before we bow out.* ● **Step down** means almost the same as **bow out.** V+ADV: ALSO+*of*

bow to. If you **bow to** someone's wishes, or **bow to** pressure from someone, you change your plans and do what they want you to do. EG *They are inclined to bow to all her wishes... The Minister seems to be bowing to pressure from industry to ignore the recommendations.* ● **Yield to** means almost the same as **bow to.** V+PREP

bowl, bowls, bowling, bowled

bowl out. To **bowl out** a team in cricket means to get all their players out and end their innings. EG *We were bowled out for 220 runs.* ● **Dismiss** is a more formal word for **bowl out.** V+N+ADV, V+PRON+ADV, V+ADV+N

bowl over. 1 If you **bowl** someone **over,** you knock them down by colliding with them when you are moving very quickly. EG *They leapt aside to avoid being bowled over by three boys as they raced past.* ● **Knock over** means almost the same as **bowl over.** V+N+ADV, V+PRON+ADV, V+ADV+N

2 If you **are bowled over** by someone or something, you are very impressed or deeply affected by them because they are so surprising, different, or exciting. EG *I was bowled over by the beauty of Malawi... The sight of her just bowled him over.* ● **Overwhelm** is a more formal word for **bowl over.** V+N+ADV, V+PRON+ADV

box, boxes, boxing, boxed

box in. If you **are boxed in** somewhere, you are unable to move because you are surrounded by people, by parked cars, or other obstructions. EG *Unless you go ahead early on in the race there's a danger you'll get boxed in... Some fool parked his car too close to mine and boxed me in.* ● **Hem in** means almost the same as **box in.** V+N+ADV, V+PRON+ADV, V+ADV+N

box off. To **box off** an area means to make a small enclosed area within a larger area by building walls around it. EG *You could box off the area under the stairs to make a cupboard.* V+N+ADV, V+PRON+ADV, V+ADV+N

box up. If you **box** something **up,** you put it into boxes. EG *...boxing up medical supplies... I boxed all those books up, so I think it's your turn to do something now.* V+ADV+N, V+N+ADV, V+PRON+ADV

branch, branches, branching, branched

branch off. 1 A road or path that **branches off** from another, larger one starts from it and goes in a slightly different direction. EG *The road to Oxford branches off here... A dirt path branched off the main road.* V+ADV, V+PREP

2 If you **branch off** when you are speaking, you start talking about something slightly different. EG *Do you not think then, to branch off that subject a little, that their upbringing is important too?* V+ADV, V+PREP

branch out. If you **branch out,** you do something different from your normal activities or work, especially something unusual or risky. EG *I can't think why we didn't move years ago when we felt the urge to branch out... She decided to branch out alone and launch a concerted campaign.* V+ADV

brave, braves, braving, braved

brave out. If you **brave out** a dangerous or upsetting situation, you V+ADV+N,

face it and deal with it in a brave way. EG *We'll just have to brave out*   V+N+ADV,
the return journey on our own.   V+PRON+ADV

brazen, brazens, brazening, brazened

brazen out. If you have done something wrong and you **brazen** it   V+*it*+ADV
out, you behave confidently and show no shame or regret. EG *Of
course he'll brazen it out; he's got no scruples at all.*

break, breaks, breaking, broke, broken

break away. 1 When you **break away** from a group, you stop being   V+ADV:
part of it, for example because of a disagreement. EG *Two United*   USUALLY+*from*
*Party senators broke away to form the Federal Party... Another sect
had broken away from the long-established Plymouth Brethren.*
● **Split off** means almost the same as **break away.** ▸ A **breakaway**   ADJECTIVE
group is one that has separated from a larger group. EG *How well is
Britain's new breakaway party likely to do in the General Election?*
▸ A **breakaway** is the act of breaking away from a group. EG *The*   N COUNT
move towards a final breakaway began on 10 February.
2 If you **break away** from someone who is holding you, you move   V+ADV:
away from them suddenly. EG *She made a half-hearted attempt to*   ALSO+*from*
break away... Florrie broke away and rushed upstairs.
3 If a part of something **breaks away,** it separates and moves away.   V+ADV:
EG *Australia had broken away from Antarctica and continued to*   USUALLY+*from*
drift.
4 If you **break away** from a belief or a habit, you reject it. EG *...the*   V+ADV:
tendency to break away from tradition.   USUALLY+*from*

break down. 1 When an arrangement, plan, or discussion **breaks**   V+ADV
down, it fails because of a problem or disagreement. EG *The talks
broke down over differences on doctrine... An unhappy marriage
which eventually breaks down often results in disturbed children.*
● **Founder** is a formal word for **break down.** ▸ The **breakdown** of an   N COUNT
arrangement, plan, or discussion is the failure or collapse of it. EG
*There was a serious breakdown of communications... Politicians
blame the police for the breakdown in community relations.*
2 When a machine or a vehicle **breaks down,** it stops working. EG   V+ADV
*The telephone communication system had broken down... Mum's
TV has broken down.* ● **Pack up** and **conk out** are more informal
expressions for **break down.** ▸ If you have a **breakdown** when you   N COUNT
are travelling in a car, the car stops working. EG *Spark plugs in bad
condition make you very prone to breakdowns... We had a breakdown on the motorway.* ▸ A **broken-down** vehicle or a machine no   ADJECTIVE
longer works because it has something wrong with it. EG *...pushing a
broken-down car.*
3 To **break down** an idea, a statement, or information means to   V+ADV+N,
separate it into smaller parts in order to understand it or deal with it   V+PRON+ADV,
more easily. EG *Learn to break down large tasks into manageable*   V+N+ADV
*units... ...trying to break it down into concepts that they could cope
with... With a computer you can break the data down to suit
particular requirements.* ▸ A **breakdown** of a set of figures is a   N COUNT
simpler version of it arranged in separate sections. EG *Can you give
me the breakdown for London?*
4 When a substance **breaks down** or when something **breaks** it   V+ADV,
down, it changes as a result of a chemical or biological process. EG   V+ADV+N,
The residue breaks down before reaching the sewer... Enzymes   V+N+ADV,
break down proteins by chemical action.   V+PRON+ADV:
  ERGATIVE
5 If you **break down** a problem or obstacle, you weaken or remove it   V+ADV+N,
so that it no longer prevents you from doing something. EG *This*   V+N+ADV,
would help break down the barriers between young and old...   V+PRON+ADV
...women who play the 'little girl role' to break down a man's

resistance. ● **Overcome** means almost the same as **break down.**
▶ The **breakdown** of an idea or a tradition is the ending of it. EG   N COUNT
There had been a breakdown of class in England.
6 If someone **breaks down, 6.1** they start crying or laughing uncon-   V+ADV
trollably. EG *He was afraid he was going to break down and cry.*   **6.2**   V+ADV
they become very depressed and ill because they cannot cope with
their problems. EG *She broke down completely and had to go into
hospital... I was under enormous pressure for about 2 years before I
broke down.* ● **Crack up** means almost the same as **break down.** ▶ A   N COUNT
breakdown is an illness involving severe mental depression which
needs psychiatric treatment. EG *You'll give yourself a nervous
breakdown... I shall have another breakdown if I stay in this house.*
7 To **break down** something such as a door or wall means to hit it   V+ADV+N,
hard so that it breaks and falls to the ground. EG *...breaking down the*   V+N+ADV,
gates... The water floods their homes or breaks down the walls.   V+PRON+ADV
● **Smash down** means almost the same as **break down,** and **demol-**
ish is a more formal word. ▶ A **broken-down** building is in very bad   ADJECTIVE
condition. EG *...a narrow street of broken-down shops.*

break in. **1** If someone **breaks in,** they get into a building illegally or   V+ADV
by force. EG *The police broke in and arrested all the brothers... They
had broken in through a gardener's gate.* ▶ A **break-in** is the act of   N COUNT
getting into a building illegally or by force. EG *The break-in and
robbery had taken them only twenty minutes.*
2 If you **break in** when someone is talking or doing something, you   V+ADV:
interrupt them. EG *'Don't look at me,' Etta broke in brusquely...*   ALSO+QUOTE
'Crow—' began Spear excitedly, but his wife broke in. ● **Butt in** and
cut in mean almost the same as **break in.**
3 If you **break** someone **in,** you get them used to a new job or   V+ADV+N,
situation. EG *Chief Brody liked to break in his young men slowly.*   V+PRON+ADV,
   V+N+ADV
4 When you **break in** a new pair of shoes, you wear them for short   V+ADV+N,
periods of time until they become comfortable enough for normal   V+PRON+ADV
use. EG *...good weather recently for breaking in new boots.*
5 If you **break in** a wild or young horse, you train it to be obedient   V+ADV+N,
and unafraid of humans. EG *...her first chance to break in a pony.*   V+PRON+ADV,
   V+N+ADV
break in on. If you **break in on** a person or a conversation, you   V+ADV+PREP
interrupt them. EG *Sorry to break in on you like this, Dr Marlowe...
Could we just break in on that question?*

break into. **1** If someone **breaks into** a room or a building, they   V+PREP:
enter it illegally or by force. EG *He broke into a shop one night and*   HAS PASSIVE
killed the proprietor... Offices were broken into and files removed.
2 If you **break into** an action or activity, you suddenly start doing it.   V+PREP
EG *When Rudolph saw her, he broke into a run... Piggy broke into
noisy laughter... The boys broke into applause.* ● **Burst into** means
almost the same as **break into.**
3 If you **break into** an activity or process that is going on, you   V+PREP
interrupt it. EG *He became so pensive that she did not like to break
into his thought.* ● **Disturb** means almost the same as **break into.**
4 If you **break into** a new activity or business, you start becoming   V+PREP
involved in it. EG *...women wanting to break into the labour market.*
● **Get into** and **move into** mean almost the same as **break into.**
5 If you **break into** a sum of money that you have been saving, you   V+PREP
start to spend it. EG *She was so desperate that she broke into her
holiday money.* ● **Dip into** means almost the same as **break into.**
6 If you **break into** a container of food or drink, you open it and start   V+PREP
to eat or drink the contents. EG *Let's break into a bottle of champagne to celebrate.*
7 When you **break** something **into** smaller parts, you divide it into   V+N+PREP,
   V+PRON+PREP

smaller parts. EG *...breaking words into syllables... You can break each feeding period into several parts.*

break in upon. If one thing **breaks in upon** another, it affects it suddenly and strongly; a formal expression. EG *The Revolution broke in upon a culture which had petrified.* v+ADV+PREP

break off. 1 If a part of something **breaks off** or you **break it off**, it separates or is removed by force. EG *A little bit has broken off... I broke a branch off and stabbed at the ground with it... Garroway broke off another piece of bread.* V+ADV, V+N+ADV, V+ADV+N, V+PRON+ADV: ERGATIVE

2 If you **break off** when speaking, you suddenly stop. EG *He broke off, only to resume almost immediately... 'I thought—' he broke off, then smiled. 'Sorry, not my business.'* V+ADV

3 If you **break off** something that you are doing, you stop doing it. EG *He would break off the rehearsal... ...breaking off their game reluctantly to say goodbye.* V+ADV+N, V+PRON+ADV

4 If you **break off** a relationship or agreement, you end it. EG *Men seem to be more skilled at breaking off relationships than women.* ● **Terminate** is a more formal word for **break off**. V+ADV+N, V+PRON+ADV, V+N+ADV

break out. 1 If something unpleasant **breaks out,** it begins suddenly. EG *War broke out in Europe on 4 August... This row broke out on the eve of the Congress... A fire broke out on the third floor.* ▶ An **outbreak** of something unpleasant is a sudden occurrence of it. EG *...a severe outbreak of food poisoning... Outbreaks of looting were reported.* V+ADV: USUALLY+A / N COUNT

2 If a noise **breaks out,** it begins suddenly. EG *The clamour broke out at once... The smiles broaden, laughter breaks out.* V+ADV

3 If someone **breaks out** of a place where they are a prisoner, they escape from it. EG *He broke out one spring night in 1946 and hitched south.* ▶ A **break-out** is the act of escaping from a place. EG *We debated whether to make our break-out on Christmas Eve.* V+ADV: ALSO+from/of / N COUNT

4 If you **break out** of a routine, a habit, or a restricting situation, you manage to change it and do something different. EG *We've got to break out of this vicious circle... She has managed to break out of the mould and achieve something.* V+ADV: ALSO+of

5 If you **break out** in a rash or a sweat, or if it **breaks out** on your body, it suddenly appears on your skin. EG *She broke out in a rash... She felt the sweat break out on her forehead.* V+ADV: USUALLY+A

break through. 1 If you **break through** a barrier, you force your way through it. EG *I struggled up the side and broke through the elder bushes... Some of the crowd attempted to break through police cordons... A horse broke through the fence.* V+PREP

2 If you **break through** a problem that prevents you from doing something, you find a way to deal with it or remove it. EG *She could not break through such a barrier of indifference... They gradually broke through my reserve.* ● **Overcome** is a more formal word for **break through.** ▶ A **breakthrough** is an important development or achievement. EG *Scientists are hovering on the brink of a major breakthrough... ...a breakthrough in government-industry relations.* V+PREP / N COUNT

3 If a quality or aspect of something **breaks through,** it begins to appear or to be noticed; a literary use. EG *Sometimes the artistic impulses break through in your work... ...a young person, whose spirit is just breaking through.* V+ADV

4 If the sun **breaks through** the clouds, it becomes visible after being hidden by them. EG *The pitch will dry up quickly if the sun breaks through.* V+PREP, V+ADV

break up. 1 When something **breaks up** or when you **break it up**, it becomes divided into smaller parts. EG *The great southern land-mass eventually began to break up... Most birds still have a need to break* V+ADV, V+ADV+N, V+N+ADV, V+PRON+ADV: ERGATIVE *up their food... Here the paddy land is broken up like a jigsaw puzzle.*

▶ If the **break-up** of a ship, spacecraft, or other vehicle occurs, it suddenly breaks into two or more pieces, usually after a collision. EG *...the dramatic break-up of oil tankers.* · N COUNT

2 If a group or organization **breaks up,** or if something **breaks** it **up,** the people in it separate from each other. EG *His committee broke up into rival groups... There is nothing like sudden wealth for breaking up an ordinary family.* ● **Split up** means almost the same as **break-up.** ▶ When the **break-up** of a group, organization, or system occurs, it comes to an end. EG *We are on the brink of a break-up of the two-party system.* · V+ADV, V+ADV+N, V+N+ADV, V+PRON+ADV: ERGATIVE · N SING

3 If you **break up** with your wife, husband, boyfriend, or girlfriend, your relationship with that person ends. EG *Tim and I broke up... Their marriage is breaking up... Had you already broken up with your boyfriend?* ● **Split up** and **finish** mean almost the same as **break up.** ▶ If the **break-up** of a marriage or a relationship occurs, it comes to an end. EG *...all marriage break-ups are traumatic.* · V+ADV, V+ADV+with: RECIPROCAL · N COUNT

4 If a gathering of people **breaks up** or if you **break** it **up,** it is brought to an end. EG *The long drunken party had just broken up... The crowd broke up in panic... The rest of us were trying to break the skirmish up... ...disruptive tactics of breaking up meetings.* · V+ADV, V+N+ADV, V+ADV+N, V+PRON+ADV: ERGATIVE

5 If an event or activity **breaks up** your day, it helps to make your day less boring, because it is different from what you do the rest of the time. EG *Meals and drinks break up the hospital day... These games could be used to break up the monotony.* · V+ADV+N, V+N+ADV, V+PRON+ADV

6 If you **break up** something that is all one colour or pattern, you add new colours or patterns to make it more interesting. EG *...a modern logo at the top, breaking up what used to be slabs of grey type... ...a portrait which has been broken up into rectangles of different colours.* · V+ADV+N, V+PRON+ADV, V+N+ADV

7 When schools or schoolchildren **break up,** the school term ends and the children start their holidays; used mainly in informal British English. EG *We're lucky, we break up quite early.* · V+ADV

break with. **1** If you **break with** a friend, or a group you belong to, you disagree with them and end your association with them; a formal use. EG *In 1929 he broke with the Liberal Party over Lloyd George's policies.* · V+PREP

2 If you **break with** a custom or tradition, you reject it and do something different; a formal use. EG *We have broken irretrievably with the past... He broke with precedent by making his maiden speech on a controversial subject.* · V+PREP: HAS PASSIVE

breathe, breathes, breathing, breathed

breathe in. When you **breathe in,** you take air into your lungs through your nose or mouth. EG *Breathe in slowly... We lifted our heads to breathe in the fresh air... If you use a spray, don't breathe it in.* ● **Inhale** is a more formal word for **breathe in.** · V+ADV, V+ADV+N, V+PRON+ADV, V+N+ADV

breathe out. When you **breathe out,** you make the air in your lungs come out through your nose or mouth. EG *She breathed out through parted lips... She breathed it out slowly and spoke reasonably calmly... They breathed out smoke.* ● **Exhale** is a more formal word for **breathe out.** · V+ADV, V+PRON+ADV, V+N+ADV, V+ADV+N

breeze, breezes, breezing, breezed

breeze in. If someone **breezes in,** they enter a place in a carefree and relaxed way. EG *She just breezed in, as if nothing had happened.* · V+ADV

breeze out. If someone **breezes out,** they leave a place in a carefree and relaxed way. EG *She breezed out of the bathroom, whistling loudly.* · V+ADV

brew, brews, brewing, brewed

brew up. 1 If you **brew up**, you make a pot of tea; an informal use in British English. EG *I'll be brewing up about ten... ...brewing up their morning cuppa.*   v+ADV, v+ADV+N

2 When a difficult or unpleasant situation is **brewing up**, it starts to develop. EG *It was obvious that a big storm was brewing up.*   v+ADV

brick, bricks, bricking, bricked

brick in. If you **brick** something **in**, you build a wall of bricks to enclose it or to fill it. EG *They decided to brick the old fireplace in.*   v+N+ADV, v+PRON+ADV

brick off. If you **brick off** an area, you build a wall of bricks that separates this area from another. EG *The lift was long dead, and the shaft bricked off.*   v+ADV+N, v+N+ADV, v+PRON+ADV

brick up. If you **brick up** a hole or space, you build a wall of bricks to enclose it or to fill it. EG *To stop burglars you'd have to board or brick the windows up... Two workmen bricked up the window.*   v+N+ADV, v+ADV+N, v+PRON+ADV

brighten, brightens, brightening, brightened

brighten up. 1 If someone **brightens up**, they suddenly look or feel much happier. EG *She seemed to brighten up a bit at this.* ● **Perk up** is a more informal expression for **brighten up**.   v+ADV

2 If you **brighten** a place **up**, you make it more colourful and attractive. EG *These flowers will brighten up your garden.*   v+ADV+N, v+N+ADV, v+PRON+ADV

3 Someone or something that **brightens up** a situation, makes it more pleasant and enjoyable. EG *The music brightened things up a little... She brightened up the rather gloomy masculine atmosphere.* ● **Liven up** means almost the same as **brighten up**.   v+N+ADV, v+PRON+ADV, v+ADV+N

4 If the weather **brightens up**, it becomes clearer and sunnier. EG *It should brighten up in the afternoon.*   v+ADV

brim, brims, brimming, brimmed

brim over. 1 When a container or the liquid in it **brims over**, the liquid spills out. EG *He splashed wine into Daniel's glass until it brimmed over onto the tablecloth.* ● **Overflow** means almost the same as **brim over**.   v+ADV

2 Someone or something that **brims over** with something else is full of it. EG *...parents brimming over with joy and pride... I was brimming over with questions.*   v+ADV: ALSO+ *with*

bring, brings, bringing, brought

bring about. To **bring** something **about** means to cause it to happen. EG *The Administration helped bring about a peaceful settlement... ...the smog brought about by car exhausts... But why was all this happening? What had brought it about?... Naturally, one wonders what may have taken place to bring the separation about.*   v+ADV+N, v+PRON+ADV, v+N+ADV

bring along. If you **bring** someone or something **along**, you bring them with you when you come to a place. EG *Bring your friends along... He brought along several examples of his work.*   v+N+ADV, v+ADV+N, v+PRON+ADV

bring back. 1 If something **brings back** an event or memory from your past, it makes you think about it. EG *Losing a lover can bring back memories of childhood loss... It brings it all back... Seeing the place again would bring all the horrors back to me.*   v+ADV+N, v+PRON+ADV, v+N+ADV

2 When people **bring back** something that existed in an earlier time, they introduce it again. EG *He was all for bringing back the cane as a punishment in schools... ...bringing back old crafts.* ● **Revive** is a more formal word for **bring back**.   v+ADV+N, v+PRON+ADV

bring down. 1 If people or events **bring down** a government or ruler, they cause them to lose their power. EG *A national strike*   v+N+ADV, v+ADV+N, v+PRON+ADV

*would bring the government down... Unofficial strikes had brought
down the regime.* ● **Topple** means almost the same as **bring down**.

2 To **bring down** the level of something means to reduce it. EG *The* V+ADV+N,
promised measures included steps to bring down prices... ...to bring V+N+ADV,
population growth down further. V+PRON+ADV

3 To **bring down** someone or something with a gun means to shoot V+ADV+N,
them so that they fall to the ground. EG *A rifleman actually managed* V+PRON+ADV,
to bring down an enemy airplane... He was going to open fire from V+N+ADV
the ground and bring him down.

4 If someone **brings** a person **down,** they make them fall, or pull V+ADV+N,
them to the ground. EG *Clough scored a penalty when Sealy brought* V+N+ADV,
down Hodge... He brought the girl down rather heavily with a kind V+PRON+ADV
of rugger tackle.

5 If someone or something **brings** you **down,** they make you feel V+PRON+ADV,
unhappy, depressed, or disappointed. EG *It brings you down with a* V+N+ADV
thump... Whatever he said seemed to bring Sally down. ● **Get down**
means almost the same as **bring down**.

bring forth. To **bring forth** something means to produce it or cause V+ADV+N,
it to happen; a formal expression. EG *This brought forth a shudder of* V+PRON+ADV
revulsion... In time, this policy will bring forth new results. ● **Result
in** means almost the same as **bring forth**.

bring forward. 1 If you **bring forward** a meeting or an event, you V+ADV+N,
arrange for it to be at an earlier time or date than was planned. EG V+N+ADV,
Ask him to bring the meeting forward to eight o'clock... The match V+PRON+ADV
would have to be brought forward. ● **Put back** means the opposite of
bring forward.

2 If you **bring forward** an argument or proposal, you state it so that V+ADV+N,
people can consider it and discuss it. EG *He brought forward some* V+N+ADV,
very cogent arguments... The Government had invited us to bring V+PRON+ADV
forward proposals for the expansion of Stansted airport. ● **Put
forward** means almost the same as **bring forward**.

3 When the total at the bottom of a page or column of figures **is** PASSIVE:
brought forward, it is written at the top of the next page or column V+ADV
and added to the amounts on that page or in that column; a
technical use. EG *...reductions in public expenditure of 200m pounds
brought forward.* ● **Carry over** means almost the same as **bring
forward**.

bring in. 1 When a government or other organization **brings in** a V+ADV+N,
new law, rule, or system, they introduce it. EG *We intend to bring in* V+PRON+ADV,
legislation to control their activities... The firm has just brought in a V+N+ADV
three-shift system.

2 Someone or something that **brings in** money makes or earns it. EG V+ADV+N,
Tourism is a big industry, bringing in £7 billion a year. V+N+ADV,
V+PRON+ADV

3 If you **bring** someone **in,** you ask them to take part in an activity. V+N+ADV,
EG *Why did they wait so long before bringing Patton in to command* V+PRON+ADV,
the corps?... Police had to be brought in to protect him... It would be V+ADV+N
fatal to bring in an outsider. ● **Call in** means almost the same as
bring in.

4 If you **bring in** a particular point or subject, you include it or V+ADV+N,
mention it. EG *Try to bring in the moral points as well... Oh, the* V+N+ADV,
English always start bringing in Shakespeare! V+PRON+ADV

5 When a jury **bring in** a particular verdict, they officially give it as V+ADV+N
their verdict; a legal term. EG *A verdict was brought in of accidental
death.*

bring into. 1 If you **bring** someone **into** an event or group, you ask V+N+PREP,
them to take part in it or be part of it. EG *Jordan has got to be* V+PRON+PREP
*brought into this... He planned to bring Northcliffe into the govern-
ment.*

2 If you **bring** a subject **into** a discussion or situation, you talk about it or introduce it in order to arouse people's interest. EG *A second major function of election campaigns is to bring issues into the political arena... Advertisers always bring sex into it.*
V+N+PREP,
V+PRON+PREP

bring off. If someone **brings off** something difficult, they do it successfully; an informal expression. EG *The most brilliant manoeuvre was brought off by Japan... The Ghost is the hardest thing to bring off in 'Hamlet'.* ● **Pull off** means almost the same as **bring off.**
V+N+ADV,
V+ADV+N,
V+PRON+ADV

bring on. 1 Something that **brings on** an illness or pain causes it to occur. EG *It'll bring on his cough again... The journey had already brought on a severe attack of angina... Convulsions are brought on by irritation of the brain.*
V+ADV+N,
V+N+ADV,
V+PRON+ADV

2 To **bring** someone **on** means to improve their ability to do something. EG *I want to learn to be a coach so that I can help to bring on young cricketers.*
V+ADV+N,
V+PRON+ADV,
V+N+ADV

3 If you **bring** shame or trouble **on** someone, you cause them to experience it. EG *He brought it all on himself... Don't bring shame on the family.*
V+PRON+PREP,
V+N+PREP

bring out. 1 When a person or company **brings out** a new product, they produce it and sell it. EG *I've just brought out a little book on Dostoevski... Colin Bradbury has now brought out a second album.*
V+ADV+N,
V+PRON+ADV,
V+N+ADV

2 Something that **brings out** a particular kind of behaviour or feeling in someone causes them to reveal it although they do not normally have it or show it. EG *These dreadful circumstances bring out the worst in absolutely everybody... He brings out the animal in me.*
V+ADV+N:
USUALLY+*in*

3 If an actor or musician **brings out** a particular quality or feature in a work that they are performing, they make people aware of that quality or feature. EG *The effect is to bring out all sorts of things in the poetry... In both works, Giulini brings out a sort of serenity.*
V+ADV+N

4 To **bring** someone **out** means to encourage them to be less shy or quiet. EG *He talks to them and brings them out... It's really brought him out, and it's done him the world of good.*
V+PRON+ADV,
V+N+ADV

5 If someone **brings out** some words, they say them with difficulty or with an effort. EG *They even brought out a few English words... 'It's so typical,' Etta at last brought out.*
V+ADV+N,
V+ADV+QUOTE

bring out in. If something **brings** you **out in** a rash or in spots, it causes you to have them on your skin. EG *...if some food or other disagrees with them and brings them out in a rash... The cold was bringing her out in goose-pimples.*
V+PRON+ADV+PREP,
V+N+ADV+PREP

bring over. If you **bring** someone or something **over,** you take them with you from one place, house, or country to another. EG *...a big white china mug which she brought over to us very carefully... I brought over a nut cake... ....aircraft bringing over US military personnel.*
V+ADV+N,
V+PRON+ADV,
V+N+ADV

bring round. 1 If someone is unconscious and you **bring** them **round,** you make them conscious again. EG *Nobody was making any attempt to bring her round.* ● **Bring to** means almost the same as **bring round.**
V+PRON+ADV,
V+N+ADV

2 If someone disagrees with you and you **bring** them **round,** you cause them to change their opinion and agree with you. EG *We suggested a fox hunt; nothing was so sure to bring Alethea round... We tried to bring him round to our point of view... ...lessons to do with bringing people round.* ◑ **Win over** means almost the same as **bring round.**
V+PRON+ADV,
V+N+ADV:
USUALLY+*to*

bring to. If you **bring** someone **to,** you revive them and make them conscious again after they have been unconscious. EG *She was*
V+N+ADV,
V+PRON+ADV

eventually brought to after several minutes of unconsciousness.
● **Bring round** means almost the same as **bring to**.

bring together. If you **bring together** people who have never met, you introduce them to each other. If you **bring together** people who have quarrelled or parted, you cause them to live or work together again. EG *It's also brought together artists from diverse parts of the country... This was only just sufficient to bring them together again.* `V+ADV+N, V+PRON+ADV, V+N+ADV`

bring up. 1 When you **bring up** a child, you look after it until it is grown up and you try to give it particular beliefs and attitudes. EG *I brought up two children alone... Tony was brought up strictly.* `V+ADV+N, V+N+ADV, V+PRON+ADV`
● **Raise** means almost the same as **bring up.** ▶ Your **upbringing** is the way your parents treat you and the things that they teach you to care about and believe in. EG *Tony never rebelled against his upbringing... ...a strict upbringing.* `N SING`

2 When you **bring up** a particular subject, you mention it or introduce it into a discussion or conversation. EG *I advised her to bring the matter up at the next meeting... I am sorry to bring up the subject of politics yet again.* ● **Raise** means almost the same as **bring up.** `V+N+ADV, V+ADV+N, V+PRON+ADV`

3 When you **bring up** food, you vomit; an informal use. EG *That child is bringing up his breakfast!... I had some toast, but brought it up again soon after.* ● **Throw up** is a more informal expression for **bring up.** `V+ADV+N, V+PRON+ADV, V+N+ADV: NO PASSIVE`

bristle, bristles, bristling, bristled

bristle with. 1 Something that **bristles with** sharp, spiky things has a large number of them sticking out of it. EG *...a creature with a long nose, bristling with whiskers... ...five command ships bristling with radar and radio antennae.* `V+PREP`

2 When a place or situation **bristles with** things, it seems to be full of them; an informal use. EG *The hotel was bristling with policemen at every entrance... The porcelain and pottery section fairly bristled with exciting things.* `V+PREP`

3 If you **bristle with** an emotion, you feel uncomfortable because of it and show this in your expression or behaviour. EG *He bristled with a kind of subdued panic... She smiled and bristled with embarrassment.* `V+PREP`

broaden, broadens, broadening, broadened

broaden out. 1 When a road or river **broadens out**, it becomes wider. EG *Aldgate High Street broadens out east to Whitechapel High Street.* `V+ADV`

2 When something **broadens out** or when you **broaden** it **out**, it includes a larger number of things or people, or becomes more general. EG *The definition of antiques broadens out until it becomes things your grandmother owned... We were broadening out these struggles to attack the capitalists.* `V+ADV, V+ADV+N, V+PRON+ADV, V+N+ADV: ERGATIVE`

brood, broods, brooding, brooded

brood on. If you **brood on** or **upon** something, you think about it seriously for a period of time. EG *He brooded on this for a while, and then spoke... ...brooding on the events of the past... ...brooding upon the antiquity of the church.* ● **Dwell on** means almost the same as **brood on.** `V+PREP`

brood over. If you **brood over** something unpleasant or difficult, you think about it a lot, seriously, and often unhappily. EG *The more you sit and brood over your problems, the bigger they get... ...questions to brood over.* `V+PREP`

brood upon. See **brood on: brood upon** is more formal.

brown, browns, browning, browned

brown off. If you are **browned off** with something, you no longer feel any enthusiasm for it, and may even be annoyed about it; a rather old-fashioned expression, used in informal British English. EG *He was a bit browned off with the job.*

V+PRON+ADV,
V+N+ADV:
USUALLY PASSIVE

brush, brushes, brushing, brushed

brush aside. If you **brush aside** a remark or some information, you refuse to take any notice of it because it seems unimportant. EG *Miss Crabbe continued, brushing aside this interruption... She brushed his protests aside, politely.* ● **Ignore** and **dismiss** mean almost the same as **brush aside.**

V+ADV+N,
V+N+ADV,
V+PRON+ADV

brush away. If you **brush** an idea or thought **away**, you ignore it because you do not want to think about it. EG *She hurriedly brushed the thought away.* ● **Dismiss** is a less informal word for **brush away.**

V+N+ADV,
V+PRON+ADV,
V+ADV+N

brush by. If you **brush by** someone, you walk quickly past them, almost touching them and without stopping, usually in order to avoid talking to them. EG *I brushed by him, opened the door and stopped.*

V+PREP

brush down. If you **brush down** something you are wearing, or if you **brush** yourself **down**, you remove dirt from your clothes with quick, light strokes of your hands. EG *She crawled out and brushed down her skirt... He was brushing himself down.*

V+ADV+N,
V+REFL+ADV,
V+N+ADV,
V+PRON+ADV

brush off. 1 If you **brush** someone **off**, you avoid them or avoid speaking to them, because you want to end your relationship with them. EG *...buying her an expensive present, and then brushing her off in the nicest way possible... By brushing me off like this, she had probably done me a favour.* ▶ If you give someone the **brushoff,** you brush them off; an informal word. EG *She gave me the brushoff once too often.*

V+PRON+ADV,
V+N+ADV

N SING

2 If you **brush** someone **off** when they are talking to you, you refuse to listen to them. EG *He was not the sort of reporter to be brushed off like that.* ● **Rebuff** is a more formal word for **brush off.**

V+N+ADV,
V+PRON+ADV,
V+ADV+N

3 If you **brush off** a remark or some information, you refuse to consider or discuss it because you think it is not important. EG *President Carter brushed the story off at a press conference.* ● **Brush aside** means almost the same as **brush off,** and **dismiss** is a more formal word.

V+N+ADV,
V+PRON+ADV,
V+ADV+N

brush off on. If a quality or characteristic **brushes off on** you, it influences the way that you behave. EG *...in the hope of having some of their poise brush off on them... Something he called 'basic emotions' should inevitably brush off on him.*

V+ADV+PREP

brush out. If you **brush out** your hair, or if you **brush out** the tangles or knots, you brush your hair very thoroughly to get rid of the tangles. EG *She was brushing out my tangled hair with sharp brush strokes... ...brushing it out, washing it, drying it.*

V+ADV+N,
V+PRON+ADV,
V+N+ADV

brush past. If you **brush past** someone or something, you walk quickly past them, often nearly touching them. EG *She laughed, and brushed past me out of the room... A marine brushed past us.*

V+PREP

brush up. If you **brush up** a subject you know but have not used for a while, you revise or improve your knowledge of it. EG *I would like to brush up my zoology... ...helped them to brush up their French.*

V+ADV+N,
V+PRON+ADV,
V+N+ADV:
NO PASSIVE

brush up on. If you **brush up on** something, you improve it, or revise your knowledge of it. EG *He was in New York, brushing up on his image as an expert in foreign affairs.*

V+ADV+PREP

bubble, bubbles, bubbling, bubbled

bubble over with. If you are **bubbling over with** feelings or ideas, you are very excited and show it in your behaviour. EG *He was*

V+ADV+PREP

bubbling over with excitement... Mrs Finch was most enthusiastic and bubbled over with suggestions.

bubble up. If a liquid **bubbles up**, it rises up in the form of bubbles. eg *Champagne bubbled up over the edge of the glass... ...thermal springs, bubbling up from the core of the earth.*   v+adv

buck, bucks, bucking, bucked

buck up. 1 If you **buck up** a person or their spirits, you make them feel more cheerful. eg *J.B.Priestley bucked us all up in the war... I need something to buck my spirits up today... ...as hopeless as the attempt to buck up Mrs. Halverston.*   v+pron+adv, v+n+adv, v+adv+n

2 If you **buck up**, you become more cheerful; an informal use. eg *She bucked up a bit once she started going out with Phillip... Come on, Charlie, buck up! It's not the end of the world, is it?*   v+adv

3 You say '**buck up**' to someone when you want them to hurry up; an informal, old-fashioned use. eg *Buck up, we haven't got all day!*   imperative: v+adv

bucket, buckets, bucketing, bucketed

bucket down. If rain **buckets down**, it falls very heavily. eg *It really started bucketing down this afternoon.* ● **Pelt down** means almost the same as **bucket down**.   v+adv

buckle, buckles, buckling, buckled

buckle down. If you **buckle down** to something, you start working seriously at it. eg *I'm going to buckle down to the training course... We buckled down and got on with our work.* ● **Knuckle down** means almost the same as **buckle down**.   v+adv: also+to

buckle in. If you **buckle** someone **in**, you fasten them into a seat with a buckle. eg *You need a strap to buckle the baby in... Help me buckle him in.*   v+n+adv, v+pron+adv, v+adv+n, v+refl+adv

buckle into. If you **buckle** someone **into** a seat, you fasten them there with a buckle. eg *She was buckling her son into his harness... He was buckling himself into the seat of the plane.* ● **Strap into** means almost the same as **buckle into**.   v+n+prep, v+refl+prep, v+pron+prep

buckle on. If you **buckle** something **on**, you attach it by means of buckles. eg *He buckled his stylish belt on... He buckled on his revolver.* ● **Put on** means almost the same as **buckle on**.   v+n+adv, v+pron+adv, v+adv+n

buckle under. If you **buckle under** to a person or situation, you do what they require you to do, even though you do not want to. eg *...their unwillingness to buckle under blindly to authority... No, damn it! She wouldn't buckle under to the verdict of Wilbur Birdsall.*   v+adv: also+to

budge, budges, budging, budged

budge up. If you **budge up**, you move along a seat in order to make space for someone else to sit down; an informal expression. eg *Budge up, will you.*   v+adv: also imperative

budget, budgets, budgeting, budgeted

budget for. If you **budget for** something, you take account of it in your calculations. eg *The Chancellor budgeted for an unemployment rate of 8.5 per cent... These expenses can all be budgeted for.*   v+prep: has passive

bugger, buggers, buggering, buggered

Bugger is a rude, offensive word used in spoken British English.

bugger about. 1 If you **bugger about** or **bugger around**, you waste time doing unnecessary things. eg *What the hell do you mean by buggering about like this?*   v+adv

2 If you **bugger** someone **about** or **bugger** them **around**, you treat them badly by not being honest with them, or by continually changing plans which affect them. eg *Those Nationalists have been*   v+pron+adv, v+n+adv

buggering you around for years. ● **Mess about** means almost the same as **bugger about.**

bugger around. See **bugger about.**

bugger off. 1 If someone **buggers off,** they go away quickly or   V+ADV
suddenly. EG *His wife just buggered off.*

2 If you say '**bugger off**' to someone, you are telling them rudely to   IMPERATIVE:
go away. EG *Oh, bugger off and leave me in peace.*   V+ADV

bugger up. If you **bugger** something **up,** you ruin it or spoil it. EG *If*   V+N+ADV,
you bugger things up at this stage, I'll kill you.   V+PRON+ADV, V+ADV+N

build, builds, building, built

build in. 1 If you **build in** an idea or some information, you include it   V+ADV+N,
as part of a larger plan. EG *This will enable the designers to build in a*   V+PRON+ADV
further piece of information... ...the advantages of not having all the
traditional prejudices built in. ● **Incorporate** is a formal word for
build in. ▸ A quality that is **inbuilt** in a person or thing is one that   ADJECTIVE
they have from the time they were born or produced. EG *The child*
has got an inbuilt feeling of inferiority... This kind of thinking has
inbuilt limitations.

2 If furniture **is built in,** it is made in such a way that it is in the wall,   V+ADV+N,
or is part of it. EG *All the kitchen cupboards have been built in, of*   V+N+ADV, V+PRON+ADV
course. ▸ **Built-in** furniture is made in such a way that it is part of a   ADJECTIVE
wall and cannot be moved around. EG *...a built-in wardrobe.* ● **Fitted**
means almost the same as **built-in.** ▸ **Built-in** devices or features   ADJECTIVE
are included in something as an essential part of it. EG *...missiles*
equipped with built-in homing devices.

build into. 1 If something **is built into** a wall or space, it is made to   V+N+PREP,
be part of it or to fit in to it. EG *There was a cupboard built into the*   V+PRON+PREP
whitewashed wall... ...a bar which he had built into a corner of his
living room.

2 If you **build** something **into** a policy, system, or product, you make   V+N+PREP,
it a part of it. EG *They tried to build authoritarian principles into the*   V+PRON+PREP:
draft manifesto... ...the inequalities built into our system of financ-   HAS PASSIVE
ing... Existing political groupings could be built into the new struc-
ture of colonial rule.

build on. 1 If an organization, system, or product **is built on** or **upon**   V+N+PREP,
something, it is developed from that thing. EG *How could peace be*   V+PRON+PREP
built on a foundation of reckless science and violence?... ...an outlook
built on illusion rather than reality. ● **Base on** means almost the
same as **build on.**

2 If you **build on** or **upon** the success of something, you take   V+PREP:
advantage of it to make further progress. EG *We must try to build on*   HAS PASSIVE
the success of these growth industries... ...building on existing skills
and traditions.

build up. 1 If something **builds up** or if you **build** it **up,** it gradually   V+ADV,
increases in amount, size, or intensity. EG *Mud builds up in the lake...*   V+ADV+N, V+N+ADV,
We helped to build up the wealth of this country... We're trying to   V+PRON+ADV:
build up a collection of herbs and spices. ● **Accumulate** is a more   ERGATIVE
formal word for **build up.** ▸ A **build-up** is a gradual increase in   N COUNT
something. EG *Over the island the build-up of clouds continued... ...a*
massive build-up of nuclear weapons. ▸ **Built-up** shoes are shoes   ADJECTIVE
with very thick soles and heels that people wear in order to appear
taller than they really are. EG *I noticed that he was wearing built-up*
boots.

2 If people **build up** an organization, society, or system, they   V+ADV+N,
gradually develop it or improve it. EG *Japan successfully built up a*   V+N+ADV, V+PRON+ADV
modern capitalist economy... His organizational knowledge and
personal reputation has built the business up.

3 If you **build up** someone's trust or confidence, you gradually make them more trusting or more confident. EG *Being a cop means building up trust with the people on the streets.*

V+ADV+N,
V+N+ADV,
V+PRON+ADV

4 If you **build up** someone or something, you tell people that they are very special or important. EG *I've built up Mr Reston's credentials... He does not need to build me up.* ▶ A **build-up** is a description of a person or thing in which you tell people that the person or thing is very special or important. EG *She was getting a fair amount of publicity build-up.*

V+ADV+N,
V+PRON+ADV,
V+N+ADV

N COUNT,
N UNCOUNT

5 If you **build** someone **up** after they have been ill, you help them to get better and stronger. EG *The patient needs building up... We must build him up before he can go home.*

V+N+ADV,
V+PRON+ADV,
V+ADV+N:
NO PASSIVE

6 When an area near a city or town **is built up**, a lot of houses are built there. EG *It has been like this since the area was built up several years ago... The park and riverside are all now built up.* ▶ A **built-up** area is a part of a city or town where there are many buildings. EG *...the built-up area on the fringes of Kilmarnock.*

PASSIVE:
V+ADV

ADJECTIVE

build upon. See **build on: build upon** is more formal.

bum, bums, bumming, bummed

bum about. See **bum around.**

bum around. If you **bum around, round,** or **about, 1** you travel casually for pleasure and with very little money; an informal use. EG *I just bummed around northern Europe for a few months.* **2** you live in a very lazy way, doing very little; an informal use. EG *They've just bummed around, all of them... Are you going to bum around all summer?*

V+ADV,
V+PREP

V+ADV

bum round. See **bum around.**

bump, bumps, bumping, bumped

bump into. If you **bump into** someone you know, you meet them by chance. EG *I bumped into Mary an hour ago... I probably won't see him any more unless I bump into him on the street.* ● **Run into** means almost the same as **bump into.**

V+PREP

bump off. To **bump** someone **off** means to kill them; an informal expression. EG *In his imagination, he bumps off his wife half a dozen times.* ● **Murder** is a more formal word for **bump off.**

V+ADV+N,
V+PRON+ADV,
V+N+ADV

bump up. To **bump** something **up** means to increase it suddenly by a large amount; an informal expression. EG *She was going to charge £140, but the extra work bumped up the price to £200... This will bump up the workforce yet again.*

V+ADV+N,
V+PRON+ADV,
V+N+ADV

bump up against. If you **bump up against** someone, you meet them and get to know them by chance. EG *He rarely bumped up against anyone who approved of what he was doing... You bumped up against some miners in a pub.*

V+ADV+PREP

bunch, bunches, bunching, bunched

bunch up. If you **bunch up** a piece of material, you squash it up to make a tight bundle. EG *She was holding her skirts bunched up over one arm... His suit was bunched up over his shoulders.*

V+N+ADV,
V+PRON+ADV,
V+ADV+N

bundle, bundles, bundling, bundled

bundle off. If you **bundle** someone **off** somewhere, you send them there in a hurry. EG *My father bundled me off to school... ...making sure she is not bundled off too roughly.* ● **Pack off** means almost the same as **bundle off.**

V+PRON+ADV,
V+N+ADV,
V+ADV+N

bundle up. 1 If you **bundle up** a mass of things, you make a bundle by gathering or tying them together. EG *My mother bundled up all my comics and threw them out... She bundled up her knitting and put it away... The rest of my things were bundled up in a pillowcase.*

V+ADV+N,
V+PRON+ADV,
V+N+ADV

2 If you **bundle up,** you dress in a lot of warm clothes because the weather is very cold. EG *We bundled up warmly against the cold... She bundled them up and walked them down to the railway station... They were bundled up in tweeds and flannels.* ● **Wrap up** means almost the same as **bundle up.**

V+ADV,
V+N+ADV,
V+PRON+ADV:
ERGATIVE

bung, bungs, bunging, bunged

bung up. If you **bung up** a hole, you put something in it so that the hole is filled or blocked. EG *Don't put tea leaves down the sink, they bung it up.* ● **Block up** means almost the same as **bung up.**

V+PRON+ADV,
V+N+ADV,
V+ADV+N

buoy, buoys, buoying, buoyed

buoy up. 1 If you **buoy** someone **up,** you keep them cheerful in a situation in which they might feel depressed. EG *He did his best to buoy her up.*

V+PRON+ADV,
V+N+ADV

2 To **buoy** something **up** means to keep it afloat and stop it from sinking. EG *The float needs to be fairly big so that it buoys up the 1/2 oz of lead necessary to sink the bait.*

V+ADV+N,
V+N+ADV,
V+PRON+ADV

3 To **buoy** something **up** also means to support it and help it to survive. EG *...newspapers buoyed up with advertising... This may help to buoy up the family's motive for saving.*

V+ADV+N,
V+N+ADV,
V+PRON+ADV

burn, burns, burning, burned/burnt

burn away. If something **burns away,** or if it **is burned away,** it burns or catches fire until it disappears completely. EG *...an ashtray, where a cigarette has burned away, while they have been busy... The cardboard was burned away from the metal binding wire... We were trying to burn away the net.*

V+ADV,
V+ADV+N,
V+PRON+ADV,
V+N+ADV:
ERGATIVE

burn down. If a building **burns down** or if someone **burns** it **down,** it is completely destroyed by fire. EG *The mansion burned down four years ago... ...peasants burning down the huts of chiefs... He could have burned the place down... His school had been burned down in the riots.*

V+ADV,
V+ADV+N,
V+N+ADV,
V+PRON+ADV:
ERGATIVE

burn off. If you **burn** something **off,** you remove it by burning or heating it. EG *...burning the flaking paint off beforehand.*

V+ADV+N,
V+N+ADV,
V+PRON+ADV

burn out. 1 If a fire **burns out** or **burns** itself **out,** it stops burning because there is nothing left to burn. EG *We let the fire burn out... All the fires had now burned themselves out.* ▶ A **burnt-out** or **burned-out** vehicle or building has been very badly damaged by fire. EG *They barricaded the streets with burnt-out cars.* ● **Gutted** means almost the same as **burnt out.**

V+ADV,
V+REFL+ADV

ADJECTIVE

2 If a piece of machinery **burns out** or if you **burn** it **out,** it stops working because it has been used too much or too roughly. EG *If his points or plugs burn out, he's done for... The exhaust valve on my car has burnt out three times in 46,000 miles... He's gonna burn out the pistons for sure.*

V+ADV,
V+ADV+N,
V+PRON+ADV,
V+N+ADV:
ERGATIVE

3 If you **burn** yourself **out** or **burn out,** you become exhausted or ill by working too hard; an informal use. EG *I don't want you to burn yourself out.* ▶ Someone who is **burnt-out** or **burned-out** is unable to do things because they are too tired, weak, or ill; an informal use. EG *...an old burnt-out actor... I was burnt-out emotionally.*

V+REFL+ADV,
V+ADV

ADJECTIVE

burn up. 1 If something **burns up,** it is completely destroyed by fire or strong heat. EG *The satellite had burned up on re-entering the atmosphere... Most of it is burned up or falls as dust.*

V+ADV:
ALSO PASSIVE,
V+ADV

2 If you say that an engine **burns up** fuel, you mean that it uses a lot of fuel.

V+ADV+N

3 If you say that something **burns** you **up,** you mean that it makes you feel angry and upset; an informal use. EG *His attitude just burns me up... The girls seemed to be burned up about something.*

V+PRON+ADV,
V+N+ADV,
V+ADV+N

burst, bursts, bursting, burst

burst in on. If you **burst in on** someone, you suddenly and quickly   V+ADV+PREP
enter the room that they are in. EG *He suddenly burst in on me.*

burst into. 1 If you **burst into** tears, laughter, or song, you suddenly   V+PREP
begin to cry, laugh, or sing. EG *I keep bursting into tears... Uncle
Tony burst into song... The delegates burst into loud applause.*

2 If something **bursts into** flames, it suddenly starts to burn. EG *The*   V+PREP
newspapers burst into flames.

3 When plants **burst into** leaf, blossom, or flower, their leaves or   V+PREP
flowers open.

burst out. 1 If you **burst out** laughing or crying, you suddenly begin   V+ADV+-ING
laughing or crying, usually loudly. EG *Mrs Oliver felt a sudden desire
to burst out crying... To my amazement, he burst out laughing.* ▶ An   N COUNT
outburst is a sudden and strong expression of emotion, or a sudden
period of activity. EG *I apologize for my outburst just now... ...degrad-
ing outbursts of drunken violence.*

2 You use **burst out** when you are reporting what someone said, to   V+ADV+QUOTE
indicate that they said it suddenly and loudly. EG *Then he burst out,
'Get into the car, Phil, can't you?'*

bury, buries, burying, buried

bury away. If something **is buried** away somewhere, it is put in a   PASSIVE:
place where it is difficult to find or reach. EG *Buried away inside the*   V+ADV
paper, in a tiny paragraph, was an account of his visit.

bury in. If you **bury** yourself or your head **in** something that you are   V+REFL+PREP,
reading, you concentrate hard on it. EG *He buried himself deep in the*   V+N+PREP
wine list... Their faces were buried in their evening newspapers.
● **Immerse** is a more formal word for **bury in.**

bust, busts, busting, busted

The form **bust** is used in the present tense and can also be used as
the past tense and past participle of the verb. The verb **bust** is
always informal.

bust out of. If you **bust out of** a place, you escape from it using   V+ADV+PREP
force. EG *He bust out of jail.*

bust up. 1 If you **bust up** an event or meeting, you stop it from   V+ADV+N,
continuing by causing a disturbance or fight. EG *They busted up the*   V+PRON+ADV
*Miss America competition last November... They could come and
bust up the meeting like they did yesterday.* ● **Break up** is a less
informal expression for **bust up.**

2 If you **bust** something **up**, you break it. EG *They bought a new chair*   V+ADV+N,
to replace the one they'd busted up.   V+PRON+ADV,
   V+N+ADV

3 If you **bust up** with your boyfriend or girlfriend, you have a   V+ADV,
quarrel with them and end your relationship. EG *She's been staying*   V+ADV+with:
here since she bust up with Toby... They bust up last year. ▶ A **bust-**   RECIPROCAL
up is a serious quarrel or a fight. EG *There was a bust-up down at the*   N COUNT
pub last night.

bustle, bustles, bustling, bustled

bustle about. If you **bustle about** or **around,** you do things or move   V+ADV,
about in a busy and determined way. EG *She bustled about, humming*   V+PREP
*to herself... He bustles about with all sorts of plans to occupy him...
She was bustling around preparing a snack... She bustled around the
kitchen.*

bustle around. See **bustle about.**

butt, butts, butting, butted

butt in. If you **butt in,** you rudely interrupt a conversation or   V+ADV:
   ALSO+on

activity. EG *You can't just butt in on someone else's discussion... I was always butting in and saying the wrong thing.*

butt out. If you say 'Butt out' to someone, you are telling them angrily and rudely to go away or to stop interfering; used in American English. EG *Butt out before I throw you out.*

IMPERATIVE:
V+ADV

butter, butters, buttering, buttered

butter up. If you **butter** someone **up**, you praise or try to please them, because you want to ask them a favour. EG *I'm buttering him up for a pay rise.*

V+PRON+ADV,
V+N+ADV,
V+ADV+N

button, buttons, buttoning, buttoned

button up. If you **button up** a shirt, coat, or other piece of clothing, you fasten it by pushing its buttons through buttonholes. EG *He began to gather his papers and button up his coat... She put her blouse on and buttoned it up.* ● **Do up** means almost the same as **button up**.

V+ADV+N,
V+PRON+ADV,
V+N+ADV

buy, buys, buying, bought

buy in. If you **buy in** something such as food, you buy large amounts of it for a future occasion, or for a time when it might not be available. EG *We bought in a few loaves of bread.*

V+ADV+N,
V+N+ADV,
V+PRON+ADV

buy into. When someone **buys into** a business or organization, they buy part of it, for example in order to gain some control over it. EG *He's been trying for years to buy into the printing industry.*

V+PREP

buy off. If you **buy** someone **off**, you pay them money so that they do not act against you. EG *The workers were bought off by their employers... They have no money to buy off the police... He thought he could buy them off.*

V+ADV+N,
V+PRON+ADV,
V+N+ADV

buy out. 1 If you **buy** someone **out**, you buy their share of a property or business that you previously owned together. EG *He sold off the shops to buy out his partner... We bought him out.* ▶ A **buyout** occurs when a group of people join together to buy the company that they previously worked for. EG *Nobody has talked to us about a management buyout.*

V+N+ADV,
V+PRON+ADV,
V+ADV+N

N COUNT

2 If you **buy** yourself **out** of the armed forces, you pay a sum of money so that you can leave before the end of the period you had agreed to stay for. EG *He managed to buy himself out of the navy.*

V+REFL+ADV:
ALSO+of

buy over. If you **buy** someone **over**, you win their support by giving them money. EG *She was not able to buy him over.*

V+PRON+ADV,
V+N+ADV,
V+ADV+N

buy up. If someone **buys up** land or property, they buy large quantities of it, or all that is available. EG *They were trying to buy up every acre in sight.*

V+ADV+N,
V+PRON+ADV,
V+N+ADV

buzz, buzzes, buzzing, buzzed

buzz about. See buzz around.

buzz around. 1 If something **buzzes around, round,** or **about,** it moves along making a buzzing sound. EG *...those light planes I had seen buzzing around all day... ...a fly buzzing round her head... There was a wasp buzzing about her ear and she wanted to kill it.*

V+ADV,
V+PREP

2 If someone **buzzes around, round,** or **about,** they move around a place very quickly and busily. EG *The rickshaw drivers buzz around... He is always buzzing about the office.*

V+ADV,
V+PREP

buzz off. If someone **buzzes off,** they go away; used in informal English, often as a rude way of telling someone to go away. EG *'Now buzz off,' shouted Mrs Coggs... We'll buzz off at midday.*

V+ADV:
ALSO IMPERATIVE

C c

call, calls, calling, called

call after. If you **call** someone or something **after** a person or thing, you give them the same name as that other person or thing; used mainly in British English. EG *She was called after Caddy, a character in a William Faulkner novel.* ● **Name after** means almost the same as **call after.**

V+PRON+PREP,
V+N+PREP

call away. If you **are called away,** you are asked to stop doing something in order to go somewhere else. EG *They were called away to another case... He's been called away on business.*

V+N+PREP,
V+PRON+PREP:
USUALLY PASSIVE

call back. 1 If you **call back,** you contact someone who has contacted you previously, often by telephone, or at the place where you last saw them. EG *Pitts called back on Thursday, saying he hadn't been able to make the arrangements... You can call back and collect your shoes tomorrow.*

V+ADV

2 If you **call** someone **back,** you telephone them again in return for a telephone call they have made to you. EG *I told him I would call him back when I had some news... I shall make some enquiries and call you back.* ● **Ring back** means almost the same as **call back.**

V+PRON+ADV,
V+N+ADV:
NO PASSIVE

3 If you **call** someone **back** when they are walking away from you, you ask them to return. EG *He moved away as inconspicuously as he could, but Binta called him back, probably to reprimand him... She walked away heavily and slowly, as if waiting to be called back.*

V+PRON+ADV,
V+N+ADV

call by. If you **call by,** you visit a place for a short time, especially when you are going somewhere else afterwards. EG *I'll call by with your tape recorder this afternoon.*

V+ADV

call down on. If you **call** curses or vengeance **down on** someone, you pray that something unpleasant will happen to them; a formal expression. EG *She called God's vengeance down on her husband.*

V+N+ADV+PREP,
V+PRON+N+PREP:
NO PASSIVE

call for. 1 If you **call for** someone or something, you go to the building where they are to collect them. EG *I'll call for you about eight... The parcel was kept at the Post Office until someone called for it.*

V+PREP:
HAS PASSIVE

2 If you **call for** an action, you demand that it should be done. EG *The declaration called for an immediate cease-fire... Democrats are calling for a two-year tax cut... New automatic gates and assurances on safety have been called for.*

V+PREP:
HAS PASSIVE

3 If something **calls for** a particular action or quality, it needs it in order to be successful. EG *Controlling a class calls for all your skill as a teacher... The script called for the whole story to be shot in darkness... Mountaineering ability was not called for.* ● **Require** means almost the same as **call for.**

V+PREP:
HAS PASSIVE

4 You describe a remark or criticism as **uncalled-for** when you think that it should not have been made, because it was unkind or unfair. EG *That last remark was uncalled-for... ...an uncalled-for outburst.*

ADJECTIVE

5 If you **call** someone or something **for** a person or thing, you give them the same name as that other person or thing; used in American English. EG *They're going to call it the Bentley Mulsanne for the name of that stretch of the track at Le Mans.* ● **Name for** means almost the same as **call for.**

V+N+PREP,
V+PRON+PREP

call forth. If you **call** something **forth,** you make it exist; a formal expression. EG *He is not capable of calling forth much emotion in his*

V+ADV+N,
V+PRON+ADV

*readers... Excitement is hardly likely to be called forth by a series of
scales and arpeggios.* ● **Inspire** means almost the same as **call
forth.**

call in. 1 If you **call** someone **in,** you ask them to come and help you
or do something for you. EG *Before you call in the water board,
check that the pipes are not frozen... They called me in for questioning... The Army was called in to quell the rioting.* ● **Send for** means
almost the same as **call in.**

V+ADV+N,
V+PRON+ADV,
V+N+ADV

2 If you **call in,** you contact someone you know by visiting them, or
by telephoning them. EG *He hadn't called in to see the Duke after he
had left us... He called in to say he was feeling ill.*

V+ADV

3 If someone **calls** something **in,** they ask for it to be returned, for
example because it might be dangerous or because it is needed. EG
*Ford are calling some of their Escorts in to check their brakes...
The university called in all library books for stocktaking.* ● **Recall** is
a more formal word for **call in.**

V+ADV+N,
V+N+ADV,
V+PRON+ADV

call off. 1 If you **call off** an event or an arrangement that has been
planned, you cancel it. EG *I can't call off the ceremony now... If you
can't behave yourself, we might as well call the whole thing off...
Classes will be called off on Thursday and Friday.*

V+ADV+N,
V+N+ADV,
V+PRON+ADV

2 If you **call** a dog or a person **off,** you order them to stop attacking
something or someone else. EG *He called his dog off when he saw
that mine was frightened of it.*

V+N+ADV,
V+PRON+ADV,
V+ADV+N

call on. 1 If you **call on** someone, you pay them a short visit. EG *Don't
bother to call on me or ring me... Mrs Knight seldom seemed to call
on Charlotte... The four of us called on him in his room.*

V+PREP:
HAS PASSIVE

2 If you **call on** someone to do something, you appeal to them to do
it. EG *The Opposition called on the Prime Minister to stop the arms
deal... She was never called on to testify.*

V+PREP:
WITH to-INF,
HAS PASSIVE

3 If you **call on** or **upon** something, you use it in order to achieve
something; a fairly formal use. EG *The woman has to call on her
willpower... ...calling on the assistance of my parents... You will have
plenty of reserves to call upon.*

V+PREP

call out. 1 If you **call** something **out,** you shout it. EG *'Don't jump,' she
called out... She turned into the yard, calling out to the porter that
she'd arrived... Karen called out and told us to be quiet... One boy
rushed forward, calling out his father's name.*

V+ADV+QUOTE,
V+ADV+REPORT,
V+ADV,
V+ADV+N,
V+N+ADV,
V+PRON+ADV

2 If you **call** someone **out,** you ask them to come to help, especially
in an emergency. EG *I called the coastguard out... The National
Guard has been called out by Governor Duck... The ambulance had
been called out.*

V+N+ADV,
V+PRON+ADV,
V+ADV+N

3 If you **call out** a group of workers, you order them to go on strike.
EG *They were called out for half a day.*

V+ADV+N,
V+N+ADV,
V+PRON+ADV

call out for. If a situation **calls out for** a particular action, there is a
very strong need for that action. EG *Even the smallest act of
oppression calls out for universal condemnation.*

V+ADV+PREP

call over. 1 If you **call** someone **over,** you ask them to come to you,
usually in order to speak with them or to give them something. EG *I
called the waitress over and said, 'Bring us a bottle of red wine'... He
called over the producer to speak to her.*

V+N+ADV,
V+PRON+ADV,
V+ADV+N

2 If you **call over,** you visit someone for a short time. EG *It's OK, we'll
be calling over shortly anyway.* ● **Call round** means almost the
same as **call over.**

V+ADV

call round. If you **call round** to a place, you visit it for a short time.
EG *I called round to a dozen places to get the proper size of bulb.*

V+ADV:
ALSO+to

call up. 1 If you **call** someone **up,** you telephone them. EG *People call
me up to talk about what's on their minds... About ten minutes after
I had checked in, I called her up... The radio station had an open line*

V+PRON+ADV,
V+N+ADV,
V+ADV:
NO PASSIVE

on which listeners could call up to discuss various issues. ● **Phone up**
and **ring up** mean almost the same as **call up.**

2 If someone **is called up,** they are ordered to join the army, navy,
or air force. EG *I was extremely lucky not to be called up at the
time... The reserves began to be called up.* ● **Draft** means almost the
same as **call up.** ▶ If a person gets their **call-up** papers, they receive
an official order to join the army, navy, or air force; a British use.
▶ A **call-up** is the number of people who are ordered to report for
service in the armed forces.

3 If someone in authority in an activity or event **calls up** someone,
they ask them to take part, or choose them to do a particular task.
EG *He has ample time to call up replacements... The captain called
up Geffin to take the next kick... Jack Charlton called him up for the
World Cup qualifier in Spain.* ● **Call in** and **send for** mean almost the
same as **call up.**

4 If something **calls up** a memory or an idea of something, it makes
you think about them. EG *The museum called up memories of my
childhood... The city called up images of the emperors of China.*
● **Conjure up** means almost the same as **call up,** and **evoke** is a
more formal word.

5 If you **call up** information from a computer, you obtain it. EG *He
was able to call up the information he needed... ...data lodged in the
computer which can be called up at the press of a button.*

call upon. **1** If you **are called upon** to do something, you are asked
to do it; a fairly formal use. EG *Lord Shawcross was called upon to
declare the hotel open... The chairman will call upon me for my
appraisal of the domestic and international situation.*
2 See **call on.**

calm, calms, calming, calmed

calm down. **1** If you **calm down** or if someone **calms** you **down,** you
become less upset, excited, or lively. EG *'Please, Mrs Kinter,' said
Brody. 'Calm down. Let me explain'... An officer tried to calm them
down but had no success... When she had calmed herself down, she
started the engine.*
2 If a situation **calms down** or if you **calm** it **down,** it becomes
quieter and less tense. EG *He told me that things appeared to be
calming down a bit... Dad managed to calm things down.* ● **Settle
down** means almost the same as **calm down.**

camp, camps, camping, camped

camp out. If you **camp out,** you sleep outdoors in a tent. EG *All right,
tonight we'll camp out.*

camp up. If you **camp** it **up,** you deliberately act in an exaggerated
or affected way; used in informal and slightly old-fashioned English.
EG *They were really camping it up.*

cancel, cancels, cancelling, cancelled

American English uses the spellings **canceling** and **canceled.**

cancel out. If one thing **cancels** another thing **out** or if two things
cancel each other **out,** they have opposite effects, so that when they
are combined no real effect is produced. EG *The drug produces side
effects, tending to cancel out the benefits... Increased productivity
and generous staffing could be said to cancel each other out... Noise
would be reduced but this would be cancelled out by extra traffic at
Luton airport.*

care, cares, caring, cared

care for. **1** If you **care for** someone or something, you look after
them and keep them in a good state or condition. EG *Only £65 million*

Right margin grammar codes:

V+N+ADV,
V+PRON+ADV,
V+ADV+N:
USUALLY PASSIVE

ADJECTIVE

N COUNT

V+ADV+N,
V+N+ADV,
V+PRON+ADV

V+ADV+N

V+ADV+N,
V+N+ADV,
V+PRON+ADV

V+PREP:
HAS PASSIVE,
USUALLY PASSIVE

V+ADV,
V+PRON+ADV,
V+REFL+ADV,
V+N+ADV:
ERGATIVE

V+ADV,
V+N+ADV,
V+PRON+ADV,
V+ADV+N:
ERGATIVE

V+ADV

V+it+ADV

V+ADV+N,
V+N+ADV,
V+PRON+ADV

V+PREP:
HAS PASSIVE

was given to help care for the mentally retarded... Who would care for the farm when they were away?... Pets must be properly cared for. ▶ **Uncared-for** people or animals have not been looked after ADJECTIVE properly and as a result are hungry, dirty, or ill. EG *Thousands of children were left uncared-for... ...uncared-for cats.*

2 If you do not **care for** something, you do not like it; a rather old V+PREP: fashioned use. EG *He didn't drink, he didn't care for the taste of it... I* WITH NEGATIVE *did not care for the play.*

3 If you **care for** someone, you love them; an old-fashioned use. EG V+PREP *Here is a young man whom I care for and who cares for me.*

carry, carries, carrying, carried

carry away. If you get **carried away,** you are so enthusiastic about PASSIVE: something that you behave in a silly or hasty way. EG *They can't be* V+ADV *allowed to be carried away by their feelings... She can get so carried away making the design that she forgets to put the dinner on.*

carry back. If something **carries** you **back,** it reminds you of V+N+ADV, something that happened in the past. EG *That marvellous smile* V+PRON+ADV *carried me back nearly twenty-four years.* ● **Take back** means almost the same as **carry back.**

carry forward. When the sum of the figures on a page or in a V+N+ADV, column **is carried forward,** it is written at the top of the next page V+PRON+ADV: or column so that it can be added to the figures on that page or in USUALLY PASSIVE that column. EG *The total is then carried forward for next month's accounts.* ● **Bring forward** means almost the same as **carry forward.**

carry off. 1 If you **carry off** something that is difficult to do, you V+N+ADV, succeed in doing it. EG *She would have carried everything off* V+PRON+ADV, *beautifully... He looked at her to see how she was carrying off the* V+ADV+N: *lie.* ● **Bring off** means almost the same as **carry off.** NO PASSIVE

2 If you **carry off** a prize or an award, you win it. EG *Vita carried off* V+ADV+N, *all the prizes... Liane Aukin carried off the Best Play Adaptation.* V+N+ADV, V+PRON+ADV

carry on. 1 If you **carry on** with an activity, you continue doing it. EG V+ADV+with, *Are you telling me to carry on with my investigation?... The guest* V+ADV+N/-ING *speaker was not in the least disturbed, but carried on reading from his prepared script... It was the worst possible place to carry on his research.*

2 If you **carry on** when you are in a difficult or unpleasant situation, V+ADV you manage to continue with your normal, everyday activities. EG *A few carry on as if nothing had happened... I could never have carried on without their support.* ● **Go on** means almost the same as **carry on.**

3 If you **carry on** a particular kind of work, activity, or a conversa- V+ADV+N tion, you take part in it. EG *Our work is carried on in an informal atmosphere... She could not carry on a normal conversation.* ● **Conduct** is a more formal word for **carry on.**

4 If you **carry on** about something, you make a fuss about it; an V+ADV informal use. EG *The child was screaming and carrying on.* ▶ A N SING **carry-on** is behaviour that you think is annoying and unnecessary; an informal word used in British English showing disapproval. EG *Well, what a carry-on.*

5 If you **carry on** with someone, you have a love affair with them; an V+ADV+with, old-fashioned, informal use which shows disapproval. EG *Helen was* V+ADV: *carrying on with Hogan.* RECIPROCAL

carry out. 1 If you **carry out** a task, you do it. EG *They have to carry* V+ADV+N, *out many administrative duties... 'Woman' magazine has just carried* V+N+ADV, *a survey out... The first experiments were carried out by Dr Preston* V+PRON+ADV *McLendon.*

2 If you **carry out** an idea, suggestion, or instruction, you put it into practice. EG *He explained that he was simply carrying out instructions... Men at the top make the decisions, men at the bottom carry them out... He gave guarantees that such a policy will be carried out if his Party achieves office.*

V+ADV+N,
V+PRON+ADV,
V+N+ADV

carry over. 1 If you **carry** something **over** from one situation to another, you allow it to continue to exist in the new situation. EG *Small children live a life of fantasy and they carry this fantasy over into action... ...large deficits customarily carried over to next year's budget.*

V+N+ADV,
V+PRON+ADV,
V+ADV+N

2 If a set of figures on a page **is carried over,** it is written at the top of the next page. EG *The sum total to be carried over amounts to £76.* ● **Be brought forward** means almost the same as **be carried over.**

PASSIVE:
V+ADV

carry through. 1 If you **carry through** a plan, you succeed in putting it into practice. EG *...the task of carrying through the necessary reforms... We are united on these policies and determined to carry them through.*

V+ADV+N,
V+PRON+ADV,
V+N+ADV

2 If something **carries** you **through** a period of time, it makes it possible for you to survive or endure something unpleasant during that time. EG *They stole some grain—not much—but enough to carry them through a few weeks... A rich season meant prosperity enough to carry the town through a lean winter.*

V+PRON+PREP,
V+N+PREP:
NO PASSIVE

cart, carts, carting, carted

cart off. If you **cart** someone **off,** you take them somewhere without asking them whether they want to go there or not. EG *His father was carted off to jail... I was terrified they'd get me carted off to a police hospital.* ● **Pack off** means almost the same as **cart off.**

V+N+ADV,
V+PRON+ADV,
V+ADV+N

carve, carves, carving, carved

carve out. 1 If something or someone **carves out** something such as a particular area, they create it in a large area, often with difficulty. EG *It has taken the Colorado River a century to carve a canyon out of the red clay soil... The river sliced through sediments, carving out the gorge... A small airport had been carved out of the forest.*

V+N+ADV,
V+ADV+N,
V+PRON+ADV:
USUALLY+*of*

2 If you **carve out** something for yourself, you create or obtain it, often with difficulty. EG *The company is carving out a huge slice of the electronics market... He stayed to carve out a kingdom for himself and his followers... ...the role that green politics is carving out for itself.*

V+ADV+N,
V+N+ADV,
V+PRON+ADV:
NO PASSIVE

carve up. 1 If you **carve up** an area, you divide it into smaller areas. EG *The junta would carve up that vast region into a number of slaveholdings... They prepared to carve up the British Empire.*

V+ADV+N,
V+N+ADV,
V+PRON+ADV

2 If you **carve** someone **up,** you wound them badly with a knife; an informal use. EG *He'd probably carve the victim up in the end.* ● **Cut up** means almost the same as **carve up.**

V+N+ADV,
V+PRON+ADV

cash, cashes, cashing, cashed

cash in. 1 If you **cash in** an investment such as shares or premium bonds, you exchange them for money. EG *She had to cash in her premium bonds to raise a bit of money... I used to have a few shares, but I cashed them in last year.*

V+ADV+N,
V+PRON+ADV,
V+N+ADV

2 If you **cash in** on a situation, you take advantage of it, especially by doing something slightly unfair or dishonest. EG *...cashing in on other's people's inequality... I don't blame businessmen for cashing in.*

V+ADV:
ALSO+*on*

cast, casts, casting

The form **cast** is used in the present tense and is the past tense and past participle of the verb.

cast about. If you **cast about, around,** or **round** for something, you   V+ADV:
look for it; a formal expression. EG *Jack cast about on the bare rock*   ALSO+*for*
and looked anxious... I cast around for a place to live.

cast around. See **cast about.**

cast aside. If you **cast** someone or something **aside,** you get rid of   V+ADV+N,
them because you no longer like them or approve of them; a formal   V+N+ADV,
expression. EG *The figure who is an honour to his country is cast*   V+PRON+ADV
aside and disgraced... Her son cast aside his Christian forbearance.

cast away. 1 If you **cast** something **away,** you get rid of it   V+PRON+ADV,
completely; a literary use. EG *He says he finds his life of little*   V+N+ADV,
account and is proud to cast it away.   V+ADV+N

2 A **castaway** is a person who has managed to swim or float to a   N COUNT
lonely island or shore after their ship has been wrecked. EG *...cast-*
aways marooned on a desert island.

cast back. If you **cast** your mind **back** to something that happened   V+N+ADV:
in the past, you think about it again and try to remember it. EG *He*   NO PASSIVE
cast his mind back over the day.

cast down. 1 If someone is **cast down,** they lose their social status;   PASSIVE:
a formal use. EG *Men of high status were cast down... Why were we*   V+ADV
cast down so far? ● **Raise** means the opposite of **cast down.**

2 If you **cast** your eyes **down,** you look downwards; a formal use. EG   V+N+ADV,
Her eyes were cast down. ● **Lower** is a less formal word for **cast**   V+ADV+N
down.

3 If you are **downcast** you are feeling sad and pessimistic; a formal   ADJECTIVE
word. EG *Cameron seemed unusually downcast and taciturn.*

cast off. 1 If you **cast** something **off,** you get rid of it because you no   V+ADV+N,
longer want it or because it is preventing you from making pro-   V+N+ADV,
gress. EG *Organizations must cast off those bureaucratic practices.*   V+PRON+ADV
● **Discard** is a more formal word for **cast off.** ▶ **Cast-off** clothes or   ADJECTIVE,
cast-offs are clothes which you give to someone else, because they   N PLURAL
do not fit you or you do not like them. EG *...the embarrassing position*
of wearing cast-off shoes or sports jackets... They had dressed up in
Winifred's cast-offs. ▶ **Cast-off** is also used to describe something   ADJECTIVE
which people have got rid of because it is no longer wanted or it has
become a nuisance. EG *...cast-off ideas.*

2 When you **cast off,** you remove or untie the rope fastening a boat   V+ADV+N,
to a harbour wall so that the boat can move away. EG *Hendricks cast*   V+ADV:
off the bow line and walked to the stern... She gave the order to cast   NO PASSIVE
off.

3 In knitting, when you **cast off** stitches, you remove them from the   V+ADV+N,
needle after doing a special stitch, especially in order to finish a   V+ADV
piece of knitting.

cast on. In knitting, when you **cast on** stitches, you make them on a   V+ADV+N,
needle in order to begin a piece of knitting. EG *Using 4mm needles*   V+ADV
cast on 53 stitches... I'm just casting on.

cast out. If you **cast** someone **out,** you get rid of them or make   V+PRON+ADV,
them leave a place; a formal expression. EG *She had abandoned him,*   V+N+ADV,
she had cast him out... What will such vulnerable creatures do when   V+ADV+N
they are cast out into the open? ▶ An **outcast** is someone who is   N COUNT
rejected and ignored by other people. EG *...a social outcast who has*
spent some time in jail.

cast round. See **cast about.**

cast up. If something is **cast up** on the shore or on a beach, it is left   V+N+ADV,
there by the sea at high tide. EG *His body was cast up onto the shore.*   V+PRON+ADV,
● **Wash up** means almost the same as **cast up.**   V+ADV+N

catch, catches, catching, caught

catch on. 1 If someone **catches on** to something, they understand   V+ADV:
  ALSO+*to*

cave in

and learn it. EG *He'll catch on eventually... They finally caught on to our game.* ● **Cotton on** means almost the same as **catch on**.

2 If something **catches on**, it becomes popular. EG *The idea is catching on... Ballroom dancing caught on.* `V+ADV`

catch out. 1 If you **catch** someone **out**, you make them make a mistake, often by an unfair trick. EG *Fancy trying to catch me out!* `V+N+ADV, V+PRON+ADV`

2 If you **are caught out** by something that happens unexpectedly, you find yourself in an unfortunate situation or weak position. EG *He had also been caught out by the nationalization of Britain's oil industry... I am not going to be caught out by a new war.* `PASSIVE: V+ADV`

catch up. 1 If you **catch up** with someone who is in front of you, you reach them by walking faster than they are walking. EG *He is dawdling behind, not wanting to catch up... Simon tried to catch up with the others... She stood still, allowing him to catch her up.* `V+ADV, USUALLY+with: V+PRON+ADV, V+N+ADV`

2 If you **catch up** with someone, you reach the same standard or level as they are. EG *Most leaders were obsessed with catching up with the West.* `V+ADV: ALSO+with`

catch up in. 1 If you **are caught up in** something, you are involved in it, usually unwillingly. EG *...a society caught up in complex, high-speed change... You are bound to be caught up in events.* `PASSIVE: V+ADV+PREP`

2 You can also say that you **are caught up in** something when it prevents you from moving. EG *I got caught up in the traffic... A bird had got caught up in the net.* `PASSIVE: V+ADV+PREP`

catch up on. When you **catch up on** something, you spend time doing something that you have not had time to do properly until now. EG *I was just catching up on my sleep... They would be going to the office to catch up on some correspondence.* `V+ADV+PREP`

catch up with. 1 If the police or the authorities **catch up with** someone who has done something wrong, they succeed in finding them, especially in order to arrest or punish them. EG *When Birmingham authorities finally caught up with her, she had spent all the money.* `V+ADV+PREP`

2 If something **catches up with** you, you find yourself in an unpleasant situation which you have been able to avoid but which you are now forced to deal with. EG *I am sure that the truth will catch up with him... Poverty may catch up with the apparently most secure.* `V+ADV+PREP`

cater, caters, catering, catered

cater for. To **cater for** a person or group means to provide all the things that they need or want in a particular situation. EG *We can cater for all age groups in our summer schools... Newspapers cater for a variety of tastes... In a consumer society no effort is made to cater for the needs of the elderly... Hotels like this are not geared to cater for parties like ours.* `V+PREP: HAS PASSIVE`

cater to. To **cater to** a need or taste means to provide things which satisfy it. EG *Terry catered to the public taste for new plays.* `V+PREP`

cave, caves, caving, caved

cave in. 1 When something such as a roof or a ceiling **caves in** or when something **caves** it **in**, it collapses inwards. EG *In order to prevent the sides caving in, it is usually lined with bricks... The blow caved in his skull.* ▸ A **cave-in** is the sudden collapse of a roof or ceiling into a building or room below it. `V+ADV, V+ADV+N, V+PRON+ADV: ERGATIVE` `N COUNT`

2 If you **cave in**, you give in or surrender to someone or something, especially when you are under pressure. EG *I more or less caved in, though I still defended my explanation... The spies had given the invaders a few days to cave in.* ● **Capitulate** is a more formal word for **cave in**. `V+ADV`

centre, centres, centring, centred

American English uses the spellings **center, centers, centering** and **centered.**

centre around. If something **centres around** or **centres round** a person or thing, they are the main feature or subject of attention; usually used when you are generalizing rather than describing the specific details of a subject. EG *The workers' demands centred around pay and conditions... Our holidays centred very much round horse-racing.*
`V+PREP,`
`V+N+PREP,`
`V+PRON+PREP:`
`ERGATIVE`

centre on. If something **centres on** or **upon** a person or thing, it concentrates on them; usually used when you are describing specific details rather than generalizing. EG *Attention was for the moment centred on Michael Striker... The struggle was now centred upon Pennsylvania.*
`V+PREP,`
`V+N+PREP,`
`V+PRON+PREP:`
`ERGATIVE`

centre round. See centre around.
centre upon. See centre on.

chain, chains, chaining, chained

chain up. If you **chain up** someone or something, you fasten them to something using a chain. EG *The rowing boats were chained up.*
`V+N+ADV,`
`V+PRON+ADV,`
`V+ADV+N`

chalk, chalks, chalking, chalked

chalk up. If you **chalk up** a victory, a success, or a number of points in a game, you achieve it. EG *They chalked up several victories... She's chalked up four wins already this season.* ● **Notch up** means almost the same as **chalk up.**
`V+ADV+N`

chance, chances, chancing, chanced

chance on. If you **chance on** or **chance upon** something or someone, you meet or discover them unexpectedly. EG *I chanced on an old friend in the street... He'd chanced upon an old book.*
`V+PREP:`
`HAS PASSIVE`

chance upon. See chance on: **chance upon** is more formal.

change, changes, changing, changed

change down. When you **change down,** you move the gear lever on a car or bicycle in order to use a lower gear. EG *You'll have to change down into second to get round the corner.*
`V+ADV`

change over. 1 To **change over** from one thing to another means to stop doing, using, or having one thing and start doing, using, or having something else. EG *The school changed over from having a system of streaming to having mixed ability classes... They had been Liberal till several years ago, then they changed over to Conservative.* ▸ A **changeover** is a change from one activity, system, or way of working to another one. EG *The changeover took place at Easter.*
`V+ADV:`
`USUALLY`
`WITH from/to`

`N COUNT`

2 You say that two people **change over** when each of them does what the other person was previously doing or when each of them goes to where the other person was. EG *Let's change over—you paint the wall and I'll paint the door.*
`V+ADV`

change up. When you **change up,** you move the gear lever on a car or bicycle in order to use a higher gear. EG *She changed up into fourth.*
`V+ADV`

chase, chases, chasing, chased

chase after. 1 If you **chase after** someone, you run after them or follow them quickly in order to catch them. EG *...hundreds of warriors chasing after a fugitive... I couldn't chase after them; they were too quick for me.*
`V+PREP`

2 If you **chase after** something you want or need, such as work, money, or the solution to a problem, you try very hard to obtain it.
`V+PREP`

EG *His work involves a hunt for ideas—he chases after solutions... I had chased after easy alternatives.*

chase off. If you **chase** someone **off,** you run after them in order to frighten them or force them to go away. EG *Male birds use harsh, rattling cries to chase off other thrushes... There was another snake. The dog chased it off.*

V+ADV+N,
V+PRON+ADV,
V+N+ADV

chase up. 1 If you **chase** someone **up,** you contact them to remind them to do something for you, or to ask them something. EG *I'll chase her up for those reports... I've been trying to find you, chasing up people you'd worked with.*

V+PRON+ADV,
V+ADV+N,
V+N+ADV

2 If you **chase** something **up,** you try to find it because it is needed. EG *You'd better chase those addresses up tomorrow... Someone else is in charge of chasing up the missing books.* ● **Track down** means almost the same as **chase up.**

V+N+ADV,
V+PRON+ADV,
V+ADV+N

chat, chats, chatting, chatted

chat up. If you **chat** someone **up,** you talk to them in a friendly way because you are sexually attracted to them; used mainly in informal British English. EG *He would rather be chatting the stewardess up... How could Sheila be so stupid, chatting up two louts like that?... The last I saw of her she was being chatted up by this bloke.*

V+N+ADV,
V+PRON+ADV,
V+ADV+N

cheat, cheats, cheating, cheated

cheat on. 1 If you **cheat on** your sexual partner, you behave dishonestly towards them by secretly having a relationship with someone else. EG *A private detective has been assigned to find out whether she's cheating on her husband.* ● **Deceive** means almost the same as **cheat on.**

V+PREP

2 To **cheat on** someone also means to lie to them or behave dishonestly towards them. EG *He can cheat on us, but he's smart enough to say somebody else did it.*

V+PREP:
HAS PASSIVE

check, checks, checking, checked

check in. 1 When you **check in** or when someone **checks** you **in** at a hotel, you arrive at the hotel, collect the key to your room, and fill in any forms which are necessary. EG *I checked in at the Gordon Hotel... He worked at the front desk checking in the guests when they arrived.*

V+ADV,
V+ADV+N,
V+N+ADV,
V+PRON+ADV:
ERGATIVE

2 When you **check in** at an airport or when someone **checks** you **in,** you show your ticket before getting on the plane. EG *He checked in without baggage for a flight to Rome... The remaining passengers were still being checked in.* ▶ A **check-in** is the place in an airport where you check in. EG *We were supposed to notice damaged bags at the check-in but seldom did... ...a check-in counter.*

V+ADV,
V+N+ADV,
V+PRON+ADV,
V+ADV+N:
ERGATIVE

N COUNT

check into. When you **check into** a hotel or if someone **checks** you **into** it, you arrive at the hotel, collect the key to your room, and fill in any forms which are necessary. EG *With no money, we could hardly think about checking into a motel.*

V+PREP,
V+N+PREP,
V+PRON+PREP:
ERGATIVE

check off. When you **check off** a list of things, you count them to make sure everything is right. EG *We waited while Mr Wilde checked off the things on the list... I store the details in a file to check off when I am ready to go.*

V+ADV+N,
V+N+ADV,
V+PRON+ADV

check out. 1 When you **check out** of a hotel where you have been staying, you pay the bill and leave. EG *The following morning he checked out... She checked out of the hotel and took the train to Paris.*

V+ADV:
ALSO+of

2 If you **check** something **out,** you find out about it or examine it because you want to make sure that everything is correct or safe. EG *An officer would be checking out the statement Mrs. Mossman just*

V+ADV+N,
V+PRON+ADV,
V+N+ADV

made... *Frank was going to check out the restaurant floor to see whether anything unusual was going on... It might be difficult to transfer your money, so check it out with the manager.*

3 If you **check** someone **out,** you obtain information about them secretly to find out if they are telling the truth. EG *They knew his habits, Luca thought, they must have been checking him out... Jenny was reserving judgement until she could check out the two men who had called her.* ● **Check up** means almost the same as **check out.**

V+PRON+ADV,
V+ADV+N,
V+N+ADV

4 In a shop, if you **check out** the things you want to buy, you pay for them at a special counter; used mainly in American English. EG *Wait before you check those cards out, and I'll get some too.* ▷ In a supermarket, a **checkout** is a counter where you pay for the things you have bought. EG *Only two checkouts were operating... ...queueing at the checkout counter.*

V+N+ADV,
V+PRON+ADV,
V+ADV+N

N COUNT

check up. If you **check up** on someone or something, you obtain information about them, often secretly. EG *The council had checked up on her and decided that she was unsuitable for employment... He had been aware that they would be checking up on him... They think there is a security leak and are trying to check up.* ● **Check out** means almost the same **check up.** ▷ A **check-up** is an examination by a doctor to see that your health is all right. EG *See the doctor for a blood test and check-up.*

V+ADV:
USUALLY+*on*

N COUNT

cheer, cheers, cheering, cheered

cheer on. If you **cheer** someone **on,** you cheer loudly in order to encourage them. EG *Some students stood on the roof, cheering the rioters on... There was no one there to cheer him on or applaud.*

V+N+ADV,
V+PRON+ADV,
V+ADV+N

cheer up. When you **cheer up** or when someone or something **cheers** you **up,** you stop feeling depressed and become more cheerful. EG *She cheered up a little as Miss Livingstone went out... Her friends tried to cheer her up, telling her she wasn't missing much... She bought strawberries to cheer herself up.* ● **Buck up** means almost the same as **cheer up.**

V+ADV,
V+PRON+ADV,
V+REFL+ADV,
V+N+ADV,
V+ADV+N:
ERGATIVE

cheese, cheeses, cheesing, cheesed

cheese off. If you are **cheesed off** with something, you are annoyed, bored, or disappointed with it; an informal expression, used in British English. EG *I was really cheesed off when he didn't turn up.*

V+PRON+ADV,
V+N+ADV:
USUALLY PASSIVE

chew, chews, chewing, chewed

chew on. If you **chew on** an idea or a problem, you think about it carefully for a long time. EG *He chewed on the idea that his brother had suggested... You've given me a lot to chew on.* ● **Consider** is a more formal word for **chew on.**

V+PREP

chew over. If you **chew** something **over,** you think carefully about it. EG *In discussion we chew over problems and work out possible solutions... ...chewing over the happenings of the day.* ● **Mull over** means almost the same as **chew over.**

V+ADV+N,
V+N+ADV,
V+PRON+ADV

chew up. If you **chew** food **up,** you chew it until it is completely crushed or softened. EG *Lally put it into her mouth and chewed it up happily... Peas and beans are too tough to be chewed up.*

V+PRON+ADV,
V+N+ADV,
V+ADV+N

chicken, chickens, chickening, chickened

chicken out. If you **chicken out** of something, you decide not to do it because you are afraid; an informal expression which is used showing disapproval. EG *He didn't want to look as if he was chickening out... ...trying to chicken out of going to the dentist.*

V+ADV:
ALSO+*of*

chime, chimes, chiming, chimed

chime in. If someone **chimes in,** they say something just after someone else has spoken. EG *Bill Henderson chimed in with 'This is an emergency situation...' 'Yes,' he chimed in, 'there's where the future of this wretched country lies.'* · V+ADV: ALSO+*with*, USUALLY+QUOTE

chime in with. If one thing **chimes in with** another thing, the two things are consistent with each other and seem to belong together. EG *These influences could only chime in with the growing feeling of despair.* · V+ADV+PREP

chip, chips, chipping, chipped

chip in. 1 If you **chip in** to pay for something, you contribute part of the cost so that you and several other people pay for it together; an informal use. EG *If anyone was ill, they all chipped in to pay the doctor's bill... They all ought to chip in and buy a present.* • **Club together** means almost the same as **chip in.** · V+ADV

2 If someone **chips in** during a conversation, they interrupt it by saying something. EG *'Do you know,' said Mrs Oliver, chipping in again, 'whether Celia was there or not?'... 'Come on, back to work' chipped in the older man.* · V+ADV: ALSO+QUOTE

chip off. If a coating **chips off** a surface, or if you **chip** it **off,** it gradually becomes detached from the surface. EG *He had been compelled to earn his living chipping rust off bridges... With extreme care, she began chipping off the white paint... The car was only two years old, and already the paint had started to chip off.* · V+N+PREP/ADV, V+PRON+PREP/ADV, V+ADV+N, V+ADV: ERGATIVE

choke, chokes, choking, choked

choke back. 1 If you **choke back** a strong emotion, you force yourself not to show it. EG *I choked back the sobs... She spoke with difficulty, choking back the tears.* • **Suppress** means almost the same as **choke back.** · V+ADV+N: NO PASSIVE

2 If you **choke back** something you are saying, you stop yourself from saying it. EG *'I'm—' she choked back the word... He turned to yell for Helen, but choked it back.* · V+ADV+N, V+N+ADV, V+PRON+ADV

chop, chops, chopping, chopped

chop down. If you **chop down** a tree, you cut through its trunk with an axe so that it falls to the ground. EG *...trying to chop down the stump of a small holly tree... I chopped the saplings down every year, but they always grew back.* · V+ADV+N, V+N+ADV, V+PRON+ADV

chop off. If you **chop** something **off,** you cut it off with a sudden or decisive stroke, using something such as a knife. EG *Keep your foot still, or I'll chop it off at the knee... ...women in the fields, chopping off the long golden stalks of corn.* · V+PRON+ADV, V+ADV+N, V+N+ADV

chop up. If you **chop** something **up,** you cut it into small pieces. EG *Soak the plants, then chop them up as small as you can... Fruit tastes delicious when chopped up and sprinkled with wine.* · V+PRON+ADV, V+N+ADV, V+ADV+N

chuck, chucks, chucking, chucked

chuck away. If you **chuck** something **away,** you throw it away, because you do not want it or cannot use it any longer. EG *'What are you going to do with all those old clothes?'—'Oh, just chuck them away I think'... This heater had to be chucked away because it didn't work.* • **Chuck out** means almost the same as **chuck away.** · V+PRON+ADV, V+N+ADV, V+ADV+N

chuck in. If you **chuck in** your job or other activity, you stop doing it; an informal expression. EG *He got a new job, but when he found out that he paid as much tax as Paddy earned, he chucked it in.* • **Jack in** and **pack in** mean almost the same as **chuck in.** · V+PRON+ADV, V+N+ADV, V+ADV+N: NO PASSIVE

chuck out. 1 If you **chuck** someone **out** of a place, you force them · V+PRON+ADV, to leave. EG *I could never forgive them for chucking me out... Why did you leave? Were you chucked out?* ● **Throw out** means almost the same as **chuck out**. ▶ **Chucking-out** time is the time when public houses close; an informal word used in British English. EG *Is it chucking-out time already?*

`V+N+ADV,`
`V+ADV+N`

`ADJECTIVE`

2 If you **chuck** something **out**, you throw it away because you do not want it any longer. EG *Chuck those old boots out, for goodness sake... She chucked out loads of books that could have been given to Oxfam.* ● **Chuck away** means almost the same as **chuck out**.

`V+N+ADV,`
`V+PRON+ADV,`
`V+ADV+N`

chuck up. If you **chuck up** a job or other activity, you stop doing it; an informal expression. EG *He was just one of the lads who had chucked his job up.* ● **Chuck in** means almost the same as **chuck up**.

`V+N+ADV,`
`V+PRON+ADV,`
`V+ADV+N`

churn, churns, churning, churned

churn out. To **churn** things **out** means to produce them in large numbers very quickly. EG *His campaign organization began churning out tracts and posters... My brain was churning out objections at an incredible rate... The routine calculations that had to be churned out grew and grew.* ● **Pump out** means almost the same as **churn out**.

`V+ADV+N,`
`V+N+ADV,`
`V+PRON+ADV`

churn up. **1** If something **churns up** mud or water, it moves it about violently. EG *The wind churned up the water into a swirling foam... The silt in the lakes has been churned up by motorboats.*

`V+ADV+N,`
`V+N+ADV,`
`V+PRON+ADV`

2 If something **churns** you **up**, it makes you feel worried or frightened. EG *Something seemed to be churning her up inside... I would be churned up and destroyed inside by irrepressible desires.*

`V+PRON+ADV,`
`V+N+ADV`

clam, clams, clamming, clammed

clam up. If someone **clams up**, they refuse to say anything about a subject; an informal expression. EG *Lonnie just clammed up as if he had already said too much... We had a row, and I clammed up and said nothing for a complete half-hour.*

`V+ADV`

clamp, clamps, clamping, clamped

clamp down. To **clamp down** on people or activities means to take strong official action to stop or control them. EG *The authorities have got to clamp down on these trouble-makers... The Federal Reserve clamped down on bank lending.* ● **Crack down** means almost the same as **clamp down**. ▶ A **clampdown** is a sudden restriction on an activity by a government or other authority. EG *...a clampdown on wasteful spending.*

`V+ADV:`
`USUALLY+on`

`N COUNT`

clap, claps, clapping, clapped

clap out. **1** If you **clap out** a tune, you produce it by hitting your hands together in a way which matches the rhythm of the tune. EG *A leader is selected, and he or she begins to clap out a rhythm which the others quickly duplicate... The actor claps out a beat, which fits into the collective rhythm... You clap it out, and I'll join in when I get the hang of it.*

`V+ADV+N,`
`V+N+ADV,`
`V+PRON+ADV`

2 Something such as a machine that is **clapped-out** is old and no longer working properly; used in informal British English. EG *The last car was a clapped-out old Ford.* ● **Worn-out** means almost the same as **clapped-out**.

`ADJECTIVE`

class, classes, classing, classed

class among. If you **class** someone or something **among** a particular group, you consider them to be a member of that group. EG *At one time the arts of reading and writing were classed among the great mysteries of life for the majority of people... Would you class young Paddy Martyn among the best?*

`V+N+PREP,`
`V+PRON+PREP`

claw, claws, clawing, clawed

claw at. When people or animals **claw at** something, they try to get   V+PREP
hold of it or damage it by using their nails or claws. EG ...*shaking her
head and clawing at my trousers*... ...*scrabbling with my hands,
clawing at the rock as I fell.*

claw back. If an organization **claws back** money, it finds a way of   V+ADV+N,
getting money back which it has spent earlier. EG *The Government*   V+N+ADV,
was determined to claw back the extra supplementary benefit. ▶ A   N COUNT
clawback is a method of getting money back which was spent
earlier. EG *Debts offset by £285 million in clawback arrangements.*

clean, cleans, cleaning, cleaned

clean down. If you **clean down** a building or part of a building, you   V+ADV+N,
clean or wash it thoroughly. EG *First, clean down the walls*... *Nicola*   V+N+ADV,
cleaned the windows down, while Alan made a cup of tea.   V+PRON+ADV

clean out. 1 If you **clean** something **out,** you clean it very thorough-   V+N+ADV,
ly and remove anything that is not wanted or needed. EG *I spent*   V+PRON+ADV,
three days cleaning our flat out... *I was to massage the wound and*   V+ADV+N
clean it out every day... *I was cleaning out my desk at the office on
my last day there.* ▶ A **clean-out** is the activity of cleaning a place   N COUNT
very thoroughly and throwing away things you do not want or need.
EG *I was just having a little clean-out in the kitchen.*

2 If you **clean out** a person, you take all the money they have. If you   V+ADV+N,
clean out a place, you take everything of value that is in it; an   V+N+ADV,
informal use. EG *I've got no more money—they cleaned me out*...   V+PRON+ADV
Thomas thought idly of cleaning out the cash register.

clean up. 1 If you **clean up** someone or something, you clean them   V+ADV+N,
fairly thoroughly. EG *Clean up food spills at once*... *He winced as I*   V+N+ADV,
cleaned up his face... ...*the costs of cleaning up rivers and beaches.*   V+PRON+ADV

2 If you **clean up** a place, you clean it thoroughly and make it tidy.   V+ADV,
EG *It must be very depressing to spend your life cleaning up after*   V+ADV+N,
people you never see... *They would stay behind to help me clean up*   V+N+ADV,
the classroom... *He cleaned the room up before leaving.* ● **Clear up**   V+PRON+ADV
means almost the same as **clean up.** ▶ A **clean-up** is a good,   N COUNT
thorough clean. EG *This room could do with a good clean-up.*

3 If the police or the authorities **clean up** a place, they make it free   V+ADV+N,
from crime. EG *Then they can begin to clean up the cities*... *City*   V+N+ADV,
authorities have long wanted to clean up Times Square.   V+PRON+ADV

4 If people **clean up,** they make a large profit from a business deal.   V+ADV
EG *People who buy shares now will clean up when the price rises.*

clear, clears, clearing, cleared

clear away. When you **clear away,** you put away the things that   V+ADV,
you have been using. EG *After dinner, when we had cleared away*   V+ADV+N,
and washed up, we went for a walk... *Brody stood up and began to*   V+N+ADV,
clear away the soup bowls... *Clear the cutlery away.* ● **Tidy away**   V+PRON+ADV
means almost the same as **clear away.**

clear off. If you say '**clear off**' to someone, you are telling them in a   IMPERATIVE:
rude way to go away; used mainly in informal British English. EG   V+ADV
Now you clear off and leave me alone... *He was told to clear off by
the publican.* ● **Buzz off** means almost the same as **clear off.**

clear out. 1 If you **clear out** of a place, you leave it; an informal use.   V+ADV:
EG *I've got to clear out of my place by next week*... *I woke one night*   ALSO+*of,*
around midnight and decided to clear out... *Just clear out and leave*   ALSO IMPERATIVE
me in peace! ● **Get out** means almost the same as **clear out.**

2 If you **clear out** a cupboard, a room, or a house, or if you **clear**   V+ADV+N,
things **out** of it, you tidy it and throw away the things you no longer   V+N+ADV,
need. EG *It's about time I cleared out the kitchen cupboards*... *These*   V+PRON+ADV

cards had to be cleared out at fairly short intervals. ▶ A **clear-out** is the activity of collecting together all the things that you do not want and throwing them away; an informal word used in British English. EG *...a general clear-out of our archives.* | N COUNT

clear up. 1 When you **clear up** or **clear** something **up**, you tidy things and put them away. EG *I was too tired to clear up... I wonder who clears all this up... Go and clear up your room.* | V+ADV, V+N+ADV, V+PRON+ADV, V+ADV+N

2 If you **clear up** a problem, disagreement, or misunderstanding, you settle it or give a satisfactory explanation for it. EG *Inspector Standish was trying to clear up a tiresome problem... I went to clear the matter up with him.* ● **Sort out** means almost the same as **clear up.** | V+ADV+N, V+N+ADV, V+PRON+ADV

3 If someone's illness **clears up**, they recover from it. EG *I was very lucky, it was only a minor infection and it all cleared up in a week... The neck pains could clear up on their own.* | V+ADV

4 When bad weather **clears up**, it stops raining or being cloudy. EG *I'm going back till this weather clears up.* ● **Brighten up** means almost the same as **clear up.** | V+ADV

climb, climbs, climbing, climbed

climb down. If you **climb down** in an argument or dispute, you admit that you are wrong. EG *Even after these facts were published, he was unwilling to climb down.* ● **Back down** means almost the same as **climb down.** ▶ A **climb-down** is the act of admitting that you are wrong and agreeing to accept what someone else wants. EG *Many strikes end in a climb-down on the part of the management.* | V+ADV, N COUNT

clock, clocks, clocking, clocked

clock in. 1 When workers **clock in** or **clock on** at a factory or office, they record the time that they arrive by putting a special card into a device. EG *If they are late clocking in, they lose pay.* | V+ADV

2 If someone or something **clocks in** at a particular weight, they register that amount after being weighed. EG *The van clocked in at 2,000 pounds.* ● **Weigh in** means almost the same as **clock in.** | V+ADV: USUALLY+at

clock off. See **clock out.**

clock on. See **clock in.**

clock out. When workers **clock out** or **clock off** in a factory or office, they record the time that they leave by putting a special card into a device. EG *It's time to clock out.* | V+ADV

clock up. To **clock up** a large number or total means to reach that total. EG *He has clocked up more than 171,750 miles in a lifetime of running... Manufactured exports clocked up an average 5% increase in volume.* ● **Notch up** means almost the same as **clock up.** | V+ADV+N

clog, clogs, clogging, clogged

clog up. If something **clogs up** or **is clogged up**, it becomes blocked and no longer works properly. EG *We have to call a mechanic every time the waste disposal unit clogs up... If the cooling unit is clogged up it can't do its job efficiently.* | V+ADV, OR PASSIVE, V+ADV: ERGATIVE

close, closes, closing, closed

close down. 1 If someone **closes down** a factory or an organization, or if it **closes down**, all work or activity stops there, usually for ever. EG *They're closing down my old school... The mines had been closed down following a geological survey... If the firms failed to make enough money, they would close down.* ● **Shut down** means almost the same as **close down.** | V+ADV+N, V+N+ADV, V+PRON+ADV, V+ADV: ERGATIVE

2 When a television or radio channel **closes down**, it stops broadcasting for the day; used in British English. EG *Channel 4 closes down* | V+ADV

at midnight. ▸ **Closedown** is the end of broadcasting for the day on the television or radio.   N UNCOUNT

close in. 1 If a group of people **close in** on a person or a place, they come nearer and nearer to them and gradually surround them. EG *They closed in on the struggling pig... Several of the onlookers closed in upon the group... Now the police were closing in.*   V+ADV: ALSO+*on/upon*

2 If something **closes in** on a person or a place, it approaches or is present in a threatening way. EG *I can feel the danger closing in... As night closed in, the invasion force continued to wait... The heat was closing in on the island.*   V+ADV: ALSO+*on/upon*

3 When the days **close in,** there are gradually fewer hours of daylight as winter gets nearer.   V+ADV

close off. If an area **is closed off,** a barrier is put round it or a door is shut, so that nobody can get into it. EG *They lived in a castle in which most of the rooms were permanently closed off... He hadn't been down that road since they closed it off... The iron door closing off our section slid open.* ● **Seal off** means almost the same as **close off.**   V+N+ADV, V+PRON+ADV, V+ADV+N: USUALLY PASSIVE

close on. If you **close on** something or someone, you gradually get nearer and nearer to them, often in a threatening way. EG *The fish closed on the woman and hurtled past... ...Soviet T-34s closing on the camp so suddenly... Snodin brought down Olsen as he closed on the Everton goal.* ● **Close in on** means almost the same as **close on.**   V+PREP

close out. If you **close out** light or sound, you prevent it from reaching a place, for example by using a screen of some kind. EG *Then the canvas flap dropped shut, closing out the light from the middle ground between their trenches and ours... She shut the window, closing out the sound of the midday traffic.*   V+ADV+N

close up. 1 When you **close up** a building or a business, you close it completely and securely. EG *The big house was closed up for the holidays... The officials had closed up for the day.*   V+ADV+N, V+N+ADV, V+PRON+ADV, V+ADV

2 If something **closes up** or if you **close** it **up,** it closes completely. EG *One of his eyes seemed to be closing up... She closed up the atlas and put it back on the shelf... He closed the luggage up and stored it by the door.*   V+ADV, V+ADV+N, V+N+ADV, V+PRON+ADV: ERGATIVE

3 If people **close up,** they move nearer to each other. EG *She told the children to close up to allow everyone into the hall... The two motor cycle riders closed up.*   V+ADV

cloud, clouds, clouding, clouded

cloud over. 1 If it **clouds over** or if the sky **clouds over,** the sky becomes covered with clouds. EG *The sky had clouded over completely... It was clouding over and we thought it was going to rain.*   V+ADV

2 If your face **clouds over,** you suddenly look sad or angry. EG *I saw Hamish's face cloud over... His face clouded over with anguish.*   V+ADV

3 If your eyes **cloud over,** they become dull and blank. EG *As we watched, his eyes clouded over; he twitched and then lay still.* ● **Mist over** means almost the same as **cloud over.**   V+ADV

club, clubs, clubbing, clubbed

club together. If people **club together** to do or buy something, they all give money in order to share the cost of it. EG *We all clubbed together to buy her a present when she retired.*   V+ADV: ALSO+*to*-INF

clue, clues, clueing, clued

clue up. If you **are clued up** about something, you know about it and understand it; an informal expression. EG *You need to have good leaders who are all clued up.*   V+PRON+ADV, V+N+ADV: USUALLY PASSIVE

cluster, clusters, clustering, clustered

cluster around. If people **cluster around** or **round** a place, they   V+PREP,
stand around it in a tight group. EG *He watched the happy parents*   V+ADV
cluster around their darling sons... Sometimes they stop and cluster
round a patch of ground. ● **Gather around** means almost the same
as **cluster around.**

cluster round. See **cluster around.**

clutter, clutters, cluttering, cluttered

clutter up. If you **clutter up** a place, you fill it untidily with a lot of   V+ADV+N,
unnecessary things. EG *The room was cluttered up with all kinds of*   V+N+ADV,
things.   V+PRON+ADV

coax, coaxes, coaxing, coaxed

coax into. If you **coax** someone **into** doing something, you persuade   V+N+PREP,
them to do it by speaking in a gentle and pleasant way to them. EG   V+PRON+PREP
You just coax them into doing it... Even Dr Cox was coaxed into
having some mutton.

cobble, cobbles, cobbling, cobbled

cobble together. If you **cobble** something **together**, you make or   V+ADV+N,
produce it roughly or quickly, by using things that are available to   V+N+ADV,
you. EG *Its author has cobbled together a guide to the islands.*   V+PRON+ADV

cock, cocks, cocking, cocked

cock up. If you **cock** something **up**, you do it so badly that you   V+N+ADV,
completely ruin or spoil it; a very informal expression used in   V+PRON+ADV,
British English. EG *We don't want to cock the whole thing up.* ▸ A   V+ADV+N
cock-up is something that is done very badly; a very informal word   N COUNT
used in British English. EG *There has been a series of cock-ups.*

coil, coils, coiling, coiled

coil up. If you **coil** something **up**, you wind it into a continuous series   V+ADV+N,
of loops. EG *He coiled up the garden hose.*   V+N+ADV,
  V+PRON+ADV

collect, collects, collecting, collected

collect up. If you **collect** things **up**, you collect them all together. EG   V+ADV+N,
They collected up their gear... She was asked to collect up the   V+N+ADV,
briefcases and the books.   V+PRON+ADV

colour, colours, colouring, coloured

American English uses the spellings **color, colors, coloring** and
colored.

colour in. If you **colour in** a shape or outline that is drawn on paper,   V+ADV+N,
you give it different colours using paints or crayons. EG *His little girl*   V+N+ADV,
was busy colouring in her picture.   V+PRON+ADV

colour up. When someone **colours up**, their face becomes red   V+ADV
because they are angry or embarrassed. ● **Blush** means almost the
same as **colour up.**

comb, combs, combing, combed

comb out. If you **comb out** your hair, or if you **comb** something **out**   V+PRON+ADV,
of it, you comb it very thoroughly in order to remove anything that   V+N+ADV,
should not be there, such as tangles or knots. EG *Head lice attach*   V+ADV+N
their eggs to the base of your hair, and you can't comb them out.

come, comes, coming, came

The form **come** is used in the present tense and is the past participle
of the verb.

come about. When you say how something **comes about**, you   V+ADV
explain how it happens. EG *The discovery of adrenalin came about*
through a mistake... How did the invitation come about?

come across. 1 When someone **comes across**, they cross a room, water, or other area towards the place where you are. EG *At that point he came across the room and took her firmly by the shoulder... Some people have been coming across in aeroplanes.*
  `V+PREP,`
  `V+ADV`

2 If you **come across** someone or something, you find or meet them by chance, without having expected to or without having thought about it. EG *Everyone has come across the sort of problem which seems impossible to solve... I came across a man hoeing a field... I've never come across anything like this.*
  `V+PREP`

3 If someone or something **comes across** as having a particular characteristic, they give you the impression of having that characteristic. EG *He wasn't coming across as the idiot I had expected him to be... This was the image that was coming across.*
  `V+ADV:`
  `USUALLY+as`

4 When an idea or meaning **comes across**, you understand exactly what was meant. EG *Do you think this idea comes across in the play?... Did you think that this came across well?* ● **Come over** means almost the same as **come across.**
  `V+ADV`

come after. 1 When something **comes after** a particular event or point in time, it happens later than that event or time. EG *Learning should come after play... It was not looked on, by the generations that came after, as the high point of their civilization.* ● **Follow** means almost the same as **come after.**
  `V+PREP,`
  `V+ADV`

2 If someone **comes after** you, they chase you or hunt you. EG *The faster I retreated, the faster they came after me.*
  `V+PREP`

come along. 1 When someone **comes along** a road or other area of ground, they move along it towards you. EG *The children came along the beach... Ralph was coming along, holding his spear.*
  `V+PREP,`
  `V+ADV`

2 If someone **comes along**, they go somewhere with you or go to the same place as you. EG *Thank you for coming along at this somewhat inconvenient time... But why don't you come along with us?*
  `V+ADV:`
  `ALSO+with`

3 When something or someone **comes along**, they happen or arrive, without your having thought much about it beforehand. EG *When the harvest came along, the boy who was doing the milking fell ill... A new generation of planners came along who were much more scientifically based.*
  `V+ADV`

4 If something or someone **is coming along**, they are making progress or developing in the way you want. EG *There are even cookers which tell you how the meat is coming along.* ● **Come on** means almost the same as **come along.**
  `V+ADV`

5 You say 'come along' to someone 5.1 when you want them to hurry up. EG *Come along now, little ones, off to bed.* ● **Come on** and **hurry up** mean almost the same as **come along.** 5.2 when you want to encourage them to do something. EG *He took out a flask of brandy and poured a measure. 'Come along now, old chap. Put this down.'* 5.3 when you think that they are saying something untrue or unreasonable. EG *Come along now, Marsha, the personal sphere is political as well.*
  `IMPERATIVE:`
  `V+ADV`
  `IMPERATIVE:`
  `V+ADV`
  `IMPERATIVE:`
  `V+ADV`

come apart. If something **comes apart**, it breaks or collapses. EG *He pulled both ends of the stick, and it came apart in two pieces.*
  `V+ADV`

come around. See **come round.**

come at. 1 If someone **comes at** you, they move towards you in order to attack you. EG *The bear came at me.*
  `V+PREP`

2 If things such as questions, ideas, or events **come at** you, they are all presented to you at the same time in a way that you find threatening, confusing, or exciting. EG *A new question was coming at him... ...particularly encouraged by all of this information coming at them at once.*
  `V+PREP`

come away. 1 If you **come away** from a place, you leave it. EG *He*
  `V+ADV:`
  `ALSO IMPERATIVE`

came away with the uncomfortable feeling that he had been brain-washed... Come away. There's going to be trouble.

2 When something **comes away** from something else, it becomes separated or detached from it very easily and without needing force. EG *She picked up the book. The cover had come away from the spine... They dissect it, everything comes away very neatly.*   V+ADV: ALSO+*from*

come back. **1** When someone or something **comes back,** they return to the place where you are. EG *He came back from the war... Are you ever coming back home?*   V+ADV

2 When something **comes back** after a period of inactivity, it starts to happen again. EG *That shelter might fall down if the rain comes back... The strange feeling comes back.*   V+ADV

3 When something **comes back** after being unfashionable for a time, it becomes fashionable again. EG *Ostrich feathers never really came back... At last reliability and efficiency seem to be coming back into fashion.* ● **Go out** means the opposite of **come back.** ▶ If something makes a **comeback,** it becomes fashionable again. EG *Body painting made a brief comeback in the 1960s.* ▶ If someone makes or stages a **comeback,** they become successful again at something where they were successful before. EG *I tried to make a comeback.*   V+ADV / N COUNT / N COUNT

4 When a person, answer, or message **comes back,** you get a response to something you have said or done. EG *Lally's voice came back from the dark... The message which came back was that I could order books from the library.*   V+ADV

5 If something that you had forgotten **comes back** to you, you remember it, often quite suddenly. EG *Then the scene of their encounter came back to him with a sense of embarrassment... Against his will, it all came back to him.*   V+ADV: USUALLY+*to*

come back to. If you **come back to** a particular topic or idea, you mention or start to discuss it again. EG *He always came back to this point... We'll come back to that question a little later... ...to come back to what Brian was saying.*   V+ADV+PREP

come before. If people, problems, or cases **come before** a judge, court of law, or other authority, they are brought or discussed there as part of an official process, so that a decision can be made about them. EG *His case came before a tribunal... The major came before the Armed Services Committee.*   V+PREP

come between. If something **comes between** two people, it causes trouble between them and so spoils their friendship. EG *I had come between him and his girlfriend... Nothing like that came between me and the people I met.*   V+PREP

come by. **1** When someone **comes by,** they come to see you for a short time, on a casual or informal basis. EG *Tom had said he would come by at five... Students, astonished, came by his office.*   V+ADV, V+PREP

2 If you **come by** something, you obtain it by chance or without much thought or planning. EG *He had not come by these things through his own labour... Good jobs were hard to come by.*   V+PREP: HAS PASSIVE

come down. **1** When someone or something **comes down,** they move from a higher position to a lower one, or move towards the place where you are. EG *We came down the aircraft steps... A taxi came down the street... After supper, she came down to the pump with me... They came down from the bridge.*   V+PREP, V+ADV

2 When someone in a building **comes down,** they move downstairs towards you. EG *I showered, dressed and came down for breakfast... I heard you come down the stairs with him.* ● **Descend** is a more formal word for **come down.**   V+ADV, V+PREP

3 If someone **comes down** to a place near you, they visit it or move there; used when the place is farther south or is in the country. EG *He*   V+ADV: USUALLY+A *said he wanted his mother to come down to New York... This is Mr Stuart. He's come down from London to talk to me.*

4 When something **comes down,** it collapses or falls to the ground, or someone dismantles it or moves it to a lower position. EG *In the storm a tree came down... Bricks flew in all directions as walls came down... Then, when they reached a deep creek, the big, red-ochred sails came down... Her cheeks were flushed, and her top-knot had come down.* V+ADV

5 If a plane **comes down,** it lands or crashes. EG *Almost all the division's gliders came down on or close to the field... The plane circled and came down in flames.* V+ADV

6 If the cost, level, or amount of something **comes down,** it becomes cheaper or less than it was before. EG *Prices could come down only if wages came down... Local government expenditure has come down by 20% since 1975.* ● **Decrease** is a more formal word for **come down,** and **go up** means the opposite. V+ADV

7 If you **come down** when you are making an offer or suggesting an amount, you decrease the original offer or amount. EG *Get on the phone at once, please, and offer to come down a couple of hundred dollars.* V+ADV, V+ADV+N

8 Something that **comes down** to a particular point extends downwards as far as that point. EG *The window came down almost to the ground... His eyebrows came down over his nose.* V+ADV: WITH A

9 If something such as a tradition, belief, or land **comes down** to a group of people, it is passed to that generation of people from a previous one. EG *...the religious doctrines which have come down to us... ...one of the most moving objects that has come down to us from the distant past.* ● **Be handed down** means almost the same as **come down.** V+ADV: ALSO+*to*

10 If a sign, message, or noise **comes down** to you, you receive it or hear it. EG *Now word had come down that a large mass of activists was in the vicinity... An instruction came down from Paris to investigate him... A cry came down from above.* V+ADV: USUALLY+A

11 If rain or snow or fog **comes down,** it falls heavily. EG *...when the monsoon breaks, and the rain comes down... Five inches of snow had fallen and more was coming down... But then the fog came down.* V+ADV

12 When university students **come down,** they leave university, especially at the end of their degree course, or at the end of term; used in British English. EG *He came down from Oxford in 1958.* ● **Go up** means the opposite of **come down.** V+ADV

13 If you **come down** in favour of something or on the side of something, you decide that that is the right or appropriate thing to do. EG *The subcommittees both came down in favour of the conservation programme... They came down strongly on the side of Pigott.* V+ADV: WITH A

14 You say that something is a **come-down** if you think that it is not as good as something else that you have just done or had. EG *Professionally it is considered a come-down to work in portrait classes... What a comedown!* N SING

come down on. If you **come down on** someone, you blame them for something, and criticize them severely for allowing it to happen. EG *Social workers like me come down harder on parents than on their children... Don't come down on me before you understand.* V+ADV+PREP

come down to. If a problem or question **comes down to** a particular thing, that is the most important or relevant factor to be considered. EG *Your final choice of kitchen may well come down to cost... It all comes down to the mathematics taught in schools... When it comes down to it, that's what I hired him for.* V+ADV+PREP

come down with. If you **come down with** an illness or disease, you   V+ADV+PREP
catch it or develop it. EG *She came down with pneumonia... He came
down with appendicitis.* ● **Contract** is a more formal word for **come
down with.**

come for. 1 When someone **comes for** a person or thing, they come   V+PREP
to where you are in order to get them and take them away. EG *I said
I would come for Dolly in the afternoon... The police came for
Humboldt... I'll come for the sandwiches later.*

2 If someone **is coming for** you, they move towards you in a   V+PREP
threatening way, as if they might attack you. EG *Jake was coming for
me with a knife.*

come forth. 1 If you **come forth** with a suggestion or with informa-   V+ADV:
tion, you make that suggestion or give the information; a literary   ALSO+*with*
use. EG *The British came forth with a second proposal... A witness
came forth to testify that the young man had been present.* ● **Come
forward** means almost the same as **come forth.** ▸ Someone who is   ADJECTIVE
forthcoming willingly gives information when you ask them about
something. EG *He was disinclined to talk about that: nor was he
forthcoming on the way in which he had risen to power.* ▸ If   ADJECTIVE
something is **forthcoming,** it is given or made available. EG *No
evidence of this was forthcoming.*

2 If something **comes forth,** it appears and moves towards you; a   V+ADV
literary use. EG *Great rockets of flame came forth... ...casting spells
before the hunt to make the animals come forth.*

3 A **forthcoming** event is planned to happen soon. EG *I wrote to the*   ADJECTIVE
Minister asking his advice on the forthcoming presidential election.

come forward. If someone **comes forward** to do something, they   V+ADV
offer to do it. EG *When we first came here people came forward to
help us... Many people came forward to accuse her of various
misdemeanours.*

come forward with. If you **come forward with** a suggestion,   V+ADV+PREP
proposal, or idea, you make that suggestion or proposal, or state
your idea. EG *They came forward with ambitious plans for the
centre.*

come from. 1 If you **come from** a particular place, you were born   V+PREP
there or grew up there. You can also say that someone **comes from**
a particular type of family or a particular social class when they
have experienced the type of life that is usually associated with that
type of family or social class. EG *'Where do you come
from?'—'India'... They all came from well-off families... Julie does
not come from a very theatrical background.*

2 If one thing **comes from** another thing, the second thing is its   V+PREP
source or origin. EG *Did you know the word 'idea' comes from
Greek?... Where is the money to come from?... There was a smell of
something cooking coming from the oven.*

3 If you say that you know where someone **is coming from,** you   V+PREP
mean that you understand their situation, attitude, or emotional
state; an informal use. EG *I just don't get where he's coming from,
that guy.*

come in. 1 When someone **comes in,** they enter the room or   V+ADV,
building where you are. EG *There was a knock on the door. 'Come*   V+PREP
in'... Jeremy came in looking worried... 'Come in the house,' she said.

2 When someone **comes in** somewhere such as a place of work or   V+ADV
business or hospital, they arrive there in order to work, carry out
business, receive treatment, and so on. EG *I came in early today... I
was asked to come in for a few days to help out... Someone came in
with undiagnosable bleeding.*

3 When someone such as a builder or cleaner **comes in,** they come   V+ADV

to your house in order to carry out work there. EG *I can't get anybody to come in and do anything in my house... I've also telephoned the local builder to come in tomorrow morning.*

4 When someone or something **comes in** from another place, they   V+ADV
arrive at or approach the place where you are. EG *...the businessman who came in from the capital by air... ...the vast import of processed fish, coming in through the commercial docks.*

5 When a plane, ship, train, or bus **comes in,** it arrives at its   V+ADV
destination or a station or bus stop. EG *Father and son could see the planes coming in over the fields... A ship had just come in from Turkey... She waited near the bus terminus until the last bus came in.* ▸ An **incoming** plane or passenger is travelling towards a place   ADJECTIVE
and about to arrive. EG *...the incoming passengers at London Airport.*
● **Outward** means the opposite of **incoming.**

6 When light, sound, air, or rain **comes in,** it penetrates a barrier or   V+ADV
hole and reaches the place where you are. EG *It was dark inside the wood. No sunlight came in at all... The wind was strong, rain was coming in, she thought it wiser to close the shutters.*

7 If something such as information, a report, or a letter **comes in,**   V+ADV
you receive it. EG *...in the reports that are coming in from Thailand... I'm waiting for some new orders coming in any time... A call had come in telling us that arrests had been made.* ● **Arrive** means almost the same as **come in,** and **go out** means the opposite. ▸ An   ADJECTIVE
incoming message, letter, or phonecall has been sent to you or is received by you. EG *I throw incoming mail in a wicker basket.*
● **Outgoing** means the opposite of **incoming.**

8 If you have money **coming in,** you earn it or receive it as your   V+ADV
normal income. EG *The taxman is entitled to details of the money you have coming in... There is practically no money coming in to buy food, furniture or clothing.* ▸ Your **income** is the amount of   N COUNT
money that you earn from your work or business, or from other sources such as pension or investments. EG *My monthly income was over two hundred pounds.*

9 When something such as a fashion **comes in,** it becomes fashion-   V+ADV
able. EG *Thicker fabrics and darker colors came in.* ● **Go out** means the opposite of **come in.**

10 When something new such as an invention or law **comes in,** it is   V+ADV
introduced and begins to have an effect. EG *We used coal gas before natural gas came in... ...with the Health and Safety at Work Act coming in last year.*

11 When something in a shop **comes in,** a supply of it reaches the   V+ADV
shop and it becomes available. EG *...when copies of George Jackson's 'Soledad Brother' came in... We're waiting for the new brochures to come in.*

12 If someone **comes in** on a discussion, they join in, sometimes   V+ADV:
interrupting someone who is already speaking. EG *Let me just come*   ALSO+*on*
in on this, because Clive is not giving the whole story... Could I come in here?

13 If someone **comes in** on an arrangement, they join a group of   V+ADV:
other people and take part in what they are planning to do. EG *He*   ALSO+*on/with*
should come in on the deal... He was sorry that he had asked Fred Caldwell to come in with him.

14 When a government **comes in,** it wins an election and starts   V+ADV
governing the country. EG *Labour governments come in promising to expand public expenditure... Mrs Thatcher's government came in pledged to arrest and reverse this trend.* ▸ An **incoming** official or   ADJECTIVE
administration is one that has just been newly appointed or elected.

EG *They gave their loyalty to the incoming Government... The outgoing and incoming Administrations will not agree.*

15 You ask or mention where something or someone **comes in** when you are talking about how they are involved in a situation. EG *I still don't see where you come in... 'It's highly illogical.'—'Well logic doesn't come in anyway does it?'* V+ADV

16 When the tide **comes in,** it rises, so that the water reaches higher up the shore. EG *The tide was coming in and all the muddy banks were being covered.* ● **Go out** means the opposite of **come in.** ▸ An **incoming** tide or wave is coming towards you. V+ADV / ADJECTIVE

17 When a season, month, or period of weather **comes in,** it begins. EG *Winter came in with a dark, hungry sadness... We have some improved weather coming in here soon.* V+ADV

18 If something **comes in** useful or handy, it is a useful thing to have. EG *Savings may come in useful for holidays... A toothbrush would come in handy.* V+ADV+ADJ

19 When someone or something **comes in** a particular position or rank, they are in that position or rank in a sequence or at the end of a competition. EG *David had begun the day well by coming in third in the junior riding class.* V+ADV+C

20 When cricketers, baseball players, and so on **come in,** they begin to bat. EG *He made a Test century only a week ago, coming in at number nine.* V+ADV

come in for. If someone or something **comes in for** criticism, blame, or abuse, they are criticized, blamed, or insulted. EG *British industry does come in for a great deal of criticism... The officers often came in for abuse... The Unions come in for a lot of knocking.* V+ADV+PREP

come into. **1** If someone **comes into** a room, house, or other place, they enter it. EG *Boylan came silently into the room.... They came into the bookstore.* ● **Leave** means the opposite of **come into.** V+PREP

2 If someone or something **comes into** being, sight, use, force, and so on, they begin to exist, be noticed or used, have an effect, and so on. EG *Christianity came into being in a hostile environment... Some people stared at me when I came into sight... This technique is rapidly coming into use today... New legislation came into force in 1981.* V+PREP

3 If you say that something **comes into** it or **comes into** a situation or subject, you mean that it is relevant to the situation or subject that you are talking about. EG *I don't quite see how the wigs come into it... Where does money come into it?... ...psychological factors that come into it... The judge decided that it was not discrimination, since sex did not come into the overt reason given for the action.* V+PREP+*it,* V+PREP

4 When a government **comes into** office or power, it wins an election and starts governing the country. EG *...before the present Conservative Government came into office... The Labour Government came into power in March 1974.* V+PREP

5 If someone **comes into** money, property, or a title, they inherit it. EG *She came into some money on her mother's death.* V+PREP

come of. **1** You talk about something **coming of** a situation when you are mentioning its result or consequences. EG *I'll let you know what comes of the meeting... I'm relieved to learn no great harm came of it.* V+PREP

2 If a person **comes of** a particular family or group of ancestors, he or she is descended from them; a slightly literary use. EG *She came of a family that had lived there for many years... The boys came of a sea-faring line.* V+PREP

come off. **1** If someone or something **comes off** an area, place, or V+PREP, V+ADV vehicle, they leave it. EG *She saw him come off the plane with Tom Hagen... The umpires came off after just one ball.*

2 When something **comes off,** it becomes unfastened or unstuck, or it is removed. EG *All the wallpaper's coming off... He tugged at the metal handle and it came off in his hand.* V+ADV, V+PREP

3 If an event or action **comes off,** it is successful or effective. EG *Gary tried to smile but it didn't come off, his heart wasn't in it... I hope this business comes off all right.* V+ADV

4 If you **come off** well or badly at the end of a process, you are in a good or bad position as a result of it. EG *As usual, he came off second best... Families in the wealthier classes come off comparatively better.* ● **End up** means almost the same as **come off.** V+ADV: WITH A/C

5 When a play or film **comes off,** it stops being performed or shown in a particular theatre, cinema, etc. EG *The production had to come off because the theatre was already booked for a pantomime.* V+ADV

6 If something such as mist, wind, or a smell **comes off** a particular place or thing, it originates or radiates from that place or thing. EG *There was a mist coming off the water... It was a warm day, and even with the wind that came off the river his father was sweating.* V+PREP

7 If someone **comes off** something such as a drug, medicine, or alcohol, they stop taking it. EG *...the therapeutic community where she finally came off drugs... It's about time you came off the booze.* V+PREP

8 If you say **'Come off it!'** to someone, you are indicating that you do not believe what they have just said, or think it is unreasonable; an informal use. EG *Come off it, Mr Davis. The oil was ordered three months ago... 'Oh, come off it,' Freya said. 'Nazir hated him'... Come off it, Jim, that's not a letter.* IMPERATIVE: V+PREP+*it*

come on. **1** You say **'come on'** to someone **1.1** when you want to encourage them or comfort them. EG *Come on, I'll help you back to the hotel... Come on, Mike, say you'll do it.* **1.2** when you want them to hurry up. EG *There's something I want you to see. Come on, child, come on!* ● **Come along** means almost the same as **come on.** IMPERATIVE: V+ADV / IMPERATIVE: V+ADV

2 When you **come on** somewhere, you go there. EG *'Hello, there,' said Brody. 'Come on in.'... Gertrude had come on to Rome instead of staying in France... Come on over—quick as you can.* ▶ **Oncoming** means moving towards you. EG *...oncoming traffic.* V+ADV: WITH A / ADJECTIVE

3 When an actor or actress **comes on,** he or she appears on a stage or in a scene of a film. EG *...shuffling in the wings, waiting to come on... Olivier dominated the play from the moment he came on the stage.* V+ADV, V+PREP

4 If someone **comes on** the phone, they begin speaking to you. EG *One of the most powerful men in France came on the line... There was this silence and then my mother came on.* V+PREP, V+ADV

5 If you **come on** something, you find it unexpectedly or by chance. EG *I came on the idea by pure chance... It was half an hour before he came on the note in his tray.* ● **Chance on** means almost the same as **come on.** V+PREP

6 When a power supply or device **comes on,** it starts functioning. EG *At nine the street lights came on... The loudspeaker came on with a soft popping noise.* ● **Go off** means the opposite of **come on.** V+ADV

7 When a programme or film **comes on,** it starts to be broadcast or screened. EG *At seven the Swiss news came on.* V+ADV

8 When a season or period of time or weather **comes on,** it approaches or begins. EG *...on a fall evening, as the twilight came on... Christmas came on... ...as though a terrible heat was coming on.* V+ADV

9 If a cold, headache, or some other medical condition **is coming on,** it is just starting. EG *I felt a cold coming on... At lunch a bad headache came on, and he went home.* V+ADV

10 If something **is coming on,** it is making progress or developing. EG *My new book is coming on quite well now... He must've come on a bit in eight hours!* ● **Come along** means almost the same as **come on.**

V+ADV

11 If someone **comes on** in a particular way, they behave in that way; an informal use. EG *...really coming on hard, solid and uncompromising... Williams doesn't come on too strong.*

V+ADV: WITH ADJ

12 When someone **comes on** to someone else, they behave in an openly sexual way towards them; an informal use. EG *She comes on like a cheap hooker, hips swaying... I get scared when men come on to me.* ▸ A **come-on** is a openly sexual remark or action which is intended to attract someone; an informal word. EG *Remarks like this are a tease, a come-on.*

V+ADV: ALSO+to

N COUNT

come on to, come onto. **1** When someone **comes on to** a stage, court, or other area, they enter it. EG *She has something. Whenever she came on to the stage everybody held their breath... Fifteen minutes later Sinclair came onto the court and beat his opponent hollow.*

V+ADV+PREP

2 If you **come on to** a particular topic or idea, you start discussing it. EG *I want to come on to the question of disease in a minute... Now here we come onto another contentious subject.* ● **Turn to** means almost the same as **come on to.**

V+ADV+PREP

3 If something **comes onto** the market, it becomes available. EG *Very little top grade land came onto the market.*

V+PREP

come out. **1** When someone **comes out** of their house or room, or a place where they were hidden, they leave it or appear from it. EG *After an hour or so he comes out into a small clearing... We came out of the tunnel.*

V+ADV: ALSO+of

2 If someone **comes out** with you, you go somewhere together socially. EG *Let's ring him up and see if he'll come out for a pint... Would you like to come out with me?*

V+ADV: USUALLY+with

3 If someone **comes out** to the country where you are, they visit you there. EG *Maybe one day soon, I'll come out and visit you... ...when she came out to Egypt, or Malaya or wherever it was.*

V+ADV: ALSO+to

4 If someone **comes out** of an organization or institution, they leave it. EG *She had deteriorated after coming out of hospital... He came out of the army with a lump sum.* ● **Go in** means the opposite of **come out.**

V+ADV: ALSO+of

5 If something **comes out** of a particular place or source, it originates there or is produced there. EG *Dance music started coming out of the radiogram... She opened her mouth to scream, but no sounds came out. She was pale with rage... There were flames coming out of the engine... Information coming out of the country was unreliable.*

V+ADV: USUALLY+of

6 If something **comes out** of a container, you remove it from there. EG *I pulled the trigger as the gun came out of the case... He was frightened. One hand came out of his pocket.*

V+ADV: USUALLY+of

7 When something **comes out** from or onto a particular point, it joins something else at that point. EG *...the four big arteries and the two veins coming out from the base of the heart... The road comes out onto a broad paved drive.*

V+ADV

8 If something **is coming out,** it is becoming separated from the thing that it was attached to. EG *My shirt had come out of the top of my shorts... I had noticed then that her hair was coming out in patches.*

V+ADV

9 When information **comes out,** it is revealed or made public. EG *All the facts came out after Seery's death... It came out that the more money you make the less tax you are likely to pay... Tess burst into tears, and the story came out.*

V+ADV

10 You say that someone **comes out** when they admit something   v+adv
about themselves that they were ashamed of or keeping secret, for
example that they are homosexual; an informal use.

11 If you **come out** for or against something, you declare that you do   v+adv:
or do not support it. EG *He came out in support of the claim... Most*   WITH A
Trade Union Group members came out against the document.

12 When something such as a book **comes out,** it is published or   v+adv
becomes available to the public. EG *Over the summer his book had*
come out... He asked me to send him any new stamps which might
come out. ● **Appear** means almost the same as **come out.**

13 If something **comes out** in a particular position or in a particular   v+adv:
way, it is in that position or condition at the end of a competition,   WITH A/C
process, or period of time. EG *Who do you think will come out on*
top?... The press was coming out of the affair very badly... The
numbers came out exactly right. ▶ The **outcome** of something such   N COUNT
as an action or process is its result. EG *There were not many people*
who dared predict the outcome of the general election... It was a
complicated sequence of events that led to this most extraordinary
outcome.

14 If what you say **comes out** in a particular way, it is said in that   v+adv:
way. EG *The words came out more harshly than she had intended...*   WITH A
'I'm sorry,' said Tim. It came out in a whisper.

15 If workers **come out,** they go on strike; used in British English. EG   v+adv
The work force promptly came out... The whole of London Trans-
port came out in protest when a conductor got the sack.

16 When the sun, moon, or a star **comes out,** it appears in the sky. EG   v+adv
It was cold and the sun never came out once.

17 If colours, stains, or marks **come out,** they disappear or fade. EG   v+adv
Be careful when you're washing that towel or the colour will come
out... The stains just would not come out. It was blood.

18 If a photograph or something that has been photographed **comes**   v+adv:
out, it is successful. EG *He is an excellent photographer. All his*   USUALLY+A
pictures come out very well. Every detail shows... Annabel did not
come out well.

19 When flowers, leaves, or plants **come out,** the flowers or leaves   v+adv
develop and open. EG *As soon as the leaves came out, the blossoms*
appeared.

come out in. If you or your body **comes out in** spots or rashes, they   v+adv+prep
develop all over your body. ● **Break out** means almost the same as
come out in.

come out of. If one thing **comes out of** something else, the first   v+adv+prep
thing results from the second. EG *Expert systems have come out of*
artificial intelligence research.

come out with. If someone **comes out with** something, they say it,   v+adv+prep
often unexpectedly. EG *Occasionally they come out with fascinating*
snippets of gossip... John came out with an unusual proposal.

come over. 1 When someone **comes over, 1.1** they move across a   v+adv
room or other place towards you. EG *He came over and stood beside*
me... Come over here, George, and I'll tell you... The bartender
came over and put her drink down in front of her. **1.2** they come to   v+adv
the country which you are talking about from a country overseas. EG
He'd come over on leave from Northern Ireland... He'd met her on
the plane coming over... Do you fancy coming over for 2 weeks? **1.3**   v+adv
they call at your house to see you for a short time. EG *You can come*
over tomorrow at four... He wanted me to come over for lunch... I've
got some friends coming over. ● **Come round** means almost the
same as **come over.**

2 If someone **comes over** to a grouping or organization, they leave   v+adv their old grouping or organization and join a rival one. EG *They all came over to the new party... ...the five who came over from Labour.* ● **Defect** is a more formal word for **come over.**

3 If a voice, sound, or message **comes over** a phone, radio, or loudspeaker, it is transmitted or broadcast and you hear it. EG *The voice that came over the phone was unrecognizable... The news came over the radio... Captain Walker's voice came over at full strength.* V+PREP, V+ADV

4 If a change or feeling **comes over** you, it affects you or happens to you, perhaps making you behave in an uncharacteristic way. EG *A great change had come over me since the previous night... A look of contentment came over her face.* V+PREP

5 If you **come over** dizzy, shy, funny, and so on, you start feeling that way; an informal use. EG *She comes over all shy when she has to meet new people.* V+ADV: WITH ADJ

6 When an idea or meaning **comes over,** you understand exactly what was meant. EG *I don't think that the larger symbolic purpose really comes over in this particular painting... The message of the opera came over with unmistakeable power.* ● **Come across** means almost the same as **come over.** V+ADV

7 If someone or something **comes over** as having a particular characteristic, they give you the impression of having that characteristic. EG *It came over as a clear US victory... He actually does come over as someone who really would like to do this.* ● **Come across** means almost the same as **come over.** V+ADV: USUALLY+*as*

come round. **1** When someone **comes round** or **around, 1.1** they call at your house to see you for a short time. EG *I could come round this evening if you like... Don't call. Come round. About eleven... He abruptly stopped calling or coming around to visit.* ● **Come over** means almost the same as **come round.** **1.2** they visit or attend to you as part of a series of visits or as part of a routine. EG *The driver came around to collect fares... The stewardess came around with the local paper.* V+ADV

2 When letters or other things **come round** or **around,** they are circulated or sent to a group of people. EG *A departmental memo just came round to say that Mangel's coming here.* V+ADV

3 If you **come round** or **around** to someone or to an idea, belief, or suggestion, you change your mind and start to like them or agree with it. EG *He knew I would have to come round to his way of thinking in the end... You two used to be such friends. You'll come around to his side in the end... But you'll find she'll come round. Parents always do.* V+ADV: USUALLY+*to*

4 If something **comes round** or **around,** it happens as a regular or predictable event. EG *Don't wait for April to come round before planning your vegetable garden... She'll be a jolly tough candidate to beat when the election comes round... ...when the new academic year came around in the autumn.* V+ADV

5 When someone **comes round,** they recover consciousness. EG *She was bending over him as he came round.* ● **Pass out** means the opposite of **come round.** V+ADV

come through. **1** When someone **comes through** the room where you are, they enter the room and cross it. EG *He came through from an inner office... She's poorly. Would you come through, Doctor... I came through the hall and heard him talking.* V+PREP, V+ADV

2 When someone **comes through** the town or place where you are, they travel through it, perhaps stopping there briefly. EG *Bob had recently come through Frankfurt, and stayed awhile... I told him so quite frankly when he came through town last year.* V+PREP, V+ADV

3 When something such as a phone call, message, document, or authorization **comes through,** you receive it, often after some procedure has been carried out. EG *A call came through asking for assistance... Has my visa come through yet?... She intended to look for a car as soon as the money came through.* V+ADV

4 If you **come through** with something, you produce or do something that is expected of you. EG *He finally came through with the documents... The state legislature, for its part, came through with $9.4 million.* V+ADV: USUALLY+*with*

5 If a quality, impression, or idea **comes through,** you perceive it in what has been said or done. EG *I think the teacher's own personality has got to come through... What came through most forcibly was a sense of excitement... He was an intellectual charmer. His charm comes through in his letters.* ● **Come across** means almost the same as **come through.** V+ADV: ALSO+*as*

6 If you **come through** a dangerous or difficult situation, you survive it and recover from it. EG *Most of the troops came through the fighting unharmed... They are going to come through all right.* V+PREP, V+ADV

7 When the sun or moon **comes through,** you begin to see it through the clouds. EG *The sun was struggling to come through... There was a wisp of sun coming through the mist.* ● **Break through** means almost the same as **come through.** V+ADV, V+PREP

come to. 1 If someone **comes to,** they recover consciousness. EG *That's about all I remember, until I came to in a lifeboat.* ● **Come round** means almost the same as **come to,** and **pass out** means the opposite. V+ADV

2 If something **comes to** a particular number or amount, its total is that number or amount. EG *My income now comes to £65 a week.* V+PREP

come under. 1 If you **come under** criticism, attack, pressure, and so on, you are criticized or attacked, or put under pressure. EG *The premier came under severe criticism... The housing strategy is almost certain to come under increasing attack... British produce came under pressure from foreign competition.* V+PREP

2 If something **comes under** a particular authority or control, it is managed, controlled, or owned by it. EG *Day Nurseries come under the Department of Health and Social Security... ...popular demand that health care should come under public ownership.* V+PREP

3 If one thing **comes under** a particular heading or category, it is in that class or category. EG *Records and tapes come under published material... The loss sustained by the statue came under the heading of fair wear and tear.* V+PREP

come up. 1 When someone or something **comes up,** they move from a lower position to a higher one, or move towards the place where you are. EG *Daintry came up the great staircase towards them... I came up the garden... His head went down then, but his heels came up.* V+PREP, V+ADV

2 When someone in a building **comes up,** they move upstairs towards you. EG *I was about to come up and wake you... You'd better come up to my room afterwards.* V+ADV

3 If someone **comes up** to you, they approach you until they are standing next to you. EG *An man came up and spoke to him... Bill came up to Ralph... She came up to him and threw her arms around him.* V+ADV: ALSO+*to*

4 If someone **comes up** to a place near you, they visit it or move there; used when the place is farther north or is in a city. EG *I will come up to see you one of these days... A couple of months ago we sold the farm and came up north here.* V+ADV: WITH A

5 If someone **comes up** when they are underwater, they rise to the V+ADV surface of the water. EG *I came up, and swam across a few yards... An instant later he came up spluttering.*

6 If something **comes up** in a conversation or meeting, it is mentioned or discussed. EG *His name came up at a buffet lunch... Egyptian art came up as a topic... An interesting point came up here.*   V+ADV

7 If something **comes up** for discussion or sale, it is put forward for discussion or is sold. If someone **comes up** for election, they are put forward as a candidate in an election. EG *The pension scheme has come up for review... An adjacent twenty-seven-acre field came up for sale... A third of my colleagues will come up for election next May.*   V+ADV: ALSO+*for*

8 If a job **comes up,** it becomes available. EG *When I applied here, I didn't know this post in Oxford would come up... He was willing to take any job that came up.*   V+ADV

9 If something **is coming up,** it is about to happen or take place. EG *There's a royal wedding coming up... The SDP are fighting any election that comes up anywhere... It was just coming up to ten o'clock in the morning.*   V+ADV

10 When a problem, situation, or event **comes up,** it happens, perhaps unexpectedly. EG *I can't see you tonight. Something's come up... If anything urgent comes up you can always get me on the phone... A rather delicate assignment has come up.* ● **Crop up** means almost the same as **come up.**   V+ADV

11 In a court of law, if a case **comes up,** it is presented to the magistrates or judge. EG *A case on Corporate fraud came up in the Chancery Courts recently.*   V+ADV

12 If something **comes up** to or as far as a particular point or level, it reaches that point or level. EG *Measure how far the water comes up... Few of them come up to its quality.*   V+ADV: USUALLY+*to*

13 When the sun or moon or a star **comes up,** it rises. When the dawn **comes up,** it begins to grow light. EG *The sun comes up in the East... Slowly a full moon comes up from the horizon... ...as dawn came up over the New Jersey skyline.* ● **Go down** means almost the opposite of **come up.**   V+ADV

14 If a wind, sound, or light, and so on **comes up,** it appears and grows stronger, louder, or brighter. EG *By ten o'clock a breeze had come up—not strong, but fresh... A roar of applause came up as the spotlight hit me... The film had ended and the lights came up.*   V+ADV

15 When a seed, plant, or bulb **comes up,** it grows and pushes through the soil. EG *The grass was high and had come up with a rush.*   V+ADV

16 You talk about information **coming up** when it appears, for example on a computer screen, or on announcement boards in stations and airports. EG *It didn't come up on their computer.*   V+ADV

17 If someone **comes up** in society or their profession, they achieve a higher status in it. EG *Boulton was a Birmingham craftsman who came up the hard way... Evie and her mother had come up in the world.* ● **Go down** means the opposite of **come up.** ▶ Someone or something that is **up-and-coming** is likely to be very successful in the future. EG *He was one of the up-and-coming young businessmen in town.*   V+ADV: USUALLY+A

ADJECTIVE

18 If you say that someone or something **comes up** a particular thing, you mean that they appear that way at the end of a process or period of time or activity. EG *Dorothy always came up smiling... He went to Harvard a shy young boy and came up a mature man... ... especially rabbit skins, which come up beautifully.*   V+ADV: WITH C/A

come up against. If you **come up against** a problem or difficulty, you are faced with it and have to deal with it. EG *Everyone comes up*   V+ADV+PREP *against discrimination sooner or later... The first time I did this I came up against an unforeseen problem.*

come upon. 1 If you **come upon** someone or something, you meet   v+prep
or find them unexpectedly. eg *They rounded a turn and came upon a family of lions... She had been thrown into confusion by suddenly coming upon a photo of Terry.* ● **Come across** means almost the same as **come upon.**

2 If an idea or feeling **comes upon** you, it develops without your   v+prep
really being aware of it. eg *His new outlook on life had come upon him gradually... Embarrassment came upon me... Suddenly there came upon me once again the memory of that afternoon.*

come up to. 1 If something does not **come up to** expectations or a   v+adv+prep:
particular standard, it is not as good as people expected it to be. eg *It*   WITH NEGATIVE
must be said that it never really came up to expectations... I think perhaps Christine wasn't coming up to scratch.

2 To **be coming up to** a time or state means to be getting near to it.   v+adv+prep
eg *Some of them are coming up to retirement... It was just coming up to ten o'clock.* ● **Approach** means almost the same as **come up to.**

come up with. 1 If you **come up with** a plan, idea, or solution, you   v+adv+prep
think of it and suggest it. eg *I hope to come up with some of the answers... It didn't take her long to come up with a very convincing example... The EEC commission came up with a compromise.*

2 If you **come up with** a sum of money, you provide it when it is   v+adv+prep
needed. eg *You have no choice but to come up with the £120,000... Revlon came up with $750,000 to fund a research program.*

cone, cones, coning, coned

cone off. To **cone off** a road or an area of ground means to place a   v+adv+n,
line of large plastic cones there to prevent people driving on part of   v+n+adv;
it. eg *The police were busy coning off the road where the accident*   v+pron+adv
had taken place. ● **Close off** means almost the same as **cone off.**

confide, confides, confiding, confided

confide in. If you **confide in** someone, you tell them about a private   v+prep
problem or some other secret matter. eg *His father probably doesn't confide in him a great deal... May I confide in you?... ...men friends in whom he can confide... People don't confide much in a security officer.*

conjure, conjures, conjuring, conjured

conjure up. If you **conjure up** a particular picture or idea of   v+adv+n,
something, or if your words **conjure** them **up,** you make other   v+n+adv;
people imagine that idea or picture. eg *They listened in astonish-*   v+pron+adv
ment while James conjured up pictures of fantastic machines... The word 'unemployment' still conjures up an image of men in cloth caps. ● **Evoke** is a more formal word for **conjure up.**

conk, conks, conking, conked

conk out. If something, such as a machine or vehicle, **conks out,** it   v+adv
stops working or breaks down; an informal expression used mainly in British English. eg *The washing machine has finally conked out.*

contract, contracts, contracting, contracted

contract in. If you **contract in** to a scheme or arrangement, you   v+adv:
formally say that you want to take part in it; a legal or formal   ALSO+*to*
expression. eg *You have to contract in if you want to participate in the scheme.*

contract out. 1 If you **contract out** of a scheme or arrangement,   v+adv:
you formally say that you do not want to take part in it; a legal or   ALSO+*of*

formal use. EG *You can apply to the Pensions Board to contract out...
She wants to contract out of the private health scheme.*

2 If you **contract out** of something that you are expected to do or   V+ADV:
take part in, you withdraw from it or fail to do it. EG *Generally, the*   USUALLY+*of*
*unions have contracted out of their responsibilities... ...contracting
out of defence arrangements.*

3 If a company **contracts out** work to another company, it employs   V+ADV+N,
that company to do it, rather than doing it itself. EG *...a move towards*   V+N+ADV
*contracting out more work to private firms... We've now started
contracting out some of these services.*

cook, cooks, cooking, cooked

cook up. 1 If you **cook up** a meal, you make it, often quickly. EG *She*   V+ADV+N,
could really cook up a good meal... He cooked up a very good   V+N+ADV,
mushroom omelette. ● **Rustle up** means almost the same as **cook**   V+PRON+ADV
up.

2 If someone **cooks up** a dishonest scheme, they plan it; an informal   V+ADV+N,
use which shows disapproval. EG *They tend to cook up all sorts of*   V+N+ADV,
little deals... The Ministry cooked up a meaningless mission to   V+PRON+ADV
Canada. ● **Concoct** is a more formal word for **cook up.**

cool, cools, cooling, cooled

cool down. 1 If something **cools down** or if you **cool** it **down,** it   V+ADV,
becomes cooler until it reaches the temperature that you want it to   V+PRON+ADV,
be at. EG *The engine will take half an hour to cool down... Rinse the*   V+N+ADV,
bowl in cold water to cool it down.   V+ADV+N:
    ERGATIVE

2 If someone **cools down** or if you **cool** them **down,** they become less   V+ADV,
angry. EG *Tom had cooled down considerably... I had changed, and*   V+PRON+ADV,
was cooling down slightly... I had the greatest difficulty in cooling   V+N+ADV:
him down. ● **Calm down** means almost the same as **cool down.**   ERGATIVE

cool off. 1 If someone or something that is too hot **cools off,** they   V+ADV
become cooler. EG *We cooled off from the heat with a refreshing
swim... These metal attachments normally take longer than that to
cool off... As the weather cooled off he exchanged the robe for a
thick blanket.*

2 If you **cool off,** you become less excited or enthusiastic about   V+ADV
something. EG *He seems to have cooled off on the negotiation idea...
Vita's love for him was cooling off.* ▶ A **cooling-off** period is an   ADJECTIVE
agreed period of time during which unions and management will try
to resolve a dispute before taking any serious action. EG *Our union is
opposed to any cooling-off period.*

coop, coops, cooping, cooped

coop up. If someone is **cooped up** in a place, they are kept in a   PASSIVE:
place which is too small or which does not give them much   V+ADV
freedom. EG *...a prisoner cooped up in a cell... She had been cooped
up in her aunt's house for ten days... After being cooped up for so
long, it was pleasant to be out driving.*

cop, cops, copping, copped

cop out. If you **cop out** of doing something, you avoid doing it   V+ADV:
because you are afraid or embarrassed about it; an informal expres-   ALSO+*of*
sion used showing disapproval. EG *My friend and I simply copped out
of the plan altogether... You're the one that's copping out, not me.*
● **Duck out** means almost the same as **cop out.** ▶ If you say that   N COUNT
something is a **cop-out,** you think that someone is not doing what
they should do; an informal word used showing disapproval. EG *Such
international co-operation is often merely a cop-out.*

copy, copies, copying, copied

copy down. If you **copy down** what someone has said or written, you write it on a piece of paper. EG *Can you copy down his address for me?*

V+ADV+N,
V+N+ADV,
V+PRON+ADV

copy in. If you **copy** someone **in**, you make sure that they receive a letter, memo, or other piece of written information that you are sending to several people. EG *We've copied in all interested parties... Make sure you're copied in.*

V+ADV+N,
V+N+ADV,
V+PRON+ADV

copy out. If you **copy out** a piece of writing, you write it down exactly as it was written before. EG *I remember copying out the whole play... He jotted down each entry then copied it out with abbreviations... ...the words of a pop song, copied out and stuck above the bed.*

V+ADV+N,
V+PRON+ADV,
V+N+ADV

cordon, cordons, cordoning, cordoned

cordon off. If someone in authority **cordons off** an area, they prevent people from entering or leaving it by putting up a barrier. EG *I remember the officials having to cordon off an area in White-hall... The city was split into areas, cordoned off by barbed wire.*
• **Close off** means almost the same as **cordon off.**

V+ADV+N,
V+N+ADV,
V+PRON+ADV

cork, corks, corking, corked

cork up. If you **cork up** a bottle, you close it by putting a cork in it. EG *Let Miss Drew have what she wants; then cork up the bottle.*

V+ADV+N,
V+N+ADV,
V+PRON+ADV

cotton, cottons, cottoning, cottoned

cotton on. If you **cotton on** to something, you understand it or realize it; an informal expression. EG *At long last he has cottoned on to the fact that I'm not interested in him!... The other man cottoned on and came running.* • **Catch on** means almost the same as **cotton on.**

V+ADV:
ALSO+*to*

couch, couches, couching, couched

couch in. If something is **couched in** a particular type of language, it is expressed in that type of language. EG *Here was a resolution couched in forthright terms... It was all couched in legal jargon.*

PASSIVE:
V+PREP

cough, coughs, coughing, coughed

cough up. 1 If you **cough up** or if you **cough up** an amount of money, you give someone money that they need or that you owe them; an informal use. EG *They'll cough up the hundred million... Come on, cough up.* • **Pay up** means almost the same as **cough up.**

V+ADV,
V+ADV+N

2 If you **cough up** something such as blood or phlegm, you get rid of it from inside your throat by forcing it out of your mouth with a sudden, harsh noise. EG *She coughed up phlegm... He sounded as if he was coughing his insides up.*

V+ADV+N,
V+N+ADV,
V+PRON+ADV

count, counts, counting, counted

count against. If an action or characteristic **counts against** you, it is a disadvantage to you and may help to cause you to be punished, rejected, or defeated. EG *It would count heavily against me if I got the Director into trouble.*

V+PREP

count among. If you **count** someone or something **among** a particular group, you consider them to be a member of that group. EG *Gradually, these youngsters became decent, honest citizens, many of whom I used to count among my friends... My mother had admitted that people who had counted themselves among her friends had broken down under the pressure.*

V+N+PREP,
V+REFL+PREP,
V+PRON+PREP

count down. If you **count down**, you count numbers aloud in reverse order until you reach zero, especially before something

V+ADV

happens, such as a spacecraft being launched. EG *We have begun counting down to lift-off.* ▶ A **countdown** is the counting aloud of numbers in reverse order before something happens, especially before a spacecraft is launched. EG *Millions stand transfixed as the countdown begins.* N COUNT

count for. If you say that a particular thing **counts for** something, you mean that it is valuable or important. EG *I felt that all my years there counted for nothing... They feel they don't count for anything.* V+PREP

count in. If you **count** someone **in**, you include them in a particular activity. EG *You can count me in for the next outing.* ● **Count out** means the opposite of **count in**. V+PRON+ADV, V+N+ADV

count on. 1 If you **count on** or **upon** something, you expect it to happen and include it in your plans. EG *Doctors could now count on a regular salary... The campaign can count on the public support of a few Labour MPs... I didn't count on meeting you here... At least it could be counted upon to stay in one place.* ● **Rely on** means almost the same as **count on**. V+PREP, V+PREP+-ING: HAS PASSIVE

2 If you **count on** or **upon** someone, you rely on them to support you or help you. EG *You can count on me... They count upon their parents for leadership and love... He cannot always be counted on.* ● **Depend on** means almost the same as **count on**. V+PREP: HAS PASSIVE

count out. 1 If you **count out** coins or banknotes, you count them as you move them one by one from one pile to another or as you give them to someone else. EG *She counted out the money... He counted out five wads of twenty notes each.* V+ADV+N, V+N+ADV, V+PRON+ADV

2 If someone **counts** you **out**, they exclude you from a particular activity. EG *If you're going to gossip, you can count me out.* V+PRON+ADV

3 When a referee **counts out** a boxer who has been knocked down, he or she counts to ten before the boxer can get up, and the boxer loses the match. V+N+ADV, V+ADV+N, V+PRON+ADV

count towards. If something **counts towards** something that you want, it adds to the things that give you the right to have it. EG *Any contributions you have paid will count towards your pension.* V+PREP

count up. If you **count up** all the things in a group, you count them in order to find how many there are. EG *I counted up my years of teaching experience.* ● **Add up** means almost the same as **count up**. V+ADV+N, V+N+ADV, V+PRON+ADV

count upon. See count on: **count upon** is more formal.

cover, covers, covering, covered

cover over. To **cover** something **over** means to cover it completely with something else. EG *The sky was covered over with cloud.* ● **Obscure** is a more formal word for **cover over**. V+N+ADV, V+ADV+N, V+PRON+ADV

cover up. 1 If you **cover** something **up**, you place or spread something else over it in order to protect it or hide it. EG *Cover yourself up with this sheet... She took a blanket out of the car and covered up the windows.* V+REFL+ADV, V+ADV+N, V+N+ADV, V+PRON+ADV

2 If you **cover up** something that you do not want people to know about, you hide it from them. EG *She tried to cover up for Willie... She hoped to cover up anything unpleasant that might be said... He alleged that the President knew about Watergate and tried to cover it up.* ● **Conceal** is a more formal word for **cover up**. ▶ A **cover-up** is an attempt to hide the truth so that people do not realize that there has been a crime or mistake. EG *He denied that he took any part in the cover-up.* V+ADV, V+ADV+N, V+PRON+ADV, V+N+ADV — N COUNT

crack, cracks, cracking, cracked

crack down. To **crack down** on a group of people means to become stricter in making them obey rules or laws and in punishing those who do not obey the rules. EG *The police cracked down on* V+ADV: USUALLY+*on* *vandals and drug offenders... Her first reaction to the riots was to crack down hard.* ● **Clamp down** means almost the same as **crack down.** ► A **crackdown** is strong official action taken to punish people who break laws or rules in order to make sure that the laws or rules are obeyed in future. EG *...a crackdown on criminals.*

N COUNT

crack up. 1 If someone **cracks up,** they lose control of themselves and become mentally ill. EG *I'd crack up if there wasn't someone I could talk to.* ● **Break down** means almost the same as **crack up.** ► If someone has a **crack-up,** they lose control of themselves and become mentally ill; an informal word. EG *People gossiped about his crack-up.* ● **Breakdown** means almost the same as **crack-up.**

V+ADV

N COUNT

2 You can also say that someone **cracks up** when they start to laugh uncontrollably; an informal use. EG *When I told her about everything that had happened, she just cracked up.* ● **Crease up** means almost the same as **crack up.**

V+ADV

crank, cranks, cranking, cranked

crank up. If you **crank up** an engine, you make it start by turning a handle. EG *The car's owner cranked it up and drove away.*

V+ADV+N,
V+N+ADV,
V+PRON+ADV

crash, crashes, crashing, crashed

crash about. To **crash about** or **around** means to move about and make a lot of loud noises; an informal expression. EG *We heard thundering booms as the boilers started crashing about... What on earth is she doing, crashing around upstairs like that?*

V+ADV

crash around. See **crash about.**

crash out. 1 If a noise **crashes out,** it starts and is very loud. EG *The applause crashed out... The opening chords crashed out.* ● **Ring out** means almost the same as **crash out.**

V+ADV

2 If you **crash out,** you fall asleep; an informal use. EG *She had crashed out on the floor.* ● **Flake out** means almost the same as **crash out.**

V+ADV

crate, crates, crating, crated

crate up. To **crate** something **up** means to put it into a crate so that it can be stored or taken somewhere. EG *We decided to keep the painting, rather than crate it up with everything else... They can't carry that machine unless it's properly crated up.*

V+PRON+ADV,
V+N+ADV,
V+ADV+N

cream, creams, creaming, creamed

cream off. To **cream off** people from a group means to take them away and treat them in a special way, because you think that they are better than the rest of the group. EG *The best pupils would be creamed off and given a superior training... They decided to cream part of the staff off for more complicated tasks.*

V+N+ADV,
V+ADV+N,
V+PRON+ADV

crease, creases, creasing, creased

crease up. If someone or something **creases** you **up,** they make you laugh a lot; an informal expression. EG *She creased me up with her tall stories!... We were all creased up with laughter.*

V+PRON+ADV

creep, creeps, creeping, crept

creep in. If something such as a word or custom **creeps in,** it gradually becomes used by people. EG *New gestures do occasionally manage to creep in and establish themselves... The word 'intelligence' is beginning to creep back in... Elements of military uniform creep in.* ● **Slip in** means almost the same as **creep in.**

V+ADV

creep into. If an attitude or a feeling **creeps into** something, it begins to be expressed or felt gradually. EG *A certain lassitude is creeping into our meetings... A note of impatience creeps into her voice... The shadow of doubt began to creep into her mind.*

V+PREP

creep up on. 1 If you **creep up on** someone, you move slowly closer   v+ADV+PREP
to them without being seen by them. EG *One child stands facing a
wall while all the others creep up on him... He was aware of
something dangerous creeping up on them under cover of the bush.*
2 If a feeling or state **creeps up on** you, you begin to experience it   v+ADV+PREP
very slowly. EG *She paused, fighting the dizziness that was creeping
up on her... A sense of unreality was beginning to creep up on me.*
● **Come over** means almost the same as **creep up on**.

crop, crops, cropping, cropped

crop up. If something **crops up**, it happens or appears suddenly and   v+ADV
unexpectedly. EG *There was one word that cropped up in each of the
reports... I can come now, unless any other problems crop up.*
● **Come up** means almost the same as **crop up**.

cross, crosses, crossing, crossed

cross off. If you **cross off** one or more words on a list, you draw a   v+N+PREP/ADV,
line through them to indicate that they are no longer on the list. EG *I*   v+PRON+PREP/ADV,
crossed my name off the list... You should cross it off. ● **Delete**   v+ADV+N
means almost the same as **cross off**.

cross out. If you **cross out** one or more words on a page, you draw   v+N+ADV,
a line through them, usually because they are wrong or because you   v+ADV+N,
do not want people to read them. EG *Now and then he frowned,*   v+PRON+ADV
*crossed something out and rewrote it... I crossed out 'Unpublished'
and made it 'Works in preparation'... I would promptly write it down
and then cross it out again.* ● **Delete** means almost the same as
cross out.

cross over. 1 When you **cross over**, you go across to the other side   v+ADV,
of something such as a road, room, or border. EG *We crossed over*   v+PREP
*into Tennessee... I crossed over to a grocery store... The car had
crossed over the river.*
2 If you **cross over** to a different side in a disagreement, you change   v+ADV:
to that side. EG *If we ever crossed over to their side, war would be*   ALSO+*to*
declared. ● **Come over** means almost the same as **cross over**.

crouch, crouches, crouching, crouched

crouch down. If you **crouch down**, you move to a position in which   v+ADV
your legs are bent under you so that you are close to the ground and
slightly leaning forward. EG *Two of them crouched down behind the
car... She passed quite close to him, but he crouched down, and did
not see her face.*

crowd, crowds, crowding, crowded

crowd around. If a group of people **crowd around** or **round**   v+PREP,
someone or something, they gather closely together around that   v+ADV
person or thing. EG *Children were always crowded around the ticket
booth... The boys crowded round him... We crowded round eagerly,
then felt disappointed.* ● **Surround** is a more formal word for **crowd
around**.

crowd in. If a group of people or things **crowd in**, a lot of them try   v+ADV
to get into a place at the same time. EG *The TV men crowded in,
examining our equipment.* ● **Pile in** means almost the same as
crowd in.

crowd in on. If a lot of things **crowd in on** you, you have to think   v+ADV+PREP
about them all at once and they upset you or worry you. EG *Other
worries were crowding in on Gavin... All the things and places that I
loved so well keep crowding in on me now in this gloomy bedroom.*

crowd into. If a group of people or things **crowd into** a place, or if   v+PREP,
you **crowd** them **into** it, they are all pushed or squeezed into a place   v+N+PREP,
that is too small for them. EG *Outside, shiny cars crowded into the*   v+PRON+PREP

courtyard... He helped his dad and brother crowd the animals into a truck... Reporters and photographers were crowded into the lobby.

crowd out. To **crowd** someone or something **out** means to deliber- ately take up so much space that they are forced to leave or move away. EG *I tried to keep my place in the queue, but they crowded me out.* • **Push out** and **squeeze out** mean almost the same as **crowd out.**   V+N+ADV, V+PRON+ADV, V+ADV+N

crumple, crumples, crumpling, crumpled

crumple up. If you **crumple up** a piece of paper, you squash it into a ball. EG *She looked at the scrap of paper, crumpled it up, and threw it into the wastebasket.* • **Screw up** means almost the same as **crumple up.**   V+PRON+ADV, V+N+ADV, V+ADV+N

cry, cries, crying, cried

cry off. If you **cry off**, you change your mind and decide not to do something that you had arranged or agreed to do; an informal expression. EG *She cried off at the last moment... He was engaged once, but he cried off.*   V+ADV

cry out. If you **cry out**, you suddenly shout or cry loudly because you are surprised or in pain. EG *She cried out in terror... Ralph cried out: 'Oh God, Oh God!'... They cried out their greetings.*   V+ADV, V+ADV+QUOTE, V+ADV+N: NO PASSIVE

cry out against. If you **cry out against** something, you complain about it because you do not approve of it. EG *People are crying out against the new laws.* ▶ An **outcry** is a reaction of strong disapprov- al and anger shown by the public or media about an event, a government policy, etc. EG *There was a public outcry about selling arms to the rebels.*   V+ADV+PREP

N COUNT

cry out for. If one thing **is crying out for** another, it needs it very much. EG *There is a vast surplus of workers crying out for employ- ment... Its controls were crying out for adjustment.*   V+ADV+PREP

cuddle, cuddles, cuddling, cuddled

cuddle up. When you **cuddle up** to someone, you sit or lie as near to them as possible and you cuddle them; an informal expression. EG *They tried to cuddle up and get warm under the bedclothes... There was a woman cuddled up close to him.* • **Snuggle up** means almost the same as **cuddle up.**   V+ADV

curl, curls, curling, curled

curl up. 1 If you **curl up**, you lie down bringing your arms, legs, and head in towards your stomach, for example because you sleep in that position. EG *He curled up in the chair... She could see the cat curled up asleep on the sofa.*   V+ADV

2 When something flat, such as a leaf or a piece of paper, **curls up**, its edges bend towards its centre. EG *As the tree bark dries it curls up into sticks.*   V+ADV

curtain, curtains, curtaining, curtained

curtain off. If part of a room is **curtained off**, it is separated from the rest of the room by a curtain. EG *The rear of the passenger cabin was curtained off... We need to curtain off a section of the altar.*   V+ADV+N, V+N+ADV, V+PRON+ADV

cut, cuts, cutting

The form **cut** is used in the present tense and is the past tense and past participle of the verb.

cut across. 1 If you **cut across** a place, you go across it because it is the shortest route to another place. EG *I wanted to cut across country for the next hundred miles.*   V+PREP

2 If an issue or problem **cuts across** divisions or differences be- tween people, the people agree about it although they disagree   V+PREP

about most other things. EG *Issues, however, tended to cut across party lines... ...the development of institutional arrangements cutting across ethnic barriers.*

3 If something **cuts across** a rule or law, it contradicts or breaks it. V+PREP EG *...a religion that does not cut across scientific laws.*

cut away. If you **cut away** a part of something, you remove it by V+N+ADV, cutting it, using a knife, saw, scissors, and so on. EG *All the rotten* V+PRON+ADV, *wood must be cut away and burned... Cut it away with a sharp knife.* V+ADV+N

cut back. If you **cut back** something such as expenditure, you V+ADV+N, reduce it. EG *Congress cut back the funds for NASA's space pro-* V+N+ADV, *gramme... The factory has cut back its work force by 50%... We are* V+PRON+ADV, *all having to cut back.* ▸ A **cutback** is a reduction in something, N COUNT especially in the number of people that a firm or organization employs. EG *...the cutback in public services.*

cut back on. If you **cut back on** something such as expenditure, V+ADV+PREP you try to reduce it, often because you can no longer afford it. EG *The government has had to cut back on public expenditure... They had to cut back on their charitable donations.*

cut down. 1 If you **cut** something **down**, you reduce it or do it less V+ADV+N, often. EG *...the need to cut down pollution... Save time for yourself by* V+N+ADV, *cutting your shopping down to twice a week... The text was too long* V+PRON+ADV, *so we cut it down... 'I wouldn't drink that whisky if I were you,' he* V+ADV *said. 'Cut down.'*

2 If you **cut down** a tree, you cut through its trunk so that it falls to V+N+ADV, the ground. EG *A quarter of forestry reserves had been cut down by* V+PRON+ADV, *1974... How much is it going to cost us to cut all these trees down?* V+ADV+N
● **Fell** means almost the same as **cut down.**

cut down on. If you **cut down on** something, you try to reduce it or V+ADV+PREP do it less often. EG *She had cut down on smoking... ...how to cut down on housework.*

cut in. 1 If you **cut in**, you interrupt someone when they are V+ADV: speaking. EG *'You have to employ a professional,' cut in the English-* ALSO+QUOTE *man quietly... Mrs Travers began a reply, but Mrs Patel cut in again.*
● **Break in** means almost the same as **cut in.**

2 If you **cut** someone **in**, you give them a share of the profits you V+N+ADV, have made on a business deal or sale. EG *We haven't got to cut Sam* V+PRON+ADV, *in have we? He didn't help much... I think we should cut in all those* V+ADV+N *who helped us organize the auction in the first place.*

cut into. If you **cut into** something, you push a knife or similar tool V+PREP into it in order to mark it, damage it, or remove something from it. EG *I cut into the meat and felt a sudden twinge of nausea.*

cut off. 1 If you **cut** a part of something **off**, you remove it V+ADV+N, completely by cutting it, using a knife, saw, scissors, and so on. EG V+N+ADV, *They held a gun to his head and threatened to cut off his ears.* ▸ An V+PRON+ADV **off-cut** is a piece of something that has been removed by cutting. EG N COUNT *You can make your own frames from Perspex off-cuts... ...burning the off-cuts and chippings.* ▸ **Cut-off** jeans or trousers have been ADJECTIVE shortened by cutting off a large part of the legs. EG *...wearing cut-off jeans and a t-shirt.*

2 If someone is **cut off**, they are separated and isolated from other V+N+ADV, people. EG *The battalions found themselves pinned down and cut* V+ADV+N, *off... Many mothers feel cut off during the day... The town was cut* V+REFL+ADV, *off by the floods... We have cut ourselves off from the old ways of* V+PRON+ADV: *thinking.* ALSO+*from*, USUALLY PASSIVE

3 To **cut off** the supply of something means to stop it. EG *People have* V+ADV+N, *been suggesting that we should cut off economic aid... Gas supplies* V+N+ADV, *had now been cut off.* ▸ A **cut-off** or a **cut-off point** is the level or V+PRON+ADV limit at which you decide that something should stop happening. EG N COUNT, ADJECTIVE

Forty-five pounds is our cut-off, and we'll only go that high if we really have to... We thought it was already past the cut-off point.

4 If you **cut** someone **off** or **cut off** what they are saying, you stop them saying it. EG *I waved my hand to cut him off... 'Jenny, I'm sorry.'—'Stop.' She cut off my apology.* ● **Silence** is a more formal word for **cut off**.

V+PRON+ADV,
V+ADV+N,
V+N+ADV

5 To **cut** someone **off** also means to disconnect them when they are having a telephone conversation. EG *Don't complain when they cut you off by mistake.*

V+PRON+ADV,
V+N+ADV

cut out. 1 If you **cut out** part of something, you remove it by cutting it. EG *Badly decayed timber should be cut out and replaced... There were pictures of animals cut out of magazines and tacked to the wall.* ▶ A **cut-out** is a shape that has been cut from card or cardboard. EG *...a cut-out of a girl... ...two cardboard cut-outs.*

V+N+ADV,
V+ADV+N,
V+PRON+ADV

N COUNT

2 If you **cut out** part of something that someone has written, you remove it from the text and do not print or broadcast it. EG *He cut out all references to the Baron being ugly... Her publishers insisted on cutting several stories out of her memoirs.*

V+ADV+N,
V+N+ADV,
V+PRON+ADV:
ALSO+of

3 If you **cut out** something that you are doing or saying, you stop doing or saying it. If you tell someone to **cut** it **out,** you are telling them angrily to stop misbehaving, joking, or being unreasonable. EG *He ought to cut out the drinking... 'Look,' he said, 'let's cut out all this encounter-group rubbish'... She said in a shrill brief whine: 'Cut it out!'* ● **Desist** is a very formal word for **cut out.**

V+ADV+N,
V+N+ADV,
V+PRON+ADV:
ALSO
IMPERATIVE,
V+it+ADV

4 If you **cut** someone **out** of an activity or job, you do not allow them to do it. EG *He'll cut you out of the operation completely... I don't think I should be cut out of the trip.*

V+PRON+ADV,
V+N+ADV:
USUALLY+of

5 If an object **cuts out** the light, it is between you and the light, so that you are in the dark or shade. EG *Great trees soar above to cut out most of the light.*

V+ADV+N,
V+N+ADV,
V+PRON+ADV

6 If an engine **cuts out,** it suddenly stops working. EG *The engine's cut out again.* ▶ A **cut-out** is an automatic device that turns off a motor or engine, for example because there is something wrong with it. EG *...a cut-out to prevent the battery from overcharging.*

V+ADV

N COUNT

cut through. 1 To **cut** through something such as water means to move or pass through it easily and smoothly. EG *The big canoe was cutting through the water.*

V+PREP

2 If a path **cuts through** a forest or jungle, it goes through it. EG *We were making our way down a path that cut through the pine forest.*

V+PREP

3 If you **cut through** a place, you go through it because it is the shortest route to another place. EG *We cut through a field of cows.*

V+PREP

cut up. 1 If you **cut** something **up,** you cut it into several pieces. EG *You start the lesson by cutting up a worm... He has to have his food cut up for him.* ● **Slice up** means almost the same as **cut up.**

V+ADV+N,
V+N+ADV,
V+PRON+ADV

2 If you **are cut up** about something, you are upset or angry about it. EG *She's really cut up about getting a D in Maths.*

PASSIVE:
V+ADV

D d

dab, dabs, dabbing, dabbed

dab at. If you **dab at** something, you touch it several times with
quick, stabbing movements. EG *She dabbed at her mouth with the
lace handkerchief... 'You're horrid!' Sarah said, shaking her finger at
them and dabbing at her eyes.*   V+PREP

dab on. If you **dab** a substance **on** a surface, you put it on with quick,
light strokes. EG *She dabbed some powder on her nose... Dab some
antiseptic on the wound... The liquid has to be dabbed on three times
a day.*   V+N+PREP, V+PRON+PREP, V+N+ADV, V+PRON+ADV

dabble, dabbles, dabbling, dabbled

dabble in. If you **dabble in** an activity or subject, you take part in it
or study it occasionally, but not seriously. EG *They wear heavy boots
and dabble in right-wing politics... He had dabbled in composition,
but now devoted himself wholly to his piano playing... Despite my
having dabbled in psychiatry and social work, I really know very
little about people.*   V+PREP

dally, dallies, dallying, dallied

dally with. If you **dally with** an idea or plan, you think about it but
not in a serious way. EG *I'm dallying with the idea of giving up my
job... She dallies with mischievous half-truths.* ● **Toy with** means
almost the same as **dally with**.   V+PREP

dam, dams, damming, dammed

dam up. 1 To **dam up** a river means to put something across it to
hold back the water. EG *The boards dammed up the creek enough to
form a huge bath tub... The old channels are dammed up in the hope
that the water will seek out a new course.*   V+ADV+N, V+N+ADV, V+PRON+ADV

2 If you **dam up** your feelings and emotions, you prevent yourself
from expressing them. EG *...passions too long dammed up by society
and its laws.* ● **Bottle up** means almost the same as **dam up**.   V+N+ADV, V+PRON+ADV, V+ADV+N

damp, damps, damping, damped

damp down. 1 To **damp down** a situation that involves a great deal
of emotion, growth, or change means to reduce the amount of effort
and intensity in it. EG *Neighbouring countries had been of little or no
help in damping down the crisis... ...increasing strength abroad at
the cost, if necessary, of damping down progress at home... Missiles
were fired at stand-off ranges by the Tornados to damp things down
a little.* ● **Dampen down** means almost the same as **damp down**.   V+ADV+N, V+N+ADV, V+PRON+ADV

2 If you **damp down** a fire, you make it burn more slowly by
reducing the flow of air.   V+ADV+N, V+PRON+ADV, V+N+ADV

3 If you **damp down** a surface, you spray it with a small amount of
water. EG *The surface had been smoothed over, levelled out and
damped down with water... His hair was damped down as if it had
been wet.* ● **Dampen down** means almost the same as **damp down**.   V+ADV+N, V+N+ADV, V+PRON+ADV

dampen, dampens, dampening, dampened

dampen down. 1 To **dampen down** a situation that involves a
great deal of emotion, growth, or change means to reduce the
amount of effort and intensity in it. EG *A policy of high interest rates
has the effect of further dampening down the economy.* ● **Damp
down** means almost the same as **dampen down**.   V+ADV+N, V+N+ADV, V+PRON+ADV

2 If you **dampen down** a surface, you spray a small amount of water over it. ● **Damp down** means almost the same as **dampen down**.

V+ADV+N,
V+N+ADV,
V+PRON+ADV

dash, dashes, dashing, dashed

dash off. If you **dash off** a short piece of writing, you write it quickly and without careful thought. EG *She bombarded the market with letters, dashing off several each week... She dashed off a note to the ASA... ...others seemed to have been dashed off in seconds.* ● **Scribble** means almost the same as **dash off.**

V+ADV+N

date, dates, dating, dated

date back. If something **dates back** to a particular time, it has existed since that time. EG *...a Jewish burial ground dating back to the New Testament period... The current idea for defending western Europe dates back to 1967... ...cultures that date back much further than the era of colonization... Much of this debt dated back many years.*

V+ADV:
WITH A

dawn, dawns, dawning, dawned

dawn on. If a fact or idea **dawns on** or **upon** you, you suddenly begin to realize what is happening or what the real nature of your situation is. EG *It never dawned on her that her life was in danger... It slowly dawned on me that something unusual was happening... The awful truth dawned upon him.* ● **Strike** means almost the same as **dawn on.**

V+PREP

dawn upon. See dawn on: **dawn upon** is more formal.

deal, deals, dealing, dealt

deal in. 1 If a company or shop **deals in** a particular type of goods, it buys and sells those goods. EG *...the shop that deals only in trousers... Julie's father owned a business that dealt in bulk orders of paper.* ● **Handle** means almost the same as **deal in.**

V+PREP

2 Someone who **deals in** a particular activity or subject is involved with it or knowledgeable about it. EG *Go to the legal adviser who deals in road accidents.* ● **Deal with** means almost the same as **deal in.**

V+PREP

deal out. 1 If you **deal out** punishment to someone, you inflict it on them. EG *Beatings and other cruelties were dealt out to those who had been captured... And the same punishment would be dealt out to any boy who was ever late for his class.* ● **Mete out** and **administer** are more formal ways of saying **deal out.**

V+ADV+N:
ALSO+to

2 When you **deal out** playing cards, you give each player a number of cards. EG *He drank the last of his whisky, then swiftly dealt out the next hand.*

V+ADV+N,
V+N+ADV,
V+PRON+ADV

deal with. 1 When you **deal with** something that needs attention, you do what is necessary in order to achieve the result that is wanted. EG *They learned to deal with any sort of emergency... The Finance Officer deals with all the finances of the university... The work is dealt with by a Stipendiary Magistrate.* ● **Handle** and **tackle** mean almost the same as **deal with.**

V+PREP:
HAS PASSIVE

2 If a book, speech, film or theory **deals with** a particular topic or idea, this is one of the subjects that is discussed or expressed in it. EG *There are some issues you just can't deal with in a popular magazine... ...a motion dealing with the educational training of the nation... These questions will be dealt with in chapter 7.* ● **Cover** means almost the same as **deal with.**

V+PREP:
HAS PASSIVE

3 If you **deal with** a person or organization, you do business with them. EG *I planned to deal with this bank for many years.*

V+PREP

debar, debars, debarring, debarred

debar from. If you **are debarred from** doing something, you are prevented from doing it by a regulation or law; a formal expression. EG *She saw no reason why public industries alone should be debarred from the normal commercial right to expand... This state of affairs effectively debars us from full and equal participation.*

V+N+PREP,
V+PRON+PREP

decide, decides, deciding, decided

decide on. If you **decide on** or **upon** something, you choose it or make up your mind about it after careful thought. EG *He decided on a career in the army... They are due to meet on 22 August to decide on further action... The men would be selected according to criteria which had to be decided upon.* ● **Settle on** is a more informal expression for **decide on**.

V+PREP:
HAS PASSIVE

decide upon. See **decide on**: **decide upon** is slightly more formal.

deck, decks, decking, decked

deck out. If you **are decked out** in something, you put on very grand clothes for a special occasion. EG *He enjoyed being at his father's side, decked out in embroidered coats stiff with gold... I decked myself out in a suit and tie, and set off.* ● **Dress up** means almost the same as **deck out**.

V+REFL+ADV,
V+PRON+ADV:
ALSO+in/with

defer, defers, deferring, deferred

defer to. If you **defer to** someone, you accept their opinion or do what they want you to do, even though you do not agree with it. EG *No longer did MPs defer to the Speaker... He's a medical man and we'd be fools not to defer to him in medical matters... Despite being one of the most powerful industrialists in the world, he was in no way deferred to by his Swiss guests.*

V+PREP:
HAS PASSIVE

delight, delights, delighting, delighted

delight in. If you **delight in** something, you get a lot of pleasure from it. EG *Morris delighted in hard manual work... Be prepared for friends who delight in breaking bad news... ...someone who delights in controversy... He has his favourite sources and delights in their academic approach.*

V+PREP

deliver, delivers, delivering, delivered

deliver of. 1 If you **deliver** yourself **of** an opinion, you express it in a confident way; a formal use. EG *He delivered himself of a judgment lifting the ban... She delivered herself of her view of that morning's events... Having arrived at a measured opinion, he delivered himself of it.*

V+REFL+PREP

2 If a woman **is delivered of** a baby, she gives birth to it; an old-fashioned use. EG *After twelve hours of labour she was delivered of a son.*

PASSIVE:
V+PREP

deliver up. If you **deliver** something **up**, you surrender it or give it to someone because you have been ordered to do so. EG *The Court ordered three weeks ago that he must deliver up the evidence.*

V+ADV+N,
V+N+ADV,
V+PRON+ADV

delve, delves, delving, delved

delve in. See **delve into**.

delve into. 1 If you **delve into** or **in** something, you search vigorously deep inside it. EG *They delved into their desks for their pens... She walked to a cavity in the wall and delved about in it... I held the basket while she delved in the boxes.*

V+PREP

2 If you **delve into** something, you try in a determined way to discover more information about it. EG *...a good source for anyone interested in delving into the history of London... To find out, one*

V+PREP

really needs to delve into the past... ...delving into the secrets of nature.

depart, departs, departing, departed

depart from. If you **depart from** an accepted belief, method, or type of behaviour, you do or believe something different. EG *Children born in this country are British and we ought not to depart from that principle... Lenin departed from Marx on the role of the peasantry... In the next couple of hours, we departed from the script to produce a completely unorthodox finish.*   V+PREP: HAS PASSIVE

depend, depends, depending, depended

depend on. 1 If you **depend on** or **upon** someone or something, you need them in order to be able to exist, survive or continue. EG *Our lives and those of all other animals depend on oxygen... These factories depend upon natural resources.... They do benefit from adult attention which can always be depended on.* ● **Rely on** means almost the same as **depend on.**   V+PREP: HAS PASSIVE

2 If you can **depend on** or **upon** someone or something, you know that you can trust them to provide help or do something reliably. EG *I knew I could depend on you... This country is an ally you can depend on... Can he be depended upon to provide regular deliveries?* ● **Rely on** and **trust** mean almost the same as **depend on.**   V+PREP: HAS PASSIVE

3 If a result or situation **depends on** or **upon** particular circumstances, it will be affected or changed according to what those circumstances are. EG *The success of the meeting depends largely on whether the chairman is efficient... What you saw depended on where you were... The amount of money you make depends on the amount of sweat you put in... The screens on which the text is displayed will vary in size depending upon what one wants to do with it.*   V+PREP: USUALLY+WH

depend upon. See depend on.

deprive, deprives, depriving, deprived

deprive of. If you **deprive** someone **of** something, you take it away from them or prevent them from having it. EG *Imprisonment deprives the offender of his liberty... When the heart stops, the brain is deprived of fresh blood and oxygen... 'I'm not trying to deprive you of the necessities of life,' I explained.*   V+N+PREP, V+PRON+PREP

derive, derives, deriving, derived

derive from. 1 If you **derive** pleasure or benefit **from** something, it gives you pleasure or some advantage. EG *They derive enormous pleasure from their grand-children... They nest near the house where they derive some protection from the harsh weather.*   V+N+PREP, V+PRON+PREP

2 If something **derives from** or **is derived from** something else, it develops or comes from that thing. EG *This argument derives from a belief in the importance of education... We may expect that economics must derive its aims and objectives from a study of man... The word 'detergent' is derived from the Latin word for 'cleaner'.*   V+PREP, V+N+PREP, V+PRON+PREP: ERGATIVE

descend, descends, descending, descended

descend on. If you **descend on** or **upon** a place or person, you arrive suddenly without being invited. EG *I gather that I'm the second uninvited guest to descend upon your house today!... Were FBI agents really lurking around waiting to descend on him?... The Vikings descended on the Saxon coast.*   V+PREP

descend to. If you **descend to** something, you behave in a way that is considered unacceptable or unworthy of you. EG *All too soon they*   V+PREP

will descend to spreading scandal and gossip... Gareth was vexed that he should descend to such a fatuous remark.
descend upon. See descend on: **descend upon** is more formal.

despair, despairs, despairing, despaired

despair of. If you **despair of** something, you feel that there is no hope that it will happen, improve, or survive. EG *He despaired of ever having the courage to ask her... ...people who despair of American society... At many times, both during and after the birth, her life was despaired of.*

V+PREP:
HAS PASSIVE

deter, deters, deterring, deterred

deter from. If someone or something **deters** you **from** doing something, they persuade you not to do it by showing that it is difficult or unpleasant. EG *Such discrimination may deter more women from seeking work... The punishment did not deter you from committing further offences?... He stole my gold watch, but this did not deter him from telephoning a few weeks later to chat about old times.* ● **Put off** is a more informal expression for **deter from.**

V+N+PREP,
V+PRON+PREP

detract, detracts, detracting, detracted

detract from. If something **detracts from** something else, it makes that thing seem less good or reduces its effect. EG *Although these may not be harmful to health, they certainly detract from the quality of life.* ● **Diminish** means almost the same as **detract from.**

V+PREP

deviate, deviates, deviating, deviated

deviate from. If someone or something **deviates from** normal or expected behaviour or ways of doing something, they behave or act differently. EG *...people who deviate from society's ideas of what is normal... I do not see any reason to deviate from the classical view.* ● **Depart from** means almost the same as **deviate from.**

V+PREP

devolve, devolves, devolving, devolved

devolve on. See devolve to.
devolve to. If someone in authority **devolves** a job, duty, or privilege **to, on,** or **upon** another person or group, they transfer it to that person or group. EG *...the methods by which authority can be devolved to local and regional communities... It is facing growing pressures to devolve authority on sub-sections within the organization... From now on the task must devolve upon us all.*
devolve upon. See devolve to.

V+N+PREP,
V+PRON+PREP,
V+PREP:
ERGATIVE

dictate, dictates, dictating, dictated

dictate to. If you **dictate to** someone, you tell them what they should do. EG *They are hardly in a position to dictate to the Labour party... They found themselves dominated and dictated to by nations smaller than themselves.*

V+PREP:
HAS PASSIVE

die, dies, dying, died

die away. If a sound or emotion **dies away,** it gradually becomes weaker or fainter and finally disappears. EG *Now that the cheers and excitement had died away, it seemed oddly quiet.* ● **Fade** means almost the same as **die away.**

V+ADV

die back. If a plant **dies back,** its leaves die but its roots remain alive. EG *Cut the leaves when the plant starts to die back after flowering.*

V+ADV

die down. If something **dies down,** it becomes much quieter or less intense. EG *She waited until the laughter had died down... The wind has died down now.* ● **Subside** is a more formal word for **die down.**

V+ADV

die off. If a group of people or animals **dies off,** all the people or

V+ADV

animals in that group die, often over a short period of time. EG *Even the wild animals were dying off... Their children are dying off like flies.*

die out. If something **dies out**, it becomes less common and eventu- V+ADV
ally disappears. EG *Traditional grocers' shops are fast dying out... Use of the abacus has only recently died out in Japan.... Many species died out.*

dig, digs, digging, dug

dig in. 1 When you are gardening, if you **dig** a substance **in**, you mix V+N+ADV,
it deep into the soil. EG *Dig the compost in thoroughly and make sure* V+PRON+ADV,
you give it plenty of water in the evening. V+ADV+N

2 If soldiers **dig in** or **dig** themselves **in**, they dig trenches for V+ADV,
protection and prepare for an attack by the enemy. EG *...the 2nd* V+REFL+ADV
Battalion which was dug in along the northern perimeter.

3 If you tell someone to **dig in**, you are telling them to start eating; V+ADV:
an informal use. • **Tuck in** means almost the same as **dig in**. USUALLY
 IMPERATIVE

dig into. If you **dig into** something, you put your hand in it to search V+PREP
for something. EG *He dug into his pocket for his money.* • **Delve into**
means almost the same as **dig into**.

dig out. If you **dig** something **out**, you find it and get it out after it V+PRON+ADV,
has been hidden, covered with things or stored for a long time. EG V+N+ADV,
I've had it for years; I just dug it out because it goes with this suit... V+ADV+N:
We had dug out our tour books and maps ready for the holiday... ALSO+from/of
Could you dig out the infant mortality figures for 1957?... ...an old monograph which was dug out for me from a dusty storage room.
• **Fish out** means almost the same as **dig out**.

dig over. If you **dig over** the earth, you break it up with a fork or V+ADV+N,
spade so that plants can grow there. EG *Dad spent most of the* V+PRON+ADV,
afternoon digging over the old vegetable patch. V+N+ADV

dig up. 1 If you **dig up** something that has been buried or that is V+ADV+N,
growing, you remove it from the ground. EG *...digging up potatoes in* V+N+ADV,
the vegetable garden. V+PRON+ADV

2 If you **dig up** information that is not widely known, you discover it V+ADV+N,
after a determined search. EG *Journalists had dug up some hair-* V+N+ADV,
raising facts about the company. • **Unearth** means almost the same V+PRON+ADV
as **dig up**.

din, dins, dinning, dinned

din into. If someone **dins** something **into** you, they repeat it in a V+N+PREP,
forceful way to make you remember it. EG *At school, it was dinned* V+PRON+PREP
into us that we mustn't talk to strangers. • **Drum into** means almost
the same as **din into**.

dine, dines, dining, dined

dine off. See dine on.

dine on. If you **dine on** or **dine off** a particular sort of food, you eat V+PREP
it for dinner; an old-fashioned or formal expression. EG *I stayed in the compartment and dined on a chocolate bar... ...creatures that are only too glad to dine off a prairie dog if given a chance.*

dine out. If you **dine out**, you have dinner away from your home at V+ADV
a restaurant or at someone else's home. EG *By seven he was showering in his own flat before dining out in the West End.* • **Eat out** means almost the same as **dine out**.

dip, dips, dipping, dipped

dip in. If you tell someone to **dip in**, you are inviting them to take V+ADV
their share of something, especially food. EG *Dip in, everybody!—The food's on the table.*

dip into. 1 If you **dip into** a book or subject, you look at it V+PREP occasionally and briefly without reading or studying it seriously. EG *If you want to know more, I suggest you dip into 'The English Legal System' by K.T. Eddey.*

2 If you **dip into** your savings or your pocket, you spend some money   V+PREP
which you had intended to keep. EG *He would be compelled to dip into capital to maintain his standard of living... This could be secured by restoring the grant and dipping into reserves.*

disabuse, disabuses, disabusing, disabused

disabuse of. If you **disabuse** someone **of** something, you persuade   V+N+PREP,
them that what they believe is untrue; a formal expression. EG *'Well,*   V+PRON+PREP
I think I can disabuse you of that notion,' he said solemnly.

disagree, disagrees, disagreeing, disagreed

disagree with. **1** If you **disagree with** a particular action or   V+PREP
proposal, you disapprove of it and believe that it is wrong. EG *He said he was resigning because he disagreed with the company's labour policies... If the farmer disagreed with the decision, he could take the case to court.*

2 If a particular food or drink **disagrees with** you, it makes you feel   V+PREP
unwell. EG *They'd both eaten something that disagreed with them... Oranges and chocolate disagree with me, they give me migraine.*
● **Upset** means almost the same as **disagree with.**

disapprove, disapproves, disapproving, disapproved

disapprove of. If you **disapprove of** something or someone, you   V+PREP:
feel or show that you do not like them or do not approve of them. EG   HAS PASSIVE
The other directors disapproved of his methods... Gluttonous drinking was especially disapproved of.

dish, dishes, dishing, dished

dish out. **1** If you **dish out** something, you give an amount of it to   V+ADV+N,
each person in a group; an informal use. EG *...dishing out presents in*   V+N+ADV,
the Christmas bazaar... He was burdened with endless paperwork   V+PRON+ADV
dished out by bureaucrats, and he hated it. ● **Dole out** means almost the same as **dish out.**

2 To **dish out** a punishment or criticism means to punish or criticize   V+ADV+N,
someone; an informal use. EG *I had to be able to withstand anything*   V+PRON+ADV,
the warder could dish out... See, you can dish it out, but you can't   V+N+ADV
take it!

3 When you **dish out** food, you serve it to people. EG *We could not*   V+ADV+N,
wash the saucepans until the food was dished out... The amount of   V+N+ADV,
food dished out to each person varied according to his rank. ● **Dish**   V+PRON+ADV:
up means almost the same as **dish out.**   ALSO+to

dish up. When you **dish up** food, you put it into serving dishes or   V+ADV,
onto plates so that it is ready to eat; an informal expression. EG *We*   V+ADV+N,
tried dishing up earlier, but people complained... Collect these plates   V+PRON+ADV,
while I go and dish up the main course... Until I've dished it up and   V+N+ADV,
we've eaten it, I won't be able to relax... I dare say she will dish you   V+PRON+ADV+N
up something nice for dinner. ● **Serve** is a more formal word for **dish up.**

dispense, dispenses, dispensing, dispensed

dispense with. If you **dispense with** something, you stop using it   V+PREP:
or get rid of it because you no longer need it; a formal expression. EG   HAS PASSIVE
Should we not dispense with the services of Mrs. Baggot?... The weather had turned warm enough for her to dispense with her fur coat... His knowledge of foreign affairs is too precious to be dispensed with.

dispose, disposes, disposing, disposed

dispose of. 1 If you **dispose of** something, you get rid of it, for example, by throwing it away or selling it. EG *They had no authority to dispose of the land... It may cost industry more to dispose of its waste in a safer manner... I've got a houseful of things in Chicago to dispose of... Miles of telex tape had to be disposed of.*   V+PREP: HAS PASSIVE

2 If you **dispose of** a problem, task, or question, you deal with it. EG *That, then, is the first point disposed of... Medical evidence would be enough to dispose of any suggestion that I was guilty... They soon got down to business, once the formalities were disposed of.*   V+PREP: HAS PASSIVE

3 To **dispose of** a person or an animal means to kill them; a formal use. EG *I disposed of one of the rats that came nosing round the hut... Stein will have to be disposed of; you realize that, don't you?* ● **Destroy** means almost the same as **dispose of.**   V+PREP: HAS PASSIVE

dissociate, dissociates, dissociating, dissociated

dissociate from. If you **dissociate** yourself **from** something or someone, you show that you are not connected with them in order to avoid trouble or blame; a formal expression. EG *Bailey dissociated himself from this group... As a member of the Community, it is impossible to dissociate ourselves from this problem.*   V+REFL+PREP

dive, dives, diving, dived

American English uses the form **dove** as the past tense and past participle of the verb.

dive in. If you **dive in** when you start something new, you start doing it enthusiastically and without any preparation. EG *He just dived in before I could get there and caused absolute havoc.* ● **Rush in** means almost the same as **dive in.**   V+ADV

dive into. 1 If you **dive into** something such as a bag, you put your hand into it quickly in order to get something out. EG *He suddenly dived into the chest and produced a wig.*   V+PREP

2 If you **dive into** an activity, you start doing it enthusiastically and without any preparation. EG *Don't dive headlong into a task which you know you can't complete.* ● **Rush into** means almost the same as **dive into.**   V+PREP

divest, divests, divesting, divested

divest of. 1 If you **divest** yourself **of** a belief or attitude, you realize that you were wrong; a formal use. EG *They will have to divest themselves of the notion that they have that power.* ● **Rid of** means almost the same as **divest of.**   V+REFL+PREP

2 If you **divest** yourself **of** something that you are carrying or wearing, you take it off or put it down; a formal use. EG *She divested herself of her bag... He began thankfully to divest himself of his suit.*   V+REFL+PREP

3 If you **divest** someone or something **of** a role, function, or quality, you cause them to lose it. EG *...divesting public housing of its welfare role... If they were honourable, they would resign and divest themselves of their status as Christian ministers.* ● **Strip of** means almost the same as **divest of.**   V+N+PREP, V+PRON+PREP

divide, divides, dividing, divided

divide by. If you **divide** a larger number **by** a smaller number, you calculate how many times the smaller number can fit into the larger number. EG *Divide 35 by 7... 35 divided by 7 is 5... Add 7 and 5, divide by 3 and add 2... This total is then divided by 52 to arrive at your weekly payment.*   V+N+PREP, V+PRON+PREP, V+PREP

divide into. If you **divide** a smaller number **into** a larger number,   V+N+PREP, V+PRON+PREP you calculate how many times the smaller number can fit into the larger number. EG *Divide 7 into 35.*

divide off. If something **divides** things **off,** it forms a barrier that keeps them separate. EG *Huge iron gates divide off the east end of the church.* ● **Separate off** means almost the same as **divide off.**

V+ADV+N,
V+N+ADV,
V+PRON+ADV

divide up. 1 If you **divide** something **up,** you separate it into completely separate groups or parts. EG *Film divides motion up into a series of static images... We're dividing our group up... The imagination can divide up the stick into a number of different sections... The house has been divided up and used as flats.* ● **Split up** means almost the same as **divide up.**

V+N+ADV,
V+PRON+ADV,
V+ADV+N

2 If you **divide up** a quantity of something, you share it out among a number of people or groups. EG *The Spanish and Portuguese divided up Latin America between them... We divided the meat up amongst you so it could all be eaten before it went bad... The proceeds had to be divided up among about four hundred people.* ● **Parcel up** means almost the same as **divide up.**

V+ADV+N,
V+N+ADV,
V+PRON+ADV

divvy, divvies, divvying, divvied

divvy up. If you **divvy up,** you share out the profits from what you have been doing with other people; an informal expression. EG *We'll divvy up as soon as we get back to the club.*

V+ADV

do, does, doing, did, done

do as. See **do for.**

do away with. 1 To **do away with** something means to get rid of it. EG *Our medicines have not done away with disease... You cannot do away with violence by using violence... At the sight of all the food, thoughts of diets were done away with.* ● **Eliminate** is a more formal word for **do away with.**

V+ADV+PREP:
HAS PASSIVE

2 To **do away with** someone means to kill them; an informal use. EG *Who on earth would want to do away with a harmless boy like Antonio?... They were prepared to do away with Denton, and anyone else who stood in the way... I was afraid of being done away with.* ● **Do in** means almost the same as **do away with.**

V+ADV+PREP:
HAS PASSIVE

do down. If you **do** someone **down,** you make them appear stupid, unpleasant or unsuccessful by criticizing them. EG *Jeanette remained determined to do Armand down one way or another... You enjoy trying to do each other down... She argued out of sheer spite and desire to do him down... Don't do yourself down.*

V+N+ADV,
V+PRON+ADV,
V+REFL+ADV

do for. 1 If you **are done for** or if something **does for** you, your life or chance of success has been ruined; an informal use. EG *If his battery fails, he's done for... She tried with her right hand, but she couldn't work it. She was done for.*

V+PREP:
HAS PASSIVE,
USUALLY PASSIVE

2 If you say that something will **do for** or **do as** another thing, you mean that you can use it instead of the other thing; an informal use. EG *A few lamps did for the lighting... They could buy nothing, and sacks had to do for raincoats.* ● **Serve for** means almost the same as **do for.**

V+PREP

3 If someone **does for** another person, they are employed by that person to clean their house or flat; an informal use. EG *Agnes did for us for thirteen years before retiring.*

V+PREP

do in. 1 To **do** someone **in** means to kill them; an informal use. EG *They might do you in while you're sleeping... They had decided to do their victim in... Be careful!—He'll do himself in!* ● **Bump off** means almost the same as **do in.**

V+PRON+ADV,
V+N+ADV,
V+REFL+ADV

2 If you say that you **are done in,** you mean that you are completely exhausted. EG *Not to put too fine a point on in, you seem done in...*

V+N+ADV,
V+PRON+ADV

'We need a rest. I feel done in,' he said untruthfully... Walking up that hill just about did me in, I can tell you.

do out. If you **do out** a cupboard or room, you clean and tidy it thoroughly; an informal expression. EG *She offered to do out the cell for me... I must do these cupboards out tomorrow... It still isn't right—I'll have to do it out again.*

V+ADV+N,
V+N+ADV,
V+PRON+ADV

do out in. If a room or building is **done out in** a particular colour or style, it is decorated or furnished in that way; an informal expression. EG *The bedroom was done out in pale pink... I'm thinking of having it done out in yellow and blue... ...a modernistic place done out in oiled pinewood.*

V+N+ADV,
V+PRON+ADV:
USUALLY PASSIVE

do out of. If you **do** someone **out of** something, you unfairly prevent them from having or getting it; an informal expression. EG *They asked if I was trying to do Miss Claybon out of a job... ...assurances that the worker is not being done out of wage increases... ...an investment which they tried to do me out of.*

V+N+ADV+PREP,
V+PRON+ADV+PREP

do over. 1 If you **do** something **over**, you do it again from the beginning; used mainly in informal American English. EG *'Do we have to do this over?' I said... That essay was no good, I'll have to do it over.* ● **Redo** is a more formal word for **do over**.

V+N+ADV,
V+PRON+ADV

2 If you **do over** a house, you clean or redecorate it and change its furnishings; used mainly in informal American English. EG *Mrs Kennedy did over the White House... The hall looked as if it had been done over for a school prom.* ● **Do out** means almost the same as **do over**.

V+ADV+N

3 If someone's house **has been done over**, burglars have broken in and stolen things from it; an informal use. EG *That place has been done over a few times.*

V+N+ADV,
V+PRON+ADV:
USUALLY PASSIVE

4 To **do** someone **over** means to hit and kick them in order to hurt and injure them; an informal use. EG *He was done over by a gang of youths.* ● **Beat up** and **duff up** mean almost the same as **do over**.

V+PRON+ADV,
V+N+ADV

do up. 1 If you **do** something **up**, you fasten it. EG *I can't do my top button up... He started to do up his boots, pulling fiercely at the laces... 'Don't talk to me like that,' she said, doing up her suitcase... He would undo a window cord, do it up again and walk back.*

V+N+ADV,
V+ADV+N,
V+PRON+ADV

2 If a woman **does** her hair **up**, she arranges it so that it is tied or fastened close to her head rather than hanging loosely. EG *She did her hair up in a knot on top of her head... Her hair was done up in a neat bun at the back of her head.*

V+N+ADV,
V+PRON+ADV,
V+ADV+N

3 If you **do up** an old building, you repair and decorate it and put in modern facilities. EG *...huge old houses in the south east that people are doing up... The theatre was horrible, done up as cheaply as possible... They wanted payment in cash for doing up the kitchen of one of his cottages.* ● **Renovate** is a more formal word for **do up**.

V+ADV+N,
V+N+ADV,
V+PRON+ADV

4 If something **is done up** in a parcel or bundle, it is wrapped in material or paper or tied together. EG *I gave her a box, nicely done up in flowered paper... ...a big bunch of flowers done up in white tissue and tied with a blue ribbon.*

V+N+ADV,
V+ADV+N:
USUALLY PASSIVE

do with. 1 If you explain that one thing **has** something **to do with** or is **to do with** another thing, you mean that the two things are related or connected in some way. EG *My interest in MPs had nothing to do with Parliament at all... Lateral thinking is to do with new ideas... What's his job? He's something to do with the Foreign Office... Mind your own business; it's got nothing to do with you.*

V+PREP:
ONLY AS *to*-INF

2 If you say you could **do with** something, you mean that you need it or would like it. EG *I think we could all do with a good night's sleep... The staff could probably do with some more money.*

V+PREP

do without. If you **do without** something, you manage or survive in

V+PREP,
V+ADV

spite of not having it. EG *Many Victorian households did without a bathroom altogether... If you don't have cigarettes, you must simply do without.* ● **Go without** means almost the same as **do without**.

dob, dobs, dobbing, dobbed

dob in. 1 When someone has done something wrong, if you **dob** them **in**, you get them into trouble by telling a person in authority what they did; an informal use. EG *If you dob me in, I'll get you. That's a promise.*
V+PRON+ADV,
V+N+ADV

2 If people **dob in**, they all contribute some money so that they can buy something together; an informal use. EG *We all dobbed in to buy her a present.*
V+ADV

dole, doles, doling, doled

dole out. If you **dole** something **out**, you give an amount of it to each person or animal in a group; an informal expression. EG *From the bridge, children dole out their sandwich crusts to the ducks... Gus was doling out crumbled cookies from a large tin box... The problem had something to do with how the money was doled out; only three of the six had actually received anything.* ● **Dish out** and **hand out** mean almost the same as **dole out**.
V+ADV+N,
V+N+ADV,
V+PRON+ADV

doll, dolls, dolling, dolled

doll up. If you **doll** yourself **up**, you put on smart or fashionable clothes; an informal expression. EG *He was all dolled up in the latest gear... She started dolling herself up to go out.* ● **Dress up** means almost the same as **doll up**.
V+REFL+ADV:
USUALLY PASSIVE

dope, dopes, doping, doped

dope up. If someone is **doped up**, they are in a state where they cannot think clearly because they are under the influence of drugs. EG *Irene gave evidence that Mackie and Bell were doped up... They were all so doped up they wouldn't even know the war had started until it was too late... That's right, dope them up, keep them quiet.* ● **Drugged** means almost the same as **doped up**.
V+N+ADV,
V+PRON+ADV:
USUALLY PASSIVE

dose, doses, dosing, dosed

dose up. If you **dose** someone **up**, you give them the full amount of a medicine or a drug that can be given at one time. EG *We'll dose her up with it and see how she responds.*
V+PRON+ADV,
V+N+ADV,
V+REFL+ADV

doss, dosses, dossing, dossed

doss down. If you **doss down** in a temporary bed or unusual place, you sleep there for a short time; an informal expression used in British English. EG *...a rusty stretcher where he had dossed down once or twice... He'll be dossing down in the living room for a couple of weeks.* ● **Kip down** means almost the same as **doss down**.
V+ADV

dote, dotes, doting, doted

dote on. If you **dote on** or **upon** someone, you love them so much that you cannot see their faults. EG *This guy she's just married, he dotes on her.* ● **Adore** means almost the same as **dote on**.
V+PREP:
HAS PASSIVE

dote upon. See **dote on**.

double, doubles, doubling, doubled

double back. 1 If you **double back**, you turn and go back in the direction that you came from. EG *When nobody was watching, they doubled back.* ● **Turn back** means almost the same as **double back**.
V+ADV

2 When a line **doubles back** on itself, it bends in the middle, so that the second part is parallel to the first part. EG *The queue doubled back on itself.*
V+ADV:
USUALLY
WITH *on*+REFL

double over. See **double up**.

double up. 1 If two people **double up,** they both use the same thing   v+ADV
because there is not enough for them to have one each. EG *There
weren't enough offices for everyone, so we had to double up...
Families who had previously doubled up in the same accommodation were housed in the new units.*

2 If you **double up** or **double over,** you bend your body quickly, for   V+ADV,
example because you are laughing a lot or because you are in pain.   V+N+ADV,
EG *His companion doubled up with laughter, holding his stomach...   V+PRON+ADV:
She was doubled over, her whole face distorted with pain... The pain   ERGATIVE
caught me and doubled me over in agony.*

doze, dozes, dozing, dozed

doze off. If you **doze off,** you fall into a light sleep. EG *I leant back   v+ADV
against the sunny wall and dozed off... It was about midnight and
she'd just dozed off.* ● **Nod off** means almost the same as **doze off.**

drag, drags, dragging, dragged

drag along. See drag on.

drag down. 1 Someone who **drags** someone else **down,** reduces   V+N+ADV,
them to an inferior social status or to lower standards of behaviour.   V+PRON+ADV
EG *His mother hates me. She thinks I drag him down.*

2 Something that **drags** you **down** makes you feel weak or de-   V+N+ADV,
pressed. EG *That bout of flu really dragged me down... I felt dragged   V+PRON+ADV
down by the obligations of making the film.*

drag in. When you are talking, if you **drag in** a particular subject   V+ADV+N,
you mention something that is not relevant and that other people do   V+PRON+ADV,
not want to discuss. EG *They disapproved of my dragging in his   V+N+ADV
wealth.*

drag into. To **drag** something or someone **into** an event or situation   V+N+PREP,
means to involve them in it when it is not necessary or not   V+PRON+PREP
desirable. EG *It was the politicians who were dragging politics into
sport, not the sportsmen... That's no reason for dragging you into it.*

drag on. If an event or process **drags on** or **drags along,** it   v+ADV
progresses very slowly and takes longer than seems necessary. EG
*Some legal cases have dragged on for eight years... The civil war
dragged on... His divorce was dragging along... The weeks dragged
on, but no one ever came.*

drag out. 1 If you **drag** something **out,** you make it last for longer   V+ADV+N,
than is necessary. EG *We did not know how to prevent them from   V+N+ADV,
dragging out the talks.* ● **Spin out** means almost the same as **drag**   V+PRON+ADV
out, and **prolong** is a more formal word for it.

2 If you **drag** something **out** of someone, you persuade them to tell   V+N+ADV,
you something that they do not want to tell you. EG *The truth had to   V+PRON+ADV:
be dragged out of him... It was hard to drag this sort of stuff out of   USUALLY+of
him.*

drag up. If someone **drags up** an unpleasant event or an old story   V+PRON+ADV,
from the past, they mention it when people do not want to be   V+N+ADV,
reminded of it. EG *There's no need to drag that up again.* ● **Bring up**   V+ADV+N
is a more general expression for **drag up.**

draw, draws, drawing, drew, drawn

draw back. If you **draw back,** you move away from something   v+ADV
because you are surprised or because you do not like it. EG *A little
blood dribbled down the stick. Instinctively the boys drew back.*
● **Recoil** is a more formal word for **draw back.** ▶ A **drawback** is a   N COUNT
disadvantage caused by an unpleasant or unhelpful characteristic
that someone or something has. EG *Her only drawback is that she's
so stupid... This machine has a major drawback from the technological point of view.*

draw down. If you **draw down** an unpleasant reaction, you do V+ADV+N
something which makes other people criticize you. EG *In doing so, he
drew down the anger of the senior members of the party.*

draw in. 1 When the days or evenings **are drawing in,** it is getting V+ADV
dark at an earlier time each evening because autumn or winter is
approaching.

2 When a train **draws in** at a station, it arrives there and stops. V+ADV
● **Pull in** and **come in** mean almost the same as **draw in.**

3 If you **draw in** breath, you breathe deeply. EG *He moved closer to* V+ADV+N
her and drew in a deep breath. ● **Take in** means almost the same as
draw in.

draw into. If you **draw** someone **into** an activity or situation, you V+PRON+PREP,
cause them to become involved in it. EG *Quite by chance I got drawn* V+N+PREP
into a kind of party downstairs... Peter drew her into the discussion.

draw off. If you **draw off** a quantity of liquid from a larger amount, V+ADV+N,
you remove that quantity, usually through a pipe or tube. EG *She* V+N+ADV,
drew off some of the beer, to see if it was ready to drink. V+PRON+ADV

draw on. 1 As a period of time **draws on,** it gets nearer or passes V+ADV
gradually. EG *As the winter months draw on, the leaves fall and the
days get shorter... The evening drew on, and Andrew and I got
drunk.* ● **Wear on** means almost the same as **draw on.**

2 If you **draw on** or **upon** something, you make use of it in order to V+PREP:
do something. EG *He was able to draw on vast reserves of talent...* HAS PASSIVE
*...the subconscious information the expert draws on without even
realizing that he has it... They draw upon a variety of sources in
developing their theory.*

3 When someone **draws on** a cigarette, they breathe in through it V+PREP
and inhale the smoke deeply.

draw out. 1 When a train **draws out,** it moves out of the station. V+ADV
● **Pull out** means almost the same as **draw out.**

2 If you **draw out** a sound, you make it longer. EG *'Ah,' she said,* V+ADV+N,
smiling, drawing out the 'ah'. V+PRON+ADV,
V+N+ADV

3 If something **is drawn out** it takes much longer than is normal or V+ADV+N,
necessary. EG *I wonder whether this debate is going to be short and* V+N+ADV,
decisive, or drawn out by a reluctance to use nuclear weapons. V+PRON+ADV:
USUALLY PASSIVE

4 If someone or something **draws out** information or an emotion V+ADV+N,
from you, they make you say or express it. EG *...the way in which its* V+N+ADV,
forms and colours draw out certain emotions in the viewer... It was V+PRON+ADV:
impossible to draw the truth out of him. ● **Elicit** means almost the ALSO+*of*
same as **draw out.**

5 If you **draw** someone **out,** you make them feel less nervous and V+N+ADV,
more willing to talk. EG *Why not make conversation with them, draw* V+PRON+ADV
them out, make them laugh and feel at ease?

6 When the days or evenings **are drawing out,** it is getting dark later V+ADV
each evening because spring or summer is approaching.

draw up. 1 When you **draw up** a document, list, or plan, you V+ADV+N,
prepare it and write it out. EG *A charter was drawn up, setting out* V+N+ADV,
their policies... The committee drew up a five-point plan to revive V+PRON+ADV
the economy. ● **Formulate** is a formal word for **draw up.**

2 When a vehicle **draws up,** it comes to a particular place and stops. V+ADV
EG *Just before eleven a bus drew up... The taxi drew up before the
house on Sixty-second Street.* ● **Pull up** means almost the same as
draw up.

3 If you **draw up** a chair, you bring it nearer to a person or place, so V+ADV+N,
that you can sit close to them. EG *Draw up a chair, and we'll go* V+N+ADV,
through these notes of yours... He drew his stool up to the table. V+PRON+ADV
● **Pull up** means almost the same as **draw up.**

4 If you **draw** yourself **up,** you make your back very straight so that V+REFL+ADV you look as tall as possible. EG *He drew himself up. 'I apologise,' he said... Its whiskers began to twitch. Slowly, it drew itself up to an extreme height.*

draw upon. See draw on.

dream, dreams, dreaming, dreamed/dreamt

dream of. 1 If you say you would not **dream of** doing something, you are emphasizing that you would never do it in any circumstances. EG *I wouldn't dream of asking my mother to look after her.*

V+PREP:
WITH NEGATIVE,
HAS PASSIVE

2 Something that is **undreamed of** is much better, worse, or more unusual than you ever imagined or thought was possible. EG *People now have achieved a physical mobility previously undreamed of.*

ADJECTIVE

dream up. If you **dream up** a plan or idea, you work it out or create it in your mind. EG *He would never dream up a desperate scheme like that on his own... The jamboree had been dreamed up by the Duke.*

V+ADV+N,
V+PRON+ADV

dredge, dredges, dredging, dredged

dredge up. If you **dredge up** something from the past, you remember it with some difficulty and perhaps without much enthusiasm. EG *...all these old verses that we seem to dredge up from early memories.* ● **Dig up** means almost the same as **dredge up.**

V+ADV+N,
V+N+ADV,
V+PRON+ADV

dress, dresses, dressing, dressed

dress down. To **dress** someone **down** means to punish them by telling them angrily that they have done something wrong. EG *The Foreign Minister was dressed down in public.* ● **Reprimand** means almost the same as **dress down,** and **tell off** is a more informal expression. ▶ If someone gives you a **dressing-down,** they punish you by telling you angrily that you have behaved badly. EG *The Duke gave him a severe dressing-down for his drunkenness.* ● **Reprimand** and **telling-off** mean almost the same as **dressing-down.**

V+N+ADV,
V+PRON+ADV

N SING

dress up. 1 If you **dress up** or **dress** yourself **up,** you put on clothes that are smarter than the ones you usually wear because you are going somewhere special. EG *Rather than sit at home, they all get dressed up and go out... She was glad that she was all dressed up and had done her hair that morning.*

V+ADV,
V+REFL+ADV

2 When people or children **dress up** or when they **are dressed up,** they wear old fashioned clothes or costumes to disguise themselves, to play a game, or to go to a fancy-dress party. EG *You could get someone to dress up as a pig... ...an actor dressed up like a U.S. GI.* ▶ **Dressing-up** is a game in which children put on old or unusual clothes and pretend to be different people.

V+ADV:
ALSO PASSIVE,
V+ADV

N UNCOUNT

3 If you **dress** something **up,** you make it seem more attractive, interesting, or acceptable than it really is. EG *The offer was simply an old one dressed up for gullible European socialists.* ● **Tart up** is a more informal expression for **dress up.**

V+N+ADV,
V+PRON+ADV,
V+ADV+N

drift, drifts, drifting, drifted

drift about. See drift around.

drift along. See drift around.

drift apart. If people who have had a close relationship **drift apart,** they become less close and the relationship gradually comes to an end. EG *Back home again, we more or less drifted apart... ...the feeling that they had drifted apart during those previous months... European and American politics seem to be drifting apart.*

V+ADV

drift around. Someone who **drifts around, drifts about,** or **drifts along,** does not have a settled way of life and has no definite plans or aims. EG *He drifted about from job to job for over a year... She sort*

V+ADV

of drifts around and doesn't do anything much... They feel they may as well drift along through adolescence.

drift off. If you **drift off**, you gradually fall asleep. EG *Finally, he gave up worrying and drifted off to sleep... I slept again, drifting off to the sound of the bells... Occasionally he would drift off into fitful, moaning sleep.* ● **Doze off** means almost the same as **drift off.**

V+ADV:
ALSO+*to/into*

drill, drills, drilling, drilled

drill into. If you **drill** something **into** someone, you teach it to them by making them repeat it many times. EG *...the rigid training rules that had been drilled into him at the academy... It was drilled into them that no matter what happens they must never drop the paddle.* ● **Drum into** means almost the same as **drill into.**

V+N+PREP,
V+PRON+PREP

drink, drinks, drinking, drank, drunk

drink down. If you **drink down** a liquid in a glass, cup, or other container, you drink it all quickly, often without stopping. EG *I drank down my double Scotch eagerly... He drank the bourbon down in two long draughts... Come on, you'd better drink that down.*

V+ADV+N,
V+N+ADV,
V+PRON+ADV

drink in. If you **drink in** something that you see or hear, you concentrate all your attention on it and experience the strong effect that it has on you. EG *He stood still, drinking in the beauty of the countryside... She sat listening attentively to the speaker, drinking it all in.* ● **Take in** means almost the same as **drink in.**

V+ADV+N,
V+N+ADV,
V+PRON+ADV

drink to. When you **drink to** someone or something, you raise your glass and say their name before drinking, to show that you hope they will be happy or successful. EG *The barman set their glasses in front of them and they drank to Mary Jane... They agreed on their plan and drank to it.*

V+PREP

drink up. When you **drink up**, you finish what you are drinking completely. EG *Drink up. Here comes another bottle of wine... Drink your milk up and then you can go out to play.*

V+ADV,
V+N+ADV,
V+PRON+ADV,
V+ADV+N

drive, drives, driving, drove, driven

drive at. If you ask what someone **is driving at,** you are asking what they are trying to say. EG *What are you driving at?... She knew at once what I was driving at... I can see what you're driving at, but I'm still not convinced.* ● **Get at** means almost the same as **drive at.**

V+PREP

drive away. To **drive** someone or something **away** means to behave in a way that forces them to leave. EG *'Flies!' Etta cried and attempted to drive them away by waving her hand... ...spectators whose habits and foul language drive others away... The terrorist campaign has tended to drive away foreign correspondents.*

V+PRON+ADV,
V+N+ADV,
V+ADV+N

drive off. If you **drive off** someone or something that you see as a threat, you force them to go away. EG *The crowd pelted the spies, driving them off before they'd seen anything... They claimed they had driven off a major force.*

V+PRON+ADV,
V+ADV+N,
V+N+ADV

drive out. To **drive** someone or something **out** means to force them to leave or disappear. EG *Some people want to drive others out of the party... The magic man came to Juffure to drive out evil spirits... The system seemed to drive out all love and liberty.* ● **Expel** is a more formal word for **drive out.**

V+N+ADV,
V+ADV+N,
V+PRON+ADV:
ALSO+*of*

drone, drones, droning, droned

drone on. If someone **drones on**, they talk in a boring way for a long time in a low, monotonous voice. EG *I remember him droning on about how important it was to study literature... The President droned on, not daring to look at the camera.*

V+ADV:
ALSO+*about*

drool, drools, drooling, drooled

drool over. If you **drool over** someone or something, you look at them with desire because you find them very attractive. EG *You go round in that bikini and he's drooling over you all the time... ...youths drooling over pornographic pictures.*   V+PREP

drop, drops, dropping, dropped

drop away. If support or interest **drops away**, it becomes less strong. EG *Public interest in the royal marriage has dropped away... Trade Union support dropped away.*   V+ADV

drop back. If someone who is moving along **drops back**, they go slower to allow other people to pass them. EG *The two motor-cycles dropped back to take up position at the rear of the convoy.* ● **Fall behind** means almost the same as **drop back**.   V+ADV

drop by. To **drop by** means to visit someone informally without having arranged the visit. EG *If there's anything you want to see, just drop by.* ● **Drop in** and **drop round** mean almost the same as **drop by**.   V+ADV

drop in. If you **drop in** on someone, you visit them without making any formal arrangement to do so. EG *I thought I'd just drop in and see how you were... I dropped in on her during the afternoon.* ● **Drop by, drop round** and **pop in** mean almost the same as **drop in**. ▸ A **drop-in** centre is a building provided by a local authority where people can go during the day or evening and use the facilities or get help with welfare problems. EG *I've been working at the drop-in centre for the last three months.*   V+ADV: ALSO+*on*

ADJECTIVE

drop off. 1 If you **drop off** to sleep, you go to sleep. EG *I come to see him, and what does he do? He drops off to sleep!... I couldn't get to sleep, and when I did eventually drop off, I was assaulted by dreams.* ● **Doze off** means almost the same as **drop off**.   V+ADV

2 When you are driving, if you **drop** one of your passengers **off**, you take them to where they want to go and leave them there. EG *I can drop Daisy off on my way home.*   V+N+ADV, V+PRON+ADV, V+ADV+N

3 If support or interest **drops off**, it becomes less strong. EG *Three days later interest had dropped off, and we could walk the streets without being recognised.*   V+ADV

drop out. 1 If you **drop out** of a group, you stop belonging to it. If you **drop out** of school or college, you leave before finishing your course. EG *Four of the original thirty five dropped out of the group because they decided they couldn't afford the fare... Some are thrown out and some drop out voluntarily... He had dropped out of college in the first term.* ▸ A **drop-out** is someone who leaves school or college before finishing their course; sometimes used showing disapproval. EG *This part of town is full of hippies and dropouts.*   V+ADV: ALSO+*of*

N COUNT

2 If a word or expression **drops out** of the language, it is no longer used. EG *Today the word 'teeny-bopper' has virtually dropped out of usage.*   V+ADV: USUALLY+*of*

drop round. 1 To **drop round** means to visit someone without making any formal arrangement to do so. EG *I'll drop round when I've finished the shopping.* ● **Drop in** and **drop by** mean almost the same as **drop round**.   V+ADV

2 If you **drop** something **round**, you take it to a person's home for them. EG *Bill can drop your books round on his way home.*   V+N+ADV, V+PRON+ADV

drown, drowns, drowning, drowned

drown out. If something **drowns out** a sound, it makes so much noise that it is impossible to hear that sound properly. EG *The noise*   V+ADV+N, V+N+ADV, V+PRON+ADV

*from the plane drowned out the noise of the guns... The music had
been blaring all evening, drowning out the speakers in the tent.*

drum, drums, drumming, drummed

drum into. If you **drum** something **into** someone, you make them   V+N+PREP,
remember it by repeating it to them regularly. EG *I have had the art*   V+PRON+PREP
of tidiness drummed into me... Such expectations are drummed into
every growing child. ● **Din into** means almost the same as **drum**
into.

drum out. To **drum** someone **out** of an organization means to force   V+N+ADV,
them to leave it; a rather old-fashioned expression. EG *He had been*   V+PRON+ADV:
drummed out of the club for indecent behaviour. ● **Kick out** means   USUALLY+of
almost the same as **drum out**, and **expel** is a more formal word.

drum up. If you **drum up** support for a cause or campaign, you do   V+ADV+N
things to get people's support for it. EG *We were busy canvassing and*
drumming up support... They attempted to drum up support from
students... His bandwagon rolled from state to state, drumming up
radical delegates to support him. ● **Gather** means almost the same
as **drum up.**

dry, dries, drying, dried

dry off. When something wet **dries off**, the moisture that was on its   V+ADV,
surface disappears. EG *I'll walk the dog for a while till she dries off...*   V+N+ADV,
As soon as the sweat dries off, you get hot... She took one of the big   V+PRON+ADV:
towels and dried him off.   ERGATIVE

dry out. 1 If something that contains moisture **dries out**, it loses all   V+ADV,
the moisture that was in it and becomes hard and completely dry. EG   V+ADV+N,
The soil gets as hard as brick when it dries out... How could the eggs   V+N+ADV,
be prevented from drying out?... ...drying out wet boards before   V+PRON+ADV:
laying a floor.   ERGATIVE

2 If someone who has been an alcoholic **dries out**, they are cured of   V+ADV
alcoholism; an informal use.

dry up. 1 If something **dries up** or if something **dries** it **up**, it loses   V+ADV,
all the moisture that was in it. EG *My mouth always dries up under*   V+PRON+ADV,
stress... She tried drying her hair in front of the gas fire, but the gas   V+N+ADV,
dried it up and frizzled the ends... It dried up the ends.   V+ADV+N:
   ERGATIVE

2 If a river, lake, or well **dries up**, it becomes empty of water,   V+ADV
usually because of hot weather or lack of rain. EG *In the dry season*
these wells dry up and water has to be bought from vendors... On
Wednesday, his goldfish pond dried up in mysterious circumstances.

▶ A **dried-up** river or lake is completely empty of water. EG *...dried-*   ADJECTIVE
up river-beds.

3 When you **dry up** or **dry up** the dishes after they have been   V+ADV+N,
washed, you wipe the water off them with a cloth. EG *I started to dry*   V+N+ADV,
up a cup rather slowly... If you use two washing up racks, you rarely   V+PRON+ADV,
need to dry up. ▶ **Drying-up** or the **drying-up** is the job of drying   V+ADV
dishes and cutlery after they have been washed; also used to refer to   N UNCOUNT,
the things that need to be dried. EG *We helped with the drying-up in a*   N SING
thoughtful silence... I can't come yet, I've got all this drying up to do.

4 If you **dry up** when you are speaking, you stop in the middle of   V+ADV
what you were saying because you cannot think what to say next. EG
Halfway through the speech she dried up completely... We did a new
play every week and we all used to dry up and make mistakes.

5 If something **dries up**, it stops being productive. EG *They had not*   V+ADV
contemplated the possibility of supplies drying up... They found their
business drying up and were finally forced to close... The market for
luxury goods dried up during the recession. ● **Fail** means almost the
same as **dry up.**

6 If you say '**dry up**' to someone, you are telling them in a rather   IMPERATIVE:
   V+ADV

rude way to stop talking and be quiet. ● **Shut up** and **belt up** mean almost the same as **dry up**.

7 Someone who is **dried-up** looks old, small, wrinkled, and perhaps bad-tempered. EG *...a sour, dried-up man with gold-rimmed spectacles.* ● **Wizened** and **withered** mean almost the same as **dried-up**.

ADJECTIVE

dub, dubs, dubbing, dubbed

dub in. When film-makers **dub in** a voice, they use the recorded voice of one actor in place of the voice of the actor who appears on the film. EG *Later on, probably, a different voice will be dubbed in.*

V+N+ADV,
V+PRON+ADV,
V+ADV+N

dub into. If a film **is dubbed into** another language, the sound is replaced by a different recording so that the actors appear to be speaking in a different language. EG *Hawaii-five-O sells in forty-seven countries and is dubbed into seven languages.*

V+N+PREP,
V+PRON+PREP:
USUALLY PASSIVE

dub over. When a sound **is dubbed over** a film, a different recording is used so that the sound is not the original one. EG *Many sequences showed wounded prisoners pleading, whether genuinely or with false voices dubbed over, for peace.*

PASSIVE:
V+ADV,
V+PREP

duck, ducks, ducking, ducked

duck out. If you **duck out** of something that you are supposed to do, you avoid doing it; an informal expression. EG *He ducked out of an appointment as aide to a General... They are used by adults to duck out of their responsibilities... He got her into this mess in the first place and is now ducking out without providing her with essential support.* ● **Back out** means almost the same as **duck out**.

V+ADV:
USUALLY+*of*

duff, duffs, duffing, duffed

duff up. To **duff** someone **up** means to hit and kick them in order to injure them; an informal expression used in British English. EG *Well, I put the boot in and duffed him up... He would have liked to have duffed up half the people in the club.* ● **Beat up** and **do over** mean almost the same as **duff up**.

V+PRON+ADV,
V+ADV+N,
V+N+ADV

dummy, dummies, dummying, dummied

dummy up. If someone **dummies up**, they keep a secret by pretending not to know anything about it when they are asked; an informal expression. EG *I dummied up, and I believe the police approved of this.*

V+ADV

dump, dumps, dumping, dumped

dump on. If you **dump on** someone or something, you treat them unfairly, for example by criticizing them too severely or giving them unpleasant tasks to do. EG *You let people dump on you... I could dump on my home town, but no outsider had better try... Housework and child-rearing were being roundly dumped on... White House officials thought it best not to dump on him gratuitously.*

V+PREP:
HAS PASSIVE

dust, dusts, dusting, dusted

dust down. If you **dust** something **down**, you remove dust from it with a brush or dry cloth. EG *Dust down the walls and wipe paintwork thoroughly before starting... ...the distracted mother, dusting down the frills and trimmings.*

V+ADV+N,
V+PRON+ADV,
V+N+ADV

dust off. If you **dust off** your clothes or your hands, you brush the dust from them. EG *'What a mess!' she said dusting off her hands... He dusts off his trousers and gets in the car.*

V+ADV+N,
V+N+ADV,
V+PRON+ADV

dwell, dwells, dwelling, dwelled/dwelt

dwell on. If you **dwell on** or **upon** something, you think or speak about it a great deal. EG *Accept the pleasures of past experiences*

V+PREP

without dwelling upon the miseries... People are reluctant to dwell on the subject of death.

dwell upon. See dwell on: dwell upon is more formal.

E e

earmark, earmarks, earmarking, earmarked

earmark for. If sums of money or other resources **are earmarked for** a purpose, people in authority have decided that they should be used for that purpose. EG *At least $100,000 in CRP's budget was earmarked for 'Convention Security'... Two sites have been earmarked for industrial use... Some satellites are already earmarked for person-to-person calls.*

V+N+PREP,
V+PRON+PREP:
USUALLY PASSIVE

earth, earths, earthing, earthed

earth up. If you **earth up** vegetables or plants, you pile more soil around them in order to protect their roots or to encourage the roots to grow. EG *I went and earthed up my celery... ...planted by dropping them straight onto muck, then earthing them up... We didn't earth the clumps up until later in the year.*

V+ADV+N,
V+PRON+ADV,
V+N+ADV

ease, eases, easing, eased

ease off. 1 If something **eases off,** it becomes slower or less intense. EG *The pace of our activity gradually eased off... The headaches eased off and mum decided she had better continue her treatment... The rain had eased off.*

V+ADV

2 If you **ease off** clothes that you are wearing, you take them off carefully and gently. EG *She bent down and eased off her shoes... We got him onto a couch and I eased off his right boot... She took hold of the bandage and eased it off.*

V+ADV+N,
V+PRON+ADV,
V+N+ADV:
NO PASSIVE

ease up. If you **ease up,** you stop putting so much energy or effort into what you are doing. EG *You're working too hard and need to ease up... We aren't going to ease up—we are going to increase the pressure.* ● **Slow down** means almost the same as **ease up.**

V+ADV

eat, eats, eating, ate, eaten

eat away. 1 If an animal **eats** something **away,** it eats it gradually and partially destroys it. EG *...who let cockroaches and rats eat away his walls without lifting a hand to preserve his property... I feel as if worms are eating away my brain.*

V+ADV+N,
V+N+ADV,
V+PRON+ADV

2 If something **is eaten away** by water or chemicals, it is gradually destroyed by the physical force of the water or the action of the chemicals. EG *...a sandbank that was already eaten away by the advancing water... ...such chrome as had not yet been eaten away by rust... As the rain fell, water rushed down every gully, eating away the road... He watches the crumbling walls while the waves eat them away.*

V+ADV+N,
V+N+ADV,
V+PRON+ADV:
USUALLY PASSIVE

3 If a disease or a feeling **eats** someone **away,** it causes them physical or mental harm. EG *You have this cancer inside you eating you away.*

V+PRON+ADV,
V+N+ADV

eat away at. 1 If water or chemicals **eat away at** something solid, they gradually destroy it. EG *...rivulets eating away at the foundations.*

V+ADV+PREP

2 To **eat away at** someone's hopes, aims, or feelings means to

V+ADV+PREP

gradually destroy or weaken them. EG *Inflation eats away at any advantage which might have been gained by lower-paid workers... She eats away at their resolve... Corruption eats away at the foundations of trust between people.* ● **Undermine** means almost the same as **eat away at.**

eat in. When you **eat in,** you have a meal at home rather than going out to a restaurant. EG *'We won't be eating in tonight,' Shoshana said.* ● **Eat out** means the opposite of **eat in.**   V+ADV

eat into. 1 If something **eats into** a part of your body, it presses or pokes hard into it and may cause you pain. EG *He could see where the stockings ended and the garters ate into the flesh... There was a nail eating into his toe.*   V+PREP

2 If a chemical or a chemical process **eats into** a physical object, it affects the object and gradually destroys it. EG *Iron pans are not suitable as vinegar eats into them.*   V+PREP

3 If something **eats into** resources such as money or land, it gradually uses more of them than was expected. EG *Repayment of past loans has been eating increasingly into aid transfers.* ● **Encroach on** means almost the same as **eat into.**   V+PREP

4 If a feeling or an event **eats into** you, it upsets you deeply and you cannot forget about it. EG *That laughter constantly rang in his ears and ate into him... The problems ate into all their affections.*   V+PREP

eat out. 1 When you **eat out,** you have a meal at a restaurant instead of at home. EG *Do you eat out a lot in London?... Willie liked to eat out in restaurants and stay up late in bars.* ● **Eat in** means the opposite of **eat out.** ▸ **Eating out** is the activity of having a meal in a restaurant. EG *Eating out was beyond their means.*   V+ADV

N UNCOUNT

2 If an area or a crop **is eaten out,** all the plants there have been eaten by animals. EG *The country was ruined. Broken. Eaten out by cattle... Many of the plants they favour become eaten out.*   PASSIVE: V+ADV

eat up. 1 If people or animals **eat up** food, they eat all the food that they have been given or all that is available. EG *If you eat up all your cereal, I'll give you a piece of chocolate... ...if your animals stray away and eat up the crops growing in another man's field... She sat on my bed and made me eat it all up.* ● **Polish off** is a more informal expression for **eat up.**   V+ADV+N, V+PRON+ADV, V+N+ADV

2 If you say **'Eat up'** to someone, you are encouraging them to eat as much as they can and to enjoy their food. EG *He also took a strange pleasure in watching me eat. 'Eat up, girl, that's it,' he would say.*   IMPERATIVE: V+ADV

3 If water or chemicals **eat up** something, they destroy it gradually, by physical force or by a chemical process. EG *Nothing at all would be left to stop the wind and the rain eating up the land... The beautiful islands were eaten up by sand and erosion.*   V+ADV+N, V+PRON+ADV, V+N+ADV

4 If you **are eaten up** by a negative feeling, you feel it very deeply and you cannot stop yourself from feeling it. EG *Many of the older country folk are eaten up with jealousy of the young... It's what we all do, shamelessly, when we're eaten up by suspicion... Cynicism was his stock in trade, but now it seemed to be eating him up.* ● **Consume** is a more formal word for **eat up.**   V+ADV+N, V+N+ADV, V+PRON+ADV: USUALLY PASSIVE

5 If something **eats up** money, time, or other resources, it gradually uses the entire amount that is available. EG *Gambling had eaten up his fortune... Housing estates were eating up good agricultural land.*   V+ADV+N, V+PRON+ADV, V+N+ADV

ebb, ebbs, ebbing, ebbed

ebb away. If a feeling or your strength **ebbs away,** it gradually becomes weaker until it disappears completely. EG *Their rage ebbed away, to be replaced by fear... Their confidence in him seems to be ebbing away.*   V+ADV

edit, edits, editing, edited

edit out. If you **edit out** parts of a film or a piece of writing, you remove them because they are not necessary or because they might offend some people. EG *They'll have to edit all the names out... 'Don't worry, Irv,' said Middleton. 'We can edit that out.'*

V+N+ADV,
V+PRON+ADV,
V+ADV+N

egg, eggs, egging, egged

egg on. If you **egg** someone **on**, you encourage them to do something foolish or daring. EG *Some egged him on, while the more sober did their best to lead him away... Egged on by Iago, Othello makes up his mind to kill Desdemona.*

V+PRON+ADV,
V+N+ADV,
V+ADV+N

eke, ekes, eking, eked

eke out. 1 If you **eke** something **out**, you make it last as long as possible, by using it carefully. EG *Migrants send home cash that helps eke out low village incomes... ...eking out rations and fuel and quietly waiting to die... ...a whole packet and not just the halves we've been using to eke it out.*

V+ADV+N,
V+PRON+ADV,
V+N+ADV:
NO PASSIVE

2 If you **eke out** a living or an existence, you obtain with difficulty the food or money that you need in order to live. EG *...people trying to eke out a living in forest areas... She eked out a poor existence by boiling and selling toffee.*

V+ADV+N:
NO PASSIVE

elaborate, elaborates, elaborating, elaborated

elaborate on. If you **elaborate on** or **upon** something already mentioned, you give more details about it or explain it more clearly. EG *Cook confirmed what Mr Cowie had said, and elaborated on it... ...a myth which was gleefully elaborated upon by several generations of science-fiction writers.*

V+PREP:
HAS PASSIVE

elaborate upon. See elaborate on: **elaborate upon** is more formal.

emanate, emanates, emanating, emanated

emanate from. If something **emanates from** a particular person or thing, they started it or caused it; a formal expression. EG *These ideas are said to emanate from Henry Kissinger... A dim glow of light still emanated from the room.*

V+PREP

embark, embarks, embarking, embarked

embark on. 1 If you **embark on** or **upon** something new, difficult, or exciting, you start doing it. EG *Peru embarked on a massive programme of reform... ...to embark upon a new translation of the Bible.*

V+PREP:
HAS PASSIVE

2 If you **are embarked on** or **upon** a course of action, you have already started doing it. EG *We are already embarked on a course which might have quite sweeping consequences... We knew that you were embarked upon some more special undertaking.*

PASSIVE:
V+PREP

embark upon. See embark on: **embark upon** is more formal.

embroider, embroiders, embroidering, embroidered

embroider on. If you **embroider on** a story or account, you add details to it from your imagination in order to try and make it more interesting. EG *Other ancient writers have embroidered on these early reports.* ● **Embellish** is a more formal word for **embroider on.**

V+PREP:
HAS PASSIVE

empty, empties, emptying, emptied

empty out. If you **empty out** a container, or **empty** something **out** of it, you remove the contents from it. EG *They emptied out their sacks... We'd take his pipe and empty out the tobacco... You ought to empty the water out of those boots... I took the bag and emptied it out on the bed.*

V+ADV+N,
V+N+ADV,
V+PRON+ADV

encroach, encroaches, encroaching, encroached

encroach on. 1 To **encroach on** or **upon** something means to change it gradually by taking away parts of it, or by taking more and more of it; a formal use which shows disapproval. EG *This new law doesn't encroach on the rights of the citizen... The Populists saw the village as a natural society upon which capitalism was encroaching.*

V+PREP:
HAS PASSIVE

2 If someone or something **encroaches on** or **upon** an area of land, they gradually occupy more and more of it. EG *The invading army were encroaching on national territory... ...tropical countries where the forest is being encroached upon.*

V+PREP:
HAS PASSIVE

encroach upon. See encroach on.

end, ends, ending, ended

end up. 1 If you **end up** in a particular place or situation, you are in that place or situation after a series of events, even though you did not originally intend to be. EG *Many of their friends and neighbours have ended up in prison for terrorist activities... Sylvia ended up with no money, no husband and no house and a two-year-old child... If we go on in this way, we shall end up with millions and millions of unemployed.* ● **Wind up** and **finish up** mean almost the same as **end up.**

V+ADV:
WITH A

2 If you **end up** doing something after a period of time, you do it even though you did not originally intend to. EG *We ended up taking a taxi there... We always end up arguing.* ● **Finish up** means almost the same as **end up.**

V+ADV:
WITH -ING

endow, endows, endowing, endowed

endow with. If someone or something **is endowed with** a particular quality or talent, they have it or are given it; a fairly formal expression. EG *Nature has endowed the Cobra Lily with the means of catching its own food... ...a man endowed with great leadership talents.*

V+N+PREP,
V+PRON+PREP:
USUALLY PASSIVE

engage, engages, engaging, engaged

engage in. If you **engage in** an activity, you take part in it. If you **are engaged in** it, you are involved in it. EG *It was considered inappropriate for a former President to engage in commerce... Often he would engage in conversation with complete strangers.*

V+PREP

engage on. If you **are engaged on** or **upon** an activity, you are doing it. EG *Accountants engaged on this kind of work rarely have expense accounts... We would just like to know what you're engaged on at the moment... The artist engaged upon a quest for the 'essence' of painting.*

PASSIVE:
V+PREP

engage upon. See engage on.

enlarge, enlarges, enlarging, enlarged

enlarge on. If you **enlarge on** or **upon** a subject, you give more details about it; a formal expression. EG *This thought has only just occurred to me—I can't enlarge on it!... I went on to enlarge upon the difficulties of naming a cat.* ● **Expand on** means almost the same as **enlarge on.**

V+PREP:
HAS PASSIVE

enlarge upon. See enlarge on.

enquire, enquires, enquiring, enquired

Enquire is another spelling of **inquire.**

enter, enters, entering, entered

enter for. If you **enter for** a competition, race, or examination, or if someone enters you **for** it, you take part in it. EG *She fully intends to*

V+PREP,
V+N+PREP,
V+PRON+PREP:
ERGATIVE

enter for it... At least four Republicans are officially entered for the race.

enter into. 1 If you **enter into** an agreement or arrangement, you take part in it. EG *The company had entered into unprofitable contracts... ...a suicide pact entered into by the mother's sister and her husband... ...young people who enter into a trial marriage.*

V+PREP:
HAS PASSIVE

2 If you **enter into** a discussion with someone, you start it or become involved in it. EG *The Labour Government refused to enter into negotiations... Airlines found it cheaper to pay up rather than enter into a prolonged dispute... No correspondence will be entered into.*

V+PREP:
HAS PASSIVE

3 If something **enters into** something else, it affects it and is an important factor in it. EG *All sorts of emotional factors enter into the relationship... Repression enters into every aspect of human life.*

V+PREP

enter on. See **enter upon.**

enter upon. When you **enter upon** or **on** something, you start to do it; a rather formal expression. EG *Brandt entered upon this new policy in the 1960s... She knew she had entered upon her sentence of life imprisonment.* ● **Embark on** means almost the same as **enter upon.**

V+PREP:
HAS PASSIVE

enthuse, enthuses, enthusing, enthused

enthuse over. If you **enthuse over** something, you talk about it in a way that shows that you are excited and pleased about it. EG *She was enthusing over something that had caught her eye... ...enthusing over a weekend spent in the Lake District... ...a piece of good fortune that could not be enthused over enough.*

V+PREP:
HAS PASSIVE

erode, erodes, eroding, eroded

erode away. 1 If rock or soil **is eroded away** or if it **erodes away,** wind, water, or the weather causes it to crumble and break, and eventually disappear. EG *The central pueblo there has eroded away to little more than a circular wall... The deposits that had accumulated on the mountainside were eroded away.* ● **Wear away** means almost the same as **erode away.**

V+ADV,
OR PASSIVE,
V+ADV:
ERGATIVE

2 If someone's power, authority, or freedom **erodes away** or **is eroded away,** it gradually becomes weaker until it is no longer significant. EG *You would think colonialism of this kind would have eroded away... Our sovereign right to legislate has been eroded away.*

V+ADV,
OR PASSIVE,
V+ADV:
ERGATIVE

even, evens, evening, evened

even out. If you **even** something **out** or if it **evens out,** its distribution becomes more equal because some of it moves from one place to another. EG *In Asia, irrigation systems help to even out the supply of water over the growing season... No amount of 'social engineering' will even out the world's unfairness.* ● **Balance out** means almost the same as **even out.**

V+ADV+N,
V+N+ADV,
V+PRON+ADV,
V+ADV:
ERGATIVE

even up. To **even up** a game or competition means to make it more equally balanced than it was, by making the weaker side stronger than it was, or by making the stronger side weaker than it was. EG *Frank and I will change sides. That should even things up a bit... The straight answer to unequal competition is to even up access to capital and government services for all levels of producer.* ● **Balance** means almost the same as **even up.**

V+N+ADV,
V+PRON+ADV,
V+ADV+N

expand, expands, expanding, expanded

expand on. If you **expand on** or **upon** a topic you have already mentioned, you give more information or details about it. EG *I went on to expand upon this theme... This highly relevant observation is*

V+PREP:
HAS PASSIVE

expanded on by Dr. White. ● **Enlarge on** means almost the same as **expand on.**

expand upon. See expand on: **expand upon** is more formal.

explain, explains, explaining, explained

explain away. If you **explain** away a mistake or unpleasant situation, you give reasons to show that it is not as bad or important as people think. EG *Mr Stewart tried to explain away the Police interest in Waddell... There is a difference, but I cannot really explain it away... All this can, of course, be explained away for other reasons.* ● **Excuse** means almost the same as **explain away.**

V+ADV+N,
V+PRON+ADV,
V+N+ADV

eye, eyes, eyeing, eyed

eye up. If someone **eyes** you **up,** they look at you carefully because they find you sexually attractive; an informal expression. EG *I made tea while she sat there eyeing me up... ...eyeing up the girl in the corner.* ● **Ogle** means almost the same as **eye up.**

V+PRON+ADV,
V+N+ADV,
V+ADV+N

F f

face, faces, facing, faced

face about. If you **face about,** you turn so that you are looking in the opposite direction. EG *She walked backwards a couple of steps, and then faced about, and walked toward me.*

V+ADV

face down. In a situation of conflict or disagreement, if you **face** someone **down,** you gain the advantage by acting confidently and looking at them boldly; used in American English. EG *She was intent on facing down the terrorists.*

V+ADV+N,
V+PRON+ADV,
V+N+ADV

face out. If you **face out** a difficult situation, you deal with it by behaving firmly or defiantly; used in British English. EG *We'll just have to face this crisis out.* ● **See through** means almost the same as **face out.**

V+ADV+N,
V+N+ADV,
V+PRON+ADV

face up to. If you **face up to** a difficult situation, you accept it and deal with it. EG *We may as well face up to the fact that it isn't going to work... His situation was desperate, but he faced up to it... Issues like these simply cannot be ignored; the problems have to be faced up to.*

V+ADV+PREP:
HAS PASSIVE

fade, fades, fading, faded

fade away. 1 If something **fades away,** it slowly becomes less intense, frequent or common until it ends or disappears completely. EG *The sun's warmth began to fade away... Your new-found enthusiasm for running will soon fade away... ...a vague rumour which would fade away and be forgotten.*

V+ADV

2 If a sound or sight **fades away,** it gradually becomes quieter or less easy to see and eventually disappears. EG *On the right were the hills fading away into the misty morning... The music and laughter gradually faded away as the procession moved off down the street.* ● **Recede** is a more formal word for **fade away.**

V+ADV

3 If someone **fades away,** they become weaker and die. EG *He was fading quietly away day by day... She'd fade away and die.*

V+ADV

fade in. To **fade in** or **fade up** a picture or sound on television, film, record or radio means to introduce it gradually and make it brighter

V+ADV+N,
V+PRON+ADV,
V+N+ADV

or louder until people can see it or hear it properly; a technical expression.

fade out. 1 If something **fades out**, it slowly becomes less intense, frequent or common until it ends or disappears completely. EG *This sort of protest tends to fade out... Childhood diseases tend to fade out as the child reaches adolescence.* ● **Fizzle out** means almost the same as **fade out**.   V+ADV

2 When a sound or radio signal **fades out,** it slowly becomes less loud or strong until you can no longer hear it or receive it. EG *The sound of the chopper had faded out.*   V+ADV

3 To **fade out** a picture or sound on television, film, record or radio means to make it disappear gradually; a technical use.   V+ADV+N, V+PRON+ADV, V+N+ADV

fade up. See fade in.

faff, faffs, faffing, faffed

faff about. If someone is **faffing about** or **around,** they are doing unnecessary things in a fussy or disorganized way and not really achieving very much; used in informal British English.   V+ADV

faff around. See faff about.

fag, fags, fagging, fagged

fag out. If something **fags** you **out,** it makes you feel tired and exhausted; an informal expression used in British English. EG *That last game really fagged me out!* ● **Wear out** is a less informal expression for **fag out.** ▷ If you are **fagged out,** you feel tired and exhausted; an informal expression used in British English.   V+PRON+ADV, V+REFL+ADV, V+N+ADV   ADJECTIVE

fall, falls, falling, fell, fallen

fall about. If you say that people **are falling about,** you mean that they are laughing uncontrollably; an informal expression. EG *When we complained, they fell about laughing.*   V+ADV

fall apart. 1 If something **falls apart,** it breaks into pieces, usually because it is weak, old, or badly made. EG *...clothing which lasts a little while and then falls apart... ...a flimsy shack that was falling apart.* ● **Disintegrate** is a more formal word for **fall apart.**   V+ADV

2 If an organization, system or relationship **falls apart,** it no longer works effectively and eventually fails or ends completely. EG *The conference was to have taken place in 1932, but it fell apart when France and Italy refused to participate... Their marriage began to fall apart.* ● **Collapse** means almost the same as **fall apart.**   V+ADV

3 If someone **is falling apart,** they are unable to think or behave normally and calmly because they are in such a difficult or unpleasant situation; an informal use. EG *It was something to do, it kept you from falling apart.* ● **Crack up** means almost the same as **fall apart.**   V+ADV

fall away. 1 If something **falls away,** it breaks off from the surface that it was attached to. EG *Patches of plaster had fallen away between the windows... The bark was curling and falling away... The rock fell away and exposed the skeletons.* ● **Fall off** means almost the same as **fall away.**   V+ADV: USUALLY+PREP

2 Where land **falls away,** it slopes gently downwards. EG *I got to the ridge expecting to see a gentle slope falling away in front of me... A long field that fell away from the house towards thick woods.*   V+ADV: USUALLY+PREP

3 If an unpleasant quality or a difficulty **falls away,** it disappears and no longer affects you; a literary use. EG *His film star affectations had fallen away... All practical difficulties fell away.*   V+ADV

4 If the degree, amount, or strength of something **falls away,** it becomes less or smaller. EG *During the general strike, the party's membership fell away... Student support fell away.* ● **Fall off** means almost the same as **fall away.**   V+ADV

5 If a sound **falls away**, it gradually becomes quieter until you can   V+ADV
no longer hear it. EG *The drone of the engine falls away again... His
voice fell away and I couldn't catch his next few words.* ● **Die away**
and **fade away** mean almost the same as **fall away**.

fall back. 1 If an army **falls back** during a battle or war, it retreats.   V+ADV
EG *They fell back in confusion, surprised by the direction of attack.*

2 If you **fall back**, you suddenly move backwards away from   V+ADV:
someone or something because they have upset or frightened you.   ALSO+*in*
EG *I watched him fall back in horror... He fell back with a scream.*
● **Recoil** is a more formal word for **fall back**.

fall back on. If you **fall back on** or **upon** something that you know   V+ADV+PREP
you can rely on, you use it or do it when other things have failed. EG
*We have a written script to fall back on if we run out of things to
discuss... He invariably falls back on sentimental clichés about
peace and love... Teachers fall back upon authority.* ● **Resort to**
means almost the same as **fall back on.** ▸ A **fall-back** method, plan,   ADJECTIVE
or system, is one which you have in case the first method, plan, or
system you use is unsatisfactory or fails to work. EG *...the fall-back
proposals of his opponents.* ● **Back-up** means almost the same as
fall-back.

fall back upon. See **fall back on.**

fall behind. 1 If you **fall behind** when moving with a group of   V+ADV,
people, you move more slowly than them, so they get ahead of you.   V+PREP
EG *He began to limp and fell so far behind that I decided to let him
rest... Don't fall behind the leaders or you'll never catch up.* ● **Lag
behind** means almost the same as **fall behind.**

2 If someone or something **falls behind**, they do not achieve the   V+ADV,
standard that is expected of them or that is achieved by similar   V+PREP
people or things. EG *...children who fall behind with their reading...
Vicars' salaries have fallen behind those of many of the laity.*

3 If you **fall behind** with something that you have to do by a certain   V+ADV:
time, you fail to do it and gradually get later and later with it. EG *The*   ALSO+*with*
*programme had fallen so far behind that there was little chance of
meeting the deadline... Unfortunately, we have fallen behind with
the payments.*

fall down. 1 If someone or something **falls down** when they have   V+ADV,
been in an upright or standing position, they become unbalanced   V+PREP
and drop to the ground. EG *He tripped and fell down... The pile of
hymn books fell down and scattered all over the floor... I remember
him falling down the cellar steps.*

2 If something such as a building or bridge **falls down**, it collapses   V+ADV
and breaks into pieces because it is old, weak, or damaged. EG *That
shelter might fall down if the rain comes back... ...a one room
wooden shack, part of which fell down while I was there.*

3 If a building **is falling down**, it is in very bad condition and may   V+ADV
collapse. EG *The house was cheap because it was falling down.*

4 If something such as an argument, idea, or method **falls down**, it   V+ADV
has a weakness in it which is likely to make it fail. EG *In one area
only did the comparison fall down... This is where a lot of teachers
fall down.*

5 The **downfall** of a successful or powerful institution or person is   N UNCOUNT
their failure or ruin. EG *...the downfall of a dictator.* ▸ Something that   N UNCOUNT
is the **downfall** of a particular person or thing is the thing that
causes the person or thing to be ruined or to fail. EG *Bad publicity
was our downfall.*

fall for. 1 If you **fall for** someone or something, you are attracted   V+PREP
towards them and like them very much. EG *He fell for her the*

*moment he set eyes on her... I bought it yesterday, falling for it
because it was extremely simple.*

2 If you **fall for** something that is not true, you are tricked into   v+PREP
believing it. EG *It was a stupid trick and I fell for it... The working
class were not going to fall for this one.*

fall in. 1 If a roof or ceiling **falls in,** it collapses and falls to the   v+ADV
ground. ● **Cave in** means almost the same as **fall in.**

2 If soldiers, scouts, or other people in a procession **fall in,** they get   v+ADV:
into a line one behind the other. EG *Pick up your gear and fall in... As   ALSO+behind
he began to march around the lawn, people fell in behind him.* ● **Fall
out** means the opposite of **fall in.**

fall into. 1 If something or someone **falls into** a particular state,   v+PREP
they begin to be in that state. EG *The practice had fallen into disuse
and been forgotten... He fell into disfavour with his superiors... She
fell into debt.*

2 If you **fall into** an activity or way of behaving, you start to do it,   v+PREP
often without intending to. EG *His colleagues refused to support him
and fell into disagreements with the union leadership... We fell into
fits of hysteria at each other's antics.*

3 If something **falls into** a particular group or category, it is   v+PREP
classified as belonging to that group or category. EG *The main thesis
of the book was that human beings fall into two opposing types... My
work really falls into three parts.*

fall in with. 1 If you **fall in with** an existing idea, plan or system,   v+ADV+PREP
you accept it and do not try to change it. EG *I didn't know whether to
fall in with this arrangement... Instead of challenging the lie she
falls in with it.* ● **Go along with** means almost the same as **fall in
with.**

2 If you **fall in with** someone, you meet them by chance and often   v+ADV+PREP
become friends with them. EG *He had the luck to fall in with the
American humorist, Tom Lehrer.*

fall off. 1 If something **falls off,** it separates from the thing to which   v+ADV,
it was attached. EG *Their scales fall off and the fish die... Some rotten   v+PREP
apples fall off the bough.* ● **Drop off** means almost the same as **fall
off.**

2 If the degree, amount, or standard of something **falls off,** it   v+ADV
becomes less or lower. EG *The flow of western capital is falling off
just when it is most needed... We knew that the numbers of overseas
students would fall off drastically... Economic growth will fall off
only slightly.* ● **Drop** means almost the same as **fall off.** ▶ If there is   N SING
a **falling-off** of something, there is a decrease in the degree or
intensity of it. EG *There was a definite falling-off of active interest... A
falling-off in business was expected.*

fall on. 1 If a responsibility or duty **falls on** or **upon** someone, it   v+PREP
becomes their responsibility or duty. EG *It would fall on her to make
the final decision... Without a producer, the weight of responsibility
fell upon me.* ● **Fall to** means almost the same as **fall on.**

2 If something unpleasant **falls on** or **upon** someone, it happens to   v+PREP
them; a literary use. EG *All of these ills have fallen upon us.* ● **Befall**
means almost the same as **fall on.**

3 If someone **falls on** you, they hug you eagerly because they are   v+PREP
very happy or excited. EG *People were falling on each other in
delight and tears.*

4 If someone **falls on** or **upon** you, they attack you suddenly and   v+PREP
violently. EG *Terrorist groups were falling indiscriminately upon
men and women in the street.* ● **Set upon** means almost the same as
fall on.

5 If your eyes **fall on** or **upon** someone or something, you see or   v+PREP

notice them. EG *His gaze fell on a small white bundle... His eyes fell on Laing, who was hunched in a corner.*

6 If a date **falls on** a certain day of the week, it occurs on that day. EG *My birthday falls on a Thursday this year.* V+PREP

fall out. 1 If something **falls out** of a container, it leaves the container and drops towards the ground. EG *...tobacco cans falling out of the cupboard... He had to cling to Melanie to avoid falling out.* V+ADV: ALSO+of

2 If something such as hair or a tooth **falls out,** it becomes loose and separates from your body. EG *After about two weeks, your hair starts to fall out... ...baby teeth which get loose and then fall out.* V+ADV

3 If you **fall out** with someone, you have an argument and are no longer friendly with them. EG *I've fallen out with certain members of the band... Everybody stands to lose if the partners fall out... Fancy falling out over something as trivial as that!* V+ADV, V+ADV+with: RECIPROCAL

4 When soldiers or people in a parade or formation **fall out,** they leave their positions and the formation is broken up. ● **Fall in** means the opposite of **fall out.** V+ADV

5 **Fallout** is the radiation that affects a particular place or area after a nuclear explosion has taken place. EG *Exposure to radioactive fallout would be much worse than previously anticipated.* N UNCOUNT

fall over. 1 If someone or something that is standing **falls over,** they become unbalanced and end up lying on the ground. EG *He pushed back his chair so hard that it fell over... 'Look at me!' He pretended to fall over... He nearly fell over an old lady in a wheelchair.* ● **Topple over** means almost the same as **fall over.** V+ADV, V+PREP

2 If people **are falling over** themselves to do something, they are very eager to do it; an informal use. EG *Of course, they were all falling over to serve us... Governments were falling over each other to win these valuable contracts.* V+ADV, V+PREP+REFL, V+PREP

fall through. If an arrangement or plan **falls through,** something goes wrong before it can be completed and it has to be abandoned. EG *We arranged to book a villa and it fell through... Any number of things could lead to a sale falling through.* V+ADV

fall to. 1 If a responsibility or duty **falls to** someone, it becomes their responsibility or duty. EG *That task fell to Mrs Isabel Travers... It fell to Philip Crow to act the part of host.* ● **Fall on** means almost the same as **fall to.** V+PREP

2 If someone **falls to** doing something, they start doing it; a literary or old-fashioned use. EG *The party fell instead to blaming the voters... I fell to musing on the revolution.* V+PREP: USUALLY+-ING

fall under. If something **falls under** a particular category, it belongs in that category. EG *'Portrait of an Artist' falls under autobiography, not fiction.* V+PREP

fall upon. See fall on: **fall upon** is more formal.

fan, fans, fanning, fanned

fan out. 1 If a group of people or things **fan out,** they move forwards together from the same point and gradually spread farther away from each other. EG *The five of us fanned out at intervals of not more than fifteen feet.* V+ADV

2 If something **fans out,** or if it **is fanned out,** it has or forms a shape which is narrow at one end and wide at the other. EG *They were already waiting where the little valley fanned out into the savannah... The birds lay with their wings fanned out and their beaks open.* V+ADV, V+ADV+N, V+N+ADV, V+PRON+ADV: ERGATIVE

farm, farms, farming, farmed

farm out. If you **farm out** something that is your responsibility, you send it to other people for them to deal with or look after. EG *Many* V+ADV+N, V+N+ADV, V+PRON+ADV

European businesses found it satisfactory to farm out big clerical
jobs to London agencies... She may have farmed the child out in
order to remarry.

fart, farts, farting, farted

Fart is a rude word used mainly in very informal British English.

fart about. If someone is farting about or around, they are wasting
time doing silly things instead of doing what needs to be done.
● Mess about is a less rude expression for fart about. `V+ADV`

fart around. See fart about.

fasten, fastens, fastening, fastened

fasten on. 1 If you fasten on to something or fasten your attention
on or upon it, you concentrate all your attention or efforts on it. EG
Once she had fastened on to a scheme she did not let go... Your
attention is fastened on that... They cannot fasten on profit as the
only object of their work... Such goods are fastened on as symbols of
high status... His mind fastened upon it now: escape. ● Latch on to
means almost the same as fasten on. `V+ADV+to, V+N+PREP: ALSO V+PREP, HAS PASSIVE`

2 If someone fastens on to you, they keep following you or wanting
to be with you when you want them to go away. EG The doctor had
fastened on to an official of the Yugoslav embassy. `V+ADV+to`

fasten up. If you fasten something up, you close it using buttons,
straps, and so on. EG Fasten your coat up. ● Do up means almost the
same as fasten up. `V+N+ADV, V+PRON+ADV, V+ADV+N`

fasten upon. See fasten on.

fathom, fathoms, fathoming, fathomed

fathom out. If you fathom something out, you eventually understand it as a result of thinking carefully about it. EG What I can't
fathom out is why he did it. ● Work out means almost the same as
fathom out. `V+ADV+N, V+N+ADV, V+PRON+ADV`

fatten, fattens, fattening, fattened

fatten up. If you fatten up an animal, you give it a lot of food so that
it reaches the weight that you want it to be. EG They take twice as
long to fatten up as European cattle. `V+ADV+N, V+N+ADV, V+PRON+ADV`

fear, fears, fearing, feared

fear for. If you fear for someone or something, you are very
worried that they might be in danger. EG Morris began to fear for the
life of Mrs Reilly... She feared for her daughters. `V+PREP`

feed, feeds, feeding, fed

feed off. See feed on.

feed on. If an idea, feeling, system or process feeds on or off
something, it continues to exist or grow because of that thing. EG
Creativity and curiosity are part of the same thing, they feed on
each other... Art feeds off life. `V+PREP`

feed up. 1 Someone who is fed up is unhappy, bored, or tired of
something. EG I should think they're getting pretty fed up with him
by now... You sound a bit fed up. `ADJECTIVE`

2 If you feed up an animal, child, or invalid, you give them plenty of
nourishing food to eat in order to make them strong and healthy. EG
It costs 18,000 soles to feed up a heifer or bullock into a saleable two-
year old... 'She can have her baby here. Harriet'll feed her up, won't
you Harriet?' ● Build up means almost the same as feed up. `V+ADV+N, V+N+ADV, V+PRON+ADV`

feel, feels, feeling, felt

feel for. If you feel for someone who has a problem or is upset, you `V+PREP` have sympathy for them. EG *Boy, I feel for you guys.* ● **Sympathize with** means almost the same as **feel for.**

feel out. If you **feel** someone **out,** you carefully try to discover their opinions, attitudes, or ideas, without asking them directly; a rather informal expression. EG *We felt him out, he wasn't willing.* ● **Sound out** means almost the same as **feel out.**

V+PRON+ADV,
V+N+ADV

feel up. To **feel up** someone means to touch their body in order to gain sexual excitement. ● **Touch up** means almost the same as **feel up.**

V+PRON+ADV,
V+N+ADV,
V+ADV+N'

feel up to. If you **feel up to** doing something, you feel physically and mentally able to do it. EG *'I just hope I feel up to eating,' said Dr Cox... I require an assistant. Feeling up to it now?... We set out for a climb that I don't think any of us felt up to.*

V+ADV+PREP

fence, fences, fencing, fenced

fence in. If something **is fenced in,** it is surrounded by a fence. EG *...a sloping area which is fenced in by iron railings... My little vegetable garden was fenced in with wire mesh.*

V+N+ADV,
V+PRON+ADV,
V+ADV+N:
USUALLY PASSIVE

fence off. If an area **is fenced off,** it is separated from other areas by a fence. EG *By the nineteenth century, almost all land had been fenced off and made private... They had found a plot of land and fenced it off.*

V+ADV+N,
V+N+ADV,
V+PRON+ADV

fend, fends, fending, fended

fend off. 1 If you **fend off** someone who is attacking you, you try to prevent them from hurting you by putting your arms or an object in front of you. EG *He fended him off with his shovel... He raised his arms to fend off the blows.* ● **Ward off** means almost the same as **fend off.**

V+PRON+ADV,
V+ADV+N,
V+N+ADV

2 If you **fend off** questions, problems or things that you do not want, you avoid dealing with them or refuse to accept them. EG *It was the first time Daniel had spoken, except to fend off questions... He was continually fending off unwanted meals.*

V+ADV+N,
V+PRON+ADV

ferret, ferrets, ferreting, ferreted

ferret out. If you **ferret out** information or the location of someone, you discover it by searching thoroughly in a determined way; an informal expression. EG *...ferreting out the details of private lives... He demonstrated his competence at ferreting out errors... We had taken the decision to try and ferret him out.* ● **Unearth** means almost the same as **ferret out.**

V+ADV+N,
V+N+ADV,
V+PRON+ADV

fetch, fetches, fetching, fetched

fetch up. If you **fetch up** somewhere, you arrive there, usually without intending to; an informal expression. ● **Land up** means almost the same as **fetch up.**

V+ADV

fiddle, fiddles, fiddling, fiddled

fiddle about. If you **fiddle about** or **around,** you do small tasks without effort or interest and do not achieve very much. EG *He was fiddling about in the parlour... I spent two hours fiddling about with this table... Eddie and I were fiddling around making last-minute adjustments.* ● **Mess about** means almost the same as **fiddle about.**
fiddle around. See **fiddle about.**

V+ADV:
USUALLY+A

fight, fights, fighting, fought

fight back. 1 If you **fight back** when someone attacks you or causes you problems, you defend yourself and try to beat them or stop them. EG *Our forces were fighting back desperately... If we did that, the importing countries could fight back with laws of their own.* ● **Retaliate** and **resist** are more formal words for **fight back.**

V+ADV

2 If you **fight back** an emotion, you try very hard not to let it affect you. EG *I waited, fighting back my fear... ...standing in the early morning silence, fighting back my unease... She fought back the tears.*   V+ADV+N, V+PRON+ADV

fight down. If you **fight down** a desire or temptation, you try very hard to resist it. EG *He had to fight down the impulse to sneak out.*   V+ADV+N, V+PRON+ADV

fight off. If you **fight off** something unpleasant or unwanted, you succeed in getting rid of it or overcoming it. EG *...the ailments we can fight off if we are enjoying ourselves... ...grieving over his sons and fighting off despair... You shouldn't have to fight off too much competition for the job... We'll need help to fight off the bandits!*   V+ADV+N, V+PRON+ADV

fight out. When two people or groups **fight** something **out** or **fight it out**, they fight or argue until one of them wins. EG *The European nations were fighting it out on the battlefields... These decisions were fought out between contending groups.*   V+N+ADV, V+it+ADV, V+ADV+N

figure, figures, figuring, figured

figure on. If you **figure on** something, you assume or plan that it will happen; an informal expression used mainly in American English. EG *How soon are you figuring on getting married?... I figured on going out tonight.* ● **Reckon on** and **count on** mean almost the same as **figure on**.   V+PREP

figure out. If you **figure out** the solution to a problem, the answer to a question, or the reason for something, you work it out and understand it; an informal expression. EG *I've figured out what the trouble is... We tried to figure out a way to get to Wimbledon... You've got everything figured out, haven't you?... I just can't figure him out.*   V+ADV+N, V+N+ADV, V+PRON+ADV

file, files, filing, filed

file away. If you **file away** a fact or idea, you make an effort to remember it because you think it might be useful. EG *Dan carefully filed away this added reason for hating Joe Parker.*   V+N+ADV, V+PRON+ADV, V+ADV+N

fill, fills, filling, filled

fill in. **1** If you **fill in** a crack or a hole, you put a substance into it so that the surface becomes level. EG *She bought a packet of cement mix and began, herself, to fill in some holes.*   V+ADV+N, V+N+ADV, V+PRON+ADV

2 If you **fill in** a form or the details on a form, you write all the information that is requested in the appropriate spaces. EG *We filled in all the customs forms... Ask for a claim form, fill it in and send it to the social security office... Fill in your name and address here.* ● **Fill out** and **fill up** mean almost the same as **fill in**.   V+ADV+N, V+PRON+ADV, V+N+ADV

3 If you **fill in** a shape, you paint or draw all over the space inside the lines so that it becomes covered with colour. EG *You could get the kids to fill in the various pieces in different colours... She drew a circle and filled it in.* ● **Colour in** means almost the same as **fill in**.   V+ADV+N, V+PRON+ADV, V+N+ADV

4 If you **fill** someone **in** on a situation or event, you give them more information about it so that they have all the details. EG *I'll fill you in on the details now... Come back to the office and I'll fill you in.*   V+PRON+ADV, V+N+ADV: ALSO+*on*

5 If you **fill in** a period of time in which you are inactive or bored, you find things to do during it. EG *They then drove to Girvan to fill in time... There were ten long days to fill in... He obviously said it to fill in an awkward pause.*   V+ADV+N, V+PRON+ADV, V+N+ADV

6 If you **fill in** for someone, you do the work that they normally do because they are temporarily unable to do it. EG *One of the other girls is sick and I said I'd fill in.* ● **Stand in** means almost the same as **fill in**.   V+ADV: ALSO+*for*

fill out. **1** If you **fill out** a form, you write all the information that is   V+ADV+N, requested in the spaces on the form. EG *Brody was filling out forms about the accident... I found the death certificate forms and filled them out.* ● **Fill in** and **fill up** mean almost the same as **fill out**.

V+PRON+ADV,
V+N+ADV

2 If a thin person **fills out**, they become fatter. EG *He'd filled out a lot since I'd last seen him.*

V+ADV

fill up. 1 If you **fill up** a container, you put a large amount of something into it, so that it becomes full. EG *Fill the tank up, please... I filled up a test tube with potassium permanganate... ...when you filled it up to the brim.*

V+N+ADV,
V+ADV+N,
V+PRON+ADV:
ALSO+with

2 If something **fills up** a space or area, it is so big or is present in such large numbers that the whole space seems to be occupied. EG *The computer was massive, filling up a whole room.*

V+ADV+N,
V+N+ADV,
V+PRON+ADV

3 If a place, area or container **fills up**, it becomes crowded or full. EG *His office began to fill up with people... Belfast hotels filled up with journalists from around the world.*

V+ADV:
ALSO+with

4 If you **fill up** a period of time with a particular activity, you spend the time in this way. EG *The point was to fill up the day with meaningless activities.* ● **Take up** means almost the same as **fill up**.

V+ADV+N,
V+N+ADV,
V+PRON+ADV:
USUALLY+with

5 If you **fill** yourself **up**, you eat as much as you can. EG *No filling yourselves up with sandwiches, beer, and chips!... You would see the boys and girls filling themselves up before they left.*

V+REFL+ADV,
V+PRON+ADV,
V+N+ADV:
ALSO+with

6 If you **fill up** a form, you complete it, giving all the information that is requested. EG *Sorry to interrupt, but I've some forms to fill up.* ● **Fill in** and **fill out** mean almost the same as **fill up**.

V+ADV+N,
V+N+ADV,
V+PRON+ADV

film, films, filming, filmed

film over. If your eyes **film over**, they become covered with a very thin layer of tears.

V+ADV

filter, filters, filtering, filtered

filter out. To **filter out** something from a substance means to remove it by passing the substance through an obstacle such as a net, or through another substance such as sand. EG *The problem would involve filtering out some of the tar... Any excess is filtered out of the blood stream by the kidneys... This forms a protective screen around the planet, filtering out damaging ultra-violet radiation.*

V+ADV+N,
V+PRON+ADV,
V+N+ADV:
ALSO+of

find, finds, finding, found

find against. When a judge **finds against** one of the people contesting a court case, he or she comes to a judgment in favour of the other person; a legal expression.

V+PREP:
HAS PASSIVE

find for. When a judge **finds for** one of the people contesting a court case, he or she comes to a judgement in favour of this person; a legal expression. EG *The judge had found for the husband, describing him as a caring and responsible father.*

V+PREP:
HAS PASSIVE

find out. 1 If you **find out** something, you learn something that you did not already know. EG *I found out the train times... I'm only interested in finding out what the facts are... I've just found out that I won't have to start until Wednesday... I've been trying to find this out for weeks.* ● **Discover** means almost the same as **find out**.

V+ADV+N,
V+ADV+REPORT,
V+N+ADV,
V+PRON+ADV

2 If someone is **found out**, another person discovers that they have been dishonest or have done something wrong. EG *The manager had found him out and was going to sack him... I'm the sort of man who's always found out... Our lies are found out but remain unchallenged.* ● **Rumble** is an informal word for **find out**.

V+PRON+ADV,
V+N+ADV:
USUALLY PASSIVE

finish, finishes, finishing, finished

finish off. 1 When you **finish off** something that you are doing, you complete it by doing the last part. EG *He had finished off his thesis...*

V+ADV+N,
V+PRON+ADV,
V+N+ADV

The herdsmen were just finishing off the milking... We had to work until midnight to finish them off.

2 When you **finish off** by doing a particular thing, you do it as the last part of an event or series of actions. EG *He used to play the piano on Saturday nights and always finished off with 'Spread A Little Happiness'... Can I finish off by asking you one question?* ● **Conclude** is a more formal word for **finish off**.

V+ADV:
USUALLY+A

3 When you **finish off** food or drink, you eat or drink the last bit of it, so that there is none left. EG *We decided to go back and finish off the wine... He had cooked a chicken and they'd finished it off together in one afternoon.* ● **Polish off** is an informal expression for **finish off**.

V+ADV+N,
V+PRON+ADV,
V+N+ADV

4 If something **is finished off** in a particular way, it is decorated in that way or made to look neat and attractive by this method. EG *The shirt had a silver cross on the left breast and the neck was finished off with a frill.*

V+N+ADV,
V+PRON+ADV,
V+ADV+N:
USUALLY PASSIVE

5 To **finish off** a person or animal means to kill them. EG *Now was the time to go ahead and finish the intruders off... I'll never go there again as long as I live. It nearly finished me off.*

V+PRON+ADV,
V+N+ADV,
V+ADV+N

finish up. **1** If you **finish up** in a particular place or situation, you are in it at the end of an event or process. EG *She'll be going on tour, starting in Southampton and finishing up in London... They all finished up stranded on the beaches... They finished up serving in a shop... Maybe you too will finish up as Prime Minister.* ● **End up** and **wind up** mean almost the same as **finish up**.

V+ADV:
USUALLY+A

2 When you **finish up** something that you have been eating or drinking. you eat or drink the last part of it. EG *They were just finishing up their lunch... They never finish up their puddings.*

V+ADV+N,
V+PRON+ADV,
V+N+ADV

3 When you **finish up** something that you are doing, you complete it by doing the last part of it; used in American English. EG *Hendricks was finishing up his paper work when Brady walked in... I was just finishing up work on some Schubert manuscripts.* ● **Finish off** means almost the same as **finish up**.

V+ADV+N

finish up with. If you **finish up with** something, this is the result of your activity or efforts. EG *Whichever way you do it, you must finish up with the same voltage drop... If you deleted that, you would finish up with a two sentence paragraph.*

V+ADV+PREP

finish with. If you **finish with** someone or something, or **are finished with** them, you stop dealing with them or end your involvement or connection with them. EG *I haven't finished with you yet... I thought I had finished with the play for ever... He had decided several years before that he was finished with marriage.*

V+PREP,
HAS PASSIVE:
ALSO PASSIVE,
V+PREP

fire, fires, firing, fired

fire away. You say to someone **'Fire away'** to indicate that you are ready for them to begin speaking; an informal expression. ● **Shoot** means almost the same as **fire away**.

IMPERATIVE:
V+ADV

fire off. **1** If you **fire off** a shot, you press the mechanism which causes a bullet or other missile to be released from a gun. EG *The sniper popped up and fired off a single round... He pointed the pistol and fired off a shot.*

V+ADV+N

2 If you **fire off** questions or suggestions, you say a lot of them quickly, one after the other. EG *Tony used to fire off his own suggestions faster than I could write them down.*

V+ADV+N,
V+N+ADV,
V+PRON+ADV

firm, firms, firming, firmed

firm up. **1** If you **firm up** part of your body, you exercise to improve the condition of the muscles and reduce the amount of fat. EG *This exercise will help to firm up those flabby thighs.* ● **Tone up** means almost the same as **firm up**.

V+ADV+N,
V+N+ADV,
V+PRON+ADV

2 If you **firm up** an idea or plan, you make decisions about all the   V+ADV+N,
details that have not yet been arranged. EG *I think we're all agreed*   V+N+ADV,
on the basic approach; we can firm up the details at next week's   V+PRON+ADV
meeting.

fish, fishes, fishing, fished

fish for. If you **fish for** information or praise, you try and get it from   V+PREP
someone in an indirect way. EG *I think he was just fishing for*
compliments... I was never invited, and I never fished for an
invitation... ...questions that fished for some indication as to how
they were doing. ● **Angle for** means almost the same as **fish for.**

fish out. If you **fish** something **out** of a liquid, substance, or   V+ADV+N,
container, you pull it out or take it out. EG *Patterson had brought his*   V+PRON+ADV,
briefcase, and he fished out a package which he gave to Amsburg...   V+N+ADV:
One of her earrings dropped into her scrambled egg, and she fished   ALSO+*of*
it out and screwed it back on... ...corpses being fished out of the
water.

fit, fits, fitting, fitted

Fit is sometimes used in American English as the past tense and
past participle.

fit in. **1** If you manage to **fit in** a person or task, you manage to find   V+ADV+N,
time to deal with them. EG *You seem to fit in an enormous amount*   V+PRON+ADV,
every day... They can't do it today, so they will fit it in when they   V+N+ADV
have a van in that area... I'm on holiday next week, but I can fit you
in on the 9th. ● **Squeeze in** means almost the same as **fit in.**

2 If you **fit in** as part of a group, you seem to belong there because   V+ADV
you are similar to the other people in it. EG *You can't bring outsiders*
into a place like this; they wouldn't fit in; they would upset the whole
atmosphere... You would have to try to adapt yourself to fit in.

3 If you say that something or someone **fits in,** you understand how   V+ADV
they form part of a particular situation or system. EG *It's difficult to*
know where these books fit in.

fit into. **1** If you **fit into** a particular group, you seem to belong there   V+PREP
because you are similar to the other people in it. EG *These children*
are unable to fit into ordinary society... I would have to exercise
great effort to fit into a predominantly white world.

2 If something or someone **fits into** a category, classification, or   V+PREP
explanation, you can see that they belong to it or are part of it and
understand why. EG *...odd things that don't fit into any category...*
Where does David fit into all this?

fit in with. If something **fits in with** a system, method, idea, or   V+ADV+PREP,
situation, it is suitable and works successfully as part of it. EG *The old*   V+N+ADV+PREP,
sort of love no longer fits in with our changing needs... They   V+PRON+ADV+PREP:
manufacture mild steel to fit in with modern methods of produc-   ERGATIVE
tion... I'm willing to fit in with your way of doing things.

fit out. If you **fit** someone or something **out,** you provide them with   V+ADV+N,
equipment and other things that they need. EG *He started to fit out a*   V+PRON+ADV,
ship in secret till the British Ambassador found out about it... When   V+N+ADV,
the men arrive, they fit them out in combat uniforms and jungle   V+REFL+ADV:
boots. ● **Kit out** means almost the same as **fit out.**   ALSO+*in/with*

fit up. **1** If you **fit** someone or something **up,** you provide them with   V+PRON+ADV,
equipment or other things that they need. EG *Dr Bell was wanting to*   V+REFL+ADV,
fit you up with a contraceptive... He could fit himself up at modest   V+N+ADV,
cost.   V+ADV+N

2 If someone **fits** you **up,** they provide false evidence and convince   V+PRON+ADV,
other people that you are guilty of a crime or other serious offence,   V+N+ADV,
although you are innocent; mainly used in very informal British   V+ADV+N
English. ● **Frame** is a more formal word for **fit up.**

fix, fixes, fixing, fixed

fix on. If you **fix on** a particular thing, you decide that this is what you will have or do; an informal expression. EG *Have you fixed on a date for the party yet?... We seem to have fixed on the same day for supermarket shopping.* ● **Set** means almost the same as **fix on.**   V+PREP: HAS PASSIVE

fix up. 1 If you **fix** someone **up** with something they need, you provide it for them; an informal use. EG *They told me that they could fix me up with tickets for the opera... 'Can I stay at your place for a short time,' she said appealingly, 'till I get fixed up?'*   V+PRON+ADV, V+N+ADV, V+ADV+N, V+REFL+ADV: ALSO+with

2 If you **fix** something **up**, you make the arrangements that are necessary to achieve it. EG *Have you done anything about fixing up a meeting place?... We'll fix up a nice meal for the three of us... I'll talk to Sonny about fixing things up.* ● **Arrange** is a more formal word for **fix up.**   V+ADV+N, V+N+ADV, V+PRON+ADV

3 If you **fix up** something, you build it quickly and roughly because you need it immediately. EG *We tried to fix up a shelter from the wind... I've fixed up this sort of wire barricade.* ● **Rig up** is a more informal expression for **fix up.**   V+ADV+N, V+PRON+ADV, V+N+ADV

4 If you **fix up** something that needs repair or attention, you do the work that is necessary to improve it or make it suitable. EG *He was fixing up the flat, ready to move in... You promised us money to fix up the streets and alleys.* ● **Do up** means almost the same as **fix up.**   V+ADV+N, V+N+ADV, V+PRON+ADV

fizzle, fizzles, fizzling, fizzled

fizzle out. If something **fizzles out**, it ends in a weak or disappointing way, often after starting strongly. EG *The strike fizzled out after three days... It wasn't long before interest in it fizzled out... The discussion fizzled out after a few minutes.* ● **Peter out** means almost the same as **fizzle out.**   V+ADV

flag, flags, flagging, flagged

flag down. If you **flag down** a vehicle, you wave at it as a signal for the driver to stop. EG *We flagged down the tractor and clambered aboard.*   V+ADV+N, V+N+ADV, V+PRON+ADV

flake, flakes, flaking, flaked

flake off. If something **flakes off**, it separates from the surface it was attached to. EG *The paint was flaking off the walls of the shop.*   V+ADV

flake out. If you **flake out**, you collapse or fall asleep, usually because you are exhausted; an informal expression. EG *When I got to the top I just flaked out... I flaked out on my bed.*   V+ADV

flare, flares, flaring, flared

flare out. Something that **flares out** spreads outwards at one end to form a wide shape. EG *She pirouetted, making the skirt flare out... The long feathered tail flared out behind it.* ● **Fan out** means almost the same as **flare out.**   V+ADV

flare up. 1 If fire or a flame **flares up**, it suddenly burns very fiercely and brightly. EG *The fire flared up high and showed up their little group clearly... He set fire to it, then stood watching it flare up.* ● **Blaze** means almost the same as **flare up.**   V+ADV

2 If something such as violence, conflict, or an emotion **flares up**, it suddenly becomes very intense or serious. EG *The argument between the two groups flared up at the meeting... The conflict flared up into civil war... Panic flared up in her.* ● **Erupt** is a more formal word for **flare up.** ▸ If there is a **flare-up** of a previous situation, condition, or emotion, it suddenly occurs again. EG *...the incident which produced this new flare-up of anxiety... The disease had shown occasional flare-ups, particularly in the South West.*   V+ADV   N COUNT

3 If someone **flares up** at you, they suddenly get very angry with you, often without good reason. EG *He was being thoroughly objectionable, flaring up at her over quite reasonable requests... She would sometimes flare up at me as a way of relieving her own panic.* ▸ A **flare-up** is a sudden argument or situation of conflict. EG *Ian found himself in another flare-up over umpiring.*

V+ADV:
ALSO+*at*

N COUNT

flash, flashes, flashing, flashed

flash back. If your mind **flashes back** to an event in your past, you suddenly remember it very forcefully. EG *My mind flashed back to past demonstrations... His mind flashed back to what the sisters had said... Soshnick's mind flashed back to the notorious lipstick murders in Chicago.* ▸ A **flashback** is an occasion, especially in a film or a play, when someone suddenly remembers an event in their past. EG *Then follows a brief flashback to the four earlier murders.*

V+ADV

N COUNT

flatten, flattens, flattening, flattened

flatten out. **1** If you flatten something **out** or if it **flattens out**, it becomes flat or flatter. EG *...a bulldozer flattening out the ruts in the road... ...where the foothills flattened out to meet the Bay shore... To the north of the ridge, the country flattened out into a blue expanse.*
2 If something **flattens out** differences or variations in things, it reduces the differences or variations and the things become more like each other. EG *Comprehensive schools assisted in flattening out all regional accents.*

V+ADV+N,
V+N+ADV,
V+PRON+ADV,
V+ADV:
ERGATIVE

V+ADV+N,
V+N+ADV,
V+PRON+ADV

flesh, fleshes, fleshing, fleshed

flesh out. If you **flesh** something **out**, you give more information about it or add details to make it complete. EG *Those are the main points I'll be talking about. Now I'll flesh them out for you... We had several ideas for the initial concept of the scene and we are now seeing them fleshed out for the first time.*

V+PRON+ADV,
V+N+ADV,
V+ADV+N

flick, flicks, flicking, flicked

flick over. If you **flick over** the pages of a magazine or book, you turn the pages quickly. EG *He put his head down at once, flicking over the pages with a practised hand.*

V+ADV+N,
V+N+ADV,
V+PRON+ADV:
NO PASSIVE

flick through. If you **flick through** a magazine, book, or pile of papers or cards, you turn over pages or individual items quickly to get a brief idea of what they contain. EG *He flicked through the passport, not understanding a word... The interviewer started flicking through job cards on her desk.* ● **Leaf through** means almost the same as **flick through.**

V+PREP

fling, flings, flinging, flung

fling into. If you **fling** yourself **into** an activity, you begin to do it with a lot of enthusiasm, energy and effort. EG *...before we fling ourselves into the mad world of pleasure... She flung herself into her work.* ● **Throw into** means almost the same as **fling into.**

V+REFL+PREP

fling off. If you **fling off** your clothes, you take them off very quickly and carelessly. EG *She ran into the bedroom, where she flung off her dress and took out a clean one.* ● **Throw off** means almost the same as **fling off.**

V+N+ADV,
V+PRON+ADV

fling out. If you **fling out** a remark, you say it quickly in a rather aggressive way. EG *...lurking in an office somewhere, ready to fling out their routine insults in response to any enquiry... 'I told you,' she flung out, 'I won't hear anything more about Mr Edwards.'*

V+ADV+N,
V+ADV+QUOTE,
V+PRON+ADV,
V+N+ADV

flip, flips, flipping, flipped

flip through. If you **flip through** a magazine, book, or pile of papers or cards, you turn over pages or individual items quickly to get a

V+PREP,
V+ADV

brief idea of what they contain. EG *Renshaw flipped through the book... She flipped through a card-index... 'Read it yourself,' he said, flipping through until he found the page.* ● **Flick through** means almost the same as **flip through.**

flirt, flirts, flirting, flirted

flirt with. 1 If you **flirt with** someone, you behave towards them in a   V+PREP
teasing way that suggests you are sexually attracted to them. EG *Now Belinda was flirting shamelessly with another man.*
2 If you **flirt with** the idea of doing or having something, you   V+PREP:
consider the idea without making any definite plans. EG *Burlington*   HAS PASSIVE
has flirted with the idea of a wood-burning electrical generator... Channon flirted with the idea of running for the Presidency. ● **Toy with** and **dally with** mean almost the same as **flirt with.**

float, floats, floating, floated

float around. 1 If a rumour or idea **is floating around,** it is being   V+ADV
discussed or thought about in a general, rather vague way. EG *There are a lot of weird ideas floating around... I have a lot of ideas floating around between books that don't come to anything.*
2 If you say that something **is floating around,** you mean that you   V+ADV
have seen it recently somewhere nearby, but you do not know exactly where; an informal use. EG *There's a bag of sweets floating around somewhere. Would you like one?*

flood, floods, flooding, flooded

flood in. If people or things **flood in** somewhere, they arrive there   V+ADV:
in large numbers. EG *Cheap sandals began to flood in from Korea...*   ALSO+*to*
US reinforcements were now flooding in... Letters flooded in to MPs.
flood into. If people or things **flood into** a place, large numbers of   V+PREP
them arrive in a short space of time. EG *Nine million people a year were flooding into the Third World cities... By now, messages were flooding into command posts all over Normandy.* ● **Pour into** means almost the same as **flood into.**
flood out. If people **are flooded out,** they have to leave their homes   V+N+ADV,
because river or sea water has risen to an unusually high level and   V+PRON+ADV,
come into the buildings. EG *If the rain continued, we'd be flooded out.*   V+ADV+N:
   USUALLY PASSIVE

flop, flops, flopping, flopped

flop down. If you **flop down,** you let your body fall quickly   V+ADV:
downwards, usually because you are exhausted. EG *They flop down,*   USUALLY+A
yelling, and pound with their hands and feet... Jimmie flopped down in the chair... He flopped down next to her.

flounder, flounders, floundering, floundered

flounder about. 1 If someone or something **flounders about** or   V+ADV
around in a place, they move very unsteadily, and perhaps keep falling over. EG *They had flown aboard and floundered about in vain trying to escape.*
2 If someone **flounders about** or **around** in a situation, they are   V+ADV
confused and cannot think or express themselves clearly. EG *He was floundering about, patently trying to organize some kind of argument.*

flow, flows, flowing, flowed

flow from. If a situation, product, or quality **flows from** something,   V+PREP
it occurs as a natural result of it. EG *The consequences that flow from this view are endless... Films and television programmes would flow from this collaboration.* ● **Stem from** means almost the same as **flow from.**
flow over. If a feeling **flows over** you, you suddenly feel it very   V+PREP

fog up

strongly. EG *He couldn't suppress the contempt that flowed over him... A wash of sympathy for Simmonds flowed over him.*

fluff, fluffs, fluffing, fluffed

fluff out. If you **fluff** something **out** or **up**, you make it softer, looser, or lighter, for example by shaking or brushing it. EG *She fluffed her hair out in big waves... Put the mashed potato in the oven for 20 minutes, fluff it up with a fork and serve.*
V+N+ADV,
V+PRON+ADV,
V+ADV+N

fluff up. See fluff out.

flunk, flunks, flunking, flunked

flunk out. If you **flunk out**, you are dismissed from a school or college because your work is not good enough; an informal expression used in American English. EG *You're gonna flunk out if you just sit there watching me study!*
V+ADV

flush, flushes, flushing, flushed

flush out. If you **flush out** someone or something, you find them and force them to come out or be revealed. EG *They went into the area to flush out guerrillas who were sheltering there... ...secrets which Cobb will painstakingly flush out.*
V+ADV+N,
V+N+ADV,
V+PRON+ADV

flutter, flutters, fluttering, fluttered

flutter about. If someone **flutters about** or **around**, they move about quickly and nervously without seeming to have any definite purpose. EG *Unable to sit down, she would flutter about from room to room... They wasted half their time fluttering around the invalid.*
V+ADV,
V+PREP

flutter around. See flutter about.

flutter down. If something light **flutters down**, it moves slowly and gently through the air towards the ground. EG *The pieces of paper flutter down like large butterflies in the darkness... The first flakes of snow began to flutter down early in the afternoon.*
V+ADV

fly, flies, flying, flew, flown

fly at. If you **fly at** someone, you suddenly get very angry with them and express this, either in words or by attacking them. EG *One day the man flew at me in a temper... She looked at him as though she were about to fly at his face.* ● **Go for** means almost the same as **fly at**.
V+PREP

fly in. If someone **flies in**, or people or things **are flown in**, they arrive in a place by aeroplane. EG *Howard had flown in from Atlanta at my request... Portable units had been flown in.*
V+ADV,
V+ADV+N:
ERGATIVE

fly into. If you **fly into** a rage or a panic, you suddenly become very angry or start to panic. EG *She flies into a temper if I make a mistake... Something dropped onto his back and he flew into a flat panic.*
V+PREP

fly out. If someone **flies out**, or people or things **are flown out**, they go or are sent somewhere by aeroplane. EG *I decided to fly out to Bombay in order to help... The RAF had flown out the vital equipment.*
V+ADV,
V+ADV+N:
ERGATIVE

fob, fobs, fobbing, fobbed

fob off. If you **fob** someone **off** with something, you persuade them to accept it, although it is not what they wanted or asked for. EG *He may try to fob you off with a prescription for pills... She felt she was being fobbed off.*
V+PRON+ADV,
V+N+ADV,
V+ADV+N:
USUALLY+with

fog, fogs, fogging, fogged

fog up. If something made of glass **fogs up**, it becomes difficult to see through because it is covered with tiny drops of water that make
V+ADV

it cloudy; an informal expression. ● **Steam up** means almost the same as **fog up**.

foist, foists, foisting, foisted

foist on. If you **foist** something **on** or **upon** someone, you force them to have it or experience it. EG *They were not out to lead, to foist their ideas and views on the people... We do not want to foist answers on anyone... ...the kinds of ideas foisted upon us all our lives.* — V+N+PREP, V+PRON+PREP

foist upon. See **foist on**: **foist upon** is more formal.

fold, folds, folding, folded

fold in. In cooking, if you **fold** something **in**, you mix it gently and carefully into a mixture, keeping as much air in the mixture as possible. EG *When the batter is ready, fold in the egg white with a metal spoon.* — V+ADV+N, V+N+ADV, V+PRON+ADV

fold into. In cooking, if you **fold** one substance **into** another, you mix them gently and carefully, keeping as much air in the mixture as possible. EG *Beat the egg whites until stiff and then fold them carefully into the sauce... Using a metal spoon, fold the dry ingredients into the cream.* — V+PREP

fold up. 1 If you **fold** something **up**, you make it into a smaller, neat shape by folding it several times. EG *She began to fold up the blanket... He was just folding the map up when he spotted it.* ● **Unfold** means the opposite of **fold up**. — V+ADV+N, V+N+ADV, V+PRON+ADV

2 If the petals of a flower **fold up**, they close and come together in the centre of the flower. EG *The buds had folded up against the light.* ● **Close up** means almost the same as **fold up**. — V+ADV, V+REFL+ADV

3 If a business or organization **folds up**, it closes or comes to an end because it has been unsuccessful. EG *She had known too many businesses fold up through bad management... They had no choice but to fold up their offshore operations.* ● **Pack up** means almost the same as **fold up**. — V+ADV, V+ADV+N, V+N+ADV, V+PRON+ADV: ERGATIVE

follow, follows, following, followed

follow out. If you **follow out** instructions you do exactly what you have been told to do. EG *She knew she could trust him to follow out her instructions... ...following out the teachings of their religious leaders.* ● **Carry out** means almost the same as **follow out**. — V+ADV+N, V+PRON+ADV

follow through. 1 If you **follow** an idea **through**, you carefully consider how it would work and what its effects would be. EG *Tempting though it may be to follow this point through, it is not really relevant.* — V+N+ADV, V+PRON+ADV, V+ADV+N

2 If you **follow through** a series of actions, you complete all the stages to achieve something or to get to the end. EG *She was the only journalist to follow the story through... The offensive action was swiftly followed through to the early attainment of victory.* ▶ An action that completes something or is a natural continuation of it is called the **follow-through**. EG *This wouldn't halt the attack but it would at least blunt the follow-through.* — V+N+ADV, V+ADV+N, V+PRON+ADV / N COUNT

3 In a sport such as golf, tennis, or football, to **follow through** means to complete the movement after hitting the ball by continuing to move your arm or leg in the same curve. EG *You're not following through after playing the stroke.* ▶ In sport, the **follow-through** is the completion of a movement after hitting the ball. EG *The follow-through is part of the kick.* — V+ADV / N COUNT

follow up. 1 If you **follow** something **up**, you try to find out more about it and perhaps do something about it. EG *It's an idea which has been followed up by the local council... I followed up an advertisement for a second-hand Volkswagen... ...according to the fisherman* — V+N+ADV, V+ADV+N, V+PRON+ADV

who followed up the reports. ● **Investigate** is a more formal word
for **follow up.**

2 If you **follow up** one action with another, you do the second action
soon after the first. EG *The President followed up the first round of
voting by challenging his opponent to a public debate... They must
attend the course, and this is followed up by personal visits... He
murmured the word quietly and with great venom, following up with
a string of oaths.* ▷ A **follow-up** or a **follow-up** activity is done as a
continuation or second part of something done previously. EG *This
conference is a follow-up to an earlier one in Gabon... He needed
follow-up treatment from a specialist doctor.*

V+ADV+N,
V+N+ADV,
V+PRON+ADV,
V+ADV:
USUALLY+with/by

N COUNT,
ADJECTIVE

fool, fools, fooling, fooled

fool about. See **fool around.**

fool around. 1 If you **fool around** or **about,** you behave in a playful
or childish way. EG *The boys passed them, laughing and fooling
around and talking loudly... He was always fooling about.*

V+ADV

2 If you **fool around** or **about** with something dangerous, you behave
in a careless or irresponsible way. EG *Chemicals are very dangerous
things to fool around with... I don't want to have to fool around
trying to dock two boats in the dark.* ● **Mess around** means almost
the same as **fool around.**

V+ADV:
ALSO+with

3 If someone **fools around** with another person, especially when one
of them is married, they have a casual sexual relationship with
them; used mainly in American English. EG *I'll bet you were fooling
around with Miss Roach... ...that fellow who's fooling around with
your wife.*

V+ADV:
ALSO+with

force, forces, forcing, forced

force back. If you **force back** an emotion or desire, you manage,
with an effort, to prevent it from affecting you. EG *He forced back
the strong urge to stroke her.* ● **Suppress** and **fight back** mean
almost the same as **force back.**

V+ADV+N,
V+PRON+ADV

force into. If you **force** someone **into** doing something, you make
them do it, although they do not want to. EG *...to force landlords into
increasing their wages... ...forcing him into the role of confidant...
'No one's forcing you into it,' Joyce said.*

V+N+PREP,
V+PRON+PREP

force on. If you **force** something **on** or **upon** someone, you make
them accept, use, or deal with it when they would prefer not to. EG
*...the missiles which the Americans are forcing, he believes, upon
Britain... I forced some more of the salt and water on him.*

V+N+PREP,
V+PRON+PREP

force upon. See **force on: force upon** is more formal.

forge, forges, forging, forged

forge ahead. If you **forge ahead,** you make a lot of progress, or
more progress than someone else. EG *The company has made use of
the absence of competition to forge ahead... They could see the
army forging ahead along the road.*

V+ADV

fork, forks, forking, forked

fork out. If you **fork out** for something, you pay money for it; an
informal expression. EG *It's likely that she will be prepared to fork
out extra cash to install a tape player... His old man's forked out at
last... ...the fortune I had already had to fork out on her education.*
● **Cough up** means almost the same as **fork out.**

V+ADV,
V+ADV+N:
USUALLY+A

form, forms, forming, formed

form up. When a group of people or things **form up,** they move into
position in lines. EG *The yachts formed up in Hampton Roads... The*

V+ADV,
V+REFL+ADV,

police arrived as the procession was forming up... *Form yourselves up into two columns and follow me!*   `V+N+ADV,`
`V+PRON+ADV:`
`ERGATIVE`

foul, fouls, fouling, fouled

foul up. If someone **fouls up** a plan, situation, or relationship, they   `V+ADV+N,`
spoil it by doing something wrong or stupid; an informal expression.   `V+N+ADV,`
`V+PRON+ADV`
EG *So many good projects have been fouled up by elementary
mistakes in planning... He does seem to have fouled up negotiating
practice in the docks.* ● **Mess up** means almost the same as **foul up.**
▶ A **foul-up** is a state of disorder or trouble which is the result of   `N COUNT`
mistakes or carelessness; used in informal English. EG *The Centre
hates that kind of foul-up.*

freak, freaks, freaking, freaked

freak out. If someone **freaks out,** they suddenly behave in a very   `V+ADV,`
strange and uncontrolled way, for example because of a sudden   `V+N+ADV,`
shock or the effect of drugs; an informal expression. EG *When I gave*   `V+PRON+ADV:`
`ERGATIVE`
*him an application form, he just freaked out completely... He was
freaking the colonel out a little bit... Well, I'm freaked out by what
we're seeing... It freaks him out every time.*

freeze, freezes, freezing, froze, frozen

freeze out. If you **freeze** someone **out** of an activity or situation,   `V+ADV+N,`
you prevent them from being involved in it by creating difficulties   `V+N+ADV,`
or being unfriendly. EG *Producers try to freeze out parasitic middle*   `V+PRON+ADV:`
`ALSO+of`
men. ● **Squeeze out** means almost the same as **freeze out.**

freeze over. If a pond, lake or river **freezes over** or **is frozen over,**   `V+ADV:`
it becomes covered with a layer of ice. EG *In really hard winters, the*   `ALSO PASSIVE,`
`V+ADV`
*Thames has been known to freeze over.... ...when the Lakes were
frozen over.* ● **Ice over** and **ice up** mean almost the same as **freeze
over.**

freeze up. If an area of water or a pipe or machine **freezes up** or **is**   `V+ADV:`
frozen up, it becomes completely blocked or covered with ice. EG *It*   `ALSO PASSIVE,`
`V+ADV`
*was so cold last winter that even the river froze up... The lock has
frozen up.* ● **Ice up** means almost the same as **freeze up.** ▶ If there is   `N COUNT`
a **freeze-up,** it is so cold that pipes and areas of water become
blocked with ice.

freshen, freshens, freshening, freshened

freshen up. 1 If you **freshen up** or **freshen** yourself **up,** you wash   `V+ADV,`
and make yourself look neat and tidy. EG *Sarah and Barry returned*   `V+REFL+ADV`
*to their hotel to freshen up... I shall just have time to change and
freshen up.*
2 If you **freshen** something **up,** you make it look cleaner, brighter   `V+N+ADV,`
and more attractive. EG *New wallpaper and curtains will freshen up*   `V+PRON+ADV,`
`V+ADV+N`
the place.

frig, frigs, frigging, frigged

frig about. If someone says that you are **frigging about** or **around,**   `V+ADV`
they mean that you are wasting time when you should be doing
something; a very informal expression. ● **Mess about** is a less
informal expression for **frig about.**
frig around. See **frig about.**

frighten, frightens, frightening, frightened

frighten away. 1 If you **frighten away** a person or animal or   `V+ADV+N,`
frighten them **off,** you make them afraid so that they run away and   `V+N+ADV,`
do not harm you. EG *He waved his torch to frighten away some*   `V+PRON+ADV`
*animal, probably a hyena... It flaps its wings and flashes a huge pair
of eye spots which frighten the killer away... We were waving our*

arms to frighten them off. ● **Scare off** means almost the same as **frighten away.**

2 To **frighten away** or **off** someone who is expressing an interest in a person or activity means to make them doubtful or nervous so that they decide to withdraw their interest or support. EG *He managed to woo the Communists on his left without frightening off the middle-of-the-road voters... ...so as not to frighten away the potential middle-class allies.* ● **Scare off** means almost the same as **frighten away.**
V+N+ADV,
V+ADV+N,
V+PRON+ADV

frighten into. If you **frighten** someone **into** something, you make them so frightened that they do something which they might not otherwise have done. EG *'Don't you dare,' he said, frightening her into silence.*
V+N+PREP,
V+PRON+PREP

frighten off. See **frighten away.**

frighten out of. If you **frighten** someone **out of** something, you make them so afraid that they do not do something that they had intended to do. EG *She refused to be frightened out of going.*
V+N+ADV+PREP,
V+PRON+ADV+PREP

fritter, fritters, frittering, frittered

fritter away. If you **fritter away** time or money, you waste it by spending it in a foolish way, a little bit at a time. EG *It is all too easy to fritter away the best hours of the day shopping... She was determined she would not fritter away her vacation... The money just goes though, doesn't it; you just fritter it away.* ● **Squander** is a more formal word for **fritter away.**
V+ADV+N,
V+PRON+ADV,
V+N+ADV

frost, frosts, frosting, frosted

frost over. When something made of glass **frosts over** or **up**, or is **frosted over** or **up**, it becomes covered with frost. EG *It must have been cold last night, my windscreen's frosted over.*
V+ADV:
ALSO PASSIVE,
V+ADV

frost up. See **frost over.**

frown, frowns, frowning, frowned

frown on. See **frown upon.**

frown upon. If something is **frowned upon** or is **frowned on**, people disapprove of it. EG *Broadway's licentious plays were frowned upon... Society frowns upon such behaviour.*
V+PREP:
HAS PASSIVE,
USUALLY PASSIVE

fry, fries, frying, fried

fry up. If you **fry up** food, you fry it to make a quick, casual meal; an informal expression. EG *Make yourself useful and fry up some bacon.*
V+ADV+N,
V+PRON+ADV

▶ A **fry-up** is a quick, casual meal consisting of fried food; an informal word in British English.
N COUNT

fuck, fucks, fucking, fucked

Fuck is an extremely rude word, which most people find very offensive.

fuck about. To **fuck about** or **fuck around** means to behave in a way that is silly, stupid, or unnecessary and annoys other people. ● **Mess about** is a more polite, informal expression for **fuck about.**
V+ADV,
V+N+ADV,
V+PRON+ADV

fuck off. 'Fuck off' is a very insulting way of telling someone to go away or to stop interfering. ● **Get lost** is a less offensive expression for **fuck off.**
IMPERATIVE:
V+ADV

fuck up. If someone **fucks** something **up**, they make a mess of it. ● **Mess up** is a more polite, informal expression for **fuck up.** ▶ A **fuck-up** occurs when someone does something completely wrong.
V+N+ADV,
V+PRON+ADV,
V+ADV+N

N COUNT

fur, furs, furring, furred

fur up. If a kettle or water pipe **furs up**, the inside of it becomes covered with a hard grey layer of calcium carbonate and other chemicals in the water.
V+ADV

fuss, fusses, fussing, fussed

fuss over. If you **fuss over** someone or something, you pay a lot of attention to them, showing too much concern or affection. EG *He was fed the best pieces and fussed over by his admiring brothers... His mother fussed over him a bit too much, I think... Matty was inclined to fuss over her health.*

V+PREP: HAS PASSIVE

G g

gad, gads, gadding, gadded

gad about. If you **gad about** or **around,** you go to a lot of different places looking for amusement and entertainment; an informal and old-fashioned expression. EG *I begrudged them gadding about while I did all the work... This is hardly the time to be gadding around.*
● **Gallivant** means almost the same as **gad about.** ▶ If you describe someone as a **gadabout,** you mean that they do not take things seriously, and spend their time looking for amusement and entertainment. EG *Henry's been very good. He may be quiet and not very pushing, but no one could call him a gadabout.*

V+ADV

N COUNT

gad around. See gad about.

gain, gains, gaining, gained

gain on. If you **gain on** someone or something that you are chasing, you gradually get nearer to them. EG *You'll have to drive faster—they're gaining on us... We were gaining on him towards the end of the race.*

V+PREP

gamble, gambles, gambling, gambled

gamble away. If you **gamble** money **away,** you lose it by betting on the result of a game or a competition. EG *Fred gambled his profits away... He's only just received the money, but now Tim will gamble all of it away.*

V+N+ADV, V+PRON+ADV, V+ADV+N

gamble on. 1 If you **gamble on** the result of a game or a competition, you bet money on that result. EG *He gambled heavily on the horses... He still gambled modestly on the football pools.*

V+PREP

2 If you **gamble on** something, you take a risky action or decision in the hope of gaining money, success, or an advantage. EG *...gambling on the assumption that the file had been lost... I gambled on immunity from the law and lost.*

V+PREP: HAS PASSIVE

gang, gangs, ganging, ganged

gang up. If people **gang up** on someone else, they unite against them in a fight or argument; used in informal English. EG *Telling dirty jokes is a way that men gang up on women... They are ganging up against you... National groups are ganging up to claim their rights.*

V+ADV: USUALLY WITH on/against

gather, gathers, gathering, gathered

gather around. If people **gather around** or **round** someone or something, they come together in a group and surround them. EG *The boys gathered around the old man to hear his stories... Little crowds would gather around them to clap and listen... The boys gathered round the fire.* ● **Cluster around** means almost the same as **gather around.**

V+PREP, V+ADV

gather in. If you **gather in** a group of people or things, you bring them safely together into one place; a slightly old-fashioned expression. EG *The men have three weeks to gather their harvest in... Emergency teams were organized to gather in all the unattended casualties... The main crops have to be gathered in and stored for the winter.*

V+N+ADV,
V+ADV+N,
V+PRON+ADV

gather round. See gather around.

gather up. If you **gather up** a number of things, you bring them together into a group. EG *She watched Willie gather up the papers and stuff them carelessly in his pocket... Gather up all the tools and put them away... I saw her gathering her bits and pieces up for the move to the new flat.* ● **Get together** means almost the same as **gather up,** and **assemble** is a more formal word.

V+ADV+N,
V+N+ADV,
V+PRON+ADV

gear, gears, gearing, geared

gear to. If something **is geared to** or **towards** a particular purpose, it is organized or designed to be suitable for that purpose. EG *...a system of values geared to man's needs... ...gearing our efforts to what the market really wants... Higher education is increasingly geared towards careers.*

V+N+PREP,
V+PRON+PREP

gear towards. See gear to.

gear up. If someone or something **is geared up** to do something, or if they **gear** themselves **up** to do it, they are prepared and able to do it. EG *Many football teams are not geared up to attack... Science is not geared up to cope with the problems of human development... Martin and Liz were gearing themselves up to a full-time job.*

V+PRON+ADV,
V+N+ADV,
V+REFL+ADV:
USUALLY PASSIVE
WITH to/to-INF

gen, gens, genning, genned

gen up. If you **gen up** on something, you find out as much information about it as you can. EG *He's genning up on the legal position before he signs the contract... She genned up on the character before taking on the role.* ● **Swot up** means almost the same as **gen up.** ▷ If you are **genned up** on a subject, you know a lot about it. EG *She's really genned up on all these old customs and traditions.* ● **Well-informed** is a more formal word for **genned up.**

V+ADV:
USUALLY+on

ADJECTIVE

get, gets, getting, got

Gotten is used in American English as the past participle. Most of the phrasal verbs with get are informal.

get about. 1 If you can **get about** after you have been ill or when you are old, you are able to move around without much difficulty. EG *I can't get about as much as I used to... She gets Stuart to help her, otherwise she just couldn't get about, she'd just be stuck there... I can get about with a stick.*

V+ADV

2 See get around 2.

get above. If you say that someone **is getting above** themselves, you mean that they are behaving as if they are better than everyone else. EG *She was restrained from getting above herself by a natural modesty.*

V+PREP+REFL

get across. If an idea or argument **gets across,** or if you **get** it **across,** you succeed in making other people understand it. EG *The speaker needs to know that his words are getting across... We managed to get our message across... It was difficult to get across the basic idea.* ● **Get over** and **put across** mean almost the same as **get across.**

V+ADV,
V+N+ADV,
V+ADV+N,
V+PRON+ADV:
ERGATIVE

get after. If you **get after** someone, you try to catch them, especially after they have committed a crime. EG *It is their job to get after the villains as fast as possible.* ● **Pursue** is a more formal word for **get after.**

V+PREP

get ahead. If you **get ahead,** you are successful in your career. EG   V+ADV
*The bright young man can get ahead quickly in industry... You've
got to be sharp to get ahead.* ● **Get on** means almost the same as **get
ahead.**

get along. 1 If you **get along** with someone, you have a friendly   V+ADV+*with,*
relationship with them; a very informal use. EG *He worked hard and*   V+ADV+*together,*
was easy to get along with... They just can't get along together... The   V+ADV:
two men do get along well. ● **Get on** means almost the same as **get**   RECIPROCAL
along.

2 If you **are getting along** in a situation, you are coping with it or   V+ADV:
making progress in it, although it may be difficult. EG *Some parents*   ALSO+*with*
*never ask how their children are getting along... With his ninety
dollars a week and her sixty they got along well enough... How are
you getting along with the German course?... You can get along fine
without a washing machine.* ● **Get on** means almost the same as **get
along,** and **manage** is a less informal word.

3 If you say that you must **get along,** you mean that you must leave,   V+ADV
because you have to go somewhere else. EG *Well, I'd better be
getting along, the train's due.*

get around. 1 If you **get around,** you go to a lot of different places   V+ADV
as part of your way of life. EG *Getting around will help to increase
your experience.*

2 If you say that someone **gets around,** you mean that they have   V+ADV
many casual sexual relationships; a very informal use. EG *She's that
kind of person; she gets around.*

3 If news **gets around, about,** or **round,** a lot of people hear about it   V+ADV,
and it becomes well-known. EG *The news got around, and there were*   V+ADV+REPORT,
always plenty of visitors to the exhibition... Startling rumours began   V+PREP
*to get about... The word got round that Morris was going to Eng-
land... Gossip gets round the film industry much faster than in other
places.*

4 See **get round.**

get around to. See **get round to.**

get at. 1 If you **get at** something, you manage to reach or obtain it.   V+PREP:
EG *Keep your tool box where you can get at it... The bull was trying*   HAS PASSIVE
*to smash the fence so that he could get at me... You can't get at the
public records until one hundred years has elapsed.*

2 If you **get at** something that is secret, you succeed in discovering   V+PREP
the truth about it. EG *He does attempt to get at the underlying truth
of the situation... He wanted to get at the heart of this puzzling
episode... ...a determination to get at the facts.* ● **Find out** means
almost the same as **get at.**

3 If you ask someone what they **are getting at,** you are asking them   V+PREP
to explain what they mean; a very informal use. EG *I don't know
what you are getting at... The audience had no idea what we were
getting at... I know what you're getting at, and you're right.* ● **Drive
at** means almost the same as **get at.**

4 If you say that someone **is getting at** you, you mean that they keep   V+PREP:
criticizing you in an unkind way; a very informal use. EG *You're*   HAS PASSIVE
*always getting at me... His attitude only strengthened my resolve
not to let him get at me.* ● **Pick on** means almost the same as **get at.**

5 If someone **has been got at,** they have been persuaded by threats   V+PREP:
or bribes to say something untrue or to act in an unfair way. EG *He*   HAS PASSIVE,
allowed the Foreign Office to be got at by the Prime Minister... I   USUALLY PASSIVE
should have won; I'm sure the judges had been got at.

get away. 1 If you **get away** from a place or a person's company,   V+ADV:
you succeed in leaving them. EG *You've got to get away from home...*   USUALLY+*from*

I wish you could get away from all those people... She wanted to get away, but didn't want to appear rude.

2 If you **get away**, you go away to have a holiday. EG *Is there any*   V+ADV
*chance of you getting away this summer?... I might crack up if I
don't get away for a while... It's nice to get away in the autumn.*

3 When someone or something **gets away** from a place, or when you   V+ADV,
get them **away**, they escape. EG *They got away through Mrs*   V+PRON+ADV,
Barnett's garden... I was determined not to let him get away... I   ERGATIVE
prayed for a helicopter to come and get me away from there. ▶ If   N COUNT,
someone makes a **getaway**, they leave a place in a hurry, often   ADJECTIVE
after committing a crime. EG *Duffield had already made his getaway
down the stairs... They leapt aboard the getaway cars.*

4 People sometimes say **'Get away'** to show that they do not believe   IMPERATIVE:
what has just been said; an informal use. EG *Get away! We can't have*   V+ADV
that... 'I've been arrested' I said—'Get away with you!' he laughed.
• **Go on** means almost the same as **get away**.

get away from. If you **get away from** a common or existing way   V+ADV+PREP
of behaving or doing something, you start behaving or doing things
in a different way. EG *We need to get away from the idea that
technology is essential... They wanted to get away from the rigid
timetables of the past... I thought he'd got away from that film star
image.* • **Break away from** means almost the same as **get away
from**.

get away with. If you **get away with** something that you should   V+ADV+PREP
not have done, you are not criticized or punished for doing it. EG *I'm
not going to allow Anne to get away with an offensive remark like
that... He might have bribed her—and got away with it.*

get back. 1 If you **get back** to a place or position, you return there   V+ADV:
after you have been somewhere else. EG *I've got to get back to*   USUALLY+A
*London... What time have you got to get back?... You're shivering.
Get back to bed.*

2 If you **get** someone or something **back** to a place, you take them   V+PRON+ADV,
there after they have been away from it. EG *We're going to get you*   V+N+ADV:
right back home where we can look after you properly... Did you get   USUALLY+A,
your books back to the library in time?   NO PASSIVE

3 If you **get** something **back** after you have lost it, you have it once   V+N+ADV,
again. EG *All he wants to do is get his girlfriend back... She had all*   V+PRON+ADV,
her antique jewellery stolen, and I don't think she'll get it back   V+ADV+N:
now... He would get back his old job.   NO PASSIVE

4 When you **get** your breath **back**, you pause and relax after a very   V+N+ADV
tiring or exciting activity, until you start feeling normal again. EG
*...trying to get her breath back after a spell of coughs... I got my
breath back and tried to work it out.*

5 If you tell someone to **get back**, you are telling them to move away   IMPERATIVE:
from someone or something. EG *If you come near, I'll scream. Get*   V+ADV
back! • **Stand back** and **back off** mean almost the same as **get back**.

6 If you **get** someone **back**, you punish or hurt them in return for   V+PRON+ADV,
something unpleasant that they have done to you. EG *I'll get him*   V+N+ADV
back for all the nasty things he said. • **Pay back** means almost the
same as **get back**.

get back at. If you **get back at** someone, you criticize or punish   V+ADV+PREP
them in return for something unpleasant that they have done or said
to you. EG *He hated meanness, and seemed to consider it his duty to
get back at those guilty of this.*

get back into. If you **get back into** an activity that you were doing   V+ADV+PREP
before, you start being involved in it again. EG *Maybe you could get
back into journalism... Japanese investors are getting back into the*

market... Now her kids are grown up, she'd like to get back into research.

get back to. 1 If you **get back to** what you were doing or talking   V+ADV+PREP
about before, you start doing it or talking about it again. EG *Eddie
wanted to get back to sleep... Now I really must get back to work...
Let's just get back to the argument.* ● **Go back to** means almost the
same as **get back to.**

2 If you **get back to** someone, you contact them again after a short   V+ADV+PREP
period of time, often by telephone. EG *Leave a message and I'll get
back to you... I couldn't get back to you in time to tell you the new
arrangements.*

get behind. 1 If you **get behind** with some work that you are doing,   V+ADV:
you are slow and do not make as much progress as other people   ALSO+*with*
who are doing the same sort of work. EG *I'm not surprised Sarah gets
behind at school—her parents just aren't interested... If you get
behind with your reading in your final year, you'll never catch up.*
● **Fall behind** means almost the same as **get behind.**

2 If you **get behind** someone or something, you support them and try   V+PREP
to help them to succeed; used mainly in American English. EG *'It's a
pity they don't get behind us,' Fleck said... They will support reform
if it sticks, but will not get behind it until it does.*

get beyond. If you **get beyond** a particular thing, you make   V+PREP
progress so that you are no longer concerned with that thing. EG *In
some schools, you never get beyond counting coloured pips... She
had got beyond the stage of prizing what was rare or expensive... As
a musician, he has not got beyond playing Le Sacre du Printemps.*
● **Go beyond** means almost the same as **get beyond.**

get by. 1 If you **get by**, you just manage to survive and have a fairly   V+ADV
satisfactory life. EG *He had managed to get by without much reading
or writing... They slide through life, getting by as best they can...
Khan's father had just enough land to get by.*

2 If you **get by** in a difficult situation, you manage to cope with it. EG   V+ADV:
*You can get by in any English conversation with a very limited   ALSO+*in*
vocabulary... It's possible to get by in a job interview by just talking
about your interests.*

3 If someone or something that is moving **gets by**, they manage to   V+ADV
get past an obstacle. EG *The truck began hooting to get by... I moved
away from the doorway to let her get by.* ● **Pass** means almost the
same as **get by.**

get down. 1 When someone or something **gets down** they move   V+ADV/PREP,
from a higher position or level to a lower one. To **get** someone or   V+N+ADV/PREP,
something **down** means to move them from a higher position or   V+PRON+ADV/PREP:
level to a lower one. EG *When we eventually got down the mountain,*   ERGATIVE
*he was rushed to hospital... Wait until the temperature gets down to
zero!... You'll never get the piano down the stairs.*

2 If you **get down** from an object that you are sitting, standing, or   V+ADV:
lying on, you move off it and on to the ground. EG *He got down from*   USUALLY+*from*
*the step ladder... George has climbed up that tree, and now he can't
get down.*

3 If children ask to **get down** when they have been sitting at a table   V+ADV
and eating a meal, they are asking permission to get down from
their chair and leave the table, because they have finished eating.

4 If you are standing somewhere and **get down,** you bend down and   V+ADV:
sit, kneel or lie on the ground. EG *The soldiers shouted to us to get*   ALSO+*on*
*down... The woman got down on her knees and peered at the baby...
They got down on the ground.*

5 If you **get down** to a place, you go there; a very informal use. EG   V+ADV:
Get down there and find out what they're planning... ...people who   ALSO+*to*

can't get down to the seaside as often as they want... I rushed my lunch to get down to the garage by half past one.

6 If you **get** food **down,** you swallow it, especially with difficulty; an informal use. EG *I felt better yesterday, but I'm finding it hard to get food down... He spat it out because he couldn't get it down.*

V+N+ADV,
V+PRON+ADV:
NO PASSIVE

7 If you **get down** what someone is saying, you write it down. EG *They'd have to get all the conversation down... Have you got the details down?... I keep repeating myself so that you can get it down.*
● **Take down** means almost the same as **get down.**

V+N+ADV,
V+PRON+ADV,
V+ADV+N:
NO PASSIVE

8 If something **gets** you **down,** it makes you unhappy. EG *It isn't just the work that gets her down... He said I shouldn't let my circumstances get me down... The loneliness really started to get my mother down after a few months.* ● **Depress** is a slightly less informal word for **get down.**

V+PRON+ADV,
V+N+ADV:
NO PASSIVE

get down to. When you **get down to** something, you start doing it seriously and with a lot of attention. EG *I got down to work... Let's get down to business... These are problems that we have never got down to tackling.*

V+ADV+PREP

get in. **1** If you **get in** a place such as a car, house, or room, you go inside it. EG *Never get in a stranger's car... He nearly knocked me over in his eagerness to get in the house... I walked to the van, got in and drove away.*

V+PREP,
V+ADV

2 When someone or something **gets in,** they arrive at a place where people are expecting them to be. EG *He asked if you'd ring back when you got in... What time does the coach get in, do you know?... He's got an obsession about staff getting in on time.*

V+ADV

3 If you **get in** a building, you succeed in gaining admission to it. EG *Nobody could get in or out without a pass... 'We went to the late show.'—'Oh, you managed to get in, did you?'... It cost three pounds to get in.*

V+ADV,
V+PREP

4 If you **get** something **in** from outside, you bring it inside to protect it from the weather. EG *You might at least have got the washing in... Boss, we must get in the barley.*

V+N+ADV,
V+ADV+N,
V+PRON+ADV

5 If you **get in** some provisions or supplies, you buy them when you go shopping, because you have no more left. EG *We must remember to get some more coffee in.*

V+N+ADV,
V+ADV+N

6 If you **get** someone **in,** you ask them to come and help you or to do something for you. EG *Get an expert in to deal with faulty wiring... I'll get in the police if they keep up this racket much longer.* ● **Call in** means almost the same as **get in.**

V+N+ADV,
V+ADV+N,
V+PRON+ADV

7 When a political party or a politician **gets in,** they are elected. EG *What would Labour do if they got in ?... She got in by more than 5,000 votes.*

V+ADV

8 If you **get in** something such as work, practice, or exercise, you arrange your time so that you are able to do it, even though you are very busy doing other things. EG *The idea was to get in a little golf... They get in all the work they can... I really need to get some practice in before the performance.* ● **Fit in** means almost the same as **get in.**

V+ADV+N,
V+N+ADV,
V+PRON+ADV:
NO PASSIVE

9 If you **get** something **in** when lots of people are talking at the same time, you eventually succeed in saying something. EG *Phillip got a question in about the rates... Tinker had to get in the last word... 'What I wanted to say,' I finally got in, 'is that I've a set of instructions at home.'*

V+N+ADV,
V+ADV+N,
V+ADV+QUOTE,
V+PRON+ADV

get in on. If you **get in on** an activity that is already taking place, you start taking part in it, often without being asked or invited to. EG *'He even gets in on the photography shows,' she said indignantly...*

V+ADV+PREP

...studio assistants who got in on the act... ...getting in on the satellite system.

get into. 1 If you **get into** a place, you enter it or reach it. EG *They*   V+PREP
*got into the hut through a hole in the wall... I turned off the lights
and got into bed... We got into the village at about one o'clock.*

2 If you **get into** an activity, you start being involved in it. EG *I always*   V+PREP
*get into arguments with people... He was determined to get into
politics... He had got into the campaign right at the end.*

3 If you **get into** a difficult situation, or if someone **gets** you **into** it,   V+PREP,
you are involved in it, often without intending to be. EG *Make sure*   V+PRON+PREP,
you don't overspend and get into debt... There was no telling what   V+REFL+PREP,
sort of trouble she'd get into... 'I'm in trouble,' said Carmen, 'and you   V+N+PREP:
got me into it.'... He got himself into a frightful muddle recently.   ERGATIVE,
    NO PASSIVE

4 If you **get into** a particular habit or way of behaving, you start to   V+PREP
have that habit or behave in that way. EG *She'd got into the habit of
sulking... We tend to get into a certain way of thinking... I really
need to get into a routine.*

5 If you **get into** a subject, you start getting interested in it; a very   V+PREP
informal use. EG *She got into health foods and astrology... I just can't
get into those sort of books.*

6 If you **get into** an organization such as a school, team, or club, you   V+PREP
are accepted as a member of that organization. EG *There was no
chance of her getting into University... Darwin failed to get into
medical school at Cambridge... If I don't get into the first team this
year, I'm not playing at all.*

7 If you **get into** your clothes, you put them on rather awkwardly or   V+PREP
with difficulty. EG *I became so fat I couldn't get into any of my
clothes... ...hopping on one foot to get into her shorts.*

8 You ask what **has got into** someone when you mean that they are   V+PREP
behaving in a strange or unexpected way; a very informal use. EG
*What's got into her these days?... I don't know what's got into you,
Laing.*

get in with. If you **get in with** someone, you flatter them and   V+ADV+PREP
become friendly with them, often because you think that they can
help you; a very informal expression, used showing disapproval. EG
*She takes good care to get in with the people who matter... She had
been married and divorced, and this chap got in with her.*

get off. 1 If you **get off** something that you have been standing,   V+PREP
sitting, or lying on, you move your body from it, usually onto the
ground. EG *She started to get off the table... He got off his bicycle...
She was getting off the bed.*

2 If you **get off** a bus, train, or plane, you leave it. EG *When the train*   V+ADV,
stopped, he got off... Get off at Mayfield Church... I had no reason for   V+PREP
getting off the bus near the Palais. ● **Get out** means almost the same
as **get off.**

3 When you **get off,** you leave a place. EG *I can't get off for another*   V+ADV
*hour and a half... I have to be getting off now... Did Myra get off all
right?* ● **Get away** means almost the same as **get off.**

4 If you **get** someone **off** to a place, you send them there, or take   V+N+ADV,
them part of the way there. EG *I can't stay, I've got to get the*   V+PRON+ADV:
children off to school... We'll get these two young men off first, then   ALSO+to
*we can sort things out... Some of the mothers wanted to get their
kids off to bed.*

5 If you **get** a letter, parcel, or message **off,** you send it. EG *He*   V+N+ADV,
eventually got his letter off... Get this message off to the addressee.   V+PRON+ADV,
    V+ADV+N

6 If you tell someone to **get off** a piece of land, you are telling them   V+PREP
to leave a place where they should not be. EG *I told them to get off*

the university playing fields... A cop would tell the noisy kids to get off the street.

7 If you tell someone to **get off** the phone, you are telling them to stop using it. EG *I told him to get off the phone... Will you kindly get off the phone—you've been on for hours.* `V+PREP`

8 You say '**Get off**' to someone when you are telling them not to touch you, or not to touch something; a very informal use. EG *Colin kept trying to kiss me, so I told him to get off... Get off that cake, it's for tomorrow!* `IMPERATIVE: V+ADV, V+PREP`

9 If you **get** something **off,** you remove it. EG *Get your shirt off... The top's stuck and I can't get it off... ...stains you can't get off your skin.* `V+N+ADV/PREP, V+PRON+ADV/PREP`

10 If you **get** something **off** someone, you succeed in persuading them to give it to you; a very informal use. EG *They're more concerned with getting a meal off us... I'll get some money off my dad.* `V+N+PREP, V+PRON+PREP`

11 If you **get** time **off,** you do not have to go to work during that period. EG *Years ago, a nanny was lucky to get an afternoon off a week... I wouldn't get next Monday off... She can't get time off to go to the clinic.* `V+N+ADV, V+PRON+ADV: NO PASSIVE`

12 If you **get off** when you have done something wrong, or if someone **gets** you **off,** you receive only a small punishment for what you have done. EG *He got off with a £50 fine... She had her suspicions that she would not get off so easily... 'Do you think you'll get her off?—'I'm not a lawyer!'.* `V+ADV, V+PRON+ADV, V+N+ADV: ERGATIVE`

13 If you **get off** the subject that you are talking about, you change it and start to talk about something else instead. If you **get off** the point in a discussion or argument, you start talking about things that are not relevant to it. EG *I think we'd better get off this subject... Let's get off politics and get onto the real issues here... Michael, you're getting off the point.* `V+PREP`

14 If you **get off** or **get off** to sleep, you succeed in falling asleep in spite of something that makes it difficult for you to sleep. EG *I just couldn't get off last night.* `V+ADV: USUALLY+to`

get off on. If you **get off on** something, you become very excited by it; a very informal expression. EG *I saw you watching the fight and getting off on it... Rock-climbing is such a high—I really get off on it.* `V+ADV+PREP`

get off with. If you **get off with** someone, you begin a romantic or sexual relationship with them; an informal expression. EG *Mike thinks I'm trying to get off with his girlfriend... If a man's getting off with a girl, people notice it.* `V+ADV+PREP`

get on. 1 If you **get on** an object, you move your body so that you are sitting, standing, or lying on it. EG *I'd get on my horse and go out to her place... He tried to get on the wall but it was too high.* `V+PREP`

2 If you **get on** a bus, train, or plane, you get into it. EG *She got on the bus every morning... Some new passengers were getting on.* ● **Board** is a more formal word for **get on.** `V+PREP, V+ADV`

3 If you **get on** the telephone to someone, or if you **get** them **on** it, you talk to them on the telephone. EG *He got on the phone to President Thompson... Mrs. Callahan spent days trying to get Lieutenant Donovan on the phone... Get him on the phone at once!* `V+PREP, V+N+PREP, V+PRON+PREP: NO PASSIVE`

4 If you **get** a piece of clothing **on,** you dress yourself in it. EG *Get your coat on... I left the pyjamas on the bed and told him to get them on... Amy told Paul to get on his sandals.* ● **Put on** means almost the same as **get on.** `V+N+ADV, V+PRON+ADV, V+ADV+N`

5 If you **get on** with an activity, you start doing it or continue doing it. EG *Let me get on with my dinner... Perhaps we can get on with the meeting... He suggested to his colleague that perhaps they should get on.* `V+ADV: USUALLY+with`

6 If you ask how someone **is getting on** with an activity, you are asking about their progress. EG *Sylvia asked politely how Paul was getting on at school... How are you getting on?... It's all to do with how he's getting on with his painting.* ● **Get along** means almost the same as **get on**.
`V+ADV: ALSO+with`

7 If you **get on** in your career, you are successful. EG *She's got to study to get on... I must get on in my job because of the children... You have to push yourself to get on in the academic world.* ● **Get ahead** means almost the same as **get on**.
`V+ADV: ALSO+in`

8 To **get on** without someone or something means to manage to continue or succeed without them. EG *The party will get on better without him... If they cannot get on without help, what's the point of employing them?... We'll just have to get on as best we can.*
`V+ADV: ALSO+without`

9 If you **get on** with someone, you like them and have a friendly relationship with them. EG *It's funny how they don't get on, Mark and Cyril... You seem to be getting on well with the Chairman... The two communities are not prepared to get on together.* ● **Get along** means almost the same as **get on**.
`V+ADV, V+ADV+with, V+ADV+together: RECIPROCAL`

10 If someone **gets on** a committee or a television or radio programme, or **gets** themselves **on** it, they are successful in being accepted to take part in it. EG *Ford is likely to get on the board of the new financial company... Perhaps they would even get on the Ed Sullivan show... She's hoping to get herself on the panel for 'Any Questions'.*
`V+PREP, V+REFL+PREP`

11 If you say that someone **is getting on,** you mean that they are old. EG *Now I'm getting on, these stairs are a little difficult for me... They were getting on in years now.*
`V+ADV`

12 If you say that time **is getting on,** you mean that there is not much time left before something is expected to happen, or before something must be done.
`V+ADV`

get on at. If you **get on at** someone, you continually criticize them in an unkind way. EG *I didn't want him getting on at you.* ● **Keep on at** means almost the same as **get on at**.
`V+ADV+PREP`

get on for. If something **is getting on for** an amount, it is nearly that amount. EG *This building must be getting on for four hundred years old... I am getting on for twenty and have become engaged... It was getting on for four o' clock.*
`V+ADV+PREP`

get on to, get onto. 1 If you **get on to** a particular topic, you start talking about it in a lecture or conversation after you have been talking about something else. EG *That's something we'll get on to in the future... Bobby and Denise got on to talking about old movies... I don't know how we got onto this.*
`V+ADV+PREP`

2 If you **get on to** someone, you contact them. EG *I'll get on to her right away... Get straight on to the department chief about it... John, I want you to get on to Central Records.*
`V+ADV+PREP`

3 If someone in authority **gets onto** you, they find out about something that you have been trying to keep secret. EG *The police got on to the infiltrators... I don't imagine they will get on to this if we keep quiet... It wasn't long before the Ministry of Information got on to him.*
`V+ADV+PREP`

get out. 1 If you **get out** of a place, you leave it. EG *We got out of the car... Brody got out of bed... I'm going to get out of New York... She got out and slammed the door.*
`V+ADV: USUALLY+of`

2 If you **get** someone **out** of a place, you help or order them to leave it. EG *Mr Profumo had been instrumental in getting Miss Keeler out of the country... It would take hours for the Marines to get their wounded out... Get me out of here!*
`V+N+ADV, V+PRON+ADV: USUALLY+of`

3 If you **get** someone **out** of a difficult or dangerous situation, you
`V+PRON+ADV,`

get over

help them to escape from it. EG *Who got you out of that mess in Omaha?... I got you into this and now I must get you out.* ▶ A **getout** is something which helps you to avoid or prevent an unwanted situation. EG *What we need is a safe getout... Insurance companies always have a getout clause of some kind.*

V+N+ADV: USUALLY+*of*
N COUNT, ADJECTIVE

4 If you **get out**, you go to places and meet people, because you want to have an enjoyable and interesting life. EG *Get out and enjoy yourself... You've got to get out and make friends.* ● **Go out** means almost the same as **get out**.

V+ADV

5 If you **get** something **out**, you take it out of the place or container that it is in. EG *I got my little wireless out of the rucksack... 'Where's my mug?'—'I thought you just got it out.'... He got out his book and started to read.*

V+N+ADV, V+PRON+ADV, V+ADV+N: ALSO+*of*

6 If you **get** dirt or other unwanted substances **out** of something, you remove them from it. EG *I couldn't get the stain out of your green dress.*

V+N+ADV, V+PRON+ADV: ALSO+*of*

7 If you **get out** a product or a piece of work, you manufacture it or produce it so that it is available to people. EG *The American Cancer Society got out its first report in 1954... They can't get the book out before Christmas.* ● **Bring out** means almost the same as **get out**.

V+ADV+N, V+N+ADV, V+PRON+ADV

8 If you **get** something **out** that you are trying to say, you manage to say it. EG *She couldn't get a word out for the moment... He was sobbing so hard he couldn't get anything out.*

V+N+ADV, V+PRON+ADV

9 If news or information **gets out**, it becomes known. EG *The news got out in the end... The word got out that he would go ahead.* ● **Leak out** and **come out** mean almost the same as **get out**.

V+ADV, V+ADV+REPORT

10 If you **get out** of something such as an organization or club, you leave it and stop being a member of it. EG *The Common Market? The sooner we get out the better.* ● **Pull out** means almost the same as **get out**.

V+ADV: USUALLY+*of*

11 In cricket, if you **get** a batsman **out**, you end their innings, for example by bowling the ball and hitting the wicket, or catching the ball after they have hit it.

V+N+ADV, V+PRON+ADV

get out of. 1 If you **get** pleasure or satisfaction **out of** something that you do or experience, you enjoy it and think that it is worthwhile. EG *We all got a great deal of pleasure out of our school days... She got a lot of fun out of sweeping the front porch of the restaurant... I think she got more out of the course than I did.*

V+N+ADV+PREP

2 If you **get out of** doing something, you avoid doing it; a very informal use. EG *She always got out of washing up... We'll do anything to get out of work... I had to go to school, and if I could have got out of it, I would.* ● **Wriggle out of** means almost the same as **get out of**.

V+ADV+PREP

3 If you **get** something **out of** someone, you persuade them to give it you, even though they do not really want to. EG *Next time Jim turns up we can get a few pounds out of him... ...trying to get some kind of confession out of me.*

V+N+ADV+PREP, V+PRON+ADV+PREP

4 If you **get out of** a habit or an activity that you do regularly, you stop doing it. EG *If I get out of my routine, I'm finished!*

V+ADV+PREP

get over. 1 If you **get over** an illness or other unpleasant experience, you recover from it. EG *Have you got over the shock?... George did not get over his homesickness for some time... I'm glad to hear you have got over your cold.*

V+PREP

2 If you **get over** a problem or difficulty, you find a way of dealing with it. EG *One mother got over this problem by leaving her baby with someone else... The unhappy situation in the Labour Party could be got over if we changed to the American system.*

V+PREP

3 If you say that you cannot **get over** an unexpected event or a surprising fact, you mean that you find it difficult to believe that it

V+PREP: WITH NEGATIVE

happened or is true. ᴇɢ *Sergeant Brown couldn't get over it as Evans solemnly handed over the money he had stolen... She could not get over the fact that someone so handsome could be so unlikeable.*

4 If you **get** an idea, argument, or suggestion **over**, you succeed in making other people understand it. ᴇɢ *This is the only way I know of getting my message over to you clearly... One must first get over the idea that this method is completely new... How do I get it over to you?* ● **Get across** means almost the same as **get over**.

V+N+ADV,
V+ADV+N,
V+PRON+ADV:
USUALLY+*to*

5 If you **get over** to a place, you go there or arrive there. If you **get** someone **over** to it, you arrange for them to come and visit you. ᴇɢ *We could get over to your house by about six o'clock... I thought I might get him over to dinner one evening... ...the bureaucratic obstacles to getting her son over from Jamaica.*

V+ADV,
V+PRON+ADV,
V+N+ADV:
ERGATIVE,
NO PASSIVE

get over with. If you **get** something **over with,** you do and complete something unpleasant that must be done. ᴇɢ *Can we just get this questioning over with?... He wanted to get this miserable business over with as quickly as possible... Give Woods his final warning now and get it over with.*

V+N+ADV+*with*,
V+PRON+ADV+*with*

get round. **1** If you **get round** or **around** a difficulty or restriction, you find a way of avoiding it or of escaping its effects. ᴇɢ *Irving got round the problem in a novel way... To get round the law their plays were staged in private houses... An impasse has developed and I don't know how to get around it.* ● **Bypass** is a more formal word for **get round.**

V+PREP:
HAS PASSIVE

2 If you **get round** someone, you persuade them to let you do or have something, by flattering them. ᴇɢ *She could always get round him in the end... Bryan failed to get round Joan.* ● **Win over** means almost the same as **get round.**

V+PREP:
HAS PASSIVE

3 If you **get round** when you are in a race, you manage to finish it. ᴇɢ *I felt really tired, but I did get round the course... Lauder got round in just over two hours and twenty minutes.*

V+ADV,
V+PREP

4 See **get around.**

get round to. If you **get round to** or **around to** doing something, you do it after a long delay because you were previously too busy or reluctant to do it. ᴇɢ *I didn't get round to taking the examination... It took her two years to get around to buying a car.*

V+ADV+PREP

get through. **1** If you **get through** a task, you succeed in finishing it. ᴇɢ *It is difficult to get through this amount of work in such a short time... We managed to get through our meeting early... Exercises are not a chore to be got through, but a means of training your body... As soon as I get through with this washing, I'll help you.*

V+PREP:
HAS PASSIVE,
ALSO+*with*

2 If you **get through** a difficult or unpleasant experience, or someone or something **gets** you **through** it, you survive it. ᴇɢ *He was going to get through the war and go home... She needs her coffee to get through the day... My wits got me through... ...the pain of adolescence that she got me through.*

V+ADV/PREP,
V+PRON+ADV/PREP,
V+N+ADV/PREP:
ERGATIVE,
NO PASSIVE

3 If a person or an idea **gets through** to you, you understand what they say or mean. ᴇɢ *Howard, how do I get through to you?... The actor really got through to the audience that night... As the idea got through, she smiled... ...words which somehow will get through to the child.*

V+ADV:
USUALLY+*to*

4 If you **get through** to someone on the telephone, you succeed in contacting them. ᴇɢ *I telephoned Juliet in hospital and got through without difficulty... Sorry you couldn't get through on the phone last week... I've been trying for a whole hour to get through to you.*

V+ADV:
ALSO+*to*

5 If something **gets through** to a place, it finally succeeds in reaching that place. ᴇɢ *...information that got through to Russia... I*

V+ADV:
ALSO+*to*

expect the letters just aren't getting through... The real emergencies were not getting through to the hospital.

6 If you **get through** an examination, or if someone or something gets you **through** it, you pass it. EG *They haven't got a chance of getting through... He qualifies if he gets through his two subjects this year... It's hard work and nothing else that gets you through.*

V+ADV/PREP, V+PRON+ADV/PREP, V+N+ADV/PREP: ERGATIVE, NO PASSIVE

7 If you **get through** to a particular stage in a competition, or if someone or something **gets** you **through** to it, you succeed in reaching that stage. EG *Steve Davis has got through to the final again... It was only luck that got us through to the next round... ...if United get through the 6th Round of the cup.*

V+ADV, V+PRON+ADV, V+N+ADV: ERGATIVE, NO PASSIVE

8 If you **get through** an amount of something, you use it completely. EG *When he got through all his money he went back to Canada... I got through about six pounds' worth of drink.* ● **Run through** means almost the same as **get through.**

V+PREP

9 If a law or proposal **gets through,** it is officially approved by something such as a parliament or committee. EG *If this new White Paper gets through, there will be no subsidized meals... The proposals might not have been able to get through Congress... The Bill got through all its stages and became law... The opposition got the amendment through with a majority of 117.*

V+ADV/PREP, V+N+ADV/PREP, V+PRON+ADV/PREP: ERGATIVE

get to. **1** When you **get to** a place, you arrive there. EG *It was midnight before we got to the village.*

V+PREP

2 If you **get to** doing something, you gradually begin to do it without intending to; a very informal use. EG *I got to thinking how lonely she must be.* ● **Fall to** is a literary expression for **get to.**

V+PREP

3 If an experience or emotion **gets to** you, it affects you strongly, although you try not to let it; a very informal use. EG *Don't let it get to you... The horror of war was beginning to get to me.*

V+PREP

get together. **1** When people **get together,** they meet in order to discuss something or to spend time together. EG *Workers and supervisors get together to discuss their grievances... Do you think we could get together at Christmas?... ...getting childminders together in local self-help groups... He got together a band of thieves.* ► A **get-together** is an informal meeting or party. EG *We're having a little get-together to celebrate Helen's promotion.*

V+ADV, V+N+ADV, V+ADV+N, V+PRON+ADV: ERGATIVE

N COUNT

2 If you **get** several things **together,** you collect them and put them all in one place. EG *I got my letters and papers together... Well, as long as you've got all your own stuff together, too... I got together the rest of the notes and fastened them with rubber bands.* ● **Gather up** means almost the same as **get together,** and **assemble is a** more formal word.

V+N+ADV, V+ADV+N, V+PRON+ADV

3 If you **get together** a plan or a meeting of some kind, you organize it or arrange for other people to take part in it. EG *The Defense Front got together a sizeable demonstration of support... Have you got that syllabus together yet?... I don't know whether he's got the time to get anything together yet.*

V+ADV+N, V+N+ADV, V+PRON+ADV

4 If you **get** money **together,** you succeed in getting all the money that you need in order to pay for something. EG *Almost all of the children had got the money together themselves... Somehow we have to get the fees together.* ● **Scrape up** means almost the same as **get together,** and **raise** is a more formal word.

V+N+ADV, V+PRON+ADV, V+ADV+N

5 If you **get** yourself **together,** you succeed in controlling your feelings so that you behave calmly and reasonably. EG *Gladys got herself together enough to see a lawyer.* ● **Pull together** means almost the same as **get together.**

V+REFL+ADV

get up. **1** When someone or something **gets up,** they move from a lower position or level to a higher one. To **get** someone or some-

V+ADV/PREP, V+N+ADV/PREP, V+PRON+ADV/PREP: ERGATIVE

thing **up** means to move them from a lower position or level to a higher one. EG *I knew they'd have difficulty getting up that mountain... This car can get up to 100 mph on a straight road... You'll never get him up those stairs.*

2 If you **get up**, you rise to a standing position after you have been sitting or lying down. EG *I had to get up from my stool... He got up off the floor... She got up and strode across the room.* — V+ADV

3 When you **get up**, or when someone **gets** you **up**, you get out of bed. EG *Morris decided it was time to get up... Don't get me up in the morning... We had until 7.15 to get ourselves up... Then we had to get the children up and dressed.* — V+ADV, V+PRON+ADV, V+REFL+ADV, V+N+ADV: ERGATIVE

4 If you **get up** to a place, you visit it or travel there; often used when the place is farther north than you or is in a city. EG *He'll have to get up to London for the day... I want to get up there again this summer... You'd better get up to his flat and sort things out.* — V+ADV: WITH A

5 If you **get up** something such as a public event or meeting, you arrange it or organize it, especially with very little preparation; a rather old-fashioned use. EG *The women got up a march and picket to move them out of the school... An impromptu dance was got up in his honour.* ● **Fix up** means almost the same as **get up**. — V+ADV+N, V+N+ADV, V+PRON+ADV

6 If someone **has got** themselves **up** in unusual or strange clothes, or if they **are got up** in them, they are dressed in unusual or strange clothes. EG *...the days when band leaders got themselves up in braided jackets... Several people were got up as frontiersmen... ...children got up in spaceman outfits.* ● **Rig out** means almost the same as **get up**. ▶ A **get-up** is an unusual or strange set of clothes. EG *Who does she think she is, in that get-up?* — V+REFL+ADV, OR PASSIVE, V+ADV: USUALLY+A — N COUNT

7 If the wind or a storm **gets up**, it starts to blow very strongly. — V+ADV

get up to. When you talk about what someone **gets up to,** you are referring to what they do, especially when it is something you do not approve of; a very informal expression. EG *What did you get up to while I was away?... When I found out what they used to get up to I was absolutely horrified... I don't really think he'd get up to anything behind my back.* — V+ADV+PREP

get with. If you **get with** it, you become aware of the latest events, developments, or ideas; an informal expression which is rather old-fashioned. EG *Get with it. Go and see Tess, take your partner.* — V+PREP+*it*

ginger, gingers, gingering, gingered

ginger up. If you **ginger** something **up**, you make it more interesting and exciting; an informal expression. EG *...sharply gingering up what was left.* ● **Spice up** means almost the same as **ginger up**. — V+ADV+N, V+PRON+ADV, V+N+ADV

give, gives, giving, gave, given

give away. **1** If you **give** something **away**, you give it to someone without taking money in return. EG *She has given away jewellery worth millions of pounds... I could not decide whether to keep the money he left me or give it away... Her little boy had cried so when they had given the dog away.* ▶ A **give-away** is something which you are given free, for example a free gift that you get when you buy something else. EG *There was a give-away calendar on the wall.* — V+ADV+N, V+PRON+ADV, V+N+ADV — N COUNT, ADJECTIVE

2 If you **give away** information that is meant to be secret, you let other people know about it, sometimes by mistake. EG *I didn't feel like giving away more information than I had to... Don't give the story away, silly!... He often wondered what the twins thought of him, but they gave nothing away.* ● **Reveal** is a more formal word for **give away**. ▶ A **give-away** is an action or remark by someone which reveals something that they were trying to keep secret. — V+ADV+N, V+N+ADV, V+PRON+ADV — N SING

3 If you **give** yourself **away**, your actions or words accidentally — V+REFL+ADV, reveal something about you which you wanted to keep hidden. If you **give** someone else **away,** you reveal something about them. EG *I was too afraid that I might give myself away by saying or doing something incomprehensible... His hands were beginning to give him away.* ● **Betray** is a formal or literary word for **give away.**

V+PRON+ADV,
V+N+ADV

4 When people get married in a church, the person who officially presents the bride to her husband during the ceremony **gives** her **away.** EG *She asked her uncle to give her away... He was going to give his daughter away.*

V+PRON+ADV,
V+N+ADV,
V+ADV+N

give back. 1 If you **give** something **back,** you return it to the person who gave it to you or who it belongs to. EG *I gave the trowel back... You've got to give them back... He gave them back to her... I gave the book back to Indhar... I gave back his ring and his jacket... I gave her back her newspaper... He gave the driver back his license... Did you give me the keys back?*

V+N+ADV,
V+PRON+ADV,
ALSO+*to*:
OR
V+ADV+N,
V+PRON+ADV+N,
V+N+ADV+N,
V+PRON+N+ADV

2 If something **gives back** a quality, characteristic, or freedom that someone has lost, it restores to them that quality, characteristic, or freedom. EG *The new Parliament at last gave back a voice to those who had been silent for a generation... ...so that we can give hope back to young people... He brought before them all the warriors he had defeated and gave them back their freedom.*

V+ADV+N,
V+N+ADV,
USUALLY+*to*:
ALSO
V+PRON+ADV+N,
V+N+ADV+N

give in. 1 If you **give in,** you admit that you will have to do something you have been trying not to do, or that you will not be able to do something you wanted to do. EG *I resolved not to give in... We mustn't give in to threats... They will argue and fight against it, but they will give in if they see that you are sure it's the right thing to do.* ● **Surrender** means almost the same as **give in.**

V+ADV:
ALSO+*to*

2 If you **give in** a piece of work, you hand it to a teacher or to someone who will assess it. EG *...students giving in dissertations... You have to give in any project-based work by the end of next week.* ● **Hand in** means almost the same as **give in.**

V+ADV+N,
V+N+ADV,
V+PRON+ADV

give off. 1 When objects or processes **give off** heat, light, smoke, or sound, they release it into the air. EG *...the tremendous heat given off by the fire... This gas, in the presence of oxygen, gives off an intensely hot flame... The brake-pads started to melt, giving off a smell like burnt toast.* ● **Produce** means almost the same as **give off.**

V+ADV+N

2 If a person **gives off** a particular quality, you notice it very easily in their appearance or actions. EG *Politicians always give off an air of importance... He gave off a tremendous intellectual aura.* ● **Radiate** means almost the same as **give off.**

V+ADV+N

3 If you **give off** doing something, you completely stop doing it; an informal use in British English. EG *Chaplin never gave off doing bits of business for the amusement of friends or guests.* ● **Give over** means almost the same as **give off.**

V+ADV+N/-ING:
NO PASSIVE

give onto. If a door or window **gives onto** a particular place, it leads straight there, or has a view over it. EG *The narrow steps give onto St. James's Park... The door gave onto a path which skirted the house.* ● **Open onto** means almost the same as **give onto.**

V+PREP

give out. 1 If you **give out** a number of things, you distribute them among a number of different people. EG *They also give out information about courses for teachers of English... We made the tea and I gave it out, watched by her mother... Large sheets of paper were given out.* ● **Hand out** means almost the same as **give out.**

V+ADV+N,
V+PRON+ADV,
V+N+ADV

2 If something **gives out,** it stops working, because it is old, damaged, or tired. EG *The fuse in a plug will give out occasionally... Both tyres had finally given out... My voice was about to give out.* ● **Pack up** is a more informal expression for **give out.**

V+ADV

3 When a supply of something **gives out,** there is no more left. EG

V+ADV

Turn all the taps on until the water gives out... The oxygen gave out.
● **Run out** means almost the same as **give out**.

4 When news or information **is given out**, it is announced, sometimes unofficially. EG *On the same day it was given out that fresh documents had been discovered... Uncle Nick stopped going to church, and gave it out that he was writing a book.*

PASSIVE,
V+ADV+REPORT:
ALSO
V+IT+ADV

5 When someone or something **gives out** light, heat, or a sound, they produce light, heat, or sound in a noticeable way; a rather literary use. EG *Tail lights give out red reflections onto the wet road... The stove still gave out a dying heat... She hugged her knees closer and gave out a loud girlish laugh.*

V+ADV+N

give over. **1** If you **give over** an activity, you suddenly stop doing it; an informal use. EG *I gave over my restless re-arranging and sat by the windows.* ● **Give off** means almost the same as **give over**.

V+ADV+N:
NO PASSIVE

2 If you tell someone to **give over,** you want them to stop doing something that is annoying you; a very informal use. EG *If you don't give over, I'll smack you... She asked me to give over humming.*
● **Leave off** means almost the same as **give over**.

V+ADV:
ALSO+-ING

give over to. **1** If something **is given over to** a particular activity or purpose, it is used only for that activity or purpose. EG *The response was so great that a whole page had to be given over to readers' letters... The hills of the north and west are given over mainly to sheep farming... They gave over the remaining lodgings to her senior courtiers.*

V+ADV+N+PREP,
V+N+ADV+PREP,
V+PRON+ADV+PREP:
USUALLY PASSIVE

2 If you **give** yourself **over to** an activity, you spend all your time and effort doing it. EG *During this period Tim gave himself over to an orgy of pleasure... I gave myself over to dreams for a few minutes.*
● **Give up to** means almost the same as **give over to**.

V+REFL+ADV+PREP

3 If you **give** something **over to** someone, you let them have it, so that they can look after it or have responsibility for it. EG *I'm quite thankful to give the business over to the girls now... We had it formally given over to us about three weeks ago.*

V+N+ADV+PREP,
V+PRON+ADV+PREP

give up. **1** If you **give up** an activity or belief, you stop doing it or believing in it. EG *She never completely gave up hope... I'll never be able to give up smoking.* '*Sugar?*'—'*No, I gave it up during the war.*'

V+ADV+N,
V+ADV+-ING,
V+PRON+ADV,
V+N+ADV

2 If you **give up** a task, you stop doing it because it is too difficult, or because you are no longer interested in it. EG *Even Ruskin gave up the attempt in despair... Gaskell considered ways of making a kite and gave it up... You couldn't keep it clean, although they never gave up trying... ...but the main thing is not to give up.*

V+ADV+N,
V+PRON+ADV,
V+ADV+-ING,
V+ADV

3 If you **give** someone **up,** you allow someone else to have it, because you no longer need it or they need it more than you do. EG *They expect men to give their seats up to them in buses... He even gave up his bed, while he and Eddie slept outside.* ● **Relinquish** is a formal word for **give up**.

V+N+ADV,
V+ADV+N,
V+PRON+ADV:
ALSO+to

4 If police or enemy troops are looking for you and you **give** yourself **up,** you allow yourself to be arrested or captured. EG *Griffiths replied that he could not give himself up... Goodall again urged him to give himself up.* ● **Surrender** means almost the same as **give up**.

V+REFL+ADV

5 To **give** someone **up** who is wanted by the police means to tell the police where that person is so that they can be arrested. EG *They interrogated her forcefully, but still she wouldn't give me up.*
● **Betray** means almost the same as **give up**.

V+PRON+ADV,
V+N+ADV

6 If you **give** someone **up** that you are having a relationship with, you decide to end the relationship. EG *You haven't tried to make her give him up?... Really, Daisy and I gave each other up years ago.*
● **Throw over** is a more informal expression for **give up**.

V+PRON+ADV,
V+N+ADV

7 If you **give up** your time to do something for someone else, you

V+ADV+N

spend a lot of your own time doing it. EG ...*a very elderly man known as George who gave up his Saturday mornings to play for the team... She got advice from the more established runners who gave up their time to help the newcomers like herself.*

8 If you **give up** your job, you resign from it. EG *She'd had to give up her job... I see that you gave up teaching to nurse your mother... He had to work so hard for £30 a week that he gave it up, and looked for another job.* ● **Quit** means almost the same as **give up**.

    V+ADV+N,
    V+PRON+ADV,
    V+N+ADV

give up on. If you **give up on** someone or something, you stop trying to do something that involves them, because you think you will never succeed or understand them; an informal expression. EG *Ever hopeful, McKellen never gave up on the cinema... So many women give up on men after pursuing them... ...a kind of mystery that one gives up on.* ● **Abandon** means almost the same as **give up on**.

    V+ADV+PREP

give up to. If you **give** yourself or your life **up to** a particular thing, you devote all your time, thought, and energy to it. EG *She gave herself up to an inner vision of happiness... For months after this happened I gave myself up to dreams of revenge... ...a life given up to sexual excess.* ● **Give over to** means almost the same as **give up to**.

    V+REFL+ADV+PREP,
    V+N+ADV+PREP

glance, glances, glancing, glanced

glance off. If something **glances off** an object, it hits the object at an angle and bounces away in another direction. EG *The ball glanced off his foot into the net... The light glanced off her teeth and her thick glasses.*

    V+PREP,
    V+ADV

glaze, glazes, glazing, glazed

glaze over. If your eyes **glaze over**, they become dull in appearance and your expression shows that you are not paying attention. EG *I can see people's eyes start to glaze over at this point... It is obvious that their eyes glaze over at long lists of technical terms.*

    V+ADV

glory, glories, glorying, gloried

glory in. If you **glory in** a situation or activity, you behave in a way which shows that you enjoy it very much. EG *The women were glorying in this new-found freedom... ...a beard of the brightest carrot-orange, a beard that any pirate could have gloried in.* ● **Revel in** means almost the same as **glory in**.

    V+PREP

gloss, glosses, glossing, glossed

gloss over. If you **gloss over** a problem, a mistake, or an embarrassing moment, you ignore it or deal with it quickly in order to try and make it seem unimportant. EG *'I was leaving anyway,' I said, to gloss over the tense moment... Truffaut glosses over such contradictions... In an election campaign much of this could be glossed over.*

    V+PREP:
    HAS PASSIVE

go, goes, going, went, gone

go about. 1 The way you **go about** a task or problem is the way you deal with it. EG *I'd been wondering how to go about it... Clearly we've gone about this the wrong way... ...a guide on how to go about setting up a committee.* ● **Tackle** means almost the same as **go about**.

    V+PREP

2 When you **go about** a job or regular activity, you continue doing it in your usual way. EG *He wanted to be left alone to go about his business... All along the coast, people went about their usual daily chores.*

    V+PREP

3 When you **go about** a place, you move wherever you want to in it. EG *I could go about the house as freely as I liked... I learned with difficulty to go about the streets amid cat-calls... He'd have liked to*

    V+PREP,
    V+ADV

keep me at home, to stop me going about, but he couldn't do anything about it.

4 If you **go about** doing something, you do it regularly. EG *...learning that one cannot go about hurting others.* ● **Go round** means almost the same as **go about.**   V+ADV+-ING

5 If you **go about** in a particular way, you usually dress or behave in that way. EG *Why couldn't he be like other men and go about in his shirt sleeves?... Traders like our grandfathers went about on foot.* ● **Go round** means almost the same as **go about.**   V+ADV: WITH A

6 If you **go about** with someone, or if you **go about** together, you regularly meet them and go to different places with them. EG *You used to go about with him very frequently... They seldom went about together.*   V+ADV+*with,* V+ADV+*together:* RECIPROCAL

7 If a story or piece of news **is going about,** a lot of people hear it or talk about it. EG *Blood-curdling stories were going about concerning what they intended to do... The rumour went about that he had had some hand in getting her the sack.* ● **Go round** means almost the same as **go about,** and **circulate** is a more formal word.   V+ADV

go after. **1** If you **go after** someone, you follow them or chase them, sometimes in order to attack them. EG *Don't you think you should go after Frederica? She seemed quite upset... Luca Brasi went after them and the story is that he killed six men.*   V+PREP

2 If you **go after** something, you try to get it. EG *My husband had gone after a job... Go after a better deal... ...a goal, something he can go after.*   V+PREP

go against. **1** If something **goes against** an idea, principle, or rule, it conflicts with it or contradicts it. EG *The teaching of the Bible clearly goes against it... She'll just say something that goes against everything I've been trying to say.*   V+PREP

2 If you **go against** someone or their advice or wishes, you do something different from what they have advised you or want you to do. EG *One thing must be understood. I will never go against you... They want to assert themselves, even if it means going against their parents' wishes at times.*   V+PREP

3 If a decision or judgement **goes against** someone, for example in a court of law, it is unfavourable to them, and they lose the case. EG *The verdict went against his brother... We would have abided by the Inspector's decision if it had gone against us.* ● **Favour** means the opposite of **go against.**   V+PREP

4 If something **goes against** you, it happens in a way that is bad or unfortunate for you. EG *We have got one more chance. One more. But if it goes against us next time... He indicated that the war was going against them and would soon be brought to a close.*   V+PREP

5 If one group of soldiers **goes against** another, they attack them or prepare to attack. EG *We have picked three hundred to go against the British... Crazy Horse told the young men not to go against those other Indians far away.*   V+PREP

go ahead. **1** When someone **goes ahead** with something which they planned, promised, or asked permission to do, they begin to do it. If a plan or project **goes ahead,** the work involved starts to be done. EG *They are going ahead with the missile... The case will be discussed and he will be told whether or not he can go ahead... The unloading had gone ahead very briskly... The ballot will go ahead immediately.*   V+ADV: ALSO+*with*

● **Proceed** is a more formal word for **go ahead.** ▶ If you give the **go-ahead** for a plan or project, or give someone the **go-ahead,** you give permission or approval to someone to start doing something. EG *You have the go-ahead from the Prime Minister.*   N SING

2 You tell someone to **go ahead** when you are suggesting that they   V+ADV: ALSO IMPERATIVE do something, or are permitting or challenging them to do it. EG *He said to go ahead if we arrived before him... 'Would you like to hear it?'—'Go ahead.'... He threatened to prosecute us, and I told him to go ahead.*

3 If someone **goes ahead,** they go in front of someone else who is going in the same direction or to the same place. EG *You go ahead this time, we'll stay behind... The minibus went ahead of us.*   V+ADV: ALSO+*of*

4 A **go-ahead** person or organization is ambitious and tries hard to succeed, often by using new methods. EG *...its go-ahead young secretary... ...promising a 'dynamic and go-ahead Britain'.* ● **Enterprising** means almost the same as **go-ahead.**   ADJECTIVE

go along. **1** If you **go along** in a particular direction or manner, you move in that direction or manner. EG *I went along to the recording room... I went along the corridor until I found a door open... We were going along fast on this dirt road when my car had a blow-out.*   V+ADV, V+PREP

2 When you **go along** to an event or to do something, you go there, often in a fairly casual way; an informal use. EG *Go along and talk to a solicitor... It's a sort of party, that's all, and I said I might go along.*   V+ADV

3 If you do something as you **go along,** you do it while you are doing something else and often without any planning, rather than doing it as a separate task. EG *Record your answers as you go along... You have to add everything up as you go along... I recited poems that I made up as I went along.*   V+ADV

4 If you describe how something **is going along,** you describe how it is progressing. EG *It was going along nicely, as it had every night so far.*   V+ADV: WITH A

go along with. **1** If you **go along with** a person or idea, you agree with the person or idea, and accept that what they are saying is true. EG *I am willing to go along with Celli... I go along with the view that languages are essentially communication systems.* ● **Support** means almost the same as **go along with.**   V+ADV+PREP

2 If you **go along with** a rule, decision, or policy, you accept it and obey it. EG *You agreed to go along with the decision... He is convinced that Rogers will go along with the deal voluntarily.* ● **Abide by** is a more formal expression for **go along with.**   V+ADV+PREP

go around. See **go round: go around** is slightly more formal.

go at. If you **go at** a task or activity, you start doing it in an energetic or enthusiastic way. EG *The breakfast arrived and he went at it like a starving refugee... He handed me the cables and I went at them for the customary hour... I went at it flat-out today.*   V+PREP

go away. **1** If you **go away,** you leave a place or a person's company. If you **go away** from home, you leave it and spend time somewhere else, especially as a holiday. EG *She went away to think about it... I want to be alone now. Just go away... She had gone away for a few days... What did you do over the summer? Did you go away?... Daddy is to go away on a business trip.* ▶ A bride's **going-away** outfit is the set of clothes which she puts on after the wedding before leaving on honeymoon. EG *I changed into my going-away outfit.*   V+ADV

ADJECTIVE

2 If something, especially a problem, **goes away,** it disappears. EG *Sometimes the fever lasts for a day or two and then goes away... The sounds seemed to be going away... ...those thoughts which came at night and would not go away.* ● **Come back** means the opposite of **go away.**   V+ADV

go back. **1** If you **go back,** you return to a place where you were before. EG *In six weeks we've got to go back to West Africa... I went back to the kitchen and poured my coffee... It started to rain but I had not the strength to go back for an umbrella.*   V+ADV: ALSO+*to*

2 If something **goes back** to a particular time in the past, it was made, built, or started at that time. EG *The shop goes back to 1707...* *...French national leaders, going back at least as far as Joan of Arc... The countryman's recollections go back a long way.* ● **Date back** means almost the same as **go back**.

V+ADV: WITH A

3 If you are discussing something and **go back** to a time in the past, you begin to consider things that happened at that time. EG *To trace its origins, we have to go back some thirty million years... T understand how this state of affairs came about, we have to go back to colonial days.*

V+ADV: ALSO+*to*

4 If you say that someone cannot **go back,** you mean that they can never again be in a situation that they were in before, because too many things have changed. EG *However much he wished it, he couldn't go back. He had shed the past... He had left home and there was no going back.*

V+ADV: WITH NEGATIVE

5 If someone **goes back** to a partner that they had previously left, they start living with them again or having a relationship with them again. EG *Her lover went back to his wife.*

V+ADV: USUALLY+*to*

6 When schools or schoolchildren **go back,** they start a new term after the holidays. ● **Break up** means the opposite of **go back**.

V+ADV

7 When people on strike **go back,** they end the strike and start working again. EG *I say to those men, if you give in and go back now, many of you will lose your jobs.* ● **Come out** means the opposite of **go back**.

V+ADV

8 When something which you have bought or borrowed **goes back,** you take it to the place where you got it, sometimes in order to change it. EG *These shoes will have to go back... The glasses have gone back to the wineshop.*

V+ADV: ALSO+*to*

9 When the clocks **go back** in Britain in the autumn, everyone sets their clocks one hour later, to Greenwich Mean Time. ● **Go forward** means the opposite of **go back**.

V+ADV

go back on. If you **go back on** a promise, agreement, or statement, you do not do what you promised or agreed, or you deny what you said. EG *It wouldn't be fair, wouldn't be right, to go back on those promises... I can't go back on my word... Now you're going back on what you told me earlier.*

V+ADV+PREP

go back over. If you **go back over** something, you consider it again. EG *He went back over the accounts of the inquest... There was no point in going back over it.*

V+ADV+PREP

go back to. **1** If you **go back to** something which you stopped doing or using, you start doing or using it again. EG *She had gone back to staring out of the window... No, I'm all right, go back to sleep... Now go back to your work!*

V+ADV+PREP

2 If you **go back to** a point in a discussion or conversation, you start talking about it again. EG *I think that goes back to what we were talking about earlier on... Going back to this point, there is a limited amount of government aid available.*

V+ADV+PREP

3 If things **go back to** normal or **go back to** a state, they return to the state they were in before something else happened. EG *Despite such feelings things soon went back to normal... The temperature went back to normal... Things will merely go back to being as bad as they were a month ago.* ● **Revert to** is a more formal expression for **go back to**.

V+ADV+PREP

go before. **1** You refer to what **has gone before** when you are referring to previous events, for example when you are comparing a situation with one in the past. EG *The meeting was different from any that had gone before... ...a topic which had nothing to do with*

V+ADV

what had gone before... Each stage depends on what has gone before.

2 If people, problems, or cases **go before** a judge, court of law, or other authority, they are officially considered or investigated so that a decision or judgement can be made. EG *The matter has gone before a grand jury.*   V+PREP

go below. On a boat, if you **go below,** you go down the stairs into the living or sleeping area. EG *Quint went below and returned with two coils of rope... When the other three had gone below decks, Mandria turned to Ari.*   V+ADV, V+PREP

go beyond. To **go beyond** a particular thing means to do something more extreme, more serious, greater, or better. EG *They wanted to go beyond one-day strikes... In this series I have tried to go beyond the narrower meaning of the word civilised.... His interests went beyond political economy.*   V+PREP

go by. **1** If you say that a period of time **has gone by,** you mean that it has passed. EG *Eight years went by... As time goes by more devices come on to the market... Sometimes hours go by without him saying a word... In years gone by, many disappointments came my way.*   V+ADV

▶ **Bygone** means happening or existing a very long time ago. EG *...a home built to the standards of a bygone age... ...empires established in bygone centuries.*   ADJECTIVE

2 If someone or something **goes by,** they pass you without stopping. EG *I saw a car come along the street and I paused to let it go by... It was like watching a parade go by... The small blue car goes by the opening between the shed and the end of the wall.*   V+ADV, V+PREP

3 If someone **goes by** a place, they go there for a short time in order to do or get something. EG *Let's go by the store for a minute... I can go by and ask her.* ● **Drop by** means almost the same as **go by.**   V+PREP, V+ADV

4 If you **go by** a particular thing, you use the information or guidance that it gives you in order to do or understand something. EG *I try to go by reason as far as possible... 'It's not much to go by.'—'All the same I'm pretty sure of it.'* ● **Go on** means almost the same as **go by.**   V+PREP

5 If you let someone's remarks or actions **go by,** you do not let them affect you. EG *He was able to let these go by without feeling any anxiety... I let this comment on my meanness go by me.*   V+ADV, V+PREP

go down. **1** When someone or something **goes down, 1.1** they move from a higher position to a lower one. EG *Frank quickly turned to go down the hill as fast as he could... She had heard the song break out as she was going down the stairs... At a colliery in Leicestershire the miners refused to go down the pit... ...like a diver going down to the bottom of the ocean.* **1.2** they collapse or fall over. EG *He heard a mine explode and saw Jefferson go down... He let out a great howl and went down in a heap.* ● **Fall down** means almost the same as **go down.**   V+PREP, V+ADV / V+ADV

2 If you **go down** in a building, you move downstairs. EG *I must go down and put on my necklace... Together they went down to breakfast.*   V+ADV

3 If you **go down** to a place, you visit it or travel there; often used when the place is farther south than you or is in the country. EG *I have to go down to Brighton... I didn't go down to see Mother during this time... I think you ought to go down there tomorrow morning.*   V+ADV: USUALLY+A

4 If you **go down** the shop, bank, pub, and so on, you go there for a short while; an informal use. EG *Let's go down the bank then... ...decide to go down to the rope shop and look at samples.*   V+PREP, V+ADV

5 Something that **goes down** to a particular point or in a particular direction extends as far as that point or in that direction. EG *One*   V+ADV: WITH A *road goes north, the other one goes down to Ullapool... The steps go down in the direction of the river... ...a steep slope that went down towards open meadows.*

6 If you **go down** on your knees or on all fours, you lower your body until it is supported by your knees, or by your hands and knees. EG *Ferdinand began to go down on one knee... He turned sharply to the right, went down on his hands and knees and crawled forward slowly.* ● **Get down** means almost the same as **go down.** V+ADV: WITH *on*

7 If the cost, level, standard, or amount of something **goes down,** it becomes cheaper, lower, or less than it was before. EG *We expect the price of food in real terms to go down, not up... The Conservative vote actually went down by 1.6 per cent... He knew that the water level had gone down.* ● **Decrease** is a more formal word for **go down,** and **go up** means the opposite. V+ADV

8 If you say that something **has gone down,** you mean that its quality or standard has become worse. EG *It's gone down a lot, the food... The neighbourhood has gone down since we came.* ● **Deteriorate** is a more formal word for **go down.** V+ADV

9 If a tyre, balloon, or something else which has been inflated **goes down,** air is lost from it, and it becomes flatter or smaller. ● **Deflate** is a more formal word for **go down.** V+ADV

10 If a swelling on your body or skin **goes down,** it becomes less swollen or disappears completely. EG *She discovered that the inflammation had gone down.* V+ADV

11 When something **goes down** in a particular way, it gets a particular kind of reaction from a person or group of people. EG *He gave a humorous account, which went down quite well, of how he had done it... This ruling would go down badly in Britain and Germany.* V+ADV: WITH A

12 If you talk about food or drink **going down** well, you mean that it is eaten or drunk with enjoyment; an informal use. EG *A cup of tea would go down nicely.* V+ADV: WITH A

13 When the sun or moon **goes down,** it sets. EG *We ought to be moving. The sun's going down... After the moon went down the noise grew louder.* ● **Come up** means the opposite of **go down.** V+ADV

14 If a ship **goes down,** it sinks. If a plane **goes down,** it crashes. EG *He came to the surface yards away from where his boat had gone down.* V+ADV

15 You say that you will **go down** in a particular way when you expect the consequences of your actions to be serious, but you still intend to do what you have planned. EG *I thought I might as well go down truculently, so I replied: 'I'm not prepared to discuss this'... She was determined to go down fighting.* V+ADV: WITH A/C/-ING

16 In sport, if a person or team **goes down, 16.1** they are defeated in a match or contest. EG *Lendl went down by three sets to one.* ● **Lose** means almost the same as **go down. 16.2** they move to a lower position in an official list, or to a lower division in a league. ● **Go up** means the opposite of **go down.** V+ADV

V+ADV

17 If something **goes down** in writing, it is written down. EG *They were interested in whatever we had to say, and I have no doubt it went down in their notes afterwards.* V+ADV: WITH A

18 If a computer **goes down,** it stops functioning temporarily. V+ADV

19 When university students **go down,** they leave university, especially at the end of their degree course, or at the end of term; used in British English. ● **Go up** means the opposite of **go down.** V+ADV

20 When someone having sex **goes down,** they start kissing or sucking their partner's genitals; a very informal use. V+ADV

go down as. If someone or something **goes down as** a particular V+ADV+PREP

thing, they are regarded, remembered, or recorded as that thing. EG
*Helping your neighbour can go down in the teacher's view as
cheating... Although this will go down as my day, he and Neil Foster
were the real heroes... You, Freneau, would go down in history as
his assassin.*

go down with. If you **go down with** an illness, you catch it or
develop it. EG *I was feeling tired and ill and finally went down with
gastric flu.* ● **Contract** is a more formal word for **go down with.** V+ADV+PREP

go for. 1 If you **go for** a particular thing, you choose it or aim to
achieve it. If you say '**Go for** it' to someone, you are encouraging
them to choose a particular thing or to attempt to do something
difficult. EG *They urged the Chancellor to go for the first option... ...a
tendency to go for even grander projects... We'd better just hope for
the best, and hope they don't go for our route.* V+PREP: ALSO IMPERATIVE, V+PREP+*it*

2 If you **go for** someone or something, you like them very much; an
informal use. EG *I don't go for talk like that... His eyes were too fixed
and pale, I never really went for them.* V+PREP

3 If you **go for** someone or something, you attack them. EG *He went
for me with the bread-knife... I have been twice attacked by owls.
They go for the eyes, you know, and flap their wings in your face.* V+PREP

4 If you say that a statement you have made about one person or
thing **goes for** another person or thing, you mean that the statement
is also true of the second person or thing. EG *The same goes for
Bardolph... The Alliance was the most important thing there was,
and that went for America as well as Europe.* V+PREP

5 If you have a particular thing **going for** you, it gives you an
advantage in a situation; an informal use. EG *He's got a lot more
going for him than just his store. The store's just a beginning...
Davey, our captain, had this incredible streak going for him: seven
years and he'd never played on a losing side.* V+PREP

go forth. When someone **goes forth,** they leave the place where
they were, usually in order to carry out some task or plan; a literary
expression. EG *...going forth in triumph from slavery into freedom.* V+ADV

go forward. 1 If something **goes forward,** it makes progress and
begins to happen. EG *If our present plans go forward we shall bring
in an assistant for you... Preparations were going forward for the
annual Caxley Musical Festival.* V+ADV

2 If someone's name **goes forward** as a candidate for a job or in a
election, they are proposed as a candidate. EG *He has allowed his
name to go forward.* V+ADV

3 When the clocks **go forward** in Britain in the spring, everyone sets
their clocks one hour earlier, to British Summer Time. ● **Go back**
means the opposite of **go forward.** V+ADV

go in. 1 When you **go in** somewhere, especially your own house, you
enter it. EG *Let's go in and have some coffee... I pushed open the door
of the office and went in... As you go in the door, remember that
coffee table I told you about.* V+ADV, V+PREP

2 When people, especially soldiers, **go in,** they enter a place or area
of conflict, and become involved in the situation there. EG *...an
instruction to warriors to go in and kill... The third American
seaborne attack was going in.* ● **Pull out** means the opposite of **go
in.** V+ADV

3 When you **go in** somewhere such as a place of work or business or
hospital, you go there in order to work, to carry out business, to
receive treatment, and so on. EG *He'll still be in hospital then. He's
going in for a minor operation... She hadn't the strength to go in to
work more than two or three mornings a week.* V+ADV

4 When someone **goes in** an organization, they join it; an informal V+PREP, V+ADV

use. EG *I'm not qualified enough to go in on a high level, not young enough to start near the bottom... I thought you were going in the Navy.* ● **Come out** means the opposite of **go in.**

5 If something **goes in** a container, object, or opening, it fits into it. EG *I think the thing's too big to go in the car... All those things could easily go in the dining-room cupboard... The key wouldn't go in.*   V+PREP, V+ADV

6 You talk about structures or equipment **going in** when they are being built or installed. EG *...after the new breakwater went in and the municipal pier... A new paved street went in.*   V+ADV

7 If the sun goes in, it goes behind a cloud and can no longer be seen. ● **Come out** means the opposite of **go in.**   V+ADV

8 You talk about information or a fact **going in** when you mean that you have understood it and remembered it; an informal use. EG *Nothing seemed to go in.* ● **Sink in** means almost the same as **go in.**   V+ADV

go in for. 1 If you **go in for** a particular kind of thing, you like it and regularly do it, wear it, use it, and so on. EG *I don't go in for that sort of fishing... ...the fruit-trees some previous owner had gone in for... I've never gone in for jewellery.*   V+ADV+PREP

2 If you decide to **go in for** a particular kind of work, you decide to do it as your job or career. EG *I thought of going in for teaching... She was better educated than I was; there was some talk of her going in for accountancy or law.* ● **Go into** and **take up** mean almost the same as **go in for.**   V+ADV+PREP

3 If you **go in for** a competition, you take part in it. EG *...the people who went in for the Olympic Games.* ● **Enter** is a more formal word for **go in for.**   V+ADV+PREP

go into. 1 When you **go into** a room, building, or other place, you enter it or go there. EG *She went into the bedroom and shut the door... He was unwilling to go into the garden... Clem had to go into town on business... We were going into China through Shumchun.*   V+PREP

2 When people, especially soldiers, **go into** a place or area of conflict, they go there and become involved in the situation there. EG *...the troops who were ready to go into Sicily... The police were not going into the barricaded areas.*   V+PREP

3 When you **go into** work, hospital, school, and so on, you go there in order to work, receive treatment, or study. EG *She was now far from well, and had to go into hospital for blood transfusions.*   V+PREP

4 If you **go into** a particular kind of work, you decide to do it as your job or career. EG *Ever thought of going into journalism?... I didn't want to go into politics, but I felt I had to.* ● **Go in for** and **take up** mean almost the same as **go into.**   V+PREP

5 If you **go into** an organization, you join it. EG *There are so few coloured recruits going into the police force... He went into the army and I never heard from him again.... There was no serious dissent over Britain going into Europe.*   V+PREP

6 If you **go into** a particular matter, **6.1** you describe it fully or in detail. EG *I've gone into this example in some detail... The problems involved are highly technical and I won't go into them... There was no time to go into the question of the rights and wrongs of the struggle.* ● **Discuss** means almost the same as **go into.** **6.2** you examine or investigate it in detail. EG *My solicitors are going into the question of my jewellery... ...as one goes more deeply into a subject.*   V+PREP: HAS PASSIVE

7 If someone **goes into** a long speech, outburst of laughter, piece of music, and so on, they start speaking, laughing, or playing; often used showing disapproval. EG *He went into a long monologue... ...the other boys, who at first went into screams of derisive laughter... He was deaf and had to be nudged whenever the band went into the national anthem.* ● **Launch into** means almost the same as **go into.**   V+PREP

8 When someone or something **goes into** a particular state or situation, they begin being in that state or situation. EG *Hours passed and he just went into a coma... The police were looking for Paddy and he had gone into hiding... New weapons were ready to go into service... Don went into the lead.* V+PREP

9 If you **go into** an election, competition, or exam and so on, you start taking part in it. EG *The SDP will go into the next election with two serious handicaps... It would have been reckless to go into a Test with only six batsmen.* V+PREP: USUALLY+A

10 If time, effort, or money **goes into** something, it is spent or used to do it, get it, or make it. If particular ingredients **go into** something, they are used to make it. EG *Three years of research went into the making of those films... Money and effort has gone into improving their performance... ...the information that goes into the reports of FBI operations.* V+PREP

11 If things **go into** a container, they fit in it or they are put there. EG *I put my main stuff into a rucksack, while my money and passport went into a small canvas shoulder-bag... We are looking for a different box for these to go into.* V+PREP

12 If someone or something **goes into** a particular kind of movement, they start moving in the way mentioned. EG *The plane went into a nose dive... I went into a skid.* V+PREP

13 If a vehicle or its driver **goes into** another vehicle, it hits the other vehicle. EG *Three cars went into me... I went into the mini in front.* ● **Crash into** means almost the same as **go into**. V+PREP

go in with. If you **go in with** someone, you form a business partnership or working relationship with them. EG *As a matter of business I would go in with him... They must choose whether to accept British Aerospace's homegrown version, or to go in with the Americans.* V+ADV+PREP

go off. 1 If you **go off** somewhere, you leave the place where you were, usually in order to do something. EG *He had gone off to work... She went off to look at the flowers... Eileen decided to go off on a visit of her own... He went off to his room and had a cold shower.* ● **Go away** means almost the same as **go off**. V+ADV: USUALLY+A

2 If a gun **goes off**, it is fired. If a bomb **goes off**, it explodes. EG *The gun went off as he was putting it away... I could hear the bombs going off... The probability of a nuclear weapon going off by accident is slight.* V+ADV

3 If something such as an alarm, bell, or flashbulb **goes off**, it operates, making a sudden loud noise or flash. EG *Every Sunday morning Donald's alarm went off in time for him to go to early Mass... The hall-buzzer went off... ...smiling as flashbulbs go off on all sides.* V+ADV

4 If a light, heating system, broadcasting station, or electric device **goes off**, it stops operating. EG *The light only goes off at night... The heating's gone off and I'm freezing in this draughty old place... ...until the music station went off the air.* ● **Come on** means the opposite of **go off**. V+ADV

5 If an event or arrangement **goes off** well, smoothly, or without problems, it is successful or happens without any problems. EG *The meeting went off well... They wanted all the arrangements to go off smoothly... The ceremony at the Arc de Triomphe went off exactly as planned.* V+ADV: WITH A

6 If something such as a road or line **goes off** from another, it separates from it and extends in a different direction. EG *There's a little road goes off to the right... ...a pencilled diary, the writing going off in all directions.* V+ADV: WITH A

7 You talk about people **going off** in a different direction or at a
tangent, when they start discussing or doing something different,
unexpected, or unuseful. EG *Without them a campaign can go off in
the wrong direction... He suddenly went off at a tangent and came
out with some fascinating stories about his life out East.*

V+ADV:
WITH A

8 If you **go off** someone or something, you stop liking them; an
informal use. EG *He's gone off the idea... I'm into home-made silver
jewellery, none of your musty old filigree, I've gone off that... I think
she's going off him a bit.*

V+PREP

9 If you **go off** a drug, you stop taking it. EG *There has been such bad
publicity about the pill lately that a lot of us are going off it.* ● **Come
off** means almost the same as **do off,** and **go on** means the opposite.

V+PREP

10 If you **go off,** you fall asleep; an informal use. EG *A moment later
she said: 'Oh, I nearly went off again.'... They were all quiet, and
went off to sleep at 10.00.* ● **Drop off** means almost the same as **go
off.**

V+ADV:
ALSO+*to*

11 If food or drink **goes off,** it becomes stale, sour, or rotten. EG *You
must drink it up within a fortnight or it will go off... Food that has
'gone off' has been infected with bacteria that cause illness.* ● **Decay**
is a more formal word for **go off.**

V+ADV

go off with. 1 If someone **goes off with** another person, they leave
their husband, wife, or lover and have a relationship with that
person. EG *My boyfriend went off with my best friend... ...going off
with another man after being married eight years.* ● **Run off with**
means almost the same as **go off with.**

V+ADV+PREP

2 If someone **goes off with** something that belongs to someone else,
they leave a place, taking that thing with them. EG *She had let him go
off with her papers... He had gone off with a large sum belonging to
Uncle Nick.* ● **Make off with** means almost the same as **go off with.**

V+ADV+PREP

go on. 1 If you **go on** doing something, or **go on** with an activity, you
continue to do it. EG *I went on writing... While she was pouring out
their drinks, she went on talking... The BAA argues that air traffic is
increasing and will go on doing so... They can't go on with their
examinations... I would have liked to have gone on with this method.*
● **Carry on** means almost the same as **go on.**

V+ADV:
WITH -ING/*with*

2 If something **goes on** throughout a period of time, it continues to
happen or exist. EG *The fighting had gone on all through the night...
The noise went on and on... How long do you think the rain will go
on?... He seems quite happy to let things go on as they are... The
strike went on for over a year before it was finally settled.* ▶ An
ongoing situation has been happening for quite a long time and is
continuing to happen. EG *...an ongoing economic crisis... ...an ongoing
discussion.*

V+ADV:
USUALLY+A

ADJECTIVE

3 If you say that something **is going on,** you mean that it is taking
place at the present time. EG *There's a big argument going on...
When I asked what was going on, she refused to say anything...
Something very odd was going on.* ● **Happen** means almost the same
as **go on.** ▶ You use the word **goings-on** to refer to activities that
you think are strange or amusing or that you do not approve of. EG
...an amusing story about goings-on at Harry's Bar.

V+ADV

N PLURAL

4 If you **go on** to do something, you do it after you have finished
something else. EG *He later went on to form a successful computer
company... I finished by describing Jeremy in some detail, and then
going on to talk of his cousin Monty... Once you have given the
correct answer to the problem in step one you can go on to step two.*

V+ADV:
WITH *to*-INF/*to*

5 If you **go on** in a particular direction, you continue to travel or
move in that direction. If you **go on** to a place, you go to it from the
place that you have reached. EG *I went on up the hill... You can't go*

V+ADV:
USUALLY+A

on, there's a diversion... Are you sure you don't want to go on to Italy?... Go on home... Please go on ahead of me, and I will follow slowly.

6 You say that land, rock, or a road **goes on** when you are referring to the way which it extends or its direction. EG *...incredible canyons and vast, flat, moon valleys that seem to go on for ever... Below the subsoil lies rock, and rock goes on down to the centre of the Earth.* `V+ADV`

7 You refer to a period of time **going on** when you mean that it passes and when you are describing events during that period. EG *I get more depressed, as time goes on... As the afternoon went on the strike became total in both cities.* ● **Wear on** means almost the same as **go on**. `V+ADV`

8 If someone **goes on** in a conversation, they continue talking, perhaps after an interruption. EG *'You know,' he went on, 'it's extraordinary.'... 'Sounds serious,' I said, 'go on.'... She knew he wasn't listening, but she went on all the same.... He went on for 35 minutes without a pause.* `V+ADV: ALSO+QUOTE`

9 If someone **goes on** about something, or **goes on** at you, they continue talking to you about the same thing, often in an annoying way; an informal use. EG *I went on at my father to have safety belts fitted... Don't go on about it... Although his long book is funny, most of it is familiar, and it does go on.* `V+ADV: ALSO+about/at`

10 In informal English, you say **'Go on'** to someone **10.1** to persuade or encourage them to do something. EG *Go on, have a biscuit... Well, phone them up, go on! Go on, get on the phone.* ● **Come on** means almost the same as **go on**. **10.2** to indicate that you do not believe what they have said. EG *Go on—you're kidding.* ● **Get away** means almost the same as **go on**. `IMPERATIVE: V+ADV` `IMPERATIVE: V+ADV`

11 If you say, for example, that you have something to **go on,** you mean that you have some information on which you can base an opinion or judgement. EG *I'm only going on what I've seen at Mr Gladwell's... He had nothing to go on. There were no clues.* `V+PREP`

12 If a light, machine, or other device **goes on,** it begins operating. EG *The light goes on automatically... The tape recorder went on and he started to talk.* ● **Go off** means the opposite of **go on**. `V+ADV`

13 If one object **goes on** another, the first object fits or is put onto the second. EG *He went back to the rifle. The silencer went on easily, swivelling round the end of the barrel... He sat down to put on his shoes and socks. The shoes would hardly go on.* ● **Come off** means the opposite of **go on**. `V+ADV, V+PREP`

14 If an amount of money or a commodity **goes on** something, it is spent or used on that thing. EG *A fair amount of money goes on equipment and research expenditure... Nearly half of French aid went on technical cooperation... Over 40 per cent of fuel used in agriculture goes on heating greenhouses.* `V+PREP`

15 When an actor or actress **goes on,** they appear in a play or make an entrance onto the stage. EG *I'm going to be sick. I can't go on tonight. Get my understudy... I went on in one of the crowd scenes for five pounds a week... The second girl now showed no eagerness to go on stage.* `V+ADV, V+PREP`

16 If you **go on** a drug, you start taking it. EG *They went on the Pill and suffered side-effects.* ● **Come off** means the opposite of **go on**. `V+PREP`

17 If you say that someone **is going on** a particular age, you mean that they are approaching that age; an informal use. EG *Renata was going on thirty, divorced... I am thirty-four now, going on thirty-five.* `V+PREP: WITH NUMBER`

18 If you **are gone on** someone, you are infatuated with them; an informal, rather old-fashioned use. EG *I was a bit flattered because he was so gone on me.* `PASSIVE: V+PREP`

go on with. If you say that you have enough **to be going on with,** you mean that you have enough for the present time; an informal expression. EG *Don't bother, that's enough to be going on with... With her three children, it'll make a nice little family to be going on with.* `V+ADV+with`

go out. 1 When you **go out** of a room, building, or other place, you leave it. EG *He picks up his camera bag and goes out, locking the door... Why don't we go out into the garden?... She went out of the building and through the main gate.* ● **Come in** means the opposite of **go out.** `V+ADV: ALSO+of`

2 When you **go out,** you leave your house and go somewhere else, for example in order to shop, visit friends, see a film, and so on. EG *I have to go out. I'll be back late tonight... ...all dressed up to go out to a party... ...an invitation to actually go out climbing.* ● **Stay in** means the opposite of **go out.** `V+ADV`

3 If you **are going out** with someone, you spend time with them socially and have a romantic or sexual relationship with them. EG *My parents wouldn't let me go out with boys... David used to say that you were the best dancer he ever went out with... Your daughter and Michael Corleone have been going out together for over a year.* ● **Date** means almost the same as **go out.** `V+ADV, V+ADV+with, V+ADV+together: RECIPROCAL`

4 If you **go out** to a place, especially somewhere abroad or far away, you travel there. EG *She had decided to get married and stay in England and not go out to Africa... They want me to go out West and do a movie... They might find you a seat on some flight going out tonight.* ▶ **Outgoing** traffic or an **outgoing** plane or passenger is travelling away from the place where you are. EG *They searched all outgoing traffic... ...incoming and outgoing passengers.* `V+ADV: USUALLY+A` `ADJECTIVE`

5 If you talk about people **going out** and doing something, you mean that they do it by making an effort and after planning to do it; an informal use. EG *Saying that we need something is very different from going out and fighting for it... Violence on television actually incites people to go out and do violent acts... I told your father I'd go out and get a job.* `V+ADV: WITH and+VERB`

6 If news, a message, or a letter **goes out,** it is announced, published, or sent, often officially. EG *The news went out from Washington that he was dead... Word went out that he'd arrived... That is the instruction that's gone out to our members.* ● **Come in** means the opposite of **go out.** ▶ An **outgoing** message, letter, or phone call is one sent or made from the place where you are. EG *Wouldn't that cause less of a delay in outgoing mail?* ● **Incoming** means the opposite of **outgoing.** `V+ADV` `ADJECTIVE`

7 Money that **goes out** is spent on bills and regular expenses. EG *Even though you are earning a good salary you probably find the money going out virtually as fast as it comes in.* ● **Come in** means the opposite of **go out.** ▶ You use **outgoings** to refer to the money which you have to spend regularly, for example in order to pay your rent or bills. EG *...approving payment of the bills for her regular outgoings.* ● **Expenses** means almost the same as **outgoings.** `V+ADV` `N PLURAL`

8 If a television or radio programme **goes out,** it is broadcast. EG *The series goes out on Tuesday evenings on BBC 2... We need to record it on video-tape the day before it actually goes out on the air.* `V+ADV`

9 If a light **goes out,** it stops shining. EG *The lights went out in the big tent... Stay there. The light's gone out and I won't be able to find you if you move around.* ● **Come on** means the opposite of **go out.** `V+ADV`

10 If a fire or something that is burning **goes out,** it stops burning. EG *His room was freezing. His fire had gone out, and I sat there shivering... I'm afraid my cigarette has gone out again.* `V+ADV`

11 If something **goes out,** 11.1 it stops being fashionable or used, and `V+ADV: ALSO+of`

is replaced with something else. EG *Steam went out and diesel was introduced... Shoes can sometimes go out of fashion overnight... I think it's rapidly going out of use.* ● **Come in** means the opposite of **go out.** 11.2 it is unwanted and someone gets rid of it. EG *All these* V+ADV *desks go out! This is an apartment house not an office building!*

12 When the tide **goes out,** it falls, so that the water reaches lower V+ADV up the shore. EG *...just after the tide has gone out over the vast salt-marshes.* ● **Come in** means the opposite of **go out.**

13 You use **outgoing** to describe a person 13.1 who is very friendly ADJECTIVE and open in their behaviour; used showing approval. EG *Adler was an outgoing, sociable kind of man... She became very outgoing and popular.* ● **Extrovert** means almost the same as **outgoing.** 13.2 who ADJECTIVE has held an office or position and who is just about to be replaced by someone else. EG *Congress opens with an address by the outgoing president... ...the outgoing government.* ● **Incoming** means the opposite of **outgoing.**

go out of. If you say that a quality, especially a positive quality, **has** V+ADV+PREP **gone out of** someone or something, you mean that they no longer have it. EG *Some of the urgency has gone out of the market... All the heart seemed to have gone out of him... It is still discussed in general terms, but the vigour has gone out of the debate.*

go over. 1 When you **go over** to someone or something, you move V+ADV: towards them and reach them. EG *'Mabel,' he said, going over to* USUALLY+*to/and* *her... She got up and went over to her suitcase, opened it, and took out an envelope... There was a phone on the desk. Eva went over and lifted the receiver and dialled.*

2 If you **go over** to someone's house, you visit them for a short time. V+ADV: EG *When I got home I found a phone message from Jeremy, asking* USUALLY+*to/and* *me to go over the next evening... Can we go over to Ann's today?... Mr Steinberg had often invited me to go over and stay.* ● **Go round** means almost the same as **go over.**

3 If you **go over** to a place overseas, you travel there. EG *My editor* V+ADV: *asked me to go over to England to cover a British general election...* USUALLY+*to* *...just to save yourself the trouble of going over to Paris.*

4 If you **go over** something, you examine, discuss, or think about it V+PREP: very carefully and systematically. EG *We could go over the whole* HAS PASSIVE *project and see if there are any problems... What's the point of going over all that?... He knew that every square inch had already been gone over with microscopic care.* ▶ If you give something a **going-** N SING **over,** you examine it carefully; a fairly informal use. EG *They had been giving our report a careful going-over... His room had received a thorough going-over.*

5 If someone gives you a **going-over,** they attack you violently, N SING usually as a punishment or a warning; a very informal use. EG *Someone had given young Allen a very thorough going-over indeed. 'What happened this time?' I asked.*

6 If something **goes over** well or badly, people react favourably or V+ADV unfavourably to it. EG *I got him to sing 'Sonny Boy', but it did not go over very well... I wondered how such a session would go over in America.*

go overboard. If someone **goes overboard,** they react more V+ADV strongly or act more extremely than you think they should have done. EG *You're going a little bit overboard... They went rather overboard and said that it was the best film they'd ever seen.*

go over to. 1 In a conflict, if someone **goes over to** a group of V+ADV+PREP people, they join them after previously belonging to a rival group. EG *The traitor Jan went over to the side of the very people who had* *assassinated his brothers... Who was loyal and who had gone over to the other group?... They had gone over to the enemy.*

2 If someone or something **goes over to** a different way of doing things, they change to it. EG *We went over to the American system... The school will go over to mixed ability teaching.* | V+ADV+PREP

go round. 1 If you **go round** to someone's house, you visit them for a short time. EG *I'll go round and see Nell later... Manfred rang up and asked me to go round to see him... It wasn't until Friday evening that I was able to go round to Clive's house.* ● **Go over** means almost the same as **go round.** | V+ADV

2 If you **go round** or **around** a group of people or places, you visit them, or you attend to each of them in turn. EG *Michelle, will you quickly go round and collect the exercise books up?... If you're in London you can go round the art galleries and things like that.* | V+ADV, V+PREP

3 If you **go round** or **around** a country or other place, you travel in that place and visit a lot of different things. EG *I'd like to go round Africa myself... One of them went around the world as a ship's steward... Interlaken was a very good centre for going round and seeing things.* | V+PREP, V+ADV

4 If you **go round** or **around** a room, building, or other area, you walk through every part of it or make a circuit of it. EG *Bond went round the room and examined the windows... She went around the house making sure that all doors were locked... Let's go around the block before we go in... He took four hours to go round the golf course.* | V+PREP, V+ADV

5 If you **go round** in a circle or **go around** a bend, you move in a circular or curving direction. EG *The speedboat driver has to stop or go round in circles... The car goes around a curve, and vanishes behind the trees.* | V+ADV, V+PREP

6 If you **go round** or **around** an object or obstacle, you move in a circular direction so that you can get past it or get to the other side. EG *He went round the table... When the rifle was assembled he laid it on the bonnet of the car and went round to the boot again.* | V+PREP, V+ADV

7 If something **goes round,** it spins or turns continuously like a wheel. EG *The wheels of the bicycle were going round so fast that the spokes blurred into one... The tape is still going round... The blue light is going round and round on top of the police car.* ● **Revolve** is a more formal word for **go round.** | V+ADV

8 If you **go round** or **around** in a particular way, you dress or behave in that way very often or regularly. EG *The kids go around barefoot... They go round in stockinged feet to see who is in and who is out... Ann says Auntie Jo goes around the house with no clothes on in the mornings.* ● **Go about** means almost the same as **go round.** | V+ADV, V+PREP: WITH A

9 If you **go round** or **around** doing something, often something that other people disapprove of, you are in the habit of doing it or do it repeatedly. EG *I don't go around deliberately hurting people's feelings... They're always going round sticking posters on walls... You mustn't go around telling people things that aren't true.* ● **Go about** means almost the same as **go round.** | V+ADV+-ING

10 If you **go round** or **around** with someone, or if you **go round** together, you regularly meet them and go to different places with them. EG *Don't go around with them... They go round with their fellow countrymen... Do you think it's wise for us to go round together like this?* ● **Go about** means almost the same as **go round.** | V+ADV+*with*, V+ADV+*together*: RECIPROCAL

11 If a story or piece of news **is going round** or **around,** a lot of people hear it or talk about it. EG *A rumour went round that he had after all survived... A lot of spooky stories began going around... But* | V+ADV, V+PREP *these days there are fewer jokes than usual going around this grim, grey city.* ● **Go about** means almost the same as **go round.**

12 If an illness **is going round** or **around** a group of people, a lot of them catch it. EG *'There's a virus going around,' he said. 'My wife had it last week.'*   V+ADV, V+PREP

13 If there is enough of something to **go round** or **around,** there is enough of it to be shared among a group of people, or to do all the things for which it is needed. EG *There were never enough textbooks to go around... The money just won't go round... But the fact remains that there is plenty of food to go around.*   V+ADV, V+PREP

go through. **1** If you **go through** an event or period of time, especially an unpleasant one, you experience it. EG *Not all girls go through this stage... I'm too old to go through that again... Doctors and teachers both have to go through a long period of expensive professional training.* ● **Undergo** means almost the same as **go through.**   V+PREP

2 If someone or something **goes through** an official procedure, they are made to do all the things that are required. EG *She would have to go through all the legal formalities... You did not have to go through a passport check in Mulhouse airport... If the set procedure is not gone through, then the machine cuts out.*   V+PREP: HAS PASSIVE

3 If you **go through** someone in order to do something, that person must deal with the matter before you can continue or get approval for it. EG *You have to go through the Head of Department... Industrial matters go through the regional trade group machinery.*   V+PREP

4 If a law, agreement, or official decision **goes through,** it is approved by the people who have the power or authority to do so. EG *The adoption went through... We believed the deal would not be allowed to go through.*   V+ADV

5 If you **go through** a room, you enter it and cross it. EG *She went through the kitchen and out of the back door... We went through a large room into a smaller one... Eva went through to the galley.*   V+PREP, V+ADV

6 If you **go through** a town or country, you cross it or stop there briefly on your way to somewhere else. EG *You must be going through Frankfurt anyway... To go through Germany would be to risk suspicion.*   V+ADV

7 If you **go through** a lot of things such as papers or clothes, you examine them carefully, usually in order to sort them into groups or to search for something. EG *They went through her things... He went through Guy's books to find something about Poland... I began going through my pockets. Nothing was missing... Her correspondence had been gone through. Why?* ● **Look through** means almost the same as **go through.**   V+PREP: HAS PASSIVE

8 If you **go through** a list, story, or plan, you say, describe, or discuss it from beginning to end. EG *You'd better go through the names... Could you go through roughly what's required?... Secretary Cox went through the treaty point by point.* ● **Run through** means almost the same as **go through.**   V+PREP: HAS PASSIVE

9 If someone **goes through** something such as a series of actions or movements, they perform it. EG *They watched Pat going through some of the movements she had learned.... The music started and we went through a series of warm-up exercises.*   V+PREP: HAS PASSIVE

10 If you **go through** a supply of something, you use it all so that there is none left. EG *Somehow, they had gone through the whole bottle of wine.* ● **Get through** means almost the same as **go through,** and **consume** is a more formal word.   V+PREP

11 If something such as a piece of clothing **has gone through,** there is a hole in it, because you have worn or used it so much. EG *...an old*   V+ADV *suit whose jacket had gone through at the elbows.* ● **Wear through** means almost the same as **go through**.

go through with. If you **go through with** a decision or an action, you continue to do what is necessary in order to achieve it or complete it, although this may be difficult or unpleasant. EG *Landy was already taking it for granted that I was going to go through with this business, and I resented his attitude... The government was determined to go through with that legislation.* V+ADV+PREP

go together. 1 If two things **go together,** they are often found in association with each other. EG *This had been the basis of both wealth and military power; the two went together... Fear and hatred seem to go together.* V+ADV

2 If two people **go together,** they spend time with each other and have a romantic or sexual relationship; used mainly in American English. EG *We've been going together for two years.* ● **Go out** means almost the same as **go together**. V+ADV

go towards. If one thing **goes towards** another, it contributes part of it. If an amount of money **goes towards** something, it is used as part of its cost. EG *My bonus will go towards a deposit on the flat... Any money received from now on will go towards aid for future victims... Most of the calories in our food go towards maintaining our body temperature... ...the thinking that went towards the basic ideas.* V+PREP

go under. 1 If someone or something, especially a business, **goes under,** they fail, lose power, become bankrupt, and so on. EG *Ten thousand small businesses have gone under... The high civilizations of the East went under one by one... ...but it was Ramsay Macdonald who went under, while the party survived.* ● **Collapse** means almost the same as **go under**. V+ADV

2 If someone or something in the water **goes under,** they sink below the surface of the water. EG *He thrashed about for some time before he went under... The lifeboat will sink and we shall all go under.* ● **Come up** means the opposite of **go under**. V+ADV

3 You talk about land **going under** the plough, the mower, the axe, and so on when you mean that it is being ploughed, mown, or cut down, and often when you want to suggest that it is being completely changed or destroyed. EG *The park had largely gone under the plough... The first fields of winter wheat were going under the combine... Woods were going under the chain-saw right across the country.* V+PREP

go up. 1 When someone or something **goes up,** they move from a lower position to a higher one. EG *...a party of mountaineers going up the mountain... When I tried to go up the stairs he pushed me aside... Rockets went up to the moon.* V+PREP, V+ADV

2 If you **go up** in a building, you move upstairs. EG *She went up to her bedroom... We can go up in the elevator... If you'll excuse me a moment, I'll go up and change for dinner.* V+ADV

3 If you **go up** to someone or something, you move towards them until you are standing next to them. EG *I went up to Clem where he sat smoking... Go up and introduce yourself, after the meeting is over... They walked along a gravel drive and went up to the car.* V+ADV: ALSO+*to*

4 If you **go up** to a place, you visit it or travel there; often used when the place is farther north than you or is in a city. EG *We all went up to the pub... Whatever do you want to go up there for, on a dreadful afternoon like this?... We'll go up to London early next week.* V+ADV: USUALLY+A

5 Something that **goes up** to a particular point or in a particular direction, extends as far as that point or in that direction. EG *...a dark mat of greenish-black pine trees going up to a high ridge... One road* V+ADV: WITH A

goes up north to Durness... These timetables only go up to the 30th of March.

6 If the cost, level, standard, or amount of something **goes up**, it V+ADV becomes more expensive, higher, or greater than it was before. EG *The price of petrol and oil related products will go up steadily... The expenditure on relief will go up to $400 million... That's why the crime rate is going up the way it is—seventeen per cent in Houston.* ● **Rise** means almost the same as **go up**, and **come down** and **go down** mean the opposite.

7 If you **go up** when you are making an offer or suggesting an V+ADV, amount, you increase the original offer or amount. EG *I'm being* V+ADV+N: *rather reckless, I can't help it—I'll go up as high as fifteen pounds.* NO PASSIVE

8 If a building, wall, or other structure **goes up**, it is built or fixed in V+ADV place. EG *Small blocks of flats are going up... Steel crowd barriers go up several hours before each ceremony... Billboards went up all over town.* ● **Come down** means the opposite of **go up**.

9 If something such as a curtain **goes up**, it is raised. EG *There was a* V+ADV *burst of applause as the curtain went up... It had the effect of a blind going up too quickly.* ● **Come down** means the opposite of **go up**.

10 If something **goes up**, it explodes or suddenly starts to burn. EG *In* V+ADV *seconds it had gone up in flames... I'm surprised the whole place didn't go up... Another fuel-tank went up and the first fire-bells began sounding from the distance.*

11 If a cheer, shout, or other noise **goes up**, a lot of people cheer, V+ADV shout, or make that sound at the same time. EG *A huge cheer went up... ...that afternoon when her sister had heard the shout of 'Fire!' go up at the Caxley cinema... A kind of gasp went up from the tables.*

12 When university students **go up**, they begin a degree course or V+ADV: return to university at the start of term; used in British English. EG ALSO+*to* *She said why didn't I do some exams and go up to University with her... Before going up to Oxford, I started a diary.* ● **Go down** means the opposite of **go up**.

13 In sport, if a person or team **goes up**, they move to a higher V+ADV position in a list, or to a higher division in a league. EG *I think Stoke will go up this season.* ● **Go down** means the opposite of **go up**.

go with. **1** If one thing **goes with** another, **1.1** the two things are V+PREP often found in association together. EG *...the sigh of satisfaction that goes with pleasant tiredness... ...wealth and the considerable potential power that goes with it... ...a girl with the temperament that goes with being a redhead.* ● **Attend** is a formal word for **go with**. **1.2** the V+PREP two things officially or properly belong together, so that if you get one, you also get the other. EG *...the house which went with his old job... ...the two essays I wrote to go with Peter's photographs... I did not want the thirty acres of pasture that went with the place.*

2 If you **go with** a plan, idea, or the people who are proposing it, you V+PREP decide to support them and try to make them succeed; used mainly in American English. EG *We have to go with the White House and Mr Muller on this one... North Carolina was not going with abortion to embarrass McGovern.*

3 If someone **goes with** another person, they have sex with that V+PREP person; an informal, slightly old-fashioned use. EG *He never went with other women. He never looked at another woman.* ● **Sleep with** means almost the same as **go with**.

go without. If you **go without** something, you do not have it or do it. V+PREP, EG *The family went without food all day... How long could you go* V+ADV *without sleep?... If they couldn't get coal, they had to go without.* ● **Do without** means almost the same as **go without**.

goad, goads, goading, goaded

goad into. If you **goad** someone **into** doing something they did not want to do, you make them angry so that they do it. EG *He and his editor were goading the President into war... She was being goaded into denouncing and mocking her best friend.*

V+N+PREP, V+PRON+PREP

goad on. If you **are goaded on** by someone or something, they encourage you to do more than you intended to or to do it more energetically. EG *They could always be goaded on to one more patrol... Clement had played a prominent part in the suppression of the Templars, goaded on by the French king.* ● **Spur on** means almost the same as **goad on.**

V+N+ADV, V+PRON+ADV, V+ADV+N: USUALLY PASSIVE

gobble, gobbles, gobbling, gobbled

gobble down. If you **gobble down** food or **gobble** it **up,** you very quickly eat all of it; an informal expression. EG *He gobbled down the two remaining eggs... ...truck drivers gobbling up hot dogs dripping with mustard... He had a huge sack of apples and he was gobbling them down.* ● **Wolf down** means almost the same as **gobble down.**

V+ADV+N, V+PRON+ADV, V+N+ADV

gobble up. 1 If something **gobbles up** money, property, or resources, it uses or takes more of them than seems reasonable; an informal use. EG *Research and development now gobble up a sizeable chunk of the military budget... Bigger neighbours gobbled up territories that our country couldn't defend... British agriculture gobbled up more energy than it produced.*
2 See **gobble down.**

V+ADV+N

goof, goofs, goofing, goofed

goof off. If you **goof off,** you spend your time in a lazy or foolish way when you are supposed to be doing something more important; an informal expression, used mainly in American English. EG *He never goofed off into restaurants when he was on patrol... He was always flirting with all the waitresses and letting them goof off on the job.* ● **Skive off** is an informal British English expression for **goof off.**

V+ADV

gouge, gouges, gouging, gouged

gouge out. If you **gouge** something **out,** you force it violently from the place where it is, using your fingers, a tool, or a machine. EG *...bulldozers gouging out basements... Her eyes had been gouged out.*

V+ADV+N, V+N+ADV, V+PRON+ADV

grab, grabs, grabbing, grabbed

grab at. 1 If you **grab at** an object or person, you make a desperate attempt to hold on to them. EG *She fell on her knees to grab at the money... I grabbed at it with both hands... Marsha grabbed at her hair like a lifeline.*
2 If you **grab at** a chance or opportunity, you take advantage of it eagerly. EG *Why didn't you grab at the chance to go to New York?*

V+PREP

V+PREP

grapple, grapples, grappling, grappled

grapple with. If you **grapple with** a problem or difficult task, you try many different methods to solve it or do it. EG *I grappled with this moral dilemma... He was one of the few scientists who had seriously grappled with these problems.* ● **Wrestle with** means almost the same as **grapple with.**

V+PREP: HAS PASSIVE

grasp, grasps, grasping, grasped

grasp at. 1 If you **grasp at** something, you take it with your hands and hold it very firmly. EG *He raised his hands above his head, grasping at the escape hatch.* ● **Grab at** means almost the same as **grasp at.**

V+PREP

2 If you **grasp** at an opportunity, you try to take advantage of it, even though you are not very likely to succeed. EG *The specialists had given him some slight hope, but he was not grasping at it.* ● **Clutch at** means almost the same as **grasp at.**

V+PREP

grass, grasses, grassing, grassed

grass on. If someone **grasses on** you, they give information to people in authority that causes you to be punished or to have problems; an informal expression. EG *The rumour had started that I had grassed on the lesbians, and had been moved away.* ● **Inform on** is a more formal expression for **grass on.**

V+PREP

grass over. To **grass over** an area of ground means to plant grass all over it. EG *You've grassed over the back garden, I see... There had been a path to it but the farmer had let it grass over.*

V+ADV+N,
V+PRON+ADV,
V+ADV

grind, grinds, grinding, ground

grind away. To **grind away** means to work very hard, but in an uninteresting way; an informal expression. EG *The old machinery is still grinding away... Millions of children today are forced to spend precious hours of their lives grinding away at pointless tasks.* ● **Plug away** means almost the same as **grind away.**

V+ADV:
ALSO+*at*

grind down. **1** If someone **grinds** you **down**, they persistently attack you, annoy you, or treat you cruelly until you can no longer fight back or defend yourself. EG *The sheer weight of numbers and arms began to grind them down... Rich men are always grinding down poor men... See how the working people of Britain are ground down.* ● **Wear down** means almost the same as **grind down.**

V+PRON+ADV,
V+ADV+N,
V+N+ADV

2 If you **grind** something **down**, you rub it against a hard surface or on a machine in order to make it smooth or sharp. EG *First, you must grind the components down fine... You put it on the grindstone and grind it down to shape... The hardest rock in the world will be ground down in time.*

V+N+ADV,
V+PRON+ADV,
V+ADV+N

grind on. When something **grinds on,** it continues in a very boring way for a long time. EG *Slowly the meeting ground on... I wished I could stop his voice grinding on and on.*

V+ADV

grind out. **1** If a person or machine **grinds out** information or work, they produce it in a boring or routine manner; an informal expression. EG *...a computer which grinds out decisions after computing the information... ...a printing press which ground out leaflets in several colours.* ● **Churn out** means almost the same as **grind out.**

V+ADV+N,
V+N+ADV,
V+PRON+ADV

2 If you **grind out** a lighted cigarette, you press it down firmly with your hand or foot in order to stop it burning. EG *She ground out her cigarette too soon... ...cigarette ends ground out on the carpet.* ● **Stub out** means almost the same as **grind out.**

V+ADV+N,
V+N+ADV,
V+PRON+ADV

grind up. If you **grind** something **up,** you completely crush it until it becomes a fine powder. EG *The seeds are ground up for commercial mustards... They would smash the bottles with a hammer until they were ground up... It is not easy to grind it up in a coffee grinder.*

V+N+ADV,
V+ADV+N,
V+PRON+ADV

grow, grows, growing, grew, grown

grow apart. If people who have a close relationship **grow apart,** they gradually start to have different interests and opinions from each other, and their relationship starts to fail. EG *As we travelled together, we started to grow apart... The brothers grew further and further apart.* ● **Drift apart** means almost the same as **grow apart.**

V+ADV

grow away from. If you **grow away from** someone, you develop different views and opinions so that you gradually have less in common with them. EG *There have been times when I feared that*

V+ADV+PREP

you might grow away from us and be reluctant to return... In truth, also, she had grown away from her friends.

grow into. 1 If you **grow into** a job or situation, you gradually learn   V+PREP
how to do it or deal with it skilfully. EG *Mr Mzali has grown into the job.*

2 If a child **grows into** an item of clothing, he or she becomes taller   V+PREP
or bigger so that the clothing fits properly. EG *It's a bit big, but she'll soon grow into it.*

grow on. If someone or something **grows on** you, you start to like   V+PREP
them, although you did not like them at first; an informal expression. EG *She was someone whose charm grew very slowly on you... I hated to give up my apartment. It had really grown on me over the last seven months... The hill has an enduring beauty which grows on you.*

grow out of. 1 When you **grow out of** childish behaviour or   V+ADV+PREP
interests, you become more mature and stop behaving immaturely or having those interests. EG *I've rather grown out of my taste for ice cream... She had never grown out of the beliefs acquired in childhood.* ● **Outgrow** means almost the same as **grow out of.**

2 If a child **grows out of** an item of clothing, he or she becomes so   V+ADV+PREP
tall or big that the clothing no longer fits them properly. EG *It cost a small fortune and she grew out of it in three months.*

3 If one idea or plan **grows out of** another, it develops from it. EG   V+ADV+PREP
She'd had an idea for a story that grew out of a dream... Out of this would grow a broad socialist programme. ▶ An **outgrowth** of   N SING
something is a natural development from it or result of it. EG *This theory was an outgrowth of Einstein's 'unified field theory'.*

grow up. 1 As you **grow up,** you gradually change from being a   V+ADV
child to being an adult. EG *I had grown up in the district... They grew up in the early days of television... Children should grow up with a fond attitude towards all humanity.* ▶ A **grown-up** is an adult; an   N COUNT,
informal word used especially by children or by adults when talking   ADJECTIVE
to children. EG *We could see a grown-up coming... ...older couples, with grown-up children of their own.* ▶ If you say that a child is   ADJECTIVE
being **grown-up,** you mean that he or she is behaving in a mature way. EG *Your brother's awfully grown-up for his age.*

2 If you tell someone to **grow up,** you want them to stop behaving in   V+ADV:
a silly or childish way; an informal use. EG *'Grow up, Mother.'*   USUALLY
Jeannie's voice was harsh... Lally said that it was time we all grew   IMPERATIVE
up.

3 When a place, organization, or idea **grows up,** it starts to exist and   V+ADV
becomes larger or more important. EG *Cities grew up as markets, centres of religion or trade... The idea has grown up that science cannot be wrong... Complaints and controversy grew up around the scene.* ● **Develop** means almost the same as **grow up.**

grow up on. If you **grew up on** something, it was always present   V+ADV+PREP
during your childhood and has had a strong influence on you. EG *Tony grew up on tales of London politics.*

grub, grubs, grubbing, grubbed

grub about. If you **grub about** or **around** for something, you search   V+ADV
for it with effort, for example by moving things or by digging. EG *He was tired of grubbing about in the public library for material... ...hunched up and grubbing around in the mud.* ● **Root about** means almost the same as **grub about.**

grub around. See **grub about.**

grub up. If you **grub** something **up,** you dig it out of the ground. EG   V+ADV+N,

...grubbing up hedgerows... They grubbed up roots and gathered berries... ...birds grubbing up insects.

V+N+ADV,
V+PRON+ADV

guard, guards, guarding, guarded

guard against. If you **guard against** something, you do what is necessary to make sure that it does not happen or does not affect you. EG *They need to guard against eating too much if they want to keep fit... It does suggest some ways in which we can guard against the same mistakes in the future... Jealousy is something to be particularly guarded against.*

V+PREP:
HAS PASSIVE

guess, guesses, guessing, guessed

guess at. If you **guess at** something, you try to give an answer or opinion when you do not really have enough information. EG *We can only guess at the number of deaths it has caused... We'll have to guess at what went on there... Its shape and size were not yet known or even guessed at.*

V+PREP:
HAS PASSIVE

gulp, gulps, gulping, gulped

gulp down. If you **gulp down** food or drink, you eat or drink it all very quickly by swallowing large quantities of it at a time. EG *After gulping down his breakfast in the morning, he hurried to the station... The old man gulped down his coffee... Obediently, Scylla gulped it down.*

V+ADV+N,
V+PRON+ADV,
V+N+ADV

gum, gums, gumming, gummed

gum up. If your eyes or nose **are gummed up**, they are blocked by mucus so that it is difficult to open your eyes or to breathe easily. EG *When he woke in the morning his eyes were all gummed up... Cliff, too, was gummed up.*

V+N+ADV:
USUALLY PASSIVE

gun, guns, gunning, gunned

gun down. To **gun** someone **down** means to shoot them when they are not in a position to defend themselves. EG *Nobody has ever gunned down a New York police captain and gotten away with it... They can gun him down without the police intervening... Sonny's father was gunned down on the street.*

V+ADV+N,
V+PRON+ADV,
V+N+ADV

gun for. If someone **is gunning for** you, they are trying in a very determined way to harm you or cause you trouble; an informal expression. EG *I do not wish to have half the school gunning for me.*

V+PREP

H h

hack, hacks, hacking, hacked

hack about. If someone **hacks about** the wording of a text, they change it and cut parts out, without caring much about what was originally written. EG *My book's been hacked about terribly by the editor... Her prompt-books show how she used to hack about plays.*

V+N+ADV,
V+ADV+N,
V+PRON+ADV

hack at. If you **hack at** something, you try to cut it using strong, rough strokes of an axe or knife. EG *They hacked at the jungle undergrowth with machetes.*

V+PREP

hack down. If you **hack down** something such as a tree, you cut it down roughly. EG *The thick brush was hacked down and burned... ...if a mad axe-man was hacking down the door.*

V+N+ADV,
V+ADV+N,
V+PRON+ADV

hack off. If you **hack** something **off**, you remove it by cutting it

V+N+ADV,

roughly or violently. EG *Someone had hacked his head off... He hacked off three of the branches in a rage.* ● **Chop off** means almost the same as **hack off**.

V+ADV+N,
V+PRON+ADV

hack through. If you **hack through** a wood, jungle, scrub, and so on, you move through it by cutting down branches, bushes, and other things. EG *The undergrowth becomes so thick we have to hack through it.*

V+PREP

hail, hails, hailing, hailed

hail as. If a person, event, or achievement **is hailed as** important or successful, they are praised publicly and said to be important or successful. EG *They were hailed as heroes by the entire Labour movement... The discovery was hailed as the scientific sensation of the century.*

V+N+PREP,
V+PRON+PREP:
USUALLY PASSIVE

hail from. Someone who **hails from** a particular place was born there or lives there; a formal expression. EG *I hail from America.*

V+PREP

ham, hams, hamming, hammed

ham up. If an actor, actress or other performer **hams** it **up,** they exaggerate every word and gesture as they perform, often deliberately in order to amuse the audience. EG *She was obviously hamming it up for the benefit of the watching tourists... ...like a bad actor, blustering, hamming it up.*

V+*it*+ADV

hammer, hammers, hammering, hammered

hammer away at. If you **hammer away at** something, you work at it constantly and with great energy. EG *They were all hammering away at their work.*

V+ADV+PREP

hammer out. If you **hammer out** an agreement, you achieve it after a long or difficult discussion. EG *There will be trouble unless we actually sit down together and hammer out an agreement for the future... ...procedures hammered out over recent years.*

V+ADV+N,
V+N+ADV,
V+PRON+ADV

hand, hands, handing, handed

hand back. 1 If you **hand** something **back** to someone, you return it to them after you have borrowed or taken it from them. EG *He handed back his room key to the receptionist... I examined the lighter, then handed it back... The girl handed him back his card.* ● **Give back** means almost the same as **hand back**.

V+ADV+N,
V+PRON+ADV,
V+N+ADV,
ALSO+*to*:
OR
V+PRON+ADV+N

2 If someone presenting a television or radio programme **hands** the viewers or listeners **back,** they move the transmission to the place or studio where the broadcast began. EG *...handing you back now to Jeremy Stevens at the scene of the accident... I'm now going to hand our audience back to the newsroom for a bulletin.*

V+PRON+ADV,
V+N+ADV:
USUALLY+*to*

hand down. 1 If possessions, skills, or knowledge **are handed down,** they are given or left to people who are younger or belong to a younger generation. EG *...a house, a plot of land or durable goods which can be handed down from generation to generation... Technical skills such as blacksmithing are usually handed down from father to son as a family tradition.* ● **Pass on** means almost the same as **hand down.** ▶ **Hand-me-downs** are things, especially clothing, which have been used by other people before you and which have been given to you for your use. EG *...my elder sister's hand-me-downs.*

V+N+ADV,
V+ADV+N,
V+PRON+ADV:
USUALLY PASSIVE

N PLURAL

2 If a decision or judgement **is handed down,** it is given publicly by a court or other official body; used mainly in American English. EG *Late the next day, September 15, the indictments were handed down by the grand jury.*

V+N+ADV,
V+ADV+N,
V+PRON+ADV:
USUALLY PASSIVE

hand in. 1 If you **hand in** a piece of work, you give it to someone so that they can read, correct, or deal with it. EG *In July he handed in*

V+ADV+N,
V+N+ADV,
V+PRON+ADV

the finished version of the novel to the publishers... At half-past
eleven they finished, handed their papers in, and smiled with relief.

2 If you **hand** something **in**, you give it to someone in authority
because it belongs to them or because it is their responsibility to
deal with it. EG All the knives had to be handed in with the keys to
the larder and the fridge... I had hidden my books and not handed
them in... He took off his protective shoes and overalls, handed in his
radiation film badge, and walked out.
(V+N+ADV, V+PRON+ADV, V+ADV+N)

3 If you **hand in** your notice or your resignation, you resign from
your job. EG I was tempted to hand in my resignation at once... I
handed in my notice and left.
(V+ADV+N, V+N+ADV, V+PRON+ADV)

hand on. If you **hand** something **on** to someone, you give it or leave
it to them. EG Property is something handed on from generation to
generation... They handed on their knowledge to their children.
● **Pass on** means almost the same as **hand on.**
(V+N+ADV, V+PRON+ADV)

hand out. **1** If you **hand** something **out** to people, you give each
person in a group one of a set of similar or identical things. EG They
handed out questionnaires to the participants... There were helpers
outside and inside the Cathedral to guide visitors, hand out leaflets,
and control queues... Make a list of names, see if they're all present,
and hand the books out. ▶ A **handout** is a gift of money, clothing, or
food, which is given free to poor people by people who are richer
than they are or by an organization or charity. EG We said that we
wouldn't be relying on handouts from anyone for our future. ▶ A
handout is also a document which gives information about something and is given to people free. EG The handout explains what that
means... ...public relations handouts.
(V+ADV+N, V+N+ADV, V+PRON+ADV: ALSO+to)
(N COUNT)
(N COUNT)

2 If you **hand out** advice to someone, you give them advice and
expect them to follow it. EG She answers the phone and hands out
advice and help to overseas students.
(V+ADV+N, V+N+ADV, V+PRON+ADV)

3 If a judge or person in authority **hands out** a sentence or penalty,
they say that somebody should be punished in that way. EG The
penalties which he handed out last week were extremely unfair...
...the jail sentence handed out to the Czech dramatist.
(V+N+ADV, V+ADV+N, V+PRON+ADV: ALSO+to)

hand over. **1** If you **hand** something **over** to someone, you give it to
them so that they own it. EG Samuel was about to hand over large
sums of money to his local hospital... If you don't do what I ask, I'll
take the money and hand it over to him.
(V+N+ADV, V+PRON+ADV, V+ADV+N: ALSO+to)

2 When you **hand over** someone such as a prisoner to someone else,
you give the control of and responsibility for them to that other
person. EG Britain was under no obligation to hand him over to
America... Children are often handed over to the child-minder at
seven a.m.... I was handed over to two Police sergeants. ▶ A
handover is the official transfer of responsibility for something from
one organization or person to another. EG ...a refusal to countenance
a hand-over of power.
(V+PRON+ADV, V+N+ADV, V+ADV+N: ALSO+to)
(N SING)

3 If you **hand over** to someone or **hand** something **over** to them, you
give them the responsibility for dealing with a particular situation
or problem. EG Sir John handed over to his deputy and left... In 1977
the problem was handed over to a computer... I will willingly retire
from this investigation and hand it over.
(V+ADV, V+N+ADV, V+ADV+N, V+PRON+ADV: ALSO+to)

hand over to. If you **hand over to** someone during a discussion or
debate, you invite or allow them to start talking after you have
finished saying something. EG Now let's hand over to Kate in the
newsroom.
(V+ADV+PREP)

hand round. When you **hand round** something such as food, you
pass it from one person to another in a group. EG She handed round
the cakes... He took the tray in and handed the glasses round... They
(V+ADV+N, V+N+ADV, V+PRON+ADV)

were in the kitchen making coffee and tea. Mr Thomas handed it round.

hand to. If you say that you have got to **hand** it **to** someone, you   v+*it*+PREP
mean that you admire their skill or achievements, and that you
think they deserve a lot of praise; an informal expression. EG *You
have to hand it to them, they're wonderful entertainers.*

hang, hangs, hanging, hung

hang about. 1 See hang around.

2 If you ask someone to **hang about,** you ask them to wait or stop for   IMPERATIVE:
a moment what they are doing or saying; an informal use. EG *Now*   V+ADV
*hang about, I'm not going to let you get away with a statement like
that.*

hang around. 1 If you **hang around, about,** or **round,** you stay in   V+ADV,
the same place doing nothing, usually because you are waiting for   V+PREP
something or someone; an informal use. EG *We would have to hang
around for a while... When I got to school I·hung round outside the
classroom plucking up courage to go in... She was left to hang about
the platform on her own.*

2 If you **hang around, about** or **round** a place, you spend a lot of   V+PREP
time there, often doing very little. EG *They hang around street
corners... They hang about the bus shelters, waiting for an unsus-
pecting victim... ...little flies that hang round rotting fruit.*

3 If you **hang around, about** or **round** someone or **hang round** with   V+PREP:
them, you spend a lot of time with them; an informal use. EG *He was*   ALSO
always hanging around his bigger brother... You needn't think you   V+ADV+*with,*
can hang about with us... I was becoming more cynical, probably   V+ADV+*together,*
from hanging around with newspapermen.   RECIPROCAL

hang back. 1 If you **hang back** in a place such as a school or office,   V+ADV
you stay there after everyone else has gone home. EG *Often I hung
back after classes to ask more questions.* ● **Stay behind** means
almost the same as **hang back.**

2 If you **hang back** before doing something, you hesitate before   V+ADV
doing it, for example because you are unwilling or afraid to do it. EG
*The driver was hanging back, still flashing his lights... The rest of
the children hung back, watching her.*

hang on. 1 If you **hang on,** you wait for a short while; an informal   V+ADV:
use. EG *Hang on a minute... I hung on a bit longer.* ● **Hold on** means   ALSO IMPERATIVE
almost the same as **hang on.**

2 Something that **hangs on** something else depends on it in order to   V+PREP
be successful. EG *Everything hangs on money at the moment... It was
a tricky area and his own political future hung on it.* ● **Hinge on**
means almost the same as **hang on.**

3 If you **hang on,** you hold something very tightly in order to support   V+ADV:
yourself or protect yourself. EG *Hang on tight, folks!... Waves rolled*   ALSO IMPERATIVE
*over the little deck and he had to hang on to avoid being washed
overboard.* ● **Hold on** means almost the same as **hang on.**

hang onto, hang on to. 1 If you **hang onto** something, you hold it   V+ADV+PREP
very tightly in your hands. EG *We were both hanging onto the side of
the boat... Claude moaned, and hung on to Tom's shoulder.*

2 You can also say that you **hang onto** something when you keep it   V+ADV+PREP
even though it may not be useful or valuable. EG *We can hang onto
the old jacket for another season.*

3 If you **hang onto** a position or condition that you have such as   V+ADV+PREP
power or safety, you try hard to keep it when something is threatening it. EG *...patients who managed to hang onto life for three to four
months... He is desperately hanging on to his job.*

hang out. 1 If you **hang out** clothes that you have washed, you hang   V+ADV+N,

them on a clothes line to dry. ᴇɢ *Mrs Poulter was hanging out her* V+N+ADV,
washing. ● **Peg out** means almost the same as **hang out.** V+PRON+ADV

2 If you **hang out** somewhere, you live there or spend a lot of time V+ADV:
there; an informal use. ᴇɢ *I don't hang out at the factory... He spends* WITH A
a lot of time hanging out with friends. ▶ A **hangout** is a place where N COUNT
you like spending a lot of time because you can relax there and
meet other people; an informal word. ᴇɢ *This bar became one of my
favourite hangouts.*

hang over. 1 If something such as a problem **hangs over** you, it V+PREP
worries you a lot. ᴇɢ *I had the Open University examination hanging
over me... ...the threat of deportation hanging over me.*

2 A **hangover** is an idea, attitude, or state of mind which existed in N COUNT
the past but which is no longer important or relevant now. ᴇɢ *You've
still got this hangover of ideas... That sort of thinking is a hangover
from the past.*

3 Someone who is **hungover** feels tired and ill because they have ADJECTIVE
drunk too much alcohol; an informal word. ᴇɢ *I felt really hungover
this morning, although I only had two pints last night.*

4 If you have a **hangover,** you feel tired and ill because you have N COUNT
drunk too much alcohol.

hang round. See **hang around.**

hang together. 1 Two people or groups that **hang together** stay V+ADV
with each other and support each other even though they may
disagree on some things. ᴇɢ *We have argued. But we have in the end
hung together... Scientists within a specialty tend to hang together.*

2 Things such as ideas that **hang together** are properly organized V+ADV
and fit reasonably to form a whole or unit. ᴇɢ *All aspects of the
struggle hang together... The play doesn't hang together yet.*

hang up. 1 If you **hang** something **up** in a high place or position, you V+ADV+N,
attach it there so that it does not touch the ground. ᴇɢ *Howard hangs* V+N+ADV,
up his scarf on the hook behind the door... In the rush to get the job V+PRON+ADV
done he didn't hang his notice up.

2 Something that **is hanging up** in a high place or position is V+ADV
attached there so that it does not touch the ground. ᴇɢ *There are
some old tools hanging up in the shed.*

3 If you **hang up** or you **hang up** the phone, you end a phone call and V+ADV,
put back the receiver. ᴇɢ *'Thank you. Goodbye.' He hung up... 'Good* V+ADV+N
night.' He hung up the phone.

4 If you **hang up** something that you use for a particular activity, you V+ADV+N:
stop using it because you are giving up the activity. ᴇɢ *If your one joy* NO PASSIVE
is playing squash, don't hang up your racquet.

5 Someone who is **hung up** finds it difficult to deal with certain ADJECTIVE
situations and ideas and so becomes nervous or worried; an informal
word. ᴇɢ *You're hung up about your father.* ▶ A **hang-up** is a feeling N COUNT
of fear or embarrassment about something that makes it very
difficult for you to deal with certain situations and ideas; an informal
word. ᴇɢ *He's got a hang-up about flying... ...adolescent hang-ups.*

hang up on. If you **hang up on** someone who you are speaking to on V+ADV+PREP
the phone, you end the phone call suddenly and unexpectedly by
putting back the receiver. ᴇɢ *He didn't answer. He just hung up on
me.*

hanker, hankers, hankering, hankered

hanker after. If you **hanker after** or **for** something, you have a V+PREP
great desire or longing for it. ᴇɢ *We always hankered after a
bungalow of our own.* ● **Crave** is a more formal word for **hanker
after.**

hanker for. See **hanker after.**

happen, happens, happening, happened

happen along. If something or someone **happens along,** they V+ADV
arrive or appear unexpectedly and by chance. EG *I hadn't been very
observant myself. But then, I hadn't been expecting a murder to
happen along... She just happened along while we were waiting for
the bus.*

happen on. If you **happen on** someone or something, you find them V+PREP:
or meet them by chance; an old-fashioned literary expression. EG *We* HAS PASSIVE
happened on them in the street. ● **Come across** is a more common
expression for **happen on.**

hare, hares, haring, hared

hare off. If you **hare off,** you run or move quickly away from a V+ADV
place. EG *Lebel was haring off down the street, yelling.*

hark, harks, harking, harked

hark back to; a literary expression. 1 If you **hark back to** some- V+ADV+PREP
thing in the past, you remember it or remind someone of it. EG
*Increasingly she harked back to our 'dear little' mews... He consist-
ently harked back to St. Thomas Aquinas.*

2 If something **harks back** to another thing in the past, it is similar V+ADV+PREP
to it. EG *...the decorative use of brick harking back to the old
farmhouse style.*

harp, harps, harping, harped

harp on. If you **harp on** a subject, you keep on talking about it V+PREP,
although other people may not want you to. EG *But you were the one* V+ADV
who kept harping on death, Mother... You do harp on so.

hash, hashes, hashing, hashed

hash over. If people **hash over** a subject or problem, they discuss it V+ADV+N,
in great detail; used in informal American English. EG *Meetings of* V+N+ADV,
situational groups should not be devoted to hashing over the past. V+PRON+ADV

hatch, hatches, hatching, hatched

hatch out. When a baby bird, insect, or other animal **hatches out** or V+ADV:
an egg **hatches out,** the baby animal comes out of the egg by ALSO+*into*
breaking the shell. EG *The larva hatches out and lives in the soil...
Each of these eggs hatches out into a tiny grub.*

haul, hauls, hauling, hauled

haul in. If the police or authorities **haul** someone **in,** they arrest V+N+ADV,
them. EG *...boys were regularly hauled in drunk... Wait and get your* V+PRON+ADV,
evidence before you go hauling him in. V+ADV+N

haul off. If someone is **hauled off,** they are taken to a place against V+N+ADV,
their will. EG *Youths are being dragged off buses and hauled off to* V+PRON+ADV,
jail... They tried to haul me off but I resisted. ● **Cart off** means V+ADV+N
almost the same as **haul off.**

haul up. If you are **hauled up** in a court of law or before someone in PASSIVE:
authority, you are forced to appear in that court or before that V+ADV,
person, because you are thought to have broken the law or dis- WITH A
obeyed orders. EG *He got hauled up in court for assaulting a student...
Galileo was hauled up before the Inquisition on charges of heresy.*

have, has, having, had

Have got is often used in informal English to mean the same as
have.

have against. If you **have** something **against** someone or some- V+N+PREP
thing, you disapprove of them because of something you think they
did wrong in the past. EG *I asked what you had against him... I've
never had anything personal against you.*

have away. See have off.

have in. If you **have in** workers or experts, you ask them to come to your home or workplace to do some work for you. EG *They are having a maid in to care for the house... It's not a normal routine to have Special Branch men in to search when one of us dies.*

V+N+ADV,
V+PRON+ADV

have off. If someone **has** it **off** or **has** it **away** with another person, they have sex with them; an informal expression. EG *Mary had had it off with a waiter in a Greek restaurant... ...love orgies, teenagers having it off and all that.*

V+*it*+ADV,
V+*it*+ADV+*with*:
RECIPROCAL

have on. 1 If you **have on** a piece of clothing, you are wearing it. EG *She had on an old bathrobe... Perhaps it had been a nightdress after all, she had certainly had nothing on underneath it.*

V+ADV+N,
V+N+ADV,
V+PRON+ADV:
NO PASSIVE

2 If you **have** a radio, television, or hi-fi **on**, it is switched on and you are usually listening to it or watching it. EG *...having the radio on at full blast till all hours of the night.*

V+N+ADV,
V+PRON+ADV:
NO PASSIVE

3 If you **have** someone **on**, you tease them by pretending that something is true when it is not true. EG *Or was he having me on? I didn't like to ask.*

V+PRON+ADV,
V+N+ADV,
V+ADV+N

4 If you **have** information **on** someone, you know something about them that you can use to influence them, blackmail them, or prove them guilty in a court. EG *'Are you sure Central Records have got nothing on him?' Inspector Flint shook his head.*

V+N+PREP:
NO PASSIVE

have out. 1 If you **have out** a tooth, your appendix, your tonsils and so on, a dentist or doctor removes them from your body. EG *I had gone to hospital to have my tonsils out... ...having a tooth out on the National Health.*

V+N+ADV,
V+PRON+ADV:
NO PASSIVE

2 If you **have** something **out** with someone, you talk to them about something that has been causing disagreement or unpleasantness between you for some time. EG *He felt like picking up the telephone and having it out with him there and then.*

V+PRON+ADV,
V+N+ADV:
ALSO+*with*

hawk, hawks, hawking, hawked

hawk about. See hawk around.

hawk around. If something is **hawked around**, **round**, or **about** a place or a group of people, it is offered for sale. EG *It was hawked around the city streets... For years after her son's death, his mother hawked his manuscript around until she managed to persuade a publisher to accept it.*

V+N+PREP/ADV,
V+PRON+PREP/ADV,
V+ADV+N:
USUALLY PASSIVE

hawk round. See hawk around.

head, heads, heading, headed

head back. If you **head back**, you stop travelling or moving forward and begin your return journey to the place that you came from. EG *I didn't head back at once but swam parallel with the shore towards the rocks... We wanted him to turn around and head back to L.A.*

V+ADV:
USUALLY+A

head for. 1 If you **head for** a place, you start moving or travelling towards it. EG *We had decided to head for Miami... I headed for the door.* ● **Make for** means almost the same as **head for.**

V+PREP

2 If you **are heading for** or **are headed for** a situation, that situation is becoming more and more likely. EG *Mr Reagan was heading for a personal triumph.*

V+PREP:
ALSO PASSIVE,
V+PREP

head into. If you **are heading into** a situation or a period of time, especially an unpleasant one, you are starting to experience it. EG *She was heading into another of her bad times by the looks of things.*

V+PREP

head off. 1 If you **head off** a person, animal, or vehicle, you try to stop them moving in a particular direction, for example by standing in their way. EG *The boys fanned out, trying to head off the goats... I leapt to my feet with the purpose of heading him off.*

V+ADV+N,
V+PRON+ADV,
V+N+ADV

2 If you **head off** something unpleasant, you prevent it from happening. EG *Governments may allow wages to rise faster than productivity in order to head off possible unrest... We do too little to head off disaster.* V+ADV+N, V+PRON+ADV

3 If you **head off** in a particular direction, you go in that direction. EG *She headed off towards the garage.* V+ADV: WITH A

head towards. If you **are heading towards** or **are headed towards** a situation or a period of time, the situation or period of time is slowly getting nearer or becoming more likely. EG *We were heading towards the General Election.* V+PREP: ALSO PASSIVE, V+PREP

head up. If you **head up** a group or team, you take charge of it and are responsible for it; used in American English. EG *I headed up the basketball team at high school.* V+ADV+N, V+N+ADV, V+PRON+ADV

heal, heals, healing, healed

heal over. When a wound **heals over,** the wounded part of your body becomes healthy and normal again. EG *When the cord falls off it may leave a raw spot, which takes a number of days to heal over.* V+ADV

heal up. When a wound or other injury **heals up,** the injured part of your body becomes healthy and normal again. EG *After his hoof had healed up, Boxer worked harder than ever.* V+ADV

heap, heaps, heaping, heaped

heap on. If you heap praise or criticism **on** or **upon** a person or thing, you praise or criticize them a lot. EG *Film director Kenneth Loach heaped praise on the Young Socialists... ...his silent acceptance of the abuse that was being heaped upon him.* V+N+PREP

heap up. If you **heap** things **up,** you put them on top of each other in a large pile. EG *Swearing hoarsely, he heaped up the pillows... We saw garbage heaped up almost to the top.* ● **Pile up** means almost the same as **heap up.** ▶ If you refer to **heaped-up** things, you mean that they are on top of each other in a large pile. EG *...heaped-up piles of rice.* V+ADV+N, V+N+ADV, V+PRON+ADV / ADJECTIVE

heap upon. See heap on: **heap upon** is more formal.

hear, hears, hearing, heard

hear about. If you **hear about** something or someone, you get news or information concerning them. EG *The more I hear about him, the less I like him... I heard about the bomb from Mr Zapp.* V+PREP

hear from. **1** If you **hear from** someone, you receive a letter or telephone call from them. EG *Very occasionally I hear from her.* V+PREP: HAS PASSIVE

2 If you **hear from** someone in a meeting or debate, you listen to their opinions. EG *I would have liked to hear more from the patient.* V+PREP

hear of. If you **hear of** someone or something, you get news or information about them for the first time. EG *I heard of his death as I was walking into the hospital... I have never heard of him.* ▶ An event or situation which is **unheard of** rarely happens, and is therefore very surprising or shocking when it does happen. EG *Contracts and written agreements are quite unheard of... This is an unheard-of outrage.* ▶ Someone who is **unheard of** is not famous or well-known. EG *...an unheard-of author.* V+PREP: HAS PASSIVE / ADJECTIVE / ADJECTIVE

hear out. If you **hear** someone **out,** you listen without interrupting until they have finished speaking. EG *This time you're going to hear me out... Do not be afraid to hear her out.* V+PRON+ADV, V+N+ADV

heat, heats, heating, heated

heat up. **1** When something **heats up,** it gradually becomes hotter. EG *The air over the great land mass heats up in summer and rises... Leave a space for hot air to escape as the bottles heat up.* V+ADV

2 If you **heat up** cooked food after it has become cold, you make it V+ADV+N,

hot again. EG *He debated heating up the pot roast... It should be*   V+PRON+ADV,
delicious cold. Or shall we heat it up? ● **Warm up** means almost the   V+N+ADV
same as **heat up.**

3 If a situation **heats up,** it starts to change very quickly. EG *Things*   V+ADV
were heating up so fast in the US that I did not want to make any
rash predictions.

heave, heaves, heaving, heaved, hove

You use **heaved** as the past tense and past participle for **heave up,**
and **hove** for **heave to.**

heave to. In a boat or ship with sails, if the crew **heave to,** they stop   V+ADV
the boat, using the sails instead of the anchor. EG *Couldn't we heave*
to, or whatever it is you do?

heave up. If you **heave up,** you vomit. EG *He had heaved up his*   V+ADV+N,
dinner... He heaved up all over the carpet, lay back on the sofa, and   V+N+ADV,
fell fast asleep. ● **Throw up** means almost the same as **heave up.**   V+ADV:
                                       NO PASSIVE

hedge, hedges, hedging, hedged

hedge about with. See **hedge around with.**

hedge against. If you **hedge against** something unpleasant, you do   V+PREP
something to try and prevent it from affecting you. EG *This deposit*
provides a way of hedging against fluctuating interest rates.

hedge around with. If something **is hedged around, about,** or   PASSIVE:
round with problems or restrictions, they cause it to be very   V+ADV+PREP
difficult or complicated. EG *The concessions were hedged around*
with so many restrictions... Her freedom was hedged round with
duties and restrictions.

hedge in. If someone or something **is hedged in** by problems or   V+ADV+N,
restrictions, the problems or restrictions prevent them from being   V+N+ADV,
effective or acting freely. EG *The proposals were hedged in with*   V+PRON+ADV:
legal niceties.   USUALLY PASSIVE

hedge round with. See **hedge around with.**

heel, heels, heeling, heeled

heel over. When someone or something **heels over,** they lean very   V+ADV:
far to one side, as if they are about to fall. EG *At this point, they both*   USUALLY+A
heeled over sharply in the crowd.

help, helps, helping, helped

help along. To **help** a process **along** means to cause it to take place   V+N+ADV,
more quickly or more easily. EG *You may need to help the process*   V+PRON+ADV
along by pressing with a spoon... Respiratory diseases are often
helped along by malnutrition.

help off with. If you **help** someone **off with** a piece of clothing, you   V+PRON+ADV+PREP,
help them to remove it. EG *I went to help her off with her cloak...*   V+N+ADV+PREP
Help me off with my boots... Let me help you off with your coat.

help on with. If you **help** someone **on with** a piece of clothing, you   V+PRON+ADV+PREP,
help them to dress. EG *Mrs Bixby followed her husband to the door*   V+N+ADV+PREP
and helped him on with his coat.

help out. If you **help out** or **help** someone **out,** you do them a   V+ADV+N,
favour, such as lending them money or doing some of their work. EG   V+PRON+ADV,
Neighbourhood associations help out the poor with funeral ex-   V+ADV:
penses... I was asked to come in for a few days to help them out.   ALSO+ with

help to. If you **help** someone **to** food or drink, you serve it to them.   V+PRON+PREP,
EG *I helped him to some more scotch... She was in the kitchen,*   V+REFL+PREP,
helping herself to my biscuits.   V+N+PREP

help up. If you **help** someone **up,** you help them to stand up again   V+PRON+ADV,
after they have been sitting down or after they have fallen. EG *Please*   V+N+ADV,
help me up. Thank you... She had taken him by the hand, and was   V+ADV+N

helping him up... Howard fastens the button, and helps Henry up from the bench.

hem, hems, hemming, hemmed

hem in. 1 If a place **is hemmed in** by things, it is enclosed by them. EG *...these roads, being wide and not hemmed in by buildings... ...the fields in the valley bottom, hemmed in by hedges.*

V+ADV+N,
V+N+ADV,
V+PRON+ADV:
USUALLY PASSIVE

2 If people **are hemmed in** by something, they feel that it prevents them from doing what they want to do. EG *...men and women whose lives are hemmed in by bureaucracy... ...in our case, hemmed in by so many illusions... ...other dimensions than those which seem to hem us in.*

V+N+ADV,
V+PRON+ADV,
V+ADV+N:
USUALLY PASSIVE

herd, herds, herding, herded

herd together. If you **herd** people or animals **together,** you gather them into a group. EG *The dogs rushed about trying to herd them together... Panic gripped me as they herded us together like sheep.*

V+PRON+ADV,
V+N+ADV,
V+ADV+N'

herd up. If you **herd** people or animals **up,** you make them move together to form a group. EG *Their dogs helped to herd them up again before any damage was done... Kunta herded up his goats as quickly as he could.* ● **Round up** means almost the same as **herd up.**

V+PRON+ADV,
V+ADV+N,
V+N+ADV

hew, hews, hewing, hewed/hewn

hew down. If you **hew down** something that is standing, such as a tree, you cut through it so that it falls down; a literary expression. EG *They had to hew down several trees and make a raft.* ● **Chop down** means almost the same as **hew down.**

V+ADV+N,
V+N+ADV,
V+PRON+ADV

hew out. If you **hew out** something, you make it by cutting it roughly from a large piece of stone, wood, or ground; a literary expression. EG *Excavators have hewn out an underground car park for 1,000 cars.* ● **Carve out** means almost the same as **hew out.**

V+ADV+N,
V+N+ADV,
V+PRON+ADV

hide, hides, hiding, hid, hidden

hide away. 1 If you **hide** something **away,** you put it in a place where nobody else can find it. EG *He looked at his drawings of the rocks and hid them away... I've kept it, but hidden away in a secret place.* ● **Stash away** means almost the same as **hide away.**

V+PRON+ADV,
V+N+ADV,
V+ADV+N

2 If you **hide away,** you go somewhere without telling people where you are going, because you do not want them to find you. EG *You see, I may need somewhere to hide away for a week or two... ...a small, inexpensive apartment where I could hide away during the hours I wanted to work.* ▶ A **hideaway** is a place where you go without telling other people, because you do not want them to find you. EG *...a Hollywood producer's desert hideaway.*

V+ADV

N COUNT

3 If someone or something **is hidden away,** they are very far from places where people live or often go. EG *...Rhodes' impressive tomb, hidden away in the depths of the country.*

PASSIVE:
V+ADV

hide behind. 1 If you **hide behind** something, you use it as an excuse to conceal your real ideas or feelings. EG *We can always hide behind the fact that he has no statistical evidence.*

V+PREP

2 If you **hide** a feeling or characteristic **behind** something, you try to hide the fact that you have it. EG *He hid his feelings behind a gruff abruptness... An astute and lively mind lay hidden behind his slow movements.*

V+N+PREP,
V+PRON+PREP

hide from. 1 If you **hide from** someone, you go somewhere where they cannot see you. EG *They hid from him among the trees.*

V+PREP:
HAS PASSIVE

2 If you **hide from** something, you try to pretend that you do not know it although you do. EG *All I could do was to hide from the truth.*

V+PREP

3 If you **hide** something **from** someone, you try to prevent them from seeing it or noticing it. EG *He hid the ignition key from her...*

V+N+PREP,
V+REFL+PREP,
V+PRON+PREP

After Jesus said this, he went off and hid himself from them... The truth was being hidden from the public.

hide out. If you **hide out,** you go somewhere without telling people where you are going, because you do not want them to find you. ᴇɢ *If the press were really after me it would be better to hide out until it all blew over... He has been hiding out in a provincial village.* ► A **hideout** is a place where you go without telling people where you are going, because you do not want them to find you. ᴇɢ *Perhaps they used this house as a hide-out?... Their leaders took to hideouts in the Pondoland hills.*   v+ADV: USUALLY+A   N COUNT

hide up. If you **hide up,** you go somewhere without telling people where you are going, because you do not want them to find you. ᴇɢ *Kitty, we know that Dov Landau is safe. He is hiding up at Gera.*   v+ADV

hike, hikes, hiking, hiked

hike up. 1 If you **hike up** a piece of clothing that you are wearing, you pull it up with a quick movement. ᴇɢ *He hiked up his trouser leg... Mrs Halverston hiked up her skirt and sprang onto the tailgate.* ● **Hitch up** means almost the same as **hike up.**   v+ADV+N, V+N+ADV, V+PRON+ADV

2 If someone **hikes up** a price or other sum of money, they increase it suddenly and by a large amount. ᴇɢ *...buy up supplies while they are cheap and hence hike the price up... The newly installed government hiked the timber export royalty up.* ● **Push up** means almost the same as **hike up.**   v+N+ADV, V+ADV+N, V+PRON+ADV

hinge, hinges, hinging, hinged

hinge on. If one thing **hinges on** or **upon** another, its existence or qualities depend entirely on the existence or qualities of the other thing. ᴇɢ *He said everything hinged on what happened to the United States economy... Their future well-being hinged upon victory.* ● **Hang on** means almost the same as **hinge on.**   v+PREP

hinge upon. See hinge on.

hint, hints, hinting, hinted

hint at. If you **hint at** something, you suggest in a very indirect way that it is true or likely. ᴇɢ *It was the only time Natalie had hinted at the possibility of their marriage breaking up... The weather forecast has already hinted at snow showers in the north... Marriage had already been hinted at.* ● **Imply** means almost the same as **hint at.**   v+PREP: HAS PASSIVE

hire, hires, hiring, hired

hire out. If you **hire out** something such as a car or a person's services, you allow them to be used in return for payment. ᴇɢ *Holborn library hires out reproductions and original pictures... ...labourers whom they would be glad to hire out on moderate terms.* ● **Rent out** means almost the same as **hire out.**   v+ADV+N, V+N+ADV, V+PRON+ADV

hit, hits, hitting

Hit is used in the present tense and is the past tense and past participle of the verb.

hit at. 1 If you **hit at** someone, you aim a blow at them. ᴇɢ *When I refused he hit at my shoulders and arms with the strap.*   v+PREP

2 If you **hit at** something, you try to damage it. ᴇɢ *To begin with, little effort was made to hit at the morale of the Russians themselves.*   v+PREP

hit back. 1 If you **hit back** or **hit** someone **back,** you hit them after they have hit you. ᴇɢ *Thomas staggered and then hit back... I still refused, and felt ready to hit back if he hit me again... Then Marks will pretend to hit the child back.*   v+ADV, V+N+ADV, V+PRON+ADV

2 If you **hit back** at someone, you criticize or harm them after they   v+ADV: ALSO+at

have criticized or harmed you. EG *John was obsessed with hitting back at those who had wronged him... If someone infringes upon your personal freedom, you hit back.*

hit off. If two people **hit** it **off,** they like each other and become friends as soon as they meet. EG *They had hit it off from the first evening... My mother-in-law and Tom did not hit it off.*

V+*it*+ADV,
ALSO+*with*:
RECIPROCAL

hit on. If you **hit on** or **upon** an idea, you think of it, especially when it is a solution to a problem. EG *Tired of letting the cat in and out, he hit on the idea of cutting a hole in the door... Many ideas were considered and rejected before he finally hit on the plan he decided to adopt... The architects independently hit upon the same idea for the chief feature.* ● **Stumble on** means almost the same as **hit on.**

V+PREP

hit out. 1 If you **hit out** in a fight, you aim punches in all directions around you, trying to hit the person or people who are fighting you or trying to capture you. EG *Ralph hit out; then he and a dozen others were rolling over, hitting, biting, scratching... A sick fear and rage swept him. Fiercely he hit out at the filthy thing in front of him.* ● **Lash out** means almost the same as **hit out.**

V+ADV:
ALSO+*at*

2 If you **hit out** at someone you disagree with, you attack or criticize them strongly. EG *The Prime Minister hit out at her colleagues in Europe... ...hitting out with the full might of state apparatus.* ● **Lash out** means almost the same as **hit out.**

V+ADV:
ALSO+*at*

hit upon. See **hit on.**

hitch, hitches, hitching, hitched

hitch up. If you **hitch up** a piece of clothing, you pull it up to a higher position on your body. EG *Stein hitched up his trousers and tucked in his shirt... Hitching her dress up she lay back in the chair.*

V+ADV+N,
V+N+ADV,
V+PRON+ADV

hive, hives, hiving, hived

hive off. If you **hive off** a business or a part of a business, you sell it or transfer it to someone, usually for a large profit. EG *...included a provision to hive off London Transport to the LCC... In 1968 he tried an alternative approach, hiving off the nuclear research lab.* ● **Sell off** means almost the same as **hive off.**

V+ADV+N,
V+N+ADV,
V+PRON+ADV

hoard, hoards, hoarding, hoarded

hoard away. If you **hoard** something **away,** you hide it and keep it hidden until you want it. EG *All we could think about sometimes was chocolate: we used to hoard it away in our lockers.*

V+PRON+ADV,
V+N+ADV,
V+ADV+N

hoard up. If you **hoard up** something, you try to keep a lot of it, so that you can use it later. EG *You always seem to hoard up stuff.*

V+ADV+N,
V+N+ADV,
V+PRON+ADV

hoke, hokes, hoking, hoked

hoke up. If you **hoke** something **up,** you pretend that it exists and make it seem to be more important than it really is; used in informal American English. EG *It suited Humboldt to hoke that up.*

V+N+ADV,
V+ADV+N,
V+PRON+ADV

hold, holds, holding, held

hold against. If you **hold** something **against** someone, you allow something that they did wrong in the past to influence you and cause you to deal harshly with them. EG *Nationalising for the wrong reasons will be held against him when the crunch comes... He's a good friend of mine. He won't hold it against us.*

V+N+PREP,
V+PRON+PREP

hold back. 1 If you **hold back,** or if something **holds** you **back,** you hesitate before you act or speak, because you are not sure what to do or say. EG *Police have held back from going into a holy place to arrest him... I have noticed that you do not hold back in our discussions... She couldn't quite say what it was that held her back.*

V+ADV,
V+PRON+ADV,
V+N+ADV,
V+REFL+ADV

2 If you **hold** someone **back,** you prevent them from leaving a place.

V+PRON+ADV,

EG *Judy held him back. 'Don't, Bal,' she said... They were doubtful as to how far they would be able to hold back all their units.* `V+ADV+N, V+N+ADV`

3 If you **hold** a person or their career **back,** you prevent them from making progress. EG *If she is ambitious, don't try to hold her back... ...the prejudices which are holding you back in your career.* `V+PRON+ADV, V+N+ADV, V+ADV+N`

4 If you **hold back** an event or development, you prevent it from taking place or cause it to happen more slowly. EG *The rise in living standards has been held back for so long... Worry about the environment has been one of the key restraints in holding back economic development... ...holding back on the spread of consumer non-essentials.* `V+N+ADV, V+ADV+N, V+PRON+ADV: ALSO+on`

5 If you **hold back** resources, you keep them in reserve to use later. EG *They need the money immediately and cannot hold back their goods to push the price up... 20 per cent of the aircraft must be held back and preserved for the time when nuclear strike operations might be necessary.* `V+ADV+N, V+N+ADV, V+PRON+ADV`

6 If you **hold back** information, you do not reveal it. EG *'You knew Gareth quite well at one time, then?' He could hold it back no longer. 'Yes, at Oxford.'... I can see you are holding certain things back, things you haven't said.* ● **Suppress** is a more formal word for **hold back.** `V+PRON+ADV, V+N+ADV, V+ADV+N`

7 If you **hold back** tears or laughter, you do not allow yourself to cry or laugh, because you do not want to show your emotions. EG *Most of us were either crying or doing our best to hold back the tears.* ● **Keep back** means almost the same as **hold back,** and **contain** is a more formal word. `V+ADV+N, V+N+ADV, V+PRON+ADV: NO PASSIVE`

hold down. **1** If you **hold** someone or something **down,** you use force to keep them in a particular place and to stop them from moving. EG *Ash was barely eight years old, but it had taken four men to hold him down, for he was strong and wiry... I was trying all the time to hold down the lid of the box with one hand.* `V+PRON+ADV, V+ADV+N, V+N+ADV`

2 If someone **holds down** a group of people, they do not allow them to have freedom, power, or rights. EG *There would still not be enough forces to hold down the previously subject peoples... Levi put up a rather better show, holding the Romans down till November.* ● **Keep down** means almost the same as **hold down.** `V+ADV+N, V+N+ADV, V+PRON+ADV`

3 If you **hold down** a job, you manage to keep it, although it may be difficult for you to do so. EG *There is nothing surprising about finding a woman holding down a successful job in high finance... You have to rely on reason, not authority, if you hold down a job.* `V+ADV+N, V+N+ADV, V+PRON+ADV`

4 If you **hold down** wages, prices, or costs, you prevent them from increasing very much. EG *Did they think that Sir Geoffrey's policy would hold down inflation?... Such fights are unavoidable if long-term costs are to be held down.* ● **Keep down** means almost the same as **hold down.** `V+ADV+N, V+N+ADV, V+PRON+ADV`

5 If you **hold down** an emotion such as fear or hysteria, you do not allow yourself to show or express it. EG *I could hold my emotions down no longer... The figure fades and I hold panic down.* `V+N+ADV, V+ADV+N, V+PRON+ADV: NO PASSIVE`

6 If you cannot **hold down** food, you are unable to eat it without vomiting. EG *The patient loses his appetite and cannot hold down some kinds of food.* ● **Keep down** means almost the same as **hold down.** `V+ADV+N, V+N+ADV, V+PRON+ADV: NO PASSIVE`

hold forth. If you **hold forth** on a topic, you talk about it for a long time, often in a rather boring way. EG *He was busy holding forth on the pleasures of travel... ...holding forth about the duty of Christian missionaries... I was holding forth to the actors when I suddenly heard peals of laughter.* `V+ADV: USUALLY WITH on/about`

hold in. If you **hold in** an emotion, you do not allow yourself to `V+ADV+N,`

express it. EG *Women are expected to hold in their anger... She*   v+PRON+ADV,
wanted to cry but held in the tears... 'Running about naked in a   v+N+ADV
garden!' The old woman could hold it in no longer: such a mixture of
impropriety and carelessness was unbearable.

hold off. 1 If you **hold off** an enemy, an opponent, or an attack, you   v+N+ADV,
prevent them from successfully attacking you or competing against   v+ADV+N,
you. EG *The warriors tried to hold the soldiers off until the women*   v+PRON+ADV
and children could escape... ...watching my teammates try to hold
off Al Redding's determined efforts to score... The French and
British wanted to hold off Portuguese textile competition. ● **Fight**
off means almost the same as **hold off.**

2 If you **hold off** doing something, you delay doing it or making a   v+ADV+N,
decision about it. EG *He might be so scared that he'll hold off our*   v+ADV+-ING,
offer too... Everyone holds off buying as long as they can, if they   v+ADV:
think the price still has a way to drop.   NO PASSIVE

3 If the rain **holds off,** it does not rain, although you had expected it   v+ADV
to. EG *That storm was really something. We were just blessed that it*
held off for the picnic.

hold on. 1 If you **hold on,** you grasp something firmly or lean   v+ADV:
against it, in order to prevent yourself from falling over. EG *I*   ALSO+to
grabbed hold of the front and held on for dear life... Someone was
standing behind the ladder and holding on to it for support.

2 If you are in a difficult situation but **hold on,** you force yourself to   v+ADV
continue doing something or to stick to a decision you have made. EG
The thought depressed her violently. But she held on. It would pass.
She had to breathe deeply... I would find myself again if I could just
hold on, be quiet, and lie down. ● **Give up** means the opposite of **hold**
on.

3 If you ask someone to **hold on,** you want them to wait for a short   v+ADV:
time. EG *Hold on a moment, please... Do you mind holding on while I*   USUALLY+A
find out?... Hold on! Hold on! One at a time! ● **Hang on** means almost
the same as **hold on.**

hold on to, hold onto. 1 If you **hold on to** something that is in   v+ADV+PREP
your hand, you grip it tightly so that it cannot fall or cannot be taken
away from you. EG *Jordache took a step back, holding on to the*
drawing... They all held firmly on to their brief-cases.

2 If you **hold on to** someone, you keep your arms round them so that   v+ADV+PREP
they cannot move or go away. EG *I stayed where I was on the sofa*
and held on to Humboldt... Then suddenly they stopped, holding on
to each other and laughing.

3 If you **hold on to** something that you have, you keep it for yourself   v+ADV+PREP
and do not let anyone else have it. EG *He permitted Rudolph to hold*
on to the money he earned... ...politicians like himself who want to
hold on to power at all costs... He could sell off blocks of stock while
holding on to the controlling interest in the corporation.

4 If you **hold on to** something that is old-fashioned, you continue to   v+ADV+PREP
keep it or use it. EG *...where people hold on to unmarketable skills...*
...developing electric cars instead of holding on to the old-fashioned
internal combustion engine.

5 If you ask someone to **hold on to** something for you, you want   v+ADV+PREP
them to look after it until you ask for it back. EG *Will you hold on to*
this for me for a couple of days?

6 If you **hold on to** a belief, idea, or principle, you continue to believe   v+ADV+PREP
in it and do not change or abandon it. EG *If enough people can hold*
on to their dream, this will become possible... Helen spoke carefully,
no longer holding on to the delusion that she was engaged in a
casual conversation.

hold out. 1 If you **hold out** your hand, you stretch it out in front of   v+ADV+N, you, usually in order to take something from someone or to shake hands with them. EG *Daintry held out his hand for the briefcase... She held out a hand and he shook it.* `V+N+ADV,` `V+PRON+ADV`

2 If you **hold** something **out**, you hold it in front of you, so that someone can take it or look at it. EG *He held out his plate for a second portion... He held out his arm. 'Look.'... He took off his glasses and held them out to Ralph.* `V+ADV+N,` `V+PRON+ADV,` `V+N+ADV:` `ALSO+to`

3 If you **hold out**, you manage to resist an enemy, an opponent, or an attack. EG *They could either surrender or hold out, risking starvation or death at the hands of Carson's soldiers... But even he began to despair of holding out indefinitely against the pressures building up... It was just a matter of holding out one day at a time.* ● **Give in** means the opposite of **hold out**. ▷ A **holdout** is someone who resists an enemy, an opponent, or an attack. EG *The only holdout at first was the old Afrikaner... Manuelito was the last of the holdouts.* `V+ADV:` `ALSO+against` `N COUNT`

4 If you **hold out** hope of something, you are hopeful that it will happen or succeed. EG *Benn himself held out no hopes for victory... Science may hold out some prospect of feeding the hungry multitudes... ...a programme which held out the possibility of a successful attack on poverty and inequality.* `V+ADV+N:` `NO PASSIVE`

5 If supplies of something **hold out**, there is enough for you to use for a certain period of time. EG *I decided to stay in that place as long as the water held out... The room was expensive, but my cash was holding out better than I had expected.* ● **Last out** means almost the same as **hold out**. `V+ADV`

hold out for. If you **hold out for** something, you insist on having it and refuse to accept anything less than you are asking for. EG *Jamaica was holding out for a higher sugar price... ...every Cheyenne and Arapaho chief who had held out for peace with the white men... Tanya offered thirty-five dollars; the passenger held out for forty-five.* `V+ADV+PREP`

hold out on. If you **hold out on** someone, you refuse to tell them something that you know or give them something that you promised to give them. EG *I couldn't hold out on him any more.* `V+ADV+PREP`

hold over. **1** If you **hold** something **over** someone, you use it in order to threaten them or make them do what you want. EG *He held the Will over her like a threat... 'Now I've got something to hold over you!' he said.* `V+N+PREP,` `V+PRON+PREP`

2 If you **hold** something **over**, you decide not to discuss it or deal with it until a future date. EG *Its proposals should be held over until everyone has had a good think... The prize may be held over until a subsequent year when two awards may be awarded.* ● **Defer** is a more formal word for **hold over**. `V+N+ADV,` `V+PRON+ADV,` `V+ADV+N`

3 A **holdover** is something that exists after the time that it was intended for or when it was appropriate. EG *...a holdover from early infancy... The present curriculum is a holdover from the past.* `N SING`

hold to. **1** When you **hold** one thing **to** another, you take it in your hands, put it next to the other thing, and keep it there. EG *I struggled on, holding the cage tight to my chest.* `V+N+PREP,` `V+PRON+PREP`

2 If you **hold to** an opinion, belief, or habit, you will not or cannot change it. EG *The country must not hold to rigid concepts of international alignments... Later at a brief meeting, he would hold to his decision... ...if all the points which were raised were held to by the British government.* ● **Stick to** means almost the same as **hold to**. `V+PREP:` `HAS PASSIVE`

hold together. **1** When you **hold** people **together** or when they **hold together**, they manage to live or work together without arguing or disagreeing, although they have different ideas, interests, or `V+N+ADV,` `V+ADV+N,` `V+ADV,` `V+PRON+ADV:` `ERGATIVE` opinions. EG *...if the parents hold the family together in spite of friction... Chiang's design was simply to hold together some sort of Nationalist Army... A group can hold together unless there's a general exodus.*

2 If something **holds together,** it stays in good condition. EG *The problem now seemed to be whether the car would hold together... ...the original bag, which held together long enough.*   V+ADV

hold up. **1** If you **hold up** your hand or something you have in your hand, you move it upwards into a particular position and keep it there. EG *Ralph held up his hand. 'Why shouldn't we get our own?'... The Englishman held up the rifle... The children were meant to hold up the President's book.* ● **Raise** is a more formal word for **hold up.**   V+ADV+N,
V+N+ADV,
V+PRON+ADV

2 If one thing **holds up** another, it is placed under the other thing in order to support it and prevent it from falling. EG *...steel girders to hold up skyscrapers... These books hold the bed up.* ● **Prop up** means almost the same as **hold up.**   V+ADV+N,
V+N+ADV,
V+PRON+ADV

3 If something or someone **holds up** an activity or arrangement, they delay it or make it late. EG *These slogans persuaded her to hold up the procession... The EEC threatened to hold up the negotiations... The whole thing was held up about half an hour.* ▶ A **hold-up** is a delay or something which causes a delay. EG *I nearly missed my flight owing to a traffic hold-up.*   V+ADV+N,
V+N+ADV,
V+PRON+ADV

N COUNT

4 If someone **holds** you **up,** they point a weapon at you in order to make you give them money or valuables. EG *He held me up at the point of a gun... Banks were held up with pistols and sawn-off shotguns.* ● **Rob** means almost the same as **hold up.** ▶ A **holdup** is a robbery in which weapons are used to force people to give their money or valuables to the robbers. EG *Seven people were wounded towards the end of July in different hold-ups.*   V+N+ADV,
V+PRON+ADV,
V+ADV+N

N COUNT

5 If you **hold up** someone or their behaviour or habits, you use them as an example to tell people your opinion about them and persuade them to agree with you. EG *What do you hold up to the children as being desirable goals?... He would hold them up to contempt and ridicule... I don't hold myself up as a good churchgoer... I wasn't the sort of child anyone would ever hold up as an example to others.*   V+N+ADV,
V+PRON+ADV,
V+REFL+ADV,
V+ADV+N:
USUALLY+A

6 If equipment or clothing **holds up,** it remains in good condition after rough use. EG *How did your boots hold up?*   V+ADV

7 If ideas, systems, or plans **hold up,** they remain convincing or effective after examination or use. EG *Your argument, though appealing, doesn't hold up... None of his stories would hold up in public.* ● **Stand up** means almost the same as **hold up.**   V+ADV

hold with. If you do not **hold with** an activity or idea,, you do not approve of it. EG *You know I don't hold with letter-writing... ...a man who did not hold with the notion that it was necessary.* ● **Agree with** means almost the same as **hold with.**   V+PREP:
WITH NEGATIVE

hole, holes, holing, holed

hole out. In golf, if you **hole out** in a certain number of points, you finish one of the holes or the course with that number of points. EG *In the six rounds he played, he never holed out in less than 92.*   V+ADV:
USUALLY+*in*

hole up. If you **hole up** somewhere, you hide yourself there; an informal expression. EG *The men were holed up on the top floor of the hotel... San Francisco was where she holed up... I was ready to hole up there indefinitely.*   V+ADV,
ALSO PASSIVE,
V+ADV:
USUALLY+A

hollow, hollows, hollowing, hollowed

hollow out. If you **hollow out** something that is solid, you make a space in it by removing the inside part of it. EG *Some kids had hollowed out tunnels in a maize field... Then we hollow it out a*   V+ADV+N,
V+PRON+ADV,
V+N+ADV *little... They spent the night in a small snow hole they had hollowed out under a rock.* ▶ Something that is **hollowed-out** has had the ADJECTIVE inside part of it removed. EG *...a hollowed-out tree-stump.*

home, homes, homing, homed

home in. 1 If something which is travelling through the air or through water **homes in** on something else, it moves directly towards it very rapidly. EG *The missile can thus home in on the target with pinpoint accuracy... The shark turned, homing in on the stream of blood.*   V+ADV: USUALLY+*on*

2 If you **home in** on a particular subject or topic, you pay more attention to it and deal with it in detail. EG *She homed in on the things we were discussing.*   V+ADV: USUALLY+*on*

hook, hooks, hooking, hooked

hook up. 1 If a computer or other electronic machine is **hooked up,** it is connected to similar machines or a central power supply. EG *...receivers, hooked up to screens and displaying information immediately... The loud-speaker system was hooked up... ...hooking it up to an electronic typewriter.* ● **Link up** means almost the same as **hook up.** ▶ A **hook-up** is an electronic or radio connection between computers or other electronic machines. EG *...telephone and TV antenna hook-ups.*   V+N+ADV, V+PRON+ADV, V+ADV+N: ALSO+*to*, USUALLY PASSIVE   N COUNT

2 If you **hook** something **up,** you hang or fix it in a particular position, using a hook. EG *Hook up that hose, Lucius... We had to hook the log chains up to the axle.*   V+ADV+N, V+N+ADV, V+PRON+ADV

hoot, hoots, hooting, hooted

hoot down. If someone who is making a speech is **hooted down,** the people in the audience force them to stop talking by shouting at them. EG *Scientists who tried to speak at the recent meeting were hooted down... One of the Presidents of the Royal Society was hooted down when he gave a talk.* ● **Boo** and **shout down** mean almost the same as **hoot down.**   V+N+ADV, V+PRON+ADV, V+ADV+N: USUALLY PASSIVE

hoot off. If someone who is performing on stage is **hooted off,** the people in the audience force them to stop performing and to leave the stage by shouting at them. EG *The comic was hooted off after ten minutes... He was hooted off the stage.* ● **Boo** means almost the same as **hoot off.**   V+N+ADV, V+PRON+ADV, V+N+PREP, V+PRON+PREP

hop, hops, hopping, hopped

hop off. If you tell someone to **hop off,** you are telling them rather rudely to go away; an informal expression. EG *Hop off, I'm busy.* ● **Buzz off** means almost the same as **hop off.**   IMPERATIVE: V+ADV

hope, hopes, hoping, hoped

hope for. If you **hope for** something, you want it and expect to have it. EG *They cannot hope for a rise bigger than two per cent... He paused, hoping for evidence of interest... It's already too late to hope for a good summer.*   V+PREP: HAS PASSIVE

horn, horns, horning, horned

horn in. If you **horn in** on an activity or situation, you force your way into it when you are not welcome; used in American English. EG *...horning in on all the exciting bits.*   V+ADV: USUALLY+*on*

horse, horses, horsing, horsed

horse about. See **horse around.**

horse around. If you **horse around** or **about,** you play roughly and rather carelessly; an informal expression. EG *He loved to horse*   V+ADV *around with them... ...having all the fun, horsing around.* ● **Fool around** means almost the same as **horse around.**

hose, hoses, hosing, hosed

hose down. If you **hose** something **down,** you clean it using water   V+N+ADV,
from a hose. EG *Could you not get the sanitation department to hose*   V+ADV+N,
the place down?... Joseph was hosing down the new tractor... He had   V+PRON+ADV
to enter the chamber and hose it down. ● **Wash down** means almost
the same as **hose down.**

hose out. When you **hose** something **out,** you clean the inside of it   V+N+ADV,
using water from a hose. EG *Would you mind hosing the bins out this*   V+ADV+N,
afternoon?... She hosed out the barn. ● **Wash out** means almost the   V+PRON+ADV
same as **hose out.**

hot, hots, hotting, hotted

hot up. When an event **hots up** or when you **hot** it **up,** there begins   V+ADV,
to be a lot of activity and excitement. EG *Now the pace really began*   V+N+ADV,
to hot up... The U.S. election campaign was hotting up... The docu-   V+PRON+ADV,
ments finally arrived, and the investigation was hotted up.   V+ADV+N:
                                                                     ERGATIVE

hound, hounds, hounding, hounded

hound out. If someone is **hounded out** of a place, they are forced to   V+N+ADV,
leave it. EG *They were hounded out of their small shack... The police*   V+PRON+ADV,
had hounded the gypsies out mercilessly... ...hounding him out of   V+ADV+N:
house and home.   ALSO+*of*

howl, howls, howling, howled

howl down. If someone is **howled down,** they are prevented from   V+N+ADV,
speaking by other people who shout at them. EG *He was howled*   V+PRON+ADV,
down by monarchists. ● **Shout down** means almost the same as **howl**   V+ADV+N:
down.   USUALLY PASSIVE

huddle, huddles, huddling, huddled

huddle about. See huddle around.

huddle around. If people **huddle around, about** or **round** some-   V+PREP/ADV:
thing, they gather near it and stand or sit close to it. EG *They huddled*   ALSO PASSIVE,
about their crackling fires... They huddled around to listen... The   V+PREP/ADV
actors were all huddled round the director. ● **Cluster around** means
almost the same as **huddle around.**

huddle down. If you **huddle down,** you move your body so that   V+ADV
your legs are bent under you and you are close to the ground. EG
Kunta then huddled down as well... What a pair of idiots you must
have looked, huddled down there.

huddle round. See huddle around.

huddle together. 1 If people **huddle together,** they stand, sit, or lie   V+ADV:
close to each other because they are cold or frightened. EG *All we did*   ALSO PASSIVE,
was huddle together for warmth... We can huddle together while we   V+ADV
wait... ...evacuees, huddled together on railways stations.

2 If a group of buildings **are huddled together,** they are very close   PASSIVE:
each other. EG *...a row of old houses huddled together... I passed a*   V+ADV
small group of caravans, huddled together a hundred yards from the
main road.

huddle up. When people **huddle up,** they sit or stand very close to   V+ADV
each other, for example because they are frightened or cold. EG
When she left her seat it was to huddle up with her sister... There
was a figure standing close to me, huddled up against the wind.

hunger, hungers, hungering, hungered

hunger after. If you **hunger after** something, you want it very   V+PREP
much and try to get it. EG *What makes people hunger after power?*
● **Hanker after** means almost the same as **hunger after.**

hunger for. If you **hunger for** something, you want it very much, usually because you have not been able to have it for a long time. EG ...*a meeting place for Spaniards who hunger for Flamenco music...* ...*all that she had hungered for so fiercely.* v+PREP

hunker, hunkers, hunkering, hunkered

hunker down. If you **hunker down**, you sit close to the ground so that you are balanced on your feet with your legs bent; used in American English. EG *He hunkered down by the open door... I hunkered down for the long wait.* ● **Crouch down** means almost the same as **hunker down.** v+ADV

hunt, hunts, hunting, hunted

hunt down. If you **hunt** someone or something **down**, you succeed in finding them after you have been searching for them. EG *I hid, but they hunted me down in the end... If there's a beast, we'll hunt it down!... It was obvious that the militia had hunted down their victims.* ● **Track down** means almost the same as **hunt down.** v+PRON+ADV, v+ADV+N, v+N+ADV

hunt out. If you **hunt out** something, you succeed in finding it after you have been looking for it. EG *I hunted out our Christmas tree lights... The women set out to hunt out feminist centres... Just let me hunt my bag out—it's here somewhere.* ● **Dig out** means almost the same as **hunt out.** v+ADV+N, v+N+ADV, v+PRON+ADV

hunt up. If you **hunt up** something that is needed, you manage to find it. EG *The staff there aren't very good at hunting up information for you... I trusted he wasn't likely to hunt up that particular page again.* ● **Chase up** means almost the same as **hunt up.** v+ADV+N, v+N+ADV, v+PRON+ADV: NO PASSIVE

hurl, hurls, hurling, hurled

hurl about. If you **hurl** things **about, around** or **round**, you throw them forcefully in lots of different directions. EG *She overturned the chairs and hurled the cushions about... ...food she could hurl around the kitchen... It looked like someone had been hurling bottles of ink around.* v+N+PREP/ADV, v+PRON+PREP/ADV

hurl around. See **hurl about.**

hurl round. See **hurl about.**

hurry, hurries, hurrying, hurried

hurry on. 1 If you **hurry on**, you continue walking quickly or running without stopping. EG *Their staring eyes made me hurry on... The man hurried on with a preoccupied look on his face.* v+ADV

2 If you **hurry on** to say something, you quickly continue speaking and do not allow anyone else to stop you. EG *Having admitted this, Robertson hurried on to say that it was not intentional... Before hurrying on to other aspects of Beaverbrook's career, he explained the background.* v+ADV: USUALLY+to

hurry up. 1 If you tell someone to **hurry up**, you are telling them to do something more quickly. EG *Hurry up, Bill... She yelled down to Robin to hurry up... I can't hurry up! Not if you keep on shouting!* ● **Buck up** means almost the same as **hurry up.** v+ADV: ALSO IMPERATIVE

2 If you **hurry** someone **up**, you make them do something more quickly than they would have done. EG *The nurse stood outside the washrooms to hurry us up... The man burst in on the general, hurrying him up for their lunch date.* v+PRON+ADV, v+N+ADV

3 If you **hurry** something **up**, you make it happen faster or sooner than it would have done. EG *Can't you hurry things up a bit?... If you want the ice in a fridge to melt more quickly, you can hurry it up by leaving the door open.* ● **Speed up** means almost the same as **hurry up.** v+N+ADV, v+PRON+ADV, v+ADV+N

hush, hushes, hushing, hushed

hush up. 1 If people in authority **hush** something **up**, they prevent the public from knowing about it. EG *The police had hushed the matter up... My association with these men had been hushed up... The incident didn't remain altogether hushed up.* ● **Cover up** means almost the same as **hush up**, and **suppress** is a more formal word. — V+N+ADV, V+PRON+ADV, V+ADV+N

2 If you **hush** someone up, you persuade them in a nice way to be quiet. EG *She hushed him up as only she could.* — V+PRON+ADV, V+N+ADV

hype, hypes, hyping, hyped

hype up. 1 If you **hype** someone **up**, you make them excited and eager to do something. EG *I realized the job was not to hype up the team, but to calm them down.* ● **Psych up** means almost the same as **hype up**. — V+N+ADV, V+ADV+N, V+PRON+ADV

2 If you **hype** something **up**, you make it seem more attractive or interesting. EG *The ad-men try to hype up even the silliest little media event... It's been hyped up out of all proportion.* — V+ADV+N, V+N+ADV, V+PRON+ADV

I i

ice, ices, icing, iced

ice over. When something **ices over** or **is iced over**, it becomes covered with a layer of ice. EG *The lake began to ice over... The road becomes treacherous when it is iced over.* ● **Freeze over** means almost the same as **ice over**. — V+ADV: ALSO PASSIVE, V+ADV

ice up. When something **ices up** or **is iced up**, it becomes so cold that ice forms around it or inside it so that it cannot function properly. EG *The lock, in these conditions, may ice up and become unusable.* ● **Freeze up** means almost the same as **ice up**. — V+ADV, OR PASSIVE: V+ADV

identify, identifies, identifying, identified

identify with. 1 If you **are identified with** something, you are very closely involved or associated with it. EG *During the 1950's he was identified with certain radical causes... Of the 34 candidates nearly a third were identified with revolutionary groups.* — PASSIVE: V+PREP

2 If you **identify with** someone, you feel that you have something in common with them and can understand them better because of this similarity. EG *They find it much harder to identify with the boss... He couldn't identify with other people's troubles.* — V+PREP

idle, idles, idling, idled

idle about. If you **idle about** or **around**, you spend your time relaxing or doing nothing. EG *I can't have you idling around the house all afternoon.* — V+PREP, V+ADV

idle around. See **idle about**.

idle away. If you **idle away** a period of time, you relax by sitting or lying somewhere and doing nothing. EG *...three old men, idling away the summer afternoon under the trees.* ● **While away** means almost the same as **idle away**. — V+ADV+N

impinge, impinges, impinging, impinged

impinge on. If something **impinges on** or **upon** you, it forces you to change the way you normally behave; a formal expression. EG *Your political opinions will necessarily impinge on your public life...* — V+PREP: HAS PASSIVE

Economic circumstances impinge on them... ...the quarrels and antagonisms whose development does not impinge upon the historical development of Africa. ● **Affect** is a less formal word for **impinge on.**

impinge upon. See **impinge on.**

impose, imposes, imposing, imposed

impose on. 1 If you **impose** something **on** or **upon** people, you use your authority to force them to accept it. EG *She was a harsh mother and imposed severe discipline on her children... The Government tried to impose a five per cent limit on public employees... Peace terms were imposed upon Germany.*   V+N+PREP, V+PRON+PREP

2 If someone **imposes on** or **upon** you, they unreasonably expect you to do something for them or to spend time with them when you do not really want to. EG *Clarissa was like that, she imposed on people... Relatives have imposed enormously upon you lately.*   V+PREP: HAS PASSIVE

impose upon. See **impose on.**

impress, impresses, impressing, impressed

impress on. 1 If you **impress** something **on** or **upon** someone, you talk about it emphatically in order to make them understand its importance. EG *The following day he impressed on the Government the danger of 45,000 redundancies... The authorities impressed on him the need for a psychiatric consultation... They are still trying to impress it upon us that we have not yet succeeded.*   V+N+PREP: ALSO V+PREP, V+it+PREP, WITH REPORT

2 If something **impresses** itself **on** or **upon** a situation, it has a powerful effect on the situation. EG *...the enduring menace which clings to the place and impresses itself on strangers.*   V+REFL+PREP

3 If you **impress** something **on** or **upon** something else, you cause the image or memory of it to remain on the other thing. EG *I repeated the last verse several times, hoping to impress it on my memory.*   V+PRON+PREP, V+N+PREP, V+PREP

impress upon. See **impress on.**

improve, improves, improving, improved

improve on. To **improve on** or **upon** a previous achievement means to reach a better standard or achieve a better result than previously. EG *I found that the film improved on the book... For social justice, this system could hardly be improved upon.*   V+PREP: HAS PASSIVE

improve upon. See **improve on.**

impute, imputes, imputing, imputed

impute to. If you **impute** blame or an unpleasant action **to** someone or something, you suggest that they were responsible for it or caused it; a formal expression. EG *No blame can be imputed to him... They had been guilty not of the crimes imputed to them but of uttering falsehoods about their order... It is hard to impute a rise in output to any one factor.* ● **Attribute** means almost the same as **impute to.**   V+N+PREP, V+PRON+PREP

include, includes, including, included

include in. 1 If you **include** someone **in** a particular plan or activity, you allow them to take part in it. EG *Governments found themselves forced to include employees in the dialogue... He sought to include them in what had happened.*   V+N+PREP, V+PRON+PREP

2 If you **include** one thing **in** with another thing, you make it a part of that other thing. EG *Most restaurants now include the tip in with the price of the meal... Nothing should be included in the curriculum unless it is relevant... Few novelists would have dared include it in a work of fiction.* ● **Incorporate** is a more formal word for **include in.**   V+N+PREP, V+PRON+PREP: ALSO+with

include out. If you say to someone 'include me out', you mean that   V+PRON+ADV
you do not want to join them in a particular activity; an informal or
humorous expression. EG *If you're going to carry on like this, you can
include me out!*

indulge, indulges, indulging, indulged

indulge in. If you **indulge in** a particular activity, you take great   V+PREP:
pleasure in doing it because it is something you really enjoy; a fairly   HAS PASSIVE
formal expression. EG *He indulged heavily in conversation and
drink... Could I still indulge in outdoor activities like sailing and fell
walking?... A social pastime may be indulged in for its own sake.*

inform, informs, informing, informed

inform on. If you **inform on** someone, you give information about   V+PREP:
them to the police or other authority so that they are accused of   HAS PASSIVE
having done something wrong because of what you said. EG *It can be
difficult for a child to inform on someone he knows... ...to inform on
an acquaintance who had allegedly engaged in treasonable activities.* ● **Betray** means almost the same as **inform on.**

infringe, infringes, infringing, infringed

infringe on. If something **infringes on** or **upon** you, it affects your   V+PREP:
behaviour by making it difficult for you to do what you want. EG *No   HAS PASSIVE
man was allowed to infringe on the livelihood of his neighbour...
They infringe on our own children's right to freedom... ...citizens
with legal rights which were being infringed upon.* ● **Encroach on**
and **restrict** mean almost the same as **infringe on.**
infringe upon. See **infringe on.**

ink, inks, inking, inked

ink in. 1 If you **ink** something **in**, you write it in ink to show that it is   V+N+ADV,
now your definite or final version, having previously written it in   V+PRON+ADV,
pencil. EG *The revisions can now be inked in... Then you go over it   V+ADV+N
later and ink them in.* ● **Pencil in** means the opposite of **ink in.**

2 If you **ink** someone or something **in**, you decide that they will   V+N+ADV,
definitely be used for a particular purpose after you have discussed   V+PRON+ADV,
various possibilities; an informal use. EG *Gooch was the opener we   V+ADV+N
had inked in after his tour of West Indies.*

inquire, inquires, inquiring, inquired

Inquire is also spelled **enquire.**

inquire after. If you **inquire after** someone, you ask how they are   V+PREP
or what they are doing. EG *She enquired after Mrs Carstair's daughter... I enquired after Mrs. Merry's health.* ● **Ask after** means almost
the same as **inquire after.**

inquire into. When a person or committee **inquires into** a matter,   V+PREP:
they make a thorough, formal investigation of the matter. EG *A   HAS PASSIVE
Royal Commission was established in 1919 to enquire into all aspects
of income tax... When he got back to Berlin he would inquire into
the whole business again... It will not, one guesses, be much inquired
into.*

insist, insists, insisting, insisted

insist on. If you **insist on** or **upon** something, you ask for it firmly   V+PREP:
and refuse to accept any alternative. EG *Most universities insist on   HAS PASSIVE
an interview before they accept a student... I insisted on a contract
that gave me some sort of security... He insisted on paying for the
meal... Crawford insisted upon carrying Billy's bag.*
insist upon. See **insist on.**

insure, insures, insuring, insured

insure against. 1 If you **insure against** something unpleasant, you   v+prep
take action to prevent it happening or affecting you. eg *During years
of good rainfall they expand their stocks to insure against drought...
Attempts were made to insure against that possibility.*

2 If you **are insured against** something happening, you have bought   passive:
an insurance policy so that you will be paid compensation if it   v+prep
happens. eg *If you bring your bicycle you must have it insured
against theft... I don't even know if I'm insured against this kind of
thing... His neighbour's house is not insured against fire.*

interfere, interferes, interfering, interfered

interfere in. If you **interfere in** something, you become involved in   v+prep
it and start changing it when it is not really your business. eg *Well
next time, don't interfere in things that don't concern you... It makes
him furious to have anyone interfere in one of his jobs.* ● **Meddle in**
means almost the same as **interfere in.**

interfere with. 1 If something **interferes with** a process or situa-   v+prep
tion, it prevents the process or situation from continuing efficiently
or successfully. eg *Problems of obtaining spare parts for mines are
likely to interfere with production... His father-in-law had interfered
with his marriage right from the very beginning.*

2 When sound or radio waves **interfere with** each other, they   v+prep
interrupt each other so that they cannot be heard or received easily.
eg *Why did their calls not interfere with one another, jamming the
signals?... There was evidence of pirate radios interfering with
shipping.*

3 Someone who **interferes with** a child touches the child's sexual   v+prep:
organs or tries to have sex with the child; used showing disapproval.   has passive
eg *They were interfered with by their babysitter.* ● **Molest** means
almost the same as **interfere with.**

intrude, intrudes, intruding, intruded

intrude on. If something **intrudes on** or **upon** your mood or way of   v+prep:
life, it has an unwelcome or unpleasant effect on it. eg *Nothing was   has passive
allowed to intrude on their evening ritual... A park would intrude on
the region's way of life... Some women would feel intruded upon.*
intrude upon. See **intrude on.**

inure, inures, inuring, inured

inure to. If you **are inured to** something unpleasant, you are used to   v+n+prep,
it and accept it as being unavoidable; a formal expression. eg *...a*   v+refl+prep,
child so inured to punishment that he no longer cares... To such a   v+pron+prep:
din I was already inured... They inure themselves to a lifetime of   usually passive
self-restraint.

inveigh, inveighs, inveighing, inveighed

inveigh against. If you **inveigh against** something, you strongly   v+prep
criticize it; a formal expression. eg *It is fashionable in some quarters
to inveigh against a 'competitive ladder' society.* ● **Rail against** is a
less formal expression for **inveigh against.**

invite, invites, inviting, invited

invite around. See **invite round.**
invite in. If you **invite** someone **in,** you ask them politely to come   v+pron+adv,
into your house, usually when they have knocked on the door or   v+n+adv
rung the bell. eg *Aren't you even going to invite me in?... ...inviting
her friends in to play poker.*

invite out. If you **invite** someone **out,** you ask them to go with you   v+pron+adv,
to a play, show, party, and so on. eg *To cheer her up, Morris invited*   v+n+adv

her out for a meal... Once he had invited Frederica out for a ride on
his motorbike. ● **Ask out** is a more informal expression for **invite
out**.

invite over. If you **invite** someone **over**, you ask them to come and   V+N+ADV,
visit you in your home. EG *The neighbours felt free to invite one of*   V+PRON+ADV
them over for a party... I've invited them over on Thursday for the
barbecue.

invite round. If you **invite** someone **round** or **around,** you ask them   V+PRON+ADV,
to come and visit you in your home. EG *He hoped the Count would*   V+N+ADV
invite him round, but he didn't... She invited a few friends around for
drinks.

iron, irons, ironing, ironed

iron out. If you **iron out** small problems or difficulties, you find a   V+ADV+N,
way to solve them or overcome them. EG *The point of practice is, of*   V+N+ADV,
course, to iron out such problems... I thought most of our problems   V+PRON+ADV
were ironed out.

itch, itches, itching, itched

itch for. If you **itch for** something, you want it very much. EG   V+PREP
...Democrats itching for more vigorous opposition... ...itching for a
fight.

J j

jab, jabs, jabbing, jabbed

jab at. If you **jab at** something, you make repeated, short, stabbing   V+PREP,
movements at it with something long and thin. EG *She could hear*   V+N+PREP,
him jabbing viciously at the keys of the typewriter... He grabbed   V+PRON+PREP:
Eric's spear and jabbed at Robert with it... He raised his voice and   NO PASSIVE
jabbed his finger at me. ● **Poke at** means almost the same as **jab at**.

jabber, jabbers, jabbering, jabbered

jabber away. If someone **jabbers away,** they talk so quickly that it   V+ADV
is difficult to understand what they say. EG *My German's pretty*
rusty, but it acted like magic—he started jabbering away.

jack, jacks, jacking, jacked

jack in. If you **jack in** a job, course, or other regular activity, you   V+N+ADV,
stop doing it altogether; used in informal British English. EG *One of*   V+PRON+ADV,
these days I'm going to jack this job in and sail round the world...   V+ADV+N:
There is simply no answer. You might as well jack it in then and   NO PASSIVE
there. ● **Pack in** means almost the same as **jack in**.

jack off. If someone **jacks off,** they masturbate; a rude expression   V+ADV
used mainly in American English. ● **Jerk off** and **toss off** mean
almost the same as **jack off**.

jack up. 1 If you **jack up** a car or heavy object, you raise it off the   V+N+ADV,
ground using a jack or other lifting device. EG *Make sure you've got*   V+PRON+ADV,
the tools ready before you jack up the car.   V+ADV+N

2 If prices **are jacked up,** they are higher than you expect them to   V+ADV+N,
be or think they ought to be. EG *The price of the part is jacked up*   V+N+ADV
way beyond its old price... In 1973 the oil producing countries jacked
up prices by 400%. ● **Inflate** is a more formal word for **jack up**.

3 If someone **jacks up,** they take a drug such as heroin or cocaine by injecting it; an informal use. `v+ADV`

jam, jams, jamming, jammed

jam on. If you **jam on** the brakes while you are driving, you stop suddenly and with a lot of force; an informal expression. EG *Suddenly she jammed on the jeep brakes.* `v+ADV+N, v+N+ADV`

jam up. If people or things **are jammed up** against an object, they are placed very close to the object so that they cannot move easily. EG *Gareth's bed now sat jammed up against the French windows.* `PASSIVE: v+ADV, ALSO+against`

jazz, jazzes, jazzing, jazzed

jazz up. If you **jazz** something **up,** you make it more interesting or exciting; an informal expression. EG *They've certainly jazzed this place up since the last time I was here.* ● **Liven up** means almost the same as **jazz up.** ▶ Music that is **jazzed-up** has been changed or re-arranged in order to sound more like popular music or jazz; an informal word. EG *...a jazzed-up version of one of the Brandenburg Concertos.* `v+N+ADV, v+PRON+ADV, v+ADV+N` `ADJECTIVE`

jerk, jerks, jerking, jerked

jerk off. If someone **jerks off,** they masturbate; a rude expression used mainly in American English. ● **Jack off** and **toss off** mean almost the same as **jerk off.** `v+ADV, v+PRON+ADV, v+ADV+N, v+N+ADV`

jerk out. If you **jerk out** a remark, you say it very abruptly after first hesitating. EG *'I can't argue—with you—' he jerked out... 'Dead flowers?' jerked out Mr. Roberts with extreme surprise... 'Enough to drive you mad!' His words jerked out as he darted breathlessly about.* `v+ADV+QUOTE, v+ADV+N, v+ADV: NO PASSIVE`

jib, jibs, jibbing, jibbed

jib at. If you **jib at** doing something, you are reluctant to do it; a rather old-fashioned expression. EG *He had begun to jib at carrying out the orders of his masters... 'I hope I may be struck blind'. He jibbed at using the word 'dead'.* `v+PREP`

jockey, jockeys, jockeying, jockeyed

jockey for. If someone **jockeys for** position or status, they compete against other people to improve their own position or status. EG *Rival trade unions continuously jockey for position... People jockeyed for status, in the social vacuum created by independence.* `v+PREP`

jog, jogs, jogging, jogged

jog along. If you **jog along** in a situation, you continue in it and accept what happens to you, without trying to change it. EG *They assume that any job carries with it daily stretches of boredom, so they jog along for thirty, forty years without complaint... The human animal jogs happily along in this way.* `v+ADV`

join, joins, joining, joined

join in. If you **join in** an activity with other people, such as a meeting, you become involved in what they are doing. EG *He took his coat off and joined in the work... Several people joined in the applause... Is this a private fight or can anyone join in?... Then they began to sing and in a moment all the voices joined in.* `v+PREP, v+ADV`

join up. 1 If one person **joins up** with another or if two people **join up,** they decide to go somewhere together. EG *We joined up with two young men and went along to a road-house... The French division joined up with the rest of the Southern Army Group... The two families joined up for the rest of the holiday.* ● **Get together** means almost the same as **join up.** `v+ADV+with, v+ADV: RECIPROCAL`

2 If someone **joins up**, they become a member of the army, the navy, or the air force; used in British English. EG *I didn't join up until 1940 in the end... Just before joining up and going abroad I met Elizabeth.* ● **Enlist** means almost the same as **join up**. `V+ADV`

3 If you **join up** two things or if they **join up**, they become fastened together. EG *I used to join up all his paper clips in a long chain... ...busy trying to join them up... This takes place when two cells join up and exchange genes.* ● **Link up** means almost the same as **join up**. `V+ADV+N,` `V+PRON+ADV,` `V+N+ADV,` `V+ADV:` `ERGATIVE`

jolly, jollies, jollying, jollied

jolly along. If you **jolly** someone **along**, you keep them in a good mood, often so that they will continue to do something for you, such as work. EG *It's no good jollying her along, telling her to take it easy... Harold, you've been jollying me along for quite long enough.* `V+PRON+ADV,` `V+N+ADV`

jot, jots, jotting, jotted

jot down. If you **jot** something **down**, you write it down briefly in the form of a short informal note. EG *Renshaw jotted down a few particulars in his notebook... He jotted some notes down on a pad... She noted the exact time of the call and jotted it down on the tablecloth.* ● **Note down** means almost the same as **jot down**. `V+ADV+N,` `V+N+ADV,` `V+PRON+ADV`

juggle, juggles, juggling, juggled

juggle with. **1** If you **juggle with** things such as numbers or ideas, you keep adjusting them slightly until they fit together in the best possible way. EG *Still juggling with figures and possibilities, she remained alert... He was juggling with formulae and documents.* `V+PREP:` `HAS PASSIVE`

2 If you **are juggling with** several objects, you are having difficulty holding onto all of them. EG *He juggled with the controls... His wife emerged, juggling with peas and wiping up a broken bottle of wine.* `V+PREP`

jumble, jumbles, jumbling, jumbled

jumble up. If things **are jumbled up**, they are mixed together or confused, so that it is difficult to tell them apart. EG *The bits and pieces were jumbled up with a lot of stuff that would never be needed again... They range from grade 5 to grade 1, and they're all jumbled up.* ● **Mix up** means almost the same as **jumble up**. `PASSIVE:` `V+ADV`

jump, jumps, jumping, jumped

jump at. If you **jump at** an opportunity or offer, you accept it immediately. EG *Any one of them would jump at the chance of being with Dolly Clare... Private companies have not exactly jumped at the opportunity... They have to persuade their own members not to jump at superficially attractive offers.* ● **Leap at** means almost the same as **jump at**. `V+PREP:` `HAS PASSIVE`

jump in. During a conversation or discussion with someone, if you **jump in**, you interrupt them or say something that they do not want you to say. EG *Before Brian jumps in I would like to say something... Goldsmith jumped in with a public rebuke for Beckett's 'irresponsibility'.* ● **Butt in** means almost the same as **jump in**. `V+ADV`

jump on. If you **jump on** someone, you criticize them as soon as you notice that they have said or done something wrong. EG *You don't need to jump on a child for making up stories occasionally... He felt no matter how I qualified the term, I would be jumped on.* `V+PREP:` `HAS PASSIVE`

jump out at. If something **jumps out at** you, it is so obvious that you notice it immediately. EG *The quality of the prose jumps out at you from the start of chapter one.* `V+ADV+PREP`

jump up. **1** If someone who is sitting down **jumps up**, they suddenly `V+ADV` stand up. EG *He slumped back into his chair and then jumped up again... 'Mabel!' he cried, jumping up from his chair.*

2 Jumped-up people consider themselves to be more important than they really are; an informal word in British English, used showing disapproval. EG *...a jumped-up office boy.*

ADJECTIVE

jut, juts, jutting, jutted

jut out. 1 If an area of land or an object **juts out,** it sticks out so that it is more obvious. EG *The pillar leaned into a steady overhang, jutting out at least twenty feet from the wave-washed base... The road climbs to a high point that apparently juts out into the ocean.* ● **Protrude** is a more formal word for **jut out.**

V+ADV

2 If you **jut out** your chin, you thrust it forwards, often to show your determination to do something. EG *She jutted out her chin and went out into the street with a little flouncing movement of disdain... Bond's jaw was jutting out dangerously.* ● **Stick out** means almost the same as **jut out.**

V+ADV+N, V+ADV: ERGATIVE

K k

keel, keels, keeling, keeled

keel over. If someone **keels over,** they fall over sideways. EG *One of the middle-aged athletes keeled over and was rushed to hospital... He suddenly keeled over with a heavily-loaded tray... The others had either keeled over or were laughing hysterically.*

V+ADV

keep, keeps, keeping, kept

keep at. If you **keep at** it, or **keep** someone **at** it, you continue, or make them continue, working at a job or task or trying hard, even if it is very difficult or unpleasant. EG *It is hard, but you've just got to keep at it... I kept at it for another hour... Necessity had kept her at it... Ron told me to keep her at it till Monday.* ● **Persevere** is a more formal word for **keep at,** and **stick at** and **stick to** mean almost the same.

V+PREP+*it*, V+PRON+PREP+*it*, V+N+PREP+*it*: ERGATIVE

keep away. 1 If you **keep away** from somewhere, you avoid going there. EG *They kept away from the forest... It would be better to keep away and not attempt to enter the city until she knew what was happening there... The more you keep away from the shops the less money you'll spend.* ● **Stay away** means almost the same as **keep away.**

V+ADV: ALSO+*from*

2 If you **keep** someone **away** from somewhere, you prevent them from going near there. EG *Keep your kids away from those bulls... The male takes extreme measures to keep raiders away from the eggs... If you don't keep them away, they'll take over.*

V+N+ADV, V+PRON+ADV, V+ADV+N: ALSO+*from*

3 If you **keep** something unpleasant or unwanted **away,** you prevent it from affecting and harming you. EG *...a dog shampoo that kept away lice and ticks.*

V+ADV+N, V+N+ADV, V+PRON+ADV

keep back. 1 If you **keep** part of something **back,** you make sure that you do not use or give away all of it, so that you still have some to use at a later time. EG *Remember to keep back enough cream to make the topping... She did keep some things back for when Pam came.* ● **Reserve** is a more formal word for **keep back.**

V+ADV+N, V+N+ADV, V+PRON+ADV

2 If you **keep** some information **back,** you do not tell all that you

V+N+ADV,

know about something. EG *You can't write an autobiography without* V+ADV+N,
keeping something back... ...keeping back the existence of the V+PRON+ADV
documents. ● **Withhold** is a more formal word for **keep back.**

3 If you **keep back** your emotions, feelings, or ideas, you try not to V+ADV+N
let other people know about them. EG *When I looked at Charlene,*
Kendra, Franklin, Margaret, Howard—I couldn't keep back the
tears... ...keeping back our innermost thoughts and plans. ● **Hold**
back means almost the same as **keep back.**

keep down. 1 If you **keep** the number, size, or amount of some- V+N+ADV,
thing **down,** you stop it increasing and try to keep it at a low level. EG V+ADV+N,
The French too are very concerned to try and keep costs down... V+PRON+ADV
This keeps prices down... Can you keep the noise down... ...the need
to keep down public borrowing.

2 If you **keep down** or if you **keep** your head **down,** you stay in a V+ADV,
lying or low position in order to avoid being seen or attacked. EG V+N+ADV:
Keep down!... They kept their heads down. NO PASSIVE

3 If someone **keeps** a group of people or a nation **down,** they keep V+N+ADV,
them in a state of powerlessness, and prevent them from being V+PRON+ADV,
completely free. EG *For centuries men have been trying to keep* V+ADV+N
women down. ● **Oppress** is a more formal word for **keep down.**

4 If you can't **keep** food or drink **down,** you are unwell, and vomit if V+N+ADV,
you try to eat or drink. EG *I can't keep anything down, not even* V+ADV+N,
water... He took a drink and kept it down. ● **Hold down** means V+PRON+ADV:
almost the same as **keep down.** NO PASSIVE

keep from. 1 If you **keep** someone **from** doing something, you stop V+PRON+PREP,
them doing it. EG *The sergeant tried to keep me from going... We tied* V+N+PREP
rope round the bundles to keep them from falling off... These long
discussions kept me from my studies.

2 If you **keep from** doing something, you manage with difficulty to V+PREP+-ING
stop yourself doing it. EG *I have managed to keep from revealing it...*
I could not keep from stepping in. ● **Resist** is a more formal word
for **keep from.**

3 If you **keep** information **from** someone, you do not tell them about V+N+PREP,
it. EG *There was something so simple and innocent about James then* V+PRON+PREP
that keeping anything from him seemed utterly wrong.

keep in. 1 If a parent or teacher **keeps** children **in,** they make them V+N+ADV,
stay indoors or they make them stay late at school, usually as a V+PRON+ADV,
punishment. EG *John was kept in at school one day last week... We'll* V+ADV+N
all be kept in after school writing telegrams.

2 If you **keep in** when you are walking, cycling, or driving along a V+ADV
road or path, you stay near the edge of the road or path, instead of
being in the middle of it. EG *Keep in! You'll be run over if you don't*
watch it!

keep in with. If you **keep in with** someone, you stay friendly with V+ADV+PREP
them, often in order to gain some advantage for yourself. EG *If I*
wanted to stay with the firm I ought to try to keep in with him...
They kept in with each other and had secrets.

keep off. 1 If you **keep** someone or something **off** a particular area, V+N+PREP/ADV,
you prevent them from going onto it. If you **keep off** an area, you do V+PRON+PREP/ADV,
not go there yourself. EG *In Scotland you have no right to keep* V+ADV+N,
people off your land unless they are doing damage... Having a job V+PREP/ADV
helps keep them off the streets... If you don't keep off the street with
your bicycle, I'll take it away... He kept off the fell... Christopher was
warned to keep off.

2 If you **keep** something **off** someone, you prevent it from touching, V+N+PREP/ADV,
harming, or attacking them. EG *Keep those dogs off her!... ...a* V+ADV+N,
bamboo shelter to keep the rain off... She had a veil pulled down all V+PRON+PREP/ADV
round her hat to keep off the flies.

3 If you **keep off** a particular food or drink, you avoid eating or drinking it, usually because you know that it will make you ill. EG *She can drink skimmed milk, but she has to keep off butter... Keep him off the booze, that's all.* `V+PREP, V+PRON+PREP, V+N+PREP`

4 If you **keep off** a particular subject, you deliberately do not talk about it. EG *He kept off the question of whose fault it was.* ● **Avoid** means almost the same as **keep off**. `V+PREP`

5 If rain or snow **keeps off**, it does not begin. EG *Luckily the rain kept off.* ● **Hold off** means almost the same as **keep off**. `V+ADV`

keep on. **1** If you **keep on** doing something, you continue to do it and do not stop. EG *Mike reckoned he could keep on talking for one and a half hours... Keep on rinsing until the water is clear... He kept on staring at me... We just keep on collecting the stuff for ever.* ● **Carry on** means almost the same as **keep on**. `V+ADV+-ING`

2 If you **keep** someone **on** at work or school, you continue to employ them although their contract has ended or they are old enough to retire, or you continue to educate them although they are old enough to leave. EG *I think Bessie likes to keep Isabel on for the sake of her family... Only half the workforce will be kept on after this order has been completed... She had to start work while her brothers were kept on at expensive private schools.* `V+N+ADV, V+PRON+ADV, V+ADV+N`

3 If you **keep on** about something, you continue to talk about it in a boring or repetitive way. EG *She kept on about the stupid car.* ● **Go on** and **harp on** mean almost the same as **keep on**. `V+ADV: ALSO+about`

keep on at. If you **keep on** at someone, you repeatedly ask them something or tell them something in a way that annoys them. EG *I made no reply, but he kept on at me... They will not ask, so we have to keep on and on at them.* `V+ADV+PREP`

keep out. **1** To **keep** someone or something **out** of a place means to prevent them from entering it or being there. EG *...a guard dog to keep out intruders... This should keep them out.* `V+ADV+N, V+PRON+ADV, V+N+ADV`

2 If a sign says **'Keep Out'**, it is warning you not to go onto that piece of land. EG *'Private property. Keep out.'* `IMPERATIVE: V+ADV`

keep out of. **1** If you **keep** someone **out of** an unpleasant situation, you avoid involving them in it. EG *You should try and keep him out of it, or it will only complicate things further... We should bend over backwards to keep young people out of prison... Keep Piggy out of danger.* `V+PRON+ADV+PREP, V+N+ADV+PREP`

2 If you **keep out of** an unpleasant situation, you avoid becoming involved in it. EG *You keep out of this. It's got nothing to do with you... I kept out of trouble as best I could... We kept out of her way and never spoke to her again.* ● **Stay out of** means almost the same as **keep out of**. `V+ADV+PREP`

keep to. **1** If you **keep to** a regulation or agreement, you do exactly what you are expected or supposed to do. EG *We must keep to the deadlines... Keep to the letter of the law... Try to keep to a routine.* ● **Stick to** means almost the same as **keep to**. `V+PREP: HAS PASSIVE`

2 If you **keep to** a particular subject, you talk only about that subject, and do not talk about anything else. EG *I wish you'd keep to the point.* ● **Stick to** means almost the same as **keep to** and **get off** means the opposite. `V+PREP: HAS PASSIVE`

3 If you **keep** something **to** a particular number or amount, you limit it to that number or amount. EG *Keep it to a minimum... It has been kept to an extremely tempting price... ...the kind of play whose casts you keep to a minimum... We can easily keep to single figures.* `V+PRON+PREP, V+N+PREP, V+PREP`

4 If you **keep to** a place such as your bed or a room in your home, you stay there for a period of time, for example if you are ill or if the weather is bad. EG *He kept to his bed when he had flu... ...a shy boy* `V+PREP` *who keeps to his bedroom practising magic tricks.* ● **Stay in** means almost the same as **keep to.**

5 If you **keep** something **to** yourself, you do not tell anyone about it. EG *If I tell her, she won't keep it to herself... People may get embarrassed, so keep it to yourself.*   V+PRON+PREP, V+N+PREP: WITH REFL:

keep under. If someone **keeps** you **under,** they keep you in a state of unconsciousness by giving you drugs. EG *She was kept under with a mixture of morphine and chloroform.*   V+PRON+ADV, V+N+ADV

keep up. 1 If you **keep up** an activity, you continue to do it and do not let it stop or end. EG *I tried to keep up the conversation... He was unable to keep up the payments... The tanks kept up a steady fire... A wildebeest can run at the same speed and keep it up for much longer.* ● **Maintain** is a more formal word for **keep up.**   V+ADV+N, V+PRON+ADV, V+N+ADV

2 If you **keep up** with a situation in which things are changing quickly or greatly, you manage to deal with it. EG *...the struggle to keep up with inflation... It has increased so much that our imagination can't keep up... The flow of decisions could be accelerated to keep up with the faster pace of life.*   V+ADV: USUALLY+with

3 If you **keep up,** you work at the necessary speed so that you do as well as other people or so that you get all your work done in the required time. EG *They appear to be able to keep up with the class... I shall be taking work home every night, you know, to keep up... I never quite manage to keep up with the rest.* ● **Fall behind** means the opposite of **keep up.**   V+ADV: ALSO+with

4 If you **keep** it **up,** you continue working hard, trying hard, or achieving the standard that you have in the past. EG *Being human, he can only keep it up for eight hours a day... He kept it up until they had gone... It's no good. I can't keep it up, you see... This is good. Keep it up!*   V+it+ADV

5 If you **keep up** with someone else, you move at the same speed as them. EG *I started to run a bit so that she had to hurry to keep up with me... They will have to get off the highway because they can't keep up.*   V+ADV: ALSO+with

6 If you **keep** something **up,** you prevent it from growing less in amount or size, or worse in quality. EG *I can't see how we can keep this pace up for more than a day or two... Morris could keep up the pace no longer... It's important to keep up the standard.*   V+N+ADV, V+PRON+ADV, V+ADV+N

7 If you **keep up** a subject or skill that you learned a long time ago, you continue to study, practise, or use it. EG *I do try and keep up my physics... He's managed to keep his Spanish up quite well.*   V+ADV+N, V+N+ADV, V+PRON+ADV

8 If one process **keeps up** with another, it increases at the same speed and in the same way as the other is increasing. EG *Supply could never have kept up with consumption... Pensions were increased to keep up with the rise in prices.*   V+ADV: USUALLY+with

9 If you **keep up** with a situation, you learn all the most recent facts about it. EG *They kept up with what was happening in their work... Even friends have trouble keeping up with each other's whereabouts.*   V+ADV: USUALLY+with

10 If you **keep** someone **up,** you delay them going to bed. EG *I ought never to have kept you up so late... I am sorry. I won't keep you up a minute longer.*   V+PRON+ADV, V+N+ADV

11 If you **keep up** a building, you look after it and make sure that it remains in good condition. EG *I'd never get any of the estate people to live in it now. If you'll keep it up you're welcome to it.* ● **Maintain** means almost the same as **keep up.** ▸ The **upkeep** of a building is the continual process of keeping it in good condition. EG *We have to pay for the upkeep of the chapel.* ● **Maintenance** means almost the same as **upkeep.**   V+PRON+ADV, V+N+ADV, V+ADV+N

N UNCOUNT

keep up with. If you **keep up with** a friend, you stay in contact with them by writing, telephoning, or seeing them regularly. EG *We've kept up with each other ever since we left school.* V+ADV+PREP

key, keys, keying, keyed

key in. When you are using a computer and you **key** something **in**, you give the computer instructions by typing something on the keyboard. EG *To extract information you key in the word you require... Key in the appropriate words.* ● **Enter** and **type in** mean almost the same as **key in,** and **input** is a more technical word. V+ADV+N, V+N+ADV, V+PRON+ADV

key up. If you **are keyed up,** you are very excited or nervous because something important or dangerous is about to happen. EG *His anger surprised him: he was more keyed up than he had anticipated... ...consciously look for signs of being keyed up too much.* ● **Tense** means almost the same as **keyed up.** PASSIVE: V+ADV

kick, kicks, kicking, kicked

kick about. See **kick around.**

kick against. If you **kick against** a situation you cannot control, you show your dislike and impatience by reacting against it. EG *He's always kicking against the system.* ● **Kick out against** means almost the same as **kick against.** V+PREP

kick around. 1 You say that something is **kicking around** or **about** or **round** somewhere when you mean that it is lying there and does not seem wanted or important. EG *His old bike has been kicking about among the bushes for days... There's a lot of difference between a fresh herring and one which may have been kicking around in a deep freeze for months.* ● **Lie around** means almost the same as **kick around.** V+ADV

2 When people **kick around** ideas or suggestions, they discuss them informally. EG *The first step was to call in some writers and kick around ideas.* V+ADV+N, V+N+ADV

3 If someone **kicks** you **around, kicks** you **round,** or **kicks** you **about,** they treat you very badly or roughly. EG *She shouldn't let her brother kick her around like that.* ● **Push around** means almost the same as **kick around.** V+PRON+ADV, V+N+ADV

kick back. If someone **kicks back** an amount of money, they illegally return some money to a person who is buying something as a bribe in order to encourage them to buy it. EG *The doctors kicked back a percentage of the fee.* ▶ A **kickback** is a bribe paid to a representative of a government or firm to encourage them to place an order. EG *He's systematically taken kickbacks from the hiring agencies he works through.* V+ADV+N

N COUNT

kick down. If you **kick down** a door or other structure, you kick it violently with your foot so that it falls or collapses. EG *They tried to kick down the front door... I nearly kicked the door down in my fury.* ● **Break down** and **smash down** mean almost the same as **kick down.** V+ADV+N, V+N+ADV, V+PRON+ADV

kick in. If you **kick in** something such as a door or window, you kick it violently with your foot so that it breaks into pieces. EG *The fireman kicked in one of the windows... Doors and windows were smashed with sledge-hammers, television sets kicked in, and clothes slashed to ribbons.* ● **Smash in** means almost the same as **kick in.** V+ADV+N, V+N+ADV, V+PRON+ADV

kick off. 1 When you **kick off** your shoes, you shake your feet so that your shoes come off. EG *He became conscious of the weight of his clothes and kicked his shoes off fiercely... Mark kicked off his shoes and climbed down into the stream.* V+ADV+N, V+N+ADV, V+PRON+ADV

2 When you **kick off** an event or discussion, you start it. EG *At 10 p.m. Prince Charles kicks off 45 minutes of fireworks... They kicked off a* V+ADV+N, V+ADV

two-month tour of the U.S. with a party in Washington... Are we ready for the debate? Right. Who kicks off?

3 When football players **kick off,** they start the game by kicking the ball from the centre of the pitch. EG *The first goal was scored within twenty seconds of kicking off.* ▸ The **kick-off** is the kick that officially starts a game of football, or the time that the game starts. EG *The kick-off's at 3 o'clock.* `V+ADV`

`N SING`

kick out. If you **kick** someone **out** of a place or an organization, you force them to leave it. EG *I'm afraid I'm going to have to kick you out into the rain... They kicked her out of her house... Franklin had been unilaterally kicked out of the organization... He started off at university but he got kicked out.* ● **Throw out** means almost the same as **kick out.** `V+PRON+ADV, V+N+ADV, V+ADV+N: ALSO+of`

kick out against. If you **kick out against** a situation that you cannot control, you show your dislike and impatience by reacting against it in a violent or extreme way. EG *...a lorry-driver called John who suddenly kicked out against the daily grind of his life.* ● **Kick against** means almost the same as **kick out against.** `V+ADV+PREP`

kick over. If someone **kicks** something **over,** they kick it so that it falls to the ground. EG *John, beside himself with rage, had kicked over the table and grabbed at her... Roger led the way through the sand castles, kicking them over.* ● **Knock over** means almost the same as **kick over.** `V+ADV+N, V+PRON+ADV, V+N+ADV`

kick round. See **kick around.**

kick up. **1** If someone **kicks up** a fuss or a row, they get very annoyed or upset about something, especially when this seems unnecessary to you. EG *He kicked up a great fuss and swore our friendship was at an end... Why are you kicking up all this fuss?* `V+ADV+N`

2 If you **kick up** dust or dirt with your feet, you create a cloud of dust or dirt as you move along a dusty road. EG *They struggled amid the dust clouds that their feet kicked up... ...turf kicked up by flying hoofs.* ● **Raise** means almost the same as **kick up.** `V+ADV+N, V+N+ADV`

kill, kills, killing, killed

kill off. If you **kill** something **off,** you completely destroy it. EG *This discovery killed off one of the last surviving romances about the place... The bacteria had been killed off.* ● **Wipe out** means almost the same as **kill off,** and **eradicate** is a more formal word. `V+ADV+N, V+N+ADV, V+PRON+ADV`

kip, kips, kipping, kipped

kip down. If you **kip down** at someone's house, you sleep there for the night instead of going home; an informal expression. EG *Why don't you take one of these mattresses and kip down here?* ● **Doss down** means almost the same as **kip down.** `V+ADV`

kiss, kisses, kissing, kissed

kiss away. If you **kiss** something unpleasant **away,** you try to sympathize with someone by kissing them; an informal expression. EG *I would have kissed the fever away if I had been closer to you.* `V+N+ADV, V+PRON+ADV`

kit, kits, kitting, kitted

kit out. If someone or something **is kitted out** or **kitted up,** they are provided with everything they need for a particular situation, for example with clothing, equipment, or furniture. EG *Beginners can be kitted out for less than a hundred pounds... The range of electronic equipment with which they will be kitted out will be phenomenal.* ● **Fit out** means almost the same as **kit out.** `PASSIVE: V+ADV`

kit up. See **kit out.**

kneel, kneels, kneeling, kneeled/knelt

kneel down. When you **kneel down,** you sit with your legs bent   V+ADV
underneath you and your weight on your knees. EG *He knelt down
beside the unconscious girl... He kneeled down and prayed to Allah...
My sister was kneeling down, peering over the floor.*

knit, knits, knitting, knitted
The form **knit** is used in the present tense, and can also be used as
the past tense and past participle of the verb.

knit together. When two things **knit together,** or are **knit** or   V+ADV,
knitted together, they join together to form a whole. EG *After a lot of*   V+ADV+N,
practice the side begins to knit together... Knit together the parts of   V+ADV,
each speech... Telephone reservation systems have not been knitted   V+PRON+ADV:
together... The Slav world has become unified and knit together.   ERGATIVE
● **Fuse** means almost the same as **knit together.**

knit up. If you **knit up** something such as a jumper, you knit the   V+ADV+N,
whole of it. EG *I knitted up the front of a cardigan this evening.*   V+N+ADV,
                                                                        V+PRON+ADV

knock, knocks, knocking, knocked

knock about; an informal expression. 1 If a person **is knocked**   V+N+ADV,
about or **around,** someone hits or kicks them several times. EG *One*   V+PRON+ADV:
of them was knocked about and wounded... This fellow has been   USUALLY PASSIVE
knocking a policeman about in the gutter.

2 If you **knock** an idea **about** or **around,** you discuss it with other   V+N+ADV,
people so that they can suggest ways of improving it. EG *The*   V+ADV+N
document was knocked about and redrafted by a dozen hands.

3 If someone **knocks around** or **knocks about,** they get experience   V+ADV,
in a lot of different situations, especially by travelling to different   V+PREP
places and meeting people. EG *I knocked around for a few years
after university... I'm a bachelor, I've knocked about the world a bit,
known a few women.*

4 If someone or something **is knocking around** or **about** some-   V+ADV
where, they are present there, usually not doing anything in particular. EG *My brothers should be knocking around somewhere... There's
the odd Scotsman knocking about here who's looking for someone to
play golf.* ● **Hang around** means almost the same as **knock around.**

knock about with. See **knock around with.**
knock around. See **knock about.**

knock around with. If you **knock around with** someone or **knock**   V+ADV:
about with them, you spend your spare time with them, either   USUALLY + *with*
because you are one of their friends or because you are their special
boyfriend or girlfriend. EG *Who's she knocking around with now?...
He's knocking about with a gang from the next village.* ● **Consort
with** is a more formal expression for **knock around with.**

knock back. 1 If you **knock back** an alcoholic drink, you drink it   V+ADV+N,
fairly quickly. EG *He won't be too happy when he comes up here and*   V+N+ADV,
finds me knocking back his favourite whisky... Davis knocked the   V+PRON+ADV
*drinks back with a fine abandon... She had poured Eva another
Tequila, and insisted she take a bite of lemon before knocking it
back.* ● **Swig** means almost the same as **knock back.**

2 If something **knocks** you **back** a particular amount of money, it   V+PRON+ADV+N
costs you that amount of money; an informal use. EG *How much did
that car knock you back? A few thousand?* ● **Set back** means almost
the same as **knock back.**

knock down. 1 If you **knock** someone **down,** you hit them or push   V+N+ADV,
them, deliberately or accidentally, so that they fall to the ground. EG   V+PRON+ADV,
I bumped into and nearly knocked down a person at the bus stop... I   V+ADV+N

was nearly knocked down by a hefty slap on the back. ● **Knock over** means almost the same as **knock down.**

2 If a car or other vehicle **knocks** someone **down,** it hits them so that they fall to the ground and may be injured or killed. EG *A bus came screeching to a stop, practically knocking him down... ...knocked down by cars as they dash among the traffic.* ● **Knock over** means almost the same as **knock down.**
V+PRON+ADV,
V+N+ADV,
V+ADV+N

3 To **knock down** a building or part of a building means to demolish it. EG *...their plan to knock down once and for all the hated Berlin Wall... I'd knock the wall down between the front room and dining room.* ● **Pull down** means almost the same as **knock down.**
V+ADV+N,
V+N+ADV,
V+PRON+ADV

4 If you **knock down** an idea or opinion, you argue successfully against it, so that it is no longer considered valid. EG *Jane has systematically knocked down every one of her friend's suggestions... The argument is in a form in which you can easily knock it down.* ● **Demolish** means almost the same as **knock down.** ▶ A **knockdown** argument or piece of reasoning is very powerful and difficult to argue against. EG *Opponents of expansion believe they have a knockdown argument.*
V+ADV+N,
V+PRON+ADV,
V+N+ADV

ADJECTIVE

5 If you **knock** someone **down** when they are selling you something, or if you get a price **knocked down,** you persuade the seller to reduce the price. EG *I tried to knock him down a few pounds but he wouldn't have it... We managed to knock the price down quite a lot because it was torn... The bust had been knocked down for £5 to the antique dealer.* ▶ A **knockdown** price is one that is a lot lower than it would be normally. EG *I got it for a knockdown price.* ● **Reduced** is a less informal word for **knockdown.**
V+PRON+ADV+N,
V+N+ADV,
V+PRON+ADV,
V+N+ADV+N

ADJECTIVE

knock off.

1 If you **knock** something **off** a shelf or other surface, you hit it so that it falls to the ground. EG *A stone was placed on a brick and had to be knocked off by another stone when it was aimed at.*
V+N+ADV/PREP,
V+PRON+ADV/PREP,
V+ADV+N

2 If a seller **knocks off** an amount from the price or cost of something, he or she reduces the price or cost by that amount. EG *He said he'd knock £50 off the price... They offered to pay back about a million pounds of it by knocking it off the price of future work.*
V+N+PREP/ADV,
V+PRON+PREP/ADV,
V+ADV+N

3 When you **knock off,** you finish work at the end of the day or before a break; an informal use in British English. EG *We knock off at 5... About half past six we knocked off.*
V+ADV

4 In very informal English, to **knock** someone **off** means to murder them. EG *I think he had one of his elderly relatives knocked off so that he could inherit the fortune.* ● **Bump off** means almost the same as **knock off.**
V+N+ADV,
V+PRON+ADV,
V+ADV+N

5 If you **knock off** a piece of work, you finish it very quickly and easily; an informal use. EG *I thought I could knock off a couple of essays in no time.*
V+ADV+N,
V+N+ADV,
V+PRON+ADV

6 If someone **knocks** something **off,** they steal it; a very informal use. EG *He was planning to knock off a few videos, but the boss found out and got there just in time to stop him.* ● **Nick** means almost the same as **knock off.**
V+ADV+N,
V+N+ADV,
V+PRON+ADV

7 If someone **knocks off** a bank or a shop, they carry out a robbery there; a very informal use. EG *He'd knocked off three banks before they caught up with him.*
V+ADV+N

8 To **knock** someone **off** also means to have sex with them; an informal and rude use in British English.
V+N+ADV,
V+PRON+ADV,
V+ADV+N

9 If you say '**Knock it off!**' to someone, you are telling them to stop doing something which is annoying you; an informal use. EG *'Knock it off, Pyle,' said the boy... Knock it off. Anyhow, who the hell do you think you're laughing at?*
IMPERATIVE:
V+it+ADV

knock out. 1 To **knock** someone **out** means to cause them to become unconscious or to fall asleep. EG *The old man hit him so hard that he knocked him out... The tablet had knocked her out for four solid hours... The explosion hurt no one, except that it knocked out Colonel Lacour.* ● **Bring round** means the opposite of **knock out.** ▶ A **knock-out** dose of medicine or injection makes you become unconscious or fall asleep. EG *...knock-out drops.* ▶ In boxing or wrestling, a **knockout** is a blow that makes your opponent fall to the ground and unable to stand up before the referee has counted to ten. EG *Davies won by a knockout.* `V+PRON+ADV, V+N+ADV, V+ADV+N` `ADJECTIVE` `N COUNT`

2 If a person or team **is knocked out** of a competition, they are defeated, so that they take no more part in the competition. EG *Connors just avoided being knocked out in the second round... ...their aim is for the Social Democrats to knock out the Labour Party.* ● **Eliminate** is a more formal word for **knock out.** ▶ A **knockout** competition is one in which several competitors or teams take part, and the winner of each match goes on to the next round while the loser drops out, until one competitor or team is the winner. `V+ADV+N, V+N+ADV, V+PRON+ADV: ALSO+of` `ADJECTIVE`

3 In war, if something **is knocked out** by enemy action, it is destroyed or damaged enough to prevent it from working properly. EG *Radars were knocked out, aircraft were shot down... Almost 2000 tanks had been knocked out of action by missiles.* ▶ A **knockout** blow or victory is one that completely destroys an opponent. `PASSIVE: V+ADV` `ADJECTIVE`

4 If you **knock out** a piece of work, you do it very quickly without paying much attention to detail. EG *He can knock out a short story in less than a day.* `V+ADV+N, V+N+ADV, V+PRON+ADV`

5 If an event or piece of news **knocks** you **out,** it shocks you so much that you cannot think clearly or react immediately. EG *I didn't mean to be rude. I was sort of knocked out... The news absolutely knocked me out.* ● **Stun** means almost the same as **knock out.** `V+PRON+ADV, V+N+ADV`

6 If something **knocks** you **out,** it impresses you greatly and is much better than you had expected. EG *Her performance completely knocked me out.* ● **Astound** and **stun** are more formal words for **knock out.** ▶ If you say that someone is a **knockout,** you mean that they are extremely attractive or clever. EG *Sandra looked a knockout in her new dress... He lives in the cutest little house you ever saw, with a knockout wife and two daughters.* `V+PRON+ADV, V+N+ADV` `N SING, ADJECTIVE`

7 If a characteristic **is knocked out** of someone, they are influenced very strongly so that they lose the characteristic. EG *His natural flair was in danger of being knocked out of him... You're not really at your best because has been knocked out of you.* `PASSIVE: V+ADV, ALSO+of`

knock over. To **knock** someone or something **over** means to push them or hit them so that they fall or turn on their side. EG *I got knocked over by a car when I was six... Careful you don't knock the paint over... He managed to knock over a box.* `V+N+ADV, V+PRON+ADV, V+ADV+N`

knock together. See knock up.

knock up. 1 If you **knock** something **up** or **knock** it **together,** you make it or build it very quickly, using whatever materials are available. EG *They do not ask official permission to knock up a ramshackle home to live in... Do you want me to knock up a meal for you?... The residents here pay rents to the landlords who knocked the shacks together.* `V+ADV+N, V+N+ADV, V+PRON+ADV`

2 In British English, if you **knock** someone **up,** you knock on the door of their bedroom or of their house during the night in order to wake them. EG *He knocked me up at 4 to ring for an ambulance.* ● **Rouse** is a formal word for **knock up.** `V+PRON+ADV, V+N+ADV`

3 In very informal American English, if a man **knocks** a woman **up,** he makes her pregnant. `V+ADV+N, V+PRON+ADV, V+N+ADV`

4 In a game such as tennis, squash, or badminton, when the players **knock up,** they practise hitting the ball or shuttlecock to each other before they begin a game. ▶ A **knock-up** is a period of time in which the players practise hitting the ball or shuttlecock to each other before beginning a game of tennis, squash, or badminton. EG *Let's have a knock-up before we start.*

V+ADV

N COUNT

know, knows, knowing, knew, known

know about. If you **know about** a subject, you have studied it and understand part or all of it. EG *What do you know about the film industry?... She knew a bit about acoustics.*

V+PREP

know as. If someone or something **is known as** a particular name, they are called by that name. EG *...Lev Davidovitch Bronstein, otherwise known as Leon Trotsky... ...William Kent, known to his friends and family as Will... In South America they are known as army ants, in Africa as drivers.*

V+PRON+PREP,
V+N+PREP:
USUALLY PASSIVE

know of. If you **know of** something, you have heard of it but you do not necessarily have a lot of information about it. EG *I know of one girl who moved into a flat with two others... Many people did not even know of their existence.*

V+PREP

knuckle, knuckles, knuckling, knuckled

knuckle down. If someone **knuckles down,** they begin to work or study very hard, especially after a period when they have done very little. EG *It's high time you knuckled down to some hard study... Don't you think you ought to knuckle down a bit?... The thought of knuckling down to a mundane routine was quite frightening.* ● **Buckle down** means almost the same as **knuckle down.**

V+ADV:
ALSO+*to*

knuckle under. If you **knuckle under,** you do what someone else tells you to do or what a situation forces you to do, because you realize that you have no choice. EG *He refused to knuckle under and was asked to leave.* ● **Buckle under** means almost the same as **knuckle under.**

V+ADV

L l

lace, laces, lacing, laced

lace up. If you **lace up** something with laces attached to it, you fasten it by pulling the ends of the laces tight and tying them together. EG *He bent and laced up his shoes.* ● **Do up** is a more informal, general expression for **lace up.** ▶ **Lace-ups** are shoes which fasten with laces. EG *Maria's lace-ups had got holes in the toes.*

V+ADV+N,
V+N+ADV,
V+PRON+ADV

N PLURAL

ladle, ladles, ladling, ladled

ladle out. 1 To **ladle out** something such as money, information or advice means to give it freely and in large quantities; an informal use. EG *...the knowledge that is ladled out daily in high schools.* ● **Dish out** and **dole out** mean almost the same as **ladle out.**

V+ADV+N,
V+N+ADV,
V+PRON+ADV

2 If you **ladle out** soup, stew, and so on, you serve it into dishes, using a large spoon or ladle. EG *Ladle it out into jars lined with coarse cheesecloth... She was just ladling out the spaghetti which was liberally covered with olive oil, tomato sauce and basil.*

V+PRON+ADV,
V+N+ADV,
V+N+ADV

lag, lags, lagging, lagged

lag behind. 1 When two or more people are moving along, if someone **lags behind,** that person moves more slowly than the others and so fails to keep with them. EG *He set off at a brisk walk, Kate lagging behind... ...not to lag behind the others, but to keep in close, compact formation.* ● **Fall behind** means almost the same as **lag behind.** — V+ADV, V+PREP

2 If someone or something **lags behind** another person or thing, they fail to achieve as much. EG *Britain's economic development must lag behind that of almost every other industrial nation... In recent months increases in earnings have lagged behind the tax and price index.* ● **Fall behind** means almost the same as **lag behind.** — V+PREP, V+ADV

lam, lams, lamming, lammed

lam into. To lam into someone means to attack them violently. EG *The men lammed into him brutally, kicking and punching.* ● **Lay into** means almost the same as **lam into.** — V+PREP

land, lands, landing, landed

land in. If someone or something **lands** you **in** trouble or a difficult situation, you find yourself in a difficult situation because of them. EG *How do we get out of the terrible situation this Government has landed us in?... You know, I wouldn't be surprised if he'd landed himself in prison... They said I had better give them the information they wanted or I would land in 'a lot of trouble'.* ● **Get into** means almost the same as **land in.** — V+PRON+PREP, V+REFL+PREP, V+N+PREP, V+PREP

land up. If you **land up** in a place or situation, you arrive at that place or are in that situation, often without having intended to; an informal expression. EG *He landed up in the special hospital in Leningrad... ...a bunch of social misfits who have landed up teaching English.* ● **End up** and **wind up** mean almost the same as **land up.** — V+ADV: USUALLY+A

land with. If you are **landed with** a difficult or unpleasant situation, you have to deal with it or accept it because you cannot avoid it; an informal expression. EG *...a clergyman landed with a rectory the size of a mansion... You landed us with that awful Hector whom I'd never seen in my life.* ● **Saddle with** and **lumber with** mean almost the same as **land with.** — V+N+PREP, V+PRON+PREP: USUALLY PASSIVE

lap, laps, lapping, lapped

lap up. 1 When an animal **laps up** a drink, it drinks it. EG *The cat lapped up the milk as if it had not been fed for days.* — V+ADV+N, V+N+ADV, V+PRON+ADV

2 If someone **laps up** praise, attention or information, they accept it eagerly and with great enjoyment. EG *He continued looking round, smiling, lapping up the attention... Jago sparkled with charm and Dolly lapped it up... The feud was instantly lapped up by the press.* — V+ADV+N, V+PRON+ADV, V+N+ADV

lapse, lapses, lapsing, lapsed

lapse into. If you **lapse into** a more relaxed or less acceptable kind of behaviour, you start behaving in that way because you have relaxed your self control. EG *He sat down and lapsed into an unhappy silence... She seemed to lapse into a troubled sleep... ...fearing my voice might go out of control and lapse into croaks of broken English.* ● **Sink into** means almost the same as **lapse into.** — V+PREP

lark, larks, larking, larked

lark about. If you **lark about,** you enjoy yourself by doing silly things; used in informal British English. EG *We had a lovely holiday, sunbathing and larking about... ...their favourite spare-time activity, larking about at the Club.* ● **Fool around** and **mess about** mean almost the same as **lark about.** — V+ADV

lash, lashes, lashing, lashed

lash down. 1 If you **lash** someone or something **down**, you fasten them firmly in a particular position, using ropes. EG *It was lashed down by at least a dozen steel cables... It doesn't weigh much, and I can lash it down out of the way.*
V+N+ADV, V+PRON+ADV, V+ADV+N

2 If rain **lashes down**, it falls very heavily. EG *The rain lashed down so fiercely that we could hardly see.*
V+ADV

lash into. If you **lash into** someone, you criticize or scold that person very angrily and severely. EG *They listened to Jimmie lashing into the extremists... ...even as I opened my mouth to lash into him.*
● Lay into means almost the same as **lash into.**
V+PREP: HAS PASSIVE

lash out. 1 If you **lash out**, you attempt to hit someone with sudden violent movements of your arms or legs or with a weapon. EG *When cornered, they lash out with savage kicks... He tried to pin Kitty to the wall, but she lashed out and tore from his grasp.* ● Hit out means almost the same as **lash out.**
V+ADV: ALSO+with

2 If you **lash out** at someone, you speak to them very angrily or cruelly, criticizing or scolding them. EG *I lashed out at Kurt, calling him every name under the sun... Harris used the opportunity to lash out against the Committee.*
V+ADV: USUALLY WITH at/against

3 If you **lash out** on something, you spend a lot of money to buy it. EG *I should have to consider carefully before lashing out on something much dearer.* ● Splash out means almost the same as **lash out.**
V+ADV: ALSO+on

last, lasts, lasting, lasted

last out. 1 To **last out** a period of time means to manage to stay alive, to continue functioning or to reach the end of a difficult experience. EG *I'm afraid she might not last out the winter... I don't think I can last out without any cigarettes... Do you think the car will last out until the end of the year?*
V+ADV: USUALLY+A

2 If a supply of something **lasts out** a period of time, there is enough of it for as long as it is needed or for that period of time. EG *The heater in the village hall needed two bottles of fuel to last out a full meeting... How long will our coal reserves last out?* ● Hold out means almost the same as **last out.**
V+ADV+N, V+N+ADV, V+ADV: NO PASSIVE

latch, latches, latching, latched

latch on to, latch onto. 1 If someone **latches on to** you, they demand your attention and expect you to spend a lot of time with them. EG *These kids know what they like and latch on to adults who can provide surprises and suggest new games... Just as he was about to leave, he was latched on to by a girl he'd met that morning.*
V+ADV+PREP: HAS PASSIVE

2 If someone **latches onto** something, they realize it or learn about it. EG *They never once latched onto the fact that he was using his own code... Once the landlords latched on to what was happening, out they went.*
V+ADV+PREP: HAS PASSIVE

3 If something **latches onto** something else, it attaches itself firmly to that thing. EG *The grubs hatch and make their way underground where they latch onto plant stems and hack them open.*
V+ADV+PREP

laugh, laughs, laughing, laughed

laugh at. If you **laugh at** someone or something, you make jokes about them. EG *I don't think it's nice to laugh at people's disabilities... Not even a saint enjoys being laughed at in this kind of misfortune... The noise of the bells is said to fracture the towers but architects laugh at this and say it is rubbish.* ● Ridicule is a more formal word for **laugh at.**
V+PREP: HAS PASSIVE

laugh off. If you **laugh off** a difficult or serious situation, you try to suggest that it is amusing and unimportant. EG *Despite being in*
V+N+ADV, V+ADV+N, V+PRON+ADV

serious trouble with the Government, Northcliffe attempted to laugh the matter off... Smith laughed off the insult by telling reporters that he was flattered that someone had taken notice of his work.

launch, launches, launching, launched

launch into. If you **launch into** something such as a speech, task, or fight, you start it with enthusiasm. EG *She launched into a long speech about duty and patriotism... It was ironic that the movement should have launched itself into battle at this time... Then the chorus launches into an ecstatic song.*

V+PREP,
V+REFL+PREP

lavish, lavishes, lavishing, lavished

lavish on. If you **lavish** money, time or affection **on** or **upon** someone, you spend a lot of money or time on them or give them a lot of affection. EG *Everything was lavished on her one and only child... Why do the media lavish so much attention on people like Hinckley?... I'm not about to lavish money on you; I have little enough myself.* ● **Heap on** means almost the same as **lavish on**.
lavish upon. See lavish on.

V+N+PREP

lay, lays, laying, laid

Lay is also the past tense of the verb **lie**.

lay about. 1 If someone **lays about** with a weapon, they use it to hit anyone who is nearby in a violent, uncontrolled way. You can also say that someone **lays about** themselves with a weapon when they attack other people in this way. EG *His two assistants sprang forwards and began to lay about the boys with sticks... He rushed out of his house, armed with a sword and a hatchet, and laid about himself fiercely, killing two of the animals.*

V+PREP,
V+ADV+REFL:
USUALLY+*with*

2 If someone is described as a **layabout**, that person is very lazy and never does any work. EG *'Perhaps your assistant could do it?'—'Charlie? That bone idle layabout. Not him.'*

N COUNT

lay aside. 1 If you **lay aside** something that you have been using or dealing with, you leave it for a while to do something else. EG *He laid the newspaper aside and turned his attention to breakfast... I've been reading this instead of doing my work; I can't seem to lay it aside... She was more restless than Anne and laid aside her books sooner.* ● **Put aside** means almost the same as **lay aside**.

V+N+ADV,
V+PRON+ADV,
V+ADV+N

2 If you **lay aside** a feeling, belief or attitude that you have experienced, you stop or reject it so that it no longer affects you. EG *They tried to lay aside their usual inhibitions and say whatever came into their heads... People found the performances gave them a great deal of pleasure once prejudices against this kind of music were laid aside.* ● **Set aside** means almost the same as **lay aside**.

V+ADV+N,
V+N+ADV,
V+PRON+ADV

lay before. If you **lay** an idea or a problem **before** someone, you present it to them in detail for them to consider and give their advice, opinion, or judgement. EG *If you have any proof of that allegation, I advise you to lay it before the police... The Wildlife and Countryside Bill had been laid before Parliament in October 1979.* ● **Put before** means almost the same as **lay before**.

V+PRON+PREP,
V+N+PREP

lay by. 1 If you **lay** a store of something **by**, you save it for future use. EG *I've got some savings laid by for my old age.* ● **Put by** means almost the same as **lay by**.

V+N+ADV,
V+PRON+ADV,
V+ADV+N

2 A **lay-by** is a short strip of road by the side of a main road, where cars can stop for a while. EG *Pull into the next lay-by.*

N COUNT

lay down. 1 If you **lay** something **down**, you put it down on a surface. If you **lay** yourself **down**, you move your body so that you are lying flat on a surface. EG *Albert laid his pipe down carefully on the table beside him... She took the key out of his pocket and*

V+N+ADV,
V+PRON+ADV,
V+REFL+ADV,
V+ADV+N

said,'Here. You keep it. I might lay it down somewhere and mislay it.'... She laid herself down on a long seat... Uncle Nick laid down his pencil and pushed the sheet of paper away from him.

2 If laws, rules, or people in authority **lay down** what people should do, they state that this is what must be done. EG ...laws which lay down what employers and employees must and must not do... As institutions they lay down no formal entry requirements... A government should lay down national policy for various sectors of education. ● **Stipulate** is a more formal word for **lay down**. `V+ADV+N, V+PRON+ADV`

3 If something such as food **is laid down**, it is stored for future use. EG Wine that is too young to drink now should be laid down for a few years to allow it to mature... Carbohydrate not used up in work during the day will get laid down by the body as fat. `V+N+ADV, V+PRON+ADV, V+ADV+N: USUALLY PASSIVE`

4 To **lay down** something new means to establish or create it. EG Adolescence is important because the habits that are laid down then seem to last for a lifetime... After injury the haematoma is invaded by repair cells which lay down scar tissue. `V+ADV+N, V+PRON+ADV, V+N+ADV`

5 If something such as an area of grass or a path or airstrip **is laid down**, it is constructed covering an area of ground. EG A new golf course has been laid down over a swamp... The Seabees laid down a 600-metre tarmac airstrip and built a beer hall. `V+ADV+N, V+N+ADV, V+PRON+ADV: USUALLY PASSIVE`

6 When layers of sediment, sand or rock **are laid down**, the layers settle and form into a solid mass over a long period of time. EG Most sedimentary stone has been laid down in layers under water and therefore splits easily. `V+ADV+N, V+PRON+ADV: USUALLY PASSIVE`

7 If you **lay down** something such as an attitude, belief, or position that you have held, you give it up or reject it; a formal or literary use. EG It had been a great relief to be able to lay down the mantle of authority which I had borne for so long... The Law Lords concluded that a peer could not lay down his title. ● **Lay aside** means almost the same as **lay down**. `V+ADV+N, V+N+ADV, V+PRON+ADV`

8 If people who have been at war **lay down** their arms or weapons, they stop fighting and make peace; a literary use. EG There was no guarantee that the members of these units would lay down their arms. `V+ADV+N`

9 If someone **lays down** their life for a cause, they are killed because they are involved in it or support it; a literary use. EG Not so many people today are willing to lay down their lives for their country any more. ● **Give** means almost the same as **lay down**. `V+ADV+N`

lay in. If you **lay in** an amount of something, you buy it and store it to be used later. EG The Governor has laid in a plentiful supply of champagne and Havana cigars... ...people responsible for laying in food stocks for a city full of children. ● **Buy in** means almost the same as **lay in**. `V+ADV+N, V+N+ADV, V+PRON+ADV`

lay into. **1** If someone **lays into** another person, they start to hit and kick that person violently. EG The special patrol group laid into them, forcing them to run into the near-by park... I was going to lay into her but the other two girls grabbed my arms. `V+PREP: HAS PASSIVE`

2 If someone **lays into** you, they start to criticize you severely. EG Before we went out Bob really laid into us: 'You're not even trying! For heaven's sake put some effort into it.'... I was wearing one brown shoe and one black. He loved that, seeing the chance to lay into me: 'Been getting up in the dark again, eh?' ● **Lash into** means almost the same as **lay into**. `V+PREP: HAS PASSIVE`

3 If you **lay into** food or drink, you eat or drink it very eagerly and in large quantities; an informal use. ● **Tuck into** means almost the same as **lay into**. `V+PREP`

lay off. **1** If workers **are laid off**, they are told by their employer `V+N+ADV,`

that they have to leave their jobs, either for a period of time or V+ADV+N,
permanently, because there is no more work for them to do. EG *So if* V+PRON+ADV:
demand falls, the company lays men off... City workers are being USUALLY PASSIVE
laid off at the rate of 100 a week. ▶ If there is a **layoff,** workers are N COUNT
told by their employer to leave their jobs. EG *Textile companies*
announced 2,000 fresh layoffs last week. ▶ A **layoff** is also a period of N COUNT
time in which people do not work or take part in their normal
activities, often because they are resting or are injured. EG *He was*
bowling badly after his long lay-off.

2 If you tell someone to **lay off,** you are telling them to leave you V+ADV,
alone, to stop criticizing you, or to stop doing something which is V+PREP:
annoying you; an informal use. EG *They had warned him to lay off,* ALSO IMPERATIVE
but he'd kept cutting in just the same... Anyway, I don't do it
indiscriminately. You know that, but lay off me, or I might.

3 If you **lay off** something or **lay off** doing something, you give it up V+ADV+N,
or stop doing it; an informal use. EG *Cut down on the starches, lay off* V+ADV:
the fudge sundaes and milk shakes... Tom, lay off that sherry—it's NO PASSIVE
terrible... 'Why not lay off till Monday?'—'I can't. I've got to hand it
in tomorrow.'

lay on. **1** If you **lay on** something such as food, entertainment, or a V+ADV+N,
service, you provide or supply it. EG *The organisers had laid on buses* V+N+ADV,
to transport people from the city... Early this evening, the press laid V+PRON+ADV
on an informal drinks party for us... Every kind of facility was laid
on for their amusement.

2 To **lay** blame or responsibility **on** or **upon** someone means to state V+N+PREP,
officially that they are responsible for something. EG *So far, women* V+PRON+PREP
have been able to lay most of the blame on men... ...administrative
duties laid upon them by Acts of Parliament... Responsibility for
these people was therefore laid on the Assistance Committees.

3 To **lay** stress or emphasis **on** or **upon** something means to stress or V+N+PREP
emphasize it. EG *Less emphasis is laid on rivalry and competition,*
and more on co-operation... The Government has laid great stress
on harnessing private enterprise and voluntary help. ● **Put on**
means almost the same as **lay on.**

4 If you **lay** it **on,** you deliberately exaggerate a statement, gesture, V+*it*+ADV
or emotion in order to try to impress people or draw their attention
to it; an informal use. EG *He moved his chair all the while to make*
sure we didn't exchange eye-signals. He laid it on so thick that we
were bound to try to outwit him... I used grander expressions and
laid it on much more thickly than I should have done.

lay out. **1** If you **lay** something **out,** you put it in a particular place, V+ADV+N,
spread out and neatly arranged. EG *Lally was setting the table, laying* V+N+ADV,
out the plates and cups... I watched him start to lay the papers out V+PRON+ADV
on the table in the conference room... Handle the paper very
carefully, then lay it out on racks to dry. ● **Put out** means almost the
same as **lay out.**

2 If you **lay out** an idea or information, you express or present it V+ADV+N,
clearly and thoroughly. EG *The situation is laid out very clearly in a* V+PRON+ADV
briefing paper from the Ramblers Association... ...laying out the
relationship between racism today and the problems experienced in
the past. ● **Set out** means almost the same as **lay out.**

3 If a garden, building, town, and so on **is laid out** in a particular PASSIVE:
way, it is designed or arranged in that way. EG *The homestead, shop* V+ADV,
and outbuildings were spaciously laid out... ...a garden laid out with USUALLY+A
terraces, fountains and shady walks. ▶ The **layout** of something such N COUNT
as a garden, building, or piece of writing is the way in which the
parts of it are arranged. EG *...the general layout of the farm... ...the*
poor layout and organization of the report.

4 To **lay out** a dead person means to clean their body and dress them for the funeral. EG *After her death, no one could be found to lay her out.* V+PRON+ADV, V+N+ADV, V+ADV+N

5 If someone **lays** a person **out,** they knock that person unconscious by hitting them violently; an informal use. EG *Someone crept up behind Allen and laid him out with some heavy and solid object... Mother leapt out of bed. 'No one's going to lay out our Laurie!'* ● **Knock out** means almost the same as **lay out.** V+PRON+ADV, V+ADV+N, V+N+ADV

6 If you **lay out** money on something, you spend a large amount of money on it; an informal use. EG *Some people might be too hard up midweek to lay out large sums... ...a notebook in which he kept a record of petty expenses he laid out on errands.* ● **Shell out** and **fork out** mean almost the same as **lay out.** V+ADV+N, V+N+ADV

lay up. 1 If an illness **lays** you **up,** or if you **are laid up** with it, it causes you to stay in bed; an informal use. EG *The baby was just beginning to walk when an illness laid her up... The gentleman had been laid up for five days with a bad cold.* V+PRON+ADV, V+N+ADV, OR PASSIVE: V+ADV+ with

2 If a car, boat, or piece of equipment **is laid up,** it is not in use, usually because it is being repaired. EG *The boats which took crews to Arctic waters had been laid up... The car had been laid up after Guy's death, but it was quite easy to get back on the road again.* V+N+ADV, V+ADV+N, V+PRON+PREP: USUALLY PASSIVE

3 If you **lay up** something, you gradually save quantities of it for future use; a rather old-fashioned use. EG *Hunter-gatherers simply do not lay up stocks against future shortages... This is one of those golden days to lay up as treasure for the future.* V+ADV+N

4 If a person or animal **lays up** somewhere, they go there to hide or do nothing for a while; an informal use. EG *If the fox does lay up, you can dig him out... There are ways and means of recapturing a ferret if he lays up... For two pins I'd lay up today, but I don't like to let Miss Read down.* V+ADV

lay upon. See **lay on: lay upon** is a more formal expression.

laze, lazes, lazing, lazed

laze about. If you **laze about,** you relax and enjoy yourself, not doing any work or anything that requires effort. EG *...cleaning and washing up while the other women laze about... They read and listened to records and sometimes just lazed about without a care.* ● **Lounge about** means almost the same as **laze about.** V+ADV

lead, leads, leading, led

lead in. If you **lead in,** you start a formal discussion or meeting by making a short speech. EG *She led in with a few introductory remarks, then handed over to the main speaker.* ▶ A **lead-in** is a short introductory speech at the beginning of a formal discussion or meeting. EG *Six people missed the lead-in.* V+ADV N COUNT

lead off. 1 If a road, path, corridor, or room **leads off** a place, it connects directly with that place. EG *From the lift shaft four straight corridors lead off at right angles... There is a lane leading off right beside the Restaurant du Canal... Two tiny rooms led off the living-room... ...two doors leading off the hallway.* V+ADV+A, V+PREP

2 If someone **leads off** in a meeting, performance, or event, they start it. EG *The chairman led off with a financial statement... He said, 'Join in with me, if you will, in singing ...' And then he led off in a different key from the one in which the organist was playing.* V+ADV

lead on. If someone **leads** you **on,** they deceive you by giving you false information or by behaving in a misleading way. EG *A girl doesn't indulge in antics like that unless she's been led on artfully by a man... ...cunningly leading them on; never letting them see that you know.* V+N+ADV, V+PRON+ADV, V+ADV+N

lead up to. 1 The events and periods of time that **lead up to** a final   V+ADV+PREP
situation happen one after the other until that situation is reached.
EG *Witnesses gave their testimony of events leading up to and
following Gregory's death... ...the riots of the early 1830s that led up
to the reform bill... ...during the days leading up to the special
conference.*
2 If someone **leads up to** a particular subject in a conversation, they   V+ADV+PREP
gradually guide the conversation to a point where they can intro-
duce the subject. EG *Ever since you came in you've been leading up
to this one question... What was he leading up to, in his deliberate,
Scottish way?*

leaf, leafs, leafing, leafed

leaf through. If you **leaf through** a book or magazine, you turn the   V+PREP
pages quickly without reading or looking at them carefully. EG *While
he is waiting he leafs through a magazine... She took another volume
out of the bookcase and began leafing through the pages.* ● **Thumb
through** means almost the same as **leaf through.**

leak, leaks, leaking, leaked

leak out. If information or news that should have been kept secret   V+ADV
leaks out, it becomes known to other people. EG *News of their
engagement leaked out just before Christmas... Terrible stories
were leaking out about the cruelties.* ● **Get out** means almost the
same as **leak out.**

lean, leans, leaning, leaned/leant

lean on. 1 If someone **leans on** you, they try to influence you by   V+PREP:
putting pressure on you or threatening you. EG *They can lean on the*   HAS PASSIVE
*administration by threatening to withhold their subscriptions... Film
production is an enormously competitive business, so the producers
lean on the writers and the writers have a straight choice.*
● **Pressurize** is a more formal word for **lean on.**
2 If you **lean on** a particular person or thing, you depend on them for   V+PREP
support and encouragement. EG *He leant on the calm and steadfast
Kathy... They lean heavily upon each other for support... During this
transition period, the world is likely to lean increasingly on the solid
fossil fuels (coal and shale).* ● **Rely on** means almost the same as
lean on.

lean out. If you **lean out** of an open window or other opening, you   V+ADV:
put your head and shoulders through the gap so that you are looking   ALSO+of
outside. EG *She leaned out and waved at him... A large number of
people seemed to be leaning out of the window.*

lean over. If someone or something **leans over,** they bend in a   V+ADV,
particular direction. EG *You'll have to lean over to see it... He was*   V+PREP
leaning over me.

leap, leaps, leaping, leaped/leapt

leap at. If you **leap at** a chance or opportunity, you accept it quickly   V+PREP
and eagerly. EG *I can't understand why you didn't want to go; I would
have leaped at the chance.* ● **Jump at** means almost the same as
leap at.

leap on. 1 If someone **leaps on** or **upon** you, they suddenly move   V+PREP:
towards you and take hold of you roughly or violently. EG *And then,*   HAS PASSIVE
*before I could leap on Derek, I saw a little blind kid... He had been
leapt upon by a wolf while out hunting.*
2 If you **leap on** or **upon** an idea or suggestion, you suddenly become   V+PREP:
interested in it or enthusiastic about it. EG *They leap on the sugges-*   HAS PASSIVE
tion with artificial enthusiasm... This is something you should leap

upon and become involved with. ● **Seize on** means almost the same as **leap on.**

leap out. If someone or something **leaps out,** they suddenly appear   V+ADV
from a place where they have been hiding. EG *They opened the gate,
and I leapt out... ...when a rapist leaps out on a victim.*

leap out at. If something such as an idea or something that is   V+ADV+PREP
written down **leaps out** at you, it suddenly becomes very obvious or
striking. EG *Her name leapt out at me from the list of applicants.*

leap upon. See **leap on.**

leave, leaves, leaving, left

leave aside. If you **leave aside** an idea or suggestion, you do not   V+N+ADV,
think or talk about it straight away, although you intend to think   V+ADV+N,
about it or discuss it later. EG *Let's leave generalities aside and get*   V+PRON+ADV
*back to Mr. Bashton... ...leaving aside the question of Meehan's guilt
or innocence, the general view was that the Crown's evidence was
not strong enough to convict.*

leave behind. 1 If you **leave** someone or something **behind,** you do   V+N+ADV,
not take them with you when you go somewhere. EG *'I can't carry*   V+PRON+ADV,
this,' I said. 'We'll have to leave some behind.'... I couldn't leave   V+ADV+N
*Hilary behind to cope on her own. Not for six months... He sat there,
glancing at the newspaper that had been left behind.*

2 To **leave behind** an object or situation means to cause or allow it   V+ADV+N,
to remain after leaving a place. EG *The police departed, leaving*   V+N+ADV/PREP,
behind an unsolved mystery... The truck chugged away leaving a   V+PRON+ADV/PREP
*trail of debris behind it... When the water retreated the silt that it
had left behind had coated the surface of the road... I worried a good
deal about the debts I would leave behind if I were killed.*

3 If you **leave** a particular idea, attitude or state **behind,** you reject   V+N+ADV,
or abandon it in order to develop or progress. EG *We must leave*   V+ADV+N,
adolescence behind and grow up... To escape from the vicious circle   V+PRON+ADV
*in which he finds himself trapped he will have to leave behind a
whole complex of thoughts and prejudices.*

4 If someone **is left behind,** for example in their work or studies,   V+N+ADV,
they do not progress or develop as successfully as other people. EG   V+PRON+ADV:
You had to follow closely if you wanted to avoid being left behind...   USUALLY PASSIVE
*If you don't know your technical jargon, you're going to be left
behind.*

leave off. 1 If you **leave** someone or something **off** a list, you do not   V+N+PREP,
include them in that list. EG *Hopper was too important to be left off*   V+PRON+PREP
the guest list.

2 If you **leave off** a piece of clothing, you do not wear it on a   V+N+ADV,
particular occasion. EG *It's so hot I feel like leaving this helmet off...*   V+ADV+N,
She had, in the excitement of the moment, left off some crucial   V+PRON+ADV
garment.

3 If you **leave off** doing something, you stop doing it. EG *Waddell left*   V+ADV:
off hitting Mrs Ross and came over and struck Mr Ross... He sat   ALSO+-ING
*down at the piano again and started playing from where he left off...
She will take over where the midwife leaves off.*

4 If something **leaves off** at a particular point, it stops or ends there.   V+ADV
EG *It picks up where the earlier story leaves off.*

5 If you tell someone to **leave off,** you are telling them to stop   IMPERATIVE:
annoying you; an informal use. EG *Just leave off, will you!* ● **Lay off**   V+ADV
means almost the same as **leave off.**

leave out. 1 If you **leave** someone or something **out,** you do not   V+N+ADV,
include them in an activity or group. EG *One or two scenes in the*   V+ADV+N,
play were left out of the performance... I'm aware that we've had to   V+PRON+ADV:
   ALSO+of

leave out much interesting and important work... 'I shan't be avail-able' said our host, 'so you will have to leave me out.'

2 If you tell someone to **leave** it **out**, you are telling them that you do not believe what they are saying; used in informal British English.   V+*it*+ADV

leave over. If something such as money or food is **left over**, it remains when the rest has been taken away or used. EG *'What's left over then Tony?'—'About forty-five pence.'... Mothers and children usually get what is left over.* ▶ A **leftover** is something that belongs to a past period of time and surprisingly still exists, although most other things of that period no longer do. EG *...a leftover from our hunting past.* ▶ **Leftovers** are the food that remains uneaten after a meal. EG *The leftovers were thrown to the village dogs.* ▶ **Leftover** is used to describe an amount of something that remains after you have finished using it. EG *...a bottle of left-over perfume.*   PASSIVE: V+ADV   N COUNT   N PLURAL   ADJECTIVE

lend, lends, lending, lent

lend out. If you **lend** something **out,** you allow someone to borrow it for a particular period of time. EG *She had lent out her camera and never got it back... Sorry, that book's been lent out.*   V+ADV+N, V+N+ADV, V+PRON+ADV

let, lets, letting

The form **let** is used in the present tense and is the past tense and past participle of the verb.

let down. **1** If someone or something **lets** you **down,** they fail to do something that you have been relying on them to do. EG *He would never let a mate down... Charlie's never let me down yet.... You're so silly. You regularly let yourself down, don't you?... It would be best to run away now but she could not let down Jimmie: he needed help.*   V+N+ADV, V+PRON+ADV, V+REFL+ADV, V+ADV+N

▶ If you say that something is a **letdown,** you mean that it is disappointing. EG *For the visitor expecting something special, it is a bit of a let-down.*   N COUNT

2 If you **let down** something that is filled with air, such as a tyre, you allow air to escape from it. EG *June said, 'I dare you to go in and let down the tyres.'* ● **Deflate** is a more formal word for **let down.**   V+ADV+N, V+N+ADV, V+PRON+ADV

3 If you **let down** a garment such as a dress, skirt, or pair of trousers, you undo the hem at the bottom and sew it up again in a different place to make the garment longer. ● **Lengthen** means almost the same as **let down.**   V+ADV+N, V+N+ADV, V+PRON+ADV

let in. **1** If you **let** someone **in,** you allow them to come into a place, usually by opening the door for them. EG *Go and let them in, Howard... Lock the door and don't let anyone in... Evidently she had let herself in with a front-door key.* ● **Admit** is a more formal word for **let in.**   V+PRON+ADV, V+N+ADV, V+REFL+ADV, V+ADV+N

2 If something **lets in** water, mud, air, or light, it has a hole or crack which allows the water, mud, air, or light to get into it. EG *My old boots had been letting in water... I jump out of bed and pull up the shade and let all that sunlight in... Punch two holes, one to let the milk out, the other to let air in.*   V+ADV+N, V+N+ADV, V+PRON+ADV: NO PASSIVE

3 An **inlet** is a narrow strip of water which goes from a sea or lake into the land or between two islands. EG *The inlet was a cleft in the gorge, open on both sides.*   N COUNT

let in for. If you **let** someone **in for** something, you involve them in something that causes them difficulty, unpleasantness, or unneces-sary expense; an informal expression. EG *You don't realize, darling, what you've let me in for... We stood in front of that awful hotel and thought, what have we let ourselves in for?*   V+PRON+ADV+PREP, V+REFL+ADV+PREP, V+N+ADV+PREP

let in on. If you **let** someone **in on** something that is secret or not generally known, you tell them about it or allow them to become   V+N+ADV+PREP, V+PRON+ADV+PREP involved; an informal expression. EG *He didn't let Uncle Harold in on the news... They are going to let all of us in on their little secret.*

let into. 1 If you **let** someone **into** a building or room, you allow them to go into it, especially by opening the door for them. EG *Mr Thomas had let him into the church with the spare key... Irene Cameron let herself into Griffiths's flat at about mid-day... You let a boy like that into your house!... Then I was let into the inner office.* `V+PRON+PREP, V+REFL+PREP, V+N+PREP`

2 If you **let** someone **into** a secret or your confidence, you allow them to know something that you have not told anyone else. EG *They agreed to let him into their secret... No one else can be let into this plan.* ● **Let in on** means almost the same as **let into.** `V+PRON+PREP, V+N+PREP`

3 If something **has been let into** a surface, it has been fixed into a hollow or hole in the surface so that it does not stick out. EG *...around the places where the hot water radiators were let into the floor... She adjusted the lace front let into her dress.* ● **Set into** means almost the same as **let into.** `V+N+PREP, V+PRON+PREP: USUALLY PASSIVE`

let off. 1 If you **let** someone **off** a job or task that they should be doing, you say that they need not do it. EG *They tried to get the teacher to let them off homework... He believes that if he works all day he should be let off domestic chores.* `V+PRON+PREP, V+N+PREP, V+N+ADV, V+PRON+ADV`

2 If you **let** someone **off,** you give them a lighter punishment than was expected or no punishment at all. EG *He let me off with a reprimand... They'll tell you to be more careful next time and let you off... It never occurred to me to ask to be let off.* `V+PRON+ADV, V+N+ADV, V+ADV+N: ALSO+with`

3 If you **let off** a gun, a bomb, or a firework, you fire it or cause it to explode. EG *His hearing is so poor that you could let off a gun within inches of him and he wouldn't flinch... I paid for those rockets and I'm going to let them off.* `V+ADV+N, V+PRON+ADV, V+N+ADV`

4 If something or someone **lets off** a sound or energy, they suddenly make the sound or release the energy. EG *Just then my kettle let off a shrill whistle... Malcolm's cot squeaked as he jumped spiritedly up and down, letting off the final ounce or two of energy.* `V+ADV+N`

5 If someone **lets off,** they release air from their anus; a very informal or rude use. `V+ADV`

6 If the driver of a vehicle **lets** someone **off,** he or she stops to allow that person to get out of the vehicle. EG *We drove home slowly. He stopped in front of the porch to let me off.* `V+PRON+ADV, V+N+ADV, V+ADV+N`

let on. If you **let on** about something, you tell someone about something that was intended to be kept secret, or express an emotion that you wanted to hide; an informal expression. EG *Don't let on we went to that dance... 'Oh,' Jules said. He didn't let on that he knew the whole story... Mary was shaken by the news, I could tell, although she didn't let on in the tone of her response.* `V+ADV, V+ADV+REPORT`

let out. 1 If you **let** someone **out,** you allow them to leave a place, especially by opening or unlocking a door. EG *The other prisoners were locked into their cells before I was let out of mine... I began to long to be released. 'Please let me out,' I kept pleading with the doctors... If I'm still asleep in the morning, just let yourself out.* `V+N+ADV, V+PRON+ADV, V+REFL+ADV, V+ADV+N`

2 To **let out** something such as water, air, or breath means to allow it to flow out freely. EG *He let the water out and refilled the bath with cold water... Piggy let out his breath with a gasp.* ▶ An **outlet** is a hole or pipe through which water or air can flow out. EG *Clean the sink outlet.* `V+N+ADV, V+ADV+N, V+PRON+ADV` `N COUNT`

3 If you **let out** a particular sound, you make that sound; a formal or literary use. EG *He had slipped and fallen on the uneven ground and was letting out loud uncontrolled shrieks and wails... The dogs picked up a scent and broke into a fast run, letting out excited* `V+ADV+N: NO PASSIVE`

yelps... Montclair let out a low whistle. ● **Emit** is a more formal word for **let out.**

4 If you **let** something **out,** you say something that you should have kept secret. EG *'She's gone to buy a paper.' As soon as I said this I cursed myself for letting it out.* ▸ An **outlet is** a means of expressing and releasing emotions, feelings, or ideas which you have inside you. EG *...outlets for political expression.*

V+PRON+ADV,
V+N+ADV,
V+ADV+N

N COUNT

5 If you **let out** a house, room, or flat, you make it available for people to rent. EG *My father owned two houses which he let out as rooms to his friends... Rents received from letting out your home are liable to tax.* ● **Rent out** means almost the same as **let out.**

V+ADV+N,
V+N+ADV,
V+PRON+ADV

6 If you **let out** a garment such as a dress or pair of trousers, you make it larger by undoing the seams and sewing closer to the edge of the material. EG *I'll have to let this dress out a bit before the wedding next week.* ● **Take in** means almost the same as **let out.**

V+ADV+N,
V+N+ADV,
V+PRON+ADV

7 If something **lets** you **out,** it frees you from getting involved in a difficult or unpleasant situation; an informal use. EG *'What now?'—'Recorders, I think.'—'Well, that lets me out, anyway. I can't play them.'... Mark Rutland's suggestion had let me out nicely.* ▸ A **let-out** is something that allows you to avoid an unpleasant or difficult situation. EG *There are a few let-outs from this impossible situation.*

V+PRON+ADV,
V+N+ADV :
NO PASSIVE

N COUNT

8 An **outlet is** a shop or organization which sells the goods made by a particular manufacturer. EG *Several commercial outlets had already expressed an interest.*

N COUNT

let through. To let someone or something **through** means to allow them to pass a control point or move through something that is blocking the way. EG *To my astonishment, the group opened up politely and let us through... Police at the entrance refused to let me through... It was raining heavily and I guessed that the skylight would be letting through a regular steady trickle into my classroom.*

V+PRON+ADV,
V+ADV+N,
V+N+ADV :
NO PASSIVE

let up. If something **lets up,** it stops or becomes less in degree or intensity. EG *Day followed day and still the heat did not let up... We thought that the rain would probably let up after a while.* ● **Ease off** means almost the same as **let up.** ▸ If there is a **let-up,** the degree or intensity of something becomes less. EG *There was a noticeable let-up of police violence in the community.*

V+ADV

N COUNT

level, levels, levelling, levelled

American English uses the spellings **leveling** and **leveled.**

level against. See **level at.**

level at. If you **level** a criticism or accusation at or **against** someone, you criticize or accuse them. EG *...accusations which he could have levelled against Christopher... This criticism has been levelled at the government... A number of unfriendly glances were levelled at him.*

V+N+PREP,
V+PRON+PREP

level off. 1 If something that is increasing, decreasing, or developing **levels off** or **out,** it stops changing or developing and stays at the point it has reached. EG *Economic growth has almost certainly started to level off... This growth in demand for fossil fuels levelled off after 1973... The population will probably reach 320 millions before levelling out.* ● **Stabilize** means almost the same as **level off.**

V+ADV

2 If you **level** a surface **off** or **level** it **out,** you make it flat by smoothing or cutting off any lumps or bumps. EG *Fill the scoop with the powder and level it off with a knife... Using a smooth stone, he levelled off the mound into a plate-sized disk... A scraper can be used for levelling out small humps of earth.*

V+PRON+ADV,
V+ADV+N,
V+N+ADV

3 If an aircraft or boat **levels off** or **out,** it travels horizontally after

V+ADV

travelling upwards or downwards. EG *The planes levelled off at 20,000 feet and headed north... The boat angled slightly upwards and levelled off.*

level out. See level off.

level up. To **level** things **up** means to make them more equal by adjusting the position or standard of one or more of them. EG *Their lead was lost in the next match when New Zealand's historic win levelled things up.* ● **Even up** means almost the same as **level up.**   V+N+ADV, V+PRON+ADV, V+ADV+N

level with. If you **level with** someone, you tell them the truth and do not keep anything secret; an informal expression. EG *You're not levelling with me... I've always levelled with you, haven't I, Sam?*   V+PREP

lick, licks, licking, licked

lick up. If you **lick** something **up,** you remove it from a surface, using your tongue. EG *I could lick up the sauce while no-one was watching... It licks up the insects with its long tongue.*   V+ADV+N, V+N+ADV, V+PRON+ADV

lie, lies, lying, lay, lain

lie about. 1 If someone **lies about, around,** or **round,** they spend their time relaxing and being lazy; used in informal English. EG *They were lying about in the doorways... Afterward seven of us lay around on the living room floor, smoking... People lay around in the sun, mostly undressed, playing instruments.* ● **Lounge about** means almost the same as **lie about.**   V+ADV, V+PREP

2 If things are left **lying about, around** or **round,** they are left somewhere, especially in an untidy way. EG *...an old boot which some fool had carelessly left lying about... Do you have any money you don't want to leave lying around the house?... A sheet of paper could lie around for centuries without being burnt.* ● **Kick about** means almost the same as **lie about.**   V+ADV, V+PREP

lie around. See lie about.

lie back. If you **lie back,** you move from a sitting position into a horizontal position by lowering your head and shoulders backwards until you are lying on your back. EG *Now lie back and relax.*   V+ADV

lie before. If something **lies before** you, you will have to do it or experience it in the future; a fairly formal expression. EG *...the only choice that lies before him... Endless hours of pleasure lie before you... She is aware that a most formidable task lies before her.*   V+PREP

lie behind. The thing that **lies behind** a situation or event is the reason or explanation for it. EG *It's this kind of irresponsibility that lay behind the crisis... ...the real cause that lay behind the rise in divorce.* ● **Underlie** means almost the same as **lie behind.**   V+PREP

lie down. When you **lie down,** you move into a horizontal position, usually in order to rest or sleep. EG *I helped her to lie down again... We lay down side by side... Go and lie down on your bed.* ▶ If you have a **lie-down,** you lie down on a bed and have a short rest; an informal word. EG *I think I'll go and have a lie-down for a while.*   V+ADV   N SING

lie in. If you **lie in,** you intentionally stay in bed later than usual in the morning; a fairly informal expression. EG *I think I'll lie in tomorrow... Late evenings were no problem for him, as he could lie in till late morning.* ▶ If you have a **lie-in,** you stay in bed later than usual in the morning to have a rest or because you are feeling lazy; an informal word. EG *The meeting's not until ten o'clock, so I can have a lie-in.*   V+ADV   N SING

lie round. See lie about.

lie up. If you **lie up** somewhere, you go there to hide or rest for a   v+ADV
while. EG *The best thing to do would be to make for the cave. He
could lie up there safely... Small infantry detachments were still
lying up in hilly country, waiting for the weather to change.*

lie with. 1 If a duty, fault, or choice **lies with** someone, it is their   v+PREP
responsibility or choice; a formal use. EG *Are you saying that the
fault generally lies with the management?... Responsibility, they
implied, lay with the owners... So, in many cases, the decision lies
with the doctor... The burden of proof lies with the accuser.*
2 If one person **lies with** another person, they have sex with each   v+PREP
other; an old-fashioned or literary use.

lift, lifts, lifting, lifted

lift off. When an aircraft or rocket **lifts off**, it leaves the ground and   v+ADV
rises into the air. EG *The plane lifted off just as the ground seemed to
open to swallow it... The fish broke water a few yards from the boat,
like a rocket lifting off.* ● **Take off** means almost the same as **lift off.**
▶ **Lift-off** is the launching of a rocket into space, when it leaves the   N COUNT,
ground and rises into the air. EG *...lift-off from a floating launch pad.*   N UNCOUNT

lift up. 1 If you **lift** something **up**, you hold it in your hands or arms   V+ADV+N,
and move it upwards. EG *Stephen was attempting to lift up the two*   V+PRON+ADV,
pint tankards from the bar... He was only 5 feet 8 inches tall, but he   V+N+ADV
*would lift me up as if I was a featherweight... Hooper lifted the
bucket up on to the table.* ● **Lift** means almost the same as **lift up.**
2 If you **lift up** part of your body, you move it to a higher position. EG   V+ADV+N,
She lifted up her head to smile at him... I had to lift my tongue up so   V+N+ADV,
she could see whether I had swallowed anything. ● **Raise** means   V+PRON+ADV
almost the same as **lift up.**
3 If you **lift up** your voice, you speak or sing more loudly; a formal   V+ADV+N
or literary use. EG *It was John who lifted up his voice in answer.*
4 An **uplift** is **4.1** something which helps people to have a better life,   N UNCOUNT
for example by improving their social conditions. EG *He devoted his
life to their uplift.* **4.2** an increase in the rate or amount of   N UNCOUNT
something. EG *...the profit uplift.*

light, lights, lighting, lighted/lit

light on. See **light upon.**
light out. If you **light out**, you leave a place in a hurry; used in   v+ADV
informal American English. EG *The cats lit out and found safety on
the roof.*
light up. 1 If a source of brightness **lights up** something, it shines   V+ADV+N,
light on the whole of it, making it easy to see. EG *Above the town the*   V+PRON+ADV,
fire was still blazing, lighting up the sky... The match lit up her   V+N+ADV
*face... Someone turned his car around so that the headlights lit us
up.* ● **Illuminate** is a more formal word for **light up.**
2 If something **lights up**, a bulb inside it is turned on, making the   v+ADV
thing shine brightly. EG *A yellow arrow lights up to tell the driver
when the indicators are on... It's like a typewriter, but the letters
light up instead of going onto paper.* ▶ **Lighting-up** time is the time   ADJECTIVE
when car drivers are required by law to switch their car lights on.
3 If your face or your eyes **light up**, you suddenly look very happy or   v+ADV
excited. EG *His face lit up at the sight of Cynthia... He looked glum for
a minute; then I saw his face light up.*
4 If you **light up**, you put a match to a cigarette, cigar, or pipe and   V+ADV,
you start smoking it; a fairly informal use. EG *George lit up and*   V+ADV+N,
puffed away for a while... He paused to light up his pipe.   V+N+ADV
light upon. If you **light upon** or **on** something, you suddenly notice   V+PREP:
or find it, or it suddenly comes into your thoughts. EG *Her eyes then*   HAS PASSIVE
lit upon the piece of paper in the corner... The latter point was the

kind of thing that philosophers lighted upon. ● **Hit upon** means almost the same as **light upon**.

liken, likens, likening, likened

liken to. If you **liken** one thing or person to another, you show or suggest something about the nature and qualities of the first by comparing them to the second. EG *The pursuit of females has often been likened to a hunt... The botanist John Ray likened their taste to parsnip... ...likening her to a tuning fork.*

V+N+PREP,
V+PRON+PREP

limber, limbers, limbering, limbered

limber up. If you **limber up** just before taking part in an activity or sport, you prepare your body by doing a few exercises to make your muscles more flexible. EG *I had no time to limber up on the practice range... They were just limbering up.* ● **Loosen up** means almost the same as **limber up**.

V+ADV

line, lines, lining, lined

line up. 1 If people or things **line up** or if you **line** them **up,** they stand in a row or form a queue. EG *The children line up under the shade of a thatched roof... They lined us up and marched us off... He lined the three cartridges up on the edge of the table.*

V+ADV,
V+PRON+ADV,
V+N+ADV,
V+ADV+N:
ERGATIVE

2 A **line-up** is **2.1** a row or queue of people who are waiting for something; used especially in American English. EG *He was clearly unhappy about the length of the line-up ahead of him.* **2.2** a row of people who have been assembled in a police station. One of the people is a suspected criminal, and victims or witnesses of the crime try to identify that person; used mainly in British English.

N COUNT

N COUNT

3 If you **line** something **up,** you move it so that it is straight or in its correct position in relation to something else. EG *Adjust them so that the two are exactly lined up... The little plane's nose dipped and we lined up, poised above the landing strip... The exposure is automatic; he lines up the scene in the viewfinder and rotates the focus ring.*

V+N+ADV,
V+ADV,
V+ADV+N,
V+PRON+ADV:
ERGATIVE

4 If you **line up** something or someone in preparation for an event, you arrange for them to be ready and available for that event. EG *I had lined up a wonderful cast... A formal greeting party was lined up... It was weak stuff compared to what the Tories had lined up in their policy statement.* ● **Fix up** means almost the same as **line up**.

V+ADV+N

▸ A **line-up** is a series of things or group of people that are assembled for a particular activity or event. EG *The England line-up for the match against Poland was announced this morning.*

N COUNT

5 If you **line up** with, behind, or alongside someone, you support them. If you **line up** against them, you oppose them. EG *This gave the Revolutionary Socialists the perfect excuse to line up behind Arosemena... We can already see that the company will line up against Toyota and Nissan... Most of the others will line up with the Tattaglias.*

V+ADV:
WITH A

linger, lingers, lingering, lingered

linger on. If something or someone **lingers on,** they remain or continue to exist for a long time, especially longer than was expected. EG *Many of the old ways were dropped, but some of the habits lingered on... Tom lingered on after she had died.*

V+ADV

link, links, linking, linked

link up. 1 If you **link up** with someone, you meet them somewhere, usually before travelling on to another place with them. EG *We drove on from Florence and linked up with them in Rome.* ● **Meet up** means almost the same as **link up**.

V+ADV,
V+ADV+with:
RECIPROCAL

2 If you **link up** two items or places, you connect them to each other

V+N+ADV,

in some way. EG *This computer can be linked up to other comput-* | V+PRON+ADV,
ers... Should we be linking up with other movements in the UK? | V+ADV+N,
● **Join up** means almost the same as **link up**. ▸ A **link-up** is a | V+ADV
connection or meeting between two systems or machines. EG *...the* | N COUNT
link-up of the US Apollo and Soviet Soyuz spacecraft.

listen, listens, listening, listened

listen in. If you **listen in** to a conversation, radio programme, or | V+ADV:
other source of communication, you listen to it. EG *Do you really* | USUALLY+A
think they bother to listen in to us?... I was listening in last night.
The television was rubbish so I turned on your radio programme.

listen out for. If you **listen out for** something that you are | V+ADV+PREP
expecting to hear, you keep alert and make an effort to be ready to
hear it when it occurs. EG *Will you listen out for the car arriving?*
They should be here soon... Listen out for the signal to start.

listen to. When you **listen to** someone who is talking, or **listen to** a | V+PREP:
sound, you give your attention to them or to the sound. EG *He never* | HAS PASSIVE
listened to anyone... ...listening to Benny Goodman playing 'Paper
Doll'... Our ideas were listened to sympathetically.

live, lives, living, lived

live by. If you **live by** a particular rule, belief, or ideal, you always | V+PREP
behave in the way in which it says you should behave. EG *I know a*
man who really tries to live by the Ten Commandments... He
refuses to live by rules set up by others... How far would a Social
Democratic Government actually live by its principles and surren-
der much of its power? ● **Abide by** means almost the same as **live**
by.

live down. If you are unable to **live down** a mistake, failure, or | V+PRON+ADV,
foolish action, you are unable to make people forget that you did it. | V+ADV+N,
EG *'You'd be the laughing stock of the neighbourhood,' she said,* | V+N+ADV
'you'd never live it down.'... ...the story of a young girl who finds it
impossible to live down her past.

live for. If you **live for** a particular thing, it is the most important | V+PREP
thing in your life and you consider it as your reason for living. EG *...a*
man who lived for pleasure... She really lives for her work... He was
a great cricketer: he lived for it... ...people fighting off despair, with
really nothing to live for.

live in. 1 If someone such as a servant or student **lives in,** they sleep | V+ADV
and eat in the place where they work or study. EG *Would you be*
prepared to live in?... Members of staff and some senior postgradu-
ates live in as tutors to keep an eye on the welfare of students.
▸ **Live-in** servants or workers sleep and eat in the place where they | ADJECTIVE
work. EG *Martha was the live-in maid who kept house and cooked.*
▸ A **live-in** boyfriend or girlfriend lives in the same house as the | ADJECTIVE
person they are having a sexual relationship with. EG *She has a*
demanding job and a live-in unemployed boyfriend.
2 If a building or room looks **lived-in,** it looks comfortable and | ADJECTIVE
welcoming but perhaps rather untidy because it is used often. EG *His*
bedroom had a lived-in look.

live off. 1 If you **live off** another person or a particular source of | V+PREP
money, that is where you get the money that you need. EG *They*
continued to live off the rents of their farms, as they always had
done... Roland had not worked for two months when I met him, and
had been living off savings accumulated in the previous season.
2 If you **live off** a particular kind of food, it is the only kind of food | V+PREP
you eat, usually because this is all that is available. EG *He'd been*
living off pork pies since Monday... Dadda would catch fish and we

used to live off fish and scones and sweet potatoes. ● **Live on** means almost the same as **live off**.

live on. 1 If you **live on** a particular amount of money, you have that   v+prep
amount of money to buy things. eg *How do you expect me to live on £150 a year?... I don't have enough to live on... Up to now John and I had both been living on what was left of his money.*

2 If you **live on** a particular kind of food, it is the only kind of food   v+prep
you eat, usually because this is all that is available. eg *She lived on berries and wild herbs... ...the growing army of young workers who were living on peanut butter sandwiches.* ● **Live off** means almost the same as **live on**.

3 If someone or something **lives on**, they continue to exist or live. eg   v+adv
She lives on, crippled as before, but happy now... The Marilyn Monroe legend lives on in Hollywood... The tradition lives on, handed down from generation to generation... In Brazil and Guiana, African culture lived on, though not unchanged.

live out. 1 If you **live out** a particular set of things that you are fated   v+adv+n:
or intended to do, you actually do them; a formal use. eg *Each of us*   NO PASSIVE
lives out our destiny... ...allowing children to live out their natural interests. ● **Fulfil** is a more formal word for **live out**.

2 If you **live out** your life in a particular place or in particular   v+adv+n:
circumstances, you remain in that place or in those circumstances   USUALLY+A
until the end of your life. eg *He lived out the remaining 56 years of his life in London.*

live through. If you **live through** a difficult or dramatic event or   v+prep:
change, you experience it and survive it. eg *You've got to have*   HAS PASSIVE
courage to live through something like that... ...providing sufficient help to enable the children to live through the family breakup... This was essentially a period to be lived through. ● **Endure** is a more formal word for **live through**.

live together. 1 If two people **live together**, they share the same   v+adv
house and have a sexual relationship but are not married to one another. eg *Increasing numbers of young people choose to live together rather than to marry.* ● **Cohabit** is a formal word for **live together**.

2 You can also say that people **live together** when they live in the   v+adv
same house. eg *...groups of students living together.*

live up. If you **live** it **up**, you have a very enjoyable and exciting   v+it+adv
time, usually spending a lot of money and doing all the things that you want to do. eg *Next week we report to camp. We're going to live it up meanwhile... We spent a week living it up in the luxury of the Intercontinental Hotel... We had little chance of living it up on our meagre expense accounts.*

live up to. If someone or something **lives up to** people's expecta-   v+adv+prep:
tions, they are as good as they were expected to be. eg *The film*   HAS PASSIVE
didn't live up to my expectations... She succeeded, to my mind, in living up to her extraordinary reputation. ● **Match up to** means almost the same as **live up to**.

live with. 1 If you **live with** someone, you live in the same house as   v+prep
them. eg *He lived with his mother until he was thirty-seven.*

2 You can also say that you **live with** someone when you share a   v+prep
house with them and have a sexual relationship with them but are not married to them. eg *The social security found she was living with a man... She's living with somebody now.*

3 If you have to **live with** an unpleasant or unwelcome situation, you   v+prep:
have to accept it and carry on with your life or work. eg *They have*   HAS PASSIVE
to live with the consequences of their decision... The job involved a lot of stress and pressure, but you learnt to live with it... The fear of

death is something that has to be lived with. ● **Put up with** is a more informal expression for **live with**.

liven, livens, livening, livened

liven up. 1 If something **livens up** a place or event, or if it **livens up**, it becomes more interesting and exciting. EG *...arranging events that help to liven up the community... There are lots of new shops and things. The place is really livening up.*

V+ADV+N,
V+N+ADV,
V+PRON+ADV,
V+ADV:
ERGATIVE

2 If something **livens** you **up**, or if you **liven up**, you become more cheerful and energetic. EG *At least the incident had livened her up... Jane livened up then.* ● **Perk up** means almost the same as **liven up**.

V+PRON+ADV,
V+N+ADV,
V+ADV:
ERGATIVE

load, loads, loading, loaded

load down. 1 If you **load** someone **down** with things, you give them a large number of things to carry or hold. EG *She loaded her daughter down with packages... ...loaded down with two reels of cable and several field phones.*

V+N+ADV,
V+PRON+ADV,
V+ADV+N,
USUALLY+with

2 If you **are loaded down** with work or responsibilities, you have more than you can reasonably manage. EG *I'm loaded down with work at the moment.* ● **Be snowed under** means almost the same as **be loaded down**.

PASSIVE:
V+ADV,
USUALLY+with

load up. If you **load up** a vehicle or animal with things, or if you **load** things **up**, you put them into the vehicle or onto the animal, so that they can be taken somewhere. EG *They helped us load up the mule wagons with fresh meat and vegetables... Load up the dirty dishes first of all... I usually took off my coat while I was loading up.*

V+ADV+N,
V+N+ADV,
V+PRON+ADV,
V+ADV

loaf, loafs, loafing, loafed

loaf about. If you **loaf about, around** or **round**, you spend your time being lazy and doing nothing that requires effort or hard work. EG *She just loafed about for three years... We loafed around all morning.* ● **Laze about** means almost the same as **loaf about**.

V+ADV,
V+PREP

loaf around. See loaf about.

loaf round. See loaf about.

loan, loans, loaning, loaned

loan out. If you **loan** something **out**, you allow someone to borrow it for a particular period of time. EG *It serves you right for loaning your car out... The team were unable to loan out a replacement.*

V+N+ADV,
V+ADV+N,
V+PRON+ADV

lock, locks, locking, locked

lock away. 1 If you **lock** something **away**, you put it in something such as a safe, cupboard, or drawer, which you lock so that no-one else can get it. EG *He switched off the heating and locked away the food whenever he left the house... We should be able to function as a group without having to lock stuff away... Everything of value must be locked away.* ● **Shut away** means almost the same as **lock away**.

V+ADV+N,
V+N+ADV,
V+PRON+ADV

2 To **lock** someone **away** means to put them into prison or a special psychiatric hospital. EG *Her political activities had got her dismissed, then locked away.* ● **Lock up** means almost the same as **lock away**.

V+N+ADV,
V+PRON+ADV,
V+ADV+N

3 If you **are locked away** or you **lock** yourself **away** somewhere, you go there to be away from other people because you do not want to be disturbed. EG *She locked herself away in her room and wouldn't come out... When I was finishing my thesis I was locked away in my office for weeks.* ● **Shut away** means almost the same as **lock away**.

V+REFL+ADV:
ALSO PASSIVE:
V+ADV

4 If someone **locks** information **away**, they prevent it from becoming generally known. EG *...a report which the government preferred to keep locked away: but the union felt the public were entitled to know the truth.* ● **Suppress** is a more formal word for **lock away**.

V+N+ADV,
V+PRON+ADV,
V+ADV+N

lock in. If you **lock** someone **in**, you put them in a room or a

V+PRON+ADV,

building and lock the door so that they cannot get out. EG *After they* `V+N+ADV,`
had locked me in, the officer in charge came to see me... Tusker had `V+ADV+N`
dragged Bloxsaw into the garage and locked him in... The prisoners
were not locked in.

lock out. 1 If you **lock** someone **out** of a place, you prevent them `V+PRON+ADV,` `V+N+ADV,` `V+ADV+N`
from entering it by locking the doors. EG *One November night he*
locked her out of the house... One member of the delegation locked
another out of the room they shared... I went to Renata's apartment
for dinner one night and found myself locked out.

2 If you **lock** yourself **out** of a place, you go out of a door which locks `V+REFL+ADV:` `ALSO+of`
automatically, forgetting to take the keys, with the result that you
cannot get inside again. EG *I went to empty the bins and found that*
I'd locked myself out... I've locked myself out of the car again!

3 In an industrial dispute, if the management of a place of work `V+PRON+ADV,` `V+N+ADV,` `V+ADV+N`
locks out the workers, it closes the factory or office and prevents
the workers from coming in, because the workers refuse to accept
the management's proposals. EG *The miners refused; the owners*
then locked them out... Cigar workers were locked out in industrial
disputes. ▷ A **lockout** is a situation in which the management of a `N COUNT`
place of work closes it and prevents the workers from coming in
until they accept the management's proposals. EG *The Court can now*
grant an injunction to stop a strike or lockout.

lock up. 1 To **lock** someone **up** means to put them in prison or a `V+PRON+ADV,` `V+N+ADV,` `V+ADV+N`
special psychiatric hospital. EG *They locked him up as a madman...*
The idea of being locked up in jail filled her with horror. ● **Lock**
away means almost the same as **lock up.** ▷ A **lockup** is a jail or a `N COUNT`
cell in a police station; an informal word used in American English.
EG *They hustled him off and put him in the lockup.*

2 When you **lock up** or **lock** a house or building **up,** you make sure `V+ADV,` `V+PRON+ADV,` `V+N+ADV,` `V+ADV+N`
that all the doors and windows are properly closed or locked so that
burglars cannot get in. EG *I was waiting for him to leave so that I*
could lock up... He shall leave the house and lock it up for seven
days. ▷ A **lock-up** shop or garage is one that is available for rent. EG `ADJECTIVE`
The lease was for a lock-up shop on Kingsbury Road... ...a row of
lock-up garages.

3 If something is **locked up** in a particular place or state, it is in that `V+N+ADV,` `V+PRON+ADV,` `V+ADV+N:` `USUALLY PASSIVE`
place or state and cannot easily be taken out, used, or changed. EG *So*
much water locked up in the ice caps caused a lowering of the sea
level... The majority of the money required is locked up in the costs
of raw materials.

log, logs, logging, logged

log in. When someone who is using a computer **logs in** or **logs on,** `V+ADV`
they gain access to the system, usually by keying a special word.
● **Log out** means the opposite of **log in.**

log into. When someone **logs into** a computer system, they gain `V+PREP`
access to the system, usually by keying a special word.

log off. See **log out.**

log on. See **log in.**

log out. When someone **logs out,** they finish using a computer `V+ADV`
system by keying a special word. ● **Log in** means the opposite of **log**
out.

loll, lolls, lolling, lolled

loll about. If you **loll about,** **around** or **round** somewhere, you lie or `V+ADV,` `V+PREP`
stay there in a lazy way, doing nothing in particular. EG *He kept*
saying he should be at home and not lolling about in the summer
sun... ...walking up hills, taking photographs, and generally lolling

around... *They lolled about the place.* ● **Loaf about** means almost the same as **loll about.**
loll around. See **loll about.**
loll round. See **loll about.**

long, longs, longing, longed

long for. If you **long for** something, you want it very much. EG *I longed for a change of scenery... ...refugees longing for their homeland.* ▸ A **longed-for** thing or event is one that someone wants very much. EG *At last the longed-for refreshment arrived.*   V+PREP: HAS PASSIVE   ADJECTIVE

look, looks, looking, looked

look after. 1 If you **look after** someone or something, you take care of them and do what is necessary for them to stay in good condition. EG *Does your husband accept that he ought to be looking after the baby?... Look after my garden... She wasn't being well looked after at all.*   V+PREP: HAS PASSIVE

2 If you **look after** something, you are responsible for it and deal with it. EG *Do you think Walker should stay there all the time to look after things?... The duty of the local authority is to look after the interests of local people... Ventilation and drainage problems are often looked after by semi-qualified staff.* ● **Attend to** is a more formal expression for **look after.**   V+PREP: HAS PASSIVE

3 If you **look after** something that belongs to someone else, you take charge of it for them so that you can prevent it from being lost or damaged. EG *Will you look after my money for me while I go swimming?.*   V+PREP: HAS PASSIVE

4 If you say that you can **look after** yourself, you mean that you are able to avoid being harmed or cheated by other people.   V+PREP+REFL

look ahead. If you **look ahead,** you think about what is going to happen in the future and perhaps make plans. EG *We're trying to look ahead... ...if we look ahead and project existing trends ten years forward... You'll need to look ahead four or five years.*   V+ADV

look around. See **look round.**

look at. 1 If you **look at** something, you turn your eyes towards it so that you can see it. EG *She looks at him and smiles faintly... ...looking at a picture.*   V+PREP: HAS PASSIVE

2 If you **look at** a book, newspaper, or piece of writing, you read it, or parts of it, fairly quickly and not very thoroughly. EG *I've looked at your essay and I think it's very good.* ● **Look through** means almost the same as **look at.**   V+PREP: HAS PASSIVE

3 If an expert **looks at** something, they examine it and decide how it should be dealt with. EG *That leg's a bit swollen. I'd like Doctor Wells to look at it... Their mouths are forced open for their teeth and their throats to be looked at.*   V+PREP: HAS PASSIVE

4 If you **look at** a subject, problem or situation, you think carefully about it or study it. EG *Bowlby looked at children in institutions and claimed that they suffered no deprivation at all... However, there is one further category of evidence to be looked at.*   V+PREP: HAS PASSIVE

5 If you **look at** a situation in a particular way, you judge it or consider it in that way. EG *If you're a Democrat, you look at things one way, and if you're a Republican you look at them in a very different way... Look at it my way... If life had to be looked at in terms of high moments, or peaks, then nothing had happened.* ● **See** means almost the same as **look at.**   V+PREP: HAS PASSIVE

look away. If you **look away** from something, you turn your eyes away from it so that you can no longer see it. EG *Their eyes met and Ida blushed and looked away... It looked up at Mrs Bixby with bright yellow eyes, then looked away again and carried on eating.*   V+ADV

look back. 1 If you **look back,** you turn to see what is behind you. EG *Jack turned and looked back at Ralph... I looked back and saw my car moving slowly down the hill.*   V+ADV

2 If you **look back** on something, you think about something that happened in the past. EG *It all seems very pathetic when I look back, but it was painful enough at the time... The past always seems better when you look back on it... ...when I look back upon my life.*   V+ADV: ALSO+*on/upon*

look down. If you **look down,** you lower your eyes to see what is below. EG *The man looked down at his shaking legs... He paused on the narrow ledge and looked down.*   V+ADV

look down on. If you **look down on** someone or something, you think they are inferior or unimportant. EG *The farm labourer used to be looked down on... They are arrogant and aggressive people. They look down on us... Why do the English look down on everything foreign?* ● **Despise** means almost the same as **look down on.**   V+ADV+PREP: HAS PASSIVE

look for. 1 If you **are looking for** something, you are trying to find it. EG *I went to look for him there and at first could not find him... The priest had found the book he was looking for and was checking a reference... We started to look for a house with a garden.*   V+PREP

2 If you **are looking for** something such as the solution to a problem, you are trying to achieve it or think of it. EG *Britain is looking for a peaceful, diplomatic solution... What we are looking for is a firm commitment on the part of the government.* ● **Seek** is a more formal word for **look for.** ▷ **Unlooked-for** is used to describe something which you did not expect or want to happen. EG *...an unlooked-for change in the weather.*   V+PREP: HAS PASSIVE   ADJECTIVE

look forward to. If you **look forward to** something that is going to happen, you want it to happen because you expect to enjoy it. EG *I'm quite looking forward to seeing Rick again... I looked forward to leaving school... I did not look forward with any confidence to my meeting with the manager.*   V+ADV+PREP: HAS PASSIVE

look in. 1 If you **look in** on a person or **look in** at a place, you visit that person or place for a short time; used especially when your visit was not planned in advance. EG *Could I look in on Sam?... I think I'll look in on my parents on the way home from work... I'll look in at the newsagent's and pick up a paper.* ● **Drop in** and **call in** mean almost the same as **look in.**   V+ADV: USUALLY+A

2 If you are trying to take part in an activity and you do not get a **look-in,** you are unable to take part because other people are more successful or forceful than you. EG *James talks so much that all the others barely get a look-in.*   N SING

look into. If you **look into** a particular problem, subject or situation, you find out and examine the facts relating to it. EG *In 1959 a working party was set up to look into the problem... They wanted an independent financial controller to look into the city's accounts... The causes of these misunderstandings and anxieties should be looked into.* ● **Investigate** is a more formal word for **look into.**   V+PREP: HAS PASSIVE

look on. 1 If you **look on** while something happens, you watch it without taking part yourself. EG *His parents looked on with a triumphant smile as he collected his prize... Police boats appeared and sped down the river while families picnicking on the banks looked on in amazement.* ▷ **Onlookers** are the people watching an event take place, without taking part in it. EG *Reporters and on-lookers lined the fence beside the airfield... ...an accompanying ragged cheer from the crowd of onlookers.*   V+ADV   N COUNT

2 If you **look on** or **upon** something in a particular way, you think of it in that way. EG *If she went out with Mark after turning down an invitation from John, he'd look on it as the deadliest insult... Houses*   V+PREP: WITH A, HAS PASSIVE

are looked upon as investments... The nuclear powers would not look kindly upon such a development.

look out. 1 You say or shout **'look out'** to warn someone that they are in danger. EG *'Look out,' I said. 'There's someone coming.'* IMPERATIVE: V+ADV

● **Watch out** means almost the same as **look out.** ▶ A **lookout** is a place that is quite high up, from which someone can watch the area around them to see what is happening and to watch for any danger. N COUNT

▶ A **lookout** is also someone who is watching for danger. EG *Two of the burglars were tipped off by a lookout and escaped.* N COUNT

2 If you **look out** something that is stored away, you search for it, find it and take it out. EG *I had looked out my register and red and blue pens for marking it... Let me have a note saying what you want, and we'll look it out.* ● **Dig out** means almost the same as **look out.** V+ADV+N, V+PRON+ADV, V+N+ADV: NO PASSIVE

look out for. 1 If you **look out for** something that you want or expect, you pay attention to things around you so that you notice it and can take action when it occurs or is there. EG *It's a film we shall look out for in the next couple of months... 'It's worth a visit if you're interested.'—'Thank you. I'll look out for it.'... They have little or no idea of what hazards to look out for.* ● **Watch out for** means almost the same as **look out for.** V+ADV+PREP: HAS PASSIVE

2 If you **look out for** yourself or **look out for** your own interests, you make sure that you have all the advantages possible and that you protect yourself from danger. EG *As for the girl, she had to start looking out for herself one day... No! It means we all look out for each other in the family.* V+ADV+PREP

look over. If you **look** something or someone **over,** you examine or inspect them in order to get a general idea of what they are like. EG *Sometimes he would look over the article I had written, shrug, and tear it up... If you're worried, get the vet to look it over.* V+ADV+N, V+PRON+ADV, V+N+ADV

look round. 1 If you **look round** or **around,** 1.1 you turn to look at something behind you. EG *He stopped suddenly and looked round.* 1.2 you look in various directions to find something, or to see what is there. EG *He looked round again for a chair and, since there wasn't one, sat on the floor... 'What's the general feeling?' He looked round at the company.* V+ADV

V+ADV, V+PREP

2 If you **look round** a building or place, you walk round it and look at the different parts of it to see what it is like. EG *Shall we look round the Cathedral this afternoon?... We began to look round the schoolroom with nostalgia.* ● **Go round** means almost the same as **look round.** V+PREP, V+ADV

3 If you **are looking round** for something, you try to find it by making general enquiries or trying various different things, usually over a period of time. EG *Tell me when you decide to give up. Then I can look round for somebody who'd like the job!... Their group split up, and those that were left looked round for other amusement.* V+ADV: USUALLY+for

look through. 1 If you **look through** something such as a window or a doorway, you turn your eyes in that direction to see what is on the other side of it. EG *Michael looked through the window down into the street... The skipper looked through his binoculars at the long column of ships... She looked through to the garden.* V+PREP, V+ADV

2 If you **look through** a group of things or you **look through** a place such as a cupboard, box, or room, you examine all the things there, usually because you are trying to find something. EG *He looked through the clothing on the bed... They'll look through the applications and pick out the ones that seem promising... Did you look through all your drawers, darling, and cupboards?... Finally, having nothing else to do, I looked through the bookshelves.* ● **Go through** means almost the same as **look through.** V+PREP: HAS PASSIVE

3 If you **look through** something that has been written or printed, you read it, usually fairly quickly and briefly. EG *If you have revision notes you may find it helpful to look through them on the morning of the examination... He looked through the timetable. Yes, the Lima flight left at 10.00h.*   V+PREP: HAS PASSIVE

4 If someone **looks through** another person, they look at that person without showing that they have seen them or recognized them, for example because they are angry or deep in thought. EG *They looked straight through him.*   V+PREP

look to. **1** If you **look to** someone or something for something such as help or advice, you rely on them to provide it. EG *We should look to the economists for advice on how to overcome inflation... They look to others to structure time for them... People look to education to bring this about.* • **Turn to** means almost the same as **look to.**   V+PREP: HAS PASSIVE, WITH *for* OR *to* -INF

2 If you **look to** something, you make sure that you maintain it in good condition and that it is not neglected; a formal use. EG *They must look to their defences... Look to your health.* • **Attend to** means almost the same as **look to.**   V+PREP

3 If you **look to** something that will happen in the future, you think about it, often with a particular emotion. EG *Some New Englanders look to the future with a certain anxiety.*   V+PREP: USUALLY+A

look up. **1** If you **look up**, you raise your eyes to see what is above. EG *As he heard the one-word message that followed, he looked up in disbelief... I suddenly looked up and saw Mark Rutland watching me... She only grunted, not even looking up from her work.*   V+ADV

2 If you **look up** a piece of information in a book, or on a timetable or map, you look there to find the information. EG *He consulted his dictionary to look up the meaning of the word 'apotheosis'... Look up the address of the nearest children's clinic... Lally said it would help me with my geography if I went and looked it up on a map.*   V+ADV+N, V+PRON+ADV, V+N+ADV: USUALLY+A

3 If you **look** someone **up** or **look up** a place where you used to go, you visit the person or place after not having seen them for a long time. EG *Look me up when you're next in the area... She did not look me up even when her husband lost all his money and deserted her... We walked to the South Strand district to look up old haunts.*   V+PRON+ADV, V+ADV+N, V+N+ADV

4 If a situation **is looking up**, it is improving; a fairly informal use. EG *That summer of 1962, things were at last looking up in Boston.*   V+ADV

look upon. See **look on: look upon** is slightly more formal.

look up to. If you **look up to** someone, you respect and admire them. EG *She looks up to her father... The students look up to you and admire you.*   V+ADV+PREP: HAS PASSIVE

loom, looms, looming, loomed

loom ahead. If a dangerous or unpleasant situation **looms ahead,** it is approaching and is likely to happen quite soon. EG *If car production continues at its present rate, bottlenecks and virtual exhaustion loom ahead... She saw her great choice looming ahead.*   V+ADV

loom up. If something **looms up,** it appears as a large, unclear shape, often in a way that seems frightening or threatening. EG *...a huge Victorian edifice that loomed up against the skyline... Cape Perpetua loomed up out of the fog.*   V+ADV: USUALLY+A

loose, looses, loosing, loosed

loose off. If you **loose off** an explosive device, you make it explode by setting light to it or firing it; used mainly in American English. EG *Adam loosed off a magnesium flare... The enemy loosed a few grenades off.*   V+ADV+N, V+N+ADV, V+PRON+ADV

loose upon. If something unpleasant is **loosed upon** a place or person, it is allowed to affect them; a formal or literary expression.   PASSIVE: V+PREP

EG ...*anarchy is loosed upon the world*... ...*the nature of the aggression being loosed upon her.*

loosen, loosens, loosening, loosened

loosen up. 1 When you **loosen up** or **loosen up** part of your body, you make your muscles more flexible and relaxed by doing exercises. EG *Swing a couple of clubs to loosen up, or do one of these exercises... If the muscles are painful, I do exercises for a few minutes to loosen them up... There is too much tension around the joints, they need loosening up.* — V+ADV, V+PRON+ADV, V+N+ADV, V+ADV+N: ERGATIVE

2 If someone who has been tense and anxious **loosens up**, they become more relaxed and more comfortable with other people. EG *Her second drink loosened her up... At first, every word had to be wrung from him; but as the day wore on, he loosened up and became more and more talkative.* — V+PRON+ADV, V+N+ADV, V+ADV: ERGATIVE

lop, lops, lopping, lopped

lop off. 1 If you **lop** something **off**, you cut it away from what it was attached to, usually with a quick, strong stroke. EG *He swung the sword, and lopped my arm off... If the tree gets too big, you could always lop off a few branches.* ● **Chop off** means almost the same as **lop off**. — V+N+ADV, V+ADV+N, V+PRON+ADV

2 If someone **lops** an amount **off** a larger quantity, they reduce the larger quantity by that amount; an informal use. EG *Moorcroft lopped six seconds off the Rono record... To get their estimate, they took the current figure and lopped off a little to allow for energy conservation.* ● **Knock off** means almost the same as **lop off**. — V+N+PREP/ADV, V+ADV+N, V+PRON+PREP/ADV

lord, lords, lording, lorded

lord over. If someone **lords** it **over** you, they act in a way that shows that they think they are better than you, for example by telling you what to do. EG *...to be able to lord it over the boy at the bottom of the class... Isn't it enough that you have brought us here? Do you also have to lord it over us?* ● **Queen over** means almost the same as **lord over**. — V+*it*+PREP

lose, loses, losing, lost

lose out. If you **lose out**, you suffer a loss or disadvantage. EG *Children who fail at school lose out in the employment race and remain in poverty... ...to ensure that the small farmer and the part-timer do not lose out.* ● **Miss out** means almost the same as **lose out**. — V+ADV: USUALLY+A

lose out to. If you **lose out to** someone else, this person is more successful than you and puts you at a disadvantage or causes you to fail. EG *Both companies are losing out to overseas competition.* — V+ADV+PREP

lounge, lounges, lounging, lounged

lounge about. If you **lounge about, around** or **round**, you spend your time in a relaxed and lazy way, doing nothing that requires any effort. EG *...people who were lounging about, apparently with nothing to do... She had seen a couple of other men lounging around the house.* ● **Loaf about** means almost the same as **lounge about**. — V+ADV, V+PREP

lounge around. See **lounge about**.
lounge round. See **lounge about**.

louse, louses, lousing, loused

louse up. To **louse** something **up**, means to spoil it or ruin it completely; an informal expression. EG *There isn't a mechanic alive who doesn't louse up a job once in a while... It could louse up your divorce petition.* ● **Foul up** means almost the same as **louse up**. — V+ADV+N, V+N+ADV, V+PRON+ADV

luck, lucks, lucking, lucked

luck out. If you **luck out**, you are fortunate or lucky in something; used in informal American English. EG *We lucked out on our connections—we had a chopper that carried us back to base.*

V+ADV:
ALSO+*on*

lumber, lumbers, lumbering, lumbered

lumber with. If you are **lumbered with** something difficult, unpleasant, or unwanted, you have to deal with it or accept it, even though you do not want to; an informal expression. EG *I can see I'm going to get lumbered with it if I'm not careful... New families were unwilling to lumber themselves with too much land.* ● **Saddle with** means almost the same as **lumber with**.

V+N+PREP,
V+REFL+PREP:
USUALLY PASSIVE

lump, lumps, lumping, lumped

lump together. If you **lump together** different things or people, you consider them in the same way or combine them into one large group. EG *She believes it is a mistake to lump all these issues together... ...pensioners, treated as children and lumped together regardless of their right to dignity or respect.*

V+N+ADV,
V+PRON+ADV,
V+ADV+N

lust, lusts, lusting, lusted

lust after. 1 If you **lust after** or **for** something, you have a very strong desire to possess it. EG *They lusted after the gold of El Dorado... She is like a child lusting for toys.* ● **Crave** means almost the same as **lust after**.

V+PREP:
HAS PASSIVE

2 If you **lust after** or **for** someone, you feel a strong sexual desire for them. EG *She had lusted after other men... How I lusted for that girl!*

V+PREP:
HAS PASSIVE

lust for. See **lust after**.

luxuriate, luxuriates, luxuriating, luxuriated

luxuriate in. If you **luxuriate in** something, you experience great pleasure from it. EG *I luxuriated in my retirement... ...Kontarsky, luxuriating in the congratulations of his superiors.*

V+PREP

M m

magic, magics, magicking, magicked

magic away. If you **magic** something **away**, you make it disappear very quickly or unexpectedly. EG *He can magic a child's tears away in no time at all... The problem was large in his life; he could not magic it away.*

V+N+ADV,
V+PRON+ADV,
V+ADV+N

major, majors, majoring, majored

major in. If you **major in** a particular subject, you study it as your main subject at university. EG *I decided to major in French... White had majored in Chinese history at Harvard.*

V+PREP

make, makes, making, made

make after. If you **make after** someone or something, you chase them. EG *They made after him in the car.*

V+PREP

make away with. 1 If you **make away with** something, you steal it and take it away with you; an informal use. EG *He's afraid someone might make away with the takings.* ● **Make off with** means almost the same as **make away with**.

V+ADV+PREP

2 If you **make away with** someone, you kill them. If you **make away**

V+ADV+PREP:
WITH REFL

with yourself, you kill yourself. ● **Do away with** means almost the
same as **make away with**.

make for. 1 If you **make for** a place, you move towards it, usually　V+PREP
rather hurriedly. EG *The best thing now would be to make for the top
of Brill Hill... I made for my corner seat and sat down gratefully.*
● **Head for** means almost the same as **make for**.

2 If something **makes for** a particular situation, that situation is　V+PREP
likely to result from it. EG *I don't know if unilateral disarmament
would make for peace or would make for war... What are the values
that make for happy family life?* ● **Produce** is a more formal word
for **make for**.

make into. 1 If you **make** one thing **into** something else, you change　V+N+PREP,
it in some way so that it becomes that other thing. EG *...a knitwear*　V+PRON+PREP
*jersey which Mary wanted to make into a short dress... They're
having two houses made into one... They tore down nearly half that
forest to make it into farmlands.* ● **Turn into** means almost the same
as **make into**.

2 If someone or something **makes** you **into** a particular type of　V+N+PREP,
person, they influence or affect you so that you become that type of　V+PRON+PREP
person. EG *I kept trying to make Benedick into more of a soldier...
The pressures we have to live with will make us into freaks.* ● **Turn
into** means almost the same as **make into**.

make of. If you ask a person what they **make of** someone or　V+PREP
something, you want to know what their impression, understanding,
or opinion of them is. EG *I wondered what they made of it all... What
are we to make of Afghanistan?... He perplexed people—they didn't
know quite what to make of him.*

make off. If you **make off**, you leave somewhere as quickly as　V+ADV
possible, often in order to escape; a fairly informal expression. EG
*The vehicle made off at once... She released the child suddenly and
he made off.*

make off with. If you **make off with** something, you steal it and　V+ADV+PREP
take it away with you; a fairly informal expression. EG *Otto made off
with the last of the brandy... The dog ran down there and tried to
make off with one of his sausages.* ● **Make away with** means almost
the same as **make off with**.

make out. 1 If you can **make** something **out**, you manage to see or　V+ADV+N,
hear it. EG *He could just make out the number plate of the car...*　V+N+ADV,
...mumbling something she couldn't quite make out... I looked in the　V+PRON+ADV:
water, and at first I could not make her out anywhere.　USUALLY+MODAL

2 If you **make out** something that is difficult to understand, you　V+ADV+*if*,
manage to understand it. EG *I can't make out if Nell likes him or*　V+ADV+WH,
not... Sylvia could not make out how it had happened... What I　V+N+ADV,
couldn't make out was your motive... This idea perplexed me so　V+PRON+ADV,
much that I stopped for a few seconds to try to make it out. ● **Work**　V+ADV+N:
out means almost the same as **make out**.　NO PASSIVE

3 If you **make out** that something is the case, you try to cause people　V+ADV:
to believe it. EG *It really is not as easy as some of them make out...*　USUALLY
People tried to make out that the play was about Britain... The other　WITH REPORT
professors make out he hasn't published enough. ● **Imply** means
almost the same as **make out**.

4 If you **make** someone **out** to be something, you give the impression　V+PRON+ADV,
that they are that sort of person. EG *I'm not the monster you'd like to*　V+REFL+ADV,
make me out to be... Men aren't as sensible as they make them-　V+N+ADV:
selves out to be... They made a minor poet out to be a major literary　WITH *to*-INF
figure.

5 If you **make out** to do something, you pretend to do it; an informal　V+ADV+*to*-INF

use. EG *He opened a drawer and made out to be looking for something in it.*

6 When you **make out** a form or cheque, you write on it all the necessary information. EG *Did you make out a receipt?... I made a cheque out for £1200... 'Who do I make it out to?'—'Hourmont Travel Limited please.'* ● **Write out** means almost the same as **make out**. `V+ADV+N, V+N+ADV, V+PRON+ADV`

7 In informal English, if you **make out,** you manage to survive or live reasonably well. EG *'How am I going to make out alone?'... They are tough youngsters. They'll make out.* ● **Cope** and **get by** mean almost the same as **make out**. `V+ADV`

make out with. If you **make out with** another person, you succeed in persuading them to have sex with you; a very informal expression. ● **Score** means almost the same as **make out with**. `V+ADV+PREP`

make over. If you **make** something **over,** you legally transfer the ownership of it from one person to another. EG *You should make the business over to me—with enough money to carry on... I was willing to make over every acre I had.* `V+N+ADV, V+PRON+ADV, V+ADV+N: USUALLY+to`

make up. 1 The people or things that **make up** something form that thing. EG *Women now make up two-fifths of the British labour force... All substances are made up of molecules... Nearly half the Congress is made up of lawyers.* ● **Comprise** is a more formal word for **make up**. ▶ The **make-up** of something is the different parts that it consists of and the way that these are arranged. EG *...the physical make-up of computers.* ▶ Someone's **make-up** is their character. EG *There are things in my make-up which do not bear close examination.* `V+ADV+N, V+PRON+ADV: ALSO PASSIVE, V+ADV+of` `N UNCOUNT` `N UNCOUNT`

2 If you **make up** something such as a story, you invent it, sometimes in order to deceive people. EG *He was a good storyteller, and used to make up tales about animals... A person wouldn't make up a story that was so easy to check... She told herself, 'Don't be stupid, you're making things up.'... He couldn't remember the full titles but I knew he wouldn't make them up.* ▶ A **made-up** story, excuse, and so on is one which has been invented and is not actually true. EG *It's all a made-up story and you know it... ...made-up reasons.* `V+ADV+N, V+N+ADV, V+PRON+ADV` `ADJECTIVE`

3 When you **make up** your mind, you decide which of a number of possible things you will have or will do. EG *He has a hard time making up his mind... I can't decide; help me make my mind up... If you don't make your mind up soon, I'll make it up for you.* `V+ADV+N, V+N+ADV, V+PRON+ADV`

4 If you **make up** an amount, you add something to it so that it is as large as it should be. EG *Put one hundred into the firm's account out of my personal account to make up the balance... It's going to be fifteen cents short, but Mr Hogganbeck will make it up... Make this liquid up to 250 ml.* `V+ADV+N, V+PRON+ADV, V+N+ADV: ALSO+to`

5 If you **make** something **up,** you prepare it so that it is ready for someone to use it or have it. EG *She told me to make a bed up in the guest bedroom... When making up meals, select a well-balanced diet... We'll wait in the parlour while you make it up.* ▶ Something that is **made-up** has already been prepared so that you do not have to make it yourself. EG *Add 1 teaspoonful white vinegar to 1 pint made-up carpet shampoo.* `V+N+ADV, V+ADV+N, V+PRON+ADV` `ADJECTIVE`

6 If you **make up,** or if you **make** yourself **up,** you put substances such as lipstick, powder, and eye-shadow on your face. EG *It was time to start making up for the evening performance... You need to wash, change that dress, and make up... She spent two hours making herself up.* ▶ If you or your face, lips, or eyes are **made-up,** you are wearing make-up. EG *...freshly made-up lips... She had magnificent eyes, heavily made-up.* ▶ **Make-up** is substances such as lipstick, powder, and eye-shadow, which women use to make themselves `V+ADV, V+REFL+ADV` `ADJECTIVE` `N UNCOUNT` look more attractive, or which actors use when they are acting. EG *...eye make-up... ...a mirror to check their make-up in.* ● **Cosmetics** is a more formal word for **make-up**.

7 If two people **make up** with each other, or **make** it **up**, they become friends again after they have had a quarrel. EG *They'd kissed and made up... They had a quarrel but later Marsha wanted to make it up... I want you to make up with her.*

V+ADV,
V+*it*+ADV,
V+ADV+*with*:
RECIPROCAL

8 If you **make** it **up** to someone, you do something to repay a favour they have done for you, or to show that you are sorry for disappointing them in some way. EG *They can make it up to the baby in other ways... Somehow, some day, he'd make it up to his father.*

V+*it*+ADV:
USUALLY+*to*

make up for. To **make up for** something that is damaged, lost, or missing means to replace it or compensate for it. EG *Massive reductions in other areas would be required to make up for the expected shortfall in revenues... She asked me questions about my interest in mathematics, as if to make up for excluding me from the conversation... She hurried on to make up for the minutes she had lost.*

V+ADV+PREP

make up to. If you **make up to** someone, you try to get them to like you by being friendly towards them, usually because you want them to give you something. EG *...politicians making up to rich businessmen... 'Do you really think I was trying to make up to him?'—'Well, it looked very much like it.'*

V+ADV+PREP

make with. If you tell someone to **make with** something, you mean that you want them to do what is necessary or appropriate at the time; an informal expression used in American English. EG *They'll make with the jokes and forget the time.*

V+PREP:
ALSO IMPERATIVE

map, maps, mapping, mapped

map out. If you **map out** a plan or a task, you work out in detail how you will do it. EG *We began to map out plans for our counter offensive... ...the course that they have mapped out for him... I have it all mapped out, you need not worry.*

V+ADV+N,
V+N+ADV,
V+PRON+ADV

mark, marks, marking, marked

mark as. Someone or something that **marks** someone **as** a particular type of person indicates that they are that type of person. EG *They put me in jail and marked me as an enemy of society... ...a degree of self-esteem which marks them as special.* ● **Label** and **mark down as** mean almost the same as **mark as**.

V+PRON+PREP,
V+N+PREP

mark down. **1** If you **mark** something **down**, you write it down. EG *I marked the number down on a scrap of paper... If you witness an accident, mark down the licence number of the car.* ● **Jot down** means almost the same as **mark down**.

V+N+ADV,
V+ADV+N,
V+PRON+ADV

2 To **mark down** the price of something means to reduce its price. EG *The prices of beer, cigarettes, and whiskey have been marked down... Trousers are marked down from £39.95 to £20.00.* ● **Reduce** means almost the same as **mark down**, and **mark up** means the opposite. ▸ A **mark-down** is a reduction in the price of something.

V+N+ADV,
V+ADV+N,
V+PRON+ADV

N COUNT

3 If a teacher **marks** a student **down**, they put a lower grade on the student's work. EG *If you miss out a comma, they mark you down on it... He got marked down because the examiner could not read his handwriting... Wrong spellings get you marked down in exams.* ● **Mark up** means almost the opposite of **mark down**.

V+PRON+ADV,
V+N+ADV,
V+ADV+N

mark down as. If you **mark** someone **down as** a particular type of person, you consider that they have qualities which make them that type of person. EG *I would have marked him down as a genius... None of the suspects had been marked down as businessmen.* ● **Mark as** means almost the same as **mark down as**.

V+PRON+ADV+PREP,
V+N+ADV+PREP

mark off. 1 If you **mark off** a piece of ground, you separate it from everything around it, usually by making a fence or some other barrier. EG *He has marked off the area with lengths of string... We now mark off certain forests to protect them.* `V+ADV+N,` `V+N+ADV,` `V+PRON+ADV`

2 If something **marks** one thing **off** from another, it makes the two things very different from one another. EG *...the personality differences that mark her off from her brother... ...physical characteristics which marked him off clearly from other men... ...someone who is not marked off by a wholly different accent or style of life.* ● **Distinguish** is a more formal word for **mark off.** `V+PRON+ADV,` `V+N+ADV,` `V+ADV+N:` `USUALLY+from`

3 If you **mark off** an item on a list, you put a line through it or next to it, to show that it has been dealt with. EG *He bought a street map of Paris, and in a small notebook marked off the places he most wanted to see... Each day was marked off with a neat X.* ● **Cross off** and **tick off** mean almost the same as **mark off.** `V+ADV+N,` `V+N+ADV,` `V+PRON+ADV`

mark out. 1 When someone **marks out** a area of land which is to be used for a particular purpose, they indicate that area by drawing special lines on the ground. EG *He marked out a football pitch on the playing field... Many athletes now use circuits marked out on grass land, or roads... The landing strip at Lukla was marked out for the pilots of incoming aircraft.* `V+ADV+N,` `V+N+ADV,` `V+PRON+ADV`

2 If a particular quality or feature **marks** a person **out,** it makes them seem noticeably different from other people. EG *There was a stillness about Ralph that marked him out... It is this latter role which marks out management in capitalist society.* ● **Distinguish** means almost the same as **mark out.** `V+PRON+ADV,` `V+ADV+N,` `V+N+ADV`

3 If you say that someone **is marked out** to achieve a particular thing, you mean that they will probably eventually achieve it. EG *Ian was always marked out to become a musician... He thought of himself as a great man, marked out by destiny for his task.* ● **Be destined** means almost the same as **be marked out.** `PASSIVE:` `V+ADV`

mark up. 1 To **mark up** the price of something means to increase its price. EG *Corporations mark up prices 1,000 per cent in order, they say, to pay for research... These have been marked up since last week.* ● **Put up** means almost the same as **mark up,** and **mark down** means the opposite. ▷ A **mark-up** is an increase in the price of something, for example the difference between its cost and the price that you sell it for. EG *The percentage mark up is calculated by the market trader's association.* `V+ADV+N,` `V+N+ADV,` `V+PRON+ADV` `N COUNT`

2 If a teacher **marks** a student **up,** they put a higher grade on the student's work. EG *...the less able child who you might mark up.* ● **Mark down** means the opposite of **mark up.** `V+N+ADV,` `V+ADV+N,` `V+PRON+ADV`

3 If you **mark up** a number or score, you count it or record it by writing it on a surface such as a wall or board so that other people can see it. EG *Mark the score up on the whiteboard... Every time a plane flew overhead, he marked it up.* `V+N+ADV,` `V+ADV+N,` `V+PRON+ADV`

marry, marries, marrying, married

marry above. If you say that someone **has married above** themselves, you mean that they have married someone who is higher than them in social rank; a formal expression. EG *She married above herself. We all thought so at the time.* `V+PREP+REFL`

marry beneath. If you say that someone **has married beneath** themselves, you mean that they have married someone who is below them in social rank; a formal expression. EG *It is the opinion of every Greek citizen that the Duke married beneath himself.* `V+PREP+REFL`

marry into. If you **marry into** a family, especially a wealthy family, `V+PREP` you marry someone in that family and so become a part of it. eg *He had visions of marrying into the family and starting an empire.*

marry off. If you **marry** someone **off**, you find a suitable person for them to marry. eg *He had ideas about marrying off his daughter to Fouad... They wanted to marry her off to this Prince.*

V+ADV+N,
V+PRON+ADV,
V+N+ADV

marry out. If someone **marries out**, they marry someone who is not of the same religion as they are; an old-fashioned expression. eg *Her father disowned her when she told him she was marrying out.*

V+ADV

marry up. If things **marry up** or if you **marry** them **up**, they are brought together. eg *A line of hairs was inserted around the hairline, and then a part-wig was made to marry up with it... A system by which parts would be flown in from the United States to marry up with equipment pre-stocked in the Federal Republic.*

V+ADV,
V+N+ADV,
V+PRON+ADV,
ALSO+with:
ERGATIVE,
RECIPROCAL

marvel, marvels, marvelling, marvelled

American English uses the spellings **marveling** and **marveled**.

marvel at. If you **marvel at** something, you are filled with surprise and admiration by it. eg *Early travellers marvelled at the riches of Mali.*

V+PREP

mash, mashes, mashing, mashed

mash up. If you **mash up** food, you crush it until it is soft and smooth in texture. eg *Mash up the strawberries and strain the pips out... When you first serve chopped vegetables to a baby, mash them up pretty fine with a fork.*

V+ADV+N,
V+PRON+ADV,
V+N+ADV

mask, masks, masking, masked

mask out. If part of a photograph is **masked out**, it is covered so that it does not appear when the photograph is printed; a technical expression. eg *Two people had been masked out.*

V+ADV+N,
V+N+ADV,
V+PRON+ADV

masquerade, masquerades, masquerading, masqueraded

masquerade as. To **masquerade as** something means to pretend to be that thing. eg *He might try to masquerade as a policeman... There were many heated little speeches from the floor masquerading as questions.*

V+PREP

match, matches, matching, matched

match against. 1 If you **match** one thing **against** another, you make the two things compete against one another to see which one is better. eg *Many amateurs were matching themselves against the professionals... The horse had consistently beaten every horse matched against him for fifteen or twenty miles around.*

V+N+PREP,
V+PRON+PREP

2 You can also say that you **match** one thing **against** another when you compare the two things to see whether they are similar. eg *...adding up the money from the canvas sack and matching it against the list of bills... The book invites you to match your own experience against the examples we describe.*

V+PRON+PREP,
V+N+PREP

match up. If two things **match up**, or if you **match** them **up**, they are similar or compatible with each other in some way. eg *...examining the fingerprints on those documents and checking that they match up... Somehow we manage to match up our gestures with those of our companions... It is not always easy to match up individuals with counselors... You might have trouble matching them up.*

V+ADV,
V+ADV+N,
V+PRON+ADV,
V+N+ADV,
ALSO+with:
ERGATIVE,
RECIPROCAL

match up to. If something **matches up to** something else, it is good enough for it. eg *...setting themselves a challenge and then matching up to it... You do not exactly match up to the requirements here.*

V+ADV+PREP

● **Measure up to** means almost the same as **match up to**.

maul, mauls, mauling, mauled

maul around. If you maul something **around**, you handle it or pull
it roughly; an informal expression. EG *She stared at her reflection
while mauling her face around.*

V+N+ADV,
V+PRON+ADV

measure, measures, measuring, measured

measure against. If you **measure** someone or something **against**
another person or thing, you judge their value using that other
person or thing as a standard. EG *They realised how little their
mistakes really mattered when you measured them against the
crimes of the people in power... It now sounds quite sophisticated
when you measure it against other programmes.*

V+PRON+PREP,
V+N+PREP

measure out. If you **measure out** a certain amount of something,
you measure that amount and take it or mark it because it is the
amount that you want. EG *She carefully measured out a double
whisky... He watched her measure out the black leaves into the pot...
He dug into the can and measured out a small spoonful of the
powder... The material had been measured out and bought.*

V+ADV+N,
V+N+ADV,
V+PRON+ADV

measure up. 1 When you **measure up**, you measure something
such as a room or house, for example because you are going to
decorate it or buy carpets or curtains for it; an informal use. EG
*...interior decorators waiting to start measuring up for new carpets...
Hopefully we can get carpets down in the house so that we can have
somebody over to measure it up and things like that.*

V+ADV,
V+PRON+ADV,
V+ADV+N

2 If you say that someone **measures up**, you mean that they are of a
good enough standard; an informal use. EG *When we don't measure
up, we must find out why.*

V+ADV

measure up to. If you **measure up to** a standard or to someone's
expectations, you are good enough to achieve the standard or fulfil
the person's expectations. EG *...ensuring that people in jobs are
capable of measuring up to their responsibilities... He had an
uncomfortable feeling of not being able to measure up to his father's
expectations.* ● Live up to means almost the same as **measure up
to.**

V+ADV+PREP

meddle, meddles, meddling, meddled

meddle in. If you **meddle in** something, you interfere in it. EG *He's
never wanted me to meddle in his affairs... He refused to meddle in
such matters.*

V+PREP

meddle with. If you **meddle with** something, you interfere with it
or try to change it when people do not want you to. EG *What business
was it of mine to meddle with Hilary Jackson's affairs?... I don't let
anyone else meddle with my stoves... The press barons were not
unusual in meddling with the editorial policies of their papers.*

V+PREP:
HAS PASSIVE

meet, meets, meeting, met

meet up. 1 If you **meet up** with someone, you meet them, either by
chance or because you have arranged to. EG *We planned to meet up
with them later in Florence... We can all meet up again at about
10.30... She and Smithy should meet up, they'd get on famously.*

V+ADV,
V+ADV+with:
RECIPROCAL

2 If two or more things **meet up**, they join or come together at a
particular place. EG *The two wires will meet up here... This track
should meet up with the main road.*

V+ADV,
V+ADV+with:
RECIPROCAL

meet with. 1 If you **meet with** a particular experience or event, you
experience it or it happens to you. EG *...an inquest on a child who met
with an accident... Enemy troops could still expect to meet with
armed resistance... Strikes met with little success... Almost everything else in the report meets with my approval.*

V+PREP

2 If you **meet** something **with** a particular reaction, you react to it in

V+N+PREP,
V+PRON+PREP

this way. EG *The men had met this refusal with indifference... ...their determination to meet any attack with retaliation.*

3 In American English, to **meet with** someone means to meet them after you have arranged to do so. EG *We can meet with the professor Monday night... A few months later, Sir Lew came to America to meet with my agent and make a deal.* `V+PREP`

melt, melts, melting, melted

melt away. **1** When something **melts away**, it gradually disappears. EG *A great empire has melted away... ...watching his fortune melt away... My fears have long since melted away.* ● **Fade away** means almost the same as **melt away**. `V+ADV`

2 If people **melt away**, they move so that you can no longer see them; a formal use. EG *Most people melted away as if I had leprosy... After that, we just melted away through the wood... Others got up and melted away into the dark shadow of the front door.* `V+ADV`

3 If something **melts away** or if heat **melts** it **away**, it melts completely until it has disappeared. EG *...until it melted away and she could swallow... The temperatures dissolved dog collars and melted away jackets... ...melting it away entirely.* `V+ADV, V+ADV+N, V+PRON+ADV, V+N+ADV: ERGATIVE`

melt down. If you **melt down** an object, you heat it until it melts, so that you can use the material to make something else. EG *Railings were melted down for cannon... It is now economically viable to melt down old glass... ...all this talk about melting the stuff down.* `V+N+ADV, V+ADV+N, V+PRON+ADV`

▸ When there is a **meltdown** in a nuclear reactor, the fuel rods melt and radioactivity is released into the atmosphere because of a fault in the cooling system. EG *A wrong command nearly led to a meltdown of one of the ship's two nuclear reactors.* `N COUNT, N UNCOUNT`

melt into. **1** If a feeling such as anger **melts into** a more gentle feeling, it changes into it. EG *...feeling his strength and aggression melt into tender care... ...a sternness which slowly melted into a sort of maternal affection.* `V+PREP`

2 If you **melt into** something such as a crowd of people, you hide among them so that people do not notice you. EG *They often wanted to melt into the teeming millions.* `V+PREP`

merge, merges, merging, merged

merge in. If something **merges in** with its surroundings, it is difficult to see or distinguish it clearly because it is similar in colour or appearance to the other thing. EG *The furniture and carpets merge in with the wallpaper to give an overpowering impression.* ● **Blend in** means almost the same as **merge in**. `V+ADV: ALSO+with`

merge into. If one thing **merges into** another, it becomes difficult to see or distinguish it clearly because it is similar in colour or appearance to the other thing. EG *They were painted so that they would appear to merge into the landscape... Creepers came from farther above where the rock merged into leaves and shadows.* ● **Blend into** means almost the same as **merge into**. `V+PREP`

mess, messes, messing, messed

mess about. **1** If you **mess about** or **around**, you spend time doing unimportant or silly things rather than concentrating on your work; an informal use. EG *...talking, playing, messing about together... Some of the lads had been messing around when they should have been working.* ● **Muck about** means almost the same as **mess about**. `V+ADV`

2 If you **mess** someone **about** or **around**, you treat them badly, for example by not being honest with them, or by continually changing plans which affect them; an informal use. EG *He had been messing* `V+N+ADV, V+PRON+ADV`

Helen around... I think it would be awful to have a man messing you about.

mess about with. If you **mess about** or **around with** something, you touch it or interfere with it when you shouldn't. EG *She didn't want you coming and messing about with things.* ● **Tamper with** means almost the same as **mess about with.**

V+ADV+PREP:
HAS PASSIVE

mess around. See mess about.

mess around with. See mess about with.

mess up. 1 If you **mess up** something that has been carefully made or done, you spoil it; an informal use. EG *That will mess up the whole analysis... If she got caught with me now it would mess up the rest of her life... I don't think I messed it up too badly.* ▷ A **mess-up** is a situation in which something has been done very badly or wrongly; an informal word. EG *There was some mess-up over the availability of dates.*

V+ADV+N,
V+PRON+ADV,
V+N+ADV

N COUNT

2 If you **mess** something **up**, you make it untidy or dirty. EG *Most of the evening was spent in messing up the kitchen... ...children messing things up while she is busy cooking the dinner... You could wear a hat so that your hair doesn't get messed up.*

V+ADV+N,
V+N+ADV,
V+PRON+ADV

3 If you **mess up**, you do something very badly; an informal American English use.

V+ADV

mess with. If you **mess with** something or someone dangerous, you become involved with them; an informal American expression. EG *We don't mess with grass or heroin or any of that stuff... That was a silly thing to do. You can't mess with those lads.*

V+PREP:
HAS PASSIVE

mete, metes, meting, meted

mete out. If a punishment **is meted out** to someone, it is given to them; a formal expression. EG *This punishment was meted out to me because of my political beliefs... Magistrates meted out fines of as much as £1,000.* ● **Deal out** means almost the same as **mete out.**

V+ADV+N:
ALSO+to

militate, militates, militating, militated

militate against. If something **militates against** something else, it makes it less likely to happen or succeed; a formal expression. EG *Family tensions can militate against learning... Large comprehensive schools militate against individuality by their very size.* ● **Discourage** means almost the same as **militate against.**

V+PREP

mill, mills, milling, milled

mill about. See mill around.

mill around. When a crowd of people **mill around, about,** or **round,** they all move around within a particular place or area. EG *There were hundreds of boys and girls milling around on the lawn... Students and staff were milling about... ...the throng which milled about the streets of Hampstead.*

V+ADV,
V+PREP

mill round. See mill around.

mind, minds, minding, minded

mind out. If you tell someone to **mind out,** you are telling them to be careful. EG *He shouted out as Jack snatched the glasses off his face. 'Mind out! Give 'em back! I can hardly see!'* ● **Look out** and **watch out** mean almost the same as **mind out.**

IMPERATIVE:
V+ADV

minister, ministers, ministering, ministered

minister to. If you **minister to** people or their needs, you make sure that they have everything they need or want; a formal expression. EG *He needed a skilled and energetic servant to minister to his comforts... ...like those cartoon explorers being ministered to by grateful Polynesians.*

V+PREP:
HAS PASSIVE

miss, misses, missing, missed

miss out. 1 If you **miss out** something or someone, you fail to include them in something. EG *You can miss out a comma because you're writing too quickly... We missed out all the interesting bits... You could put it at the beginning rather than miss it out.* ● **Leave out** means almost the same as **miss out**.
V+ADV+N,
V+PRON+ADV,
V+N+ADV

2 If you **miss out**, you have not been involved in something which you feel would have been of interest or benefit to you. EG *This is an area where I think men miss out... People who have never read in this way continue to feel they have missed out somewhere... They can't help fearing they will miss out on promotion.*
V+ADV:
ALSO+*on*

mist, mists, misting, misted

mist over. 1 If a piece of glass **mists over** or is **misted over**, it becomes covered with tiny drops of moisture, so that you cannot see through it easily. EG *His spectacles were misting over with the exertion... The window of my cubicle was misted over with heat.* ● **Steam up** and **mist up** mean almost the same as **mist over**.
V+ADV,
OR PASSIVE:
V+ADV

2 If your eyes **mist over**, you cannot see easily because there are tears in your eyes. EG *Grandpa Hindley's eyes still misted over when he told the tale... I saw his eyes mist over when he thought no one was looking.*
V+ADV

mist up. If a piece of glass **mists up** or is **misted up**, it becomes covered with tiny drops of moisture, so that you cannot see through it easily. EG *Could you pass that cloth, the windscreen has misted up again... The windows were all misted up.* ● **Mist over** means almost the same as **mist up**.
V+ADV,
OR PASSIVE:
V+ADV

mix, mixes, mixing, mixed

mix in. 1 If you **mix** a substance **in**, you put it with another substance and stir it so that the two substances are blended together. EG *Stir the mixture gradually, mixing in the flour... I think he must have mixed in a little more sand than usual.* ● **Add in** means almost the same as **mix in**.
V+ADV+N,
V+N+ADV,
V+PRON+ADV

2 If you **mix in**, you join in an activity and talk in a friendly way to the other people there. EG *He didn't feel like mixing in.*
V+ADV

mix into. If you **mix** one substance **into** another, you put it with the other substance and stir it so that the two substances are blended together. EG *Mix a tiny pinch of it into a big jar of face cream.*
V+N+PREP,
V+PRON+PREP

mix up. 1 If you **mix up** two things or people, you confuse them, so that you think that one of them is the other one. EG *I have somehow mixed up two events... People even mix us up and greet us by each other's names.* ● **Muddle up** means almost the same as **mix up**. ▶ If you are **mixed up**, or if your mind is **mixed up**, you are confused, often because of emotional or social problems. EG *I got mixed up and forgot which one I'd gone to first... ...your mixed-up students... Tim was in a strange mixed-up frame of mind.* ▶ A **mix-up** is a mistake which causes confusion or misunderstanding. EG *Due to some administrative mix-up the letters had not been sent out.* ● **Muddle** means almost the same as **mix up**.
V+ADV+N,
V+PRON+ADV,
V+N+ADV

ADJECTIVE

N COUNT

2 If you **mix up** a number of things, you put them all together in a random way so that they are not in any particular order. EG *I'd cut a big bunch of flowers—all different kinds mixed up... He mixes up all the chromosomes and shakes them around.*
V+N+ADV,
V+ADV+N,
V+PRON+ADV

3 If you **mix up** a solution or a mixture, you make it by mixing different things together. EG *Ira mixed up a solution in a jar... Have you been mixing up paste again?*
V+ADV+N,
V+N+ADV,
V+PRON+ADV

mix up in. If you are **mixed up in** something such as a crime or a
PASSIVE:
V+ADV+PREP

scandal, you are involved in it. EG *Are you going to get mixed up in this gang war the papers are talking about?... He would rather not have to get mixed up in it.*

mix up with. If you are **mixed up with** a group of people, you are spending a lot of time with them; often used showing disapproval. EG *She had got mixed up with the son of a big Mafia chief... He felt that it had been a mistake to get mixed up with the French radicals.* PASSIVE: V+ADV+PREP

mix with. If someone **mixes** it **with** someone else, they fight them; a very informal expression. EG *Don't try mixing it with him, Ted. He'll murder you.* V+*it*+PREP

model, models, modelling, modelled
American English uses the spellings **modeling** and **modeled**.

model on. If you **model** yourself **on** someone or if you **model** your behaviour **on** their behaviour, you copy them, because you admire them and want to be like them. EG *The children have their parents on which to model themselves... Mary had modelled her hand-writing on Sister Catherine's.* ● **Base on** means almost the same as **model on**. V+N+PREP, V+REFL+PREP, V+PRON+PREP

molder, molders, moldering, moldered
molder away. see **moulder away**.

monkey, monkeys, monkeying, monkeyed

monkey about. If someone is **monkeying about** or **around**, they are behaving in a silly and playful way. EG *The twins have been monkeying about in the attic again... ...coming and monkeying about in my affairs.* V+ADV

monkey about with. If someone **monkeys about** or **around with** something, they touch it or interfere with it when they are not supposed to. EG *Have you been monkeying about with my typwriter again?* V+ADV+PREP

monkey around. See **monkey about**.
monkey around with. See **monkey about with**.

mooch, mooches, mooching, mooched

mooch about. When you **mooch about** or **around**, you wander around a place with no particular purpose or aim. EG *There was absolutely nothing to do but mooch about... He mooched about the house in his pyjamas... He was mooching around in his studio.* V+ADV, V+PREP

mooch around. See **mooch about**.

moon, moons, mooning, mooned

moon about. If you **moon about** or **around**, you spend time doing nothing because you are feeling unhappy. EG *He was mooning about by himself... Most of that afternoon he mooned around.* V+ADV

moon around. See **moon about**.
moon over. If you **moon over** someone, you spend your time just thinking about them because you are in love. V+PREP

mop, mops, mopping, mopped

mop up. 1 If you **mop up**, or if you **mop up** a liquid that has been spilt, you wipe it with a cloth so that the liquid is absorbed. EG *Mother started mopping up the oil... First mop it up, then try to remove the stain with cold water... I've mopped up with a bit of old cloth.* V+ADV+N, V+PRON+ADV, V+ADV, V+N+ADV

2 To **mop up** the last members of a group means to use them or deal with them in some way. EG *School leavers will be mopped up by youth opportunity schemes... We have new factories all along Deeside and still we can't mop up the pool of unemployed.* V+ADV+N, V+PRON+ADV

3 When an army **mops up** resistance, it deals with any people who V+ADV+N

are still fighting against it. EG *All resistance will be mopped up within two hours.* ● **Eliminate** means almost the same as **mop up**.

▶ In a **mop-up** operation, soldiers go into an area and deal with any people still there who are fighting against them. EG *Some flew back to the Dak To area and the mop-up operations there.*　　ADJECTIVE

mope, mopes, moping, moped

mope about. If you **mope about** a place or **mope around**, you wander around it aimlessly, looking and feeling unhappy. EG *I moped around the house for a few days... He was moping about the hallway.*　　V+PREP, V+ADV

mope around. See mope about.

moulder, moulders, mouldering, mouldered

Moulder is spelled **molder** in American English.

moulder away. Something that **is mouldering** away is decaying slowly in the place where it has been left. EG *In twenty years you might be down-and-out or mouldering away in some old folks' home.* ● **Rot away** means almost the same as **moulder away**.　　V+ADV

mount, mounts, mounting, mounted

mount up. If something **mounts up**, it increases, because more and more is being added to it all the time. EG *The soil becomes more and more acidic as pollution mounts up... You put a little money by each week and you'll be surprised how it mounts up.* ● **Build up** means almost the same as **mount up**.　　V+ADV

mourn, mourns, mourning, mourned

mourn for. If you **mourn for** someone, you are very sad because they have died, and you show how sad you are in the way that you behave. EG *He continued to mourn for his son Joseph.*　　V+PREP: HAS PASSIVE

mouth, mouths, mouthing, mouthed

mouth off. If you say that someone is **mouthing off**, you mean that they are talking loudly and saying something which nobody wants to hear; an informal expression. EG *...mouthing off opinions about everything under the sun... I just get fed up with him mouthing off all the time.*　　V+ADV+N, V+ADV

move, moves, moving, moved

move about. 1 When you **move about** or **around** a place, you keep going from one part of it to another part. EG *She moved about the office, her sari rustling... My game was not too good, but at least I could move around the court with relative ease... Don't you try to move around for a bit.*　　V+PREP, V+ADV

2 If you **move about, around** or **round**, you keep changing your job or keep changing the place where you live. EG *The men should move about freely, getting the best wages they can... The managers will not be required to move around from place to place... ...agitators that moved round from one meeting to the next.*　　V+ADV

3 When you **move** something **about, around,** or **round**, you move it from one position or place to another. EG *A poltergeist is a noisy and tiresome 'spirit' which moves furniture about... Don't move the injured limb around... She could not keep her body still but had to keep moving it about... Oil had to be moved about in ships.*　　V+N+ADV, V+PRON+ADV

4 If employees **are moved around, about** or **round**, their employer moves them to a different job or department. EG *Promising young executives are being moved around from one branch to another... I get moved about because I'm good... It means you can move people round and promote those who are ready.*　　V+N+ADV, V+PRON+ADV

move along. 1 When someone or something **moves along** a road or other place, or when you **move** them **along** there, they go forwards　　V+PREP/ADV, V+N+PREP/ADV, V+PRON+PREP/ADV: ERGATIVE along it. EG *He caught at a short section of ladder and began to move along it... She was obliged to hold herself upright as she moved along... We had to move the pump along the bank of the stream... When they got their appliances out, they were quite unable to move them along the roads.*

2 If someone, especially a police officer, tells you to **move along,** they mean that you should leave and not stand around in a particular place. EG *Just move along, please. Move along... He said, 'I'm afraid you girls had better move along.'*
V+ADV: USUALLY IMPERATIVE

3 If a task that you are doing **is moving along,** you are continuing with it and making good progress. EG *Things were moving along... The work moved along smoothly.*
V+ADV

move around. See **move about** and **move round.**

move away. **1** If you **move away,** you go and live in a different town or area of a country. EG *They had decided to retire from farming and move away... We had some very dear friends many years ago that moved away from this area.*
V+ADV: ALSO+*from*

2 When someone or something **moves away** from a place or position, or when you **move** them **away,** they leave it. EG *If he tried to move away now, everybody would notice... The boat moved away from the bobbing barrels... He moved the hand away but didn't release it... He demanded that I should move her away.*
V+ADV, V+N+ADV, V+PRON+ADV: ERGATIVE, ALSO+*from*

move away from. If you **move away from** a particular idea, method, or habit, you stop having it. EG *The Government had moved away from a simple concern with teacher training... From then on he began to move slowly away from the Labour Party.*
V+ADV+PREP: HAS PASSIVE

move down. **1** When someone or something **moves down,** or when you **move** them **down,** they go from a higher position to a lower one. EG *We moved down the side of the mountain... ...families that move up or down the social scale... His pen moved down to the next question on a list... Rodrigo tried to move her head down.* ● **Move up** means almost the same as **move down.**
V+ADV/PREP, V+N+ADV/PREP, V+PRON+ADV/PREP: ERGATIVE

2 If you **move down** to an area of a country, you go to live there; used when the place is farther south. EG *They're moving down from New Jersey... I moved down here on security work.*
V+ADV: USUALLY+A

3 At school or work, if you **move down,** or if someone **moves** you **down,** you go to a lower level, grade, or class. EG *If they fail their mathematics exams they move down a year, and take them again... There's a chance I might be moving you down a group.*
V+ADV, V+N+ADV, V+PRON+ADV: ERGATIVE

4 If the rate, level, or amount of something **moves down,** it decreases. EG *Do you really think the unemployment figures are moving down?* ● **Go down** and **fall** mean almost the same as **move down,** and **move up** means the opposite.
V+ADV

move in. **1** When you **move in,** you begin to live in a different house or place. EG *I couldn't move in until the first of July... We had moved in at the height of the summer.* ● **Move out** means the opposite of **move in.**
V+ADV

2 If someone **moves in** with you, they come to live with you. EG *He moved in with Mrs Camish... We had already decided that I would move in with Margaret... Are your parents going to move in?* ● **Move out** means the opposite of **move in.**
V+ADV: USUALLY+*with*

3 If a group of people **move in** on a place or person, they go towards them in order to attack them. EG *He began to move in on Tom... Five men with rifles came out of the bushes and moved in for the kill.* ● **Close in** means almost the same as **move in.**
V+ADV: USUALLY+*on*

4 If someone **moves in** on a particular activity, they start to be involved in it and take over from someone else, often in an unfair way; used showing disapproval. EG *Professional drug pushers moved*
V+ADV: ALSO+*on*

in and organized the trade... Those with the most advanced technology will soon move in to exploit the sea's resources.

move into. 1 When you **move into** a house or particular area of a   V+PREP
town, you start to live there. EG *She moved into lodgings... We were the first black family to move into that area... She'd just moved into the neighbourhood from Connecticut.*

2 When you **move** something or someone **into** a place, you take   V+N+PREP,
them to that place and leave them there. EG *I could move my things*   V+PRON+PREP
into that room... West wants to move them into the invasion areas immediately... The furniture was moved back into my cell.

3 If a group of people **move into** a particular activity or area of   V+PREP
business, they start to be involved in it. EG *About 30 companies have moved into the 'personal stereo' business... They tried to move into a market where sales are counted in hundreds rather than thousands... ...moving into the field of continuing education.*

4 If the army, police, or other group **move into** an area, they go   V+PREP
there in order to carry out a particular task. EG *...fire brigades and rescue squads moving into the area... The army had moved into Czechoslovakia on the 20th.*

move off. When vehicles or people **move off**, they start to leave a   V+ADV
place. EG *The fleet of cars prepared to move off... We move off on the cycles as fast as possible... ...cars blowing their horns at him to move off.* ● **Set off** means almost the same as **move off.**

move on. 1 When someone on a journey **moves on**, they leave a   V+ADV:
place where they had stopped briefly and continue the journey. EG   ALSO+*to*
They moved on as soon as the cloud lifted... The next night we had to move on to the third line of trenches... After three weeks in Hong Kong, we moved on to Japan. ● **Carry on** means almost the same as **move on.**

2 If you **move on,** you finish one thing and turn your attention to   V+ADV:
something else. EG *Let's leave it there, thank you very much and*   ALSO+*to/to*-INF
move on... The men moved on to talk about something else... Get the actors to move on to the next scene. ● **Go on** and **carry on** mean almost the same as **move on.**

3 If you **move on** from your present job, you leave it and start   V+ADV:
another one which will be better for you. EG *John wanted to move on*   ALSO+*from*
from the Post to a bigger paper... This training will work to your advantage when you want to move on. ● **Progress** is a more formal word for **move on.**

4 If someone such as a policeman **moves** you **on,** they order you to   V+PRON+ADV,
leave a particular place. EG *...waiting on a park bench in the winter*   V+N+ADV,
weather for a cop to come and move him on... An angry motorist   V+ADV+N
was moved on by police.

5 If people's ideas, knowledge, or beliefs **move on,** they change and   V+ADV
become more modern. EG *The world is about to move on from the era where knowledge comes in books... Public opinion had moved on... Computers moved on an evolutionary step.*

6 If time **moves on,** it passes. EG *As the months moved on, I realized*   V+ADV
how inadequate these measures were... As time moved on, the hunters clearly had in their heads an organized plan. ● **Wear on** means almost the same as **move on.**

move on to, move onto. If you **move on** to a particular topic, you   V+ADV+PREP
bring that topic into a conversation or lecture after you have been talking about something else. EG *If we now move on to voting behaviour the pattern becomes more complicated... The conference was able to move on to other matters of a wider interest... We moved on to the topic of careers... Let me move onto quite a*

different area. ● **Turn to** and **come on to** mean almost the same as **move on to**.

move out. 1 When you **move out**, you stop living in a particular house or place and go to live somewhere else. EG *The fellow that lived there moved out without a trace... I want to move out of Birmingham... People began moving out of the neighborhood.* ● **Move in** means almost the same as **move out**. | V+ADV: ALSO+*of*

2 If you **move** someone **out** of a place, you arrange for them to leave that place. EG *Mohammed Kassi had moved most of his men out of Fort Esther... The council agreed to move out families with three children... The women who got up a march and picket to move them out of the school.* | V+N+ADV, V+ADV+N, V+PRON+ADV: ALSO+*of*

3 If an organization or group of people **move out** of a particular activity or area of business, they stop being involved in it. EG *People are moving out of manufacture into the service industries... Well, the big companies are all moving out.* | V+ADV: USUALLY+*of*

move over. 1 If you **move over**, you change the system or method you are using and do things in a different way. EG *There have been suggestions that we ought to move over towards a more monetarist economy... ...moving over to solar powered energy.* | V+ADV: USUALLY+A

2 If you ask someone to **move over**, you are asking them to change their position so that there is room for you. EG *Move over a bit, will you?... Aurelia moved over and the maid sat down on the footstool.* | V+ADV

3 At work, if you **move over**, you start to do a different job in the same company in order to let someone else do the job that you originally had. EG *She decided to move over and make way for one of the younger women... They will have to move over and make room for new management.* ● **Step aside** means almost the same as **move over**. | V+ADV

4 When something **moves over** a surface such as land or water, it goes forward slowly across it; a rather literary use. EG *The ship entered Port Phillip Bay and moved over the quiet water towards Melbourne... Pockets of cloud moved over the fields... The train moved southward over the icy countryside.* | V+PREP

move round. 1 When you **move round** or **around** an obstacle, you move so that you can get past it. EG *I moved round the desk... He was lying on the sidewalk, people moving around him as if he were not there... She moved round the car and disappeared.* | V+PREP

2 If you **move round**, you change your position so that you can get closer to something. EG *Will you three sitting at the back please move round... Mrs Thorne moved round and sat down next to them.* | V+ADV

3 When you **move round** a place or a room, you go from one part of it to another part. EG *She moved round the scullery emptying the teapot... This was how prisoners moved round the building.* | V+PREP

4 See **move about**.

move towards. If you **move towards** a different way of organizing something, you make preparations to introduce the new methods. EG *The group has moved towards direct selling, cutting out agents' commission... Lawson put forward proposals for moving towards a more permanent system of managed exchange rates.* | V+PREP

move up. 1 When someone or something **moves up**, or when you **move** them **up**, they go from a lower position to a higher one. EG *Each day the tribe moved up the hill a few feet... We reached a huge rock. He moved up quickly and easily... She moved her feet up and down... Move it up a bit.* ● **Move down** means the opposite of **move up**. | V+ADV/PREP, V+N+ADV/PREP, V+PRON+ADV/PREP: ERGATIVE

2 At school or work, if you **move up**, or if someone **moves** you **up**, you go to a higher level, grade, or class. EG *This means the executive* | V+ADV, V+N+ADV,

can move up quickly... Apprentices move up to become engineers and managers.   V+PRON+ADV: ERGATIVE

3 If you ask someone to **move up**, you are asking them to change their position so that there is more room. EG *Move up, John, let the lady sit down... She moved up so close to my chair.* ● **Move over** means almost the same as **move up**.   V+ADV

4 When soldiers or policemen **move up** or when they **are moved up**, they are ordered to go to a particular position and be ready to act. EG *It would be some time before their tanks could move up... If we're expecting an invasion the squadrons should be moved up, not back!... Two army groups had been moved up.*   V+ADV, V+N+ADV, V+PRON+ADV, V+ADV+N: ERGATIVE

5 If the rate, level, or amount of something **moves up**, it increases. EG *Rates for one to 12 months have moved up recently... Peter mentioned that our salaries weren't in fact moving up.* ● **Go up** and **rise** mean almost the same as **move up**, and **go down** means the opposite.   V+ADV

mow, mows, mowing, mowed/mown

mow down. If a large number of people **are mowed down** or are **mown down**, they are all killed violently at one time. EG *Several children had strayed onto an airport runway and been mown down by a jet... Six prisoners tried to bolt. Kilver's men promptly mowed them down... Someone has purchased a machine gun and mown down a whole neighbourhood.*   V+N+ADV, V+PRON+ADV, V+ADV+N

muck, mucks, mucking, mucked

Muck is an informal word.

muck about. **1** If you **muck about** or **muck around**, you behave in a stupid way and waste time. EG *She was mucking about with a jug of flowers on the table... You mustn't start mucking around... You! What were you mucking about in the dark for?* ● **Mess about** means almost the same as **muck about**.   V+ADV

2 If you **muck** someone **about**, you annoy or upset them, especially by changing your mind about a plan or arrangement you have made. EG *The people at the housing association really muck the customers about... I've got no time for people who muck you about.* ● **Mess about** means almost the same as **muck about**.   V+N+ADV, V+PRON+ADV

muck around. See **muck about**.

muck in. If you **muck in**, you join in with an activity or you help other people with a job; an informal expression. EG *Management kept the same hours as the men and mucked in whenever it was necessary... Couldn't she muck in with David for the time being?... ...supervisors who mucked in with the workers... ...pulling our weight, mucking in together.*   V+ADV: ALSO V+ADV+with, V+ADV+together, RECIPROCAL

muck out. If you **muck out** a place where animals are kept, or you **muck** the animals **out**, you clean the place where they live. EG *...a small boy helping to muck out the pigsty at the bottom of his garden... The stables have to be mucked out and all the routine jobs done... Don't forget to muck the horses out.*   V+ADV+N, V+N+ADV, V+PRON+ADV

muck up. **1** If you **muck** something **up**, you do it so badly that you do not achieve what you wanted to. EG *That clever boy from Oxford mucked the interview up... I've taken my driving test twice, and both times I've mucked it up... I muck up even some of the simplest scales when I'm playing the piano.*   V+N+ADV, V+PRON+ADV, V+ADV+N

2 If you **muck** your clothes **up**, you make them dirty. EG *Don't you go mucking up that clean dress now.*   V+ADV+N, V+N+ADV, V+PRON+ADV

muddle, muddles, muddling, muddled

muddle along. If you **muddle along**, you live or exist without a   V+ADV proper plan or purpose in your life. EG *The church has lost its way, muddling along from Sunday to Sunday.*

muddle through. If you **muddle through,** you manage to do something even though you do not really know how to do it properly. EG *The children are left to muddle through on their own... Even top managers have to muddle through as best they can.* ● **Get by** means almost the same as **muddle through.**   V+ADV

muddle up. 1 If you **muddle** things **up,** you cause them to become mixed up or in the wrong order. EG *I'm afraid I've muddled your directions up... Later they may muddle up your names with those of your cousins... Put them so that you can reach them easily, and they will not get muddled up with the other things... You've got it all muddled up.*   V+N+ADV, V+ADV+N, V+PRON+ADV: ALSO+*with*

2 If you **muddle** someone **up,** you confuse them by what you are saying or doing. EG *Don't keep interfering, you'll muddle me up.*   V+N+ADV, V+PRON+ADV

muffle, muffles, muffling, muffled

muffle up. If you **are muffled up** or if you **muffle** yourself **up,** you are wearing a lot of heavy clothes. EG *A boy muffled up in a blue scarf was busy scribbling something in a book... Fancy muffling yourself up like that on a day like today.* ● **Wrap up** means almost the same as **muffle up.**   PASSIVE, V+ADV: ALSO V+REFL+ADV

mug, mugs, mugging, mugged

mug up. If you **mug up** a subject, you study it over a short period of time so that you can remember the main facts about it; an informal expression used mainly in British English. EG *She's upstairs mugging up history or geography or something... I must mug up my French before the exam.* ● **Swot up** means almost the same as **mug up.**   V+ADV+N, V+N+ADV, V+PRON+ADV

mull, mulls, mulling, mulled

mull over. If you **mull** something **over,** you think about it seriously and for a long time, often before deciding what to do. EG *I mulled that question over for a while... I sat there and tried to mull things over in my mind... Nell began to mull over the injustices of her new role... He returned to his office to mull over these coincidences.* ● **Chew over** means almost the same as **mull over.**   V+N+ADV, V+PRON+ADV, V+ADV+N

multiply, multiplies, multiplying, multiplied

multiply out. If you **multiply out** two numbers, you multiply them. EG *...to multiply out the two terms... ...multiply it out.*   V+ADV+N, V+PRON+ADV, V+N+ADV

muscle, muscles, muscling, muscled

muscle in. If you **muscle in** on something, you force your way into a situation where you have no right to be and where you are not welcome. EG *They are jealous of your success and resent the way you are muscling in on their territory.* ● **Push in** means almost the same as **muscle in.**   V+ADV: USUALLY+*on*

muscle out. If someone is **muscled out,** they are forced out of a situation or position where they want to be by someone who uses force or unfair methods. EG *He had a cafe by the station until he was muscled out by the Council.*   PASSIVE: V+ADV, ALSO+*of*

muss, musses, mussing, mussed

muss up. If your hair is **mussed up,** it looks untidy, as if it has not been combed. EG *You can't drag her through there without mussing up her hair in the process.*   V+ADV+N, V+N+ADV, V+PRON+ADV

muster, musters, mustering, mustered

muster up. If you **muster up** your strength, energy, or courage, you make a great effort in order to do something. EG *I mustered up*   V+ADV+N, V+N+ADV: ALSO+*to*-INF *enough courage to put in a request for a pay rise... Stanitsyn couldn't muster up the necessary forcefulness the role demanded... She mustered up spirit to put a timid question.* ● **Summon up** means almost the same as **muster up.**

N n

naff, naffs, naffing, naffed

naff off. If you tell someone to **naff off,** you are telling them rudely or angrily to go away; an informal expression.

IMPERATIVE:
V+ADV

nail, nails, nailing, nailed

nail down. 1 If something **is nailed down,** it is fastened securely by means of nails. EG *The lid of the box was nailed down... If it won't stay there we'll have to nail it down.*

V+N+ADV,
V+ADV+N,
V+PRON+ADV:
USUALLY PASSIVE

2 If you **nail** someone **down,** you force them to state clearly their opinions or intentions; an informal use. EG *We can go over to see them tomorrow and nail them down to some kind of commitment.* ● **Pin down** means almost the same as **nail down.**

V+PRON+ADV,
V+N+ADV

3 If you **nail down** something uncertain or unknown, you manage to describe it more accurately; a fairly informal use. EG *If you stay here the next few hours, we can nail it down, whether it's malignant or nonmalignant... ...an ambiguity which can never be satisfactorily nailed down.* ● **Pin down** means almost the same as **nail down.**

V+PRON+ADV,
V+N+ADV,
V+ADV+N

nail up. 1 If you **nail** something **up,** you fix it to a wall or other vertical surface so that it can be seen. EG *She passed a house with a brass plate nailed up outside... ...the warning notice that he had nailed up on the pole.*

V+ADV+N,
V+N+ADV,
V+PRON+ADV

2 If someone or something **is nailed up** in a room or other space, they are confined there, often because the entrance has been sealed using nails. EG *She was not burnt but nailed up in a barrel and thrown into the sea.*

PASSIVE:
V+ADV

name, names, naming, named

name after. If you **name** someone or something **after** a person or thing, you give them the same name as the other person or thing; used mainly in British English. EG *Then Cain built a city and named it after his son... She is named after her great-grandmother.*

V+PRON+PREP,
V+N+PREP

name for. If you **name** someone or something **for** a person or thing, you give them the same name as the person or thing; used in American English. EG *Hayman Creek was named for Charles Hayman... ...Cape Perpetua, sighted by Captain Cook in 1778 and named by him for Saint Perpetua.*

V+N+PREP,
V+PRON+PREP

narrow, narrows, narrowing, narrowed

narrow down. If you **narrow down** something such as a choice or subject, you consider only the most suitable or important parts, and eliminate the rest. EG *They narrowed the choice down to about a dozen sites... We finally narrowed down the list of candidates to three... Can we narrow it down a bit, David?.*

V+N+ADV,
V+ADV+N,
V+PRON+ADV

nestle, nestles, nestling, nestled

nestle up. If you **nestle up** to someone, you move close to them so that you are pressing against them, usually because you are cold or

V+ADV:
USUALLY+*to*

frightened. EG *Then Marsha began to nestle up to Lynn, whimpering like a dog.*

nibble, nibbles, nibbling, nibbled

nibble at. 1 When a mouse or other small animal **nibbles at**   V+PREP
something, it takes small bites out of it quickly and repeatedly. EG *I saw squirrels in the yew trees nibbling at the moist red berries.*

2 If you **nibble at** your food, you eat it slowly, taking small bites,   V+PREP
because you are not very hungry. EG *The two Belgian tourists nibble quietly at their food... Frank's father had only nibbled at the dish.*

nod, nods, nodding, nodded

nod off. If you **nod off**, you fall asleep, usually unintentionally, while   V+ADV
you are sitting down; an informal expression. EG *They just sit and chat to each other, or nod off... I nodded off with Diggity snoring in my arms as usual.* • **Doze off** means almost the same as **nod off**.

nose, noses, nosing, nosed

nose about. See nose around.

nose around. If you **nose around**, **round** or **about**, you look for   V+ADV
interesting things or information in a place which belongs to someone else; an informal expression. EG *They had nosed around for someone with a grudge against Curry but hadn't found anyone... Coal-dust covered his feet as he nosed about among the boilers.*
• **Poke around** means almost the same as **nose around**.

nose out. 1 If you **nose out** information, you discover it by search-   V+ADV+N,
ing something thoroughly; an informal use. EG *I am not interested in*   V+N+ADV,
nosing out the details of someone else's agony... He noses the truth   V+PRON+ADV
out eventually. • **Uncover** is a more formal word for **nose out**.

2 If you **nose out** other people in a competition or race, you   V+N+ADV,
gradually improve your position in relation to them so that you win.   V+PRON+ADV,
EG *Lendl was nosed out by the younger man this year.*   V+ADV+N

nose round. See nose around.

notch, notches, notching, notched

notch up. If you **notch up** something such as a score, total, or prize,   V+ADV+N
you achieve it. EG *The Tory candidate had notched up eleven hundred more votes than Mr Jones... The firm has notched up the Queen's Award for export six times.* • **Chalk up** means almost the same as **notch up**.

note, notes, noting, noted

note down. If you **note down** something, you make short notes   V+ADV+N,
about it, so that you can refer to them later. EG *...noting down his*   V+PRON+ADV,
observations as he made them... The teacher will demonstrate an   V+N+ADV
experiment to the students who will then note it down and write it up.

number, numbers, numbering, numbered

number among. If someone or something **is numbered among** a   V+N+PREP,
particular group, they are a member of that group. EG *They can each*   V+PRON+PREP
be numbered among the truly great Open Champions... Trade unions number among their members a substantial proportion of the total electorate.

O o

object, objects, objecting, objected

object to. If you **object to** something, you do not like it or approve of it. EG *The other tenants objected to Jeremy's habit of playing the piano at three in the morning... The plan has been objected to by the local residents association.*

V+PREP:
HAS PASSIVE

occur, occurs, occurring, occurred

occur to. If a thought or idea **occurs** to you, you suddenly think of it or realize it. EG *As soon as that thought occurred to him, he felt worse... It never occurred to me to ask... It had never occurred to her that he might insist on paying.*

V+PREP:
ALSO+REPORT

offend, offends, offending, offended

offend against. If something **offends against** a law, rule, or principle, it breaks it; a formal expression. EG *This would offend against the principle of fairness... To behave like that would offend against her conventions.*

V+PREP:
HAS PASSIVE

offer, offers, offering, offered

offer up. To **offer up** prayers, praise, or a sacrifice means to pray to God or praise Him, or to make a sacrifice. EG *I went through the motions of offering up the prayer... ...the five daily prayers that are offered up to Allah... They are preparing to offer me up as a sacrifice, Jordache.*

V+ADV+N,
V+N+ADV,
V+PRON+ADV

ooze, oozes, oozing, oozed

ooze out. If a gas or liquid **oozes out** from somewhere, it slowly appears or leaks there. EG *It caused dense yellow smoke to ooze out through the tiles... ...horrible to see blood oozing out... Tears oozed slowly out from between her eyelids.*

V+ADV:
USUALLY+A

open, opens, opening, opened

open off. If a place or area **opens off** a road, path, or corridor, it connects directly with it. EG *Squares and little streets open off the main road... ...the turret-room that opens off the corridor on the left.*

V+PREP

open onto. If a building or room **opens onto** another place, you can go straight from one to the other, for example through a door. EG *There are small back-to-back houses, whose doors open directly onto the street... All three doors opened onto a small private courtyard... ...the white arch that opens onto the sea terrace.* ● **Give onto** means almost the same as **open onto.**

V+PREP

open out. 1 If something that is in one piece or is packed closely together **opens out,** or if you **open** it **out,** it gradually separates. EG *The flower only opens out in full sun... ...bending the toes and opening them out... The fibres were opened out with the aid of a needle.*

V+ADV,
V+PRON+ADV,
V+ADV+N,
V+N+ADV:
ERGATIVE

2 If you **open out** something that is folded, you unfold it so that you can see or use it. EG *She opened out the board and began to set out the chessmen... He opened out the paper and began to read... He picked the letter up and opened it out.*

V+ADV+N,
V+PRON+ADV,
V+N+ADV

3 If a place **opens out** into another place, it gradually becomes wider until you reach the second place. EG *Giltspur Street opens out into West Smithfield... The mountains finally opened out into the plain... As the road opened out, Francis glanced at his watch.*

V+ADV:
USUALLY+*into*

4 If someone **opens out,** they become relaxed and start to talk more

V+ADV

freely. EG *She found it difficult to open out to people... He opened out quite dramatically... In the lounge, over his coffee, Crike opened out.*
● **Open up** means almost the same as **open out**.

5 If something such as a discussion, topic, or subject **opens out**, or if you **open** it **out**, it starts to involve more people or things than it did before. EG *Obviously, this question could open out into the justification of such action... It would certainly be desirable to open out this debate... The books and exhibitions opened it out still further.*

V+ADV,
V+ADV+N,
V+PRON+ADV,
V+N+ADV:
ERGATIVE

open up. **1** When a place or area **is opened up**, it becomes easier to get to, and there are more opportunities for development or trade. EG *The government was determined to open up the Sioux reservation for settlement... ...a fishing policy which will increase quotas and open up trawling grounds.*

V+ADV+N,
V+N+ADV,
V+PRON+ADV

2 When an opportunity **opens up**, or when a situation **opens** it **up**, that opportunity is given to you. EG *All sorts of possibilities began to open up... Fast transport and instantaneous communications open up a new dimension of freedom... A whole new world had been opened up for him by his rich American wife.*

V+ADV,
V+ADV+N:
ERGATIVE

3 If someone **opens up**, they start to relax and to say exactly what they know or think about something or someone. EG *After five or six beers Doring had opened up about Klara and Springer... We notice how new volunteers react, join in, begin to open up.* ● **Open out** means almost the same as **open up**.

V+ADV

4 When you **open up** a building, you unlock and open the door so that people can get in. EG *Open up! It's snowing out here... The police opened up for them... Paul opened up his tiny store and cafe as usual.*

V+ADV,
V+ADV+N,
V+PRON+ADV,
V+N+ADV

5 If a new shop or business **opens up** or if someone **opens** it **up**, it starts to trade. EG *Supermarkets, drugstores, and service stations will open up... Anyone can open up a cafe tomorrow provided they've got permission... I was wondering whether to open up a new factory.*

V+ADV,
V+ADV+N,
V+PRON+ADV:
ERGATIVE

6 If a surgeon **opens up** a patient, or **opens up** a part of their body, they operate on them; a fairly informal use. EG *The doctor wants to open up the Eustachian tube... She had to open me up soon or it'd be too late.*

V+ADV+N,
V+PRON+ADV,
V+N+ADV

7 If someone with a gun **opens up**, they start shooting. EG *They opened up as the convoy came abreast of them... Suddenly they heard a nearby flak battery open up.*

V+ADV

8 If you **open up** when you are driving a car, you suddenly begin to go much faster; an informal use. EG *After twenty miles he opened up... I throw my hand ahead in a 'Speed up!' gesture. He nods and opens up.* ● **Accelerate** is a more formal word for **open up**.

V+ADV

9 In a game, competition, or sporting activity, if the players **open up**, they begin to play in a more exciting and determined way. EG *Real Madrid suddenly opened up and surprisingly led by two goals to nil... It was a good hour or more before the game opened up.*

V+ADV

operate, operates, operating, operated

operate on. When doctors **operate on** a patient, they cut open their body in order to remove, repair, or replace a damaged part of it. EG *We can't operate on the vein until the ulcer is healed... I hope to operate on her on Sunday... His knees have been operated on three times.*

V+PREP:
HAS PASSIVE

oppose, opposes, opposing, opposed

oppose to. **1** If you are **opposed to** something, you disagree with it or disapprove of it. EG *I am opposed to capital punishment... It was the principles that the TUC were opposed to.*

PASSIVE:
V+PREP

2 If one thing **is opposed to** another, they are contrasted in order to

V+N+PREP,

show how different they are from each other. EG *Art, when it is opposed to Science, is often romantic... ...politics, here opposed to good works... You can oppose realism to idealism.*   V+PRON+PREP: USUALLY PASSIVE

opt, opts, opting, opted

opt for. If you **opt for** a particular thing, you decide to do or have that thing. EG *A woman who opts for a career and stays single may have greater commitment to the work than the single man who has not made the same sacrifices... Many Poles appeared to have opted for the poll boycott.*   V+PREP

opt in. If you **opt in** to a particular arrangement or activity, you take part in it. EG *The independent schools, although not yet able to opt in to grant-maintained status, can play their part... The stakes for playing the game will be increased, and some players will no longer be able to opt in.*   V+ADV: ALSO+to

opt out. If you **opt out** of something, you choose to be no longer involved in it. EG *Today there is a growing tendency for people to opt out... ...hospitals are opting out of health authority control... ...people who had opted out of the rat race.*   V+ADV: USUALLY+of

order, orders, ordering, ordered

order about. If you **order** someone **about** or **around**, you tell them what to do in an unpleasant and unsympathetic way; used showing disapproval. EG *He went on behaving as if he were a soldier, ordering everyone about... It was intolerable that those two fat slobs could order Carolyn around... They think because they've got money they can order you about.* ● **Push around** means almost the same as **order about.**   V+N+ADV, V+PRON+ADV

order around. See **order about.**

own, owns, owning, owned

own up. If you **own up** to something wrong that you have done, you admit that you did it. EG *Come on, own up! Who did it?... No-one owned up to taking the money.* ● **Confess** is a more formal word for **own up.**   V+ADV: ALSO+to

P p

pace, paces, pacing, paced

pace off. See **pace out.**

pace out. If you **pace out** or **pace off** a distance, you measure that distance by counting the number of steps you have to take. EG *Placing the gun beside a tree he paced out a hundred and fifty paces... Laverne paced off the sections and tied pieces of yarn to twigs to mark the spot for each post.*   V+ADV+N, V+PRON+ADV: NO PASSIVE

pack, packs, packing, packed

pack away. If you **pack** something **away,** you put it in a bag or suitcase. EG *He and Flecker pack everything away into the canvas bag... I packed away the shorts and vest that I had worn the previous day... The food was packed away.*   V+N+ADV, V+ADV+N, V+PRON+ADV

pack in. 1 If you **pack in** a job or activity, you completely stop doing it altogether because you have had enough; an informal British English use. EG *It's a good job. I don't think he'd pack it in... They*   V+PRON+ADV, V+ADV+N, V+N+ADV *may decide that enough is enough and just pack it all in... If you suddenly decide that pleasure is more important than business, well, pack in the business and go after the pleasure.* ● **Jack in** means almost the same as **pack in**.

2 If you **pack** someone **in**, you stop having a romantic or sexual relationship with them; an informal use. EG *She's just packed her boyfriend in.*   V+N+ADV, V+PRON+ADV

3 If something such as a film, play, or other form of entertainment **packs** people **in**, it attracts them in large numbers; an informal use. EG *...music that packs them in at South Kensington.* ● **Pull in** means almost the same as **pack in**.   V+PRON+ADV, V+N+ADV

pack off. If you **pack** someone **off** somewhere, you send them there to stay for a period of time, even though they may not want to go there; an informal expression. EG *They pack their sons off to boarding school... I packed her off to bed with a hot water bottle... Years ago he had been packed off to one of the colonies... The unfortunate sufferer might even be packed off to hospital.*   V+N+ADV, V+PRON+ADV, V+ADV+N: USUALLY+*to*

pack out. When a place **is packed out** with people, it is extremely crowded. EG *The course was run by Eleanor Macdonald whose seminar last year was packed out.*   PASSIVE: V+ADV

pack up. **1** If you **pack up** your belongings, you put all your belongings in a case or bag, often because you are leaving one place and going to another. EG *It was a sad day indeed when we had to pack up our things and board the bus... All right, pack the files up. Take them back to registry.*   V+ADV+N, V+N+ADV, V+PRON+ADV

2 If you **pack up** a job or activity, you stop what you are doing and go somewhere else or do something else; a fairly informal use. EG *Everyone packed up and went home... She packed up and left next day... I started playing cricket when I was eleven and only packed up five years ago... She says she's packing up work.*   V+ADV, V+ADV+N, V+PRON+ADV: NO PASSIVE

3 If a machine **packs up**, it stops working because it has broken; an informal use. EG *The heating in the hall packed up.* ● **Break down** means almost the same as **pack up**.   V+ADV

pad, pads, padding, padded

pad out. If you **pad out** a piece of writing or a speech with unnecessary words or pieces of information, you include them in order to make it longer and hide the fact that you have not got much to say. EG *He had to pad out his 300 pages with comments on his hero's digestive problems... She has a habit of padding out her essays with a lot of long quotes.*   V+ADV+N, V+N+ADV, V+PRON+ADV: USUALLY+*with*

paint, paints, painting, painted

paint out. If you **paint** something **out**, you cover or hide it with paint. EG *Branwell later painted his own figure out of the portrait of his sisters... The sign had been painted out, and could no longer be read.*   V+N+ADV, V+ADV+N, V+PRON+ADV

paint over. If you **paint over** something that has already been painted or drawn, you cover it with paint so that it is hidden. EG *When it was discovered, the guards painted over it in grey... You saw off the bolt and paint the door over.*   V+PREP, V+N+ADV, V+PRON+ADV, V+ADV+N

paint up. If you **paint** something **up**, you decorate it with paint, usually in a rather showy way. EG *The house has been bought and painted up... His face was all painted up.*   V+N+ADV, V+PRON+ADV, V+ADV+N

pair, pairs, pairing, paired

pair off. When two people **pair off** or when someone **pairs** them **off**, they come together for a particular purpose or activity, for example at the beginning of a romantic relationship. EG *They'll probably pair*   V+ADV, V+N+ADV, V+PRON+ADV, V+ADV+N: ERGATIVE,

off for company... They show no inclination to pair off with each   ALSO+*with*, RECIPROCAL
other... One of the girls feels the need to pair people off... People are
paired off according to their level of competence.

pair up. If you **pair up** with someone, you agree to do something   V+ADV+*with*, V+ADV:
together. EG *Statistics show that disabled women have a greater*   RECIPROCAL
chance of pairing up with able-bodied men... His enthusiasm was
infectious to anyone he was paired up with. ● **Team up** means
almost the same as **pair up.**

palm, palms, palming, palmed

palm off. 1 If someone **palms** something **off** on you, they give or sell   V+N+ADV, V+PRON+ADV:
it to you in order to get rid of it. EG *See what kind of cement those*   USUALLY+*on*
bloody crooks palmed off on me!... I said he was an expert at
palming things off... They spend their lives having children, and
then palming them off on somebody else.

2 If someone asks you something and you **palm** them **off** with an   V+PRON+ADV, V+N+ADV:
excuse or a lie, you tell them something which is not necessarily   USUALLY+*with*
true or relevant, but which you hope will satisfy them and stop them
bothering you. EG *There's no point in asking her where she's been,*
because she'll only palm you off with excuses... Don't let them palm
you off.

pan, pans, panning, panned

pan out. When you talk about the way that things **pan out,** you are   V+ADV
saying that this is the way that things develop from a particular
situation; an informal expression. EG *Things didn't pan out too well.*
● **Work out** means almost the same as **pan out.**

pander, panders, pandering, pandered

pander to. If you **pander to** someone or to their wishes, you do   V+PREP: HAS PASSIVE
everything that they want, often in order to get some advantage for
yourself. EG *Big business firms pander to the teenagers because*
they've got the money and the time to spend it... The older children
are encouraged to pander to their slightest whim... His firm was
pandering to what he called the 'swinish luxury of the rich'.

paper, papers, papering, papered

paper over. If someone **papers over** a difficulty or mistake, they   V+PREP: HAS PASSIVE
deliberately give the impression that things are going well and try
to hide the difficulty or mistake. EG *...trying to paper over the crisis...*
There is no papering over the fact that basic disputes exist... After
the General Election of 1964 the differences were papered over.

paroel, parcels, parcelling, parcelled

American English uses the spellings **parceling** and **parceled.**

parcel out. When you **parcel** something **out,** you divide it into   V+N+ADV, V+ADV+N,
several parts or amounts and give them to different people. EG *The*   V+PRON+ADV
responsibility for it had been parcelled out among them... ...the
parcelling out of the land among the delighted neighbours.

parcel up. 1 When you **parcel** something **up,** you wrap it as a   V+ADV+N, V+N+ADV,
parcel, with paper, string, tape, and so on. EG *We spent all of last*   V+PRON+ADV
night parcelling up the Christmas presents. ● **Wrap up** means
almost the same as **parcel up.**

2 When something **is parcelled up,** it is divided into separate   PASSIVE: V+ADV,
sections. EG *The Arab Near East after World War 1 was parcelled up*   USUALLY+A
into a number of new states.

pare, pares, paring, pared

pare down. When you **pare** something **down,** you reduce it and   V+ADV+N, V+PRON+ADV:
make it smaller or less extensive. EG *I want to pare down my*   USUALLY+*to*
political involvements to a minimum... The translator had done

Dostoevsky a disservice in paring down 'The Brothers Karamazov'
to essentials... I had pared my possessions down to almost nothing.

pare off. When you **pare off** the skin or outer layer of something,
you cut it off using a knife or other sharp tool. EG *The remains of the*
brown outer layer should be pared off with a knife.

V+ADV+N,
V+N+ADV,
V+PRON+ADV

part, parts, parting, parted

part from. 1 In formal English, when two people **part from** each
other, they leave each other; often used of people who are separating at the end of a relationship; a formal use. EG *I know that I should*
have parted from you long ago, except that I could not endure to...
He had parted from Gertrude in some kind of dreadful moral
muddle... I very nearly parted from her in Copenhagen.

V+PREP

2 If you **are parted from** someone or something, you cannot be with
them, even though you want to be. EG *He had never been parted*
from her before... It's perfectly natural that a mother should not
wish to be parted from her children... ...one who has been too long
parted from dear friends.

PASSIVE:
V+PREP

part with. If you **part with** something that is valuable or that you
would prefer to keep, you give it or sell it to someone else. EG *I took*
the book, thanked her, and told her I would never part with it... She
didn't want to part with the money... I might just be persuaded to
part with it. ● Hold on to means the opposite of part with.

V+PREP:
HAS PASSIVE

partake, partakes, partaking, partook, partaken

partake in. If you **partake in** an activity, you become involved in it
and take part; an old-fashioned expression. EG *Young people de-*
prived of the right to partake in social decision-making will grow
more and more unstable... I was made to partake in a good deal of
menial work.

V+PREP

partake of. 1 If you **partake of** food or drink, you eat or drink it; an
old-fashioned use. EG *He did not partake of either meal, preferring to*
sit at the table sipping whisky while we ate... He was invited to
partake of refreshment in the Senior Common Room.

V+PREP

2 If something **partakes of** a particular quality, it has that quality; a
literary and old-fashioned use. EG *Education is most vital when it*
partakes of the nature of discovery.

V+PREP

partition, partitions, partitioning, partitioned

partition off. If you **partition off** part of something, you separate
that part from the rest by placing a partition between the two parts.
EG *They were partitioned off from the chauffeur by the thick glass...*
...in the kitchenette that Miss Gilderthorp had partitioned off from
her father's original stone kitchen.

V+N+ADV,
V+PRON+ADV

pass, passes, passing, passed

pass along. 1 If something **passes along** or **down** a path or place, it
moves along there. EG *Footsteps passed along the corridor above...*
He nodded hello as he passed along the row of people at the bar...
Thousands of people must have passed down Whitehall without
seeing it.

V+PREP

2 If you **pass** something **along,** you send it or give it to someone else.
EG *I'll pass it along to the management.*

V+N+ADV,
V+PRON+ADV

pass around. If you **pass** things **around** or **round,** you give them
from one person to another in a group. EG *Her mother passed round*
plates of jelly and custard... Go on Ron, just take a light and pass the
matches round... She opened the mountain of gifts and passed them
around... I've got a couple of pictures you might like to pass around.

V+ADV+N,
V+N+ADV,
V+PRON+ADV

pass as. To **pass as** or **for** something means to appear to be that

V+PREP

thing. EG *You may pass as a remarkably witty man... ...that brief period that passes for summer in those high latitudes.*

pass away. 1 When something **passes away**, it slowly disappears. EG *A hurt look appeared in Jack's eyes and passed away... All hopes of compromise had now passed away.* V+ADV

2 If you say that someone **passed away**, you mean that they died; used especially when you want to avoid saying the word 'die'. EG *Your husband sent the letter to us shortly before he passed away... She passed away within three weeks of her sister.* ● **Pass on** means almost the same as **pass away**. V+ADV

3 If you **pass** time **away** in a particular place, you are there for that time. EG *He condescended to pass away a few days in my company... Children in inner city areas are doomed to pass away their days with illegal child-minders.* V+ADV+N, V+N+ADV

pass between. 1 You say that remarks, letters, looks, and so on **pass between** two people when those people say things, or write to each other, or look at each other. EG *...the usual greetings that passed between them... No words passed between us... ...the letters that passed between them in the final years.* V+PREP

2 When something **passes between** two people or places, it moves or is through them so that they are on either side of it. EG *She passed between the two of them... The nail has passed between the bones at the base of the foot... They then pass it between two millstones.* V+PREP, V+N+PREP, V+PRON+PREP

pass by. 1 If you **pass by** something or if you **pass** it **by**, you go past it without stopping. EG *We pass by another marker... A tall bearded silhouette passed by... I was just passing by and I saw your car... Helen flinched as the younger woman passed her by.* ▶ **passer-by, passers-by.** A **passer-by** is a person who is walking past something or someone. EG *One of the boys had stopped a passer-by and asked him to phone an ambulance... Passers-by dived in to rescue them.* V+PREP, V+ADV, V+PRON+ADV

N COUNT

▶ A **bypass** is a main road which is built to take traffic round the edge of a town rather than through the middle. EG *...the construction of a new by-pass around the ancient town of Sandwich... ...the Oxford bypass.* N COUNT

2 If something **passes** you **by**, it happens and finishes before you notice it or can take advantage of it. EG *...an old friend whose works up to now have passed me by... The great drama and passion of the world had already passed him by... Life was passing her by.* V+PRON+ADV

pass down. 1 If things such as stories, traditions, or characteristics are **passed down**, they are told, taught, or given to someone who belongs to a younger generation. EG *Reading little, they remembered the tales passed down from father to son... Our sense of the past is developed by our knowledge of history, by the accumulated heritage of art, music, literature, and science passed down to us through the years... ...stories his own father had passed down to him.* ● **Hand down** means almost the same as **pass down**. V+N+ADV, V+PRON+ADV, V+ADV+N: USUALLY PASSIVE WITH to/from

2 If you **pass** something **down**, you give it to someone who is standing or sitting below you. EG *Can you pass the receipts down, Pat?... Simon passed them down to the outstretched hands.* V+N+ADV, V+PRON+ADV, V+ADV+N

3 See **pass along**.

pass for. See **pass as**.

pass off. 1 If an event **passes off** in a particular way, especially in a satisfactory way, it happens and ends in that way. EG *Most of these situations pass off without mishap... It had passed off amicably enough.* V+ADV: WITH A

2 If you **pass** something unpleasant **off** lightly, you say or pretend that it was not really very important or serious. EG *I had thought he would pass this off lightly... She passed off his criticisms contemptu-* V+N+ADV, V+ADV+N, V+PRON+ADV: WITH A

ously, considering his opinion of little value. ● **Shrug off** means almost the same as **pass off**.

3 If something such as a feeling or condition **passes off**, it gradually disappears. EG *Fortunately the effects of the gas passed off relatively quickly... The attack, or whatever it was, had passed off just as asthma does.* ● **Wear off** means almost the same as **pass off**. `V+ADV`

pass off as. If you **pass** something **off as** a particular thing, you convince people that it is that thing, when in fact it is not so valuable or important, or does not have the right characteristics. EG *The painting had been passed off as early Flemish, or Dutch... The man who made the cabinet passed it off as an antique... He passed himself off as a Frenchman.* `V+N+ADV+PREP,` `V+PRON+ADV+PREP,` `V+REFL+ADV+PREP`

pass on. **1** If you **pass** something **on** to someone, you give it to them, for example after you have used it or after someone else has given it to you. EG *He handed a typewritten sheet to King to pass on to Smith... He only had shoes which other folk passed on to him... The union head office may be able to pass on useful information... I once made an appeal to mothers of twins to tell me what solutions they had found for their problems, so that I could pass them on.* `V+N+ADV,` `V+ADV+N,` `V+PRON+ADV:` `ALSO+to`

2 If things such as stories, traditions, or money **are passed on**, they are taught or given to someone who belongs to a younger generation. EG *Skills such as this should be passed on... The original Harris Company was founded in 1732, and father passed the business on to son for eight generations... Perhaps their own mothers do not have the time or skills to pass on these hobbies... She assumed that her mother would wish to pass on to her the bulk of her fortune... I have nothing that I can pass on to you.* ● **Hand down** means almost the same as **pass on**. `V+N+ADV,` `V+ADV+N,` `V+PRON+ADV:` `USUALLY PASSIVE,` `ALSO+to`

3 When parents **pass on** something such as a physical characteristic to their children, the children develop it or have it because of the genes that they inherit from their parents. EG *How do parents pass genes on to their offspring?... These different abilities may be passed on through several generations.* ● **Transmit** is a more formal word for **pass on**. `V+N+ADV,` `V+ADV+N,` `V+PRON+ADV:` `ALSO+to`

4 If you **pass** someone **on** to someone else, you put them in contact with the second person because you think they might be able to help. EG *If you want confirmation of my authority in this case I'll pass you right on to the Director-General... We passed him on to a fashion-designer friend... I was passed on to another doctor.* `V+PRON+ADV,` `V+N+ADV:` `ALSO+to`

5 If a company **passes on** costs or savings to their customers, they alter their prices and charge either more or less than usual to take account of changes in production costs. EG *Governments have tried to prevent firms from passing on cost increases... Any such saving will automatically be passed on to all clients.* `V+ADV+N,` `V+PRON+ADV:` `ALSO+to`

6 If you **pass on** to a new subject while you are writing or speaking, you begin to talk about it. EG *They passed on to other matters... They passed on to the matter of entertainment.* ● **Move on** means almost the same as **pass on**. `V+ADV:` `ALSO+to`

7 If you **pass on** to a different place in a journey or to a different stage in a process, you continue the journey or process. EG *We passed on to a small pantry and entered the dining room... They stay until they are eleven when they pass on to a secondary school... The man lowered his eyes and quickly passed on.* `V+ADV`

8 If you say that someone **passed on**, you mean that they died; used especially when you want to avoid using the word 'die'. EG *They say poor Miss Parr's passed on... A pity Sir Edmund's passed on... It's five years to the day since she passed on.* ● **Pass away** means almost the same as **pass on**. `V+ADV`

pass out. 1 If you **pass out,** you lose consciousness for a short time.   v+ADV
EG *I thought I was going to pass out... He passed out while I was in
the room... My head thumped solidly on a rock and I passed out.*
• **Black out** means almost the same as **pass out.**

2 If you **pass** something **out,** you distribute it among a number of   V+ADV+N,
people. EG *We all sat cross-legged on the grass, and I passed out the*   V+N+ADV,
lemonade... They passed out enormous bribes to port officials.   V+PRON+ADV
• **Hand out** means almost the same as **pass out.**

3 When a police, army, navy, or air force cadet **passes out,** he or she   V+ADV
satisfactorily finishes his or her course of training. EG *He was killed
in Belfast only two weeks after passing out from Sandhurst.*

pass over. 1 If you **are passed over** for a job or position that you   PASSIVE:
are trying to get, it is given to someone who is less well-qualified or   V+ADV
experienced than you. EG *He got it into his head he was being passed
over for promotion... Neither of us got the job. We were both passed
over.* • **Be rejected** means almost the same as **be passed over.**

2 If you **pass over** a particular topic in a conversation, you deliber-   V+PRON+ADV,
ately do not discuss it. EG *He didn't give a reason and Robertson*   V+ADV+N,
passed it over in silence... He passed over the events of that week.   V+N+ADV
• **Ignore** means almost the same as **pass over.**

3 When something **passes over,** it moves overhead without stopping.   V+PREP,
EG *The glacial winds pass over the waters... A helicopter had passed*   V+ADV
over a few moments before. ▸ An **overpass** is a main road which is   N COUNT
built like a bridge so that it is above another road. EG *They're
building a new overpass.* • **Flyover** means almost the same as
overpass.

4 **Passover** is a Jewish festival that begins in late March or early   N UNCOUNT
April and that lasts for eight days. EG *...the story of the Passover...
Passover is a family occasion.*

pass round. See **pass around.**

pass through. To **pass through** a period of time or series of stages   V+PREP
means to exist before, during, and after that period or those stages
and to develop during them. EG *Mrs Yule had to pass through a few
years of much bitterness... Humanity was believed to pass through
four great ages... The revolutionary movement has passed through a
succession of distinctive phases.*

pass to. When something **passes to** someone, it becomes their   V+PREP
property or responsibility. EG *Her property passes to her next of
kin... Responsibility for security there would now pass to Westmin-
ster.*

pass under. When someone or something **passes under** another   V+PREP
thing, they move underneath it without stopping. EG *We pass under
the trees along the road... After four miles the stream passes under
the road.* ▸ An **underpass** is a road or footpath that goes underneath   N COUNT
something, for example under another road or a railway. EG *...the
Knightsbridge Underpass... The underpass is closed because of fire.*

pass up. If you **pass up** something such as an opportunity, you do   V+ADV+N,
not take advantage of it. EG *Certainly, Mr Gerran would willingly*   V+PRON+ADV
*pass up any potential profit if the need arose... She never passed up
a chance to eat in a restaurant.*

paste, pastes, pasting, pasted

paste up. If you **paste** something **up,** you attach it to a wall or other   V+ADV+N,
vertical surface, using glue or paste. EG *Soldiers had pasted up*   V+N+ADV,
leaflets condemning the petrol bombings... A broad sheet of paper   V+PRON+ADV
was pasted up on the door of the church.

patch, patches, patching, patched

patch together. If something **is patched together,** it is made from   V+N+ADV,
                                                                          V+ADV+N,

a number of parts in a hurried or careless way. EG *A new government was patched together with the help of the military... It's just a lot of electronic modules which can be patched together... She couldn't, as some writers do, just patch together old material.* ● **Cobble together** means almost the same as **patch together.**

patch up. 1 If you **patch up** something which is damaged or broken, you mend it rather roughly so that it can be used. EG *They have to patch up the mud walls that the rains have battered... ...to do a reasonable job patching things up.* ● **Fix up** means almost the same as **patch up.**

V+ADV+N,
V+N+ADV,
V+PRON+ADV

2 If a doctor or surgeon **patches** you **up,** they temporarily bandage you or perform a small operation after you have been injured; an informal use. EG *I have spent a good deal of my time patching up the children who have been wounded... ...the little injury that cannot be patched up simply for lack of money.* ● **Treat** means almost the same as **patch up.**

V+ADV+N,
V+PRON+ADV

3 If you **patch up** a quarrel or relationship with someone, you try to be friends again and not to quarrel any more. EG *Many a village quarrel was patched up that morning... He finally decided to overlook his mates' unkindness and try to patch things up... The Labour party patched up its quarrels after the right won the battle over unilateral disarmament.*

V+N+ADV,
V+ADV+N,
V+PRON+ADV

pattern, patterns, patterning, patterned

pattern on. If something new **is patterned on** something else that already exists, it uses the original thing as a model and is designed and made to be similar to it. EG *The 'Daily Dispatch' was patterned on the British press... He always used a Hoffritz safety razor patterned on the old-fashioned heavy-toothed Gillette type.*

PASSIVE:
V+PREP

pave, paves, paving, paved

pave over. When a road or an area of ground **is paved over,** it is covered with blocks of stone, bricks, or concrete so that it is suitable for walking or travelling on. EG *The carriage paths were paved over only ten years ago... The next court, paved all over with white marble slabs, had a central fountain.*

PASSIVE:
V+ADV

paw, paws, pawing, pawed

paw at. When an animal **paws at** something, it tries to touch it with its paw or hoof. EG *Back in the yard Boxer was pawing with his hoof at the stable-lad... The dog pawed at the doorknob again and again.*

V+PREP

pay, pays, paying, paid

pay back. 1 If you **pay** money **back** to someone or **pay** them **back,** you give them money that you previously borrowed from them. EG *She thanked him for the cheque, saying that when the estate was finally settled she would pay back all the money he had sent her... I'm going to pay every penny of it back to him... With the salary you mentioned you ought to be able to pay it back in one month... Loan me a hundred dollars, I'll pay you back on Monday when I go to the bank.* ● **Repay** means almost the same as **pay back.**

V+ADV+N,
V+N+ADV,
V+PRON+ADV:
ALSO+ *to*

2 If you **pay** someone **back** for doing something unpleasant to you, you do something unpleasant to them as a form of punishment. EG *I felt that I would like to wake her up to pay her back for keeping me awake... I was now prepared to pay him back for his treacheries.*

V+PRON+ADV,
V+N+ADV:
USUALLY+ *for*

pay for. 1 If you **pay for** something, you give someone money for it. EG *They will still need an estimated $2 billion to pay for food and other 1981 imports... He allowed Rudolph to pay for the drinks... The ticket was reserved but not paid for.*

V+PREP:
HAS PASSIVE

2 If something that you buy eventually **pays for** itself, it saves you

V+PREP+REFL

more money than it originally cost because it is so efficient that you do not need to spend as much money as you used to. EG *In Sri Lanka hiring rates are so high that a tractor can pay for itself in less than two years... All these things are possible and would pay for themselves by saving on energy brought in from outside... Fix up a hand shower. It soon pays for itself by halving your bathwater bills.*

3 If you say that someone will have to **pay for** something bad that they have done, you mean that they will be punished or forced to do something else which they do not want to do. EG *The obvious implication was that Kruger would have to pay for his mistake in banning me... Maybe uniformity is one of the prices we have to pay for sociability in a more mobile society.*   v+PREP

pay in. When you **pay** money **in,** you put it or transfer it into a bank account. EG *They wanted the number of his bank account so that they might pay it in... Reginald called in at the bank to pay his first cheque in.*   v+PRON+ADV, v+N+ADV, v+ADV+N

pay into. When you **pay** money **into** a bank account, you put it or transfer it into the account. EG *...a girocheque, which you can cash at the post office, or pay into a bank account... Then I began to draw the money out in cash and pay it into my account under my own name at the Midland Bank.* ● **Deposit** means almost the same as **pay into.**   v+N+PREP, v+PRON+PREP

pay off. **1** If you **pay off** a debt or bill, you give someone the total amount of money that you owe them so that you are no longer in debt. EG *He had used the firm's money to pay off gambling debts... The most common reason for borrowing is to pay off existing loans... So she fell into debt and had to pay it off by selling her house.* ● **Repay** means almost the same as **pay off.**   v+ADV+N, v+PRON+ADV, v+N+ADV

2 If you **pay** someone **off,** you try to stop them threatening you or causing you trouble by giving them money. EG *Mr. Hagen, I can't afford to look ridiculous. I have to pay Johnny off... His lawyer raised money to pay off the convicted defendants in the Watergate case.* ● **Buy off** means almost the same as **pay off.** ▶ A **payoff** is a payment that you make to someone so that they do not cause trouble for you. EG *It was usually possible to make a payoff to a high police official to keep quiet.*   v+N+ADV, v+PRON+ADV, v+ADV+N

N COUNT

3 If you **pay off** workers, you pay them what you owe them for work that they have done for you and then dismiss them. EG *Mrs Foster persuaded the driver to carry her two large cases to the top of the steps. Then she paid him off and rang the bell... I paid the taxi off at the end of the street and walked down to my flat... All troops were immediately paid off and discharged.*   v+PRON+ADV, v+N+ADV, v+ADV+N

4 If an action **pays off,** it is successful. EG *It was a risk and it paid off... Their anti-aircraft precautions had paid off well.* ▶ A **payoff** is the useful result of an action. EG *Some carry out research without daring to hope that there could be a practical pay-off... There's a risk and payoff for both sides.*   v+ADV

N COUNT

pay out. **1** If you **pay out** a large amount of money, you spend it on a particular item or activity. EG *They pay out half of their income in rent... She had paid out good money to send Julie to school... Every Friday twelve or thirteen thousand pounds was paid out in wages.*   v+ADV+N, v+N+ADV, v+PRON+ADV

2 When you **pay out** a rope or cable, you unwind it in a controlled way. EG *Ned paid out the rope and carried the block to the tree... Then the boat is dropped back, downtide, paying out the steel anchor cable as we go.*   v+ADV+N, v+PRON+ADV

pay up. When you **pay up,** you give someone the money that you owe them, even though you would prefer not to. EG *Come on, pay up... Things might not go too well if he didn't pay up... Even when*   v+ADV, v+ADV+N *suspecting fraud, airlines found it cheaper to pay up quickly than enter into a prolonged dispute... When I was ill they paid up £500 immediately.*

peal, peals, pealing, pealed

peal out. When sounds **peal out,** they can be heard clearly over a long distance. EG *And the bells would peal out across the town and countryside... ...so many hammered tones pealing out in oppressive arpeggios.* ● **Resound** means almost the same as **peal out.**   V+ADV

peck, pecks, pecking, pecked

peck at. If you **peck at** your food, you eat only small amounts of it, because you are ill or not hungry, or because you do not like the food; an informal expression. EG *Throughout the meal, I could do no more than peck at my food, constantly watching the clock.*   V+PREP

peel, peels, peeling, peeled

peel off. 1 If you **peel** the outer layer **off** something or if it **peels off,** you remove it or it separates so that it comes away from the surface gently. EG *I peeled some moss off the wood... She peeled the wrapping paper off... ...gleaming sheets of metal that had been partly peeled off like the skin of an orange... On the statues, the gold leaf was beginning to peel off.*   V+N+PREP/ADV, V+PRON+PREP/ADV, V+ADV+N, V+ADV: ERGATIVE

2 If you **peel off** some money from a pile of banknotes, you take some of the notes from the top with your hand. EG *He took a wad of bills out of his side pocket and peeled off five tens... I was paid in small bills peeled off a thick wad of larger ones.*   V+ADV+N

3 If you **peel off** a tight piece of clothing, you remove it by pulling it slowly. EG *She peeled off her sweater... Once in the hotel, Mick and I peeled off our boots... Chris began to peel off her dress.* ● **Strip off** means almost the same as **peel off.**   V+ADV+N, V+N+ADV, V+PRON+ADV

4 If part of a group of moving vehicles or people **peel off,** they leave the group and follow a course that curves away to one side. EG *As the cars arrived, the police motorcycle escorts had to peel off and circle round the courtyard... Even as he saw this, one of the bodyguards peeled off to come ahead and see what was wrong.*   V+ADV

peg, pegs, pegging, pegged

peg away. If you **peg away** at something, you continue doing it in a very determined way, even though it is difficult or unpleasant; an informal expression. EG *He would rather keep on pegging away at a beginner's book... We found that it didn't help much to peg away at the same passage.* ● **Plug away** means almost the same as **peg away.**   V+ADV: USUALLY+at

peg out. 1 If someone **pegs out,** they die; an informal use. EG *If he leaves me he has to give me half the house money but if I peg out all she has to do is move in... If I don't warm up first, I'll just peg out halfway round the course.*   V+ADV

2 If you **peg out** clothes or sheets that you have just washed, you fasten them to a washing line with pegs. EG *She trudged up the garden and began to peg out the clothes on the line... Mrs Poulter began to peg out a bit of her washing... As soon as she had pegged it out, it began to rain.* ● **Hang out** means almost the same as **peg out.**   V+ADV+N, V+PRON+ADV, V+N+ADV

3 If you **peg** something **out,** you spread it on the ground and fasten it there with pegs. EG *...a sheepskin pegged out on the grass... We pegged the tent out with considerable difficulty.*   V+N+ADV, V+PRON+ADV, V+ADV+N

pelt, pelts, pelting, pelted

pelt down. If it **is pelting down** with rain, it is raining very hard; an informal expression. EG *He guessed that it must be rain pelting*   V+ADV down... ...*the rain pelted down outside.* ● **Pour down** means almost the same as **pelt down**.

pen, pens, penning, penned

pen in. 1 If you **pen in** animals, you make them move into an enclosed area such as a pen. EG ...*like a collie dog trying to pen in some reluctant sheep... They were penned in like cattle.*　　V+ADV+N, V+N+ADV, V+PRON+ADV

2 If a person or their abilities **are penned in,** they are restricted by the situation that they are in. EG *Clergymen can feel penned in too.*　　V+N+ADV, V+PRON+ADV, V+ADV+N

pen up. If people or animals **are penned up,** they are kept together in an enclosed area. EG *A thousand were penned up in a small building... ...the boredom of endless hours penned up in a hot and dusty railway carriage.*　　V+N+ADV, V+PRON+ADV, V+ADV+N

pencil, pencils, pencilling, pencilled

American English uses the spellings **penciled** and **penciling**.

pencil in. If something **is pencilled in,** it is written in pencil rather than ink on a piece of paper because you are not sure whether it is correct or because you want to see if it looks all right. EG *She had pencilled in a tentative title, 'The Song of the Salesman'... Two other dates were proposed, with something just pencilled in for both of those evenings as well.*　　V+ADV+N, V+N+ADV, V+PRON+ADV

pension, pensions, pensioning, pensioned

pension off. 1 If someone **is pensioned off,** they are made to retire from work and given money by their employers or the government. EG *Many people go on working as useful citizens at an age when we would pension them off... In 1958, Kleiber was pensioned off and allowed to buy the security company at a bargain price.*　　V+PRON+ADV, V+N+ADV, V+ADV+N

2 If you **pension off** something that you use regularly, you stop using it completely; a humorous use. EG *So I settled for an orange hunting hat, pensioning off the blue denim one I had started with.*　　V+ADV+N, V+N+ADV, V+PRON+ADV

pep, peps, pepping, pepped

pep up. 1 If you **pep** something **up,** you make it more lively or interesting. EG *Undoubtedly, he realised that the conference needed pepping up... Kellogg had good reason to try to pep up its product line.* ● **Liven up** means almost the same as **pep up**.　　V+N+ADV, V+PRON+ADV, V+ADV+N

2 If something **peps** you **up,** it gives you more energy. EG *Morell gave him an extra dose of glucose to pep him up.* ● **Perk up** means almost the same as **pep up**.　　V+PRON+ADV, V+N+ADV, V+ADV+N

pepper, peppers, peppering, peppered

pepper with. 1 To **pepper** something **with** small things means to throw lots of the things at it or to sprinkle them onto its surface. EG ...*peppered them with a hail of bullets from his pocket pistol... 'There,' he insisted, his abrupt English peppering the air with faint showers of spittle.*　　V+PRON+PREP, V+N+PREP

2 If something **is peppered with** things, there are a lot of the things on it or in it. EG ...*a monotonous plateau of rust red and ochre peppered with the pastel green of acacia... ...an elderly black face, its cheeks peppered with several days' growth of grey whiskers... The satellite was peppered with glittering particles.*　　PASSIVE: V+PREP

3 If you **pepper** your speech or writing **with** a particular type of language, you use a lot of that type of language when you speak or write. EG *Sir Derek peppered his speech with learned references... ...whose French is heavily peppered with such Americanisms.*　　V+N+PREP, V+PRON+PREP

perk, perks, perking, perked

perk up. 1 If someone **perks up** or if someone or something **perks** them **up,** they suddenly become more cheerful, interested, active, or　　V+ADV, V+ADV+N, V+N+ADV, exciting. EG *He was being a bore, that's why. A proper misery. He perked up when we got there, though... Peter perked up. He rose from his chair... There are more agreeable ways to perk up your appetite.* ● **Liven up** means almost the same as **perk up.**

V+PRON+ADV: ERGATIVE

2 If you **perk up** coffee, you make some coffee to drink, using a percolator; used mainly in American English. EG *Aw, let me treat you—I was going to perk some up for Muscle Man anyway.*

V+N+ADV, V+ADV+N, V+PRON+ADV

permit, permits, permitting, permitted

permit of. If something **permits of** a particular thing, it makes it possible; a very formal expression. EG *An institution like the concentration camp permits of no really successful defence.*

V+PREP

pertain, pertains, pertaining, pertained

pertain to. If one thing **pertains to** another thing, it relates to that other thing, affects it, or is only valid for it; a formal expression. EG *The rules pertaining to one set of circumstances do not necessarily pertain to another... ...to write about things that don't directly pertain to him... I was given free access to all official documents pertaining to the Revolution.*

V+PREP

peter, peters, petering, petered

peter out. If something **peters out,** it gets smaller, less intense, or less important and gradually stops completely. EG *The tracks petered out a mile or two later... The attack petered out after two hours... His rage petered out.*

V+ADV

phase, phases, phasing, phased

phase in. If you **phase in** a new product, method, or idea, you introduce it gradually. EG *Beveridge's original plan was to phase in adequate old-age pensions in the period up to 1956... There is probably more than enough time to phase in this enormous resource well before fossil fuels become exhausted.* ▶ The **phasing in** of a new product, method, or idea is its gradual introduction into a system. EG *...the phasing in of long-term alternatives... ...the phasing-in of 'market rents.'*

V+ADV+N, V+N+ADV, V+PRON+ADV

N SING

phase into. If you **phase** a new product, method, or idea **into** a system, you introduce it gradually into the system. EG *It is now under development but may require a decade or two to be phased into mass production... Vacuum tube collectors are being phased into an oil-fired district heating scheme at Uppsala.*

V+N+PREP, V+PRON+PREP

phase out. If you **phase out** a product, method, or idea, you gradually stop using it. EG *The Thatcher government is planning to phase out earnings-related supplements... Gold has been phased out of the monetary system... ...would be willing to phase out nuclear weapons.* ▶ The **phasing out** of a product, method, or idea is the process of gradually ceasing to use it. EG *1977 saw the phasing out of child tax allowances.*

V+ADV+N, V+N+ADV, V+PRON+ADV

N SING

phone, phones, phoning, phoned

phone back. If you **phone back** or **phone** someone **back,** you phone them for a second time or after they have phoned you. EG *The leader of the team phoned back... She phoned back to say that it was only an eleven-day trip... I said I'd phone them back this morning... We will know when I've phoned my agent back.* ● **Call back** and **ring back** mean almost the same as **phone back.**

V+ADV, V+PRON+ADV, V+N+ADV: NO PASSIVE

phone down. If you are in a building and you **phone down** to a person or a place, you phone someone on one of the floors below you, usually to ask them to do something for you. EG *I'll phone down to the restaurant and arrange it now... She phoned down to the desk*

V+ADV, V+PRON+ADV, V+N+ADV: ALSO+*to*

*to say she'd be keeping the suite... He phoned down an order, more
or less at random, for Haydn's Third Symphony.*

phone for. If you **phone for** something, you phone someone to ask
them to provide it for you. EG *When we've had breakfast you can
phone for a taxi... The other boy must have phoned for the ambulance.*

V+PREP:
HAS PASSIVE

phone in. 1 If you **phone in** to a radio or television station, you
phone them because you want to talk on a programme that is being
broadcast at the time. EG *It's called Fan Fare—people can phone in
and actually speak to local football managers... She phoned in to the
Charles Boon show.* ▸ A **phone-in** or **phone-in** programme is a radio
or TV programme in which members of the public can phone and
give their opinions or ask questions while the programme is being
broadcast. EG *There's a phone-in about it... ...a late-night phone-in
programme... ...the independent TV phone-in... ...the new phone-in
version.*

V+ADV:
ALSO+*to*

N COUNT,
ADJECTIVE

2 If you **phone in** to an organization that provides special help for
people who are in trouble, such as drug addicts, alcoholics, and
people contemplating suicide, you phone them because you need
their help. EG *There is a 24- hour religious service; you can phone in
and be saved any time.*

V+ADV:
ALSO+*to*

3 If you work for an organization such as a newspaper, the armed
forces, or the police and **phone in** information, you phone them to
tell them where you are or what you are doing, or to tell them the
information. EG *Within minutes, they phoned in another bulletin...
Lewis phoned the details in to a rewrite man... ...a news story which
a reporter at the meeting had just phoned in... She phoned in to say
that the situation was now improving.*

V+ADV+N,
V+N+ADV,
V+PRON+ADV,
V+ADV

4 If you have a job and **phone in,** you phone your employers, usually
to tell them that you are ill and cannot work that day. EG *Judy
phones in to say she has food poisoning... She had phoned in and said
she was sick.*

V+ADV

phone round. If you **phone round,** you phone several people or
organizations, for example to invite them to an event or to ask them
for help or information. EG *...while we were phoning round for our
survey... I think the best idea is to phone round and see if anyone
runs a bus there on Sundays.*

V+ADV

phone through. If you **phone through,** you make a phone call,
usually to get or give information or make some arrangements. EG
*At the end of the week he phoned through with the news of a
possible job... I'll be phoning through later this afternoon for the
result.*

V+ADV

phone up. When you **phone** someone **up,** you dial their phone
number and speak to them on the phone. EG *I've got to phone her up
tonight... So I phoned the place up and they said they had about 6... I
said to my father, 'Phone up the police.'... The landlord is phoning up
tomorrow to see if he's got it.* ● **Ring up** and **call up** mean almost
the same as **phone up.**

V+PRON+ADV,
V+N+ADV,
V+ADV+N,
V+ADV

pick, picks, picking, picked

pick at. 1 If you **pick at** the food that you are eating, you eat very
small amounts of it because you are not hungry. EG *'When the war is
over,' he said, picking at his plate, 'I'm going to go down there and
settle.'... She picked at her food, without appetite... ...like a hen
picking at grain.* ● **Nibble at** means almost the same as **pick at.**

V+PREP:
HAS PASSIVE

2 If you **pick at** something, you keep pulling it or scratching it with
your fingers. EG *Monkeys and apes pick at one another's fur as a
social ritual... Tortyev was content to pick at his fingernails.*

V+PREP

3 If you **pick at** a person or their work, you criticize small details in their actions, ideas, or work. EG *A work on such a scale is bound to have some weak spots to pick at.*   V+PREP

pick off. **1** If someone **picks off** animals or enemy soldiers, aircraft, or weapons, they shoot at them one at a time and kill or destroy them. EG *A single hunter attempting to pick off animals in groups usually has little luck... He circled the soldiers guarding the horses, and began picking them off one by one.*   V+ADV+N, V+PRON+ADV, V+N+ADV

2 If you **pick off** something, you remove it by pulling it or scratching it with your fingers or a tool. EG *They probe around the base of their quills to pick off fleas... Try picking it off with a comb or your finger.*   V+ADV+N, V+PRON+ADV, V+N+ADV

pick on. **1** If you **pick on** someone, you treat them badly or in an unfair way, often repeatedly. EG *'Why pick on Johan?' I said. 'John also deserted us.'... The older men pick on the boys and are always looking for faults... They'll be protected by the union from being picked on by the boss if they do complain.* ● **Get at** means almost the same as **pick on.**   V+PREP: HAS PASSIVE

2 If you **pick on** one particular person or thing, you choose that one. EG *Of all the girls in town, he picked on Mr Zapp's daughter... Why did we pick on Venice, for God's sake?*   V+PREP

pick out. **1** If you **pick out** someone or something when they are difficult to see or recognize, you manage to see or recognize them. EG *We could just barely pick it out when the light was right... Irene Burns picked out Meehan as one of the two men who gave her a lift... One could just pick out the letters AGR.* ● **Make out** means almost the same as **pick out,** and **discern** is a more formal word.   V+PRON+ADV, V+ADV+N, V+N+ADV

2 If you **pick out** one person or thing from a group, you choose them. EG *He picks out a flat spot without any rocks on it... They'll look through the applications, they'll pick out the ones they like, and invite you in for interview.* ● **Select** means almost the same as **pick out.**   V+ADV+N, V+N+ADV, V+PRON+ADV

3 If part of a painting or design **is picked out,** it is in a different material or colour so that it is very noticeable. EG *...his coronet, picked out in gloss paint... ...my name, the letters picked out in silver.*   PASSIVE: V+ADV, USUALLY+*in*

4 If someone or something **is picked out** by a light, the light shines only on them, so they are seen very clearly. EG *I saw teeth in the dimness—gleaming teeth picked out by our street light... Elizabeth was picked out by a tiny spotlight... The indirect glow from the light picked out their silhouettes.*   V+N+ADV, V+ADV+N, V+PRON+ADV: USUALLY PASSIVE

5 If you **pick out** a tune on a musical instrument, you play it slowly and awkwardly because you do not know it very well or cannot play the instrument very well. EG *He picked out a tune on the piano and after a while tried singing along to it.*   V+ADV+N, V+N+ADV, V+PRON+ADV

pick over. If you **pick over** a group of things, you examine them carefully and choose only the things you want and throw away or reject anything you do not want. EG *Never use soft or damaged fruit. Pick it over carefully and remove the stalks and hulls... I saw one old lady picking over a pile of old coats in a corner.*   V+PRON+ADV, V+ADV+N, V+N+ADV

pick through. If you **pick through** things, you examine them carefully. EG *Pick through the pieces and see if you can find one you like... ...some rather old hymn books that Angelica picked through but didn't seem to take any notice of.*   V+PREP: HAS PASSIVE

pick up. **1** If you **pick** something **up,** you lift it up from a particular place. EG *He stooped down to pick up the two pebbles... The telephone rang and Judy picked it up... The air was full of flying objects, picked up by the tearing winds.* ● **Lift up** means almost the same as **pick up.**   V+ADV+N, V+PRON+ADV, V+N+ADV

2 When you **pick** yourself **up** after you have fallen or been knocked down, you stand up again, often with difficulty. EG *Then he jumped off the horse, stumbled and fell, picked himself up and ran for cover.*   V+REFL+ADV

3 If you are driving a vehicle and you **pick** someone or something **up,** you stop the vehicle so that you can take them somewhere. EG *He had to pick a friend up that afternoon to go to Stranraer... I'll pick it up on my way to work... ...describing the bicycle and the boy on it and the woman who picked me up and what she was wearing and what I said... It was not likely that two murderers would pick up someone so soon after the crime... Melanie's mother drives by to pick up Carol.* ▸ **Pick-up** places or things are available for people to collect and take away. EG *Well-organized teams of agents see the shipments through from the pick-up point to their destinations.*   V+N+ADV, V+PRON+ADV, V+ADV+N   ADJECTIVE

4 If someone **is picked up** by the police or another group, they are arrested or taken somewhere to be asked questions. EG *He was picked up by government agents for questioning... I don't want you to be picked up for vagrancy... I could fix it so that the highway patrol pick him up for drunk driving and put him in jail all night.* ● **Take in** means almost the same as **pick up.**   V+ADV+N, V+N+ADV, V+PRON+ADV: USUALLY PASSIVE

5 If you **pick up** a skill, habit, or attitude, you learn it or start having it without making any effort. EG *Did you pick up any Swedish?... The kids pick it up really fast but lose it just as quickly... He'll soon start to pick the job up.*   V+ADV+N, V+PRON+ADV, V+N+ADV

6 If you **pick** something **up,** you find or get it by chance, often when you were not looking for it or expecting to get it. EG *I may pick up a couple of useful ideas for my book... Her mother had liked to pick up bargains in basement sales... ...the fragments of information they picked up on their night-time visits... ...some kind of food poisoning that they picked up at dinner... Babies can easily pick up thrush, a mild fungus infection.*   V+ADV+N, V+N+ADV, V+PRON+ADV

7 If you **pick up** a prize, a reputation, or something else that improves your situation, you gain it or win it. EG *It picked up the Best Musical Award... He was picking up a lot of support because the public admired his policies.*   V+ADV+N, V+PRON+ADV

8 If you say that someone **picks up** the tab, the bill, or the cheque, you mean that they pay for something. EG *Who's picking up the tab for the research?... The company lays men off and the national government picks up the bill in unemployment pay... I'm delighted, but you must really let me pick up the check.*   V+ADV+N, V+PRON+ADV

9 If someone **picks up** a particular amount of money for the work they do, they earn that amount of money; a fairly informal use. EG *A welding overseer picks up 400 pounds a week.*   V+ADV+N: NO PASSIVE

10 If you **pick up** someone you do not know, you start talking to them and being friendly towards them, usually because you want to have a sexual relationship with them. EG *I doubt whether Tony ever picked up a woman in his life... Then she went into the bar and nobody tried to pick her up.* ▸ A **pick-up** is a situation in which someone is trying to start a sexual relationship with someone they have just met. EG *But the girl clearly knows a pick-up when she sees one... ...from sexual suggestions to attempted pick-ups.*   V+ADV+N, V+PRON+ADV, V+N+ADV   N COUNT

11 If a person or animal **picks up** a faint smell or a quiet sound, they become aware of it. EG *He sniffed the air, trying to pick up their scent... Kunta's ears picked up a strange, muted sound.* ● **Detect** is a more formal word for **pick up.**   V+ADV+N, V+N+ADV, V+PRON+ADV

12 If a piece of equipment such as a radio or microphone **picks up** a signal or sound, it receives or detects it. EG *It was easier to pick up Radio Luxembourg than Radio One... ...bugging devices that were capable of picking up both telephone and room conversations...*   V+ADV+N, V+N+ADV, V+PRON+ADV

Signals from the Command Post's radio must have been picked up by Soviet direction finders.

13 If you **pick up** a mistake or other feature in something, you notice it. EG *...so that if there is a mistake you'll pick it up... She should be picking up inconsistencies as they occur.*
V+PRON+ADV,
V+ADV+N,
V+N+ADV

14 If you **pick up** a point or topic that someone has mentioned, you go back to it and say something relating to it. EG *I'd like to pick up the point David made... The President picked up the theme.*
V+ADV+N,
V+PRON+ADV

15 If you **pick up** something that you had stopped doing, you start doing it again, usually from the point where you had stopped. EG *I really do feel I'm picking up where I left off about twelve years ago... He'd love to pick up their conversation where they'd left off.*
V+ADV,
V+ADV+N,
V+N+ADV,
V+PRON+ADV
● **Resume** is a more formal word for **pick up.**

16 If trade, business, or the economy of a country **picks up,** it gradually increases or improves after a period of inactivity or decline. EG *The economy is picking up... Retail demand for diamonds has picked up in recent weeks... People like her are waiting for trade to pick up.* ▶ A **pick-up** in trade, business, or the economy of a country is an increase or improvement in it. EG *Small traders are now reporting a significant pick-up in business... ...a sales pick-up.*
V+ADV

N SING

17 A **pick-me-up** is a drink that you have in order to make you feel healthier and more energetic; a fairly informal word. ● **Tonic** means almost the same as **pick up.**
N COUNT

pick up on. **1** If you **pick up on** something, you notice it and it affects your attitude or behaviour. EG *A girl picks up on her mother's fear or dislike of sex... ...picking up on the woman's embarrassment.*
V+ADV+PREP

2 If you **pick** someone **up on** something that they have said or done, you tell them that you think that it is wrong. EG *May I just pick him up on what he said about women?* ● **Take up on** means almost the same as **pick up on.**
V+PRON+ADV+PREP,
V+N+ADV+PREP

pick up with. If you **pick up with** someone, you start meeting them regularly and doing things together. EG *Mother used to be wild with me the way I'd pick up with just anyone.*
V+ADV+PREP

piece, pieces, piecing, pieced

piece out. If you **piece out** the truth or facts about something, you gradually manage to discover them. EG *Her partner can piece out what is being said.* ● **Work out** and **suss out** mean almost the same as **piece out.**
V+ADV+N,
V+N+ADV,
V+PRON+ADV

piece together. **1** If you **piece together** the truth about something, you gradually discover it. EG *From hints and whispers we pieced together the explanation... As the questioning continued he began to piece it together... She had not yet been able to piece together exactly what had happened... Using manuscript sources, it has been possible to piece the whole story together.* ● **Work out** means almost the same as **piece together,** and **deduce** is a more formal word.
V+ADV+N,
V+PRON+ADV,
V+ADV+WH,
V+N+ADV

2 If you **piece** something **together,** you gradually make or form it by joining several things or elements together. EG *...a nation struggling to piece together a new identity... He would fish out torn love letters from waste baskets and piece them together carefully.*
V+ADV+N,
V+PRON+ADV,
V+N+ADV

pile, piles, piling, piled

pile in. If a group of people **pile in,** they all get into a place or vehicle at once in rather a disorganized way. EG *There was room for all four of us, and we piled in.* ● **Crowd in** means almost the same as **pile in.**
V+ADV

pile into. If a group of people **pile into** a place or vehicle, they all get into it at once in rather a disorganized way. EG *Hurriedly we packed up and piled into the bus... Businessmen pile into London in*
V+PREP

enormous numbers. ● **Crowd into** means almost the same as **pile into.**

pile on. 1 If people **pile on** to something such as a vehicle or   V+ADV:
platform, they all try to get on it at once in a disorganized way. EG   ALSO+*to*
*There was a crowd of schoolkids, all piling on to the train and trying
to grab the best seats.*

2 If you **pile on** something such as suggestions, instructions, or work,   V+N+ADV,
you give a lot of them to other people to deal with. EG *They really*   V+ADV+N,
  V+PRON+ADV:
pile the work on, don't they?... Responsibility is also piled on by all   ALSO+*to*
*that is written about the effects of bad parenting... She would not
want even more suggestions to pile on to the list of do's and don'ts.*

pile out. If a group of people **pile out** of a place, they all get out of it   V+ADV:
at once in rather a disorganized way. EG *The crowd of children piled*   ALSO+*of*
*out of the house... Everyone but me piled out of the car... They all
piled out with their cameras.*

pile up. 1 If things **pile up** or if you **pile** them **up,** they collect   V+ADV,
somewhere or you put them somewhere, forming a pile. EG *Masses*   V+ADV+N,
  V+PRON+ADV,
of cloud piled up in the sky over the distant hills... When magazines   V+N+ADV:
pile up on the floor, don't complain... He piled up the teacups... He   ERGATIVE
*told his men to gather some rocks and pile them up... Her hair had
been piled up on top of her head.* ● **Heap up** means almost the same
as **pile up.**

2 A **pile-up** is a road accident in which several vehicles crash into   N COUNT
each other. EG *There had been a twenty-car pile-up on the M1.*

3 If things **pile up** or if someone **piles** them **up,** more and more of   V+ADV,
them happen or are acquired. EG *All these disasters piled up on the*   V+ADV+N,
  V+PRON+ADV,
unfortunate Bangladeshis... As the bills piled up, she had not known   V+N+ADV:
where to turn... The traffic had piled up behind me... Last year   ERGATIVE
alone, the company piled up losses totalling £4 billion.

pin, pins, pinning, pinned

pin down. 1 If you try to **pin down** something which is hard to   V+ADV+N,
define or describe, you try to say exactly what it is or what it is like.   V+N+ADV,
  V+PRON+ADV
EG *He was afraid he might never be able to pin down his own
insights, let alone convey them to others... Police forces are continu-
ing inquiries to try and pin the whereabouts of the suspect down.*
● **Nail down** means almost the same as **pin down,** and **specify** is a
more formal word.

2 If you **pin** someone **down,** you force them to make an exact   V+N+ADV,
statement about something, which they have tried to avoid doing. EG   V+PRON+ADV:
  ALSO+*to*
*He was worried and anxious to pin Kishan Kumar down to some
definite commitment... The more he had tried to pin them down on
what they were talking about the vaguer they got... Try to pin him
down to a date.* ● **Nail down** means almost the same as **pin down.**

3 If someone or something **pins** you **down,** they force you into a   V+PRON+ADV,
particular position so that you cannot move. EG *The strong arms*   V+ADV+N,
  V+N+ADV
*were around me, pinning me down so that I couldn't move... Whole
battalions found themselves pinned down by German fire... They
pinned down the guards.* ● **Hold down** means almost the same as **pin
down.**

pin on. 1 If you **pin** the blame or responsibility for something **on** or   V+N+PREP,
upon someone, you say that they did it or caused it. EG *It amused*   V+PRON+PREP
*Wilf to watch him trying to pin a crime on him he hadn't commit-
ted... The Court was unable to pin responsibility upon any person...
You can't pin that on me.*

2 If you **pin** your hopes or faith **on** or **upon** something or someone,   V+N+PREP
you hope very much that they will help you to produce the result

you want. EG *He increasingly pinned his hopes on the prospect of a split in the opposition party... I pin my faith on public opinion.*

pin up. 1 If you **pin up** a poster or a notice, you fix it to a wall so that it can be seen easily. EG *I did not bother to pin either of them up on my wall... ...pinning up the letters the women send to each other... The map was pinned up and became the centre of attention... The chart for sight testing was pinned up on the partition.* ● **Put up** means almost the same as **pin up.** ▶ A **pin-up** is a large picture of an attractive woman or man, often a model wearing very few clothes, or a famous person. EG *The bathroom wall was plastered with pin-ups of film stars.*

V+N+ADV, V+ADV+N, V+PRON+ADV: ALSO+on

N COUNT, ADJECTIVE

2 If you **pin up** part of a piece of clothing or material, you use pins to fasten the bottom of it to a part of it that is higher up. EG *She was bending down, pinning up the hem of her sister's dress.*

V+ADV+N, V+N+ADV, V+PRON+ADV

3 If a woman **pins** her hair **up**, she makes it into a bun or a similar hairstyle and fixes it in place with hairpins. EG *Mrs Waites was pinning up her freshly-washed hair... Her hair was pinned up, but wisps escaped here and there.*

V+ADV+N, V+N+ADV, V+PRON+ADV

pin upon. See pin on.

pine, pines, pining, pined

pine away. If someone **pines away**, they gradually become weaker and die because they are very unhappy. EG *I believe she actually pined away—lost her will to live... A young lady found her lover was unfaithful, and pined away.* ● **Waste away** means almost the same as **pine away.**

V+ADV

pipe, pipes, piping, piped

pipe down. If you tell someone to **pipe down**, you are telling them to talk more quietly or to stop talking altogether; an informal expression. EG *Pipe down at the back there.*

IMPERATIVE: V+ADV

pipe up. If someone who has been silent for a while **pipes up**, they start speaking. EG *'It's all very well for you, Elizabeth,' he piped up... They heard Patsy's youngest pipe up: 'What about the girls?'.*

V+ADV, V+ADV+QUOTE

piss, pisses, pissing, pissed

Piss is a very rude, informal word.

piss about. If someone **pisses about** or **around**, they waste a lot of time and annoy other people by behaving in a silly or childish way.

V+ADV

piss around. See piss about.

piss down. If it **is pissing down**, it is raining very hard.

V+ADV

piss off. 1 If a person tells someone else to **piss off**, that person is telling them in a rude way to go away, usually because they have done something annoying.

IMPERATIVE: V+ADV

2 If someone **is pissed off** with something or if someone or something **pisses** them **off**, they feel bored and irritated by them. EG *This guy was beginning to piss me off... I'm thoroughly pissed off with all of them.*

V+PRON+ADV, V+N+ADV

pit, pits, pitting, pitted

pit against. If one thing **is pitted against** another thing, it is put in competition with it. EG *He was pitted against a really first-class player... ...heretical beliefs pitted against a moral philosophy... ...pitting his judgement against theirs.*

V+N+PREP, V+PRON+PREP

pitch, pitches, pitching, pitched

pitch in. If you **pitch in**, you help other people to do a task, using a lot of energy or enthusiasm. EG *They will be expected to pitch in and make their own beds... During the cane season everyone pitched in.* ● **Muck in** means almost the same as **pitch in.**

V+ADV: ALSO+with

pitch into. 1 If you **pitch into** a job that you have to do, you start   V+PREP
doing it with a lot of energy. EG *Brisk rubbing of hands here, as
though we are about to pitch into some job of work like washing a
window... Be careful not to pitch into your exercises before warming
up.* ● **Dive into** means almost the same as **pitch into**.

2 If someone **pitches into** you, they attack you, either by hitting you,   V+PREP:
or by insulting and criticizing you; an informal use. EG *The boss*   HAS PASSIVE
really pitched into me and told me I wasn't working hard enough.
● **Lay into** means almost the same as **pitch into**.

pivot, pivots, pivoting, pivoted

pivot on. If something **pivots on** or **upon** something else, it depends   V+PREP
on this thing which is very important to its success or progress. EG
Success or failure pivoted on a single exam. ● **Hang on** means
almost the same as **pivot on**.

pivot upon. See **pivot on**.

plague, plagues, plaguing, plagued

plague with. 1 If you **are plagued with** unpleasant things, they   PASSIVE:
keep happening and cause you a lot of trouble or suffering. EG *Simon*   V+PREP
*Keswick was plagued with kidney trouble while in the colony... The
inner-city school is plagued with problems... His summer cold was
one of the worst he had ever been plagued with.*

2 If you **plague** someone **with** something such as questions or   V+N+PREP,
requests, you keep bothering them by asking them for things. EG   V+PRON+PREP
*Readers were urged to plague their Congressmen with letters of
protest... He plagues her with questions.*

plan, plans, planning, planned

plan ahead. If you **plan ahead**, you make arrangements in advance   V+ADV
for something. EG *They advised him to plan ahead for an election... I
admire people who plan ahead... Few individuals or families plan
ahead systematically... They soon discover they cannot cheat by
planning ahead.*

plan for. If you **plan for** a particular thing or event, you consider it   V+PREP:
when you are making your arrangements. EG *A commission was*   HAS PASSIVE
*established in Tokyo to plan for the needs of the city... You should
also plan for the effect of Capital Transfer Tax... The number of
these was never quantified and thus never specifically planned for.*

plan on. 1 If you **plan on** doing something, you intend to do it; used   V+PREP:
in fairly informal English. EG *I plan on staying in London for the*   HAS PASSIVE
*foreseeable future... The troops were planning on attacking Poland
exactly one week later.*

2 If you **have not planned on** a particular thing, you have not   V+PREP:
realized that it might happen and so have not considered it when   HAS PASSIVE
making your arrangements. EG *I hadn't planned on the bad weather... I didn't plan on so many people coming.* ● **Expect** is a more
general word for **plan on**.

plan out. If you **plan out** a particular task or course of events, you   V+ADV+N,
decide in detail what you are going to do. EG *She planned out how she*   V+N+ADV,
would phrase the lyrics... Sit down earlier in the week to plan   V+PRON+ADV
everything out... The work of the coming week was planned out.

plan up. If a meeting or an arrangement **is planned up,** it is   PASSIVE:
prepared and people are ready to take part in it. EG *We've got all the*   V+ADV
interviews planned up now.

plant, plants, planting, planted

plant out. When you **plant out** seedlings or young plants, you plant   V+ADV+N,
them in the ground in the place where they are to be left to grow. EG   V+PRON+ADV,
   V+N+ADV

I trimmed the hornbeam hedge and planted out a bed of asters... We had to rear it in a nursery and plant it out.

play, plays, playing, played

play about. See play around.

play about with. See play around with.

play along. 1 If you **play along** with someone, you pretend to agree with them or accept what they say even though you do not really believe it. EG *With an acutely disturbed patient it may be necessary to play along during the initial phase of the treatment... He had realized I wouldn't play along with his plan to drop the union agreement.*

    V+ADV:
    USUALLY+*with*

2 If you **play** someone **along,** you deliberately keep them waiting for a decision. EG *You've been playing her along, haven't you?... Why had she been such a fool as to think she could play him along?*

    V+PRON+ADV,
    V+N+ADV

play around. 1 When children **play around** or **about** somewhere, they play there. EG *Mumma would be ironing while the kids played around... ...a little boy playing about in a sand heap... Don't play around public toilets... Didn't I tell you to play around the yard?*

    V+ADV,
    V+PREP

2 If you **play around,** you have sex with people other than your husband, wife, or partner. EG *You don't think he's playing around, do you?*

    V+ADV

play around with. 1 If you **play around** or **about with** something, you keep moving it from one place or position to another. EG *We spent the whole afternoon playing around with bits of string... I put the shells on a screen and played around with them until I got something attractive.*

    V+ADV+PREP

2 You can also say that someone **plays around** or **about with** something when they change it or interfere with it in a way which you disapprove of. EG *I think it's slightly frightening that people are going to play around with the hormone content of plants.* ● **Mess about with** and **tamper with** mean almost the same as **play around with.**

    V+ADV+PREP:
    HAS PASSIVE

3 If someone **plays around with** another person, they have a sexual relationship with them although they have have no serious feelings for them. EG *You've just been playing around with me.*

    V+ADV+PREP

play at. If someone, especially a child, **plays at** being a particular kind of person or being in a particular kind of situation, they pretend to be that person or be in that situation. EG *The children play at being French children... From time to time I have wandered into Sotheby's, playing at being a connoisseur... ...playing at soldiers.*

    V+PREP

play back. When you **play back** a tape or film on which you have recorded sound or pictures, you operate the machine it is in so that you can listen to it or watch it. EG *I played back a taped interview with Dr. Sanger... Let's play the tape back and hear the conversation again... There would be months in which they could play it back at leisure.* ▶ The **playback** of a tape is the operation of the machine it is in so that you can listen to it or watch it. EG *The conversation had been recorded for playback... Then all you have to do is press the playback button.*

    V+ADV+N,
    V+N+ADV,
    V+PRON+ADV

    N UNCOUNT

play down. If you **play** something **down,** you try to make people think that it is unimportant, or less important than it really is. EG *He played down his enhanced authority... They have urged that the authorities should play down the horrors of nuclear war... Because it was important, he wished to play it down.* ● **Exaggerate** and **play up** mean the opposite of **play down.**

    V+ADV+N,
    V+PRON+ADV,
    V+N+ADV

play off. When two people or teams who have the same number of points in a sports competition **play off,** they play a match to decide

    V+ADV

which one is the winner. EG *Liverpool and Everton will play off for third place.* ▶ A **play-off** is a match between two people or teams who have the same number of points, to decide which one is the winner. EG *...a play-off for third place.* [N COUNT]

play off against. If you **play** people **off against** each other, you cause them to compete or argue so that you gain an advantage. EG *It is easy for a child to play one parent off against the other... The multinational companies can play individual markets off against each other... Here was an example of one section of workers being played off against another.* [V+N+ADV+PREP, V+PRON+ADV+PREP]

play on. 1 If you **play on** or **upon** people's feelings, attitudes, or weaknesses, you deliberately use them in order to achieve what you want. EG *He used to play on their prejudices and their fears... Try to find your opponent's weaknesses and play on them relentlessly... She was forced to play upon the fears and resentments of others.* ● **Exploit** means almost the same as **play on.** [V+PREP]

2 If a writer or speaker **plays on** or **upon** a particular idea or word, he or she cleverly makes use of different aspects of it, often for a humorous effect. EG *Shatrov plays on a historical theme in his latest work.* [V+PREP]

3 If you **play on,** you continue playing a musical instrument. EG *She forced herself to play on.* [V+ADV]

4 If the referee tells players to **play on** during a game of football or rugby, he or she is telling them to continue playing even though someone has broken the rules of the game. EG *The referee told them to play on.* [V+ADV]

play out. 1 If you talk about people **playing out** a scene, drama, or series of events, you mean that they take part in events which seem fated to happen and over which they have no control. EG *One day this scene would have to be played out between them... Mother and father play out the roles assigned to them... The final drama was played out on June 17th.* ● **Enact** means almost the same as **play out.** [V+ADV+N]

2 When actors **play out** a scene, they act it. EG *The actors are asked to now play out the scene using only the three lines they've chosen.* [V+ADV+N]

3 You can say that people **play out** their feelings or fantasies when they express them in their actions. EG *Often unconscious anxieties get played out in our attitudes towards other people... We're just playing out fantasies.* [V+ADV+N]

4 If you feel **played out,** you feel exhausted and unable to do anything else. EG *I was very tired and feeling very played out.* ● **Worn out** means almost the same as **played out.** [ADJECTIVE]

play through. If you **play** a piece of music **through,** you play it from beginning to end. EG *Eddie Neils played all the songs through... She opened a book of Bach preludes and played one through.* [V+N+ADV, V+PRON+ADV]

play up. 1 If you **play up** a fact or feature, you emphasize it and try to make people think that it is more important than it really is. EG *The temptation is to play up the sensational aspects of the story... Newspaper reports play up the few accidents and injuries which do occur.* ● **Exaggerate** means almost the same as **play up,** and **play down** means the opposite. [V+ADV+N]

2 If a machine or a part of your body is **playing up** or is **playing** you **up,** it is not working properly or is hurting; an informal use. EG *Our phone is playing up... Is your arm playing up?... My leg's playing me up again.* [V+ADV, V+PRON+ADV, V+N+ADV]

3 If a group of children **are playing up** or **are playing** you **up,** they are being naughty and are difficult to control; an informal use. EG [V+ADV, V+PRON+ADV, V+N+ADV]

The kids are playing up again... Ian played him up a lot and nearly wore him out.

play upon. See play on; play upon is more formal.

play up to. If you **play up to** someone, you behave in a way which will please or amuse them, for example by flattering them. ᴇɢ *I think he feels that when he's got an audience he's got to play up to it and impress everyone... I played up to his vanity.*   V+ADV+PREP

play with. 1 When children **play with** a toy, they manipulate it or use it to amuse themselves, often in an imaginative way. ᴇɢ *He was hoping that I would come back and bring him some new toys to play with... ...dolls that are not played with.*   V+PREP: HAS PASSIVE

2 If you **play with** something, you keep moving it from one position or place to another without thinking about what you are doing, for example because you are bored or nervous. ᴇɢ *I sat there playing with a bottle of suntan lotion... Don't play with your napkin ring, Sam... She would sprinkle granulated sugar onto her porridge and then start idly playing with it.*   V+PREP

3 If you **play with** the idea of doing something, you consider doing it, although you will probably not do it. ᴇɢ *Thomas played with the idea of letting Coyne make all the arrangements... He had played with the idea of moving her to an apartment of her own.* ● Toy with means almost the same as play with.   V+PREP

4 If a writer or speaker **plays with** words or ideas, he or she uses them in a clever and unusual way for a special effect. ᴇɢ *He had been playing with themes of rebirth and renaissance... Novelists have often played with these ambiguities... I spend many hours playing with words.*   V+PREP

5 When a child **plays with** another child, the two children play together. ᴇɢ *You'll enjoy having other boys to play with... Go upstairs and play with your friends... Every baby needs to be smiled at, talked to, and played with.*   V+PREP: HAS PASSIVE

6 If you say that someone **is playing with** someone else, you mean that they are behaving towards them in an insincere way. ᴇɢ *'Albert,' she said, 'Stop playing with me like this.'*   V+PREP

7 If someone **plays with** himself or herself, he or she masturbates; an informal use.   V+PREP+REFL

plead, pleads, pleading, pleaded

plead for. 1 If you **plead for** something, you ask for it very strongly and in an emotional way. ᴇɢ *Mrs Hogan had phoned to plead for Philip's assistance... She would come and plead for help and comfort... The more he pleaded for mercy, the more they beat him.*   V+PREP

2 When a lawyer **pleads for** someone, they speak for them and try to defend them in court. ᴇɢ *...the difficult task of pleading for a defendant who was obviously guilty.*   V+PREP

plead with. If you **plead with** someone, you ask them for something in an intense and emotional way. ᴇɢ *I pleaded with him to tell me... They pleaded with us to pull them out of the water... I pleaded with her, but Joan didn't want to go.*   V+PREP

plod, plods, plodding, plodded

plod away. If you **plod away** at a particular job or task, you continue doing it without much enthusiasm. ᴇɢ *Oh, keep plodding away, it'll get done!*   V+ADV: ALSO+at

plod on. If you **plod on**, you continue walking or doing something at the same slow pace as before. ᴇɢ *She plodded on with her work, feeling tired and jaded.*   V+ADV

plonk, plonks, plonking, plonked

plonk down. 1 If you **plonk** something **down,** you put it down roughly or carelessly; an informal use. EG *...plonking down a whacking great tea in front of me... They just plonk their feet down.*   V+ADV+N, V+N+ADV, V+PRON+ADV

2 If you **plonk down** or **plonk** yourself **down,** you sit down heavily and clumsily; an informal use. EG *She plonked down in an armchair and lit a cigarette.*   V+ADV, V+REFL+ADV

plot, plots, plotting, plotted

plot against. If people **plot against** someone, they plan secretly to kill them or remove them from power. EG *Anyone convicted for suspicion of plotting against the king will be executed... ...people who think they're being plotted against.*   V+PREP: HAS PASSIVE

plot out. If you **plot out** a plan or course of events, you decide in advance what you will do. EG *We had plotted out a first rough plan... I had already plotted out the scenario in my mind.* ● **Plan out** means almost the same as **plot out.**   V+ADV+N, V+N+ADV, V+PRON+ADV

plough, ploughs, ploughing, ploughed

Plough is also spelled **plow** in American English.

plough ahead. If something or someone ploughs **ahead,** they increase or move ahead steadily. EG *Output continued to plough ahead.* ● **Forge ahead** means almost the same as **plough ahead.**   V+ADV

plough back. If you **plough** profits **back** into a business, you spend them on improving the business so that you can make more money. EG *He was happy to plough the first profits back into the business... ...a private rental system in which the profits are ploughed back into expanding the housing stock.*   V+N+ADV, V+ADV+N, V+PRON+ADV: USUALLY+*into*

plough in. If someone **ploughs in** a crop, they dig the plants into the ground to make the soil more fertile. EG *The stalks are left to be ploughed in for the next planting... ...grow the crop and then plough it in.*   V+N+ADV, V+ADV+N, V+PRON+ADV

plough into. 1 If something **ploughs into** something else, it crashes into it with a lot of force. EG *The car skidded before ploughing into the bank... Four tank regiments ploughed into the two brigades on the left.*   V+PREP: HAS PASSIVE

2 If money **is ploughed into** something, it is spent on it or invested in it in large amounts. EG *...huge sums of money which could be ploughed into computing... Ford has ploughed more than 400 million pounds into its Halewood operation since 1982... The days when local authorities could protect schools by ploughing more money into them are over.*   V+N+PREP, V+PRON+PREP: USUALLY PASSIVE

3 If a crop **is ploughed into** the land, someone digs the plants into the ground to make the soil more fertile. EG *The crop can be grown as green manure to be ploughed into the land... The process is helped by ploughing the muck into the garden during the autumn.*   V+N+PREP, V+PRON+PREP: USUALLY PASSIVE

plough on. If you **plough on,** you continue walking or doing something even though it is difficult for you; a fairly informal expression. EG *...as they ploughed on to their destination... Jimmie hesitated for a moment and then ploughed on... Does faith mean ploughing blindly on without learning any lessons from our experiences?*   V+ADV

plough through. 1 If you **plough through** a meal or piece of work, you eat it all or do it all, although it is difficult because there is a lot of it. EG *They must be given time to plough through their meals... ...gloomily ploughing through a plate of spaghetti... It would cost a fortune to pay someone to plough through all these.*   V+PREP

2 To **plough through** something also means to move through it,   V+PREP

sometimes with difficulty. EG *The barrels kept coming, ploughing through the water... They ploughed slowly through the deluge.*

plough up. If an area of land is **ploughed up**, the soil is turned over using a plough, especially on land which is being changed from grassland to land which will be used for growing crops. EG *They told him to plough up his meadows... They spent part of the time ploughing up the area... Nearly half of Wiltshire's chalk grassland was ploughed up to grow corn.*   V+ADV+N, V+N+ADV, V+PRON+ADV

plow, plows, plowing, plowed
Plow is an American spelling for **plough**.

pluck, plucks, plucking, plucked

pluck at. If you **pluck at** something, you take hold of it and pull it towards you with a sharp movement. EG *Lucas plucked at my blazer and asked if he could come too... He was sweating, and plucked now and then nervously at his shirt.* ● **Pull at** means almost the same as **pluck at**.   V+PREP

plug, plugs, plugging, plugged

plug away. If you **plug away** at something, you keep trying very hard to do something which you consider difficult or uninteresting. EG *He told them that they must keep plugging away... She plugged away at her maths.*   V+ADV: ALSO+*at*

plug in. If you **plug in** a piece of electrical equipment, you connect it to an electricity supply by pushing its plug into an electric socket. EG *I plugged in the kettle... He put on a record and plugged in the earphones... The lady across the aisle showed him how to plug his headphones in... A television set is a fire risk if left plugged in overnight.* ● **Unplug** means the opposite of **plug in**.   V+ADV+N, V+N+ADV, V+PRON+ADV

plug into. 1 If you **plug** a piece of electrical equipment **into** something, you connect it to the thing, for example by means of a plug. EG *She plugged an electric razor into a wall-socket... He has a flash gun plugged into his camera... Portable computers can be plugged into TV sets... Plug it into the mains.*   V+N+PREP, V+PRON+PREP

2 If a piece of electrical equipment **plugs into** a source of electricity or another piece of equipment, it is designed to be powered by electricity or to be connected to the other piece of equipment. EG *The one we have at home plugs into the mains... The telephone plugs into ordinary telephone sockets.*   V+PREP

3 If you **plug** something **into** a hole or slot, you fit it into the hole or slot. EG *...balls of wax which you plug into your ear... He has a hearing device plugged into his ear.*   V+N+PREP, V+PRON+PREP

4 If you **plug into** a group of people or their ideas, you find out about them and try to understand them; used mainly in informal American English. EG *What I'm really trying to do is to plug into people's fantasies... This gave us a chance to plug into a new network of friends.*   V+PREP

plug up. If you **plug up** a hole, you put something in it so that it is blocked. EG *The other opening was plugged up... She suggested plugging up the hole... ...plugging them up as the holes appeared.* ● **Block up** and **bung up** mean almost the same as **plug up**.   V+N+ADV, V+ADV+N, V+PRON+ADV

plumb, plumbs, plumbing, plumbed

plumb in. If you **plumb in** a bath, toilet, or washing machine, you connect it to the water and drainage pipes in a building. EG *We've bought the washing machine, but it needs to be plumbed in... If there's a leak, it may not have been plumbed in properly.*   V+N+ADV, V+PRON+ADV

plumb into. If you **plumb** something **into** the heating, water, or   V+N+PREP, V+PRON+PREP drainage system in a building, you connect it to that system. EG *The shower can be plumbed into the existing central heating system.*

plump, plumps, plumping, plumped

plump down. 1 If you **plump down** or **plump** yourself **down,** you sit down suddenly or clumsily; an informal use. EG *She plumped down with such force in one of the chairs... Clara plumped herself down on the bed.* ● **Plonk down** means almost the same as **plump down.**   V+ADV, V+REFL+ADV

2 If you **plump** something **down,** you put it down suddenly and carelessly; an informal use. EG *I plumped down my heavy paper bag and stood staring at the bar.* ● **Plonk down** means almost the same as **plump down.**   V+ADV+N, V+N+ADV, V+PRON+ADV

plump for. If you **plump for** someone or something, you choose them, often suddenly after a lot of hesitation or careful thought. EG *In the event, they plumped for a three-stage conference... The oil industry had plumped for unmanned underwater robots instead... Few gentlemen would now care to plump for an army career.* ● **Opt for** means almost the same as **plump for.**   V+PREP

plump out. If someone **plumps out,** they become fatter; an old-fashioned expression. EG *Zelly was plumping out in all the right places... Her face had plumped out.* ● **Fill out** means almost the same as **plump out.**   V+ADV

plump up. If you **plump up** something soft, you squeeze and shake it back into its proper shape; an old-fashioned expression. EG *'Serves him right,' said Mrs Waites, plumping up her pillow, 'Cathy and me took a week.'... The other woman plumped up the cushions and switched on the table lamps.*   V+ADV+N, V+N+ADV, V+PRON+ADV

plunge, plunges, plunging, plunged

plunge in. If you **plunge in,** you begin doing something suddenly, without thinking carefully or preparing for it. EG *...simply plunging in and hoping for the best... I plunged in hastily with another question... Tom hesitated, then plunged in. 'I'll start with my father.'*   V+ADV

plunge into. If you **plunge into** an activity or particular subject, you start doing it suddenly or become deeply involved in it, often without thinking carefully or preparing for it first. EG *Marx plunged immediately into political work... My father abandoned common sense and plunged into a financial gamble... The men did not plunge deeply into any subject.* ● **Dive into** means almost the same as **plunge into.**   V+PREP

ply, plies, plying, plied

ply with. 1 If you **ply** someone **with** food or drink, you keep on giving them more of it. EG *Dolly plied me with marshmallows and potato chips... They had plied him with too much drink... We sat and talked, plied with sugary tea prepared by Mum.*   V+PRON+PREP, V+N+PREP

2 If you **ply** someone **with** questions, you keep asking them questions. EG *I plied him with questions about his novel... Walking alongside, Lamin would ply Kunta with a steady stream of questions.*   V+PRON+PREP, V+N+PREP

point, points, pointing, pointed

point out. 1 If you **point** an object or person **out,** you cause people to notice them or look at them, perhaps by indicating with your hand or head. EG *I'll point Lundberg out to you... I try to point it out to Chris, but by the time he looks it's gone... They go together up the stone stairway to the street, and she points out the cafe.*   V+N+ADV, V+PRON+ADV, V+ADV+N: ALSO+to

2 If you **point** something **out,** you give people an important piece of information or correct their mistaken ideas. EG *She pointed out that he was wrong... 'It's a golden opportunity, really,' Johnson pointed out... ...as I pointed out to you in a letter published last week... Mr*   V+ADV+REPORT, V+ADV+QUOTE, V+N+ADV, V+ADV+N, V+PRON+ADV: ALSO+to

Merritt pointed this problem out to you the other day... Critics were quick to point out the weaknesses in these arguments... He points out to Patrick that the garage also sells cigarettes.

point to. 1 If you **point to** a fact or event, you use it as proof or evidence in an argument or discussion. EG *They point proudly to the administration's success... Optimistic Democrats can point to signs of change... She pointed to new opportunities in the area.*
V+PREP: HAS PASSIVE

2 If one fact or event **points to** another, it indicates that the other one is likely to be true or to happen. EG *There are many ways of defining poverty, but all point to the same conclusion... ...if the baby has any of the symptoms that point to a severe infection... Does slow talking point to slow mental development?*
V+PREP: HAS PASSIVE

point up. If you **point up** a fact or opinion, you emphasize it; a formal expression. EG *Haig's speech pointed up the gap that still exists between U.S. and Europe... Was the EEC initiative on Afghanistan designed to point up Soviet recalcitrance?... But this merely points up the differences again... The discussions seem to point up the mystical nature of the writing.*
V+ADV+N, V+PRON+ADV

poke, pokes, poking, poked

poke about. If you **poke about, around,** or **round** in a place, you look casually at the things there, often picking them up or moving them, because you want to find something but you are not sure what you want or what it looks like. EG *I found him poking about among your cupboards... Barbara poked around in the radical bookshops... 'Poke round for the matches, dear boy,' said Mother.* ► If you have a **poke about, poke around,** or **poke round,** you search for something casually. EG *I went once myself to have a poke around.*
V+ADV: USUALLY+A

N SING

poke around. See **poke about.**

poke at. If you **poke at** something or someone, you push something sharp towards them and touch them with it, often repeatedly. EG *The chef poked at his little charcoal pile... Gretchen poked at his cheek with two fingers. 'Don't look so glum,' she said.* ● **Prod at** means almost the same as **poke at.**
V+PREP: HAS PASSIVE

poke out. 1 If something **pokes out,** you only see part of it because the rest is hidden or covered. EG *A bottle of wine poked out of a silver ice bucket... We were warm under the cover, but our heads poked out and got very cold.* ● **Stick out** means almost the same as **poke out,** and **protrude** is a more formal word.
V+ADV: ALSO+of

2 If you **poke** something **out,** you move it so that it suddenly appears from a place where it was hidden or covered. EG *I poke my head out of the tent... She poked her tongue out at me.* ● **Stick out** means almost the same as **poke out.**
V+N+ADV, V+PRON+ADV, V+ADV+N: ALSO+of

poke round. See **poke about.**

poke through. If something **pokes through,** it is or becomes visible, after having pierced a surface or come through a hole. EG *His face is ruddy; white stubble is poking through... ...a wet armchair with a rusty spring poking through the fabric... He wore his tie poked through a ring... His secretary poked her head through an adjoining door.*
V+ADV/PREP, V+N+ADV/PREP, V+PRON+ADV/PREP: ERGATIVE

poke up. 1 If something **pokes up,** it is visible over the top of something else, or it becomes visible after being hidden under something. EG *Tufts of coarse grass were beginning to poke up among the gravel... Right in the middle there pokes up the Norman tower.*
V+ADV: USUALLY+A

2 If you **poke up** a fire, you use a poker or other sharp tool to remove ash and make the fire burn more strongly; an old-fashioned
V+ADV+N, V+N+ADV, V+PRON+ADV

use. EG *I tucked him up, poked up the fire and went out into the hall...*
Leland had poked the fire up and thrown on another log.

polish, polishes, polishing, polished

polish off. 1 If you **polish off** food, you eat all of it. EG *She can polish* | V+ADV+N,
off her favourite dish in 10 minutes... He'd just polished off the ham | V+PRON+ADV,
and eggs... The guests were probably deciding what they would | V+N+ADV
polish off next. ● **Eat up** means almost the same as **polish off.**

2 If you **polish off** a task, you finish it completely and quickly. EG *I* | V+ADV+N,
get all my office work ready in time for that day and it gets polished | V+PRON+ADV,
off in one go. | V+N+ADV

polish up. 1 If you **polish up** a skill, a quality you have, or a piece of | V+ADV+N,
work you have done, you improve it by spending more time or effort | V+PRON+ADV
on it. EG *Anne was polishing up her classical Greek... ...to polish up a*
fading memory before it is too late. ● **Brush up** means almost the
same as **polish up.**

2 If you **polish up** an object, you rub it with a cloth to make it shine. | V+PRON+ADV,
EG *My sister had the spoons and was polishing them up with a yellow* | V+ADV+N,
duster... I polished up the handle of the big front door. | V+N+ADV

ponce, ponces, poncing, ponced

ponce about. If you say that someone **is poncing about** or **around,** | V+ADV
you mean that they are not doing what they are supposed to be
doing or not doing it properly or seriously; an informal expression,
used showing disapproval. EG *Stop poncing around and help me with*
this box. ● **Muck about** and **lark about** mean almost the same as
ponce about.

ponce around. See **ponce about.**

pop, pops, popping, popped

pop in. If you **pop in,** you go to a friend's house or a shop casually. EG | V+ADV
They pop in for a coffee and a chat... I can pop in tomorrow perhaps
and let you know.

pop off. 1 If you **pop off** somewhere, you leave the place that you | V+ADV
are in. EG *'I've got to pop off just now,' Elizabeth said... Well, you'd*
better pop off for lunch now, Deirdre. I'll carry on.

2 If you say that someone **has popped off,** you mean that they have | V+ADV
died; an informal and old-fashioned use in British English. EG *I'll*
come to your funeral when you pop off.

pop out. 1 If someone or something that you could not see **pops out,** | V+ADV:
they suddenly appear. EG *A station wagon popped out of the leafy* | USUALLY+A
shade of the avenue... Suddenly she popped out from behind a bush.

2 If you are in a building and **pop out,** you go out of the building; an | V+ADV:
informal use. EG *I popped out for a drink... ...leaving her to pop out* | USUALLY+A
and ring you... I popped out to the car park to cool off.

pop up. 1 If someone or something **pops up,** they appear in a place | V+ADV
or situation unexpectedly. EG *Glazunov had popped up out of no-*
where... ...one of those military rebels who pops up every so often...
Problems kept popping up. ● **Surface** is a more formal word for **pop**
up.

2 If the pictures in a children's book **pop up,** they stand up from the | V+ADV
pages as you open it. EG *...such as folded pictures that pop up from a*
book. ▶ **Pop-up** describes pictures that stand up from the pages of a | ADJECTIVE
book or the books that contain such pictures. EG *Some books are toys*
in disguise, like those with pop-up pictures.

pore, pores, poring, pored

pore over. If you **pore over** writing, maps, or charts, you look at it | V+PREP:
and examine it very carefully. EG *Monks pored over ancient texts...* | HAS PASSIVE

He got out the chart and pored over it in a vain attempt to discover where they were... ...like a boy poring over a stamp album.

portion, portions, portioning, portioned

portion out. If you **portion** something **out**, you give a part of it to each person in a group. EG *...the pie that Tim was carefully portioning out... The presents were then further portioned out.* ● **Share out** means almost the same as **portion out**.

V+ADV+N,
V+N+ADV,
V+PRON+ADV

post, posts, posting, posted

post up. If you **post up** a notice or sign, you fix it to a wall or noticeboard so that people can see it. EG *The same week a holiday list was posted up in the main office... The price was posted up plain to see. Thirty New Francs... She used to post it up for all to see.*

V+N+ADV,
V+ADV+N,
V+PRON+ADV:
USUALLY+A

potter, potters, pottering, pottered

potter about. If you **potter about** or **around**, you pass the time in a gentle, unhurried way, doing small and unimportant tasks; used in British English. EG *The house was refreshingly peaceful, and I pottered about enjoying my leisure and solitude... He loved to potter around in the garden... We pottered around several antique shops.*

V+ADV,
V+PREP

potter around. See potter about.

pounce, pounces, pouncing, pounced

pounce on. 1 If someone **pounces on** or **upon** you, they suddenly come up to you and take hold of you roughly or violently. EG *Three men wearing masks pounced on Mr Culshaw... He was pounced upon by a gang of youths.*

V+PREP:
HAS PASSIVE

2 If you **pounce on** or **upon** something that someone says or does, you eagerly draw attention to it. EG *His colleagues were watching his every step ready to pounce upon any slip he made... Pouncing on an idea as soon as it appears kills the idea... Any coincidence was pounced upon and discussed avidly.* ● **Seize on** means almost the same as **pounce on**.

V+PREP:
HAS PASSIVE

pounce upon. See pounce on.

pour, pours, pouring, poured

pour away. If you **pour** a liquid **away**, you pour it out of a container because you no longer need it or cannot use it any more. EG *Instead of pouring the digested liquid food away, we absorb the food ingredients into our bloodstream... Three days' milk has been poured away so far... The dregs of powder paint had been poured away and gleaming jam jars awaited.* ● **Throw away** is a more general expression for **pour away**.

V+N+ADV,
V+PRON+ADV,
V+ADV+N

pour down. When rain **pours down**, it falls very heavily. EG *The rain poured down, the rivers overflowed, and the wind blew hard against the cabin door... The rain still poured down.* ● **Pelt down** means almost the same as **pour down**. ▶ A **downpour** is a very heavy shower of rain. EG *...sheltering from a downpour.*

V+ADV

N COUNT

pour forth. When things **pour forth**, they emerge from somewhere suddenly and in large quantities. EG *The primus poured forth a hissing cloud of noxious paraffin vapour... They poured forth from their homes, shouting and clapping.*

V+ADV,
V+ADV+N:
ERGATIVE

pour in. When people or things **pour in**, they arrive somewhere very quickly and in large numbers. EG *At first the British did not quite know what to do with these people pouring in over their border... Messages of encouragement poured in.* ● **Flood in** means almost the same as **pour in**.

V+ADV

pour into. When people or things **pour into** a place, they arrive there very quickly and in large numbers. EG *There were hundreds in*

V+PREP

our ranks as we poured into the building... In a matter of hours telegrams and telephone calls began to pour into the sheriff's office... When this drain blocked up the floods poured into our kitchen... ● **Flood into** means almost the same as **pour into**.

pour off. When you **pour off** some liquid from a container, you pour some of the liquid out and leave the rest in the container. EG *If you use this rich milk, you should pour off a little of the cream... Pour off half the quantity and add an equal amount of boiled water.*

V+ADV+N,
V+N+ADV,
V+PRON+ADV

pour on. To **pour** scorn **on** or **upon** someone means to talk about them or their ideas with contempt and show that you have a very low opinion of them. EG *He wasn't content merely to pour scorn on my arguments... But when it comes to the control of the police, he poured contempt upon elected people.*

V+N+PREP

pour out. 1 If you **pour out** a drink, you fill a cup or glass with the drink. EG *Castle poured out two glasses of whisky... Tim poured out some more wine... ...hostesses pouring tea out from silver tea pots.* ● **Serve** means almost the same as **pour out**.

V+ADV+N,
V+N+ADV,
V+PRON+ADV

2 If you **pour out** your thoughts, feelings, or experiences, you suddenly tell someone all about them, quickly and without being able to stop yourself. EG *I was on the verge of pouring out all my feelings... He poured out a horrifying story... I poured it all out to him—the arguments, fights, the hatred... My accumulated resentments poured out in response to this unwarranted attack.*

V+ADV+N,
V+N+ADV,
V+PRON+ADV,
V+ADV:
ERGATIVE

▶ **Outpourings** are things that you say or write which seem uncontrolled and irrational and indicate that you are very angry or upset about something. EG *...the hysterical outpourings of fanatics.*

N PLURAL

3 When things or people **pour out**, they come out of somewhere suddenly and in large amounts or numbers. EG *Black smoke was pouring out of the slanted chimney... Energy and enthusiasm seemed to be pouring out of people... Water was pouring out of the tap... I saw them pour out by the thousands and scurry frantically to get away... Factories poured out new plastics, cheap, sturdy and reliable.* ▶ An **outpouring** is a large quantity of things emerging from somewhere very quickly. EG *The explosion of the volcano set free a red-hot catastrophic outpouring... ...the almost inexhaustible outpouring of heat from the interior of the earth.*

V+ADV,
V+ADV+N,
V+PRON+ADV:
ERGATIVE,
ALSO+*of*

N COUNT

pour upon. See pour on.

preclude, precludes, precluding, precluded

preclude from. If a set of circumstances **precludes** you **from** doing something, they make it impossible for you to do it. EG *Its methodology would preclude critics from explaining why one book is better than another... It sets limits on the powers of the Government, and precludes it from acting unconstitutionally.*

V+N+PREP,
V+PRON+PREP

predispose, predisposes, predisposing, predisposed

predispose to. If something **predisposes** you to or **towards** a particular action, belief, or state, it has a great influence on you, and causes you to do that action, have that belief, or be in that state; a formal expression. EG *His education and his history as a Government official predispose him to bureaucratic modes of thinking and acting... It is now known that too much alcohol from any source predisposes one to a heart attack... She is predisposed towards action because she is confused by events beyond her control.*

V+PRON+PREP,
V+N+PREP

predispose towards. See predispose to.

preside, presides, presiding, presided

preside over. 1 If you **preside over** an official occasion or event, you are in charge of it and are considered by other people to be in

V+PREP:
HAS PASSIVE

control of it or responsible for it; a formal use. EG *He had presided over a seminar for theoretical physicists... I did not become His Majesty's Prime Minister in order to preside over the dissolution of the British Empire... ...the men presiding over this quiet revolution... On 31 January the two bodies held a joint rally, presided over by Lord George-Brown.*

2 If an object **presides over** a place, it is much larger or taller than anything else there, and therefore dominates the area; a formal use. EG *A large figure in stone presides massively over the approach to the museum... ...an arid landscape, presided over by looming mountains.* `V+PREP: HAS PASSIVE`

press, presses, pressing, pressed

press ahead. If you **press ahead** with an activity or task, you begin or continue doing it in a determined way, knowing that it may take a long time or be very difficult. EG *He has pressed ahead with talks... They have pressed ahead with bigger and more profitable schemes... Mrs Castle, whose pride is at stake, is determined to press ahead.* ● **Go ahead** means almost the same as **press ahead.** `V+ADV: USUALLY+with`

press for. **1** If you **press for** something, you try hard to achieve it or obtain it by working to persuade people that it is important and necessary. EG *He continued to press for a peaceful solution... The landless labourers formed a union to press for higher wages... He pressed for full public ownership... When I pressed him for an explanation his voice turned cold.* `V+PREP, V+PRON+PREP, V+N+PREP`

2 If you **are pressed for** time or money, you do not have enough of it; an informal use. EG *He was always pressed for money and usually in poor health... I told him I was a little pressed for time.* `PASSIVE: V+PREP`

press into. If you **press** someone **into** an activity, you force them to become involved in it or to take it up. EG *The expedition to capture the Brighton fishermen and press them into naval service had been a total failure... She found herself pressed into the role of assistant astronomer... I was pressed into rugby under compulsion.* `V+PRON+PREP, V+N+PREP`

press on. **1** If you **press on** with an activity or task, you continue doing it, despite the fact that it is difficult and might not succeed. EG *They courageously pressed on with their vital repair work... Babbage pressed on alone, achieving little... We are just pressing on regardless.* ● **Carry on** means almost the same as **press on,** and **give up** means the opposite. `V+ADV: ALSO+with`

2 If you **press on** with a journey, you continue it, even though it is becoming more difficult or dangerous. EG *Otto would press on with all speed for Bear Island... The rest of us said a prayer and pressed on... I wanted to press on, in spite of the weather.* ● **Carry on** means almost the same as **press on,** and **turn back** means the opposite. `V+ADV`

3 See **press upon.**

press upon. If you **press** something **upon** or **on** someone, you give it to them in a very forceful way so that they cannot avoid taking it, even if they do not really want it. EG *I pressed biscuits and lemonade upon them... They were flattered enough by the gifts that were pressed upon them... I refused the five shillings that she tried to press on me.* ● **Thrust upon** means almost the same as **press upon.** `V+N+PREP, V+PRON+PREP`

pretty, pretties, prettying, prettied

pretty up. If you **pretty** something **up,** you try to make it appear more attractive or acceptable. EG *...men starting to pretty themselves up a bit with state-of-the-art ties and socks... There was so much of it he didn't have time for prettying it up... ...robots called after film stars and all prettied up with ribbons.* `V+REFL+ADV, V+PRON+ADV, V+N+ADV, V+ADV+N`

prevail, prevails, prevailing, prevailed

prevail on. If you **prevail on** or **upon** someone to do something   v+prep:
which they are reluctant to do, you succeed in persuading them to   has passive
do it; a fairly formal expression. eg *He prevailed on the head
reception clerk to book him a single room... Finally she prevailed
upon George Clinton to allow his name to go on the ballot paper...
Ted had been prevailed upon to bring his flute.*
prevail upon. See prevail on.

prey, preys, preying, preyed

prey on. 1 An animal or bird that **preys on** or **upon** another kind of   v+prep:
creature lives by catching and eating those creatures. eg *Short-eared*   has passive
*owls prey on voles as well as small birds... It is itself preyed upon by
the cod shoals.*

2 Someone who **preys on** or **upon** other people exploits them or gets   v+prep:
satisfaction from treating them badly or violently, and is constantly   has passive
looking for new victims. eg *...successful producers, writers, directors,
actors, who preyed on beautiful women with lustful hatred... His
favourite victims are innocent young women in nightdresses; he also
preys upon young men.*

3 If something **preys on** or **upon** your mind, it worries you a lot and   v+prep
you cannot stop thinking about it. eg *Barton reluctantly agreed, but
the decision preyed on his mind... When you're not punished for it it
preys on your conscience... It's intolerable only if you let it prey
upon your mind.*
prey upon. See prey on.

prick, pricks, pricking, pricked

prick out. If you **prick out** young plants, especially seedlings, you   v+adv+n,
plant them in small holes which you make in the soil by using a thin   v+n+adv,
stick. eg *...pricking out an inch-high seedling in fine soil... Prick the   v+pron+adv
young plants out and continue feeding them each week.*

print, prints, printing, printed

print off. If you **print off** a certain number of copies of something,   v+adv+n,
you print as many as you need at that time. eg *Any items needed for   v+n+adv,
permanent reference could be printed off as soon as located on a   v+pron+adv
copying machine.* ▶ An **offprint** is a separately printed copy of an   n count
article or chapter from a book. eg *He gave me some offprints of
papers in which he expressed doubts about the Copenhagen interpretation.*

print out. When a computer, or a machine attached to a computer,   v+pron+adv,
prints out information, it reproduces it on paper. eg *He had deter-*   v+adv+n,
mined that it should not only calculate tables, but also print them   v+n+adv
*out on paper at the end... ...TV transmitters that would actually
display or print out the material in his own living room... The
projects are printed out, ready to use.* ▶ **Printout** is paper on which   n count,
information from a computer has been printed, either by the   n uncount
computer itself or by a printing machine attached to the computer.
eg *The computer printouts are on Howie's desk every morning.*

prise, prises, prising, prised

Prise is sometimes spelled **prize**.

prise out. If you **prise** something **out** of someone, you succeed in   v+n+adv,
getting it from them only with difficulty because they are very   v+adv+n,
unwilling to give it to you. eg *They hope that the growing publicity   v+pron+adv:
will prise more money out of the California State Legislature to   also+of
create more training programmes... Christopher had prized out of*

her in an unguarded moment some recollection about her early schooldays.

prize, prizes, prizing, prized

Prize is a less common spelling for **prise**.

proceed, proceeds, proceeding, proceeded

proceed against. To **proceed against** a person or organization means to begin a legal action against them. EG *Card reaffirmed that he would give evidence if the State proceeded against me... The Inquisition proceeded against all those whose allegiance was in question... The publishers sought to take action so that the offenders might be proceeded against with all speed and dignity.* • **Prosecute** means almost the same as **proceed against.** [V+PREP: HAS PASSIVE]

proceed from. If something **proceeds from** a particular idea, it starts there and seems to be a logical conclusion. EG *...a conviction which proceeds from the belief that they possess absolute truth... Optimism was proceeding from the sort of results that were coming through.* [V+PREP]

prod, prods, prodding, prodded

prod at. If you **prod at** something, you hit it with your fingertip or with a long instrument such as a stick or spoon. EG *She prodded at the contents of the pan... They would prod at the cows with sticks to get them moving.* • **Poke at** means almost the same as **prod at.** [V+PREP]

pronounce, pronounces, pronouncing, pronounced

pronounce on. If you **pronounce on** or **upon** something, you give an expert opinion or judgment about it; a formal expression. EG *She was asked to pronounce on the merits of an eighteenth century table... ...an official body set up to pronounce upon questions of national economic planning.* [V+PREP]

pronounce upon. See **pronounce on.**

prop, props, propping, propped

prop up. 1 If you **prop** something **up,** you support it in a particular position by putting something underneath it or resting it against something. EG *So we left off the door in the summer and just propped it up in the winter... ...like the timbers that are sometimes used to prop a building up during alterations... He propped himself up on an elbow and watched her... Anne lay in bed, propped up with pillows.* [V+PRON+ADV, V+N+ADV, V+REFL+ADV, V+ADV+N]

2 If a government or group of people **props up** an organization or country which is unlikely to survive on its own, they give it support and help it to survive. EG *The Government does not intend to prop up declining industries... Between 1975-79 Labour propped up the old order and papered over the cracks with the TUC by means of a compromise... We should prop up countries run on more or less liberal lines.* [V+ADV+N, V+PRON+ADV]

protect, protects, protecting, protected

protect against. 1 To **protect** someone or something **against** an unpleasant event or situation means to prevent the unpleasant event or situation from happening, or from having a harmful effect. EG *Mr. Reagan said his plan would stimulate the economy and protect against inflation... Babies are protected against diseases like measles by their mothers' milk... Tanning lotions may help a little, but they can't protect you against a large amount of sunshine.* • **Protect from** means almost the same as **protect against.** [V+PREP, V+N+PREP, V+PRON+PREP]

2 If an insurance policy **protects** you **against** events such as death, injury, or theft, it promises to give money to you or your family if that event happens. EG *Lloyds Bank travellers cheques protect your* [V+N+PREP, V+PRON+PREP, V+PREP]

money against loss and theft... Part of the deal would protect the
consumer against serious injury. ● **Insure against** means almost the
same as **protect against.**

protect from. To **protect** someone or something **from** an unpleas-   V+PRON+PREP,
ant event or situation means to prevent that event or situation from   V+REFL+PREP,
having a harmful effect. EG *His hat was pulled down over his face to*   V+N+PREP
protect it from the sun... Any animal will struggle to protect itself
from a threat of death... He's probably a nice old gentleman who
simply wants to be protected from the irritations of everyday
existence. ● **Protect against** means almost the same as **protect**
from.

provide, provides, providing, provided

provide against. To **provide against** a particular event, situation,   V+PREP:
or circumstance means to prevent it from happening; a fairly   HAS PASSIVE
formal expression. EG *The landlord insisted on a covenant to provide*
against the client's insolvency... It is not always possible to ensure
that all risks are provided against.

provide for. 1 If you **provide for** someone, you give them money,   V+PREP:
clothes, and the other things they need. EG *Parents are expected to*   HAS PASSIVE
provide for their children... Our nursery provides for all the needs of
very young children... Is he provided for financially?

2 If you **provide for** a possible future event, you make arrangements   V+PREP:
to deal with it; a fairly formal use. EG *The original estimates did*   HAS PASSIVE
provide for 3 per cent per annum inflation... In economics, the
solution offered may provide for freedom... The original agreement
had indeed provided for the possibility of a review. ● **Allow for**
means almost the same as **provide for.**

3 If a law or decision **provides for** a course of action, it makes that   V+PREP:
course of action possible; a formal use. EG *The Act provided for*   HAS PASSIVE
financial penalties to be imposed on all offenders.

provide with. If you **provide** someone **with** something, you give it   V+PRON+PREP,
to them or lend it to them so that they have it when they need it. EG   V+N+PREP
Your brother Rudolph was good enough to provide me with your
address in New York... I provided him with money and a basket...
The first aim is to provide readers with a comprehensive text.

psych, psychs, psyching, psyched

Psych and psychs are also spelled **psyche** and **psyches.**

psych out. If you **psych out** your opponent in a contest, you try to   V+PRON+ADV,
make them feel less confident by behaving in a very confident or   V+N+ADV,
aggressive way; an informal expression. EG *'What's psyching you*   V+ADV+N
out?' What could I tell her that she didn't already know?

psych up. If you **psych** yourself **up** before a contest or a difficult   V+REFL+ADV
task, you prepare yourself for it mentally by telling yourself that you
can win or succeed; an informal expression. EG *As usual, they spent*
an hour before the kick-off psyching themselves up.

psyche, psyches, psyching, psyched

Psyche is another spelling for **psych.**

puff, puffs, puffing, puffed

puff away. If someone **puffs away** when they are smoking a   V+ADV
cigarette or a pipe, they keep sucking smoke into their mouth and
blowing it out again. EG *George would light up and puff away for a*
while... Richie nodded and puffed away on his pipe.

puff out. 1 When part of your body **puffs out**, or when you **puff** it   V+ADV,
out, it becomes larger and rounder as if it is filled with air. EG *A*   V+ADV+N,
swelling that puffs out quickly on a child's skull after a fall doesn't   V+N+ADV,
mean anything serious in itself if there are no other symptoms... He   V+PRON+ADV:
                                                                          ERGATIVE

sat back and puffed out his cheeks... Mr Willet puffed out his moustache with disgust.

2 If you are **puffed out**, you are tired and short of breath because you have just done some hard physical exercise. EG *I had a couple of jogs and was very puffed out... By the time we had climbed up to the top of Long Burgh Hill I was pretty well puffed out.*   ADJECTIVE

puff up. 1 If part of your body **puffs up** as a result of an injury or allergy, it becomes swollen. EG *Her whole body was puffing up like a balloon from the steroids.... He could feel the side of his head puff up.* ● **Swell up** means almost the same as **puff up**.   V+ADV

2 Someone who is **puffed up** is very proud of themselves because they think that they are very important; used showing disapproval. EG *I was expecting that he would return all puffed up with himself.*   ADJECTIVE

pull, pulls, pulling, pulled

pull about. If you **pull** someone or something **about** or **around**, you move or handle them in a rough, violent way. EG *A novice rider often pulls the horse about to hurry it out of its stride... Stop pulling me about. Who do you think you are?... Treat the dough fiercely when you make bread—push and pull it about.*   V+N+ADV, V+PRON+ADV

pull ahead. 1 If you **pull ahead**, you manage to pass someone or something that is travelling in front of you. EG *The cars climbed to higher and higher speeds, each straining to pull ahead... I spurted towards the foot of the hill and pulled ahead of Robin.* ● **Fall behind** means the opposite of **pull ahead**.   V+ADV: ALSO+of

2 If you **pull ahead** of other people, you gradually become more skilful or successful than they are. EG *Fiona seemed clever and would probably pull ahead of him.* ● **Get ahead** means almost the same as **pull ahead**, and **fall behind** means the opposite.   V+ADV: USUALLY+of

pull apart. 1 When you **pull** something **apart** or when it **pulls apart**, it separates into two or more pieces. EG *Cameron pulled the soft dough apart... She joined her thumb and index finger, and then pulled them gently apart... ...if you pull apart one of those calculators... The flesh pulled apart, and bloody entrails spilled out.*   V+N+ADV, V+PRON+ADV, V+ADV+N, V+ADV: ERGATIVE

2 If you **pull** people or animals **apart** when they are fighting, you separate them using force. EG *I rushed in and tried to pull the dogs apart... William got hurt trying to pull them apart.*   V+N+ADV, V+PRON+ADV

3 If someone **pulls apart** something that you have written or said, they criticize it severely. EG *The critics just pulled his last novel apart... She just pulled my argument apart in about five minutes.* ● **Take apart** means almost the same as **pull apart**.   V+N+ADV, V+PRON+ADV

4 To **pull** someone **apart** can cause them great mental suffering. EG *Their rows are enough to pull that child apart... She was pulled apart by his thoughtlessness.* ● **Tear apart** means almost the same as **pull apart**.   V+N+ADV, V+PRON+ADV

pull around. See **pull about** and **pull round**.

pull aside. If you **pull** someone **aside**, you take them away to a different part of a room in order to have a private conversation with them. EG *Willie would pull him aside by the elbow and whisper to him... The Major pulled me aside and said, 'Listen.'* ● **Take aside** means almost the same as **pull aside**.   V+N+ADV, V+PRON+ADV

pull at. 1 If you **pull at** something, you hold it and move it towards you and then let it go again. EG *They walked along the path in silence, pulling at the tall summer grasses... 'Come home now, Jim,' she said, pulling at his sleeve.*   V+PREP

2 If you **pull at** a cigarette or pipe, you take a long, deep breath when it is in your mouth. EG *'Oh, I'm not complaining,' Arnold said, pulling at his cigarette.*   V+PREP

pull for

pull away. 1 When a vehicle **pulls away**, it starts moving forward. V+ADV:
EG *The bus pulled away... He shoved the truck into gear and pulled* ALSO+*from*
away from the scene of the accident. ● **Pull off** means almost the
same as **pull away.**

2 If you **pull away** from someone who is holding you, you suddenly V+ADV:
move away from them. EG *She bent and kissed the top of his head,* ALSO+*from*
but he pulled away... He burst into tears and pulled away from me.
● **Pull back** means almost the same as **pull away.**

3 If you **pull** someone or something **away**, you take hold of them and V+N+ADV,
remove them using force. EG *Hendricks bent down to pull some of* V+ADV+N,
the weed away... I pulled away her hands which covered her face... I V+PRON+ADV
was impressed by his bookshelves, but he pulled me away before I
could examine them too closely.

4 If something **pulls away** from something else, it becomes separat- V+ADV:
ed or detached from it. EG *The sole had pulled away from the shoe.* ALSO+*from*
● **Come away** means almost the same as **pull away.**

pull back. 1 If you **pull back**, you suddenly move away from V+ADV:
someone or something. EG *He tried to kiss her but she pulled back...* ALSO+*from*
She pulled back from the window. ● **Draw back** means almost the
same as **pull back.**

2 When you **pull** someone or something **back,** you hold them and V+N+ADV,
move them backwards. EG *He pulled his chair back... The women* V+PRON+ADV,
pulled their children back in fear... He unexpectedly laid his hand on V+ADV+N:
my arm and pulled me back... He walked over to the bed and pulled ALSO+*from*
back the covers.

3 When an army **pulls back** or **is pulled back,** it leaves its position V+ADV,
and retreats. EG *The troops were being hard pressed as they pulled* V+N+ADV,
back... The enemy is not willing to pull back from any of its present V+PRON+ADV,
positions... ...a Marine who'd just pulled his whole squad back. V+ADV+N:
● **Withdraw** means almost the same as **pull back.** ERGATIVE

4 If you **pull back** from something, you decide not to proceed with it, V+ADV:
because you are afraid of what might happen. EG *It is hard to believe* ALSO+*from*
they will pull back from this deal... He knows when to pull back. It
has always been one of his great virtues. ● **Back out** and **draw back**
mean almost the same as **pull back.**

pull down. 1 If you **pull** something **down,** you move it from a higher V+N+ADV,
position to a lower one. EG *She pulled his head down to kiss him...* V+ADV+N,
They pulled down the window shades... She pulled up a sleeve to V+PRON+ADV
show him; then she pulled it down again... He wore a brown cloth
cap with the peak pulled down over his eyes. ● **Pull up** means the
opposite of **pull down.**

2 If a building or other structure **is pulled down,** it is deliberately V+N+ADV,
destroyed, so that the land that it is on can be used. EG *Why did they* V+ADV+N,
pull all those houses down?... It was proposed to pull down Chartres V+PRON+ADV
Cathedral... The council said it would close the flats and pull them
down. ● **Demolish** is a more formal word for **pull down,** and **put up**
means the opposite.

3 If someone or something **pulls** you **down,** they make you feel V+PRON+ADV,
depressed and cause you to fail or do badly at something; an V+N+ADV
informal use. EG *Those snobs are going to pull me down if they can...*
I'm not being pulled down by anybody. ● **Drag down** means almost
the same as **pull down.**

4 The amount of money someone **pulls down** is the amount of V+ADV+N
money they earn regularly from their job; an informal use in
American English. EG *Daniel was pulling down a weekly income of*
fifty dollars.

pull for. If you **are pulling for** someone, you help or support them V+PREP
when they are having problems; an informal expression. EG *A lot of*

officers here have been pulling for you... We were really pulling for the kid. ● **Root for** means almost the same as **pull for**.

pull in. 1 When a car, lorry, or bus **pulls in**, it is driven to the side of the road or to a place where it can stop. EG *He pulls in behind a Citroen... They decided to pull in at the first small taverna in the next village... They saw a filling station and pulled in.* ● **Pull up** means almost the same as **pull in.** ▷ A **pull-in** is a cafe on a main road where you can get cheap meals; an informal word in British English. EG *We stopped at a pull-in on the way.*
V+ADV:
USUALLY+A

N COUNT

2 When a train **pulls in**, it arrives at a station and stops. EG *As the 4.30 to Newcastle pulled in, there was a mad scramble to get on.* ● **Pull out** means the opposite of **pull in.**
V+ADV

3 To **pull** people **in** means to attract them in large numbers. EG *Higher wages in the cities pull in the rural poor... The football matches pulled in big crowds... Let's face it, it's not the low prices that's pulling them in, is it?*
V+ADV+N,
V+PRON+ADV,
V+N+ADV

4 When the police **pull** someone **in,** they go to find them and arrest them; an informal British English use. EG *The police decided to pull the suspects in... ...asking about the identity of that man we pulled in... Police pulled in the elusive Jonathan Logan.*
V+N+ADV,
V+ADV+N,
V+PRON+ADV

5 If you **pull in** a particular amount of money, especially a large amount, you earn it; an informal use. EG *I got greedy. I was pulling in money hand over fist.* ● **Rake in** means almost the same as **pull in.**
V+ADV+N,
V+N+ADV,
V+PRON+ADV:
NO PASSIVE

pull into. 1 When a car, train, or other vehicle **pulls into** a place, it arrives there and stops. EG *He pulled into the small parking lot... The car had pulled into the side... The London train pulled into the branch line station... At Barog, the train pulled into a siding.*
V+PREP

2 If someone or something **pulls** you **into** a particular situation, activity, or arrangement, they involve you in it. EG *Harbouring refugees can pull a neutral country into a conflict... ...pulling Britain into the mainstream of digital telephones... We have been pulled into an arrangement against our will.*
V+N+PREP,
V+PRON+PREP

pull off. 1 When you **pull** your clothes **off,** you take them off quickly. EG *I managed to pull my boots off... Anne had already kicked off her shoes and was pulling off her socks... Thomas unlaced the gloves and pulled them off Dominic's hands... Waddell noticed the watch on her wrist, and pulled it forcibly off her.*
V+N+ADV/PREP,
V+ADV+N,
V+PRON+ADV/PREP

2 If you **pull** something **off,** you succeed in doing something which is very difficult to achieve. EG *She had succeeded, triumphantly: she had pulled it off... You have just pulled off one of the biggest arms deals in the twentieth century... Bradlee was one of the few persons who could pull that kind of thing off.* ● **Carry off** means almost the same as **pull off.**
V+PRON+ADV,
V+ADV+N,
V+N+ADV

3 When a vehicle **pulls off** the road, it is driven a little way off the road so that it can stop. EG *We pull off the road and stop... ...looking for a restful place to pull off... I pulled off the road and stopped to see what was wrong.*
V+PREP,
V+ADV

4 When a stationary vehicle **pulls off,** it starts moving forward. EG *The car pulled off. 'Where are we going?' I asked brightly... I left the house, just as the man had pulled off to circle the block once again.* ● **Pull away** means almost the same as **pull off.**
V+ADV

5 If you **pull off** a person or animal that is attacking someone, you take hold of them and move them away, using force. EG *I hit her about the head and my dad had to pull me off... My fingers itched to pull her off, but they were pretty evenly matched.*
V+PRON+ADV,
V+N+ADV,
V+ADV+N

pull on. 1 When you **pull on** your clothes, you put them on quickly. EG *He started to pull on his tattered shorts... Still sitting, he pulled his shirt and trousers on... I dragged my dress out and pulled it on.*
V+ADV+N,
V+N+ADV,
V+PRON+ADV

2 If you **pull on** something, you take hold of it firmly and move it towards you. EG *He began to pull on the rope... He noticed an electrical cord, and pulled on it... Push the fishhook clean through instead of pulling on it.* `V+PREP`

3 If you **pull on** a cigarette or pipe, you draw smoke into your mouth by breathing in when the pipe or cigarette is between your lips. EG *The vicar pulled on his pipe and resumed the story.* `V+PREP`

pull out. **1** When a vehicle **pulls out**, it is driven out of a place and into the road. You also say that the vehicle **pulls out** when it is driven into a different traffic lane. EG *Ellen waited at the door until the last of the cars had pulled out of the driveway... I saw a bus pull out in front of us... Ginny revved up the Jeep again and pulled out.* `V+ADV`

2 When a train **pulls out** of a station, it leaves the station. EG *He turned in his seat as the train pulled out... Her parents were beaming approval as the train pulled out of the station.* ● **Draw out** means almost the same as **pull out**. `V+ADV: ALSO+of`

3 If you **pull out** of an activity or agreement, you decide not to continue it. EG *We've invested too much money and manpower to pull out now... Gary Player once had to pull out of an important championship because he hurt his neck... The Swedish conglomerate have pulled out of the bidding... He pulled his party out of the coalition.* ● **Back out** means almost the same as **pull out**. `V+ADV, V+N+ADV, V+PRON+ADV: ERGATIVE, USUALLY+of`

4 If an army **pulls out** of a place or region or if it **is pulled out**, it leaves the place or region and no longer operates there. EG *Troops had begun to pull out of the area... They ordered me to pull my men out of Fort Esther immediately... The Prime Minister has reaffirmed his intention of pulling all 10,000 of them out by the end of June.* ● **Withdraw** means almost the same as **pull out**. ▶ When there is a **pull-out**, soldiers leave a place which they have occupied or where they have been fighting. EG *United Nations officers supervising the pull-out said they expected 3,000 to be out by the weekend... ...an impending pull-out.* `V+ADV, V+N+ADV, V+PRON+ADV, V+PRON+ADV+N: ERGATIVE, ALSO+of` `N SING`

5 When you **pull** something **out** of a place, you remove it from that place. EG *Pull the baby's arms out of the sleeves first... She almost pulled him out of his chair... I watched her pull herself out of the sand... He would pull out his notebook and begin writing.* ▶ A **pull-out** section in a magazine is a separate part in the middle that you can remove easily. `V+N+ADV, V+PRON+ADV, V+REFL+ADV, V+ADV+N: ALSO+of` `ADJECTIVE`

6 If you **pull out** information or ideas from a lot of other things, you separate them from those things so that you can use them on their own. EG *The computer does a search through its file and pulls out all information relevant to that word.* ● **Take out** means almost the same as **pull out**, and **extract** is a more formal word. `V+ADV+N, V+N+ADV, V+PRON+ADV`

pull out of. If you **pull out of** a difficult or unhappy situation or if someone **pulls** you **out of** it, you succeed in getting out of it. EG *I know I've got to pull out of this relationship somehow, but I can't... We must pull the country out of this 'economic calamity'.* `V+ADV+PREP, V+N+ADV+PREP, V+PRON+ADV+PREP: ERGATIVE`

pull over. **1** When a vehicle **pulls over**, it moves closer to the side of the road. EG *The patrolmen put their spotlight on the car, and told me to pull over... A green VW pulled over next to me.* `V+ADV`

2 If the police **pull** a car **over**, they signal to the driver to drive the car to the side of the road and stop. EG *He had been pulled over for going through a red light... ...a police car pulling over a lorry.* `V+N+ADV, V+ADV+N, V+PRON+ADV`

3 A **pullover** is a woollen piece of clothing that covers the upper part of your body and your arms. EG *...a very smart black pullover.* ● **Sweater** and **jumper** mean almost the same as **pullover**. `N COUNT`

pull round. **1** If you **pull round** after you have been ill or uncon- `V+ADV`

pull through 270

scious, you start to recover. EG *He'll pull round, don't worry... She's beginning to pull round.*

2 When you **pull** someone or something **round** or **around,** you turn them so that they are now facing in the opposite direction. EG *I pulled her round to face me... The helicopter pulled round in a tight circle... She pulled her car around to the side of the station.* `V+N+ADV, V+PRON+ADV`

pull through. **1** When someone who is very ill **pulls through** or when a doctor **pulls** them **through,** they recover. EG *The doctors said he'll pull through... I can't thank the nurses enough for pulling her through.* `V+ADV, V+N+ADV, V+PRON+ADV: ERGATIVE`

2 If you **pull through** a difficult situation or if something **pulls** you **through** it, you manage to survive it. EG *I had a rough old time from then on, I can tell you! But I pulled through... This was Vanessa's plan for pulling me through... He got a loan to pull him through a bad patch.* `V+ADV/PREP, V+PRON+ADV/PREP, V+N+ADV/PREP: ERGATIVE`

pull to. When you **pull** a door **to,** you move it so that it is closed or very nearly closed. EG *Pull the door to, will you. I want to talk to you... She pulled the blinds to when I came in.* ● **Shut** means almost the same as **pull to.** `V+N+ADV, V+PRON+ADV`

pull together. **1** When you **pull** yourself **together,** you control your feelings and behave calmly after you have been upset or angry. EG *That's quite enough of that. Pull yourself together now and stop this at once... He had taken some minutes alone in his room to pull himself together.* `V+REFL+ADV`

2 If people **pull together,** they co-operate with each other because they share the same aims, and ignore the things which they disagree about. EG *We all pulled together during the war... This is one thing we must all pull together on.* ● **Band together** means almost the same as **pull together.** `V+ADV`

3 If you **pull together** several different topics or ideas, you bring them into a lecture or article in an orderly or interesting way. EG *I want to pull together the threads of earlier programmes... To understand this syndrome, we must pull facts together from such fields as psychology and neurology... Write a series of articles on the events and try to pull them together.* `V+ADV+N, V+N+ADV, V+PRON+ADV`

4 If you **pull** an event or meeting **together,** you organize it for other people. EG *I helped to pull a committee together down there... In the meantime, a campus-wide rally was being pulled together... ...the art auction we pulled together... ...pulling together a challenge to this repression.* ● **Set up** means almost the same as **pull together.** `V+N+ADV, V+ADV+N, V+PRON+ADV`

pull under. If someone or something **pulls** you **under** when you are in water, they pull you down so that the water completely covers you. EG *As the rope came tight it pulled him under... One of our girl pupils delighted in pulling other pupils under the water.* `V+PRON+ADV, V+N+ADV, V+N+PREP, V+PRON+PREP`

pull up. **1** When a vehicle **pulls up,** it slows down and stops. EG *The rain stopped as we pulled up to the hotel... The ambulance was just pulling up... Braun shifted forward and told the driver to pull up.* `V+ADV`

2 If you **pull up** a chair, you move it so that you can sit close to something. EG *I pulled up a chair and sat back to watch the news... She looked at me indifferently as I pulled up a stool... Gertrude took another chair and pulled it up near Tim's.* ● **Draw up** means almost the same as **pull up.** `V+ADV+N, V+N+ADV, V+PRON+ADV`

3 When you **pull** something **up,** you raise it from a lower position to a higher one. EG *She pulled the sheet up... He had to pull up his pants which had started slipping... He laid hold of the branch to pull himself up... ...buckets that were pulled up from the well.* `V+N+ADV, V+ADV+N, V+PRON+ADV`

4 If you **pull up** something which is fixed to the ground or the floor, you remove it with force. EG *They started pulling up the floor-* `V+ADV+N, V+N+ADV, V+PRON+ADV` *boards... They lowered the tent pole and pulled up the stakes... Don't pull the plants up... Either dig the weeds out, or pull them up.*

5 If someone **pulls** you **up** on something, they scold or criticize you severely for something that you have done; an informal use. EG *If they don't like what you're doing they'll soon pull you up on it... When I asked about the photographs, the young man pulled me up quite sharply.*
V+PRON+ADV, V+N+ADV: ALSO+*on*

6 If someone or something **pulls** you **up**, they do or say something that suddenly makes you stop moving or talking. EG *Mr Wright pulled me up as soon as I left the classroom... Kate pulled herself up short and shouted: 'Don't start that again.'*
V+PRON+ADV, V+REFL+ADV

7 If you tell someone to **pull up**, you are telling them to rest more; an informal use. EG *He said if I didn't pull up a bit I was in danger of a complete breakdown.* ● **Ease up** means almost the same as **pull up.**
V+ADV

8 If you **pull up** in something that you are doing, you improve at it and reach the same standard as other people. EG *These marks seem to be satisfactory so that means you've pulled up quite a bit... It's taken ten years of investment to pull up to present U.S. standards.* ● **Catch up** means almost the same as **pull up.**
V+ADV

pump, pumps, pumping, pumped

pump away. **1** To **pump away** means to move vigorously and continuously in and out or up and down. EG *His heart was pumping away... This machine is pumping away all the time... John pumped away on the starter.*
V+ADV

2 To **pump** a liquid or gas **away** means to remove it by forcing it to flow in a particular direction, using a pump. EG *We had pumped most of the water away by the afternoon... The oil spillage was pumped away, but most of the damage had already been done... ...pumping sewage away.*
V+N+ADV, V+ADV+N, V+PRON+ADV

pump in. If you **pump** money or resources **in**, you contribute a lot of money or resources towards a particular organization, plan, or project; a fairly informal expression. EG *We had to pump a lot of money in to get the scheme to work... They needed to pump more supplies in... The Government could pump in funds to help improve technology.* ● **Inject** is a more formal word for **pump in.**
V+N+ADV, V+ADV+N

pump into. If you **pump** money or resources **into** a particular organization, plan, or project, you put a lot of money or resources into it; a fairly informal expression. EG *Commercial organizations will have to pump colossal funds into new technology... Investors pumped £5 billion into the Stock Exchange last year.*
V+N+PREP, V+PRON+PREP

pump out. **1** To **pump** a liquid or gas **out** means to remove it from a place by forcing it to flow in a particular direction, using a pump. EG *...steam engines, developed originally to pump water out of the mines... This machine pumps unwanted salt water out and then replaces it with fresh... We seal one of the tubes and pump out all the air.*
V+N+ADV, V+ADV+N, V+PRON+ADV: ALSO+*of*

2 To **pump out** someone's stomach means to remove the contents of their stomach using a pump, because they have swallowed poison or taken an overdose of drugs. EG *I became conscious again as they pumped out my stomach.*
V+N+ADV, V+ADV+N, V+PRON+ADV

3 To **pump** things **out** means to produce or supply them continually in large amounts; a fairly informal use. EG *...a radio station pumping out pop music... He automatically pumps three articles out each week... They fired continuously, each gun pumping out four or five rounds a minute.* ● **Churn out** means almost the same as **pump out.**
V+ADV+N, V+N+ADV, V+PRON+ADV

pump out of. If you **pump** information **out of** someone, you force
V+PRON+ADV+PREP, V+N+ADV+PREP

them to tell you something that they want to keep secret. EG *I tried to pump it out of him, but he wouldn't say a word.*

pump up. 1 If you **pump up** something such as a tyre, you fill it with air, using a pump. EG *Do your tyres need pumping up?... I don't know how long it took to pump up the dinghy... Not having pumped up his tyres, the effort was too much for him.* ● **Blow up** means almost the same as **pump up,** and **inflate** is a more formal word.   V+ADV+N,
V+N+ADV,
V+PRON+ADV

2 To **pump** liquid **up** from a place underground means to force it out of that place to the surface, using a pump. EG *Oil has to be pumped up from deep boreholes... You could use a windmill to pump up water from the well.*   V+N+ADV,
V+N+ADV,
V+PRON+ADV:
USUALLY+*from*

punch, punches, punching, punched

punch in. When workers **punch in** at a factory or office, they record the time that they arrive by putting a special card into a machine; used in American English. ● **Clock in** means almost the same as **punch in,** and **punch out** means the opposite.   V+ADV

punch out. 1 When you **punch** something **out** of a substance such as wood, metal, or paper, you make it out of that substance by making a hole or other shape in it using a special machine or tool. EG *...an old-fashioned machine that punches out coins... We had a copy punched out on the telex tape ready for transmission.*   V+N+ADV,
V+ADV+N,
V+PRON+ADV

2 When workers **punch out** at a factory or office, they record the time that they leave by putting a special card into a machine; used in American English. ● **Clock out** means almost the same as **punch out,** and **punch in** means the opposite.   V+ADV

punch up. 1 In a shop, when someone **punches** an amount of money **up** on the cash register, they press the keys of the cash register in order to add up the figures. EG *It was only after he'd punched it up that I realized I'd lost my purse.*   V+PRON+ADV,
V+N+ADV,
V+ADV+N

2 A **punch-up** is a fight; an informal word used in British English. EG *'Looks as though you've been in a real punch-up,' says the barmaid... An employee said it was 'a very big punch-up.'*   N COUNT

push, pushes, pushing, pushed

push about. See push around.

push ahead. 1 When you **push ahead,** you continue doing something, using a lot of energy or enthusiasm. EG *Now was the time to push ahead and finish the enemy off... By the time dinner was finished, he was clearly in a mood to push ahead.* ● **Push on** and **press on** mean almost the same as **push ahead.**   V+ADV

2 If you **push ahead** with a plan, arrangement, or event, you continue with it, often when there are problems, or when other people want you to stop. EG *The Government was anxious to push ahead with a fresh round of negotiations... Michael Ward is pushing ahead with loans and help for projects... Djibouti has pushed ahead with an optimistic development strategy.*   V+ADV:
USUALLY+*with*

push along. If you say that you must **push along,** you mean that you must leave a place; an informal expression. EG *I must be pushing along now, it's getting late.* ● **Push off** means almost the same as **push along.**   V+ADV

push around. 1 When you **push** something **around, about,** or **round,** you move it from one position to another without lifting it away from the surface that it is on. EG *The boy pushed bits of lamb chop and lettuce around his plate... Tony was playing with cotton reels, pushing them slowly round the table... She stared at the china pieces and pushed them about.*   V+N+PREP/ADV,
V+PRON+PREP/ADV

2 If someone **pushes** you **around** or **about,** they tell you what to do in a rude and insulting way. EG *If we let them push us around on the*   V+PRON+ADV,
V+N+ADV

little things they'll want to take over everything... He began to push people around intellectually... I'm sick and tired of being pushed around.

push aside. 1 When you **push** something or someone **aside**, you move them to a position where they are not in your way. EG *As soon as we had finished our tea, we pushed all the crockery aside... Stuart pushed him aside and climbed behind the wheel... He leaned forward and pushed aside his notes.*   V+N+ADV, V+PRON+ADV, V+ADV+N

2 If you **push** something **aside**, you treat it as unimportant and pay attention to something else instead. EG *He quickly pushed all thought of it aside... These issues tend to get pushed aside and forgotten... Teaching is pushed aside as a non-starter.* ● **Brush aside** means almost the same as **push aside**.   V+N+ADV, V+PRON+ADV, V+ADV+N

push back. 1 When a group of people such as a crowd or an army is **pushed back**, they are forced to move backwards. EG *The Allied forces were pushed back... People protested but the police pushed them back.*   V+N+ADV, V+PRON+ADV, V+ADV+N

2 When you **push** something or someone **back**, you move them backwards. EG *She had pushed her sunglasses back, so they rested on her hair... His hair was over his eyebrows and he pushed it back... He had pushed back his chair so hard that it fell over.*   V+N+ADV, V+PRON+ADV, V+ADV+N

push by. If someone **pushes by**, they press roughly and rudely into other people as they go past them. EG *...ignorant old men who just push by to get on the bus... She just pushed by us without so much as an 'excuse me'.* ● **Push past** means almost the same as **push by**.   V+ADV, V+PREP

push for. If you **push for** something, you constantly encourage other people to help you achieve it. EG *Winston Churchill had pushed for the creation of an Arab state... He is pushing for secret balloting in Communist Party elections.* ● **Press for** means almost the same as **push for**.   V+PREP

push forward. 1 If you **push forward** your ideas, opinions, or beliefs, you try very hard to get other people to pay attention to them. EG *...the most effective means of pushing forward the interests of workers... He always pushed forward his own and, as he saw it, the Party's principles.* ● **Promote** is a more formal word for **push forward**.   V+ADV+N, V+PRON+ADV

2 If someone **pushes** themselves **forward**, they try rather unpleasantly to make other people pay attention to them. EG *We didn't like to push ourselves forward... ...that new woman pushing herself forward!... ...pushing himself forward in an unseemly manner.*   V+REFL+ADV

push in. 1 When someone who is waiting in a queue **pushes in**, they come into the queue in front of other people; used showing disapproval. EG *Felicity pushed in next to Howard... If she pushed in again, I would say something to her... No-one was allowed to push in.*   V+ADV

2 When someone **pushes in**, they force their way into a group, situation, or activity where they are not welcome. EG *Arthur Coggs isn't the sort that pushes in where he's not wanted! ... The wife can push in and take over the man's place.*   V+ADV

push into. 1 If you **push** someone **into** doing something, you use your influence to persuade or force them to do it. EG *...trying to push government into giving money for scientific research... ...determination not to be pushed into acceptance of nuclear missiles.*   V+N+PREP, V+PRON+PREP

2 If you **are pushed into** a difficult or unpleasant situation, you are forced into it by other people or by your circumstances. EG *You may well find yourself being pushed into this role... Children at this age are easily alarmed by being pushed into an unfamiliar situation.*   V+N+PREP, V+PRON+PREP: USUALLY PASSIVE

push off. 1 When you **push off**, you leave the person or place that   V+ADV you are visiting; an informal use. EG *I gave him a good talking-to. Then I pushed off... He must have pushed off when he heard us.*

2 If someone tells you to **push off**, they are telling you in a rude way to go away. EG *'I've got something to show you.'—'You push off,' I said... 'What do you want me to do?' she said. 'Nothing. You can push off now.'*

IMPERATIVE:
V+ADV

3 When something such as a boat or a sledge **pushes off** from its starting point, or when you **push** it **off**, it starts to go forwards. EG *As the launch pushed off, the sea turned from smooth to choppy... The boats were pushed off and drifted down the river.*

V+ADV,
V+N+ADV,
V+PRON+ADV:
ERGATIVE

push on. **1** When you **push on**, you continue travelling somewhere. EG *I felt restless and wanted to push on... If we want to get in before dark we must push on.*

V+ADV

2 When you **push on** with something that you are doing, you continue doing it with a lot of energy or enthusiasm. EG *...as we push on with our explanations... I must push on with these enquiries as fast as I can... He must push on through the timetable.* ● **Carry on** means almost the same as **push on**.

V+ADV:
USUALLY+with

3 If someone **pushes** something **on**, **onto**, or **upon** you, they insist on giving or selling it to you even though you do not really want it. EG *...an insurance salesman persistently trying to push an unwanted policy on him... Several boxes will be sold, and many more can be pushed upon the public.*

V+N+PREP,
V+PRON+PREP

push onto. See **push on**.

push out. **1** When you **push** someone or something **out** of a place, you use force to remove them from there. EG *He pushed Minnie out and slammed the door... The blue car has been pushed out of the garage... I was pushed out of the door before I could put on my shoes.*

V+N+ADV,
V+PRON+ADV,
V+ADV+N:
ALSO+of

2 If people **push** you **out** of an organization or an activity, they force you to leave it by being very unpleasant to you. EG *You're having a bad time and now you push me out... She was practically pushed out of the society for political reasons.*

V+PRON+ADV,
V+N+ADV:
ALSO+of

3 To **push out** something means to produce a lot of it and send it out somewhere; an informal use. EG *Computers can push out information to the external world in a variety of ways... ...the shoddy culture pushed out by TV films and magazines.* ● **Churn out** means almost the same as **push out**.

V+ADV+N,
V+N+ADV,
V+PRON+ADV

push over. **1** If you **push** someone or something **over**, you push them so that they fall onto the ground. EG *The children were pushing each other over on the sand... No one knew who pushed the guard over the wall... They knocked all the books off the shelves, pushed over the table and left.* ● **Knock over** means almost the same as **push over**.

V+N+ADV/PREP,
V+ADV+N,
V+PRON+ADV/PREP

2 You say that something is a **pushover** when it is easy to do or easy to get. EG *'I'm supposed to give my views on Europe.'—'Sounds like a pushover.'*

N SING

3 You say that someone is a **pushover** when they are easy to persuade or influence. EG *You won't have much trouble with her—she's a pushover.*

N SING

push past. If someone **pushes past** you, they press into you rather roughly or push you out of the way as they go past you. EG *People entering or leaving had to push past them... She began to push past him to the door but Arthur stopped her... He began to push past after Margaret.* ● **Push by** means almost the same as **push past**.

V+PREP,
V+ADV

push round. See **push around**.

push through. **1** If you **push** something **through**, you succeed in getting it accepted, often with difficulty. EG *The Government were*

V+N+ADV/PREP,
V+ADV+N,
V+PRON+ADV/PREP

determined to push the legislation through... The administration pushed four measures through Congress... ...the confidence to push through a long-term project.

2 If you **push through** things that are blocking your path, you use force in order to be able to move past them. EG *She was certainly not going to push through any of those people... I pushed through the turnstile... Everyone turned silent as they saw Ari approach. He pushed through and stared at the ground.*   V+PREP, V+ADV

3 If you **push** someone **through** an examination or course, you help them to pass or finish it. EG *...constant pressure to push everyone through the exam... His mother had pushed him through Junior and Grammar School to Oxford... It takes determination and guts to push yourself through a hard running schedule.* ● **Get through** means almost the same as **push through**.   V+N+PREP, V+PRON+PREP, V+REFL+PREP

push to. When you **push** a door or window **to,** you close it or partially close it by pushing it away from you. EG *Push that gate to before the dog gets out... No, don't shut it, just push it to a bit.*   V+N+ADV, V+PRON+ADV

push towards. If you **push towards** a particular aim, you try very hard to achieve something or to get other people to accept it. EG *The forces pushing towards standardization will probably be contained... In early pieces, he seemed to be pushing towards a new form of expression.*   V+PREP

push up. **1** To **push up** the price, rate, or amount of something means to increase it. EG *...shortages that have helped push up inflation... That might push the price up astronomically... ...techniques which push the temperature up to 200° C.*   V+ADV+N, V+N+ADV, V+PRON+ADV

2 If you do **push-ups,** you exercise by lying flat on your stomach, then pushing your body up using your arms and keeping your back and legs straight. EG *George got out of bed and did fifty push-ups.*   N COUNT

push upon. See push on.

put, puts, putting

The form **put** is used in the present tense and is the past tense and past participle of the verb.

put about. **1** If you **put about** something that is untrue or uncertain, you tell it to people and cause it to become well-known. EG *A rumour was put about to the effect that he had been drunk... They had an even harder struggle to counteract the lies put about by Mr. Jones... His mother put it about that he had robbed her of everything.*   V+PRON+ADV, V+ADV+N, USUALLY PASSIVE: ALSO V+it+ADV, WITH REPORT

2 If you **put** one thing **about** another, you place it so that it surrounds or encloses the other thing. EG *She knelt beside him and put her arms about him and soothed away the boy's tears... He sat her down in the chair and put a blanket about her shoulders.*   V+N+PREP, V+PRON+PREP

3 When a ship **puts about** or when it **is put about,** it changes its path and begins to sail in the opposite direction. EG *Three hours out of Southampton we had to put about and go back.*   V+ADV, V+N+ADV, V+PRON+ADV: ERGATIVE

put above. If you **put** one thing **above** another, you consider it to be more important than the other thing. EG *...a tradition which put freedom of conscience above the law and authority.* ● **Put before** means almost the same as **put above**.   V+N+PREP

put across. **1** If you **put across** information, ideas, or opinions, you succeed in telling them or explaining them to someone. EG *I was grateful that I had been given the chance to put across my point of view... ...an attempt to put a message across to the public... I try to put that across every time I write.* ● **Convey** is a more formal word for **put across**.   V+ADV+N, V+N+ADV, V+PRON+ADV

2 If you **put** one thing **across** another, you place it on top of the other thing or against it, so that it reaches from one side to the   V+N+PREP other. EG *Somebody put some boards across the stream... ...putting my fingers across her lips.*

put around. See **put round: put around** is slightly more formal.

put aside. 1 If you **put aside** an activity, a problem, or an attitude, you stop doing it, thinking about it, or showing it. EG *Brigit Stott puts aside her own work and dedicates herself to Albert... ...putting aside for the moment the fact that you may not get the job... I put the idea aside, and for a year thought no more of it.* ● **Set aside** means almost the same as **put aside**.   V+ADV+N, V+N+ADV, V+PRON+ADV

2 If you **put aside** an object you were using or looking at, you place it somewhere next to you because you do not need it for the moment. EG *Jimmie put aside his pipe... The old man put his books aside and spoke to us... He put it aside along with the envelope.* ● **Lay aside** means almost the same as **put aside**.   V+ADV+N, V+N+ADV, V+PRON+ADV

3 If you **put aside** money or other resources, you save it for a particular purpose or until you need it. EG *Perhaps you want to put money aside towards the cost of a house or a car... Whatever is left should be put aside and kept for tomorrow... Many women find it hard to put aside this time for themselves.* ● **Put by** means almost the same as **put aside**.   V+N+ADV, V+ADV+N, V+PRON+ADV

put at. If the cost, age, or value of something is **put at** a particular amount, it is estimated to be that amount. EG *The pipeline's cost is now put at 2.7 billion pounds... The consensus of opinion put the date at 1900.*   V+N+PREP, V+PRON+PREP: USUALLY PASSIVE

put away. 1 If you **put** something **away**, you place it tidily somewhere, for example in a cupboard, drawer, or pocket. EG *She put her shopping away in the kitchen... The girl, bent over her notebook, closed it and put away her pen... Albert folded the newspaper neatly and put it away on the side table.*   V+N+ADV, V+ADV+N, V+PRON+ADV

2 If you **put away** food or drink, you eat or drink a lot of it; an informal use. EG *I've put away more white wine than is good for my digestion... I had put away half a bottle of tequila during the evening... He put away sandwiches and coffee and was still hungry.*   V+ADV+N, V+PRON+ADV

3 If you **put** money **away**, you save it. EG *...the regular sums that you put away for holidays... You may just want to put something away for a rainy day... ...a child putting away some pocket money each week.* ● **Put by** means almost the same as **put away**.   V+ADV+N, V+N+ADV, V+PRON+ADV

4 If someone is **put away** by people in authority, they are sent to prison or a mental hospital; an informal use. EG *They were put away in prisons and labour camps... They had to put him away again. The poor man is crazy.* ● **Lock away** means almost the same as **put away**.   V+N+ADV, V+PRON+ADV, V+ADV+N: USUALLY PASSIVE

5 If someone is **put away**, they are killed; an informal use. EG *...the story of one Marine putting a wounded friend away with a pistol shot... He probably deserved being put away by a bullet.*   V+N+ADV, V+PRON+ADV, V+ADV+N

put back. 1 If you **put** something **back** somewhere, you place it in the position it was in before it was moved. EG *She put the telephone back and stood absolutely still... I put it back as soon as I ate... Shall I put it back in the box for you?... I was put back into the cell.* ● **Replace** is a more formal word for **put back**.   V+N+ADV, V+PRON+ADV, V+ADV+N: USUALLY+A

2 If you **put** your head **back**, you move it so that your face is pointing upwards. EG *He put his head back and closed his eyes... He put his head back and smiled up into the rain... Sponge put his head back and roared with laughter... I was lost. I put back my head and howled.*   V+N+ADV, V+ADV+N

3 If you **put** someone or something **back** in their previous state, you change them so that they are in that state again. EG *He puts the car*   V+N+ADV, V+PRON+ADV: USUALLY+A

back in gear and drives on... This is enough to put them back to sleep... 'Programme for Action' must be put back on the agenda.

4 To **put back** an event, appointment, or task means to postpone it happening or being done until a later time. EG *The effect is to put back the date of opening of the third airport... These bills have to be put back to a day when there will be time.* ● **Defer** is a more formal word for **put back,** and **bring forward** means the opposite.

V+ADV+N,
V+N+ADV,
V+PRON+ADV:
USUALLY+A

5 To **put back** the progress or development of something means to slow it down. EG *It is easy to risk the progress you have made and put your training back a week or two.* ● **Set back** means almost the same as **put back.**

V+N+ADV,
V+PRON+ADV,
V+ADV+N:
USUALLY+A

6 If you **put** a clock or watch **back,** you adjust it so that it shows an earlier time, for example when you travel from one time zone to another. EG *I put my watch back an hour before we landed at Kennedy Airport.* ● **Put forward** means the opposite of **put back.**

V+N+ADV,
V+PRON+ADV,
V+ADV+N

7 If you **put back** alcoholic drink, you drink a large amount of it in a short time; an informal use. EG *I'd put back a fair amount of gin the night before.* ● **Knock back** means almost the same as **put back.**

V+ADV+N,
V+N+ADV,
V+PRON+ADV

put back into. If you **put** money **back into** a business or a country's economy, you use some of the profits or taxes to pay for new development. EG *The Government didn't put any money back into the economy... Only a small percentage of this revenue is being put back into maintaining roads... We were all looking for a hopeful budget to put some money back into our operations.*

V+N+ADV+PREP,
V+PRON+ADV+PREP,
V+ADV+N+PREP

put back on. If you **put** clothes **back on,** you dress in them and wear them again after taking them off. EG *She has put her shirt back on but not her jeans... Put your clothes back on, Sara... Ben took off his glasses, wiped them, and put them back on.*

V+N+ADV+ADV,
V+PRON+ADV+ADV

put before. **1** If you **put** food **before** someone, you place it in front of them so that they can eat it. EG *Put the food before the child, say nothing... I eat what's put before me... Billy looked at the supper tray she had put before him ... The waiter put cherry cake before Klaus.*

V+N+PREP,
V+PRON+PREP

2 If you **put** facts or ideas **before** someone in authority, you officially present them to them. EG *Grant did not put any of this evidence before the jury... ...the plan he wished to put before them... Have you put the consequences before her?*

V+N+PREP,
V+PRON+PREP

3 If you **put** one thing **before** another, you give it more importance than the other thing. EG *Industry was put before agriculture... He is generally expected to put his work before his family... ...a disciplined man who will put duty before pleasure.*

V+N+PREP,
V+PRON+PREP

put behind. **1** If you **put** an unhappy event **behind** you, you try to forget it and not allow it to affect you now or in the future. EG *I thought when I went to England I would put all that behind me... She spoke of him as part of a life she had put behind her... Some people seem to be able to put it behind them, but I cannot help remembering.*

V+N+PREP,
V+PRON+PREP

2 If you **put** effort or resources **behind** a person or project, you use them to support that person or project. EG *Be sure to investigate thoroughly any such schemes before putting your money behind them... We're putting our professional expertise behind it... How many women trade unionists might put their weight behind women's struggles in the community?*

V+N+PREP,
V+PRON+PREP

put by. If you **put by** a sum of money or a supply of something, you save it so that you can use it later. EG *I put by a few shillings in order to buy that... Arthur Coggs had prudently put it by for future use.* ● **Put aside** means almost the same as **put by.**

V+ADV+N,
V+PRON+ADV,
V+N+ADV

put down. **1** If you **put down** something that you are holding or carrying, you place it somewhere. EG *Greene put his drink down on*

V+N+ADV/PREP,
V+PRON+ADV/PREP,
V+ADV+N

the table... Put it down there, Mrs Meynard, that's lovely... She puts down her case, and kisses him. ● **Set down** means almost the same as **put down**, and **pick up** means the opposite.

2 You can say that you **put down** the phone or the receiver when you replace it after you have finished speaking to someone. EG *'Oh God,' she muttered and put the phone down hurriedly... She put down the receiver and went to find Mrs Castle.*

V+N+ADV,
V+PRON+ADV,
V+ADV+N

3 If you **put down** a lawn, a carpet, or other covering, you place it so that it covers the ground or a flat surface. EG *Before we move in we want to put carpets down... We put down a bed of chippings... Large plantations of beech were put down in the eighteenth and nineteenth centuries.*

V+N+ADV,
V+ADV+N,
V+PRON+ADV

4 If someone **puts down** poison, they spread it on the ground to kill pests. EG *Badgers may be the innocent victims of poison put down to kill foxes... How do they get rid of these rats and mice? Do they put down poison?*

V+ADV+N,
V+N+ADV,
V+PRON+ADV

5 If you **put down** a part of your body, you move it to a lower position. EG *He put his face down and sniffed the rose... She puts down her head, and starts reading... Then she put one hand down into the box... ...yet you can put your foot down and touch it any time.* ● **Lower** is a more formal word for **put down**.

V+N+ADV,
V+ADV+N,
V+PRON+ADV:
NO PASSIVE

6 If you **put down** money when you are buying something, you pay some of the money when you take it, and pay the rest of the money in regular amounts after that. EG *You will often be required to put down a deposit on a car or a house... ...before putting down the first month's rent.*

V+ADV+N,
V+N+ADV,
V+PRON+ADV

7 When you **put down** words or numbers, you write or type them somewhere. EG *All you have to do is put down exactly what we've just said... You haven't put Professor Mangel's name down on the list... They're very difficult to put down on paper.*

V+ADV+N,
V+N+ADV,
V+PRON+ADV

8 If someone in a meeting **puts down** a question, motion, or amendment, they officially ask for it to be discussed and voted on; a technical use. EG *The Tribune Group had put down a motion condemning the Government's policy... We could therefore expect hundreds of amendments to be put down by the Tories.* ● **Table** is a more formal word for **put down**.

V+ADV+N,
V+N+ADV

9 If people in authority **put down** opposition, they oppose it and stop it by using force. EG *The rebellion was put down by European troops... He urged his princely patrons to put it down with the utmost ferocity... ...successfully putting down a series of revolts.* ● **Suppress** is a more formal word for **put down**.

V+N+ADV,
V+PRON+ADV,
V+ADV+N

10 If you **put down** a person or their ideas, you criticize them and make them appear foolish or unimportant. EG *We've been encouraged all our life to put down women's talk... ...her infuriating habit of putting people down in small ways... ...if someone puts you down and is really mean and rotten to you... It is very hard not to feel put down and ugly and undesirable.* ● **Slag off** is a very informal expression for **put down**. ▸ A **put-down** is a statement or action that is intended to criticize a person or their ideas and make them appear foolish or unimportant. EG *...all the put-downs you have to contend with... ... a dismissive put-down.*

V+ADV+N,
V+N+ADV,
V+PRON+ADV

N COUNT

11 When someone **puts** a baby **down**, they put it to sleep in a bed or cot. EG *After Ira had left, I fed Wendy and put her down for her nap... ...a woman who has just put the baby down for a rest.*

V+PRON+ADV,
V+N+ADV

12 If you **put** someone **down** for something or to do something, you make an official choice, application, or decision so that they can have it or do it. EG *He ended up putting his name down for architecture instead... Morris had recommended putting Philip*

V+N+ADV,
V+PRON+ADV:
USUALLY+*for*
OR *to*-INF

*down to teach English... ...having a father rich enough to put you
down for Eton the moment you're born.*

13 If you **put down** or **put** yourself **down** for something, you formally   V+ADV,
apply to have it or do it. EG *There were morning sessions for women.*   V+REFL+ADV:
My wife put down for Tuesdays and Thursdays... I've put myself   OR to-INF
down to teach Russian.

14 If a vet **puts down** an animal, he or she kills it, for example   V+ADV+N,
because it is old, seriously ill, or dangerous. EG *The Canine Defence*   V+N+ADV,
League will not put down healthy animals. ● **Destroy** means almost   V+PRON+ADV
the same as **put down.**

15 When the driver of a vehicle **puts down** passengers, he or she   V+ADV+N,
stops in order to let them get out. EG *The bus was stopping to put*   V+N+ADV,
someone down... The taxi put me down in the Unter den Eichen...   V+PRON+ADV
...the place where the girls had been put down. ● **Pick up** means the
opposite of **put down.** ▶ A **put-down** point is a place where a bus or   ADJECTIVE
coach stops in order to let people get off. EG *The bus had used
Smith's as its pick-up and put-down point... ...a put-down point in the
village.*

16 When an aeroplane **puts down** somewhere, it lands and stops   V+ADV:
there for a short time. EG *We ought to put down at Aumont some*   USUALLY+A
*time between five thirty and six... They will put down in Rome to
refuel.*

put down as. If you **put** someone or something **down as** a   V+N+ADV+PREP,
particular type of person or thing, you decide, often wrongly, that   V+PRON+ADV+PREP,
they are of that type. EG *I'd have put you down as somebody*   V+ADV+N+PREP
*reasonably successful in most things... He looked fat and respectful,
and was put down by those above him as willing, but slow.*

put down to. If you **put** one thing **down** to another thing, you   V+N+ADV+PREP,
believe that it is caused by the other thing. EG *Most bad shots can be*   V+ADV+N+PREP,
put down to one of half a dozen basic faults... It seemed unsafe to put   V+PRON+ADV+PREP
*down anything to coincidence... He puts it down to a deep fear of
change.*

put forth. If you **put forth** an idea or theory, you state it or publish   V+ADV+N,
it so that people can consider it and discuss it; an old-fashioned,   V+N+ADV
formal expression. EG *The Japanese physicist Yukawa put forth a
successful theory of the nuclear force... English and Welsh bishops
met, discussed the matter, and put forth their conclusions.* ● **Set
forth** means almost the same as **put forth.**

put forward. **1** If you **put forward** an idea or proposal, you state it   V+ADV+N,
or publish it so that people can consider it and discuss it. EG *The TUC*   V+N+ADV
*put forward a plan for national recovery... The idea was first put
forward by J.Good... Lipset does not put the proposition forward as a
universal truth.* ● **Set out** means almost the same as **put forward.**

2 If you **put forward** a person or their name, you officially suggest   V+ADV+N,
that they should be considered for a particular job or position. EG   V+N+ADV,
The organization put forward eight candidates for the NUS execu-   V+PRON+ADV,
tive... ...a woman who hesitates to put her own name forward... No   V+REFL+ADV:
one put me forward as a possible alternative to Jefferson... ...this   ALSO+for
consistent pattern of people putting themselves forward.
● **Nominate** is a more formal word for **put forward.**

3 If you **put forward** an event, you cause it to take place earlier than   V+ADV+N,
planned. EG *It was decided to put forward the dancing display.*   V+N+ADV,
● **Bring forward** means almost the same as **put forward.**   V+PRON+ADV

4 If you **put** a clock or watch **forward,** you adjust it so that it shows a   V+N+ADV,
later time, for example when you travel from one time zone to   V+PRON+ADV,
another. EG *Don't forget to put your clocks forward tonight; it's the*   V+ADV+N
start of British Summer Time. ● **Put back** means the opposite of **put
forward.**

put in. 1 If you **put** one thing **in** another, you place it inside the other thing. EG *If you pour hot water into a glass, put a spoon in first to absorb the heat... 'I don't know,' said Murdo, putting a spoonful of sugar in his tea... I folded my apron and put it in the drawer... He puts in the coins and dials the number in Toulouse.* ▸ An **input** is a quantity of something that is placed inside something else, or the act of placing it there; used mainly in American English. EG *...decline in soil fertility even without chemical inputs... ...a high fluid input.* V+N+ADV/PREP,
V+PRON+ADV/PREP,
V+ADV+N
N COUNT,
N UNCOUNT

2 If you **put in** plants or crops, you plant them in the ground. EG *Brazilian farmers put in a few hundred more coffee bushes... I'll put the cabbages in... You can put them in after peas or beans or early potatoes.* V+ADV+N,
V+N+ADV,
V+PRON+ADV

3 If you **put in** new equipment or new parts, you fix them in place in a building or a machine. EG *The designer could put in a more powerful engine... I had a new lock put in... Jim put that door in himself.* ● **Install** is a more formal word for **put in.** V+ADV+N,
V+N+ADV/PREP,
V+PRON+ADV/PREP

4 If you **put** money **in** a bank or an account, you give the money to the bank, which will look after it for you. EG *His father put the money in for him... She took twenty-five rupees out of it and put it in a deposit account... With a Giro account you can put in and draw out cash during normal Post Office opening hours.* ● **Deposit** is a more formal word for **put in,** and **pay in** means almost the same. V+N+ADV/PREP,
V+PRON+ADV/PREP,
V+ADV+N

5 If you **put** money **in** a business, a project, or a country, you provide money that it needs, and receive a profit if it is successful. EG *I have put money in shows, including Evita... They were putting in new investment.* ● **Invest** is a more formal word for **put in.** V+N+ADV/PREP,
V+PRON+ADV/PREP,
V+ADV+N

6 If you **put in** time or effort doing something, you spend time or work hard doing it. EG *Half of them were putting in forty-five hours a week or more... I was certainly pleased by the level of effort everyone put in today.* ▸ The **input** in an activity is the time or effort spent on it. EG *...requiring the input of more labour... Input from the workers is vital.* V+ADV+N,
V+N+ADV
N COUNT,
N UNCOUNT

7 If you **put in** a remark or comment, you interrupt someone when they are speaking in order to add some information or to give your opinion. EG *'We're not talking about women now, dear,' Alison put in smartly... 'But didn't you hear what I said?' put in Sally Jones.* ● **Interject** is a more formal word for **put in,** and **chip in** means almost the same. V+ADV+QUOTE

8 If you **put** something **in** a piece of writing, speech, or a drawing, you include it or cause it to be included. EG *When she read my story, she suggested I put in a description of the girl... ...putting advertisements in the London papers... When we got to camp he put it in his report.* ▸ Someone's **input** to a conversation consists of all that they say; a technical word. EG *...comparing the speech intention with the perceived speech input.* V+ADV+N,
V+N+ADV/PREP,
V+PRON+ADV/PREP
N COUNT,
N UNCOUNT

9 If you **put in** an order, a bill, or a request, you officially ask someone to give you goods or money, or to do something for you. EG *You'll put in an immediate request for transfer to Singapore... Your printers put in a hefty wage claim... ...even if every bill you put in is absolutely genuine... ...if we put another order in perhaps.* V+ADV+N,
V+N+ADV,
V+PRON+ADV

10 If you **put in** a phone call or a signal, you contact someone using a telephone or radio. EG *He put in the call and made himself another drink... I'll try to put a signal in to Control.* V+ADV+N,
V+N+ADV,
V+PRON+ADV:
ALSO+to

11 To **put** someone or something **in** a particular state means to cause them to be in that state. EG *'I know,' said Meadows. 'It puts me in a rather difficult position.'... He has put me in charge of everything... Put yourself in a cool and patient frame of mind.* V+PRON+PREP,
V+REFL+PREP,
V+N+PREP

12 If you **put** someone or something **in** a particular class or range, V+N+PREP,
V+PRON+PREP

you estimate or judge them to belong in that class or range. EG *In America the microchip industry has been put in the 'top ten' industries for urgent attention... That would have put him in his eighties... Many people wouldn't put him in the same class as Verdi.*

13 When people **put in** a person or group, they elect or appoint that person or group to do a particular job. EG *The French preferred the system of direct rule, putting in their own governors... They're putting me in as editor.* ● **Bring in** means almost the same as **put in**.

V+ADV+N,
V+PRON+ADV,
V+N+ADV:
ALSO+*as*

14 If you **put** someone **in** an institution such as a jail, a hospital, or a special type of school, you cause them to go there or be there. EG *Should he put his elderly father-in-law in a nursing home?... They will declare me insane and put me in a psychiatric clinic... This was before John had been put in prison.*

V+N+PREP,
V+PRON+PREP

15 If you **put** someone **in** a particular room in a building, you ask them or allow them to be there or sleep there. EG *I was still in my room downstairs, and Sarah was put in the room above me... There's someone to see you, Sarah. I've put him in the study.*

V+N+PREP,
V+PRON+PREP

16 If you **put** someone **in** particular clothes, you cause them to be dressed in them. EG *You're not thinking of putting him in shorts and a shirt?... After this unfortunate event, the inspectors were put in uniform and given truncheons.*

V+PRON+PREP,
V+N+PREP

17 If you **put** faith, trust, or hope **in** someone or something, you feel confident or hopeful that they will do or be what you want. EG *They betrayed the people who put faith in them... Abram put his trust in the Lord.*

V+N+PREP

18 When a ship **puts in** at a place, it stops in that place for a short time. EG *Sooner or later a ship will put in here... We were refused permission to put in at Corfu.*

V+ADV:
ALSO+*at*

19 The **input** of electricity or other form of energy into a machine or system is the act of supplying it, the amount that is supplied, or the place where it enters the machine or system. EG *The energy input rate is so vast... ...the input current... ...the industry's over-reliance on high fuel inputs.*

N COUNT,
N UNCOUNT

20 The **input** of data or information into a computer system is the act of supplying it, the amount that is supplied, or the place where it enters the machine or system. EG *He replaced the keyboard input... It had a set of input devices... ...the paper tape input.*

N COUNT,
N UNCOUNT

put in for. If you **put in for** something, you formally apply to have it. EG *'I didn't even know he applied.'—'Oh he puts in for everything.'... After the gamekeeper John Daniel died, father put in for his job... He put in for leave, just to go to the funeral.*

V+ADV+PREP

put into. **1** If you **put** one thing **into** another, you place it inside the other thing. EG *He put both his hands into his trouser pockets... I folded it carefully and put it into my shirt pocket.*

V+N+PREP,
V+PRON+PREP

2 If you **put** money **into** a bank or an account, you give the money to the bank, which will look after it for you. EG *How do I put money into my account?... My wife told me she was putting her salary into a savings account .*

V+N+PREP,
V+PRON+PREP

3 If you **put** money **into** a business or a project, you provide money that it needs, and receive a profit if it is successful. EG *I put a lot of money into it... State funding is not put into alternative research... He had insisted on putting it into jewellery and pictures.*

V+N+PREP,
V+PRON+PREP

4 If you **put** time, effort, or other resources **into** an activity, you use it for doing that activity. EG *She put all her energy into tidying the place up... ...a feeling that resources need not be put into health and safety... All her imagination is put into her garden.*

V+N+PREP,
V+PRON+PREP

5 If you **put** an item **into** a piece of writing, a speech, or a drawing, you include that item or cause it to be included. EG *He tried but failed*

V+N+PREP,
V+PRON+PREP

to put amendments into Callaghan's speech... ...all the American place-names that had been put into the titles of songs: 'Missouri Waltz', 'My Old Kentucky Home'.

6 To **put** a feeling or attitude **into** someone or something means to cause them to feel it or have it. EG *...a noise that put fear into Frank's pounding heart... ...the passion put into the performance... ...a band of commanders whose successes put heart into the British people.* | V+N+PREP, V+PRON+PREP

7 To **put** someone or something **into** another form or state means to cause them to be in that new form or state. EG *She wanted desperately to put her insight into words... It is not always easy to put it into modern English... Other people feel obliged to compete and put themselves into debt to do so.* | V+N+PREP, V+PRON+PREP, V+REFL+PREP

8 To **put** someone or something **into** a particular class or type means to judge that they belong to that class or type. EG *This would put her into the category of a participant... He has told me that he puts the 'Gang of Four' into the same category as Ramsay MacDonald.* | V+PRON+PREP, V+N+PREP

9 To **put** someone **into** a job or position means to appoint or elect them. EG *It was part of the plan to put Eisenhower into the job of Supreme Commander.* | V+N+PREP, V+PRON+PREP

10 If someone **is put into** an institution such as a prison or mental hospital, they are sent to stay there by someone in authority. EG *She was about to be put into prison for a year... Put a child into an institution and all he wants is to go home.* | V+N+PREP, V+PRON+PREP

11 If someone **is put into** a particular room in a building, they are told or allowed to be there or stay there. EG *When Josie returned, she was put into a room on the ground floor... I was put into a cell opposite the one I had been in all those months.* | V+N+PREP, V+PRON+PREP: USUALLY PASSIVE

12 If you **put** someone **into** particular clothes, you cause them to dress them in those clothes. EG *Even tiny children were put into black frocks... ...putting him into grubby overalls... They were put into uniform and flown from Washington to Frankfurt.* | V+N+PREP, V+PRON+PREP

13 If a ship **puts into** a port, it stops there for a short time. EG *We might have to put into Hammerfest for shelter.* | V+PREP

put off. **1** If you **put off** an event or appointment, you delay or postpone it. If you **put** a person **off,** you delay seeing them or doing what they want you to do by telling them that you are too busy. EG *He had intended to put off seeing Daisy until after he had seen Gertrude... Don't put it off till tomorrow... She'll be here soon, unless I can put her off somehow... That would have put the end off for a while... Sollozzo can't be put off any more. You'll have to see him this week.* | V+ADV+N, V+PRON+ADV, V+N+ADV

2 To **put** someone **off** doing something or having something means to cause them to change their mind so that they no longer want to do it or have it. EG *I would not put anybody off wine-making... Nothing would put her off once she had made up her mind... Don't be put off because something doesn't have instant results.* | V+N+ADV/PREP, V+PRON+ADV/PREP, V+ADV+N

3 If something or someone **puts** you **off** what you are doing, they cause you to stop concentrating by making a sudden noise or distracting you in some other way. EG *Play stopped for nearly a minute when McEnroe was put off by a low-flying plane.* | V+N+ADV, V+PRON+ADV

4 To **put** someone **off** another person means to cause them to dislike that person. EG *I thought it more likely to put Gertrude off you... A number of people were put off Mike and termed him arrogant... ...a young actress who puts one off at first with her American briskness.* | V+N+ADV/PREP, V+PRON+ADV/PREP, V+ADV+N

▶ A **put-off** is something that causes you to dislike someone; used mainly in American English. EG *They are always alert for the slight put-off, the well-timed provocation.* ▶ Someone or something that is | N COUNT

ADJECTIVE

off-putting causes you to dislike them. EG *...her rather off-putting manner... Those glasses are most off-putting... ...an off-putting mixture of affectation and stupidity.*

5 If you **put** a light **off,** you move a switch so that it no longer shines. EG *I put the light off again... Don't forget to put all the lights off before you go to bed.* ● **Switch off** and **put out** mean almost the same as **put off.**   V+N+ADV, V+PRON+ADV, V+ADV+N

6 When a ship or vehicle **puts** someone **off,** it stops somewhere in order to let them get off. EG *He was put off at Singapore.*   V+N+ADV, V+PRON+ADV, V+ADV+N

7 If you **put off** clothes, especially a uniform of some kind, you take them off and never wear them again EG *...unwilling to put off the lovely dress for the last time... When a boy came of age in ancient Rome he put off his short tunic and assumed the toga virilis.*   V+ADV+N: NO PASSIVE

put on. 1 If you **put** something **on** a horizontal surface, you place it above the surface, which supports it. EG *He put a hand on my shoulder... ...how the Americans ever managed to put a man on the moon... When it was all ready, she put it on a tray.*   V+N+PREP, V+PRON+PREP

2 If you **put** one thing **on** another, you attach or fix it to the other thing. EG *We put a new lock on the bedroom door... He took the ring and put it on Joseph's finger.*   V+N+PREP, V+PRON+PREP

3 When you **put on** a piece of clothing, you place it over a part of your body and wear it. EG *I put on my jacket... She put her glasses on... She zipped up the dress with difficulty. She had only put it on twice before... They stripped off his clothes and put a scarlet robe on him.* ● **Take off** means the opposite of **put on.**   V+ADV+N, V+N+ADV/PREP, V+PRON+ADV/PREP

4 When you **put on** make-up or ointment, you spread it over a part of your body. EG *She put lipstick on before every class... They must have put ointment on my burns... She has put on too much perfume.*   V+N+ADV/PREP, V+PRON+ADV/PREP, V+ADV+N

5 When a person or group **puts on** a play, concert, or other entertainment, they organize it or perform it. EG *He put on a play that closed after only eight performances... A production of A Midsummer Night's Dream was being put on at the school... We took nearly a year to put it on because Pamela was not available.* ● **Stage** is a more formal word for **put on.**   V+ADV+N, V+N+ADV, V+PRON+ADV

6 When a person or organization **puts on** a service, they provide it. EG *Courses in History are put on at the request of other departments... They're putting on a special train service.* ● **Lay on** means almost the same as **put on,** and **take off** means the opposite.   V+ADV+N, V+N+ADV, V+PRON+ADV

7 If someone **puts on** weight, they become heavier. EG *She put on over a stone... I can quickly spot whether they are putting weight on or losing it.* ● **Gain** means almost the same as **put on,** and **lose** means the opposite.   V+ADV+N, V+N+ADV, V+PRON+ADV: NO PASSIVE

8 If you **put on** an electrical or gas device, you cause it to work by pressing a switch or turning a knob. EG *He put on the light... Shall I put the fire on?... They put the kettle on to make a cup of tea.* ● **Turn on** and **switch on** mean almost the same as **put on.**   V+ADV+N, V+N+ADV, V+PRON+ADV

9 If you are driving a vehicle and **put on** the brake, you operate it. EG *She had to put on her brake rather suddenly... Put the brake on and leave the car in gear.* ● **Apply** is a more formal word for **put on.**   V+ADV+N, V+N+ADV, V+PRON+ADV

10 If you **put on** a record, tape, or video, you place it on the record player or in the tape machine so that you can hear it or see it. EG *She put on the Brahms Second Piano Concerto... Morris fixed himself a stiff drink and put an Aretha Franklin LP on the hi-fi.*   V+ADV+N, V+N+ADV/PREP, V+PRON+ADV/PREP

11 If you **put on** food, you begin to cook it. EG *She forgets to put the dinner on... He went into the kitchen and put on some potatoes to boil.*   V+N+ADV/PREP, V+PRON+ADV/PREP

12 If you **put** money **on** a race, a competition, or one of the competitors, you make a bet about who will win. EG *The only time I*   V+N+ADV/PREP, V+PRON+ADV/PREP

ever put a pound on a horse I felt sick... Nobody actually put any
money on at those odds... I put a pound on for you.

13 If you **put** money **on** something, you are confident or sure that it   v+N+PREP
is true, will happen, or will be successful. EG Who would have put
money on atomic energy in 1940?... He would have put money on it.

14 To **put** an amount **on** the cost or value of something means to add   v+N+PREP
it to the cost or value. EG That decision will put another 5p a gallon
on petrol... They have been known to put a tax on salt. ● **Knock off**
means the opposite of **put on**.

15 To **put** a restriction **on** something means to make laws which   v+N+PREP
stop people from doing it. EG MAFF could help things along by
putting an embargo on all grant aid... The United States put an
immediate ban on all television coverage.

16 If you **put** emphasis or reliance **on** something, you emphasize it   v+N+PREP
or rely on it. If you **put** the blame for something **on** someone, you
blame them for it. EG Too much reliance was put on human nature...
...a system which would put more emphasis on individual freedom.

17 If you **put** extra work, responsibility, or pressure **on** someone, you   v+N+PREP
cause them to do it, have it, or feel it. EG It puts a tremendous
responsibility on us... People felt free to put more demands on the
system.

18 If you **put on** a look or a way of speaking or behaving, you look,   v+ADV+N,
speak, or behave in a way that is not natural to you or does not show   v+N+ADV,
what you really feel or think. If you say that someone **is putting** it   v+PRON+ADV,
on, you mean that they are pretending to feel something or to be   v+it+ADV
something, or that they are exaggerating how ill or upset they are.
EG I don't see why you put on a phoney English accent... ...the grin
she had put on for the cameras... I wondered if Clive was putting it
on to avoid starting work.

19 If someone **is putting** you **on,** they are teasing you by trying to   v+PRON+ADV,
make you believe something that is not true; used mainly in infor-   v+N+ADV:
mal American English. EG 'You're putting me on,' said Deirdre... I   NO PASSIVE
also like the way you put me on a while ago. About his half a million.
● **Have on** and **kid** mean almost the same as **put on**. ▶ A **put-on** is an   N SING
action that is intended to tease or deceive someone. EG I bet the
whole thing was a put-on for those TV guys.

20 If you **put** someone **on** a bus, plane, train, or ship, you take them   v+N+PREP,
to it and make sure they get onto it. EG Mummy put me on the train   v+PRON+PREP
at Victoria... We put him on a plane to California this morning.

21 If you **put** someone **on** a committee or a particular job, you   v+N+PREP,
officially decide that they should have that position or do that work.   v+PRON+PREP
EG ...companies that put trade union representatives on their
boards... They put me on security work again at the weekends... 'Put
him on the night shift,' Mr Ballott said.

22 If you **put** someone **on** the phone, you pass the phone to them so   v+N+ADV/PREP,
that they can speak to someone. EG I asked him to put Lloyd on the   v+PRON+ADV/PREP,
phone... 'Can you put her on the phone?'—'Oh, she's in the hospital.'...   v+ADV+N
Just put on Nell for one moment more, will you?

23 If someone **is put on** a particular type of food, medical treatment,   v+N+PREP,
or punishment, they are given that food, treatment, or punishment.   v+PRON+PREP:
EG After a while Laura saw the doctor and was put on a diet... They   USUALLY PASSIVE
had to put him on oxygen... When they first came in they'd be put on
pills.

put on to, put onto. **1** If you **put** one thing **onto** another, you place   v+N+PREP,
it on top of the other thing or attach it to the other thing. EG So she   v+PRON+PREP
put a cloth onto her head, went into the church, and prayed... I put
her back onto the bed.

2 If you **put** someone **onto** a bus, plane, train, or plane, you take   v+PRON+PREP,
                                                                         v+N+PREP

them to it and make sure they get on it. EG *...putting me onto a French inter-village bus the next morning.*

3 If you **put** someone **on to** someone or something, you tell them about someone or something that could help them. EG *Directory Enquiries put him on to the International Exchange... An accident put me on to the work of Husserl... I can put you onto a good thing, Charlie.*   V+PRON+PREP, V+N+PREP

put out. 1 If a statement or story **is put out,** it is officially told to people. EG *The World Wildlife Fund put out a press release... The story that the committee will put out has nothing to do with the truth... He put something out to the Press Association.* ● **Issue** means almost the same as **put out.**   V+ADV+N, V+N+ADV, V+PRON+ADV

2 If a message or programme **is put out** on radio or television, it is sent or broadcast. EG *The pilot put out a radio message giving the exact position... The Open University courses were actually putting some of them out on the television screen... It was put out by the non-commercial network OXYZ.* ● **Broadcast** is a more formal word for **put out.**   V+ADV+N, V+N+ADV, V+PRON+ADV: ALSO+*on*

3 If you **put out** something that is burning, you cause it to stop burning. EG *He put the fire out... ...putting out the candles... The fire could not be put out too easily... I lit another cigarette, but immediately put it out.* ● **Extinguish** is a more formal word for **put out.**   V+N+ADV, V+ADV+N, V+PRON+ADV

4 If you **put out** a light, you cause it to stop shining by pressing or turning a switch. EG *Castle undressed and put out the light... He put his torch out... 'Will you put the lights out or shall I?'—'You put them out, dear.'* ● **Switch off** and **turn off** mean almost the same as **put out.**   V+ADV+N, V+N+ADV, V+PRON+ADV

5 If you are at home and **put** something **out,** you take it out of the house and leave it there for someone to collect. EG *She still can't remember to put out the milk bottles... You must not put your dustbin out before 7.30 a.m.* ● **Bring in** means the opposite of **put out.**   V+ADV+N, V+N+ADV, V+PRON+ADV

6 If you **put out** babies, invalids, or animals, you take them from a building and leave them outside for a while. EG *She used to put the babies out in the pram... They put their horses out to graze... I do everything from washing up dishes to putting out the cat at night.*   V+N+ADV, V+ADV+N, V+PRON+ADV

7 If you **put** things **out** for someone, you put them somewhere where they will be noticed and used. EG *I put clean clothes out for you on the bed... All equipment and materials are put out at the beginning... I went into his office, opened his post and put it out on his desk... Now he goes about, putting out ashtrays and dishes, cushions and chairs.* ● **Lay out** means almost the same as **put out,** and **collect up** means the opposite.   V+N+ADV, V+PRON+ADV, V+ADV+N

8 If you **put out** a hand, an arm, or a foot, you move it forward and away from your body. EG *I slipped and put out my arm to save myself... Judy put out her hands and held Lynn tight... Put your left foot out... Denise put her hand out to restrain him.* ● **Hold out** means almost the same as **put out.**   V+ADV+N, V+N+ADV, V+PRON+ADV: NO PASSIVE

9 If you **put** your tongue **out,** you poke it through your lips, usually as a rude gesture. EG *He put his tongue out at his daughter playfully... 'Put out your tongue,' she said, and I obeyed.* ● **Stick out** means almost the same as **put out.**   V+N+ADV, V+ADV+N, V+PRON+ADV: NO PASSIVE

10 If you **put** your back or a joint in your body **out,** you accidentally cause a bone to be moved from its normal position. EG *More backs have been put out cleaning baths than in any other activity... It becomes weak and puts the kneecap out.* ● **Dislocate** is a more formal word for **put out.**   V+N+ADV, V+PRON+ADV

11 If you **are put out,** someone or something has upset or annoyed   PASSIVE: V+ADV

you. EG *Lally looked a bit put out... He didn't appear at all put out by the news... 'So?' asked von Amsburg, obviously put out by the general's answer.* ● **Be disconcerted** is a more formal expression for **be put out.** ▶ Someone's **put-out** expression indicates that they have been upset or annoyed. EG *'He'll be right back,' she said in a slightly put-out tone.*   ADJECTIVE

12 If you **put** yourself **out,** you make an effort to do something or help someone, although it may be inconvenient for you. EG *He was putting himself out to please her... 'He would not put himself out to do a thing', Dot said.*   V+REFL+ADV

13 If you **put** someone **out,** you cause them trouble or inconvenience; a rather old-fashioned use. EG *Don't think you're putting her out in any way. She likes nothing better.*   V+PRON+ADV, V+N+ADV

14 If you **put** someone **out** of a place, vehicle, or job, you make them leave it, sometimes by force. EG *I was put out of the school on the ground that I was useless... You can be put out on your ear at the end of the month... We put him out of the house... Irving stopped the cab and put his wife out of it..*   V+PRON+ADV, V+N+ADV, V+ADV+N: ALSO+of

15 When a boat or ship **puts out,** it leaves its harbour and sails into the sea. EG *We could see the boats putting out for the first of the summer herring... Occasionally it is too rough for the launch to put out.*   V+ADV

16 If someone **puts out,** they agree to have sex; a very informal use.   V+ADV

17 To **put** someone **out** means to cause them to become unconscious. EG *The doctor agreed to put her out altogether during the birth.*   V+PRON+ADV, V+N+ADV

18 When a plant or tree **puts out** buds, leaves or flowers, the buds, leaves or flowers grow and become visible on it. EG *When it starts putting out leaves, you know that summer is near... The dead stakes rot and disappear, but the hedge puts out new growth... It put out an exquisite spring blossom.*   V+ADV+N, V+N+ADV, V+PRON+ADV

19 If a company **puts out** products, it manufactures them, publishes them, or sells them. EG *...a small publishing firm that put out expensively bound reprints... Behind the gramophone there were some records put out by an American company.* ● **Produce** means almost the same as **put out.**   V+ADV+N, V+N+ADV, V+PRON+ADV

20 The **output** of someone or something is the amount of something that they produce, or the thing that they produce. EG *...a 3 per cent fall in industrial output... Her rapid output of novels and poetry encouraged him.*   N UNCOUNT

21 Computer **output** is the information which a computer produces as the result of a particular program or operation. EG *...output data... There's something wrong with this output.*   N UNCOUNT

put out of. To **put** someone or something **out of** a state or condition, means to stop them being in it. EG *All three tanks were very quickly put out of action... Always put poisons out of reach... Technological developments may put them completely out of business.*   V+N+ADV+PREP

put over. 1 If you **put** one thing **over** another, you place it so that it covers the other thing. EG *The postmistress put a rug over her knees... She put a hand over his... He took off his anorak and put it over the back of the chair.*   V+N+PREP, V+PRON+PREP

2 If you **put** one thing **over** another on a vertical surface or on a piece of paper, you place or write it above the other thing. EG *Alan put a sign over the entrance gate... ...put dots over each letter.*   V+N+PREP, V+PRON+PREP

3 When you **put** an idea **over,** you succeed in describing or explaining it to someone. EG *There are enough of them to put over their point of view... The university's prospectuses didn't put it over the way I wanted to... With the modern resources available, you can put*   V+ADV+N, V+PRON+ADV, V+N+ADV an article over nationally or world-wide. ● **Put across** and **get across** mean almost the same as **put over**.

put past. If you would not **put** something **past** someone, you think that they are likely to do it or are capable of doing it, even though you disapprove of it. EG *I wouldn't put anything past her in the company she's keeping now... I wouldn't put it past you to hop on a plane and go after Liebermann yourself.*

V+N+PREP,
V+PRON+PREP:
WITH NEGATIVE

put round. 1 If you **put** something **round** or **around** another thing, you place it so that it surrounds the other thing. EG *He was in his garden putting the compost round his roses... He had to put it round my waist and tie it... She put her arms around me... I knelt on the floor beside her and put an arm round her shoulders.*

V+N+PREP,
V+PRON+PREP

2 If information or a story **is put round,** it becomes known by many people. EG *The report had been put round by the Left to cause trouble... It's just a rumour put round by students... I hope she puts round a letter of thanks.*

V+N+ADV,
V+PRON+ADV,
V+ADV+N:
USUALLY PASSIVE

put through. 1 If you **put** something **through** a solid object, you pass it from one side to the other either by pushing it through a hole, or by by making a hole through it by force. EG *She simply put her hand through the letter-box and opened the door from the inside... Put an iron rod through at each end to hold the ladder together... Put them through the rings on each side of the box... He put his foot through the plaster.*

V+N+ADV/PREP,
V+PRON+ADV/PREP

2 If you **put** your arm **through** someone else's arm, you link arms with them to show affection or to control their movements. EG *The trainer caught him up and put his arm through the boy's... Gertrude put her arm through Tim's and led him away.*

V+N+PREP,
V+PRON+PREP

3 If you **put** objects or substances **through** a machine or a mechanical, electrical, or chemical process, you cause them to be affected and changed by it. EG *Put cooked vegetables and fruit through the blender... In the factories, they were put through an elaborate process to produce syrup.* ▶ The **throughput** of a machine or factory is the amount of material that it deals with or the rate at which it does so; a technical word. EG *...machines that can handle a rapid throughput of raw materials.*

V+N+PREP,
V+PRON+PREP

N COUNT

4 If you **put** plans, proposals, or problems **through** an official system, organization or person, you ask them for advice, approval or support. EG *...putting our case through the normal media channels... No need to put it through my department at all. I'll handle it personally.*

V+N+PREP,
V+PRON+PREP

5 If people in authority **put through** a proposal or plan, they formally agree to it. EG *They put through the first nuclear arms agreements... He was planning to put through his arms deal, despite official US disapproval... They had at last succeeded in putting a meaningful reform through.*

V+ADV+N,
V+N+ADV,
V+PRON+ADV

6 If you **put** a message **through** to someone, you succeed in sending it to them. EG *I've put a teleprinter request through to Washington... It would do no harm to put through the enquiry without revealing why it was being made... Yes, that would save putting it through the post.*

V+N+ADV/PREP,
V+PRON+ADV/PREP,
V+ADV+N

7 If you **put through** a phone call or the person making the call, you connect them with the person they want to speak to. EG *Please don't put any calls through until this class is over... Who? Martha? Okay. Yes, put her through... Warlimont put through a call to Blumentritt at OB West... Townsend picked up the receiver and was put through to the Laboratory.*

V+N+ADV,
V+PRON+ADV,
V+ADV+N:
ALSO+to

8 If you **put** someone **through** school or college, you pay their fees and expenses for them. EG *He only put his daughter through college*

V+N+PREP,
V+PRON+PREP,
V+REFL+PREP

by selling off his wife's jewellery... His grandparents offered to put him through dental school... While working as a civil servant in Natal, he put himself through several diploma courses.

9 If you **put** someone or something **through** an event or experience, you make them do it or suffer it. EG *It's not right to put him through a lot of tests... I'm sorry to put you through this again... Hoffmann put the lorry through a series of rough manoeuvres.*   V+PRON+PREP, V+N+PREP

10 The **throughput** of people in an organization or system is the number of people that it deals with. EG *...Gatwick, with an annual throughput rising to 10 million passengers a year... The organization has a faster throughput of people as well... Total passenger throughput is expected to rise.*   N COUNT

put to. **1** If you **put** one thing **to** another, you place or hold it next to the other thing and touching it. EG *He put a finger to his lips in a gesture of silence... Don did this by putting a pistol to the forehead of the band leader... He struck a match and put it to his pipe.*   V+N+PREP, V+PRON+PREP

2 If you **put** a name, figure, date, or face **to** something or someone, you are able to remember, calculate, or estimate who, what, or how much they are. EG *He recognised the face, but he couldn't put a name to it... They might even put a figure to the resources required... Most people, when asked to put a date to it, assume that it was designed during the last century.*   V+N+PREP

3 If you **put** an idea, question, or problem **to** someone, you ask them to consider it or react to it. EG *...the sort of questions that I'll be putting to the scientists... They formally put the demand to me... ...a motion to be put to the next party Conference... He put it to you that Griffiths was driving.*   V+N+PREP, V+PRON+PREP

4 If something **puts** you **to** a lot of trouble or expense, it makes you spend a lot of your time or money doing something that you would prefer not to have to do. EG *But if we refuse to confirm it, it'll put you to the trouble of proving it for the court record... I'm only sorry that I put you to so much trouble.*   V+PRON+PREP, V+N+PREP

put together. **1** If you **put together** an object or its parts, you join its parts to each other so that it can be used. EG *The shipyards possess years of expertise in putting together such big metal structures... Grease the valve thoroughly and put the parts together again... Anyone can put it together in a few hours.* ● **Assemble** is a more formal word for **put together,** and **take apart** means the opposite.   V+ADV+N, V+N+ADV, V+PRON+ADV

2 If you **put together** similar things, objects, or substances, or a particular combination of them, you place them near each other, in the same container, or touching each other. EG *Three tables were put together for them... They put them together in a test-tube... She put together a fresh fruit salad.*   V+N+ADV, V+PRON+ADV, V+ADV+N

3 If you **put together** a group of people, you choose them and form them into a team or group for a particular purpose. EG *This time Crook had put together a mighty army... They put together a small baseball team... The lawyers had put together an impressive assembly of defense witnesses.*   V+ADV+N, V+N+ADV, V+PRON+ADV

4 If you **put together** a project or a piece of work, you organize it or arrange it. EG *The agency has put together the biggest ever campaign for a new car... The whole production was somewhat hastily put together.*   V+ADV+N, V+N+ADV, V+PRON+ADV

5 If you **put together** words, facts, figures, or ideas, you consider them carefully and use them to create a piece of writing, a speech, a plan, or a theory. EG *He found it difficult to put a dozen words together at a time... I was busy writing a new play and I had to put my thoughts together... Beverley Nichols put together a collection of*   V+N+ADV, V+ADV+N, V+PRON+ADV *interviews with famous people... I have a lot of talent, if only I can put it together.*

6 If you say that one person or thing is better, or greater in size, amount or importance than a group of other people or things **put together** you are emphasizing how much better or greater they are. EG *He is smarter than all your colonels put together... The schools spend as much as the rest of the city put together... She was wiser than the other two put together.*   ADJECTIVE

put towards. If you **put** money **towards** something that you want to buy, you save the money until you have enough to buy it. EG *If I do win, I'll put the money towards a new car.*   V+N+PREP, V+PRON+PREP

put up. **1** If you **put** something **up**, or **put** it **up** somewhere, you move it to a higher position or place it farther away from the ground. EG *He put up the collar of his jacket... I put the window up to hear this speech... I got a box and put it up against the wall... He put his hands up over his face and cried.*   V+N+ADV, V+N+ADV, V+PRON+ADV

2 If you **put** one thing **up** another, you push it so that it is inside the other thing. EG *He put his hand up her coat and pulled out the pin.*   V+N+PREP, V+PRON+PREP

3 If you **put up** a building, wall, shelf, or similar structure, you build it or fix it in place. EG *We shall have to put up a fence... They're going to put up a whole block of apartments... It was always collapsing on my toes because I hadn't put it up properly.* ● **Erect** and **construct** are more formal words for **put up,** and **pull down** means the opposite.   V+ADV+N, V+PRON+ADV, V+N+ADV

4 If you **put up** something that is folded, such as an umbrella, tent, or hood, you open it or spread it out so that it can be used. EG *Put your umbrella up... Why doesn't she put the hood up?... Take the tent and put it up some distance away from the camp.*   V+N+ADV, V+PRON+ADV, V+ADV+N

5 If you **put up** a notice, sign, or poster, you stick or fasten it to a wall, post, or noticeboard so that people can see it. EG *She put up a large sign outside her house... We would put the signs up for his inspection, then take them down... I cut his notes out and put them up in the classroom... These posters were put up all over the area.* ● **Stick up** and **post up** mean almost the same as **put up,** and **take down** means the opposite.   V+ADV+N, V+N+ADV, V+PRON+ADV

6 If you **put up** opposition, resistance, or a fight, you oppose, resist, or fight something. EG *America has put up so much resistance to Concord... We had put up a fierce struggle.*   V+ADV+N

7 If you **put up** an idea, argument, or proposal, you tell it or suggest it to people so that they can consider it and discuss it. EG *...the argument that the Vatican is putting up all the time... He wouldn't have put up such a good case for himself... Why not check and then we'll put it up to the others?* ● **Put forward** and **put forth** mean almost the same as **put up.**   V+ADV+N, V+N+ADV, V+PRON+ADV

8 If you **put up** money for something, you provide the money that is needed to pay for it. EG *The banks will not put up money without government backing... They put up their own cash... The National Endowment for the Arts put up half the cost.*   V+ADV+N

9 To **put up** the price or rate of something means to cause it to increase. EG *In about 1920, he put the price up to 2 shillings per pound... They will not put it up a lot because of the old people... Their governments put up prices too far... The mortgage rate had been put up on the house.* ● **Raise** means almost the same as **put up,** and **bring down** means the opposite.   V+N+ADV, V+PRON+ADV, V+ADV+N

10 If someone **puts** you **up** or if you **put up** somewhere, you stay with them or stay there for one or more nights. EG *The Murrays had put him up for the night... We can't put him up here... She was put up at the Grand Hotel... We put up at Chestnut Court.*   V+PRON+ADV, V+N+ADV, V+ADV+N, V+ADV

11 If you **put up** or **are put up** in an election or contest, you are chosen to be a candidate or competitor in it. EG *They put up several candidates in Cornwall... He put up as an independent candidate... Jack is effective enough in his way; but put him up against a real boxer like Brood and he wouldn't stand a chance.*

V+ADV+N,
V+ADV:
ERGATIVE

12 A **put-up** job is something that has been arranged beforehand in order to cheat or deceive someone; an informal word. EG *It was a put-up job, if ever there was one.*

ADJECTIVE

put upon. **1** If you **put** one object **upon** another, you place it on top of the other thing; an old-fashioned or literary use. EG *He put his hand gently upon it and felt the coolness... A red cloth had been put upon the table.* ● **Put on** means almost the same as **put upon.**

V+N+PREP,
V+PRON+PREP

2 If you **put** a particular value or interpretation **upon** something, you think it has that value or meaning; an old-fashioned or literary use. EG *What value would they put upon her?... ...the unfortunate interpretation you put upon my laughter.*

V+N+PREP,
V+PRON+PREP

3 To **put** pressure, demands, or restrictions **upon** someone means to cause them to suffer by what you ask them to do or not to do; an old-fashioned or literary use. EG *His parents put demands upon him that are not in his interest... ...the pressures put upon them to prescribe more drugs... ...restrictions put upon them by their culture and religion.*

V+N+PREP,
V+PRON+PREP

4 If you **are put upon,** someone unfairly asks or expects you to do more than you originally offered or agreed to do; an old-fashioned or literary use. EG *We are not prepared to be put upon... Thank you, Ibrahim. I really am sorry to put upon you.* ● **Impose on** means almost the same as **put upon.** ▶ A **put-upon** person has been unfairly asked or expected to do too much. Their **put-upon** expression shows this. EG *...Halliwell, Orton's put-upon friend... ...an expression as mild and put-upon as his father's... ...the poor, put-upon, innocent soul!*

V+PREP:
HAS PASSIVE

ADJECTIVE

put up to. If you **put** someone **up to** something, you ask and encourage them to do something wrong or foolish. EG *He wondered if Benny hadn't put Fitzsimmons up to it... Someone put Sid up to this... Julie herself had probably put them up to it... Ma put you up to asking that!*

V+N+ADV+PREP,
V+PRON+ADV+PREP

put up with. If you **put up with** something or someone, you tolerate or accept them, even though you find it difficult or unpleasant. EG *I'm prepared to put up with it for the time being... The visitors could put up with any amount of boredom... 'Why do the people put up with it?' demanded Hilary.* ● **Endure** is a more formal word for **put up with.**

V+ADV+PREP

puzzle, puzzles, puzzling, puzzled

puzzle out. If you **puzzle** a problem **out,** you think hard about it and usually find the answer. EG *If you have time to puzzle it out... I leave them to puzzle it out... They understand how a child puzzles things out... Children pause to puzzle out the nature of the task.* ● **Solve** is a more formal word for **puzzle out.**

V+PRON+ADV,
V+N+ADV,
V+ADV+N

puzzle over. If you **puzzle over** something, you think hard about it in order to try to understand it. EG *There was scarcely time to puzzle over these features... They puzzled over what could be inside the houses... She puzzled over it, then recalled the conversation they had... He frowned and puzzled the matter over.* ● **Ponder** is a more formal word for **puzzle over.**

V+PREP:
HAS PASSIVE,
ALSO
V+N+ADV

Q q

quarrel, quarrels, quarrelling, quarrelled

American English uses the spellings **quarreling** and **quarreled**.

quarrel with. 1 If you **quarrel with** someone, you disagree with them strongly and argue or sometimes fight with them. EG *'I don't want to quarrel with her,' she said. 'She's my oldest friend.'... She quarrelled with Christopher over the lease.*

V+PREP:
ALSO+*over/about*

2 If you **quarrel with** an idea, statement, or opinion, you disagree with it; a slightly formal use. EG *One may quarrel with McHale's contention... I think Canetti would quarrel with the use of the word madness... Royalty is intimacy. Nobody could quarrel with that.*

V+PREP:
HAS PASSIVE,
USUALLY
WITH MODAL

queen, queens, queening, queened

queen over. If someone **queens** it **over** you, they act in a way that shows that they think they are better than you, for example by telling you what to do. EG *...a dozen cats queened over by the mother... All right, but don't you try to queen it over me.* ● **Lord over** means almost the same as **queen over**.

V+*it*+PREP

queue, queues, queueing/queuing, queued

queue up. If you **queue up**, you stand in a line of people and wait for something. EG *Supaya had to queue up at the factory every morning to see if there was any work... People were queueing up for his autograph.*

V+ADV

quicken, quickens, quickening, quickened

quicken up. If you **quicken** something **up** or if it **quickens up**, its speed increases. EG *Start these movements slowly and then quicken them up... Then the pace began to quicken up.* ● **Speed up** means almost the same as **quicken up**.

V+PRON+ADV,
V+N+ADV,
V+ADV+N,
V+ADV:
ERGATIVE

quiet, quiets, quieting, quieted

quiet down. If someone or something **quiets down**, or if you **quiet** them **down**, they become less noisy or active, or more calm; used in American English. EG *When he quieted down, I began to tell him the simple truth... Meanwhile, things quieted down in Los Angeles.* ● **Calm down** means almost the same as **quiet down**.

V+ADV,
V+ADV+N,
V+N+ADV,
V+PRON+ADV:
ERGATIVE

quieten, quietens, quietening, quietened

quieten down. If something or someone **quietens down** or if you **quieten** them **down**, they become less noisy or active, or more calm; used in British English. EG *He had matured and quietened down considerably... ...a cunning stratagem to quieten down the rebellious peasants.* ● **Calm down** means almost the same as **quieten down**.

V+ADV,
V+ADV+N,
V+N+ADV,
V+PRON+ADV:
ERGATIVE

R r

rabbit, rabbits, rabbiting, rabbited

rabbit on. If someone **rabbits on** about something, they talk about it for a long time in a rather boring way; an informal expression. EG *...liberals on both sides rabbiting on endlessly about underprivilege... ...TV commentators with the ability to keep rabbiting on about whatever is happening.*

V+ADV:
USUALLY+*about*

rage, rages, raging, raged

rage against. If you **rage against** a person or situation, you express

V+PREP

your great anger about them; a rather literary expression. EG
Postmen rage against the handwriting of correspondents.

rail, rails, railing, railed

rail against. If you **rail against** a person or situation, you express   V+PREP
your great anger about them; a literary expression. EG *He railed
against the doctors for forbidding it.*

rain, rains, raining, rained

rain down. If a lot of things **rain down** on a person or place, they   V+ADV
fall rapidly on them; a literary expression. EG *Millions of tons of
volcanic ash rained down over a huge area... Their sticks rained
down even harder.*

rain off. If a sports match **is rained off,** it has to stop, or it is not   PASSIVE:
able to start, because of rain. EG *Today's match between Yorkshire*   V+ADV
and Kent has been rained off.

rake, rakes, raking, raked

rake in. If someone **is raking in** money, they are earning a lot of   V+ADV+N,
money fairly easily; an informal expression. EG *Western countries*   V+PRON+ADV,
raked in 78 per cent of the income... They've got so many shops,   V+N+ADV
they must be raking it in!

rake over. If someone **rakes over** an unpleasant event in the past,   V+ADV+N
they keep talking about it even though it would be better to forget it.
EG *Why travel back into the past to rake over old worries?... It is too
early to rake over the reputations of those so recently dead.*

rake up. 1 If someone **rakes up** something unpleasant or embar-   V+ADV+N,
rassing that happened to you in the past, they find out about it and   V+PRON+ADV,
tell other people in order to cause trouble; an informal use. EG *...if*   V+N+ADV
*one political Party was allowed to rake up all the misdeeds or
mistakes of another party... Don't go raking up that filth that
happened thirteen years ago.*

2 If you **rake up** people or things, you find them and bring them   V+ADV+N,
together for a particular purpose; an informal use. EG *I'll see if I can*   V+PRON+ADV,
rake up a few people to help you.   V+N+ADV

rally, rallies, rallying, rallied

rally round. If people **rally round** you, they work together to   V+ADV,
support you at a difficult time. EG *Yes, I'm very lucky. Everyone has*   V+PREP
*rallied round... The girls have rallied round and coped magnificent-
ly... The party rallied round him after his election defeat.*

ram, rams, ramming, rammed

ram down. 1 If you **ram** an object **down,** you push it hard and   V+N+ADV,
suddenly towards the ground. EG *Ram the stick down and it lifts up*   V+ADV+N,
the catch... Reload it with gunpowder and ram down the wad.   V+PRON+ADV

2 If you **ram** a fact or idea **down** someone's throat, especially when   V+N+PREP,
they know it already or do not want to know it, you tell them about it   V+PRON+PREP
forcefully and repeatedly. EG *...wanting to ram his world record
down their throats... Weinberger takes a harder line. He wants to
ram it down their throats.*

ram in. If you **ram** an object **in,** you push it very hard and suddenly   V+PRON+ADV,
into a container. EG *Why don't we lift the lot up in the sheet and ram*   V+ADV+N,
it all in?... He took out his pipe, rammed in some tobacco and lit up...   V+N+ADV
The old man rammed the key in with a trembling finger.

ram into. 1 If you **ram into** something, you hit it very hard after   V+PREP,
moving towards it very quickly. If you **ram** one object **into** another,   V+N+PREP,
you move it quickly so that it hits the other object very hard. EG   V+PRON+PREP:
Drivers still drunkenly ram into trees... He rammed his fist into   ERGATIVE
Hooper's throat.

2 If you **ram** ideas or facts **into** someone, you force that person to learn them or remember them. EG *He felt that he had rammed it into a few minds sufficiently hard.* · $\quad$ V+PRON+PREP, V+N+PREP

ramble, rambles, rambling, rambled

ramble on. If someone **rambles on**, they talk or write for a long time in a rather confused and disordered way. EG *...listening to Miriam as she rambled on... He needed to ramble on about his financial affairs... But there I go, rambling on. Please forgive me.* $\quad$ V+ADV

range, ranges, ranging, ranged

range against. If one person or thing **is ranged against** another, they are opposed to or in conflict with the other one. EG *The forces of reaction will be strongly ranged against the next Labour Government... ...his rage at finding the system ranged against him.* $\quad$ PASSIVE: V+PREP

rank, ranks, ranking, ranked

rank among. If a person or thing **ranks among** a particular type or group, they have the qualities of that type or group. EG *Academically, Tony never ranked among the scholars... This county ranks among the wealthiest in the country.* $\quad$ V+PREP

rap, raps, rapping, rapped

rap out. If you **rap out** something, especially an order or a question, you say it quickly and sharply. EG *'Is that the truth?' he suddenly rapped out... She rapped out the orders urgently... ...and rapped out the announcement.* $\quad$ V+ADV+QUOTE, V+ADV+N, V+PRON+ADV, V+N+ADV

rat, rats, ratting, ratted

rat on. If someone **rats on** you, they give information to people in authority that causes you to be punished or to have problems; an informal expression. EG *So you ratted on Gertrude?... If they got caught, it wouldn't be because of Quiller ratting on them.* $\quad$ V+PREP: HAS PASSIVE

ration, rations, rationing, rationed

ration out. If you **ration out** something that you have very little of, you distribute it in small amounts among a group of people. EG *I rationed out the last of the food... They will ration it out, and you will accept what you're given... The limited funds available have to be rationed out among local groups.* $\quad$ V+ADV+N, V+PRON+ADV, V+N+ADV

rattle, rattles, rattling, rattled

rattle off. To **rattle** something **off** means to say or do it quickly and without effort; an informal expression. EG *...a machine capable of rattling off thousands of calculations per second... Rhoda, surprisingly, rattled off the Mozart sonata with ease.* ● **Reel off** means almost the same as **rattle off**. $\quad$ V+ADV+N, V+PRON+ADV, V+N+ADV

rattle on. If someone **rattles on** about something, they talk about it for a long time, speaking quickly and in a rather irritating way. EG *Some of the women would rattle on about sex... She rattled on excitedly about Mrs Moffat... Denise was rattling on: 'I looked and you weren't there.'* ● **Rabbit on** means almost the same as **rattle on**. $\quad$ V+ADV: USUALLY+*about*

rattle through. If you **rattle through** something, you deal with it very quickly in order to finish it; an informal expression. EG *They rattled through the rest of the meeting... He rattled through his envelopes again.* $\quad$ V+PREP

rave, raves, raving, raved

rave up. If you **rave it up**, you enjoy yourself by drinking and dancing and behaving in a noisy and uncontrolled way; a rather old-fashioned expression. EG *...a huge audience raving it up under the stars.* ▸ A **rave-up** is an event at which people drink, dance, and $\quad$ V+*it*+ADV

$\quad$ N COUNT

behave in a noisy and uncontrolled way. EG *I was looking forward to a real rave-up... ...a rave-up holiday.*

reach, reaches, reaching, reached

reach down. 1 If you **reach down,** you bend your body towards the ground and stretch your arms in order to touch or grasp something. EG *I remove a glove with my teeth, reach down and and feel the cover... Dick reached down and grabbed his wrists.*   V+ADV

2 If something **reaches down** to a particular level, it extends downwards as far as that level. EG *Only expensive tube-wells can reach down to the reserves of water... ...a long blue skirt reaching down to the ground.*   V+ADV: ALSO+*to*

reach out. If you **reach out,** or **reach out** a hand, you stretch your arm, and sometimes your body, in order to do something slightly far away from you. EG *Otto reached out for the bottle of wine... Howard reaches out of the window and hands the ticket to him... ...reach out a hand and touch the man's arm.*   V+ADV, V+ADV+N

reach out for. If people **reach out for** better things, they make great efforts to get or achieve them. EG *They now reach out for further satisfactions... ...reaching out for new standards... ...a society reaching out for a better quality of life.*   V+ADV+PREP

reach out to. If you **reach out to** people, you give them help, advice, or comfort, or ask them for it. EG *His phenomenal capacity to reach out to people... They may reach out to another person for reassurance.* ▶ **Outreach** workers are employed by local government to find people who need help and persuade them to apply for it, so that social problems can be dealt with before they become severe. EG *...vacancies for outreach workers.*   V+ADV+PREP / ADJECTIVE

reach up. 1 If you **reach up,** you stretch your body and arms upwards in order to touch or grasp something. EG *He reached up and slid the top bolt... ...reaching up to pull the lavatory chain.*   V+ADV

2 If something **reaches up** to a particular level, it extends upwards as far as that level. EG *...ferns reaching up like twelve-feet high umbrellas.*   V+ADV

read, reads, reading

The form **read** is used in the present tense and is the past tense and past participle of the verb.

read back. If you **read** a piece of writing **back,** you read it again after writing it, in order to check that it is correct or acceptable. EG *The sentence was easy to read back... ...reading back some of what you have just said.*   V+N+ADV, V+ADV+N, V+PRON+ADV

read for. If you **read for** a university degree, you do the studying and work required to obtain it; a rather old-fashioned expression. EG *Two students reading for the same degree may cover very different ground.*   V+PREP

read into. If you **read** a meaning or importance **into** something, you think it has that meaning or importance, but it may not. EG *It would be a mistake to read too much significance into the local election result... The authors warn us about reading too much into the figures... Jeremy was reading into it something that I never intended... Any religious crank can read his own meanings into the Bible.*   V+N+PREP, V+PRON+PREP

read off. If you **read off** a measurement on a machine or other device, you look carefully and note the exact measurement shown on it; a rather technical expression. EG *You read off, on that centre line, your mean viability... You read off the number at the top of the bar.*   V+ADV+N, V+PRON+ADV, V+N+ADV

read out. 1 If you **read out** a piece of writing, you say the words aloud as you read it. EG *John Tyme read out a statement on behalf of*   V+ADV+N, V+N+ADV, V+PRON+ADV: ALSO+*to*

600 objectors... Lecturers who read their scripts out can be terribly dull... One of them then writes a paper and reads it out to the rest of us.

2 The **read-out** from a computer or similar machine is the printed information that it produces. EG *...machines that give an extremely fast, efficient read-out and are low in cost... Check that computer read-out to see if you're on target this time.*   N COUNT

read over. If you **read over** a piece of writing, you read it in order to check it or comment on it before it is used or published. EG *When my director read over what I had written, he was puzzled... The typescript is taken back to them, read over, discussed.*   V+ADV+N, V+PRON+ADV, V+N+ADV

read through. If you **read through** a piece of writing, you read it from beginning to end. EG *I've read through your letter very careful-ly... Ask the student to read it through first.*   V+PREP, V+PRON+ADV, V+N+ADV

read up. If you **read up** on a subject, you read a lot about it because you want to know it thoroughly. EG *...having read up the answer to this question in Whitaker's Almanack... I got out the encyclopaedia and read up about uranium... Lucas had read up on Mother Shipton just in case he was asked.*   V+ADV+N, V+PRON+ADV: ALSO V+ADV+*on*

rear, rears, rearing, reared

rear up. When an animal such as a horse **rears up,** it suddenly lifts its front legs in the air and stands on its hind legs. EG *...a deer, rearing up with her ears back... ...Boxer, rearing up on his hind legs and striking out.*   V+ADV

reason, reasons, reasoning, reasoned

reason out. If you **reason out** a problem or puzzle, you solve it by thinking about it carefully. EG *She was able to reason out many of the passages and their meanings... She decided that she would reason out the whole matter... Leave it to me. I can reason it out later.* ● **Work out** and **figure out** mean almost the same as **reason out.**   V+ADV+N, V+PRON+ADV, V+N+ADV

reason with. If you **reason with** someone, you use sensible, logical arguments in order to persuade them to agree with you or to do something. EG *If he tries to leave, try to reason with him... Couldn't you reason with her?... I had to reason with myself like this to soothe my nervousness.*   V+PREP: HAS PASSIVE

rebound, rebounds, rebounding, rebounded

rebound on. If someone's action or attitude **rebounds on** or **upon** you, it affects you, although it was intended only to affect someone else. EG *I didn't dare tell you what I thought of you, because I knew it would only rebound on her... His resentment and ill temper re-bounded upon Cal.*   V+PREP

rebound upon. See **rebound on.**

reckon, reckons, reckoning, reckoned

reckon in. If you are calculating something and **reckon** an item **in,** you include it. EG *When everything is reckoned in, they are not so badly paid... Don't forget to reckon in the service charge... If you reckon them in, I'm sure we've got at least twenty.*   V+N+ADV, V+ADV+N, V+PRON+ADV

reckon on. If you **reckon on** something, you feel certain that it will happen and include it in your plans. EG *This was far beyond the four figure sum she had reckoned on... I reckoned on his support... They could not reckon on our neutrality... They had not reckoned on such a fight.* ● **Bank on** means almost the same as **reckon on.**   V+PREP: HAS PASSIVE

reckon up. If you **reckon up** a set of figures, you add them together to find the total. EG *I'll have to reckon it up, I can't say off-hand... She couldn't face reckoning up the length of time.* ● **Tot up** means almost the same as **reckon up,** and **calculate** is a more formal word.   V+PRON+ADV, V+ADV+N, V+N+ADV

reckon with. 1 If you had not **reckoned with** an event, you had not
expected it and so were not prepared for it. EG *She had not reckoned
with a surprise of this sort.* ● **Bargain for** means almost the same as
reckon with.

V+PREP:
HAS PASSIVE

2 If you say that someone or something is to be **reckoned with,** you
mean that they are a difficulty or threat to you. EG *There was also
Gertrude to be reckoned with... The union had become a force to be
reckoned with.*

PASSIVE:
V+with

reckon without. If you had **reckoned without** something, you had
not expected it and so were not prepared for it; an informal
expression. EG *...but the bishops reckoned without Margaret's determination... They reckoned without the keen instincts of Terry.*

V+PREP

reduce, reduces, reducing, reduced

reduce to. 1 If you **reduce** an amount **to** a lower amount, you
decrease it to the lower amount. EG *My father's wages had been
reduced to 10 shillings a week... ...reduces the number of cancer
tumours to less than half.*

V+N+PREP,
V+PRON+PREP:
USUALLY PASSIVE

2 If something or someone **is reduced to** a bad state or condition,
they are caused to be in it. EG *...every building being reduced to
rubble... A tough reporter was reduced to tears at the sight...
...flattening everything in its path, reducing it to dust.*

V+N+PREP,
V+PRON+PREP:
USUALLY PASSIVE

reek, reeks, reeking, reeked

reek of. 1 If an object or place **reeks of** a substance, it smells very
strongly of that substance. EG *His breath reeked of gin... ...ware-
houses reeking of rotten bananas.*

V+PREP

2 If a product or piece of work **reeks of** an unpleasant quality, that
quality is strongly noticeable in it. EG *Their song titles reek of
portentousness... The article reeked of deception and evasiveness.*

V+PREP

reel, reels, reeling, reeled

reel back. If you **reel back,** you move backwards suddenly and
unsteadily. EG *Daisy reeled back against the wooden partition...
...pushing against her tormentors, who reeled back in surprise.*

V+ADV

reel in. If you **reel in** a fish or a fishing line, you pull it towards you
by turning the handle of the reel to shorten the line. EG *A small blue
shark took the line: Brody reeled it in... He reeled in his line.*

V+PRON+ADV,
V+ADV+N,
V+N+ADV

reel off. If you **reel off** a speech or some information, you repeat it
from memory quickly and easily; an informal expression. EG *He
could reel off the names of all the capitals of Europe... He gets up
and reels off the same speech every time... I have to memorize all
this so I can reel it off to people I meet.* ● **Rattle off** means almost
the same as **reel off.**

V+ADV+N,
V+PRON+ADV,
V+N+ADV

refer, refers, referring, referred

refer to. 1 If you **refer to** a particular subject or person, you talk
about them or mention them. EG *In his letters to Vita he rarely
referred to political events... I am not allowed to describe the
officers or refer to them by name.*

V+PREP:
HAS PASSIVE

2 If you **refer to** something or someone as a particular thing, this is
the name or expression you use to describe them or talk about
them. EG *...the decline of what I refer to as the industrial working
class... This kind of art is often referred to as 'minimal art'.*

V+PREP:
USUALLY+as,
HAS PASSIVE

3 If a word or code **refers to** something, it relates to it or describes it
in some way. EG *The serial number refers to the country of origin...
Until the end of the 18th Century, 'antique' referred specifically to
Greek and Roman antiquities.*

V+PREP:
HAS PASSIVE

4 If you **refer to** a source of information such as a reference book,
you look at it in order to find something out. EG *She could make a*

V+PREP:
HAS PASSIVE

new dish without referring to any cookery books... ...information which can be referred to on future occasions. ● **Consult** means almost the same as **refer to.**

5 If you **refer** someone **to** a source of information, you suggest that they look there because it contains useful information. EG *I refer you to a paper by Sutherland... On two occasions at least Gray refers us to Chekhov.*   V+PRON+PREP, V+N+PREP

6 If someone **refers** a person or problem **to** a specialist or an organization, they ask the specialist or organization to deal with the person or problem. EG *She referred the matter to the European Court of Justice... She was referred by her doctor to a consultant... The death has been referred to the coroner.*   V+N+PREP, V+PRON+PREP

reflect, reflects, reflecting, reflected

reflect on. If you **reflect on** or **upon** something, you spend a lot of time thinking about it. EG *He reflected on how different things might have been... ...reflecting upon the coming of Western culture.*   V+PREP: HAS PASSIVE

reflect upon. See reflect on.

refrain, refrains, refraining, refrained

refrain from. If you **refrain from** doing something, you do not do it, although you may want to. EG *This will cause France to refrain from hostile action... He had to refrain from speaking when adults were speaking... Mary could not refrain from a faint smile.*   V+PREP: HAS PASSIVE

rein, reins, reining, reined

rein in. **1** If you are riding and you **rein in** the horse, you make it stop or go more slowly by pulling its reins. EG *He reined in his horse to a walk... They proudly reined in their horses before the park gates.*   V+ADV+N, V+N+ADV, V+PRON+ADV

2 To **rein in** someone who is behaving in an extreme or unacceptable way means to control them and make them behave properly; a formal use. EG *The colonels were going too far and would have to be reined in... They wanted to rein in the excesses of private landowners... He was reined in so severely that he almost resigned.*   V+ADV+N, V+N+ADV, V+PRON+ADV

relate, relates, relating, related

relate to. **1** If something **relates to** a particular subject, it concerns that subject or is connected with it. EG *I wanted to ask you a question that relates to electricity... The present negotiations do not relate to disarmament... ...the law relating to pet ownership.*   V+PREP

2 If you can **relate to** other people, you can understand how they feel and communicate with them or deal with them easily. EG *Children need to learn to relate to other children... ...the way we think, structure our feelings, and relate to one another.*   V+PREP

relieve, relieves, relieving, relieved

relieve of. If you **relieve** someone **of** something, you cause them not to have it any longer. EG *He relieved her of the plates she was holding... He wished to relieve her of financial anxiety... I was relieved of my position as director.*   V+PREP: HAS PASSIVE

rely, relies, relying, relied

rely on. **1** To **rely on** or **upon** something or someone means to need them in order to survive or be successful. EG *She is forced to rely on her mother's money... Hong Kong's prosperity relies heavily on foreign businesses... There were no facilities for analysing food, so I had to rely on sight, taste and smell.* ● **Depend on** means almost the same as **rely on.**   V+PREP: HAS PASSIVE

2 If you **rely on** or **upon** someone or something to work or behave in a particular way, you trust them to do this. EG *One could always rely*   V+PREP: HAS PASSIVE, USUALLY+*to*-INF on him to be polite and do the right thing... *They cannot be relied upon to offer much support or advice.* ● **Count on** is a more informal expression for **rely on**.

rely upon. See **rely on**.

remark, remarks, remarking, remarked

remark on. If you **remark on** or **upon** something, you say or write something that shows you have noticed it. EG *His friends remarked on his sudden failure to appear... This is the most remarked upon aspect of overcrowding.*

V+PREP:
HAS PASSIVE

remark upon. See **remark on**.

remember, remembers, remembering, remembered

remember to. If you ask someone to **remember** you **to** another person, you are asking them to pass your greetings to that person. EG *Don't forget to remember me to your father.*

V+PRON+PREP

remind, reminds, reminding, reminded

remind of. 1 If you **remind** someone **of** something, you tell them about it so that they remember it. EG *Howard comes to the door to remind him of their appointment... May I remind you of something you said earlier... The idea is to remind you of your proper role in life.*

V+PRON+PREP,
V+N+PREP

2 If one person or thing **reminds** you **of** another, they make you think of the other person or thing, because they are both similar in some way. EG *You remind me of my friend Baxter... His political writings remind me of those of Sartre... I am reminded of a story about Captain Hardy.*

V+PRON+PREP,
V+N+PREP

render, renders, rendering, rendered

render down. If fat **is rendered down**, it is turned into liquid, usually by heating it. EG *The whale fat is rendered down to make soap... Render the lard down for a rich stock.*

PASSIVE:
V+ADV

rent, rents, renting, rented

rent out. If someone **rents out** something such as a room or a piece of land, they allow it to be used for a period of time in return for payment. EG *They had to rent out the upstairs room for years... ...land that the farmer had previously rented out to tenants... Councils have sold a large proportion of new dwellings instead of renting them out.* ● **Let out** means almost the same as **rent out**.

V+ADV+N,
V+N+ADV,
V+PRON+ADV:
ALSO+to

report, reports, reporting, reported

report back. If you **report back** to someone, you give them an account of something that you were asked to find out about. EG *This scene would make him late reporting back to the Governor... Attend the meeting and report back on their activities... It will be days before any leak can be reported back.*

V+ADV,
ALSO+to/on:
ALSO PASSIVE,
V+ADV

repose, reposes, reposing, reposed

repose in. 1 If you say someone **reposes in** a place, you mean they are buried there; a literary use. EG *All his uncles were now reposing in the local churchyard.*

V+PREP

2 If you **repose** your trust **in** someone, you trust them; a formal use. EG *...the trust reposed in him by Crewe.*

V+N+PREP,
V+PRON+PREP

reside, resides, residing, resided

reside in. If a quality **resides in** something, it exists or is present in that thing. EG *Strength resides in the gun... Real power resides in the workshop and the office... Memory has been shown to reside in many different organisms.*

V+PREP

resort, resorts, resorting, resorted

resort to. If you **resort to** a course of action that you do not really think is right or acceptable, you adopt it because you cannot see any other way of achieving what you want. EG *Eventually the police resorted to CS gas to quell the rioters... Some factions have resorted to terrorism.*
`V+PREP: HAS PASSIVE`

rest, rests, resting, rested

rest with. If a duty or decision **rests with** a person, that person is responsible for it; a formal expression. EG *The responsibility rests with the Committee... The decision was not his, but rested with his boss.*
`V+PREP`

result, results, resulting, resulted

result from. If a situation **results from** an event or action, it is caused by that event or action. EG *Most of the damage resulted from bombing... Inflation results from an excess of demand over supply.*
`V+PREP`

result in. If something **results in** a particular situation or event, it causes that situation or event to happen. EG *A warming of the earth's surface might result in the melting of the polar ice caps... ...an accident which resulted in the death of a child... Such behaviour may result in the executive being asked to leave.*
`V+PREP`

return, returns, returning, returned

return to. 1 When you **return to** a place, you go back there after you have been away. EG *I returned to my hotel.*
`V+PREP`

2 If you **return** something **to** someone, you give it back to them after having it for a time. EG *Will you be so good as to return the drawing to me.*
`V+N+PREP, V+PRON+PREP`

3 If you **return** something **to** a place, you put it back there after removing it for a time. EG *He returned the gun to its holster.*
`V+N+PREP, V+PRON+PREP`

4 If you **return to** a previous topic when talking or writing, you mention it or discuss it again. EG *Now let me return to the question of inflation... We shall return to this theme in Chapter 7.*
`V+PREP: HAS PASSIVE`

5 If you **return to** a previous activity or state, you start doing it again or being in it again after a break. EG *After lunch, Edward returned to his gardening... The Labour Party seems poised to return to power.*
`V+PREP`

rev, revs, revving, revved

rev up. If you **rev up** a car or vehicle, you increase the speed of its engine by pressing the accelerator. EG *Moses revved up and the car shot forward... ...revving up at the lights... I told you not to rev it up like that... Victor revved up his motorbike.*
`V+ADV, V+PRON+ADV, V+N+ADV, V+ADV+N`

revel, revels, revelling, revelled

American English uses the spellings **reveling** and **reveled**.

revel in. If you **revel in** a situation or experience, it gives you a feeling of great joy and you really enjoy this feeling. EG *She seemed to revel in her success... ...schoolchildren revelling in the bright sunshine.* ● **Glory in** means almost the same as **revel in**.
`V+PREP: HAS PASSIVE`

revert, reverts, reverting, reverted

revert to. 1 If people or things **revert to** a previous state or condition, often a worse or less developed one, they change and start being in it again. EG *Pastures which yielded good grass are reverting to marsh and bracken... He was reverting rapidly to adolescence.* ● **Return to** and **go back to** mean almost the same as **revert to**.
`V+PREP`

2 If you **revert to** something that was mentioned earlier, you begin
`V+PREP: HAS PASSIVE`

talking about it again; a fairly formal use. EG *At this point in the discussion I reverted to money matters... Can I revert to one other point before you continue?*

3 When money or property **reverts to** someone, it becomes their   V+PREP
property because they owned it before or because they are a
descendant of the previous owner; a technical term in law.

revolve, revolves, revolving, revolved

revolve around. If a discussion **revolves around** or **round** a   V+PREP
particular subject, it mainly concerns that subject. EG *The discussion
revolved round three topics... The argument would revolve around
what was considered 'reasonable'.* ● **Centre around** means almost
the same as **revolve around**.

revolve round. See revolve around.

rid, rids, ridding

The form **rid** is used in the present tense and is the past tense and
past participle of the verb.

rid of. If you **rid** a place, thing, or person **of** something unpleasant or   V+N+PREP,
unwanted, you remove it completely; a formal expression. EG *It is*   V+PRON+PREP,
difficult to rid clothes of cooking smells... Occupiers must rid their   V+REFL+PREP
*premises of rats and mice... The aim is to rid the world of the risk of
total war... He had rid himself of his illusions.* ● **Get rid of** is an
informal way of saying **rid** yourself **of**.

ride, rides, riding, rode, ridden

ride out. If you **ride out** a period of difficulty or danger, you manage   V+ADV+N,
to survive it without suffering serious harm. EG *We knew that we*   V+PRON+ADV,
would be able to ride out the storm... The company can ride out the   V+N+ADV
recession and do well again. ● **Weather** means almost the same as
ride out.

ride up. If a skirt or dress **rides up**, it moves upwards, out of its   V+ADV
proper position. EG *This new petticoat is awful—it keeps riding up.*

riffle, riffles, riffling, riffled

riffle through.
This verb is mainly used in American English. 1 If you **riffle through**   V+PREP
sheets of paper or the pages of a book, you look at them briefly,
turning the pages quickly. EG *I riffled through four or five newspapers, trying to find the article.*

2 If you **riffle through** someone's belongings, you examine them   V+PREP:
quickly because you are trying to find something. EG *Tom passed the*   HAS PASSIVE
handbag to me. I riffled quickly through it.

rifle, rifles, rifling, rifled

rifle through. 1 If you **rifle through** sheets of paper or the pages of   V+PREP
a book, you look at them briefly, turning the pages quickly. EG *She
had picked up Amy's book and was rifling through it.* ● **Leaf through**
means almost the same as **rifle through**.

2 If you **rifle through** someone's belongings, you examine them   V+PREP:
quickly because you are trying to find something. EG *Jean rifled*   HAS PASSIVE
through her desk.

rig, rigs, rigging, rigged

rig out. If you **rig** yourself **out** or **are rigged out** in special or   V+REFL+ADV,
unusual clothes, you are wearing that particular kind of clothing; an   USUALLY+A:
informal expression. EG *...a photo showing them rigged out in black*   ALSO PASSIVE,
hats and stiff white collars... He had rigged himself out as a Red   V+ADV+A
Indian. ● **Get up** means almost the same as **rig out**. ▶ A **rig-out** is a   N COUNT
set of clothes that someone is wearing, especially unusual or very

fashionable clothes; an informal word. EG *Of course, she'd got herself a whole new rig-out for the trip... What an amazing rig-out!*

rig up. If you **rig up** a device or piece of equipment, you make it and fix it in place using whatever you have available; an informal expression. EG *He had rigged up a listening device... Some of the men had rigged up tents with their ponchos... If you haven't got a press, you can rig one up with a car jack.*

V+ADV+N,
V+N+ADV,
V+PRON+ADV

ring, rings, ringing, rang, rung

ring around. See **ring round**.

ring back. If you **ring back** or **ring** someone **back**, you telephone them for a second time or after they have telephoned you. EG *Tell her to ring back later... He asked if you'd ring him back when you got in.* ● **Call back** and **phone back** mean almost the same as **ring back**.

V+ADV,
V+PRON+ADV,
V+N+ADV:
NO PASSIVE

ring in. If you **ring in**, you report to someone at your place of work by telephoning them. EG *I rang in to say I was ill.* ● **Phone in** means almost the same as **ring in**.

V+ADV

ring off. When you **ring off** at the end of a telephone conversation, you put the telephone receiver back in its place to close the line. EG *The girl laughed and rang off... With a last 'Fine', Hogan had rung off.* ● **Hang up** means almost the same as **ring off**.

V+ADV

ring out. If a sound **rings out**, it is heard loudly and clearly. EG *The celebrations were suddenly interrupted when the voice of an elder rang out, 'Hear me!'... The old stable clock rings out ten o'clock.*

V+ADV,
V+ADV+N:
NO PASSIVE

ring round. If you **ring round** or **around**, you telephone several people to discuss or ask about a particular thing. EG *I got out the telephone book and began ringing round to heating contractors for estimates... I'll ring around and see what I can get.*

V+ADV,
V+PREP

ring up. 1 If you **ring** someone **up**, you telephone them. EG *I rang her up to thank her... She had rung up Emily and had told her all about it... He was rung up in the night and asked if he'd come down... It's advisable to ring up first to make an appointment.* ● **Phone up** means almost the same as **ring up**.

V+PRON+ADV,
V+ADV+N,
V+N+ADV,
V+ADV

2 When a sales assistant in a shop **rings up** an amount on the till, he or she records the amount of money that is being paid into the till by pressing the buttons. EG *She rang up £10.47 and gave me the receipt... He rang up the sale on the register.*

V+ADV+N,
V+PRON+ADV,
V+N+ADV

rinse, rinses, rinsing, rinsed

rinse out. 1 When you **rinse out** something that you have washed in soap, you get rid of the soap by washing the thing in clean water. EG *She left them in detergent overnight, then rinsed them out the next morning.* ● **Rinse** means almost the same as **rinse out**.

V+PRON+ADV,
V+N+ADV,
V+ADV+N

2 If you **rinse** something **out**, you wash it quickly, often without using soap. EG *She rinsed out the glass.* ● **Wash out** means almost the same as **rinse out**.

V+ADV+N,
V+N+ADV,
V+PRON+ADV

3 If you **rinse** your mouth **out**, you wash it by holding a mouthful of liquid in it, for example to get rid of an unpleasant taste. ● **Wash out** means almost the same as **rinse out**.

V+N+ADV,
V+PRON+ADV,
V+ADV+N

rip, rips, ripping, ripped

rip off. 1 If someone **rips** you **off**, they cheat you by charging you too much money for something; an informal use. EG *The local shopkeepers were all trying to rip off the tourists... The court wastes my time and the lawyers rip me off!* ● **Fleece** means almost the same as **rip off**. ▶ If you say that something that you bought was a **rip-off**, you mean that you were cheated into paying too much for it; an informal word. EG *They knew it was a rip-off.*

V+ADV+N,
V+PRON+ADV,
V+N+ADV

N COUNT

2 To **rip** something **off** means to steal it; an informal use. ● Nick is a V+ADV+N,
very informal word for **rip off**. V+N+ADV,
 V+PRON+ADV

rip through. If an object or sound **rips through** a place, it moves V+PREP
through it very quickly and violently. EG *A roaring explosion ripped*
through the house... His parachute crumpled as the bullets ripped
through the silk.

rip up. If you **rip up** a piece of paper or cloth, you tear it into small V+ADV+N,
pieces. EG *I wanted to rip up my schedule and fill out a new one.* V+N+ADV,
● Tear up means almost the same as **rip up**. V+PRON+ADV

rise, rises, rising, rose, risen

rise above. If you **rise above** a difficulty or problem, you manage V+PREP:
to deal with it without letting it affect you. EG *A woman who can rise* HAS PASSIVE
above such disadvantages is clearly exceptional... She was the
victim of continual pain, but magnificently she rose above it.

rise up. 1 If something **rises up**, it moves upwards. EG *He could see* V+ADV
the smoke from his bonfire rising up in a white column... A whole
flock of blackbirds rose up suddenly when we went by. ● Rise means
almost the same as **rise up**.

2 You can say that something **rises up** when it appears as a large, V+ADV
tall shape. EG *The hills rose up in the distance... Sheer mountainsides*
rise up on either shore.

3 If a thought, image, or feeling **rises up,** you suddenly think about it V+ADV:
or feel it. EG *When she said these words, the image of the boy Tom* USUALLY+A
Barter rose up... All of a sudden, a different figure from Mary's rose
up in his mind... Old humiliations and terrors rose up within him.

4 If people **rise up,** they start to rebel or fight against people in V+ADV
authority. EG *They will rise up and overthrow your imperialist*
government... The non-whites are one of these days going to rise up
and demand their rights. ▶ An **uprising** is an occasion when many N COUNT
people start to rebel or fight against people in authority. EG *...an*
uprising of the German masses... ...an armed uprising.

roll, rolls, rolling, rolled

roll about. If you **roll about** or **roll around,** you move in a lying V+ADV
position by turning your body over and over in different directions.
EG *Next moment they were rolling about the floor... Two smallish*
children were rolling around fighting.

roll around. See **roll about**.

roll back. If you **roll back** something that has been increasing in V+ADV+N,
amount or importance, you cause it to start decreasing. EG *You had* V+PRON+ADV
to do it by rolling back the power of the trade unions... The gains of
last year will be in danger of being rolled back.

roll down. If you **roll down** a piece of clothing or material that has V+ADV+N,
been folded over and over, you unfold the edge of it, in order to V+N+ADV,
make it longer. EG *He began rolling down his sleeves.* V+PRON+ADV

roll in. 1 If something such as money **is rolling in,** you receive it in V+ADV
large quantities; an informal use. EG *Orders roll in... Once we get*
there the money will just start rolling in.

2 If you say that someone **is rolling in** money, you mean that they V+PREP
are very rich. EG *They're all rolling in money. And we haven't any...*
Hearing him talk, you'd think he was rolling in dough.

3 If someone **rolls in,** they arrive somewhere in a very casual way; V+ADV
an informal use. EG *Ultimately, audiences rolled in from York and*
Scarborough... He rolled in, smoking a fag.

roll into. If you **roll** a piece of a substance or material **into** a round V+N+PREP,
shape, you fold it so that it is in that shape. EG *She started to roll the* V+PRON+PREP
socks into a ball... He found a piece of cheese, rolled it into a ball,
and popped it in his mouth.

2 If you say that a person **rolls into** a place, you mean that they　v+PREP
arrive there in a casual way; an informal use. EG *They rolled into the*
town at a quarter to seven.

roll on. **1** If an activity or process **rolls on,** it continues to happen in　v+ADV
a rather unexciting way. EG *So the jokes and laughter rolled on... Life*
was automatically rolling on with all its routine pleasures.

2 If you say **roll on** something, you mean that you want it to happen　IMPERATIVE:
soon; an informal use. EG *All I can say is roll on a government like*　v+ADV
the German government... Roll on four o' clock!

3 **Roll-on** deodorant is sold in a container with a round ball in the　ADJECTIVE
top. You use the deodorant by rubbing the ball onto your skin.

4 **Roll-on roll-off** ferries are designed with a ramp in the side so that　ADJECTIVE
vehicles can be driven onto them and off them.

roll out. If a new vehicle **rolls out,** or a company **rolls** it **out,** it is　v+ADV,
produced and is shown or made available to the public; used mainly　v+ADV+N,
in American English. EG *The first of the C-SA's rolled out of the shop*　v+PRON+ADV:
exactly on schedule... It rolled out the X-car compacts—the　ERGATIVE
Chevrolet Citation, Buick Skylark and so on.

roll over. If you are lying down and you **roll over,** you turn your　v+ADV
body so that a different part of you is facing upwards. EG *I rolled over*
on my stomach... He rolled over and peered into Jack's face. ● **Turn**
over means almost the same as **roll over.**

roll up. **1** If you **roll up** something such as a piece of paper or　v+ADV+N,
material, you wrap it several times around itself in the shape of a　v+PRON+ADV,
cylinder or a ball. EG *You sort out the tent while I roll up the sleeping*　v+N+ADV
bags. ▸ A **rolled-up** piece of paper or material has been folded or　ADJECTIVE
wrapped into a cylinder or ball shape. EG *He lunged at the wasp with*
a rolled-up newspaper... Another man carries a rolled-up stretcher.
▸ **Roll-up** describes things which can be folded or rolled into a　ADJECTIVE
cylindrical shape. EG *...a roll-up garage door... ...a roll-up map.* ▸ A　N COUNT
roll-up is a cigarette that you make yourself with tobacco and paper
with a gummed edge. EG *She gave me one of her roll-ups.*

2 If a person or animal **rolls up,** they curl their bodies into a round　v+ADV,
shape. EG *...which enable the animal to roll itself up into a ball.*　v+REFL+ADV

3 If you **roll up** your sleeves or trouser legs, you fold the edges over　v+N+ADV,
several times to make them shorter. EG *Just roll your trousers up*　v+ADV+N,
and have a paddle... His father had his sleeves rolled up.　v+PRON+ADV

4 If people **roll up** somewhere, they arrive in large numbers; an　v+ADV:
informal use. EG *I was desperate for a quiet weekend, but all these*　ALSO IMPERATIVE
visitors kept rolling up... Roll up! Roll up! Come and see the
Elephant Man.

romp, romps, romping, romped

romp through. If you **romp through** something, you do it quickly　v+PREP:
and easily; an informal expression. EG *This is easy stuff, you'll romp*　HAS PASSIVE
through this... The National Anthem was romped through.

root, roots, rooting, rooted

root about. If you **root about** or **around** among things, you look　v+ADV,
among them, moving them all about, usually because you are　v+PREP:
searching for something; an informal expression. EG *My sister was*　USUALLY+A
rooting about in the tins and bits of old iron bedstead... The inhabit-
ants were nervous of having the bears rooting around their dustbins.

root for. If you **are rooting for** someone, you are giving them your　v+PREP
support while they are doing something difficult; an informal expression. EG *Editorial friends on the newspapers were rooting for*
us... Good luck in the interview—I'll be rooting for you.

root out. If you **root** someone or something **out,** you find them and　v+PRON+ADV,
remove them in a determined way from a place or organization. EG　v+ADV+N,
　v+N+ADV

He's in the library somewhere. Let's go and root him out... A special detachment of investigators was formed to root out the leadership... He was determined to root out corruption in his department.

root up. If you **root up** a plant, you dig it up from the ground. EG *I had to root up all the plants and burn them.* ● **Uproot** means almost the same as **root up.**

V+ADV+N,
V+N+ADV,
V+PRON+ADV

rope, ropes, roping, roped

rope in. If you **rope** someone **in** to do something, you persuade them to help you to do it; an informal expression. EG *Some amazing people were roped in to work on these books... So you're roping me in?*

V+N+ADV,
V+ADV+N,
V+PRON+ADV

rope off. If an area **is roped off**, it is separated from another area by a rope tied between posts to keep people away from it. EG *The track was roped off from the rest of the field... Much of the shop is roped off because they are doing major alterations.*

V+ADV+N,
V+N+ADV,
V+PRON+ADV:
USUALLY PASSIVE

rot, rots, rotting, rotted

rot away. When something **rots away**, it gradually decays until it falls to pieces or disappears completely. EG *His body is rotting away... ...ships that would certainly have rotted away under normal atmospheric conditions... The shack rotted away.*

V+ADV

rough, roughs, roughing, roughed

rough out. If you **rough out** a drawing or idea, you draw or list the main features of it before you do it in detail. EG *I've roughed out a scene for my new play... I had roughed out a lead topic for the following day's chat show... She roughed out a sketch of the harbour.*

V+ADV+N,
V+N+ADV,
V+PRON+ADV

rough up. If someone **roughs** you **up**, they attack you by hitting or beating you; an informal expression. EG *Pushers moved in and roughed up the young junkies... They roughed me up a bit.*

V+ADV+N,
V+PRON+ADV,
V+N+ADV

round, rounds, rounding, rounded

round down. If you **round down** a figure or total, you change it by lowering it to the nearest whole number, the nearest 10, or the nearest 100, and so on. EG *We make a delivery charge of 15p in the pound, rounded down to the nearest pound.*

V+ADV+N,
V+N+ADV,
V+PRON+ADV:
ALSO+to

round off. 1 If you **round** something **off**, you do something to complete it in a satisfactory way. EG *I think you ought to see London, Paris, Rome—round off your education a bit... We'll round it off with some observations on Indian history... At the end of a lunch, the managers round off with a brandy or a liqueur.* ● **Finish off** means almost the same as **round off.**

V+ADV+N,
V+PRON+ADV,
V+N+ADV,
V+ADV:
ALSO+with

2 If a point or shape **is rounded off**, it has been made into a smooth, curved shape by shaving or rubbing part of it away.

PASSIVE:
V+ADV

round on. If you **round on** someone who is criticizing you, attacking you, or causing you difficulties, you suddenly respond angrily by criticizing or attacking that person yourself. EG *In Denver, he rounded on his critics... The girl rounded on me furiously. 'Do you think I'm ashamed?'*

V+PREP:
HAS PASSIVE

round up. 1 If you **round up** animals or people, you gather them together. EG *A dog catcher's main job is to round up strays... I rounded up some volunteers... Fifteen thousand rebels were rounded up in prison camps... They rounded everybody up and herded us into police vans.* ▶ A **round-up** is an occasion when many people are arrested or captured. EG *In a massive roundup they arrested several hundred prominent leaders... ...the nightly round-ups of hostages.*

V+ADV+N,
V+N+ADV,
V+PRON+ADV

N COUNT

2 If you **round up** a figure or total, you change it by increasing it to the nearest whole number, the nearest 10, or the nearest hundred, and so on. EG *Round up any odd half unit to the next whole number... We round the monthly total up to the nearest ten pounds.*

V+ADV+N,
V+N+ADV,
V+PRON+ADV:
ALSO+to

3 A **round-up** on radio or television, or in a newspaper, is a brief
summary of news. EG *...the eleven o'clock news followed by the
sports round-up... ...the round-up of world news on the front page...
...some television programmes, such as the news round-up.* N COUNT

rout, routs, routing, routed

rout out. If you **rout** someone or something **out**, you make them
come out from where they are. EG *Sometimes, the boys would rout
out little squirrels and chase them... Rafferty appeared to have been
routed out of bed.* V+ADV+N,
V+PRON+ADV,
V+N+ADV

rub, rubs, rubbing, rubbed

rub along. If two people **rub along** together, they are able to live or
work together in a reasonably friendly way; an informal expression. V+ADV:
ALSO+*together*
● **Get on** means almost the same as **rub along.**

rub down. 1 If you **rub down** a surface, you prepare it by rubbing it
with something such as sandpaper. EG *The boards have been rubbed
down several times to get that gleaming finish... Eliminate bad
marks by rubbing down the area gently with wire wool.* V+ADV+N,
V+N+ADV,
V+PRON+ADV
2 If you **rub** a person or animal **down**, you rub them hard with a
towel or a cloth, usually to dry them. EG *...rubbing him down and
brushing and combing his mane and tail... She rubbed me down with
a towel... He would jump out and rub himself down frantically.* V+PRON+ADV,
V+REFL+ADV,
V+N+ADV

rub in. If you feel upset, guilty, or embarrassed about something and
someone **rubs it in,** they remind you about it, often deliberately in
order to make you feel worse. EG *When the child fails, never rub it
in... 'How old are you, Mr Sharpe?'—'All right, no need to rub it in.'* V+*it*+ADV

rub off. 1 If you **rub** something **off** a surface, you remove it by
rubbing the surface with something. EG *She rubbed off the dirt with
her hand... Use a soft pencil because you can, if necessary, rub it
off... The dye in the ink stays on the paper and does not rub off.* V+ADV+N,
V+PRON+ADV,
V+N+ADV,
V+ADV:
ERGATIVE
2 If someone else's quality or mood **rubs off** on you, it affects you
and you start to have it or feel it. EG *A kind of aura of happiness was
being generated. It rubbed off on people... They hoped that some of
his prowess might rub off on them.* V+ADV:
USUALLY+*on*

rub out. 1 If you **rub out** something that you have written in pencil
or chalk, you remove it by rubbing it with a rubber or a cloth. V+ADV+N,
V+N+ADV,
V+PRON+ADV
● **Erase** is a more formal word for **rub out.**
2 To **rub** someone **out** means to kill or destroy them; an informal
use. EG *He has decided to destroy the documents, and rub out anyone
who knows about them... He would have gladly rubbed him out as he
saw him as a threat.* V+ADV+N,
V+PRON+ADV,
V+N+ADV

ruck, rucks, rucking, rucked

ruck up. If cloth or a person's clothing **rucks up,** it moves upwards,
out of its correct position. EG *...the shirt, rucked up under his braces...
There she was, with her jumper rucking up at the back.* ● **Bunch up**
means almost the same as **ruck up.** V+ADV:
USUALLY+A

rule, rules, ruling, ruled

rule off. If you **rule off** a section on a piece of paper, you draw a
straight line below it on the paper to divide it from the next section. V+ADV+N,
V+N+ADV,
V+PRON+ADV
rule out. 1 If you **rule out** an idea or a course of action, you decide
that it is impossible or unsuitable. EG *Washington need not rule out a
selective military aid program... They can't rule out the possibility
that he was kidnapped... Do not rule these out as gimmicks.* V+ADV+N,
V+PRON+ADV,
V+N+ADV
● **Dismiss** means almost the same as **rule out.**
2 If one thing **rules out** another, it prevents it from happening or
being possible. EG *A search had ruled out the possibility of further
bombs... The radio was on, effectively ruling out conversation...* V+ADV+N,
V+PRON+ADV,
V+N+ADV

These results rule out the claim that the Shroud is merely a painting. ● **Preclude** is a formal word for **rule out**.

rumble, rumbles, rumbling, rumbled

rumble on. If a person, discussion, or process **rumbles on,** they continue speaking or happening in a boring way for a long time. EG *He rumbled on in this vein for some time... The argument rumbled on.*   V+ADV

run, runs, running, ran

The form **run** is used in the present tense and is also the past participle of the verb.

run about. 1 See **run around.**

2 A **runabout** is a small car that you use mainly for short journeys; an informal word. EG *It makes an ideal shopping runabout.*   N COUNT

run across. 1 If you **run across** a place or area, you run from one side of it to the other. EG *Then they all run across the street to the church... ...used in toy cars to make them run across the floor.*   V+PREP

2 If you **run across** someone, you meet them unexpectedly. EG *He had not ‚seen him for two days when he ran across him at the Palace... It is very unusual to run across Americans in this part of the world.* ● **Come across, bump into,** and **run into** mean almost the same as **run across.**   V+PREP

run after. 1 If you **run after** someone or something that is moving, you chase them in order to catch them or stop them. EG *Thomas ran after him, yelling to him to stop.*   V+PREP

2 If you **run after** something you want, you keep trying very hard to obtain it or to achieve it. EG *He's always running after something, hoping for something... ...running after a goal which always eludes us.* ● **Pursue** is a formal word for **run after.**   V+PREP

3 If you **run after** someone, you try hard to persuade them to have a romantic or sexual relationship with you; an informal use. EG *Maybe father drank or ran after other women... Beautiful women run after me and I can't resist them.*   V+PREP

run along. If you tell a child to **run along,** you are telling him or her to go away. EG *Run along and play... Run along up to bed now, Sam.*   V+ADV: USUALLY IMPERATIVE

run around. 1 If you **run around** or **about,** you run excitedly and in different directions in a particular area. EG *We needed a large garden where the kids could run around freely... A dog was running around in the yard... She let them run about the place just as they pleased.*   V+ADV, V+PREP

2 If you **run around** doing something, you visit several places or do many different things in order to achieve something. EG *I ran around looking for work... ...after all the feverish running around to make sure we arrived on time.* ▶ If you ask someone for help or information and they give you the **runaround,** they deliberately mislead you or cause you difficulties. EG *I have been trying to make a phone call, and everybody I ask gives me the run-around.*   V+ADV

N SING

run around with. If you **run around with** a person or group of people, you spend a lot of time with them socially; an informal expression. EG *In the 1960s he used to run around a lot with Prince Bernhardt... What's his name—that guy you run around with?* ● **Go about** means almost the same as **run around.**   V+ADV+PREP

run away. 1 If you **run away,** you move quickly and farther from a place or person. EG *The children run away like frightened deer if you approach them... She ran away laughing up the road.*   V+ADV

2 If you **run away** from somewhere, you leave secretly because you are unhappy. EG *She ran away one night, leaving these pictures... Some ran away to Canada... He had run away from home... Why did*   V+ADV: ALSO+*from*

you run away from me? ▸ A **runaway** is a person who leaves their N COUNT,
home secretly. EG *They failed to find any trace of the runaways...* ADJECTIVE
...runaway slaves.

3 If you **run away** with someone, you secretly leave your home in V+ADV+*with*,
order to live with them or marry them. EG *They ran away and got* V+ADV+*together*:
married... *She had divorced him and run away with another man...* RECIPROCAL
He and Belinda were planning to run away together.

4 If you **run away** from something difficult or unpleasant, you try to V+ADV:
avoid dealing with it. EG *We cannot run away from technology... ...the* USUALLY+*from*
truth that I had been running away from.

5 A **runaway** animal or vehicle is moving but is no longer under the ADJECTIVE
control of its rider or driver. EG *...her attempt to stop a runaway*
horse... *...a runaway tractor.*

6 A **runaway** situation happens very rapidly or forcefully and cannot ADJECTIVE
be controlled. EG *...the runaway success of 'Nicholas Nickleby'... ...the*
runaway inflation after the war.

run away with. 1 If you let your feelings **run away with** you, you V+ADV+PREP
fail to control them, and they affect you so strongly that you cannot
think or behave sensibly. EG *They let their emotions run away with*
them... *They did not allow youthful zeal to run away with them.*

2 If you **run away with** a prize or competition, you win it very easily. V+ADV+PREP
EG *Her sister ran away with every prize at school.* ● **Walk off with**
means almost the same as **run away with.**

run down. 1 To **run down** somewhere means to move quickly to a V+ADV,
lower level or away from a place. EG *Marion, run down to the post* V+PREP
box with this letter... She runs down the steps... The old man stood
up with tears running down his face.

2 If you **run down** someone or something, you criticize them V+ADV+N,
strongly. EG *She was not used to people running down their own* V+PRON+ADV
families... *She began to run down everything. 'This is all rubbish.'*

3 If an industry or organization **is run down,** its size, importance, or V+ADV+N,
activity is deliberately reduced. EG *Hospitals were being run down* V+N+ADV,
because of the spending cuts... *Our forces are so run down they don't* V+PRON+ADV
deter anybody any more... This Government will go on running
down the railways. ▸ The **run-down** of an industry or organization is N SING
the deliberate reduction of its size, importance or activity. EG *Union*
leaders fought against the run-down of the coal industry.

4 If someone **runs down** their stock or supply of something, they V+ADV+N,
reduce the amount. EG *Start to run down any freezer supplies as soon* V+N+ADV,
as possible... People reacted to inflation by running down their V+PRON+ADV
savings and buying goods instead.

5 If a machine or device **runs down,** it gradually loses power or V+ADV
works more slowly. EG *The batteries in your radio are running*
down... *Hey, the clock's working now. Did it just run down yesterday,*
or what?

6 If a vehicle or its driver **runs** someone **down,** the vehicle hits and V+PRON+ADV,
injures that person. EG *A coach nearly ran us down in front of Trinity* V+ADV+N,
Church... *A car with Frankfurt license plates had run down and* V+N+ADV
killed a French border patrolman... Then in March he tried to run
Kathleen down. ● **Knock down** and **run over** mean almost the same
as **run down.**

7 If you **run down** something you have been searching for, you find V+ADV+N,
it after a lot of effort; an informal use. EG *'We haven't run down your* V+N+ADV,
man,' he began... ...taking a book out, running down a reference and V+PRON+ADV
walking out again. ● **Track down** and **trace** mean almost the same
as **run down.**

8 If you **run down** a list of items, you read or mention them briefly V+PREP
and quickly. EG *Bradlee listened attentively as Woodward ran down*

what details the reporters had given him. ● **Run through** means almost the same as **run down.** ▶ If you give someone a **rundown** on   N SING a situation or subject, you give them a summary of the important facts. EG *We've had a rundown on everyone connected with Olympus... I can give you a quick run-down.*

9 If someone is **run down**, they are very tired and unwell after   ADJECTIVE working too hard or not having enough sleep for a while. EG *'You're probably run down,' Clarissa said. 'You need a holiday.'*

10 A building or area that is **run down** is in poor condition, because   ADJECTIVE it has not been looked after. EG *...two small rooms in a run-down building... ...a run down urban area.*

run in. **1** If someone **runs in** from outside a room or building, they   V+ADV enter it, moving fast. EG *He ran in through the open glass doors of the sitting-room... I'll run in and get them.*

2 If someone is **run in** by the police, they are arrested; an informal   V+N+ADV,
use. EG *Shortly afterwards Mascall was run in... It was the kind of*   V+PRON+ADV,
behaviour that gets motorists run in at this time of year... I could run   V+ADV+N:
you in for that.   USUALLY PASSIVE

3 If you have a **run-in** with someone, you have an argument or   N COUNT quarrel with them; an informal use. EG *He's probably had a run-in at work with Ted.*

4 The **run-in** to an event is the period of preparation just before it   N COUNT takes place. EG *We did it for two weeks in Birmingham as a run-in for the main season... ...the run-in to the next general election.*

run into. **1** To **run into** a place means to enter it, moving fast. EG   V+PREP *...running into the playroom in tears... They had run into the nearest flat and taken the people hostage.*

2 If you **run into** problems or difficulties, you unexpectedly begin to   V+PREP:
experience them. EG *He ran into trouble with his economic policies...*   HAS PASSIVE
Once Beveridge revealed these proposals, he ran into considerable opposition.

3 If you **run into** someone, you meet them unexpectedly. EG *You*   V+PREP
might run into him one of these days... I first ran into him at the theatre. ● **Bump into, run across,** and **come across** mean almost the same as **run into.**

4 If something **runs into** a large number or amount, it reaches that   V+PREP number or amount. EG *If you include dams used for power, it runs into the thousands... ...exports running into billions of dollars.*

5 If a vehicle or its driver **runs into** something, the vehicle acciden-   V+PREP:
tally hits it. EG *The bus ran into a car in St. Andrew's Square... He ran*   HAS PASSIVE
into the back of a van at a zebra crossing.

6 If one thing **runs into** another, it becomes difficult to detect the   V+PREP division between them. EG *...a streak of red running into purple... The words run into each other.* ● **Merge into** means almost the same as **run into.**

run off. **1** If you **run off**, you move quickly away from a place or   V+ADV person. EG *She gave a brief wave and ran off across the lawn... He dumped the stones he was carrying and ran off to look for more.*

2 If you **run off** from somewhere, you leave secretly. EG *'That'd be*   V+ADV
the chap that ran off from Abbotsleigh yesterday'—our local mental home... All the servants have run off and they have taken our horses. ● **Run away** means almost the same as **run off.**

3 If you **run off** with someone, you secretly go away with them to   V+ADV,
live with them or marry them. EG *His wife ran off with another*   V+ADV+with:
man... She ran off to Paris with a chap ten years her junior.   RECIPROCAL

4 If a path, track, or corridor **runs off** from a place, it starts at that   V+ADV:
place and goes away from it. EG *...a narrow track running off into the*   USUALLY+A

forest... Another tunnel ran off on one side; this was dry, dusty and obviously little used. ● **Lead off** means almost the same as **run off**.

5 If you **run off** copies of a piece of writing, you produce them using a machine such as a photocopier or a printer; an informal use. EG *Could you run off five copies of this article for me, please.*   V+ADV+N, V+N+ADV, V+PRON+ADV

6 If you tell a child to **run off,** you are telling them to go away. EG *Run off and play with the others.*   V+ADV: USUALLY IMPERATIVE

7 If a liquid **runs off,** it flows out of a container. EG *The rainwater may run off in sudden sheets which can do tremendous damage.*   V+ADV

8 If a machine or system **runs off** a particular supply of power, it uses that power in order to make it work. EG *In Brazil, all new vehicles now run off fuel alcohol from the waste of sugar production... It was the size of a London bus, but you could run it off a mains plug.*   V+PREP, V+N+PREP: ERGATIVE

run off with. If someone **runs off with** something, they steal it. EG *They aim to grab as much as possible and run off with it to somewhere safe.*   V+ADV+PREP

run on. **1** If you **run on,** you continue to run in the same direction. EG *She darted from tree to tree, stopping and waiting and listening and running on again... She said: 'Where are the others?'—'Just a few minutes behind. I ran on ahead.'*   V+ADV

2 If a road or track **runs on** to a particular place, it continues in that direction. EG *From here, the railway line runs on to Gloucester... The main dusty track ran on towards Lesotho.*   V+ADV: WITH A

3 If someone **runs on,** they continue talking for a long time. EG *'How I run on, don't I?' Percival said... Sometimes she let him run on for what seemed hours.*   V+ADV: USUALLY+A

4 If something **runs on,** it continues to exist or operate longer than expected. EG *The list of British troops in Palestine ran on and on... Do you think that he tends to let his jokes run on too long?*   V+ADV

5 If a machine or system **runs on** a particular type of power, it uses it in order to work. EG *Many cars can run on unleaded petrol... The heating system was extremely economical because it ran on half-price electricity... The refrigerator ran on gas.*   V+PREP, V+N+PREP, V+PRON+PREP: ERGATIVE

run out. **1** If you **run out** of a room or building, you leave it as fast as you can. EG *I ran out and slammed the door... Mrs Todd came running out into the garden... He ran out of the room and down the stairs.*   V+ADV: ALSO+of

2 If a substance **runs out** from somewhere, it flows from there. EG *It is passed through a disc with holes in it to let the milk run out but retain the cream.*   V+ADV

3 If you **run out** of something, you have no more of it left. EG *We were rapidly running out of money... Mankind is running out of time.*   V+ADV: USUALLY+of

4 If something **runs out,** it becomes used up so that there is no more left. EG *Time is running out fast... My luck seemed to have run out... Their money ran out.*   V+ADV

5 If a legal document or contract **runs out,** it is no longer valid. EG *My passport's run out... The patent on APM runs out in 1987.*   V+ADV ● **Expire** is a more formal word for **run out.**

6 If someone **runs out** on a person they have a relationship with, they suddenly leave that person. EG *You know me well enough to know I wouldn't run out on you... I'm seeing her tonight, if she doesn't run out on me.*   V+ADV: USUALLY+on

7 In cricket, if you are batting and **are run out,** your innings is ended, because the other team manage to get the ball to the wicket before you reach it. EG *Howarth was unluckily run out... He ran himself out in the last Test against Pakistan.*   V+N+ADV, V+REFL+ADV, V+PRON+ADV, V+ADV+N

8 If you **run out** a length of rope, you unwind some of it and let it   V+ADV+N,

pass away from you. EG *It was certainly magnificent climbing. I ran*   V+N+ADV,
out 130 feet of rope to bring Rusty up... I often run the line out   V+PRON+ADV,
behind the boat... The line is allowed to run out until it bumps the   ERGATIVE
bottom.

run out of. If someone **runs** another person **out of** a place, they use   V+N+ADV+PREP,
force to make that person leave. EG *My father will kill you and run*   V+PRON+ADV+PREP
your family out of town... He grabbed the shotgun, fired back, and
ran them out of the house.

run over. 1 If you **run over** to someone or something, you move   V+ADV:
quickly to them. EG *She ran over and clutched her mother's hand...*   ALSO+*to*
She ran over to the cooker where the pan was boiling over... Ellen
ran over to the bed and threw herself across it.

2 If a vehicle or its driver **runs over** someone or something, the   V+PREP,
vehicle hits them or drives over them causing injury or damage. EG   V+PRON+ADV,
We almost ran over a fox that was crossing the road... I'm sure he   V+N+ADV
would have run us over... What would happen if I were to become ill
or get run over by a bus? ● **Run down** and **knock down** mean almost
the same as **run over.**

3 If a container of liquid **runs over,** it is too full and the liquid flows   V+ADV
over its sides. EG *Turn the tap off—the sink's running over.*
● **Overflow** is a more formal word for **run over.**

4 If you **run over** something, you repeat it or read it quickly, in order   V+PREP:
to practise it or check it. EG *He asked her to come into his dressing*   HAS PASSIVE
room to run over some lines... Now I would just like to run over the
arrangements again with you... He ran over his plans. ● **Go over** and
run through mean almost the same as **run over.**

run through. 1 If an idea, piece of news, or emotion **runs through** a   V+PREP
group of people, it spreads through the group quickly, so that they
all know it or feel it. EG *A kind of shock-wave ran through the room...*
A tremor of excitement ran through the ship as Bill announced that
they had sighted land.

2 If a quality or feeling **runs through** something, it affects every   V+PREP
part of it or is present everywhere within it. EG *...the deep-rooted*
prejudice that runs through our society... I was impressed with the
concept of fairness that ran through the report. ● **Pervade** is a
formal word for **run through.**

3 If you **run through** something, you repeat it or read it quickly, in   V+PREP:
order to practise it or check it. EG *You could hear the performers*   HAS PASSIVE
running through the whole programme in the background... Some of
you won't know this so I'll just run through it rather briefly...
Dawlish ran through the notes that he had prepared. ● **Go through**
and **run over** mean almost the same as **run through.** ▸ A **run-**   N COUNT
through for an event or performance is a rehearsal or practice for
it. EG *He agreed to come to a run-through... Run-throughs are time-*
consuming and irrelevant.

4 If you **run through** a large amount of money, you spend it quickly   V+PREP:
and in a wasteful way. EG *How he managed to run through £100,000*   HAS PASSIVE
so quickly I will never understand!

5 If someone **runs** a person **through** with a sharp weapon, they push   V+PRON+ADV,
it violently into the person's body; a literary use. EG *As he turned I*   V+N+ADV:
ran him through with my sword.   USUALLY+*with*

run to. 1 If you **run** to someone, you go to them for help, advice or   V+PREP
protection. EG *I didn't think he'd run to you with the story... We must*
learn to trust our own intuition and judgment, and not always run to
the experts.

2 If something **runs to** a particular amount or size, it is that amount   V+PREP
or size. EG *A housewife's work can run to ten or twelve hours a day if*
she has small children... The transcript runs to 1,200 pages.

3 If you say that someone **runs to** a particular thing, you mean that V+PREP
they are able to afford it. EG *He doesn't even run to a car. He cycles
to work... ...even if your company can only run to an ordinary
'security man'.*

4 If someone's taste **runs to** a particular kind of thing, that is what V+PREP
they like. EG *Unfortunately, O'Shea's tastes in TV ran to situation
comedy and sentimental serials... His taste for the arts also ran to
poetry.*

run up. **1** To **run up** means to move quickly from a lower position to V+PREP,
a higher one. EG *These small tropical lizards can run up walls... I* V+ADV
*heard her running up the stairs... ...people from downstairs running
up to see what was happening.*

2 If someone **runs up** to you, they come quickly to where you are. EG V+ADV:
They ran up and started to attack me... I ran up to him and asked, ALSO+*to*
'Did you see two ladies come by?' ▶ In sport, a **run-up** is the running N SING
approach by an athlete or player to gather speed before jumping,
throwing something, or kicking a ball. EG *He had no rhythm or speed
in his run-up... ...a sprinting run-up.*

3 If a set of steps or a road **runs up** to a place, or **runs up** an area of V+ADV+A,
land, it leads in that direction. EG *Wooden steps ran up to an open* V+PREP
front door... At first the road ran up a wide flat valley.

4 If someone **runs up** bills or debts, they start to owe a lot of money V+ADV+N,
because they fail to pay their bills. EG *He ran up a thousand dollars* V+PRON+ADV
*worth of bills in her name... She ran up a telephone bill of two
hundred pounds!*

5 If you **run up** a piece of clothing, you make it quickly. EG *'We could* V+PRON+ADV,
go to the party as clowns,' I replied, wondering if Mrs Moffat could V+ADV+N,
run me up a costume... ...a dreadful fellow whose wife had a hideous ALSO+*for*:
blazer run up for him. ALSO
V+PRON+ADV+N

6 If a flag **is run up**, it is raised to the top of a flag pole or mast. EG V+ADV+N,
Soldiers on the quay stood speechless as the flag was run up on the V+N+ADV,
mast... The flag was run up and the National Anthem was sung. V+PRON+ADV:
USUALLY PASSIVE

7 The **run-up** to an event is the period of time and the things that N SING
happen just before it. EG *The run-up to the election has been a time
of confrontation.*

run up against. If you **run up against** problems or difficulties, you V+ADV+PREP:
suddenly and unexpectedly begin to experience them. EG *You never* HAS PASSIVE
*know what you're liable to run up against... Economic growth would
sooner or later run up against major problems.* ● **Run into** and **come
up against** mean almost the same as **run up against.**

rush, rushes, rushing, rushed

rush in. If you **rush in,** you do or decide something too quickly, V+ADV
without thinking about it carefully enough. EG *...the fool who rushes
in.*

rush into. If you **rush into** something, you do it or decide about it V+PREP:
too quickly, without thinking about it carefully enough. EG *Don't rush* HAS PASSIVE
into marriage... We should not rush into the armed struggle.

rush out. If a company **rushes out** a product, it produces the V+N+ADV,
product quickly in a very short period of time. EG *Three books on the* V+ADV+N,
General Election were rushed out within a couple of weeks. V+PRON+ADV

rush through. If you **rush** something **through,** you deal with it V+N+ADV,
quickly so that it is ready in a shorter time than usual. EG *The* V+PRON+ADV,
government rushed the legislation through before the summer V+ADV+N
recess... Could you rush this application through? ● **Push through**
means almost the same as **rush through.**

rustle, rustles, rustling, rustled

rustle up. If you **rustle up** a meal, you cook it quickly, using V+N+ADV, whatever food you have available at the time. EG *I'll rustle some-thing up... We could rustle up an omelette.*

`V+ADV+N,`
`V+PRON+ADV`

S s

saddle, saddles, saddling, saddled

saddle up. If you **saddle up**, you put a saddle on a horse or pony. EG *Tell him to catch the ponies and saddle up... I saddled up and rode off... Mopani must have saddled up horses numberless times.*

`V+ADV,`
`V+ADV+N,`
`V+N+ADV,`
`V+PRON+ADV`

saddle with. If you **are saddled with** a problem or responsibility which you do not want, you have to deal with it. EG *They were in danger of being saddled with more responsibility than power... They were saddled with the task of finding the whereabouts of Calthrop... The last thing I want is to saddle myself with a second mortgage.* ● **Land with** and **lumber with** mean almost the same as **saddle with.**

`V+N+PREP,`
`V+PRON+PREP,`
`V+REFL+PREP:`
`USUALLY PASSIVE`

sail, sails, sailing, sailed

sail through. If you **sail through** a difficult experience or situation, you deal with it easily and successfully. EG *Some women just sail through their pregnancies... At the rehearsal, she had sailed through, knowing every line.* ● **Romp through** means almost the same as **sail through.**

`V+PREP,`
`V+ADV`

sally, sallies, sallying, sallied

sally forth. If someone **sallies forth**, they go to a place quickly or energetically; a literary expression. EG *Boldly they sallied forth to meet them... ...the safe place from which the child sallies forth to explore the world.*

`V+ADV`

sally out. If someone **sallies out**, they leave a place in order to go somewhere; a literary expression. EG *He was able to sally out and return undetected.*

`V+ADV`

salt, salts, salting, salted

salt away. If you **salt away** money, you do not spend it, but save it or keep it somewhere for the future; an informal expression. EG *He was said to have salted away £4 million... They salt their funds away in numbered Swiss bank accounts... People don't know how much he's got salted away.* ● **Stash away** means almost the same as **salt away.**

`V+ADV+N,`
`V+N+ADV,`
`V+PRON+ADV`

sand, sands, sanding, sanded

sand down. If you **sand down** a wood or metal surface, you rub it with sandpaper until it is completely smooth. EG *Sand down that bit before you start painting it... It took us ages to sand the doors down.*

`V+ADV+N,`
`V+N+ADV,`
`V+PRON+ADV`

save, saves, saving, saved

save up. 1 If you **save up**, or **save up** money, you collect money by not spending it, usually so that you can buy something you want. EG *The relatives will all save up to put a child through secondary school... The main purpose of his travel is to save up enough money for a bicycle... They're saving some money up for a holiday... At least he had something saved up.*

`V+ADV,`
`V+ADV+N,`
`V+N+ADV,`
`V+PRON+ADV:`
`ALSO+for`

2 If you **save** something **up**, you keep it so that you can use it or deal with it later. EG *Do you read through the children's work every time*

`V+PRON+ADV,`
`V+ADV+N,`
`V+N+ADV`

it's produced, or do you tend to save it up?... ...if you'd saved up your stamps instead of throwing them away... Mother had dozens of poems, saved up in a small black notebook.

savour, savours, savouring, savoured
Savour is also spelled **savor** in American English.

savour of. If something **savours of** a particular quality or thing, it   V+PREP
reminds you of it; often used showing disapproval. EG *To do a good deed a day savours of priggishness... She had an aversion to anything that savoured of the supernatural.* ● **Smack of** means almost the same as **savour of.**

saw, saws, sawing, sawed, sawn
The past participle is either **sawed** or **sawn.**

saw off. To **saw** something **off** means to cut a piece from some-   V+N+ADV/PREP,
thing, using a saw. EG *We sawed the legs off the table... Jack had*   V+ADV+N,
sawn off the broken ash bough... The lock on the door had been   V+PRON+ADV/PREP
sawed off... Her wedding ring had to be sawn off her finger.
▶ Something that is **sawn-off** has been made shorter by being cut   ADJECTIVE
with a saw. EG *...sawn-off shotguns... ...sawn-off lengths of scaffolding... ...a sawn-off shell case that served as an ashtray.*

saw up. To **saw** something **up** means to cut it into pieces, using a   V+N+ADV,
saw. EG *We had to saw the chairs up for firewood... He spent all day*   V+PRON+ADV,
sawing up the dead wood.   V+ADV+N

scale, scales, scaling, scaled
scale down. If something **is scaled down,** it is made smaller in   PASSIVE:
size, amount, or extent than it used to be. EG *The project has been*   V+ADV
scaled down by about half of the original estimate... Overall goals must be scaled down in importance.

scare, scares, scaring, scared
scare away. 1 To **scare** animals or people **away** means to frighten   V+N+ADV,
them so that they go away. EG *The least shadow or movement would*   V+ADV+N,
scare the fish away... ...words and magic lights to scare away   V+PRON+ADV
ghosts... The smaller predators would sometimes be scared away by shouts and screams. ● **Scare off** means almost the same as **scare away.**
2 If something **scares** people **away,** it makes them so nervous that   V+ADV+N,
they decide not to do something that they were planning to do. EG   V+N+ADV,
The dispute has scared away potential investors... The economy   V+PRON+ADV
would suffer if a threat to imports scared Europeans away.
● **Discourage** is a more formal word for **scare away.**

scare off. 1 If you **scare** people or animals **off,** you frighten them so   V+PRON+ADV,
that they go away. EG *I thought of scaring them off with a few*   V+ADV+N,
shotgun pellets... The boys made enough noise to scare off a forest of   V+N+ADV
animals. ● **Scare away** means almost the same as **scare off.**
2 If something **scares** people **off,** it makes them so nervous that they   V+N+ADV,
change their minds about something they were planning to do or   V+PRON+ADV,
have. EG *The damage caused by the pills had scared women off... He*   V+ADV+N
named a price he thought would scare me off... ...intimidating bureaucracy that scares off many people who are entitled to benefits. ● **Deter** is a more formal word for **scare off.**

scatter, scatters, scattering, scattered
scatter about. 1 If you **scatter** things **about** or **around,** you throw   V+N+ADV,
or drop them over a large area in rather a careless way. EG *Parrots*   V+PRON+ADV,
scatter their food about and make a mess... ...papers scattered   V+N+PREP,
around and the remains of a campfire... Tea was scattered about the   V+PRON+PREP
table.

2 If things or people **are scattered about** or **around** an area, they are spread over that area in rather a disorganized way. EG *She now has five shops scattered around the town... People are scattered about the countryside.*

PASSIVE:
V+PREP,
V+ADV

scatter around. See **scatter about.**

scoop, scoops, scooping, scooped

scoop out. If you **scoop out** something that is solid, or if you **scoop** something **out** of it, you make it hollow by removing the inside part of it, using a special tool such as a scoop or a spoon. EG *He showed me a skull, which he'd scooped out and dried... Slice the tops off the tomatoes and scoop out the seeds... We found the cave and began to scoop the earth out.*

V+ADV+N,
V+N+ADV,
V+PRON+ADV

scoop up. If you **scoop** something **up**, you put your hands under it and lift it in a quick movement. EG *Stephanie scooped one of the lizards up... I watched Patrick scoop up a handful of snow from the window ledge... I had to scoop it up with my fingers.*

V+N+ADV,
V+ADV+N,
V+PRON+ADV

score, scores, scoring, scored

score off. **1** If you **score off** someone, you make a clever or insulting reply to something they have said. EG *They spent the whole evening scoring off each other... Teachers could not refrain from scoring off me.*

V+PREP

2 If you **score off** something that is written down, you draw a line through it to indicate that it is not wanted or needed. EG *Score off each number as it is read out... You'll find it easier if you score them off when you've answered them... I asked him to score my name off the list of players next Saturday.* ● **Cross off** means almost the same as **score off.**

V+ADV+N,
V+PRON+ADV/PREP,
V+N+ADV/PREP

score out. If you **score out** something that is written down, you draw a line through it so that people cannot read it. EG *The rest of the sentence is heavily scored out... The article was too long, and I had to score a couple of paragraphs out.* ● **Cross out** means almost the same as **score out,** and **delete** is a more formal word.

V+ADV+N,
V+N+ADV,
V+PRON+ADV

scour, scours, scouring, scoured

scour away. If water or wind **scours away** a piece of land, the force of the water or wind gradually removes it. EG *Rainwater had scoured away the hillsides... Rivers scoured the soft sandstone away.* ● **Erode** means almost the same as **scour away.**

V+ADV+N,
V+N+ADV,
V+PRON+ADV

scout, scouts, scouting, scouted

scout around. See **scout round.**

scout round. If you **scout round** or **around** for something, you go to different places looking for it. EG *I spend most of my time scouting round for books... We'd scout around to see if anyone was in the rooms nearby.*

V+ADV:
USUALLY+for

scrabble, scrabbles, scrabbling, scrabbled

scrabble about. If you **scrabble about** or **around,** you use your hands in order to try to find something on the ground that you cannot see. EG *We scrabbled about in the grass and leaves and found the packet... Kate scrabbled around, looking for stones.*

V+ADV:
USUALLY+A

scrabble around. See **scrabble about.**

scrape, scrapes, scraping, scraped

scrape along. If you **scrape along,** you just manage to survive and have a fairly comfortable life. EG *...content to scrape along in life.* ● **Get by** means almost the same as **scrape along.**

V+ADV

scrape away. If you **scrape away** a substance, you remove it completely by means of a knife or other sharp object. EG *I dug the*

V+ADV+N,
V+N+ADV,
V+PRON+ADV

knife-blade in and scraped away an inch of the lead... The paint had been scraped away. ● **Scrape off** means almost the same as **scrape away.**

scrape by. If you **scrape by** on a particular amount of money, you just manage to survive using that money. EG *No household can hope to scrape by on forty pounds a week... We scrape by, but we never have much fun.* ● **Get by** means almost the same as **scrape by.**

V+ADV:
ALSO+*on*

scrape into. If you **scrape into** a school, university, or profession, you only just manage to be accepted there as a student or employee. EG *He only just scraped into university because of poor A levels.*

V+PREP

scrape off. If you **scrape** a substance **off,** you remove it from a surface by rubbing or scratching it with something sharp. EG *Scrape as much wax as possible off with your fingernails... They would scrape it all off... The stiff brush bristles scraped off some of the encrusted filth... ...scraping snow off railway tracks with shovels.*

V+N+ADV/PREP,
V+PRON+ADV/PREP,
V+ADV+N

scrape out. When you **scrape out** a container such as a bowl or a jar, you remove all the contents that are left in it with a special tool such as a spoon or knife. EG *She scraped out her bowl greedily... He scraped the tub out until every last bit of ice-cream was gone.*

V+ADV+N,
V+N+ADV,
V+PRON+ADV

scrape through. If you **scrape through** an examination or a course of some kind, you just succeed in passing it with a very low grade. EG *...scholars who scrape through college or university... He was lucky to scrape through because he never did any work.*

V+PREP,
V+ADV

scrape together. If you **scrape together** an amount of money or a number of things that you need, you manage with difficulty to obtain them. EG *If we could scrape together a dozen people, we could hire a minibus... ...scraping the funds together from their hard-won budgets.* ● **Scrape up** means almost the same as **scrape together.**

V+ADV+N,
V+N+ADV,
V+PRON+ADV

scrape up. 1 If you **scrape up** an amount of money, you manage with difficulty to get the money you need. EG *He scraped up the money to start his Hollywood restaurant... I can give you a few shillings that I scraped up... ...scraping the fees up to send their boys to school.* ● **Scrape together** and **get together** mean almost the same as **scrape up.**

V+ADV+N,
V+N+ADV,
V+PRON+ADV

2 If you **scrape** something **up,** you remove it from the ground using a tool with a sharp edge, such as a shovel. EG *She took a scoop from her pocket and scraped up as much of the scattered seed as she could... They scraped up the dust and put it into bags.*

V+ADV+N,
V+N+ADV,
V+PRON+ADV

scratch, scratches, scratching, scratched

scratch about. See **scratch around.**

scratch around. If you **scratch around** or **about** a place, you look for something that you cannot see on the ground, using your hands or something sharp such as a stick. EG *Chickens will scratch about in the dung of other animals and will salvage any undigested grain... So far, only a dozen men have scratched around in a few kilometres of an area the size of Africa.*

V+ADV,
V+PREP

scratch out. If you **scratch out** something that is written down, you draw a line through it with a pen or a sharp instrument so that it cannot be seen. EG *Mayhew took off his helmet and scratched out something written on the side... He scribbled down lines and then scratched them out again.* ● **Cross out** means almost the same as **scratch out.**

V+ADV+N,
V+PRON+ADV,
V+N+ADV

screen, screens, screening, screened

screen off. If a part of a room is **screened off,** it has been separated from the rest of the room by a screen or partition. EG *It was one long room that had a sleeping area screened off... He was in a little cabin screened off from the open space... ...torn curtains*

V+N+ADV,
V+PRON+ADV,
V+ADV+N:
ALSO+*from*,
USUALLY PASSIVE

screening off the bunks from the rest of the cabin. ● **Partition off** means almost the same as **screen off**.

screw, screws, screwing, screwed

screw down. If you **screw** something **down**, you close or fasten it firmly, using screws or using something which has a screw-top. EG *When the bottles are warm, screw the caps down tightly and place in the refrigerator... The lid had not been screwed down properly.*
V+N+ADV,
V+ADV+N,
V+PRON+ADV

screw out of. If you **screw** something **out of** someone, you persuade them to give it to you using force or strong arguments; a very informal expression. EG *I managed to screw a bit more money out of him... Don't worry, they'll never screw a confession out of my father.*
V+N+ADV+PREP,
V+PRON+ADV+PREP

screw up. 1 If you **screw up** your face or eyes, you move or twist them so that they no longer have their natural shape. EG *The man screwed up his face in disgust... She screwed up her eyes as she faced the sun.*
V+ADV+N,
V+N+ADV,
V+PRON+ADV

2 If you **screw up** something such as paper or material, you bend or twist it in your hands so that it is creased and crumpled. EG *She laughed and, screwing up the piece of newspaper, tossed it into a corner... My clothes were screwed up in a white plastic bag.* ● **Scrunch up** means almost the same as **screw up**.
V+ADV+N,
V+N+ADV,
V+PRON+ADV

3 If you **screw up** or if you **screw** something **up**, you cause a plan or arrangement to fail or go wrong; a very informal use. EG *She could screw things up for us... He can't do that; that screws up all my arrangements... In 1983, the cereal farmers screwed it up... What I do best is out there in the boxing ring, even if I've screwed up outside it.*
V+N+ADV,
V+ADV+N,
V+PRON+ADV,
V+ADV

4 Something that **screws** you **up** makes you nervous, worried, or confused; a very informal use. EG *Her mother's screwed her up and given her values she despises... ...a laborious series of investigations that might screw me up for weeks.* ▶ Someone who is **screwed-up** is very confused, worried, or nervous, often over a long period of time. EG *I guess I'm just a screwed-up cop... ...a screwed-up, suffering man.*
V+PRON+ADV,
V+N+ADV

ADJECTIVE

scrub, scrubs, scrubbing, scrubbed

scrub off. If you **scrub** dirt or stains **off** something, you remove them by rubbing hard. EG *Mrs Sturgill scrubbed the caked blood off her cheeks... He tried without success to scrub it off... ...sponges for scrubbing off the dirt.*
V+N+PREP/ADV,
V+PRON+PREP/ADV,
V+ADV+N

scrub out. If you **scrub** a place **out**, you clean it very thoroughly. EG *Not much of a holiday for me, scrubbing this whole place out!... She agreed to scrub out the hall in return for lessons... ...the awful job in the laundry, scrubbing it out every day.* ● **Clean out** means almost the same as **scrub out**.
V+N+ADV,
V+ADV+N,
V+PRON+ADV

scrunch, scrunches, scrunching, scrunched

scrunch up. If you **scrunch** something **up** or if it **scrunches up**, it is bent or twisted so that it no longer has its natural shape. EG *She started to read it, then scrunched it up and threw it in the bin... ...looking for a ten-pound note, which would be all scrunched up... She turns her back and scrunches up into an awkward position... I'd lain scrunched up for hours in a flimsy bunker.*
V+PRON+ADV,
V+N+ADV,
V+ADV+N,
V+ADV:
ERGATIVE

seal, seals, sealing, sealed

seal off. 1 If you **seal off** a place, you prevent people from getting into it or out of it by blocking all the entrances. EG *Police had already sealed off one of the entrances... They sealed the main road off... The meeting was in a locked school building sealed off by hundreds of police.* ● **Cordon off** means almost the same as **seal off**.
V+ADV+N,
V+N+ADV,
V+PRON+ADV

2 If someone **is sealed off** from something that they would normally be involved in, or if they **seal** themselves **off,** they are separated from it. EG *...people sealed off from social influences... He is the proverbial recluse, sealed off from the rest of the world... They have sealed themselves off from further development.* ● **Cut off** means almost the same as **seal off.**

PASSIVE,
V+ADV,
ALSO
V+REFL+ADV:
USUALLY+*from*

seal up. If you **seal** something **up,** you close it so that nothing can get in or out. EG *They were already sealing up the exits... The windows on the west side were sealed up... The box had been examined but they had sealed it up again.* ● **Close up** means almost the same as **seal up.**

V+ADV+N,
V+N+ADV,
V+PRON+ADV

search, searches, searching, searched

search out. If you **search** something or someone **out,** you keep looking for them until you find them. EG *I have been searching out old sewing patterns... Paul McAlinden searched out the illustrations for these pages... He sent a company of soldiers to search them out and destroy them.* ● **Hunt out** and **unearth** mean almost the same as **search out.**

V+ADV+N,
V+PRON+ADV,
V+N+ADV

see, sees, seeing, saw, seen

see about. When you **see about** something, you arrange for it to be done or provided. EG *Rudolph went to the station to see about Thomas's ticket... The superintendent sent me to see about painting your apartment.*

V+PREP

see as. If you **see** someone or something **as** a particular thing, you regard them in a way which suggests that they are that thing. EG *He saw her as a holy woman, innocent, calm, untouchable... The committee saw higher education as an activity with its own values and aims... He no longer saw himself as a contender in the 1908 Presidential stakes.* ● **Consider** is a more formal word for **see as.**

V+PRON+PREP,
V+N+PREP,
V+REFL+PREP

see in. If you **see** a particular quality or characteristic **in** someone or something, you believe that they have that quality or characteristic. EG *I saw a delicacy in him that I had never seen before... She saw something in me that she didn't like... No one had understood what she saw in Dave.*

V+N+PREP,
V+PRON+PREP

see into. If you **see** someone **into** a place, you go with them and make sure that they go in there. EG *He saw me into a taxi... I helped Kate undress and saw her into bed... Hattie left after seeing me safely into David's apartment.*

V+PRON+PREP,
V+N+PREP

see off. **1** When you **see** someone **off,** you go with them to the station, airport, or port that they are leaving from, and say goodbye to them there. EG *She saw him off at the station... I came to see you off at Heathrow... Also there to see us off was John Ryan... 'Are you seeing someone off too?'* ● **Wave off** means almost the same as **see off.**

V+PRON+ADV,
V+N+ADV,
V+ADV+N

2 To **see** someone or something **off** means to force them to leave a place. EG *Up and at them!—We'll see them off yet!... I saw off those children who were hanging around the sheds... They were to see off the Germans and then resist the Russians.*

V+PRON+ADV,
V+ADV+N,
V+N+ADV

3 In a game or competition, if you **see off** your opponents, you succeed in improving your position so that you win it. EG *Burgess relied on his change of pace to see off the opposition.*

V+ADV+N,
V+PRON+ADV

see out. **1** If you **see** someone **out** of a room or a building, you go with them to the door as they leave. EG *As I saw the cops out I was trembling... She saw him out of the kitchen.*

V+N+ADV,
V+PRON+ADV

2 If you **see out** a period of time, you continue with what you are doing until that period of time is over. EG *The war was over. I was seeing out my time in the army... He has decided to see out one last*

V+ADV+N,
V+N+ADV,
V+PRON+ADV

term in his teaching job. ● **Stick out** means almost the same as **see out.**

3 If something **sees** a period of time **out**, it lasts until the end of that time; an informal use. EG *I bought some food yesterday to see the week out... Somehow, I don't think these sandals are going to see out the holiday, do you?* ● **Last out** means almost the same as **see out.**   V+N+ADV, V+ADV+N

see over. **1** If you **see over** a house, building, exhibition, and so on, you go there to look at the different parts of it. EG *We've seen over two houses today, but I didn't like either of them.* ● **Look round** means almost the same as **see over.**   V+PREP

2 An **overseer** is someone who watches work being done to make sure that it is done properly.   N COUNT

see round. If you **see round** a building, town, exhibition, and so on, you visit it and look at the different parts of it. EG *We spent the best part of the morning seeing round the museum... I'm going to see round a house this afternoon... Would you like to see round?* ● **Look round** means almost the same as **see round.**   V+PREP, V+ADV

see through. **1** If you can **see through** something, you are able to look from one side of it to the other. EG *He couldn't see through the clouds of white dust... I managed to see four prisoners through a wire net... She saw him through the kitchen window.* ▶ **See-through** clothes are made of thin cloth, so that you can see a person's body or underclothes through them. EG *...a see-through blouse... ...a see-through bra of black net and lace.*   V+PREP, V+N+PREP, V+PRON+PREP   ADJECTIVE

2 If you **see through** a person or **see through** what they are doing, you realize what their intentions are, even though they are trying to hide them. EG *She had learned to see through him... The jailers saw through my scheme... Her excuses were lame but he did not see through them.*   V+PREP: HAS PASSIVE

3 If someone or something **sees** you **through** a difficult time in your life, they support you during this time. EG *He was a great friend of mine and saw me through all the hard times... I must see Gertrude through this awful trial... I now have fifteen thousand dollars to see me through until my book is published.* ● **Get through** means almost the same as **see through.**   V+PRON+PREP, V+N+PREP, V+PRON+ADV, V+N+ADV

4 If you **see** a task, plan, or project **through**, you continue to do it until it is successfully completed. EG *...the joy that comes from seeing each job right through... He began his hunger strike on March 1 and he vowed to see it through.* ● **Stick out** means almost the same as **see through.**   V+N+ADV, V+PRON+ADV

see to. If you **see to** something or someone that needs attention, you deal with them. EG *Don't you worry about that. I'll see to that... A man was there to see to our luggage... Is this lady being seen to?*   V+PREP: HAS PASSIVE

seek, seeks, seeking, sought

seek out. If you **seek out** someone or something, you try to find them; a fairly formal expression. EG *It was unusual for anyone to seek out her husband unnecessarily... Laura used to seek Gillian out when she had quarrelled with all her friends... I used to seek her out on her way home from school.*   V+ADV+N, V+N+ADV, V+PRON+ADV: USUALLY+A

seize, seizes, seizing, seized

seize on. If you **seize on** or **upon** something, you show great interest in it, often because it is useful to you. EG *The Administration immediately seized on the idea of sending the forces back into the Gulf... This was one of the points that Vasiliou seized upon with some force.*   V+PREP: HAS PASSIVE

seize up. If a part of your body **seizes up**, it suddenly stops functioning properly, usually because you have used or exercised it   V+ADV too much. You can also say that something such as a machine, engine, or system **seizes up** when it stops working altogether. EG *Your back may seize up... I had done enough to prevent my heart and lungs seizing up... My minivan just seized up, and we couldn't get it started again.*

seize upon. See seize on.

select, selects, selecting, selected

select out. If you **select out** things from a group, you choose the things you want from that group. EG *Clough selected out the team members he wanted for the match on Tuesday... Try to select unbruised fruit out for jam-making.*

V+ADV+N,
V+N+ADV,
V+PRON+ADV

sell, sells, selling, sold

sell off. If you **sell** something **off,** you get rid of it by selling it, usually because you need some money. EG *He had to sell his cattle off at derisory prices... She was forced to sell off her land... We'll have to sell it off bit by bit.* ▸ A **sell-off** is the sale of something such as a business as a way of raising money. EG *The sell-off has to be approved by the European Commission... ..the sell-off of British coal... ...sell-offs to private interests.*

V+N+ADV,
V+ADV+N,
V+PRON+ADV

N COUNT

sell on. If someone **is sold on** something, they are very enthusiastic about it; an informal expression. EG *I'm not really sold on Mahler... He was totally sold on the ethic of free enterprise... I've tried to sell this film on you before.*

V+N+PREP,
V+PRON+PREP:
USUALLY PASSIVE

sell out. 1 If a shop **is sold out** of something, or **has sold out** of it, it has all been sold, and there is none of it left in the shop. EG *Shops almost immediately sold out of the advertised goods... Sold out of baguettes by 5.00 pm? That was unheard of. French bakers are never sold out of baguettes... I'm sorry, we've sold out of that particular brand.*

V+ADV,
OR PASSIVE,
V+ADV:
USUALLY+of

2 If a performance of a play, film, or other form of entertainment **is sold out,** all the tickets have been sold. EG *The first performance was sold out and the play became a tremendous hit... The show is already sold out at Hammersmith.* ▸ If you describe a play, concert, or other event as a **sell-out,** you mean that it is very successful because all the tickets for it have been sold. EG *The show was a sell-out... Tomorrow's race would be a sell-out... ...a sell-out crowd.*

PASSIVE:
V+ADV

N SING

3 If you **sell out,** you sell almost everything you have, usually because you need some money. EG *He had to sell out and reinvest the money in land... ...selling out our interests in the olive oil business... When I married I sold out my share of the shop to Jo.*

V+ADV,
V+ADV+N,
V+PRON+ADV:
ALSO+to

4 If you **sell** somebody **out,** you betray them in order to gain an advantage for yourself; an informal use. EG *They would sell out their country rather than take a stand... So you sold him out for eighty-five cents... All but my landlady gradually sold out to the other side... They thought of him as one who had sold out and was no longer to be regarded as a friend.* ▸ If you describe someone's behaviour as a **sell-out,** you mean that they have betrayed you in order to gain an advantage; an informal word. EG *This meeting was just another sell-out to the management... ...a sell-out that perverted the people's will... ...a sell-out of socialism.*

V+ADV+N,
V+PRON+ADV,
V+N+ADV,
V+ADV:
ALSO+to

N COUNT

sell up. If you **sell up,** you sell everything you have, such as your house or your business, because you need some money. EG *Farmers sell up in order to survive... The owners have sold up and gone.*

V+ADV

send, sends, sending, sent

send ahead. If you **send** something **ahead** when you are going on a journey, you arrange for it to be taken to your destination before

V+N+ADV,
V+PRON+ADV

you arrive there. EG *He had sent his baggage wagons ahead... ...the small trunk that they had sent ahead with Billy's belongings.*
● **Forward** is a more formal word for **send ahead.**

send away. 1 If you **send** someone **away,** you tell them to go away   V+PRON+ADV,
from you, or you arrange for them to go somewhere. EG *'What are*   V+N+ADV
you doing here?'—'Don't send me away again!'... They persuaded me
to send her away to a convalescent home... Sending their children
away meant an appreciable increase in fees.

2 If you **send away** for something, you write to a firm or organiza-   V+ADV,
tion and ask them to send it to you. EG *She was going to send away*   USUALLY+*for*
for the samples... I'm thinking of sending away for one of those dolls.

send back. If you **send** something **back,** you return it to the place   V+PRON+ADV,
that it came from, usually because there is something wrong with it,   V+ADV+N,
or because you do not want it. EG *My aunt had a wig, but she sent it*   V+N+ADV
back to be redressed... She sent back her breakfast tray untouched...
He sent back the Booker prize money he won.

send down. 1 If a student **is sent down,** he or she is made to leave   PASSIVE:
a university or college because of bad behaviour; used in British   V+ADV
English. EG *He was sent down from Trinity College for sexual*
misdemeanors.

2 If someone convicted of a crime **is sent down,** they are sent to   V+N+ADV,
prison; an informal use. EG *Clive's brother had been brought to court*   V+PRON+ADV:
and sent down for larceny... His fingerprints were all over it—that   USUALLY PASSIVE
would be enough to send him down for several more years.

send for. 1 If you **send for** someone, you ask them to come and see   V+PREP:
you by sending a message. EG *'Shall I send for Doctor Rajendra,*   HAS PASSIVE
Lila?' he asked... I explained that I had been sent for.

2 If you **send for** something, you ask for it to be sent to you by   V+PREP:
sending a request. EG *You can send for a copy by writing to UCCA,*   HAS PASSIVE
PO Box 28, Cheltenham... Mechanical resuscitation equipment was
sent for, but no-one knew how to operate it.

send forth. If you **send** someone **forth,** you arrange or tell them to   V+N+ADV,
go somewhere for you; a literary expression. EG *I'm sending you*   V+PRON+ADV,
forth on your voyage of discovery... A sudden fine morning would   V+ADV+N
send us forth for a day's nutting or blackberrying.

send in. 1 If you **send in** a report or an application, you send it to a   V+ADV+N,
place where it can be dealt with officially. EG *I was expected to send*   V+N+ADV,
in a written report every two months... Humboldt sent in his   V+PRON+ADV
resignation... He's sending some big orders in again. ● **Submit** means
almost the same as **send in.**

2 If you **send in** for something, you ask for it to be posted to you by a   V+ADV:
firm, business, or other organization. EG *Don't forget to send in for*   USUALLY+*for*
your free information packs.

3 When a group of people, especially soldiers or police, **are sent in,**   V+ADV+N,
they are sent to a place in order to deal with a dangerous or difficult   V+N+ADV,
situation. EG *The army was going to be sent in to quell the rioting...*   V+PRON+ADV
The Government threatened to send in agents to collect the tax.

4 When you **send** someone **in,** you tell them to go into a room where   V+N+ADV,
someone else is waiting to see them. EG *Send Clemenza in to me...*   V+PRON+ADV,
Clare was sent in to tell me the news... The door opened, and the   V+ADV+N
secretary sent in a tall thin man.

send off. 1 If you **send off** a letter, telegram, or parcel, you post it   V+ADV+N,
somewhere. EG *He had sent off the rest of the family's belongings the*   V+N+ADV,
day before... Write the stories and send the lot off to the office... I   V+PRON+ADV
won't send it off just yet.

2 If you **send off** for something, you write to someone and ask them   V+ADV:
to post it to you. EG *Send off for lists of jobs... Can we have time to*   USUALLY+*for*

note down where to send off for them? ● **Send away** means almost the same as **send off.**

3 If you **send** someone **off,** you ask or tell them to go somewhere else. EG *I sent Georgie off with strict instructions not to come back till later... He told Virginia to send the girls off to the ranch... She sent him off to her sister's so we could talk in private.* ● **Send away** means almost the same as **send off.**

V+N+ADV,
V+PRON+ADV :
ALSO+to

4 If a football player **is sent off,** the player is made to leave the field during a game as a punishment for seriously breaking the rules. EG *Henry was sent off after allegedly punching Garnham... Referee! Send him off!*

V+N+ADV,
V+PRON+ADV :
USUALLY PASSIVE

5 A **send-off** is an occasion when people come together to say goodbye to someone who is starting a journey or going away to live in another place; an informal word. EG *They certainly gave us a fine send-off.*

N COUNT

send on. If you **send on** letters or parcels, you send them to someone else after you have received them. EG *Do you still want me to send on 'Let's Write a Novel'?... Send the letter on to your accountant... If she sends it to me I'll send it on to you... His form had been sent on to us.* ● **Forward** is a more formal word for **send on.**

V+ADV+N,
V+N+ADV,
V+PRON+ADV :
ALSO+to

send out. 1 If you **send out** something such as letters or leaflets, you send copies of them to a lot of people. EG *...sending out questionnaires to 34000 doctors... We sent out a leaflet to every household... I send letters out to all the landladies and landlords who have offered accommodation.*

V+ADV+N,
V+PRON+ADV,
V+N+ADV :
ALSO+to

2 If a machine **sends out** a sound or a light, it causes sound or light to travel in a particular direction. EG *...a small but powerful searchlight that could send out a flashing beam... An automatic radio beacon capable of sending out a continuous signal was to be switched on.* ● **Give out** means almost the same as **send out,** and **emit** is a more formal word.

V+ADV+N,
V+N+ADV,
V+PRON+ADV

send up. If you **send** someone **up,** you imitate them in a way that makes them appear foolish; an informal expression. EG *He walked behind me so as to be able to send me up for the amusement of passers-by... ...the sort of person it is only too easy to send up.* ● **Take off** means almost the same as **send up.** ▸ A **send-up** is a piece of writing or acting in which someone or something is imitated in order to make them appear foolish; an informal word. EG *...his cheeky send-up of the scene... ...Victoria Wood's fly-on-the-wall send-ups.*

V+PRON+ADV,
V+N+ADV

N COUNT

separate, separates, separating, separated

separate off. If you **separate** something **off** from a large group of things, you remove it completely from that group. EG *They have taken great care to separate off groups for slaughter from the main herd... The literacy campaign has been separated off from mainstream adult education.*

V+ADV+N,
V+N+ADV,
V+PRON+ADV :
ALSO+from

separate out. If you **separate out** a group of things or people, you divide them into smaller groups in order to make them easier to deal with. EG *Most schools decide to separate out their pupils into different groups according to age... ...separating out bits of paper, some white, some orange... When they play with language, children separate it out for a special kind of attention.*

V+ADV+N,
V+PRON+ADV,
V+N+ADV

serve, serves, serving, served

serve as. If one thing **serves as** or **for** another thing, it is used instead of that other thing, often because nothing more suitable is available. EG *There was a long, grey building that served as a cafeteria... ...an old car tyre which evidently served as a children's*

V+PREP

swing... ...*a sawn-off shell case that served for an ashtray.* ● **Do for**
means almost the same as **serve as**.

serve for. See **serve as**.

serve on. 1 If you **serve on** a committee or other organized group,   V+PREP
you are a member of it. EG *He has not served on a council before... I
have been pretty disillusioned with juries ever since I served on one.*

2 If you **serve** a legal document **on** or **upon** someone, you deliver it   V+N+PREP,
to them. The document usually orders them to appear in a court of   V+PRON+PREP
law or to do something that they have previously refused to do. EG *A
House Committee tried to serve a subpoena on Harry Truman... This
notice had been served on her six weeks before.*

serve out. When you **serve out** food, you give it to people at the   V+ADV+N,
beginning of a meal, or during it. EG *Miss Clare and I served out*   V+N+ADV,
slices of cold meat... We spend about two hours a day serving out the   V+PRON+ADV
children's dinners. ● **Serve up** and **dish up** mean almost the same as
serve out.

serve up. 1 When you **serve up** food, you give it to people at the   V+ADV+N,
beginning of a meal. EG *They serve up far more food than could*   V+PRON+ADV,
possibly be eaten... When you want them to try something new,   V+N+ADV
serve it up casually. ● **Dish up** means almost the same as **serve up**.

2 If a particular type of entertainment **is served up**, it is presented   V+ADV+N,
to people. EG *The amount of music served up at the Proms is truly*   V+N+ADV,
staggering... ...turgid patriotic and religious programmes served up   V+PRON+ADV:
by the authorities... What I find hard to stomach is the rubbish   USUALLY PASSIVE
served up on television and radio these days.

serve upon. See **serve on**.

set, sets, setting

The form **set** is used in the present tense and is the past tense and
past participle of the verb.

set about. If you **set about** doing something, you start to do it in an   V+PREP:
energetic or purposeful way. EG *The next morning they awoke and*   ALSO+-ING
*set about cleaning and sweeping the house... I set about finding a flat
bit of ground on which to pitch my tent... Vespasian set about his
small task very seriously.*

set against. 1 When one fact or argument **is set against** another, it   V+N+PREP,
is compared with the other one in order to be more easily under-   V+PRON+PREP:
stood. EG *This slight improvement has to be set against an enormous*   USUALLY PASSIVE
*increase in crime... Set against that time-span, writing is very much
a new invention.* ● **Balance against** means almost the same as **set
against**.

2 If you **set** an amount of money **against** tax or **against** another   V+N+PREP,
source of income or debt, you tell the tax authorities that that   V+PRON+PREP:
amount was spent in connection with your job or business in order   USUALLY PASSIVE
to reduce the amount of tax you have to pay. EG *This allows them to
set the net loss against taxable income earned elsewhere... The
Green Paper laid down proposals for tax credits which could be set
against tax liability.* ● **Set off against** means almost the same as **set
against**.

3 To **set** one person **against** another means to make them become   V+PRON+PREP,
enemies or rivals. EG *The last thing I wanted to do was to set her*   V+N+PREP
*against me... As a result of this war, parent had been set against
child and child against parent.*

4 If you **are set against** something, you have firmly decided that you   PASSIVE:
do not want to have it, or do not want it to happen. EG *He had wanted*   V+PREP
*to go into the army, but his mother had been so set against it that he
had given up the idea... He seemed set against most of the key*

*people in the company except me... That's partly why my husband's
so set against drink.*

5 If something **is set against** a particular background, it is placed
there so that it is clearly visible and contrasts with what is behind it.
EG *There, set against a huge ochre-coloured screen, was the Shroud...
...faces in black and dark brown carved wood set against white
emulsion.*

V+N+PREP,
V+PRON+PREP:
USUALLY PASSIVE

6 If a play, film, or story **is set against** a particular background, the
action of the story takes place in a particular setting which is
always present and which is an important part of the whole work. EG
*The career of one deadbeat rock group of the early '60s is set
against a tapestry of teenage life in the provinces... Set against the
background of the Russian Revolution, Reds is 'an historical romantic movie'.*

PASSIVE:
V+PREP

set apart. If something **is set apart** for a special use or purpose, it
is kept for that use or purpose and not used for anything else. EG *One
day of the week should be set apart for relaxation... There are no
rooms specifically set apart for quiet study.*

V+PRON+ADV,
V+N+ADV:
USUALLY PASSIVE

set apart from. If a feature or characteristic **sets** you **apart from**
other people it makes you noticeably different from the others. EG
*He had gained a lot of weight and it set him apart from the rest of
the men... These attributes set humans apart from even the highest
primates.*

V+PRON+ADV+PREP,
V+N+ADV+PREP

set aside. **1** If you **set aside** something such as time or money, you
do not use it immediately but keep it for a special use or purpose. EG
*With a separate budget account you set aside equal monthly sums to
cover your total yearly expenditure... Try to set some money aside
for this... Some time should be set aside for reading and writing and
maths.* ● **Put aside** means almost the same as **set aside.**

V+ADV+N,
V+N+ADV,
V+PRON+ADV:
ALSO+for

2 If you **set aside** a belief, principle, or feeling, you decide that you
will not be influenced by it because there are other, more important
considerations at the time. EG *...a coalition of patriots that would set
aside party dogma and lead the nation towards recovery... It would
be good for the morale of the entire village if we set our personal
feelings aside.* ● **Put aside** means almost the same as **set aside.**

V+ADV+N,
V+N+ADV,
V+PRON+ADV

3 If a judge or court **sets aside** a decision or judgement, they state
that it is not legally valid or has no legal force. EG *Marshall believes
that the courts have the right to set aside acts of Congress... He at
last won a fresh hearing before the Court of Criminal Appeal, which
declined to set aside his original conviction.* ● **Overturn** means
almost the same as **set aside.**

V+ADV+N,
V+N+ADV,
V+PRON+ADV

4 If you **set** something **aside,** you move it out of your way for a while
with the intention of going back to it later. EG *The mixture concerned should be set aside in a cool place... Set it aside to dry... He
gazed at the bottle longingly, then set it firmly aside.* ● **Put aside**
and **lay aside** mean almost the same as **set aside.**

V+PRON+ADV,
V+N+ADV,
V+ADV+N

set back. **1** If something **sets** you **back** or **sets back** your plans, it
causes a delay and makes you wait before you can continue with
what you want to do. EG *This has set back the whole programme of
nuclear power in America... The unusual cold of the early spring
had set them back with the painting.* ● **Hold up** means almost the
same as **set back.** ▶ A **setback** is an event that delays your progress
or makes your position less favourable than it was before. EG *The by-
election result is being interpreted as a serious setback for the
government... She recovered from the initial setback... The Union
suffered a serious setback.*

V+ADV+N,
V+PRON+ADV,
V+N+ADV

N COUNT

2 If a building **is set back,** it is positioned at some distance from the
road or from the edge of the area where it stands. EG *The farms*

PASSIVE:
V+ADV,
USUALLY+A

were all set back a mile or so from the road... The new station will be set back five hundred metres from the present site.

3 If something **sets** you **back** a certain amount of money, it costs you that much; an informal use. EG *The legal costs of the case set him back something in the order of £10,000... Even two nights at any reasonable hotel was going to set me back enough to hurt... It did set us back a bit.* ● **Knock back** means almost the same as **set back**.

V+PRON+ADV+N,
V+N+ADV+N

set down. **1** If you **set down** something that you have been holding, you put it on a table or on the ground. EG *She set his dinner down and handed him a napkin... The colonel lifted his cup, glared at it, set it down again... Jeremy also noticed this as he set down the coffee pot.* ● **Put down** means almost the same as **set down**.

V+N+ADV,
V+PRON+ADV,
V+ADV+N:
ALSO+*on*

2 If you **set down** your thoughts, feelings, or a series of events, you write them all down because you want to keep a record of them. EG *They were asked to set down a summary of their views... When he retired to Britain he set down the story of his career... There was a serious political conversation and Herr Ballin set it down with reasonable accuracy.*

V+ADV+N,
V+PRON+ADV,
V+N+ADV

3 When something **is** officially **set down**, it is recorded as being a law or regulation. EG *There would have to be a limit set down by statute... These Cheyennes expected to live on the reservation with the Sioux as set down in the treaty of 1868... There are laws which attempt to set down standards whereby the animal is properly protected.* ● **Lay down** means almost the same as **set down**.

V+ADV+N,
V+PRON+ADV:
USUALLY PASSIVE

4 If a bus or train **sets** you **down**, it stops and lets you get out. EG *Can you set me down here?... They set me down at the door... He soon made an excuse and asked to be set down.* ● **Put down** means almost the same as **set down**.

V+PRON+ADV,
V+N+ADV:
USUALLY+A

5 If a plane or helicopter **sets down**, it lands somewhere. EG *A Chinook, forty feet long with rotors front and back, set down on the airstrip... You can get a look at the terrain out the window and pick your place to set down.*

V+ADV

set down as. If you **set** someone **down as** a particular kind of person, you decide that you know what they are like and firmly believe it, even though you might be wrong. EG *I had quite set her down as being of the other persuasion... People who told jokes, even very good jokes, were automatically set down as bores.*

V+PRON+ADV+PREP,
V+N+ADV+PREP

set forth. **1** If you **set forth** facts, ideas, or opinions, you explain them either in writing or in speech in a clear and organized way; a formal use. EG *She led them into a parlour and Bartolomeo set forth the purpose of their visit... The plan set forth long-term proposals... Our projections for these four groups of nations are set forth in Figure 5.* ● **Expound** is a more formal word for **set forth**.

V+ADV+N,
V+PRON+ADV

2 When you **set forth**, you start a journey; a literary use. EG *Four thousand set forth and three thousand did not return... He and Lamin set forth on the trail.* ● **Set out** and **set off** mean almost the same as **set forth**.

V+ADV

set in. **1** If something unpleasant **sets in**, it begins and seems likely to continue or develop. EG *By the time he had got it back in place, panic had set in... A feeling of anti-climax set in... They had to find a roof to live under before the cold weather set in.*

V+ADV

2 If something **is set in** or **into** a surface, it has been fixed into a hollow or hole in the surface so that it does not stick out. EG *He had virtually lived in the small office with his bunk set in an alcove to one side... ...nine large panels set in a rich framework... He dropped the keys down a large drain set into the pavement.* ▶ If something is **inset** with a decoration or piece of material, the decoration or material has been fixed into its surface and can be seen but does not

PASSIVE:
V+PREP

ADJECTIVE

stick out. EG ...*gold or silver inset with gems...* ...*little panels inset on the facade.*

set into. See **set in.**

set off. 1 When you **set off,** you start a journey. EG *She reversed off the grass and set off down the road... He set off on another of his European pleasure tours... We set off for Knebworth under grey skies... At exactly four minutes to three they set off.* ● **Set out** means almost the same as **set off.**

> V+ADV: USUALLY+A

2 If something **sets off** a process or series of events, it causes the process or events to start happening. EG *The broadcast was to set off a train of thoughts and actions... The biggest event of the previous winter had been an electrical storm that had set off all the alarms... Rioting in Brixton last month was set off by charges of police harassment.* ● **Trigger off** means almost the same as **set off.**

> V+ADV+N, V+PRON+ADV

3 If you **set off** a bomb or firework, you cause it to explode. EG *The mines blew three holes in the ship's sides but failed to set off the explosives as they had hoped... Two bombs were set off by someone in the crowd.*

> V+ADV+N, V+PRON+ADV

4 If something **sets** someone **off,** it makes them start doing something such as laughing, complaining, or telling stories. EG *From then on any glimpse of the moon was enough to set Hank off on his singing... Marcus looked green, as though the mention of vertigo had set him off.*

> V+N+ADV, V+PRON+ADV: ALSO+*on*

5 If one thing **sets** something else **off,** it provides a contrast that makes the other thing look more attractive or more noticeable than it would on its own. EG *The uniform set off his figure to advantage... It was very fine soft hair of a dusty brown shade that set off her darker eyebrows...* ...*the way the bands of design set each other off to advantage by contrast.* ● **Show off** means almost the same as **set off,** and **enhance** is a more formal word.

> V+ADV+N, V+N+ADV, V+PRON+ADV

set off against. If you **set** an amount of money **off against** a source of income or debt, you tell the tax authorities that that amount was spent in connection with your job or business in order to reduce the amount of tax you have to pay. EG *The loss on one venture can be set off against the taxable profits on another... A non-producing plantation appears on the tax return as a loss to be set off against a wealthy investor's other taxable income.* ● **Set against** means almost the same as **set off against.**

> V+N+ADV+PREP, V+PRON+ADV+PREP: USUALLY PASSIVE

set on. 1 If animals or people **set on** you, or if you **are set upon** by them, they make a sudden and unexpected physical attack on you. EG *Some rival gang set on them... He was set on by toughs, hunted by girls and warned several times by the police... I was being set upon by older boys and given a beating every morning.*

> V+PREP: HAS PASSIVE

2 If someone **sets** animals or people **on** or **upon** you, they cause the animals or people to attack you. EG *He knew, as we did, the answer to that one: we set our dogs on the gypsies... This so angered her that she set his own hounds upon him.*

> V+N+PREP, V+PRON+PREP

3 The **onset** of an unpleasant situation or event is its beginning. EG ...*the onset of war...* ...*his response to the onset of blindness.*

> N SING

set out. 1 When you **set out,** you start a journey. EG *We set out along the beach... Shortly after seven they set out on bicycles... She longed to set out for Europe, to see England, her father's country... Mr Dekker and his son set out to walk to Whitelake River.* ● **Set off** means almost the same as **set out.** ▷ If you talk about the **outset** of an event, process, or period of time, you mean its beginning, before anything else has happened. EG *You should explain this to him at the outset... The police had participated from the outset.*

> V+ADV

> N SING

2 If you **set out** to do something, you start taking action or making

> V+ADV: WITH *to*-INF

plans with the intention of achieving a particular result. EG *They had failed in what they had set out to do... There he had set out to establish his own business... This chapter sets out to explain some of the relevant terms and principles.*

3 If you **set out** facts, ideas, or opinions, you explain them either in writing or in speech in a clear and organized way. EG *Darwin set out his theory in detail in 'The Origin of Species'... Keynes set it all out in a famous series of letters to The Times... His conclusions were set out in his booklet 'Greener Grass'.* `V+ADV+N, V+PRON+ADV, V+N+ADV`

4 If you **set** things **out,** you put them somewhere in an organized way so that they can be used or so that they can be seen easily. EG *She had set out wine and a jug of water... I took off my boots and socks and set them out to dry on a rock... Tim had already cleared the plates away, and the chess board had been set out between the wine glasses.* ● **Lay out** means almost the same as **set out.** `V+ADV+N, V+PRON+ADV, V+N+ADV`

set to. **1** If you **set to,** you start working or dealing with something busily and energetically. EG *I cleaned my room, then I set to to help my parents... I knew the nurses would set to, scrubbing my room.* `V+ADV`

2 If two people **set to,** they begin arguing or fighting; a slightly old-fashioned use. EG *For a minute, it looked as if they'd set to, but things calmed down.* ▸ A **set-to** is a fight or violent argument. EG *On the following Tuesday we had a real set-to.* `V+ADV` `N COUNT`

set up. **1** If you **set up** something such as a structure, monument, or piece of equipment, you place it or build it somewhere. EG *They occupied buildings and set up road blocks and machine-gun posts... A fund was launched to set up a monument in memory of the dead men... They took the tent down and set it up again at each new camping site... Set the tea table up, it will be more convenient.* `V+ADV+N, V+PRON+ADV, V+N+ADV`

2 If you **set** something **up,** you make the arrangements and preparations that are necessary for it to start. EG *The newspaper correctly reported that the government had set up an investigation... The first thing to do in a crisis is to set up a committee... They had been trained in a special school set up by Brigadier James Gavin... Laboratory experiments on the transmission of infection have been set up.* ▸ A particular **set-up** is a particular system or way of organizing something. EG *I've only been here a couple of days and I don't quite know the set-up... ...the British political set-up.* `V+ADV+N, V+N+ADV, V+PRON+ADV` `N COUNT`

3 If you **set up** somewhere or **set** yourself **up** doing something, you start a firm, business, or company. EG *The firm is run by a former IBM designer who set up on his own... Anyone with an old lorry can set up as a contractor... He's probably set himself up in business... I persuaded him to set me up in a photocopying shop.* `V+ADV, V+REFL+ADV, V+PRON+ADV, V+N+ADV: WITH A`

4 If something **sets** you **up,** it puts you in a satisfactory condition or position, for example by providing you with money or by making you feel healthy and energetic. EG *He insisted on a contract that would set him up for life... There was no porridge to set them up for the cold winter's day.* `V+PRON+ADV, V+N+ADV`

5 If something **sets up** a process or series of events, it causes the events to begin and continue. EG *It may become possible to set up a nuclear chain reaction... Unfortunately physical appearances automatically set up prejudices in our minds.* `V+ADV+N, V+PRON+ADV`

6 If someone **sets** you **up,** they make people think that you have done something wrong when you have not, or they deceive you into a situation in which you might be harmed; an informal use. EG *He and Pearson have been working together from the very beginning trying to set you up... He was paid to set the Mayor up.* ● **Frame** means almost the same as **set up.** ▸ A **set-up** is a situation in which someone makes it seem as if an innocent person has committed a `V+PRON+ADV, V+N+ADV` `N COUNT`

crime; an informal word. EG *The whole thing was just a set-up,*
organised by Jim and his cronies.

set upon. See set on.

settle, settles, settling, settled

settle down. 1 If you **settle down** to something, you start doing it,   v+ADV
with the intention of doing it seriously and for quite a while. EG *We*
settled down to wait... He had settled down to watch a sports
programme... At eight o'clock he settles down for supper.

2 When someone **settles down,** they start living a quiet life in one   v+ADV
place, especially when they get married or buy a house. EG *Alan told*
her that after this, he would settle down and marry her... You have
to get a job and settle down.

3 If people **settle down** or if you **settle** them **down,** they stop talking   v+ADV,
or being worried and become calm, peaceful, or quiet. EG *It took her*   v+PRON+ADV,
some time to settle down... The meeting settled down again...   v+N+ADV:
Eddie's presence settled me down. ● **Calm down** means almost the   ERGATIVE
same as **settle down.**

4 If something **settles down,** it becomes calmer and more stable. EG   v+ADV
His stomach had settled down enough to permit him a beer or two...
Her life had settled down.

settle for. If you **settle for** something, you choose or accept it, even   v+PREP
though it is not what you really want, because nothing else is
available. EG *Don't settle for second best... When in doubt he settled*
for hamburgers.

settle in. If you **settle in** or **are settled in,** you become used to   v+ADV:
living in a new house or town or doing a new job. EG *Madame gave*   ALSO PASSIVE,
her three weeks to settle in... And how are you settling in, Mr   v+ADV
Swallow?... There's plenty of time to get settled in.

settle into. If you **settle into** a routine, activity, or a way of   v+PREP
behaving, you start doing it in a way that suggests that it will
continue for some time. EG *Some babies are slow to settle into a*
routine... The boat settled into a slow side-to-side roll... ...just as I was
settling into normal conversation.

settle on. 1 If you **settle on** or **upon** something, you decide to have   v+PREP:
it or use it after thinking or talking about it. EG *A week ahead of the*   HAS PASSIVE
joint negotiations, exporters settled on a figure of 52.1 million... Have
you settled on a name for him yet? ● **Decide on** means almost the
same as **settle on.**

2 If money is **settled on** someone, it is left to them in a will; a formal   PASSIVE:
use. EG *Some money was settled on him when he was adopted.*   v+PREP

settle up. When you **settle up** with someone, you pay them what   v+ADV+*with*,
you owe them. EG *As soon as the money arrived I was able to settle*   v+ADV:
up with him... We settled up last week. ● **Square up** means almost   RECIPROCAL
the same as **settle up.**

settle upon. See settle on: settle upon is more formal.

sew, sews, sewing, sewed, sewn

sew on. If you **sew** something **on,** you attach it to something else by   v+N+ADV/PREP,
sewing it. EG *I had to sew on a couple of buttons that were coming*   v+ADV+N,
loose... I'll sew the button on your coat.   v+PRON+ADV/PREP

sew up. 1 If you **sew up** something that has been torn, you join it   v+ADV+N,
back together by sewing it. EG *She could find no needle or thread to*   v+N+ADV,
sew up the torn lacing... A doctor was sewing up the cut over his   v+PRON+ADV
eye.

2 If you **sew up** something such as a business deal or an election, you   v+ADV+N,
arrange it in such a way that you can be sure of favourable results; a   v+PRON+ADV
fairly informal use. EG *We thought that everything was sewn up so*

*we were surprised when they didn't sign the contract... ...the local
organizations that sewed up this year's elections.*

shack, shacks, shacking, shacked

shack up. When someone **shacks up** with someone else or when
two people **shack up** together, they start living together as lovers;
an informal expression. EG *He wants to shack up with me... If we'd
been five years younger, we'd just have shacked up together.*

V+ADV,
V+ADV+*with*,
V+ADV+*together*:
RECIPROCAL

shade, shades, shading, shaded

shade in. If you **shade in** an area in a drawing or painting, you
make it appear dark, for example by filling it in with pencil lines or
with a dark colour. EG *He was shading in the straps on the ankles.*
● **Colour in** means almost the same as **shade in.**

V+ADV+N,
V+N+ADV,
V+PRON+ADV

shade into. When something **shades into** something else, there is
no clear division between the two things, so that you cannot tell
where one thing ends and the other begins. EG *...reds shading into
pinks... Professor Wilson now sees instinct and culture as shading
into one another.* ● **Merge into** and **blend into** mean almost the
same as **shade into.**

V+PREP

shake, shakes, shaking, shook, shaken

shake down. 1 If you **shake down** somewhere, for example on the
floor or on a settee, you sleep there temporarily; an informal use. EG
You can shake down at my place for tonight. ● **Bed down** means
almost the same as **shake down.**

V+ADV:
WITH A

2 If you **shake down,** you become used to a new situation, such as a
job or course. EG *The third division had just arrived, but was at low
strength and had not yet shaken down.*

V+ADV

shake off. If you **shake off** someone or something that you do not
want, you get rid of them or get away from them. EG *It had taken
Franklin several hours to shake off the police... Such habits cannot
be shaken off in the course of a few decades.*

V+ADV+N,
V+N+ADV,
V+PRON+ADV

shake out. If you **shake out** something such as a piece of cloth, you
hold it by one of its edges and move it about vigorously, for example
in order to open it out or to make it flat. EG *...a napkin which she
shook out and spread on the table... ...shaking out her umbrella.*

V+N+ADV,
V+ADV+N,
V+PRON+ADV

shake up. 1 If something bad, unexpected, or frightening **shakes**
you **up,** it makes you feel very shocked and upset. EG *Did that
lightning shake you up?... I'm a little shaken up at the moment.*

V+N+ADV,
V+PRON+ADV

2 If you **shake** things **up,** you mix them together by shaking the
container that they are in. EG *Here are the raffle tickets; shake them
up well before you pick one.* ● **Mix up** means almost the same as
shake up.

V+PRON+ADV,
V+N+ADV,
V+ADV+N

3 If you **shake up** something such as an organization, institution, or
business, you make major changes in it, usually in order to improve
it. EG *The management aims to shake up its newly acquired companies... A rival bid is always good for shaking up the board of
directors.* ▶ A **shake-up** is a major change that affects the whole of
something such as an organization. EG *Many were eager for a shake-
up in the two-party system... I felt my life needed a shake-up.*

V+ADV+N,
V+N+ADV,
V+PRON+ADV

N COUNT

shame, shames, shaming, shamed

shame into. If you **shame** someone **into** doing something, you force
them to do it by making them feel ashamed. EG *Father was shamed
into an admission.*

V+N+PREP,
V+PRON+PREP

shape, shapes, shaping, shaped

shape up. 1 If someone or something is **shaping up** in a particular
way, they are developing or progressing in that way. EG *The summer*

V+ADV:
WITH A

was shaping up as a mediocre one... The Campaign is shaping up as one of the most intensive sales campaigns ever.

2 If you **shape up**, you become fit, healthy, or prepared for some-   V+ADV
thing; a fairly informal use. EG *We were shaping up for the attack on the Tories.*

share, shares, sharing, shared

share out. If you **share** something **out** between a group of people,   V+ADV+N,
you divide it into parts and give some to each person. EG *...sharing*   V+N+ADV,
out the money and possessions... ...the way housework and childcare   V+PRON+ADV
is shared out... Elizabeth cut the cake, then shared it out. ▸ If there   N SING
is a **share-out** of something, several people are given equal or fair
parts of it. EG *...a share-out of the profits.*

sharpen, sharpens, sharpening, sharpened

sharpen up. **1** If you **sharpen up** a knife or other tool, you make it   V+ADV+N,
sharper. EG *I was practical enough to sharpen up my knives... My*   V+PRON+ADV,
tools were blunt so I had to sharpen them up.   V+N+ADV

2 If something **sharpens up** or if you **sharpen** it **up,** it becomes   V+ADV,
better or more active. EG *The struggle against the Bill was sharpen-*   V+ADV+N,
ing up... It sharpened up her hearing... ...three useful games for   V+N+ADV,
sharpening up your mental calculating ability.   V+PRON+ADV:
  ERGATIVE

shave, shaves, shaving, shaved

shave off. **1** If someone **shaves off** their hair or beard, they remove   V+ADV+N,
it by shaving. EG *He had shaved off his beard... A small patch of his*   V+N+ADV,
hair was shaved off... As the grey hairs appear, shave them off.   V+PRON+ADV

2 If you **shave off** a thin piece of wood from a larger piece, you cut it   V+ADV+N,
off. EG *Use a plane to shave off a small amount from the bottom of*   V+N+ADV,
the door.   V+PRON+ADV

shear, shears, shearing, sheared, shorn

The past participle can be either **sheared** or **shorn.**

shear off. If something such as a piece of metal **shears off,** it   V+ADV
breaks off, for example because of pressure or old age; used
especially of metal machine parts. EG *The aeroplane's wing sheared
off.*

shell, shells, shelling, shelled

shell out. If you **shell out** for something, you spend an amount of   V+ADV+N:
money on it, especially when you do not really want to; an informal   ALSO+*on/for*
expression. EG *He's going to have to shell out another three hundred
million dollars for public transport facilities... ...any time he shells
out fifty bucks... I shelled out sixty quid on that carpet.* ● **Fork out**
means almost the same as **shell out.**

shin, shins, shinning, shinned

shin down. If you **shin down** something such as a tree or pole, you   V+PREP
climb down it quickly and easily by using both hands and legs to grip
it. EG *She shinned down the drainpipe to the lawn.*

shin up. If you **shin up** something such as a tree or a pole, you climb   V+PREP
up it quickly and easily by using both hands and legs to grip it. EG *I
shinned up a lamp post to get a better view of the procession.*

shine, shines, shining, shone

shine out. If something **shines out,** it shines brightly and so can be   V+ADV
seen very easily. EG *The town shines out as though it were golden...
...which makes its jewel shine out more brightly.*

shine through. If a quality **shines through** in a situation, it can be   V+ADV,
seen clearly. EG *...so that goodness can shine through... Two steady*   V+PREP
rays of lucidity shone through the confusion.

ship, ships, shipping, shipped

ship in. If goods **are shipped in,** they are brought into a place by boat. EG *...components shipped in from industrialized countries... Weapons are freely shipped in for commercial gain.*
V+N+ADV,
V+ADV+N,
V+PRON+ADV:
USUALLY PASSIVE

ship off. If people or things **are shipped off** to a place, they are taken there, especially by boat; an informal expression. EG *These pigs are shipped off to another farmer and he fattens them up... A giraffe was being shipped off to Dublin.*
V+N+ADV,
V+ADV+N,
V+PRON+ADV:
USUALLY PASSIVE

ship out. If people or things **are shipped out** to a place, they are taken there. EG *Everything will have to be shipped out from England... They were shipped out by rail.*
V+N+ADV,
V+ADV+N,
V+PRON+ADV:
USUALLY PASSIVE

shock, shocks, shocking, shocked

shock into. If you **are shocked into** doing something, you are so shocked or surprised that you do it. EG *The assembly was shocked into silence... He was shocked into withdrawing his request.*
V+N+PREP,
V+PRON+PREP:
USUALLY PASSIVE

shoo, shoos, shooing, shooed

shoo away. If you **shoo away** a person or an animal, you wave your arms or hands at them to make them go away. EG *We were not allowed to shoo away the pigs... The visitors were politely shooed away... They'd shooed her away as if she were a dog.*
V+ADV+N,
V+N+ADV,
V+PRON+ADV

shoot, shoots, shooting, shot

shoot away. If a part of someone's body **is shot away,** a bullet or explosion destroys or seriously damages that part of their body. EG *Half his face had been shot away.* ● **Blow away** and **blow off** mean almost the same as **shoot away.**
V+N+ADV,
V+ADV+N,
V+PRON+ADV

shoot down. 1 If someone **shoots** something or someone **down,** they make them fall to the ground by hitting them with a bullet or missile. EG *The enemy claimed to have shot down 22 of our planes... If he is intercepted, he shoots down one or two policemen... Their helicopter was shot down in flames... A firing squad will shoot him down.* ● **Bring down** means almost the same as **shoot down.**
V+ADV+N,
V+N+ADV,
V+PRON+ADV

2 If you **shoot** someone **down** or **shoot down** their ideas, you show that their ideas are wrong or foolish; an informal use. EG *No doubt you could shoot me down by all kinds of quotations... My suggestion was immediately shot down by everyone else at the meeting.*
V+N+ADV,
V+ADV+N,
V+PRON+ADV

shoot off. 1 If someone or something **shoots off,** they leave very quickly. EG *We saw the bus shoot off at a terrific speed... Brooks has gone shooting off in the other direction.*
V+ADV

2 If a part of someone's body **is shot off,** a bullet or explosion destroys or seriously damages that part of their body. EG *...poor devils on the outside getting their arms and legs shot off.* ● **Blow off** and **blow away** mean almost the same as **shoot off.**
V+N+ADV,
V+ADV+N,
V+PRON+ADV

shoot out. 1 If someone **shoots out,** they leave a room very quickly. EG *He just shot out of the room before I could say anything.*
V+ADV

2 If something **shoots out,** it moves suddenly so that it is sticking out. EG *His arm shot out to point at her... ...its tongue shoots out.*
V+ADV

3 A **shoot-out** is a fight in which people shoot at each other with guns. EG *He was wounded during a shoot-out with British troops.*
N COUNT

shoot through. If something **shoots through** a barrier of some kind, it suddenly moves through it so that it is on the other side of it. EG *Later, witnesses said that they saw the truck shoot through the police cordon without stopping.*
V+PREP

shoot up. 1 If something **shoots up,** it grows or increases very quickly. EG *...when the rents shoot up in December... Nancy began to run a fever which eventually shot up to 43 degrees... Your children have really shot up since the last time I saw them.*
V+ADV

2 If someone **shoots up** a place, they move around in it shooting a gun. ᴇɢ *He has his own reasons to shoot up the place... ...coming out at night and shooting up the area.*   `V+ADV+N, V+N+ADV, V+PRON+ADV`

3 If someone **shoots up**, they inject illegal drugs into themselves; an informal use.   `V+ADV`

shop, shops, shopping, shopped

shop around. 1 If you **shop around**, you go to different shops in order to compare the prices and quality of something before you decide to buy it. ᴇɢ *The prices are variable so shop around... There are plenty of savings if you're prepared to shop around.*   `V+ADV`

2 If you **shop around** for a particular deal, contract, or arrangement, you try to get what you want by comparing the value and quality of several similar deals or contracts before deciding which one to accept. ᴇɢ *She can shop around for the job where her chances of promotion are best... The would-be student is free to shop around... We'll shop around the building societies to find the best terms.*   `V+ADV, V+PREP`

shore, shores, shoring, shored

shore up. 1 If you **shore up** something that is weak or about to fail, you do something in order to strengthen it. ᴇɢ *Lewis and his men were already moving to shore up public confidence in the system... The nine million pounds provided by the Government to shore the group up was not enough.*   `V+ADV+N, V+N+ADV, V+PRON+ADV`

2 If you **shore up** a wall or a building, you put a strong support next to it or under it in order to stop it from falling down. ᴇɢ *The villagers shored up sagging huts... Perched on this cliff, shored up on girders, was the Marine Cafe.* ● **Prop up** means almost the same as **shore up**.   `V+ADV+N, V+N+ADV, V+PRON+ADV`

shout, shouts, shouting, shouted

shout down. If people **shout** a person **down**, they prevent the person from being heard by shouting at them. ᴇɢ *The crowd shouted the speaker down... ...the attempt to shout down the Prime Minister... ...jeering and more or less shouting them down.* ● **Hoot down** and **howl down** mean almost the same as **shout down**.   `V+N+ADV, V+ADV+N, V+PRON+ADV`

shout out. If you **shout** something **out**, you suddenly shout it. ᴇɢ *I just had time to shout out and warn them not to cross the road... They began to dance and shout out praises to God because they were cured... We began to shout out that we wanted our money back... She shouted out that she was unjustly imprisoned... Kate applauded and shouted out, 'Bravo!'* ● **Call out** means almost the same as **shout out**.   `V+ADV, V+ADV+N, V+ADV+REPORT, V+ADV+QUOTE, V+N+ADV, V+PRON+ADV`

shove, shoves, shoving, shoved

shove off. If you tell someone to **shove off**, you are telling them angrily to go away; used in very informal English. ᴇɢ *You shove off. See?* ● **Buzz off** and **push off** mean almost the same as **shove off**.   `IMPERATIVE: V+ADV`

shove up. If you tell someone to **shove up**, you are telling them in rather a rude way to move in order to make room for someone else; used in informal English. ᴇɢ *Shove up, make room for him over here.* ● **Budge up** means almost the same as **shove up**.   `IMPERATIVE: V+ADV`

show, shows, showing, showed, shown

show around. 1 If you **show** someone **around** or **round** a place, you go there with them, pointing out all the interesting or important features. ᴇɢ *I was showing a group of visitors around the school... It was Ivan's job to show him around the city... Karen showed Kitty around with obvious pride... We'll eat now and then I'll show you round—OK?* ● **Take round** means almost the same as **show around**.   `V+N+PREP, V+PRON+PREP, V+N+ADV, V+PRON+ADV`

2 If you **show** something **around**, you give it to several people to   `V+N+ADV, V+PRON+ADV` look at. EG *I showed my holiday snaps around when I got into work... His son found a hundred-pound note and ecstatically showed it around to his family.*

show in. When you **show** someone **in**, you lead them into a room or building. EG *A servant came to the door and showed me in... Miss Livingstone showed in a guest.* ● **Show out** means the opposite of **show in.**
V+PRON+ADV, V+ADV+N, V+N+ADV

show off. 1 If you **show off,** you try to impress people by making your skills or good qualities very obvious; used showing disapproval. EG *Don't show off... He was afraid the others might think he was showing off or being superior... ...kids showing off on the diving board.* ▶ If you say that someone is a **show-off,** you mean that they try to impress people by behaving in a way that shows their skills or abilities very obviously; an informal word used showing disapproval. EG *Even in those days, I was a show-off.*
V+ADV

N COUNT

2 If you **show off** something that you own, you show it to a lot of people because you are proud of it. EG *He was eager to show off the new car... ...tossing their heads and arms, showing off their jewellery... It had given me intense pleasure to show my trophies off to her.*
V+ADV+N, V+N+ADV, V+PRON+ADV: NO PASSIVE

3 If something **shows off** another thing, it makes the other thing seem more attractive or effective because it emphasizes the good qualities of that other thing. EG *...a most becoming tan that showed off her white hair beautifully... Set up situations which will show off these skills to the best advantage of the team.* ● **Set off** means almost the same as **show off,** and **enhance** is a more formal word.
V+ADV+N, V+N+ADV, V+PRON+ADV: NO PASSIVE

show out. When you **show** someone **out,** you go with them to the door as they leave a room or building. EG *Will you show Miss Nester out please?... He was just being shown out as I arrived... After she had shown him out of the office, she sat down wearily.* ● **Show in** means the opposite of **show out.**
V+N+ADV, V+ADV+N, V+PRON+ADV: ALSO+*of*

show round. See **show around.**

show through. 1 If something **shows through** a barrier of some kind, it is noticeable behind that barrier. EG *A chink of light showed through the curtains... Few buildings showed through the trees... The light showed through into the next room.*
V+PREP, V+ADV

2 If your feelings **show through,** you reveal them to other people, often without intending to. EG *I know that my sadness may show through... His eagerness and willingness to participate showed through right from the start.*
V+ADV

show up. 1 If you **show up,** you arrive at a place where people are expecting you; an informal use. EG *Over a hundred people showed up at the meeting... How would his three new friends feel about it if he showed up with his little brother?* ● **Turn up** means almost the same as **show up.**
V+ADV: USUALLY+A

2 When something **shows up,** it can be seen clearly. EG *Dark colours will not show up against a similar background... Bloodstains show up as white on the negative... The redness of sunburn doesn't show up until several hours after the damage is done.*
V+ADV

3 If a particular result or observation **is shown up** in a test or experiment, it is made noticeable as part of the result of that experiment. EG *Small differences in temperament are bound to show up... This distortion of the patient's time sense shows up in a revealing experiment... ...the intensity of past infection shown up by blood tests... It isn't always easy to show up this trend.*
V+ADV, V+N+ADV, V+ADV+N, V+PRON+ADV: ERGATIVE

4 If someone is with you and they **show** you **up,** they make you feel embarrassed and ashamed of them. EG *Don't make a big thing of it—don't show him up.*
V+PRON+ADV, V+N+ADV

show up as. If something or someone **is shown up** as being bad, unpleasant, and so on, people start to realize that they are bad, unpleasant, and so on. EG *Their air combat skills were shown up as inferior to those of the NATO pilots... They have been shown up as being very undemocratic.*

V+N+ADV+PREP, V+PRON+ADV+PREP

shrink, shrinks, shrinking, shrank, shrunk

shrink away. If you **shrink away**, you move away from something that has frightened or horrified you. EG *The circle of boys shrank away in horror... It would be impossible for him not to shrink away from any physical contact.*

V+ADV: ALSO+*from*

shrink from. If you **shrink from** doing something, you are reluctant to do it because you find it unpleasant. EG *I kept wanting to yawn, but shrank from lifting my grimy hands to my face... He shrank from giving Frank a direct answer.* ● **Shy away from** means almost the same as **shrink from**.

V+PREP

shrivel, shrivels, shrivelling, shrivelled

American English uses the spellings **shriveling** and **shriveled**.

shrivel up. When something **shrivels up**, it becomes dry and wrinkled because it loses moisture. EG *The fish had shrivelled up a bit... I was late for tea, and mine would be shrivelled up in the oven... ...shrivelling up like old apples... The sun had shrivelled the tomatoes up.* ● **Wither** means almost the same as **shrivel up**.

V+ADV, V+N+ADV, V+PRON+ADV, V+ADV+N: ERGATIVE

shrug, shrugs, shrugging, shrugged

shrug off. If you **shrug** something **off**, you ignore it or treat it as if it is not really important or serious. EG *Designers tend to shrug this problem off... The Chairman shrugs off any criticism that their operations are unscrupulous.* ● **Brush off** means almost the same as **shrug off**.

V+N+ADV, V+ADV+N, V+PRON+ADV

shuffle, shuffles, shuffling, shuffled

shuffle off. If you **shuffle** something **off**, you try to avoid talking about it or dealing with it because you find it difficult or embarrassing. EG *He shuffled the question off and changed the topic... The Government should not try to shuffle the responsibility off onto the public.*

V+N+ADV, V+PRON+ADV, V+ADV+N

shut, shuts, shutting

The form **shut** is used in the present tense and is the past tense and past participle of the verb.

shut away. 1 If you **shut** someone or something **away**, you put them in a special place where people cannot see them or take them away. EG *The dog and cats were shut away in case they ran off... ...shutting the elderly away in geriatric hospitals... I kept it shut away in a spare, unfurnished room.* ● **Lock away** means almost the same as **shut away**.

V+N+ADV, V+PRON+ADV, V+ADV+N

2 If you **shut** yourself **away**, you stay in one building or room for a long time and avoid meeting people. EG *He became an intensely private man, shutting himself away in his hotel room... I shut myself away in a library that night and wrote a letter.*

V+REFL+ADV

shut down. 1 If someone **shuts down** a factory or business or if it **shuts down**, it closes and stops working. EG *British Petroleum has permanently shut down its massive refinery in Kent... If they walked out that would shut the whole factory down... More than 10 per cent of the country's 301 production plants have shut down this year.* ● **Close down** means almost the same as **shut down**. ▷ A **shutdown** is the closing of a factory, shop, or other business. EG *Irish bar proprietors called for a shutdown between 3 and 5 pm.*

V+ADV+N, V+N+ADV, V+PRON+ADV, V+ADV: ERGATIVE

N COUNT

2 If a machine or engine **shuts down** or if it **is shut down,** it stops working altogether for a short time. EG *Computers supplying the information had automatically shut down... There was supposed to be a foolproof system for shutting down the system... One of the 747's four engines had been shut down after showing a fault.* ● **Shut off** means almost the same as **shut down.**

V+ADV,
V+ADV+N,
V+N+ADV,
V+PRON+ADV:
ERGATIVE

shut in. **1** If someone **shuts** you **in** a room or other confined space, they close the door so that you cannot leave. EG *She just shut her husband in the garage by mistake... His brother shut him in a wooden chest... We were shut in for the night.* ● **Imprison** is a more formal word for **shut in.**

V+N+PREP,
V+PRON+PREP,
V+N+ADV,
V+PRON+ADV

2 If you **shut** yourself **in** a room, you go in there and shut the door so that nobody else can get in. EG *She shut herself in the bathroom and wept... She slammed the door and shut herself in the kitchen.* ● **Shut up** means almost the same as **shut in.**

V+REFL+PREP,
V+REFL+ADV

shut off. **1** If you **shut off** an engine or the power supply to a machine, you turn it off to stop it working. EG *I stopped the car and shut off the engine... Foster shut off the heat in the main cabin... When I shut the motor off I could hear the birds.* ● **Turn off** means almost the same as **shut off.**

V+ADV+N,
V+N+ADV,
V+PRON+ADV

2 If someone **shuts off** the supply of a particular commodity or type of goods, they stop sending the commodity or goods to the people who normally use them. EG *Some nations had shut off oil or coffee as a means of blackmail... And that was when they shut off funds, saying they did not believe the programme could work.* ● **Cut off** means almost the same as **shut off.**

V+ADV+N,
V+N+ADV,
V+PRON+ADV

3 Something that **shuts off** a view prevents it from being seen by obscuring it. EG *A row of trees shut off the scene... She closed the curtains to shut off the view of the valley... The sun's rays are shut off by soot.* ● **Block out** means almost the same as **shut off.**

V+ADV+N,
V+N+ADV,
V+PRON+ADV

4 If you **shut** yourself **off,** you avoid talking to other people or getting involved with them. EG *Why have you shut yourself off from your mother and me for two years?... They use a variety of devices to shut themselves off from the other patients.*

V+REFL+ADV:
USUALLY+from

shut out. **1** If you **shut** something or someone **out,** you prevent them from getting into a place, for example by closing the doors. EG *...owners who shut their dogs out all day... They had covered the holes to shut out the water.*

V+N+ADV,
V+ADV+N,
V+PRON+ADV

2 To **shut out** sound or light means to prevent it from reaching a place. EG *He put his hands over his ears to shut out the noise... Walls rising on either side shut out the sunlight... All direct light is shut out from the forest floor.*

V+ADV+N,
V+PRON+ADV,
V+N+ADV

3 If you **shut out** a thought or feeling, you try to stop yourself from thinking about it. EG *I did not even try to shut out the speculations about my future... She found it impossible to shut out the pain... He decided to shut it out of his mind.* ● **Block out** and **blot out** mean almost the same as **shut out.**

V+ADV+N,
V+PRON+ADV,
V+N+ADV

shut up. **1** If you **shut up,** you stop talking; an informal use. If you tell someone to **shut up,** you are telling them to stop talking in rather a rude, abrupt way. EG *Everybody shuts up as soon as you mention it... Oh, shut up about yourself!*

V+ADV:
ALSO IMPERATIVE

2 If someone **shuts** you **up,** they prevent you from talking; an informal use. EG *Turn the television on. That usually shuts them up... I just said it to her one day to shut her up.* ● **Silence** is a more formal word for **shut up.**

V+PRON+ADV,
V+N+ADV

3 If you **are shut up** in a building, room, or other confined space, you are kept in there and cannot get out. EG *They wanted to shut Sarah up in a mental hospital... He was shut up for life as a dangerous*

V+N+ADV,
V+PRON+ADV:
USUALLY+A

criminal... They shut her up in the remand centre for a whole year.
● **Shut in** means almost the same as **shut up,** and **imprison** and **confine** are more formal words.

shy, shies, shying, shied

shy away from. If you **shy away from** doing something, you avoid   V+ADV+PREP
doing it, often because you are afraid or not confident enough. EG
*Some mothers shy away from breast-feeding... A few have shied
away from careers in big industry.* ● **Shrink from** means almost the
same as **shy away from.**

sick, sicks, sicking, sicked

sick up. When you **sick** food **up,** you vomit; an informal expression.   V+N+ADV,
EG *She promptly sicked everything up all over poor Karen... Look*   V+PRON+ADV,
out, the dog is sicking up his dinner. ● **Bring up** and **throw up** mean   V+ADV+N
almost the same as **sick up.**

side, sides, siding, sided

side against. If people **side against** you, they join together in order   V+PREP
to defeat you in a quarrel or an argument. EG *Her supporters sided
against me.* ● **Gang up** means almost the same as **side against,** and
side with means the opposite.

side with. If you **side with** someone, you support them in a quarrel   V+PREP
or argument. EG *The daughters sided with their mothers... ...siding
with people who encouraged civil disobedience... He may have sided
with them for personal gain.* ● **Side against** means the opposite of
side with.

sidle, sidles, sidling, sidled

sidle up. If someone **sidles up** to you, they approach you in a   V+ADV:
cautious or uncertain way, as if they do not want anyone to notice.   USUALLY+to
EG *Sylvia had managed to sidle up to Gertrude... I sidled up and
touched her with a finger.*

sift, sifts, sifting, sifted

sift through. If you **sift through** a large collection of something,   V+PREP:
you examine it carefully and thoroughly, usually because you need   HAS PASSIVE
to organize it or find something out. EG *Every day he sifted through
the reports... A computer could sift through a huge number of
records... There are archives and documents to be sifted through.*

sign, signs, signing, signed

sign away. If you **sign** something **away** or **over,** you sign an official   V+ADV+N,
document stating that you no longer own it or have a right to it. EG   V+N+ADV,
Chiefs were encouraged to sign away land that appeared to be   V+PRON+ADV
*unoccupied... That means that you sign away your right to claim
more money if your illness gets worse... One way of avoiding death
duties might be to sign the house over to your son now.*

sign in. 1 If you **sign in** or if someone **signs** you **in,** you sign your   V+ADV,
name in a book or on a special form in a hotel, club, or other   V+REFL+ADV,
institution when you arrive. EG *They sign in at the reception desk...*   V+ADV+N,
Humboldt went to Mount Sinai Hospital and signed himself in... A   V+PRON+ADV:
smiling middle-aged lady was behind the desk, signing in the new   ERGATIVE
students. ● **Book in** means almost the same as **sign in,** and **register**
is a more formal word.

2 If you **sign** someone **in** at a club or other institution of which you   V+PRON+ADV,
are a member but they are not, you sign your name in a special   V+N+ADV,
book to say that they are there as your guest. EG *Just get someone to*   V+ADV+N
sign you in... I don't think you'll have to be signed in.

sign off. 1 If you **sign off** at the end of a letter or a radio   V+ADV conversation, you write or say your final message. EG *It's just about tea time so I'll sign off now—with love, take care. Dad.*

2 If you are ill and a doctor **signs** you **off,** he or she writes a note to your employer, saying that you are not able to go to work for a particular period of time. EG *Shall we sign her off for a week?* `V+PRON+ADV, V+N+ADV`

sign on. 1 If you **sign on** at a government unemployment office, you go there and sign your name on a form to confirm that you are unemployed, so that you can receive state unemployment benefit; used mainly in British English. EG *You will have to go on calling at the UBO every fortnight to sign on while you are getting supplementary benefit.* `V+ADV`

2 If you **sign on** or if someone **signs** you **on** with a company or for an academic course, you sign a contract or form in which you agree to work for the company or to do the course. EG *You could sign on for a full-time course... The boys' ambitions were to sign on with the whaling fleet... Well, maybe I can sign you on for one run—to try out the new ship.* ● **Sign up** means almost the same as **sign on.** `V+ADV, V+PRON+ADV, V+ADV+N, V+N+ADV: ERGATIVE`

sign out. 1 If you **sign out** of a hotel, club, or other institution, you sign your name in a book or on a special form when you leave. EG *That Friday I signed out for a weekend... Signing out of our dormitory, we indicated that we had permission from our parents to visit a family in New York.* `V+ADV: ALSO+of`

2 If you **sign** something **out,** you sign your name in a book or on a card to say that you have taken it or borrowed it from an organization or institution that you belong to. EG *Bernstein signed out a company car and drove to McLean.* `V+ADV+N, V+N+ADV, V+PRON+ADV`

sign over. See **sign away.**

sign up. If you **sign up,** or if someone **signs** you **up,** you sign an official document saying that you will do something, such as a job or a course of study. EG *He signed up as a painter on the Federal Art Project... Richard Boot was signed up to play the lead in Miroslav's new film... The picture editor of the Telegraph magazine had signed up Don Whillans... Who's that wonderful man? Sign him up immediately!* `V+ADV, V+N+ADV, V+ADV+N, V+PRON+ADV: ERGATIVE`

silt, silts, silting, silted

silt up. If a river, lake, or other area of water **silts up** or is **silted up,** it becomes blocked with silt. EG *The lake silted up... The channels have been silted up... ...simply scoured away the hillsides, silting up the riverbeds and causing floods.* `V+ADV, V+ADV+N: ERGATIVE`

simmer, simmers, simmering, simmered

simmer down. If you **simmer down,** you stop being angry about something. EG *The others sat around, giving me time to simmer down; someone handed me a water-bottle... 'Simmer down,' I said. 'It's not our problem.'* ● **Calm down** and **cool down** mean almost the same as **simmer down.** `V+ADV`

sing, sings, singing, sang, sung

sing out. 1 If you **sing out,** you sing loudly. EG *He sang full out as if he were singing in public... The strains of heavenly harmony sang out for the third time... You didn't have to sing out quite as loud as you did.* `V+ADV`

2 If you **sing** something **out,** you say it suddenly and loudly, often from a distance. EG *'That's right,' Etta sang out cheerfully... Her old friends would, sooner or later, sing out 'Has he married you yet, then?'* `V+ADV: WITH QUOTE`

sing up. If you **sing up,** you sing more loudly, so that people can hear you better. EG *You boys at the back! Can you sing up?* `V+ADV`

single, singles, singling, singled

single out. If you **single out** someone or something from a group, you choose them for special attention or treatment. EG *Neither Belinda nor Mrs Harlowe made any move to single him out for attention... ...to single out the key problems for each continent... Why have badgers been singled out as culprits?... She singled this one out as being the only possible one.* ● **Pick out** means almost the same as **single out.**

V+PRON+ADV,
V+N+ADV,
V+ADV+N:
ALSO+*for/as*

sink, sinks, sinking, sank, sunk

sink back. 1 If you **sink back,** you lean backwards or lie down after being in a more upright or sitting position. EG *She sank back on her pillows... Sonny sank back in the leather armchair... I sank back and tried to think.*

V+ADV:
USUALLY+A

2 To **sink back** into a former state or habit means to return to being in that state or having that habit. EG *He would sink back again into bitterness... There is a continual battle against sinking back into the old ways... There'll be no field officers, so everything will sink back. But that happens everywhere; you take one step forward and two steps back.*

V+ADV:
USUALLY+*into*

sink down. 1 If something **sinks down,** it moves downwards. EG *The jet turns in a wide circle, sinking down through the clear air toward the hills below... The bird sank down, kicking and fluttering.*

V+ADV

2 If you **sink down,** you sit or let yourself fall gently from an upright position. EG *Hagen sank down on the grass and sighed... She sank down in the chair, with her legs wide apart... They lit cigarettes and sank down to lie on the grass.*

V+ADV:
USUALLY+A

sink in. 1 If something **sinks in,** it goes deeper into the ground, water, or other substance. EG *It sunk in up to the hilt... The rain sinks in and there is no mud.*

V+ADV

2 When a fact or idea, usually an unpleasant one, **sinks in,** it gradually becomes recognized or understood. EG *It took a moment or two to sink in... The implications of this did not at first sink in... The prisoners had nothing to do but let their situation sink in.*

V+ADV

3 If you **are sunk in** a state or mood, especially a dull or inactive one, you are completely in it. EG *She remained sunk in silent contemplation... The nation seemed sunk in lethargy.*

PASSIVE:
V+ADV

4 If you **sink** something sharp **in** something solid, you cause it to pierce the surface and go deep into the solid. EG *The cat suddenly leapt off a roof and sank her claws in his neck... The other hyena lunges at its belly, sinks in its teeth and holds on.*

V+N+PREP/ADV,
V+ADV+N,
V+PRON+PREP/ADV

5 If you **sink** money **in** a product or project, you provide money for it, hoping to get a profit later. EG *Enormous sums of capital had to be sunk in a modern building... Fired by his enthusiasm, I sank all our savings in a second-hand camera.*

V+N+PREP,
V+PRON+PREP

sink into. 1 If something **sinks into** the ground, water, or other substance, it moves downwards and deeper into it. EG *The weight will sink into the wax... Her chair, her cello, and she herself were sinking into the sand... I prefer to sink the rod tip well into the water.*

V+PREP,
V+N+PREP,
V+PRON+PREP:
ERGATIVE

2 If you **sink into** a chair, a bed, or other soft furniture, you sit in it or lie on it and let your body relax so that you are completely supported by it. EG *Floyd sank into a comfortable leather chair... ...sinking deeper and deeper into the cushions... She sank herself, with evident relief, into a soft armchair.*

V+PREP,
V+REFL+PREP

3 If you **sink** something sharp **into** something solid, you cause it to pierce the surface and go into the solid. EG *She sank her teeth so*

V+N+PREP,
V+PRON+PREP,
V+PREP:
ERGATIVE

deeply into his finger that he loosened his grip... The cat's long claws
sank into the shoulder of Hallam's suit.

4 If you **sink into** a state or mood, especially a dull or inactive one,   v+PREP
you pass gradually into it. EG He sinks into a period of extreme
depression... I sank into sleep with a sigh of satisfaction... The poor
man sinks further into debt.

5 If you **sink** money **into** a business or project, you spend money on   v+N+PREP,
it in the hope of making more money. EG He's going to sink a lot of   v+PRON+PREP
money into that theatre group... No company is likely to sink large
sums into such a poor investment. ● **Plough into** means almost the
same as **sink into**.

sip, sips, sipping, sipped

sip at. If you **sip at** a drink or a container, you drink a small amount   v+PREP
at a time. EG Sandra decides to sip at her drink and behave as if
nothing were wrong... He sipped compulsively at a plastic mug of
cheap machine coffee.

siphon, siphons, siphoning, siphoned

Siphon is also spelled **syphon**.

siphon off. 1 If you **siphon off** a liquid, you get it out of a container   v+N+ADV,
through a tube using atmospheric pressure. EG Then you siphon the   v+ADV+N,
water off... Claude pushed it out of the garage, after siphoning off a   v+PRON+ADV
little gas from the family's second car... If you want a sweet cider,
syphon it off without disturbing the sediment.

2 If you **siphon off** money or other resources from a source or   v+N+ADV,
supply, you separate or remove them from the rest, often in order to   v+ADV+N,
use them for a purpose for which they were not intended. EG Money   v+PRON+ADV
being poured into scientific work should be syphoned off for this
purpose... ...strategically placed to siphon off trade from both
towns... Substantial numbers of students should be siphoned off to
the Junior Colleges.

sit, sits, sitting, sat

sit about. See sit around.

sit around. If you **sit around, about** or **round,** you stay in the same   v+ADV,
place and do very little except sit. EG The rest of us sat around   v+PREP:
happily in the hotel dining room... We sat about drinking wine...   USUALLY+A
They sit round and discuss the results... All I ever did was sit around
the house reading.

sit back. 1 If you **sit back,** you lean backwards so that the back of   v+ADV:
your body is supported by something and you can sit more comfort-   USUALLY+A
ably. EG He sat back and took a deep breath... She sits back in her
chair... The little Bushman was sitting back against a wall.

2 If you **sit back** while something is happening or while other people   v+ADV:
are doing something, you deliberately do not become involved in it.   USUALLY
EG We cannot afford just to sit back and wait for the next industrial   WITH and+VERB
crisis... Maureen was sitting back and letting Kate get on with it...
All they have to do is sit back and enjoy the fun.

sit by. If you **sit by** while something is happening, especially   v+ADV
something that you think is wrong, you allow it to happen and do not
do anything about it. EG ...those who sit idly by while you slave over a
hot stove... The two remaining members of the committee sat by
half dozing... I felt I couldn't sit by and see you deceived... You don't
sit by and watch a small child destroy something. ● **Stand by** means
almost the same as **sit by**.

sit down. 1 If you **sit down** or **sit** yourself **down,** you lower your   v+ADV,
body until you are sitting on something. EG We were both looking for   v+REFL+ADV:
a place to sit down... He sat down on the edge of the bed... After a bit   ALSO+A/to-INF

we all sat down to tea... She sat herself down beside me. ● **Stand up** means the opposite of **sit down.** ▸ If you have a **sit-down,** you sit   N SING
down and rest for a short time. EG *When we got to Firle Beacon we had a bit of a sit down.* ▸ A **sit-down** meal is a large or formal meal   ADJECTIVE
eaten while sitting at a table. EG *...a snack bar where you go when there is not time for a sit-down meal before a theatre.* ▸ A **sit-down**   ADJECTIVE,
strike or a **sit-down** is a strike or protest in which people sit down in   N COUNT
their workplace or in a public place and refuse to move until they get what they are asking for. EG *...staging sit-down strikes that paralysed the traffic... ...civil rights marches and demonstrations, sit-downs, rent and rate strikes.*

2 If you **sit** someone **down,** you make them sit down, by persuasion,   V+PRON+ADV,
force, or by placing them in a sitting position because they are   V+N+ADV
unable to do it by themselves. EG *I helped him to the door and sat him down on a convenient seat... I sat Kate down and pointed the rifle at her head.*

3 If you **sit down** and do something, you spend a lot of time and   V+ADV:
effort doing it, in order to try to achieve something. EG *They are not*   WITH and+VERB
willing to sit down and negotiate... I sat down and wrote my first book... The bright ones will sit down and tackle the work necessary.

sit for. **1** If you **sit for** an artist, a photographer, a painting, or a   V+PREP
photograph, you place yourself in a particular position so that the artist can paint your picture or the photographer can take your photograph. EG *She had sat for painters like Rossetti... I have sat for my portrait before.*

2 If you **sit for** an examination, you do the things that are required   V+PREP
by the institution that organizes it, such as answering questions or doing practical tests. EG *Ash never sat for an examination again... Keynes sat for the Civil Service examinations and did badly.*

sit in. **1** If you **sit in** on a meeting or similar event, you are allowed   V+ADV:
to be present but are not expected to take part. EG *He suggested that*   USUALLY+A/on
Kissinger be invited to come over from Georgetown and sit in on the meeting... I was asked by Asian friends to sit in on a conference... At meetings of the Midland Employers' Federation, I used to sit in as an observer... We will arrange for you to sit in with an experienced worker during sessions.

2 A **sit-in** is an event in which people protest against something by   N COUNT
staying in a place until they get what they want. EG *Since his success in ending the sit-in, Morris had become well-known... There was a sit-in in the administration building.*

sit on. **1** If you **sit on** a committee, board, or panel, you are an   V+PREP
official member of it. EG *She does a lot of welfare work and sits on various committees... Representatives of the workers should sit on the boards of directors... Women didn't sit on local juries.*

2 If you say that someone **is sitting on** a task or resource, you mean   V+PREP:
that they are not doing it quickly enough or using it enough. EG *He's*   HAS PASSIVE
been sitting on those applications for over a week... ...countries sitting on scarce and valuable commodities.

sit out. **1** If you **sit out** somewhere, you sit outside rather than inside   V+ADV:
a building. EG *Groups of people were sitting out on the grass during*   USUALLY+A
their lunch hour... We sat out at metal tables and drank white wine... They'd sit out there in the sun and watch.

2 If you **sit out** an event or a period of time, you wait for it to finish,   V+ADV+N,
rather than continuing with what you were doing. EG *Don tried to*   V+PRON+ADV:
persuade him to sit out the night there... ...spending two more days   NO PASSIVE
sitting out the bad weather.*

3 If you are at a dance and **sit out,** you do not dance, but sit at the   V+ADV side of the room; an old-fashioned use. EG *In the old days a girl could go to a dance and sit out... We'll be able to sit out together, then.*

sit over. 1 If you **sit over** an object or activity, you spend a long   v+PREP time occupied with it or doing it. EG *Tim and Gertrude were sitting over a long lunch... We sat over it for the rest of the evening.*

2 If you **sit over** someone, you watch them very carefully, for   v+PREP example because they are ill or because you want to make sure that they do not do anything wrong. EG *Fanny tried to make him drink, sat over him.*

sit round. See sit around.

sit through. If you **sit through** an event or period of time, especial-   v+PREP ly an unpleasant one, you stay until it is finished. EG *The professor sat through the entire monologue with growing impatience... I've sat through many weary hours as a delegate.*

sit up. 1 If you **sit up,** you move into an upright sitting position when   v+ADV you have been leaning back or lying down. EG *I tried to sit up to take off my jacket... The baby was sitting up unaided... Marie is awake now and sits up in the seat.* ▶ **Sit-ups** are an exercise in which you   N COUNT repeatedly move from lying down on the floor to a sitting position. EG *We did all the exercises with the class, push-ups, sit-ups, knee bending... Sit-ups are an advanced exercise for athletic training.*

2 If you **sit up** at night, you do not go to bed although it is very late.   v+ADV EG *She had sat up all night... Ellen would sit up working on his plans and drawings... Breaking the bedtime rules by sitting up far too late.* ● **Stay up** means almost the same as **sit up.**

3 If something makes you **sit up,** it makes you suddenly pay   v+ADV attention to what is happening. EG *The whole audience began to sit up and take notice... Right now you sit up and listen.*

size, sizes, sizing, sized

size up. If you **size up** people or situations, you look at them or think   v+N+ADV, about them, in order to judge them in some way. EG *We went over to*   v+PRON+ADV *size up our potential rivals... ...a man who could size up a chaotic situation... He had sized me up wrongly.* ● **Weigh up** means almost the same as **size up.**

skate, skates, skating, skated

skate around. See skate over.

skate over. If you **skate over, round,** or **around** a subject or   v+PREP: problem, you avoid discussing it or dealing fully with it, because you   HAS PASSIVE find it too difficult or embarrassing. EG *Girls' books skate over the technicalities of adult life... He skated warily round the subject once or twice... Women prefer to skate around the issue of sexual preference.* ● **Skirt round** means almost the same as **skate round,** and **evade** is a more formal word.

skate round. See skate over.

sketch, sketches, sketching, sketched

sketch in. 1 If someone who is drawing **sketches in** something, they   v+ADV+N, add it quickly and roughly to the drawing, usually before deciding   v+PRON+ADV, whether to keep it, rub it out, or change it. EG *...a huge sign,*   v+N+ADV *CALDERWOOD'S, that the architects had sketched in at the entrance... Scylla rapidly sketched in England, adding Ireland off to the left.*

2 If you **sketch in** an idea or fact, you add a few details about it, but   v+ADV+N, do not deal with it fully. EG *Here it is only necessary to sketch in the*   v+PRON+ADV, *broad outlines of the reform... I'm going to sketch in a bit of the*   v+N+ADV *background by way of introduction.*

sketch out. 1 If someone who is drawing **sketches out** something,   v+ADV+N,

they draw all the main features, but do not put in the details. EG *With* V+PRON+ADV,
V+N+ADV
a pencil and ruler he sketches out the route.
2 If you **sketch out** an idea, situation, or incident, you give a brief, V+ADV+N,
V+PRON+ADV,
V+N+ADV
general description of it, not including the details. EG *We will just*
sketch out the outline of the two systems... I'll just sketch out what
happened... The background to this incident is sketched out by
Oliver Goldsmith. ● **Outline** is a more formal word for **sketch out**.

skim, skims, skimming, skimmed

skim off. If you **skim off** a substance which is floating on the top of V+ADV+N,
V+N+ADV,
V+PRON+ADV
a liquid, you remove it. EG *Skim off the froth, and strain the beer into*
a wooden barrel... Skim the scum off from time to time.

skim through. If you **skim through** a piece of writing, you read V+PREP
through it quickly without looking at the details. EG *I thought I would*
skim through a few of the letters. ● **Flick through** means almost the
same as **skim through**.

skimp, skimps, skimping, skimped

skimp on. If you **skimp on** something, you use less time, money, or V+PREP:
HAS PASSIVE
material for it than you really need, so that the result is unsatisfac-
tory. EG *Never skimp on your warm-up exercises... She was skimping*
on food.

skirt, skirts, skirting, skirted

skirt around. 1 If you **skirt around** or **round** something, you go V+PREP
around the edge or the outside of it. EG *They skirted round a bus...*
The path skirts around a large pond.
2 If you **skirt around** or **round** a subject or question, you avoid V+PREP:
HAS PASSIVE
dealing with it, usually because it is difficult or controversial. EG *We*
spent a lot of time skirting around the main issues... Leading figures
accused NATO of trying to skirt round the Treaty.
skirt round. See **skirt around**.

skive, skives, skiving, skived

skive off. If you **skive off** your work or studies, you avoid doing V+ADV,
V+PREP
your work by staying away from the place where you should be
working; an informal expression. EG *He's skiving off again... ...skiving*
off school.

slacken, slackens, slackening, slackened

slacken off. If something **slackens off**, it becomes slower, less V+ADV
active, or less intense. EG *Business finally slackened off... ...when the*
tourist boom slackens off. ● **Slow down** and **ease off** mean almost
the same as **slacken off**.

slag, slags, slagging, slagged

slag off. If you **slag** someone **off**, you criticize them in an unpleas- V+N+ADV,
V+ADV+N,
V+PRON+ADV
ant way; an informal expression. EG *He's always slagging people off*
behind their backs... The only reason he won the Nobel prize was
because he slagged off Russia.

slam, slams, slamming, slammed

slam down. 1 If you **slam** something **down**, you put it down with a V+N+ADV,
V+ADV+N,
V+PRON+ADV
lot of force, often because you are angry. EG *She slammed the jug*
down onto the tray... ...slamming the lid down on my fingers.
2 If you **slam down** the phone, you end a conversation suddenly by V+ADV+N,
V+N+ADV
putting the receiver back down, often because you are angry. EG *She*
slammed down the phone... ...She was almost moved to slam down
the receiver... That's one good reason to slam the phone down.

slap, slaps, slapping, slapped

slap around. If someone **slaps** you **around**, they hit you a few V+N+ADV,
V+PRON+ADV times. EG *I'll just slap him around a little.* ● **Rough up** means almost the same as **slap around.**

slap down. 1 If you **slap** something **down,** you put it forcefully onto a surface, making a loud noise. EG *She shuffled the cards loudly and slapped them down... She slapped down a thick white cup and saucer.*
V+N+ADV, V+ADV+N, V+PRON+ADV

2 If you **slap** someone **down,** you speak to them unkindly or harshly, usually in order to prevent them from doing or saying something. EG *Men are afraid to be romantic because women slap them down... Rather than slapping down newcomers, we ought to be encouraging them.*
V+PRON+ADV, V+ADV+N, V+N+ADV

slap on. If you **slap** a substance **on,** you put it carelessly onto something. EG *I smear the toast with butter, then slap on a spoonful of marmalade... You mix the paint and just slap it on the cleaned metal.*
V+ADV+N, V+N+ADV/PREP, V+PRON+ADV/PREP

slave, slaves, slaving, slaved

slave away. If you **slave away,** you work hard at something for a long time. EG *Here I am, slaving away, running a house and family... Joseph slaved away at cutting the grass.* ● **Slog away** means almost the same as **slave away.**
V+ADV

sleep, sleeps, sleeping, slept

sleep around. If someone **sleeps around,** they have sex with a lot of different people rather than having a sexual relationship with only one person ; an informal expression used showing disapproval. EG *I did everything I could to hurt her, including sleeping around... Young people today do not sleep around, drink alcohol, or smoke, according to a survey published today.*
V+ADV

sleep in. If you **sleep in,** you stay asleep in the morning for longer than you usually do; used in British English. EG *...the guilt I felt if I slept in.* ● **Lie in** means almost the same as **sleep in.**
V+ADV

sleep off. If you **sleep off** the effects of eating or drinking too much, you recover from it by sleeping. EG *...sleeping off his drinks in one of the wicker chairs... We went back to our room to sleep it off... He claimed he was drunk and was looking for somewhere to sleep it off.*
V+ADV+N, V+N+ADV, V+PRON+ADV

sleep on. If you **sleep on** an idea, you delay making a decision about it until the next day. EG *Are you sure you don't want to sleep on it? You may have changed your mind by tomorrow.*
V+PREP

sleep out. If you **sleep out,** you sleep outdoors. EG *There were all kinds of reasons why they slept out... The inspector went round asking why the men sleep out in this bitter weather.*
V+ADV

sleep through. If you **sleep through** a noise or disturbance, you fail to wake up in spite of it. EG *The girl slept through everything.*
V+PREP

sleep together. 1 If two people **sleep together,** they have a sexual relationship, especially when they are not married to each other. EG *They were presumably sleeping together... She assumed that we should sleep together.*
V+ADV

2 You can also say that two people **sleep together** when they sleep in the same bed or room. EG *He and his mother slept together in her bed until he was nearly four..... The children sleep together to keep warm.*
V+ADV

sleep with. 1 If you **sleep with** someone, you have sex with them, especially when you are not married to them. EG *I heard all the gossip about who was sleeping with whom... Do you think I should sleep with David?*
V+PREP

2 To **sleep with** someone also means to sleep in the same bed or room as them. EG *The baby sleeps with mother.*
V+PREP

slice, slices, slicing, sliced

slice off. If you **slice** something **off,** you remove it by cutting it. EG *She sliced off another chunk... The bottom half of the main hull was sliced off and replaced with a new section.*
V+ADV+N, V+N+ADV, V+PRON+ADV

slice up. If you **slice** something **up,** you cut it into smaller pieces. EG *Surely we could feed ourselves without slicing up animals... ...slicing the bread up... This area was sliced up to suit the developers.*
V+ADV+N, V+N+ADV, V+PRON+ADV

slick, slicks, slicking, slicked

slick down. If you **slick** your hair **down,** you make it smooth and shiny by putting water or hair oil on it. EG *Their hair was neatly combed and slicked down.* ● **Smooth down** means almost the same as **slick down.**
V+N+ADV, V+ADV+N, V+PRON+ADV

slip, slips, slipping, slipped

slip away. 1 If you **slip away,** you leave a place quietly, often so that people do not notice you. EG *I hope we can slip away before she notices... I slipped away down a side street.* ● **Slip off** means almost the same as **slip away.**
V+ADV

2 If something **slips away,** it disappears gradually or without effort. EG *You can feel the stresses and strains of the day slipping away as you run... I feel my life is slipping away to no purpose.*
V+ADV

slip by. 1 If you say that time or an event **slips by,** you mean that it passes and so is gone. EG *We should not allow the time to slip by without making renewed efforts... The occasion slipped by... The days slipped by without any sign of the promised spell of fine weather.*
V+ADV

2 To **slip by** also means to go past someone or something quietly, so that people do not notice. EG *The canoe underneath slips by quite slowly... I managed to slip by him.*
V+ADV, V+PREP

slip down. 1 To **slip down** means to fall down by sliding. EG *She slipped down... She pulled up her sock which had slipped down.*
V+ADV

2 If you say that a drink **slips down** easily, you mean that it is pleasant to drink and you could drink a lot of it; an informal use. EG *The beer slipped down very easily.*
V+ADV

slip in. 1 If you **slip** something **in,** you put it somewhere or include it quietly, often without telling anyone. EG *We thought it was time to slip in the odd phoney headline... We prevented the bartender from slipping in any vodka.*
V+ADV+N, V+N+ADV, V+PRON+ADV

2 If you **slip in,** you go into a place quietly, often so that people do not notice you. EG *You should be able to slip in unnoticed by him... They slip in and out of the office.*
V+ADV

slip into. 1 If you **slip into** a place, you go into it quietly, often so that people do not notice you. EG *He must have slipped into the house... Cordelia slipped into the kitchen.*
V+PREP

2 If you **slip** something **into** a place, you put it there quietly, often so that people do not notice. EG *The man in white picked the letter up and slipped it into his jacket pocket.*
V+PRON+PREP, V+N+PREP

3 If you **slip into** a piece of clothing, you put it on quickly; an informal use. EG *I slipped into my pyjamas.*
V+PREP

4 If you **slip into** a particular situation or way of behaving, that situation gradually starts happening, or you begin behaving in that way. EG *He tries to slip into the parental role... The country was slipping into recession... We frequently slip into the habit of telling lies.*
V+PREP

slip off. 1 If you **slip off,** you leave a place quietly, often so that people do not notice you. EG *Then slip off and ask the usherette for*
V+ADV

the manager... The ship slipped off to a Spanish port. ● **Slip away** means almost the same as **slip off.**

2 To **slip off** something means to fall off it by slipping. EG *The fruit knife slipped off the table... Soon the thatch begins to slip off.*   V+PREP, V+ADV

3 If you **slip off** a piece of clothing, you take it off quickly. EG *She slipped off her dress... I slipped off my coat, poured myself a drink, and tried to look relaxed.*   V+ADV+N, V+N+ADV, V+PRON+ADV

slip on. If you **slip on** a piece of clothing, you put it on quickly. EG *He slipped on his shoes and went out... Just let me slip on my jacket and I'll come with you.*   V+ADV+N, V+N+ADV, V+PRON+ADV

slip out. 1 If you **slip out** of a place, you leave it for a short while, usually quietly. EG *I slipped out to phone the police... I just slipped out for a packet of fags... She had slipped out of her seat and escaped.*   V+ADV: USUALLY+A/of

2 If you say that a piece of information **slipped out,** you mean that you told it to someone without meaning to. EG *I'm sorry. It slipped out.*   V+ADV

3 If you **slip out** of a piece of clothing, you take it off quickly; an informal use. EG *She slips out of her working clothes.*   V+ADV: USUALLY+of

slip up. If you **slip up,** you make a mistake; an informal expression. EG *We must have slipped up somewhere... She's slipped up in the calculations; I don't think it can be as much as that.* ▶ A **slip-up** is a mistake, especially one that is small or unimportant; an informal word. EG *There must have been a slip-up... A similar slip-up occurred later in the week.*   V+ADV

    N COUNT

slog, slogs, slogging, slogged

slog away. If you **slog away** at something, you continue to work hard at it for a long time. EG *The second group are slogging away at revision... Having got the job, he likes to really slog away at it.* ● **Slave away** and **beaver away** mean almost the same as **slog away.**   V+ADV: USUALLY+at

slog through. If you **slog through** something difficult, you continue moving through it or working at it with a lot of effort. EG *He preferred to slog through long lists of spelling... ...slogging through twenty feet of snow.* ● **Plough through** means almost the same as slog through.   V+PREP: HAS PASSIVE

slop, slops, slopping, slopped

slop about. See slop around.

slop around. If you **slop around** or **about,** you spend time in a place being lazy and doing nothing. EG *...slopping around in the university for a year or two... ...inviting us to slop around all afternoon.* ● **Slouch about** means almost the same as **slop around.**   V+ADV

slop out. To **slop out** in a prison means to empty the buckets that the prisoners use as toilets. EG *...first thing in the morning, when they are slopping out... Slopping out at Reading prison continues to be disgusting, the Board says.*   V+ADV

slop over. If a liquid **slops over,** it spills over the edge of the container it is in. EG *Some of the milk slopped over onto the grass... ...made the rain in the gutters slop over and stream down the glass... The stew slopped over the container.*   V+ADV, V+PREP

slope, slopes, sloping, sloped

slope off. If you **slope off,** you go away quickly and quietly, as if you are trying to escape or avoid something; an informal expression. EG *I have a feeling that most of them have sloped off... He'll be sloping off home to his supper.*   V+ADV

slot, slots, slotting, slotted

slot into. 1 If you **slot** someone or something **into** a schedule, scheme, or organization, you find a place for them within it. EG *The*   V+N+PREP, V+PRON+PREP, V+PREP: ERGATIVE

unions are slotted into the state apparatus... All the components of a
full terrestrial ecosystem begin to slot into place.

2 If you **slot** something **into** a narrow opening, you put it carefully   v+n+prep,
into the opening. eg *They slotted the papers neatly back into the*   v+pron+prep,
file... The woman took the gun and showed how the cylinder slotted   v+prep:
into the barrel.   ERGATIVE

slouch, slouches, slouching, slouched

slouch about. If you **slouch about** or **around,** you spend time being   v+adv
lazy and not doing anything. eg *She slouched about in a dressing*
gown. ● **Slop around** means almost the same as **slouch about.**
slouch around. See **slouch about.**

slough, sloughs, sloughing, sloughed

slough off. 1 If you **slough off** something that you no longer need,   v+adv+n
you get rid of it; a formal use. eg *Women are less willing than their*
husbands to slough off a friendship after a move.

2 If an animal such as a snake **sloughs off** its outer skin, it goes   v+adv+n,
through a natural process which causes this skin to come off. eg *A*   v+n+adv,
new skin grows beneath the old which is then sloughed off... As the   v+pron+adv
dead cells are sloughed off, the skin becomes red and irritated.
● **Shed** means almost the same as **slough off.**

slow, slows, slowing, slowed

slow down. 1 If something **slows down** or if you **slow** it **down,** it   v+adv,
starts to move or happen more slowly. eg *Economic growth has*   v+adv+n,
slowed down dramatically... The van slowed down... Governments   v+n+adv,
have sought to slow down the inflationary spiral... Harold slowed the   v+pron+adv:
car down... We did not stop his southward advance but did much to   ERGATIVE
slow it down. ● **Slow up** means almost the same as **slow down,** and
speed up means the opposite. ▶ A **slowdown** is a reduction in speed   n count
or activity. eg *He projects a slowdown in the rate of expansion of*
world trade. ▶ A **slowdown** is also a protest by workers in which   n count
they deliberately work slowly and cause problems for their employers; used in American English. eg *There were peace marches, rent*
strikes, and work slowdowns.

2 If someone **slows down,** they become less active, when they have   v+adv
been working very hard or have been very energetic. eg *He needs to*
slow down a little or he'll get an ulcer. ● **Relax** means almost the
same as **slow down.**

slow up. If something **slows up** or if you **slow** it **up,** it starts to move   v+n+adv,
or happen more slowly. eg *Steep hills slow them up... Instability*   v+adv+n,
slows up a country's development... The resistor slows the current   v+pron+adv,
up... 'Car broken down?' bawled the driver as he slowed up. ● **Slow**   v+adv:
down means almost the same as **slow up,** and **speed up** means the   ERGATIVE
opposite.

smack, smacks, smacking, smacked

smack of. If something **smacks of** something unpleasant, it is   v+prep
similar and it reminds you of it. eg *Any literature other than*
romantic novels smacked to her of school... ...secret consultations
which smacked of a cover-up. ● **Savour of** means almost the same
as **smack of.**

smarten, smartens, smartening, smartened

smarten up. To **smarten up** a person or place means to make   v+adv,
them look neater and tidier. eg *We could smarten up a bit and then*   v+adv+n,
go... He resists every suggestion for smartening up his personal   v+n+adv,
appearance... The New Electric Cinema has been smartened up.   v+pron+adv:
● **Spruce up** means almost the same as **smarten up.**   ERGATIVE

smash, smashes, smashing, smashed

smash down. If you **smash down** something such as a door, you hit it and break it so that it falls onto the ground. EG *I'm going to smash this door down if you don't come out... King Kong lurched around smashing down skyscrapers.*
  V+N+ADV,
V+ADV+N,
V+PRON+ADV

smash in. To **smash** something **in** means to hit it very hard so that it breaks and often so that the pieces fall inwards. EG *We'll smash the window in... This was what had been used to smash in the back of Stryker's skull.*
  V+N+ADV,
V+ADV+N,
V+PRON+ADV

smash up. If you **smash** something **up**, you hit it so that it breaks into many pieces and is completely destroyed. EG *He started smashing up all the furniture... Six students smashed up a car... They smashed the place up.* ▸ A **smash-up** is a bad car crash; an informal word. EG *We saw a terrible smash-up on the way home.*
  V+ADV+N,
V+N+ADV,
V+PRON+ADV

  N COUNT

smell, smells, smelling, smelled/smelt

smell of. 1 If something **smells of** a particular thing, it has a smell like that thing. EG *The room was hot and smelled of hospitals... She smelled of soap and talcum powder.*
  V+PREP

2 You can say that something **smells of** an unpleasant quality when it seems to have that quality. EG *Such an action would have smelt, to her, of defeat.* ● **Smack of** and **savour of** mean almost the same as **smell of.**
  V+PREP

smell out. 1 If you **smell** someone **out**, you discover where they are even though they may be hiding or doing something in secret. EG *Maggie could smell out evildoers and cast spells on them.* ● **Root out** means almost the same as **smell out.**
  V+ADV+N,
V+N+ADV,
V+PRON+ADV

2 If an animal **smells** something **out**, it finds where it is by following its smell. EG *We'll take the dog—she'll smell those rabbits out.*
  V+N+ADV,
V+ADV+N,
V+PRON+ADV

smoke, smokes, smoking, smoked

smoke out. 1 If you **smoke out** a person or animal, you force them to come out of a place by filling it with smoke. EG *...smoking out a bees' nest.*
  V+ADV+N,
V+N+ADV,
V+PRON+ADV

2 If you **smoke** someone **out**, you manage to find them or force them to reveal themselves. EG *The governor's staff yesterday claimed they had smoked out Mr. Bush from his isolation... You've got to smoke him out like a rat or a snake.*
  V+ADV+N,
V+PRON+ADV,
V+N+ADV

smooth, smooths, smoothing, smoothed

smooth down. If you **smooth down** your hair or your clothes, you press them with your hands to make them flat. EG *Gertrude smoothed down her dress... She smoothed down her short blonde hair.* ● **Flatten** means almost the same as **smooth down.**
  V+ADV+N,
V+PRON+ADV,
V+N+ADV

smooth out. 1 If you **smooth out** a surface, you press it down with something in order to make it flat. EG *Martha smoothed out the newspaper on the table... Using the flat side, smooth out any rough surfaces.* ● **Flatten** means almost the same as **smooth out.**
  V+ADV+N,
V+PRON+ADV

2 If you **smooth out** a process or situation, you make it more even and regular. EG *Daily fluctuations in power output could be smoothed out... We need more cash to smooth out the monthly outgoings.* ● **Even out** means almost the same as **smooth out.**
  V+ADV+N,
V+PRON+ADV

smooth over. If you **smooth over** a problem or difficulty, you talk about it in a way that makes it seem less serious and easier to deal with. EG *I tried to smooth over the awkwardness of this first meeting... He was grateful for her help in smoothing over what could have become an embarrassing scene.* ● **Gloss over** means almost the same as **smooth over.**
  V+ADV+N,
V+PRON+ADV

snap, snaps, snapping, snapped

snap out. If speech or a sound **snaps out**, it is heard suddenly and loudly. EG *The sound snapped out in the night like a pistol shot... 'Halt!' her voice snapped out.*
V+ADV

snap out of. If you **snap out of** a sad mood or a moment of concentration, you quickly change by forcing yourself to act more cheerfully or sociably. If you tell someone to **snap out of it,** you want them to stop being being sad or depressed; an informal expression. EG *I snapped out of this melancholy the moment a friend called... 'Do you mind if I ask what you live on?' Abruptly I snapped out of my calculations. 'Yes, I do.'... She's had this before and has snapped right out of it.*
V+ADV+PREP,
V+ADV+PREP+*it*

snap up. 1 If you **snap** something **up,** you buy it quickly while it is cheap before anyone else can buy it; an informal use. EG *U.S. and European pension funds have been snapping up shares of steel companies... He snapped it up for £2,000 after the British Museum had felt it beyond their resources... All these houses were snapped up as soon as they were offered for sale.*
V+ADV+N,
V+PRON+ADV,
V+N+ADV

2 If you **snap up** a chance or opportunity, you take advantage of it quickly before it becomes too late; an informal use. EG *There was a time when Morris would have snapped up a chance like this.*
V+ADV+N,
V+PRON+ADV,
V+N+ADV

snarl, snarls, snarling, snarled

snarl up. When traffic **is snarled up,** the road is blocked so that the traffic cannot move freely. When a process **is snarled up,** it becomes blocked or overworked so that it cannot continue smoothly. EG *The traffic was snarled up due to riots on the campus... He had eaten a bowl of cereals, drunk half a cup of coffee and was snarled up in a traffic jam at the roundabout... The distributors are snarled up.*
V+N+ADV:
USUALLY PASSIVE

snatch, snatches, snatching, snatched

snatch away. If you **snatch** something **away** from someone, you take it from them forcefully with a sudden movement. EG *Then he snatched away his coat, which I was still holding for him... He suddenly reached over and snatched it away from me... I don't mean that you have to snatch the bottle away.* ● **Grab** means almost the same as **snatch away.**
V+PRON+ADV,
V+ADV+N,
V+N+ADV:
ALSO+*from*

snatch up. If you **snatch** something **up,** you pick it up very quickly and with a violent movement. EG *I snatched up Otto's glass just as it began to topple off the table... She snatched up an oil-can and threw it all on the fire... He snatched her up as if she were made of straw.* ● **Grab** means almost the same as **snatch up.**
V+ADV+N,
V+PRON+ADV

sniff, sniffs, sniffing, sniffed

sniff out. If you **sniff** something **out,** you discover it by looking for it, often by guessing where it might be; an informal expression. EG *Gordon and his two friends sniffed out some lovely little quiet beaches... He'd told me that he was sniffing out more books.* ● **Nose out** means almost the same as **sniff out.**
V+ADV+N,
V+PRON+ADV

snow, snows, snowing, snowed

snow in. If you are **snowed in,** you are prevented from leaving your house or travelling anywhere because there is so much snow on the ground. EG *'Perhaps we'll be snowed in for a week!' cried Liz gleefully.*
PASSIVE:
V+ADV

snow under. If you are **snowed under,** you have more pieces of work to deal with than you can manage, especially paperwork. EG *I've been snowed under by reports from over 200 organisations... At*
V+PRON+ADV,
V+N+ADV:
USUALLY PASSIVE

*present we're snowed under with an irrational expansion of blind
data-gathering.*

snow up. If you **are snowed up,** you are prevented from leaving
your house or travelling anywhere because there is so much snow
on the ground. EG *Were you snowed up in Dawlish at all?... We were
snowed up for a week.*

PASSIVE:
V+ADV

snuff, snuffs, snuffing, snuffed

snuff out. 1 If someone **snuffs out** something such as a rebellion or
disagreement, they put an end to it by using violence or other
oppressive means. EG *In the past the voice of dissension has been
quickly snuffed out.* ● **Crush** means almost the same as **snuff out.**

V+ADV+N:
USUALLY PASSIVE

2 If you **snuff out** a candle or a flame, you put it out by pinching it
with your fingers or by putting a cover over it for a few seconds. EG
She snuffed out the candle and closed her eyes. ● **Extinguish** is a
formal word for **snuff out.**

V+ADV+N,
V+PRON+ADV,
V+N+ADV

snuggle, snuggles, snuggling, snuggled

snuggle down. If you **snuggle down,** you move deeper into your
bedclothes in order to get warm and comfortable; an informal
expression. EG *We got sleeping bags out and snuggled down... Just as
I was snuggling down I heard a scratching sound on the tent door.*

V+ADV

snuggle up. If you **snuggle up** to someone, you settle yourself into
a warm, comfortable position by sitting or lying so that your body is
against theirs; an informal expression. EG *Sally snuggled up to him...
Geraldine snuggled up against him on the front seat.* ● **Cuddle up**
means almost the same as **snuggle up.**

V+ADV:
USUALLY+A

soak, soaks, soaking, soaked

soak in. If you **soak** yourself **in** a particular subject, you study it
very intensely in order to learn as much about it as possible. EG *I
soaked myself in the works of Dickens and George Eliot.*

V+REFL+PREP

soak off. If you **soak** something **off** a surface, you remove it by
using water to loosen it. EG *He's going to soak all the paint off it...
They can soak them off with pieces of wet cotton wool... None of the
paint had soaked off.*

V+N+ADV,
V+PRON+ADV,
V+ADV

soak through. If someone or something **is soaked through,** they
are completely wet, usually because they have been outside in the
pouring rain. EG *By morning, their gear was soaked through.*

PASSIVE:
V+ADV

soak up. 1 If something **soaks up** a liquid, it gradually absorbs the
liquid. EG *The parched soil soaked up what seemed like a huge
volume of water... Leave it for about 5 minutes during which time
the granules will soak up the water.* ● **Absorb** means almost the
same as **soak up.**

V+ADV+N,
V+PRON+ADV,
V+N+ADV

2 If you **soak up** sunshine, you sit or lie for a long time in the sun
because you enjoy it; an informal use. EG *She sat on the edge of her
seat, leaning back to soak up the sun... She liked to soak up the
Mediterranean sunshine.*

V+ADV+N:
NO PASSIVE

3 If something **soaks up** money or resources, it uses more than you
consider reasonable or practical. EG *Population growth soaked up 70
per cent of the increase in national incomes... Expanded production
is soaked up by worsening terms of trade.*

V+ADV+N,
V+PRON+ADV

sob, sobs, sobbing, sobbed

sob out. If someone **sobs out** something, they try to say it while
they are crying. EG *They were scarcely speaking to each other
except to sob out some extra insult... He sobbed out the story of what
had happened... She sobbed out some of her anxieties and troubles.*

V+ADV+N:
NO PASSIVE

sober, sobers, sobering, sobered

sober up. When someone who is drunk **sobers up,** the effect of the alcohol disappears and they become sober again. EG *When you sober up you may be ashamed of what you've done... I caught Mrs Mawne's eye and sobered up almost immediately... He'll have to be sobered up, and quickly.*

V+ADV,
V+PRON+ADV:
ERGATIVE

sod, sods, sodding, sodded

sod off. Sod off is an insulting and offensive way of telling someone to go away.

IMPERATIVE:
V+ADV

soften, softens, softening, softened

soften up. 1 If you **soften** someone **up,** you praise them or try to please them because you want to ask them to do something for you which they do not really want to do. EG *I wondered if there was any hope of softening him up... The Ambassador is also trying to soften up Velasco on the Cuban problem.* ● **Butter up** means almost the same as **soften up.**

V+PRON+ADV,
V+ADV+N

2 When soldiers or sailors **soften up** a target, they make a preliminary attack to weaken the target before the main attack is launched. EG *I watched two helicopters soften up a mountainside with their machine guns and bombs.*

V+ADV+N,
V+PRON+ADV

soldier, soldiers, soldiering, soldiered

soldier on. If you **soldier on,** you continue doing something and working hard at it, even though it is difficult and unpleasant. EG *You have to admire them as they soldier on smiling in the face of adversity... One simply soldiered on becoming older and balder.*

V+ADV

sop, sops, sopping, sopped

sop up. To **sop up** a liquid means to force it off a surface by using an absorbent cloth or material. EG *My bandage would sop it up all right.*

V+PRON+ADV,
V+ADV+N

sort, sorts, sorting, sorted

sort out. 1 If you **sort out** a group of things that are in a mess or are not ready, you arrange them so that they become organized or ready. EG *It took quite a while to sort out all our luggage... Sort them out alphabetically... Couldn't you have washed up and sorted the place out before coming down?... With Mum and Dad in one bedroom, the six of them had to sort themselves out in the remaining rooms for sleeping.... Mrs Kirk and I got everything sorted out.* ● **Arrange** means almost the same as **sort out.**

V+ADV+N,
V+PRON+ADV,
V+N+ADV,
V+REFL+ADV

2 If you **sort out** a group of things, you consider them carefully and divide them into categories that are clearly different from each other. EG *It was an intelligence test, intended to sort out the children capable of attempting the papers... Some secondary schools begin at once to sort out children who read with less confidence or skill... It is difficult to sort out fact from fiction.*

V+ADV+N,
V+N+ADV,
V+PRON+ADV:
ALSO+*from*

3 If you **sort out** a problem or misunderstanding, you deal with it and find a solution to it. EG *We'd just have to sort it out for ourselves... We have to sort things out between us... ...a network of affection and support within which we were able to sort out our personal problems... I've seen problems like this sort themselves out again and again.* ● **Resolve** is a more formal word for **sort out.**

V+PRON+ADV,
V+N+ADV,
V+ADV+N,
V+REFL+ADV

4 If you **sort** someone **out,** you punish them very forcefully or violently; a very informal use. EG *He was bigger and stronger than I was, and no doubt would have sorted me out very quickly had we actually come to blows.*

V+PRON+ADV,
V+N+ADV

sound, sounds, sounding, sounded

sound off. If you **sound off**, you express your opinions strongly and   v+ADV
loudly without being asked; a fairly informal expression. EG *On most
matters she's quite prepared to sound off without inhibition... He
found himself sounding off about the cost of living.*

sound out. 1 If you **sound** someone **out**, you ask them questions in   V+ADV+N,
order to find out their views, especially about what should or will   V+PRON+ADV,
happen in a particular situation. EG *Joining in gave me a chance to*   V+N+ADV
*sound out their attitudes... Kids at school were always sounding her
out about their chances of being moved to the top of the list... All the
members of the English Department who have been sounded out on
the subject suggested your name.*

2 When a noise **sounds out**, it can be heard clearly above all the   V+ADV
other sounds that are present. EG *The hooter sounded out like a
lighthouse foghorn... The ambulance klaxon sounds out as it drives
off.*

soup, soups, souping, souped

soup up. If you **soup up** a car, you make it more powerful by   V+ADV+N,
adjusting the engine or adding special parts; an informal expression.   V+PRON+ADV
EG *The boy who is lazy in class will spend hours souping up motor
engines.* ▸ A **souped-up** car has had its engine altered so that it is   ADJECTIVE
more powerful. EG *On weekends he drove a souped-up MG in the
California races.*

space, spaces, spacing, spaced

space out. 1 If you **space** things **out**, you arrange them so that they   V+ADV+N,
are not all grouped together, but have gaps or intervals of time   V+PRON+ADV,
between them. EG *We began to space out our meetings... This is a*   V+N+ADV
*rough copy which will give you the chance to space it out well...
These books should have large print well spaced out on the page.*

2 Someone who is **spaced out** cannot think clearly because they are   ADJECTIVE
under the influence of drugs; an informal expression. EG *I gathered
up my belongings and said good-bye to the women, even though
most were totally spaced out.*

spark, sparks, sparking, sparked

spark off. If one thing **sparks off** a state or event, it causes the   V+ADV+N,
state or event to exist or happen, often by accident rather than   V+PRON+ADV,
deliberately. EG *There was a risk that the decision would spark off a*   V+N+ADV
*conflict... His letter of praise and support at that time had sparked
off a friendship between the two men... Can they meet the demand
sparked off by the boom in TV video?*

speak, speaks, speaking, spoke, spoken

speak for. 1 If you **speak for** a group of people, you represent them   V+PREP
and explain their views. EG *We believe that in putting forward our
policies we are speaking for the majority of the British people.*

2 If you **speak for** an idea, a proposal, or a set of beliefs, you support   V+PREP
it by explaining it and saying what is good about it. EG *I spoke for
going south.* ● **Stand up for** means almost the same as **speak for.**

3 If you **speak for** yourself, you say what you think, even though you   V+PREP+REFL:
know that it is not what other people think. EG *Speak for yourself,*   ALSO IMPERATIVE
*Chas. I drive just to get from place to place... I'm only speaking for
myself, not for my colleagues.*

4 If something **speaks for** itself, it has qualities which are so   V+PREP
apparent that you can easily see what they are. EG *The facts in
Samsonov's case speak for themselves.*

5 If you say that someone is **spoken for**, you mean that they are   ADJECTIVE

married or already have a boyfriend or girlfriend; an informal
expression. EG *Sorry Jan. He's spoken for.*

speak out. If you **speak out**, you express your views forcefully and V+ADV:
publicly, especially in order to criticize or oppose something. EG ALSO+*against*
*Garrett wouldn't dare speak out against Byrne... He spoke out early
and clearly against the war in Vietnam... But neither Asquith nor
Grey spoke out in public to clear Haldane's name.* ▸ If you are ADJECTIVE
outspoken, you give your opinions about things openly and honestly,
even if they are likely to shock or offend people. EG *...an outspoken
critic of extremists.*

speak up. 1 If you **speak up** about something, you say publicly what V+ADV:
you believe, especially in support of a person or an idea. EG *Never be* USUALLY+*for*
*frightened of speaking up for your beliefs... The cricketers them-
selves should speak up in favour of non-racial cricket... Why do they
not speak up for themselves?*

2 If you **speak up,** you begin to speak more loudly. EG *Could you* V+ADV
please speak up. We can't hear you at the back.

speed, speeds, speeding, speeded

speed up. When something **speeds up** or when you **speed** it **up,** its V+ADV+N,
speed increases so that it moves or happens more quickly. EG *Bad* V+PRON+ADV,
housing and poverty speed up the breakdown of family life... You V+N+ADV,
can do some slower movements, then speed them up a bit... Making V+ADV:
notes in this way will enable you to speed up even more. ERGATIVE
● **Accelerate** is a more formal word for **speed up.**

spell, spells, spelling, spelled/spelt

spell out. 1 If you **spell** something **out,** you explain it in detail or in V+ADV+N,
a very clear way. EG *Let me try and spell out what I mean by that...* V+PRON+ADV,
But the doctor had merely been spelling it all out for us... The first V+N+ADV
person to spell this out was Alvin Toffler in his book Future Shock.
● **Explicate** is a more formal word for **spell out.**

2 If you **spell out** a word, you write or speak each letter in the word V+ADV+N,
one after the other. EG *We had to spell out the words we heard... At* V+N+ADV
*the head of the quay, dull brass letters spelled out LENINGRAD...
To communicate with her you have to spell words out on her hand.*

spew, spews, spewing, spewed

spew out. When a machine **spews** something **out,** it produces it V+ADV+N
very quickly; an informal expression. EG *More and more, airline
weather forecasts and flight plans were being spewed out by computers.*

spew up. If someone **spews up,** they vomit; a very informal V+ADV
expression. EG *He spewed up as soon as he got outside.* ● **Throw up**
means almost the same as **spew up.**

spice, spices, spicing, spiced

spice up. If you **spice up** something that you do or say, you make it V+N+ADV,
more exciting or lively. EG *John, not content with dragging up a story* V+PRON+ADV,
more dead than dated, has spiced it up with all kinds of innuendoes. V+ADV+N:
 ALSO+*with*

spill, spills, spilling, spilled/spilt

spill out. 1 When liquids or objects **spill out** of a container, they V+ADV:
splash, pour, or fall out of it. EG *Water spilled out of the vase... Be* USUALLY+*of*/A
careful, so that the contents don't spill out or break the fragile box.

2 You talk about people or things **spilling out** of a place when large V+ADV:
numbers of them come from it in a hurried, disorganized, or untidy ALSO+*of*
way. EG *...thousands of visitors who spilled out of the hotels and lined
the processional route... Chairs from the tavernas on either side of*

the street spill out until there is only a narrow pathway left. ● **Pour out** means almost the same as **spill out**.

3 If you **spill out** information or a secret, you tell it to someone in a hurried way. EG *He will talk to anyone and spill out his life story to a total stranger... He was tempted to spill out everything he had been thinking... ...the overwhelming urge to spill it all out and be done with it... The words just spill out.*

V+ADV+N,
V+PRON+ADV,
V+ADV:
ERGATIVE

spill over. **1** If the liquid in a container **spills over**, it flows or is accidentally poured over its edge. EG *...like a bucket full of water, almost spilling over... ...so startled that his steady hand trembled and some coffee spilt over the edge of his cup.*

V+ADV,
V+PREP

2 If people or things **spill over** from one place to another, there are too many of them to fit or stay in the first place. EG *These dark-suited figures were filling the pavements and spilling over into the roadways... Most of them live outside China but some spill over the northern and southern borders.* ▸ The **overspill** from an overcrowded city or place consists of the people or parts of it which do not fit in and so have to go somewhere else. EG *The overspill from Heathrow became concentrated on Gatwick... These flats are an overspill development..*

V+ADV+A,
V+PREP

N SING,
ADJECTIVE

3 If something in one situation **spills over** into another, it has an accidental or negative effect on it. EG *Any troubles at work could also spill over into your private life... ...hatred for Daniel's father, some of which always spilled over onto Daniel.*

V+ADV:
WITH+*into/onto*

spin, spins, spinning, spun

The form **span** is sometimes used in old-fashioned English as the past tense.

spin around. See **spin round**.

spin off. If a part of something **is spun off**, it is separated from the whole, because it is not relevant or important, or because it would be more useful in another place. EG *...a minor Conoco chemical division that could easily be spun off... ...autonomous, semi-attached units which can be spun off, and destroyed.* ▸ A **spin-off** is something useful that develops unexpectedly as a result of activities which were intended to achieve something else. EG *The search for knowledge frequently has beneficial spin-offs for mankind... They come into commercial or domestic use as a result of spin-off from the space program.* ▸ A **spin-off** is also a book, film, or television series that is derived from a similar book, film, or television series which has been very successful.

PASSIVE:
V+ADV

N COUNT,
N UNCOUNT

N COUNT

spin out. If you **spin** something **out**, you make it last as long as possible. EG *We found it exhausting spinning out the conversation... The Mudpore thing carried extra pay, so I spun it out as long as I could.*

V+ADV+N,
V+PRON+ADV,
V+N+ADV

spin round. If something or someone **spins round** or **around**, they turn quickly around a central point, and face in another direction, or continue turning. EG *'Right, that's it, then,' he said firmly, spinning round from the window... ...the part of the engine that was spinning around... She started spinning round and round.*

V+ADV

spirit, spirits, spiriting, spirited

spirit away. If you **spirit** someone **away** or **off**, you quickly and secretly take them from the place where they were. EG *Heissman was spirited away because Otto had arranged it... They simply spirited him away at the end of the war for his own safety.*

V+ADV+N,
V+PRON+ADV,
V+N+ADV

spirit off. See **spirit away**.

spit, spits, spitting, spat

spit out. 1 If you **spit** something **out**, you get rid of it from your   v+ADV+N,
mouth by blowing hard. EG *He sipped at it cautiously. He spat out the*   V+PRON+ADV, V+N+ADV
first few drops at once; the taste was terrible... They insisted that it
was drinkable, even after spitting it out time and time again.

2 If you **spit out** words, you say them in an angry way, so that you   V+ADV+N,
seem to be forcing them out of your mouth. EG *He spat out his*   V+ADV+QUOTE, V+N+ADV
answer... 'Economy!' Mr Willet spat out, with disgust. 'I don't call
that economy!'... 'Don't tell me anything Vulkan said.' He spat the
words out like bloody teeth.

3 You say '**spit it out**' to someone as a way of encouraging them to   IMPERATIVE:
say something which they seem reluctant to say; an informal use. EG   V+*it*+ADV
'But just to find out—to be—truly, I mean—'—'Spit it out.'

splash, splashes, splashing, splashed

splash down. When a space vehicle **splashes down**, it lands in the   V+ADV
sea at the end of a space flight. EG *The three astronauts splashed*
down safely at nine o'clock this morning. ▸ A **splashdown** is the   N COUNT
landing of a space vehicle in the sea after a flight.

splash out. If you **splash out** on something, especially on a luxury,   V+ADV:
you spend a lot of money on it; an informal expression. EG *We*   ALSO+*on*
splashed out on a colour television... Once in Pankot she would
splash out by using the whole of her allowance.

split, splits, splitting

The form **split** is used in the present tense and is the past tense and
past participle of the verb.

split off. 1 If you **split off** a part of something, or if it **splits off**, it   V+ADV+N,
becomes separated from the rest, for example by being cut or   V+N+ADV, V+PRON+ADV,
divided, or by breaking. EG *If you are splitting off a big piece you can*   V+ADV: ERGATIVE
use an axe... Such policies divide families. They split the suburbs off
from the city... ...the failure of the attempt to split them off... A chain
reaction comes about when a particle splits off from one atom
nucleus. ● **Break off** means almost the same as **split off.**

2 When people **split off** from a group, they stop being members of   V+ADV:
that group, and form a separate one. EG *The Marxist wing split off to*   ALSO+*from*
form a separate faction... They united with the Socialists in the 1960s
and split off again at the end of the decade ● **Break away** means
almost the same as **split off.**

split on. If you **split on** someone, you betray them by revealing a   V+PREP
secret about them to other people; an informal expression, used in
British English. ● **Tell on** means almost the same as **split on.**

split up. 1 If you **split** something **up**, or if it **splits up**, it is divided   V+PRON+ADV,
into several smaller sections or parts EG *You might achieve more by*   V+N+ADV, V+ADV+N,
splitting them up into small groups... I was splitting the cycle up into   V+ADV: ERGATIVE,
finer and finer pieces... One idea is to split up the session into a   USUALLY+*into*
series of sets... I think it will be appropriate if we split up into
working groups. ● **Separate** means almost the same as **split up.**

2 If a group of people **split up** or if they get **split up**, they go away in   V+ADV:
different directions. EG *In Hamburg the girls split up... They drove to*   ALSO PASSIVE, V+ADV
London, where the party split up... A large group of us went from the
village but we soon got split up. I never saw most of them again.

3 If two people **split up**, they end their relationship or marriage. EG *I*   V+ADV,
went out with him for a year and then we split up for three months...   V+ADV+*with*: RECIPROCAL
After he split up with his wife, he went to Arizona.

spoil, spoils, spoiling, spoiled/spoilt

spoil for. If you are **spoiling for** trouble or a fight, you are ready or   V+PREP eager for it. EG *The unions are spoiling for a fight about pay and conditions once again.*

sponge, sponges, sponging, sponged

sponge down. If you **sponge** something **down**, you clean it by wiping or rubbing it gently with a wet sponge or cloth. EG *Sponge down the work surface with a wet cloth... She bathed the wound and laid a bandage over it. Then she sponged Ari down.*   V+ADV+N, V+N+ADV, V+PRON+ADV

sponge off. See **sponge on.**

sponge on. Someone who **sponges on** other people or **sponges off** them takes advantage of them by getting money and other things from them without giving back anything in return; an informal expression, used showing disapproval. EG *She found it distasteful the way Clarissa sponged on them... The young unemployed are not simply layabouts who sponge off the Welfare State.*   V+PREP

spoon, spoons, spooning, spooned

spoon out. If you **spoon out** food, you give someone a portion of it, using a spoon. EG *Rey spooned out a small portion of the pudding for himself... ...spooning it out of paper cups.* ● **Serve out** means almost the same as **spoon out.**   V+ADV+N, V+PRON+ADV, V+N+ADV: ALSO+*of*

spoon up. If you **spoon up** food, you eat it or pick it up, using a spoon. EG *...spooning up milk puddings.*   V+ADV+N, V+PRON+ADV

spout, spouts, spouting, spouted

spout out. If someone **spouts out** words, they say something in a dull way, as if they are not thinking about what they are saying. EG *The answer was mechanically spouted out to us: 'obstructing pedestrian traffic'... ...spouting out rubbish about love and loyalty.*   V+ADV+N

sprawl, sprawls, sprawling, sprawled

sprawl out. If you **sprawl out** somewhere or if you **are sprawled out**, you sit or lie down, spreading your legs and arms in a relaxed or careless manner. EG *Segal sprawled out on the couch... Thomas was sitting on a bench under a tree, his legs sprawled out in a V.* ● **Stretch out** means almost the same as **sprawl out.**   V+ADV, USUALLY+A: ALSO PASSIVE, V+ADV

spread, spreads, spreading

The form **spread** is used in the present tense and is the past tense and past participle of the verb.

spread out. 1 If something **spreads out** or **is spread out,** it grows wider or covers a wider area than before. EG *Sunlight can be spread out by an instrument called a spectroscope... If the temperature goes above 68°F (20°C) spread it out more thinly and turn it often... The damage is scarcely apparent because it is spread out over such a long period of time.*   V+N+ADV, V+PRON+ADV, V+ADV+N, V+ADV: ERGATIVE

2 If people **spread out,** they move away from each other so that they are far apart. EG *They followed him and spread out, nervously, in the forest... When they saw him coming, the gang spread out across the pavement, completely blocking it.*   V+ADV

3 If people or things **are spread out,** they are scattered or far apart, and cover a large area. EG *There in the harbour was a line of dark battleships spread out under the night sky... These American villages are far more spread out than the German ones ever were.*   PASSIVE: V+ADV

4 If a city, building, or land **is spread out** or **spreads out,** it covers a large area; often used when you are looking down on it from a higher point, or when the place seems very spacious. EG *I turned around at the top of the hill. The farmland spread out below me... Out through the window, you can see the town spread out below...*   V+ADV: ALSO PASSIVE, V+ADV

The embassy itself is more palatial, spread out over the second floor of Eagle House.

5 If you **spread** something **out** over a surface, you open or arrange it there, so that you can use it or see it easily. EG *They took seats directly opposite me and spread out their newspapers... She took the folded blanket from its corner and spread it out... He sipped at the drink as he spread the sheets of stiff paper out on the desk.* ● **Lay out** means almost the same as **spread out**. V+ADV+N,
V+PRON+ADV,
V+N+ADV

6 If you **spread out** your fingers, arms, legs, and so on, you stretch them and move them so that they are far apart. If you **are spread out,** you lie or stand somewhere with your arms and legs apart. EG *Then he spread his hand out... She threw herself on the bed and spread out her limbs... She lifted up a hand and held it there, the fingers spread out... We caught sight of a figure spread out against a wall, being searched by a policeman.* V+N+ADV,
V+ADV+N,
V+PRON+ADV

spread over. If something **is spread over** a period of time, it happens throughout that period, rather than at a single point. EG *The job losses may not seem catastrophic when spread over a period... You can spread repayments over 6, 12, 18, 24 or 30 months... We had to space the stuff out bit by bit; spread it over a few weeks... They had experience spreading over twenty years.* V+N+PREP,
V+PRON+PREP,
V+PREP:
ERGATIVE

spring, springs, springing, sprang, sprung

spring back. If something **springs back** after being stretched or pushed, it quickly returns to its original position or shape. EG *The more you stretch a muscle, the more it will spring back into place.* V+ADV

spring from. **1** If one thing **springs from** another or **springs out of** it, it is the result of that other thing or it originated there. EG *Almost all the psychological ills that a man can suffer spring from self-doubt... Her hostility to him sprang out of sheer envy.* V+PREP

2 You ask where someone or something **has sprung from** when you are surprised at their unexpected appearance. EG *Well, well, Niccolo, where have you sprung from?... So where had all these other towns suddenly sprung from?* V+PREP

spring on. **1** If you **spring** a remark or action **on** or **upon** someone, you suddenly say or do something which surprises them. EG *I wondered what he was going to spring on me next... At what point are you going to spring the news on him?* V+N+PREP,
V+PRON+PREP

2 If a person or animal **springs on** you, they suddenly attack you; a fairly old-fashioned use. EG *They had opened the door of a tiger's cage, and the beast had sprung on me.* ● **Leap on** means almost the same as **spring on**. V+PREP

spring out of. See **spring from**

spring up. **1** If something **springs up**, it suddenly appears or comes into existence. EG *Here where it only rains once every five or ten years, grass will spring up within days of a rainstorm... A fresh wind had sprung up... These friendships spring up and very often don't last.* V+ADV

2 If someone **springs up**, they stand up very quickly with a jumping movement. EG *He kept having thoughts of springing up and running away... Feet together, spring up and touch the wall as high as you can.* ● **Jump up** means almost the same as **spring up**. V+ADV

spring upon. See **spring on**: **spring upon** is more formal.

sprout, sprouts, sprouting, sprouted

sprout up. If things **sprout up**, large numbers of them suddenly appear. EG *Caravans had suddenly sprouted up in the fields... ...the magazines that sprouted up as part of the youth culture of the sixties.* ● **Spring up** means almost the same as **sprout up**. V+ADV

spruce, spruces, sprucing, spruced

spruce up. If you **spruce** yourself **up** or if you get **spruced up**, you make yourself look neat and smart. If you **spruce up** an object or place, you improve its appearance. EG *Spruce yourself up a bit—you look a mess!... If you spruce the bodywork up and the interior, you'll have no trouble selling it.*

V+REFL+ADV,
V+N+ADV,
V+PRON+ADV,
V+ADV+N

spur, spurs, spurring, spurred

spur on. If something **spurs** you **on**, it encourages you to act in a particular way. EG *It was personal ambition that spurred him on... The development of British industry, in its turn, was spurred on by the existence of vast captive markets... ...spurred on by success.*
● **Urge on** means almost the same as **spur on**.

V+PRON+ADV,
V+N+ADV,
V+ADV+N

spurt, spurts, spurting, spurted

spurt out. If liquid **spurts out**, it comes out quickly and suddenly in a series of quick, pulsing movements. EG *More tears spurted out... I cut my wrist and the blood spurted out.*

V+ADV

sputter, sputters, sputtering, sputtered

sputter out. If something **sputters out**, it stops functioning, happening, or existing, often in a rather feeble way. EG *Hughes rose to begin his talk just as the engine sputtered out and the hall was plunged into darkness.* ● **Die** means almost the same as **sputter out**.

V+ADV

spy, spies, spying, spied

spy on. If you **spy on** someone or **spy upon** them, you watch them secretly. EG *They spied on us to see how many turned up to the meetings... She hid behind a bush to spy upon him.*

V+PREP

spy out. If you **spy** something **out**, you get information about it secretly or while pretending to do something else. EG *You've probably been sent here to spy out my latest designs... Shaw was one of the first to spy out her talent at this performance.*

V+ADV+N,
V+PRON+ADV

spy upon. See **spy on**: **spy upon** is more formal.

square, squares, squaring, squared

square up. 1 If you **square up** to a person, you stand facing them in a threatening way. EG *...two girls squaring up to one another... ...squaring up for a fight.* ● **Confront** is a more formal word for **square up**.

V+ADV:
USUALLY+*to*

2 If you **square up** to a problem or difficult situation, you accept that you have to deal with it. EG *You've got to square up to failure and try to carry on.*

V+ADV:
USUALLY+*to*

3 If you **square up** with someone, you pay the bills or money that you owe them; an informal use. EG *Do you want to square up now or later?... I've got to square up with the bank before I can pay you.*
● **Settle up** means almost the same as **square up**.

V+ADV,
V+ADV+*with*:
RECIPROCAL

squash, squashes, squashing, squashed

squash in. If you **squash in**, you manage to get into a place where there is not much room for you. EG *The crowd rushed under the trees, squashing in under the shelter.* ● **Squeeze in** means almost the same as **squash in**.

V+ADV:
USUALLY+A

squash into. If you **squash into** a place, you manage to get in there, even though there is not much room. EG *We all squashed into the room to hear him give his talk.* ● **Squeeze into** means almost the same as **squash into**.

V+PREP

squash up. If something or someone is **squashed up**, they are forced into a very small space. EG *Lally and the others sat squashed up inside the car... Her dress was squashed up in her case.*

V+N+ADV,
V+PRON+ADV,
V+ADV+N:
USUALLY PASSIVE

squeal, squeals, squealing, squealed

squeal on. If someone **squeals on** a person who has committed a crime, they inform the police about it; an informal expression. EG *Nobody's squealed on us, so just calm down.* V+PREP

squeeze, squeezes, squeezing, squeezed

squeeze in. 1 If you **squeeze in**, you manage to sit or stand in a place where there is not much room for you. EG *She squeezed in beside me... Can I just squeeze in there?... Two could squeeze in if they weren't too large.* V+ADV

2 If you **squeeze** something **in**, you manage to find time to do it, even though you are busy doing other things. EG *You can squeeze in your hobbies and reading... The programme had been his idea, and would be squeezed in amongst his other work.* ● **Fit in** means almost the same as **squeeze in.** V+ADV+N, V+N+ADV, V+PRON+ADV

squeeze into. If you **squeeze into** a place, you manage to get in there, even though there is not much room. EG *There were so many children you could hardly squeeze into the room... Jill squeezes into the seat beside you.* ● **Squash into** means almost the same as **squeeze into.** V+PREP

squeeze out. 1 If you **squeeze** liquid or air **out** of something, you remove it by pressing it very hard. EG *Squeeze the surplus water out... The breath was being squeezed out of his lungs... ...squeezing out the final few drops.* V+N+ADV, V+ADV+N, V+PRON+ADV

2 If you **squeeze** money **out** of someone, you manage to persuade them to give it to you. EG *Has he been able to squeeze extra cash out of his tight-fisted employer?... I bet they squeeze more out of the Welfare State than we do... ...an effort to squeeze out a little more money for wages.* V+N+ADV, V+ADV+N, V+PRON+ADV: USUALLY+*of*

3 If you **squeeze** someone **out** of a particular activity, you prevent them from taking part in it. EG *New settlement is beginning to squeeze the farmers out... Large scale bureaucracies have undoubtedly squeezed out the individual entrepreneur.* ● **Exclude** is a more formal word for **squeeze out.** V+N+ADV, V+ADV+N, V+PRON+ADV

squeeze through. If you **squeeze through**, you manage to get through a small space. EG *The doorway was merely a gap, barely enough to squeeze through... She opened the gate and squeezed through... They can't squeeze through the window.* V+ADV, V+PREP

squirrel, squirrels, squirrelling, squirrelled

American English uses the spellings **squirreling** and **squirreled.**

squirrel away. If you **squirrel away** something, especially money, you put it somewhere secret or safe, so that you can use it in the future. EG *...funds that the chairman of the board of my company had managed to squirrel away in Switzerland.* ● **Stash away** and **hoard** mean almost the same as **squirrel away.** V+ADV+N, V+N+ADV, V+PRON+ADV

stack, stacks, stacking, stacked

stack up. If you **stack up** a number of things, you arrange them in a tall pile. EG *Melanie stacked up the plates and carried them to the sink... He stacked up a few rows of stones.* ● **Pile up** means almost the same as **stack up.** V+ADV+N, V+N+ADV, V+PRON+ADV

staff, staffs, staffing, staffed

staff up. When a firm **staffs up**, it increases the number of people it employs until it has the right number. EG *It's vital that we finish staffing up by the end of the year.* V+ADV

stake, stakes, staking, staked

stake on. If you **stake** money, your reputation, or something V+N+PREP, V+PRON+PREP valuable **on** or **upon** the result of something, you risk losing your money or your reputation if it does not work as you thought it would. EG *He has staked his reputation as a prophet on this assertion... She has staked everything on what will happen when she gets there... I wouldn't like to stake my life on that.*

stake out. 1 If you **stake out** a particular area of land, or **stake out** a claim to it, you make it clear that you have a special interest in that piece of land, although you may not actually own it. EG *The settlers were staking out ranches and land claims on territory in the South... ...the geographical area they staked out for themselves.*

V+ADV+N,
V+N+ADV,
V+PRON+ADV

2 If you **stake out** your attitude or position on a particular issue, you define the limits or boundaries of that attitude or position. EG *The committee's report stakes out the new frontiers of acceptable advance... We need to challenge the position they have staked out for themselves.*

V+ADV+N,
V+N+ADV,
V+PRON+ADV

3 If someone **stakes out** a building, they stay hidden near the building in order to watch anyone who enters or leaves it; a fairly informal use. EG *You staked out the house to watch me walk into your trap... The police staked the flat out for twelve hours before moving in to make arrests.* ▶ A **stake-out** is a situation in which someone stays hidden near a building in order to watch anyone who enters or leaves it; an informal word. EG *...a police stake-out.*

V+ADV+N,
V+N+ADV,
V+PRON+ADV

N COUNT

stake upon. See stake on.

stammer, stammers, stammering, stammered

stammer out. If you **stammer** something **out,** you say it with difficulty, hesitating and repeating words or sounds because you are nervous. EG *Before he could stammer out his thanks, she walked away... I stammer out some sort of explanation... 'I think she's lovely,' Marsha stammered out... The father was just able to stammer out that perhaps the son should leave the room.*

V+ADV+N,
V+ADV+QUOTE,
V+ADV+REPORT,
V+N+ADV,
V+PRON+ADV

stamp, stamps, stamping, stamped

stamp down. If you **stamp** something **down,** you lift your feet one after the other and put them down very hard on it in order to make it flatter or firmer. EG *She buried the money, stamping down the earth over it... He put dirt around the base of the cross, and stamped it down hard with his feet... He put the cardboard boxes in a heap and stamped them down.*

V+ADV+N,
V+PRON+ADV,
V+N+ADV

stamp on. 1 If you **stamp on** something, you put your foot down on it very hard, usually in order to damage it or hurt it. EG *...boys who stamped on beetles when they found them... I stamped heavily on her foot and muttered, 'Shut up.'... I was kicked, struck and stamped on.*

V+PREP:
HAS PASSIVE

2 If someone or something **stamps** themselves **on** or **upon** another thing, they have a strong effect on it. EG *Britain was to stamp itself upon India in a way that was to shape history for many years... He had already stamped his presence on the face of science... His class background and schooling were indelibly stamped upon his work.*

V+REFL+PREP,
V+N+PREP,
V+PRON+PREP

stamp out. 1 If you **stamp** something **out,** you put an end to it or destroy it completely. EG *They are determined to stamp out political extremism... The rail strike was stamped out with particular brutality... The language was stamped out.* ● **Eliminate** and **eradicate** are more formal words for **stamp out.**

V+ADV+N,
V+N+ADV,
V+PRON+ADV

2 If you **stamp out** something that is burning, you keep treading on it with your feet in order to stop it burning. EG *I stamped out the flaming paper with my foot... A small fire was going and he stamped it out... The hardly touched cigarette had been stamped out.* ● **Extinguish** is a more formal word for **stamp out.**

V+ADV+N,
V+PRON+ADV,
V+N+ADV

3 If something **is stamped out** by a machine or tool, it is cut out from a substance such as wood, metal, or paper. EG *It appears to have been stamped out by a machine.* ● **Punch out** means almost the same as **stamp out**.

V+N+ADV,
V+ADV+N,
V+PRON+ADV:
USUALLY PASSIVE

stamp upon. See stamp on: **stamp upon** is more formal.

stand, stands, standing, stood

stand about. See stand around.

stand around. If you **stand around, about,** or **round,** you stand rather aimlessly in a place because you have nothing to do. EG *They seemed content to stand around for a time chatting... He stood about for a little, then he went to his room... ...disconsolate passengers standing around the ticket counters.*

V+ADV,
V+PREP

stand aside. 1 If you **stand aside,** you move to a position where you will not block other people. EG *Gareth stood aside to let him pass... I told the girls to stand aside to make way... She made them stand aside while the more important guests were served.*

V+ADV

2 If you **stand aside** from a disagreement or difficult situation, you separate yourself from it and refuse to become involved in it. EG *We wish to stand aside from these quarrels... He had, in the past, stood aside quite passively during any arguments.*

V+ADV:
ALSO+*from*

stand back. 1 If you **stand back,** you move away from something or someone. EG *'Will you ladies kindly stand back a minute, please,'* Ned said... Karin stood back a little and paused... He stood back from the doorway, allowing her to enter.*

V+ADV:
ALSO+*from*

2 If you **stand back** from a situation, you put yourself in a position in which you are not too closely involved in it. EG *I think someone ought to stand back and look critically at this issue... It can be difficult to stand back from your problems in an objective way.*

V+ADV:
ALSO+*from*

3 If a building **stands back** from a road or other area, it is some distance away from it. EG *...the Royal Hospital, standing back behind the trees... The village was hidden away, standing back from the bigger hills.* ● **Set back** means almost the same as **stand back**.

V+ADV:
ALSO+*from*

stand between. If something or someone **stands between** you and a likely situation, it prevents that situation from arising. EG *...the men who stand between you and the top jobs... ...the barriers which stand between the average person and this knowledge... Damages awarded by the courts were all that stood between the family and destitution.*

V+PREP

stand by. 1 If you **stand by** and let something unpleasant happen, you do not try to do anything to stop it. EG *We cannot stand by and watch while our allies are attacked... We watched the troops standing by while strikers wrecked a bus... The police were just standing by and looking on.* ● **Sit by** means almost the same as **stand by**. ▶ A **bystander** is a person who is present when something happens, and who sees it but does not take part in it. EG *Innocent bystanders can get hurt, but that is the price one has to pay in a free society.* ● **Onlooker** means almost the same as **bystander**.

V+ADV:
USUALLY+A

N COUNT

2 If you **stand by,** you are ready to provide help or take action if it becomes necessary. EG *Government engineers were standing by to provide emergency repairs... Stand by with lots of water in case a fire breaks out.* ▶ A **stand-by** is something that is always ready to be used instead of another thing if the other thing is not available. EG *There's always that old stand-by, cheese on toast... ...emergency stand-by services... It was one of three Boeings put on standby for the trip.* ▶ A **standby** ticket for something such as the theatre or a plane journey is a cheap ticket that you buy just before the perfor-

V+ADV

N SING,
N UNCOUNT

ADJECTIVE

mance starts or the plane takes off, if there are any seats left. EG *I've got a standby booking on a Caravelle to Brussels.*

3 If you **stand by** someone, you continue to give them help or support, especially when they are in trouble. EG *If they try to make you resign, we'll stand by you... He considered it his duty to stand by her.* ● **Stick by** means almost the same as **stand by.**   V+PREP

4 If you **stand by** an earlier decision, promise, or agreement, you continue to support it or keep it. EG *I said I would do it and I stand by my promise... He confirmed that his Government would stand by the NATO decision.* ● **Abide by** and **adhere to** are more formal expressions for **stand by,** and **go back on** means the opposite.   V+PREP

stand down. **1** If someone **stands down,** they resign from an important position, often in order to let someone else take their place. EG *She was asked if she was prepared to stand down in favour of a younger candidate... There were rumours that he would stand down after 1982.* ● **Step down** means almost the same as **stand down.**   V+ADV

2 In a courtroom, if a witness is asked to **stand down,** they are asked to leave the witness box. EG *The defendant may now stand down.*   V+ADV

stand for. **1** If you say that a letter or initial **stands for** a particular word or name, you mean that it is an abbreviation for that word or name. EG *What does GCSE stand for?... T.E.C. stands for Technical Education Certificate.*   V+PREP

2 The ideas or attitudes that someone **stands for** are the ones that they support or represent. EG *I disagreed so fundamentally with what the party stood for... Everything you'd stood for had been condemned and ridiculed.*   V+PREP

3 If someone **stands for** election or **stands for** a post that is decided by an election, they are a candidate for that post. EG *No-one would stand for election... He stood for Governor of New York... It is very difficult to stand for local government as an independent.*   V+PREP

4 If you will not **stand for** something, you will not allow it to happen or continue. EG *He warned that the Army would not stand for it much longer... They would not stand for their obstruction by secretive bureaucratic means.* ● **Put up with** means almost the same as **stand for,** and **tolerate** is a more formal word.   V+PREP: WITH NEGATIVE

stand in. If you **stand in** for someone, you take their place or do their job, because they are ill or not there. EG *You will stand in for me at the meeting?... Goin had volunteered to stand in for the now absent Heyter... She stood in for me several times.* ▸ A **stand-in** is a person who takes someone else's place or does someone else's job because the other person is ill or not there. EG *If you employ a home help, make sure your stand-in is liked by the children.*   V+ADV: USUALLY+*for*

N COUNT

stand off. If you **stand** someone **off,** you stop them from coming close to you or interfering with what you are doing. EG *She stood off curious intruders by day and by night... You were the only one who could stand off the old man.*   V+ADV+N, V+N+ADV, V+PRON+ADV: NO PASSIVE

stand out. **1** If something **stands out,** it can be seen very clearly. EG *The name on the van stood out clearly... The bones of his face stood out like a skeleton's.*   V+ADV

2 If something **stands out** from other things of the same kind, it is much better or much more important than those other things. EG *Two findings stand out as particularly significant... The Australian tour stands out as the most satisfying and enjoyable of them all... There was one episode which stood out from the rest.* ▸ Something or someone that is **outstanding** is much better or more important than other things of the same kind. EG *She would never be an*   V+ADV: ALSO+*from*

ADJECTIVE

outstanding actress... There are significant exceptions, of which oil is the outstanding example.

3 If a debt or a problem is still **outstanding,** it has not yet been paid or solved. EG *There is fifty pounds outstanding, I believe... ...an outstanding problem that needs working on.*   ADJECTIVE

stand out against. If you **stand out against** something, you remain opposed to it, even though a lot of other people do not agree with you. EG *It's no easy thing for a politician to stand out against the tide of materialism... He alone had stood out against the hunting of whales.*   V+ADV+PREP

stand out for. If you **stand out for** something, you want it and refuse to accept anything else. EG *The union decided to stand out for its original claim.* ● **Hold out for** and **stick out for** mean almost the same as **stand out for.**   V+ADV+PREP

stand over. If you **stand over** someone, you stand very close to them, usually because you want to watch what they are doing. EG *He wasn't hungry, but she stood over him and made him eat his lunch... The wardens had to stand over them while they scrubbed it.*   V+PREP

stand round. See **stand around.**

stand up. **1** If you **stand up,** you change your position so that you are standing rather than sitting or lying. EG *Lewis Jones refused to stand up when he came into the room... Can you imagine standing up in the middle of a hall and saying what you think?... I put down my glass and stood up.* ● **Get up** means almost the same as **stand up.**   V+ADV

▶ **Stand-up** comedy is comedy in which a comedian stands alone in front of an audience and tells jokes. EG *...a stand-up comedian.* ▶ A **stand-up** fight or argument is one in which people hit or shout at each other in an unrestrained way. EG *It started as a quarrel but turned into a stand-up fight.*   ADJECTIVE   ADJECTIVE

2 If something such as a claim or piece of evidence **stands up,** it is accepted as true. EG *The prosecution had no evidence which would stand up in a court of law... These claims just don't stand up.*   V+ADV

3 If you **stand** someone **up,** especially someone you are just beginning a romantic relationship with, you fail to keep an arrangement to meet them; an informal use. EG *I feel really bad about standing you up that day... I think I've been stood up.*   V+PRON+ADV, V+N+ADV

stand up for. If you **stand up for** a person or principle that is being attacked or criticized, you take forceful action in order to defend that person or principle. EG *I'm glad to see that he's standing up for himself... Only one man stood up for me and he was jeered... ...people who stood up for human rights... Don't be afraid to stand up for your rights.* ● **Defend** means almost the same as **stand up for.**   V+ADV+PREP

stand up to. **1** If something or someone **stands up to** rough treatment, they survive it and remain unharmed. EG *This carpet stands up to the wear and tear of continual use... The economy would not stand up to wartime pressures... My mother stood up to the whole ordeal.*   V+ADV+PREP

2 If you **stand up to** someone, especially someone more powerful than you are, you defend yourself against their attacks or demands. EG *He's too weak to stand up to her... Why didn't you stand up to Phillip more if you dislike him so much?.*   V+ADV+PREP

stare, stares, staring, stared

stare down. See **stare out.**

stare out. If you **stare** someone **out** or **stare** them **down,** you stare into their eyes intensely until you make them look away, thus showing that they accept your authority or superiority. EG *Wasps*   V+N+ADV, V+PRON+ADV *should be either stared out or engaged in mortal combat... Her mother tried to stare Hagen down.*

start, starts, starting, started

start back. 1 If you **start back** somewhere, you begin returning to or towards the place where you have come from. EG *She started slowly back to the bedroom... We started back on the long journey home... Some were fearful of starting back north.*   V+ADV: USUALLY+A

2 If you **start back,** you move suddenly backwards because something has shocked or startled you. EG *I might cause her to start back in revulsion and terror... The next moment she started back and I heard her catch her breath sharply.*   V+ADV

start in. If you **start in** on a task or subject, you begin to do it or to deal with it. EG *It proves if you start in early enough, you can do it... We went back into the living-room and started in on breakfast.*   V+ADV: ALSO+*on*

start off. 1 When people or vehicles **start off,** they begin to move and go somewhere. EG *When they started off again he was unconscious... It started off down Cresta Ridge Drive, negotiating each hairpin... We were due to start off for Branscombe Castle at eleven sharp.* ● **Move off** and **set off** mean almost the same as **start off.**   V+ADV: USUALLY+A

2 To **start off** in a particular state, position, or manner means to be in that state or position or to act in that manner at the beginning of a process, existence, or career. EG *...those who start off at the very bottom of the social scale... All rice starts off brown... I started off as a bookseller in Bristol... Let's start off by sorting out who is involved.*   V+ADV: USUALLY+A

3 To **start** someone **off** means to cause them to begin doing something. EG *I shall start them off and let them finish four or five tasks... The mention of their names could start her off again.* ● **Set off** means almost the same as **start off.**   V+PRON+ADV, V+N+ADV

4 To **start** a process **off** means to cause it to begin. EG *...the event which starts off the growth of a cancer tumour... I asked a simple little question to start the interview off... I suspect she started it off—picked the poor beast up wrongly.* ▸ The **starting-off** point of a process or project is the time or the stage of development when it begins. EG *...the starting-off point for a fairer housing policy.*   V+ADV+N, V+N+ADV, V+PRON+ADV   ADJECTIVE

start on. 1 If you **start on** something that needs to be done, you begin doing it or dealing with it. EG *She put the forks in a neat pile and started on the knives... We want to start her on music lessons soon... ...a bad day on which to start on anything of importance.*   V+PREP: HAS PASSIVE

2 If you **start on** someone, you treat them severely or unfairly, for example by criticizing them, teasing them, or hitting them; an informal use. EG *I warn you, don't start on my father!... They started on Jim over the Welsh business... They start on him and he gets so embarrassed.*   V+PREP

start out. 1 If you **start out,** you begin to move and go somewhere. EG *They started out to church... ...longing to start out for Hayport.* ● **Set off, set out** and **start off** mean almost the same as **start out.**   V+ADV: USUALLY+A

2 To **start out** doing something or being something means to do it or be it at the beginning of a situation, process, career, or existence. EG *What started out as fun for the parents becomes an endless chore... We have to start out by understanding managers... A bruise would start out black and blue, then become purple.* ● **Start off** means almost the same as **start out,** and **end up** means the opposite.   V+ADV: USUALLY+A

3 If you **start out** to do something, you intend to do it. EG *You've done what you started out to do... She doesn't have anything to do with what I originally started out to say.* ● **Set out** means almost the same as **start out.**   V+ADV: WITH *to*-INF

start over. If you **start over,** you begin doing something right from   V+ADV the beginning again, for example because you did it wrong last time or you have decided to do something different. EG *You must go back to the beginning and start over again... How will you earn your living then, starting over at thirty, thirty-five, even?*

start up. 1 If you **start up** a new business or organization, or if it **starts up,** you organize or arrange it and it begins to operate. EG *She wanted to start up a little country pub... They've just started up a discussion group in Plotinus... Every year many people decide to start up in business.* ● **Set up** means almost the same as **start up.**   ADJECTIVE
▶ **Start-up** money is used to organize or arrange a new business, organization, or activity. EG *...start-up costs.*

V+ADV+N,
V+N+ADV,
V+PRON+ADV,
V+ADV:
ERGATIVE

2 If you **start up** an engine or a motor vehicle, or if it **starts up,** you make it begin to operate. EG *The officer got in and started up the motor... He limped back to the cycle, leapt on and started it up... There was a car starting up in the background.*

V+ADV+N,
V+PRON+ADV,
V+N+ADV,
V+ADV:
ERGATIVE

3 If you are sitting quietly or sleeping and **start up,** you move suddenly into a sitting or standing position because you are startled or surprised by something. EG *'Oh no!' she cried, starting up suddenly from the pillow... They dozed off until Michael suddenly started up anxiously and looked at his watch.*

V+ADV:
USUALLY+A

4 If a sound, activity, or event **starts up** or if you **start** it **up,** it begins to be heard or to take place. EG *The music started up in the Ballroom... ...months of waiting for trade to start up again... The rain has started up again... The book, when published, would start up a literary controversy.*

V+ADV,
V+ADV+N,
V+PRON+ADV:
ERGATIVE

5 You refer to someone as an **upstart** when they behave as if they are important, but you think that they are too new in a place or job to be treated as important; used showing disapproval. EG *We have to put this upstart in his place.*

N COUNT

starve, starves, starving, starved

starve for. If you **are starved for** something, you have not had much of it for some time and you want some. EG *I was so starved for a bit of natural light... I'm starved for the taste of rare midwestern beef... They were starved for some kind of affection which he never gave.*

PASSIVE:
V+PREP

starve into. If someone **is starved into** a state or action, they are given no food and so are forced to enter that state or do that action. EG *They can be starved into retreat, but not into submission... ...damage their health by starving themselves into a state of emaciation.*

V+N+PREP,
V+PRON+PREP:
USUALLY PASSIVE

starve of. If someone or something **is starved of** something they need, they do not get enough of it and therefore suffer. EG *He was obviously starved of decent home cooking... By neglecting black talent, the British theatre could be starving itself of a vital new force.*

V+N+PREP,
V+PRON+PREP:
USUALLY PASSIVE

starve out. To **starve out** a group of people means to force them to surrender or leave a place by not giving them any food. EG *In a short time the soldiers starved us out... ...the inhumanity of starving out a civilian population.*

V+PRON+ADV,
V+ADV+N,
V+N+ADV

stash, stashes, stashing, stashed

stash away. 1 If you **stash away** money or valuable things, you hide them or put them somewhere because you are saving the money or collecting the things. EG *...those who stash away their funds in Swiss bank accounts... She rose early and hurried to stash the bills away in safety... I stashed it away with all the others.*

V+ADV+N,
V+N+ADV,
V+PRON+ADV

2 If you **stash** someone **away,** you hide them somewhere, for example because they are in danger. EG *The kid was stashed away*

V+ADV+N,
V+PRON+ADV,
V+N+ADV:
USUALLY PASSIVE

with her sister in the Bronx... Mel suspected she had a lover somewhere, stashed away.

stave, staves, staving, staved

stave off. To **stave off** an unpleasant event means to prevent it happening. EG *There wasn't much that Abel could have done to stave off disaster... Batik cannot stave off the challenge from cheaper machine-made prints... Chrysler staved off bankruptcy earlier this year.* ● **Avert** is a more formal word for **stave off**.

V+ADV+N,
V+PRON+ADV,
V+N+ADV

stay, stays, staying, stayed

stay ahead of. If you **stay ahead** of someone or something, you manage to remain in a better position than them. EG *That way you'll only just stay ahead of inflation... To stay ahead of them would cost money... What I seek to do is to stay ahead of the rest.*

V+ADV:
USUALLY+of

stay away. If you **stay away** from a place, you do not go there. EG *As yet he had never stayed away for a night... This town is unsafe: stay away from here... You get fed up being picked on, so you stay away from school.*

V+ADV:
ALSO+from

stay away from. 1 If you **stay away from** a person, you try to avoid meeting them or talking to them. EG *My instructions are to stay away from him.*

V+ADV+PREP

2 If you **stay away from** an activity or subject, you avoid doing the activity or talking about the subject. EG *Underdeveloped countries will focus on economic issues and stay away from politics... I had stayed away from problems of definition.*

V+ADV+PREP

stay back. If you **stay back** in a place, you remain there and do not move forward or leave, even if other people do. EG *Stay back here a moment with me until you get used to it... I stayed back home, studying half-heartedly... Stay back behind the barrier.*

V+ADV:
USUALLY+A

stay behind. If you **stay behind**, you remain in a place after most of the other people have gone. EG *You can just stay behind and do it over again... Why had she not stayed behind to talk to them?... ...the people who had stayed behind after independence.* ● **Remain** is a more formal word for **stay behind**.

V+ADV

stay down. 1 If a swimmer or diver **stays down**, they remain underwater. EG *If he controlled his breathing, he could stay down for at least half an hour more... I was eventually able to stay down for over three and a half minutes.*

V+ADV

2 If food that you have eaten **stays down**, you do not vomit. EG *Meals stay down better when they consist entirely of solids... If this stays down and she begs for more, let her have it.*

V+ADV

stay in. If you **stay in**, you remain at home rather than going out and enjoying yourself. EG *She had to stay in and do the dishes... We stayed in the whole evening, didn't go to the disco at all.* ● **Stop in** means almost the same as **stay in**, and **go out** means the opposite.

V+ADV

stay off. If you **stay off**, you do not go to work or school, for example because you are ill. EG *If I'm not better, I think I shall stay off tomorrow.*

V+ADV

stay on. If you **stay on** somewhere, you remain there longer than other people, longer than in the past, or longer than you planned. EG *Pupils have to stay on at school till they are 16... He can stay on for three months... He had stayed on to have a drink.* ● **Leave** means the opposite of **stay on**.

V+ADV

stay out. 1 If you **stay out**, you remain away from home, especially when you are expected to be there. EG *We stayed out all night... Her mother didn't like her to stay out late.* ● **Stop out** means almost the same as **stay out**.

V+ADV

2 If workers who are on strike **stay out**, they remain on strike. EG

V+ADV

The men stayed out for the best part of a year... The 400 women at the factory stayed out on strike for eleven weeks.

stay out of. 1 If you **stay out of** a place, you do not enter it. EG *His* V+ADV+PREP
family paid him to stay out of Britain... Tell everybody to stay out of the bathroom for the next half an hour.

2 If you **stay out of** a situation or activity, you do not get involved or V+ADV+PREP
take part in it. EG *We've begged them a thousand times to stay out of this fight... I stayed out of the social life of the school... You made a wise choice by staying out of this thing.* ● **Keep out of** means almost the same as **stay out of.**

stay over. If you visit someone and decide to **stay over,** you spend V+ADV
the night there instead of leaving; used mainly in American English.
EG *Better yet, come Monday, stay over, and go on from here Tuesday.*

stay up. If you **stay up,** you go to bed much later than usual. EG V+ADV
Nobody would stay up to give us any supper when we got back... They seem to stay up until the parents themselves go to bed... He must have stayed up working all night. ● **Stop up** means almost the same as **stay up.**

stay with. If you **stay with** a fact, a task, an attitude, or a situation, V+PREP
you continue using it, doing it, having it, or being involved with it, rather than changing it or doing something else. EG *Let us stay with the official figure for the Flanders campaign... ...the discipline to keep persevering, to stay with the battle... We cannot stay with that questioning mood for long.*

steal, steals, stealing, stole, stolen

steal away. If you **steal away** from a place or a task, you leave it V+ADV:
quietly or secretly. EG *Ralph stole away through the branches...* USUALLY+A
...whenever he could steal away from his duties.

steal over. If light **steals over** a place, it gradually shines more V+PREP
brightly on it; a literary expression. EG *We'll have dinner and talk until the dawn steals over the Blue Mountains... The sun rose and a broad streak of light stole over the ship.*

steal up. If you **steal up** on someone, you move quietly until you are V+ADV:
next to them, and surprise them or attack them. EG *We could steal up* ALSO+on
on one—paint our faces so they wouldn't see... 'Nice view,' said the youth, who had stolen up silently behind him.

steam, steams, steaming, steamed

steam away. If a kettle or saucepan is **steaming away,** it is V+ADV
producing steam continually, often because someone has forgotten to switch it off or reduce the heat. EG *The kettle was steaming away on the Primus stove.*

steam off. If one thing is stuck to another and you **steam** it **off,** you V+N+ADV/PREP,
remove it from the other thing by using steam to melt the glue. EG V+PRON+ADV/PREP
You can steam the stamps off the envelopes.

steam up. 1 If something made of glass such as a window or mirror V+ADV,
steams up, it becomes covered with steam or mist. EG *My glasses* V+ADV+N:
steamed up as soon as I walked into the room... The windows always ERGATIVE
get steamed up when I'm cooking... 'You saved?' he bellowed suspiciously to the newcomer, steaming up the glass as he spoke.
● **Mist up** means almost the same as **steam up.**

2 If someone is **steamed up,** they are very annoyed, angry, or ADJECTIVE
excited about something. EG *My friend was very steamed up about this project... What was she getting so steamed up about?* ● **Het up** means almost the same as **steamed up.**

steer, steers, steering, steered

steer away from. If you steer away from a subject or action, you
avoid talking about it or doing it. EG *I like to steer away from serious
topics... Kitty was steering all the conversation away from any talk
of herself... The reporters had some information that he had to steer
them away from.*

V+ADV+PREP,
V+N+ADV+PREP,
V+PRON+ADV+PREP

stem, stems, stemming, stemmed

stem from. If a situation or problem **stems from** something, it was
caused by that thing. EG *Attitudes like these stem from ignorance...
...the obvious risks which stem from regular alcohol drinking.*

V+PREP

step, steps, stepping, stepped

step aside. See step down.

step back. 1 If you **step back** from a problem or situation, you try
to think about it again in a fresh way, ignoring previous ideas or
personal feelings. EG *Step back and look at how little a young adult
often has to spend... It is tempting to step back and ask whether it is
worth introducing such a complicated scheme.* ● **Stand back** means
almost the same as **step back.**

V+ADV

2 If you **step back** into a previous situation, you return to being in it
or feel as if you have returned to it. EG *Many women would willingly
step back into the manual or service work in which they started...
You feel, as you land, that you have stepped back two hundred
million years.*

V+ADV

step down. If you **step down** or **step aside** from an important job
or position, you resign from it, often in order to let someone else
take your place. EG *Robert offered to step down if that would
promote negotiations... ...before stepping down last month because
of illness... ...if I stepped aside as vice-presidential candidate.* ● **Stand
down** means almost the same as **step down.**

V+ADV

step forward. In a difficult situation, if someone **steps forward,**
they offer to help. EG *The Russians stepped forward and offered to
pay the entire cost... Close relatives immediately stepped forward to
take their place.*

V+ADV

step in. In a difficult situation, if you **step in,** you get involved in it
and try to help. EG *She really appreciates the way you stepped in and
saw to things... The government has often had to step in to protect
employees from employers... David stepped in quickly. 'I think you
had better apologize.'* ● **Intervene** is a more formal word for **step in.**

V+ADV

step on. If you tell the driver of a car to **step on** it, you are telling
him or her to drive fast, because you are in a hurry.

IMPERATIVE:
V+PREP+*it*

step up. If you **step up** something, you increase the speed, amount,
or extent of it. EG *...when a nation decides to step up arms production... Now if you want to step your voltage up it's quite simple...
Congress have been stepping up their preparations for the final
showdown.* ▸ A **step-up** in something is an increase in its speed,
amount, or extent. EG *...a step-up in the pace of life... There has been
a marked step-up in police activity.*

V+ADV+N,
V+N+ADV,
V+PRON+ADV

N SING

stick, sticks, sticking, stuck

Most of the phrasal verbs with **stick** are informal.

stick around. If you **stick around,** you stay where you are, often
because you are waiting for something. EG *Mike wanted me to stick
around for a couple of days... Maybe I'll just stick around here a
while... There's nothing else to stick around for.* ● **Hang around**
means almost the same as **stick around.**

V+ADV,
V+PREP

stick at. 1 To **stick at** a particular amount, stage, or point in a
process means to stop and not increase, decrease, change, or

V+PREP:
ALSO PASSIVE,
V+PREP

progress. EG *These will probably stick at roughly the same levels as in 1975... If he sticks at a word or stumbles over a phrase, don't rush in... We all seemed to be stuck at this level of development.*

2 If you **stick at** a task or job, you continue working at it or trying as hard as you can, even if it is very difficult or unpleasant. EG *It's been very tricky and I've had to stick at it... If she stuck at it she would have her degree in two years... Their grandfather never stuck at one job for more than a week.* ● **Persevere** is a more formal word for **stick at,** and **keep at** and **stick to** mean almost the same. `V+PREP, V+PREP+it`

3 If you say that someone will **stick at** nothing to achieve something, you mean that they are prepared to do whatever is necessary, even if it involves doing bad things. EG *Orestes didn't stick at anything to revenge his family... Its members stuck at nothing in their determination to help the Government.* `V+PREP: WITH NEGATIVE`

stick back. If you **stick** something **back** somewhere, you put it there or attach it there again, after it has fallen off, broken off, or been taken away for a while. EG *He stuck the knife back in his belt... She closed up the big atlas and stuck it back on the shelf... They mixed some glue and stuck it back on the handle.* `V+N+ADV, V+PRON+ADV: USUALLY+A`

stick by. 1 If you **stick by** someone, you continue to give them help or support, especially when they are in difficulty. EG *It was her duty to stick by dear James through thick and thin... Despite her husband's appalling life of crime, she had stuck faithfully by him... He was a good officer who stuck by his men when they got into trouble.* ● **Stand by** means almost the same as **stick by,** and **abandon** and **desert** mean the opposite. `V+PREP`

2 If you **stick by** something, you continue to use it or believe in it and do not change your mind. EG *We stick by what we have argued all through this book... I stick by the traditional club which has stood the test of time.* ● **Adhere to** is a more formal expression for **stick by,** and **abandon** means the opposite. `V+PREP`

stick down. 1 If you **stick** something **down** somewhere, you put it there. EG *I saw him stick two fingers down into it and withdraw a white peppermint... I just stuck this thing down here as I left... Tell me precisely why you stuck that doll down that hole.* `V+N+ADV/PREP, V+PRON+ADV/PREP`

2 If you **stick** something **down,** you seal it or attach it firmly to something else, usually by using glue or tape and then pressing it. EG *Fill out the coupons, copy the address, add the five pounds, and stick down the envelope... Pictures could be stuck down at odd angles, and the page could be assembled.* `V+ADV+N, V+N+ADV, V+PRON+ADV`

3 If you **stick** something **down** on paper, you write or draw it quickly or roughly. EG *Just stick it down and we'll look at it properly later... I saw that he'd stuck my name down on the list.* `V+PRON+ADV, V+N+ADV, V+ADV+N`

stick in. 1 If you **stick** someone or something **in** a place or container, you cause them to go in there or put them in there. EG *No, don't just stick it in your pocket... I do sometimes stick papers and books in there... We didn't stick them in hospital... Her thumb was stuck firmly in her mouth and she was fast asleep.* `V+PRON+PREP, V+N+PREP`

2 If you **stick** something sharp **in** something solid, you cause it to pierce the surface and stay there. EG *These darts are rigged. Some of them don't stick in the board... A garden fork had been left sticking in the newly-dug ground... I hit him! The spear stuck in... One of them stuck a needle in its spine.* `V+ADV, V+PREP, V+N+ADV/PREP, V+PRON+ADV/PREP: ERGATIVE`

3 If you **stick** something **in** something, you attach it there firmly using glue or tape. EG *I soon tired of sticking in the stamps on the wrong pages... He stuck a Labour poster in his window.* `V+ADV+N, V+N+PREP/ADV, V+PRON+PREP/ADV`

4 If something **sticks in** your mind or memory, you continue to remember it very clearly. EG *This strange conversation was to stick* `V+PREP`

in Meehan's mind... ...behaviour which sticks in the popular consciousness... They stuck in your memory... They haunted my eyes and stuck in my dreams.

5 If you are writing or drawing and **stick** something **in,** you write it or draw it roughly or quickly. EG *Better stick in there: 'possibility of Birmingham'... I've endeavoured to avoid boring legal jargon in this book; I stick it in only when it is vital.* ● **Take out** and **remove** mean the opposite of **stick in.**   V+N+ADV/PREP, V+PRON+ADV/PREP

6 If you have a difficult task or a lot of work to do and get **stuck in,** you start doing it, usually with a lot of energy or enthusiasm; a very informal use. EG *We rolled up our sleeves, got stuck in and made a start... This means that they have to get stuck in for once. It is no good waiting.*   ADJECTIVE

stick on. 1 If you **stick** something **on** a surface, you attach it to the surface using glue, tape, or drawing pins. EG *Stick a numbered label on each case... Cut out interesting items from newspapers and stick them on noticeboards... He saw a picture of Stanley Baldwin stuck on the wall... The hat seems to be stuck on with glue... Bandages won't stick on the palm.* ▶ **Stick-on** things have a layer of glue on one side so that they can be attached to surfaces easily. EG *Label fuses with stick-on labels.* ▶ **Stuck-on** things have been attached to a surface with glue or adhesive. EG *...the first page covered by a stuck-on tab of paper.*   V+N+PREP/ADV, V+PRON+PREP/ADV, V+ADV+N, V+ADV: ERGATIVE

ADJECTIVE

ADJECTIVE

2 If you **stick** one thing **on** another, you place it on there casually or carelessly. EG *She poked away at the fire, stuck on another lump of coal... ...the bottles going clink clink as Pa stuck them on the stack... ...an orange hat stuck on her dark red curls.*   V+ADV+N, V+PRON+ADV/PREP, V+N+ADV/PREP

3 If you **are stuck on** an object or idea, you like it very much; a very informal use. EG *...after it was all arranged, and they were absolutely stuck on it... The government isn't going to get stuck on any set of fancy doctrinaire ideas.*   PASSIVE: V+PREP

stick out. 1 If you **stick** something **out,** you push it so that it appears from inside or behind something else. EG *Lally stuck her head out of a window... Lynn stuck out her tongue... Is that tummy really all fat or do you stick it out when you are standing?*   V+N+ADV, V+ADV+N, V+PRON+ADV

2 If something **sticks out,** it extends beyond something else, because of its length or because of the direction in which it is pointing. EG *...if the arm is sticking out... There was a little chimney sticking out of the roof... She sat on the beach, her bony legs sticking straight out in front of her... He looked at the crumpled bills sticking out between his fingers.* ● **Protrude** is a more formal word for **stick out.**   V+ADV: USUALLY+A

3 If a quality or feature of someone or something **sticks out,** it is very obvious or noticeable. EG *...a home that would not stick out on a European or North American estate... She was going out with someone else tonight: that had stuck out a mile.* ● **Stand out** means almost the same as **stick out.**   V+ADV

4 If you **stick out** a difficult or unpleasant situation, you continue being involved in it, rather than leaving it. EG *Sometimes I wonder if I can stick this job out much longer... I stuck it out until the situation became ugly... The women have stuck it out and won what they were fighting for.* ● **Endure** is a more formal word for **stick out.**   V+N+ADV, V+PRON+ADV

stick out for. If you **stick out for** something, you keep demanding it until you get it, and do not accept anything different or less than you have asked for. EG *He stuck out for twice the usual salary, and got it.* ● **Hold out for** means almost the same as **stick out for.**   V+ADV+PREP

stick to. 1 If a substance or object **sticks to** a surface, it becomes accidentally attached to it and is difficult to remove. EG *...powdered sand that sticks to your hair and skin... ...the invalid, whose clothes*   V+PREP

were sticking to him... The eggs scorched and stuck to the pan.
● **Adhere to** is a more formal word for **stick to.**

2 If you **stick to** what you have decided to do or what you are   V+PREP
expected to do, you continue doing it in the same way, even if you
would prefer not to or if people try to make you change. EG *I was
pleased to see the lads were sticking to their task... 'Of course we'll
stick to our policy,' said McPherson... ...unless they stick to their
promise... Stick strictly to the diet to gain full relief... I have my own
likes and dislikes and choose to stick to them... I didn't have to stick
to any set route.* ● **Keep to** means almost the same as **stick to.**

3 If you are talking and **stick to** a subject, you talk only about that   V+PREP
subject, and not about anything else. EG *Let me stick to painting for a
moment... I think we should stick to the point... Stick to the facts.*
● **Keep to** means almost the same as **stick to.**

4 If you **stick to** someone, you keep supporting and trusting them,   V+PREP
especially when they are in a difficult situation. EG *She is sticking to
her husband through thick and thin... ...under the circumstances
Dolores had better stick to her old man.* ● **Stand by** and **stick by**
mean almost the same as **stick to.**

stick together. 1 If you **stick** things or parts **together,** you attach   V+PRON+ADV,
or fix them to each other. EG *When I come back, we'll stick them*   V+ADV+N,
together again... Once they'd made all the bits it would be cheaper   V+N+ADV
*to stick them together in the factory... I have struggled like that to
stick together different materials with unsuitable glue.*

2 If things **stick together,** they become attached to each other and   V+ADV
are difficult to separate. EG *Their feathers stick together if they don't
keep them warm... I don't want to move in case my nails stick
together... ...shaking the chips to loosen the few which had stuck
together.*

3 If people **stick together,** they stay with each other and support   V+ADV
each other, especially when they are in a difficult situation. EG *We
have to stick together to guard against outside meddlers... Life was
none too easy in the colony, but the boys learnt to stick together...
Only by sticking together will they improve conditions.*

stick up. 1 If you **stick up** a picture, notice, or object, you attach it   V+ADV+N,
to a wall or noticeboard so that it can be seen. EG *They stick up*   V+PRON+ADV,
pictures of women all round the rooms... She suggests that women   V+N+ADV
*stick up a notice in their Welfare Clinic... 'You don't mind if I stick
this up?' Donald held up a crucifix.*

2 If something long **sticks up,** it points upwards in an upright   V+ADV:
position. EG *...a nail sticking up from a board... ...his long legs bent,*   USUALLY+A
*his knees sticking up towards his chin... Above the forehead the tufts
of grey hair stuck up at all angles.* ● **Protrude** and **project** are more
formal words for **stick up.**

3 If you **stick** something **up** somewhere, you push it inside there   V+N+PREP,
with some force. EG *They're always sticking potatoes up my exhaust*   V+PRON+PREP
pipe.

4 If someone **sticks up** a bank, a shop, or a person, they rob them,   V+ADV+N,
using a gun as a threat; an old-fashioned or American use. EG *If I*   V+N+ADV
*wanted to stick up a bank, I'd do it just before a long weekend... Did
they ever catch the robbers that stuck up your friend?... I didn't
think the bank was going to get stuck up today.* ● **Hold up** means
almost the same as **stick up.** ▶ A **stick-up** is a robbery in which the   N COUNT
thieves use guns; an old-fashioned or American word. EG *Poor guy.
Was it a stick-up?*

5 If you describe someone as **stuck-up,** you mean that they think   ADJECTIVE
they are very important or high class and are not friendly. EG *...a
small company where no one is stuck-up.*

stick up for. If you **stick up for** a person, a principle, or a belief, V+ADV+PREP
you support or defend them, using force if necessary. EG *I'll stick up
for you... I was too small to stick up for my rights... ...at a public
school you have to be able to stick up for yourself.* ● **Stand up for**
means almost the same as **stick up for.**

stick with. 1 If you **stick with** something, you continue to use it or V+PREP
do it, and do not change to something else. EG *I stuck with what was
to be my staple diet: brown rice... Will they stick with the business
or run off to start something else?... Jim and Ginny had such
difficulty ever sticking with anything.* ● **Stick at** and **stick to** mean
almost the same as **stick with.**

2 If you **stick with** someone, you stay close to them. EG *Stick with me* V+PREP
*and you'll be okay, don't you worry... Ducret shouted to the driver to
stick with the President... I'll stick with him, step by step.*

3 If you **are stuck with** someone or something, you feel that you did PASSIVE:
not choose them and do not like them or want them, but you do not V+PREP
have the power to change the situation. EG *...some useless secretary
he was stuck with... They sell everything they have got for fear of
being stuck with a load of cheap goods.*

4 If an idea or memory **sticks with** you, you continue to remember V+PREP
it for a long time. EG *One note of memory stuck with him: singing
with Nino Valenti... That idea stuck with me. It's simple, but it is
dynamic... It's funny how some things stick with you.*

stir, stirs, stirring, stirred

stir in. If you **stir** a substance **in**, you mix it with another substance, V+N+ADV,
using a tool such as a spoon. EG *When the yeast is dissolved, stir the* V+ADV+N,
flour in gradually... She had stirred in the sugar. ● **Mix in** means V+PRON+ADV
almost the same as **stir in.**

stir into. If you **stir** one substance **into** another, you mix it with the V+N+PREP,
other substance so that the two substances are blended together. EG V+PRON+PREP
*He stirred some cream into his coffee... Strain the liquid and stir this
into the margarine and flour... The gelatine can be stirred into a hot
liquid or custard until dissolved.* ● **Mix into** means almost the same
as **stir into.**

stir up. 1 If something **stirs up** dust or mud, it causes it to rise and V+ADV+N,
move around. EG *Some gentle winds stirred up the dust.* ● **Disturb** is V+N+ADV,
a more formal word for **stir up.** V+PRON+ADV

2 To **stir up** trouble or **stir up** a feeling means to cause trouble or to V+ADV+N,
cause people to have the feeling. EG *He was prevented from speak-* V+N+ADV,
ing on the grounds that it would 'stir up trouble'... ...a rally called to V+PRON+ADV
*stir up popular support for nuclear disarmament... Being back in the
hospital stirred up unpleasant memories... She was one of those
people who likes stirring things up.* ● **Provoke** and **incite** are more
formal words for **stir up.**

stitch, stitches, stitching, stitched

stitch up. When doctors **stitch up** an open wound, they use a special V+ADV+N,
needle and thread to join the edges of it together so that it is V+N+ADV,
completely closed. EG *My mother took a needle in her hand to stitch* V+PRON+ADV
*up terrible wounds... She scraped the dirt out of my wounds and
stitched up one finger.* ● **Sew up** means almost the same as **stitch
up,** and **suture** is a more technical word.

stock, stocks, stocking, stocked

stock up. If you **stock up** with things, you buy a lot of them in case V+ADV:
you cannot get them later. EG *Stock up with groceries and canned* USUALLY+*with*,
foods once a fortnight... I stocked up on some gourmet frozen ALSO+*on*
dishes... All the lads were keen to stock up in case of shortages.

stoke, stokes, stoking, stoked

stoke up. 1 If you **stoke up** a fire you make it burn faster by adding more fuel and poking it with a stick or a poker. EG *He crouched to stoke up the flames... The servants were there to stoke up coal fires... Miss Jackson and I stoked the fire up.* V+ADV+N, V+N+ADV, V+PRON+ADV

2 If you **stoke up** a particular feeling or idea, you encourage people to feel more excited, angry, or enthusiastic about something. EG *...stoking up popular prejudice... He stoked up their anger with his insensitive remarks.* ● **Stir up** means almost the same as **stoke up**. V+ADV+N, V+N+ADV, V+PRON+ADV

stop, stops, stopping, stopped

stop away. If you **stop away**, you deliberately do not go to a place. EG *The roads have been clear so people are stopping away or they're coming in some other way... She's been stopping away from school.* ● **Stay away** means almost the same as **stop away**. V+ADV: ALSO+*from*

stop behind. If you **stop behind**, you stay in a place after other people have left. EG *Mr. Piggott made the whole class stop behind.* ● **Stay behind** means almost the same as **stop behind**. V+ADV

stop by. If you **stop by**, you visit a place for a short time; an informal expression. EG *I thought I might stop by and say hello... They invited us to stop by the house for coffee... All day long people stopped by Barak's hotel room to pay their respects to him.* ● **Drop by** means almost the same as **stop by**. V+ADV, V+PREP

stop in. 1 If you **stop in**, you stay at home rather than going out. EG *I stop in each morning to read... I'd rather stop in, thanks.* ● **Stay in** means almost the same as **stop in**. V+ADV

2 If you **stop in** at a place, you visit it for a short time. EG *Yesterday, I stopped in to visit a friend of mine... I stopped in at the restaurant... We stopped in at Wingelinna to say goodbye.* ● **Stop by** and **stop off** mean almost the same as **stop in**. V+ADV: USUALLY+*at*

stop off. If you **stop off** somewhere, you stay there for a short time in the middle of a journey. EG *On the way home I stopped off in London to attend a conference... Do you mind if I stop off for some groceries?... I'll stop off at headquarters and give his wife a call.* V+ADV: USUALLY+A

stop out. If you say that someone **stopped out**, you mean that they stayed out late at night when you thought they ought to have come home. EG *Billie stopped out all night last Saturday.* ● **Stay out** means almost the same as **stop out**. ▶ If you say that someone is a **stop-out**, you mean that they are the sort of person who likes to stay out late; used showing disapproval. EG *...dirty little stop-out.* V+ADV

N COUNT

stop over. 1 If you **stop over** somewhere, you stay there for one or more nights in between two parts of a journey, especially a plane journey. EG *I stopped over in Paris on my way here.* ● **Stop off** means almost the same as **stop over**. ▶ A **stopover** is a short stay in a particular place between parts of a long journey. EG *...a five-week tour abroad with a three-day stopover in the United States.* V+ADV

N COUNT

2 If you **stop over**, you visit a place for a short time. EG *Stop over for coffee in the morning... Why don't you stop over sometime? Doreen would love to see you.* ● **Stop by** and **come over** mean almost the same as **stop over**. V+ADV

stop up. 1 If you **stop up** something, you cover or fill a hole or gap in it so that nothing can get through it. EG *Stop up each crack as it occurs... They shut every door and window in the house, and stopped up every chimney.* ● **Block up** means almost the same as **stop up**. V+ADV+N, V+N+ADV, V+PRON+ADV

2 If you **stop up**, you go to bed much later than usual. EG *I stopped up to watch the match.* ● **Stay up** means almost the same as **stop up**. V+ADV

store, stores, storing, stored

store away. To store things away means to put them in a safe place and keep them until they are needed. EG *They stored their tackle away during the winter... The body takes the energy-value it needs and stores away the rest... The goods were stored away at the back of the warehouse.* ● **Stow away** means almost the same as **store away.**   `V+N+ADV,` `V+ADV+N,` `V+PRON+ADV`

store up. To store something up means to keep it until the time is right to use it. EG *She had some sausage carefully stored up for the occasion... Jane had noticed what he said, and stored it up as a weapon... Plants store up energy in the summer.* ● **Save up** means almost the same as **store up.**   `V+N+ADV,` `V+PRON+ADV,` `V+ADV+N`

storm, storms, storming, stormed

storm in. If you storm in, you rush into a place suddenly and noisily, often because you are very angry. EG *Geoffrey looked up as Peter stormed in, more excited than anyone had seen him before.*   `V+ADV`

storm into. If you storm into a place, you rush into it suddenly and noisily, often because you are very angry. EG *John stormed into his room... Ira came storming into the clinic.*   `V+PREP`

storm off. If you storm off, you go away suddenly because you are very angry. EG *Within minutes, he'd stormed off angrily... In a rage I stormed off to the police station.*   `V+ADV`

storm out. If you storm out, you leave a place very suddenly because you are very angry. EG *He said a few strong words to the owner and stormed out... It was all too much for Alec, who stormed out of the room.*   `V+ADV:` `ALSO+of`

stow, stows, stowing, stowed

stow away. 1 If you stow something away, you put it carefully in a place until it is needed. EG *She had stowed her canvasses away... He accepted the money gratefully and stowed it away in his suitcase... His baggage was safely stowed away in the plane... Bill instructed the driver to stow away the white ribbons.* ● **Store away** means almost the same as **stow away.**   `V+N+ADV,` `V+PRON+ADV,` `V+ADV+N`

2 If someone stows away, they hide in a ship, aeroplane, or other vehicle in order to make the journey secretly and without paying the fare. EG *She had not forgotten her original objective—to stow away on a flight to New York... He made his escape and stowed away to America.* ▸ A **stowaway** is a person who hides in a ship, aeroplane, or other vehicle in order to make the journey secretly without paying the fare. EG *There's a stowaway on Flight 80.*   `V+ADV`   `N COUNT`

straighten, straightens, straightening, straightened

straighten out. 1 If you straighten out something that is twisted, bent, or crumpled or if it straightens out, it becomes completely straight. EG *Sylvia sits down on the wooden picnic bench and straightens out her legs... He straightened out the paper... The road through the canyon doesn't straighten out.*   `V+ADV+N,` `V+N+ADV,` `V+PRON+ADV,` `V+ADV:` `ERGATIVE`

2 If you straighten out a confused situation, you succeed in organizing it and putting it in order. EG *A legal contract does help to straighten out the mess when things go wrong... The baby sitter had straightened out the room... It'll take six weeks to get things straightened out... Everything will be straightened out before we leave.* ● **Sort out** and **straighten up** mean almost the same as **straighten out.**   `V+ADV+N,` `V+N+ADV,` `V+PRON+ADV`

3 If you straighten someone out, you help them with their problems and stop them from being worried or confused. EG *Geoff had his problems, but I straightened him out and we got married... You*   `V+PRON+ADV,` `V+N+ADV`

straightened the kid out, stopped him going bad. ● **Help out** means almost the same as **straighten out.**

straighten up. 1 When you **straighten up,** you make your back or body completely straight and you stand upright. EG *He straightens up, combs his hair, and walks into the meeting... He released his grip and let Breslow straighten up.* · V+ADV

2 If you **straighten up** a confused situation, you succeed in organizing it and putting it in order. EG *We must get it all straightened up soon... As soon as we can straighten up matters here we will book a passage to America.* ● **Sort out** and **straighten out** mean almost the same as **straighten up.** · V+ADV+N, V+N+ADV, V+PRON+ADV

strain, strains, straining, strained

strain at. If you **strain at** a rope or cord of some kind, you pull very hard on it. EG *They strained at the ropes... ...vicious dogs straining at their leashes.* · V+PREP

strain off. If you **strain** a liquid **off,** you separate it from something solid using something such as a sieve or a funnel. EG *When the mixture is boiling, strain it off into jars... Strain off the water and dry the sediment.* · V+PRON+ADV, V+ADV+N, V+N+ADV

strap, straps, strapping, strapped

strap in. If you **strap** someone **in,** you fasten them firmly into a seat, using a belt or strap. EG *Gwen pulled down a folding seat and strapped herself in... Check to see that the children are strapped in securely.* ● **Buckle in** means almost the same as **strap in.** · V+REFL+ADV, V+N+ADV, V+PRON+ADV

strap into. If you **strap** someone **into** a seat, you fasten them firmly there, using a belt or strap. EG *Quite a few of them knew how to strap themselves into the helicopter... The twins were strapped into their seats... ...a plastic seat into which the baby can be strapped.* ● **Buckle into** means almost the same as **strap into.** · V+REFL+PREP, V+N+PREP, V+PRON+PREP

strap on. If you **strap** something **on,** you fasten it in position, using a belt or strap. EG *Mona hastily strapped on her skis... He strapped on his new watch.* · V+ADV+N, V+N+ADV, V+PRON+ADV

strap up. If someone **straps up** a part of their body, they put a bandage or support around it in order to avoid using it. EG *They strapped it up for me at hospital... ...the harness that kept his right leg strapped up.* · V+N+ADV, V+PRON+ADV, V+ADV+N

stretch, stretches, stretching, stretched

stretch away. If a flat area of land **stretches away,** it extends for some distance. EG *The beach stretched away before them in a gentle curve... The coast stretching away straight and black... He observes sunny lawns stretching away to mountains.* · V+ADV: USUALLY+A

stretch out. 1 If you **stretch out** or **stretch** yourself **out** somewhere, you lie there with your legs and body in a straight line. EG *I just want to stretch out in my own bed... Stretch out in comfort... She groaned and stretched herself out flat on the sofa.* · V+ADV, V+REFL+ADV

2 If you **stretch out** your arm or leg, you hold it out straight. EG *He stretched out a thin arm and took our hands... She stretched out her hand for the money... ...stretching one leg out sideways.* · V+ADV+N, V+N+ADV, V+PRON+ADV

strike, strikes, striking, struck

strike at. If you **strike at** someone or something, you do or say something which attacks them. EG *The opposition had struck at the root of Labour's strategy... They are using this alliance to strike at the Palestinians... McPherson saw a chance to strike at Barber.* · V+PREP

strike back. If you **strike back,** you attempt to harm someone because they have harmed you. EG *As he grows older he begins to* · V+ADV

strike back... ...striking back against the contempt of their enemies.
● **Hit back** means almost the same as **strike back.**

strike down. If someone **is struck down,** they are badly injured or killed. EG *President Kennedy was struck down by an assassin's bullet... It would be so awful to be struck down before one's time... Polio struck him down.*

V+N+ADV,
V+PRON+ADV,
V+ADV+N:
USUALLY PASSIVE

strike off. 1 If someone such as a doctor or lawyer **is struck off,** their name is taken off the official register and they are not allowed to do medical or legal work any more. EG *'You should be struck off!' Dr Leon shouted... You can be struck off the roll for that.*

PASSIVE:
V+ADV,
V+PREP

2 See **strike out.**

strike on. If you **strike on** or **upon** a solution, answer, or idea, you think of it unexpectedly and suddenly. EG *He had for once struck on a quite shrewd judgement... Then they struck upon the idea of making their own yoghurt.* ● **Hit on** means almost the same as **strike on.**

V+PREP

strike out. 1 If you **strike out,** you begin to do something different, often because you want to become more independent. EG *He decided to strike out on his own... The company was striking out in new directions in the field of drama.*

V+ADV:
USUALLY+A

2 If you **strike out** or **off** somewhere, you start to move in a determined way in a particular direction. EG *He decided to leave the path and strike out across the grass... We struck off northward through the woods... He covered another twenty yards beside the rail and then struck off left into the mangroves.*

V+ADV:
USUALLY+A

3 If you **strike out** at someone, you aim a blow or punch at them. EG *He strikes out blindly, trying to get away.* ● **Hit out** means almost the same as **strike out.**

V+ADV:
USUALLY+A

4 If you **strike out** something that is written down, you put a line through it because it is wrong or because you do not want it to be seen. EG *Strike out the questions which do not apply to you... She read through her essay and struck a few words out here and there.* ● **Cross out** means almost the same as **strike out,** and **delete** is a more formal word.

V+ADV+N,
V+N+ADV,
V+PRON+ADV

strike up. 1 When you **strike up** a conversation or friendship with someone, you begin it. EG *Alice and I struck up a friendship immediately... They began to try and strike up contacts with sympathizers... As soon as she struck up any kind of acquaintance he felt jealous.*

V+ADV+N

2 When musicians **strike up,** they begin to play music. EG *The band strikes up at noon... The orchestra struck up the national anthem... The band had just struck up Duke Ellington's 'Satin Doll'.*

V+ADV,
V+ADV+N

strike upon. See **strike on.**

string, strings, stringing, strung

string along. 1 If you **string** someone **along,** you deceive them by encouraging them to believe that you both have the same desires, beliefs, or hopes; used in informal English showing disapproval. EG *He dreamed of being Vice-President, and Roosevelt had strung him along... Gareth's just strung you along; he won't marry you.*

V+PRON+ADV,
V+N+ADV

2 If you **string along** with someone, you go somewhere with them rather casually for a short time; an informal use. EG *I'll string along with you... He'll string along if he gets bored.* ● **Tag along** means almost the same as **string along.**

V+ADV:
ALSO+ *with*

string out. If things **are strung out,** they are spread out in a long line. EG *...boom towns which are strung out along dirt roads... The genes are strung out along the chromosomes... The soldiers were hammering in concrete posts and stringing out the wire... The Indians strung them out in a fifteen mile line.*

V+N+ADV,
V+ADV+N,
V+PRON+ADV:
USUALLY PASSIVE

string together. If you **string** things **together,** you make them into

V+N+ADV,

one thing by adding them to each other, one at a time. EG ...*a knack for stringing sentences together... I sang her a wistful ballad and strung together some rhymes to amuse her... No sooner are two thoughts strung together than there is an interruption.* V+ADV+N,
V+PRON+ADV

string up. 1 If you **string** something **up,** you hang or tie it high in the air between two or more objects. EG *They had strung the straw man up between two poles... He took down the red lights and strung up the blue ones... Core the apples and string up the slices.* ● **Put up** means almost the same as **string up.** V+N+ADV,
V+ADV+N,
V+PRON+ADV

2 To **string** someone **up** means to kill them by hanging them; an informal use. EG ...*stringing you up from the nearest lamp post... ...a little corpse, strung up as a warning... She found a dead cat strung up on her porch.* V+PRON+ADV,
V+N+ADV,
V+ADV+N

3 If you **are strung up,** you feel tense and nervous; an informal use. EG *I was too strung up to eat anything... I began to get strung up.* PASSIVE:
V+ADV

strip, strips, stripping, stripped

strip away. 1 If you **strip away** something that is attached to a surface, you remove it completely. EG *Someone got on the roof and stripped away the lead... The pale grey wallpaper had been stripped away.* ● **Strip off** means almost the same as **strip away.** V+ADV+N,
V+N+ADV,
V+PRON+ADV

2 To **strip away** people's rights, beliefs, or attitudes means to get rid of them completely. EG ...*stripping away the symbols of individuality... ...stripping away their remaining civil rights... This pretence is to be stripped away on the Day of Judgement.* V+ADV+N,
V+N+ADV,
V+PRON+ADV

strip down. If you **strip down** an engine or piece of equipment, you take it to pieces, usually in order to clean it or repair it. EG *She offered to help them in dismantling and stripping down the bike... Can you lubricate the engine without stripping it down?* V+ADV+N,
V+PRON+ADV,
V+N+ADV

strip of. If someone **is stripped of** something such as their property, rights, or title, those things are taken away from them. EG *She was rejected by her husband and automatically stripped of all her property and possessions... ...a group stripped of its civil rights... They stripped the bodies of their gear.* V+N+PREP,
V+PRON+PREP:
USUALLY PASSIVE

strip off. 1 When you **strip off** your clothes, you undress. EG *Casson stripped off his raincoat... Gertrude was unlacing her plimsolls and stripping off her socks... They stripped off and dived in.* V+ADV+N,
V+PRON+ADV,
V+N+ADV,
V+ADV

2 If you **strip off** something that is attached to a surface, you remove it completely. EG *They spent two weeks stripping off all the brown paint... ...stripping off the tarpaulins... The bark could easily be stripped off.* ● **Strip away** means almost the same as **strip off.** V+ADV+N,
V+N+ADV,
V+PRON+ADV

strip out. 1 If you **strip** a place **out,** you take out everything that is inside it so that you can decorate it or rebuild it. EG *The nursery was stripped out and painted white.* V+N+ADV,
V+PRON+ADV,
V+ADV+N

2 If you **strip out** information from a financial or statistical calculation, you ignore it because it is not relevant to what you are trying to discover. EG *After stripping out all acquisitions and other factors to gain a fair comparison with 1987, domestic profits have risen by a disappointing 3 per cent.* V+ADV+N,
V+N+ADV,
V+PRON+ADV

struggle, struggles, struggling, struggled

struggle on. If you **struggle on,** you manage with great difficulty to continue doing something. EG *Some struggled on, but those who couldn't were left for dead... Fifteen years older than Gladys, he struggled on manfully only for a few years longer.* ● **Soldier on** means almost the same as **struggle on.** V+ADV

stub, stubs, stubbing, stubbed

stub out. When someone **stubs out** a cigarette or cigar, they stop it V+ADV+N,

burning by pressing the end against something hard. EG *Phillip stubs* V+N+ADV,
out his cigarette and lights another... ...stubbing her half-smoked V+PRON+ADV
cigarette out in one of the tin lids... ...rolling their own cigarettes and
stubbing them out on the furniture. ● **Extinguish** is a more formal
word for **stub out**.

stumble, stumbles, stumbling, stumbled

stumble across. If you **stumble across** something or someone, V+PREP
you discover or meet them unexpectedly. EG *In the course of their*
search they may stumble across something quite different... Had I
stumbled across another human being, I would have hidden. ● **Come**
across means almost the same as **stumble across**.

stumble on. If you **stumble on** or **upon** something or someone, you V+PREP:
discover or meet them unexpectedly. EG *Sir Alexander Fleming* HAS PASSIVE
stumbled on his great discovery of penicillin quite by accident...
Kairi stumbled upon something that was to alter their lives... If a
solution ever happens it will be stumbled upon. ● **Come across**
means almost the same as **stumble on**.
stumble upon. See **stumble on**.

stump, stumps, stumping, stumped

stump up. If you **stump up** a sum of money, you pay the money that V+ADV+N
is required for something, often reluctantly. EG *The government is*
being asked to stump up the rest of the cash... ...asking investors to
stump up £50m to help finance the films. ● **Cough up** means almost
the same as **stump up**.

subject, subjects, subjecting, subjected

subject to. If you **subject** someone to something unpleasant, you V+N+PREP,
make them experience it. EG *A court order was obtained, permitting* V+PRON+PREP
the police to subject Arthur to a lie detector test... They stayed at
home rather than subject themselves to bureaucratic checks at the
border... The air bases were subjected to intense air attack.

subscribe, subscribes, subscribing, subscribed

subscribe to. 1 If you **subscribe to** an opinion or belief, you have V+PREP:
this opinion or belief and share it with a number of other people. EG HAS PASSIVE
A large number of them now subscribe to the Mohammedan faith...
They find they cannot subscribe to the values of an older genera-
tion... The rest of us do not subscribe to this theory.
2 If you **subscribe to** a magazine or a newspaper, you pay to receive V+PREP
copies of it regularly. EG *She subscribed to Reader's Digest and TV*
Guide... I started subscribing to a morning newspaper.

suck, sucks, sucking, sucked

suck off. If someone having sex **sucks** their partner **off**, they lick or V+N+ADV,
suck their partner's genitals until their partner has an orgasm; a V+PRON+ADV,
very informal expression. V+ADV+N

suck up to. If you **suck up to** someone in a position of authority, V+ADV+PREP
you try to please them by flattering them or by doing things for
them, especially in order to gain some advantage for yourself; an
informal expression, used showing disapproval. EG *There was no*
need for them to suck up to Mrs Norberg so much... 'They were
trying to be amiable and agreeable.'—'Sucking up to me, you mean?'

sum, sums, summing, summed

sum up. 1 If you **sum up** a situation, you state or describe briefly its V+ADV+N,
most important aspects or characteristics. EG *I can't sum up his* V+N+ADV,
whole philosophy in one sentence... To sum all this up, what we need V+PRON+ADV
is a reform of the grant-aid system... She was searching for the

words that would sum it up. ● **Summarize** means almost the same as **sum up,** and **encapsulate** is a more formal word.

2 When someone **sums up** at the end of a speech, argument, or   V+ADV
debate, they state briefly and clearly its main points as a conclusion.
When a judge **sums up** at the end of a trial, he or she makes a
speech to the jury reminding them of the evidence and the main
arguments of the case; a technical use. EG *At the end of the
discussion, he summed up, and added a few points... To sum up:
within our society there still exist rampant inequalities.*
● **Summarize** means almost the same as **sum up.** ▸ **summing-up,**   N COUNT
summings-up. The **summing-up** at the end of a trial is a speech in
which the judge reminds the jury of the evidence and the main
arguments of the case. EG *In his summing up, the judge again
returned to the motive.*

3 If something **sums up** a situation, it represents or suggests to you   V+ADV+N,
the most important and typical features of that situation. EG *...a*   V+N+ADV,
                                              V+PRON+ADV
*crusade which summed up one aspect of the Sixties... His attitude
was summed up by another incident a little later last winter.*
● **Epitomize** is a more formal word for **sum up.**

4 If you **sum up** someone or something, you pass an opinion on them   V+PRON+ADV,
or make an accurate judgement of them. EG *He was able to sum us*   V+ADV+N,
                                              V+N+ADV
*up in a very short time... She asked him to sum himself up, and he
allowed that he had an easy temperament... It was as though she
was summing up the differences between her world and ours.* ● **Size
up** means almost the same as **sum up.** ▸ A **summing up** is an   N SING
opinion or judgement about something or someone. EG *It seemed a
pretty fair summing up of two thousand years of Western civilization... 'She was all right,' was Lester's summing up.*

summon, summons, summoning, summoned

summon up. 1 If you **summon up** your strength, energy, courage,   V+ADV+N:
and so on, you make a great effort in order to do something. EG *...if*   USUALLY+*to*-INF
*you can't summon up enough energy to get up early... She did not
seem able to summon up the effort to return to London... He
eventually summoned up the courage to ask them if Melanie was all
right.* ● **Muster up** means almost the same as **summon up.**

2 If you **summon up** support, help, or resources, you persuade   V+ADV+N,
people to give you support or help. EG *He was hoping to summon up*   V+N+ADV,
                                             V+PRON+ADV
*support for his measures... Almost overnight Wren seems to have
summoned up a team of craftsmen of the necessary talent.* ● **Drum
up** means almost the same as **summon up.**

3 If you **summon** someone **up,** you order them to come to you; a   V+ADV+N,
fairly formal use. EG *She summoned up the remainder of the family...*   V+PRON+ADV
A short time later we were summoned up. ● **Call up** means almost
the same as **summon up.**

4 If something **summons up** a memory or thought, it causes you to   V+ADV+N,
remember, feel, or think a particular thing. EG *The odour summoned*   V+PRON+ADV
*up memories of my childhood... ...all the emotions to be summoned
up during their work.* ● **Conjure up** and **evoke** mean almost the
same as **summon up.**

surge, surges, surging, surged

surge up. 1 If an emotion or sensation **surges up** in you, you   V+ADV:
suddenly feel it very intensely; a literary use. EG *His true feelings*   USUALLY+A
*keep surging up inside him... The impulses of anarchy and madness
surge up to challenge the rule of reason and convention.* ● **Well up**
means almost the same as **surge up.**

2 If a sound **surges up,** you suddenly hear it very loudly and   V+ADV:
powerfully; a literary use. EG *A huge roar of applause and cheers*   USUALLY+A

surged up from the crowd... Chords of smooth music surged up in my head. ● **Rise up** means almost the same as **surge up.**

3 An **upsurge** in something is a sudden and serious increase in it. EG N SING *...a massive upsurge of social unrest... ...an upsurge in industrial production... ...the inflationary upsurge.*

suss, susses, sussing, sussed

suss out. 1 If you **suss out** someone or something, you discover V+PRON+ADV, what they are really like; an informal use. EG *She had me sussed out* V+ADV+N, *in ten minutes... How long it took to suss out the true nature of that lovely stuff!* ● **Work out** means almost the same as **suss out.**

2 If you **suss out** a problem, you discover how to do it or solve it; an V+ADV+N, informal use. EG *At last she sussed out the reason for this.* ● **Sort out** V+PRON+ADV, means almost the same as **suss out.** V+N+ADV

swab, swabs, swabbing, swabbed

Swab is also spelled **swob** in American English.

swab down. If you **swab down** a floor or wall, you clean it V+PRON+ADV, thoroughly with a wet mop or brush and water. EG *A relatively easy* V+ADV+N, *way to swab it down is with a softish brush.* ● **Wash down** means almost the same as **swab down.**

swab out. If you **swab out** a room or container, you clean it V+PRON+ADV, thoroughly with a wet mop or brush and water. EG *Swab it out with* V+ADV+N, *hot water and a little disinfectant.* ● **Wash out** means almost the same as **swab out.**

swallow, swallows, swallowing, swallowed

swallow down. If you **swallow down** something that is in your V+PRON+ADV, mouth, you cause it to pass from your mouth into your stomach. EG V+ADV+N, *'Go on and drink,' he said. She swallowed it down... He swallowed* V+N+ADV *down the last lump of bread... The fish may have swallowed the bait down.* ● **Gulp down** means almost the same as **swallow down.**

swallow up. 1 If you **swallow** something **up,** you take it into your V+PRON+ADV, mouth and cause it to pass into your stomach; often used in contexts V+ADV+N, when you are talking about the idea of something being swallowed, V+N+ADV rather than something actually being eaten. EG *...opening her eyes wider and wider, as if to swallow him up... They believed at that time that sinners in general were literally swallowed up by hell, which they entered through the mouth of the Devil.*

2 If something **is swallowed up** by something else, it becomes part V+ADV+N, of it and no longer has a separate identity of its own. EG *The* V+N+ADV, *members would not tolerate the Liberal Party being swallowed up* V+PRON+ADV: *by the SDP... The residents in the square feared the Museum was* USUALLY PASSIVE *going to swallow it all up.* ● **Be absorbed** means almost the same as **be swallowed up.**

3 If someone or something **is swallowed up,** for example by a crowd V+ADV+N, or cloud, they are hidden by it or disappear into it, and you cannot V+PRON+ADV, see them any more. EG *And then the mist came down. In no time at* V+N+ADV: *all, every object in sight had been swallowed up—bushes, rocks,* USUALLY PASSIVE *trees, fences... A moment later she moved away, and was instantly swallowed up in the crowd of passengers around the Trans America counters.* ● **Be engulfed** means almost the same as **be swallowed up.**

4 If something **swallows up** money or resources, it uses them V+ADV+N, entirely, and they have hardly any effect on it. EG *These livestock* V+PRON+ADV *units swallowed up 22.4% of the money... It is very expensive, and is inclined to swallow up all available resources.* ● **Use up** means almost the same as **swallow up.**

swap, swaps, swapping, swapped
Swap is also spelled **swop**.

swap around. See swap round.

swap over. If you **swap** two things **over,** you take them and put each one in the place where the other one was before. EG *You can always swap it over at a later stage... See if you can swap them over.* V+PRON+ADV, V+N+ADV, V+ADV+N

swap round. If you **swap** things **round** or **around,** you move them so that each one is in a place where one of the others was before. EG *I swapped them round when he wasn't looking... ...swapping around the beds for the night at 5.30.*

swear, swears, swearing, swore, sworn

swear by. If you **swear by** something, you believe that it is especially effective, reliable, or useful for a particular purpose. EG *Gas is better than electricity for cooking, I always swear by it... Some swear by vitamin tablets, and others put their trust in pints of milk.* V+PREP

swear in. When someone **is sworn in,** they make a solemn promise or promises, either at the beginning of a trial in a court of law or when they are starting a new official appointment. EG *The jury was sworn in on March 14... General Figueiredo will be sworn in on Wednesday.* ▶ The **swearing-in** at the beginning of a trial or official appointment is the act of making a solemn promise or promises. EG *I took the bus to Baltimore for the medical examination and swearing in.* V+ADV+N, V+PRON+ADV: USUALLY PASSIVE / N SING

swear off. If you **swear off** something such as alcohol or smoking, you decide not to drink alcohol or to smoke any more; an informal expression. EG *I've sworn off alcohol for the time being.* ● **Give up** means almost the same as **swear off,** and **renounce** is a more formal word. V+PREP

sweat, sweats, sweating, sweated

sweat off. 1 If you **sweat off** weight, you lose weight by causing yourself to sweat heavily, for example through violent exercise or steam baths. EG *He managed to sweat off five pounds before the weigh-in.* V+ADV+N, V+PRON+ADV

2 If you **sweat off** a fever or other illness, you get rid of it by keeping yourself very warm and causing yourself to sweat heavily. EG *Just go to bed and try to sweat it off.* V+PRON+ADV, V+ADV+N

sweat out. 1 If you **sweat out** a period of time or **sweat** it **out,** you endure a difficult situation, waiting patiently for it to end; an informal use. EG *Cut off from the remainder of the country, the invasion force sweated it out... He sweated it out to the end... The problem was how to sweat out the next six weeks.* V+it+ADV, V+ADV+N, V+N+ADV

2 If you **sweat out** something, you get rid of it from your body or system by causing yourself to sweat heavily. EG *You could always go running. That way, you could sweat out the gin.* V+ADV+N, V+PRON+ADV

sweat over. If you **sweat over** something, you work very hard at it. EG *They sweated over every move... I really sweated over it.* V+PREP

sweep, sweeps, sweeping, swept

sweep aside. To sweep something **aside** means to make it seem unimportant and irrelevant, or to treat it as if it does not matter at all. EG *The realities of the war swept those doubts aside... His Parliamentary genius swept aside many obstacles... He himself dismissed his work, you know. Swept it aside... My suggestion was swept aside.* V+N+ADV, V+ADV+N, V+PRON+ADV

sweep away. 1 To sweep something **away** means to destroy or remove it entirely, usually because it is considered outdated or V+ADV+N, V+N+ADV, V+PRON+ADV wrong. EG *...to eliminate traditional landscapes entirely, sweeping away the hedges, valley meadows, old woods, and footpaths... ...the rush to sweep the old away and bring in the new... Almost the entire manufacturing base has been swept away.* ● **Eradicate** is a more formal word for **sweep away**.

2 When someone or something **is swept away** by a river or the sea, the current is so strong that it pulls them from the place where they were and carries them off or destroys them. EG *...a memorial tablet to the Paget family, swept away by a huge wave... We were finally brought to a halt: the entire road had been swept away.*
V+N+ADV,
V+ADV+N,
V+PRON+ADV:
USUALLY PASSIVE

3 If someone **is swept away,** their emotions are so strong that they cannot behave calmly and sensibly. EG *His life was too well regulated to be affected by affairs of the heart, while she always allowed herself to be swept away... He was suddenly swept away by the full force of her wild irresponsible seduction.* ● **Be carried away** means almost the same as **be swept away**.
PASSIVE:
V+ADV

sweep out. If you **sweep out** a room, you clean it thoroughly with a broom, getting rid of all the dust and so on. EG *...clearing the tables after each meal and sweeping out the dining rooms... They're in Grandfather's old room. I've swept it out and put some sheets on the beds... Mrs Pringle appeared, on her way to sweep the school out.*
V+ADV+N,
V+PRON+ADV,
V+N+ADV

sweep up. **1** If you **sweep up** things from a place, you collect them with a broom in order to get rid of them. EG *Kathy was in the middle of the crossing, sweeping up the glass from my broken headlights... The gardening girls were sweeping up leaves and cutting the grass... They can sweep up afterwards.*
V+ADV+N,
V+N+ADV,
V+PRON+ADV,
V+ADV

2 If you **are swept up** in something, you become very involved in it, and perhaps cannot think about anything else. EG *After Karen learned her father was alive she, too, became swept up in the desire to return home... I had not yet been swept up into the Civil Rights Movement... She was swept up by a passion of creativity.* ● **Be caught up** means almost the same as **be swept up**.
PASSIVE:
V+ADV,
USUALLY+A

sweeten, sweetens, sweetening, sweetened

sweeten up. If you **sweeten** someone **up,** you do something nice for them or give them something, in order to prepare them for something unpleasant or to persuade them to do something. EG *They sweetened him up by offering him another £1000 a year.* ● **Butter up** and **soften up** mean almost the same as **sweeten up**.
V+PRON+ADV,
V+ADV+N,
V+N+ADV

swell, swells, swelling, swelled, swollen

The past participle can be either **swelled** or **swollen**.

swell up. **1** If a part of your body **swells up,** it becomes larger and rounder than normal, usually as a result of an injury or illness. EG *A mosquito had bitten her and her whole arm had swollen up... After a few minutes my throat started to swell up.* ● **Puff up** means almost the same as **swell up**, and **go down** means the opposite.
V+ADV

2 If something such as reaction, feeling, or sound **swells up,** it suddenly becomes much stronger or more noticeable. EG *...the protests that swelled up in the 1950s against Britain's possession of nuclear weapons... And why shouldn't he? Resentment swelled up inside his breast... ...standing there as the chorus swelled up.*
V+ADV

3 If the sea **swells up,** the waves become larger and stronger; a rather literary use. EG *We stood together on the brink. The sea was not far below us; it swelled up towards us like a beckoning arm.*
V+ADV

swill, swills, swilling, swilled

swill down. If you **swill down** a drink, you drink it quite fast. If you **swill down** food, you drink something at the same time as you are
V+ADV+N,
V+PRON+ADV

eating; a fairly informal expression. EG *Everyone laughed and swilled down another drink... ...the choicest of meats to eat and swill down with claret.*

swing, swings, swinging, swung
swing around. See swing round.

swing round. If you **swing round** or **around,** you suddenly turn and   v+ADV
face in the opposite direction. EG *There was a knock on his door. He swung round startled... Marianne touched Gareth on the arm and he swung around fiercely, ready to attack.* ● **Turn round** means almost the same as **swing round.**

swing round to. If a conversation **swings round to** a particular   v+ADV+PREP,
topic, you start talking about something different, often without   V+N+ADV+PREP,
appearing to change topic completely. EG *These remarks were*   V+PRON+ADV+PREP:
apparently about David's character, but subtly they swung round to   ERGATIVE
being about our relationship... After a time he swung the conversa-
tion round to discussing the police. ● **Turn to** means almost the same as **swing round to.**

switch, switches, switching, switched
switch around. See switch round.

switch off. 1 If you **switch off** an electrical device, engine, and so   V+N+ADV,
on, you stop it working by pressing a switch. EG *He switched the*   V+ADV+N,
radio off... He drew his car into the side of the lane, and switched off   V+PRON+ADV,
the engine... Let's switch it off now, we've finished... A man banged   V+ADV
on his door to tell him to switch off. ● **Turn off** means almost the same as **switch off,** and **switch on** means the opposite.

2 If you **switch off** a television or radio programme, you stop   V+ADV+N,
watching or listening to it by pressing a switch on your set. EG *I could*   V+N+ADV,
not even summon the energy to switch off the ballet... It was a   V+PRON+ADV,
programme about minorities in a late stage of industrial capitalism.   V+ADV
Philip switched off. ● **Switch on** means the opposite of **switch off.**

3 If you **switch off** a particular kind of behaviour, you suddenly stop   V+ADV+N,
behaving in that way. EG *...attempts simply to switch off an unwanted*   V+PRON+ADV
mood... She had suddenly switched off the emotional and physical
warmth with which I associated her. ● **Switch on** means the opposite of **switch off.**

4 If you **switch off** when you are listening to something, you stop   V+ADV
paying attention to it, because you are no longer interested; an informal use. EG *The lecture was so boring I just switched off... I listened to him for perhaps a couple of minutes and then switched off.*

switch on. 1 If you **switch on** an electrical device, engine, and so   V+ADV+N,
on, you start it working by pressing a switch. EG *He ran up the stairs*   V+N+ADV,
and switched on the light on the landing... She had switched a fire on   V+PRON+ADV,
because she felt rather cold... 'Here's the electric light.'—'All right.   V+ADV
Don't switch it on.'... When the child switches on he listens to the
story and then answers a series of questions. ● **Turn on** means almost the same as **switch on,** and **switch off** means the opposite.

2 If you **switch on** a television or radio programme, you start   V+ADV+N,
watching or listening to it by pressing a switch on your set. EG *I*   V+N+ADV,
switched on the news... ...people who switch on five minutes after   V+PRON+ADV,
the beginning of the programme. ● **Switch off** means the opposite of   V+ADV
switch on.

3 If you **switch on** a particular kind of behaviour, you suddenly start   V+ADV+N,
behaving in that way; often used showing disapproval. EG *He had the*   V+PRON+ADV
ability to switch on the concentration when necessary... The girl
behind the counter switched on an automatic smile as he ap-
proached. ● **Switch off** means the opposite of **switch on.**

switch over. 1 If you **switch over** from one thing to another, you v+ADV
change from using or doing the first to the second. EG *Airline and
chain-hotel bookings switched over to computers... They will switch
over completely in a few weeks.*

2 When you are watching television, if you **switch over,** you change v+ADV
the setting on the television set in order to see something on a
different channel. EG *My father always switches over during the
adverts.*

switch round. If you **switch** things **round** or **around,** you move v+N+ADV,
them or change them so that each one is in a place where one of the v+PRON+ADV,
others was before. EG *You might have warned me that you switched* v+ADV+N
the men's and women's toilets around last night in your building.

swivel, swivels, swivelling, swivelled
American English uses the spellings **swiveling** and **swiveled.**

swivel around. See **swivel round.**

swivel round. If you **swivel round** or **around,** especially when you v+ADV,
are sitting, you turn quickly and face in another direction, or v+N+ADV,
continue turning. If you **swivel** something **round,** you turn it quickly. v+PRON+ADV:
EG *I swivelled right round in my chair... He swivelled around to greet* ERGATIVE
her as she came in... Michael slowly swivelled his chair round.
● **Turn round** means almost the same as **swivel round.**

swob, swobs, swobbing, swobbed
Swob is another spelling for **swab,** mainly used in American English.

swoop, swoops, swooping, swooped
swoop down. 1 When a bird **swoops down,** it suddenly moves v+ADV
downwards through the air towards the ground. EG *An adult swift
swooped down and glided across the roof.*

2 If a group of soldiers, policemen, or other people **swoops down** on v+ADV
you, they suddenly move towards you and attack you. EG *British
troops swooped down twice in pre-dawn raids on their headquarters... Whenever a rancher or miner got careless a band of
raiders would swoop down to capture horses or cattle.*

swop, swops, swopping, swopped
Swop is another spelling for **swap.**

swot, swots, swotting, swotted
swot up. If you **swot up** a subject or **swot up** on it, you read as v+ADV+N,
much as you can about it, usually because you are going to be asked v+PRON+ADV,
questions about it or take an examination; an informal expression. v+ADV+*on*
EG *He attended sessions in Congress, swotted up American history,
and met some politicians... They have to swot it all up... I was
swotting up on my transformational grammar.* ● **Mug up** means
almost the same as **swot up,** and **revise** is a more formal word.

syphon, syphons, syphoning, syphoned
Syphon is another spelling for **siphon.**

T t

tack, tacks, tacking, tacked

tack down. If you **tack** something **down**, you fix it to a floor or surface by using tacks. EG *...tacking floorboards down... Carpets should always be tacked down securely.*

V+N+ADV,
V+ADV+N,
V+PRON+ADV

tack on. If something **is tacked on**, it is added to something else that is already complete, often in a way that seems unsatisfactory. EG *The second legal point is tacked on to the end of Regulation 4(i)i... Bank End Cottage was on a lane through two gates, tacked on to the end of a farm.*

V+N+ADV,
V+PRON+ADV,
V+ADV+N:
USUALLY PASSIVE

tack up. If you **tack** something **up**, you fasten it to a vertical surface by using tacks. EG *Perhaps fifty men and women were at work, tacking up curtains and hoovering carpets... I'd seen advertisements for them tacked up in many rural areas.*

V+ADV+N,
V+N+ADV,
V+PRON+ADV

tag, tags, tagging, tagged

tag along. If you **tag along** with someone, you go with them, especially when they have not asked you to. EG *Our younger sisters always wanted to tag along when we went somewhere with our friends... Do you mind if I tag along?*

V+ADV

tag on. If a remark **is tagged on**, it is added to the end of something that you have said or written. EG *This information was revealed in a casual phrase, tagged on to the end of the conversation.* ● **Tack on** means almost the same as **tag on.**

V+ADV+N,
V+N+ADV,
V+PRON+ADV:
USUALLY PASSIVE

tail, tails, tailing, tailed

tail away. When a person's voice or what they are saying **tails away** or **off**, they gradually become quieter and then silent. EG *As I walked in her voice tailed away... Conversation tended to tail off when he approached.*

V+ADV

tail back. When traffic **tails back**, a long queue of it forms along a road, moving very slowly or not at all, for example because of road works or an accident. EG *Traffic tailed back from the roundabout to the M4 junction.* ▶ A **tailback** is a long queue of stationary or slowly-moving traffic that forms, for example, because of road works or an accident. EG *Almost at once they hit a tailback of rush hour traffic in the Midland Road.*

V+ADV

N COUNT

tail off. 1 When something **tails off**, it gradually becomes less in amount or value, often before coming to an end completely. EG *The rains tail off in September... The average figure has tailed off in the last few years... For many manual workers, income tails off as retirement approaches.*

2 See **tail away.**

V+ADV

take, takes, taking, took, taken

take aback. If you **are taken aback** by something, you are so surprised or shocked by it that you stop what you are doing and cannot think or behave normally. EG *I was a bit taken aback by this sudden reversal... He caught sight of my appearance for the first time and was taken aback at how different I looked... The sound of her voice took him aback.*

V+PRON+ADV,
V+N+ADV:
USUALLY PASSIVE

take after. If you **take after** a member of your family, you resemble them in your appearance, behaviour, or character. EG *You don't take after your sister... He took after his grandfather where*

V+PREP

character was concerned... If Cathy took after him she'd be a real good looking girl.

take against. If you **take against** someone or something, you start   V+PREP
to dislike them, often for no good reason. EG *The Producer started taking against Dan and the whole script... ...a person whom it was indeed easy to take against.* ● **Take to** means the opposite of **take against.**

take along. If you **take** someone or something **along** when you are   V+PRON+ADV,
going somewhere, they accompany you there or you have them   V+N+ADV, V+ADV+N
with you. EG *I asked Mr Sutton to take me along to the club... She always took her children along... I also take along a small black bag.*

take apart. 1 If you **take** something **apart,** you separate it into the   V+N+ADV,
different parts that it is made from. EG *They were the hands of a*   V+ADV+N, V+PRON+ADV
man who liked to take engines apart... Most of these machines have to be taken apart to be cleaned... Their tasks include taking apart and reassembling large bits of furniture. ● **Dismantle** is a more formal word for **take apart,** and **put together** means the opposite.

2 If you **take apart** something such as an argument or an essay, you   V+ADV+N,
analyse it carefully in order to show what its weaknesses are. EG *He*   V+PRON+ADV, V+N+ADV
had read the material and was prepared to take apart the statement that rhetoric is an art... The essay had not been a particularly great success and I'd taken it apart somewhat.

take around. See **take round**; **take around** is slightly more formal.

take aside. If you **take** someone **aside,** you separate them from the   V+N+ADV,
rest of a group in order to talk to them privately. EG *He made a point*   V+PRON+ADV, V+ADV+N
of taking Daniel aside and telling him not to worry... He took me aside and began to talk to me about his boyhood in London... ...taking aside the boy or girl who is causing trouble.

take away. 1 If you **take** something **away** from a place or position,   V+N+ADV,
you remove it and put it somewhere else. EG *Do you want to take any*   V+ADV+N, V+PRON+ADV:
of this away with you, Ian?... Take your hands away... A maid came   ALSO+*from*
to take away the tray... I took the camera away from my eye and gazed unbelievingly... ...but the rug had been taken away for cleaning. ● **Put back** means the opposite of **take away.** ▷ In British   N COUNT
English, a **takeaway** is a shop or restaurant which sells cooked food that you eat somewhere else, for example at home. EG *...the man behind the counter at the Chinese takeaway.* ▷ **Takeaway** food or a   ADJECTIVE,
takeaway is hot cooked food that is sold to be eaten somewhere   N COUNT
else. EG *I really fancy an Indian takeaway... ...takeaway pizzas.*
● **Take-out** is used in American English for **takeaway.**

2 If you **take** something **away** from a person, you remove it and   V+ADV+N,
prevent them from having it any more. EG *They took my name and*   V+N+ADV, V+PRON+ADV:
address, took away all my possessions, and sent me down to the   ALSO+*from*
cells... I took the knife away from him. I don't know how... These men wanted to help them keep their land, not take it away from them... Even his rights as a citizen had been taken away from him... ...people from whom everything has been taken away.

3 If someone **takes** you **away,** 3.1 you go with them to stay in   V+N+ADV,
another place. EG *She had taken the children away with her to her*   V+PRON+ADV: ALSO+*with/A*
parents' house... I want to take Billy away with me... It seemed a pity to take her away from it all... My parents took me away to Vermont.
3.2 they force you to go with them, for example to prison or a   V+N+ADV,
mental hospital; a fairly informal use. EG *His parents were taken*   V+ADV+N, V+PRON+ADV
away in a dark van... She was taken away by a doctor... Two officers took him away to Glasgow Central Police Station... They had taken her away. They had kidnapped her.

4 If something **takes** you **away** from a person, place, or activity, it   V+PRON+ADV,
prevents you from being with that person, being in that place, or   V+N+ADV: USUALLY+*from*

continuing that activity. EG *My husband's job took him away a lot...* *She enjoys her work but it takes her away from her family... Do you have to take a working man away from his Sunday dinner?*

5 To **take away** something such as a quality or idea means to destroy it, spoil it, or get rid of it in some way. EG *This would take away the justification for it... Nothing seems to take away your appetite... His teasing remark did take away some of the terror from the operation.*

V+ADV+N;
ALSO+*from*

6 If something **takes** your breath **away,** it is so beautiful, exciting, or surprising that you are unable to speak or breathe normally for a moment. EG *It was so beautiful it took her breath away... Aurelia's beauty had taken his breath away... The idea fairly took my breath away.*

V+N+ADV

7 If you **take** something **away** from an experience or situation, it has a lasting effect or influence on you in that respect; a fairly informal use. EG *But, as with the lecture, it is not clear what they take away from it... It's the one thing you really took away from that gloomy convent.*

V+N+ADV;
USUALLY+*from*

8 If you **take** one number or amount **away** from another, you subtract the first from the second. EG *He could add up numbers up to ten and take them away too, though this was hard sometimes... This last amount is then taken away from each annual figure of earnings.*

V+PRON+ADV,
V+ADV+N,
V+N+ADV;
ALSO+*from*

take away from. 1 If someone takes you **away from** your husband, wife, or lover, they cause you to leave your husband, wife, or lover, and have a relationship with them instead. EG *He would kill anyone who tried to take her away from him... I always knew she'd take you away from me... ...though you took Bruno away from me.*

V+PRON+ADV,
V+N+ADV

2 To **take away from** something means to make it lower in value, standard, or amount than it should be or than it was. EG *Whatever he may have been like as a person, nothing can take away from his achievements as a scientist... ...joking about alcohol increasing the desire but taking away from the performance.* ● **Detract from** is a more formal expression for **take away from.**

V+ADV+PREP

take back. 1 When you **take** something **back** to the place where you were or where it was before, you go to that place with it. EG *'More hot coffee?' She shook her head so he took the tray back... ...spending an hour shopping for gifts to take back with me... ...trying to store up impressions to take back to her stepdaughters... The courier was to take it back to Florence the next day.*

V+N+ADV,
V+ADV+N,
V+PRON+ADV;
ALSO+*to*

2 If you **take back** something which you borrowed or bought, you return it to the place or person that you got it from, for example because you have finished using it or because it is damaged. EG *We're going to take the typewriter back to the shop... You will take this book back to Father Huismans... They were totally useless, but he wouldn't take them back to the shop.*

V+N+ADV,
V+PRON+ADV,
V+ADV+N;
ALSO+*to*

3 If you **take back** something which you gave to someone, you agree to accept it from them. If a shop or person **takes back** something which they sold you, they agree to accept it again and to return your money, for example because it is unsuitable or does not work. EG *Belinda would not promise anything. Nor would she take back the ring... Shops are often reluctant to take back unsatisfactory goods.*

V+ADV+N,
V+PRON+ADV,
V+N+ADV

4 If you **take back** something which you had before, you act forcefully so that you have it again. EG *You should just have taken your money back and then let me go... We should take back our lost territories in Staten Island... They had taken that amount from his father and he was taking it back from them.* ● **Repossess** is a formal word for **take back.**

V+N+ADV,
V+ADV+N,
V+PRON+ADV

5 If you **take** someone **back** to the place where they were or to your

V+N+ADV,
V+PRON+ADV

home, you go with them there, usually after arranging to do so. EG *How could I take Billy back to York and then arrive in Whitby on time?... I may be taking a friend back with me... They offered to take her back to the hotel.*

6 If you **take** someone **back** after a quarrel or separation, you agree to let them live with you or work with you again. EG *Her father would never take her back... She is grateful that he takes her back after her affair... The bank was persuaded to take me back... She wrote to Mrs Cox saying she would be willing to take back the child.*   V+PRON+ADV, V+N+ADV, V+ADV+N

7 If you **take back** something that you have said or thought, you admit that you were wrong. EG *I'm going to have to take back all those things I thought about you... Shirley said, 'Take that back or I'll slap your face.'* ● **Retract** is a more formal word for **take back**.   V+ADV+N, V+PRON+ADV, V+N+ADV

8 If you **take** someone or something **back** to the past, you start discussing or considering what happened then. EG *Helen then takes us back to her childhood... We can then use these studies to take us further back in time... ...to take the historical record further back.*   V+PRON+ADV, V+N+ADV

9 If you say that something **takes** you **back,** you mean that it reminds you of a period in your past, and makes you think about it again; a fairly informal use. EG *There was a smell of hot jam that took Tom back to his childhood... Then they sang some sort of Revolutionary ballad. It took us back thirty years to another time.*   V+N+ADV, V+PRON+ADV

take down. **1** If you **take** someone or something **down,** you go with them, or make them go with you, to a lower level, position, or place. You also use **take down** when you are going with them to a different part of a building, town, or country. EG *The judge sent the jury away to consider their verdict, and I was taken down to the cells again... She had taken her washing down to the laundry... I thought I'd take a sleeping-bag down to the beach and spend the night there... Their parents took them down to New York City... Hold his hand and take him down the steps carefully.* ● **Take up** means the opposite of **take down.**   V+ADV+N, V+N+ADV/PREP, V+PRON+ADV/PREP

2 If you **take** something **down** from a high place such as a shelf, you reach up and get it, so that you can use it. EG *I went over to a shelf and took down a can... He took down a volume of verse... She took down a suitcase from the top of the wardrobe, and opened it.* ● **Put back** means the opposite of **take down.**   V+ADV+N, V+PRON+ADV, V+N+ADV

3 If you **take down** something that is attached to a wall, post, or other object, you unfasten or disconnect it, and remove it. EG *The removal men won't take down electrical fittings if wired up to the mains... The saddest moment of course is when on Twelfth Night one has to take down all the Christmas decorations... He was prosecuted for refusing to take the sign down.* ● **Put up** means the opposite of **take down.**   V+ADV+N, V+N+ADV, V+PRON+ADV

4 If you **take down** a barrier, tent, or other structure, you undo or unfasten it, and remove it or put it away. EG *Wendy and I took the tent down, packed the van and set out for home... They've taken all the swings down... The scaffolding won't be taken down until next year.* ● **Dismantle** is a more formal word for **take down,** and **put up** means the opposite.   V+N+ADV, V+ADV+N, V+PRON+ADV

5 If you **take down** what someone is saying, you listen to them and write it down or record it. EG *The postmistress began to take down the message... He set up a tape recorder at Peter's bed to take down anything he might say... ...as if he was about to take the story down for his newspaper... Is this true? I don't know. I am simply taking it all down.* ● **Get down** means almost the same as **take down.**   V+ADV+N, V+N+ADV, V+PRON+ADV

6 If someone or something **takes** you **down,** they make you feel less confident or less happy with yourself; a very informal use. EG *Did*   V+PRON+ADV, V+N+ADV *some rotten cow take you down?... She was almost taken down, but not quite, by an English accent.* ● **Demoralize** is a less informal word for **take down.**

take in. 1 If you **take** someone or something **in,** you go with them into a room, building, or other place, such as the centre of a town. EG *She said that she would take her drink in with her to dinner... I drove him to the centre of the town—he said he didn't want to take his car in... I took him in to meet Miss Gray... I took in the coffee.* `V+N+ADV, V+PRON+ADV, V+ADV+N`

2 If you **take** someone **in** your arms, you put your arms around them. If you **take** something **in** your hand, you hold it. EG *I took her in my arms, and kissed her... Jenny came, then, and took the child in her arms... He takes the glass in his left hand still holding the gun in his right.* `V+PRON+PREP, V+N+PREP`

3 If you **take** someone **in** to your house, you allow them to live there, either as a favour or in return for payment. EG *It was kind of her to take me in... ...houses in which the owner regularly takes in several lodgers... I do you a favour and take Freddie in when you're having a bad time, don't I?* `V+PRON+ADV, V+ADV+N, V+N+ADV`

4 If an organization, school, or hospital **takes** you **in,** they accept you or have you as a member, student, patient, and so on. EG *He told me that unfortunately they couldn't take me in... The Department take in between 80 and 90 undergraduates a year... We ought to be expanding in order to take in new people.* ▶ The **intake** of an institution or organization is the number of people who come into it at a particular time. EG *...huge intakes of new recruits.* `V+PRON+ADV, V+ADV+N, V+N+ADV` `N COUNT`

5 If the police **take** you **in,** they make you go with them to a police station in order to answer questions or to arrest you. EG *First we take him in for questioning... 'Just a moment, you,' they said. 'We are taking you in.'* `V+PRON+ADV, V+N+ADV`

6 If you **are taken in** by someone, they deceive or trick you in some way; a fairly informal use. EG *I had given him the money before I was conscious of having been taken in... I wasn't going to be taken in by this kind of sentimentality... Even after years of close acquaintance he could take you in.* `V+PRON+ADV, V+N+ADV, V+ADV+N: USUALLY PASSIVE`

7 If you **take in** something that you see, hear, or read, you pay attention to it and are able to understand it, remember it, or evaluate it. EG *I didn't take in all that he was saying... Mrs Stannard shook hands, her eyes taking in Karin from head to foot... 'Anticlimax, old boy,' he said, taking in the situation at a glance... Alex had been the perfect pupil, listening and watching and taking it in.* `V+ADV+N, V+PRON+ADV, V+N+ADV`

8 To **take** something **in** means to include it. EG *...a worldwide empire that may soon take in Western Europe and Latin America... The truth takes in both extremes... His talk took in Freud, Wagner, and Goethe.* ● **Embrace** is a more formal word for **take in.** `V+ADV+N, V+PRON+ADV, V+N+ADV`

9 If you **take in** something such as a film, a museum, or a place, while you are on holiday or travelling somewhere, you go to see it or visit it. EG *He told them of week-ends in London where one could always take in a show... We had taken in all the movies... I flew on to California, deciding to take in Florida on the way home.* `V+ADV+N, V+N+ADV, V+PRON+ADV`

10 If you **take in** the milk, the washing, the newspaper, and so on, you bring it into your house from outside. EG *...fifteen minutes later, when she took in the milk... She got up to take in the washing.* `V+ADV+N, V+N+ADV, V+PRON+ADV`

11 If you **take in** washing, sewing, typing, and so on, you earn money at home by washing, sewing, or typing for other people. EG *All this while she continued taking in washing for the well-off people in neighbouring streets... I thought I'd take in dressmaking in a small way... Jane took in clerical work at home.* `V+ADV+N, V+N+ADV`

12 If you **take in** your car, a machine, and so on, you go with it to a `V+N+ADV,`

place where it can be serviced or repaired. EG *I had to take the car in this morning... We took in the sewing machine to be repaired.* V+ADV+N,
V+PRON+ADV

13 When people or animals **take in** air, drink, food, and so on, it enters their bodies, for example because they breathe it or swallow it. EG *Sharks take in water through the mouth... She sat taking in breaths of fresh air.* ▸ Someone's **intake** of food, drink, or air is the amount that enters their body, or the process of it entering their body. EG *...the average daily intake of iron in a normal diet... ...oxygen intake.* ▸ You talk about an **intake** of breath when someone breathes in quickly and deeply, perhaps because they are shocked at something. EG *There is an intake of breath and some of us look at each other.* V+ADV+N,
V+N+ADV,
V+PRON+ADV

N UNCOUNT

N COUNT

14 If you **take in** a dress, jacket, or other item of clothing, you make it smaller and tighter by altering its seams. EG *He lost so much weight that he had to take in all his trousers.* ● **Let out** means the opposite of **take in**. V+ADV+N,
V+N+ADV,
V+PRON+ADV

take into. 1 If you **take** someone or something **into** a place, you go with them there. EG *I took my cup of tea into the sitting room and sat there wondering... I took him into the nearest pub... We must get a message to her mother, before I take her into Caxley.* V+N+PREP,
V+PRON+PREP

2 If you **take** someone **into** an organization, school, or hospital, you accept them as a member, student, patient, and so on. EG *Mr Phillips would have taken Simon into the business, had he so wanted... If I had been taken into the local psychiatric hospital they could only have prescribed further drugs... Then my boss offered to take me into the firm as a full time member of her staff.* V+N+PREP,
V+PRON+PREP

3 When people or animals **take** something **into** their bodies, it enters their bodies, for example because they breathe it or swallow it. EG *...feeling as if I'd rather not breathe than take the dust into my lungs... The fish will hit the bait hard, as it takes it into its mouth.* V+N+PREP,
V+PRON+PREP

4 If something **takes** you **into** a particular subject or activity, it causes you to consider it or become involved in it. EG *These thoughts could take me into places I didn't want to be... To do this, I have to take you into the relations existing between ideology and politics... What had taken him into politics in the first place?* V+PRON+PREP,
V+N+PREP

5 To **take** something **into** a new state or situation means to cause it to be in that state or situation. EG *Successive administrations had been forced to take firms into public ownership... Years of low investment had re-enforced low profits, taking Britain into a spiral of decline... Women have succeeded in taking women's studies into the university curriculum.* V+N+PREP,
V+PRON+PREP

6 If you say that something will **take** you **into** a future period of time, you mean that it will last or continue to be effective until that time. EG *...a package of policies which will take farming into the next century in a prosperous state... Coal will take us into the next century and may go on for another hundred years or so... ...a preliminary season of ten weeks which would take him into May.* V+N+PREP,
V+PRON+PREP

take off. 1 If you **take** something **off**, you remove it or separate it from the place where it was. EG *Without moving the packing case from its position he took off the top... ...as soon as you take off the pressure... How do you measure the social costs of taking traffic off London roads?... Bring the water to the boil, then take it off the heat and leave it to cool down.* ● **Put on** means the opposite of **take off**. V+ADV+N,
V+N+ADV/PREP,
V+PRON+ADV/PREP

2 If you **take off** your clothes or something that you are wearing, you undress or remove it. EG *She took off the amber necklace and put it on the dressing-table... I had taken my clothes off because of the heat... She stood up, undid her skirt and took it off.* ● **Put on** means the opposite of **take off**. V+ADV+N,
V+N+ADV,
V+PRON+ADV

3 If you **take** something **off** someone, you use force or your authority to get it from them; a fairly informal use. EG *We were defending the principle that you cannot take things off other people by force... They were going to take some money off you... If I had a gun I'd go and take it off them.* [V+N+PREP, V+PRON+PREP]

4 When an aeroplane or bird **takes off,** it leaves the ground and starts flying. EG *A steady stream of aircraft was taking off and landing... After refuelling we took off... The swans took off from the lake.* ● **Land** means the opposite of **take off.** ▸ **Takeoff** is the beginning of a flight, when an aircraft leaves the ground. EG *Ninety per cent of all aircraft accidents occur at either take-off or landing... ...the overwhelming din of takeoffs.* [V+ADV] [N UNCOUNT, N COUNT]

5 If something such as a product or activity **takes off,** it suddenly becomes very successful and popular. EG *When the micro market really takes off, the Japanese will once again be its principal competitors... It will be interesting to see how the campaign takes off.* ▸ **Takeoff** is the stage in the development of a product or activity when it begins to be successful. EG *The government had already provided the groundwork for economic take-off by creating almost full employment.* [V+ADV] [N UNCOUNT]

6 If you **take off** or **take** yourself **off,** you go away, often suddenly and unexpectedly; a fairly informal use. EG *They took off for a weekend in the country... He lived with her for a bit, but then took off again, to the Far East this time... I thought I would take myself off on a little trip.* [V+ADV, V+REFL+ADV: USUALLY+A]

7 If you **take** someone **off** to a particular place or institution, you make them go there with you. EG *She came down with pneumonia and was taken off to hospital... Then they took him off to prison.* [V+N+ADV, V+PRON+ADV]

8 If you **take** someone **off** a task or list, you stop them doing that task or being on that list. EG *The Police will take every one of its detectives off whatever he is on... He was taken off the case on orders from headquarters... The next day, I found Laura had taken me off the list.* [V+N+PREP, V+PRON+PREP]

9 If you **take** time **off,** you spend it doing something different from your normal routine or job. EG *Bill and I took time off from work and flew to France... You have to take off Christmas Day as a holiday... They could not afford to take a day off work.* [V+N+ADV, V+ADV+N, V+N+PREP]

10 If you **take off** something such as an amount of money or a mark, you subtract it from a total. EG *Your employer will take off some of your wages to pay your national insurance contribution... Half a point would be taken off for a mistake in spelling.* ● **Add on** means the opposite of **take off.** [V+ADV+N, V+N+ADV, V+PRON+ADV]

11 If you **take** someone **off,** you imitate their appearance or behaviour, usually in order to make other people laugh; an informal use. EG *Mike can take off his father to perfection.* ● **Mimic** means almost the same as **take off.** ▸ A **takeoff** of someone is an imitation of their appearance or behaviour that is done in order to make people laugh. EG *He did a very amusing take-off of the headmaster.* [V+ADV+N, V+N+ADV, V+PRON+ADV] [N COUNT]

12 If someone in authority **takes** you **off** a particular type of food, medical treatment, or punishment, they stop it from being given to you. EG *The doctor took her off insulin... ...people being forcibly taken off drugs.* ● **Put on** means the opposite of **take off.** [V+PRON+PREP, V+N+PREP]

13 If a bus, train, or plane service **is taken off,** it stops operating and is no longer available for people to use. EG *The 7.18 London train was taken off for the winter.* ● **Be withdrawn** is a more formal expression for **be taken off.** [V+ADV+N, V+N+ADV, V+PRON+ADV: USUALLY PASSIVE]

14 If a play **is taken off** at a particular theatre, its performances [V+N+ADV, V+PRON+ADV,] there end. EG *'My Fair Lady' was taken off when it was at the peak of its success... I've no idea why it was taken off.* V+ADV+N: USUALLY PASSIVE

take on. 1 If you **take on** a job, task, or responsibility, you accept it and try to do what is required. EG *She takes on more work than is good for her... He should have had it attended to before he took the job on... I must say I think it's very nice of him to take it on.* V+ADV+N, V+N+ADV, V+PRON+ADV

2 If something **takes on** a new quality or appearance, it develops that quality or appearance. EG *His voice took on a new note of uncertainty... From this point on, the whole scheme began to take on a more practical aspect... The word 'profession' is taking on a new meaning.* ● **Assume** is a more formal word for **take on.** V+ADV+N

3 If someone **takes** you **on** at a place of work, they employ you. EG *They took me on because I was a good mathematician... I was keen to take him on to my editorial staff... Employers take on fewer young people.* V+PRON+ADV, V+ADV+N, V+N+ADV

4 If you **take on** a rival or opponent, especially one who is bigger or more powerful than you, you fight or compete against them. EG *British Leyland plans to take on the competition at home and abroad... ...the Government's decision to take on the unions... They wouldn't let him take me on.* ● **Tackle** means almost the same as **take on.** V+ADV+N, V+PRON+ADV, V+N+ADV

5 If a bus, train, ship, or plane **takes on** passengers, goods, or fuel, it stops in order to allow the passengers to get on or the goods or fuel to be loaded. EG *Buses stopped by request to take on more passengers... We sailed to Ajaccio in order to take on fresh lobster... We're only stopping briefly to take on fuel.* ● **Put off** means the opposite of **take on.** V+ADV+N, V+PRON+ADV, V+N+ADV

6 If you **take** something **on** or **upon** yourself, or if you **take** it **upon** yourself to do something, you decide to do it without asking anyone for permission or approval. EG *Mrs Cook took matters upon herself... Mrs Kaul took it upon herself to turn round and say 'Be quiet!'... I couldn't take it on myself to provide you with that information.* V+N+PREP+REFL: ALSO V+it+PREP+REFL, WITH to-INF

7 If you say **'Don't take on'** to someone, you mean that they should not get angry or upset about a situation, or make a fuss about it; an informal use. EG *Now don't take on, darling! Honestly, I won't be any time at all... No need to take on so, ma!* V+ADV: USUALLY WITH NEGATIVE

take out. 1 When you **take** something **out,** you remove it from a container or from the place where it was. EG *Emma opened her bag and took out her comb... Davis was taking a report out of the office... I felt in my jacket for my address book, and took it out.* ● **Put back** means the opposite of **take out.** ▷ In American English, a **take-out** or **take-out** food is hot cooked food that is sold to be eaten somewhere else. EG *...the Chinese takeout dinner... ...a take-out of spaghetti sauce.* ● **Takeaway** is used in British English for **take-out.** V+ADV+N, V+N+ADV, V+PRON+ADV: ALSO+of/from

N COUNT, ADJECTIVE

2 To **take** something **out** also means to remove it for ever from the place where it was, for example because it is unwanted or damaged. EG *They could edit that film, take bits out... ...to take the sulphur out of natural gas... If you don't like the fireplace you can take it out... The only way to get the sculptures into the museum would be to take out the ground floor windows on Fifth Avenue.* V+N+ADV, V+PRON+ADV, V+ADV+N: ALSO+of

3 If you **take** someone **out,** for example to a restaurant or a film, they go there with you, and you pay for everything. EG *I took Andrea out to dinner one evening... Why don't you take the children out?... He offered to take us out for a drink or something.* V+N+ADV, V+PRON+ADV, V+ADV+N

4 In very informal English, if you **take** someone **out,** you kill them. If you **take** something **out,** you destroy it or damage it so that it can no longer be used. EG *He and his brother have taken out 58 enemy soldiers between them... 'You see that gun?' he said. 'Now, that'll* V+ADV+N, V+N+ADV, V+PRON+ADV

take out a police station for you.'... Several miles of railway line were taken out by bombs that went off at six hundred yard intervals.
● **Wipe out** means almost the same as **take out.**

5 If you **take out** something such as a licence, an insurance policy, or a bank loan, you arrange to get it from a court of law, an insurance company, or a bank. EG *I want to take out a mortgage... He had lived seventeen years in Chicago, but he had never taken out naturalisation papers... The policy gives life cover, so if you took it out on your husband's life, you'd get a lump sum if he died.* `V+ADV+N, V+PRON+ADV`

6 If you **take out** money from a bank or a bank account, you obtain it by writing a cheque or filling in a form. EG *Where can I take cash out and how much can I withdraw at any one time?... You can also take out money at any other branch of your own bank... You get interest even on the amount withdrawn right up to the time you take it out.* `V+N+ADV, V+ADV+N, V+PRON+ADV`
● **Withdraw** is a more formal word for **take out.**

7 If you **take out** a book from a library, you borrow it for a time. EG *Can I take a book out right away?... She would recommend titles that he could ask his mother to take out for him from the adult section of the library... The book had been on the shelves for several months, but so far no one had taken it out.* `V+N+ADV, V+ADV+N, V+PRON+ADV`

8 If you **take** time **out,** you spend time doing something different from what you are supposed to be doing, or from what you normally do; a fairly informal use. EG *In the middle of the campaign, he took time out to attend a meeting of local officials... The plumber was taking time out for a cigarette... She would have to take a day out from her bread baking.* ● **Take off** means almost the same as **take out.** `V+N+ADV`

take out of. **1** If something **takes** a lot **out of** you, or **takes** it **out of** you, it makes you feel exhausted; an informal use. EG *I find that people take so much out of me... The work an artist does takes so much out of him, in the way of feeling and emotion... A five-block walk in that heat could take it out of you.* `V+N+ADV+PREP, V+it+ADV+PREP`

2 If something **takes** you **out of** yourself, it makes you stop thinking about your problems or the situation you are in. EG *People will adore this film: it takes you right out of yourself... That cheered me up, took me out of myself, cured my depression... The glory of the play and its magnificent poetry took you out of yourself.* `V+PRON+PREP, V+N+PREP: WITH REFL`

take out on. If you **take** something **out on** someone, you behave in an unpleasant way towards them because you feel angry or upset, even though it is not their fault. EG *I was in a depressed and hostile mood, needing to take my bad feelings out on someone... When Kurt was in one of his moods, he took it out on everyone... She took out most of her unhappiness on her husband.* `V+N+ADV+PREP, V+it+ADV+PREP, V+ADV+N+PREP`

take over. **1** To **take over** a company or business means to gain control of it by buying it or buying a majority of its shares. EG *Some people wanted to take over my father's oil importing business... The I.P.C. was taken over by the huge Reed Paper Group... No tycoon has ever been able to take it over.* ● **Buy out** means almost the same as **take over.** ▶ A **takeover** is the act of gaining control of a company by buying it or buying a majority of its shares. EG *The trend towards takeovers has intensified... All middle-size oil companies are likely candidates for takeover... His firm might be vulnerable to a takeover bid.* `V+ADV+N, V+N+ADV, V+PRON+ADV` / `N COUNT, N UNCOUNT, ADJECTIVE`

2 If people **take over** a country, region, or city, they gain control of it, usually with the help of an army. EG *Once again the military had taken over... Well-trained and equipped troops could probably take over the country... They had preferred to destroy the town rather than take it over... ...wanting to send in the National Guard and take* `V+ADV, V+ADV+N, V+PRON+ADV, V+N+ADV`

the city over. ▸ A **takeover** is the act of gaining control of a country,   N COUNT
region, or city, usually with the help of an army. EG *...the danger of a
military takeover.*

3 If people who are protesting about something **take over** a factory   V+ADV+N,
or other building, they enter it and stay there, preventing it from   V+PRON+ADV, V+N+ADV
being used normally, as part of their protest. EG *The television
station was taken over and held for some hours by technicians...
Feminists in Italy took over hospital clinics... They took over the
university for a week in protest.* ● **Occupy** is a more formal word for
take over. ▸ A **takeover** is the act of occupying a factory or other   N COUNT
building as a form of protest. EG *The student takeover was just the
beginning.*

4 If you **take over** a house, flat, or room, you start living in it or using   V+N+ADV,
it. EG *She had taken the house over some months before... She*   V+ADV+N, V+PRON+ADV
*wanted a flat of her own, but I suggested she take over mine while I
was in California... Doctor Ford had taken it over, possibly the only
place available in the house.*

5 If you **take over** a job or a responsibility, you start doing it or being   V+ADV,
responsible for it after someone else has finished. EG *Thornaby took*   ALSO+as/from: ALSO V+ADV+N,
over as secretary in 1976... I took over from a man who was brilliant   V+N+ADV, V+PRON+ADV
*at recruiting agents... Heever returned to take over the question-
ing... Relatives took their debts over.*

6 If you **take** trouble, care, or time **over** something, you do it slowly,   V+N+PREP
carefully, and thoroughly. EG *He had taken particular pains over the
report... This is a purchase which it is worth taking a lot of trouble
over... She washed herself most carefully and took a long time over
it.*

7 If you **take** something or someone **over** to a place or person, you   V+PRON+ADV,
carry them or lead them to that place or person. EG *Leave the door*   V+N+ADV, V+ADV+N:
open while I take him over to the house... The woman took two full   ALSO+to
*bottles over to the group round the big table... Then he takes a chair
over and sits down to look at her.*

8 If a feeling, thought, or activity **takes** you **over,** it affects you so   V+PRON+ADV,
strongly or takes so much of your time that you find it difficult to do   V+N+ADV
anything else. EG *If the woman feels there are forces which took her
over, she is confirmed in her role of dependency... I let the thought
take me over... So often his busy life took him over for weeks on end
and he lost all contact with us.*

9 If one thing **takes over** from another, it becomes more important,   V+ADV:
successful, or powerful than the other thing, and eventually replaces   USUALLY+from
it. EG *Microfilms might even take over from libraries... Reading to
learn now seems to take over from learning to read... The science of
medicine took over from the art of healing.*

take round. If you **take** someone **round** or **around** a place, you go   V+N+ADV/PREP,
there with them and show them all the interesting or important   V+PRON+ADV/PREP
features. EG *I took my godson around my laboratory... Parties of
visitors are taken round on Saturday afternoons... Why don't you just
take me round now and tell me what's been happening.* ● **Show
round** means almost the same as **take round.**

take through. If you **take** someone **through** a procedure or task,   V+N+PREP,
you discuss it or do it with them, so that they know what to do. EG   V+PRON+PREP
*Helen, would you be kind enough to take Elaine through the
schedule... Lodge took the actors through the scene again... If you
wish, someone will take you through the sums.*

take to. **1** If you **take to** someone or something, you begin to like   V+PREP
them. EG *It was impossible to tell whether he had taken to Rose or
not... I didn't think at first I'd take to him—but I did... I was taught*

Geography at school but never took to it. ● **Take against** means the opposite of **take to.**

2 If you **take to** doing something, you begin to do it as a regular habit. EG *He took to wearing black leather jackets... As they grow larger, they take to eating fish... This he had achieved by taking to a life of crime.* `V+PREP+-ING, V+PREP`

3 If you **take to** a place, you go there, usually as a result of a difficult or dangerous situation. EG *Their leaders took to hideouts in the Pondoland hills... I took to my bed with a fever that lasted two weeks... The local inhabitants took to the streets to defend themselves and their property.* `V+PREP`

take up. 1 If you **take** someone or something **up,** you go with them, or make them go with you, to a higher level, position, or place. You also use **take up** when you are going with them to a different part of a building, town, or country. EG *If you'll excuse me, I'll take her tea up... I will take Fanny up to my room now... A guard took them up the hill... I went downstairs again, and Aunt Bertha took up the beer.* ● **Take down** means the opposite of **take up.** `V+N+ADV/PREP, V+PRON+ADV/PREP, V+ADV+N`

2 If you **take up** an object, you begin to hold it or carry it; a fairly old-fashioned use. EG *She took up the box and tapped the lid... When they had finished eating, the men took up their tools again... She took it up, and threw it.* ● **Pick up** means almost the same as **take up.** `V+ADV+N, V+PRON+ADV`

3 If you **take up** an activity or job, you start doing it. EG *I thought I'd take up fishing... She decided to take up medicine as a career... I might take it up professionally.* ● **Go in for** means almost the same as **take up.** `V+ADV+N, V+PRON+ADV, V+N+ADV`

4 If you **take up** a point, idea, or issue that you think is important, you draw attention to it and cause it to be discussed or dealt with. EG *The committee is expected to take up the question of the government's role in the arts... Mr Biffen took this point up by harking back to his own career... He declined the offer and took the matter up with his shop steward... We took this up with the social worker.* ● **Pick up** means almost the same as **take up,** and **pursue** is a more formal word. ▶ If you are quick on the **uptake,** you understand an idea or situation quickly. EG *She was not very quick on the uptake and needed time to register and take everything in.* `V+ADV+N, V+N+ADV, V+PRON+ADV: ALSO+with` `N SING`

5 If you **take up** an offer, challenge, or opportunity, you accept it. EG *She wished Jane would take up Derek's offer to decorate the house... Harlech television took up the challenge and made a splendid documentary about it... Lionel allowed a pause for elaboration but she did not take it up.* ● **Refuse** means the opposite of **take up.** ▶ **Take-up** is the rate at which people apply for or buy something which is being offered to them. EG *Initially, there wasn't much take-up of the home improvement offers.* `V+ADV+N, V+PRON+ADV, V+N+ADV` `N UNCOUNT`

6 If you **take up** a particular attitude, belief, or way of doing something, you start to have it. EG *He hated to see her taking up this hard, uncompromising attitude... They had abandoned Californian living patterns and had taken up European ones... Such styles may later be taken up by the media.* ● **Adopt** is a less informal word for **take up.** `V+ADV+N`

7 If you **take up** an activity that was interrupted, you continue doing it from the point where it had stopped. EG *Sam took up the story... Nicola was taking up where she had left off... ...the plan to kill him, which she had abandoned, or had she taken it up again?* ● **Pick up** means almost the same as **take up.** `V+ADV+N, V+PRON+ADV, V+N+ADV`

8 If you **take up** a song or chant that other people are singing or shouting, you start singing it or shouting it with them. EG *The other* `V+ADV+N, V+PRON+ADV, V+N+ADV`

boys took up the cry till the mountain rang... She intoned a song and the other women took it up.

9 If something **takes up** a particular amount of time, space, or effort, it uses that amount. EG *Dresses don't take up much space... The baby took up all her energy and attention... At the moment 'Oliver' is taking a lot of my time up.* ● **Occupy** is a more formal word for **take up.** `V+ADV+N, V+N+ADV, V+PRON+ADV`

10 If you **take up** a particular position, you move to it, because you have been told to or because it is the best position for what you want to do. EG *The fire engines had taken up position by the runway... As the herd gallops away, he takes up the rear... Machine-gunners were to take up positions to cover the main charge.* `V+ADV+N, V+N+ADV, V+PRON+ADV`

11 If something that is fixed to a surface **is taken up,** it is removed from that surface by force. EG *The rails were taken up and used to make weapons... Then she takes the lino up, and scrubs the boards underneath.* ● **Pull up** means almost the same as **take up.** `V+N+ADV, V+PRON+ADV, V+ADV+N`

12 If you **take up** something such as a dress or a pair of trousers, you shorten it by folding up the bottom edge and stitching it in place. EG *You can always take that skirt up if you don't like it that long... I've taken it up twice, and it still looks wrong.* ● **Let down** means the opposite of **take up.** `V+ADV+N, V+N+ADV, V+PRON+ADV`

13 If someone **takes** you **up** when you are starting a career, they help, support, and encourage you to succeed. EG *He was my agent—a dealer who took me up, and stuck to me... Stanley and Guy had taken up young Balintoy... You're lucky to have been taken up by a clergyman.* ● **Patronize** is a more formal word for **take up.** `V+N+ADV, V+PRON+ADV, V+ADV+N`

14 To **take up** moisture, gas, or other substance means to absorb it. EG *Red blood cells take up oxygen... A growing crop will take up and store the nitrogen and other elements in the soil.* ▷ A person's or machine's **uptake** of something is the amount of it that they use; a technical term. EG *An athlete has a maximum oxygen uptake of four litres per minute... She increased the water uptake.* ● **Intake** means almost the same as **uptake.** `V+ADV+N, V+N+ADV, V+PRON+ADV` `N SING`

15 If you **take up** a collection of money, you collect it from people. EG *He took up a collection and sent the money to Jerusalem.* `V+ADV+N`

take up on. **1** If you **take** someone **up on** an offer they have made, you accept their offer. EG *She paused a while, in case he might care to take her up on her offer... But this suggestion is absurd, and no one takes him up on it... That's very kind of you, Mr Zapp, I'll take you up on that generous invitation.* `V+PRON+ADV+PREP, V+N+ADV+PREP`

2 If you **take** someone **up on** something they have said or done, you ask them to explain or justify what they have said or done, because you think that they are wrong. EG *I think I would like to take Tony up on something that he said... I'm going to be very unkind and very rude and take you up on this.* ● **Pick up on** means almost the same as **take up on.** `V+N+ADV+PREP, V+PRON+ADV+PREP`

take upon. See take on: take upon is slightly more formal.

take up with. **1** If you **take up with** someone, you begin to be friendly with them and spend a lot of time with them. EG *For a little time after she took up with Mr Marvin she went on singing in public... ...Doreen being the first girl he'd taken up with after Ginny.* `V+ADV+PREP`

2 If you **are taken up with** something, it keeps you busy or fully occupied. EG *She was too taken up with her own feelings to pay much attention to his... The meeting I attended was taken up with discussion of the group's failure to attract new members.* `PASSIVE: V+ADV+PREP`

talk, talks, talking, talked

talk around. If people **talk around** or **round** a subject or problem, `V+PREP` they discuss it in a general way, often failing to deal with the main points. EG *I just have a feeling that I've somehow talked around the point.*

talk at. If you **talk at** someone, you talk to them without letting them speak or without listening to their opinions. EG *Charles had been talking at him for hours, permitting few interruptions... I've kept you too long, I've talked at you too much.* | V+PREP: HAS PASSIVE

talk away. If you **talk away**, you talk continuously for a period of time. EG *You were talking away like a nine-year-old kid... Along she came, wagging her stick and talking away to herself.* | V+ADV

talk back. If you **talk back** to someone in authority such as a parent or teacher, you answer them in a bold or rude way. EG *Don't talk back to me like that!... He, however, talked back firmly to his generals... She was shocked to hear me talking back so forcefully.* • **Answer back** means almost the same as **talk back**. | V+ADV: USUALLY+*to*

talk down. 1 If someone **talks** you **down**, they talk longer or louder than you do and so make you stop talking. EG *I objected to the proposal, but they talked me down... He made another weak protest and was talked down by Jenny.* | V+PRON+ADV, V+N+ADV

2 To **talk down** the pilot of an aircraft means to give them instructions over the radio so that they can land the aircraft, for example in bad weather or in an emergency. | V+N+ADV, V+PRON+ADV, V+ADV+N

talk down to. If someone **talks down to** you, they talk to you in a way that shows that they think that they are more important or more clever than you. EG *Parents can't dictate to their adolescent children or talk down to them... I think some of the teachers felt they were being talked down to.* • **Patronize** is a more formal word for **talk down to**. | V+ADV+PREP: HAS PASSIVE

talk into. If you **talk** someone **into** doing something, you persuade them to do it. EG *She talked me into taking a week's holiday... He talked the Pondo leaders into ending the uprising... We can talk ourselves into anything.* • **Talk out of** means the opposite of **talk into**. | V+PRON+PREP, V+N+PREP, V+REFL+PREP

talk out. 1 If people **talk out** a problem, plan, or idea, they discuss it thoroughly. EG *Marianne had come to talk out her plan of campaign... ...listening to other people talk out their problems... They began talking things out between themselves... They helped me by letting me talk it out over several days.* | V+ADV+N, V+N+ADV, V+PRON+ADV

2 If you **talk** yourself **out**, you talk so much that you feel that you have nothing more to say. EG *He said little, simply letting me talk myself out each time... We were enjoying the kind of relationship we had, talking ourselves out and not feeling bored.* | V+REFL+ADV

talk out of. If you **talk** someone **out of** doing something, you persuade them not to do it. EG *He tried to talk me out of buying such a big car... Fortunately, Faye Seidel talked her husband out of his plan... She managed to talk herself out of going.* • **Talk into** means the opposite of **talk out of**. | V+PRON+ADV+PREP, V+N+ADV+PREP, V+REFL+ADV+PREP

talk over. If you **talk** something **over**, you discuss it with someone. EG *I'll talk it over with Len tonight and let you know tomorrow... There's plenty of opportunity for you to talk your problems over... We all met in Pat's room, to talk over what we had seen.* | V+PRON+ADV, V+N+ADV, V+ADV+N: USUALLY+*with*

talk round. 1 If you **talk** someone **round**, you persuade them to agree with you or to do what you want them to do. EG *I must talk Daddy round. He won't like it... He didn't really want to go to France, but I managed to talk him round.* | V+N+ADV, V+PRON+ADV

2 See **talk around**.

talk through. 1 If people **talk through** a problem, plan, or idea, they discuss it thoroughly until some sort of agreement is made. EG | V+PREP, V+PRON+ADV, V+N+ADV

We had already talked through many problematic areas and wanted to move on... At breakfast, I talked through the options with Jennifer... We often find that people like to talk it through with someone. ● **Talk over** means almost the same as **talk through.**

2 If you **talk** someone **through** a difficult situation, you help or support them by talking to them and reassuring them. EG *Boon had talked a pregnant mother through her first labour pains... You may find your coach talking you through certain phases of the training session.*

V+N+PREP,
V+PRON+PREP

talk to. **1** If you **talk to** someone, you have a conversation with them. EG *I just wanted to talk to you... I was talking to Mike about this... I find her so easy to talk to... You were talking to her at the party... The child wants to be talked to and reassured.*

V+PREP:
HAS PASSIVE

2 If you give someone a **talking-to,** you speak to them seriously or forcefully, especially about something they have failed to do or have done wrong. EG *Grab them, hold them face to face, and give them a talking-to.*

N SING

talk with. If you **talk with** someone, you have a conversation with them; used mainly in American English. EG *I'd like to talk with you about your husband... I'd spent an hour talking with a new student called Kathleen... ...every time we meet and talk with a companion... Grout had often talked with the farmers.*

V+PREP

tamp, tamps, tamping, tamped

tamp down. If you **tamp** something **down,** you press it down several times so that it becomes more solid and compact. EG *It will probably be necessary to tamp the clay down... One man shovelled tarmac into the hole, the other tamped it down.*

V+N+ADV,
V+PRON+ADV,
V+ADV+N

tamper, tampers, tampering, tampered

tamper with. If you **tamper with** something, you try to change it in some way when you have no right to do so. EG *Someone had tampered with the register of the church and changed the christening records... I'm against tampering with nature in such a vital matter... He claimed that his briefcase had been tampered with on the flight.* ● **Interfere with** means almost the same as **tamper with.**

V+PREP:
HAS PASSIVE

tangle, tangles, tangling, tangled

tangle up. **1** If something such as string or wire **is tangled up,** it is twisted into an untidy mass which is difficult to separate or sort out. EG *Use a light cord rather than a string which gets tangled up... Don't do that; you're tangling them up!... It ripped the hinges and tangled up the barbed wire.*

V+N+ADV,
V+PRON+ADV,
V+ADV+N

2 If someone or something **is tangled up** in wires or ropes, they are caught or trapped in them so that it is difficult to free them. EG *He's out there tangled up in the wire... He was tangled up in a mess of chains.*

PASSIVE:
V+ADV,
USUALLY+*in*

tangle with. If you **tangle with** someone, you get involved in a fight or quarrel with them. EG *I wouldn't tangle with him if I were you... I'm tangling with some tough guys, Jerry.* ● **Mess with** means almost the same as **tangle with.**

V+PREP:
HAS PASSIVE

tap, taps, tapping, tapped

tap for. If you **tap** someone **for** something, you persuade them to give you something you want, especially money or information; an informal expression. EG *I'll tap my Dad for a couple of hundred... Get to know the neighbours fast so that you can tap them for sugar, milk and teabags.*

V+N+PREP,
V+PRON+PREP

tap in. **1** If you **tap in** something sharp such as a nail, you force it into a surface by hitting it with quick, light blows. EG *I found a spot*

V+ADV+N,
V+N+ADV,
V+PRON+ADV

close to the tepee, and started to tap in the pegs... He tapped the drawing pins in gently with a book.

2 If you **tap** numbers or letters **in**, you type them into a machine by pressing the keys or buttons with your fingers. EG *Simply put your card into the machine, tap in your personal number and you can withdraw up to £100 a day... Presumably there are codes that you have to tap in before you can get access to the information.* ● **Key in** means almost the same as **tap in.**
V+N+ADV, V+PRON+ADV, V+ADV+N

tap into. If someone or something **taps into** a source of something such as energy, information, or money, they manage to obtain energy, information, or money from it, sometimes illegally. EG *You have to find the right places to tap into the heat sources... ...tapping into the body's reserve energy... ...tapped into the university's private funds.*
V+PREP

tap out. To **tap out** a sound means to produce it by hitting a surface lightly and repeatedly. EG *I could hear the telegraph instrument tapping out morse... ...tapping out the rhythm.*
V+ADV+N, V+N+ADV, V+PRON+ADV

tape, tapes, taping, taped

tape up. If you **tape** something **up**, you fasten tape around it firmly, in order to protect it or to hold it in a certain position. EG *I cleaned and disinfected the scratches and taped them up carefully... Tape the windows up and leave the room.*
V+PRON+ADV, V+N+ADV, V+ADV+N

taper, tapers, tapering, tapered

taper off. If something **tapers off** or if you **taper** it **off**, it gradually becomes greatly reduced in size, quantity, or amount. EG *...in the 1970s, as the economic boom tapered off... Patterson's voice kind of tapered off... Keep this diet up for several days, then taper it off... The plan was to inject the drugs, then taper off the dosage.*
V+ADV, V+PRON+ADV, V+ADV+N, V+N+ADV: ERGATIVE

tart, tarts, tarting, tarted

tart up. **1** If a woman **tarts** herself **up**, she tries to make herself look especially smart and attractive; used in informal British English. EG *I didn't know whether to tart myself up or just go in my normal clothes.* ● **Doll up** means almost the same as **tart up.**
V+REFL+ADV

2 If someone **tarts up** a room or building, they try to improve its appearance, often in a way that you consider vulgar; used in informal British English. EG *They put in furniture, antiques, fabrics, anything to tart up the place... ...a monstrosity of a house he tarted up with a tennis court and swimming pool... It was a nice old pub till they decided to tart it up.*
V+ADV+N, V+N+ADV, V+PRON+ADV

tax, taxes, taxing, taxed

tax with. If you **tax** someone **with** something wrong that you think they have done, you show them the evidence and ask them for an explanation. EG *An old friend advised him not to tax Mr Profumo with the information... Mr Wigg contemplated for a moment taxing the Minister with it.*
V+N+PREP, V+PRON+PREP

team, teams, teaming, teamed

team up. If you **team up** with someone, you join them so that you can do something together. EG *Tom and Joe were now due to go home, and so I teamed up with two Americans... Conservatives teamed up with Opposition Peers... It's strange that such a good producer and a great artist have not really teamed up well.*
V+ADV+ with, V+ADV: RECIPROCAL

tear, tears, tearing, tore, torn

tear apart. **1** To **tear** something **apart** means to pull it into pieces violently. EG *...lions and panthers which could tear a goat apart in*
V+N+ADV, V+PRON+ADV

*seconds... I saw a jacket so torn apart that no one would ever want it
again.*

2 If something **tears** a person, organization, or country **apart,** it
causes them to experience great conflicts or disturbances. EG *He
was fighting against the 'anarchy' which he insisted was tearing the
Church apart... She is torn apart by conflicting pressures... ...agonies
which tear him apart.*   V+N+ADV, V+PRON+ADV

3 If someone **tears** an idea or theory **apart,** they criticize it severely.
EG *I can imagine a Marxist tearing the theory apart as elitist and
sentimental.* ● **Pull apart** and **take apart** mean almost the same as
tear apart.   V+N+ADV, V+PRON+ADV

tear at. To **tear at** something means to try violently to pull it into   V+PREP
pieces. EG *He took the meat that Sam had given him and began to
tear at it... Without any warning, the two animals were tearing at
each other's throats.*

tear away. **1** If you **tear** someone **away** from a place or activity,
you force them to leave the place or stop doing the activity. EG *What
a shame it was to tear Dolly away from the play... I tore myself
away and came to Paris... I would like to tear you away from Italy
and take you on a trip.*   V+N+ADV, V+REFL+ADV, V+PRON+ADV: USUALLY+*from*

2 To **tear** something **away** means to pull it violently from the thing
that it is attached to. EG *The road was covered in leaves which had
been torn away by the strong winds... Grasp the flesh and tear it
away from the shell... I could always tear away a piece of the wall.*   V+N+ADV, V+PRON+ADV, V+ADV+N: ALSO+*from*

3 A **tearaway** is a young person who behaves in a wild and   N COUNT
uncontrolled way; a rather old-fashioned word used in British English. EG *Colin was a bit of a tearaway in his youth.*

tear down. If you **tear down** something such as a building, tree, or
statue, you destroy it completely. EG *It is often cheaper to tear down
the buildings than to repair them... ...tearing down woodlands... We
have a theatre in town, but they're tearing it down next year.* ● **Pull
down** means almost the same as **tear down,** and **demolish** is a more
formal word.   V+N+ADV, V+PRON+ADV, V+ADV+N

tear into. If you **tear into** someone, their work, or their behaviour,   V+PREP
you criticize them very strongly; an informal expression. EG *In a
rage I tore into the demonstrators, asking why they were there... I
didn't like the way you tore into Dempsey's paper at the seminar.*
● **Lay into** means almost the same as **tear into.**

tear off. **1** If you **tear off** your clothes, you take them off quickly
and violently. EG *I opened the window and tore off my shirt... They
raced round the reservation tearing off their clothes... She tore her
sandals off and jumped in.*   V+ADV+N, V+N+ADV, V+PRON+ADV

2 If you **tear** something **off,** you remove it from the thing it is
attached to by pulling it violently. EG *I like to get a new loaf and tear
the crust off and eat it... He tore the metal tab off his beer can... He
leans back on an elbow, tears off a grass-stalk,and bites its end.*   V+N+ADV/PREP, V+ADV+N, V+PRON+ADV/PREP

3 If you **tear off** somewhere, you go there very quickly; an informal
use. EG *He tore off home... I watched them tearing off into the
distance... He jumps into the car and tears off like a race driver.*   V+ADV: USUALLY+A

tear out. If you **tear out** something that is attached to another thing,
you separate it with your hands, using force. EG *I write the list in my
book, tear out the top copy, and send it with the laundry... She tore
several sheets of paper out of the back of the book.*   V+ADV+N, V+N+ADV, V+PRON+ADV

tear up. **1** If you **tear up** paper or material, you pull it into a lot of
small pieces with your hands. EG *He hadn't torn up Caldicott's
cheque... We bought bandages rather than tearing up a large sheet
for this purpose... She smiled and folded the letter, intending to tear*   V+ADV+N, V+PRON+ADV, V+N+ADV

tell on

it up and throw it out of the window. ● **Rip up** means almost the same as **tear up**.

2 If something **is torn up**, it is damaged or destroyed. EG *Thousands of trees have been torn up in recent years... Parks, once bursting with flowers, were now being torn up in favour of factories... We do not yet have baseball crowds tearing up the grounds or breaking up trains.*

V+N+ADV,
V+ADV+N,
V+PRON+ADV

tease, teases, teasing, teased

tease out. If you **tease** something **out,** you separate it very carefully from the thing that contains it. EG *Jimmy leant across and tried to tease it out of the packet... Break up the food or tease out the hard bits... In an autobiography it is often difficult to tease out fact from literary expression.* ● **Extract** is a more formal word for **tease out.**

V+PRON+ADV,
V+ADV+N,
V+N+ADV

tee, tees, teeing, teed

tee off. When a golfer **tees off,** he or she hits the first shot at the start of a round of golf. EG *Hit a few practice shots before you tee off just to warm off.*

V+ADV

tee up. To **tee up** means to place a golf ball on a tee so that it is ready for you to hit it at the start of a hole. EG *After he has teed up the ball, Nicklaus walks behind it to check the line of the shot.*

V+ADV,
V+ADV+N

teem, teems, teeming, teemed

teem down. If it **is teeming down,** it is raining very heavily. EG *It was teeming down and we all got soaked.* ● **Pour** means almost the same as **teem down.**

V+ADV

tell, tells, telling, told

tell against. If facts or opinions **tell against** a person or plan, they indicate that the person or plan is unlikely to succeed. EG *The figures, therefore, told against Concorde... These facts, if put in the report, would tell against the woman.* ● **Count against** means almost the same as **tell against.**

V+PREP

tell apart. If you can **tell** similar people or things **apart,** you can identify them individually because you can recognize the differences between them. EG *It is impossible to tell the packing cases apart... His relatives were starting to drift in. I couldn't tell them apart.*

V+N+ADV,
V+PRON+ADV

tell off. If you **tell** someone **off,** you speak to them angrily because they have done something wrong. EG *All the senior mistress does is to tell the girls off for wearing the wrong colour blouse... He had a reputation for telling off generals... If I was told off by my parents, I could come along to the kitchen.* ● **Reprimand** is a formal word for **tell off.** ▶ **telling-off, tellings-off/telling-offs.** If you give someone a **telling-off,** you speak to them angrily because they have done something wrong. EG *When she got back she would give him such a telling-off about that doll.* ● **Ticking-off** means almost the same as **telling-off.**

V+PRON+ADV,
V+N+ADV,
V+ADV+N

N COUNT

tell on. 1 If you **tell on** someone who has done something wrong, you inform someone in authority about it; an informal use. EG *Do you think it's right to make a man tell on his friends to save himself?... But honour was satisfied, I hadn't told on them.* ● **Grass on** means almost the same as **tell on.**

V+PREP

2 If pressure or strain **tells on** you, people begin to realize that you cannot cope with it. EG *But the pressure was beginning to tell on him too... He had been there for a long time now, and it was beginning to tell on his face... The strain of year-round cricket is telling on many of the world's top players.*

V+PREP

tend, tends, tending, tended

tend to. If you **tend to** someone or something, you pay attention to   v+PREP
them and deal with their problems and needs. EG *Excuse me, I have
to tend to the other guests... In his spare time he tends to the family
business.* ● **Attend to** means almost the same as **tend to.**

tend towards. If something **tends towards** a quality, it shows   v+PREP
more of that quality than others. EG *It is no doubt inevitable that the
'neutral' society should tend towards uniformity... In some countries,
the military hierarchy tends towards the right.*

tense, tenses, tensing, tensed

tense up. If you or the muscles in your body **tense up,** your muscles   v+ADV
stiffen and stretch tight, usually because you are afraid or are
preparing yourself to make a movement. EG *Try to relax while
you're saying it. Don't tense up... 'What are you talking about?' I
asked, the skin of my cheekbones tensing up.* ● **Tighten up** means
almost the same as **tense up.** ▸ If you are **tensed up,** you feel   ADJECTIVE
nervous and worried and cannot relax properly. EG *Relax. You're all
tensed up... When night came I was all tensed up for another
argument.* ● **Worked up** means almost the same as **tensed up.**

thaw, thaws, thawing, thawed

thaw out. 1 When you **thaw out** frozen food, or when it **thaws out,**   V+N+ADV,
you take it out of the freezer for some time so that it it is no longer   V+ADV+N,
frozen. EG *Pre-cooked food can be thawed out quicker than a joint or*   V+PRON+ADV,
poultry... There was a joint thawing out on the kitchen table.   V+ADV:
● **Defrost** means almost the same as **thaw out.**   ERGATIVE

2 If you **thaw out,** you get warm by a fire after you have got very   v+ADV
cold outside; an informal use. EG *What joy to take refuge in a stove-
heated cabin and thaw out with a mug of steaming tea.*

thin, thins, thinning, thinned

thin down. When you **thin down** a liquid, you add water or another   V+ADV+N,
liquid to make it weaker and less thick. EG *Meanwhile, thin down the*   V+PRON+ADV
*mayonnaise with the cream... The paint has been thinned down too
much.*

thin out. If someone **thins out** an area or the people or things in it,   V+ADV+N,
the area becomes less crowded as some of the things or people   V+PRON+ADV,
move away or are removed. EG *The wood had been neglected and a*   V+ADV:
programme has begun to thin out the mature trees... The trees thin   ERGATIVE
*out to a bare spot at the summit... Western cities are thinning out as
people move to the suburbs.*

think, thinks, thinking, thought

think ahead. If you **think ahead,** you make plans or arrangements   v+ADV
for the things you want to do in the future. EG *We need to analyse the
situation and think ahead... Holland is one of those countries which
think ahead.* ● **Plan ahead** means almost the same as **think ahead.**

think back. If you **think back,** you make an effort to remember   V+ADV:
things that happened to you in the past. EG *Think back to some of*   ALSO+*to/over*
*your history lessons... It gives you an opportunity to think back over
the year... Thinking back later I often regretted not staying to talk
with him.* ● **Look back** means almost the same as **think back.**

think of. 1 If you can **think of** something that exists or is a fact, you   V+PREP:
know it and can therefore suggest it to other people. EG *I can think of*   WITH MODAL
*at least two examples of this Government's stupidity... He can think
of no reason for going on living... He had examined every argument
he could think of.*

2 If you **think of** an idea, you use your imagination and intelligence   V+PREP:
   HAS PASSIVE

to create it or develop it. EG ...*a scheme which, so far as he knew, had never even been thought of before... So I began to think of new methods.*

3 If you **think of** doing something, you consider the possibility of   V+PREP
doing it. EG *We began to think of moving... I'm also thinking of buying you a fur coat... His family have discovered that he is thinking of adopting his two nephews.*

think out. If you **think out** a plan or a piece of writing, you prepare   V+ADV+N,
it fully and in detail before doing anything. EG *She needed time to*   V+PRON+ADV,
think out a strategy to deal with Gareth... I'm too tired to try to think   V+N+ADV
it out... He's a great believer in thinking things out. ● **Work out**
means almost the same as **think out.**

think over. If you **think** something **over,** you consider it carefully   V+ADV+N,
before making a decision. EG *I wanted to think over one or two*   V+N+ADV,
business problems... He said he would leave me alone to think things   V+PRON+ADV
over for five minutes.

think through. If you **think** a situation **through,** you consider it   V+N+ADV,
thoroughly, together with all its possible effects or consequences. EG   V+PRON+ADV,
I haven't really thought the whole business through in my own   V+ADV+N
mind... I've been thinking it all through and I do just want to see for
myself... ...the desire to think through a difficulty.

think up. If you **think up** a clever idea, you use your imagination or   V+ADV+N,
intelligence to create it. EG *I kept thinking up ways I could murder*   V+N+ADV,
him without getting caught... He informed me of a new financial   V+PRON+ADV
agreement he had thought up... 'Some suggestion.' Calderwood snort-
ed. 'Did you think this up all by yourself?' ● **Devise** means almost
the same as **think up.**

thirst, thirsts, thirsting, thirsted

thirst for. If you **thirst for** something, you want it very much; a   V+PREP:
literary expression. EG *The story is so exciting it makes you thirst for*   HAS PASSIVE
the next episode.

thrash, thrashes, thrashing, thrashed

thrash out. If you **thrash out** a difficult problem or idea, you discuss   V+ADV+N,
it in detail until you reach an agreement or arrive at a solution. EG   V+PRON+ADV,
Try and see how many of these questions you can thrash out   V+N+ADV
between the three of you... We'll thrash this out after dinner... A new
economic strategy is being thrashed out.

throttle, throttles, throttling, throttled

throttle back. If you **throttle back** or **down** when you are driving a   V+N+ADV,
motor vehicle or aircraft, you make it go slower by reducing the   V+PRON+ADV,
pressure on the accelerator. EG *I throttled the motor right back...*   V+ADV
Hendricks throttled down, and the boat settled into a slow drift.
throttle down. See **throttle back.**

throw, throws, throwing, threw, thrown

throw about. 1 If you **throw** your arm or arms **about, around** or   V+N+PREP
round someone, you embrace them or hug them to show your
affection for them. EG *I wanted to throw my arms about him... She*
threw her arms around his neck... He threw his arms round his
brother and began to cry.

2 If you **throw** things **about** or **around,** you throw them in different   V+N+ADV/PREP,
directions in an angry way. EG *The boy began to throw bread about*   V+PRON+ADV/PREP
the dining room... He had terrorized everyone by throwing things
about... ...throwing bits of stuff around in a blind fury.

3 If people **throw** something **about** or **around,** they throw it from   V+N+ADV
one person to the other, usually as part of a game. EG *I saw him*

throwing a cricket ball about with some other boys... He doesn't join any of the games. He doesn't even throw a football around.

4 If you **throw** yourself **about,** you move your body suddenly and in different directions, usually because you are ill or angry. EG *David had thrown himself about wildly... The animal is throwing its head about.*　　V+REFL+ADV, V+N+ADV

5 If you **throw** money **about** or **around,** you spend it freely and in large amounts, especially on things that are not necessary, useful or sensible. EG *Ford, however, does not have money to throw about... If you throw enough money around you don't have enemies.*　　V+N+ADV, V+PRON+ADV

throw around. 1 If you **throw** one thing **around** or **round** another, you place it so that it surrounds or encircles the other thing. EG *...with a rope thrown around his waist... 'Coming!' said she, throwing a scarf round her neck.*　　V+N+PREP, V+PRON+PREP

2 See **throw about.**

throw aside. 1 If you **throw** a covering or curtain **aside,** you move it quickly to one side so that it is no longer in your way. EG *She threw the bedclothes aside and jumped out of bed... ...throwing aside the mosquito netting.*　　V+N+ADV, V+PRON+ADV, V+ADV+N

2 If you **throw aside** an attitude, principle, or idea, you suddenly abandon it, reject it, or change it. EG *The time came to throw aside all indecisiveness... ...a lesson eagerly learned but then carelessly thrown aside.*　　V+ADV+N, V+N+ADV, V+PRON+ADV

throw at. 1 If you **throw** an object **at** someone or something, you try to make the object hit them, by moving your hand forward very fast and letting go of the object. EG *He threw a dart, hard, at the board... Roger stooped, picked up a stone, aimed, and threw it at Henry... ...terrorists who threw a petrol bomb at the Cultural Institute.*　　V+N+PREP, V+PRON+PREP

2 If you **throw** a look, remark, or question **at** someone, you look at them, or say something to them, suddenly and often aggressively. EG *She threw nervous glances at him every now and again... He sang, whistled, threw remarks at the silent Ralph... 'It's where your father works.' She threw this at him just a little too casually.*　　V+N+PREP, V+PRON+PREP

3 To **throw** something **at** an enemy or opponent means to attack or challenge them with it. EG *The silliest soldier would not throw his whole strength at a break-through without tanks... ...other laws they could throw at me if they chose.*　　V+N+PREP, V+PRON+PREP

4 If you **throw** money **at** a difficult situation or problem, you try to solve it by spending more money rather than by thinking of new ways that might work better. EG *The Prime Minister is against throwing money at the inner cities... The response of the West at present is simply to throw pound notes at them.*　　V+N+PREP, V+PRON+PREP

5 If you **throw** yourself **at** someone or something, you run or jump quickly and desperately towards them. EG *Kairi threw herself at him, wailing with terror... He abruptly throws himself at Gaspar and seizes the barrel of the gun.*　　V+REFL+PREP

6 If you **throw** yourself **at** someone you are attracted to, you behave in a way that makes it obvious that you want to have a relationship with them, and do not care that other people find your behaviour unacceptable or embarrassing. EG *...hundreds of girls who would be more than honoured to throw themselves at his head... Connie had thrown herself at his feet and he had rejected her.*　　V+REFL+PREP

throw away. 1 If you **throw away** from you an object you were holding, you move your hand suddenly and let go of it, so that it moves rapidly away. EG *He threw away his brush, but stopped to pick it up... He threw her away from him... He read one page and then threw the paper away from him.*　　V+ADV+N, V+PRON+ADV, V+N+ADV: ALSO+*from*

2 When you **throw away** something that you no longer want or need,　　V+PRON+ADV,

you get rid of it, for example by putting it in a dustbin. ᴇɢ *You should* V+ADV+N,
throw those away and get a pair of these... Throw away medicine V+N+ADV
after an illness is over... 30 million tonnes of refuse are thrown away
in the UK. ● **Discard** is a more formal word for **throw away**, and
keep means the opposite. ▸ A **throw-away** product is intended to be ADJECTIVE
used only once, or only for a short time, before being got rid of. ᴇɢ
...a throw-away toothbrush... ...throw-away chopsticks. ● **Disposable**
means almost the same as **throw-away.**

3 If someone **throws away** something valuable that they have, they V+N+ADV,
waste it rather than using it sensibly. ᴇɢ *He is evidently prepared to* V+PRON+ADV,
throw his money away... To throw it all away when we're so near!... V+ADV+N
They threw away their advantage... Throw away his career for a
girl?

4 A **throwaway** remark is spoken casually and quietly, although it is ADJECTIVE
important, and therefore only people who are listening carefully
will hear it or realize its importance. ᴇɢ *...making your point in a*
throwaway line.

throw back. **1** If you **throw** something or someone **back** some- V+N+ADV,
where, you put them carelessly in the place where they were before V+PRON+ADV,
or force them to return there. ᴇɢ *Hagen threw his papers back into* V+REFL+ADV:
the basket... ...catching fish, weighing them and throwing them USUALLY+A
back... I was collared by the police and thrown back onto Schenk
Street... I would have thrown myself back under the covers in a
blind panic.

2 If you **throw back** a covering such as a piece of cloth, you pull it or V+ADV+N,
fold it, so that the thing that was covered becomes visible. ᴇɢ *She* V+N+ADV,
threw back the covers on the bed... He threw back the curtains... ...a V+PRON+ADV
veil, which she threw back over her hat.

3 If you **throw back** your head or arms, you move them backwards V+ADV+N,
suddenly. ᴇɢ *I threw back my head and yelled 'Help!'... He sleeps still* V+N+ADV,
with his arms thrown back... Valentino threw himself back in his V+REFL+ADV,
chair and roared with laughter. V+PRON+ADV

4 If you **throw back** a drink, you drink it quickly, often in one gulp. V+ADV+N,
ᴇɢ *Stock threw back two vodkas in quick succession.* ● **Knock back** V+N+ADV,
and **put back** mean almost the same as **throw back.** V+PRON+ADV

5 If something **throws back** light or sound, it reflects the light or V+N+ADV,
causes the sound to echo. ᴇɢ *...a shirt so white it threw the sun's light* V+ADV+N,
back... ...drifting fog that would suddenly throw the headlight beam V+PRON+ADV
back through the windscreen... Mirage fighters take off from the
airport, throwing back a sound like a crack of thunder.

6 To **throw** someone **back** to an earlier time means to cause them to V+PRON+ADV,
remember it. ᴇɢ *The scene threatened to throw me back eight years,* V+N+ADV,
to the time I had been beaten up... That headline threw our little V+REFL+ADV
group back on memories of the Thirties... ...throwing ourselves back
to a simpler time.

7 If you say that something is a **throwback** to something that existed N SING
or was common a long time ago, you mean that it is very similar to
it. ᴇɢ *His pro-British sentiments were a throwback to the old colonial*
days.

8 If you **are thrown back** on someone or something, you have to rely V+N+ADV,
on them once more, after a period of not needing them. ᴇɢ *Ethnic* V+PRON+ADV:
groups were thrown back on their own resources... We are thrown WITH PREP,
back onto mother... I feel very strongly that this throws him back USUALLY PASSIVE
upon himself.

throw back at. If you **throw** a mistake or weakness **back at** V+N+ADV+PREP,
someone, you remind them of it, usually in order to hurt them. ᴇɢ V+PRON+ADV+PREP
Satisfying, isn't it, to throw everything back at him?... ...throwing
their childless marriage right back at her.

throw down. 1 If you **throw down** something you are holding, you move your hand downwards and let go of it so that it falls rapidly downwards. EG *He threw down his napkin and went out of the room... He threw the gun down on the floor... She went to throw garbage down the incinerator... Take this stick and throw it down in front of the king.*

V+ADV+N,
V+N+ADV/PREP,
V+PRON+ADV/PREP

2 If you **throw** yourself **down,** you deliberately fall or move rapidly towards the ground. EG *She threw herself down on her knees and prayed... He threw himself down beside me and closed his eyes.*

V+REFL+ADV

3 If soldiers **throw down** their arms, they surrender or stop fighting. EG *The soldiers often looked as if they would like to throw down their arms and join the protesting students.*

V+ADV+N,
V+N+ADV,
V+PRON+ADV

4 If you **throw down** something you are eating or drinking, you eat or drink it very quickly, often in one gulp. EG *He threw down the rest of his coffee and stood up... The whole thing was a ghastly mistake. I thought I'd throw down a few pills and—zap!—instant answers.*

V+ADV+N,
V+N+ADV,
V+PRON+ADV

throw in. 1 If you **throw** an object **in** a container or other place, you put it there casually, sometimes with force. EG *She threw both letters in the bin... Add a teaspoonful of salt, and throw in the rice... They threw it in the river, and went home.*

V+N+ADV/PREP,
V+ADV+N,
V+PRON+ADV/PREP

2 If someone **throws** a person **in** jail, prison or a cell, they force them to enter it and stay there. EG *The cop threatened to throw all of us in jail.*

V+N+PREP

3 If you **throw in** a word or comment when talking or writing, you add it in a casual or unexpected way. EG *...Mr Edgar H. Humbert (I threw in the 'Edgar' just for fun)... 'It's simply disgraceful of you, Philip,' threw in Ann.* ● **Toss in** means almost the same as **throw in.**

V+ADV+N,
V+ADV+QUOTE,
V+N+ADV,
V+PRON+ADV

4 If you **throw in** an extra item when you are selling something or arranging something, you add it or include it in order to persuade people to buy the thing or accept the arrangement. EG *They threw in the matching handbag for another hundred... ...a few minor reforms thrown in to sweeten the temper of the local people.*

V+ADV+N,
V+N+ADV,
V+PRON+ADV

5 If someone in authority **throws in** soldiers or workers, they order them to go somewhere and start fighting or working. EG *He could not throw in his final reserves on the Central Front... ...throwing in different shifts of carpenters and masons.*

V+ADV+N,
V+N+ADV,
V+PRON+ADV

6 If your team in a football match has a **throw-in** because the other team has kicked the ball off the pitch, one of your players stands at the edge of the pitch and throws the ball to one of your team. EG *A quick throw-in gave the State players a chance to score.*

N COUNT

throw into. 1 If you **throw** an object **into** a container or place, you put it there casually, sometimes with force. EG *Hagen threw his papers into the basket... Mrs Haze threw it into a cupboard.*

V+N+PREP,
V+PRON+PREP

2 If someone **throws** a person **into** jail, prison or a cell, they force them to enter it and stay there. EG *They arrested several leaders and threw them into prison.*

V+N+PREP

3 If you **throw** yourself **into** a place, you move there quickly and forcefully. EG *She threw herself into Rudolph's arms... She threw herself into the street... Peggy threw herself into a chair.*

V+REFL+PREP

4 To **throw** someone or something **into** a particular state means to cause them suddenly to be in that state. EG *The driver threw the car into reverse... He turned out the light, throwing the room into blackness... Her voice threw me into a rage.*

V+N+PREP,
V+PRON+PREP

5 If you **throw** yourself **into** a task, activity, or situation, you begin to do it with a lot of effort and energy. EG *Mrs Kaul threw herself into her work... He threw himself into the battle against Chamberlain... Everyone threw themselves energetically into clearing it away.*

V+REFL+PREP

6 If you **throw** energy or resources **into** an activity or enterprise,

V+N+PREP,
V+PRON+PREP

you use a lot of energy or resources to try and make it succeed. EG
*Many women throw all of their energies into a career... ...throwing
an estimated 100,000 troops into the manoeuvres.*

throw off. 1 If you **throw off** your clothes or something covering
you, you remove them from your body quickly and carelessly. EG
*Laverne threw off her T-shirt... ...throwing it off and handing it to
him... He threw off his blanket and lay still.*

V+ADV+N,
V+N+ADV,
V+PRON+ADV

2 If you **throw off** someone or something that is restricting you, you
free yourself from them. EG *Throw off the chains of the
slavemaster... Britain threw off some of the illusions... Some children throw off their ailments quickly.*

V+ADV+N,
V+N+ADV,
V+PRON+ADV

3 If something **throws off** heat, light, or other form of energy, it
releases it. EG *...a little furnace, throwing off a haze of visible heat...
The thinking brain throws off electrical and chemical discharges...
Other particles will be thrown off in all directions.* ● **Emit** is a
formal word for **throw off.**

V+ADV+N,
V+N+ADV,
V+PRON+ADV

4 To **throw** someone or something **off** means to cause them to make
a mistake or to fail. EG *He had been thrown off by an ambiguity in
the term 'quality'... A faulty gauge can throw your calculations way
off... ...throwing the building programme off schedule.*

V+N+ADV/PREP,
V+PRON+ADV/PREP,
V+ADV+N

5 To **throw** someone **off** the scent, track, or trail means to deliberately deceive, confuse, or mislead them. EG *I will change transportation to throw them off, and use back roads... That should throw him
off the track or at least leave him uncertain... The story threw the
police off the right scent.*

V+PRON+ADV/PREP,
V+N+ADV/PREP,
V+ADV+N

throw on. 1 If you **throw on** your clothes, you put them on quickly
and carelessly. EG *He threw on his clothes and went downstairs... I
threw Clem's red jacket on over my straight black dress.*

V+ADV+N,
V+N+ADV,
V+PRON+ADV

2 If you **throw** yourself **on** or **upon** someone or something, you rush
at them, deliberately fall on top of them, or attack them. EG *She
threw herself on the bed... Joseph threw himself on his father,
crying and kissing his face.*

V+REFL+PREP

3 If something **throws** light or shadow **on** or **upon** someone or
something, it causes them to be covered in light or shadow; a
literary use. EG *Its light threw a faint radiance on the sleeping girl...
A large beech tree threw its shadow upon the grass.*

V+N+PREP

4 To **throw** light **on** or **upon** a problem means to help people to
understand it or solve it. EG *...an attempt to throw light on this
perplexing situation... Can't Mrs. Welch throw any light on the
matter?... The diaries throw a new light upon certain incidents.*

V+N+PREP

5 To **throw** doubt or suspicion **on** or **upon** someone or something
means to cause people to doubt them or suspect them. EG *A re-
examination of the evidence has thrown doubts on this view...
Meehan tried to throw suspicion on the two youths... Recent research has tended to throw doubt upon this concept.*

V+N+PREP

throw onto, throw on to. If you **throw** one thing **onto** or **on to**
another, you cause it to fall with force on top of the other thing. EG
*She threw her books violently onto the floor... She threw it on to the
porcelain tiles and smashed it... Kitty threw herself onto the bed.*

V+N+PREP,
V+PRON+PREP,
V+REFL+PREP

throw out. 1 If you **throw out** an object you are holding, you cause
it to move away from you by moving your hand forward and letting
go of it. EG *They threw the net out and could not pull it back in... He
threw it out into the sunlight... He looked again at the papers and
threw them out of the window... She threw out handfuls of wheat.*

V+N+ADV,
V+PRON+ADV,
V+ADV+N:
ALSO+*of*

2 If you **throw out** an object you no longer want, you get rid of it, for
example by putting it in a dustbin. EG *...throwing out their rubbish on
to the courtyards... I can remember my parents throwing out their*

V+ADV+N,
V+PRON+ADV,
V+N+ADV

old furniture... What's this? Should I throw it out and wash the pot?
● **Throw away** means almost the same as **throw out**.

3 If you **throw out** someone's ideas, proposals, or work, you reject them because you find them unacceptable. EG *At first he threw out almost every headline I wrote... The Grand Jury threw out the Bill... New societies may be tempted to throw out the principles of democracy.*

V+ADV+N,
V+N+ADV,
V+PRON+ADV

4 If you **throw** someone **out** of a place, job, or institution, you force them to leave it. EG *They'll throw out their councillor if he doesn't vote for it... Axel threw his brother out of the house... He was nearly thrown out of college... They'll throw me out of Britain.*

V+ADV+N,
V+N+ADV,
V+PRON+ADV:
ALSO+of

5 If you are speaking and **throw out** ideas or suggestions, you mention them for people to consider. EG *Bernstein threw out a name he had never heard before... Whiting would only throw out hints... Actors worked from suggestions thrown out to them from the floor.*

V+ADV+N,
V+N+ADV,
V+PRON+ADV

6 If something **throws out** smoke, light, heat, or a smell, it produces it and releases it, usually in large quantities. EG *...chimneys throwing out huge plumes of black smoke... ...throwing out beams and rays... It throws out an intense smell of tea-leaves.* ● **Emit** is a formal word for **throw out**.

V+ADV+N,
V+N+ADV,
V+PRON+ADV

7 If you **throw out** a hand, arm, or leg, you move it suddenly away from your body. EG *Bond stumbled and threw out his right hand for support... She threw out her hands, laughing.*

V+ADV+N,
V+N+ADV,
V+PRON+ADV

throw over. **1** If you **throw** one thing **over** another, **1.1** you cause it to move above and past the other thing until it is on the other side of it. EG *I threw my brief-case over the wall... She ran to the low fence and threw herself over it... He was frightened he might throw himself over.* **1.2** you place it so that it covers the other thing or is supported by it. EG *Covers were hastily thrown over the stalls... He threw his sweater over the chair... Thomas picked Claude up and threw him over his shoulder.*

V+N+ADV/PREP,
V+PRON+ADV/PREP,
V+REFL+ADV/PREP

V+N+PREP,
V+PRON+PREP

2 If you **throw** something **over** to someone, you pass it to them casually or carelessly. EG *He threw over a newspaper... They're in the chest there. And throw those beers over, too.*

V+ADV+N,
V+N+ADV,
V+PRON+ADV

3 If you **throw over** a boyfriend or girlfriend, you end your relationship with them; a rather old-fashioned use. EG *Eventually the girl threw him over for a young minister... ...just after he'd been thrown over by Claudia.* ● **Jilt** and **chuck** mean almost the same as **throw over.**

V+PRON+ADV,
V+N+ADV,
V+ADV+N

throw overboard. **1** If you are on a ship and **throw** something **overboard,** you throw it over the side of the ship into the water. EG *Throw them overboard to lighten the ship... They threatened to throw themselves overboard.*

V+PRON+ADV,
V+REFL+ADV,
V+N+ADV,
V+ADV+N

2 If you **throw** an idea or plan **overboard,** you reject it completely. EG *The country threw Baldwin's policy overboard... You had to throw overboard everything known, good, loving, and trusted.*

V+N+ADV,
V+ADV+N,
V+PRON+ADV

throw round. See **throw about** and **throw around.**

throw together. **1** If you **throw** something **together,** you make it or arrange it quickly and not very carefully. EG *...throwing together an alcoholic mixture which left them breathless... This is no crisis measure hastily thrown together... ...a small building, recently thrown together.*

V+ADV+N,
V+N+ADV,
V+PRON+ADV

2 If people **are thrown together** by a situation or event, it causes them to meet each other and get to know each other. EG *They were thrown together in Paris in the Thirties... ...manage things so that he and the woman are thrown together.*

PASSIVE:
V+ADV

throw up. **1** If something **throws up** small particles such as dust, stones, or water, it causes them to rise upwards into the air. EG *A*

V+ADV+N,
V+N+ADV,
V+PRON+ADV

passing car threw up a cloud of white dust... ...throwing up a shower of wood chips... The wheels would throw sparks up into our faces.

2 If you **throw up** something you are holding, you cause it to move upwards into the air by moving your hand quickly and letting go of it. EG *Adam threw the ball up and they started to play... Howarth threw up his lucky 20-cent piece.*   V+N+ADV, V+PRON+ADV, V+ADV+N

3 If you **throw up** your arms or hands, you lift them quickly from your sides and move them upwards. If you **throw up** your head, you move it upwards and tilt it backwards. EG *Mrs Pringle threw her hands up in astonishment... Bond threw up an arm to protect himself... She threw up her head with a little laugh.*   V+N+ADV, V+ADV+N, V+PRON+ADV

4 If people **throw up** a building or structure, they build or make it very quickly. EG *...travelling actors throw up a canvas-and-wood stage... ...throw up a ranch house.*   V+ADV+N, V+PRON+ADV

5 If a situation, country, or activity **throws up** particular types of things or people, it produces them or causes them to become well-known. EG *The new equipment threw up major problems over safety... Neither country has thrown up class-based parties... Your research has thrown up some very fascinating facts, hasn't it?*   V+ADV+N, V+N+ADV, V+PRON+ADV

6 If you **throw up** a job, position, or activity you leave it or stop doing it suddenly and unexpectedly. EG *Even if I'd thrown up my job, it wouldn't have worried me... He considered throwing it up for something easier.* ● **Chuck in** means almost the same as **throw up**.   V+ADV+N, V+PRON+ADV, V+N+ADV

7 If someone **throws up,** they vomit. EG *Halfway through the meal, I collapsed and crawled outside to throw up.*   V+ADV

throw upon. See throw on.

thrust, thrusts, thrusting

The form **thrust** is used in the present tense and is the past tense and past participle of the verb.

thrust up. If something tall or pointed **thrusts up** somewhere, it is higher than the surrounding things and can be clearly seen; a literary expression. EG *...the bell-tower thrusting bravely up beside it... ...an imposing rock needle thrusting up at least 250 feet.*   V+ADV: USUALLY+A

thrust upon. To **thrust** something **upon** someone means to force them to have it, deal with it, or experience it. EG *An enormous political responsibility had been thrust upon me... She had thrust herself upon him.*   V+N+PREP, V+REFL+PREP, V+PRON+PREP

thumb, thumbs, thumbing, thumbed

thumb through. If you **thumb through** a book or other written material, you glance at the pages briefly and turn them over, rather than reading each page carefully. EG *Bernstein thumbed through a local afternoon paper... She picks it up and thumbs through its pages.*   V+PREP: HAS PASSIVE

thump, thumps, thumping, thumped

thump out. **1** If you **thump out** a tune on a piano, you play it by hitting the keys very hard.   V+ADV+N, V+PRON+ADV

2 If a message **is thumped out,** it is expressed very forcefully. EG *The message was thumped out in his newspapers' editorials week after week.*   V+ADV+N, V+N+ADV, V+PRON+ADV

tick, ticks, ticking, ticked

tick away. If a clock or other mechanical device **ticks away** or **ticks on,** it makes a continual ticking noise. EG *I could hear my wristwatch ticking away... ...a time-bomb ticking away in a safe... The metronome ticked on slowly.*   V+ADV

tick by. If you say that time, especially seconds or minutes, **ticked by,** you are emphasizing the fact that time was passing, usually just   V+ADV

before something important or exciting was expected to happen; a
literary expression. EG *The minutes ticked by. Then Eisenhower
announced his decision.*

tick off. 1 If you **tick off** items on a list, you write a tick or other   V+ADV+N,
mark next to them, in order to show that they have been dealt with.   V+PRON+ADV/PREP,
EG *I tick off the items in my book... Tick them off as each job is   V+N+ADV/PREP
finished... ...ticking the names off the Electoral Roll.*

2 If you **tick off** items on your fingers, you say them one by one and   V+PRON+ADV,
touch your fingers with another finger at the same time, usually to   V+ADV+N,
make sure you have not forgotten an item. EG *'I want three things   V+N+ADV
out of this.' He ticked them off on his fingers... I have ticked off the
months on my fingers... She ticked the items off on her fingers.*

3 If you **tick** someone **off,** you speak angrily to them because they   V+PRON+ADV,
have done something wrong. EG *David had ticked her off for not   V+ADV+N,
getting some work right... 'Not much good ticking off the children,'   V+N+ADV:
she remarked, 'when the parents are just as rude.* ● **Scold** is a more   ALSO+*for*
formal word for **tick off,** and **tell off** means almost the same.

▶ **ticking-off, tickings-off/ticking-offs.** If you give someone a   N COUNT
ticking-off, you speak angrily to them because they have done
something wrong. EG *Then Lally confessed and got a ticking-off.*
● **Telling-off** means almost the same as **ticking-off.**

4 If you say that a clock **ticks off** time, or that the time **ticks off,** you   V+ADV+N,
are emphasizing that the time is passing, especially before some-   V+ADV:
thing important is expected to happen. EG *The clock ticked off the   ERGATIVE
seconds to the meeting... ...the seconds ticking off inside his head.*

tick on. 1 See **tick away.**

2 If you say that an idea or system **ticks on,** you mean that it   V+ADV
continues to exist or to be accepted and does not stop or get
changed. EG *Thoughts of this sort did go ticking on, useless or not...
The universe of Newton ticked on without a hitch for about two
hundred years.*

tick over. 1 If an engine or similar device **is ticking over,** it is   V+ADV
operating steadily or slowly, because it is not being used much. EG
*Now the reactor was merely ticking over as it generated electrical
power for the ship... With transistors, the computer had shrunk and
a ten-kilowatt generator would have kept it ticking over.* ● **Idle** is a
more technical word for **tick over.**

2 If a person, a system, or a business **is ticking over,** they are   V+ADV
working, but not producing very much or making much progress. EG
*The company can generate enough money to keep it ticking over...
Keep all the essential processes ticking over... Putting your money
in a building society is just ticking over, playing safe.*

tide, tides, tiding, tided

tide over. If you give someone money or help in order to **tide** them   V+PRON+ADV/PREP,
over, you do it so that they can get through a period of time when   V+N+ADV/PREP:
they are having problems. EG *I only want to borrow enough to tide   NO PASSIVE
me over till Monday... ...if you need a few dollars to tide you over...
...the huge grain surpluses that helped tide the world over the
1972-74 shortages.*

tidy, tidies, tidying, tidied

tidy away. When you **tidy** things **away,** you put them somewhere   V+N+ADV,
neatly after using them or dealing with them. EG *She tidied the box   V+PRON+ADV,
away in her dressing-table... I suggested we tidied them away, but   V+ADV+N
she's got more than a hundred... ...to tidy away letters before locking
up.*

tidy out. When you **tidy out** a cupboard or a room, you take   V+ADV+N, everything out of it, get rid of the things you do not want, and put the rest back neatly. `V+N+ADV, V+PRON+ADV`

tidy up. 1 When you **tidy up** a place, a container, or the things in them, you put all the things back in their proper places so that the place or container is neat again. EG *I started to tidy up the drawers... He went back to the studio and tidied it up... Tidy everything up and put it away in my locker... Eva was tidying up after lunch.* `V+ADV+N, V+PRON+ADV, V+N+ADV, V+ADV`

2 If you **tidy up** a person, you quickly make them look cleaner or smarter, for example by washing their hands and face, brushing their hair, or straightening their clothes. EG *I tidied myself up before we landed... ...when Deanna had tidied him up... Leggett tidied up his friend and asked what the quarrel was about.* `V+REFL+ADV, V+PRON+ADV, V+ADV+N`

3 If you **tidy up** a piece of work, a project, or a situation, you deal with the small unfinished or unsatisfactory parts of it, so that it is completely ready or finished. EG *I had a week to tidy up all last-minute details... You haven't made any serious errors, it's just a question of tidying it up.* `V+ADV+N, V+PRON+ADV, V+N+ADV`

tie, ties, tying, tied

tie back. If you **tie** something **back,** you fasten it into a position so that it cannot move and is not in the way. EG *Her hair was long and tied back... ...brushing her hair and tying it back.* `V+N+ADV, V+ADV+N, V+PRON+ADV`

tie down. 1 If you **tie** someone or something **down,** you tie them to the ground or in a low position. EG *I wasn't sure whether I should tie the camels down or not... One of the prison guards was confining him and tying him down.* `V+N+ADV, V+ADV+N, V+PRON+ADV`

2 A person or thing that **ties** someone **down** restricts their freedom. EG *You're not tied down to a date... He. doesn't like to tie himself down... She doesn't want children because she says they tie you down.* `V+N+ADV, V+PRON+ADV, V+REFL+ADV`

3 To **tie down** enemy troops means to force them to stay in one place for a while so that they cannot take action against you; a technical use. EG *The Berlin garrison would be capable of tying down large numbers of Warsaw Pact troops.* `V+ADV+N, V+N+ADV, V+PRON+ADV`

tie in with. If one thing **ties in with** another, it is closely connected to it, fits in with it, or agrees with it. EG *His beliefs didn't seem to tie in at all with reality... Estimates from the World Bank tie in well with these figures... The first letter seemed to tie in with the other... Does this tie in with what you were doing on 'Quality'?* `V+ADV+PREP`

tie up. 1 If you **tie** something **up,** you put string or rope round it so that it is firm or secure. EG *Clarissa came in, carrying some canvases tied up in brown paper... ...with their lunch tied up in white paper.* `V+N+ADV, V+ADV+N, V+PRON+ADV`

2 If you **tie up** a person or an animal, you fasten ropes or chains around them so that they cannot move or escape. EG *I tied my goat up during the day... I tied him up to a fence.* `V+N+ADV, V+ADV+N, V+PRON+ADV`

3 When you **tie up** laces, you fasten them in a bow. EG *He saw the man bending down and tying up his shoelace.* ● **Do up** means almost the same as **tie up.** `V+ADV+N, V+N+ADV, V+PRON+ADV`

4 When a boat **ties up** or **is tied up,** it is attached to something with a rope or chain, for example in a harbour. EG *The ships made for port and tied up... The Morning Rose was tied up alongside the harbour wall.* ● **Moor** is a more formal word for **tie up.** `V+ADV, ALSO PASSIVE, V+ADV: ERGATIVE`

5 To **tie** something **up** also means to use it in some way, with the result that it is not available for other people or other purposes. EG *The big companies were tying up supplies of minerals in long-term contracts... People don't want to tie their money up for long periods... They marched on the expressway, tied up two tunnels and blocked a bridge.* `V+ADV+N, V+N+ADV, V+PRON+ADV`

6 If you are **tied up**, you are busy, with the result that you are not free to do anything else. EG *I'm tied up right now, can you call me back later?*

PASSIVE:
V+ADV

7 If you **tie up** an issue or problem, you deal with it in a way that gives definite conclusions or answers. EG *Cobb ties it up in 100 pages of the book.*

V+N+ADV,
V+ADV+N,
V+PRON+ADV

8 Something that **ties up** with something else or **is tied up** with it is closely linked with it. EG *The vulnerability of the professions is tied up with their special strength... It supposedly tied up with her interest in dance.*

V+ADV,
OR PASSIVE,
V+ADV:
ALSO+with,
RECIPROCAL

tighten, tightens, tightening, tightened

tighten up. 1 When you **tighten up** a fastening, you move it so that it is more firmly in place or holds something more firmly. EG *The steward would get out on the wing to tighten up some loose wire... You'd better tighten those screws up... Tighten it up with a spanner.*
● **Loosen** means the opposite of **tighten up.**

V+ADV+N,
V+N+ADV,
V+PRON+ADV

2 If a muscle in your body **tightens up** or if you **tighten** it **up**, it becomes tense and stiff rather than being relaxed. EG *These exercises are to tighten up the abdominal muscles... No woman wants to make these muscles more relaxed, instead she wants to tighten them up and get rid of the surrounding fat... As your arm straightens back, the back of the arm tightens up.*

V+ADV+N,
V+N+ADV,
V+PRON+ADV,
V+ADV:
ERGATIVE

3 If someone **tightens up** a rule or system, they make it stricter or more efficient. EG *...as regulations on the testing of drugs are tightened up in the rich countries... He said he would take steps to tighten up the administration... There has been a demand to tighten up the law.*

V+ADV+N,
V+N+ADV,
V+PRON+ADV

tinker, tinkers, tinkering, tinkered

tinker about. If you **tinker about** with something or **tinker around** with it, you play with it and make small alterations and adjustments to it. EG *Some of the kids tinker about in the workshop... ...tinkering around with machines.*

V+ADV:
ALSO+with

tinker around. See tinker about.

tinker with. If you **tinker with** something, you try to mend it or improve it in some way by making a lot of small alterations and adjustments to it. EG *They have no desire to tinker with engines... I like tinkering with figures.*

V+PREP:
HAS PASSIVE

tip, tips, tipping, tipped

tip off. If you **tip** someone **off**, you tell them that something has happened or that it is going to happen when other people were trying to keep it secret. EG *The burglars were tipped off by a lookout and escaped... They tipped the police off.* ▶ A **tip-off** is a piece of information that you give to someone, usually as a warning that something is going to happen. EG *The building was evacuated as the result of a tip-off.*

V+N+ADV,
V+PRON+ADV

N COUNT

tip over. When you **tip** an object **over** or when it **tips over**, it falls or turns onto its side or upside down. EG *The last of the glasses broke when Sean tipped over the sideboard... She tipped the pan over and a dozen fish fell out... The boat transporting them had somehow tipped over.* ● **Overturn** means almost the same as **tip over.**

V+ADV+N,
V+N+ADV,
V+PRON+ADV,
V+ADV:
ERGATIVE

tip up. If you **tip up** a container such as a bucket or glass, you make it lean to one side so that its contents begin to pour out of it. EG *She tipped up the sherry glass... I had to hold the can to his mouth and tip it up as his head went back.* ● **Tilt** means almost the same as **tip up.**

V+ADV+N,
V+N+ADV,
V+PRON+ADV

tire, tires, tiring, tired

tire of. If you **tire of** something, you become bored with it and are   v+PREP
no longer interested in it. EG *They will tire of the sport soon enough...*
Father would simply stop talking when he tired of my questions.

tire out. If something **tires** you **out,** it makes you exhausted. EG *Even*   V+PRON+ADV,
climbing up the stairs would tire him out... He would walk back in   V+REFL+ADV,
the evening, and so tire himself out and be able to sleep... It is   V+N+ADV
necessary to keep the cough from being so frequent that it tires the
person out or interferes with sleep. ● **Wear out** means almost the
same as **tire out.** ▸ If you are **tired out,** you are exhausted. EG *By the*   ADJECTIVE
time he got round to them he was tired out... ...tired-out parents.

tog, togs, togging, togged

tog out. If you **tog** yourself **out** or **are togged out,** you are dressed in   V+REFL+ADV:
special or unusual clothes. EG *The kids had togged themselves out in*   USUALLY+A
their best clothes... Every year they arrive, togged out for the party.
● **Rig out** means almost the same as **tog out.**

tog up. If you **are togged up,** you are dressed in the right clothing   PASSIVE:
for a particular activity; an informal expression. EG *Sheila was all*   V+ADV
togged up like a camper.

toil, toils, toiling, toiled

toil away. If you **toil away,** you work hard at something continuous-   V+ADV
ly over a long period of time, especially something that is unpleasant and physically very tiring. EG *...the coalminer toiling away in the*
black deeps... Our mothers toiled away in the kitchen most of their
lives. ● **Slave away** means almost the same as **toil away.**

tone, tones, toning, toned

tone down. If you **tone** something **down,** you make it less strong,   V+ADV+N,
severe, or offensive. EG *He advised me to tone down my article...*   V+N+ADV,
Tone down that language!... The accent seemed to have been toned   V+PRON+ADV
down. ● **Moderate** means almost the same as **tone down.**

tone in. If something **tones in** with something else, it looks nice with   V+ADV:
it because their colours are similar. EG *The hat toned in with the*   ALSO+*with*
dress Nance was wearing... That carpet doesn't really tone in with
the curtains. ● **Match** means almost the same as **tone in.**

tone up. If something **tones up** your muscles, it makes them firm   V+ADV+N,
and strong. EG *This exercise should help to tone up the stomach*   V+N+ADV,
muscles.   V+PRON+ADV

tool, tools, tooling, tooled

tool up. When a factory **tools up** or **is tooled up,** it gets its   V+ADV,
machinery ready to produce things. EG *The costs of tooling up for*   OR PASSIVE:
this new model were $50 million... We are tooled up to produce now.   V+ADV

top, tops, topping, topped

top off. If you **top** something **off,** you do something to complete it in   V+ADV+N,
a satisfactory way. EG *The discovery of the volcanoes topped off an*   V+N+ADV,
exciting week... We topped the evening off with a few drinks... He   V+PRON+ADV
ate a plate of steak and eggs and then topped it off with ice cream
and loganberries. ● **Round off** means almost the same as **top off.**

top up. If you **top up** something such as a container or a drink, you   V+ADV+N,
fill it up again when it has been partly emptied. EG *Philip topped up*   V+N+ADV,
his gin and tonic... Shall I top your glass up?... The radiator will have   V+PRON+ADV
to be topped up because of evaporation. ▸ A **top-up** is another   N COUNT
serving of a drink in the same glass that you have just used. EG
Anyone ready for another top-up?

topple, topples, toppling, toppled

topple over. If something **topples over**, it becomes unsteady and falls. EG *She looked at the young tree nervously, as if expecting it to topple over.* ● **Keel over** means almost the same as **topple over.**   V+ADV

toss, tosses, tossing, tossed

toss about. 1 To **toss** something **about** or **around** means to move or shake it roughly. EG *She started to toss her head about... ...tossing her hair around a lot... The plane was tossed about like a small boat in a storm... They were too old now for pillow fights or to be tossed around.*   V+N+ADV, V+PRON+ADV

2 If you **toss** an idea or phrase **about** or **around,** you mention or suggest it, but not in a very serious way. EG *London newspapers started tossing around phrases like 'The big three'... We tossed a few ideas around.*   V+ADV+N, V+N+ADV, V+PRON+ADV

toss around. See **toss about.**

toss away. If you **toss** something **away**, you get rid of it in a casual or careless way. EG *She tossed away her cigarette... He made a gesture of tossing something away.*   V+ADV+N, V+PRON+ADV, V+N+ADV

toss back. 1 If you **toss back** your head, you move it back sharply. If you **toss back** your hair, you move your head back sharply so that your hair is no longer over your face. EG *He tosses his head back... ...rubbing his hand on his chest and tossing back his head... He removed his hand from the table and tossed back his blond hair.*   V+N+ADV, V+ADV+N, V+PRON+ADV

2 If you **toss back**, **toss down**, or **toss off** a drink, you drink it quickly. EG *He tossed back another glass of wine... When the drink came, he tossed it down in one gulp... She tossed her second sherry off even quicker than the first.*   V+ADV+N, V+PRON+ADV, V+N+ADV

toss down. See **toss back.**

toss in. If you **toss in** a comment or a piece of information, you give it casually in the middle of a conversation. EG *...tossing in the odd juicy titbit... I tossed a few comments in.* ● **Toss out** means almost the same as **toss in.**   V+ADV+N, V+N+ADV, V+PRON+ADV

toss off. 1 See **toss back.**

2 If you **toss off** something such as a letter or an article, you write it very quickly. EG *I tossed off a letter to my parents.* ● **Dash off** means almost the same as **toss off.**   V+ADV+N, V+N+ADV, V+PRON+ADV

3 To **toss** someone **off** means to give them an orgasm by rubbing their genitals; a rude and very informal use.   V+N+ADV, V+PRON+ADV, V+REFL+ADV

toss out. If you **toss out** an idea or a comment, you give it casually or without being asked. EG *She would toss out an idea that they'd never expected from her... I tossed a few suggestions out to see how they'd react.* ● **Toss in** means almost the same as **toss out.**   V+ADV+N, V+N+ADV, V+PRON+ADV

toss up. If you **toss up**, you make a decision about something by throwing a coin into the air and guessing which side of the coin will be on top when it falls. EG *We tossed up to decide who should pay the bill.* ▸ A **toss-up** is a situation in which either of two results seems equally likely. EG *It was a toss-up who would get there first.*   V+ADV   N SING

tot, tots, totting, totted

tot up. To **tot up** numbers means to add them together in order to get the total number or amount of something. EG *I'll just tot up what you owe me... We totted all the figures up.*   V+ADV+N, V+N+ADV, V+PRON+ADV

touch, touches, touching, touched

touch down. When an aircraft **touches down**, it lands. EG *He watched the plane as it touched down... We touched down at Heathrow.* ● **Take off** means the opposite of **touch down.** ▸ **Touchdown** is the landing of an aircraft. EG *Failure of any*   V+ADV   N UNCOUNT, N COUNT

*mechanical system to function after touchdown could destroy hu-
man lives.*

touch off. If something **touches off** a situation or series of events, it   V+ADV+N
causes it to start happening. EG *The police action touched off another
night of rioting... A new 'Cuba' type crisis could touch off a nuclear
war.* ● **Spark off** means almost the same as **touch off.**

touch on. If you **touch on** or **upon** a subject, you mention it or write   V+PREP:
briefly about it. EG *I've touched on a couple of topics already... They*   HAS PASSIVE
*had touched on the possibility of an atomic bomb... ...the themes
which have been touched upon in this chapter.*

touch up. 1 If you **touch** something **up,** you improve its appearance   V+N+ADV,
by covering up small marks with paint or another substance. EG *He*   V+ADV+N,
touched the car up a bit and sold it... For dark scratches try touching   V+PRON+ADV
up woodwork with shoe polish... She touches up her hair. ▶ **Touched-**   ADJECTIVE
up means improved by having small marks painted over. EG *...a
touched-up photo of President Nixon.*

2 To **touch up** someone means to touch their body in order to gain   V+PRON+ADV,
sexual excitement. EG *You've been touching her up, haven't you?...*   V+N+ADV,
...touching up girls on country buses. ● **Feel up** means almost the   V+ADV+N
same as **touch up.**

touch upon. See touch on: touch upon is more formal.

toughen, toughens, toughening, toughened

toughen up. If you **toughen up,** or if you **are toughened up,** you   V+ADV,
become stronger and harder, and less gentle or sensitive. EG *He told*   V+REFL+ADV,
me that I would have to toughen up... It was time to toughen   V+N+ADV,
ourselves up... He was toughened up by all his physical labour.   V+PRON+ADV

tout, touts, touting, touted

tout around. See tout round.

tout round. If you **tout round** or **around** for something, you try to   V+ADV:
obtain it by asking a lot of different people. EG *...touting round for*   ALSO+*for*
books.

tow, tows, towing, towed

tow away. If a vehicle is **towed away,** it is removed from a place   V+N+ADV,
by being attached to another vehicle and pulled along. EG *If your car*   V+ADV+N,
breaks down on the motorway, you can have it towed away... He   V+PRON+ADV
found his van had been towed away by the police.

tower, towers, towering, towered

tower above. If someone or something **towers above** or **over** you,   V+PREP
they are a lot taller than you and make you seem small. EG *The old
chief towered above everybody... The trees towered above me... The
sides of the great ship towered over them.*

tower over. See tower above.

tower up. If something **towers up,** it is very tall and impressive. EG   V+ADV
*The Catholic church was towering up behind her... She towered up
immense and strong.*

toy, toys, toying, toyed

toy with. 1 If you **toy with** an idea or suggestion, you consider it   V+PREP:
casually, without making any decisions about it. EG *I've been toying*   HAS PASSIVE
*with the idea for some time... The United States is still toying with
military solutions... ...toying with the possibility of leaving.*

2 If you **toy with** an object, you keep moving it about with small   V+PREP
movements, usually while you are thinking about something else. EG
*She toyed with the one shrimp remaining on her plate... He reached
for his spectacles and toyed with them.* ● **Play with** means almost
the same as **toy with.**

trace, traces, tracing, traced

trace out. If you **trace** something **out**, you write it or mark it
clearly and carefully. EG *The names were traced out in stark black*
print... She traced out a bow on the envelope... She traced out A, B, C,
and D in the dust with a stick.

V+N+ADV,
V+ADV+N,
V+PRON+ADV

track, tracks, tracking, tracked

track down. If you **track down** someone or something, you find
them after searching for them with effort. EG *You have to cover a*
wide area to have any hope of tracking down the submarine...
...driving miles to track down parts for his tractor... One journalist
succeeded in tracking the victims down and finding out what had
happened to them... He eventually tracked the book down in the
university library... If he refused, they would not hesitate to track
him down. ● **Hunt down** means almost the same as **track down.**

V+ADV+N,
V+N+ADV,
V+PRON+ADV

trade, trades, trading, traded

trade in. If you **trade in** an old car, machine, or piece of equipment,
you give it to a dealer when you buy a new one so that you get a
reduction on the price. EG *We wanted to trade in the piano for one*
with a better tone... You might trade the car in for a smaller one... It
will cost £21 to repair. Is it worth it, or shall I trade it in for a new
one? ▸ A **trade-in** is a business deal in which someone exchanges an
old car, machine, or piece of equipment for a new one at a reduced
price.

V+ADV+N,
V+N+ADV,
V+PRON+ADV:
USUALLY+*for*

N COUNT

trade on. If someone **trades on** something such as another person's
weakness, they make use of it in an unfair way to gain an advantage
for themselves. EG *...people who trade on the hopes of the desperate-*
ly ill... The Democrats traded on the unpopularity of the two main
parties. ● **Exploit** means almost the same as **trade on.**

V+PREP:
HAS PASSIVE

trail, trails, trailing, trailed

trail away. If a speaker's voice **trails away**, it gradually becomes
quieter or more hesitant until it stops completely. EG *He didn't finish*
what he'd intended saying. His voice trailed away.

V+ADV

trail off. If someone who is speaking **trails off** or if their voice **trails**
off, they gradually speak more quietly and hesitantly until they stop
completely. EG *'You see, there are circumstances——' He trailed*
off... His voice trailed off as he reached the landing.

V+ADV

train, trains, training, trained

train on. If you **train** something such as a gun, light, or camera **on**
or **upon** someone or something, you aim it at them and keep it
pointing steadily towards them. EG *She trained her binoculars on the*
car speeding towards them... One gun was trained on Jo... All the
searchlights were trained upon a single aircraft.

V+N+PREP,
V+PRON+PREP

train up. If you **train up** a person, you teach them how to do
something so that they reach a particular standard. EG *They need to*
train up large numbers of local people as clerks and accountants...
They rented a shop, hired some lads, and trained them up... ...begin-
ners who were going to be trained up for the National Dancing
Championships.

V+ADV+N,
V+PRON+ADV,
V+N+ADV

train upon. See train on: train upon is more formal.

trample, tramples, trampling, trampled

trample on. 1 If you **trample on** or **upon** something, you tread on it
heavily so that it is damaged. EG *He knocked the statue over and*
trampled on it... They were kicked, bitten, and trampled on... He
found his new plants trampled upon.

V+PREP:
HAS PASSIVE

2 If you **trample on** or **upon** a person, their rights, or their feelings,

V+PREP:
HAS PASSIVE

you behave towards them in an unfair, insensitive, or cruel way. EG
*Half the population trample on the rights of the other half... Neither
will we allow ourselves to be trampled on... National distinctions
cannot be trampled upon.*

trample upon. See trample on: trample upon is more formal.

trap, traps, trapping, trapped

trap into. If you **trap** someone **into** saying or doing something, you
make them say or do it by tricking them or misleading them. EG
*...trying to trap Vita into an admission about her past... The student
was finally trapped into making a mistake.* ● **Trick into** means
almost the same as **trap into.**

V+N+PREP,
V+PRON+PREP

trespass, trespasses, trespassing, trespassed

trespass upon. If you **trespass upon** someone's generosity or
friendship, you take advantage of them by asking too much from
them; a formal and old-fashioned expression. EG *May I trespass upon
your sense of justice?*

V+PREP:
HAS PASSIVE

trick, tricks, tricking, tricked

trick into. If you **trick** someone **into** doing something, you manage
to get them to do it by misleading them or not telling them the truth.
EG *She has been tricked into marriage... ...girls tricked by promises
of work into leaving home... She tricked me into thinking it was gold.*

V+N+PREP,
V+PRON+PREP

trick out. If someone or something **is tricked out** in a particular
way, they are made to look that way. EG *...cupboards with sliding
doors tricked out to look like Georgian cocktail cabinets... She'd be a
funny kind of tailor not to have tricked me out better.*

V+N+ADV,
V+PRON+ADV:
USUALLY PASSIVE

trifle, trifles, trifling, trifled

trifle with. If you **trifle with** someone or something, you treat them
in a frivolous or disrespectful way. EG *Mitchell was not someone to
be trifled with... He was in no mood to be trifled with... One does not
trifle with history.*

V+PREP:
HAS PASSIVE

trigger, triggers, triggering, triggered

trigger off. If something **triggers off** an event or particular reaction, it causes it to happen. EG *The report triggered off a parliamentary debate... Radiation can damage DNA and trigger off cancer...
Many of the ideas were triggered off by things which were not
actively looked for.* ● **Spark off** and **set off** mean almost the same as
trigger off.

V+ADV+N,
V+PRON+ADV,
V+N+ADV

trim, trims, trimming, trimmed

trim away. If you **trim away** a part of something, you cut it off,
because it is not needed. EG *Kellner was trimming away the excess
carpet... You can trim the flesh away a little so that you can see the
ribs.*

V+ADV+N,
V+N+ADV,
V+PRON+ADV

trim off. If you **trim off** parts of something, you cut them off,
because they are not needed. EG *Remove as many bones as possible,
and trim off the fins... Thread them through the hole, then trim the
ends off... ...a book with all its margins trimmed off to save weight.*

V+ADV+N,
V+N+ADV,
V+PRON+ADV

trip, trips, tripping, tripped

trip over. 1 If you **trip over** something, you knock your leg against it
and fall over or nearly fall over. EG *He stuck out his foot, and I
tripped over it, but recovered... He tripped over and came down
with a crash.*

V+PREP,
V+ADV

2 If you **trip over** something you are saying, you say it hesitantly or
make mistakes because you are nervous. EG *Children understand the*

V+PREP

meaning even when they trip over unexpected words... Frederica spoke a few lines, tripping over words and recovering her dignity.

trip up. 1 If someone or something **trips** you **up**, they cause you to fall over or nearly fall over by obstructing your feet when you are walking. EG *When people run after you, your friends trip them up or threaten them... The road was full of holes and rocks which could trip you up... ...walking cautiously to avoid tripping up.*
V+PRON+ADV, V+N+ADV, V+ADV: ERGATIVE

2 To **trip** someone **up** also means to make them confused so that they say something that they did not intend to say; an informal use. EG *The judges' questions tripped him up completely... Even the cleverest of us can be tripped up from time to time.* ● **Catch out** means almost the same as **trip up.**
V+PRON+ADV, V+N+ADV

trot, trots, trotting, trotted

trot off. If you **trot off** somewhere, you go there fairly quickly and in a purposeful way. EG *He described his little girl trotting off to school in her new blazer... He trotted off to tell his grandmother all about it.*
V+ADV: USUALLY+A

trot out. If you **trot out** old ideas, excuses, or pieces of information, you repeat or produce them in a boring way that shows that you have not really thought about them seriously. EG *...politicians who could be guaranteed to trot out the party line... Alison can hear it when I do, and you're not trotting it all out twice... We heard the usual excuses trotted out by the man in charge.*
V+ADV+N, V+PRON+ADV, V+N+ADV

truckle, truckles, truckling, truckled

truckle to. If you **truckle to** someone, you behave in a humble way towards them and do whatever they tell you to do; a fairly formal and old-fashioned expression. EG *I am sick of having to truckle to the professors... Only a weak and spineless man would truckle to the powerful and ruthless.*
V+PREP: HAS PASSIVE

truss, trusses, trussing, trussed

truss up. If you **truss** someone **up**, you tie them with ropes very tightly so that they cannot move; a rather old-fashioned expression. EG *Finally I had to truss him up like a turkey to get at his foot... The bulls were trussed up with ropes... Madame Berte was trussed up hand and foot with the clothes line.*
V+PRON+ADV, V+N+ADV

trust, trusts, trusting, trusted

trust to. If you **trust to** someone or something, you rely on them to do something for you or to take care of you. EG *The people of England are discovering that it is no good trusting to the old politicians... He would just have to trust to luck.*
V+PREP

try, tries, trying, tried

try for. If you **try for** something, you make an effort to get it or achieve it. EG *The Government tried for this two-thirds majority and failed... The school advised Mr Denby to let his son try for university.*
V+PREP

try on. 1 If you **try on** a piece of clothing, you put it on to see if it fits you or if it looks nice. EG *Poppy Green came to the house to try on her party dress... She tried it on for size... Always try shorts on in the shop.*
V+ADV+N, V+PRON+ADV, V+N+ADV

2 If someone is **trying** it **on**, they are attempting to trick you or make you angry. EG *So don't try it on, my poor misguided boy, or else... She is probably trying it on to see how far she can go with you... I was only trying it on, Mary. All right, let's start again.*
V+*it*+ADV

try out. 1 If you **try** something **out**, you test it in order to find out how useful or effective it is. EG *Oxford is trying out another idea to*
V+N+ADV, V+PRON+ADV: ALSO+*on*

help working parents... First they tried it out on a small group of children. ▶ If you give something a **try-out**, you test it so that you N COUNT can find out how useful or effective it is. EG *A neighbour had given the machine a good try-out.*

2 If you **try** someone **out**, you ask them to do a small task, so that V+PRON+ADV, you can see how good or useful they are before you ask them to do a V+N+ADV particular job. EG *Just try me out for a week, you'll see... You can try your horse out in a local competition first.*

tuck, tucks, tucking, tucked

tuck away. 1 If you **tuck away** something that is valuable, you store V+ADV+N, it in a safe place. EG *She had a bit of money tucked away... The bike* V+PRON+ADV, *can be folded and tucked away in a suitcase... ...rolling up the bill* V+N+ADV *and tucking it away for safety.* ● **Stash away** means almost the same as **tuck away.**

2 If something **is tucked away**, it is in a quiet place where very few PASSIVE: people go. EG *The parish church is tucked away behind the ca-* V+ADV *thedral... He is tucked away in a tiny office.* ● **Be hidden away** means almost the same as **be tucked away.**

tuck in. 1 If you **tuck** someone **in** or **up**, especially a child, you make V+PRON+ADV, them comfortable in bed by straightening their sheets and blankets V+ADV+N, and pushing the loose ends firmly under the mattress. EG *He was* V+N+ADV *asleep before I tucked him in... Get her to tuck you up in bed... She bent over, pretending to be tucking in the child.*

2 If you **tuck in** material such as a sheet, or the clothes you are V+N+ADV, wearing, you push the loose ends into a narrow space, in order to V+PRON+ADV, hold them in position. EG *I tucked my blouse in at the waist... She* V+ADV+N *began buttoning up her shirt and stood up to tuck it in... He tucked in his shirt tails.*

3 If you **tuck in,** you eat something with a lot of pleasure; an V+ADV informal use. EG *Well, there we are, tuck in... Mary put a plate of scrambled eggs and bacon in front of Morris and he tucked in appreciatively.*

4 If you **tuck** a part of your body **in,** you use your muscles and move V+N+ADV, it inwards rather stiffly. EG *Tuck your elbows in and sit up straight...* V+ADV+N, *He hunched his shoulders and tucked in his stomach.* V+PRON+ADV

tuck into. 1 If you **tuck** something **into** a narrow space, you press or V+N+PREP, push it into that space. EG *'Oh, do stand still!' she said, tucking Paul's* V+PRON+PREP *shirt into his shorts... Madeline crumpled the note and tucked it into her glove... He wore hiking boots into which he tucked the bottom of his jeans.*

2 If you **tuck into** food, you eat it with a lot of pleasure; an informal V+PREP use. EG *'Was that a helicopter?' she asked, tucking into her break-fast... ...tucking into mountains of greasy chips and sticky buns.* ● **Lay into** means almost the same as **tuck into.**

tuck up. 1 See **tuck in.**

2 If you **tuck** your legs or your feet **up** when you are sitting down, V+N+ADV, you move them underneath your body so that you are sitting on V+ADV+N, them. EG *'That's where you're wrong,' said Ellen, tucking her feet up* V+PRON+ADV *under her black skirt... She tucked up her feet and gazed at him... Her restless, elegant legs were tucked up onto the sofa.*

tug, tugs, tugging, tugged

tug at. If you **tug at** something, you give it a quick and usually V+PREP strong pull. EG *He tugged at the metal handle, and it came off in his hand... I had to tug at his hand to loosen it... He began to tug at the grass.* ● **Yank** means almost the same as **tug at.**

tumble, tumbles, tumbling, tumbled

tumble down. If someone or something **tumbles down,** they fall   v+ADV
down. EG *It only needed a push and the whole building would come
tumbling down... Did the walls really come tumbling down?* ▸ A   ADJECTIVE
tumbledown building is in such a bad condition that it is partly
falling down or has holes in it. EG *...a deserted, tumbledown building.*

tumble over. If someone or something **tumbles over,** they fall   v+ADV,
down. EG *She tumbled over and hit her head on the concrete... ...a*   v+PREP
barrier designed to stop cars tumbling over a steep drop.

tumble to. If you **tumble to** something, you suddenly understand it   v+PREP:
or realize what is happening. EG *I soon tumbled to the fact that I was*   HAS PASSIVE
*wasting my time... At least nobody tumbled to what these pipes were
for a long time... I can't guarantee to get you out of trouble if he
tumbles to what's going on.*

tune, tunes, tuning, tuned

tune in. If you **tune in,** you set the controls of your radio or   v+ADV
television so that you can listen to or watch a particular programme. EG *Tune in next week to hear how English is taught in
China... There must be millions of people tuning in to see the World
Snooker Championships.*

tune into. 1 If you **tune into** a particular channel or station, you set   v+PREP
the controls on your radio or television so that you can listen to or
watch that channel or station. EG *Film enthusiasts can tune into their
own channels... I've been listening to the early morning radio, tuned
into Delhi.*

2 If you **are tuned into** someone or something, you understand them   PASSIVE:
very well and are sympathetic towards them; an informal use. EG   v+PREP
*She was so tuned into you that she could 'read' your mind... People
are becoming more tuned into what computers can actually do.*

tune up. 1 When a group of musicians **tune up,** they adjust their   v+ADV
instruments so that they produce the right notes. EG *The orchestra
was tuning up for its regular Sunday afternoon broadcast... The
sound suggests they are tuning up.*

2 If you **tune up** a car, you adjust its engine so that it goes faster or   v+ADV+N,
more efficiently.   v+N+ADV,
  v+PRON+ADV

turf, turfs, turfing, turfed

turf out. 1 If you **turf** someone **out,** you force them to leave a   v+PRON+ADV,
particular place; an informal use. EG *Settlers are aware that the chief*   v+N+ADV
*can turf them out if he takes a dislike to them... When I turfed him
out, he told me he was going straight to your place.* ● **Kick out** and
chuck out mean almost the same as **turf out.**

2 If you **turf out** unwanted things, you get rid of them; an informal   v+ADV+N
use. EG *I turfed out a lot of stuff last week.*

turn, turns, turning, turned

turn about. 1 If something or someone **turns about** or if you **turn**   v+ADV,
them **about,** they move so that they are facing in a different   v+PRON+ADV,
direction. EG *He turned about and tiptoed away... The old method of*   v+N+ADV:
harvesting barley is to turn it about until it is quite dry. ● **Turn**   ERGATIVE
around means almost the same as **turn about.** ▸ **About-turn** is a   IMPERATIVE
command which is used to tell a group of people who are marching
in a particular direction to turn round and march in the opposite
direction. EG *Right about-turn—Quick march!*

2 A **turnabout** is a complete change in opinion or attitude. EG *I was*   N COUNT
eager to know what had caused the turnabout.

3 An **about turn** is an unexpected and complete change in opinion or   N COUNT
attitude. EG *Sandy Lyle yesterday did an about-turn and agreed to*

play... One of the reasons prompting the about-turn was the increasing expense.

turn against. If someone **turns against** or **is turned against** you, they start to dislike you or disapprove of you. EG *They might at any time turn against their masters... Public opinion turned against Hearst... You turn everyone against me... My daughter, who I was very close to, has been turned against me by her father.*   V+PREP, V+N+PREP, V+PRON+PREP: ERGATIVE

turn around. 1 See **turn round**.

2 If something such as a plan, project, or business that is failing **turns around** or if you **turn** it **around**, it becomes successful and profitable. EG *...if the economy turns around and the prices go up... ...an attempt to turn around last year's losses of £20 million... The company were in such bad shape that nobody could have turned things around in four years.* ▶ A **turnaround** is a sudden improvement, especially in the success of a business or country's economy. EG *There is little prospect of a sudden turnaround.* • **Turnround** means almost the same as **turnaround**.   V+ADV, V+ADV+N, V+N+ADV, V+PRON+ADV: ERGATIVE   N COUNT

turn aside. If you **turn aside** from someone or something, you move away from them or avoid them. EG *He turned discreetly aside to wipe his nose... The Government has turned aside from its collision course with the unions.*   V+PREP: ALSO+*from*

turn away. 1 If you **turn away** from someone or something, you move away from them so that you are no longer facing them. EG *I had to turn away to avoid letting him see my smile... Kunta turned away from the water's edge.*   V+ADV: ALSO+*from*

2 If you **turn** something **away** from someone or something, you move it to a different position so that it is no longer facing them. EG *She turned his chair away from the window... Karen turned her eyes away from Kitty.*   V+N+ADV, V+PRON+ADV: ALSO+*from*

3 If you **turn** someone **away,** you refuse to allow them to enter a place, or refuse to help them. EG *We don't turn anybody away because the old business was built up on friendship... The college has been forced to turn away 300 prospective students... Clerical workers and secretaries were turned away by gangs of men when they arrived at work.*   V+N+ADV, V+ADV+N, V+PRON+ADV

turn away from. If you **turn away from** something, or **are turned away from** it, you reject it or lose interest in it. EG *Women are turning away from hand-made clothes to machine printed dresses... ...stores which had done so much to turn people away from processed food... Mrs Norberg threw out a challenge that Daniel did not turn away from.*   V+ADV+PREP, V+N+ADV+PREP, V+PRON+ADV+PREP: ERGATIVE

turn back. 1 If you **turn back** or **are turned back** when you are travelling somewhere, you stop and return to the place you started from. EG *The snow started to fall, so we turned back... The police were turning back thousands of mourners... A lot of the cars had been turned back at the border... We were turned back by machine-gun fire.*   V+ADV, V+ADV+N, V+N+ADV, V+PRON+ADV: ERGATIVE

2 If you say that you cannot **turn back,** you mean that you cannot change your plans and decide not to do something, because of the action that you have already taken. EG *She had made her decision and from that point there could be no turning back.*   V+ADV: WITH NEGATIVE

3 If you **turn back** material or paper, you fold one part of it over so that it is covering the other part. EG *He leaped out of the bed and turned back the blankets... She was holding two papers but they were turned back so I couldn't see.*   V+ADV+N, V+N+ADV, V+PRON+ADV

turn down. 1 If you **turn down** a person, their request, or their offer, you refuse their request or offer. EG *I turned down an invitation for Saturday... I couldn't very well turn him down... She applied*   V+ADV+N, V+PRON+ADV, V+N+ADV

*for a job in a restaurant, but was turned down... Their claim has
been turned down.* ● **Reject** means almost the same as **turn down.**

2 When you **turn down** something such as a radio or a heater, you
adjust the controls and reduce the amount of sound or heat being
produced. EG *Turn the sound down... It's a bit hot in here—turn it
down... She turned down the gas fire.* ● **Turn up** means the opposite
of **turn down.**
V+N+ADV,
V+PRON+ADV,
V+ADV+N

3 If there is a **downturn** in the rate, level, or success of something, it
decreases or becomes less successful. EG *The downturn in inflation
has only taken place in the last three months... The company
blamed its downturn on interest rates.* ● **Upturn** means the opposite
of **downturn.**
N COUNT

4 If you **turn down** material or paper, you fold it so that one part of
it is covering the other part. EG *The room bearer had turned down
their bedcovers... Some of the cards were turned down at the
edges... She won't turn down the collar of her coat.*
V+ADV+N,
V+N+ADV,
V+PRON+ADV

turn in. 1 When you **turn in**, you go to bed; an informal use. EG
*Before turning in for the night he asked for an early morning call...
I'd like to wait until they've all turned in for a good night's sleep,
then I'd stage a riot.* ● **Retire** is a more formal word for **turn in.**
V+ADV

2 If you **turn in** someone who is suspected of a crime, you take them
to the police; an informal use. EG *Can you trust him? Do you think he
might turn you in?... They had been turned in by one of their own
sons... ...escapees who turned themselves in.* ● **Turn over** means
almost the same as **turn in.**
V+PRON+ADV,
V+N+ADV,
V+REFL+ADV,
V+ADV+N

3 If you **turn** something **in**, you give it to someone in authority
because it is their responsibility to deal with it. EG *They agreed to
turn in their guns... He was sure he had turned his uniform in when
he left the force... Meehan bought a car and then had to turn it in
because it had been stolen.*
V+ADV+N,
V+N+ADV,
V+PRON+ADV

4 When you **turn in** a completed piece of work, especially written
work, you give it to the person who asked you to do it. EG *Some of the
students began to turn in superb work... David and Chris turned in
the type of workmanlike results I had expected of them.* ● **Hand in**
and **give in** mean almost the same as **turn in.**
V+ADV+N,
V+PRON+ADV

turn into. If someone or something **turns into** another thing or if
you **turn** them **into** it, they change and become that other thing. EG
*Maggots turn into flies, and caterpillars into butterflies... Having a
gun can turn a coward into a dangerous criminal... The novel had
been turned into a television series.*
V+PREP,
V+N+PREP,
V+PRON+PREP:
ERGATIVE

turn off. 1 When you **turn off** a device, machine, or appliance, you
adjust the controls in order to stop it working. EG *Turn the gas fire
off when you leave the room... How do you turn it off?... He must
have turned off the radio.* ● **Switch off** means almost the same as
turn off, and **turn on** means the opposite.
V+N+ADV,
V+PRON+ADV,
V+ADV+N

2 If you **turn off** the road or path you are going along, you start
going along a different road or path which leads away from it. EG
*They turned off the main road... Small groups occasionally would
turn off the trail to hunt... This is where I turn off.* ▶ A **turn-off** is a
road which leads away from the side of another road. EG *Be careful,
or you'll miss the turn-off.*
V+PREP,
V+ADV

N COUNT

3 If something **turns** you **off** or if you **turn off,** you stop being
excited or interested; an informal use. EG *Had I turned her off by not
being daring enough?... ...customers turned off by poor advertising
techniques... The lecture was so boring that I just turned off.*
▶ Something that is a **turn-off** causes you to lose interest or
enthusiasm; an informal word. EG *All this legal stuff is a total turn-off
for us.*
V+PRON+ADV,
V+N+ADV,
V+ADV

N COUNT

turn on. 1 When you **turn on** a device, machine, or appliance, you adjust the controls so that it starts working. EG *Shall I turn the fire on?... I have a radio too, but I seldom turn it on except for concerts... She turned on the shower.* ● **Switch on** means almost the same as **turn on,** and **turn off** means the opposite.

V+N+ADV,
V+PRON+ADV,
V+ADV+N

2 If someone or something **turns** you **on,** they make you interested or excited; an informal use. EG *I don't really turn you on, do I?... It says some women are turned on by the smell and feel of leather.*

V+PRON+ADV,
V+N+ADV

▶ Something or someone that is a **turn-on** makes you interested or excited; an informal word. EG *I find long hair a real turn-on.* ● **Turn-off** means the opposite of **turn-on.**

N COUNT

3 If you **turn on** a particular way of behaving, you suddenly start behaving in that way; an informal use. EG *...a kid who knew how to turn on the charm... Maternal behaviour couldn't be turned on and off at will.* ● **Switch on** means almost the same as **turn on.**

V+ADV+N,
V+PRON+ADV

4 If a person or animal **turns on** or **upon** you, they suddenly attack you or speak angrily to you. EG *She turned on the men. 'How can you treat your daughters like this!'... Amir's dogs turned upon their master and tore him to pieces.* ● **Round on** means almost the same as **turn on.**

V+PREP

5 If something **turns on** or **upon** a particular thing, its success or truth depends on that thing. EG *His own future will turn on whether or not he can convince enough voters... The whole issue turns on the question of finances.* ● **Hinge on** means almost the same as **turn on.**

V+PREP

6 If your thoughts or a conversation **turn on** or **upon** a particular subject, they are concerned with that subject. EG *For a moment my thoughts turned on that gross and stupid man... Her mind turned upon the horrors depicted in the film... The conversation turned on the question of athleticism.*

V+PREP

7 If you **turn** something such as a gun, light, or a type of look **on** or **upon** someone or something, you aim it at them or keep it pointing steadily at them. EG *She turned a flashlight on Karen... Firefighters turned their hoses on the flames... Mrs Mawne turned a frosty glance upon Mr Willet.* ● **Train on** means almost the same as **turn on.**

V+N+PREP,
V+PRON+PREP

turn out. 1 If something **turns out** a particular way, it happens in that way. EG *Nothing ever turned out right... It turned out to be a fairly sensational evening... That's the way things turn out.* ● **Work out** means almost the same as **turn out.**

V+ADV:
WITH+A/to-INF

2 If something or someone **turns out** to be a particular thing, they are discovered to be that thing. EG *The Marvins' house turned out to be an old converted barn... Mrs Moffat had turned out to be the perfect landlady... It turned out that the message sent to him had been intercepted.*

V+ADV:
WITH to-INF
OR REPORT

3 When you **turn out** a light or a gas fire, you adjust the controls so that it stops giving out light or heat. EG *She didn't bother to turn the light out when she went out of the room... Pa had turned out the gas in the kitchen... His hand was on the light to turn it out again.* ● **Turn off** means almost the same as **turn out,** and **turn on** means the opposite.

V+N+ADV,
V+ADV+N,
V+PRON+ADV

4 If you **turn** someone **out** of a place, you force them to leave it. EG *I wouldn't want to turn you out of the house with the child ill... There's rumours going that she'll be turned out of the school-house... There are plenty of others likely to find themselves turned out on the streets after closing-time.* ● **Turf out, kick out** and **chuck out** mean almost the same as **turn out.**

V+PRON+ADV,
V+N+ADV:
USUALLY+of

5 If you **turn out** a container or **turn** its contents **out,** you empty it completely. EG *I have turned out the cupboard under the stairs... She*

V+ADV+N,
V+N+ADV,
V+PRON+ADV

opened her purse and turned out the contents onto the table... Come on, turn your pockets out! ▸ If you have a **turnout,** you sort through the things in a room or other place and throw away the unwanted things. EG *On Saturday I began my usual turnout.*   N COUNT

6 If a business or other organization **turns out** something, it produces it, usually in large quantities. EG *Salford was turning out the type of graduate they wanted... Better-quality goods were being turned out at lower prices.* ● **Churn out** means almost the same as **turn out.**   V+ADV+N, V+PRON+ADV

7 If people **turn out** for a particular event or activity, they go and take part in it or watch it. EG *Voters turned out in extraordinary numbers for the election... 50,000 people turned out during the bank holiday weekend to watch the airshow.* ● **Turn up** means almost the same as **turn out.** ▸ The **turnout** at an event is the number of people who go to it or take part in it. EG *It was such a small turnout!*   V+ADV: USUALLY+A

N COUNT

8 If you say that someone **is turned out** smartly, nicely, neatly, and so on, you mean that they are dressed in that way. EG *...attractive-looking girls, well turned out and smart... ...Soviet officers, elegantly turned out in black hats.* ▸ Someone's **turnout** is the way that they are dressed and how neat they are. EG *Claude approved of Daniel's turnout, with the exception of his tie.*   PASSIVE: V+ADV

N COUNT

turn over. 1 If something or someone **turns over** or if you **turn** them **over,** they move so that they are facing in a different direction. EG *She turned over and went to sleep... He turned the novel over to see the title... When the pancake is set, turn it over and cook the other side... The students were asked to turn over their papers and begin the exam.*   V+ADV, V+N+ADV, V+PRON+ADV, V+ADV+N: ERGATIVE

2 If you **turn over** someone suspected of a crime to the police or the authorities, you take them to the police or authorities. EG *If he'd suspected him, he'd have turned the man over right away... If you turn me over to the police I'll tell them nothing... They were caught by security patrols and turned over to the police.* ● **Turn in** means almost the same as **turn over.**   V+N+ADV, V+PRON+ADV, V+ADV+N: USUALLY+to

3 If you **turn** something **over** to someone, you give it to them or make them responsible for it. EG *He had refused to turn over funds that belonged to Potter... ...turning over control of the schools to local authorities... I turned the cheque over to the Treasurer.* ● **Hand over** means almost the same as **turn over.**   V+ADV+N, V+N+ADV, V+PRON+ADV: USUALLY+to

4 If you **turn** something **over** to a different function or use, you change its function or use. EG *The automobile industry had to turn their production facilities over to the creation of weapons... Soon afterwards I turned over part of the shop to antiques.*   V+N+ADV, V+PRON+ADV, V+ADV+N: USUALLY+to

5 If you **turn over** when you are watching television, you change the programme you are watching and watch another one instead. EG *I turned over and it was Kojak... Turn over, I can't stand this programme.* ● **Switch over** means almost the same as **turn over.**   V+ADV

6 When you talk about the rate that people or things **turn over** in a particular place, you are talking about how long they stay there before moving or being sent somewhere else. EG *In a grocery store, milk turns over more rapidly than, say, canned asparagus.* ▸ The **turnover** of people in an organization is the rate at which people leave and are replaced by others. EG *The group has an extremely high turnover of members.* ▸ The **turnover** of a company is the value of the goods or services that it has sold during a particular period of time. EG *Annual turnover is about £9,000 million.*   V+ADV

N UNCOUNT

N UNCOUNT

7 If you **turn** something **over** in your mind, you think carefully about it. EG *I had thought about the problem all day, turning it over in my mind... Going home that night, Dr Renshaw turned over the facts of*   V+N+ADV, V+PRON+ADV, V+ADV+N the case... We ate in silence, turning over this uncomfortable rumour in our minds. ● **Chew over** and **mull over** mean almost the same as **turn over**, and **consider** is a more general word.

8 When an engine **turns over**, it continues running steadily at a low speed. EG *The car engines turn over, ready for the race.* ● **Tick over** means almost the same as **turn over**. `v+ADV`

9 If someone **turns over** a place, they search it thoroughly or steal things from it in an organized way, usually causing a lot of damage at the same time; an informal use. EG *Half the school is on probation for turning over a supermarket... They turned room 37 over—it looked as if a tornado had hit it.* ● **Do over** means almost the same as **turn over**. `v+ADV+N,` `v+N+ADV,` `v+PRON+ADV`

10 A **turnover** is a small piece of pastry that has been filled with fruit or jam, folded over, and baked. EG *...an apple turnover.* `N COUNT`

turn round. 1 If someone or something **turns round** or **around**, or you **turn** them **round** or **around**, they move so that they are facing in the opposite direction. EG *She would turn round and whisper jokes with the others... Toby turned her round to face me... After much effort, he manages to turn the car around... She'd turn her hat around so that the ribbons hung over her face.* `v+ADV,` `v+PRON+ADV,` `v+N+ADV:` `ERGATIVE`

2 If you **turn round** a plan, project, or business that is failing, you change it so that it becomes successful and profitable. EG *It's a cruel deception to pretend that you could turn round the economy in a week... The engineering group is at last fighting to turn round its business.* ▶ A **turnround** is a sudden improvement, especially in the success of a business or country's economy. EG *With so little room to move, the turnround will be gradual.* ● **Turnaround** means almost the same as **turnround**. `v+ADV+N,` `v+N+ADV,` `v+PRON+ADV` `N COUNT`

3 If you **turn** a sentence or idea **round** or **around**, you change the way in which it is expressed or considered. EG *When you first asked me about this I turned the whole question round... So by putting it in the third person I can turn it round a bit and make it funny.* `v+N+ADV,` `v+PRON+ADV`

4 If someone **turns round** or **around** and does something, they do something unexpectedly or unfairly; an informal use. EG *Won't the child turn round and blame the school?... He left her, then turned around and went out with her best friend!* `v+ADV:` `WITH and+VERB`

turn to. 1 If you **turn to** someone, you ask them for something such as help, advice, or information. EG *If they feel they've been wronged, they'll turn to a solicitor... Thank you, Geoff. Now we turn to John Venables to see what he thinks... Children can get along well without having to turn to an adult for support... I have no other friend to turn to.* `v+PREP:` `HAS PASSIVE`

2 If you **turn to** a particular topic when you are talking or writing, you start to talk or write about it. EG *Let us turn to a completely different country, Japan... Now I can turn to what prison did to you.* `v+PREP`

turn up. 1 If someone **turns up**, they arrive somewhere. EG *He turned up at rehearsal the next day looking awful... If it's a boring game the crowds won't turn up next time... When you didn't turn up on Friday we tried to get in touch with you.* ● **Show up** means almost the same as **turn up**. `v+ADV`

2 If something **turns up** or **is turned up**, it is found, discovered, or noticed. EG *You must be willing to take a job as soon as one turns up... Protein turns up in almost every food... Scientists have turned up no useful information on how best to treat it... If I turn anything up, I'll let you know.* `v+ADV,` `v+ADV+N,` `v+N+ADV,` `v+PRON+ADV:` `ERGATIVE`

3 When you **turn up** something such as a radio or heater, you increase the amount of sound or heat being produced, by adjusting the controls. EG *Turn the volume control up... Turn up the heat and* `v+N+ADV,` `v+ADV+N,` `v+PRON+ADV` *stir in the soy sauce... The TV was turned up loudly so that no-one would hear them talking.* ● **Turn down** means the opposite of **turn up.**

4 When someone **turns up** something such as a dress, skirt, or pair of trousers, they shorten it by folding up the bottom edge, sometimes stitching it in place. EG *Will you turn my jeans up for me, mum?... I turned it up but the hem is all crooked now.* ● **Let down** means the opposite of **turn up.** ▶ The **turn-ups** of someone's trousers are the ends of the trouser legs, which are folded upwards so that they show on the outside.

V+N+ADV,
V+PRON+ADV,
V+ADV+N

N PLURAL

5 If you **turn** something **up,** you move it so that it is pointing in an upward direction. EG *She turned up her collar before facing the bad weather... She turned up the palm of one hand in a gesture of resignation... Her blonde plaits were turned up and tied with a neat black velvet bow.*

V+ADV+N,
V+N+ADV,
V+PRON+ADV

6 If there is an **upturn** in something such as a country's economy, it starts to improve. EG *When the upturn comes in world trade... ...an upturn in demand.* ● **Downturn** means the opposite of **upturn.**

N COUNT

turn upon. See **turn on: turn upon** is more formal.

type, types, typing, typed

type away. If you **type away,** you type busily and for a long time. EG *Gerald was typing away in his office.*

V+ADV

type in. If you **type in** a name, word, letter, and so on, you use a computer or word processor to record it. EG *If you want the dictionary, you type in the letter D... She's typed the wrong name in... Fresh details will be typed in by the doctor on the spot.* ● **Key in** means almost the same as **type in.**

V+ADV+N,
V+N+ADV,
V+PRON+ADV

type into. If you **type** something **into** a computer or word processor, you put information or text into it by pressing the keys on the keyboard. EG *You can throw a program by typing nonsense into the computer... Your responses will be typed into the system.*

V+N+PREP,
V+PRON+PREP

type out. If you **type** something **out,** you produce a copy of it on a typewriter. EG *I'm typing out my tape script... If I stopped to type them out, they would never get done... I'll get this play typed out in the next few days.*

V+ADV+N,
V+PRON+ADV,
V+N+ADV

type up. If you **type up** your ideas, notes, or handwritten text, you produce a completed version of it on a typewriter. EG *I'll go and type up these notes... After thinking about it, she typed it up, then we both read it... The report was typed up by the secretary.*

V+ADV+N,
V+PRON+ADV,
V+N+ADV

U u

urge, urges, urging, urged

urge on. **1** If you **urge** someone **on,** you encourage them to do something. EG *Both decisions urged the Tartars on to new forms of protest... I am trying to urge him on to 'try things out for himself'... The President, reportedly urged on by his vice-president, has decided to attend the talks.* ● **Egg on** means almost the same as **urge on,** and **encourage** is a more formal word.

V+N+ADV,
V+PRON+ADV,
V+ADV+N

2 If you **urge** something **on** or **upon** someone, you try to persuade them to accept it, even though they do not really want to. EG *Frank had another reason for urging caution on them both at this mo-*

V+N+PREP,
V+PRON+PREP

ment... That's a wise thought and I urge it on them... Mr.Profumo accepted the wording urged upon him by his colleagues.
urge upon. See **urge on: urge upon** is slightly more formal.

use, uses, using, used

use up. If you **use up** a supply of something, you finish it so that none of it is left. EG *She did use up a tremendous amount of energy... He used up all the coins he had... Put the leftovers in a tub and use it all up the next day.*   V+ADV+N, V+PRON+ADV, V+N+ADV

usher, ushers, ushering, ushered

usher in. If one thing **ushers in** another thing, it indicates that the other thing is about to begin; a formal expression. EG *The French Revolution ushered in a new age... He entered the Polytechnic, ushering in an illustrious career in military science.*   V+ADV+N, V+PRON+ADV

V v

vamp, vamps, vamping, vamped

vamp up. If you **vamp** something **up**, you make it seem as if it is new and exciting by adding things to it. EG *...a musical comedy vamped up for the audience... We can always vamp it up a bit, then we'd sell it all right.*   V+N+ADV, V+PRON+ADV, V+ADV+N

varnish, varnishes, varnishing, varnished

varnish over. If you **varnish over** a situation or an event, you hide unpleasant aspects of it or pretend that they do not exist. EG *Conflict is varnished over with polite words.* ● **Gloss over** and **paper over** mean almost the same as **varnish over.**   V+PREP: HAS PASSIVE

veer, veers, veering, veered

veer off. If something that is moving in a particular direction **veers off**, it suddenly changes direction. EG *The general direction of the gulls is southwards, but they will always veer off to follow a shoal of herring or mackerel.*   V+ADV

venture, ventures, venturing, ventured

venture forth. If you **venture forth**, you go somewhere, especially somewhere that might be dangerous; an old-fashioned expression. EG *I did indeed venture forth again that night.* ● **Sally forth** means almost the same as **venture forth.**   V+ADV

verge, verges, verging, verged

verge on. If a particular quality **verges on** or **verges upon** another, it begins to be very similar to it. EG *I had a feeling of distrust verging on panic... It was the kind of smile that verged on laughter... ...games which verge on criminality.* ● **Border on** means almost the same as **verge on.**   V+PREP

vie, vies, vying, vied

vie with. If you **vie with** someone, you try hard to get something before they do, or do something better than they do. EG *Pressure is mounting as a number of companies and entrepreneurs vie with each other for the coveted trophies... Manufacturers are vying with each other to produce the first CFC-free fridge.*   V+PREP

visit, visits, visiting, visited

visit with. If you **visit with** someone, you go and see them and spend time with them; an American expression. EG *He had not visited with the rascal since 1946.* — V+PREP

vote, votes, voting, voted

vote down. If something or someone **is voted down,** they are rejected, especially as a result of a formal vote. EG *My proposal was voted down... This particular group got voted down... The committee decided to advise Parliament to vote down the measure.* — V+N+ADV, V+ADV+N, V+PRON+ADV

vote in. When people **vote in** a person or group of people, they give them enough votes in an election for them to hold a position of power. EG *There are already enough pensioners to vote a government in or out... So they voted him in, did they?... All the directors were voted in by proxies.* ● **Elect** means almost the same as **vote in.** — V+N+ADV, V+PRON+ADV, V+ADV+N

vote out. When people **vote out** a person or group of people, they do not give them enough votes in an election to allow them to continue holding a position of power. EG *They voted Councillor Hitchcock out of her seat... No-one ever wanted to vote you out of office... He was voted out in 1983.* — V+N+ADV, V+PRON+ADV, V+ADV+N: ALSO+*of*

vote through. If a law or proposal **is voted through,** a majority of people accept it in a formal election. EG *...the land reform programme was voted through the Phillipine Congress... The new measures were voted through, but only by a small margin... The committee voted the motion through by an overwhelming majority.* — V+N+ADV/PREP, V+PRON+ADV/PREP, V+ADV+N: USUALLY PASSIVE

vouch, vouches, vouching, vouched

vouch for. 1 If you say that you can or will **vouch for** someone, you mean that you are sure that they will behave correctly, and that you take responsibility for their good behaviour. EG *Don Tomassino vouched for you personally... He said you'd vouch for him.* — V+PREP

2 If you say that you can **vouch for** something, you mean that you know from your own personal experience or knowledge that it is true or correct. EG *I can vouch for the accuracy of my information... She was down there all right. I'll vouch for that.* — V+PREP: HAS PASSIVE

W w

wade, wades, wading, waded

wade in. If you are faced with a difficult situation or a lot of work and **wade in,** you start dealing with it in a determined and energetic way. EG *Bill itched to wade in and 'sort them out'... Get to San Francisco at once and watch him wade in.* — V+ADV

wade into. If you **wade into** someone or something that is causing problems, you start dealing with them in a determined and energetic way. EG *Only he had sufficient vitality to wade into the three-hundred page report.* — V+PREP

wade through. If you **wade through** a lot of written material, you spend a lot of time and effort reading it. EG *A lawyer was wading through the three-hundred-page file... ...to start wading through the mass of paper-work.* ● **Plough through** means almost the same as **wade through.** — V+PREP

wait, waits, waiting, waited

wait about. See wait around.

wait around. If you **wait around** or **about,** you spend a long period of time doing very little before something happens or before you can do something or see someone. EG *Julie had waited around for nearly a whole year... Two detectives were waiting around to question the old man... ...waiting about while Mr Wilde checked off the things on the list.*

V+ADV:
USUALLY+A

wait behind. If you **wait behind,** you deliberately stay in a place after everyone else has left, for example because you want to talk to someone alone. EG *She walked out, leaving Doctor Percival to wait behind for the bill.*

V+ADV

wait in. If you **wait in,** you deliberately stay at home and do not go out, for example because someone is coming to see you. EG *I waited in all the afternoon... 'I'll wait in for it.'—'No need for that.'* ● **Stay in** means almost the same as **wait in.**

V+ADV

wait on. 1 If someone **waits on** you in a restaurant or at a formal party, they serve you food and drink. EG *...sitting around a dinner table, being waited on by uniformed waitresses... 'Help yourself,' I say. 'I'm not waiting on you.'*

V+PREP:
HAS PASSIVE

2 If you **wait on** or **upon** someone, you take care of all their needs and do anything that they ask you to do. EG *Ever since the world started, men have been waited on by women... I found it a remarkable experience to be waited upon by eight servants.*

V+PREP:
HAS PASSIVE

3 If you **wait on** someone, you wait somewhere until they have finished what they are doing and can talk to you or go with you; used in American English. EG *I've got some good news. That's why I waited on you out here... Get your chores done, Miss Jordache. We'll be waiting on you... 'Wait on, Mr South!' a child called.*

V+PREP,
V+ADV

4 If you **wait on** or **upon** an event, you wait until it happens before doing or deciding something; used in American English and old-fashioned British English. EG *The company is prepared to delay the deal and wait on events... She laughed—but waited on his response none the less... ...the future of a world waiting upon their decision.*

V+PREP

wait out. If you **wait out** a period of time or an event, especially a difficult one, you wait for it to pass or to happen. EG *So we chatted as we waited out the ten minutes... They erected a small stockade, dug in, and waited out the night... A large assembly had gathered to wait out the hearing... Anne calmed her and persuaded her to sit and wait it out.* ● **Sit out** means almost the same as **wait out.**

V+ADV+N,
V+PRON+ADV:
NO PASSIVE

wait up. 1 If you **wait up,** you deliberately do not go to bed, because you know that someone who lives in the same place as you will be returning home late at night. EG *I can't make it home until late. Tell her not to wait up... He was waiting up for me when I got in last night.*

V+ADV:
ALSO+*for*

2 If you say **'Wait up'** to someone, you want them to wait until you reach them or finish what you are doing; used in American English. EG *Wait up—I'm coming.* ● **Hang on** is a British English expression for **wait up.**

IMPERATIVE:
V+ADV

wait upon. See wait on.

wake, wakes, waking, woke, woken

American English also uses the form **waked** for the past tense and past participle of the verb.

wake up. 1 When you **wake up,** or someone or something **wakes** you **up,** you become conscious again after being asleep. EG *Ralph, wake up!... ...young babies waking up at night and crying... I'll wake Buller up... I won't wake him up yet... ...enough racket to wake up*

V+ADV,
V+N+ADV,
V+PRON+ADV,
V+ADV+N:
ERGATIVE

half the occupants of the cabin. ▸ A **wake-up** call is a telephone call that you ask someone to make to you so that it wakes you up, for example because you do not have an alarm clock. EG *...New York's most prestigious wake-up service.* ADJECTIVE

2 If an activity or event **wakes** you **up** after you have been inactive or bored, it makes you more active or interested. EG *Some of the students challenge him a little to wake him up... Those exercises woke Donald up, I can tell you... I once waked up a dull meeting by proposing that... The other two students wake up briefly, exchange glances and snigger.* V+PRON+ADV, V+N+ADV, V+ADV+N, V+ADV: ERGATIVE

wake up to. If you **wake up to** a problem or a dangerous situation, you become aware of it. EG *The West began to wake up to the danger it faced... The Church must wake up to the financial problems of the clergy... ...by the time they woke up to the fact that they needed our technology.* ● **Realize** is a more formal word for **wake up to.** V+ADV+PREP

walk, walks, walking, walked

walk away from. If someone **walks away from** a difficult or unpleasant situation, they leave it rather than trying to deal with it; used showing disapproval. EG *'You can't walk away from this, Frank,' Patterson said... So many customers have walked away from its $40-per-barrel contracts.* V+ADV+PREP

walk away with. See walk off with.

walk in on. If you **walk in on** someone when they are doing something private or secret, you enter the place where they are and interrupt them, and embarrass them or yourself, usually unintentionally because you did not know they were there. EG *...as adolescents, they had walked in on their parents' embraces and caresses... I imagine their embarrassment at walking in on me.* V+ADV+PREP

walk into. **1** If you **walk into** an unpleasant or dangerous situation, you become involved in it unexpectedly, sometimes because you are careless. EG *He had walked into a trap... You might be walking into an ambush... How come you can walk into a situation like this?* V+PREP

2 If you **walk into** a job, you manage to get it very easily. EG *He just walked into the job without even an interview... ...how Cockburn came to walk straight out of The Times and into the Daily Worker.* V+PREP

walk off. If you **walk off** an unpleasant feeling, you go for a walk in order to stop having the feeling. EG *He went out to walk off his disquiet in the night air... She managed to walk off her headache... It is better for you to walk it off.* V+ADV+N, V+PRON+ADV: NO PASSIVE

walk off with. **1** If someone **walks off with** something, they take it without asking the person to whom it belongs. EG *Not realizing what she was doing, she had walked off with it... She wants to know what to do about the man who has walked off with her pruning hook.* ● **Go off with** means almost the same as **walk off with.** V+ADV+PREP

2 If you **walk off with** something such as a prize, or **walk away with** it, you win it or achieve it very easily. EG *He walked away with $1,200 in cash... She will walk away with the title.* V+ADV+PREP

walk on. If you **walk on** in a play, you have a very minor part in it, often one that does not require you to speak at all; a technical expression. EG *Why don't you come and walk on in 'The High Bid', at Her Majesty's Theatre?... She desperately wants a part in the play, whether she has a leading role or is only walking on.* ▸ A **walk-on** part is a very minor part in a play. EG *My sister had a walk-on part.* V+ADV / ADJECTIVE

walk out. **1** If you **walk out** of a meeting, a performance, or an unpleasant situation, you leave it suddenly, as a way of showing that you dislike it or that you are angry. EG *Haig walked out of the conference... Many of the audience walked out through sheer bore-* V+ADV: ALSO+*of*

dom... *'You did not,'* I said sourly, standing up and walking out. ▶ A   N COUNT
walk-out is a protest in which you leave a meeting or performance
to show your dislike or anger. EG *The students had called for a*
walkout.

2 If workers **walk out,** they suddenly go on strike. EG *The firemen*   V+ADV
voted to walk out in support... When 160 men walked out in August,
union officials were taken aback. ▶ A **walk-out** by workers is a   N COUNT
sudden strike. EG *...ending the 43-day walk-out.*

walk out on. If you **walk out on** someone with whom you have a   V+ADV+PREP
close relationship, you leave them suddenly and end the relationship. EG *His girlfriend walked out on him... They had walked out on*
me after the scene at Inge's flat... If I try to discipline him, he just
walks out on me without listening.

walk over. **1** If someone **walks over** you, they treat you very badly,   V+PREP:
especially by telling you what to do all the time. EG *...allow officials*   HAS PASSIVE
to walk all over them... Father is much less inclined to lie back and
allow himself to be walked over. ● **Trample on** means almost the
same as **walk over.**

2 A **walkover** is a success or victory that is achieved without much   N SING
effort. EG *By yielding to a forceful Government, those victims allow*
injustice a walkover.

wall, walls, walling, walled

wall in. If someone or something **is walled in,** they are surrounded   V+ADV+N,
or enclosed by a wall or barrier. EG *They walled in the front of their*   V+PRON+ADV:
cave and built steps from it... Once in it you are enclosed, walled in   USUALLY PASSIVE
by tombs of kings.

wall off. If part of a place **is walled off,** it is separated from the rest   PASSIVE:
of the place by a wall. EG *The area was walled off... It had an end*   V+ADV
walled off to form a gas chamber.

wall up. If someone **is walled up,** they are put in a place and   V+N+ADV,
prevented from leaving it by blocking every exit with a wall. EG *...a*   V+PRON+ADV,
peasant-girl, who's had herself walled up in a specially prepared cell   V+ADV+N
in her local church... Creon punishes Antigone by walling her up
alive in a tomb... ...get the horse in and wall him up in one corner
with planks so he can't slip down.

wallow, wallows, wallowing, wallowed

wallow in. If you **wallow in** a situation or emotion, you think about   V+PREP
it or remain in it for a long time, because you are enjoying it. EG
...wallowing in self-pity.

waltz, waltzes, waltzing, waltzed

waltz off with. If you **waltz off with** something such as a prize or   V+ADV+PREP
award, you win it. EG *She swept the board, waltzing off with three*
gold medals.

want, wants, wanting, wanted

want for. If you do not **want for** something, you have or get as   V+PREP:
much of it as you need. EG *Now the responsibility was ours to see*   WITH NEGATIVE
that she did not want for understanding and sympathy... As long as
Alan was here, he would not want for hot food.

want in. If someone is arranging a plan, project, or business deal   V+ADV:
and you **want in,** you want to be involved or have a share in it; used   ALSO+*on*
mainly in American English and informal British English. EG *They*
all want in... The Swiss wanted in on whatever deal Patterson was
trying to put together. ● **Want out** means the opposite of **want in.**

want out. **1** If you **want out,** you no longer want to be involved in a   V+ADV
plan, project, or business deal that you are part of; used mainly in
American English and informal British English. EG *I want out. I want*

to sell up... If you want out, right now, just say so, and I'll under-stand... The main flaw in this package, I now see, is the fact that City Bank wants out. ● **Want in** means the opposite of **want out.**

2 If you **want out** of a place, you want to leave it; used mainly in American English and informal British English. EG *He knew he was in the hospital and really wanted out... The cat ran in; he patted it and it wanted out again... I want out of here right now.*

V+ADV:
ALSO+*of*

ward, wards, warding, warded

ward off. 1 To **ward off** something unpleasant or dangerous means to prevent it from affecting you or harming you. EG *...sufficient food and clothing to ward off starvation and ill-health... ...the ornaments at the head of the bed, placed there to ward off evil spirits... ...before anti-aircraft equipment arrived to ward off further attacks.*

V+ADV+N,
V+PRON+ADV

2 If you **ward** someone **off,** you prevent them going somewhere or doing something. EG *'I'm sorry the room's such a mess,' Elaine said, warding him off... I turned to him in amazement, but he warded me off. 'No, no, enough revelations for one evening.'*

V+PRON+ADV,
V+N+ADV

warm, warms, warming, warmed

warm to. If you **warm to** or **towards** a person, you become fonder of them. If you **warm to** or **towards** an idea or task, you become more interested in the idea, or more keen to do the task. EG *I warmed to him in the bar... Tom found himself warming towards Vic... Bricklayers warmed to the work—it was at last an opportunity to use their skills.*

V+PREP

warm towards. See warm to.

warm up. 1 If you **warm up** cold food, you put it on a cooker and heat it until it is ready to be eaten. EG *Start warming up the soup now... ...scooped one of the cold slices into the oven to warm it up... I keep lots of food that's quickly thawed and easily warmed up.* ● **Heat up** means almost the same as **warm up.**

V+ADV+N,
V+PRON+ADV,
V+N+ADV

2 If the weather, the day, or part of the earth **warms up,** the temperature rises and it gradually gets hotter. EG *The weather was warming up... Scientists believe the earth is warming up as a result of gases trapping the sun's heat into the atmosphere.*

V+ADV

3 If you **warm up** or if something **warms** you **up,** you start to feel warm again after you have been cold. EG *She began to warm up... Come in and warm up by the stove... You're a whisky man, Doc. That's the stuff to warm you up.* ● **Thaw out** means almost the same as **warm up.**

V+ADV,
V+PRON+ADV,
V+N+ADV:
ERGATIVE

4 If you **warm up** just before a physical activity or event such as a race, you prepare yourself for it, usually by practising or doing some exercises. EG *They jogged around the track twice, warming up... ...while the singers were warming up.* ● **Limber up** means almost the same as **warm up.** ▷ A **warm-up** is preparation which you do just before a physical activity or event. EG *During the warm-up exercises, I was still shaking.*

V+ADV

N SING,
ADJECTIVE

5 If a situation, event, or activity **warms up,** or you **warm** it **up,** it becomes more intense or exciting. EG *The campaign against the brothers began to warm up... Business'll be warming up soon... The studio has been warming up America to go film-mad for most of this year.* ● **Hot up** means almost the same as **warm up.**

V+ADV,
V+ADV+N,
V+N+ADV,
V+PRON+ADV:
ERGATIVE

6 When a machine, engine, or electrical device **warms up** or you **warm** it **up,** it starts working and becomes ready for use. EG *...a muffled roaring sound, like the engines of jet planes warming up on a distant runway... Mr McElrea then gave final instructions to Richie as he warmed up the engines... I went across and switched on the TV and waited for it to warm up.*

V+ADV,
V+ADV+N,
V+PRON+ADV:
ERGATIVE

warn, warns, warning, warned

warn away. If you **warn** someone **away**, you tell them to leave a place because it is dangerous for them to be there. EG *F-14s circled the exercise area to warn aircraft away from the firing zone... They were warning us away, waving frantically and shouting... They were warned away from the firing range by one of the soldiers.*

V+N+ADV, V+PRON+ADV, V+ADV+N: ALSO+*from*

warn off. If you **warn** someone **off**, you tell them to go away or to stop doing something because of possible danger or punishment. EG *She makes agitated signs to warn him off, whispering that 'Mr Shaw is at work.'... I thought you were warning me off the drink... Lansing may discover that fact and warn off our friends.*

V+PRON+ADV/PREP, V+ADV+N, V+N+ADV/PREP: ALSO+*from*

wash, washes, washing, washed

wash away. 1 If rains, floods, or waves **wash away** something, they carry it away by force, usually causing a lot of damage or destruction. EG *The dam collapsed, washing away twenty-five villages... The big flood washed it away and then they put the swing bridge up... The tidal wave washed everything away.* ● **Sweep away** means almost the same as **wash away.** ▸ A **washaway** is a hollow area caused by the earth being washed away by rain or floods; used mainly in Australian English. EG *I camped in a washaway near the ruin of a cottage.*

V+ADV+N, V+PRON+ADV, V+N+ADV

N COUNT

2 To **wash away** smells, tastes, or other qualities of an object or substance means to remove them, usually using water. EG *Soaps wash away the natural odors of the human body... He drank the scotch, then washed the taste away with water.*

V+ADV+N, V+N+ADV, V+PRON+ADV

3 To **wash away** a problem, feeling, or situation means to cause it to end or to be forgotten. EG *All that had happened in the past was washed away... We will never be able to wash away the taint... ...trying to wash your troubles away... ...and then it just seemed to wash away.*

V+ADV+N, V+N+ADV, V+ADV: ERGATIVE

wash down. 1 If you **wash down** food, you drink something after eating it or while eating it. EG *...washing each mouthful down with coffee... He washed it down with whisky... ...if you wash down your meal with cola... ...chips, washed down with milk shakes.*

V+N+ADV, V+PRON+ADV, V+ADV+N: USUALLY+*with*

2 If you **wash down** an object or surface, you wash all of it. EG *I mopped up the kitchen, washed down the walls... ...washed him down and dried him... He washed the windshield down.*

V+ADV+N, V+PRON+ADV, V+N+ADV

3 If rocks or soil **are washed down** by rains or floods, they are carried by the water to another place. EG *A row of stone kept the soil from being washed down the steep hills in heavy rain... Boulders and scree were washed down by the floods... Soil from the mountains washes down in the rivers.*

V+ADV+N, V+PRON+ADV, USUALLY PASSIVE, ALSO V+ADV: ERGATIVE

wash off. 1 If you **wash** dirt or other unwanted things **off**, you remove them from the surface of something using water. EG *Take them home and wash off the mud and sand... She washed the blood off... Wash all the bleach off the sides... She was told not to wash it off... It does not rub off or, if allowed to dry, wash off either.*

V+ADV+N, V+N+ADV/PREP, V+PRON+ADV/PREP, V+ADV: ERGATIVE

2 If you **wash** someone **off**, you remove the dirt or blood from their body, using water. EG *Let Sally wash you off... Wash yourself off and put these clothes on... He washed himself off.*

V+PRON+ADV, V+REFL+ADV, V+N+ADV

wash out. 1 If you **wash out** clothes, you clean them using water. EG *...a mother washing out her baby's nappies... Go down to the stream and wash your underwear out.... She let me wear it for a few days before she made me wash it out.*

V+ADV+N, V+N+ADV, V+PRON+ADV

2 If you **wash out** a container, you clean the inside of it with water. EG *I washed out the coffee things... Wash it out well and fill it with*

V+ADV+N, V+N+ADV, V+PRON+ADV

clear water... A milky bottle is easily washed out with cold water.
● **Rinse out** means almost the same as **wash out.**

3 If you **wash out** dirt, stains, or other unwanted things, or if they **wash out,** they are removed, using water. EG *Wash the sand out of them in shallow water... This is good because it washes out some of the germs... Dominic had tried to wash it all out... The grey dye was washed out with the aid of a solvent... The ink, surprisingly, washed out easily.*

V+N+ADV,
V+ADV+N,
V+PRON+ADV,
V+ADV:
ERGATIVE,
ALSO+*of*

4 If you **wash out** a feeling or thought, you cause it to end or to be forgotten. EG *...preparing his breakfast with her own hands to wash out the guilt she felt... I ought to try to forget it, wash it out of my mind... ...an unclean feeling that you can't wash out of your head.*

V+ADV+N,
V+PRON+ADV,
V+N+ADV:
ALSO+*of*

5 If something **washes** you **out,** it causes you to feel exhausted or to fail to do what you were trying to do. EG *Only an utter catastrophe can wash me out... The trip just washed all of them out.* ▶ If someone is or looks **washed-out,** they are or look very tired and lacking in energy. EG *I returned to Chamonix, washed out and depressed.* ● **Run down** means almost the same as **washed out.**

V+PRON+ADV,
V+N+ADV,
V+ADV+N

ADJECTIVE

6 A **washed-out** colour is pale and dull. EG *...eyes of washed-out grey... ...a canopy of washed-out blue.*

ADJECTIVE

7 If a game, event, or activity **is washed out,** it is prevented from taking place, usually because it rains. EG *The first day of play was washed out after only 90 minutes.* ▶ If an attempt, event, or project is a **washout,** it is a total failure. EG *The whole thing will be a washout if we don't arrive before sunset.*

PASSIVE:
V+ADV

N COUNT

8 If someone or something **is washed out** from a place by rain or floods, they are carried away by force. EG *...prevent the seed from being washed out... Her home collapsed and she was washed out on the tide... The next tides will wash the hatched fish out to sea again... Another 40,000 tons of oil washed out of the damaged tanker.*

V+N+ADV,
V+PRON+ADV,
V+ADV+N,
USUALLY PASSIVE,
ALSO V+ADV:
ERGATIVE

wash up. **1** If you **wash up** the things such as pans, plates, and knives that have been used to cook and eat a meal, you clean them using water and detergent. EG *He insisted on helping me wash up... We cleared the table and washed up the dishes... Tim carried the plates to the kitchen and washed them up.* ▶ If you do the **washing-up,** you clean the things that have been used to cook and eat a meal, using water and detergent. EG *There was enough water to do all the washing-up... Clean the sink with hot water and washing-up liquid.*

V+ADV,
V+ADV+N,
V+PRON+ADV,
V+N+ADV

N SING

2 If you are dirty and **wash up,** you clean yourself, especially your hands and face; used in American English. EG *I washed up as best I could in the adjacent bathroom... He went to the bathroom to wash up and comb his hair.*

V+ADV

3 If someone or something **is washed up** on a piece of land, or **washes up** there, they are carried by the water of a river or the sea and left there. EG *Their boat was washed up ten miles to the south... ...pieces of wood have been washed up on the shores... Pyle's body washed up under the bridge at Dakao.*

V+N+ADV,
V+PRON+ADV,
USUALLY PASSIVE,
ALSO V+ADV:
ERGATIVE

4 If you say that someone is **washed up,** you mean that they are at the end of their career and no longer of any use; used mainly in informal American English. EG *I was not going to be all washed up, an ex-sportsman with nothing to do at 35.*

ADJECTIVE

waste, wastes, wasting, wasted

waste away. **1** If someone **wastes away** or **is wasted away,** they become extremely thin or weak because they are ill or worried and they are not eating properly. EG *I don't want you to waste away... I hope your flesh will waste away... He was wasted away to no more than a skeleton.*

V+ADV:
ALSO PASSIVE,
V+ADV

2 If something **wastes away**, it becomes smaller or weaker until it eventually disappears because it is not being properly looked after. ᴇɢ *Whenever muscles are rested they start to waste away and rapidly lose strength... Our planners have allowed rural communities to waste away.* — V+ADV

watch, watches, watching, watched

watch for. If you **watch for** something which is likely to happen in the future, you wait carefully for it because it might be important or unpleasant. ᴇɢ *You have to watch for the union problem... Watch carefully for signs of growth... Watch our travel pages for final details.* — V+PREP: HAS PASSIVE

watch out. If you tell someone to **watch out,** you are warning them to be careful because something unpleasant might happen to them. ᴇɢ *If you don't watch out, he might stick a knife into you... You behave yourself or you'd better watch out... The mood was gentle, and yet, I had been told to watch out.* ● **Look out** means almost the same as **watch out.** — V+ADV: ALSO IMPERATIVE

watch out for. If you **watch out for** something, you stay alert so that you will notice it when it appears or happens because it is likely to be important. ᴇɢ *Watch out for the warning signs of depression like insomnia... This is a good place to watch out for wild animals.* ● **Look out for** means almost the same as **watch out for.** — V+ADV+PREP

watch over. If you **watch over** someone or something, you take care of them because you are responsible for them. ᴇɢ *The wives took turns to watch over the children... From this point on the two tribes would be watched over and controlled by the Army.* ● **Guard** means almost the same as **watch over.** — V+PREP: HAS PASSIVE

water, waters, watering, watered

water down. **1** If a speech or written statement **is watered down,** it is made much weaker and less forceful or controversial. ᴇɢ *The paragraph had in any case been watered down, and the final draft was a compromise... He watered down the article guaranteeing the right to strike.* — V+ADV+N, V+PRON+ADV: USUALLY PASSIVE

2 If you **water down** food or drink, you add water to it to make it weaker. ᴇɢ *No, it's not watered down. It's quite potent stuff for beer.* ● **Dilute** is a less informal word for **water down.** — V+ADV+N, V+N+ADV, V+PRON+ADV

wave, waves, waving, waved

wave aside. If you **wave aside** an idea, reason, or objection, you show that you do not want to consider it because you do not think it is important enough. ᴇɢ *The Chief waved his objection aside... Miss Jackson waved aside these little difficulties.* ● **Brush aside** means almost the same as **wave aside,** and **dismiss** is a less informal word. — V+N+ADV, V+ADV+N, V+PRON+ADV

wave away. If you **wave** someone or something **away,** you signal with your hand that you do not want them near you at the moment. ᴇɢ *She waved him away when he ventured near her desk... Another mistake many businessmen make at lunch is to wave away the sweets trolley but indulge in cheese and biscuits.* — V+PRON+ADV, V+ADV+N, V+N+ADV

wave down. **1** If you **wave down** a vehicle, you stand by the road or in the road and signal with your hands for the driver to stop. ᴇɢ *At Napoleon's Hill, a policeman waved them down and told them to get off the main road.* ● **Flag down** means almost the same as **wave down.** — V+PRON+ADV, V+N+ADV, V+ADV+N

2 If you **wave down** people's reactions to you, you signal to them that you do not want to be interrupted and that you wish to continue what you are saying. ᴇɢ *The Prime Minister waved down the* — V+ADV+N, V+PRON+ADV

*applause and seemed to forget all about the cameras as he leaned
forward... He waved down my protest with a limp palm.*

wave off. 1 If you **wave** someone **off,** you wave to them as they
leave somewhere. EG *They go to wave their boys off on the troop
trains... At ten o'clock Mr Bhoolabhoy said goodnight, they waved
him off and then told Ibrahim he could lock up.* ● **See off** means
almost the same as **wave off.**

V+N+ADV,
V+PRON+ADV,
V+ADV+N

2 If you **wave** someone or something **off,** you wave your arms as a
signal that you do not want them to come any closer. EG *...a man
waving off the flies.* ● **Ward off** and **fend off** mean almost the same
as **wave off.**

V+ADV+N,
V+PRON+ADV,
V+N+ADV

wave on. If someone in authority **waves** traffic **on,** they signal with
their hands for the traffic to continue going forwards. EG *A soldier
asked the driver in front of us to open the boot of her car, but he
waved us on... Policemen were everywhere, waving drivers on and
sometimes flagging them down.*

V+PRON+ADV,
V+N+ADV,
V+ADV+N

wave through. If someone in authority **waves** you **through,** they
allow you to enter a place. EG *...a lone official waving vehicles
through... They waved us through the gate, and there was already no
room there... ...arriving at an airport and being waved through
immigration control by mistake.*

V+N+ADV/PREP,
V+PRON+ADV/PREP

wear, wears, wearing, wore, worn

wear away. 1 If you **wear** something **away** or if it **wears away,** it
becomes thin and eventually disappears because it is used a lot or
rubbed a lot. EG *Like fingernails, they are made of a dead horny
material and gradually wear away... ...the smell and sound of the
chalk wearing itself away to nothing... The grass was still worn
away where the children used to play.* ● **Wear down** means almost
the same as **wear away.**

V+ADV,
V+N+ADV,
V+PRON+ADV,
V+ADV+N:
ERGATIVE

2 If something **wears away** emotions or characteristics, it gradually
weakens them until they are no longer noticeable. EG *Time and
absence wear away pain and grief... Hard work and bad food
appeared to have worn away her feminine characteristics.*

V+ADV+N,
V+PRON+ADV

3 If a period of time **wears away,** it passes slowly. EG *The shadows
slowly lengthened again as the afternoon wore away and the sun
moved down towards the far horizon.* ● **Wear on** means almost the
same as **wear away.**

V+ADV

wear down. 1 If you **wear** people **down,** you weaken them or their
position by being more persistent than they are. EG *It was one of the
recognised nuisance-tactics designed to wear down the patience of
the court... These night calls are wearing me down... He fought with
a kind of hideous, heedless, mechanical energy, slowly wearing his
man down... Let him wear himself down.*

V+ADV+N,
V+PRON+ADV,
V+N+ADV,
V+REFL+ADV

2 If you **wear** something **down** or if it **wears down,** the top gradually
disappears because its surface is constantly rubbed. EG *As the teeth
wear down, new ones start growing... All the green crayons were
wearing down fast... No one could deny that large numbers of
visitors had worn down the top of Helvellyn in the Lake District...
The stairs were worn down like the doorstep.*

V+ADV,
V+ADV+N,
V+N+ADV,
V+PRON+ADV:
ERGATIVE

wear off. When a feeling **wears off,** it disappears slowly until it no
longer exists or has any effect. EG *By the next afternoon the shock
had worn off... The effect of the aspirin had worn off and her
toothache had come back... The pain soon wears off.*

V+ADV

wear on. If time **wears on,** it seems to pass very slowly. EG *So the
day wore on and still they sat, drinking, smoking, talking... As the
night wore on the absence of electricity made matters worse... As
Monday wore on they discussed Helen's absence.*

V+ADV

wear out. 1 When something **wears out** or when you **wear** it **out,** it is used so much that it becomes thin or weak and unable to be used any more. ᴇɢ *Sooner or later the soles of your favourite shoes are going to wear out... The wardrobe contained only clothes she had worn out or rejected... I just played the record it until it was worn out.* ▸ Something that is **worn-out** has become so old, damaged, or thin that it cannot be used any more. ᴇɢ *...a worn-out sofa.*

   V+ADV,
V+N+ADV,
V+PRON+ADV,
V+ADV+N:
ERGATIVE

   ADJECTIVE

2 If something **wears** you **out,** it makes you become so tired that you cannot continue what you were doing. ᴇɢ *Visitors wear us out more than the children do... There is no point in wearing yourself out... That isn't show jumping. It's a marathon designed to wear the horse out.* ● **Exhaust** means almost the same as **wear out.** ▸ Someone who is **worn-out** is extremely tired. ᴇɢ *She certainly had looked worn out when he came home.*

   V+PRON+ADV,
V+REFL+ADV,
V+N+ADV

   ADJECTIVE

wear through. If something such as a piece of clothing **wears through** or is **worn through,** it develops a hole where the material has become weak and thin. ᴇɢ *When holes began to wear through the soles of my shoes we went downtown to select a new pair... The carpeting through the hall and up the spiral staircase was almost worn through in spots.*

   V+ADV:
ALSO V+PREP,
HAS PASSIVE

weary, wearies, wearying, wearied

weary of. If you **weary of** something, you become very bored with it and lose interest in it; a formal expression. ᴇɢ *He is beginning to weary of sitting still... I never weary of books that I like... Life may be hated or wearied of, but never despised.* ● **Tire of** means almost the same as **weary of.**

   V+PREP:
HAS PASSIVE

weed, weeds, weeding, weeded

weed out. If you **weed out** things that are useless or unwanted in a group, you get rid of them. ᴇɢ *Natural selection has weeded out the weakest... Teachers should report on their own incompetent colleagues if they want to weed them out of the profession... I sometimes think it's their way of weeding the rest of us out.*

   V+ADV+N,
V+PRON+ADV,
V+N+ADV

weigh, weighs, weighing, weighed

weigh against. 1 If you **weigh** one thing **against** another, you consider the relative importance of each of them in order to decide what you should do. ᴇɢ *However, you must weigh the benefits against the potential hazards... Nevertheless, there will be real difficulties in weighing local priorities against national ones... These factors have to be weighed against the dangers and anxiety of pregnancy.* ● **Balance against** and **set against** mean almost the same as **weigh against.**

   V+N+PREP,
V+PRON+PREP

2 If something **weighs against** a situation, it makes the situation seem more dangerous or difficult. ᴇɢ *Political events weighed heavily against having children... But weighing against this comforting thought is the fact that he is travelling on a charter flight.*

   V+PREP

weigh down. 1 If you **are weighed down** by something heavy, you cannot move easily because it is so heavy. ᴇɢ *...a leaking boat which was weighed down by five men... The pearls weighing down her ears were hitting her savagely on the cheek... The sand in his shoes weighed him down.*

   V+N+ADV,
V+ADV+N,
V+PRON+ADV:
USUALLY PASSIVE

2 If you **are weighed down** by a difficulty or problem, it causes you to worry a great deal. ᴇɢ *So you're weighed down with problems... Maybe he was weighed down by the burden of state secrets... The stress of maternal responsibility was beginning to weigh her down.*

   V+N+ADV,
V+PRON+ADV:
USUALLY PASSIVE

weigh in. 1 If you **weigh in** on a discussion or a task, you begin to take part in it rather forcefully. ᴇɢ *The Queen Mother weighed in*

   V+ADV:
USUALLY+A

with some advice... When the time came to lay the concrete, we all
weighed in... The Treasury Secretary weighed in with an opinion.
● **Come in** means almost the same as **weigh in**.

2 When the competitors in a boxing match or a horse race **weigh in,**   V+ADV:
they are weighed to check their weight shortly before the event   ALSO+*at*
starts. EG *Weighing in at 200 pounds, he's a little overweight.* ▶ When   N COUNT
there is a **weigh-in** on the day of a boxing match or a horse race,
each competitor is weighed to check their weight shortly before the
event. EG *Angry words were exchanged at the weigh-in this morning.*

weigh on. If a problem **weighs on** or **upon** you, it makes you worry.   V+PREP
EG *I could still sleep at night, however serious the problems weighing
on me were... To keep silent about such a situation would weigh
heavily upon our consciences.*

weigh out. If you **weigh** something **out,** you measure a certain   V+ADV+N,
weight of it in order to make sure that you have the correct amount.   V+PRON+ADV,
EG *He weighed out a pound of tomatoes... Collect and weigh out all*   V+N+ADV
the ingredients to be used before starting.

weigh up. 1 If you **weigh** things **up,** you consider their importance   V+ADV+N,
in relation to each other in order to help you make a decision. EG *I*   V+N+ADV,
weighed up the pros and cons... Having weighed everything up, he   V+PRON+ADV
*must have decided it was the right thing to do... Next time they
thought of committing a crime they would weigh it up and think,
'Well it just isn't worth it.'*

2 If you **weigh** someone **up,** you try and find out what they are like   V+N+ADV,
and form an opinion of them by talking to them, watching them, and   V+PRON+ADV,
listening to them. EG *We argued like this for a while, weighing each*   V+ADV+N
other up. ● **Size up** means almost the same as **weigh up**.

weigh upon. See weigh on.

weight, weights, weighting, weighted

weight down. If you **weight** something **down,** you add something   V+N+ADV,
heavy to it to prevent it moving easily. EG *Put the stuff in a bag and*   V+PRON+ADV,
weight that down with old motor tyres... ...a plastic sheet weighted   V+ADV+N
down with straw bales.

well, wells, welling, welled

well up. 1 If a quantity of liquid **wells up,** it comes to the surface in   V+ADV
a sudden rush. EG *Tears welled up in his eyes and he brushed them
aside... ...where water has welled up from the ocean beneath.*

2 If an emotion **wells up** inside you, it suddenly affects you quite   V+ADV:
strongly. EG *Happiness welled up inside me... All his fury against Zoe*   USUALLY+A
welled up in him. ● **Rise up** means almost the same as **well up**.

wheel, wheels, wheeling, wheeled

wheel around. See wheel round.

wheel round. If you **wheel round** or **around,** you turn round   V+ADV
suddenly. EG *I wheeled around and shook off the hand she had placed
on my shoulder... He wheeled round with delight.*

while, whiles, whiling, whiled

while away. If you **while away** the time in a particular way, you   V+ADV+N,
spend time in that way because you are waiting for something or   V+N+ADV:
because you have nothing else to do. EG *How about whiling away the*   NO PASSIVE
*time by telling me a story?... They served food to help the passen-
gers while away the hours.*

whip, whips, whipping, whipped

whip out. If you **whip** something **out,** you produce it from a place   V+ADV+N,
very quickly and suddenly. EG *He stopped long enough to whip out a*   V+N+ADV,
  V+PRON+ADV

pencil and write on the wall... Quickly, she whipped a knife out and cut herself free.

whip up. 1 If you **whip up** an emotion in people, you deliberately encourage them to feel that emotion. You can also say that you **whip** people **up** when you deliberately cause or encourage them to feel a particular emotion. EG *The television interview whipped up half the American people into a frenzy of rage... The reporters whipped up sympathy with stories of pensioners dying from the cold... The hatred is whipped up by the continual flow of rumors.* ● **Stir up** means almost the same as **whip up**.
V+ADV+N, V+N+ADV, V+PRON+ADV

2 If the wind **whips up** dust or waves, it makes it rise up in a sudden swirling movement. EG *The wind whips up the sea forming waves which spread out across the bay... A gale can whip up waves measuring 20 to 25m from trough to crest... A cool breeze whipped up a swirl of dust.*
V+ADV+N, V+N+ADV, V+PRON+ADV

3 If you **whip up** a substance such as cream or egg, you stir it very fast until it becomes frothy, thick, or stiff. EG *I got him to grate the cheese whilst I whipped up eggs for three omelettes... To make an instant sauce from it, whip it up with some plain yoghourt and a little sugar.*
V+ADV+N, V+PRON+ADV, V+N+ADV

4 If you **whip up** something that takes time to prepare, you make or do it quickly; an informal use. EG *I could whip up a salad, if you like... You've got a day left, Audrey, you could whip up two thousand words.*
V+ADV+N, V+PRON+ADV: NO PASSIVE

5 If someone **whips up** a horse or other animal, they encourage it to move much faster. EG *At this moment the man on the box whipped up his horses and the van moved out of the yard... He had to guide the plough and whip up the oxen.*
V+ADV+N, V+PRON+ADV

whisk, whisks, whisking, whisked

whisk away. If you **whisk** someone or something **away**, you remove them from a place very quickly. EG *'It'll get burnt!' said Louisa, whisking it away and putting it clear of the flames... The royal couple were whisked away from a brief welcome at the airport... 'You mustn't let us keep you,' she said, whisking away my plate as soon as I'd finished.*
V+PRON+ADV, V+N+ADV, V+ADV+N

whittle, whittles, whittling, whittled

whittle away. To **whittle** something **away** means to gradually make it smaller or less effective over a period of time. EG *This may whittle away our liberties... Traditionalists would see the changes as whittling away the virtues of a well-established institution... Their 9-12 lead was gradually whittled away in the final quarter of the game.*
V+ADV+N, V+N+ADV, V+PRON+ADV

whittle away at. To **whittle away at** something, you gradually make it smaller or less effective over a period of time. EG *This constant hunting whittles away at the numbers of fish... They whittle away at your self-respect until there is nothing left.*
V+ADV+PREP

whittle down. To **whittle** something **down** means to gradually make it smaller or less effective over a period of time. EG *They were slyly whittling down the power of the Corleone Family... Profits are whittled down by the ever-rising cost of energy... Roskill began with 78 possible sites, whittled it down to 29, and finally to four.*
V+ADV+N, V+N+ADV, V+PRON+ADV

whoop, whoops, whooping, whooped

whoop up. If you **whoop** it **up**, you have an enjoyable and exciting time, for example by going to parties or doing all the things you like doing; an informal expression. EG *...while he and Janet were whooping it up in France.* ● **Live up** means almost the same as **whoop up**.
V+it+ADV

wimp, wimps, wimping, wimped

wimp out. If you **wimp out**, you decide not to do something because v+ADV
you are afraid; an informal expression. EG *They wimped out of doing
anything that might be even slightly risky.* ● **Chicken out** means
almost the same as **wimp out**.

win, wins, winning, won

win back. If you **win back** something that you have lost, you get it v+ADV+N,
back through your own efforts. EG *The party badly needs to find a* v+N+ADV,
v+PRON+ADV
*way to win back straying voters... Management have won back
decision-making power from the shop floor militants... How are you
going to use the horse to win the automobile back?* ● **Regain** is a
more formal word for **win back**.

win out. If something or someone **wins out**, they succeed or defeat v+ADV
others after a struggle. EG *They had fought a civil war and had won
out over fantastic odds... In the battle between reformists and
radicals, the reformists won out, because they had the weight of
European support behind them.*

win over. If you **win** someone **over** or **win** them **round**, you v+ADV+N,
persuade them to support you or agree with you. EG *Local radio* v+N+ADV,
v+PRON+ADV:
stations have done their best to win over new audiences... Benn had ALSO+*to*
*succeeded in winning over those in authority to the workers' cause...
I was completely won over by the courtesy and direct simplicity of
the people... Gentle persuasion soon won him round.*

win round. See **win over**.

win through. If you **win through** a difficult situation or experience, v+PREP,
you succeed in overcoming it. EG *I know that we will win through* v+ADV
*this terrible struggle one day... Two Birmingham companies have
won through the first two rounds of the Reed National Management
Game... Liverpool won through with a performance that was at
times dazzling.*

wind, winds, winding, winded, wound

wind back. When you **wind back** the tape in a cassette player or v+PRON+ADV,
the film in a camera, you make it move back towards its starting v+ADV+N,
v+N+ADV
position. EG *Wind it back till the counter's at 157... It'll have to be
wound back.* ● **Rewind** is a more formal word for **wind back**.

wind down. 1 When you **wind down** the window of a car, you open v+ADV+N,
it by moving it downwards, using a handle or control switch. EG v+N+ADV,
v+PRON+ADV
Philip stopped at a red light and wound down his window. ● **Wind up**
means the opposite of **wind down**.

2 If a mechanical device such as a clock **winds down**, it gradually v+ADV
works more slowly and eventually stops completely. ● **Run down**
means almost the same as **wind down**.

3 When you **wind down** after doing something that has made you v+ADV
feel tired or tense, you gradually relax. EG *We went to the local pub
to wind down.* ● **Unwind** means almost the same as **wind down**.

4 If something such as a business or institution **winds down** or if v+ADV+N,
someone **winds** it **down**, the amount of work that it does or the v+N+ADV,
v+PRON+ADV,
number of people employed is gradually reduced before it is closed v+ADV:
down completely. EG *Unfortunately, we had to wind down the* ERGATIVE
*Liverpool office... The government is winding down the National
Health Service... ...images of a nation winding down economically.*
● **Wind up** means almost the same as **wind down**.

wind forward. If you **wind forward** or **wind on** the tape in a v+PRON+ADV,
cassette player or the film in a camera, you make it move forward v+ADV+N,
v+N+ADV
to a new position. EG *Just wind it forward until you can see the
number 'one' in the little window.*

wind on. See **wind forward.**

wind up. 1 If you **wind up** a length of something, you wrap it round V+ADV+N,
itself to reduce its length and form it into a ball or roll. EG *Lift the* V+N+ADV,
rod, lower it and wind up the line... Wind the string up into a ball... V+PRON+ADV
Her long, uncut hair was wound up into a bun.

2 When you **wind up** a mechanical device such as a watch, you turn V+ADV+N,
a knob, key, or handle on it round and round in order to make it V+N+ADV,
operate. EG *Frank wound up the old gramophone... It was as though* V+PRON+ADV
two machines, wound up and synchronized, had run down at exactly
the same time. ▶ A **wind-up** device or mechanism is one that is ADJECTIVE
operated by clockwork. EG *...a wind-up racing car.*

3 When you **wind up** the window of a car, you close it by making it V+ADV+N,
move upwards, using a handle or a control switch. EG *Wind up that* V+N+ADV,
window, I'm getting a draught here. ● **Wind down** means the V+PRON+ADV
opposite of **wind up.**

4 When you **wind up** an activity, you finish it or stop doing it. EG *It* V+ADV+N,
was time to wind up the game... By the time we wound up the V+N+ADV,
conversation, I knew that I would not be going... When my turn V+PRON+ADV,
came to wind up the debate, I felt very nervous... The proceedings V+ADV:
wind up at midnight, with a conga all round the hall. ERGATIVE

5 When someone **winds up** a business or other organization, they V+ADV+N,
close it down completely. EG *The company was wound up in 1971... A* V+PRON+ADV
Bill was introduced to wind up the Shipbuilding Industry Board.
▶ The **winding-up** of a business or other organization is its official N SING
closure. EG *...provisions only applicable in a winding-up... ...compulso-*
ry winding-up.

6 If you **wind up** in a particular place or situation, you are in it as the V+ADV:
end result of a series of events or processes. EG *We wound up at the* WITH A/-ING
Szanghi restaurant... If I stay here long enough, I'll wind up marry-
ing him... He usually wound up voting for Democrats... He knew it
was going to wind up in a fight. ● **Finish up** and **end up** mean almost
the same as **wind up.**

7 If you **wind** someone **up,** you deliberately say or do things to annoy V+N+ADV,
them or get them excited; an informal use. EG *He's always winding* V+PRON+ADV
his teachers up... The team were all wound up for the big moment...
Gareth's remarks had wound him up to full pitch. ▶ A **wind-up** is a N COUNT
trick that is played on someone to make them believe something
that is not true; an informal word. EG *Is this a wind-up, or what?*

wipe, wipes, wiping, wiped

wipe away. If you **wipe away** dirt or liquid from something, or if V+ADV+N,
you **wipe** it **off,** you remove it using a cloth or your hand. EG *She* V+N+ADV,
wiped away their childish tears... ...wiping away the chalk marks... I V+PRON+ADV
need a handkerchief to wipe off the sand.

wipe down. If you **wipe** something **down,** you rub it with a damp V+N+ADV,
cloth to clean or dry its surface. EG *The walls will have to be wiped* V+ADV+N,
down... Make sure you wipe down all the work surfaces. V+PRON+ADV

wipe off. 1 See **wipe away.**

2 If you **wipe off** a debt or money that is owed to you, you accept V+N+ADV,
that the money will not be repaid. EG *Twelve million pounds was* V+ADV+N,
simply wiped off by the Government... ...wiping off the threatened V+PRON+ADV
deficit. ● **Write off** means almost the same as **wipe off.**

wipe out. 1 If you **wipe out** something that has contained liquid or V+ADV+N,
food, you rub the inside of it with a cloth or piece of paper to clean V+N+ADV,
it. EG *I carefully wipe out the wash basin with a tissue... Wipe out the* V+PRON+ADV
frying pan with kitchen paper... Wipe the bucket out when you've
finished.

2 To **wipe** someone or something **out** means to destroy or get rid of V+ADV+N,

them completely. EG *They planned one big assault to wipe out the* V+N+ADV,
remains of the ghetto... Epidemics wiped out the local population... V+PRON+ADV
Uncle Aaron was determined to wipe out the memory of his years in
Auschwitz... You can wipe clover out of a pasture by applying
artificial nitrogen. ● **Eradicate** is a more formal word for **wipe out.**

wipe up. If you **wipe up** dirt or liquid from something, you remove V+ADV+N,
it using a cloth. EG *He begins to wipe up the mess... ...throwing mud* V+PRON+ADV,
then wiping it up. V+N+ADV

wire, wires, wiring, wired

wire up. If you **wire** something **up,** you connect it to something else V+ADV+N,
with electrical wires so that electricity or electrical signals can pass V+N+ADV,
between them. EG *...electrical fittings wired up to the mains... Make* V+PRON+ADV:
sure the plug is wired up properly. ALSO+to

wise, wises, wising, wised

wise up. If someone **wises up** to a situation or state of affairs, they V+ADV:
realize or become aware of it; an informal expression in American USUALLY+to
English. EG *Christopher wised up to the fact that the whole district*
was being bought up by property developers... Of course they will
wise up and get out sooner or later... Wise up, Barrett!

wish, wishes, wishing, wished

wish away. If you **wish** something **away,** you hope to get rid of it V+ADV+N,
although you do not do anything practical to remove it. EG *It seems* V+PRON+ADV,
unlikely that the statistical errors can be wished away... Wishing V+N+ADV
them away won't get rid of your problems.

wish on. If you **wish** something **on** or **upon** someone else, you hope V+N+PREP,
very much that it will happen to them or that they will be influenced V+PRON+PREP
by it. EG *The one thing I would not wish on my worst enemy is*
eternal life... ...the nicest thing she could wish on anybody... ...a very
convenient tradition which has been wished upon the nurses.

wish upon. See **wish on: wish upon** is slightly more formal.

wither, withers, withering, withered

wither away. If something **withers away,** it gradually becomes V+ADV
weaker until eventually it no longer exists. EG *Links with the outside*
community withered away... His eagerness to fight back could not
be permitted to wither away.

wolf, wolfs, wolfing, wolfed

wolf down. If you **wolf** food **down,** you eat it all very quickly and V+ADV+N,
greedily. EG *I wolfed down an enormous meal... He wolfed the food* V+N+ADV,
down, bones and all. ● **Gobble down** means almost the same as **wolf** V+PRON+ADV
down.

wonder, wonders, wondering, wondered

wonder at. If you **wonder at** something, you are surprised or V+PREP:
puzzled by it. EG *One can only wonder at children's reserves of* HAS PASSIVE
strength when this kind of thing happens... This prosperity is more
wondered at than envied. ● **Marvel at** means almost the same as
wonder at.

work, works, working, worked

work at. See **work on.**

work away. If you **work away,** you continue working hard for a V+ADV:
long time. EG *...scientists working away at perfecting the weapons... I* ALSO+at
was able to keep warm as I worked away in the snow.

work in. 1 When you are preparing a mixture or a surface, if you V+N+ADV,
work a substance **in,** you rub or mix it gradually and carefully into V+PRON+ADV,
V+ADV+N

the mixture or surface. EG *We worked the fat in with our fingers...*
Sprinkle dry salt on the butter and work it in thoroughly.

2 If you are doing or saying something and you **work** something else **in**, you manage to include it. EG *During his speech, he managed to work in several sly remarks about the Prime Minister... I'll try and work it in some time during the day.* ● **Squeeze in** means almost the same as **work in**.

V+ADV+N,
V+PRON+ADV,
V+N+ADV

3 A **work-in** is a form of industrial action in which workers occupy buildings and take over the running of a factory or business to protest about plans to close it.

N COUNT

work into. If you **work** a substance **into** a mixture or surface, you rub it in or mix it in gradually and carefully. EG *To get the necessary lightness it should be worked into the soil with sand or ashes.*

V+N+PREP,
V+PRON+PREP

work off. **1** If you **work** something **off,** you gradually overcome the effects of it by doing something energetic or something different. EG *We should all be able to work off our stress physically... He worked off his embarrassment by harassing us with questions... He had given us as much food as we could eat, and wouldn't hear of letting us work off our meal... If parents feel irritated at their children, they may try to work it off as teasing.*

V+ADV+N,
V+PRON+ADV,
V+N+ADV

2 If someone **works off** a debt, they repay it by working without pay for the person who lent them the money. EG *They had to sell their possessions or work off the amount as the lender's slave... He agreed to go without pay until he had worked off the family debt.*

V+ADV+N,
V+PRON+ADV

3 If a piece of equipment **works off** a particular source of power, this is the source of power that it uses to make it function. EG *There is a special wire cutter which works off a battery... You can buy quite cheap and simple welding sets that work off the mains.*

V+PREP

work on. **1** If you **work on** something or **work at** it, you spend time and effort trying to improve it. EG *He has been working all season on his game... She works hard at keeping herself fit.*

V+PREP:
HAS PASSIVE

2 If you **work on** an assumption or idea, you rely on it being true or correct when you develop your own ideas or plans. EG *Mr Reagan said he was working on the assumption that formal negotiations would shortly take place... Evolution theory works on the idea that the fittest survive and produce fit offspring.*

V+PREP

3 If you **work on** someone, you spend time trying to influence them or persuade them to do something. EG *The good priest worked on me with the finest tenderness and understanding... I think he could be worked on.*

V+PREP:
HAS PASSIVE

work out. **1** If you **work out** the answer to a mathematical problem, you calculate it. EG *I've worked it out, it's 3,171.875 tons... The weekly rate is worked out by dividing by 52... Calculate how much you owe each person, then work out how much you can afford to pay each of them... He worked the sum out twenty times on the adding machine.*

V+ADV+N,
V+N+ADV,
V+PRON+ADV

2 If something **works out** at a particular amount, it is found to be that amount after all the calculations have been made. EG *It worked out about a hundred pounds in the end... Petrol prices here are among the cheapest in Europe, working out at around 52p a litre.*

V+ADV:
WITH A

3 If you **work out** a solution or a plan, you think about it carefully and find a solution or decide what to do. EG *We are always hopeful that a more peaceful solution can be worked out... We could begin to work out the best ways to help these youngsters... I stopped and sat down to work out where I would go next.*

V+ADV+N,
V+N+ADV,
V+PRON+ADV

4 If you manage to **work out** something that seems strange, you think about it and manage to understand it. EG *He couldn't at first work out why the room was at once so strange and so familiar... I'm trying to work out what's wrong... I'm not sure what's missing. We'll*

V+ADV+N,
V+N+ADV,
V+PRON+ADV

work it out when we see yours. ● **Figure out** means almost the same as **work out.**

5 If you say that you cannot **work** someone **out,** you mean that you cannot understand them; an informal use. EG *I just can't work you out, you never seem to enjoy anything.* ● **Suss out** is a more informal expression for **work out.**

V+N+ADV,
V+PRON+ADV:
USUALLY NEGATIVE

6 If a situation **works out** in a particular way, it happens or progresses in that way. EG *I asked him how he was, and how his job was working out... It's funny how life worked out.* ● **Turn out** means almost the same as **work out.**

V+ADV:
WITH A

7 If a situation, arrangement, or plan **works out,** it is successful. EG *...so it really didn't have any chance to work out at all... He's moody because things aren't working out at home.*

V+ADV

8 If a process **works** itself **out,** it reaches a conclusion or satisfactory end. EG *Popular theories depend on the great historical purpose working itself out... What she was engaged in was the dream, which worked itself out in her.* ● **Resolve** means almost the same as **work out.**

V+REFL+ADV

9 If you **work out** your service or your notice, you continue to work at your job until you have completed a specified period of time. EG *...including 30,000 conscripts still working out their reserve service... She was given a month's pay and asked to leave immediately, rather than working out her notice.*

V+ADV+N,
V+N+ADV,
V+PRON+ADV

10 If a mine **is worked out,** all the coal or metal has been removed from it. EG *As more and more seams were worked out, the danger of pit closures increased.* ● **Be exhausted** means almost the same as **be worked out.**

PASSIVE:
V+ADV

11 If you **work out,** you do physical exercises in order to make your body fit and strong. EG *She worked out in a ballet class three hours a week.* ▸ A **workout** is a period of physical exercise or training. EG *He felt relaxed because of the light workout he had just done... They go to the gym for a workout every Wednesday.*

V+ADV

N COUNT

work over. If someone **works** you **over,** they attack you, either physically or by shouting at you and criticizing you; an informal expression. EG *Morris and Richards worked Robinson over to get the truth out of him... I kept on reading as she worked me over.*

V+N+ADV,
V+PRON+ADV,
V+ADV+N

work through. If you **work through** a problem or difficulty, you deal with it carefully and thoroughly until you find a satisfactory solution. EG *They work through a series of issues and problems with key employees... While Diana disentangles that question I was able to work through the next... The teacher sets the experiment or project and the students work it through.*

V+ADV+N,
V+PRON+ADV

work towards. If you **work towards** something, you try very hard to achieve it or make it happen. EG *My mother was working towards her master's degree in education... It called for the trade union movement to work towards greater industrial democracy.*

V+PREP:
HAS PASSIVE

work up. 1 If you **work** yourself **up,** you gradually make yourself very upset or angry about something. EG *I don't want you to resign. Now tell me why you are so worked up over that editorial... Of course it's yours, my dear. There's no need to get so worked up about it.*

V+REFL+ADV:
USUALLY+A

2 If someone **works up** something such as a feeling, the energy to do something, or an appetite, they gradually develop and increase it until they have what they need. EG *It had taken months to work up the courage to participate... She went for a run to work up an appetite... I can hardly work up enough energy.*

V+ADV+N

3 If you **work** yourself **up** to do something, you get ready to do it

V+REFL+ADV:
WITH to/to-INF

because you are enthusiastic or excited about it. EG *A group of girls excitedly work themselves up to going on some wild diet.*

4 When you are doing something regularly, if you **work up** to a particular amount or level, you gradually increase or improve what you are doing until you reach that amount or level. EG *She recommends starting with a teaspoonful or less and working up gradually to 2 or 3 tablespoonfuls... Repeat movements 1, 2 and 3 four times at first and gradually work up to about six repetitions.* ● **Build up** means almost the same as **work up**.

V+ADV:
USUALLY+*to*

5 If you **work up** something, you spend time and effort on it to make it complete or successful. EG *One day I may work this idea up into a story... ...as though he were working up a character in a book... He would be able to work up a sound business.*

V+N+ADV,
V+ADV+N,
V+PRON+ADV

worm, worms, worming, wormed

worm out. If you **worm** information **out** of someone, you gradually find it out from them by constantly asking them about it. EG *He might worm the story out of her by emotional pressure... The truth had been wormed out of him by his lawyers.*

V+N+ADV,
V+PRON+ADV:
USUALLY+*of*

worry, worries, worrying, worried

worry at. 1 If you **worry at** a problem, you think about it continually and anxiously to find a way of solving it. EG *God knows the truth of the matter, there is little point in worrying at it.... But I can't just let it happen. I worry at it: I keep digging it up to find an answer.*

V+PREP

2 When a dog or other animal **worries at** something, it holds it in its teeth, continually shaking it and moving it about. EG *Bunching the towel up beneath her she would worry at it until she found a suitable part to suck.*

V+PREP

wrap, wraps, wrapping, wrapped

wrap up. 1 When you **wrap** something **up,** you fold a piece of paper, cloth, or other material round it so that it is completely covered. EG *He had bought a teapot and was waiting for them to wrap it up... He had wrapped up a parcel of his manuscripts and a few books... My hair is wrapped up in a towel because I've just washed it.* ● **Do up** means almost the same as **wrap up**.

V+PRON+ADV,
V+ADV+N,
V+N+ADV

2 If you **wrap up** or **wrap** yourself **up,** you put warm clothes on. EG *Wrap up well. It's cold outside... Wrap up warm and relax by going to bed or resting in your chair... I read somewhere that if you wrap up well in summer it insulates you against the heat... The children came to school wrapped up in coats and scarves.*

V+ADV,
V+REFL+ADV,
ALSO PASSIVE,
V+ADV:
USUALLY+A

3 If you **wrap up** something such as a job, agreement, or particular activity, you complete or end it in a satisfactory way; an informal use. EG *The whole deal was wrapped up within a few days... That about wraps it up for this week... He was wrapping up a five-week tour abroad with a three-day stopover in Paris.* ● **Wind up** means almost the same as **wrap up**.

V+N+ADV,
V+PRON+ADV,
V+ADV+N

4 If you tell someone to **wrap up,** you are telling them in a rude, informal way to stop talking.

IMPERATIVE:
V+ADV

wrap up in. If someone **is wrapped up in** a particular person or thing, they spend nearly all their time thinking about that person or thing and so have little time for anything else. EG *They are completely wrapped up in the baby... He will be wrapped up in his work, leaving little time for you... ...adolescents who are wrapped up in themselves.*

PASSIVE:
V+ADV+PREP

wrestle, wrestles, wrestling, wrestled

wrestle with. 1 If you **wrestle with** a problem or a difficult situation, you try to deal with it or find a solution to it. EG *For*

V+PREP:
HAS PASSIVE

decades, mathematicians have wrestled with this problem... Viktor was wrestling with the intricacies of international telephone calls.

2 If someone **is wrestling with** something large or heavy, they are having difficulty holding it or controlling it. EG *She wondered if she should go and help the man wrestling with the map.* `V+PREP`

wriggle, wriggles, wriggling, wriggled

wriggle out of. If you **wriggle out of** doing something that you are expected to do but that you do not want to do, you manage to avoid doing it. EG *I can't manage to wriggle out of accompanying my parents to Europe... They use classy lawyers and accountants to wriggle out of paying taxes.* ● **Get out of** means almost the same as **wriggle out of.** `V+ADV+PREP`

wring, wrings, wringing, wrung

wring out. **1** If you **wring out** a wet cloth or piece of clothing, you twist it as far as it will go to squeeze the water out of it. EG *Don't wring it out, pat it dry with a towel.* `V+PRON+ADV, V+ADV+N, V+N+ADV`

2 If you **wring** something **out of** someone, you force them to give it to you, although they do not want to. EG *His captors were obviously trying to wring out information from him... I spend a great deal of my time trying to wring the costs for this litigation out of the Legal Aid fund.* `V+ADV+N, V+N+ADV, V+PRON+ADV`

write, writes, writing, wrote, written

write away. If you **write away** or **off** to a company or organization, you send them a letter, asking them to send you a product or some information. EG *You just write away giving your name, address and enclosing three tokens... Why don't you write off to Sussex University and ask for their prospectus?* ● **Send off** and **send away** mean almost the same as **write away.** `V+ADV: USUALLY+A`

write back. If you **write back** to someone, you reply to a letter that they sent you. EG *I wrote, explaining our difficulty and asking for suggestions. Samarkand wrote back at once... First of all Christopher wrote to my father, and my father wrote back saying you must be joking... You could write a letter back saying that you don't want to go.* `V+ADV, V+N+ADV`

write down. When you **write** something **down,** you record it on a piece of paper using a pen or pencil. EG *The magistrate had to write all the evidence down... Write down any four digit number... They ask me the date and the flight number: I always write it down so I'll remember.* ● **Put down** means almost the same as **write down.** `V+N+ADV, V+ADV+N, V+PRON+ADV`

write in. **1** If you **write in** to an organization, you send them a letter. EG *We are offering a half-price holiday to the first person to write in with the correct explanation... The majority of those who had already written in to give their views had backed the idea.* `V+ADV: USUALLY+A`

2 If you **write in** a piece of information on a form or document, you add the information by writing it in the appropriate place. EG *I'll give you my diploma and write in your name so you can pretend you got through... He arranged the meeting for Tuesday and wrote it in on the kitchen calendar in red pencil.* `V+ADV+N, V+PRON+ADV, V+N+ADV: USUALLY+A`

3 If a part **is written in** to a play, or if a clause **is written in** to a contract, the part or clause is added after the play or document has been created. EG *The Prince had assumed that a special part was being written in for him... The new contract has the same clause written in.* `PASSIVE: V+ADV`

write into. If a particular rule or detail **is written into** a contract or agreement, it is included in it. EG *The new arrangements have been written into the agreement.* `PASSIVE: V+PREP`

write off. 1 See **write away.**

2 If you **write** someone or something **off,** you decide that they are unimportant, useless or unlikely to be successful and that they are not worth further consideration. EG *Do not sound harassed, or you will be written off as a hysterical woman... 'Whatever you do,' she pleaded, 'don't write off philosophy without even trying it'... ...injuries that threatened to write him off in his late twenties.* ● **Dismiss** is a more formal word for **write off.**

V+N+ADV,
V+ADV+N,
V+PRON+ADV:
ALSO+*as*

3 If someone **writes off** a vehicle, they have a crash in it and it is so badly damaged that it is not worth repairing. EG *She had crashed the car twice, writing it off completely on the second occasion... Should an insured car be written off in an accident, the insurers will usually pay the current value of the vehicle.* ▸ If a vehicle is a **write-off** after an accident, it is so badly damaged that it is not worth spending money on it to repair it. EG *The Boylan's car was a write-off so they decided to abandon the trip.*

V+PRON+ADV,
V+ADV+N,
V+N+ADV

N COUNT

4 If someone **writes off** a debt or an amount of money that has been spent on a project, they accept that they are never going to get the money back. EG *Should we not write off many of the debts that are crippling Third World countries?... Normal accounting practice is to write off the loss immediately in the year in which it is incurred... 'Last year I wrote off six thousand dollars' worth of bad debts,' he said.* ▸ A **write-off** is an official declaration that a debt is not going to be repaid. EG *The only state assistance was a write-off of 64 million pounds.*

V+ADV+N,
V+PRON+ADV,
V+N+ADV

N COUNT

write out. 1 When you **write out** something such as a report, a list, or a word, you write it on paper. EG *When you have done your reports type them or write them out very clearly... I wondered whether he wrote his material out first or just composed it in his head... The editor wrote me out a list of places I must visit... His name was Mayhew, it was written out in enormous letters.*

V+PRON+ADV,
V+N+ADV,
V+PRON+ADV+N,
V+ADV+N

2 When someone **writes out** something such as a cheque, receipt, or prescription, they write all the necessary information on it. EG *I went directly to my cabin to write out the death certificate... If you are at your own branch you simply write out a cheque and give it to the cashier... I could write you a cheque out now, or give you the cash tomorrow.*

V+ADV+N,
V+PRON+ADV+N,
V+PRON+ADV,
V+N+ADV

3 If a character in a drama series on television or radio **is written out,** the story is changed so that the character leaves or dies and is no longer part of the series.

PASSIVE:
V+ADV

write up. 1 When you **write up** something that has been done or said, you record it on paper in a neat and complete form, usually using notes that you have made. EG *He usually spent solitary evenings writing up his work... Anything I was told, I had to write up in my reports... I'm going to enjoy writing it up for the journals.* ▸ A **write-up** is an article in a newspaper or magazine, in which someone describes and gives their opinion of something such as a play, a new product, or a place they have visited, EG *Somebody told me you got a terrific write-up in the 'Guardian'.*

V+ADV+N,
V+N+ADV,
V+PRON+ADV

N COUNT

2 If you **write** something **up** somewhere, you write it on a wall, board or notice. EG *...the desire which so many people obviously have to write their names up everywhere... Yes, write it up on the board... His name was written up everywhere I looked.*

V+N+ADV,
V+PRON+ADV,
V+ADV+N:
USUALLY+A

3 When someone **writes up** something such as a cheque, receipt, or prescription, they write all the necessary information on it; used in American English. EG *I don't want you to have to write up a slip just for eighty cents... She wrote up the ticket, tore out the coupon, and*

V+ADV+N,
V+PRON+ADV+N,
V+PRON+ADV,
V+N+ADV

stuck it in the book... Write me up a cheque if you don't have the right change.

X x Y y Z z

x, x's, x'ing, x'd

x out. If you **x out** someone or something, you stop thinking about them; an informal expression. EG *When I thought of Morgan, I simply x'd her out.* ● **Blot out** means almost the same as **x out.**

V+PRON+ADV,
V+N+ADV,
V+ADV+N

yearn, yearns, yearning, yearned

yearn for. If you **yearn for** something, you have a strong desire for it; a literary expression. EG *Most people yearn for some truth in a relationship... He yearned for academic recognition.* ● **Long for** means almost the same as **yearn for.**

V+PREP

yell, yells, yelling, yelled

yell out. If you **yell out** or if you **yell** something **out,** you shout loudly, for example because you are excited, angry, or in pain. EG *The nurse hastened to her aid when she yelled out and collapsed... I yelled out, 'Come down!'... He yelled out to his leader that the job was impossible... The older boys yelled out insults... ...a voice in the office yelling my name out.* ● **Shout out** means almost the same as **yell out.**

V+ADV,
V+ADV+QUOTE,
V+ADV+REPORT,
V+ADV+N,
V+N+ADV,
V+PRON+ADV

yield, yields, yielding, yielded

yield to. 1 If you **yield to** someone or something, you stop resisting them. EG *The Chancellor yielded to the critics and halved the March Budget... She was yielding to public pressure... He was progressively yielding to American demands.*

V+PREP

2 If you say that one thing **yields to** another, you mean that the second thing replaces or gets power over the first; a formal use. EG *The wilderness of ugly warehouses is to yield to complete redevelopment... Radio has long been under pressure to yield to television... The swamp would yield to drier land.*

V+PREP

yield up. If you **yield up** a secret, you reveal it; a formal expression. EG *...methods of making the brain yield up its secrets... He must be allowed to save face by yielding them up voluntarily.* ● **Disclose** means almost the same as **yield up.**

V+ADV+N,
V+PRON+ADV,
V+N+ADV

zero, zeros/zeroes, zeroing, zeroed

zero in on. 1 To **zero in on** a target means to aim at it very accurately or move towards it. EG *The missile then zeros in on the target... ...guns so powerful they could zero in on Omaha Beach.*

V+ADV+PREP

2 If you **zero in on** a problem or subject, you concentrate all your attention on it. EG *I want to talk generally before I zero in on any one speciality... By zeroing in on a particular lifestyle, we exclude a vast number of alternatives.*

V+ADV+PREP

zip, zips, zipping, zipped

zip up. 1 When you **zip up** something such as a piece of clothing, you fasten it using a zip. EG *She zipped up the dress with difficulty... He zipped his jeans up... I had to struggle out of the dress and half zip it up and then struggle back into it.* ● **Do up** means almost the same as

V+ADV+N,
V+N+ADV,
V+PRON+ADV

zip up. ▸ A **zip-up** piece of clothing is one which fastens with a zip. ADJECTIVE
EG ...*zip-up boiler-suits.*

2 If you **zip** someone **up,** you fasten the zip on their clothes for them. V+PRON+ADV,
EG *Zip me up at the back, please.* V+N+ADV

zoom, zooms, zooming, zoomed

zoom in. If a photographer or camera **zooms in** on the person or V+ADV:
thing being photographed, they make the image larger by changing ALSO+*on*
the focus. EG *I should have zoomed in closer on the driver's face.*

zoom off. If you **zoom off** somewhere, you go there in a hurry; an V+ADV:
informal expression. EG *In the summer, we all zoom off to* USUALLY+A
Felixstowe on our bikes... He zoomed off to the USA.

zoom out. If a photographer or camera **zooms out,** they draw back V+ADV
from what is being photographed and show the things that surround
it. EG *Zoom out now, and get the overall effect.*

Particles Index

The Particles Index is an extensive guide to the way in which particles are used in English phrasal verbs. It acts as an index to the dictionary, listing phrasal verb headwords alphabetically within given categories of meaning. It also gives the actual number of occurrences of each particle, which will be of interest to teachers, who may use this information to determine which phrasal verbs to focus on.

There is an entry for each of the forty-eight particles which are found in the phrasal verb headwords. Some of the headwords contain more than one particle. In most cases, the first particle is an adverb and the second one a preposition. The index deals with two-particle combinations under the first of the particles.

Some particles occur in a large number of different phrasal verbs. Eighteen of them occur in fifty or more combinations. The commonest particles are **up, out, off, in, on,** and **down,** in descending order of frequency. **Up** and **out,** in particular, are extremely common: 28% of the phrasal verbs listed here include either **up** or **out.** In contrast, some of the particles such as **aback** and **across** occur in very few phrasal verbs: fifteen of them occur in fewer than ten combinations.

The index lists groups of phrasal verbs which share particular meanings, and thus the patterns of meaning of the particles themselves can be seen. Some of these meanings are 'literal': that is, they are the main meanings of the particle in question. These literal meanings are usually to do with physical position or direction of movement. We do not give lists of combinations which have these purely literal meanings.

The lists contain all the central and typical examples of phrasal verbs which include a particular particle. Sometimes a phrasal verb fits into more than one category of particle meaning, as the meanings may overlap, or one may be a metaphorical extension of another, and sometimes it is difficult to say exactly what meaning is contributed by the particle to the phrasal verb. Only the clearest-cut cases therefore appear in the lists. In addition, many phrasal verbs have more than one sense. Often the particle has the same meaning in all these senses, but sometimes it has different meanings. In these cases, we include the phrasal verb in more than one list, but we add a sense number where this avoids confusion.

The meanings of English phrasal verbs are not always obvious. Yet the particles index shows very clearly how phrasal verbs are not just arbitrary combinations of verbs and particles. Instead, they fit into the broad patterns of choice and selection in English. When a new combination occurs, it too fits into these patterns. The Particles Index will help you to deal with these new combinations, and phrasal verbs as a whole will become a more manageable part of the vocabulary of English.

aback is an adverb which was used in old forms of English with some of the meanings that **back** has. In modern English, it only occurs in the phrasal verb **take aback.**

about is an adverb and a preposition. It occurs in 88 phrasal verbs in this dictionary.

1 Movement

About is used in literal combinations to indicate movement in many different directions over a period of time, often without any specific aim or purpose. For example, if you **drift about,** you travel to a lot of different places; if someone **lays about** with a weapon, they move it randomly in many directions; and if you **hurl** things **about,** you throw them violently in several directions. Some combinations have the meaning of looking in many different places. These phrasal verbs are often followed by the preposition *for.* For example, if you **cast about** for something, you search for it in many places. **About** is used in a similar way in combinations which have the meaning of distributing or spreading something to many different places or people. For example, if you **scatter** things **about,** you distribute them over a wide area. If news **gets about,** it reaches many people. When **about** is used as a preposition, it has the additional meaning of 'within a particular place': you mention the place in the noun group after **about.** For example, if you **crash about** the kitchen, you move in many different directions in the kitchen, making a lot of noise. To **root about** a place means to search it thoroughly. **Around** and **round** have similar meanings: see **around 1** and **round 1.**

2 Inactivity and aimlessness

About is also used to indicate lack of activity, lack of purpose, or lack of achievement over a period of time. For example, if you **lounge about,** you spend your time being lazy and doing nothing. When **about** is used as a preposition, it has the additional meaning of 'in a particular place': you mention the place in the noun group after **about.** For example, if you **mope about** the house, you spend time in the house rather aimlessly and feeling unhappy. **About** also occurs in a few combinations indicating that something is present in a place, although you are not sure where. For example, if something **is kicking about** in a place, it is somewhere in that place, but you do not know exactly where. These phrasal verbs are usually used in continuous tenses. **About** is also used as an adverb in some informal or rude combinations to indicate wasting time or behaving foolishly. For example, if you **lark about,** you behave in a foolish or silly way. **Around** and **round** have similar meanings: see **around 2** and **round 7.**

faff about	kick about	loaf about	mope about	slop about
fiddle about	lark about	loll about	muck about	stand about
fool about	laze about	lounge about	play about	tinker about
hang about	lie about	mess about	sit about	wait about

3 Encirclement

You use **about** as a preposition in combinations which have the literal meaning of putting one thing round another, so that it forms a circle round it. You mention the second thing in the noun group after **about.** For example, if you **throw** your arms **about** someone, you throw them round the person. **Around** and **round** have similar meanings, and are more informal: see **around 4** and **round 4.**

4 Turning

You use **about** as an adverb in literal combinations such as **face about** and **turn about** ion order to say that someone or something turns until they are facing in the opposite direction. This is a formal use. **Around** and **round** have similar meanings, and are more informal: see **around 3** and **round 2.**

5 Action

About is used as an adverb in a few combinations which have the idea of an event happening or someone doing something. For example, to **bring** something **about** means to make it happen.

bring about   come about   go about   set about

6 Introduction of subject

About is used as a preposition in many combinations with the literal meaning 'concerning a particular subject'. You mention the subject in the noun group after **about**. For example, to **know about** a subject means to know things concerning that subject, and if you **hear about** something, you get information concerning it.

above

above is both a preposition and an adverb, although it is used mainly as a preposition in phrasal verbs. It occurs in 5 phrasal verbs in this dictionary. Its literal meaning is to do with position, to say that one thing is at a higher level than another. **Tower above** has the added sense of making other people or things seem smaller than they are, and **rise above** has the meaning of overcoming difficulties. The other three combinations refer to the extended meaning of **above,** implying greater importance or higher rank. For example, if you **put** one thing **above** another, you consider that the first thing is more important than the second.

get above   marry above   put above   rise above   tower above

across

across is both a preposition and an adverb. It occurs in 6 phrasal verbs in this dictionary. Its basic meaning is to do with movement from one side of an area to the other, and it occurs with this meaning in a few literal combinations with very common verbs, such as **come across 1** and **run across 1.**

1 Finding

Across is used in a few combinations which have 'find' as part of their meaning. For example if you **stumble across** something, you find it unexpectedly.

come across 2   run across 2   stumble across

2 Communicating

Across is also used in a few combinations which refer to communication and understanding. For example, if an idea **gets across,** people understand it. Over has a similar meaning: see **over 11.**

come across 4   get across   put across 1

after

after is a preposition. It occurs in 15 phrasal verbs in this dictionary. The basic meaning of **after** is to do with the sequence of events in time, indicating that one event happens later than another. Some of the meanings of **after** occur in only one combination. For example, the meaning of **after** in **look after** is different from any of its other meanings. There are three main meanings for **after** which occur in several combinations.

1 Following and hunting

After occurs with intransitive verbs in combinations which have 'follow', 'chase', or 'hunt' as part of their meaning. You mention the person or animal being chased in the noun group following **after.**

chase after   get after   go after 1   make after   run after 1
come after

2 Wanting

After also occurs with intransitive verbs in combinations which express ideas of wanting to obtain something or trying hard to obtain it. This may be regarded as a metaphorical use of the previous category. You mention the thing that you want in the noun group following **after**. Some of these verbs can be used in combination with **for** instead of **after.**

ask after	hanker after	inquire after	lust after	run after 2
go after 2	hunger after			

3 Similarity and imitation

Some combinations with **after** express the idea that one thing is similar to another in some way. For example, if you **take after** someone, you resemble them, and if you **call** something **after** another thing, you give it the same name as the other thing.

call after	name after	take after

against is a preposition. It occurs in 30 phrasal verbs in this dictionary. One meaning of **against** is to do with position, indicating that one thing is next to another and touching it, or with movement into that position, but it is also used very commonly to express ideas of opposition. **Against** occurs with two main meanings in phrasal verbs.

1 Opposition and prevention

You use **against** in combinations which have 'attack' or 'oppose' as part of their meaning. For example, if two people **side against** you, they join together in order to defeat you, and if you **kick against** something, you protest about it. You mention the person or thing being attacked or opposed in the noun group after **against**. Some combinations have 'prevent' or 'protect' as part of their meaning. The noun group after **against** refers to something potentially harmful, which you want to avoid. For example, to **guard against** something means to take action to prevent it happening or harming you.

go against 5	inveigh against	proceed against	rail against	side against
guard against	kick against	protect against	range against	take against
hedge against	offend against	provide against	set against 3	turn against
insure against	plot against	rage against		

2 Comparison and detraction

Against occurs in combinations with transitive verbs where you are comparing two things. You mention the second thing in the comparison in the noun group after **against**. For example, if you **balance** one thing **against** another, you assess their relative importance. **Against** occurs in combinations with intransitive verbs where you are saying that something is making a situation less likely, less favourable, or less successful. You mention the situation or person that is affected in the noun group after **against**. For example, if something **counts against** you, it is a disadvantage to you and may lead to your defeat, and if one thing **militates against** another, it makes it less likely to happen or succeed.

balance against	find against	match against	militate against	tell against
count against	go against 4	measure against	set against 1	weigh against

ahead is an adverb. It occurs in 14 phrasal verbs in this dictionary.

1 Progress

Ahead is most frequently used in combinations with intransitive verbs of movement to refer to progress of some kind, usually in a non-literal sense, rather than referring to actual movement. For example, if you **forge ahead,** you make rapid progress in what you are doing, but you do not have to be moving physically. You can mention the activity you are involved in after the preposition *with.* When you are saying that one person is making more progress than another, the second person is mentioned after the preposition *of.*

forge ahead	go ahead	press ahead	pull ahead	push ahead
get ahead				

2 Futurity

If you use **ahead** with verbs of thinking and looking, it often means that you are doing something in advance. For example, if you **plan ahead,** you make plans about what you may do in the future. Some combinations have the meaning of something being likely to happen in the future. For example, if something **looms ahead,** it is likely to happen soon.

lie ahead	loom ahead	plan ahead	send ahead	think ahead
look ahead				

along is an adverb and a preposition. It occurs in 23 phrasal verbs in this dictionary.

1 Travel

Along occurs most frequently in literal combinations with verbs of motion to indicate movement in a certain direction, as in **go along** or **move along,** and it is often used, usually as an adverb, to imply departure, for example in **get along** and **push along.**

2 Progress

You can use **along** as an adverb in a non-literal way with verbs of motion to indicate progress. For example, if a project **is coming along,** it is making progress. Some combinations emphasize that something is not progressing very well, so if you say that a job **is dragging along** you think it is taking you a long time to do it.

come along 4	get along 2	go along 4	help along	move along 3
drag along				

3 Accompanying

You use **along** as an adverb in some combinations with transitive verbs to indicate that you are taking someone or something with you, so if you **bring along** a friend to a party, you take them with you. **Along** can also be used in intransitive combinations to show that someone is accompanying someone else. For example, if you **tag along** with someone, you accompany them somewhere.

bring along	come along 2	tag along
		take along

4 Acceptance

Along is sometimes used as an adverb to indicate acceptance of someone or something, especially when it is followed by *with,* so if you **go along with** a plan, you agree with it and accept it, and if you **get along** with someone, you have a friendly relationship with them and accept them.

get along 1	go along with	play along	rub along

among is a preposition. It occurs in 4 phrasal verbs in this dictionary. The basic meaning of **among** is to do with physically being in the middle of a group or surrounded by them. The combinations in this dictionary use **among** in the extended sense of being included or considered as part of a particular class. For example, if someone **ranks among** the members of a particular group, they are one of those members. You mention the group in the noun group after **among.**

class among	count among	number among	rank among

apart is an adverb. It occurs in 10 phrasal verbs in this dictionary. The basic meaning of **apart** is to do with position, indicating that one thing is at a distance from another. **Together** often has opposite meanings.

1 Undoing and collapse

Apart occurs with transitive verbs in combinations which describe the process of undoing or dismantling something which was originally one piece or unit. For example, to **take** something **apart** means to undo it so that it is in separate parts. **Pull apart, take apart,** and **tear apart** also have meanings to do with analysing something and considering its individual parts. This is a metaphorical use of the 'undoing' meaning. **Apart** occurs with intransitive verbs in combinations which mean 'collapse', and refer to either the physical collapse of an object or the mental collapse of a person. For example, **fall apart** can refer either to a physical collapse or a mental breakdown.

come apart	fall apart	pull apart 1	take apart	tear apart

2 Separation

Apart is used in combinations which describe a process of separation between two or more things. The separation may involve physical movement away from each other. For example, if you **pull apart** two people or animals who are fighting, you physically separate them. But the combinations often have an extended meaning involving relationships or the act of distinguishing. If two people **grow apart,** their relationship becomes less close as they develop separate interests. **Apart** occurs in **set apart** and **tell apart** to indicate that one thing or person is distinguished from another.

drift apart	grow apart	pull apart 2	set apart	tell apart

around is an adverb and a preposition. It occurs in 104 phrasal verbs in this dictionary.

1 Movement

Around is used in literal combinations to indicate movement in many different directions over a period of time, often without any specific aim or purpose. For example, if you **run around,** you run in a lot of different directions; if you **shop around,** you go to several different shops in order to compare the price and quality of the goods; and if you **push** something **around,** you move it in several different directions. Some combinations have the meaning of looking in a lot of different places or asking several people in order to find something. These phrasal verbs are often followed by the preposition *for*. For example, if you **ask around** for something, you ask several people for it. **Around** is used in a similar way in combinations which have the meaning of distributing or spreading something to many different places or people. For example, if you **pass** things **around,** you pass them from one person to another in a group, and if you **scatter** things **around,** you spread them over a wide area. When **around** is used as a preposition, it has the additional meaning of 'within a particular place'. You mention the place in the noun group after **around.** For example, if you **run around** the room, you run in many different directions in the room; and if you **nose around** a place, you look in several different places for things in it. **About** and **round** have similar meanings: see **about 1** and **round 1.**

2 Inactivity and aimlessness

Around is used to indicate lack of activity, lack of purpose, or lack of achievement over a period of time. For example, if you **loll around,** you spend time being lazy and doing nothing. When **around** is used as a preposition, it has the additional meaning of 'in a particular place'. You mention the place in the noun group after **around.** For example, if you **hang around** a place, you spend time there doing very little. **Around** also occurs in a few combinations indicating that something is present in a place, although you are not sure where. For example, if something **is kicking around** in a place, it is somewhere in that place, but you do not know exactly where. These phrasal verbs are usually used in continuous tenses. **Around** is also used as an adverb in some informal or rude combinations to indicate wasting time or behaving in a silly way. For example, if you **mess around,** you behave in a foolish or irritating way. **About** and **round** have similar meanings: see **about 2** and **round 7.**

fiddle around	lie around	mess around	play around	stick around
fool around	loaf around	mope around	sit around	tinker around
hang around	loll around	muck around	stand around	wait around
kick around	lounge around			

3 Turning

You use **around** as an adverb in combinations which have the meaning of turning so as to be facing in the opposite direction or turning round and round in a series of circles. For example, to **spin around** means to turn quickly and face in the opposite direction, or to spin round and round in a circle. **Round** has a similar meaning: see **round 2.**

look around	spin around	swivel around	turn around	wheel around
pull around	swing around			

4 Surrounding

Around is used in many combinations with the literal meaning of surrounding or encircling someone or something. For example, when people **gather around,** they come together and surround someone or something, and when you **throw** your arms **around** someone, you put them so that they form a circle round them. **Round** and **about** have similar meanings: see **round 4** and **about 3.**

5 Avoidance

You use **around** in a few combinations which have meanings to do with avoiding something, either a physical object or a problem. For example, if you **talk around** a subject, you avoid talking about it directly. **Round** has a similar meaning: see **round 8.**

go around	skirt around	talk around

6 Focusing

You use **around** as a preposition in **centre around** and **revolve around** where the meaning is to focus on something or concentrate on it. For example, if a discussion **revolves around** a subject, it concentrates on that subject. **Round** has a similar meaning: see **round 9.**

as is a preposition. It occurs in 8 phrasal verbs in this dictionary. **As** is one of the commonest words in English, and it is especially used in comparisons. It is used in phrasal verbs in order to indicate that someone or something is considered to have a particular role or function. For example, if you **masquerade as** a particular kind of person, you pretend to be that kind of person, and if you say that one thing **serves as** another, you mean that it is used instead of it. **As** also occurs as the second particle in combinations which include two particles, for example **go down as** and **pass off as.**

do as	know as	masquerade as	see as	serve as
hail as	mark as	pass as		

aside is an adverb. It occurs in 15 phrasal verbs in this dictionary. Its basic meaning is to do with movement from a position in front of something towards the side of it.

1 Rejection

Aside is frequently used with transitive verbs of movement in combinations which mean that something is being rejected. For example, if you **brush aside** someone's comments, you reject or ignore what they say.

brush aside	lay aside 2	set aside 3	throw aside 2	wave aside
cast aside	push aside 2	sweep aside		

2 Postponing

You can use **aside** in literal combinations to show that you are moving something away from you, usually not far away and temporarily. For example, if you **lay aside** a book, you place it somewhere near you until you are ready to read it again. These combinations can also be used in a non-literal sense in relation to ideas, tasks, or emotions. For example, if you **leave aside** a suggestion, you do not deal with it immediately because you intend to consider it or discuss it later.

lay aside 1	leave aside	put aside	set aside 4

3 Yielding or vacating

Aside means 'sideways', so if you **step aside** you move sideways to get out of someone's way. You can also use this in a non-literal way, for example if you **step aside** from a job, you resign so that someone else can have your job.

stand aside	step aside	turn aside

4 Isolation and privacy

Aside sometimes gives an idea of moving somewhere in order to have a private conversation with somebody, so if you **pull** someone **aside,** you take them somewhere where other people cannot hear what you are saying.

pull aside	take aside

at is a preposition. It occurs in 45 phrasal verbs in this dictionary. The most common use of **at** is to do with indicating points in space and time, to say where something is or where or when something happens. There are two basic meanings of phrasal verbs with **at** in this dictionary, and they have the meaning of directing or focusing an action on someone or something.

1 Direction

At is used in combinations which indicate that an action is carried out in a particular direction. For example, if you **aim at** a target, you try to achieve that target, and if you **talk at** somebody, you are talking in their direction, regardless of whether they are listening to you.

aim at	go at	level at	marvel at	throw at 1
drive at	laugh at	look at	talk at	work at
get at 1				

2 Attempting, attacking, seizing, and holding

At occurs in combinations with verbs which express ideas of attacking, hitting, seizing, holding, and so on. These verbs are mainly intransitive, although they can often be used transitively too, without **at.** By using them in combinations with **at,** instead of as transitives, you imply that someone is trying to attack or seize or hold something, perhaps unsuccessfully, rather than actually doing so. For example, if you **jab at** something, you try to hit it but do not succeed, and if you **get at** someone, you attack them verbally by shouting at them or criticizing them. **At** is also used in a similar way in combinations with the meaning of breaking off or removing small pieces from something, especially in small, repeated movements. For example, if you **pick at** your food, you only eat small amounts of it, and to **tear at** something means to try and pull it into small pieces. Other combinations indicate that a person or animal suddenly seizes something, or attempts to do so. For example, if a wild animal **claws at** you, it tries to catch you in its claws. You can also use **at** in a non-literal sense of 'seizing'. For example if you **grab at** or **leap at** an opportunity or offer, you try to take advantage of it, and if you **guess at** a question or problem, you try to understand it and provide an answer, although you do not really have enough information.

claw at	guess at	nibble at	pluck at	strike at
come at	hack at	paw at	poke at	tear at
fly at	hit at	peck at	prod at	throw at 3
get at 4	jab at	pick at	pull at 1	tug at
grab at	jump at	play at	sip at	worry at
grasp at	leap at			

away is an adverb. It occurs in 134 phrasal verbs in this dictionary.

1 Movement

Away is used in literal combinations to indicate movement in a direction farther from you, or movement from the place where you are or were. You use **away** with verbs which describe movement. For example, **run away** means to run from someone or something in the opposite direction, and **pull** something

away means to pull someone or something from the place where they were. These combinations are often followed by an adjunct referring to direction or place, usually beginning with the prepositions *from* or *to*.

break away 2	get away 1,2	look away	pull away 1,2	send away 1
come away 1	go away 1	move away 1	run away 1	stretch away
fall away 2				

2 Withdrawing and non-involvement

Away occurs in combinations which have meanings to do with someone avoiding or withdrawing from an activity, or ceasing to be involved in an activity. They can be regarded as metaphorical uses of the previous group. For example, **shy away from** means to avoid doing something because you are afraid or have no confidence. Some combinations have meanings to do with avoiding a place. These combinations are often followed by the preposition *from*.

back away	keep away 1,2,3	shy away from	steal away	walk away from
break away 1,4	move away from	slip away 1	steer away from	warn away
frighten away 2	run away 2,3,4	stay away	stop away	wave away
get away from	scare away 2	stay away from 1,2	turn away from	whisk away
grow away from	shrink away			

3 Removing, transferring, and separating

Away is used in combination with transitive verbs to indicate that something is taken from the place where it was or taken from the person who had it before. For example, to **snatch** something **away** from someone means to take it from them forcefully. Some combinations have meanings to do with taking a person from one place to another. Combinations such as **give away** have meanings to do with transferring something from one person to another. These combinations are often followed by the prepositions *from* or *to*. **Away** occurs with intransitive verbs in combinations such as **break away** and **come away** to indicate that something becomes separated from the thing that it was attached to. Such combinations are often followed by the preposition *from*.

break away 3	get away 3	pull away 3,4	take away 1,2,3,4,8	throw away 1
call away	give away 1,2,4	sign away	take away from 1	tow away
come away 2	kiss away	snatch away	tear away 2	turn away 1,2
fall away 1	move away 2	spirit away		

4 Storing, hiding, and isolating

You use **away** in phrasal verbs which have meanings to do with putting things in a safe place, or storing or hiding them. For example, **pack** something **away** means to put something in a bag or other container. You also use **away** in combinations which have isolation as part of their meaning. For example, something which **is buried away** is difficult to find, and someone who **has locked** himself or herself **away** has gone somewhere where they will not be disturbed. These combinations are often followed by an adjunct in which you mention the place where the person or thing is put or hidden.

bury away	hide away 1,2,3	put away 1,3,4	squirrel away	stow away 1,2
clear away	hoard away	salt away	stash away 1,2	tidy away
file away	lock away 1,2,3,4	shut away 1,2	store away	tuck away 1,2
give away 3	pack away			

5 Getting rid of things and destroying things

Away is used in combinations, mainly with transitive verbs, where you are saying that something is removed entirely. You add **away** to the verb to show that nothing is left. Many of the combinations mean 'destroy' or 'get rid of'. For example, **strip** something **away** means to remove it completely. A few combinations mean 'use something completely', and they often also suggest ideas of wasting it.

blow away 1,2,3	drive away	pass away 2	strip away 1,2	trim away
brush away	explain away	pour away	sweep away 1,2	turn away 3
burn away	frighten away 1	pump away 2	take away 5	wash away 1,2,3

cast away	gamble away	scare away	tear away 1	while away
chuck away	idle away	scrape away	throw away 2,3	wipe away
cut away	magic away	shoot away	toss away	wish away
do away with 1,2	make away with			

6 Disappearing

You use **away** in combinations to indicate that something gradually disappears or or is gradually destroyed until it does not exist at all. For example, **fade away** means to fade entirely. The verbs in these combinations are mostly intransitive.

boil away	ebb away	go away 2	rot away	waste away 1,2
die away	erode away	melt away 1,2,3	scour away	wear away 1,2,5
drop away	fade away 1,2,3	moulder away	slip away 2	whittle away
eat away 1,2,3	fall away 3,4,5	pass away 1	tail away	whittle away at
eat away at 1,2	fritter away	pine away	trail away	wither away

7 Continuous activity

You use **away** with intransitive verbs describing processes or activities in order to indicate that the process or activity continues throughout a period of time. For example, **work away** means to work hard for a long time, and **bang away** means to continue hitting something for a long time. These verbs are often used in a continuous tense, or with words which indicate continuousness, such as *would, continue,* or *keep.* Many of the phrasal verbs have the meaning 'work', and you can mention the thing being done in an adjunct, after the preposition *at.*

bang away	grind away	plod away	slave away	tick away
beaver away	hammer away at	plug away	slog away	toil away
blast away	jabber away	puff away	steam away	type away
blaze away	peg away	pump away 1	talk away	work away

back is an adverb. It occurs in 83 phrasal verbs in this dictionary.

1 Returning and movement backwards

Back is used in literal combinations with verbs of movement to say that someone or something returns to a place that they were in before. For example, when you **start back,** you start travelling in the direction that you came from, and if something **blows back,** the wind moves it in the direction that it was coming from.

blow back	go back 1	pull back 2	sit back 1	start back 1
come back 1	head back	push back 2	spring back	toss back 1
double back 1	lie back	put back 2	stand back 1	turn back 1,3
get back 1,2	look back 1	sink back 1		

2 Position

You use **back** in combinations indicating a position at a distance from a central point or from a place where something is happening. For example, if an army **falls back,** it retreats and if you **tie back** your hair, you tie it so that it is away from your face. You can extend this use of **back** to say that you separate yourself from something that is happening when you are unwilling to get involved. For example, if you **stand back** while something is happening, you do not become involved in it.

call back 3	get back 5	reel back 2	start back 2	tail back
draw back	hang back 1,2	set back 2	stay back	throw back 3
drop back	hold back 4	sit back 2	step back 1	tie back
fall back 1,2	pull back 1,3,4	stand back 2,3		

3 Time

You use **back** in combinations which have the meaning of belonging to the past or thinking about the past. For example, if something **carries** you **back,** it makes you think about something in the past.

bring back 1,2	come back 5	go back 2,3,4	look back 2	think back
carry back	date back	hark back to 1,2	take back 8,9	throw back 6,7
cast back	flash back			

4 Returning or retrieving something

You use **back** in combinations with meanings to do with returning something to a place where it was before, or to a person who had it before. For example, if you **give** something **back,** you give it to the person who had lent it to you, and if you **get** something **back,** someone gives it to you after you had lent it to them. This use of **back** is very productive.

claw back	go back 8,9	pay back 1	send back	throw back 1,2,5,8
die back	hand back	plough back	set back 3	win back
get back 3,4	kick back	put back 1,3,6	stick back	wind back
give back 1,2	knock back 2	put back into	take back 1,2,3,4,5,7	

5 Repeating or returning to an action

You can extend the above use of **back** in combinations with the meaning of returning to or repeating an act. For example, if you **get back into** an activity, you start doing it again. Several of these combinations have the meaning of repeating the action that someone else has done. For example, if you **hit** someone **back,** you hit them after they have hit you. This is a very productive use of **back.**

answer back	fight back 1	go back on	play back	step back 2
bounce back	get back 6	go back over	put back on	strike back
call back 1,2	get back at	go back to 1,2,3	read back	talk back
come back 2,3,4	get back into	hit back 1,2	report back	take back 6
come back to	get back to	pay back 2	ring back	throw back at
fall back on	go back 5,6,7	phone back	sink back 2	write back

6 Controlling or suppressing

You use **back** in combinations with meanings to do with controlling or suppressing something, especially an emotion, or preventing something from progressing. For example, if you **choke back** tears, you suppress them and stop them from coming.

bite back	cut back on	hold back	push back 1	roll back
choke back 1,2	fight back 2	keep back 1,2,3	put back 4,5	set back 1
cut back	force back			

7 Drinking

You use **back** in a few combinations meaning to drink something quickly, often in one gulp.

knock back 1	put back 7	throw back 4	toss back 2

before is both a preposition and an adverb. It is often used to indicate that something is in front of something else. **Before** only occurs in 5 phrasal verbs in this dictionary and in them this meaning is extended to talk about presenting ideas or matters to someone, especially someone in authority. For example, if a case **goes before** a judge, the judge considers it.

come before	go before	lay before	lie before	put before

behind is an adverb and a preposition. It occurs in 10 phrasal verbs in this dictionary. Its basic meaning is to do with relative position in space or time.

1 Relative position

Behind occurs in literal combinations which refer to the position of one person or thing in relation to another. For example, if someone **stops behind,** they stay in a place after other people have left, and if you **leave** something **behind,** you do not take it with you when you go somewhere.

2 Progress

Behind is also used to indicate relative progress, and to say that one person or thing is less advanced than another. For example, if you **get behind** with your work, you do not make as much progress as you should.

fall behind	get behind	lag behind	leave behind

3 Concealment and support

Behind is used literally to indicate that something is on the other side or at the back of another thing so that it supports or hides it. However, it is used metaphorically in phrasal verbs. For example, if you **hide behind** something, you use it as an excuse so that you can conceal your feelings, and if you **get behind** someone, you help or support them.

get behind 2	hide behind	lie behind	put behind

below is both a preposition and an adverb. Its basic meaning is to do with position, to say that one thing is at a lower level than something else. It only occurs in 1 phrasal verb in this dictionary, **go below,** and this refers to movement from a higher level on a boat to a lower level.

beneath is both a preposition and an adverb. Its basic meaning is to do with position, to say that one thing is under or at a lower level than another. It only occurs in 1 phrasal verb in this dictionary, **marry beneath,** and this refers to relative position or rank in society.

between is mainly used as a preposition. Its basic meaning is to do with movement from one point to another, or position in the middle of two things. It only occurs in 3 phrasal verbs in this dictionary. It is used to indicate movement in **pass between**. It also occurs in **come between** and **stand between,** where it is used non-literally to refer to something that prevents you from doing or having something you want by appearing to interfere with it.

beyond is both a preposition and an adverb. Its basic meaning is to do with position, to indicate that one thing is farther away from something else. It only occurs in 2 phrasal verbs in this dictionary, **get beyond** and **go beyond,** where it is used metaphorically to express ideas of doing something more advanced or more extreme than before.

by is an adverb and a preposition. It occurs in 22 phrasal verbs in this dictionary. Some meanings of **by** occur in a very few combinations. For example, **get by** and **scrape by** have the meaning of managing to survive with difficulty because of limited resources. **Come by** has the meaning of acquiring or gaining. There are four main uses of **by** in phrasal verbs.

1 Movement past a person or thing

Some phrasal verbs use **by** as an adverb or a preposition with the meaning of moving past a person or thing, often passing very close to them. **Brush by** and **push by** are examples of this meaning. Some combinations do not refer to physical objects, but to situations or experiences. **By** is usually an adverb in these combinations. For example, if you let someone's remarks or actions **go by,** you let them take place without allowing them to affect you. Some similar combinations relate to the passage of time. For example if you say that time or an event **slips by,** you mean that it passes and is gone.

brush by	go by	push by	slip by	tick by
get by	pass by	sit by	stand by 1	

2 Visiting

In some phrasal verbs with **by**, the meaning is of visiting someone casually and often only for a short time. **By** is usually an adverb but can be a preposition. For example, if you **stop by,** you visit a place for a short time, and if you **go by** a place, you go there for a short time in order to do or get something.

call by	come by	drop by	go by 3	stop by

3 Consistency and loyalty

You use **by** as a preposition in some phrasal verbs to indicate that someone always obeys a rule or principle, or always supports or helps someone,

however difficult this may be. For example, if you **abide by** a law, agreement, or decision, you do what it says you should do. If you **stick by** someone, you help or support them when they are in difficulty.

abide by	live by	stand by 3	stick by	swear by
go by 4				

4 Preparation and readiness

In a few combinations with **by** as an adverb, the meaning is that people or things are kept in preparation for something that might happen. For example, if you **lay** a store of something **by,** you save it for future use. If you **stand by,** you are ready to provide help or take action if it becomes necessary.

lay by	put by	stand by 2

down is an adverb and a preposition. It occurs in 191 phrasal verbs in this dictionary. The basic meaning of **down** is to do with movement from a higher position or level to a lower one.

1 Movement and position

You use **down** in literal combinations to indicate movement from a higher position or place to a lower one. For example, if you **shin down** a tree or pole, you climb very rapidly from a higher point on it towards the ground. If a plane **comes down**, it moves towards the ground and lands. and if you say it **is pouring down,** you mean that rain is falling very heavily. **Up** can often be used instead of **down** to indicate movement in the opposite direction.

beat down 1,2	lash down 2	pull down 1	set down 4,5	talk down 2
bucket down	move down 1	put down 15,16	shin down	teem down
cast down 2	pass down 2	rain down	sink down 1	touch down
come down 1,2,3,8,11	pelt down	ram down 1	snuggle down	turn down 4
flutter down	phone down	reach down 2	splash down	wash down 3
get down 1,2,3	piss down	roll down 1	swoop down 1	wind down 1
go down 1.1,2,5,13	pour down	run down 1	take down 1,2,3	

Down occurs as an adverb in combinations where you are describing movement from an upright or standing position to a lying, sitting, or crouching position, and so on. For example, if you **lie down,** you move into a horizontal position, and if you **kneel down,** you sit with your legs bent underneath your body.

bed down 1,2	flop down	keep down 2	plump down 1	sink down 2
bend down	get down 4	kip down	put down 5,11	sit down 1,2
bow down	go down 6,20	kneel down	reach down 1	stay down 1
crouch down	huddle down	lie down	shake down 1	throw down 2
doss down	hunker down	plonk down 2		

You also use **down** as an adverb in combinations which refer to someone putting something onto a surface. For example, if you **slap** something **down** on a table, you put it on the table with a lot of force.

bang down	plonk down 1	put down 1,2	slam down 1,2	stick down 1
lay down 1,3	plump down 2	set down 1	slap down 1	throw down 1

A few combinations with **down** refer to movement towards you either horizontally or in time, rather than from a higher position to a lower one. For example, if something **bears down on** you, it approaches you, and if traditions or stories **are passed down** to you, they are taught or told to you by an older generation.

bear down upon	get down 5	hand down 1	move down 2	pass down 1,3
come down 9,10	go down 3,4			

2 Decreasing, lowering, and reducing

Down occurs as an adverb in combinations which refer to a decrease or lowering in size, degree, standard, intensity, and so on. For example, if the cost of something **goes down,** it becomes less expensive; if you **turn down** a television, radio, or record player, you make it quieter; and if you **water down** food or drink, you make it weaker.

Some of the combinations describe processes of reducing the physical size of something, perhaps by cutting or removing part of it. For example, if you **grind** something **down,** you make it smoother and smaller by rubbing it against a hard surface or on a machine. A few combinations refer to complete changes in state or shape. For example, if you **melt** something **down,** you melt it until it melts completely, and if a substance **breaks down,** it separates into the parts from which it is made.

Other combinations include verbs which are also adjectives, in particular adjectives describing qualities which are low in intensity or amount, such as *cool, narrow,* and *quiet.* These combinations express ideas of something becoming even lower in intensity or amount. For example, if something **cools down,** it becomes cooler, and if you **narrow down** a choice or subject, you make it narrower or more selective.

beat down 3	cool down 1,2	knock down 5	quiet down	slow down 1,2
boil down 1,2	count down	let down 2,3	quieten down	thin down
boil down to	cut down 1	mark down 2,3	render down	throttle down
break down 3,4	cut down on	melt down	round down	tone down
bring down 2	damp down 1,2	move down 3,4	run down 3,4,5	turn down 2,3
calm down 1,2	dampen down 1	narrow down	scale down	water down 1,2
change down	die down	pare down	settle down 3,4	whittle down
come down 6,7,14	go down 7,8,9,10	pipe down	simmer down	wind down 2,3
come down to	grind down 2	play down		

3 Fastening and fixing

You use **down** as an adverb in combinations where you are describing processes of fastening or fixing something to the ground, or making it secure. For example, if you **nail** something **down,** you use nails to fasten it to a lower surface, and when something **beds down,** it settles firmly into position so that it cannot be shaken loose. Some of these combinations have metaphorical meanings. For example, you talk about **nailing** people **down** when you mean that you are forcing them to state clearly their opinions or intentions.

batten down	lay down 5,6	put down 3	stick down 2	tie down 1,2
bed down 3	nail down 1,2,3	screw down	tack down	weight down
lash down 1	pin down 1,2	stamp down	tamp down	

4 Collapsing, attacking and destroying

You use **down** as an adverb in combinations which contain ideas of collapsing, cutting, and destruction. **Down** helps to give the idea that something falls to the ground or is forced to the ground during the process. For example, if you **chop down** a tree, you cut through its trunk until it falls, and if a building **burns down,** it is completely destroyed by fire and collapses onto the ground.

Other combinations contain ideas of attacking, destroying, and killing. For example, when people **are mown down,** they are killed in a violent way, and when someone or something **is brought down,** they are attacked and killed, and fall to the ground.

batter down	chop down	gun down	pull down 2	strike down
blow down	come down 4,5	hack down	put down 4,14	swoop down 2
break down 6,7	cut down 2	hew down	run down 6,10	take down 4
bring down 3,4	dress down	kick down	shoot down 1	tear down
burn down	fall down 1,2,3	knock down 1,2,3	slip down 1	tumble down
call down on	go down 1,2,14	mow down	smash down	

5 Defeating and suppressing

Down occurs as an adverb in combinations which have 'defeat' as part of their meaning. For example, if you **argue** someone **down,** you succeed in forcing them to accept your point of view during an argument, and if you **back down,** you accept someone else's point of view. **Down** also occurs in combinations which mean 'suppress'. For example, if someone **clamps down** on you, they take action to control you or stop you doing something, and if people **are kept down,** they are not allowed to have any power.

argue down	come down on	go down 15,16	knock down 4	stare down
back down	crack down	go down with	pin down 3	take down 6
break down 5	do down	grind down 1	pull down 3	talk down 1
bring down 1,5	drag down 1,2	hold down 1,2,3,4,5	put down 9,10	tie down 3
cast down 1	draw down	hoot down	shoot down 2	vote down
come down with	face down	howl down	shout down	wave down 2
clamp down	fight down	keep down 1,3	slap down 2	wear down 1
climb down	get down 8			

6 Completing or failing

Down is used in combinations to give an idea of thoroughness or completeness, and usually of ending or failing. It is always adverbial in these combinations. For example, if you **shut** a business **down,** it stops trading altogether, and if you **hunt** someone **down,** you hunt them and succeed in finding them. Some of the combinations mean 'stop functioning'. For example, if a machine **breaks down,** it stops operating.

break down 1,2	go down 18,19	ram down 2	stand down 1,2	turn down 1
close down 1,2	hunt down	run down 7	step down	wave down 1
come down 12	lay down 7,8,9	send down 1,2	strip down	weigh down 1,2
fall down 4,5	let down 1	settle down 2	throw down 3	wind down 4
flag down	load down 1,2	shut down 1,2	track down	

7 Eating and drinking

Down occurs as an adverb in combinations which refer to eating and drinking, and the action of food or drink passing from your mouth into your stomach. For example, if you **bolt down** your food, you eat it very quickly. **Down** also occurs in combinations such as **hold down** and **keep down,** where you are talking about food remaining in a person's stomach, for example if you are talking about someone who is ill and therefore likely to vomit.

bolt down	gobble down	keep down 4	swallow down	toss down
drink down	gulp down	slip down 2	swill down	wash down 1
get down 6	hold down 6	stay down 2	throw down 4	wolf down
go down 12				

8 Writing and recording

You use **down** as an adverb in combinations which mean 'write' or 'record'. For example, if you **note** something **down,** you write it somewhere. It also occurs in a few combinations such as **go down as** and **put down to** which express ideas of deciding that something is a particular kind of thing, or that something is caused by a particular kind of thing.

copy down	hand down 2	mark down as	put down to	stick down 3
get down 7	jot down	note down	run down 8	take down 5
go down 17	lay down 2	put down 7,8,12,13	set down 2,3	write down
go down as	mark down 1	put down as	set down as	

9 Cleaning and flattening

You use **down** as an adverb in combinations which describe processes of cleaning, smoothing, or brushing surfaces, such as walls or the outside of objects. For example, if you **wash down** a wall, you clean it thoroughly with water, and if you **smooth down** the clothes that you are wearing, you press them until they lie flat.

brush down	dampen down 2	rub down 1,2	smooth down	wash down 2
clean down	dust down	sand down	sponge down	wear down 2
damp down 3	hose down	slick down	swab down	wipe down

10 Work and activities

A few combinations which contain **down** as an adverb express ideas of starting to work at something. For example, if you **settle down** to work, you begin to work seriously.

buckle down	get down to	knuckle down	settle down 1	sit down 3

for is a preposition. It occurs in 63 phrasal verbs in this dictionary. **For** is one of the commonest words of English, and it is especially used when stating reasons, causes, purposes, aims, and so on. It often has no special use or meaning in combinations with verbs, apart from introducing a noun group in which you mention a reason, purpose, aim, and so on. For example, if you **make for** a place, you move in that direction; if you **angle for** something, you try to obtain it by indirect means; and if you **live for** something, that is the most important thing in your life.

For is also used to introduce the noun group which indicates the thing or person that you are dealing with or considering. For example, if you **allow for** something in your planning, you make sure that you will be able to deal with it; if you **root for** someone, you encourage them while they are doing something difficult; and if you **fall for** someone, you become very attracted to them or fond of them. **For** also occurs as the second particle in combinations which include two particles, for example **cry out for** and **stand up for.**

Some meanings of **for** are used in only a few combinations. For example, if an animal **goes for** you, it attacks you, and if someone **is gunning for** you, they are trying in a determined way to harm you.

forth is an adverb. It occurs in 11 phrasal verbs in this dictionary. It is a rather formal, literary, or old-fashioned word.

1 Departure
Forth occurs in literal combinations with intransitive verbs which express ideas of departing from one place and going somewhere else. For example, if someone **sallies forth,** they go somewhere quickly and energetically, and if they **venture forth,** they go somewhere that might be dangerous.

2 Production
Forth also occurs in combinations which express ideas of something being produced or stated. They can be regarded as metaphorical or extended uses of the previous category. For example, if things **pour forth,** they appear suddenly in large quantities; and if you **set forth** an opinion, you present it to people by stating it clearly.

bring forth	come forth	pour forth	put forth	set forth
call forth	hold forth			

forward is an adverb. It occurs in 10 phrasal verbs in this dictionary. Its basic meaning is to do with movement in a direction in front of you.

1 Advancement in time and position
Forward occurs in a few combinations which refer to time. For example, if you **bring** something **forward,** it happens at an earlier time than planned, and if you **look forward to** something in the future, you want it to happen and expect to enjoy it. **Forward** also occurs in a few combinations which refer to position. For example, if you **carry forward** an amount when you are doing accounts, you write it at the top of the next page or column.

bring forward 1	go forward 1	look forward to	put forward 3	wind forward
carry forward				

2 Presenting and appearing
Forward also occurs in combinations which contain ideas of something being presented or produced. These combinations sometimes refer to suggestions and offers. For example, if you **bring forward** an argument, you state it so that it can be discussed, and if you **step forward** in a difficult situation, you offer to help.

bring forward 2	come forward with	push forward	put forward 1	step forward
come forward	go forward 2			

from is a preposition. It occurs in 23 phrasal verbs in this dictionary. **From** is one of the commonest words of English, and it is especially used when mentioning sources or origins, or when indicating ideas of separation and exclusion. It is mostly used in the same ways in phrasal verb combinations.

1 Sources and origins

From is used in literal combinations with verbs which express ideas of developing, appearing, or originating. The noun group after **from** refers to the source or origins of whatever has developed, appeared, or originated. For example, if one word **derives from** another, the second word is the origin of the first, if something **emanates from** a particular person or thing, they started it, and if someone **hails from** a particular place, they were born there or live there.

2 Separation and prevention

From is used in literal combinations which express ideas of separation, prevention, difference, and exclusion. The noun group after **from** refers to the thing which is now separated, prevented, different, or excluded. For example, if you **depart from** an accepted belief or practice, you believe or do something different; if you **keep** someone **from** doing something, you stop them doing it; and if you **hide from** someone or something, you go somewhere where they cannot see you. **From** also occurs with this meaning as the second particle in combinations which include two particles, for example **get away from** and **set apart from**.

in is an adverb and a preposition. It occurs in 209 phrasal verbs in this dictionary. The basic meaning of **in** is to do with movement from the outside of an enclosed space or container to the inside of it. **Out** often has opposite meanings. **Into** is often used instead of **in** as a preposition when referring to movement, and phrasal verbs containing **into** are treated as separate entries.

1 Movement, entering, and arriving

In is used most frequently in literal combinations which express ideas of entering a place or arriving there. For example, if someone **breezes in,** they enter a place in a carefree manner, and if you **let** someone **in,** you open a door so that they can enter. When people or things **pour in,** large numbers of them arrive somewhere; if you **fly in,** you arrive at a place by aeroplane; and if a train **pulls in,** it enters the station as it arrives. A few combinations have an additional meaning of registering your arrival officially. For example, if you **book in** at a hotel, you arrive there and tell the hotel staff that you have arrived; if a competitor in a race or boxing match **weighs in,** they register their weight before the race or match begins; and if a person in authority **swears** someone **in,** they register them officially. **In** is also used in combinations where it has the meaning 'approach'. These combinations are sometimes followed by the preposition *on*. For example, if something **zeroes in on** another thing, it moves towards it.

ask in	crowd in	invite in	put in 14,15,18	squeeze in
book in 1,2	draw in 1,2	let in 1	roll in 3	stop in 2
breeze in	drop in	look in 1	run in 1	storm in
call in 2	flood in	move in 1,2,3	ship in	swear in
check in 1,2	fly in	pile in	show in	take in 1,2,12
clock in 2	get in 1,2,3,7	pop in	sign in 1,2	weigh in 2
close in 3	go in 1,2,3,4,6,7	pour in	slip in 2	zero in on 1,2
come in 1,2,3,4,5,7, 11,16,19	home in 1,2	pull in 1,2	squash in	zoom in

2 Inserting, penetrating, and absorbing

In is used in combinations which refer to the insertion of one thing inside another, sometimes going through a barrier of some kind, or to one thing absorbing another. For example, if water or air **comes in,** it penetrates a barrier and enters a place; if you **breathe in,** air moves into your lungs as you take a breath; and if you **stick** something **in,** you insert it somewhere. A few combinations with **in** are used to talk about gaining access to information, especially electronic information, after first passing through an entry system. For example, when you **log in** on a computer, you gain access to the system by typing a special word. Some of these combinations are used in an extended way. For example, you talk about information **going in** when you mean that you have understood it, as if the information had penetrated a barrier of some kind, and you say that you **soak** yourself **in** a subject when you study it intensely. It can also be used to say that you absorb something such as an atmosphere, so if you **drink in** your surroundings, you behave or feel as if you were able to take them into your body.

breathe in	drink in	plough in	ram in	take in 7,13
bury in	go in 5,8	plug in	set in 2	tap in
clock in	key in	plumb in	sink in 1,2,3,4	throw in 1,2,3
come in 6	let in 2	pump in	slip in 1	tuck in 1,2
delve in	log in	punch in	soak in	tune in
draw in 3	pay in	put in 1,2,3,4,6,19,20	stick in 1,2,3,4,5	type in

3 Collapsing, damaging, surrendering, and ending.

In occurs in combinations which have meanings to do with damage or destruction. For example, if a roof or building **caves in,** it collapses inwards, and if you **kick in** a door, you break it down by kicking it from the outside. **In** also occurs in combinations which express ideas of surrender or defeat. For example, if you **give in,** you accept that you have to do something that you did not want to do. A few combinations with **in** are used to indicate that an activity ends. For example, if you **jack in** your job, you stop doing it.

bash in 1,2	chuck in	fall in 1	jack in	pack in 1,2
break in 1	do in 1,2	give in 1	kick in	smash in
cave in 1,2				

4 Mixing and including

In occurs in phrasal verbs which express ideas of two things being combined, so that they form a single substance. For example, if you **stir** a substance **in,** you add it to another substance and mix them together. **In** also occurs in combinations which refer to things being included in a larger group. For example, if someone who is selling several things **throws** an item **in,** they agree to include it in the price of those things, and if you **reckon** an item **in** when you are calculating something, you include it in your calculations.

Some combinations with **in** are used to say that two or more things seem to belong together. These combinations are sometimes followed by the preposition *with*. For example, if one thing **chimes in with** another, they are consistent with each other.

add in	dig in 1	include in 1,2	sketch in 1	tie in with
blend in	dub in	ink in 2	squeeze in 2	tone in
build in 1,2	fit in 1,2,3	merge in	stir in	trade in
chime in with	fit in with	mix in 1	stand in	work in 1,2,3
chip in 1	fold in	put in 8	take in 8	write in 2,3
copy in	get in 8	reckon in	throw in 4	

5 Gathering, collecting, and fetching

In is used as an adverb in combinations which have meanings associated with gathering or collecting something, and fetching or taking it somewhere. For example, if you **get in** the washing, you collect it and bring it indoors, and if someone **calls** something **in,** they ask for it to be collected and returned to them. If you collect a lot of things over a period of time, you can also use **in** to talk about accumulating those things, especially money. For example, if you talk about **raking in** money, you are talking in an informal way about earning a lot of money, and if you **lay in** food, you buy it and store it to use later. **In** also occurs in combinations where you are talking about fetching people and taking them somewhere. For example, if the police **haul** you **in,** they arrest you and take you to the police station. **In** is sometimes used to talk about giving something to a person who is authorized to collect and deal with it. For example, if you **hand in** a piece of work, someone collects it from you and if you **cash** something **in,** you give it to someone in exchange for money.

bring in 2	gather in	lay in	reel in	take in 5,10,11
buy in	get in 4,5	pack in 3	roll in 1,2	trade in
call in 3	give in 2	pull in 3,4,5	run in 2	turn in 2,3,4
cash in 1	hand in 1,2,3	put in 9	send in 1,2	write in 1
come in 8,18	haul in	rake in		

6 Filling

In is used in a small number of combinations to say that you complete a shape or hole by filling it with something. For example, if you **colour** a shape or outline **in,** you fill the space with a colour, and if you **fill in** a gap in something such as a wall, you put a substance inside it to cover the gap.

block in 2	colour in	ink in 1	pencil in	shade in
brick in	fill in 1,2,3			

7 Remaining somewhere

Some phrasal verbs with **in** mean that someone stays in a particular place, or stays at home, instead of going somewhere else. For example, if you **eat in,** you have your meal at home rather than going to a restaurant for it, and if you **stop in,** you stay at home rather than going out. Some of the combinations in this category are to do with more long-term arrangements. For example, if a servant or student **lives in,** they stay in the same place to work, study, and sleep, rather than going elsewhere for some of these activities. **Out** is sometimes used with the opposite meaning, to indicate that someone goes to a different place, instead of staying at home.

dig in 2	lie in	repose in 1	stay in	take in 3
eat in	live in 1	sleep in	stop in 1	wait in
keep in 2				

8 Restricting and preventing

In occurs with a number of verbs to say that you keep someone somewhere and do not allow them to get out. For example, if you **lock** someone **in,** you put them somewhere and lock the door so that they cannot escape. Some of these combinations are usually used in the passive. For example, you talk about people being **hemmed in, snowed in,** or **walled in,** when they cannot move from a place. **In** is always an adverb with verbs like these. Some of these combinations are used metaphorically to express ideas of repressing or preventing something. For example, you can say that someone **holds in** a feeling when they do not allow themselves to show it, or that something is **hedged in** by problems when those problems put restrictions on the things that it is possible to do.

block in 1	close in 1,2	hem in 1,2	pen in 1,2	snow in
box in	crowd in on	hold in	rein in	strap in
brick in	fence in	keep in 1	shut in	wall in
buckle in	hedge in	lock in		

9 Being involved and active

A large number of combinations with **in** express ideas of involvement with activities. For example, if you **count** someone **in,** you include them in an activity or task, and if you say that you **want in,** you mean that you would like to be involved. When **in** is prepositional, the noun group after **in** refers to the activity that people are involved with. For example, if you **dabble in** an activity, you do it occasionally and not seriously. Some of these combinations are followed by the preposition *on:* the noun group after *on* refers to the activity that you are talking about. For example, if you **muscle in** *on* an activity, you get involved in a situation where you are not wanted. You can also use some combinations in this category to talk about relationships with other people. They are usually used with the preposition *with* in this case. For example, if you **keep in** with someone, you try to become involved with them and the things they are interested in, and if you **fall in with** someone, you start to become friends with them. You can use **in** in a similar way to say that you become accustomed to an activity or situation. For example, if you **break** someone **in,** you help them to get used to a new job, and if you **settle in,** you get used to living or working somewhere.

Some combinations with **in** refer to the interruption of an activity. For example, if you **butt in** when someone is talking, you enter the conversation by speaking at the same time as they do. **In** is always adverbial in these combinations. Some of them can be used with the preposition *on:* you mention the person or thing in the noun group after *on.*

barge in	dabble in	have in	muck in	send in 3,4
break in 2,3,4,5	deal in 1,2	horn in	muscle in	settle in
break in on	dip in	interfere in	opt in	sink in 5
break in upon	dive in	join in	partake in	sit in 1,2
bring in 3,4	dob in 2	jump in	phone in 1,2,3,4	start in
burst in on	drag in	keep in with	pitch in	step in
butt in	engage in	land in	plunge in	stick in 6
call in 1	fall in with	let in for	push in 1,2	take in 4,9
cash in 2	fill in 5	let in on	put in 5,7,10,11,13	throw in 5
chime in	get in 6,9	listen in	put in for	toss in
chip in 2	get in on	look in 2	ring in	wade in
come in 12,13,15	get in with	meddle in	rope in	walk in on
contract in	go in for 1,2,3	mix in	rush in	want in
count in	go in with	move in 4	run in 3	weigh in 1
cut in 1,2				

10 Beginning
A few combinations with **in** are used to indicate that an activity begins. For example, if you **lead in,** you begin a discussion by making a short speech and if a situation **sets in,** it begins to take place.

bring in 1	creep in	fade in	phase in	tuck in 3
come in 9,10,14,17,20	dig in 3	lead in	set in 1	usher in

11 Focussing: actions, attitudes, and qualities
In also occurs as a preposition in a few combinations where you are talking about actions and attitudes. The noun group after **in** refers to the focus of the action or attitude. For example, if you **glory in** something, you take great pleasure in it, and if you **put** trust or confidence **in** someone, you feel confident or hopeful about something that they are going to do. **In** can be used to indicate that someone or something has a certain quality. For example, if you say that a quality or characteristic **resides in** someone or something, you mean they have it.

believe in 1,2,3	delight in	luxuriate in	result in	see in
confide in	glory in	repose in	revel in	wallow in
couch in	indulge in	reside in		

into is a preposition. It occurs in 112 phrasal verbs in this dictionary. Its basic meanings are to do firstly with movement from the outside of something to the inside, and secondly with change. **Out of** often has opposite meanings.

1 Movement, entering, and arrival
Into is used in literal combinations which express ideas of entering a place. You mention the place in the noun group after **into.** For example, if people **crowd into** a place, they all squeeze in there; if you say that someone **rolls into** a place, you mean that they arrive there very casually; and if you **see** someone **into** a place, you enter it with them.

2 Inserting, penetrating, and placing

Into occurs in combinations which refer to the insertion of one thing inside another, sometimes going through a barrier of some kind. The noun group after **into** refers to the place where it is inserted. For example, if you **plug** an electrical appliance **into** a socket, you insert the plug in the socket, and if you **delve into** a container, you put your hand inside it. Some combinations refer to someone or something being put in a particular place, position, institution, and so on. For example, if you **buckle** someone **into** a seat, you fasten them there, for example with a safety belt, and if you **pay** money **into** a bank account, you transfer it there. Some combinations are used with metaphorical meanings. For example, if you say that someone's eyes **bored into** you, you mean that they stared at you intensely, and if you **drill** something **into** someone, you make them understand or remember it by continually repeating it, as if you are going through a barrier of some kind. A few combinations with **into** are used to talk about gaining access to information, especially electronic information, after first passing through an entry system. For example, if you **log into** a computer, you gain access to the system by typing a special word.

bore into	dip into	log into	ram into 2	take into 3
buckle into	dive into 1	pay into	sink into 3	tap into
build into 1	drill into	plug into	slip into 2	throw into
delve into	drum into	plumb into	slot into 2	tuck into 1
dig into	go into 11	put into	strap into	tune into
din into	let into 3			

3 Mixing and inclusion

Into occurs in combinations which express ideas of one thing being included as part of another: you mention the second thing in the noun group after **into**. For example, if you **build** something **into** a statement or plan, you include it in your statement or plan, and if you **marry into** a family, you marry a member of that family, and so become a part of it. **Into** is also used to suggest that one thing combines with another thing, often in a way which makes it hard to tell them apart. For example, if one colour **shades into** another, it is so similar to that other colour that it is hard to tell which is which, and if you **mix** one substance **into** another, you put it with the other substance and stir them so that they are blended together. A few combinations with **into** refer to the spending of money or other resources such as time on a particular plan or project. These combinations often imply that large amounts of money or resources are involved, so if you **pump** money **into** a business or organization, you invest large sums of money in it. **Into** is also used in a few combinations which refer to things fitting or belonging to particular categories. For example, if something **fits into** a particular group, it logically belongs to that group.

blend into	fold into	mix into	put into	slot into 1
bring into 2	marry into	phase into	run into 6	stir into
build into 2	melt into 2	plough into	shade into	work into
fall into 3	merge into	pump into	sink into 5	write into
fit into				

4 Changing

Into occurs in several combinations, which describe processes of change from one form or situation to another. The noun group after **into** refers to the new form or situation. For example, if one thing **turns into** another thing, it becomes that other thing; if something **burst into** flames, it suddenly begins to burn; and if an experience **makes** you **into** a particular type of person, you become that type of person because of that experience. A few of these combinations are used to say that someone starts behaving in a particular way. For example, if someone **bursts into** tears, they suddenly begin crying, and if they **lapse into** silence, they stop talking or making a noise.

break into	fly into	lapse into	put into 7	slip into 4
burst into	get into 4	launch into	roll into 1	take into 5
divide into	go into 7	make into	settle into	throw into 4
dub into	grow into	melt into 1	sink into 4	turn into
fall into				

5 Involvement and activities

Into occurs in combinations which express ideas of starting to be involved with an activity. You mention the activity in the noun group after **into.** For example, if you **enter into** a discussion with someone, you start to have a discussion with them, and if you **head into** a situation, you start to experience it. Some of these combinations express the idea of getting interested in a particular subject, especially in a hurried or enthusiastic way. For example, if you **pitch into** a particular task, you start to do it with a lot of energy; if you **dive into** an activity, you start to be involved without any preparation; and if you **fling** yourself **into** an activity, you begin to do it energetically and enthusiastically. A few combinations with **into** refer to the interruption of an activity. For example, if you **barge into** a conversation, you enter it by interrupting someone. **Into** also occurs in combinations which refer to the thorough investigation of something. For example, if you **delve into** a matter, you try to discover more information about it.

break into 3	enter into	head into	pitch into 1	take into 5
buy into	fling into	inquire into	plunge into	throw into 5
delve into 2	get into	look into	push into 2	wade into
dive into 2	go into 6	move into 3	rush into	walk into 1

6 Persuasion and forcing

Into occurs in combinations with transitive verbs which have the meaning of persuading or forcing someone to become involved in an activity. You mention the activity in the noun group after **into.** For example, if you **frighten** someone **into** doing something, you frighten them in order to force them to do that thing, and if you **trick** them **into** it, you get them to do it by fooling or misleading them.

bluff into	force into	press into	shame into	talk into
coax into	frighten into	pull into 2	shock into	trap into
drag into	goad into	push into 1	starve into	trick into
draw into				

7 Contact, colliding, meeting, and attacking

Into occurs in combinations which refer to contact, and mean 'collide', 'meet', or 'attack'. The noun group after **into** refers to the person or thing that you collide with, meet, or attack. Some of these combinations suggest that the collision is fairly violent, so that if one vehicle **ploughs into** another one, it hits it forcefully, and if you **ram** one object **into** another, you move it so that it hits the other thing very hard. Some of the combinations simply mean that you meet something or someone, perhaps by chance. For example, if you **bump into** someone, you meet them unexpectedly. A few combinations are used to say that one person is attacking another person, either physically or by shouting at them and criticizing them. For example, if someone **tears into** you, they criticize you very severely, and if someone **lays into** you, they start to hit or kick you.

bang into	go into 13	lay into	plough into 1	run into
barge into 3	lam into	pitch into 2	ram into	tear into
bump into	lash into			

8 Consumption and using

Into occurs in combinations which mean 'consume' or 'use'. The noun group after **into** refers to the thing which is consumed or used. Some of these combinations suggest that you are doing so for the first time. For example, if you **break into** a sum of money that you have saved, you start to spend it, and if you **tuck into** food, you start to eat it. Other combinations refer to processes of destruction and damaging. For example, if one thing **bites into** another, it presses its surface and damages it, and if clothing **eats into** your body, it is too tight and causes you pain.

bite into	cut into	eat into	lay into 3	tuck into 2
break into 5	dip into			

of is a prepositional particle. **Of** is one of the commonest words of English, and it is mainly used with nouns in order to introduce and specify relationships of belonging, possession, or connection. It also has many general uses such as stating what something is, what it contains, what it is made from, or how much of it there is.

Of occurs in 30 phrasal verbs in this dictionary. Some of its meanings occur in very few combinations, most of which are old-fashioned or formal. For example, **admit of** and **permit of** can be used when talking about the range of possibilities in a situation; and **become of** and **come of** when referring to the final result of a situation. **Of** has four main uses in phrasal verbs.

1 Knowledge and its communication
Of is used in some phrasal verbs to introduce the fact, knowledge, or piece of information that is being received or given. For example, if you **hear of** someone or something, you get news about them for the first time. If you **apprise** someone **of** something, you inform them about it, and if you **remind** them **of** it, you tell them about it so that they remember it.

apprise of	hear of	make of	remind of 1	think of
deliver of 1	know of			

2 Attributing qualities
Some phrasal verbs are used to state or claim that people or things have a particular quality or characteristic. For example, if something **partakes of** a particular quality, it has that quality, and if someone or something **reminds** you **of** another, they make you think of the other person or thing, because they are similar in some way.

partake of 2	remind of 2	savour of	smack of	smell of
reek of				

3 Evaluation, approval, and disapproval
In some phrasal verbs with **of,** the meaning involves making a judgement about something and expressing an attitude based on that judgement. For example, if you **approve of** someone or something, you like and admire them; and if you **tire of** something, you lose interest in it.

approve of	disapprove of	dream of 1	tire of	weary of
despair of				

4 Removal and elimination
You use **of** in a number of phrasal verbs with the meaning that something is removed from a person or situation, or is dealt with so that it does not remain or continue to have an effect. For example, if you **deprive** someone **of** something, you take it away from them or prevent them from having it.

deprive of	dispose of	partake of 1	rid of	strip of
disabuse of	divest of	relieve of	starve of	

off is an adverb and a preposition. It occurs in 233 phrasal verbs in this dictionary. The basic meaning of **off** is to do with movement away from something or separation from it. **On** sometimes has opposite meanings to **off.**

1 Departure
Literal verb combinations with **off** as an adverb or preposition often give an idea of departure, so when a rocket **blasts off,** it leaves the ground and starts its journey into space, and if you **get off** a bus, you leave it. When **off** is an adverb, **away** often has a similar meaning. With transitive verbs, **off** indicates that someone or something is being sent to another place. For example, if you **pack** someone **off** somewhere, you send them there.

Some combinations emphasize the manner of departure, for example casualness or even secrecy is implied in **slip off** and **slope off.** Several combinations are used as imperatives to tell someone in a rude way to go away, for example **clear off** and **bog off.** A few verbs in combination with **off** indicate that something such as heat or a smell is being released. For example, something might **give off** light or smoke, or **let off** a sound or energy. **Out** often has a similar meaning.

back off	fuck off	make off	send off 1,2,3,4,5	strike off 2
blast off	get off 1,2,3,4,5,6	move off	set off 1	take off 4,5,6,7
bog off	give off 1	naff off	shoot off 1	tear off 3
bugger off 1,2	go off 1	pack off	shove off	throw off 3
bundle off	go off with 1,2	peel off 4	slip off 1	trot off
buzz off	hare off	piss off 1	slope off	turn off 2
cart off	haul off	pop off 1,2	sod off	veer off
clear off	head off 3	push off 1,2,3	spirit off	wave off 1,2
come off 1,6	lead off 1	put off 6	start off 1	write off 1
drop off 2	let off 4,5,6	run off 1,2,3,4,6	storm off	zoom off
fire off 1	lift off	see off 1,2		

2 Removing and disposing

Off as an adverb or preposition in literal combinations often implies removing or disposing of something that you no longer need or want. For example, if you **take** your shoes **off,** you remove them, and if you **score off** an item from a list, you remove it from the list. **Off** can also be used in combinations such as **make off with** which implies stealing. In relation to people, **off** can imply removing them from your area of responsibility, so that if you **marry** your daughter or son **off,** you find a suitable person for them to marry, and if someone **is pensioned off,** their employers or the government make them retire from work. In a few combinations referring to people, **off** can mean 'kill', so if a person **knocks** somebody **off,** they kill them.

auction off	ease off 2	mark off 3	saw off	steam off
blow off 1,2	fall off 1	marry off	score off 2	strain off
break off 1	finish off 5	pare off	scrape off	strike off 1
bump off	fling off	pay off 3	scrub off	strip off 1,2
burn off	get off 9	peel off 1,2,3	sell off	sweat off 1,2
cast off 1,2,3	hack off	pension off 1	shave off 1,2	take off 1,2,3,8
check off	help off with	pick off 1,2	shear off	tear off 1,2
chip off	hive off	pour off	shoot off 2	throw off 1,2
chop off	kick off 1	put off 7	siphon off 1,2	tick off 1,2
come off 2	kill off	round off 2	skim off	trim off
cross off	knock off 1,4,6	rub off 1	slip off 2,3	walk off with 1
cut off 1	leave off 1,2	run off 7	slough off 1,2	wash off 1,2
draw off	lop off 1	run off with	soak off	wipe off 1
dust off	make off with			

3 Obstructing and separating

In several phrasal verbs with **off,** the verb indicates a type of barrier, and the combination has the meaning of obstructing, blocking, or separating. For example, if the police **cone off** a lane of a motorway, they place plastic cones on the road so that people cannot drive on that lane, and if you **partition off** part of a room, you build a partition wall to separate that part of the room. Sometimes, the verb itself conveys the sense of obstruction or separation, as in **close off** and **split off.**

block off	cone off	fence off	rule off	shut off 3
box off	cordon off	go off 6	rope off	spin off
branch off 1	curtain off	head off 1	screen off	split off 1,2
brick off	cut off 2	mark off 1	seal off 1,2	wall off
close off	divide off	partition off	separate off	

4 Rejecting

Some combinations with **off** have the meaning of rejection. Sometimes they refer to abandoning a particular habit or thing, so if you **swear off** alcohol, you decide to stop drinking it altogether. Other combinations imply that you are ignoring something. For example, if you **shrug off** or **brush off** what somebody says, you ignore it.

brush off 1,2,3	laugh off	put off 1	shuffle off	wipe off 2
fend off 2	lay off 1,3	shake off	shut off 4	write off 2,3
keep off 3,4	pass off 2	shrug off	swear off	

5 Preventing and protecting

Verb combinations with **off** often indicate that you are doing something to protect yourself or to prevent something from happening. For example, if you **ward off** something unpleasant or dangerous, you prevent it from affecting you or harming you, and if you **pay** someone **off,** you give them money in order to stop them threatening you or causing you trouble.

beat off	fend off 1	hold off 1,2	scare off 1,2	throw off 4
buy off	fight off	keep off 1,2	stand off	ward off 1,2
chase off	get off 8	pay off 2	stave off	warn off
drive off	head off 2	put off 2,3,4		

6 Beginning

You can use **off** to imply starting to do something, so if a discussion **kicks off,** it starts. Combinations with transitive verbs convey a sense of causing something to begin. For example, if something **sparks off** an argument, it causes the argument to start.

get off with	lead off 2	spark off	tee off	trigger off
kick off 2,3	set off 2,4	start off 2,3,4	touch off	

7 Stopping and cancelling

Phrasal verbs with **off** can also imply the ending of something. For example, if you **knock off** work, you stop working and if someone's voice **trails off,** it gradually stops. Sometimes the verb conveys the reason why something has stopped, so if an event **is rained off,** it stops or is cancelled because of the rain.

beg off	cut off 3,4,5	lay off 2	rain off	stop off
break off 2,3,4	get off 7,11	leave off 3,4,5	ring off	switch off 1,2,3,4
call off 1,2	go off 4,8,9	let off 1	shut off 1,2	take off 9,12,13,14
clock off	give off 3	log off	sign off 1,2	trail off
come off 5,7	hoot off	pension off 2	stay off	turn off 1,3
cry off	knock off 3,9	put off 5		

8 Decreasing

Off is frequently used to show that something decreases. For example, if a feeling **passes off** or **eases off,** it decreases. **Off** sometimes combines with verbs formed from adjectives to indicate that something gradually has less of a quality. So if a hot object **cools off,** it loses heat and becomes cooler, and if a wet object **dries off,** it loses some of its moisture and becomes drier. Some combinations, such as **sleep off** and **work off,** refer to an activity which you do in order to reduce the effect of something unpleasant.

cool off 1,2	fall off 2	level off 1,3	slacken off	taper off
die off	get off 12	lop off 2	sleep off	walk off
drop off 3	knock off 2	pass off 3	tail off 1,2	wear off
dry off	let off 2	set off against	take off 10	work off 1
ease off 1				

9 Finishing and completing

People often use **off** to indicate that an activity or process is completed. For example, if you **polish off** a piece of work, you finish it, and if an event **passes off** in a particular way, it happens and ends that way.

bring off	go off 5	play off	reel off	top off
carry off 1,2	knock off 5	polish off 1,2	round off 1	toss off 2
come off 3,4	pass off 1	print off	run off 5	work off 2
dash off	pay off 1	rattle off	see off 3	write off 4
finish off 1,2,3				

10 Consuming

Phrasal verbs with **off** as a preposition sometimes indicate that something is being consumed or used. For example if someone **lives off** a particular kind of food, they eat only that kind of food, and if a machine **runs off** a particular supply of power, it uses that power in order to make it work. You can also use some of these verbs in a pejorative way. For example, if you say that a person

is sponging off someone, it means that the person is taking advantage of their generosity. **On** can often be used with a similar meaning.

dine off	live off 2	sponge off	toss off 1	work off 3
feed off	run off 8			

11 falling asleep

There are a few phrasal verbs with **off** which refer to falling asleep, so if you **doze off** or **nod off,** you fall asleep.

doze off	drop off 1	get off 14	go off 10	nod off
drift off				

12 displaying

Verb combinations with **off** occasionally have a sense of putting on some sort of display, so if an object is **set off** by its background, the object is displayed more favourably because of its background, and if someone is **showing off** they are generally putting on some sort of display to try to impress people.

finish off	mouth off	set off 5	show off 1,2,3	sound off

13 Deceiving

Off sometimes occurs in phrasal verbs relating to deceiving or tricking. For example, if someone **fobs** something **off** on you, they deceive you into thinking it is worth having.

fob off	palm off	play off against	skive off	throw off 5
goof off	pass off as	rip off		

14 Exploding and firing

There is a small set of combinations with **off** which indicate that a weapon or an explosive device or material is fired or explodes. For example, if you **let off** a gun, a bomb, or a firework, you fire it or cause it to explode.

fire off 1	go off 2	let off 3	loose off	set off 3

on is an adverb and a preposition. It occurs in 199 phrasal verbs in this dictionary. The basic meaning of **on** is to do with position, indicating that one thing is above another, touching it and supported by it, or with movement into that position. **Onto** or **on to** is sometimes used instead of **on** as a preposition, and **upon** is a more formal alternative in some combinations. **Off** sometimes has opposite meanings to **on**.

1 Movement and position

On occurs in some literal combinations which refer to movement and position. For example, if you **get on** a bus, you **get** into it. Many of these combinations have extended meanings. For example, if an actor **walks on** in a play, he or she has a very unimportant part in it, and if someone **is sitting on** a task, they are not doing it quickly enough. To **look on** means to watch something, but with the added sense of not taking part in it. **Off** sometimes has opposite meanings.

call on 1	fall on 5	pile on 1	stamp on 1	trample on 1
come on 2,3	get on 1,2	put on 1	take on 5	wait on 3
come on to 1	go on 15	put on to 2	throw on 2	walk on
descend on	look on 1	sit on 2		

2 Holding, attaching, and adding

On is used in literal combinations which have 'hold', 'attach', or 'add' as part of their meaning. For example, if you **hang on,** you hold very tightly to something; if you **buckle** something **on,** you attach it by means of buckles; and if you **slap** paint **on,** you paint a surface carelessly. **On** also occurs in combinations which refer to dressing. For example, when you **put on** your clothes, you get dressed.

Off sometimes has opposite meanings, although often in combination with different verbs. For example, **put on** and **take off** have opposite meanings.

add on	hang on 1,3	move on 4	sew on	tack on
buckle on	have on 1	pile on 2	slap on	tag on
dab on	help on with	pull on 1,2	slip on	throw on 1
fall on 3	hold on 1,3	put on 2,3,4,7,	stick on 1,2	throw on to
get on 4	hold on to 1,2,3,5	14,20,22	strap on	try on 1
go on 13	latch on to 1,3	put on to 1		

3 Continuing

On is used in combinations which describe activities in order to say that an activity is continued or that it lasts for a long time. For example, if you **carry on** with an activity, you continue doing it, and if you **struggle on** with it, you manage to continue doing it with great difficulty. Some combinations imply that the activity continues for an unacceptably long time. For example, if you say that someone **drones on,** you mean that they talk in a boring way for a long time, and if a process **drags on,** it continues for longer than is necessary.

On is also used with verbs of movement, to indicate that a journey or movement continues. For example, if you **push on,** you continue travelling somewhere. **On** is used with transitive verbs in combinations such as **hand on** and **pass on** to indicate that something is given from one person to another, and so refers to a continuity of ownership.

bang on	grind on	linger on	press on 1,2	send on
bash on	hand on	live on 3	rabbit on	soldier on
carry on 1,2,3,4,5	harp on	move on 1,6	ramble on	stay on
drag on	hold on 2	pass on 1,2,3,5,7	rattle on	struggle on
drone on	hold on to 4,6	play on 3,4	roll on 1	tick on 1,2
get on 5,8	hurry on 1,2	plod on	rumble on	wave on
get on at	keep on 1,2,3	plough on	run on 1,2,3,4	wear on
go 1,2,4,5,6,7,8,9	keep on at	push on 1,2,3		

4 Progressing and encouraging

On is used in combinations which have progress as part of their meaning. For example, if something **is coming on,** it is making progress or developing, and if people's ideas **move on,** they change and become more modern. A few combinations are used to indicate progress in time. For example, when winter or night **draws on,** it approaches. **On** also occurs in combinations which mean 'encourage'. For example, if you **egg** someone **on,** you encourage them to do something foolish.

bring on 2	draw on 1	get on for	lead on	step on
cheer on	egg on	go on 10.1,17	move on 3,5	urge on 1
come on 1,10	get on 6,7,12	goad on	spur on	wind on

5 Beginning and operating

On is used in combinations which express ideas of beginning or starting. For example, if something **brings on** an illness, it causes it to occur. Some combinations such as **move on** to and **get on to** indicate change of topic in a conversation. **On** also occurs in combinations which refer to the operating of a machine or device. For example, when you **switch on** an electric light, you cause it to start shining, and if you **jam on** your brakes, you use them suddenly. **Off** is sometimes used with the opposite meaning, to indicate that something ceases to function.

bring on 1	cotton on	go on 12,16	log on	set on 3
cast on	embark on 1	grow on	move on 2	sign on 1,2
catch on 1,2	enter on	have on 2	move on to	start on 1
clock on	get on 5	jam on	pass on 6	switch on 1,2,3
come on 4,6,7,8,9	get on to 1	latch on to 2	put on 8,9,10,11	turn on 1,2,3
come on to 2,3				

6 Focussing: effects, actions, and feelings

On is used as a preposition in combinations which describe effects, actions, and feelings. **On** has a very general meaning or use in these combinations. Sometimes it appears to be a metaphorical use of the literal meanings of **on** to do with movement, position, or attachment, but in many cases, it has very little special meaning at all, and simply introduces a noun group which refers to the focus of the action described by the verb. This category of **on** includes a large number of combinations, and some of them are quite closely related to each other. Categories 7 to 10 of **on** are more specialized, and deal with particular groups of combinations, although **on** still has the same general meaning.

The noun group following **on** refers to the person or thing that is affected, or that the action or feeling is directed towards. For example, if you **prevail on** someone to do something, you persuade them to do it; if you **cheat on** someone, you behave dishonestly towards them; and if you **dote on** someone, you love them very much. A number of the combinations refer to actions such as giving, transferring, or aiming: after **on** you mention the person that something is given or transferred to, or the target that something is aimed at. For example, if you **lavish** money **on** someone, you spend a lot of money on them, and if someone **trains** a weapon **on** you, they aim it at you.

Upon can be substituted for **on** in many of these combinations.

bring on 3	gain on	pin on 1	seize on	stick on 3
cheat on 1,2	get on 10	play on 1,2	sell on	tell on 1,2
dawn on	grass on	pounce on 2	serve on 1,2	throw on 3,5
devolve on	heap on	pour on	sit on 1	train on
dote on	impress on 1,3	press on 3	skimp on	turn on 7
engage on	improve on	prevail on	split on	urge on 2
fall on 1	inform on	pull on 3	spring on 1	wait on 1,2
fasten on 1	lavish on	put on 15,17,18,21,23	squeal on	weigh on
foist on	lean 1	put on to 3	spy on	wish on
force on	look on 2	rat on	stamp on 2	work on 3
frown on	operate on	rebound on		

7 Attacking

On is used as a preposition in combinations which express ideas of attacking, either physically or, more often, by means of words. The verb is usually intransitive, and the noun group after **on** refers to the person or thing being attacked. For example, if an animal **turns on** you, it suddenly attacks you, and if you **round on** someone who has been criticizing you, you suddenly respond angrily. **Upon** can be substituted for **on** in some of these combinations.

beat on	jump on	pounce on 1	set on 1,2	trample on 2
dump on	lay on	prey on 1,2	spring on 2	turn on 4
fall on 4	pick on 1	round on	start on 2	

8 Closeness, interference, and connections

On is used as a preposition in combinations with intransitive verbs which express ideas of closeness and connection between two things. The noun group after **on** refers to one of the things, and the other is mentioned as the subject of the verb. Sometimes the two things are physically close. For example, if one country **borders on** another, the two countries are next to each other. In other cases, the connection is non-physical, and the combination implies interference or relevance. For example, if something **intrudes on** your way of life, it affects it in an unpleasant way, and if something such as a fact **bears on** a situation or matter, it is relevant to it. **Upon** can be substituted for **on** in some of these combinations.

bear on	encroach on 1,2	impose on	infringe on	prey on 3
border on 1,2	fasten on 2	impress on 2	intrude on	verge on
close on	impinge on			

9 Discovering

On is used as a preposition in a few combinations which have 'find' as part of their meaning. The noun group after **on** refers to the thing which you find. For example if you **stumble on** something, you find it unexpectedly, and if you **hit on** the solution to a problem, you find or think of the solution. **Upon** can be substituted for **on** in some of these combinations, and **across** has a similar meaning.

chance on	happen on	light on	strike on	stumble on
come on 5	hit on			

10 Subjects and topics

On occurs as a preposition in combinations which refer to processes of mentioning, stating, deciding, thinking, and so on. The noun group after **on** refers to the subject or topic about which you are talking, deciding, or thinking. For example, if you **pronounce on** something, you give an expert opinion or judgement about it; if you **touch on** a subject, you mention it briefly; and if you **chew on** a problem, you think about it carefully for a long time. **Upon** can be substituted for **on** in some of these combinations.

brood on	dwell on	expand on	reflect on	throw on 4
centre on	elaborate on	fix on	remark on	touch on
chew on	embroider on	insist on	settle on 1	turn on 6
decide on	enlarge on	pronounce on	sleep on	

11 Depending and expecting

On is used as a preposition in combination with verbs which express ideas of depending and expecting. The noun group which follows **on** refers to the thing which you expect or need. For example, if you **count on** something happening, you expect it to happen and include this in your plans, and if one thing **hinges on** another, the existence of the first depends entirely on the second. **Upon** can be substituted for **on** in some of these combinations.

bank on	depend on 1,2,3	hinge on	plan on 1,2	stake on
bargain on	figure on	lean on 2	put on 12,13,16	turn on 5
bet on 1,2	gamble on	pin on 2	reckon on	wait on 4
call on 2,3	hang on 2	pivot on	rely on 1,2	work on 2
count on 1,2				

12 Using

On is used as a preposition in combination with verbs which express ideas of use or basis. The noun group which follows **on** refers to the thing which you make use of or which forms the basis for something else. For example, if you **draw on** a particular thing, you make use of it in order to do something, and if something **is based on** a particular thing, it takes its general form or nature from that thing. **Upon** can be substituted for **on** in some of these combinations.

act on	build on 1,2	model on	pattern on	trade on
base on	draw on 2,3			

13 Consuming

On occurs as a preposition in combinations where you are saying that someone eats a particular thing, or that they make use of a particular thing or person. You mention the food or source in the noun group after **on.** For example, if you **dine on** a particular food, you eat it, and if you **batten on** someone, you make use of them in order to become successful or live comfortably, and so on. Similarly, if a machine or device **runs on** a particular fuel or type of power, it uses that fuel or power in order to function. Some of these verbs can be used with **off** instead of **on,** with almost the same meaning.

batten on	feed on	live on 2	run on 5	sponge on
dine on				

onto is a preposition. It can also be written as **on to.** It occurs in 12 phrasal verbs in this dictionary. In addition, it is often used instead of the preposition **on,** when **on** refers to movement and position, or to actions such as holding and attaching. For example, you can say that someone **put** something **on** a surface or **onto** a surface. By choosing **onto** instead of **on,** you make the action seem more deliberate or precise. These uses of **onto** in phrasal verbs are mostly dealt with in the entries for phrasal verbs with **on,** and the extra column indicates it by showing patterns such as ALSO + *to* or USUALLY + *to.* **Onto** has the following meanings when it occurs in phrasal verb headwords.

1 Movement and holding

Onto or **on to** occurs in combinations which mean 'move' or 'hold': these combinations are both literal and non-literal. For example, **come onto** can refer to physical movement, or you can talk about **coming onto** a new topic in a conversation. Similarly, **hang onto** can mean 'hold something tightly in your hand' or 'keep and not lose or give away'. **Get onto** and **put onto** are also used to express ideas of contacting someone. For example, if you **get onto** someone, you contact them.

come onto	hang onto	latch onto	push onto	throw onto
get onto	hold onto	move onto	put onto	

2 Direction

Onto occurs in a few combinations which indicate the direction in which a building, room, or other place faces or leads. For example, if one room **opens onto** another, you can go straight from one to the other.

back onto	give onto	open onto

out is an adverb. It occurs in 410 phrasal verbs in this dictionary. The basic meaning of **out** is to do with movement from the inside of an enclosed space or container to the outside of it. **In** often has opposite meanings.

In some varieties of English such as American English, and also in non-standard British English, **out** can also be used as a preposition with verbs of movement. So in American English you can say 'He went out the room', but in standard British English you need to add the preposition 'of' and say 'He went out of the room'.

1 Leaving

You use **out** in literal combinations to indicate movement from the inside of somewhere to the outside. For example, if you are inside a house or room and **come out,** you move so that you are outside it; if you **bail out** of an aeroplane, you jump from it into the air with a parachute; if you say that people **spill out** of a place, you mean that large numbers of them come from it in a hurried or disorganized way; and if you **break out** of prison, you escape from it. Some combinations emphasize the sense of leaving a place and going somewhere else. This may involve travelling. For example, if you **set out,** you start a journey. Other combinations express the idea of leaving a place of work or a work activity. For example, when workers **punch out,** they record the time that they leave a factory or office, and if you **log out,** you finish using a computer by typing a special word. **In** and **into** often have opposite meanings.

back out 2	clock out	light out	put out 15	sign out 1
bail out 3	come out 1,4	log out	run out 1,6	slip out 1
break out 1,3	draw out 1	move out 2,3	sally out	spill out 2
breeze out	fall out 4	pile out	see out 1	start out 1,2
bust out of	fly out	pop out 2	set out 1	storm out
buy out 2	get out 1,10	pour out 3	ship out	strike out 2
check out 1,4	go out 1,7,12	pull out 1,2	shoot out 1	want 2
clear out 1	let out 1	punch out	show out	

2 Removing, excluding, and preventing

Out occurs in a large number of combinations which mean 'remove', 'get rid of', or 'force to leave a place'. The verbs in these combinations are mainly transitive. For example, if you **squeeze out** liquid or air from a container, you remove it by squeezing the container; when you **throw** things **out,** you get rid of things that you no longer need or want; and if you **root out** someone from an organization, you force them to leave the organization. Other combinations express ideas of preventing something from being seen or heard. For example, if an object **cuts out** the light, it prevents light from reaching a place, and if a part of a photograph **is masked out,** it is covered so that it is not printed.

Some combinations express ideas of avoiding becoming involved or of preventing people from becoming involved in a situation. For example, if you get out of doing something, you avoid doing it; if you **freeze** someone **out** of an activity or situation, you prevent them from being involved; and if the management of a factory **locks out** the workers, they close the factory and prevent the workers from entering and working during an industrial dispute. Some other combinations indicate that someone or something is considered and perhaps accepted or admitted for a while, but is then rejected. For example, if you **rule out** an idea, solution, or course of action, you decide that it is impossible or unsuitable.

argue out of	cut out 1,2,4,5	include out	put out 14	strip out 1
bail out 4	do out of	keep out 1,2	root out	sweat out 2
black out 3,4	drive out	keep out of 1,2	rout out	take out 1,2
block out 1,2,3,4	drown out	kick out	rub out 1,2	talk out of
blot out 1,2,3	drum out	knock out 2,7	rule out 1,2	tear out
boot out	edit out	leave out 1	run out 2	thin out
breathe out	empty out	let out 2,7	run out of	throw out 1,2,3,4
buy out 1	fall out 1,2	lock out 1,2,3	score out	turf out 1,2
call out 3	filter out	mask out	scrape out	turn out 4,5
cancel out	flood out	miss out 1,2	scratch out	vote out
cast out	flush out	miss out on	shut out 1,2,3	walk out 1,2
chuck out 1,2	freeze out	muscle out	slip out 3	want out 1
close out	frighten out of	nose out 2	smoke out 1	wash out 3
come out 6,8,15	get out 2,5,6	opt out	spit out 1	weed out
contract out 1,2	get out of 2	paint out	squeeze out 1,3	wriggle out of
count out 2,3	go out 11.2	pull out 5	starve out	write out 3
cross out	have out 1	pump out 1,2	stay out of 1,2	x out
crowd out	hound out	push out 1,2	strike out 4	

3 Searching, finding, and obtaining

Out occurs in combinations which mean 'search', 'find', or 'obtain'. Some combinations contain an idea of removal. For example, if you **dig** something **out,** you find it and get it out of a place where it is hidden or stored, and if you **fish** something **out,** you pull it out of a liquid or a container. Other combinations are metaphorical, and refer to the obtaining of information. For example, if you **ferret out** information, you discover it after a thorough search, and if you **worm** information **out** of someone, you find it out by constantly asking them about it.

check out 2,3	find out 1,2	pick out 1	smell out 1,2	stake out 3
dig out	fish out	piece out	smoke out 2	suss out 1,2
drag out 2	get out of 3	prise out	sniff out	take out 5,6
draw out 4	hunt out	pump out of	sort out 3	try out 1,2
eke out 2	iron out	puzzle out	sound out 1	turn out 2
fathom out	look out 2	screw out of	spit out 3	work out 1,3,4,5
feel out	make out 1,2	search out	spy out	worm out
ferret out	nose out 1	seek out	squeeze out 2	wring out 2
figure out				

4 Appearing

Out also occurs in combinations which refer to the way something suddenly happens or appears. Many of these combinations contain an idea of something having been hidden or unseen, and then being revealed. For example, if something that you could not see **pops out,** it suddenly appears; if you **come out in** spots or rashes, they appear all over your body; and when a baby bird **hatches out,** it comes out of an egg by breaking the shell. Some of these combinations simply refer to how clearly something is seen. For example, if something **sticks out** or **stands out,** you can see it clearly.

break out 5	get out 9	lean out	mark out 2	slip out 2
bring out 2,3	hatch out	leap out	pick out 3,4	stand out 1,2
come out 9,10,16,19	jump out at	leap out at	poke out 1,2	stick out 3
come out in	jut out 1,2	let out 4	pop out 1	whip out

5 Locations outside and away from home

Some phrasal verbs with **out** mean that someone does not remain in a place or remain at home, but goes somewhere else. For example, if you **eat out,** you have a meal at a restaurant rather than at home. Some of the combinations indicate that the activity takes place out of doors, as in **sleep out** and **camp out.** Metaphorical uses indicate that the activity itself is unusual, different, or new for the person or group involved. For example, if you **branch out,** you do something different from your normal activities or work, and if someone **marries out,** they marry someone of a different religion to them.

ask out	camp out	go out 2,3,4	move out 1	stop out
bed out	come out 2,3	hang out 2	put out 6,10	strike out 1
board out	dine out	hide out	sit out 1	take out 3,8
branch out	eat out 1	invite out	sleep out	turn out 7
break out	get out 4	marry out	stay out 1,2	

6 Producing and creating

A number of phrasal verbs with **out** have the meaning of producing or emitting sounds, smells, light, heat, and so on. For example, when a radio or record player **blares out** noise or music, it produces loud noise or music, and if a machine **sends out** sound or light, it causes them to travel in a particular direction. Other combinations such as **ooze out** and **leak out** refer to liquids, gases, and so on being produced, leaked, or appearing. Some combinations relate specifically to the production of sounds or speech by a human voice. For example, if you **yell out,** you shout loudly, and if you **blurt** something **out,** you say it suddenly without thinking about it. You can also use **out** in combinations such as **churn out** and **turn out** that refer to producing things quickly and in large quantities.

act out 1,2	churn out	let out 3	roll out	spew out
bang out 1,2	clap out 1	ooze out	rough out	spill out 1,3
bark out	come out 5,12,14	peal out	rush out	spit out 2
bawl out 1,2	come out with	pick out 5	send out 2	spout out
beat out 1	crash out 1	play out 1,2,3	set 3	spurt out
belt out	cry out	pour out 2	shine out	stammer out
blare out	fling out	pump out 3	shout out	stamp out 3
blast out	get out 7,8	punch out 1	sing out 1,2	tap out
blow out 3.2,3.3	give out 4,5	push out 3	sketch out 1,2	throw out 5,6
blurt out	go out 6,8	put out 1,2,18,19,	snap out	thump out 1,2
boom out	grind out 1	20,21	sob out	toss out
break out 2	jerk out	rap out	sound out 2	trot out
bring out 1,5	knock out 4	read out 1	speak out	turn out 6
burst out 1,2	lay out 2	ring out	spell out 1,2	yell out
call out 1	leak out			

7 Increasing size, shape, or extent

You use **out** in phrasal verbs which indicate that something increases in physical size or extent. For example, if a thin person **fills out,** they become fatter, and if you **pad out** writing, you include unnecessary words or information in it. Often, **out** just emphasizes the action described by the verb, rather than changing its meaning, so that if something **spreads out,** it spreads and covers a wider area than before. Some combinations suggest that something is or becomes longer or more stretched, such as **stringing out** things. The increase is sometimes in terms of time rather than space. For example, if you **drag** something **out,** you make it last for longer than is necessary. Some combinations have the sense of changing the shape of something by cutting or scraping part of it away from the rest, in order to create a hole or a new shape, as in **carve out** and **hollow out. Out** also occurs in combinations which refer to something protruding or being held towards you, or to something being extended in a straight line. For example, if you **hold out** your hand, you stretch it in a straight line in front of you.

belly out	flare out	let out 6	reach out	spread out 1,2,3,4,6
broaden out 1,2	flesh out	open out 1,2,3,4,5	run out 8	stick out 1,2
carve out 1,2	fluff out	pad out	scoop out	straighten out 1
drag out 1	gouge out	pay out 2	shake out	stretch out 1,2
draw out 2,3,6	grow out of 2	plump out	shoot out 2	string out
eke out 1	hew out	puff out 1	spin out	throw out 7
fan out 1,2	hold out 1,2	put out 8,9	sprawl out	zoom out
fill out 2	hollow out			

8 Thoroughness and completeness

You use **out** in combinations with verbs which describe activities in order to indicate that the activity is done thoroughly or completely. For example, when you **argue out** an idea or plan, you discuss in detail all its aspects; if you **type out** a piece of work, you produce a complete copy of it on a typewriter; and if you **scrub out** a place, you clean it very thoroughly. Some of the combinations involve verbs that are also adjectives, such as **clean out, dry out,** and **thin out,** which mean to become or make very clean, dry, or thin. Some phrasal verbs with **out** refer to the situation at the end of an activity. For example, if things **balance out,** they are equal in amount or value, after a period of time or when they have been added up, and if a situation, arrangement, or plan **works out,** it is successful.

argue out	deck out	lay out 4	read out 2	think out
average out	do out	level out	rig out	thrash out
average out at	dry out 1,2	live out 2	rinse out 1,2,3	tidy out
balance out	even out	make out 6	scrub out	tog out
bliss out	fill out 1	make out with	set out 2	trace out
bottom out	fit out	map out	slop out	trick out
brush out	flatten out 1,2	muck out	smooth out 1,2	turn out 1,8
carry out 1,2	follow out	multiply out	stake out 2	type out
clean out 1,2	go out 5	pack out	start out	wash out 1,2
clear out 2	hammer out	pan out	swab out	wipe out 1
comb out	have out 2	plan out	sweep out	work out 2,6,7,11
come out 11,18	hear out	plot out	talk out 1	wring out 1
come out of	hose out	print out	thaw out 1,2	write out 1,2
copy out	kit out	reach out for		

9 Duration and resisting

Out is used in phrasal verbs to indicate that people or things do an activity or continue to exist until the activity is completed, until a period of time is over, or until an aim is achieved, even though this may be difficult. For example, if you **hold out,** you manage to resist an enemy, opponent or attack, and if a supply of something **lasts out,** there is enough of it for as long as it is needed or for a particular period of time.

brave out	hold out on	ride out	stand out for	sweat out 1
brazen out	last out 1,2	see out 2,3	stare out	wait out
face out	live out 1	sit out 2,3	stick out 4	win out
hold out 3,4,5	make out 7	stand out against	stick out for	work out 8,9
hold out for	mark out 3			

10 Ending or disappearing

Out occurs in combinations with verbs which refer to activities in order to indicate that the activity ends completely. Some combinations indicate that an activity cannot continue any longer, because all the things or people involved have been used up or destroyed. For example, if a shop **is sold out** of something, it has all been sold, and if a fire **burns out,** it stops burning because there is nothing left to burn. Other combinations indicate that an activity ceases gradually, as in **peter out,** or is stopped abruptly or violently, as in **stamp out.** Some combinations indicate that the activity ceases prematurely because the person involved withdraws or refuses to continue, as in **back out** and **chicken out.** Other combinations indicate that the activity ceases because the person doing it is too tired to continue. These combinations are often passive. For example, if you **are played out,** you are exhausted and feel unable to do anything. A few combinations with **out** refer to falling asleep or losing consciousness, as in **pass out** and **black out.**

back out 1	cop out	give out 2,3	phase out	stamp out 1,2
beat out 2	crash out 2	go out 9,10,11.1,13.2	play out 4	stub out
black out 1	cut out 3,6	go out of	psych out	take out 4
blow out 1,2	die out	grind out 2	puff out 2	take out of 1
bomb out	drop out 1,2	grow out of 1	pull out 3,4	talk out 2
bottle out	duck out	hole out	pull out of	tire out
bow out	eat out 2	knock out 1	put out 3,4,17	turn out 3

bowl out	fade out 1,2,3	lay out 5	put out of	walk out on
burn out 1,2,3	fag out	lose out	run out 3,4,5,7	wash out 4,5
butt out	fizzle out	lose out to	sell out 1,2,3	wear out 1,2
chicken out	flake out	luck out	snap out of	wimp out
clap out 2	flunk out	pass out 1,3	snuff out 1,2	wipe out 2
come out 13,17	get out 11	peg out 1	sputter out	work out 10
conk out	get out of 4	peter out		

11 Arranging, dividing, selecting, and distributing

Out occurs in some phrasal verbs with the meaning of arranging things in particular groups, as in **sort out**. Some combinations have the sense of dividing areas, amounts, or groups into smaller ones, for example **mark out** and **weigh out**. Others indicate that one or more items are selected from a group. For example, if you **single out** someone or something, you choose them for special attention or treatment. Other combinations refer to the distribution or sharing of things among different people, as in **give out** and **ration out,** or to the allocation of money for a specific purpose, for example **lash out** and **fork out.**

blow out 3.1	hire out	pass out 2	rent out	space out 1
contract out 3	ladle out 1,2	pay out 1	select out	splash out
count out 1	lash out 3	peg out 2,3	send out 1	spoon out
deal out 2	lay out 1,3,6	pick out 2	separate out	spread out 5
dish out 1,3	lend out	plant out	serve out	stake out 1
dole out	let out 5,8	portion out	set out 4	straighten out 2
farm out	loan out	pour out 1	share out	strip out 2
fork out	mark out 1	prick out	shell out	take out 7
give out 1	measure out	pull out 6	sign out 2	tease out
hand out 1	pace out	put out 7	single out	weigh out
hang out 1	parcel out	ration out	sort out 1,2	

12 Paying attention and awareness

In a few phrasal verbs, **out** has the sense of paying attention to something, often because of the possibility of danger as in **mind out.** If something is expected to happen, it is usually introduced by the preposition **for** as in **listen out for.**

| listen out for | look out for 1,2 | point out 1,2 | watch out | watch out for |
| look out | mind out | | | |

13 Supporting and helping

Out occurs in some phrasal verbs with the meaning of giving support to someone or helping them in some way. For example, if you **bail** someone **out,** you help them out of a difficult situation; if you **draw** someone **out,** you make them feel less nervous and more willing to talk.

bail out 1,2	call out 2	hand out 2	put out 12	straighten out 3
bear out	draw out 5	help out	reach out to	take out of 2
bring out 4	get out 3			

14 Attacking, criticizing, and protesting

In some phrasal verbs, **out** has the sense of criticizing or protesting against something or someone, either verbally or physically. For example, if you **lash out,** you criticize them very angrily or severely, or you scold them; if you **sort** someone **out,** you punish them, often using force or violence.

cry out against	fight out	kick out against	mete out	sort out 4
deal out 1	hit out 1,2	knock out 3	shoot out 3	take out on
dish out 2	lash out 1,2			

over is an adverb and a preposition. It is used in 111 phrasal verbs in this dictionary.

1 Movement and position

You use **over** in literal combinations with meanings to do with moving across a surface or being in a position above something. For example, if you **cross over** a road, you move across it from one side to the other, and if something **passes**

over, it moves overhead. **Over** is extended in meaning in a few combinations with the meaning of supervising someone or being in a position of authority over them. For example, if you **stand over** someone, you stand beside them and watch them working. **Over** is also used metaphorically to indicate that someone or something threatens or worries you. For example, if a problem **hangs over** you, it worries you a lot, and if you **hold** something **over** someone, you use it as a threat against them. You also use **over** in combinations with the meaning of moving or going towards a place, especially the place where someone is standing, or going to their house to visit them. For example, if you **run over** to someone, you run to the place where they are, and if you **call over** to see someone, you go to their house to see them. **Over** is also used in some combinations with the meaning of moving something so that it faces in another direction. For example, if you **turn** something **over,** you turn it so that it is facing in the opposite direction.

ask over	flick over	lord over	roll over	stop over 1,2
bend over	get over 5	move over 2,4	run over 1	take over 7
bring over	go over 1,2,3	pass over 3	see over 2	throw over 1.1,2
call over 1,2	hang over 1	preside over 1,2	sit over 2	tower over
come over 1	hold over 1	pull over 1,2,3	stand over	turn over 1,2,10
cross over 1	invite over	put over 2	stay over 2	watch over
double over	lean over	queen over	steal over	

2 Overflowing and overwhelming feelings

You use **over** in combinations which describe a liquid spilling out of a container because it is too full. For example, if a liquid **slops over** the edge of a container, a small amount of it spills out. You also use **over** in combinations with the meaning of having a strong feeling or reaction towards someone or something. For example, if you **enthuse over** something, you feel very enthusiastic about it; and if feelings of anger **boil over,** they become so strong that you cannot stop yourself from showing them.

boil over 1,2	come over 4,5	fall over 2	get over 3	slop over
bowl over 2	drool over	flow over	moon over	spill over 1,2,3
brim over 1,2	enthuse over	fuss over	run over 3	take over 8
bubble over with				

3 Falling and attacking

You use **over** in combinations which have the meaning of something falling or being pushed to the ground. In these combinations, **over** has the meaning of completing the action described by the verb. For example, if something **blows over,** the wind blows it and it falls to the ground; and if you **kick** something **over,** you kick it so that it falls on the ground. If someone **does** you **over,** they attack you by hitting or kicking you.

blow over 3	go over 5	kick over	run over 2	trip over 1
bowl over 1	heel over	knock over	tip over	tumble over
do over 4	keel over	push over 1	topple over	work over
fall over 1				

4 Covering and hiding

You use **over** in combinations with meanings to do with something becoming covered with a layer of something. For example, if the sky **clouds over,** it becomes covered with a layer of cloud, and if you **put** one thing **over** another, you put it on it so that it covers it. Some combinations are used metaphorically with the meaning of avoiding or hiding from something. For example, if you **varnish over** an unpleasant situation, you hide the unpleasant aspects of it; and if you **skate over** a problem, you pretend that it does not exist.

cloud over 1,2,3	frost over	heal over	paper over	skate over
cover over	glaze over	ice over	pass over 2	smooth over
dub over	gloss over	mist over 1,2	pave over	throw over 1.2
film over	grass over	paint over	put over 1	varnish over
freeze over				

5 Considering and communicating

You use **over** in combinations which have the meaning of thinking about or looking at something in a thorough and detailed way. For example, if you **mull** something **over**, you think about it carefully for a long time, and if you **pore over** something, you look at it very carefully. **Over** is also used in a few combinations to do with managing to communicate with someone and make them understand what you are saying. For example, if you **get** something **over** to someone, you manage to explain it to them so that they understand it.

brood over	hash over	pore over	read over	take over 6
chew over	look over	puzzle over	run over 4	talk over
come over 3,6,7	mull over	put over 3	see over 1	think over
get over 4	pick over	rake over	sweat over	turn over 7
go over 4,6				

6 Changing and transferring

You use **over** as an adverb in combinations which have meanings to do with changing or transferring something. For example, if you **swap** two things **over**, you exchange their positions so that each is in the position that the other was in before. Some combinations have the meaning of giving something to someone in a formal way, so that the ownership of the thing is transferred to the other person. For example, if you **sign** something **over** to someone, you sign a document which says that they now own it. A few combinations have the meaning of changing your mind or changing the group that you support. For example, if you **win** someone **over**, you persuade them to change their mind and agree with you or support you.

buy over	cross over 2	hand over to	sign over	take over 1,2,3,4,5,9
carry over 1,2	do over 2	make over	swap over	turn over 3,4,5,6
change over 1,2	go over to 1,2	move over 1,3	switch over 1,2	win over
come over 2	hand over 1,2,3			

7 Ending and recovering

You use **over** in combinations which have meanings to do with something unpleasant being finished, usually in a satisfactory way. For example, if an argument **blows over**, it ends and is forgotten about, and if you **get over** an unpleasant experience, you recover from it.

blow over 1,2	get over with	give over 1,2	throw over 3	tide over
get over 1,2			

overboard is an adverb. Its basic meaning is to do with falling from a ship into the water. It only occurs in 2 phrasal verbs in this dictionary, **go overboard** and **throw overboard,** in which it is also used non-literally to indicate extreme actions.

past is a preposition and an adverb. Its basic meanings are to do with time that has passed or is over, and movement from one side of an object to another. It only occurs in 3 phrasal verbs in this dictionary. **Brush past** and **push past** are literal combinations which refer to movement, and **put past** occurs in a semi-fixed expression. If you say 'I wouldn't put anything past her', you mean that you think she is likely to do things which you disapprove of.

round is an adverb and a preposition. It occurs in 58 phrasal verbs in this dictionary.

1 Movement

You use **round** in literal combinations which have meanings to do with going to different places or different parts of a place. For example, if you **look round** a building, you look at all the different parts of it. Some combinations have meanings to do with looking for something in a lot of different places, or talking to a lot of different people, often in order to obtain information. For example, if you **phone round,** you phone several different people; and if you hawk something **round,** you offer it for sale to many different people. **Round** is used in a similar way in combinations which have the meaning of distributing something to a lot of people. For example, if you **hand** things **round,** you give them to people in a group. If a story or information **is put round,** it is told to several people. **About** and **around** have similar meanings: see **about 1** and **around 1.**

2 Turning

You use **round** in combinations with the meaning of turning so as to be facing in the opposite direction, or turning in a complete circle or series of circles. For example, **spin round** means to spin so as to be facing in the opposite direction, or continue spinning in a circle. With this meaning, **round** is often repeated. For example, you might say that something spins round and round. **Around** has a similar meanings: see **around 3.**

go round 5	pull round 2	swing round	turn round	wheel round
look round	spin round	swivel round		

3 Visiting

You use **round** as an adverb in combinations with the meaning of visiting someone, often informally. For example, if you **drop round,** you go and visit someone informally or casually.

ask round	call round	come round 1	drop round	go round 1

4 Surrounding

Round is used in combinations with the literal meaning of surrounding or encircling someone or something. For example, when people **gather round,** they come together and surround someone or something, and if you **put** something **round** something else, you place it so that it forms a circle around it. **Around** and **about** have a similar meaning: see **around 4** and **about 3.**

5 Change of opinion

You use **round** as an adverb in a few combinations which have the meaning of changing your mind about something or being persuaded about it. For example, if you **talk** someone **round,** you persuade them about something.

bring round 2	come round 3	talk round 1	win round

6 Revival of consciousness

You use **round** as an adverb in a few combinations with the meaning of becoming conscious or well again after a period of unconsciousness or illness. For example, to **bring** someone **round** means to make them conscious again.

bring round 1	come round 5
pull round 1	

7 Inactivity and aimlessness

You use **round** in a few combinations which have the meaning of spending time in a place doing nothing. For example, if you **sit round,** you sit in a place and do nothing. **Around** and **about** have similar meanings, and are both more common: see **about 2** and **around 2.**

hang round	sit round	stand round

8 Avoidance

You use **round** in a few combinations with meanings to do with avoiding something, either a physical object or a problem. For example, if you **get round** a problem, you manage to avoid it. **Around** has a similar meaning: see **around 5.**

get round 1	go round 6	move round	skirt round	talk round 2

9 Focus

You use **round** as a preposition in two combinations, **centre round** and **revolve round,** where the meaning is to focus on or concentrate on something. For example, if a discussion **centres round** a subject, it concentrates on that subject. **Around** has a similar meaning: see **around 6.**

through is an adverb and a preposition. It occurs in 59 phrasal verbs in this dictionary.

1 Movement

You use **through** in literal combinations with the meaning of passing from one side of something to the other, for example passing from one side of a solid object to the other, often making a hole, or passing from one side of a room or other place to the other. For example, if something **pokes through** an object, it is visible because it has pierced the object; if you can **see through** something, you can look from one side of it to the other; and if you **go through** a place, you go from one side of it to the other.

2 Completion and thoroughness

You use **through** in combinations with meanings to do with completing something, for example a period of time, a piece of work, or an experience. For example, if you **pull through** after an illness, you survive and recover, and if you **rattle through** a piece of work, you complete it very quickly. Some combinations have the meaning of doing something very thoroughly, or continuing to do it until it is completely finished. For example, if you **think** something **through,** you think about it in great detail until you have understood it completely, and if you **see** something **through,** you continue to do it until it is completely finished. A few combinations have the meaning of completing a process. For example, if something **goes through** an official procedure, especially a long and complicated one, all the necessary parts of that procedure are done; and if you **push** something **through,** you succeed in getting it accepted.

blunder through	live through	push through 3	sail through	soak through
carry through 1	muddle through	put through 5	scrape through	take through
come through 4	pass through	rattle through	see through 4	talk through 1
follow through 2	play through	romp through	sit through	think through
get through 1	plough through 1	run through 3	sleep through	vote through
go through 9	pull through 2	rush through	slog through	win through

3 Reading or looking

Through is used as a preposition in combinations with meanings to do with turning the pages of a book and reading it, especially quickly, or picking up a series of things and looking at them or turning them over because you are looking for something. For example, if you **flick through** a book, you turn all its pages quickly, not reading it very carefully, and if you **rifle through** things, you pick them up and examine them because you are looking for something.

flick through	look through 2	riffle through	sift through	thumb through
go through 7	pick through	rifle through	skim through	wade through
leaf through	read through			

4 Communication

You use **through** as an adverb in combinations with the meaning of managing to communicate with someone, especially by telephone. For example, if you **put** someone **through,** you connect them on the telephone with the person they want to speak to; and if you **get through** to someone, you succeed in speaking to them on the telephone, or you succeed in making them understand you.

come through 3	get through 3	phone through	put through 7

5 Obviousness and visibility

You use **through** in a few combinations with meanings to do with a something being obvious, so that people can see it. For example, if a quality **shines through,** it can be seen clearly, and if you **see through** someone, you realize clearly what their real feelings or intentions are.

break through 3	come through 7	see through 2	shine through	show through 2

to occurs in 64 phrasal verbs in this dictionary.

To is one of the commonest words in English, and its basic uses as a preposition are to do with directions, destinations, targets, and relationships. Often, it has no special meaning when used in combination with verbs, apart from introducing the noun group which refers to the thing or person that an action or attitude is directed towards. For example, if you **get to** a place, you arrive there; if you **aspire to** something, you try very hard to achieve it; and if you **warm to** someone, you start to like them.

To is also used to introduce the noun group which indicates the thing or person that is involved or connected in a relationship. For example, if something **belongs to** you, it is yours; if something **runs to** a particular amount, it is that amount; and if you **see to** someone or something that needs attention, you deal with them.

To is used as an adverb in a few combinations. For example, if you **pull** a door **to,** you close it quietly; if someone **comes to,** they regain consciousness; and if you **set to** when doing something, you start doing it.

bring to	heave to	pull to	push to	set to
come to				

together is an adverb. It occurs in 22 phrasal verbs in this dictionary. Its meanings all include an idea of closeness, connection, or combination. **Apart** sometimes has opposite meanings. **Together** is sometimes used after other phrasal verbs, for example **go out** or **shack up,** in order to indicate that two people or groups are doing something with each other. You mention both people or groups as the subject of the verb. These phrasal verbs can also be used with *with* if you mention one of the people or groups as the subject of the verb, and the other in the noun group after *with*. Such phrasal verbs are marked RECIPROCAL in the Extra Column.

1 Nearness, position, and linking

You use **together** in literal combinations to indicate that people or things are near each other, or move near each other. For example, if people **huddle together,** they stand very close to each other; and if people **live together,** they live in the same house. Some combinations have the meaning of linking things or putting them in a group. The verb is usually transitive, and its object refers to the things which are combined. For example, if you **string** things **together,** you add them to each other, one at a time; if you **herd** animals or people **together,** you gather them in a group; and if you **add together** several numbers, you calculate their total.

2 Producing and organizing things

Together occurs in combinations which describe a process of making, collecting, or organizing something, often from a number of different parts. The verb is transitive, and its object refers to the result of the process. For example, if you **cobble** something **together,** you make it quickly and roughly.

cobble together	knock together	patch together	scrape together	throw together
get together 3				

3 Groups and unity

Together occurs in combinations which describe how people work or act as a unit. For example, if people **band together,** they act as a group in order to achieve a particular purpose. These combinations mostly include an intransitive verb. **Together** also occurs in combinations which refer to the unity of a group, or the way in which different things combine successfully to form a whole. For example, if ideas **hang together,** they are consistent and do not contradict each other.

band together	get together 1	hang together	knit together	stick together 3
club together	go together	hold together	pull together	

towards is a preposition. It occurs in 11 phrasal verbs in this dictionary. Its basic meaning is to do with movement in the direction of a particular thing, though not reaching it. **Towards** is used non-literally in phrasal verbs which express ideas of aims, tendencies, and actions in a particular direction. The noun group after **towards** refers to the goal which is aimed at, the result or situation which is likely to happen, and so on. For example, if you **work towards** something, you try to achieve it, and if you **are heading towards** a situation, it is becoming more likely. **Towards** also occurs in combinations which contain an idea of partly filling or contributing. For example, if an amount of money **goes towards** something, it is used as part of its cost.

count towards	head towards	predispose towards	put towards	warm towards
gear towards	move towards	push towards	tend towards	work towards
go towards				

under is both a preposition and an adverb. It occurs in 9 phrasal verbs in this dictionary. Its basic meaning is to do with position, to say that one thing is below something else. In **go under** and **pull under,** the combination refers to someone being below the surface of the water. **Under** is also used in phrasal verbs to indicate that someone is below someone else in rank or is controlled by them. For example, if something **comes under** a particular authority, it is managed or controlled by it; and if you **buckle under** to someone, you do what they tell you to do. **Under** is used in a few other combinations with metaphorical meanings. For example, if you **are snowed under,** you have more work to do than you can manage.

up is an adverb and a preposition. It occurs in 482 phrasal verbs in this dictionary and is the commonest of the particles used in combinations. The basic meaning of **up** is to do with movement from a lower position or level to a higher one.

1 Movement and position

You use **up** in literal combinations to indicate movement from a lower position or place to a higher one. For example, if someone **jumps up,** they raise themselves to their feet, and if you **run up** a hill, you run from the bottom of the hill towards the top. **Down** can often be used instead of **up** to indicate movement in the opposite direction.

You can also use **up** with verbs which mean 'lift' to show that you are raising something to a higher position, so if you **pick up** something from the floor, you raise it from the floor to a higher level. In these combinations, the particle **up** implies movement upwards, while the verb gives an impression of how the movement is achieved. For example, if you **dig up** an object, you remove the soil or earth from above it in order to lift it out of the ground.

back up 3,4	help up	poke up 1	scoop up	stir up 1
bob up 1,2	hike up 1	pop up 2	scrape up 2	straighten up 1
break up 5,6	hitch up	pull up 3,4	screw up 1	take up 1,2,10,11
bubble up	hold up 1,2	pump up 2	shin up	throw up 1,2,3
budge up	jack up 1	push up 2	shove up	thrust up
buoy up 2	jump up 1	put up 1,2,4	show up 1	tip up
come up 1,2,4,5,13	kick up 2	reach up 1,2	sit up 1	tower up
dig up 1	lick up	rear up	snatch up	turn up 1
double up 2	lift up 1,2	ride up	spoon up	turn up 5
draw up 2,4	look up 1	rise up 1,2	spring up 2	well up 1
get up 1,2,3,4	mark up 3	roll up 4	stand up 1	whip up 2
go up 1,2,4,5,9	move up 1,3	ruck up	start up 3	wind up 3
grub up	pick up 1,2	run up 1,3,6	stick up 2,3	write up 2

2 Increasing and improving

As well as signifying movement upwards, **up** can also be used to indicate an increase in quantity or intensity. For example, if something **speeds up,** it begins to move or work more quickly. The verb often gives an indication of the **cause or quality of the increase. For example, if a fire blazes up,** it starts to burn more fiercely, and if someone **speaks up,** they begin to speak more loudly.

back up 1,2	dose up	jazz up	polish up 1	step up
bank up 1,2	dress up 1,3	key up	pretty up	stick up for
beef up	fatten up	lift up 3,4	prop up 2	stoke up 1,2
blaze up	feed up 2	light up 1,2,3	puff up 1,2	surge up 1,2,3
blow up 3,5,6	firm up 1	line up 5	push up 1	swell up 1,2,3
boil up 1,2	fix up 4	live up	put up 9	swot up
bolster up	flare up 1,2,3	liven up 1,2	quicken up	take up 13
bone up on	fluff up	look up 4	rave up	tart up 1,2
brighten up 1,2,3,4	freshen up 1,2	loosen up 1,2	read up	tidy up 2
bring up 1	gen up	mark up 1,2	rev up	tighten up 2,3
brush up	get up 7	mount up	save up 1	tone up
brush up on	ginger up	move up 2,5	sharpen up 1,2	touch up 1
buck up 1,2,3	go up 6,7,13	mug up	shoot up 1	toughen up
buoy up 1,3	grow up 1,2,3	open up 8,9	sing up	tune up 2
build up 1,2,3,4,5	grow up on	paint up	sit up 3	turn up 3,6
bump up	ham up	patch up 1,2	smarten up	vamp up
camp up	heap up	pep up 1,2	soup up	wake up 2
change up	heat up 1,3	perk up 1	speak up 1,2	wake up to
cheer up	hike up 2	pick up 7,16,17	speed up	warm up 2,3,5
churn up 1	hoke up	pile up	spice up	well up 2
colour up	hot up	play up 1	staff up	whip up 1,5
come up 14,15,17	hurry up 1,2,3	plump up	steam up	whoop up
do up 3	hype up 1,2	point up	stand up for	work up 1,2,4,5
doll up	jack up 2	poke up 2		

3 Preparing and beginning

You can use **up** with a number of verbs to indicate that something is being prepared or is starting. For example, if athletes **train up,** they take exercise in order to be in better condition in readiness for an event. If a new shop **opens up,** it starts to trade.

book up 1	gear up	open up 4,5,7	rustle up	tense up
brew up 1,2	get up 5	patch up 1,2	saddle up	tog up
butter up	go up 12	perk up 2	set up 2,3,4,5	tool up
cook up 1	heat up 2	pick up 15	shape up 1,2	throw up 5
crank up	kit up	pipe up	soften up 1,2	tidy up 3
dish up	knock up 1,4	plan up	start up 1,2,4	train up
draw up 1	light up 4	psych up	strike up 1,2	tune up 1
feel up to	limber up	put up 12	suck up to	warm up 1,4,6
firm up 2	line up 4	rig up	sweeten up	whip up 3,4
fit up 1	make up 5,6	rise up 4	take up 3,6,7,8	wind up 2
fix up 1,2,3	move up 4	run up 5,7	tee up	work up 3
fry up				

4 Fastening and restricting

Up is used in combinations to indicate that something is being fastened or restricted in some way. The verb frequently indicates what the fastening is, so if you **bandage up** a wound, you fasten a bandage over it, and if you **brick up** a hole in a wall you fill it with bricks to stop people going through it. Some verbs with **up** are used to show that someone's movement is being restricted. For example, if you **belt up** when you get in a car or on plane, you fasten yourself in using the safety belt.

bandage up	cork up	lay up 1,2	scrunch up	sweep up 2
bang up	crumple up	let up	seal up	tack up
belt up 2	dam up 1,2	lock up 1,3	sew up 1	take up 12
bind up	do up 1,2,4	mist up	shore up 1,2	tangle up 1,2
block up 1,2	earth up	muffle up	shut up 3	tape up
board up	ease up	nail up 1,2	silt up	tense up
bottle up 1	fasten up	paste up	slow up	tie up 1,2,3,4,5,6
brick up	fog up	pen up	snarl up	tighten up 1
bundle up 1,2	freeze up	pin up 1,2,3	snow up	truss up
bung up	fur up	plug up	squash up	tuck up 1
button up	gum up	post up	steam up 1	turn up 4
catch up in 1,2	hang up 1,2	prop up 1	stick up 1	wait up 2
chain up	hook up 2	pull up 6,7	stitch up	wall up
clog up	ice up	put up 3,5	stop up 1	wind up 1
close up 1	jam up	roll up 1,2,3	strap up	wrap up 1,2
coop up	lace up	screw up 2	string up 1	zip up

5 Approaching

Up can be used in combinations to indicate that two people are moving closer together or staying close together. For example if someone **catches up with** you they get closer to you; and if someone **creeps up on** you, they approach you quietly and secretly; and if you **keep up** with someone else, you stay close to them by moving at the same speed as them. In combinations with transitive verbs, **up** indicates that things are being brought closer together, so if you **line up** some objects, you place them together in a line. Some combinations give the idea that the quality of something is close to the quality of another thing, so if something **measures up to** what was expected, its quality is as good as it was expected to be.

balance up	creep up on 1,2	lead up to 1,2	measure up 2	run up against
bump up against	cuddle up	level up	measure up to	sidle up
catch up 1,2	draw up 3	line up 1,2	nestle up	snuggle up
catch up on	even up	live up to	patch up 3	square up 1,2
catch up with 1,2	face up to	loom up	pick up 10	steal up
chat up	form up	make up 4,7	play up to	
close up 3	go up 3	make up to	pull up 2,8	
come up 3,12	keep up 1,2,3,4,5,	marry up	queue up	
come up against	6,7,8,9,11	match up	round up 2	
come up to 1,2	keep up with	match up to	run up 2	

6 Disrupting and damaging

Up is used in combinations to give the idea that something is not in its normal state, and has perhaps been spoilt or damaged in some way. For example, if you **mess up** a tidy room, you make it untidy, and if a machine **plays up,** it does not work properly. Several of these verbs can be used to refer to somebody doing a job badly, so if someone **botches up** a job, they do not do it very well.

act up 1,2	carve up 2	foul up	mix up 1,2	shake up 1,3
balls up	churn up 2	fuck up	muck up 1,2	shoot up 2,3
bash up	cock up	go up 10	muddle up 1,2	slip up
beat up 1,2	crack up 1	hang up 5	muss up	smash up
beat up on	curl up 2	hold up 3	pack up 3	stand up 3
bitch up	cut up 2	jack up 3	play up 2,3	stir up 2
blow up 1,2	dope up	jumble up	punch up 2	string up 2,3
botch up	dry up 5,7	keep up 10	rough up	tear up 2
break up 4	duff up	kick up 1	screw up 3,4	trip up 1,2
bugger up	eat up 3,4	knock up 3	seize up	wash up 4
burn up 1,3	feed up 1	louse up	set up 6	wind up 7
bust up 1,2	fit up 2	mess up 1,2,3		

7 Completing and finishing

Up is used in combinations to indicate that something has ended or been finished, so if you **hang up** when you are using the telephone, you end the conversation, and if someone **winds up** what they are doing, they finish doing it. Often, **up** indicates that something has been done thoroughly or completely. For example, if you **tear up** a piece of paper, you tear it into smaller pieces, you do not just tear the edge.

As an extension of this, you can use **up** to indicate that something has been totally consumed or **used up.** The verb often indicates how this happens, so if someone **drinks up,** they finish what they are drinking so that there is none left.

add up 1,2	count up	grind up	plough up	sum up 1,2
add up to 1,2	cover up 1,2	hang up 3	polish up 2	swallow up 1,4
belt up 1	crack up 2	hang up on	pull up 1	tear up 1
blow up 4	crease up	heal up	pump up 1	throw 6
book up 2	drink up	hush up 1,2	punch up 1	tidy up 1,3
break up 7	dry up 1,2,3,4,6	knit up	reckon up	tie up 7
burn up 2	dummy up	knock up 2	ring up 2	top up
buy up	eat up 1,2,5	land up	rip up	toss up
chalk up	end up 1,2	lap up	run up 4	tot up
check up	fetch up	load up	sew up 2	type up

chew up	fill up 1,2,3,4,5,6	lock up 2	shrivel up	use up
chuck up	finish up 1,2,3	make up 3	shut up 1,2	wake up 1
clam up	finish up with	mash up	snap up 1,2	wash up 1,2,4
clean up 1,2,3,4	fold up 2,3	measure up 1	soak up 1,3	weigh up 1
clear up 1,2,3,4	follow up 1,2	mop up 1,2,3	sober up	wind up 4,5,6
clock up	give up 1,2,8	notch up	sop up	wrap up 3,4
close up 2	gobble up	pack up 2	straighten up 2	write up 1,3
come up 18				

8 Rejecting and surrendering

There are several phrasal verbs where **up** indicates that something is being given away or rejected. For example, if you **pass up** an offer, you reject it, and if someone **pays up** or **coughs up** the money they owe you, they give it to you.

bear up 2	give up 3,4,5	hold up 7	settle up	stand up 2
bring up 3	give up on	pass up	sick up	stump up
cast up	give up to	pay up	spew up	throw up 7
cough up 1,2	hang up 4	put up with	square up 2	wash up
deliver up	heave up	sell up		

9 Happening and creating

There are a number of phrasal verbs with **up** which give the idea of something happening or being created. For example, if something **crops up,** it happens or appears; if you **think up** a clever idea, you use your imagination or intelligence to create it; and if something **comes up** in a conversation or meeting, it is mentioned or discussed.

bring up 2	conjure up	go up 8,11	rise up 3	take up 4
call up 4	cook up	make up 2	show up 3	think up
come up 6,7,8,9,	crop up	open up 2	spring up 1	throw up 5
10,11,16	drag up	pick up 5,6,14	sprout up	turn up 2
come up with 1	dream up	pop up 1	summon up 4	

10 Collecting and togetherness

Some combinations with **up** give the idea that something is being gathered together, and that it sometimes becomes smaller in the process. There is a set of such verbs where the verb tells you what sort of container is being used to collect things, so if you **bag up** some objects, you put them together in a bag, and if you **crate up** some bottles you put them together in a crate.

When this sort of verb is used to refer to people, it tends to convey an idea of involvement, so if you **sign up** with an organization, you become a member of it or you become involved with it.

bag up	drum up	link up 1,2	pile up 1,2,3	stock up
bind up with	fold up 1	look up 3	put up 10	store up
bottle up 2	gang up	make up 1	rake up 2	sweep up 1
box up	gather up	meet up 1,2	ring up 1	swallow up 2
bunch up	give up 7	mix up 3	roll up 2	take up 15
call 1,2,3	heap up	mix up with	round up 1	take up on
chase 1	herd up	muster up	save up 2	take up with 1
clutter up	hoard up	pack up 1	scrape up 1	team up
coil up	hook up 1	pair up	shack up	tie up 8
collect up	huddle up	phone up	shake up 2	tuck up 2
crate up	join up 1,2,3	pick up 3,4	sign up	wire up
curl up 1	lay up 3	pick up with	stack up	wrap up in
double up 1				

11 Revealing and discovering

Up is used in some combinations to give the idea of information being revealed or discovered. For example, if someone **digs up** a secret, they discover it, and if they **own up** to something, they reveal the fact that they did it.

call up 5	chase up 2	own up	show up 2,4	throw up
come up with 2	hunt up	pick up 11,12,13	show up as	weigh up 2
dig up 2	look up 2	rake up 1	size up	yield up
dredge up	open up 3	scrape up 1		

12 Separating

Up often indicates that a person or thing is moving away from someone or something else or is being separated from it. For example, if you **divide up** a quantity of something, you split it into smaller portions, and if a group of people **splits up,** the people go away in different directions. Some combinations indicate that a person is hiding from other people. For example, if you **lie up** somewhere, you go there to hide or rest.

break up 1,2,3	cut up 1	give up 6	lay up 4	saw up
bust up 3	divide up 1,2	hide up	lie up	slice up
carve up 1	divvy up	hole up	parcel up 2	split up 1,2,3
chop up				

upon is a preposition. It occurs in 83 phrasal verbs in this dictionary. **Upon** is a more formal alternative for the preposition **on,** and in most cases it is a simple variation of it. That is, most of the phrasal verbs which it occurs in also have variations with **on,** and these variations are nearly always more common and less formal. Phrasal verbs with **upon** are mostly treated together with the variations with **on** in this dictionary, unless the variation with **upon** is more common. You cannot substitute **upon** for **on** in all phrasal verbs with **on:** phrasal verbs which are informal are almost never used with **upon.**

Upon is used with the meanings which are explained in categories **6, 7, 8, 9, 10, 11,** and **12** of **on.** The following phrasal verbs do not have variations with **on** given in this dictionary, or have meanings where **on** cannot be substituted for **upon.**

call upon	loose upon	put upon	thrust upon	trespass upon
come upon				

with is a preposition. It occurs in 56 phrasal verbs in this dictionary. **With** is one of the commonest words of English, and it is especially used when referring to relationships and connections, when mentioning the instrument or means by which an action is carried out, and when describing attributes. It is mostly used in the same ways in phrasal verb combinations.

1 Activities and connections between people

With occurs in combinations which describe activities, relationships, and connections between people or groups of people. One person or group is mentioned as the subject of the verb, and the other is mentioned in the noun group which follows **with.** For example, if you **meet with** someone, there is a meeting between you and them, and if you **plead with** someone, you ask them for something. **With** also occurs as the second particle in similar combinations which include two particles, for example **get in with** and **run around with.**

acquaint with 2	go with 3	lie with 2	play with 5	stick with 2
break with 1	identify with 2	live with 1	plead with	tangle with
deal with 3	interfere with 3	meet with 3	reason with	trifle with
finish with	level with	mess with	sleep with 2	visit with
flirt with 1				

2 Connections and associations between things

With occurs in combinations which express ideas of connections, associations, and correspondences between things. You mention one of the things as the subject or object of the verb, and you mention the other in the noun group which follows **with.** For example, if a book **deals with** a particular topic, it is about that topic, and if one thing **goes with** another, the two things are associated in some way. **Break with** and **part with** refer to the ending of a connection. **With** also occurs as the second particle in similar combinations which include two particles, for example **chime in with** and **tie in with.**

agree with	deal with 2	do with 1	go with 1	lie with 1
break with 2	disagree with 1	finish with	identify with 1	part with

3 Dealing and involvement

With occurs in combinations which describe processes of taking action about something or getting involved in it. The noun group after **with** refers to the thing that you are taking action about or getting involved in. For example, if you **deal with** something, you do what is necessary to achieve the result that you want; if you **toy with** an idea or suggestion, you consider it; and if you **meddle with** something, you get involved in a way that other people do not approve of. **With** also occurs as the second particle in similar combinations which include two particles, for example **go through with** and **do** away with.

dally with	interfere with 1	meddle with	play with 2	tinker with
deal with 1	juggle with 1	mess with	reckon with 1	toy with 2
flirt with 2	make with	part with	tamper with	wrestle with
grapple with				

4 Supporting

You use **with** in a few literal combinations which have support as part of their meaning. You mention the person or idea that is being supported in the noun group after **with**. For example, if you do not **hold with** something, you believe that it is wrong, and if you **stick with** something, you continue to support or use it. **With** also occurs as the second particle in combinations which include two particles, for example **go along with**.

agree with	hold with	side with	stay with	stick with 1
disagree with 1	identify with 1			

5 Attributes and provision

With occurs in a large number of combinations where you are simply referring to the presence or provision of things. You mention what is present, provided, or given in the noun group after **with**. For example, if something **bristles with** things, it has a large number of them, and if you **ply** someone **with** something, you give it to them. A few of the combinations have 'say', 'believe', or 'know' as part of their meanings. You mention what is said or learned after **with**. For example, if you **tax** someone **with** something, you accuse them of it. **With** also occurs as the second particle in similar combinations which include two particles, for example **help off with** and **finish up with**.

acquaint with 2	dispense with	land with	pepper with 1	saddle with
begin with 1	do with 2	lumber with	ply with	stick with 3
bristle with	endow with	meet with 2	provide with	tax with

without is usually a preposition. It occurs in 3 phrasal verbs in this dictionary: **do without, go without,** and **reckon without.** In each case, **without** refers to an absence of something, and you mention the thing which is not present in the noun group after **without**. For example, if you **go without** something, you do not have it. In the phrasal verbs **do without** and **go without,** you can use **without** as an adverb as well as a preposition.